OPTIONS, FUTURES, AND OTHER DERIVATIVES

TENTH EDITION

OPTIONS, FUTURES, AND OTHER DERIVATIVES

John C. Hull

Maple Financial Group Professor of Derivatives and Risk Management
Joseph L. Rotman School of Management
University of Toronto

TENTH EDITION

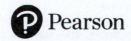 Pearson

New York, NY

Vice President, Business Publishing: Donna Battista
Director of Portfolio Management: Adrienne D'Ambrosio
Director, Courseware Portfolio Management:
  Ashley Dodge
Senior Sponsoring Editor: Neeraj Bhalla
Editorial Assistant: Kathryn Brightney
Vice President, Product Marketing: Roxanne McCarley
Director of Strategic Marketing: Brad Parkins
Strategic Marketing Manager: Deborah Strickland
Field Marketing Manager: Ramona Elmer
Product Marketing Assistant: Jessica Quazza
Vice President, Production and Digital Studio,
  Arts and Business: Etain O'Dea
Director of Production, Business: Jeff Holcomb
Managing Producer, Business: Alison Kalil
Operations Specialist: Carol Melville

Creative Director: Blair Brown
Manager, Learning Tools: Brian Surette
Content Developer, Learning Tools: Lindsey Sloan
Managing Producer, Digital Studio, Arts and Business:
  Diane Lombardo
Digital Studio Producer: Melissa Honig
Digital Studio Producer: Alana Coles
Digital Content Team Lead: Noel Lotz
Digital Content Project Lead: Miguel Leonarte
Full-Service Project Management and Composition:
  The Geometric Press
Cover Design: Laurie Entringer
Cover Art: 123rf.com
Printer/Binder: LSC Communications
Cover Printer: Phoenix Color

Library of Congress Cataloging-in-Publication Data

Hull, John, 1946–, author.
Options, futures, and other derivatives / John C. Hull, University of Toronto.
Tenth edition. New York: Pearson Education, [2018]. Revised edition of
the author's Options, futures, and other derivatives, [2015]. Includes index.
2016051230 | 013447208X
1. Futures. 2. Stock options. 3. Derivative securities.
HG6024.A3 H85 2017 | 332.64/5–dc23
LC record available at https://lccn.loc.gov/2016051230

5   18
ISBN-10: 013447208X
ISBN-13: 9780134472089

To Michelle

CONTENTS IN BRIEF

Contents

BUSINESS SNAPSHOTS

TECHNICAL NOTES

Available on the Author's Website

www-2.rotman.utoronto.ca/~hull/technicalnotes

1. Convexity Adjustments to Eurodollar Futures
2. Properties of the Lognormal Distribution
3. Warrant Valuation When Value of Equity plus Warrants Is Lognormal
4. Exact Procedure for Valuing American Calls on Stocks Paying a Single Dividend
5. Calculation of the Cumulative Probability in a Bivariate Normal Distribution
6. Differential Equation for Price of a Derivative on a Stock Paying a Known Dividend Yield
7. Differential Equation for Price of a Derivative on a Futures Price
8. Analytic Approximation for Valuing American Options
9. Generalized Tree-Building Procedure
10. The Cornish–Fisher Expansion to Estimate VaR
11. Manipulation of Credit Transition Matrices
12. Calculation of Cumulative Noncentral Chi-Square Distribution
13. Efficient Procedure for Valuing American-Style Lookback Options
14. The Hull–White Two-Factor Model
15. Valuing Options on Coupon-Bearing Bonds in a One-Factor Interest Rate Model
16. Construction of an Interest Rate Tree with Nonconstant Time Steps and Nonconstant Parameters
17. The Process for the Short Rate in an HJM Term Structure Model
18. Valuation of a Compounding Swap
19. Valuation of an Equity Swap
20. Changing the Market Price of Risk for Variables That Are Not the Prices of Traded Securities
21. Hermite Polynomials and Their Use for Integration
22. Valuation of a Variance Swap
23. The Black, Derman, Toy Model
24. Proof that Forward and Futures Prices are Equal When Interest Rates Are Constant
25. A Cash-Flow Mapping Procedure
26. A Binomial Measure of Credit Correlation
27. Calculation of Moments for Valuing Asian Options
28. Calculation of Moments for Valuing Basket Options
29. Proof of Extensions to Itô's Lemma
30. The Return of a Security Dependent on Multiple Sources of Uncertainty
31. Properties of Ho–Lee and Hull–White Interest Rate Models

Preface

It is sometimes hard for me to believe that the first edition of this book was only 330 pages and 13 chapters long! The book has grown and been adapted to keep up with the fast pace of change in derivatives markets.

Like earlier editions, the book serves several markets. It is appropriate for graduate courses in business, economics, financial mathematics, and financial engineering. It can be used on advanced undergraduate courses when students have good quantitative skills. Many practitioners who are involved in derivatives markets also find the book useful. I am delighted that the book sells equally well in the practitioner and college markets.

One of the key decisions that must be made by an author who is writing in the area of derivatives concerns the use of mathematics. If the level of mathematical sophistication is too high, the material is likely to be inaccessible to many students and practitioners. If it is too low, some important issues will inevitably be treated in a rather superficial way. I have tried to be particularly careful about the way I use mathematics in the book. Notation involving many subscripts, superscripts, or function arguments can be off-putting to a reader unfamiliar with the material and has been avoided as far as possible. Nonessential mathematical material has been either eliminated or included in the technical notes on my website and the end-of-chapter appendices. Concepts that are likely to be new to many readers have been explained carefully, and many numerical examples have been included.

Options, Futures, and Other Derivatives can be used for a first course in derivatives or for a more advanced course. There are many different ways it can be used in the classroom. Instructors teaching a first course in derivatives are likely to want to spend most classroom time on the first half of the book. Instructors teaching a more advanced course will find that many different combinations of chapters in the second half of the book can be used. I find that the material in Chapter 37 works well at the end of either an introductory or an advanced course.

What's New in the Tenth Edition?

Material has been updated and improved. OIS discounting is now used throughout the book. This makes the presentation of the material more straightforward and more theoretically appealing. The valuation of instruments such as swaps and forward rate agreements requires (a) forward rates for the rate used to calculate payments (usually LIBOR) and (b) the risk-free zero curve used for discounting (usually the OIS zero curve). The methods presented can be extended to situations where payments are dependent on any risky rate.

The changes in the tenth edition include the following:

1. A rewrite of the chapter on swaps (Chapter 7) to improve presentation and reflect changing market practices.

2. A new chapter (Chapter 9) on valuation adjustments (CVA, DVA, FVA, MVA, and KVA). Financial economists have reservations about FVA, MVA, and KVA (and these are explained), but XVAs have become such an important part of derivatives valuation that it is important to cover them.

3. Material at various points in the book on how negative interest rates can be handled in pricing models. In the no-arbitrage world that we assume when valuing derivatives, negative rates make no sense. But they are a feature of financial markets in a number of European countries and Japan and cannot be ignored.

4. A new chapter on equilibrium models of the term structure (Chapter 31). These models are important pedagogically and are widely used in long-term scenario analyses. I decided that they deserved their own chapter.

5. More details on the calculation of Greek letters and smile dynamics.

6. More discussion of the expected shortfall measure and stressed risk measures, reflecting their increasing use in regulation and risk management.

7. Coverage of the SABR model.

8. Updated material on CCPs and the regulation of OTC derivatives.

9. Improved material on martingales and measures, tailing the hedge, bootstrap methods, and convertible bonds.

10. Updating of examples to reflect current market conditions.

11. New end-of chapter problems and revisions to many old end-of-chapter problems.

12. New version of the software DerivaGem.

Software

DerivaGem 4.00 is included with this book. As before, this consists of two Excel applications: the *Options Calculator* and the *Applications Builder*. The Options Calculator consists of easy-to-use software for valuing a wide range of options. The Applications Builder consists of a number of Excel functions from which users can build their own applications. It includes a number of sample applications and enables students to explore the properties of options and numerical procedures more easily. It also allows more interesting assignments to be designed.

DerivaGem 4.00 allows a number of new models (Heston, SABR, Bachelier normal, and displaced lognormal) to be used for valuation. The software is described more fully at the end of the book. Updates to the software can be downloaded from my website:

www-2.rotman.utoronto.ca/~hull.

Slides

Several hundred PowerPoint slides can be downloaded from Pearson's Instructor Resource Center or from my website. Instructors who adopt the text are welcome to adapt the slides to meet their own needs.

Solutions Manual

End-of-chapter problems are divided into two groups: "Practice Questions" and "Further Questions." Solutions to the Practice Questions are in *Options, Futures, and Other Derivatives 10e*: *Solutions Manual* (ISBN-10: 013462999X), which is published by Pearson and can be purchased by students.

Instructors Manual

The Instructors Manual is made available online to adopting instructors by Pearson. It contains solutions to all questions (both Further Questions and Practice Questions), notes on the teaching of each chapter, test bank questions, notes on course organization, and some relevant Excel worksheets.

Technical Notes

Technical Notes are used to elaborate on points made in the text. They are referred to in the text and can be downloaded from my website:

www-2.rotman.utoronto.ca/~hull/TechnicalNotes

By not including the Technical Notes in the book, I am able to streamline the presentation of material so that it is more reader-friendly.

Acknowledgments

Many people have played a part in the development of successive editions of this book. Indeed, the list of people who have provided me with feedback on the book is now so long that it is not possible to mention everyone. I have benefited from the advice of many academics who have taught from the book and from the comments of many derivatives practitioners. I would like to thank the students on my courses at the University of Toronto who have made many suggestions on how the material can be improved. Eddie Mizzi from The Geometric Press did an excellent job editing the final manuscript and handling page composition. Emilio Barone from Luiss Guido Carli University in Rome provided many detailed comments.

Alan White, a colleague at the University of Toronto, deserves a special acknowledgment. Alan and I have been carrying out joint research and consulting in the areas of derivatives and risk management for over 30 years. During that time, we have spent many hours discussing key issues. Many of the new ideas in this book, and many of the new ways used to explain old ideas, are as much Alan's as mine. Alan has done most of the development work on the DerivaGem software.

Special thanks are due to many people at Pearson, particularly Donna Battista, Neeraj Bhalla, Nicole Suddeth, and Alison Kalil for their enthusiasm, advice and encouragement.

I welcome comments on the book from readers. My e-mail address is:

hull@rotman.utoronto.ca

John Hull

About the Author

John Hull is the Maple Financial Professor of Derivatives and Risk Management at the Joseph L. Rotman School of Management, University of Toronto. He is an internationally recognized authority on derivatives and risk management with many publications in this area. His work has an applied focus. In 1999, he was voted Financial Engineer of the Year by the International Association of Financial Engineers. He has acted as consultant to many North American, Japanese, and European financial institutions. He has won many teaching awards, including University of Toronto's prestigious Northrop Frye award.

CHAPTER 1

Introduction

In the last 40 years, derivatives have become increasingly important in finance. Futures and options are actively traded on many exchanges throughout the world. Many different types of forward contracts, swaps, options, and other derivatives are entered into by financial institutions, fund managers, and corporate treasurers in the over-the-counter market. Derivatives are added to bond issues, used in executive compensation plans, embedded in capital investment opportunities, used to transfer risks in mortgages from the original lenders to investors, and so on. We have now reached the stage where those who work in finance, and many who work outside finance, need to understand how derivatives work, how they are used, and how they are priced.

Whether you love derivatives or hate them, you cannot ignore them! The derivatives market is huge—much bigger than the stock market when measured in terms of underlying assets. The value of the assets underlying outstanding derivatives transactions is several times the world gross domestic product. As we shall see in this chapter, derivatives can be used for hedging or speculation or arbitrage. They can be used to transfer a wide range of risks in the economy from one entity to another.

A *derivative* can be defined as a financial instrument whose value depends on (or derives from) the values of other, more basic, underlying variables. Very often the variables underlying derivatives are the prices of traded assets. A stock option, for example, is a derivative whose value is dependent on the price of a stock. However, derivatives can be dependent on almost any variable, from the price of hogs to the amount of snow falling at a certain ski resort.

Since the first edition of this book was published in 1988 there have been many developments in derivatives markets. There is now active trading in credit derivatives, electricity derivatives, weather derivatives, and insurance derivatives. Many new types of interest rate, foreign exchange, and equity derivative products have been created. There have been many new ideas in risk management and risk measurement. Capital investment appraisal now often involves the evaluation of what are known as *real options*. Many new regulations have been introduced covering over-the-counter derivatives markets. The book has kept up with all these developments.

Derivatives markets have come under a great deal of criticism because of their role in the credit crisis that started in 2007. Derivative products were created from portfolios of risky mortgages in the United States using a procedure known as securitization. Many of the products that were created became worthless when house prices declined. Financial

1

institutions, and investors throughout the world, lost a huge amount of money and the world was plunged into the worst recession it had experienced in 75 years. Chapter 8 explains how securitization works and why such big losses occurred.

The way market participants trade and value derivatives has evolved through time. Regulatory requirements introduced since the crisis have had a huge effect on the over-the-counter market. Collateral and credit issues are now given much more attention than in the past.

Market participants have changed the proxy they use for the risk-free rate. They also now calculate a number of valuation adjustments to reflect funding costs and capital requirements, as well as credit risk.   This edition has been changed to keep up to date with these developments. Chapter 9 is now devoted to a discussion of how valuation adjustments work and the extent to which they are theoretically valid.

In this opening chapter, we take a first look at derivatives markets and how they are changing. We describe forward, futures, and options markets and provide an overview of how they are used by hedgers, speculators, and arbitrageurs. Later chapters will give more details and elaborate on many of the points made here.

1.1 EXCHANGE-TRADED MARKETS

A derivatives exchange is a market where individuals trade standardized contracts that have been defined by the exchange. Derivatives exchanges have existed for a long time. The Chicago Board of Trade (CBOT) was established in 1848 to bring farmers and merchants together. Initially its main task was to standardize the quantities and qualities of the grains that were traded. Within a few years, the first futures-type contract was developed. It was known as a *to-arrive contract*. Speculators soon became interested in the contract and found trading the contract to be an attractive alternative to trading the grain itself. A rival futures exchange, the Chicago Mercantile Exchange (CME), was established in 1919. Now futures exchanges exist all over the world. (See table at the end of the book.) The CME and CBOT have merged to form the CME Group (www.cmegroup.com), which also includes the New York Mercantile Exchange (NYMEX), and the Kansas City Board of Trade (KCBT).

The Chicago Board Options Exchange (CBOE, www.cboe.com) started trading call option contracts on 16 stocks in 1973. Options had traded prior to 1973, but the CBOE succeeded in creating an orderly market with well-defined contracts. Put option contracts started trading on the exchange in 1977. The CBOE now trades options on thousands of stocks and many different stock indices. Like futures, options have proved to be very popular contracts. Many other exchanges throughout the world now trade options. (See table at the end of the book.) The underlying assets include foreign currencies and futures contracts as well as stocks and stock indices.

Once two traders have agreed on a trade, it is handled by the exchange clearing house. This stands between the two traders and manages the risks. Suppose, for example, that trader A agrees to buy 100 ounces of gold from trader B at a future time for $1,250 per ounce. The result of this trade will be that A has a contract to buy 100 ounces of gold from the clearing house at $1,250 per ounce and B has a contract to sell 100 ounces of gold to the clearing house for $1,250 per ounce. The advantage of this arrangement is that traders do not have to worry about the creditworthiness of the people they are trading with. The clearing house takes care of credit risk by requiring each of the two traders to deposit funds (known as margin) with the clearing house to ensure that they will live up to their obligations. Margin requirements and the operation of clearing houses are discussed in more detail in Chapter 2.

Electronic Markets

Traditionally derivatives exchanges have used what is known as the *open outcry system*. This involves traders physically meeting on the floor of the exchange, shouting, and using a complicated set of hand signals to indicate the trades they would like to carry out. Exchanges have largely replaced the open outcry system by *electronic trading*. This involves traders entering their desired trades at a keyboard and a computer being used to match buyers and sellers. The open outcry system has its advocates, but, as time passes, it is becoming less and less used.

Electronic trading has led to a growth in high-frequency and algorithmic trading. This involves the use of computer programs to initiate trades, often without human intervention, and has become an important feature of derivatives markets.

1.2   OVER-THE-COUNTER MARKETS

Not all derivatives trading is on exchanges. Many trades take place in the *over-the-counter* (OTC) market. Banks, other large financial institutions, fund managers, and corporations are the main participants in OTC derivatives markets. Once an OTC trade has been agreed, the two parties can either present it to a central counterparty (CCP) or clear the trade bilaterally. A CCP is like an exchange clearing house. It stands between the two parties to the derivatives transaction so that one party does not have to bear the risk that the other party will default. When trades are cleared bilaterally, the two parties have usually signed an agreement covering all their transactions with each other. The issues covered in the agreement include the circumstances under which outstanding transactions can be terminated, how settlement amounts are calculated in the event of a termination, and how the collateral (if any) that must be posted by each side is calculated. CCPs and bilateral clearing are discussed in more detail in Chapter 2.

Large banks often act as market makers for the more commonly traded instruments. This means that they are always prepared to quote a bid price (at which they are prepared to take one side of a derivatives transaction) and an offer price (at which they are prepared to take the other side).

Prior to the credit crisis, which started in 2007 and is discussed in some detail in Chapter 8, OTC derivatives markets were largely unregulated. Following the credit crisis and the failure of Lehman Brothers (see Business Snapshot 1.1), we have seen the development of many new regulations affecting the operation of OTC markets. The main objectives of the regulations are to improve the transparency of OTC markets and reduce systemic risk (see Business Snapshot 1.2). The over-the-counter market in some respects is being forced to become more like the exchange-traded market. Three important changes are:

1. Standardized OTC derivatives between two financial institutions in the United States must, whenever possible, be traded on what are referred to a *swap execution*

Business Snapshot 1.1   The Lehman Bankruptcy

On September 15, 2008, Lehman Brothers filed for bankruptcy. This was the largest bankruptcy in U.S. history and its ramifications were felt throughout derivatives markets. Almost until the end, it seemed as though there was a good chance that Lehman would survive. A number of companies (e.g., the Korean Development Bank, Barclays Bank in the United Kingdom, and Bank of America) expressed interest in buying it, but none of these was able to close a deal. Many people thought that Lehman was "too big to fail" and that the U.S. government would have to bail it out if no purchaser could be found. This proved not to be the case.

How did this happen? It was a combination of high leverage, risky investments, and liquidity problems. Commercial banks that take deposits are subject to regulations on the amount of capital they must keep. Lehman was an investment bank and not subject to these regulations. By 2007, its leverage ratio had increased to 31:1, which means that a 3–4% decline in the value of its assets would wipe out its capital. Dick Fuld, Lehman's Chairman and Chief Executive Officer, encouraged an aggressive deal-making, risk-taking culture. He is reported to have told his executives: "Every day is a battle. You have to kill the enemy." The Chief Risk Officer at Lehman was competent, but did not have much influence and was even removed from the executive committee in 2007. The risks taken by Lehman included large positions in the instruments created from subprime mortgages, which will be described in Chapter 8. Lehman funded much of its operations with short-term debt. When there was a loss of confidence in the company, lenders refused to renew this funding, forcing it into bankruptcy.

Lehman was very active in the over-the-counter derivatives markets. It had over a million transactions outstanding with about 8,000 different counterparties. Lehman's counterparties were often required to post collateral and this collateral had in many cases been used by Lehman for various purposes. Litigation aimed at determining who owes what to whom continued for many years after the bankruptcy filing.

---

facilities (SEFs). These are platforms similar to exchanges where market participants can post bid and offer quotes and where market participants can trade by accepting the quotes of other market participants.

2. There is a requirement in most parts of the world that a CCP be used for most standardized derivatives transactions between financial institutions.

3. All trades must be reported to a central repository.

Market Size

Both the over-the-counter and the exchange-traded market for derivatives are huge. The number of derivatives transactions per year in OTC markets is smaller than in exchange-traded markets, but the average size of the transactions is much greater. Although the statistics that are collected for the two markets are not exactly comparable, it is clear that the volume of business in the over-the-counter market is much larger than in the exchange-traded market. The Bank for International Settlements (www.bis.org) started collecting statistics on the markets in 1998. Figure 1.1 compares (a) the estimated total

---

Business Snapshot 1.2 Systemic Risk

Systemic risk is the risk that a default by one financial institution will create a "ripple effect" that leads to defaults by other financial institutions and threatens the stability of the financial system. There are huge numbers of over-the-counter transactions between banks. If Bank A fails, Bank B may take a huge loss on the transactions it has with Bank A. This in turn could lead to Bank B failing. Bank C that has many outstanding transactions with both Bank A and Bank B might then take a large loss and experience severe financial difficulties; and so on.

The financial system has survived defaults such as Drexel in 1990 and Lehman Brothers in 2008, but regulators continue to be concerned. During the market turmoil of 2007 and 2008, many large financial institutions were bailed out, rather than being allowed to fail, because governments were concerned about systemic risk.

---

principal amounts underlying transactions that were outstanding in the over-the counter markets between June 1998 and December 2015 and (b) the estimated total value of the assets underlying exchange-traded contracts during the same period. Using these measures, the size of the over-the-counter market in December 2015 was $492.9 trillion and the size of the exchange-traded market was $63.3 trillion.[1] Figure 1.1 shows that the OTC market grew rapidly up to 2007, but has seen very little net growth since then. One reason for the lack of growth is the popularity of *compression*. This is a procedure where two or more counterparties restructure transactions with each other with the result that the underlying principal is reduced.

In interpreting Figure 1.1, we should bear in mind that the principal underlying an over-the-counter transaction is not the same as its value. An example of an over-the-counter transaction is an agreement to buy 100 million U.S. dollars with British pounds

Figure 1.1 Size of over-the-counter and exchange-traded derivatives markets.

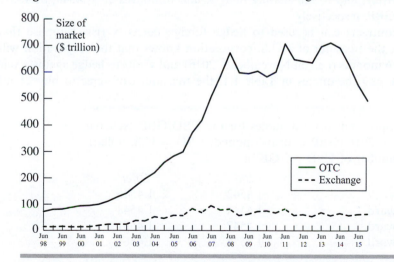

---

[1] When a CCP stands between two sides in an OTC transaction, two transactions are considered to have been created for the purposes of the BIS statistics.

at a predetermined exchange rate in 1 year. The total principal amount underlying this transaction is $100 million. However, the value of the transaction might be only $1 million. The Bank for International Settlements estimates the gross market value of all over-the-counter transactions outstanding in December 2015 to be about $14.5 trillion.[2]

1.3 FORWARD CONTRACTS

A relatively simple derivative is a *forward contract*. It is an agreement to buy or sell an asset at a certain future time for a certain price. It can be contrasted with a *spot contract*, which is an agreement to buy or sell an asset almost immediately. A forward contract is traded in the over-the-counter market—usually between two financial institutions or between a financial institution and one of its clients.

One of the parties to a forward contract assumes a *long position* and agrees to buy the underlying asset on a certain specified future date for a certain specified price. The other party assumes a *short position* and agrees to sell the asset on the same date for the same price.

Forward contracts on foreign exchange are very popular. Most large banks employ both spot and forward foreign-exchange traders. As we shall see in a later chapter, there is a relationship between forward prices, spot prices, and interest rates in the two currencies. Table 1.1 provides quotes for the exchange rate between the British pound (GBP) and the U.S. dollar (USD) that might be made by a large international bank on May 3, 2016. The quote is for the number of USD per GBP. The first row indicates that the bank is prepared to buy GBP (also known as sterling) in the spot market (i.e., for virtually immediate delivery) at the rate of $1.4542 per GBP and sell sterling in the spot market at $1.4546 per GBP. The second, third, and fourth rows indicate that the bank is prepared to buy sterling in 1, 3, and 6 months at $1.4544, $1.4547, and $1.4556 per GBP, respectively, and to sell sterling in 1, 3, and 6 months at $1.4548, $1.4551, and $1.4561 per GBP, respectively.

Forward contracts can be used to hedge foreign currency risk. Suppose that, on May 3, 2016, the treasurer of a U.S. corporation knows that the corporation will pay £1 million in 6 months (i.e., on November 3, 2016) and wants to hedge against exchange rate moves. Using the quotes in Table 1.1, the treasurer can agree to buy £1 million

Table 1.1 Spot and forward quotes for the USD/GBP exchange rate, May 3, 2016 (GBP = British pound; USD = U.S. dollar; quote is number of USD per GBP).

	Bid	*Offer*
Spot	1.4542	1.4546
1-month forward	1.4544	1.4548
3-month forward	1.4547	1.4551
6-month forward	1.4556	1.4561

---

[2] A contract that is worth $1 million to one side and −$1 million to the other side would be counted as having a gross market value of $1 million.

6 months forward at an exchange rate of 1.4561. The corporation then has a long forward contract on GBP. It has agreed that on November 3, 2016, it will buy £1 million from the bank for $1.4561 million. The bank has a short forward contract on GBP. It has agreed that on November 3, 2016, it will sell £1 million for $1.4561 million. Both sides have made a binding commitment.

Payoffs from Forward Contracts

Consider the position of the corporation in the trade we have just described. What are the possible outcomes? The forward contract obligates the corporation to buy £1 million for $1,456,100. If the spot exchange rate rose to, say, 1.5000, at the end of the 6 months, the forward contract would be worth $43,900 (= $1,500,000 − $1,456,100) to the corporation. It would enable £1 million to be purchased at an exchange rate of 1.4561 rather than 1.5000. Similarly, if the spot exchange rate fell to 1.4000 at the end of the 6 months, the forward contract would have a negative value to the corporation of $56,100 because it would lead to the corporation paying $56,100 more than the market price for the sterling.

In general, the payoff from a long position in a forward contract on one unit of an asset is

$$S_T - K$$

where K is the delivery price and S_T is the spot price of the asset at maturity of the contract. This is because the holder of the contract is obligated to buy an asset worth S_T for K. Similarly, the payoff from a short position in a forward contract on one unit of an asset is

$$K - S_T$$

These payoffs can be positive or negative. They are illustrated in Figure 1.2. Because it costs nothing to enter into a forward contract, the payoff from the contract is also the trader's total gain or loss from the contract.

Figure 1.2 Payoffs from forward contracts: (a) long position, (b) short position. Delivery price = K; price of asset at contract maturity = S_T.

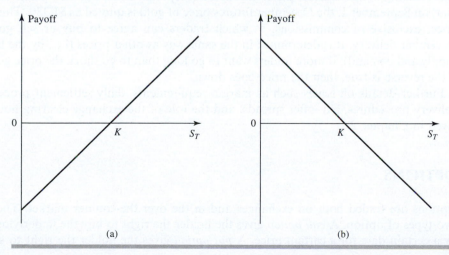

In the example just considered, $K = 1.4561$ and the corporation has a long contract. When $S_T = 1.5000$, the payoff is \$0.0439 per £1; when $S_T = 1.4000$, it is −\$0.0561 per £1.

Forward Prices and Spot Prices

We shall be discussing in some detail the relationship between spot and forward prices in Chapter 5. For a quick preview of why the two are related, consider a stock that pays no dividend and is worth \$60. You can borrow or lend money for 1 year at 5%. What should the 1-year forward price of the stock be?

The answer is \$60 grossed up at 5% for 1 year, or \$63. If the forward price is more than this, say \$67, you could borrow \$60, buy one share of the stock, and sell it forward for \$67. After paying off the loan, you would net a profit of \$4 in 1 year. If the forward price is less than \$63, say \$58, an investor owning the stock as part of a portfolio would sell the stock for \$60 and enter into a forward contract to buy it back for \$58 in 1 year. The proceeds of investment would be invested at 5% to earn \$3. The investor would end up \$5 better off than if the stock were kept in the portfolio for the year.

1.4 FUTURES CONTRACTS

Like a forward contract, a futures contract is an agreement between two parties to buy or sell an asset at a certain time in the future for a certain price. Unlike forward contracts, futures contracts are normally traded on an exchange. To make trading possible, the exchange specifies certain standardized features of the contract. As the two parties to the contract do not necessarily know each other, the exchange also provides a mechanism that gives the two parties a guarantee that the contract will be honored.

Two large exchanges on which futures contracts are traded are the Chicago Board of Trade (CBOT) and the Chicago Mercantile Exchange (CME), which have now merged to form the CME Group. On these and other exchanges throughout the world, a very wide range of commodities and financial assets form the underlying assets in the various contracts. The commodities include pork bellies, live cattle, sugar, wool, lumber, copper, aluminum, gold, and tin. The financial assets include stock indices, currencies, and Treasury bonds. Futures prices are regularly reported in the financial press. Suppose that, on September 1, the December futures price of gold is quoted as \$1,380. This is the price, exclusive of commissions, at which traders can agree to buy or sell gold for December delivery. It is determined in the same way as other prices (i.e., by the laws of supply and demand). If more traders want to go long than to go short, the price goes up; if the reverse is true, then the price goes down.

Further details on issues such as margin requirements, daily settlement procedures, delivery procedures, bid–offer spreads, and the role of the exchange clearing house are given in Chapter 2.

1.5 OPTIONS

Options are traded both on exchanges and in the over-the-counter market. There are two types of option. A *call option* gives the holder the right to buy the underlying asset by a certain date for a certain price. A *put option* gives the holder the right to sell the

Table 1.2 Prices of call options on Alphabet Inc. (Google), May 3, 2016; stock price: bid $695.86, offer $696.25 (*Source*: CBOE).

Strike price ($)	June 2016		September 2016		December 2016	
	Bid	Offer	Bid	Offer	Bid	Offer
660	43.40	45.10	60.80	62.70	72.70	76.70
680	29.20	30.60	47.70	50.70	60.90	64.70
700	18.30	18.90	37.00	39.20	49.70	52.50
720	9.90	10.50	27.50	29.50	40.10	42.80
740	4.70	5.20	19.80	21.60	31.40	34.40

underlying asset by a certain date for a certain price. The price in the contract is known as the *exercise price* or *strike price*; the date in the contract is known as the *expiration date* or *maturity*. *American options* can be exercised at any time up to the expiration date. *European options* can be exercised only on the expiration date itself.[3] Most of the options that are traded on exchanges are American. In the exchange-traded equity option market, one contract is usually an agreement to buy or sell 100 shares. European options are generally easier to analyze than American options, and some of the properties of an American option are frequently deduced from those of its European counterpart.

It should be emphasized that an option gives the holder the right to do something. The holder does not have to exercise this right. This is what distinguishes options from forwards and futures, where the holder is obligated to buy or sell the underlying asset. Whereas it costs nothing to enter into a forward or futures contract, except for margin requirements which will be discussed in Chapter 2, there is a cost to acquiring an option.

The largest exchange in the world for trading stock options is the Chicago Board Options Exchange (CBOE; www.cboe.com). Table 1.2 gives the bid and offer quotes for some of the call options trading on Google (ticker symbol: GOOG), which is now Alphabet Inc. Class C, on May 3, 2016. Table 1.3 does the same for put options trading

Table 1.3 Prices of put options on Alphabet Inc. (Google), May 3, 2016; stock price: bid $695.86, offer $696.25 (*Source*: CBOE).

Strike price ($)	June 2016		September 2016		December 2016	
	Bid	Offer	Bid	Offer	Bid	Offer
660	7.50	8.20	24.20	26.20	35.60	38.10
680	13.30	14.00	31.90	33.80	43.40	46.00
700	21.70	23.00	40.80	42.70	52.40	55.20
720	33.10	34.80	51.10	53.20	62.60	65.20
740	47.70	49.60	63.10	65.20	74.10	76.70

---

[3] Note that the terms *American* and *European* do not refer to the location of the option or the exchange. Some options trading on North American exchanges are European.

on Google on that date. The quotes are taken from the CBOE website. The Google stock price at the time of the quotes was bid 695.86, offer 696.25. The bid–offer spread for an option (as a percent of the price) is usually greater than that for the underlying stock and depends on the volume of trading. The option strike prices in Tables 1.2 and 1.3 are $660, $680, $700, $720, and $740. The maturities are June 2016, September 2016, and December 2016. The actual expiration day is the third Friday of the expiration month. The June options expire on June 17, 2016, the September options on September 16, 2016, and the December options on December 16, 2016.

The tables illustrate a number of properties of options. The price of a call option decreases as the strike price increases, while the price of a put option increases as the strike price increases. Both types of option tend to become more valuable as their time to maturity increases. These properties of options will be discussed further in Chapter 11.

Suppose a trader instructs a broker to buy one December call option contract on Google with a strike price of $700. The broker will relay these instructions to a trader at the CBOE and the deal will be done. The (offer) price indicated in Table 1.2 is $52.50. This is the price for an option to buy one share. In the United States, an option contract is a contract to buy or sell 100 shares. Therefore, the trader must arrange for $5,250 to be remitted to the exchange through the broker. The exchange will then arrange for this amount to be passed on to the party on the other side of the transaction.

In our example, the trader has obtained at a cost of $5,250 the right to buy 100 Google shares for $700 each. If the price of Google does not rise above $700 by December 16, 2016, the option is not exercised and the trader loses $5,250.[4] But if Google does well and the option is exercised when the bid price for the stock is $900, the trader is able to buy 100 shares at $700 and immediately sell them for $900 for a profit of $20,000, or $14,750 when the initial cost of the options is taken into account.[5]

An alternative trade would be to sell one September put option contract with a strike price of $660 at the bid price of $24.20. The trader receives $100 \times 24.20 = \$2,420$. If the Google stock price stays above $660, the option is not exercised and the trader makes a $2,420 profit. However, if stock price falls and the option is exercised when the stock price is $600, there is a loss. The trader must buy 100 shares at $660 when they are worth only $600. This leads to a loss of $6,000, or $3,580 when the initial amount received for the option contract is taken into account.

The stock options trading on the CBOE are American. If we assume for simplicity that they are European, so that they can be exercised only at maturity, the trader's profit as a function of the final stock price for the two trades we have considered is shown in Figure 1.3.

Further details about the operation of options markets and how prices such as those in Tables 1.2 and 1.3 are determined by traders are given in later chapters. At this stage we note that there are four types of participants in options markets:

1. Buyers of calls

2. Sellers of calls

3. Buyers of puts

4. Sellers of puts.

---

[4] The calculations here ignore any commissions paid by the trader.

[5] The calculations here ignore the effect of discounting. Theoretically, the $20,000 should be discounted from the time of exercise to the purchase date, when calculating the profit.

Figure 1.3   Net profit from (a) purchasing a contract consisting of 100 Google December call options with a strike price of $700 and (b) selling a contract consisting of 100 Google September put options with a strike price of $660.

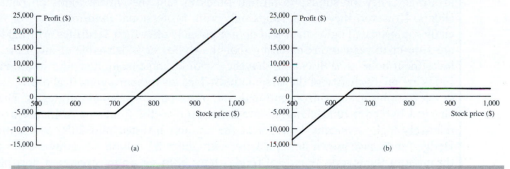

(a)   (b)

Buyers are referred to as having *long positions*; sellers are referred to as having *short positions*. Selling an option is also known as *writing the option*.

1.6   TYPES OF TRADERS

Derivatives markets have been outstandingly successful. The main reason is that they have attracted many different types of traders and have a great deal of liquidity. When a trader wants to take one side of a contract, there is usually no problem in finding someone who is prepared to take the other side.

Three broad categories of traders can be identified: hedgers, speculators, and arbitrageurs. Hedgers use derivatives to reduce the risk that they face from potential future movements in a market variable. Speculators use them to bet on the future direction of a market variable. Arbitrageurs take offsetting positions in two or more instruments to lock in a profit. As described in Business Snapshot 1.3, hedge funds have become big users of derivatives for all three purposes.

In the next few sections, we will consider the activities of each type of trader in more detail.

1.7   HEDGERS

In this section we illustrate how hedgers can reduce their risks with forward contracts and options.

Hedging Using Forward Contracts

Suppose that it is May 3, 2016, and ImportCo, a company based in the United States, knows that it will have to pay £10 million on August 3, 2016, for goods it has purchased from a British supplier. The USD–GBP exchange rate quotes made by a financial institution are shown in Table 1.1. ImportCo could hedge its foreign exchange risk by buying pounds (GBP) from the financial institution in the 3-month forward market

---

Business Snapshot 1.3   Hedge Funds

Hedge funds have become major users of derivatives for hedging, speculation, and arbitrage. They are similar to mutual funds in that they invest funds on behalf of clients. However, they accept funds only from professional fund managers or financially sophisticated individuals and do not publicly offer their securities. Mutual funds are subject to regulations requiring that the shares be redeemable at any time, that investment policies be disclosed, that the use of leverage be limited, and so on. Hedge funds are relatively free of these regulations. This gives them a great deal of freedom to develop sophisticated, unconventional, and proprietary investment strategies. The fees charged by hedge fund managers are dependent on the fund's performance and are relatively high—typically 1 to 2% of the amount invested plus 20% of the profits. Hedge funds have grown in popularity, with about $2 trillion being invested in them throughout the world. "Funds of funds" have been set up to invest in a portfolio of hedge funds.

The investment strategy followed by a hedge fund manager often involves using derivatives to set up a speculative or arbitrage position. Once the strategy has been defined, the hedge fund manager must:

1. Evaluate the risks to which the fund is exposed
2. Decide which risks are acceptable and which will be hedged
3. Devise strategies (usually involving derivatives) to hedge the unacceptable risks.

Here are some examples of the labels used for hedge funds together with the trading strategies followed:

Long/Short Equities: Purchase securities considered to be undervalued and short those considered to be overvalued in such a way that the exposure to the overall direction of the market is small.

Convertible Arbitrage: Take a long position in a thought-to-be-undervalued convertible bond combined with an actively managed short position in the underlying equity.

Distressed Securities: Buy securities issued by companies in, or close to, bankruptcy.

Emerging Markets: Invest in debt and equity of companies in developing or emerging countries and in the debt of the countries themselves.

Global Macro: Carry out trades that reflect anticipated global macroeconomic trends.

Merger Arbitrage: Trade after a possible merger or acquisition is announced so that a profit is made if the announced deal takes place.

---

at 1.4551. This would have the effect of fixing the price to be paid to the British exporter at $14,551,000.

Consider next another U.S. company, which we will refer to as ExportCo, that is exporting goods to the United Kingdom and, on May 3, 2016, knows that it will receive £30 million 3 months later. ExportCo can hedge its foreign exchange risk by selling £30 million in the 3-month forward market at an exchange rate of 1.4547. This would have the effect of locking in the U.S. dollars to be realized for the sterling at $43,641,000.

Note that a company might do better if it chooses not to hedge than if it chooses to hedge. Alternatively, it might do worse. Consider ImportCo. If the exchange rate is

1.4000 on August 3 and the company has not hedged, the £10 million that it has to pay will cost $14,000,000, which is less than $14,551,000. On the other hand, if the exchange rate is 1.5000, the £10 million will cost $15,000,000—and the company will wish that it had hedged! The position of ExportCo if it does not hedge is the reverse. If the exchange rate in August proves to be less than 1.4547, the company will wish that it had hedged; if the rate is greater than 1.4547, it will be pleased that it has not done so.

This example illustrates a key aspect of hedging. The purpose of hedging is to reduce risk. There is no guarantee that the outcome with hedging will be better than the outcome without hedging.

Hedging Using Options

Options can also be used for hedging. Consider an investor who in May of a particular year owns 1,000 shares of a particular company. The share price is $28 per share. The investor is concerned about a possible share price decline in the next 2 months and wants protection. The investor could buy ten July put option contracts on the company's stock with a strike price of $27.50. Each contract is on 100 shares, so this would give the investor the right to sell a total of 1,000 shares for a price of $27.50. If the quoted option price is $1, then each option contract would cost $100 \times \$1 = \$100$ and the total cost of the hedging strategy would be $10 \times \$100 = \$1,000$.

The strategy costs $1,000 but guarantees that the shares can be sold for at least $27.50 per share during the life of the option. If the market price of the stock falls below $27.50, the options will be exercised, so that $27,500 is realized for the entire holding. When the cost of the options is taken into account, the amount realized is $26,500. If the market price stays above $27.50, the options are not exercised and expire worthless. However, in this case the value of the holding is always above $27,500 (or above $26,500 when the cost of the options is taken into account). Figure 1.4 shows the net value of the portfolio (after taking the cost of the options into account) as a function of the stock price in 2 months. The dotted line shows the value of the portfolio assuming no hedging.

Figure 1.4 Value of the stock holding in 2 months with and without hedging.

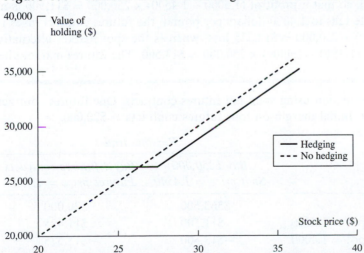

A Comparison

There is a fundamental difference between the use of forward contracts and options for hedging. Forward contracts are designed to neutralize risk by fixing the price that the hedger will pay or receive for the underlying asset. Option contracts, by contrast, provide insurance. They offer a way for investors to protect themselves against adverse price movements in the future while still allowing them to benefit from favorable price movements. Unlike forwards, options involve the payment of an up-front fee.

1.8 SPECULATORS

We now move on to consider how futures and options markets can be used by speculators. Whereas hedgers want to avoid exposure to adverse movements in the price of an asset, speculators wish to take a position in the market. Either they are betting that the price of the asset will go up or they are betting that it will go down.

Speculation Using Futures

Consider a U.S. speculator who in February thinks that the British pound will strengthen relative to the U.S. dollar over the next 2 months and is prepared to back that hunch to the tune of £250,000. One thing the speculator can do is purchase £250,000 in the spot market in the hope that the sterling can be sold later at a higher price. (The sterling once purchased would be kept in an interest-bearing account.) Another possibility is to take a long position in four CME April futures contracts on sterling. (Each futures contract is for the purchase of £62,500 in April.) Table 1.4 summarizes the two alternatives on the assumption that the current exchange rate is 1.4540 dollars per pound and the April futures price is 1.4543 dollars per pound. If the exchange rate turns out to be 1.5000 dollars per pound in April, the futures contract alternative enables the speculator to realize a profit of $(1.5000 - 1.4543) \times 250,000 = \$11,425$. The spot market alternative leads to 250,000 units of an asset being purchased for $1.4540 in February and sold for $1.5000 in April, so that a profit of $(1.5000 - 1.4540) \times 250,000 = \$11,500$ is made. If the exchange rate falls to 1.4000 dollars per pound, the futures contract gives rise to a $(1.4543 - 1.4000) \times 250,000 = \$13,575$ loss, whereas the spot market alternative gives rise to a loss of $(1.4540 - 1.4000) \times 250,000 = \$13,500$. The futures market alternative

Table 1.4 Speculation using spot and futures contracts. One futures contract is on £62,500. Initial margin on four futures contracts = $20,000.

	Possible trades	
	Buy £250,000 *Spot price = 1.4540*	*Buy 4 futures contracts* *Futures price = 1.4543*
Investment	$363,500	$20,000
Profit if April spot = 1.5000	$11,500	$11,425
Profit if April spot = 1.4000	−$13,500	−$13,575

appears to give rise to slightly worse outcomes for both scenarios. But this is because the calculations do not reflect the interest that is earned or paid.

What then is the difference between the two alternatives? The first alternative of buying sterling requires an up-front investment of $250,000 \times 1.4540 = \$363,500$. In contrast, the second alternative requires only a small amount of cash to be deposited by the speculator in what is termed a "margin account". (The operation of margin accounts is explained in Chapter 2.) In Table 1.4, the initial margin requirement is assumed to be $5,000 per contract, or $20,000 in total. The futures market allows the speculator to obtain leverage. With a relatively small initial outlay, a large speculative position can be taken.

Speculation Using Options

Options can also be used for speculation. Suppose that it is October and a speculator considers that a stock is likely to increase in value over the next 2 months. The stock price is currently $20, and a 2-month call option with a $22.50 strike price is currently selling for $1. Table 1.5 illustrates two possible alternatives, assuming that the speculator is willing to invest $2,000. One alternative is to purchase 100 shares; the other involves the purchase of 2,000 call options (i.e., 20 call option contracts). Suppose that the speculator's hunch is correct and the price of the stock rises to $27 by December. The first alternative of buying the stock yields a profit of

$$100 \times (\$27 - \$20) = \$700$$

However, the second alternative is far more profitable. A call option on the stock with a strike price of $22.50 gives a payoff of $4.50, because it enables something worth $27 to be bought for $22.50. The total payoff from the 2,000 options that are purchased under the second alternative is

$$2,000 \times \$4.50 = \$9,000$$

Subtracting the original cost of the options yields a net profit of

$$\$9,000 - \$2,000 = \$7,000$$

The options strategy is, therefore, 10 times more profitable than directly buying the stock.

Options also give rise to a greater potential loss. Suppose the stock price falls to $15 by December. The first alternative of buying stock yields a loss of

$$100 \times (\$20 - \$15) = \$500$$

Table 1.5 Comparison of profits from two alternative strategies for using $2,000 to speculate on a stock worth $20 in October.

	December stock price	
Speculator's strategy	*$15*	*$27*
Buy 100 shares	−$500	$700
Buy 2,000 call options	−$2,000	$7,000

Figure 1.5 Profit or loss from two alternative strategies for speculating on a stock currently worth $20.

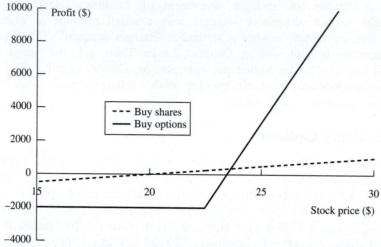

Because the call options expire without being exercised, the options strategy would lead to a loss of $2,000—the original amount paid for the options. Figure 1.5 shows the profit or loss from the two strategies as a function of the stock price in 2 months.

Options like futures provide a form of leverage. For a given investment, the use of options magnifies the financial consequences. Good outcomes become very good, while bad outcomes result in the whole initial investment being lost.

A Comparison

Futures and options are similar instruments for speculators in that they both provide a way in which a type of leverage can be obtained. However, there is an important difference between the two. When a speculator uses futures, the potential loss as well as the potential gain is very large. When options are used, no matter how bad things get, the speculator's loss is limited to the amount paid for the options.

1.9   ARBITRAGEURS

Arbitrageurs are a third important group of participants in futures, forward, and options markets. Arbitrage involves locking in a riskless profit by simultaneously entering into transactions in two or more markets. In later chapters we will see how arbitrage is sometimes possible when the futures price of an asset gets out of line with its spot price. We will also examine how arbitrage can be used in options markets. This section illustrates the concept of arbitrage with a very simple example.

Let us consider a stock that is traded on both the New York Stock Exchange (www.nyse.com) and the London Stock Exchange (www.londonstockexchange.com). Suppose that the stock price is $140 in New York and £100 in London at a time when the exchange rate is \$1.4300 per pound. An arbitrageur could simultaneously buy 100 shares of the stock in New York and sell them in London to obtain a risk-free profit of

$$100 \times [(\$1.43 \times 100) - \$140]$$

or \$300 in the absence of transactions costs. Transactions costs would probably eliminate the profit for a small trader. However, a large investment bank faces very low transactions costs in both the stock market and the foreign exchange market. It would find the arbitrage opportunity very attractive and would try to take as much advantage of it as possible.

Arbitrage opportunities such as the one just described cannot last for long. As arbitrageurs buy the stock in New York, the forces of supply and demand will cause the dollar price to rise. Similarly, as they sell the stock in London, the sterling price will be driven down. Very quickly the two prices will become equivalent at the current exchange rate. Indeed, the existence of profit-hungry arbitrageurs makes it unlikely that a major disparity between the sterling price and the dollar price could ever exist in the first place. Generalizing from this example, we can say that the very existence of arbitrageurs means that in practice only very small arbitrage opportunities are observed in the prices that are quoted in most financial markets. In this book most of the arguments concerning futures prices, forward prices, and the values of option contracts will be based on the assumption that no arbitrage opportunities exist.

1.10 DANGERS

Derivatives are very versatile instruments. As we have seen, they can be used for hedging, for speculation, and for arbitrage. It is this very versatility that can cause problems. Sometimes traders who have a mandate to hedge risks or follow an arbitrage strategy become (consciously or unconsciously) speculators. The results can be disastrous. One example of this is provided by the activities of Jérôme Kerviel at Société Général (see Business Snapshot 1.4).

To avoid the sort of problems Société Général encountered, it is very important for both financial and nonfinancial corporations to set up controls to ensure that derivatives are being used for their intended purpose. Risk limits should be set and the activities of traders should be monitored daily to ensure that these risk limits are adhered to.

Unfortunately, even when traders follow the risk limits that have been specified, big mistakes can happen. Some of the activities of traders in the derivatives market during the period leading up to the start of the credit crisis in July 2007 proved to be much riskier than they were thought to be by the financial institutions they worked for. As will be discussed in Chapter 8, house prices in the United States had been rising fast. Most people thought that the increases would continue—or, at worst, that house prices would simply level off. Very few were prepared for the steep decline that actually happened. Furthermore, very few were prepared for the high correlation between mortgage default rates in different parts of the country. Some risk managers did express reservations about the exposures of the companies for which they worked to the U.S. real estate market. But, when times are good (or appear to be good), there is an unfortunate tendency to ignore risk managers and this is what happened at many

---

Business Snapshot 1.4 SocGen's Big Loss in 2008

Derivatives are very versatile instruments. They can be used for hedging, speculation, and arbitrage. One of the risks faced by a company that trades derivatives is that an employee who has a mandate to hedge or to look for arbitrage opportunities may become a speculator.

Jérôme Kerviel joined Société Général (SocGen) in 2000 to work in the compliance area. In 2005, he was promoted and became a junior trader in the bank's Delta One products team. He traded equity indices such as the German DAX index, the French CAC 40, and the Euro Stoxx 50. His job was to look for arbitrage opportunities. These might arise if a futures contract on an equity index was trading for a different price on two different exchanges. They might also arise if equity index futures prices were not consistent with the prices of the shares constituting the index. (This type of arbitrage is discussed in Chapter 5.)

Kerviel used his knowledge of the bank's procedures to speculate while giving the appearance of arbitraging. He took big positions in equity indices and created fictitious trades to make it appear that he was hedged. In reality, he had large bets on the direction in which the indices would move. The size of his unhedged position grew over time to tens of billions of euros.

In January 2008, his unauthorized trading was uncovered by SocGen. Over a three-day period, the bank unwound his position for a loss of 4.9 billion euros. This was at the time the biggest loss created by fraudulent activity in the history of finance. (Later in the year, a much bigger loss from Bernard Madoff's Ponzi scheme came to light.)

Rogue trader losses were not unknown at banks prior to 2008. For example, in the 1990s, Nick Leeson, who worked at Barings Bank, had a mandate similar to that of Jérôme Kerviel. His job was to arbitrage between Nikkei 225 futures quotes in Singapore and Osaka. Instead he found a way to make big bets on the direction of the Nikkei 225 using futures and options, losing $1 billion and destroying the 200-year old bank in the process. In 2002, it was found that John Rusnak at Allied Irish Bank had lost $700 million from unauthorized foreign exchange trading. The lessons from these losses are that it is important to define unambiguous risk limits for traders and then to monitor what they do very carefully to make sure that the limits are adhered to.

---

financial institutions during the 2006–2007 period. The key lesson from the credit crisis is that financial institutions should always be dispassionately asking "What can go wrong?", and they should follow that up with the question "If it does go wrong, how much will we lose?"

SUMMARY

One of the exciting developments in finance over the last 40 years has been the growth of derivatives markets. In many situations, both hedgers and speculators find it more attractive to trade a derivative on an asset than to trade the asset itself. Some derivatives are traded on exchanges; others are traded by financial institutions, fund managers, and corporations in the over-the-counter market, or added to new issues of debt and equity securities. Much of this book is concerned with the valuation of derivatives. The aim is to present a unifying framework within which all derivatives—not just options or futures—can be valued.

In this chapter we have taken a first look at forward, futures, and option contracts. A forward or futures contract involves an obligation to buy or sell an asset at a certain time in the future for a certain price. There are two types of options: calls and puts. A call option gives the holder the right to buy an asset by a certain date for a certain price. A put option gives the holder the right to sell an asset by a certain date for a certain price. Forwards, futures, and options trade on a wide range of different underlying assets.

The success of derivatives can be attributed to their versatility. They can be used by: hedgers, speculators, and arbitrageurs. Hedgers are in the position where they face risk associated with the price of an asset. They use derivatives to reduce or eliminate this risk. Speculators wish to bet on future movements in the price of an asset. They use derivatives to get extra leverage. Arbitrageurs are in business to take advantage of a discrepancy between prices in two different markets. If, for example, they see the futures price of an asset getting out of line with the cash price, they will take offsetting positions in the two markets to lock in a profit.

FURTHER READING

Chancellor, E. *Devil Take the Hindmost—A History of Financial Speculation*. New York: Farra Straus Giroux, 2000.

Merton, R. C. "Finance Theory and Future Trends: The Shift to Integration," *Risk*, 12, 7 (July 1999): 48–51.

Miller, M. H. "Financial Innovation: Achievements and Prospects," *Journal of Applied Corporate Finance*, 4 (Winter 1992): 4–11.

Zingales, L., "Causes and Effects of the Lehman Bankruptcy," Testimony before Committee on Oversight and Government Reform, United States House of Representatives, October 6, 2008.

Practice Questions (Answers in Solutions Manual)

1.1. What is the difference between a long forward position and a short forward position?

1.2. Explain carefully the difference between hedging, speculation, and arbitrage.

1.3. What is the difference between entering into a long forward contract when the forward price is $50 and taking a long position in a call option with a strike price of $50?

1.4. Explain carefully the difference between selling a call option and buying a put option.

1.5. An investor enters into a short forward contract to sell 100,000 British pounds for U.S. dollars at an exchange rate of 1.5000 USD per pound. How much does the investor gain or lose if the exchange rate at the end of the contract is (a) 1.4900 and (b) 1.5200?

1.6. A trader enters into a short cotton futures contract when the futures price is 50 cents per pound. The contract is for the delivery of 50,000 pounds. How much does the trader gain or lose if the cotton price at the end of the contract is (a) 48.20 cents per pound and (b) 51.30 cents per pound?

1.7. Suppose that you write a put contract with a strike price of $40 and an expiration date in 3 months. The current stock price is $41 and the contract is on 100 shares. What have you committed yourself to? How much could you gain or lose?

1.8. What is the difference between the over-the-counter market and the exchange-traded market? What are the bid and offer quotes of a market maker in the over-the-counter or exchange-traded market?

1.9. You would like to speculate on a rise in the price of a certain stock. The current stock price is $29 and a 3-month call with a strike price of $30 costs $2.90. You have $5,800 to invest. Identify two alternative investment strategies, one in the stock and the other in an option on the stock. What are the potential gains and losses from each?

1.10. Suppose that you own 5,000 shares worth $25 each. How can put options be used to provide you with insurance against a decline in the value of your holding over the next 4 months?

1.11. When first issued, a stock provides funds for a company. Is the same true of a stock option? Discuss.

1.12. Explain why a futures contract can be used for either speculation or hedging.

1.13. Suppose that a March call option to buy a share for $50 costs $2.50 and is held until March. Under what circumstances will the holder of the option make a profit? Under what circumstances will the option be exercised? Draw a diagram illustrating how the profit from a long position in the option depends on the stock price at maturity of the option.

1.14. Suppose that a June put option to sell a share for $60 costs $4 and is held until June. Under what circumstances will the seller of the option (i.e., the party with the short position) make a profit? Under what circumstances will the option be exercised? Draw a diagram illustrating how the profit from a short position in the option depends on the stock price at maturity of the option.

1.15. It is May and a trader writes a September call option with a strike price of $20. The stock price is $18 and the option price is $2. Describe the trader's cash flows if the option is held until September and the stock price is $25 at that time.

1.16. A trader writes a December put option with a strike price of $30. The price of the option is $4. Under what circumstances does the trader make a gain?

1.17. A company knows that it is due to receive a certain amount of a foreign currency in 4 months. What type of option contract is appropriate for hedging?

1.18. A U.S. company expects to have to pay 1 million Canadian dollars in 6 months. Explain how the exchange rate risk can be hedged using (a) a forward contract and (b) an option.

1.19. A trader enters into a short forward contract on 100 million yen. The forward exchange rate is $0.0090 per yen. How much does the trader gain or lose if the exchange rate at the end of the contract is (a) $0.0084 per yen and (b) $0.0101 per yen?

1.20. The CME Group offers a futures contract on long-term Treasury bonds. Characterize the traders likely to use this contract.

1.21. "Options and futures are zero-sum games." What do you think is meant by this?

1.22. Describe the profit from the following portfolio: a long forward contract on an asset and a long European put option on the asset with the same maturity as the forward contract and a strike price that is equal to the forward price of the asset at the time the portfolio is set up.

1.23. In the 1980s, Bankers Trust developed *index currency option notes* (ICONs). These were bonds in which the amount received by the holder at maturity varied with a foreign exchange rate. One example was its trade with the Long Term Credit Bank of Japan. The ICON specified that if the yen–USD exchange rate, S_T, is greater than 169 yen per dollar at maturity (in 1995), the holder of the bond receives $1,000. If it is less than 169 yen per dollar, the amount received by the holder of the bond is

$$1,000 - \max\left[0, \; 1,000\left(\frac{169}{S_T} - 1\right)\right]$$

When the exchange rate is below 84.5, nothing is received by the holder at maturity. Show that this ICON is a combination of a regular bond and two options.

1.24. On July 1, 2017, a company enters into a forward contract to buy 10 million Japanese yen on January 1, 2018. On September 1, 2017, it enters into a forward contract to sell 10 million Japanese yen on January 1, 2018. Describe the payoff from this strategy.

1.25. Suppose that USD/sterling spot and forward exchange rates are as follows:

Spot	1.5580
90-day forward	1.5556
180-day forward	1.5518

What opportunities are open to an arbitrageur in the following situations?
(a) A 180-day European call option to buy £1 for $1.52 costs 2 cents.
(b) A 90-day European put option to sell £1 for $1.59 costs 2 cents.

1.26. A trader buys a call option with a strike price of $30 for $3. Does the trader ever exercise the option and lose money on the trade? Explain your answer.

1.27. A trader sells a put option with a strike price of $40 for $5. What is the trader's maximum gain and maximum loss? How does your answer change if it is a call option?

1.28. "Buying a put option on a stock when the stock is owned is a form of insurance." Explain this statement.

Further Questions

1.29. On May 3, 2016, as indicated in Table 1.2, the spot offer price of Google stock is $696.25 and the offer price of a call option with a strike price of $700 and a maturity date of September is $39.20. A trader is considering two alternatives: buy 100 shares of the stock and buy 100 September call options. For each alternative, what is (a) the upfront cost, (b) the total gain if the stock price in September is $800, and (c) the total loss if the stock price in September is $600. Assume that the option is not exercised before September and if the stock is purchased it is sold in September.

1.30. What is arbitrage? Explain the arbitrage opportunity when the price of a dually listed mining company stock is $50 (USD) on the New York Stock Exchange and $60 (CAD) on the Toronto Stock Exchange. Assume that the exchange rate is such that 1 U.S. dollar equals 1.21 Canadian dollars. Explain what is likely to happen to prices as traders take advantage of this opportunity.

1.31. Trader A enters into a forward contract to buy an asset for $1,000 in one year. Trader B buys a call option to buy the asset for $1,000 in one year. The cost of the option is $100. What is the difference between the positions of the traders? Show the profit as a function of the price of the asset in one year for the two traders.

1.32. In March, a U.S. investor instructs a broker to sell one July put option contract on a stock. The stock price is $42 and the strike price is $40. The option price is $3. Explain what the investor has agreed to. Under what circumstances will the trade prove to be profitable? What are the risks?

1.33. A U.S. company knows it will have to pay 3 million euros in three months. The current exchange rate is 1.1500 dollars per euro. Discuss how forward and options contracts can be used by the company to hedge its exposure.

1.34. A stock price is $29. A trader buys one call option contract on the stock with a strike price of $30 and sells a call option contract on the stock with a strike price of $32.50. The market prices of the options are $2.75 and $1.50, respectively. The options have the same maturity date. Describe the trader's position.

1.35. The price of gold is currently $1,200 per ounce. The forward price for delivery in 1 year is $1,300 per ounce. An arbitrageur can borrow money at 3% per annum. What should the arbitrageur do? Assume that the cost of storing gold is zero and that gold provides no income.

1.36. The current price of a stock is $94, and 3-month European call options with a strike price of $95 currently sell for $4.70. An investor who feels that the price of the stock will increase is trying to decide between buying 100 shares and buying 2,000 call options (= 20 contracts). Both strategies involve an investment of $9,400. What advice would you give? How high does the stock price have to rise for the option strategy to be more profitable?

1.37. On May 3, 2016, an investor owns 100 Google shares. As indicated in Table 1.3, the share price is about $696 and a December put option with a strike price of $660 costs $38.10. The investor is comparing two alternatives to limit downside risk. The first involves buying one December put option contract with a strike price of $660. The second involves instructing a broker to sell the 100 shares as soon as Google's price reaches $660. Discuss the advantages and disadvantages of the two strategies.

1.38. A bond issued by Standard Oil some time ago worked as follows. The holder received no interest. At the bond's maturity the company promised to pay $1,000 plus an additional amount based on the price of oil at that time. The additional amount was equal to the product of 170 and the excess (if any) of the price of a barrel of oil at maturity over $25. The maximum additional amount paid was $2,550 (which corresponds to a price of $40 per barrel). Show that the bond is a combination of a regular bond, a long position in call options on oil with a strike price of $25, and a short position in call options on oil with a strike price of $40.

1.39. Suppose that in the situation of Table 1.1 a corporate treasurer said: "I will have £1 million to sell in 6 months. If the exchange rate is less than 1.42, I want you to give me 1.42. If it is greater than 1.48, I will accept 1.48. If the exchange rate is between 1.42 and 1.48, I will sell the sterling for the exchange rate." How could you use options to satisfy the treasurer?

1.40. Describe how foreign currency options can be used for hedging in the situation considered in Section 1.7 so that (a) ImportCo is guaranteed that its exchange rate will be less than 1.4700, and (b) ExportCo is guaranteed that its exchange rate will be at least 1.4300. Use DerivaGem to calculate the cost of setting up the hedge in each case assuming that the exchange rate volatility is 12%, interest rates in the United States are 2%, and interest rates in Britain are 1%. Assume that the current exchange rate is the average of the bid and offer in Table 1.1.

1.41. A trader buys a European call option and sells a European put option. The options have the same underlying asset, strike price, and maturity. Describe the trader's position. Under what circumstances does the price of the call equal the price of the put?

2

Futures Markets and Central Counterparties

In Chapter 1 we explained that both futures and forward contracts are agreements to buy or sell an asset at a future time for a certain price. A futures contract is traded on an exchange, and the contract terms are standardized by that exchange. A forward contract is traded in the over-the-counter market and can be customized to meet the needs of users.

This chapter covers the details of how futures markets work. We examine issues such as the specification of contracts, the operation of margin accounts, the organization of exchanges, the regulation of markets, the way in which quotes are made, and the treatment of futures transactions for accounting and tax purposes. We explain how some of the ideas pioneered by futures exchanges have been adopted by over-the-counter markets.

2.1 BACKGROUND

As we saw in Chapter 1, futures contracts are now traded actively all over the world. The Chicago Board of Trade, the Chicago Mercantile Exchange, and the New York Mercantile Exchange have merged to form the CME Group (www.cmegroup.com). Other large exchanges include the InterContinental Exchange (www.theice.com), Eurex (www.eurexchange.com), BM&F BOVESPA (www.bmfbovespa.com.br), and the Tokyo Financial Exchange (www.tfx.co.jp). A table at the end of this book provides a more complete list of exchanges.

We examine how a futures contract comes into existence by considering the corn futures contract traded by the CME Group. On June 5 a trader in New York might call a broker with instructions to buy 5,000 bushels of corn for delivery in September of the same year. The broker would immediately issue instructions to a trader to buy (i.e., take a long position in) one September corn contract. (Each corn contract is for the delivery of exactly 5,000 bushels.) At about the same time, another trader in Kansas might instruct a broker to sell 5,000 bushels of corn for September delivery. This broker would then issue instructions to sell (i.e., take a short position in) one corn contract. A price would be determined and the deal would be done. Under the traditional open outcry system, floor traders representing each party would physically meet to determine the price. With electronic trading, a computer matches the traders.

24

Business Snapshot 2.1 The Unanticipated Delivery of a Futures Contract

This story (which may well be apocryphal) was told to the author of this book a long time ago by a senior executive of a financial institution. It concerns a new employee of the financial institution who had not previously worked in the financial sector. One of the clients of the financial institution regularly entered into a long futures contract on live cattle for hedging purposes and issued instructions to close out the position on the last day of trading. (Live cattle futures contracts are traded by the CME Group and each contract is on 40,000 pounds of cattle.) The new employee was given responsibility for handling the account.

When the time came to close out a contract the employee noted that the client was long one contract and instructed a trader at the exchange to buy (not sell) one contract. The result of this mistake was that the financial institution ended up with a long position in two live cattle futures contracts. By the time the mistake was spotted trading in the contract had ceased.

The financial institution (not the client) was responsible for the mistake. As a result, it started to look into the details of the delivery arrangements for live cattle futures contracts—something it had never done before. Under the terms of the contract, cattle could be delivered by the party with the short position to a number of different locations in the United States during the delivery month. Because it was long, the financial institution could do nothing but wait for a party with a short position to issue a *notice of intention to deliver* to the exchange and for the exchange to assign that notice to the financial institution.

It eventually received a notice from the exchange and found that it would receive live cattle at a location 2,000 miles away the following Tuesday. The new employee was sent to the location to handle things. It turned out that the location had a cattle auction every Tuesday. The party with the short position that was making delivery bought cattle at the auction and then immediately delivered them. Unfortunately the cattle could not be resold until the next cattle auction the following Tuesday. The employee was therefore faced with the problem of making arrangements for the cattle to be housed and fed for a week. This was a great start to a first job in the financial sector!

The trader in New York who agreed to buy has a *long futures position* in one contract; the trader in Kansas who agreed to sell has a *short futures position* in one contract. The price agreed to is the current *futures price* for September corn, say 600 cents per bushel. This price, like any other price, is determined by the laws of supply and demand. If, at a particular time, more traders wish to sell rather than buy September corn, the price will go down. New buyers then enter the market so that a balance between buyers and sellers is maintained. If more traders wish to buy rather than sell September corn, the price goes up. New sellers then enter the market and a balance between buyers and sellers is maintained.

Closing Out Positions

The vast majority of futures contracts do not lead to delivery. The reason is that most traders choose to close out their positions prior to the delivery period specified in the contract. Closing out a position means entering into the opposite trade to the original one. For example, the New York trader who bought a September corn futures contract on June 5 can close out the position by selling (i.e., shorting) one September corn futures contract on, say, July 20. The Kansas trader who sold (i.e., shorted) a September contract on June 5 can close out the position by buying one September contract on, say, August 25. In each case, the trader's total gain or loss is determined by the change in the futures price between June 5 and the day when the contract is closed out.

Delivery is so unusual that traders sometimes forget how the delivery process works (see Business Snapshot 2.1). Nevertheless, we will review delivery procedures later in this chapter. This is because it is the possibility of final delivery that ties the futures price to the spot price.[1]

2.2   SPECIFICATION OF A FUTURES CONTRACT

When developing a new contract, the exchange must specify in some detail the exact nature of the agreement between the two parties. In particular, it must specify the asset, the contract size (exactly how much of the asset will be delivered under one contract), where delivery can be made, and when delivery can be made.

Sometimes alternatives are specified for the grade of the asset that will be delivered or for the delivery locations. As a general rule, it is the party with the short position (the party that has agreed to sell the asset) that chooses what will happen when alternatives are specified by the exchange.[2] When the party with the short position is ready to deliver, it files a *notice of intention to deliver* with the exchange. This notice indicates any selections it has made with respect to the grade of asset that will be delivered and the delivery location.

The Asset

When the asset is a commodity, there may be quite a variation in the quality of what is available in the marketplace. When the asset is specified, it is therefore important that the exchange stipulate the grade or grades of the commodity that are acceptable. The IntercontinentalExchange (ICE) has specified the asset in its orange juice futures contract as frozen concentrates that are U.S. Grade A with Brix value of not less than 62.5 degrees.

For some commodities a range of grades can be delivered, but the price received depends on the grade chosen. For example, in the CME Group's corn futures contract, the standard grade is "No. 2 Yellow," but substitutions are allowed with the price being adjusted in a way established by the exchange. No. 1 Yellow is deliverable for 1.5 cents per bushel more than No. 2 Yellow. No. 3 Yellow is deliverable for 1.5 cents per bushel less than No. 2 Yellow.

The financial assets in futures contracts are generally well defined and unambiguous. For example, there is no need to specify the grade of a Japanese yen. However, there are

---

[1] As mentioned in Chapter 1, the spot price is the price for almost immediate delivery.

[2] There are exceptions. As pointed out by J. E. Newsome, G. H. F. Wang, M. E. Boyd, and M. J. Fuller in "Contract Modifications and the Basic Behavior of Live Cattle Futures," *Journal of Futures Markets*, 24, 6 (2004), 557–90, the CME gave the buyer some delivery options in live cattle futures starting in 1995.

some interesting features of the Treasury bond and Treasury note futures contracts traded on the Chicago Board of Trade. For example, the underlying asset in the Treasury bond contract is any U.S. Treasury bond that has a maturity between 15 and 25 years; in the 10-year Treasury note futures contract, the underlying asset is any Treasury note with a maturity of between 6.5 and 10 years. The exchange has a formula for adjusting the price received according to the coupon and maturity date of the bond delivered. This is discussed in Chapter 6.

The Contract Size

The contract size specifies the amount of the asset that has to be delivered under one contract. This is an important decision for the exchange. If the contract size is too large, many traders who wish to hedge relatively small exposures or who wish to take relatively small speculative positions will be unable to use the exchange. On the other hand, if the contract size is too small, trading may be expensive as there is a cost associated with each contract traded.

The correct size for a contract clearly depends on the likely user. Whereas the value of what is delivered under a futures contract on an agricultural product might be $10,000 to $20,000, it is much higher for some financial futures. For example, under the Treasury bond futures contract traded by the CME Group, instruments with a face value of $100,000 are delivered.

In some cases exchanges have introduced "mini" contracts to attract smaller traders. For example, the CME Group's Mini Nasdaq 100 contract is on 20 times the Nasdaq 100 index, whereas the regular contract is on 100 times the index. (We will cover futures on indices more fully in Chapter 3.)

Delivery Arrangements

The place where delivery will be made must be specified by the exchange. This is particularly important for commodities that involve significant transportation costs. In the case of the ICE frozen concentrate orange juice contract, delivery is to exchange-licensed warehouses in Florida, New Jersey, or Delaware.

When alternative delivery locations are specified, the price received by the party with the short position is sometimes adjusted according to the location chosen by that party. The price tends to be higher for delivery locations that are relatively far from the main sources of the commodity.

Delivery Months

A futures contract is referred to by its delivery month. The exchange must specify the precise period during the month when delivery can be made. For many futures contracts, the delivery period is the whole month.

The delivery months vary from contract to contract and are chosen by the exchange to meet the needs of market participants. For example, corn futures traded by the CME Group have delivery months of March, May, July, September, and December. At any given time, contracts trade for the closest delivery month and a number of subsequent delivery months. The exchange specifies when trading in a particular month's contract will begin. The exchange also specifies the last day on which trading can take place for a given contract. Trading generally ceases a few days before the last day on which delivery can be made.

Price Quotes

The exchange defines how prices will be quoted. For example, crude oil futures prices are quoted in dollars and cents. Treasury bond and Treasury note futures prices are quoted in dollars and thirty-seconds of a dollar.

Price Limits and Position Limits

For most contracts, daily price movement limits are specified by the exchange. If in a day the price moves down from the previous day's close by an amount equal to the daily price limit, the contract is said to be *limit down*. If it moves up by the limit, it is said to be *limit up*. A *limit move* is a move in either direction equal to the daily price limit. Normally, trading ceases for the day once the contract is limit up or limit down. However, in some instances the exchange has the authority to step in and change the limits.

The purpose of daily price limits is to prevent large price movements from occurring because of speculative excesses. However, limits can become an artificial barrier to trading when the price of the underlying commodity is advancing or declining rapidly. Whether price limits are, on balance, good for futures markets is controversial.

Position limits are the maximum number of contracts that a speculator may hold. The purpose of these limits is to prevent speculators from exercising undue influence on the market.

2.3   CONVERGENCE OF FUTURES PRICE TO SPOT PRICE

As the delivery period for a futures contract is approached, the futures price converges to the spot price of the underlying asset. When the delivery period is reached, the futures price equals—or is very close to—the spot price.

To see why this is so, we first suppose that the futures price is above the spot price during the delivery period. Traders then have a clear arbitrage opportunity:

1. Sell (i.e., short) a futures contract
2. Buy the asset
3. Make delivery.

These steps are certain to lead to a profit equal to the amount by which the futures price exceeds the spot price. As traders exploit this arbitrage opportunity, the futures price will fall. Suppose next that the futures price is below the spot price during the delivery period. Companies interested in acquiring the asset will find it attractive to enter into a long futures contract and then wait for delivery to be made. As they do so, the futures price will tend to rise.

The result is that the futures price is very close to the spot price during the delivery period. Figure 2.1 illustrates the convergence of the futures price to the spot price. In Figure 2.1a the futures price is above the spot price prior to the delivery period. In

Figure 2.1 Relationship between futures price and spot price as the delivery period is approached: (a) Futures price above spot price; (b) futures price below spot price.

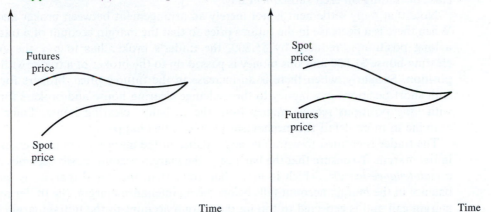

Figure 2.1b the futures price is below the spot price prior to the delivery period. The circumstances under which these two patterns are observed are discussed in Chapter 5.

2.4 THE OPERATION OF MARGIN ACCOUNTS

If two traders get in touch with each other directly and agree to trade an asset in the future for a certain price, there are obvious risks. One of the traders may regret the deal and try to back out. Alternatively, the trader simply may not have the financial resources to honor the agreement. One of the key roles of the exchange is to organize trading so that contract defaults are avoided. This is where margin accounts come in.

Daily Settlement

To illustrate how margin accounts work, we consider a trader who contacts his or her broker to buy two December gold futures contracts. We suppose that the current futures price is $1,250 per ounce. Because the contract size is 100 ounces, the trader has contracted to buy a total of 200 ounces at this price. The broker will require the trader to deposit funds in a margin account. The amount that must be deposited at the time the contract is entered into is known as the *initial margin*. We suppose this is $6,000 per contract, or $12,000 in total. At the end of each trading day, the margin account is adjusted to reflect the trader's gain or loss. This practice is referred to as *daily settlement* or *marking to market*.

Suppose, for example, that by the end of the first day the futures price has dropped by $9 from $1,250 to $1,241. The trader has a loss of $1,800 (= 200 × $9), because the 200 ounces of December gold, which the trader contracted to buy at $1,250, can now be sold for only $1,241. The balance in the margin account would therefore be reduced by $1,800 to $10,200. Similarly, if the price of December gold rose to $1,259 by the end of the first day, the balance in the margin account would be increased by $1,800 to $13,800. A trade is first settled at the close of the day on which it takes place. It is then settled at the close of trading on each subsequent day.

Note that daily settlement is not merely an arrangement between broker and client. When there is a decrease in the futures price so that the margin account of a trader with a long position is reduced by $1,800, the trader's broker has to pay the exchange clearing house $1,800 and this money is passed on to the broker of a trader with a short position. Similarly, when there is an increase in the futures price, brokers for parties with short positions pay money to the exchange clearing house and brokers for parties with long positions receive money from the exchange clearing house. Later we will examine in more detail the mechanism by which this happens.

The trader is entitled to withdraw any balance in the margin account in excess of the initial margin. To ensure that the balance in the margin account never becomes negative a *maintenance margin*, which is somewhat lower than the initial margin, is set. If the balance in the margin account falls below the maintenance margin, the trader receives a margin call and is expected to top up the margin account to the initial margin level by the end of the next day. The extra funds deposited are known as a *variation margin*. If the trader does not provide the variation margin, the broker closes out the position. In the case of the trader considered earlier, closing out the position would involve neutralizing the existing contract by selling 200 ounces of gold for delivery in December.

Table 2.1 Operation of margin account for a long position in two gold futures contracts. The initial margin is $6,000 per contract, or $12,000 in total; the maintenance margin is $4,500 per contract, or $9,000 in total. The contract is entered into on Day 1 at $1,250 and closed out on Day 16 at $1,226.90.

Day	Trade price ($)	Settlement price ($)	Daily gain ($)	Cumulative gain ($)	Margin account balance ($)	Margin call ($)
1	1,250.00				12,000	
1		1,241.00	−1,800	−1,800	10,200	
2		1,238.30	−540	−2,340	9,660	
3		1,244.60	1,260	−1,080	10,920	
4		1,241.30	−660	−1,740	10,260	
5		1,240.10	−240	−1,980	10,020	
6		1,236.20	−780	−2,760	9,240	
7		1,229.90	−1,260	−4,020	7,980	4,020
8		1,230.80	180	−3,840	12,180	
9		1,225.40	−1,080	−4,920	11,100	
10		1,228.10	540	−4,380	11,640	
11		1,211.00	−3,420	−7,800	8,220	3,780
12		1,211.00	0	−7,800	12,000	
13		1,214.30	660	−7,140	12,660	
14		1,216.10	360	−6,780	13,020	
15		1,223.00	1,380	−5,400	14,400	
16	1,226.90		780	−4,620	15,180	

Table 2.1 illustrates the operation of the margin account for one possible sequence of futures prices in the case of the trader considered earlier. The maintenance margin is assumed to be $4,500 per contract, or $9,000 in total. On Day 7, the balance in the margin account falls $1,020 below the maintenance margin level. This drop triggers a margin call from the broker for an additional $4,020 to bring the account balance up to the initial margin level of $12,000. It is assumed that the trader provides this margin by the close of trading on Day 8. On Day 11, the balance in the margin account again falls below the maintenance margin level, and a margin call for $3,780 is sent out. The trader provides this margin by the close of trading on Day 12. On Day 16, the trader decides to close out the position by selling two contracts. The futures price on that day is $1,226.90, and the trader has a cumulative loss of $4,620. Note that the trader has excess margin on Days 8, 13, 14, and 15. It is assumed that the excess is not withdrawn.

Further Details

Most brokers pay traders interest on the balance in a margin account. The balance in the account does not, therefore, represent a true cost, provided that the interest rate is competitive with what could be earned elsewhere. To satisfy the initial margin requirements, but not subsequent margin calls, a trader can usually deposit securities with the broker. Treasury bills are usually accepted in lieu of cash at about 90% of their face value. Shares are also sometimes accepted in lieu of cash, but at about 50% of their market value.

Whereas a forward contract is settled at the end of its life, a futures contract is, as we have seen, settled daily. At the end of each day, the trader's gain (loss) is added to (subtracted from) the margin account, bringing the value of the contract back to zero. A futures contract is in effect closed out and rewritten at a new price each day.

Minimum levels for the initial and maintenance margin are set by the exchange clearing house. Individual brokers may require greater margins from their clients than the minimum levels specified by the exchange clearing house. Minimum margin levels are determined by the variability of the price of the underlying asset and are revised when necessary. The higher the variability, the higher the margin levels. The maintenance margin is usually about 75% of the initial margin.

Margin requirements may depend on the objectives of the trader. A bona fide hedger, such as a company that produces the commodity on which the futures contract is written, is often subject to lower margin requirements than a speculator. The reason is that there is deemed to be less risk of default. Day trades and spread transactions often give rise to lower margin requirements than do hedge transactions. In a *day trade* the trader announces to the broker an intent to close out the position in the same day. In a *spread transaction* the trader simultaneously buys (i.e., takes a long position in) a contract on an asset for one maturity month and sells (i.e., takes a short position in) a contract on the same asset for another maturity month.

Note that margin requirements are the same on short futures positions as they are on long futures positions. It is just as easy to take a short futures position as it is to take a long one. The spot market does not have this symmetry. Taking a long position in the spot market involves buying the asset for immediate delivery and presents no problems. Taking a short position involves selling an asset that you do not own. This is a more complex transaction that may or may not be possible in a particular market. It is discussed further in Chapter 5.

The Clearing House and Its Members

A *clearing house* acts as an intermediary in futures transactions. It guarantees the performance of the parties to each transaction. The clearing house has a number of members. Brokers who are not members themselves must channel their business through a member and post margin with the member. The main task of the clearing house is to keep track of all the transactions that take place during a day, so that it can calculate the net position of each of its members.

The clearing house member is required to provide to the clearing house initial margin (sometimes referred to as clearing margin) reflecting the total number of contracts that are being cleared. There is no maintenance margin applicable to the clearing house member. At the end of each day, the transactions being handled by the clearing house member are settled through the clearing house. If in total the transactions have lost money, the member is required to provide variation margin to the exchange clearing house (usually by the beginning of the next day); if there has been a gain on the transactions, the member receives variation margin from the clearing house. Intraday variation margin payments may also be required by a clearing house from its members in times of significant price volatility or changes in position.

In determining margin requirements, the number of contracts outstanding is usually calculated on a net basis rather than a gross basis. This means that short positions the clearing house member is handling for clients are netted against long positions. Suppose, for example, that the clearing house member has two clients: one with a long position in 20 contracts, the other with a short position in 15 contracts. The initial margin would be calculated on the basis of 5 contracts. The calculation of the margin requirement is usually designed to ensure that the clearing house is about 99% certain that the margin will be sufficient to cover any losses in the event that the member defaults and has to be closed out. Clearing house members are required to contribute to a guaranty fund. This may be used by the clearing house in the event that a member defaults and the member's margin proves insufficient to cover losses.

Credit Risk

The whole purpose of the margining system is to ensure that funds are available to pay traders when they make a profit. Overall the system has been very successful. Traders entering into contracts at major exchanges have always had their contracts honored. Futures markets were tested on October 19, 1987, when the S&P 500 index declined by over 20% and traders with long positions in S&P 500 futures found they had negative margin balances with their brokers. Traders who did not meet margin calls were closed out but still owed their brokers money. Some did not pay and as a result some brokers went bankrupt because, without their clients' money, they were unable to meet margin calls on contracts they entered into on behalf of their clients. However, the clearing houses had sufficient funds to ensure that everyone who had a short futures position on the S&P 500 got paid.

2.5   OTC MARKETS

Over-the-counter (OTC) markets, introduced in Chapter 1, are markets where companies agree to derivatives transactions without involving an exchange. Credit risk has traditionally been a feature of OTC derivatives markets. Consider two companies, A and B, that have entered into a number of derivatives transactions. If A defaults when the net value of the outstanding transactions to B is positive, a loss is likely to be taken by B. Similarly, if B defaults when the net value of outstanding transactions to A is positive, a loss is likely to be taken by company A. In an attempt to reduce credit risk, the OTC market has borrowed some ideas from exchange-traded markets. We now discuss this.

Central Counterparties

We briefly mentioned CCPs in Section 1.2. These are clearing houses for standard OTC transactions that perform much the same role as exchange clearing houses. Members of the CCP, similarly to members of an exchange clearing house, have to provide both initial margin and daily variation margin. Like members of an exchange clearing house, they are also required to contribute to a guaranty fund.

Once an OTC derivative transaction has been agreed between two parties A and B, it can be presented to a CCP. Assuming the CCP accepts the transaction, it becomes the counterparty to both A and B. (This is similar to the way the clearing house for a futures exchange becomes the counterparty to the two sides of a futures trade.) For example, if the transaction is a forward contract where A has agreed to buy an asset from B in one year for a certain price, the clearing house agrees to

1. Buy the asset from B in one year for the agreed price, and
2. Sell the asset to A in one year for the agreed price.

It takes on the credit risk of both A and B.

All members of the CCP are required to provide initial margin to the CCP. Transactions are valued daily and there are daily variation margin payments to or from the member. If an OTC market participant is not itself a member of a CCP, it can arrange to clear its trades through a CCP member. It will then have to provide margin to the CCP member. Its relationship with the CCP member is similar to the relationship between a broker and a futures exchange clearing house member.

Following the credit crisis that started in 2007, regulators have become more concerned about systemic risk (see Business Snapshot 1.2). One result of this, mentioned in Section 1.2, has been legislation requiring that most standard OTC transactions between financial institutions be handled by CCPs.

Bilateral Clearing

Those OTC transactions that are not cleared through CCPs are cleared bilaterally. In the bilaterally cleared OTC market, two companies A and B usually enter into a master agreement covering all their trades.[3] This agreement usually includes an annex, referred to as the credit support annex or CSA, requiring A or B, or both, to provide collateral. The collateral is similar to the margin required by exchange clearing houses or CCPs from their members.

Collateral agreements in CSAs usually require transactions to be valued each day. A simple two-way agreement between companies A and B might work as follows. If, from one day to the next, the transactions between A and B increase in value to A by X (and

---

[3] The most common such agreement is an International Swaps and Derivatives Association (ISDA) Master Agreement.

Business Snapshot 2.2   Long-Term Capital Management's Big Loss

Long-Term Capital Management (LTCM), a hedge fund formed in the mid-1990s, always collateralized its bilaterally cleared transactions. The hedge fund's investment strategy was known as convergence arbitrage. A very simple example of what it might do is the following. It would find two bonds, X and Y, issued by the same company that promised the same payoffs, with X being less liquid (i.e., less actively traded) than Y. The market places a value on liquidity. As a result the price of X would be less than the price of Y. LTCM would buy X, short Y, and wait, expecting the prices of the two bonds to converge at some future time.

When interest rates increased, the company expected both bonds to move down in price by about the same amount, so that the collateral it paid on bond X would be about the same as the collateral it received on bond Y. Similarly, when interest rates decreased, LTCM expected both bonds to move up in price by about the same amount, so that the collateral it received on bond X would be about the same as the collateral it paid on bond Y. It therefore expected that there would be no significant outflow of funds as a result of its collateralization agreements.

In August 1998, Russia defaulted on its debt and this led to what is termed a "flight to quality" in capital markets. One result was that investors valued liquid instruments more highly than usual and the spreads between the prices of the liquid and illiquid instruments in LTCM's portfolio increased dramatically. The prices of the bonds LTCM had bought went down and the prices of those it had shorted increased. It was required to post collateral on both. The company experienced difficulties because it was highly leveraged. Positions had to be closed out and LTCM lost about $4 billion. If the company had been less highly leveraged, it would probably have been able to survive the flight to quality and could have waited for the prices of the liquid and illiquid bonds to move back closer to each other.

---

therefore decrease in value to B by X), B is required to provide collateral worth X to A. If the reverse happens and the transactions increase in value to B by X (and decrease in value to A by X), A is required to provide collateral worth X to B. (To use the terminology of exchange-traded markets, X is the variation margin provided.) Collateral agreements and the way counterparty credit risk is assessed for bilaterally cleared transactions is discussed further in Chapter 24.

It has traditionally been relatively rare for a CSA to require initial margin. This is changing. From 2016, regulations require both initial margin and variation margin to be provided for bilaterally cleared transactions between financial institutions.[4] The initial margin is posted with a third party and calculated on a gross basis (no netting).

Collateral significantly reduces credit risk in the bilaterally cleared OTC market (and so the use of CCPs for standard transactions between financial institutions and regulations requiring initial margin for transactions between financial institutions should reduce risks for the financial system). Collateral agreements were used by hedge fund Long-Term Capital Management (LTCM) for its bilaterally cleared derivatives in the 1990s. The

---

[4] For both this regulation and the regulation requiring standard transactions between financial institutions to be cleared through CCPs, "financial institutions" include banks, insurance companies, pension funds, and hedge funds. Transactions with most nonfinancial corporations and some foreign exchange transactions are exempt from the regulations.

Figure 2.2 (a) The traditional way in which OTC markets have operated: a series of bilateral agreements between market participants; (b) how OTC markets would operate with a single central counterparty (CCP) acting as a clearing house.

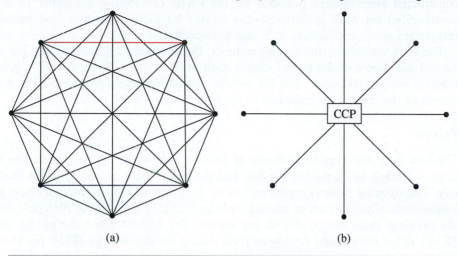

(a)   (b)

agreements allowed LTCM to be highly levered. They did provide credit protection, but as described in Business Snapshot 2.2, the high leverage left the hedge fund exposed to other risks.

Figure 2.2 illustrates the way bilateral and central clearing work. (It makes the simplifying assumption that there are only eight market participants and one CCP). Under bilateral clearing there are many different agreements between market participants, as indicated in Figure 2.2a. If all OTC contracts were cleared through a single CCP, we would move to the situation shown in Figure 2.2b. In practice, because not all OTC transactions are routed through CCPs and there is more than one CCP, the market has elements of both Figure 2.2a and Figure 2.2b.[5]

Futures Trades vs. OTC Trades

Regardless of how transactions are cleared, initial margin when provided in the form of cash usually earns interest. The daily variation margin provided by clearing house members for futures contracts does not earn interest. This is because the variation margin constitutes the daily settlement. Transactions in the OTC market, whether cleared through CCPs or cleared bilaterally, are usually not settled daily. For this reason, the daily variation margin that is provided by the member of a CCP or, as a result of a CSA, earns interest when it is in the form of cash.

Securities can be often be used to satisfy margin/collateral requirements.[6] The market value of the securities is reduced by a certain amount to determine their value for margin purposes. This reduction is known as a *haircut*.

---

[5] The impact of CCPs on credit risk depends on the number of CCPs and proportions of all trades that are cleared through them. See D. Duffie and H. Zhu, "Does a Central Clearing Counterparty Reduce Counterparty Risk?," *Review of Asset Pricing Studies*, 1 (2011): 74–95.

[6] As already mentioned, the variation margin for futures contracts must be provided in the form of cash.

2.6 MARKET QUOTES

Futures quotes are available from exchanges and several online sources. Table 2.2 is constructed from quotes provided by the CME Group for a number of different commodities on May 3, 2016. Similar quotes for index, currency, and interest rate futures are given in Chapters 3, 5, and 6, respectively.

The asset underlying the futures contract, the contract size, and the way the price is quoted are shown at the top of each section of Table 2.2. The first asset is gold. The contract size is 100 ounces and the price is quoted in dollars per ounce. The maturity month of the contract is indicated in the first column of the table.

Prices

The first three numbers in each row of Table 2.2 show the opening price, the highest price in trading so far during the day, and the lowest price in trading so far during the day. The opening price is representative of the prices at which contracts were trading immediately after the start of trading on May 3, 2016. For the June 2016 gold contract, the opening price was $1,293.40 per ounce. The highest price during the day was $1,303.90 per ounce, and the lowest price during the day was $1,284.00 per ounce.

Settlement Price

The *settlement price* is the price used for calculating daily gains and losses and margin requirements. It is usually calculated as the price at which the contract traded immediately before the end of a day's trading session. The fourth number in Table 2.2 shows the settlement price the previous day (i.e., May 2, 2016). The fifth number shows the most recent trading price, and the sixth number shows the price change from the previous day's settlement price. In the case of the June 2016 gold contract, the previous day's settlement price was $1,295.80. The most recent trade was at $1,288.10, $7.70 lower than the previous day's settlement price. If $1,288.10 proved to be the settlement price on May 3, 2016, the margin account of a trader with a long position in one contract would lose $770 on May 3 and the margin account of a trader with a short position would gain this amount on May 3.

Trading Volume and Open Interest

The final column of Table 2.2 shows the *trading volume*. The trading volume is the number of contracts traded in a day. It can be contrasted with the *open interest*, which is the number of contracts outstanding, that is, the number of long positions or, equivalently, the number of short positions.

If there is a large amount of trading by day traders (i.e., traders who enter into a position and close it out on the same day) the volume of trading in a day can be greater than either the beginning-of-day or end-of-day open interest.

Patterns of Futures

Futures prices can show a number of different patterns. In Table 2.2, gold, oil, corn, and wheat settlement futures prices are an increasing function of the maturity of the contract. This is known as a *normal market*. In the case of live cattle, settlement futures

Table 2.2 Futures quotes for a selection of CME Group contracts on commodities on May 3, 2016.

	Open	High	Low	Prior settlement	Last trade	Change	Volume
Gold 100 oz, $ per oz							
June 2016	1293.4	1303.9	1284.0	1295.8	1288.1	−7.7	202,355
Aug. 2016	1295.6	1306.0	1286.4	1298.1	1290.8	−7.3	26,736
Oct. 2016	1296.0	1307.7	1289.1	1300.0	1292.7	−7.3	1,005
Dec. 2016	1299.6	1309.1	1290.0	1301.9	1294.5	−7.4	3,465
Apr. 2017	1305.2	1305.8	1296.1	1305.7	1296.1	−9.6	250
Crude Oil 1000 barrels, $ per barrel							
June 2016	44.92	45.35	43.36	44.78	43.51	−1.27	503,259
Aug. 2016	46.02	46.45	44.63	45.91	44.82	−1.09	50,439
Dec. 2016	47.09	47.55	45.99	47.09	46.24	−0.85	41,447
Dec. 2017	48.75	49.17	47.83	48.72	48.16	−0.56	13,032
Dec. 2018	50.27	50.40	49.30	49.99	49.59	−0.40	1,618
Corn 5000 bushels, cents per bushel							
July 2016	391.75	395.00	377.00	391.75	378.25	−13.50	215,808
Sept. 2016	392.00	394.75	378.75	392.25	379.50	−12.75	34,514
Dec. 2016	396.00	398.50	384.00	396.50	385.00	−11.50	70,460
Mar. 2017	403.50	406.00	392.50	404.50	393.25	−11.25	11,131
May 2017	408.75	410.75	397.75	409.25	398.25	−11.00	1,276
July 2017	413.00	415.00	402.00	413.50	403.25	−10.25	2,555
Soybeans 5000 bushel, cents per bushel							
July 2016	1043.75	1057.00	1023.00	1043.75	1033.25	−10.50	200,456
Aug. 2016	1043.75	1057.25	1025.00	1044.00	1034.75	−9.25	22,110
Sept. 2016	1027.75	1041.75	1012.25	1029.00	1021.00	−8.00	8,753
Nov. 2016	1017.00	1030.75	1003.00	1017.75	1011.75	−6.00	87,122
Jan. 2017	1018.00	1031.25	1004.00	1019.25	1012.00	−7.25	10,937
Mar. 2017	1010.00	1021.75	995.25	1010.75	1001.25	−9.50	12,906
Wheat 5000 bushel, cents per bushel							
July 2016	487.00	492.75	468.25	487.75	473.00	−14.75	106,051
Sept. 2016	497.00	503.25	478.75	498.50	483.25	−15.25	20,043
Dec. 2016	515.20	521.25	496.25	516.75	500.50	−16.25	23,374
Mar. 2017	535.00	538.00	513.00	534.00	517.50	−16.50	2,730
Live Cattle 40,000 lbs, cents per lb							
June 2016	116.550	116.850	115.750	115.800	116.500	+0.750	16,127
Aug. 2016	114.325	114.800	113.775	113.725	114.475	+0.750	10,595
Dec. 2016	114.150	114.425	113.575	113.700	114.350	+0.650	2,350
Apr. 2017	112.900	112.925	112.250	112.450	112.750	+0.300	430

prices decline with maturity. This is referred as an *inverted market*.[7] Soybean futures show a pattern that was partly normal and partly inverted on May 3, 2016.

2.7 DELIVERY

As mentioned earlier in this chapter, very few of the futures contracts that are entered into lead to delivery of the underlying asset. Most are closed out early. Nevertheless, it is the possibility of eventual delivery that determines the futures price. An understanding of delivery procedures is therefore important.

The period during which delivery can be made is defined by the exchange and varies from contract to contract. The decision on when to deliver is made by the party with the short position, whom we shall refer to as trader A. When trader A decides to deliver, trader A's broker issues a notice of intention to deliver to the exchange clearing house. This notice states how many contracts will be delivered and, in the case of commodities, also specifies where delivery will be made and what grade will be delivered. The exchange then chooses a party with a long position to accept delivery.

Suppose that the party on the other side of trader A's futures contract when it was entered into was trader B. It is important to realize that there is no reason to expect that it will be trader B who takes delivery. Trader B may well have closed out his or her position by trading with trader C, trader C may have closed out his or her position by trading with trader D, and so on. The usual rule chosen by the exchange is to pass the notice of intention to deliver on to the party with the oldest outstanding long position. Parties with long positions must accept delivery notices. However, if the notices are transferable, traders with long positions usually have a short period of time to find another party with a long position that is prepared to take delivery in place of them.

In the case of a commodity, taking delivery usually means accepting a warehouse receipt in return for immediate payment. The party taking delivery is then responsible for all warehousing costs. In the case of livestock futures, there may be costs associated with feeding and looking after the animals (see Business Snapshot 2.1). In the case of financial futures, delivery is usually made by wire transfer. For all contracts, the price paid is usually the most recent settlement price. If specified by the exchange, this price is adjusted for grade, location of delivery, and so on. The whole delivery procedure from the issuance of the notice of intention to deliver to the delivery itself generally takes about two to three days.

There are three critical days for a contract. These are the first notice day, the last notice day, and the last trading day. The *first notice day* is the first day on which a notice of intention to make delivery can be submitted to the exchange. The *last notice day* is the last such day. The *last trading day* is generally a few days before the last notice day. To avoid the risk of having to take delivery, a trader with a long position should close out his or her contracts prior to the first notice day.

---

[7] The term *contango* is sometimes used to describe the situation where the futures price is an increasing function of maturity and the term *backwardation* is sometimes used to describe the situation where the futures price is a decreasing function of the maturity of the contract. Strictly speaking, as will be explained in Chapter 5, these terms refer to whether the price of the underlying asset is expected to increase or decrease over time.

Cash Settlement

Some financial futures, such as those on stock indices discussed in Chapter 3, are settled in cash because it is inconvenient or impossible to deliver the underlying asset. In the case of the futures contract on the S&P 500, for example, delivering the underlying asset would involve delivering a portfolio of 500 stocks. When a contract is settled in cash, all outstanding contracts are declared closed on a predetermined day. The final settlement price is set equal to the spot price of the underlying asset at either the open or close of trading on that day. For example, in the S&P 500 futures contract traded by the CME Group, the predetermined day is the third Friday of the delivery month and final settlement is at the opening price on that day.

2.8 TYPES OF TRADERS AND TYPES OF ORDERS

There are two main types of traders executing trades: *futures commission merchants* (FCMs) and *locals*. FCMs are following the instructions of their clients and charge a commission for doing so; locals are trading on their own account.

Individuals taking positions, whether locals or the clients of FCMs, can be categorized as hedgers, speculators, or arbitrageurs, as discussed in Chapter 1. Speculators can be classified as scalpers, day traders, or position traders. *Scalpers* are watching for very short-term trends and attempt to profit from small changes in the contract price. They usually hold their positions for only a few minutes. *Day traders* hold their positions for less than one trading day. They are unwilling to take the risk that adverse news will occur overnight. *Position traders* hold their positions for much longer periods of time. They hope to make significant profits from major movements in the markets.

Orders

The simplest type of order placed with a broker is a *market order*. It is a request that a trade be carried out immediately at the best price available in the market. However, there are many other types of orders. We will consider those that are more commonly used.

A *limit order* specifies a particular price. The order can be executed only at this price or at one more favorable to the trader. Thus, if the limit price is $30 for a trader wanting to buy, the order will be executed only at a price of $30 or less. There is, of course, no guarantee that the order will be executed at all, because the limit price may never be reached.

A *stop order* or *stop-loss order* also specifies a particular price. The order is executed at the best available price once a bid or offer is made at that particular price or a less-favorable price. Suppose a stop order to sell at $30 is issued when the market price is $35. It becomes an order to sell when and if the price falls to $30. In effect, a stop order becomes a market order as soon as the specified price has been hit. The purpose of a stop order is usually to close out a position if unfavorable price movements take place. It limits the loss that can be incurred.

A *stop–limit order* is a combination of a stop order and a limit order. The order becomes a limit order as soon as a bid or offer is made at a price equal to or less favorable than the stop price. Two prices must be specified in a stop–limit order: the stop price and the limit price. Suppose that at the time the market price is $35, a stop–limit order to buy is issued with a stop price of $40 and a limit price of $41. As soon as there is a bid or offer at $40, the stop–limit becomes a limit order at $41. If the stop price and the limit price are the same, the order is sometimes called a *stop-and-limit order*.

A *market-if-touched* (MIT) *order* is executed at the best available price after a trade occurs at a specified price or at a price more favorable than the specified price. In effect, an MIT becomes a market order once the specified price has been hit. An MIT is also known as a *board order*. Consider a trader who has a long position in a futures contract and is issuing instructions that would lead to closing out the contract. A stop order is designed to place a limit on the loss that can occur in the event of unfavorable price movements. By contrast, a market-if-touched order is designed to ensure that profits are taken if sufficiently favorable price movements occur.

A *discretionary order* or *market-not-held order* is traded as a market order except that execution may be delayed at the broker's discretion in an attempt to get a better price.

Some orders specify time conditions. Unless otherwise stated, an order is a day order and expires at the end of the trading day. A *time-of-day order* specifies a particular period of time during the day when the order can be executed. An *open order* or a *good-till-canceled order* is in effect until executed or until the end of trading in the particular contract. A *fill-or-kill order*, as its name implies, must be executed immediately on receipt or not at all.

2.9 REGULATION

Futures markets in the United States are currently regulated federally by the Commodity Futures Trading Commission (CFTC; www.cftc.gov), which was established in 1974.

The CFTC looks after the public interest. It is responsible for ensuring that prices are communicated to the public and that futures traders report their outstanding positions if they are above certain levels. The CFTC also licenses all individuals who offer their services to the public in futures trading. The backgrounds of these individuals are investigated, and there are minimum capital requirements. The CFTC deals with complaints brought by the public and ensures that disciplinary action is taken against individuals when appropriate. It has the authority to force exchanges to take disciplinary action against members who are in violation of exchange rules.

With the formation of the National Futures Association (NFA; www.nfa.futures.org) in 1982, some of responsibilities of the CFTC were shifted to the futures industry itself. The NFA is an organization of individuals who participate in the futures industry. Its objective is to prevent fraud and to ensure that the market operates in the best interests of the general public. It is authorized to monitor trading and take disciplinary action when appropriate. The agency has set up an efficient system for arbitrating disputes between individuals and its members.

The Dodd–Frank act, signed into law by President Obama in 2010, expanded the role of the CFTC. For example, it is now responsible for rules requiring that standard over-the-counter derivatives between financial institutions be traded on swap execution facilities and cleared through central counterparties (see Section 1.2).

Trading Irregularities

Most of the time futures markets operate efficiently and in the public interest. However, from time to time, trading irregularities do come to light. One type of trading irregularity occurs when a trader group tries to "corner the market."[8] The trader group takes a huge long futures position and also tries to exercise some control over the supply of the underlying commodity. As the maturity of the futures contracts is approached, the trader group does not close out its position, so that the number of outstanding futures contracts may exceed the amount of the commodity available for delivery. The holders of short positions realize that they will find it difficult to deliver and become desperate to close out their positions. The result is a large rise in both futures and spot prices. Regulators usually deal with this type of abuse of the market by increasing margin requirements or imposing stricter position limits or prohibiting trades that increase a speculator's open position or requiring market participants to close out their positions.

2.10 ACCOUNTING AND TAX

The full details of the accounting and tax treatment of futures contracts are beyond the scope of this book. A trader who wants detailed information on this should obtain professional advice. This section provides some general background information.

Accounting

Accounting standards require changes in the market value of a futures contract to be recognized when they occur unless the contract qualifies as a hedge. If the contract does qualify as a hedge, gains or losses are generally recognized for accounting purposes in the same period in which the gains or losses from the item being hedged are recognized. The latter treatment is referred to as *hedge accounting*.

Consider a company with a December year end. In September 2017 it buys a March 2018 corn futures contract and closes out the position at the end of February 2018. Suppose that the futures prices are 450 cents per bushel when the contract is entered into, 470 cents per bushel at the end of 2017, and 480 cents per bushel when the contract is closed out. The contract is for the delivery of 5,000 bushels. If the contract does not qualify as a hedge, the gains for accounting purposes are

$$5,000 \times (4.70 - 4.50) = \$1,000$$

in 2017 and

$$5,000 \times (4.80 - 4.70) = \$500$$

in 2018. If the company is hedging the purchase of 5,000 bushels of corn in February 2018 so that the contract qualifies for hedge accounting, the entire gain of $1,500 is realized in 2018 for accounting purposes.

---

[8] Possibly the best known example of this was the attempt by the Hunt brothers to corner the silver market in 1979–80. Between the middle of 1979 and the beginning of 1980, their activities led to a price rise from $6 per ounce to $50 per ounce.

The treatment of hedging gains and losses is sensible. If the company is hedging the purchase of 5,000 bushels of corn in February 2018, the effect of the futures contract is to ensure that the price paid (inclusive of the futures gain or loss) is close to 450 cents per bushel. The accounting treatment reflects that this price is paid in 2018.

The Financial Accounting Standards Board has issued FAS 133 and ASC 815 explaining when companies can and cannot use hedge accounting. The International Accounting Standards Board has similarly issued IAS 39 and IFRS 9.

Tax

Under the U.S. tax rules, two key issues are the nature of a taxable gain or loss and the timing of the recognition of the gain or loss. Gains or losses are either classified as capital gains or losses or alternatively as part of ordinary income.

For a corporate taxpayer, capital gains are taxed at the same rate as ordinary income, and the ability to deduct losses is restricted. Capital losses are deductible only to the extent of capital gains. A corporation may carry back a capital loss for three years and carry it forward for up to five years. For a noncorporate taxpayer, short-term capital gains are taxed at the same rate as ordinary income, but long-term capital gains are subject to a maximum capital gains tax rate of 20%. (Long-term capital gains are gains from the sale of a capital asset held for longer than one year; short-term capital gains are the gains from the sale of a capital asset held one year or less.) Starting in 2013, taxpayers earning income above certain thresholds pay an additional 3.8% on all investment income. For a noncorporate taxpayer, capital losses are deductible to the extent of capital gains plus ordinary income up to $3,000 and can be carried forward indefinitely.

Generally, positions in futures contracts are treated as if they are closed out on the last day of the tax year. For the noncorporate taxpayer, this gives rise to capital gains and losses that are treated as if they were 60% long term and 40% short term without regard to the holding period. This is referred to as the "60/40" rule. A noncorporate taxpayer may elect to carry back for three years any net losses from the 60/40 rule to offset any gains recognized under the rule in the previous three years.

Hedging transactions are exempt from this rule. The definition of a hedge transaction for tax purposes is different from that for accounting purposes. The tax regulations define a hedging transaction as a transaction entered into in the normal course of business primarily for one of the following reasons:

1. To reduce the risk of price changes or currency fluctuations with respect to property that is held or to be held by the taxpayer for the purposes of producing ordinary income

2. To reduce the risk of price or interest rate changes or currency fluctuations with respect to borrowings made by the taxpayer.

A hedging transaction must be clearly identified in a timely manner in the company's records as a hedge. Gains or losses from hedging transactions are treated as ordinary income. The timing of the recognition of gains or losses from hedging transactions generally matches the timing of the recognition of income or expense associated with the transaction being hedged.

2.11 FORWARD vs. FUTURES CONTRACTS

The main differences between forward and futures contracts are summarized in Table 2.3. Both contracts are agreements to buy or sell an asset for a certain price at a certain future time. A forward contract is traded in the over-the-counter market and there is no standard contract size or standard delivery arrangements. A single delivery date is usually specified and the contract is usually held to the end of its life and then settled. A futures contract is a standardized contract traded on an exchange. A range of delivery dates is usually specified. It is settled daily and usually closed out prior to maturity.

Profits from Forward and Futures Contracts

Suppose that the sterling exchange rate for a 90-day forward contract is 1.5000 and that this rate is also the futures price for a contract that will be delivered in exactly 90 days. What is the difference between the gains and losses under the two contracts?

Under the forward contract, the whole gain or loss is realized at the end of the life of the contract. Under the futures contract, the gain or loss is realized day by day because of the daily settlement procedures. Suppose that trader A is long £1 million in a 90-day forward contract and trader B is long £1 million in 90-day futures contracts. (Because each futures contract is for the purchase or sale of £62,500, trader B must purchase a total of 16 contracts.) Assume that the spot exchange rate in 90 days proves to be 1.7000 dollars per pound. Trader A makes a gain of $200,000 on the 90th day. Trader B makes the same gain—but spread out over the 90-day period. On some days trader B may realize a loss, whereas on other days he or she makes a gain. However, in total, when losses are netted against gains, there is a gain of $200,000 over the 90-day period.

Foreign Exchange Quotes

Both forward and futures contracts trade actively on foreign currencies. However, there is sometimes a difference in the way exchange rates are quoted in the two markets. For example, futures prices where one currency is the U.S. dollar are always quoted as the number of U.S. dollars per unit of the foreign currency or as the

Table 2.3 Comparison of forward and futures contracts.

Forward	Futures
Private contract between two parties	Traded on an exchange
Not standardized	Standardized contract
Usually one specified delivery date	Range of delivery dates
Settled at end of contract	Settled daily
Delivery or final cash settlement usually takes place	Contract is usually closed out prior to maturity
Some credit risk	Virtually no credit risk

number of U.S. cents per unit of the foreign currency. Forward prices are always quoted in the same way as spot prices. This means that, for the British pound, the euro, the Australian dollar, and the New Zealand dollar, the forward quotes show the number of U.S. dollars per unit of the foreign currency and are directly comparable with futures quotes. For other major currencies, forward quotes show the number of units of the foreign currency per U.S. dollar (USD). Consider the Canadian dollar (CAD). A futures price quote of 0.8500 USD per CAD corresponds to a forward price quote of 1.1765 CAD per USD (1.1765 = 1/0.8500).

SUMMARY

A very high proportion of the futures contracts that are traded do not lead to the delivery of the underlying asset. Traders usually enter into offsetting contracts to close out their positions before the delivery period is reached. However, it is the possibility of final delivery that drives the determination of the futures price. For each futures contract, there is a range of days during which delivery can be made and a well-defined delivery procedure. Some contracts, such as those on stock indices, are settled in cash rather than by delivery of the underlying asset.

The specification of contracts is an important activity for a futures exchange. The two sides to any contract must know what can be delivered, where delivery can take place, and when delivery can take place. They also need to know details on the trading hours, how prices will be quoted, maximum daily price movements, and so on. New contracts must be approved by the Commodity Futures Trading Commission before trading starts.

Margin accounts are an important aspect of futures markets. A trader keeps a margin account with his or her broker. The account is adjusted daily to reflect gains or losses, and from time to time the broker may require the account to be topped up if adverse price movements have taken place. The broker either must be a clearing house member or must maintain a margin account with a clearing house member. Each clearing house member maintains a margin account with the exchange clearing house. The balance in the account is adjusted daily to reflect gains and losses on the business for which the clearing house member is responsible.

In over-the-counter derivatives markets, transactions are cleared either bilaterally or centrally. When bilateral clearing is used, collateral frequently has to be posted by one or both parties to reduce credit risk. When central clearing is used, a central counter-party (CCP) stands between the two sides. It requires each side to provide margin and performs much the same function as an exchange clearing house.

Forward contracts differ from futures contracts in a number of ways. Forward contracts are private arrangements between two parties, whereas futures contracts are traded on exchanges. There is generally a single delivery date in a forward contract, whereas futures contracts frequently involve a range of such dates. Because they are not traded on exchanges, forward contracts do not need to be standardized. A forward contract is not usually settled until the end of its life, and most contracts do in fact lead to delivery of the underlying asset or a cash settlement at this time.

In the next few chapters we shall examine in more detail the ways in which forward and futures contracts can be used for hedging. We shall also look at how forward and futures prices are determined.

FURTHER READING

Duffie, D., and H. Zhu. "Does a Central Clearing Counterparty Reduce Counterparty Risk?" *Review of Asset Pricing Studies*, 1, 1 (2011): 74–95.

Gastineau, G. L., D. J. Smith, and R. Todd. *Risk Management, Derivatives, and Financial Analysis under SFAS No. 133.* The Research Foundation of AIMR and Blackwell Series in Finance, 2001.

Hull, J. C. "CCPs, Their Risks and How They Can Be Reduced," *Journal of Derivatives*, 20, 1 (Fall 2012): 26–29.

Jorion, P. "Risk Management Lessons from Long-Term Capital Management," *European Financial Management*, 6, 3 (September 2000): 277–300.

Kleinman, G. *Trading Commodities and Financial Futures.* Upper Saddle River, NJ: Pearson, 2013.

Lowenstein, R. *When Genius Failed: The Rise and Fall of Long-Term Capital Management.* New York: Random House, 2000.

Panaretou, A., M. B. Shackleton, and P. A. Taylor. "Corporate Risk Management and Hedge Accounting," *Contemporary Accounting Research*, 30, 1 (Spring 2013): 116–139.

Practice Questions (Answers in Solutions Manual)

2.1. Distinguish between the terms *open interest* and *trading volume*.

2.2. What is the difference between a *local* and a *futures commission merchant*?

2.3. Suppose that you enter into a short futures contract to sell July silver for $17.20 per ounce. The size of the contract is 5,000 ounces. The initial margin is $4,000, and the maintenance margin is $3,000. What change in the futures price will lead to a margin call? What happens if you do not meet the margin call?

2.4. Suppose that in September 2018 a company takes a long position in a contract on May 2019 crude oil futures. It closes out its position in March 2019. The futures price (per barrel) is $48.30 when it enters into the contract, $50.50 when it closes out its position, and $49.10 at the end of December 2018. One contract is for the delivery of 1,000 barrels. What is the company's total profit? When is it realized? How is it taxed if it is (a) a hedger and (b) a speculator? Assume that the company has a December 31 year end.

2.5. What does a stop order to sell at $2 mean? When might it be used? What does a limit order to sell at $2 mean? When might it be used?

2.6. What is the difference between the operation of the margin accounts administered by a clearing house and those administered by a broker?

2.7. What differences exist in the way prices are quoted in the foreign exchange futures market, the foreign exchange spot market, and the foreign exchange forward market?

2.8. The party with a short position in a futures contract sometimes has options as to the precise asset that will be delivered, where delivery will take place, when delivery will take place, and so on. Do these options increase or decrease the futures price? Explain your reasoning.

2.9. What are the most important aspects of the design of a new futures contract?

2.10. Explain how margin accounts protect futures traders against the possibility of default.

2.11. A trader buys two July futures contracts on frozen orange juice concentrate. Each contract is for the delivery of 15,000 pounds. The current futures price is 160 cents per pound, the initial margin is $6,000 per contract, and the maintenance margin is $4,500 per contract. What price change would lead to a margin call? Under what circumstances could $2,000 be withdrawn from the margin account?

2.12. Show that, if the futures price of a commodity is greater than the spot price during the delivery period, then there is an arbitrage opportunity. Does an arbitrage opportunity exist if the futures price is less than the spot price? Explain your answer.

2.13. Explain the difference between a market-if-touched order and a stop order.

2.14. Explain what a stop–limit order to sell at 20.30 with a limit of 20.10 means.

2.15. At the end of one day a clearing house member is long 100 contracts, and the settlement price is $50,000 per contract. The original margin is $2,000 per contract. On the following day the member becomes responsible for clearing an additional 20 long contracts, entered into at a price of $51,000 per contract. The settlement price at the end of this day is $50,200. How much does the member have to add to its margin account with the exchange clearing house?

2.16. Explain why collateral requirements will increase in the OTC market as a result of new regulations introduced since the 2008 credit crisis.

2.17. The forward price of the Swiss franc for delivery in 45 days is quoted as 1.1000. The futures price for a contract that will be delivered in 45 days is 0.9000. Explain these two quotes. Which is more favorable for a trader wanting to sell Swiss francs?

2.18. Suppose you call your broker and issue instructions to sell one July hogs contract. Describe what happens.

2.19. "Speculation in futures markets is pure gambling. It is not in the public interest to allow speculators to trade on a futures exchange." Discuss this viewpoint.

2.20. Explain the difference between bilateral and central clearing for OTC derivatives.

2.21. What do you think would happen if an exchange started trading a contract in which the quality of the underlying asset was incompletely specified?

2.22. "When a futures contract is traded on the floor of the exchange, it may be the case that the open interest increases by one, stays the same, or decreases by one." Explain this statement.

2.23. Suppose that, on October 24, 2018, a company sells one April 2019 live cattle futures contract. It closes out its position on January 21, 2019. The futures price (per pound) is 121.20 cents when it enters into the contract, 118.30 cents when it closes out its position, and 118.80 cents at the end of December 2018. One contract is for the delivery of 40,000 pounds of cattle. What is the total profit? How is it taxed if the company is (a) a hedger and (b) a speculator? Assume that the company has a December 31 year end.

2.24. A cattle farmer expects to have 120,000 pounds of live cattle to sell in 3 months. The live cattle futures contract traded by the CME Group is for the delivery of 40,000 pounds of cattle. How can the farmer use the contract for hedging? From the farmer's viewpoint, what are the pros and cons of hedging?

2.25. It is July 2017. A mining company has just discovered a small deposit of gold. It will take 6 months to construct the mine. The gold will then be extracted on a more or less continuous basis for 1 year. Futures contracts on gold are available with delivery months every 2 months from August 2017 to December 2018. Each contract is for the delivery of 100 ounces. Discuss how the mining company might use futures markets for hedging.

2.26. Explain how CCPs work. What are the advantages to the financial system of requiring CCPs to be used for all standardized derivatives transactions between financial institutions?

Further Questions

2.27. Trader A enters into futures contracts to buy 1 million euros for 1.1 million dollars in three months. Trader B enters in a forward contract to do the same thing. The exchange rate (dollars per euro) declines sharply during the first two months and then increases for the third month to close at 1.1300. Ignoring daily settlement, what is the total profit of each trader? When the impact of daily settlement is taken into account, which trader has done better?

2.28. Explain what is meant by open interest. Why does the open interest usually decline during the month preceding the delivery month? On a particular day, there were 2,000 trades in a particular futures contract. This means that there were 2,000 buyers (going long) and 2,000 sellers (going short). Of the 2,000 buyers, 1,400 were closing out positions and 600 were entering into new positions. Of the 2,000 sellers, 1,200 were closing out positions and 800 were entering into new positions. What is the impact of the day's trading on open interest?

2.29. One orange juice futures contract is on 15,000 pounds of frozen concentrate. Suppose that in September 2017 a company sells a March 2019 orange juice futures contract for 120 cents per pound. At the end of December 2017, the futures price is 140 cents; at the end of December 2018, it is 110 cents; and in February 2019, it is closed out at 125 cents. The company has a December 31 year end. What is the company's profit or loss on the contract? How is it realized? What is the accounting and tax treatment of the transaction if the company is classified as (a) a hedger and (b) a speculator?

2.30. A company enters into a short futures contract to sell 5,000 bushels of wheat for 750 cents per bushel. The initial margin is $3,000 and the maintenance margin is $2,000. What price change would lead to a margin call? Under what circumstances could $1,500 be withdrawn from the margin account?

2.31. Suppose that there are no storage costs for crude oil and the interest rate for borrowing or lending is 4% per annum. How could you make money if the June and December futures contracts for a particular year trade at $50 and $56, respectively?

2.32. What position is equivalent to a long forward contract to buy an asset at K on a certain date and a put option to sell it for K on that date.

2.33. A company has derivatives transactions with Banks A, B, and C that are worth +$20 million, −$15 million, and −$25 million, respectively, to the company. How much margin or collateral does the company have to provide in each of the following two situations?
(a) The transactions are cleared bilaterally and are subject to one-way collateral agreements where the company posts variation margin but no initial margin. The banks do not have to post collateral.
(b) The transactions are cleared centrally through the same CCP and the CCP requires a total initial margin of $10 million.

2.34. A bank's derivatives transactions with a counterparty are worth +$10 million to the bank and are cleared bilaterally. The counterparty has posted $10 million of cash collateral. What credit exposure does the bank have?

2.35. The author's website (www-2.rotman.utoronto.ca/~hull/data) contains daily closing prices for the crude oil futures contract and the gold futures contract. You are required to download the data for crude oil and answer the following:

(a) Assuming that daily price changes are normally distributed with zero mean, estimate the standard deviation of daily price changes. Calculate the standard deviation of two-day changes from the standard deviation of one-day changes assuming that changes are independent.

(b) Suppose that an exchange wants to set the margin requirement for a member with a long position in one contract so that it is 99% certain that the margin will not be wiped out by a two-day price move. (It chooses two days because it considers that it can take two days to close out a defaulting member.) How high does the margin have to be when the normal distribution assumption is made? Each contract is on 1,000 barrels of oil.

(c) Use the data to determine how often the margin of the member would actually be wiped out by a two-day price move. What do your results suggest about the appropriateness of the normal distribution assumption?

(d) Suppose that for retail clients the maintenance margin is equal to the amount calculated in (b) and is 75% of the initial margin. How frequently would the balance in the account of a client with a long position be negative immediately before a margin payment is due (so that the client has an incentive to default)? Assume that balances in excess of the initial margin are withdrawn by the client.

CHAPTER

Hedging Strategies Using Futures

Many of the participants in futures markets are hedgers. Their aim is to use futures markets to reduce a particular risk that they face. This risk might relate to fluctuations in the price of oil, a foreign exchange rate, the level of the stock market, or some other variable. A *perfect hedge* is one that completely eliminates the risk. Perfect hedges are rare. For the most part, therefore, a study of hedging using futures contracts is a study of the ways in which hedges can be constructed so that they perform as close to perfectly as possible.

In this chapter we consider a number of general issues associated with the way hedges are set up. When is a short futures position appropriate? When is a long futures position appropriate? Which futures contract should be used? What is the optimal size of the futures position for reducing risk? At this stage, we restrict our attention to what might be termed *hedge-and-forget* strategies. We assume that no attempt is made to adjust the hedge once it has been put in place. The hedger simply takes a futures position at the beginning of the life of the hedge and closes out the position at the end of the life of the hedge. In Chapter 19 we will examine dynamic hedging strategies in which the hedge is monitored closely and frequent adjustments are made.

The chapter initially treats futures contracts as forward contracts (that is, it ignores daily settlement). Later it explains an adjustment known as "tailing the hedge" that takes account of the difference between futures and forwards.

3.1 BASIC PRINCIPLES

When an individual or company chooses to use futures markets to hedge a risk, the objective is often to take a position that neutralizes the risk as far as possible. Consider a company that knows it will gain $10,000 for each 1 cent increase in the price of a commodity over the next 3 months and lose $10,000 for each 1 cent decrease in the price during the same period. To hedge, the company's treasurer should take a short futures position that is designed to offset this risk. The futures position should lead to a loss of $10,000 for each 1 cent increase in the price of the commodity over the 3 months and a gain of $10,000 for each 1 cent decrease in the price during this period. If the price of the commodity goes down, the gain on the futures position offsets the loss on the rest of the company's business. If the price of the commodity goes up, the loss on the futures position is offset by the gain on the rest of the company's business.

Short Hedges

A *short hedge* is a hedge, such as the one just described, that involves a short position in futures contracts. A short hedge is appropriate when the hedger already owns an asset and expects to sell it at some time in the future. For example, a short hedge could be used by a farmer who owns some hogs and knows that they will be ready for sale at the local market in two months. A short hedge can also be used when an asset is not owned right now but will be owned and ready for sale at some time in the future. Consider, for example, a U.S. exporter who knows that he or she will receive euros in 3 months. The exporter will realize a gain if the euro increases in value relative to the U.S. dollar and will sustain a loss if the euro decreases in value relative to the U.S. dollar. A short futures position leads to a loss if the euro increases in value and a gain if it decreases in value. It has the effect of offsetting the exporter's risk.

To provide a more detailed illustration of the operation of a short hedge in a specific situation, we assume that it is May 15 today and that an oil producer has just negotiated a contract to sell 1 million barrels of crude oil. It has been agreed that the price that will apply in the contract is the market price on August 15. The oil producer is therefore in the position where it will gain $10,000 for each 1 cent increase in the price of oil over the next 3 months and lose $10,000 for each 1 cent decrease in the price during this period. Suppose that on May 15 the spot price is $50 per barrel and the crude oil futures price for August delivery is $49 per barrel. Because each futures contract is for the delivery of 1,000 barrels, the company can hedge its exposure by shorting (i.e., selling) 1,000 futures contracts. If the oil producer closes out its position on August 15, the effect of the strategy should be to lock in a price close to $49 per barrel.

To illustrate what might happen, suppose that the spot price on August 15 proves to be $45 per barrel. The company realizes $45 million for the oil under its sales contract. Because August is the delivery month for the futures contract, the futures price on August 15 should be very close to the spot price of $45 on that date. The company therefore gains approximately

$$\$49 - \$45 = \$4$$

per barrel, or $4 million in total from the short futures position. The total amount realized from both the futures position and the sales contract is therefore approximately $49 per barrel, or $49 million in total.

For an alternative outcome, suppose that the price of oil on August 15 proves to be $55 per barrel. The company realizes $55 per barrel for the oil and loses approximately

$$\$55 - \$49 = \$6$$

per barrel on the short futures position. Again, the total amount realized is approximately $49 million. It is easy to see that in all cases the company ends up with approximately $49 million.

Long Hedges

Hedges that involve taking a long position in a futures contract are known as *long hedges*. A long hedge is appropriate when a company knows it will have to purchase a certain asset in the future and wants to lock in a price now.

Suppose that it is now January 15. A copper fabricator knows it will require 100,000 pounds of copper on May 15 to meet a certain contract. The spot price of copper is 340 cents per pound, and the futures price for May delivery is 320 cents per pound. The fabricator can hedge its position by taking a long position in four futures contracts offered by the CME Group and closing its position on May 15. Each contract is for the delivery of 25,000 pounds of copper. The strategy has the effect of locking in the price of the required copper at close to 320 cents per pound.

Suppose that the spot price of copper on May 15 proves to be 325 cents per pound. Because May is the delivery month for the futures contract, this should be very close to the futures price. The fabricator therefore gains approximately

$$100{,}000 \times (\$3.25 - \$3.20) = \$5{,}000$$

on the futures contracts. It pays $100{,}000 \times \$3.25 = \$325{,}000$ for the copper, making the net cost approximately $\$325{,}000 - \$5{,}000 = \$320{,}000$. For an alternative outcome, suppose that the spot price is 305 cents per pound on May 15. The fabricator then loses approximately

$$100{,}000 \times (\$3.20 - \$3.05) = \$15{,}000$$

on the futures contract and pays $100{,}000 \times \$3.05 = \$305{,}000$ for the copper. Again, the net cost is approximately \$320,000, or 320 cents per pound.

Note that, in this case, it is clearly better for the company to use futures contracts than to buy the copper on January 15 in the spot market. If it does the latter, it will pay 340 cents per pound instead of 320 cents per pound and will incur both interest costs and storage costs. For a company using copper on a regular basis, this disadvantage would be offset by the convenience of having the copper on hand.[1] However, for a company that knows it will not require the copper until May 15, the futures contract alternative is likely to be preferred.

The examples we have looked at assume that the futures position is closed out in the delivery month. The hedge has the same basic effect if delivery is allowed to happen. However, making or taking delivery can be costly and inconvenient. For this reason, delivery is not usually made even when the hedger keeps the futures contract until the delivery month. As will be discussed later, hedgers with long positions usually avoid any possibility of having to take delivery by closing out their positions before the delivery period.

We have also assumed in the two examples that there is no daily settlement. In practice, daily settlement does have a small effect on the performance of a hedge. As explained in Chapter 2, it means that the payoff from the futures contract is realized day by day throughout the life of the hedge rather than all at the end.

3.2 ARGUMENTS FOR AND AGAINST HEDGING

The arguments in favor of hedging are so obvious that they hardly need to be stated. Most nonfinancial companies are in the business of manufacturing, or retailing or wholesaling, or providing a service. They have no particular skills or expertise in predicting variables such as interest rates, exchange rates, and commodity prices.

---

[1] See Section 5.11 for a discussion of convenience yields.

(Indeed, even experts are often wrong when they make predictions about these variables.) It makes sense for them to hedge the risks associated with these variables as they become aware of them. The companies can then focus on their main activities. By hedging, they avoid unpleasant surprises such as sharp rises in the price of a commodity that is being purchased.

In practice, many risks are left unhedged. In the rest of this section we will explore some of the reasons for this.

Hedging and Shareholders

One argument sometimes put forward is that the shareholders can, if they wish, do the hedging themselves. They do not need the company to do it for them. This argument is, however, open to question. It assumes that shareholders have as much information as the company's management about the risks faced by a company. In most instances, this is not the case. The argument also ignores commissions and other transactions costs. These are less expensive per dollar of hedging for large transactions than for small transactions. Hedging is therefore likely to be less expensive when carried out by the company than when it is carried out by individual shareholders. Indeed, the size of futures contracts makes hedging by individual shareholders impossible in many situations.

One thing that shareholders can do far more easily than a corporation is diversify risk. A shareholder with a well-diversified portfolio may be immune to many of the risks faced by a corporation. For example, in addition to holding shares in a company that uses copper, a well-diversified shareholder may hold shares in a copper producer, so that there is very little overall exposure to the price of copper. If companies are acting in the best interests of well-diversified shareholders, it can be argued that hedging is unnecessary in many situations. However, the extent to which managers are in practice influenced by this type of argument is open to question.

Hedging and Competitors

If hedging is not the norm in a certain industry, it may not make sense for one particular company to choose to be different from all others. Competitive pressures within the industry may be such that the prices of the goods and services produced by the industry fluctuate to reflect raw material costs, interest rates, exchange rates, and so on. A company that does not hedge can expect its profit margins to be roughly constant. However, a company that does hedge can expect its profit margins to fluctuate!

To illustrate this point, consider two manufacturers of gold jewelry, SafeandSure Company and TakeaChance Company. We assume that most companies in the industry do not hedge against movements in the price of gold and that TakeaChance Company is no exception. However, SafeandSure Company has decided to be different from its competitors and to use futures contracts to hedge its purchase of gold over the next 18 months. If the price of gold goes up, economic pressures will tend to lead to a corresponding increase in the wholesale price of jewelry, so that TakeaChance Company's gross profit margin is unaffected. By contrast, SafeandSure Company's profit margin will increase after the effects of the hedge have been taken into account. If the price of gold goes down, economic pressures will tend to lead to a corresponding decrease in the wholesale price of jewelry. Again, TakeaChance Company's profit margin is unaffected. However, SafeandSure Company's profit margin goes down. In extreme conditions,

Table 3.1   Danger in hedging when competitors do not hedge.

Change in gold price	*Effect on price of gold jewelry*	*Effect on profits of TakeaChance Co.*	*Effect on profits of SafeandSure Co.*
Increase	Increase	None	Increase
Decrease	Decrease	None	Decrease

SafeandSure Company's profit margin could become negative as a result of the "hedging" carried out! The situation is summarized in Table 3.1.

This example emphasizes the importance of looking at the big picture when hedging. All the implications of price changes on a company's profitability should be taken into account in the design of a hedging strategy to protect against the price changes.

Hedging Can Lead to a Worse Outcome

It is important to realize that a hedge using futures contracts can result in a decrease or an increase in a company's profits relative to the position it would be in with no hedging. In the example involving the oil producer considered earlier, if the price of oil goes down, the company loses money on its sale of 1 million barrels of oil, and the futures position leads to an offsetting gain. The treasurer can be congratulated for having had the foresight to put the hedge in place. Clearly, the company is better off than it would be with no hedging. Other executives in the organization, it is hoped, will appreciate the contribution made by the treasurer. If the price of oil goes up, the company gains from its sale of the oil, and the futures position leads to an offsetting loss. The company is in a worse position than it would be with no hedging. Although the hedging decision was perfectly logical, the treasurer may in practice have a difficult time justifying it. Suppose that the price of oil at the end of the hedge is $59, so that the company loses $10 per barrel on the futures contract. We can imagine a conversation such as the following between the treasurer and the president:

President: This is terrible. We've lost $10 million in the futures market in the space of three months. How could it happen? I want a full explanation.

Treasurer: The purpose of the futures contracts was to hedge our exposure to the price of oil, not to make a profit. Don't forget we made $10 million from the favorable effect of the oil price increases on our business.

President: What's that got to do with it? That's like saying that we do not need to worry when our sales are down in California because they are up in New York.

Treasurer: If the price of oil had gone down . . .

President: I don't care what would have happened if the price of oil had gone down. The fact is that it went up. I really do not know what you were doing playing the futures markets like this. Our shareholders will expect us to have done particularly well this quarter. I'm going to have to explain to them that your actions reduced profits by $10 million. I'm afraid this is going to mean no bonus for you this year.

Business Snapshot 3.1   Hedging by Gold Mining Companies

It is natural for a gold mining company to consider hedging against changes in the price of gold. Typically it takes several years to extract all the gold from a mine. Once a gold mining company decides to go ahead with production at a particular mine, it has a big exposure to the price of gold. Indeed a mine that looks profitable at the outset could become unprofitable if the price of gold plunges.

Gold mining companies are careful to explain their hedging strategies to potential shareholders. Some gold mining companies do not hedge. They tend to attract shareholders who buy gold stocks because they want to benefit when the price of gold increases and are prepared to accept the risk of a loss from a decrease in the price of gold. Other companies choose to hedge. They estimate the number of ounces of gold they will produce each month for the next few years and enter into short futures or forward contracts to lock in the price for all or part of this.

Suppose you are Goldman Sachs and are approached by a gold mining company that wants to sell you a large amount of gold in 1 year at a fixed price. How do you set the price and then hedge your risk? The answer is that you can hedge by borrowing the gold from a central bank, selling it immediately in the spot market, and investing the proceeds at the risk-free rate. At the end of the year, you buy the gold from the gold mining company and use it to repay the central bank. The fixed forward price you set for the gold reflects the risk-free rate you can earn and the lease rate you pay the central bank for borrowing the gold.

Treasurer: That's unfair. I was only...

President: Unfair! You are lucky not to be fired. You lost $10 million.

Treasurer: It all depends on how you look at it...

It is easy to see why many treasurers are reluctant to hedge! Hedging reduces risk for the company. However, it may increase risk for the treasurer if others do not fully understand what is being done. The only real solution to this problem involves ensuring that all senior executives within the organization fully understand the nature of hedging before a hedging program is put in place. Ideally, hedging strategies are set by a company's board of directors and are clearly communicated to both the company's management and the shareholders. (See Business Snapshot 3.1 for a discussion of hedging by gold mining companies.)

3.3   BASIS RISK

The hedges in the examples considered so far have been almost too good to be true. The hedger was able to identify the precise date in the future when an asset would be bought or sold. The hedger was then able to use futures contracts to remove almost all the risk arising from the price of the asset on that date. In practice, hedging is often not quite as straightforward as this. Some of the reasons are as follows:

1. The asset whose price is to be hedged may not be exactly the same as the asset underlying the futures contract.

2. There may be uncertainty as to the exact date when the asset will be bought or sold.

3. The hedge may require the futures contract to be closed out before its delivery month.

These problems give rise to what is termed *basis risk*. This concept will now be explained.

The Basis

The *basis* in a hedging situation is as follows:[2]

Basis = Spot price of asset to be hedged − Futures price of contract used

If the asset to be hedged and the asset underlying the futures contract are the same, the basis should be zero at the expiration of the futures contract. Prior to expiration, the basis may be positive or negative. In Table 2.2, we can assume that the June futures price is close to the spot price. The table therefore indicates that the basis was negative for gold and positive live cattle on May 3, 2016.

As time passes, the spot price and the futures price for a particular month do not necessarily change by the same amount. As a result, the basis changes. An increase in the basis is referred to as a *strengthening of the basis*; a decrease in the basis is referred to as a *weakening of the basis*. Figure 3.1 illustrates how a basis might change over time in a situation where the basis is positive prior to expiration of the futures contract.

To examine the nature of basis risk, we will use the following notation:

S_1: Spot price at time t_1

S_2: Spot price at time t_2

F_1: Futures price at time t_1

F_2: Futures price at time t_2

b_1: Basis at time t_1

b_2: Basis at time t_2.

Figure 3.1 Variation of basis over time.

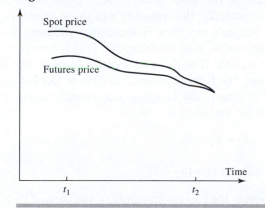

---

[2] This is the usual definition. However, the alternative definition Basis = Futures price − Spot price is sometimes used, particularly when the futures contract is on a financial asset.

We will assume that a hedge is put in place at time t_1 and closed out at time t_2. As an example, we will consider the case where the spot and futures prices at the time the hedge is initiated are \$2.50 and \$2.20, respectively, and that at the time the hedge is closed out they are \$2.00 and \$1.90, respectively. This means that $S_1 = 2.50$, $F_1 = 2.20$, $S_2 = 2.00$, and $F_2 = 1.90$.

From the definition of the basis, we have

$$b_1 = S_1 - F_1 \quad \text{and} \quad b_2 = S_2 - F_2$$

so that, in our example, $b_1 = 0.30$ and $b_2 = 0.10$.

Consider first the situation of a hedger who knows that the asset will be sold at time t_2 and takes a short futures position at time t_1. The price realized for the asset is S_2 and the profit on the futures position is $F_1 - F_2$. The effective price that is obtained for the asset with hedging is therefore

$$S_2 + F_1 - F_2 = F_1 + b_2$$

In our example, this is \$2.30. The value of F_1 is known at time t_1. If b_2 were also known at this time, a perfect hedge would result. The hedging risk is the uncertainty associated with b_2 and is known as *basis risk*. Consider next a situation where a company knows it will buy the asset at time t_2 and initiates a long hedge at time t_1. The price paid for the asset is S_2 and the loss on the hedge is $F_1 - F_2$. The effective price that is paid with hedging is therefore

$$S_2 + F_1 - F_2 = F_1 + b_2$$

This is the same expression as before and is \$2.30 in the example. The value of F_1 is known at time t_1, and the term b_2 represents basis risk.

Note that basis changes can lead to an improvement or a worsening of a hedger's position. Consider a company that uses a short hedge because it plans to sell the underlying asset. If the basis strengthens (i.e., increases) unexpectedly, the company's position improves because it will get a higher price for the asset after futures gains or losses are considered; if the basis weakens (i.e., decreases) unexpectedly, the company's position worsens. For a company using a long hedge because it plans to buy the asset, the reverse holds. If the basis strengthens unexpectedly, the company's position worsens because it will pay a higher price for the asset after futures gains or losses are considered; if the basis weakens unexpectedly, the company's position improves.

The asset that gives rise to the hedger's exposure is sometimes different from the asset underlying the futures contract that is used for hedging. This is known as *cross hedging* and is discussed in the next section. It leads to an increase in basis risk. Define S_2^* as the price of the asset underlying the futures contract at time t_2. As before, S_2 is the price of the asset being hedged at time t_2. By hedging, a company ensures that the price that will be paid (or received) for the asset is

$$S_2 + F_1 - F_2$$

This can be written as

$$F_1 + (S_2^* - F_2) + (S_2 - S_2^*)$$

The terms $S_2^* - F_2$ and $S_2 - S_2^*$ represent the two components of the basis. The $S_2^* - F_2$ term is the basis that would exist if the asset being hedged were the same as the asset underlying the futures contract. The $S_2 - S_2^*$ term is the basis arising from the difference between the two assets.

Choice of Contract

One key factor affecting basis risk is the choice of the futures contract to be used for hedging. This choice has two components:

1. The choice of the asset underlying the futures contract
2. The choice of the delivery month.

If the asset being hedged exactly matches an asset underlying a futures contract, the first choice is generally fairly easy. In other circumstances, it is necessary to carry out a careful analysis to determine which of the available futures contracts has futures prices that are most closely correlated with the price of the asset being hedged.

The choice of the delivery month is likely to be influenced by several factors. In the examples given earlier in this chapter, we assumed that, when the expiration of the hedge corresponds to a delivery month, the contract with that delivery month is chosen. In fact, a contract with a later delivery month is usually chosen in these circumstances. The reason is that futures prices are in some instances quite erratic during the delivery month. Moreover, a long hedger runs the risk of having to take delivery of the physical asset if the contract is held during the delivery month. Taking delivery can be expensive and inconvenient. (Long hedgers normally prefer to close out the futures contract and buy the asset from their usual suppliers.)

In general, basis risk increases as the time difference between the hedge expiration and the delivery month increases. A good rule of thumb is therefore to choose a delivery month that is as close as possible to, but later than, the expiration of the hedge. Suppose delivery months are March, June, September, and December for a futures contract on a particular asset. For hedge expirations in December, January, and February, the March contract will be chosen; for hedge expirations in March, April, and May, the June contract will be chosen; and so on. This rule of thumb assumes that there is sufficient liquidity in all contracts to meet the hedger's requirements. In practice, liquidity tends to be greatest in short-maturity futures contracts. Therefore, in some situations, the hedger may be inclined to use short-maturity contracts and roll them forward. This strategy is discussed later in the chapter.

Example 3.1

It is March 1. A U.S. company expects to receive 50 million Japanese yen at the end of July. Yen futures contracts on the CME Group have delivery months of March, June, September, and December. One contract is for the delivery of 12.5 million yen. The company therefore shorts four September yen futures contracts on March 1. When the yen are received at the end of July, the company closes out its position. We suppose that the futures price on March 1 in cents per yen is 1.0800 and that the spot and futures prices when the contract is closed out are 1.0200 and 1.0250, respectively.

The gain on the futures contract is $1.0800 - 1.0250 = 0.0550$ cents per yen. The basis is $1.0200 - 1.0250 = -0.0050$ cents per yen when the contract is closed out. The effective price obtained in cents per yen is the final spot price plus the gain on the futures:

$$1.0200 + 0.0550 = 1.0750$$

This can also be written as the initial futures price plus the final basis:

$$1.0800 + (-0.0050) = 1.0750$$

The total amount received by the company for the 50 million yen is 50×0.01075 million dollars, or \$537,500.

Example 3.2

It is June 8 and a company knows that it will need to purchase 20,000 barrels of crude oil at some time in October or November. Oil futures contracts are currently traded for delivery every month by the CME Group and the contract size is 1,000 barrels. The company therefore decides to use the December contract for hedging and takes a long position in 20 December contracts. The futures price on June 8 is \$48.00 per barrel. The company finds that it is ready to purchase the crude oil on November 10. It therefore closes out its futures contract on that date. The spot price and futures price on November 10 are \$50.00 per barrel and \$49.10 per barrel.

The gain on the futures contract is $49.10 - 48.00 = \$1.10$ per barrel. The basis when the contract is closed out is $50.00 - 49.10 = \$0.90$ per barrel. The effective price paid (in dollars per barrel) is the final spot price less the gain on the futures, or

$$50.00 - 1.10 = 48.90$$

This can also be calculated as the initial futures price plus the final basis,

$$48.00 + 0.90 = 48.90$$

The total price paid is $48.90 \times 20,000 = \$978,000$.

3.4 CROSS HEDGING

In Examples 3.1 and 3.2, the asset underlying the futures contract was the same as the asset whose price is being hedged. *Cross hedging* occurs when the two assets are different. Consider, for example, an airline that is concerned about the future price of jet fuel. Because jet fuel futures are not actively traded, it might choose to use heating oil futures contracts to hedge its exposure.

The *hedge ratio* is the ratio of the size of the position taken in futures contracts to the size of the exposure. When the asset underlying the futures contract is the same as the asset being hedged, it is natural to use a hedge ratio of 1.0. This is the hedge ratio we have used in the examples considered so far. For instance, in Example 3.2, the hedger's exposure was on 20,000 barrels of oil, and futures contracts were entered into for the delivery of exactly this amount of oil.

When cross hedging is used, setting the hedge ratio equal to 1.0 is not always optimal. The hedger should choose a value for the hedge ratio that minimizes the variance of the value of the hedged position. We now consider how the hedger can do this.

Calculating the Minimum Variance Hedge Ratio

We first present an analysis assuming no daily settlement of futures contracts. The minimum variance hedge ratio depends on the relationship between changes in the spot price and changes in the futures price. Define:

ΔS: Change in spot price, S, during a period of time equal to the life of the hedge

ΔF: Change in futures price, F, during a period of time equal to the life of the hedge.

We will denote the minimum variance hedge ratio by h^*. It can be shown that h^* is the slope of the best-fit line from a linear regression of ΔS against ΔF (see Figure 3.2). This result is intuitively reasonable. We would expect h^* to be the ratio of the average change in S for a particular change in F.

The formula for h^* is:

$$h^* = \rho \frac{\sigma_S}{\sigma_F} \tag{3.1}$$

where σ_S is the standard deviation of ΔS, σ_F is the standard deviation of ΔF, and ρ is the coefficient of correlation between the two.

Equation (3.1) shows that the optimal hedge ratio is the product of the coefficient of correlation between ΔS and ΔF and the ratio of the standard deviation of ΔS to the standard deviation of ΔF. Figure 3.3 shows how the variance of the value of the hedger's position depends on the hedge ratio chosen.

If $\rho = 1$ and $\sigma_F = \sigma_S$, the hedge ratio, h^*, is 1.0. This result is to be expected, because in this case the futures price mirrors the spot price perfectly. If $\rho = 1$ and $\sigma_F = 2\sigma_S$, the

Figure 3.2 Regression of change in spot price against change in futures price.

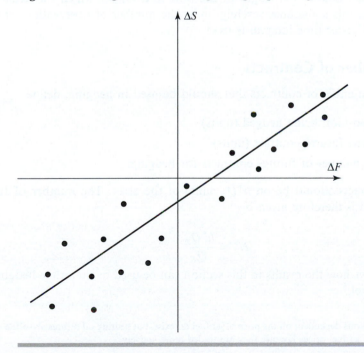

Figure 3.3   Dependence of variance of hedger's position on hedge ratio.

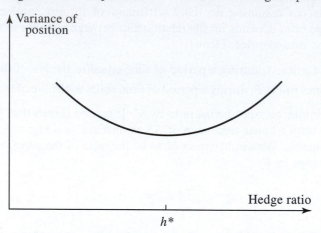

hedge ratio h^* is 0.5. This result is also as expected, because in this case the futures price always changes by twice as much as the spot price. The *hedge effectiveness* can be defined as the proportion of the variance that is eliminated by hedging. This is the R^2 from the regression of ΔS against ΔF and equals ρ^2.

The parameters ρ, σ_F, and σ_S in equation (3.1) are usually estimated from historical data on ΔS and ΔF. (The implicit assumption is that the future will in some sense be like the past.) A number of equal nonoverlapping time intervals are chosen, and the values of ΔS and ΔF for each of the intervals are observed. Ideally, the length of each time interval is the same as the length of the time interval for which the hedge is in effect. In practice, this sometimes severely limits the number of observations that are available, and a shorter time interval is used.

Optimal Number of Contracts

To calculate the number of contracts that should be used in hedging, define:

Q_A: Size of position being hedged (units)

Q_F: Size of one futures contract (units)

N^*: Optimal number of futures contracts for hedging.

The futures contracts should be on $h^* Q_A$ units of the asset. The number of futures contracts required is therefore given by

$$N^* = \frac{h^* Q_A}{Q_F} \tag{3.2}$$

Example 3.3 shows how the results in this section can be used by an airline hedging the purchase of jet fuel.[3]

---

[3] Derivatives with payoffs dependent on the price of jet fuel do exist, but heating oil futures are often used to hedge an exposure to jet fuel prices because they are traded more actively.

Example 3.3

An airline expects to purchase 2 million gallons of jet fuel in 1 month and decides to use heating oil futures for hedging. We suppose that Table 3.2 gives, for 15 successive months, data on the change, ΔS, in the jet fuel price per gallon and the corresponding change, ΔF, in the futures price for the contract on heating oil that would be used for hedging price changes during the month. In this case, the usual formulas for calculating standard deviations and correlations give $\sigma_F = 0.0313$, $\sigma_S = 0.0263$, and $\rho = 0.928$.

From equation (3.1), the minimum variance hedge ratio, h^*, is therefore

$$0.928 \times \frac{0.0263}{0.0313} = 0.78$$

Each heating oil contract traded by the CME Group is on 42,000 gallons of heating oil. From equation (3.2), the optimal number of contracts is

$$\frac{0.78 \times 2,000,000}{42,000}$$

which is 37 when rounded to the nearest whole number.

Table 3.2 Data to calculate minimum variance hedge ratio when heating oil futures contract is used to hedge purchase of jet fuel.

Month i	Change in heating oil futures price per gallon $(= \Delta F)$	Change in jet fuel price per gallon $(= \Delta S)$
1	0.021	0.029
2	0.035	0.020
3	−0.046	−0.044
4	0.001	0.008
5	0.044	0.026
6	−0.029	−0.019
7	−0.026	−0.010
8	−0.029	−0.007
9	0.048	0.043
10	−0.006	0.011
11	−0.036	−0.036
12	−0.011	−0.018
13	0.019	0.009
14	−0.027	−0.032
15	0.029	0.023

Impact of Daily Settlement

The analysis we have presented so far is appropriate when forward contracts are used for hedging. The daily settlement of futures contract means that, when futures contracts are used, there are a series of one-day hedges, not a single hedge. Define:

$\hat{\sigma}_S$: Standard deviation of percentage one-day changes in the spot price

$\hat{\sigma}_F$: Standard deviation of percentage one day changes in the futures price

$\hat{\rho}$: Correlation between percentage one-day changes in the spot and futures

The standard deviation of the one-day change in the value of the position being hedged is $V_A \sigma_S$ where V_A is the value of the position (i.e., asset price times Q_A). The standard deviation of the one-day change in the value of the futures position is $V_F \sigma_F$, where V_F is the futures price times Q_F. It follows that the optimal number of contracts for a one-day hedge is

$$N^* = \frac{\hat{h} V_A}{V_F} \qquad (3.3)$$

where $\hat{h} = \hat{\rho} \hat{\sigma}_S / \hat{\sigma}_F$.

Suppose that in Example 3.5 the futures price and the spot price are 1.99 and 1.94 dollars per gallon, respectively. Then $V_A = 2,000,000 \times 1.94 = 3,880,000$, while $V_F = 42,000 \times 1.99$. If $\hat{h} = 0.75$, the optimal number of contracts is

$$\frac{0.75 \times 3,880,000}{83,580} = 34.82$$

Rounding to the nearest whole number, the optimal number of contracts is 35. In theory the number of contracts should be adjusted as V_A and V_F change. In practice, day-to-day changes in the optimal hedge position are small and are often ignored.

The analysis just presented can be refined to take account of the interest that can be earned or paid over the remaining life of the hedge. Suppose that at time t it is calculated that 5% interest can be earned or paid over the period between t and the end of the hedge. It is then appropriate to divide the N^* calculated at time t by 1.05 to allow for this.

These refinements to equation (3.2) to allow for daily settlement are referred to as *tailing the hedge*.

3.5   STOCK INDEX FUTURES

We now move on to consider stock index futures and how they are used to hedge or manage exposures to equity prices.

A *stock index* tracks changes in the value of a hypothetical portfolio of stocks. The weight of a stock in the portfolio at a particular time equals the proportion of the hypothetical portfolio invested in the stock at that time. The percentage increase in the stock index over a small interval of time is set equal to the percentage increase in the value of the hypothetical portfolio. Dividends are usually not included in the calculation so that the index tracks the capital gain/loss from investing in the portfolio.[4]

[4] An exception to this is a *total return index*. This is calculated by assuming that dividends on the hypothetical portfolio are reinvested in the portfolio.

If the hypothetical portfolio of stocks remains fixed, the weights assigned to individual stocks in the portfolio do not remain fixed. When the price of one particular stock in the portfolio rises more sharply than others, more weight is automatically given to that stock. Sometimes indices are constructed from a hypothetical portfolio consisting of one of each of a number of stocks. The weights assigned to the stocks are then proportional to their market prices, with adjustments being made when there are stock splits. Other indices are constructed so that weights are proportional to market capitalization (stock price × number of shares outstanding). The underlying portfolio is then automatically adjusted to reflect stock splits, stock dividends, and new equity issues.

Stock Indices

Table 3.3 shows futures prices for contracts on three different stock indices on May 3, 2016.

The *Dow Jones Industrial Average* is based on a portfolio consisting of 30 blue-chip stocks in the United States. The weights given to the stocks are proportional to their prices. The CME Group trades two futures contracts on the index. One is on $10 times the index. The other (the Mini DJ Industrial Average) is on $5 times the index. The Mini contract trades most actively.

The *Standard & Poor's 500* (S&P 500) *Index* is based on a portfolio of 500 different stocks: 400 industrials, 40 utilities, 20 transportation companies, and 40 financial institutions. The weights of the stocks in the portfolio at any given time are proportional to their market capitalizations. The stocks are those of large publicly held companies that trade on NYSE Euronext or Nasdaq OMX. The CME Group trades two futures contracts on the S&P 500. One is on $250 times the index; the other (the Mini S&P 500 contract) is on $50 times the index. The Mini contract trades most actively.

The *Nasdaq-100* is based on a portfolio of 100 stocks traded on the Nasdaq exchange with weights proportional to market capitalizations. The CME Group trades two futures contracts. One is on $100 times the index; the other (the Mini Nasdaq-100 contract) is on $20 times the index. The Mini contract trades most actively.

Table 3.3 Futures quotes for a selection of CME Group contracts on stock indices on May 3, 2016.

	Open	*High*	*Low*	*Prior settlement*	*Last trade*	*Change*	*Volume*
Mini Dow Jones Industrial Average, $5 times index							
June 2016	17,806	17,814	17,585	17,799	17,697	−102	127,956
Sept. 2016	17,719	17,719	17,500	17,710	17,622	−88	106
Mini S&P 500, $50 times index							
June 2016	2,075.50	2,076.25	2,048.00	2,074.25	2,060.25	−14.00	1,314,974
Sept. 2016	2,067.00	2,068.00	2,040.25	2,066.50	2,052.00	−14.50	6,416
Dec. 2016	2,061.00	2,061.00	2,033.25	2,059.75	2,044.75	−15.00	405
Mini NASDAQ-100, $20 times index							
June 2016	4,372.00	4,374.50	4,319.50	4,369.00	4,352.50	−16.50	189,845
Sept. 2016	4,359.00	4,360.25	4,316.00	4,361.75	4,349.75	−12.00	109

Some futures contracts on indices outside the United States are also traded actively. An example is the contract on the CSI 300 index, a market-capitalization-weighted index of 300 Chinese stocks, which trades on the China Financial Futures Exchange (CFFEX, www.cffex.com.cn).

As mentioned in Chapter 2, futures contracts on stock indices are settled in cash, not by delivery of the underlying asset. All contracts are marked to market to either the opening price or the closing price of the index on the last trading day, and the positions are then deemed to be closed. For example, contracts on the S&P 500 are closed out at the opening price of the S&P 500 index on the third Friday of the delivery month.

Hedging an Equity Portfolio

Stock index futures can be used to hedge a well-diversified equity portfolio. Define:

V_A: Current value of the portfolio

V_F: Current value of one futures contract (the futures price times the contract size).

If the portfolio mirrors the index, the optimal hedge ratio can be assumed to be 1.0 and equation (3.3) shows that the number of futures contracts that should be shorted is

$$N^* = \frac{V_A}{V_F} \tag{3.4}$$

Suppose, for example, that a portfolio worth $5,050,000 mirrors a well-diversified index. The index futures price is 1,010 and each futures contract is on $250 times the index. In this case $V_A = 5,050,000$ and $V_F = 1,010 \times 250 = 252,500$, so that 20 contracts should be shorted to hedge the portfolio.

When the portfolio does not mirror the index, we can use the capital asset pricing model (see the appendix to this chapter). The parameter beta (β) from the capital asset pricing model is the slope of the best-fit line obtained when excess return on the portfolio over the risk-free rate is regressed against the excess return of the index over the risk-free rate. When $\beta = 1.0$, the return on the portfolio tends to mirror the return on the index; when $\beta = 2.0$, the excess return on the portfolio tends to be twice as great as the excess return on the index; when $\beta = 0.5$, it tends to be half as great; and so on.

A portfolio with a β of 2.0 is twice as sensitive to movements in the index as a portfolio with a beta 1.0. It is therefore necessary to use twice as many contracts to hedge the portfolio. Similarly, a portfolio with a beta of 0.5 is half as sensitive to market movements as a portfolio with a beta of 1.0 and we should use half as many contracts to hedge it. In general,

$$N^* = \beta \frac{V_A}{V_F} \tag{3.5}$$

This formula assumes that the maturity of the futures contract is close to the maturity of the hedge.

Comparing equation (3.5) with equation (3.3), we see that they imply $\hat{h} = \beta$. This is not surprising. The hedge ratio $\hat{h}$ is the slope of the best-fit line when percentage one-day changes in the portfolio are regressed against percentage one-day changes in the futures price of the index. Beta (β) is the slope of the best-fit line when the return from the portfolio is regressed against the return for the index.

We illustrate that this formula gives good results by extending our earlier example. Suppose that a futures contract with 4 months to maturity is used to hedge the value of a portfolio over the next 3 months in the following situation:

Index level = 1,000
Index futures price = 1,010
Value of portfolio = $5,050,000
Risk-free interest rate = 4% per annum
Dividend yield on index = 1% per annum
Beta of portfolio = 1.5

One futures contract is for delivery of $250 times the index. As before, $V_F = 250 \times 1,010 = 252,500$. From equation (3.5), the number of futures contracts that should be shorted to hedge the portfolio is

$$1.5 \times \frac{5,050,000}{252,500} = 30$$

Suppose the index turns out to be 900 in 3 months and the futures price is 902. The gain from the short futures position is then

$$30 \times (1010 - 902) \times 250 = \$810,000$$

The loss on the index is 10%. The index pays a dividend of 1% per annum, or 0.25% per 3 months. When dividends are taken into account, an investor in the index would therefore earn −9.75% over the 3-month period. Because the portfolio has a β of 1.5, the capital asset pricing model gives

Expected return on portfolio − Risk-free interest rate

= 1.5 × (Return on index − Risk-free interest rate)

The risk-free interest rate is approximately 1% per 3 months. It follows that the expected return (%) on the portfolio during the 3 months when the 3-month return on the index

---

Table 3.4   Performance of stock index hedge.

Value of index in three months:	900	950	1,000	1,050	1,100
Futures price of index today:	1,010	1,010	1,010	1,010	1,010
Futures price of index in three months:	902	952	1,003	1,053	1,103
Gain on futures position ($):	810,000	435,000	52,500	−322,500	−697,500
Return on market:	−9.750%	−4.750%	0.250%	5.250%	10.250%
Expected return on portfolio:	−15.125%	−7.625%	−0.125%	7.375%	14.875%
Expected portfolio value in three months including dividends ($):	4,286,187	4,664,937	5,043,687	5,422,437	5,801,187
Total value of position in three months ($):	5,096,187	5,099,937	5,096,187	5,099,937	5,103,687

is −9.75% is

$$1.0 + [1.5 \times (-9.75 - 1.0)] = -15.125$$

The expected value of the portfolio (inclusive of dividends) at the end of the 3 months is therefore

$$\$5,050,000 \times (1 - 0.15125) = \$4,286,187$$

It follows that the expected value of the hedger's position, including the gain on the hedge, is

$$\$4,286,187 + \$810,000 = \$5,096,187$$

Table 3.4 summarizes these calculations together with similar calculations for other values of the index at maturity. It can be seen that the total expected value of the hedger's position in 3 months is almost independent of the value of the index. This is what one would expect if the hedge is a good one.

The only thing we have not covered so far is the relationship between futures prices and spot prices. We will see in Chapter 5 that the 1,010 assumed for the futures price today is roughly what we would expect given the interest rate and dividend we are assuming. The same is true of the futures prices in 3 months shown in Table 3.4.[5]

Reasons for Hedging an Equity Portfolio

Table 3.4 shows that the hedging procedure results in a value for the hedger's position at the end of the 3-month period being about 1% higher than at the beginning of the 3-month period. There is no surprise here. The risk-free rate is 4% per annum, or 1% per 3 months. The hedge results in the investor's position growing at the risk-free rate.

It is natural to ask why the hedger should go to the trouble of using futures contracts. To earn the risk-free interest rate, the hedger can simply sell the portfolio and invest the proceeds in a risk-free security.

One answer to this question is that hedging can be justified if the hedger feels that the stocks in the portfolio have been chosen well. In these circumstances, the hedger might be very uncertain about the performance of the market as a whole, but confident that the stocks in the portfolio will outperform the market (after appropriate adjustments have been made for the beta of the portfolio). A hedge using index futures removes the risk arising from market moves and leaves the hedger exposed only to the performance of the portfolio relative to the market. This will be discussed further shortly. Another reason for hedging may be that the hedger is planning to hold a portfolio for a long period of time and requires short-term protection in an uncertain market situation. The alternative strategy of selling the portfolio and buying it back later might involve unacceptably high transaction costs.

Changing the Beta of a Portfolio

In the example in Table 3.4, the beta of the hedger's portfolio is reduced to zero so that the hedger's expected return is almost independent of the performance of the index.

---

[5] The calculations in Table 3.4 assume that the dividend yield on the index is predictable, the risk-free interest rate remains constant, and the return on the index over the 3-month period is perfectly correlated with the return on the portfolio. In practice, these assumptions do not hold perfectly, and the hedge works rather less well than is indicated by Table 3.4.

Sometimes futures contracts are used to change the beta of a portfolio to some value other than zero. Continuing with our earlier example:

$$\text{Index level} = 1,000$$
$$\text{Index futures price} = 1,010$$
$$\text{Value of portfolio} = \$5,050,000$$
$$\text{Beta of portfolio} = 1.5$$

As before, $V_F = 250 \times 1,010 = 252,500$ and a complete hedge requires

$$1.5 \times \frac{5,050,000}{252,500} = 30$$

contracts to be shorted. To reduce the beta of the portfolio from 1.5 to 0.75, the number of contracts shorted should be 15 rather than 30; to increase the beta of the portfolio to 2.0, a long position in 10 contracts should be taken; and so on. In general, to change the beta of the portfolio from β to β^*, where $\beta > \beta^*$, a short position in

$$(\beta - \beta^*)\frac{V_A}{V_F}$$

contracts is required. When $\beta < \beta^*$, a long position in

$$(\beta^* - \beta)\frac{V_A}{V_F}$$

contracts is required.

Locking in the Benefits of Stock Picking

Suppose you consider yourself to be good at picking stocks that will outperform the market. You own a single stock or a small portfolio of stocks. You do not know how well the market will perform over the next few months, but you are confident that your portfolio will do better than the market. What should you do?

You should short $\beta V_A/V_F$ index futures contracts, where β is the beta of your portfolio, V_A is the total value of the portfolio, and V_F is the current value of one index futures contract. If your portfolio performs better than a well-diversified portfolio with the same beta, you will then make money.

Consider an investor who in April holds 20,000 shares of a company, each worth $100. The investor feels that the market will be very volatile over the next three months but that the company has a good chance of outperforming the market. The investor decides to use the August futures contract on the Mini S&P 500 to hedge the market's return during the three-month period. The β of the company's stock is estimated at 1.1. Suppose that the current futures price for the August contract on the Mini S&P 500 is 2,100. Each contract is for delivery of $50 times the index. In this case, $V_A = 20,000 \times 100 = 2,000,000$ and $V_F = 2,100 \times 50 = 105,000$. The number of contracts that should be shorted is therefore

$$1.1 \times \frac{2,000,000}{105,000} = 20.95$$

Rounding to the nearest integer, the investor shorts 21 contracts, closing out the position in July. Suppose the company's stock price falls to $90 and the futures price of the

Mini S&P 500 falls to 1,850. The investor loses $20{,}000 \times (\$100 - \$90) = \$200{,}000$ on the stock, while gaining $21 \times 50 \times (2{,}100 - 1{,}850) = \$262{,}500$ on the futures contracts.

The overall gain to the investor in this case is \$62,500 because the company's stock price did not go down by as much as a well-diversified portfolio with a β of 1.1. If the market had gone up and the company's stock price went up by more than a portfolio with a β of 1.1 (as expected by the investor), then a profit would be made in this case as well.

3.6   STACK AND ROLL

Sometimes the expiration date of the hedge is later than the delivery dates of all the futures contracts that can be used. The hedger must then roll the hedge forward by closing out one futures contract and taking the same position in a futures contract with a later delivery date. Hedges can be rolled forward many times. The procedure is known as *stack and roll*. Consider a company that wishes to use a short hedge to reduce the risk associated with the price to be received for an asset at time T. If there are futures contracts 1, 2, 3, ..., n (not all necessarily in existence at the present time) with progressively later delivery dates, the company can use the following strategy:

Time t_1: Short futures contract 1

Time t_2: Close out futures contract 1
          Short futures contract 2

Time t_3: Close out futures contract 2
          Short futures contract 3
          $\vdots$

Time t_n: Close out futures contract $n - 1$
          Short futures contract n

Time T: Close out futures contract n.

Suppose that in April 2017 a company realizes that it will have 100,000 barrels of oil to sell in June 2018 and decides to hedge its risk with a hedge ratio of 1.0. (In this example, we do not make the adjustment for daily settlement described in Section 3.4.) The current spot price is \$49. Although futures contracts are traded with maturities stretching several years into the future, we suppose that only the first six delivery months have sufficient liquidity to meet the company's needs. The company therefore shorts 100 October 2017 contracts. In September 2017, it rolls the hedge forward into the March 2018 contract. In February 2018, it rolls the hedge forward again into the July 2018 contract.

Table 3.5   Data for the example on rolling oil hedge forward.

Date	Apr. 2017	Sept. 2017	Feb. 2018	June 2018
Oct. 2017 futures price	48.20	47.40		
Mar. 2018 futures price		47.00	46.50	
July 2018 futures price			46.30	45.90
Spot price	49.00			46.00

Business Snapshot 3.2 Metallgesellschaft: Hedging Gone Awry

Sometimes rolling hedges forward can lead to cash flow pressures. The problem was illustrated dramatically by the activities of a German company, Metallgesellschaft (MG), in the early 1990s.

  MG sold a huge volume of 5- to 10-year heating oil and gasoline fixed-price supply contracts to its customers at 6 to 8 cents above market prices. It hedged its exposure with long positions in short-dated futures contracts that were rolled forward. As it turned out, the price of oil fell and there were margin calls on the futures positions. Considerable short-term cash flow pressures were placed on MG. The members of MG who devised the hedging strategy argued that these short-term cash outflows were offset by positive cash flows that would ultimately be realized on the long-term fixed-price contracts. However, the company's senior management and its bankers became concerned about the huge cash drain. As a result, the company closed out all the hedge positions and agreed with its customers that the fixed-price contracts would be abandoned. The outcome was a loss to MG of $1.33 billion.

   One possible outcome is shown in Table 3.5. The October 2017 contract is shorted at $48.20 per barrel and closed out at $47.40 per barrel for a profit of $0.80 per barrel; the March 2018 contract is shorted at $47.00 per barrel and closed out at $46.50 per barrel for a profit of $0.50 per barrel. The July 2018 contract is shorted at $46.30 per barrel and closed out at $45.90 per barrel for a profit of $0.40 per barrel. The final spot price is $46.

   The dollar gain per barrel of oil from the short futures contracts is

$$(48.20 - 47.40) + (47.00 - 46.50) + (46.30 - 45.90) = 1.70$$

The oil price declined from $49 to $46. Receiving only $1.70 per barrel compensation for a price decline of $3.00 may appear unsatisfactory. However, we cannot expect total compensation for a price decline when futures prices are below spot prices. The best we can hope for is to lock in the futures price that would apply to a June 2018 contract if it were actively traded.

   In practice, a company usually has an exposure every month to the underlying asset and uses a 1-month futures contract for hedging because it is the most liquid. Initially it enters into ("stacks") sufficient contracts to cover its exposure to the end of its hedging horizon. One month later, it closes out all the contracts and "rolls" them into new 1-month contracts to cover its new exposure, and so on.

   As described in Business Snapshot 3.2, a German company, Metallgesellschaft, followed this strategy in the early 1990s to hedge contracts it had entered into to supply commodities at a fixed price. It ran into difficulties because the prices of the commodities declined so that there were immediate cash outflows on the futures and the expectation of eventual gains on the contracts. This mismatch between the timing of the cash flows on hedge and the timing of the cash flows from the position being hedged led to liquidity problems that could not be handled. The moral of the story is that potential liquidity problems should always be considered when a hedging strategy is being planned.

SUMMARY

This chapter has discussed various ways in which a company can take a position in futures contracts to offset an exposure to the price of an asset. If the exposure is such that the company gains when the price of the asset increases and loses when the price of the asset decreases, a short hedge is appropriate. If the exposure is the other way round (i.e., the company gains when the price of the asset decreases and loses when the price of the asset increases), a long hedge is appropriate.

Hedging is a way of reducing risk. As such, it should be welcomed by most executives. In reality, there are a number of theoretical and practical reasons why companies do not hedge. On a theoretical level, we can argue that shareholders, by holding well-diversified portfolios, can eliminate many of the risks faced by a company. They do not require the company to hedge these risks. On a practical level, a company may find that it is increasing rather than decreasing risk by hedging if none of its competitors does so. Also, a treasurer may fear criticism from other executives if the company makes a gain from movements in the price of the underlying asset and a loss on the hedge.

An important concept in hedging is basis risk. The basis is the difference between the spot price of an asset and its futures price. Basis risk arises from uncertainty as to what the basis will be at maturity of the hedge.

The hedge ratio is the ratio of the size of the position taken in futures contracts to the size of the exposure. It is not always optimal to use a hedge ratio of 1.0. If the hedger wishes to minimize the variance of a position, a hedge ratio different from 1.0 may be appropriate. The optimal hedge ratio is the slope of the best-fit line obtained when changes in the spot price are regressed against changes in the futures price.

Stock index futures can be used to hedge the systematic risk in an equity portfolio. The number of futures contracts required is the beta of the portfolio multiplied by the ratio of the value of the portfolio to the value of one futures contract. Stock index futures can also be used to change the beta of a portfolio without changing the stocks that make up the portfolio.

When there is no liquid futures contract that matures later than the expiration of the hedge, a strategy known as stack and roll may be appropriate. This involves entering into a sequence of futures contracts. When the first futures contract is near expiration, it is closed out and the hedger enters into a second contract with a later delivery month. When the second contract is close to expiration, it is closed out and the hedger enters into a third contract with a later delivery month; and so on. The result of all this is the creation of a long-dated futures contract by trading a series of short-dated contracts.

FURTHER READING

Adam, T., S. Dasgupta, and S. Titman. "Financial Constraints, Competition, and Hedging in Industry Equilibrium," *Journal of Finance*, 62, 5 (October 2007): 2445–73.

Adam, T. and C.S. Fernando. "Hedging, Speculation, and Shareholder Value," *Journal of Financial Economics*, 81, 2 (August 2006): 283–309.

Allayannis, G., and J. Weston. "The Use of Foreign Currency Derivatives and Firm Market Value," *Review of Financial Studies*, 14, 1 (Spring 2001): 243–76.

Brown, G.W. "Managing Foreign Exchange Risk with Derivatives." *Journal of Financial Economics*, 60 (2001): 401–48.

Campbell, J.Y., K. Serfaty–de Medeiros, and L.M. Viceira. "Global Currency Hedging," *Journal of Finance*, 65, 1 (February 2010): 87–121.

Campello, M., C. Lin, Y. Ma, and H. Zou. "The Real and Financial Implications of Corporate Hedging," *Journal of Finance*, 66, 5 (October 2011): 1615–47.

Cotter, J., and J. Hanly. "Hedging: Scaling and the Investor Horizon," *Journal of Risk*, 12, 2 (Winter 2009/2010): 49–77.

Culp, C. and M.H. Miller. "Metallgesellschaft and the Economics of Synthetic Storage," *Journal of Applied Corporate Finance*, 7, 4 (Winter 1995): 62–76.

Edwards, F.R. and M.S. Canter. "The Collapse of Metallgesellschaft: Unhedgeable Risks, Poor Hedging Strategy, or Just Bad Luck?" *Journal of Applied Corporate Finance*, 8, 1 (Spring 1995): 86–105.

Graham, J.R. and C.W. Smith, Jr. "Tax Incentives to Hedge," *Journal of Finance*, 54, 6 (1999): 2241–62.

Haushalter, G.D. "Financing Policy, Basis Risk, and Corporate Hedging: Evidence from Oil and Gas Producers," *Journal of Finance*, 55, 1 (2000): 107–52.

Jin, Y., and P. Jorion. "Firm Value and Hedging: Evidence from U.S. Oil and Gas Producers," *Journal of Finance*, 61, 2 (April 2006): 893–919.

Mello, A.S. and J.E. Parsons. "Hedging and Liquidity," *Review of Financial Studies*, 13 (Spring 2000): 127–53.

Neuberger, A.J. "Hedging Long-Term Exposures with Multiple Short-Term Futures Contracts," *Review of Financial Studies*, 12 (1999): 429–59.

Petersen, M.A. and S.R. Thiagarajan, "Risk Management and Hedging: With and Without Derivatives," *Financial Management*, 29, 4 (Winter 2000): 5–30.

Rendleman, R. "A Reconciliation of Potentially Conflicting Approaches to Hedging with Futures," *Advances in Futures and Options*, 6 (1993): 81–92.

Stulz, R.M. "Optimal Hedging Policies," *Journal of Financial and Quantitative Analysis*, 19 (June 1984): 127–40.

Tufano, P. "Who Manages Risk? An Empirical Examination of Risk Management Practices in the Gold Mining Industry," *Journal of Finance*, 51, 4 (1996): 1097–1138.

Practice Questions (Answers in Solutions Manual)

3.1. Under what circumstances are (a) a short hedge and (b) a long hedge appropriate?

3.2. Explain what is meant by *basis risk* when futures contracts are used for hedging.

3.3. Explain what is meant by a *perfect hedge*. Does a perfect hedge always lead to a better outcome than an imperfect hedge? Explain your answer.

3.4. Under what circumstances does a minimum variance hedge portfolio lead to no hedging at all?

3.5. Give three reasons why the treasurer of a company might not hedge the company's exposure to a particular risk.

3.6. Suppose that the standard deviation of quarterly changes in the prices of a commodity is $0.65, the standard deviation of quarterly changes in a futures price on the commodity is $0.81, and the coefficient of correlation between the two changes is 0.8. What is the optimal hedge ratio for a 3-month contract? What does it mean?

3.7. A company has a $20 million portfolio with a beta of 1.2. It would like to use futures contracts on a stock index to hedge its risk. The index futures price is currently standing at 1080, and each contract is for delivery of $250 times the index. What is the hedge that minimizes risk? What should the company do if it wants to reduce the beta of the portfolio to 0.6?

3.8. In the corn futures contract traded on an exchange, the following delivery months are available: March, May, July, September, and December. Which of the available contracts should be used for hedging when the expiration of the hedge is in (a) June, (b) July, and (c) January.

3.9. Does a perfect hedge always succeed in locking in the current spot price of an asset for a future transaction? Explain your answer.

3.10. Explain why a short hedger's position improves when the basis strengthens unexpectedly and worsens when the basis weakens unexpectedly.

3.11. Imagine you are the treasurer of a Japanese company exporting electronic equipment to the United States. Discuss how you would design a foreign exchange hedging strategy and the arguments you would use to sell the strategy to your fellow executives.

3.12. Suppose that in Example 3.2 of Section 3.3 the company decides to use a hedge ratio of 0.8. How does the decision affect the way in which the hedge is implemented and the result?

3.13. "If the minimum variance hedge ratio is calculated as 1.0, the hedge must be perfect." Is this statement true? Explain your answer.

3.14. "If there is no basis risk, the minimum variance hedge ratio is always 1.0." Is this statement true? Explain your answer.

3.15. "When the futures price of an asset is less than the spot price, long hedges are likely to be particularly attractive." Explain this statement.

3.16. The standard deviation of monthly changes in the spot price of live cattle is (in cents per pound) 1.2. The standard deviation of monthly changes in the futures price of live cattle for the closest contract is 1.4. The correlation between the futures price changes and the spot price changes is 0.7. It is now October 15. A beef producer is committed to purchasing 200,000 pounds of live cattle on November 15. The producer wants to use the December live cattle futures contracts to hedge its risk. Each contract is for the delivery of 40,000 pounds of cattle. What strategy should the beef producer follow?

3.17. A corn farmer argues "I do not use futures contracts for hedging. My real risk is not the price of corn. It is that my whole crop gets wiped out by the weather." Discuss this viewpoint. Should the farmer estimate his or her expected production of corn and hedge to try to lock in a price for expected production?

3.18. On July 1, an investor holds 50,000 shares of a certain stock. The market price is $30 per share. The investor is interested in hedging against movements in the market over the next month and decides to use an index futures contract. The index futures price is currently 1,500 and one contract is for delivery of $50 times the index. The beta of the stock is 1.3. What strategy should the investor follow? Under what circumstances will it be profitable?

3.19. Suppose that in Table 3.5 the company decides to use a hedge ratio of 1.5. How does the decision affect the way the hedge is implemented and the result?

3.20. A futures contract is used for hedging. Explain why the daily settlement of the contract can give rise to cash-flow problems.

3.21. An airline executive has argued: "There is no point in our using oil futures. There is just as much chance that the price of oil in the future will be less than the futures price as there is that it will be greater than this price." Discuss the executive's viewpoint.

3.22. Suppose that the 1-year gold lease rate is 1.5% and the 1-year risk-free rate is 5.0%. Both rates are compounded annually. Use the discussion in Business Snapshot 3.1 to calculate the maximum 1-year gold forward price Goldman Sachs should quote to the gold-mining company when the spot price is $1,200.

3.23. The expected return on the S&P 500 is 12% and the risk-free rate is 5%. What is the expected return on an investment with a beta of (a) 0.2, (b) 0.5, and (c) 1.4?

Further Questions

3.24. It is now June. A company knows that it will sell 5,000 barrels of crude oil in September. It uses the October CME Group futures contract to hedge the price it will receive. Each contract is on 1,000 barrels of "light sweet crude." What position should it take? What price risks is it still exposed to after taking the position?

3.25. Sixty futures contracts are used to hedge an exposure to the price of silver. Each futures contract is on 5,000 ounces of silver. At the time the hedge is closed out, the basis is $0.20 per ounce. What is the effect of the basis on the hedger's financial position if (a) the trader is hedging the purchase of silver and (b) the trader is hedging the sale of silver?

3.26. A trader owns 55,000 units of a particular asset and decides to hedge the value of her position with futures contracts on another related asset. Each futures contract is on 5,000 units. The spot price of the asset that is owned is $28 and the standard deviation of the change in this price over the life of the hedge is estimated to be $0.43. The futures price of the related asset is $27 and the standard deviation of the change in this over the life of the hedge is $0.40. The coefficient of correlation between the spot price change and futures price change is 0.95.
(a) What is the minimum variance hedge ratio?
(b) Should the hedger take a long or short futures position?
(c) What is the optimal number of futures contracts when adjustments for daily settlement are not considered?
(d) How can the daily settlement of futures contracts be taken into account?

3.27. A company wishes to hedge its exposure to a new fuel whose price changes have a 0.6 correlation with gasoline futures price changes. The company will lose $1 million for each 1 cent increase in the price per gallon of the new fuel over the next three months. The new fuel's price changes have a standard deviation that is 50% greater than price changes in gasoline futures prices. If gasoline futures are used to hedge the exposure, what should the hedge ratio be? What is the company's exposure measured in gallons of the new fuel? What position, measured in gallons, should the company take in gasoline futures? How many gasoline futures contracts should be traded? Each contract is on 42,000 gallons.

3.28. A portfolio manager has maintained an actively managed portfolio with a beta of 0.2. During the last year, the risk-free rate was 5% and equities performed very badly providing a return of −30%. The portfolio manager produced a return of −10% and claims that in the circumstances it was a good performance. Discuss this claim.

3.29. The following table gives data on monthly changes in the spot price and the futures price for a certain commodity. Use the data to calculate a minimum variance hedge ratio. (Do not make an adjustment for daily settlement.)

Spot price change	+0.50	+0.61	−0.22	−0.35	+0.79
Futures price change	+0.56	+0.63	−0.12	−0.44	+0.60
Spot price change	+0.04	+0.15	+0.70	−0.51	−0.41
Futures price change	−0.06	+0.01	+0.80	−0.56	−0.46

3.30. It is July 16. A company has a portfolio of stocks worth $100 million. The beta of the portfolio is 1.2. The company would like to use the December futures contract on a stock index to change the beta of the portfolio to 0.5 during the period July 16 to November 16. The index futures price is currently 2,000 and each contract is on $250 times the index.
(a) What position should the company take?
(b) Suppose that the company changes its mind and decides to increase the beta of the portfolio from 1.2 to 1.5. What position in futures contracts should it take?

3.31. A fund manager has a portfolio worth $50 million with a beta of 0.87. The manager is concerned about the performance of the market over the next 2 months and plans to use 3-month futures contracts on a well-diversified index to hedge its risk. The current level of the index is 1,250, one contract is on 250 times the index, the risk-free rate is 6% per annum, and the dividend yield on the index is 3% per annum. The current 3-month futures price is 1,259.
(a) What position should the fund manager take to hedge all exposure to the market over the next 2 months?
(b) Calculate the effect of your strategy on the fund manager's returns if the index in 2 months is 1,000, 1,100, 1,200, 1,300, and 1,400. Assume that the 1-month futures price is 0.25% higher than the index level at this time.

3.32. It is now October 2017. A company anticipates that it will purchase 1 million pounds of copper in each of February 2018, August 2018, February 2019, and August 2019. The company has decided to use the futures contracts traded by the CME Group to hedge its risk. One contract is for the delivery of 25,000 pounds of copper. The initial margin is $2,000 per contract and the maintenance margin is $1,500 per contract. The company's policy is to hedge 80% of its exposure. Contracts with maturities up to 13 months into the future are considered to have sufficient liquidity to meet the company's needs. Devise a hedging strategy for the company. (Do not make the adjustment for daily settlement described in Section 3.4.)

Assume the market prices (in cents per pound) today and at future dates are as in the following table. What is the impact of the strategy you propose on the price the company pays for copper? What is the initial margin requirement in October 2017? Is the company subject to any margin calls?

Date	Oct. 2017	Feb. 2018	Aug. 2018	Feb. 2019	Aug. 2019
Spot price	372.00	369.00	365.00	377.00	388.00
Mar. 2018 futures price	372.30	369.10			
Sept. 2018 futures price	372.80	370.20	364.80		
Mar. 2019 futures price		370.70	364.30	376.70	
Sept. 2019 futures price			364.20	376.50	388.20

APPENDIX

CAPITAL ASSET PRICING MODEL

The capital asset pricing model (CAPM) is a model that can be used to relate the expected return from an asset to the risk of the return. The risk in the return from an asset is divided into two parts. *Systematic risk* is risk related to the return from the market as a whole and cannot be diversified away. *Nonsystematic risk* is risk that is unique to the asset and can be diversified away by choosing a large portfolio of different assets. CAPM argues that the return should depend only on systematic risk. The CAPM formula is[6]

$$\text{Expected return on asset} = R_F + \beta(R_M - R_F) \qquad (3A.1)$$

where R_M is the return on the portfolio of all available investments, R_F is the return on a risk-free investment, and β (the Greek letter beta) is a parameter measuring systematic risk.

The return from the portfolio of all available investments, R_M, is referred to as the *return on the market* and is usually approximated as the return on a well-diversified stock index such as the S&P 500. The beta (β) of an asset is a measure of the sensitivity of its returns to returns from the market. It can be estimated from historical data as the slope obtained when the excess return on the asset over the risk-free rate is regressed against the excess return on the market over the risk-free rate. When $\beta = 0$, an asset's returns are not sensitive to returns from the market. In this case, it has no systematic risk and equation (3A.1) shows that its expected return is the risk-free rate; when $\beta = 0.5$, the excess return on the asset over the risk-free rate is on average half of the excess return of the market over the risk-free rate; when $\beta = 1$, the expected return on the asset equals to the return on the market; and so on.

Suppose that the risk-free rate R_F is 5% and the return on the market is 13%. Equation (3A.1) shows that, when the beta of an asset is zero, its expected return is 5%. When $\beta = 0.75$, its expected return is $0.05 + 0.75 \times (0.13 - 0.05) = 0.11$, or 11%.

The derivation of CAPM requires a number of assumptions.[7] In particular:

1. Investors care only about the expected return and standard deviation of the return from an asset.

2. The returns from two assets are correlated with each other only because of their correlation with the return from the market. This is equivalent to assuming that there is only one factor driving returns.

3. Investors focus on returns over a single period and that period is the same for all investors.

4. Investors can borrow and lend at the same risk-free rate.

5. Tax does not influence investment decisions.

6. All investors make the same estimates of expected returns, standard deviations of returns, and correlations betweeen returns.

---

[6] If the return on the market is not known, R_M is replaced by the expected value of R_M in this formula.

[7] For details on the derivation, see, for example, J.C. Hull, *Risk Management and Financial Institutions*, 4th edn. Hoboken, NJ: Wiley, 2015, Chap. 1.

These assumptions are at best only approximately true. Nevertheless CAPM has proved to be a useful tool for portfolio managers and is often used as a benchmark for assessing their performance.

When the asset is an individual stock, the expected return given by equation (3A.1) is not a particularly good predictor of the actual return. But, when the asset is a well-diversified portfolio of stocks, it is a much better predictor. As a result, the equation

$$\text{Return on diversified portfolio} = R_F + \beta(R_M - R_F)$$

can be used as a basis for hedging a diversified portfolio, as described in Section 3.5. The β in the equation is the beta of the portfolio. It can be calculated as the weighted average of the betas of the stocks in the portfolio.

CHAPTER 4

Interest Rates

Interest rates are a factor in the valuation of virtually all derivatives and will feature prominently in much of the material that will be presented in the rest of this book. This chapter introduces a number of different types of interest rate. It deals with some fundamental issues concerned with the way interest rates are measured and analyzed. It explains the compounding frequency used to define an interest rate and the meaning of continuously compounded interest rates, which are used extensively in the analysis of derivatives. It covers zero rates, par yields, and yield curves, discusses bond pricing, and outlines a "bootstrap" procedure commonly used to calculate zero-coupon interest rates. It also covers forward rates and forward rate agreements and reviews different theories of the term structure of interest rates. Finally, it explains the use of duration and convexity measures to determine the sensitivity of bond prices to interest rate changes.

Chapter 6 will cover interest rate futures and show how the duration measure can be used when interest rate exposures are hedged. For ease of exposition, day count conventions will be ignored throughout this chapter. The nature of these conventions and their impact on calculations will be discussed in Chapters 6 and 7.

4.1 TYPES OF RATES

An interest rate in a particular situation defines the amount of money a borrower promises to pay the lender. For any given currency, many different types of interest rates are regularly quoted. These include mortgage rates, deposit rates, prime borrowing rates, and so on. The interest rate applicable in a situation depends on the credit risk. This is the risk that there will be a default by the borrower of funds, so that the interest and principal are not paid to the lender as promised. The higher the credit risk, the higher the interest rate that is promised by the borrower.

Interest rates are often expressed in basis points. One basis point is 0.01% per annum.

Treasury Rates

Treasury rates are the rates an investor earns on Treasury bills and Treasury bonds. These are the instruments used by a government to borrow in its own currency. Japanese Treasury rates are the rates at which the Japanese government borrows in yen; U.S. Treasury rates are the rates at which the U.S. government borrows in U.S. dollars; and so on. It is usually assumed that there is no chance that a government will default on an obligation denominated in its own currency. Treasury rates are therefore regarded as risk-free in the sense that an investor who buys a Treasury bill or Treasury bond is certain that interest and principal payments will be made as promised.

LIBOR

LIBOR is short for *London Interbank Offered Rate*. It is an unsecured short-term borrowing rate between banks. LIBOR rates are quoted for a number of different currencies and borrowing periods. The borrowing periods range from one day to one year. LIBOR rates are used as reference rates for hundreds of trillions of dollars of transactions throughout the world. One popular derivatives transaction that uses LIBOR as a reference interest rate is an interest rate swap. (Interest rate swaps are introduced in Section 4.2 and discussed more fully in Chapter 7.) LIBOR rates are compiled by asking 18 global banks to provide quotes estimating the rate of interest at which they could borrow funds from other banks just prior to 11:00 a.m. (U.K. time). The highest four and the lowest four of the quotes for each currency/borrowing period combination are discarded and the remaining ones are averaged to determine the LIBOR fixings for a day. The banks submitting quotes typically have a AA credit rating.[1] LIBOR is therefore usually considered to be an estimate of the unsecured borrowing rate for a AA-rated bank.

Some traders working for banks have been investigated for attempting to manipulate LIBOR quotes. Why might they do this? Suppose that the payoff to a bank from a derivative depends on the LIBOR fixing on a particular day with the payoff increasing as the fixing increases. It is tempting for a trader to provide a high quote on that day and to try to persuade other banks to do the same. Tom Hayes was the first trader to be convicted of LIBOR manipulation. In August 2015, he was sentenced to 14 years (later reduced to 11 years) in prison by a court in the U.K. A problem with the system was that there was not enough interbank borrowing for banks to make accurate estimates of their borrowing rates for all the quotes that were required and some judgment was inevitably necessary. In an attempt to improve things, the number of different currencies has been reduced from 10 to 5 and the number of different borrowing periods has been reduced from 15 to 7. Also, regulatory oversight of the way the borrowing estimates are produced has been improved.

It is now recognized that LIBOR is a less-than-ideal reference rate for derivatives transactions because it is determined from estimates made by banks, not from market transactions. It is likely that the derivatives market will move to using other reference rates in the future.

Overnight Rates

Banks are required to maintain a certain amount of cash, known as a reserve, with the central bank. The reserve requirement for a bank at any time depends on its outstanding assets and liabilities. At the end of a day, some financial institutions typically have surplus funds in their accounts with the central bank while others have requirements for

---

[1] The best credit rating given to a company by the rating agencies S&P and Fitch is AAA. The second best is AA. The corresponding credit ratings for Moody's are Aaa and Aa.

funds. This leads to borrowing and lending overnight. A broker usually matches borrowers and lenders. In the United States, the central bank is the Federal Reserve (often referred to as the Fed) and the overnight rate is called the *federal funds rate*. The weighted average of the rates in brokered transactions (with weights being determined by the size of the transaction) is termed the *effective federal funds rate*. This overnight rate is monitored by the Federal Reserve, which may intervene with its own transactions in an attempt to raise or lower it. Other countries have similar systems to the United States. For example, in the United Kingdom, the average of brokered overnight rates is termed the *sterling overnight index average* (SONIA), and in the eurozone, it is termed the *euro overnight index average* (EONIA).

Repo Rates

Unlike LIBOR and the overnight federal funds rate, repo rates are secured borrowing rates. In a repo (or repurchase agreement), a financial institution that owns securities agrees to sell the securities for a certain price and buy them back at a later time for a slightly higher price. The financial institution is obtaining a loan and the interest it pays is the difference between the price at which the securities are sold and the price at which they are repurchased. The interest rate is referred to as the *repo rate*.

If structured carefully, a repo involves very little credit risk. If the borrower does not honor the agreement, the lending company simply keeps the securities. If the lending company does not keep to its side of the agreement, the original owner of the securities keeps the cash provided by the lending company. The most common type of repo is an *overnight repo*, which may be rolled over day to day. However, longer-term arrangements, known as *term repos*, are sometimes used. Because it is a secured rate, a repo rate is generally slightly below the corresponding LIBOR or fed funds rate.

4.2   SWAP RATES

Swaps are discussed in Chapter 7, but it will be useful to provide a brief introduction to them here. The most common swap is an agreement where a LIBOR interest rate is exchanged for a fixed rate of interest for a period of time. For example, two parties could agree to exchange three-month LIBOR (with the rate being reset every three months) applied to a principal of $100 million for a fixed rate of interest of 3% per annum applied to the same principal for five years. One party would pay LIBOR and receive the fixed rate of 3%; the other party would receive LIBOR and pay a fixed rate of 3%.

A swap is designed so that it has zero value initially. The fixed rate (3% in our example) is known as the swap rate. A bank can earn this five-year swap rate as follows:

1. Make a series of 20 three-month loans for $100 million (at times 0, 3 months, 6 months, . . . , 57 months) to AA-rated banks at LIBOR. The bank ensures that a borrowing bank is always rated AA at the beginning of the life of its three-month loan.

2. Enter into a swap where the three-month LIBOR rate of interest is paid and a fixed rate of interest (3% per annum in our example) is received.

Note that it would be more risky for a bank to lend money to a single AA-rated bank for five years. A bank that is initially creditworthy is unlikely to default in three months, but over a five-year period its credit quality could well decline. It is better for the lending bank to have 20 three-month credit exposures than one five-year credit exposure. (The probability that a bank initially rated AA will default over five years is more than twenty times the probability that it will default in three months.)

An interest rate that is earned by renewing loans periodically in the way we have described is referred to as a *continually refreshed rate*. The swap rate in our example is a continually refreshed rate lasting five years and based on three-month LIBOR.

Overnight Indexed Swaps

An overnight indexed swap (OIS) is a swap where an agreed fixed rate for a period (e.g., one month or three months) is exchanged for the geometric average of the overnight rates during the period. The overnight rate is the one discussed in Section 4.1 (the effective federal funds rate in the United States or a similarly defined rate in another country). If during a certain period, a bank borrows funds at the overnight rate (rolling the interest and principal forward each day), the interest rate it pays for the period is the geometric average of the overnight interest rates. Similarly, if it lends money at the overnight interest rate every day (rolling the interest and principal forward each day), the interest it earns for the period is also the geometric average of the overnight interest rates. An OIS therefore allows overnight borrowing or lending for a period to be swapped for borrowing or lending at an agreed fixed rate for the period. The agreed fixed rate in an OIS is referred to as the *OIS rate*. If this fixed rate is greater than the geometric average of daily rates for the period, there is a payment from the fixed-rate payer to the floating-rate payer at the end of the period; otherwise, there is a payment from the floating-rate payer to the fixed-rate payer. For example, suppose that in a U.S. three-month OIS the notional principal is $100 million and the fixed rate (i.e., the OIS rate) is 3% per annum. If the geometric average of overnight effective federal funds rates during the three months proves to be 2.8% per annum, the fixed rate payer has to pay $0.25 \times (0.030 - 0.028) \times \$100,000,000$ or $50,000 to the floating rate payer. (This calculation does not take account of the impact of day count conventions, which will be discussed in later chapters.)

OISs lasting 10 years or longer are now traded. An OIS lasting longer than one year is typically divided into three-month subperiods. At the end of each subperiod, the geometric average of the overnight rates during the subperiod is exchanged for the OIS rate.

The OIS rate is a continually refreshed overnight rate: it is the rate that can be earned by a financial institution when a series of overnight loans to other financial institutions are combined with a swap. The credit risk associated with a three-month OIS rate is the credit risk associated with a series of one-day loans, which is less than the credit risk associated with a single three-month loan.

4.3   THE RISK-FREE RATE

As we shall see, the usual approach to valuing derivatives involves setting up a riskless portfolio and arguing that the return on the portfolio should be the risk-free rate. The risk-free rate therefore plays a central role in derivatives pricing. It might be thought that derivatives traders would use the rates on Treasury bills and Treasury bonds as risk-free rates. In fact they do not do this. This is because there are tax and regulatory factors that lead to Treasury rates being artificially low. For example:

1. Banks are not required to keep capital for investments in a Treasury instruments, but they are required to keep capital for other very low risk instruments.

2. In the United States, Treasury instruments are given favorable tax treatment compared with other very low risk instruments because the interest earned by investors is not taxed at the state level.

Prior to the credit crisis which started in 2007, LIBOR rates were regarded as risk-free rates. It was considered extremely unlikely that a AA-rated bank would default on a loan lasting 12 months or less. During the crisis, LIBOR rates soared and financial institutions realized that it was no longer reasonable to assume that they were risk-free rates. Since the crisis, OIS rates have been used as risk-free rates. As explained in Section 4.2, the OIS rate is a continually refreshed one-day rate. There is some chance that a creditworthy bank will default in one day, but this is considered sufficiently small to be ignored.

The three-month LIBOR–OIS spread is watched carefully by market participants as a measure of stress in financial markets. It is the amount by which three-month LIBOR exceeds the three-month OIS rate. It measures the difference between the credit risk in a three-month interbank loan and the credit risk in a series of one-day interbank loans. In normal market conditions, it is less than 15 basis points. However, it rose sharply during the credit crisis because banks became less willing to lend to each other for three-month periods. In October 2008, the spread spiked to an all time high of 364 basis points, but by the end of 2009 it had returned to more normal levels. Later it rose again as a result of concerns about the financial health of Greece and some other European countries.

4.4 MEASURING INTEREST RATES

A statement by a bank that the interest rate on one-year deposits is 10% per annum sounds straightforward and unambiguous. In fact, its precise meaning depends on the way the interest rate is measured.

If the interest rate is measured with annual compounding, the bank's statement that the interest rate is 10% means that $100 grows to

$$\$100 \times 1.1 = \$110$$

at the end of 1 year. When the interest rate is measured with semiannual compounding, it means that 5% is earned every 6 months, with the interest being reinvested. In this case, $100 grows to

$$\$100 \times 1.05 \times 1.05 = \$110.25$$

at the end of 1 year. When the interest rate is measured with quarterly compounding, the bank's statement means that 2.5% is earned every 3 months, with the interest being reinvested. The $100 then grows to

$$\$100 \times 1.025^4 = \$110.38$$

Table 4.1 Effect of the compounding frequency on the value of $100 at the end of 1 year when the interest rate is 10% per annum.

Compounding frequency	Value of $100 at end of year ($)
Annually ($m = 1$)	110.00
Semiannually ($m = 2$)	110.25
Quarterly ($m = 4$)	110.38
Monthly ($m = 12$)	110.47
Weekly ($m = 52$)	110.51
Daily ($m = 365$)	110.52

at the end of 1 year. Table 4.1 shows the effect of increasing the compounding frequency further.

The compounding frequency defines the units in which an interest rate is measured. A rate expressed with one compounding frequency can be converted into an equivalent rate with a different compounding frequency. For example, from Table 4.1 we see that 10.25% with annual compounding is equivalent to 10% with semiannual compounding. We can think of the difference between one compounding frequency and another to be analogous to the difference between kilometers and miles. They are two different units of measurement.

To generalize our results, suppose that an amount A is invested for n years at an interest rate of R per annum. If the rate is compounded once per annum, the terminal value of the investment is

$$A(1 + R)^n$$

If the rate is compounded m times per annum, the terminal value of the investment is

$$A\left(1 + \frac{R}{m}\right)^{mn} \tag{4.1}$$

When $m = 1$, the rate is sometimes referred to as the *equivalent annual interest rate*.

Continuous Compounding

The limit as the compounding frequency, m, tends to infinity is known as *continuous compounding*.[2] With continuous compounding, it can be shown that an amount A invested for n years at rate R grows to

$$Ae^{Rn} \tag{4.2}$$

where e is approximately 2.71828. The exponential function, e^x, is built into most calculators, so the computation of the expression in equation (4.2) presents no problems. In the example in Table 4.1, $A = 100$, $n = 1$, and $R = 0.1$, so that the value to which A

---

[2] Actuaries sometimes refer to a continuously compounded rate as the *force of interest*.

grows with continuous compounding is

$$100e^{0.1} = \$110.52$$

This is (to two decimal places) the same as the value with daily compounding. For most practical purposes, continuous compounding can be thought of as being equivalent to daily compounding. Compounding a sum of money at a continuously compounded rate R for n years involves multiplying it by e^{Rn}. Discounting it at a continuously compounded rate R for n years involves multiplying by e^{-Rn}.

In this book, interest rates will be measured with continuous compounding except where stated otherwise. Readers used to working with interest rates that are measured with annual, semiannual, or some other compounding frequency may find this a little strange at first. However, continuously compounded interest rates are used to such a great extent in pricing derivatives that it makes sense to get used to working with them now.

Suppose that R_c is a rate of interest with continuous compounding and R_m is the equivalent rate with compounding m times per annum. From the results in equations (4.1) and (4.2), we have

$$Ae^{R_c n} = A\left(1 + \frac{R_m}{m}\right)^{mn}$$

or

$$e^{R_c} = \left(1 + \frac{R_m}{m}\right)^{m}$$

This means that

$$R_c = m \ln\left(1 + \frac{R_m}{m}\right) \qquad (4.3)$$

and

$$R_m = m(e^{R_c/m} - 1) \qquad (4.4)$$

These equations can be used to convert a rate with a compounding frequency of m times per annum to a continuously compounded rate and vice versa. The natural logarithm function $\ln x$, which is built into most calculators, is the inverse of the exponential function, so that, if $y = \ln x$, then $x = e^y$.

Example 4.1

Consider an interest rate that is quoted as 10% per annum with semiannual compounding. From equation (4.3) with $m = 2$ and $R_m = 0.1$, the equivalent rate with continuous compounding is

$$2 \ln\left(1 + \frac{0.1}{2}\right) = 0.09758$$

or 9.758% per annum.

Example 4.2

Suppose that a lender quotes the interest rate on loans as 8% per annum with continuous compounding, and that interest is actually paid quarterly. From equation (4.4) with $m = 4$ and $R_c = 0.08$, the equivalent rate with quarterly compounding is

$$4 \times (e^{0.08/4} - 1) = 0.0808$$

or 8.08% per annum. This means that on a $1,000 loan, interest payments of $20.20 would be required each quarter.

4.5 ZERO RATES

The *n*-year zero-coupon interest rate is the rate of interest earned on an investment that starts today and lasts for *n* years. All the interest and principal is realized at the end of *n* years. There are no intermediate payments. The *n*-year zero-coupon interest rate is sometimes also referred to as the *n*-year *spot rate*, the *n*-year *zero rate*, or just the *n*-year zero. Suppose a 5-year zero rate with continuous compounding is quoted as 5% per annum. This means that $100, if invested for 5 years, grows to

$$100 \times e^{0.05 \times 5} = 128.40$$

Most of the interest rates we observe directly in the market are not pure zero rates. Consider a 5-year risk-free bond that provides a 6% coupon. The price of this bond does not by itself determine the 5-year risk-free zero rate because some of the return on the bond is realized in the form of coupons prior to the end of year 5. Later in this chapter we will discuss how we can determine zero rates from the market prices of coupon-bearing instruments.

4.6 BOND PRICING

Most bonds pay coupons to the holder periodically. The bond's principal (which is also known as its par value or face value) is paid at the end of its life. The theoretical price of a bond can be calculated as the present value of all the cash flows that will be received by the owner of the bond. Sometimes bond traders use the same discount rate for all the cash flows underlying a bond, but a more accurate approach is to use a different zero rate for each cash flow.

To illustrate this, consider the situation where zero rates, measured with continuous compounding, are as in Table 4.2. (We explain later how these can be calculated.) Suppose that a 2-year bond with a principal of $100 provides coupons at the rate of 6% per annum semiannually. To calculate the present value of the first coupon of $3, we discount it at 5.0% for 6 months; to calculate the present value of the second coupon of $3, we discount it at 5.8% for 1 year; and so on. Therefore, the theoretical price of the bond is

$$3e^{-0.05 \times 0.5} + 3e^{-0.058 \times 1.0} + 3e^{-0.064 \times 1.5} + 103e^{-0.068 \times 2.0} = 98.39$$

or $98.39. (DerivaGem can be used to calculate bond prices.)

Table 4.2 Zero rates.

Maturity (years)	Zero rate (% continuously compounded)
0.5	5.0
1.0	5.8
1.5	6.4
2.0	6.8

Bond Yield

A bond's yield is the single discount rate that, when applied to all cash flows, gives a bond price equal to its market price. Suppose that the theoretical price of the bond we have been considering, $98.39, is also its market value (i.e., the market's price of the bond is in exact agreement with the data in Table 4.2). If y is the yield on the bond, expressed with continuous compounding, it must be true that

$$3e^{-y \times 0.5} + 3e^{-y \times 1.0} + 3e^{-y \times 1.5} + 103e^{-y \times 2.0} = 98.39$$

This equation can be solved using an iterative ("trial and error") procedure to give $y = 6.76\%$.[3]

Par Yield

The *par yield* for a certain bond maturity is the coupon rate that causes the bond price to equal its par value. (The par value is the same as the principal value.) Usually the bond is assumed to provide semiannual coupons. Suppose that the coupon on a 2-year bond in our example is c per annum (or $\frac{1}{2}c$ per 6 months). Using the zero rates in Table 4.2, the value of the bond is equal to its par value of 100 when

$$\frac{c}{2}e^{-0.05 \times 0.5} + \frac{c}{2}e^{-0.058 \times 1.0} + \frac{c}{2}e^{-0.064 \times 1.5} + \left(100 + \frac{c}{2}\right)e^{-0.068 \times 2.0} = 100$$

This equation can be solved in a straightforward way to give $c = 6.87$. The 2-year par yield is therefore 6.87% per annum.

More generally, if d is the present value of $1 received at the maturity of the bond, A is the value of an annuity that pays one dollar on each coupon payment date, and m is the number of coupon payments per year, then the par yield c must satisfy

$$100 = A\frac{c}{m} + 100d$$

so that

$$c = \frac{(100 - 100d)m}{A}$$

In our example, $m = 2$, $d = e^{-0.068 \times 2} = 0.87284$, and

$$A = e^{-0.05 \times 0.5} + e^{-0.058 \times 1.0} + e^{-0.064 \times 1.5} + e^{-0.068 \times 2.0} = 3.70027$$

The formula confirms that the par yield is 6.87% per annum. A bond with this coupon and semiannual payments is worth par.

4.7 DETERMINING ZERO RATES

In this section we describe a procedure known as the *bootstrap method* which can be used to determine zero rates.

---

[3] One way of solving nonlinear equations of the form $f(y) = 0$, such as this one, is to use the Newton–Raphson method. We start with an estimate y_0 of the solution and produce successively better estimates $y_1, y_2, y_3, \ldots$ using the formula $y_{i+1} = y_i - f(y_i)/f'(y_i)$, where $f'(y)$ denotes the derivative of f with respect to y.

Treasury Rates

We first show how Treasury zero rates can be calculated from Treasury bill and Treasury bond prices. Consider the data in Table 4.3 on the prices of five bonds. Because the first three bonds pay no coupons, the zero rates corresponding to the maturities of these bonds can easily be calculated. The 3-month bond has the effect of turning an investment of 99.6 into 100 in 3 months. The continuously compounded 3-month rate R is therefore given by solving

$$100 = 99.6e^{R \times 0.25}$$

It is 1.603% per annum. The 6-month continuously compounded rate is similarly given by solving

$$100 = 99.0e^{R \times 0.5}$$

It is 2.010% per annum. Similarly, the 1-year rate with continuous compounding is given by solving

$$100 = 97.8e^{R \times 1.0}$$

It is 2.225% per annum.

The fourth bond lasts 1.5 years. The cash flows it provides are as follows:

6 months: $2
1 year: $2
1.5 years: $102.

From our earlier calculations, we know that the discount rate for the payment at the end of 6 months is 2.010% and that the discount rate for the payment at the end of 1 year is 2.225%. We also know that the bond's price, $102.5, must equal the present value of all the payments received by the bondholder. Suppose the 1.5-year zero rate is denoted by R. It follows that

$$2e^{-0.02010 \times 0.5} + 2e^{-0.02225 \times 1.0} + 102e^{-R \times 1.5} = 102.5$$

This reduces to

$$e^{-1.5R} = 0.96631$$

or

$$R = -\frac{\ln(0.96631)}{1.5} = 0.02284$$

Table 4.3 Data for bootstrap method.

Bond principal ($)	Time to maturity (years)	Annual coupon* ($)	Bond price ($)	Bond yield** (%)
100	0.25	0	99.6	1.6064 (Q)
100	0.50	0	99.0	2.0202 (SA)
100	1.00	0	97.8	2.2495 (A)
100	1.50	4	102.5	2.2949 (SA)
100	2.00	5	105.0	2.4238 (SA)

*Half the stated coupon is assumed to be paid every 6 months. **Compounding frequency corresponds to payment frequency: Q = quarterly, SA = semiannual, A = annual.

Table 4.4 Continuously compounded zero rates determined from data in Table 4.3.

Maturity (years)	Zero rate (% continuously compounded)
0.25	1.603
0.50	2.010
1.00	2.225
1.50	2.284
2.00	2.416

The 1.5-year zero rate is therefore 2.284%. This is the only zero rate that is consistent with the 6-month rate, 1-year rate, and the data in Table 4.3.

The 2-year zero rate can be calculated similarly from the 6-month, 1-year, and 1.5-year zero rates, and the information on the last bond in Table 4.3. If R is the 2-year zero rate, then

$$2.5e^{-0.02010 \times 0.5} + 2.5e^{-0.02225 \times 1.0} + 2.5e^{-0.02284 \times 1.5} + 102.5e^{-R \times 2.0} = 105$$

This gives $R = 0.02416$, or 2.416%.

The rates we have calculated are summarized in Table 4.4. A chart showing the zero rate as a function of maturity is known as the *zero curve*. A common assumption is that the zero curve is linear between the points determined using the bootstrap method. (This means that the 1.25-year zero rate is $0.5 \times 2.225 + 0.5 \times 2.284 = 2.255\%$ in our example.) It is also usually assumed that the zero curve is horizontal prior to the first point and horizontal beyond the last point. Figure 4.1 shows the zero curve for our data using these assumptions. By using longer maturity bonds, the zero curve would be more accurately determined beyond 2 years.

Figure 4.1 Zero rates given by the bootstrap method.

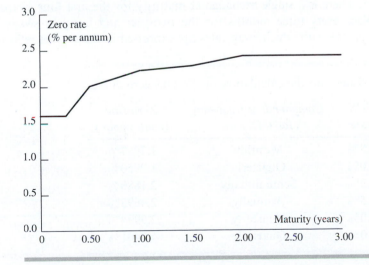

In practice, we do not usually have bonds with maturities equal to exactly 1.5 years, 2 years, 2.5 years, and so on. One approach is to interpolate between the bond price data before it is used to calculate the zero curve. For example, if it is known that a 2.3-year bond with a coupon of 6% sells for 108 and a 2.7-year bond with a coupon of 6.5% sells for 109, it might be assumed that a 2.5-year bond with a coupon of 6.25% would sell for 108.5. Another more general procedure, which we use below for the OIS example, is as follows. Define $t_1, t_2, \ldots, t_n$ as the maturities of the instruments whose prices are to be matched. Assume a piecewise linear curve with corners at these times. Use an iterative "trial and error" procedure to determine the rate at time t_1 that matches the price of the first instrument, then use a similar procedure to determine the rate at time t_2 that matches the price of the second instrument, and so on. For any trial rate, the rates used for coupons are determined by linear interpolation.

A more sophisticated approach is to use polynomial or exponential functions, rather than linear functions, for the zero curve between times t_i and t_{i+1} for all i. The functions are chosen so that they price the bonds correctly and so that the gradient of the zero curve does not change at any of the t_i. This is referred to as using a *spline function* for the zero curve.

OIS Rates

A similar bootstrap approach to that just described can be used to determine OIS zero rates. As explained in Section 4.3, OIS rates are the risk-free rates used by traders to value derivatives. An overnight indexed swap (OIS) involves exchanging a fixed rate for a floating rate. The floating rate is calculated by assuming that someone invests at the (very low risk) overnight rate, reinvesting the proceeds each day.

An OIS with a maturity of 12 months or less typically involves the fixed rate being exchanged for the floating rate just once. The (fixed) OIS rate that is exchanged for floating is therefore already a zero rate. It can therefore be treated like the three-month, six-month, and 12-month Treasury rates in Table 4.4. When an OIS has a maturity longer than 12 months, payments are usually exchanged every three months. The OIS rate can then be treated as the rate on a par yield bond.

Suppose that the fixed OIS rates that can be exchanged for floating in the market are those in Table 4.5. There is a single exchange at maturity for the first four swaps and exchanges take place every three months for the two-year and five-year swaps. The compounding frequency with which swap rates are expressed in the market reflects the

Table 4.5 OIS Rates and the calculation of the OIS zero curve.

OIS maturity	OIS rate	Compounding frequency for OIS rate	Zero rate (cont. comp.)
1 month	1.8%	Monthly	1.7987%
3 months	2.0%	Quarterly	1.9950%
6 months	2.2%	Semiannually	2.1880%
12 months	2.5%	Annually	2.4693%
2 years	3.0%	Quarterly	2.9994%
5 years	4.0%	Quarterly	4.0401%

Figure 4.2   OIS zero rates in Table 4.5.

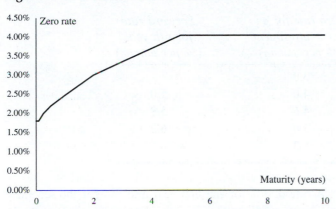

frequency of payments. The third column shows this. The one-month rate in Table 4.3 is expressed with monthly compounding; the three-month rate is expressed with quarterly compounding; and so on. We use continuous compounding for the zero rates in the final column of Table 4.5. The one-month, three-month, six-month, and 12-month OIS zero rates are the OIS rates in column 2, adjusted for the compounding frequency difference. To determine the other rates, a two-year bond with a principal of $100 paying a coupon of 3% per year ($0.75 every three months) is assumed to be worth $100; a five-year bond with a principal of $100 paying a coupon of 4% ($1 every three months) is also assumed to be worth $100; and so on. The zero rates as a function of maturity are assumed to be linear between maturities as indicated in Figure 4.2. An iterative trial and error procedure is used to determine the positions of the corners.

The calculations in Table 4.5 can be carried out by DerivaGem. As in the case of the Treasury instruments considered in Table 4.3, the calculations do not take account of complications created by statutory holidays and day count conventions.

4.8   FORWARD RATES

Forward interest rates are the rates of interest implied by current zero rates for periods of time in the future. To illustrate how they are calculated, we suppose that zero rates are as shown in the second column of Table 4.6. The rates are assumed to be continuously compounded. Thus, the 3% per annum rate for 1 year means that, in return for an investment of $100 today, an amount $100e^{0.03 \times 1} = \$103.05$ is received in 1 year; the 4% per annum rate for 2 years means that, in return for an investment of $100 today, an amount $100e^{0.04 \times 2} = \$108.33$ is received in 2 years; and so on.

The forward interest rate in Table 4.6 for year 2 is 5% per annum. This is the rate of interest that is implied by the zero rates for the period of time between the end of the first year and the end of the second year. It can be calculated from the 1-year zero interest rate of 3% per annum and the 2-year zero interest rate of 4% per annum. It is the rate of interest for year 2 that, when combined with 3% per annum for year 1, gives 4% overall for the 2 years. To show that the correct answer is 5% per annum, suppose

Table 4.6 Calculation of forward rates.

Year (n)	Zero rate for an n-year investment (% per annum)	Forward rate for nth year (% per annum)
1	3.0	
2	4.0	5.0
3	4.6	5.8
4	5.0	6.2
5	5.3	6.5

that $100 is invested. A rate of 3% for the first year and 5% for the second year gives

$$100e^{0.03 \times 1} e^{0.05 \times 1} = \$108.33$$

at the end of the second year. A rate of 4% per annum for 2 years gives

$$100e^{0.04 \times 2}$$

which is also $108.33. This example illustrates the general result that when interest rates are continuously compounded and rates in successive time periods are combined, the overall equivalent rate is simply the average rate during the whole period. In our example, 3% for the first year and 5% for the second year average to 4% over the 2 years. The result is only approximately true when the rates are not continuously compounded.

The forward rate for year 3 is the rate of interest that is implied by a 4% per annum 2-year zero rate and a 4.6% per annum 3-year zero rate. It is 5.8% per annum. The reason is that an investment for 2 years at 4% per annum combined with an investment for one year at 5.8% per annum gives an overall average return for the three years of 4.6% per annum. The other forward rates can be calculated similarly and are shown in the third column of the table. In general, if R_1 and R_2 are the zero rates for maturities T_1 and T_2, respectively, and R_F is the forward interest rate for the period of time between T_1 and T_2, then

$$R_F = \frac{R_2 T_2 - R_1 T_1}{T_2 - T_1} \tag{4.5}$$

To illustrate this formula, consider the calculation of the year-4 forward rate from the data in Table 4.6: $T_1 = 3$, $T_2 = 4$, $R_1 = 0.046$, and $R_2 = 0.05$, and the formula gives $R_F = 0.062$.

Equation (4.5) can be written as

$$R_F = R_2 + (R_2 - R_1) \frac{T_1}{T_2 - T_1} \tag{4.6}$$

This shows that, if the zero curve is upward sloping between T_1 and T_2 so that $R_2 > R_1$, then $R_F > R_2$ (i.e., the forward rate for a period of time ending at T_2 is greater than the T_2 zero rate). Similarly, if the zero curve is downward sloping with $R_2 < R_1$, then $R_F < R_2$ (i.e., the forward rate is less than the T_2 zero rate). Taking limits as T_2

Business Snapshot 4.1 Orange County's Yield Curve Plays

Suppose a large investor can borrow or lend at the rates given in Table 4.5 and thinks that 1-year interest rates will not change much over the next 5 years. The investor can borrow 1-year funds and invest for 5-years. The 1-year borrowings can be rolled over for further 1-year periods at the end of the first, second, third, and fourth years. If interest rates do stay about the same, this strategy will yield a profit of about 2.3% per year, because interest will be received at 5.3% and paid at 3%. This type of trading strategy is known as a *yield curve play*. The investor is speculating that rates in the future will be quite different from the forward rates observed in the market today. (In our example, forward rates observed in the market today for future 1-year periods are 5%, 5.8%, 6.2%, and 6.5%.)

Robert Citron, the Treasurer at Orange County, used yield curve plays similar to the one we have just described very successfully in 1992 and 1993. The profit from Mr. Citron's trades became an important contributor to Orange County's budget and he was re-elected. (No one listened to his opponent in the election, who said his trading strategy was too risky.)

In 1994 Mr. Citron expanded his yield curve plays. He invested heavily in *inverse floaters*. These pay a rate of interest equal to a fixed rate of interest minus a floating rate. He also leveraged his position by borrowing in the repo market. If short-term interest rates had remained the same or declined he would have continued to do well. As it happened, interest rates rose sharply during 1994. On December 1, 1994, Orange County announced that its investment portfolio had lost $1.5 billion and several days later it filed for bankruptcy protection.

---

approaches T_1 in equation (4.6) and letting the common value of the two be T, we obtain

$$R_F = R + T\frac{\partial R}{\partial T}$$

where R is the zero rate for a maturity of T. The value of R_F obtained in this way is known as the *instantaneous forward rate* for a maturity of T. This is the forward rate that is applicable to a very short future time period that begins at time T. Define $P(0, T)$ as the price of a zero-coupon bond maturing at time T. Because $P(0, T) = e^{-RT}$, the equation for the instantaneous forward rate can also be written as

$$R_F = -\frac{\partial}{\partial T}\ln P(0, T)$$

If a large financial institution can borrow or lend at the rates in Table 4.5, it can lock in the forward rates. For example, it can borrow $100 at 3% for 1 year and invest the money at 4% for 2 years, the result is a cash outflow of $100e^{0.03\times1} = \$103.05$ at the end of year 1 and an inflow of $100e^{0.04\times2} = \$108.33$ at the end of year 2. Since $108.33 = 103.05e^{0.05}$, a return equal to the forward rate (5%) is earned on $103.05 during the second year. Alternatively, it can borrow $100 for 4 years at 5% and invest it for 3 years at 4.6%. The result is a cash inflow of $100e^{0.046\times3} = \$114.80$ at the end of the third year and a cash outflow of $100e^{0.05\times4} = \$122.14$ at the end of the fourth year. Since $122.14 = 114.80e^{0.062}$, money is being borrowed for the fourth year at the forward rate of 6.2%.

If a large investor thinks that rates in the future will be different from today's forward rates, there are many trading strategies that the investor will find attractive (see Business Snapshot 4.1). One of these involves entering into a contract known as a *forward rate agreement*. We will now discuss how this contract works and how it is valued.

4.9   FORWARD RATE AGREEMENTS

A forward rate agreement (FRA) is an over-the-counter contract designed to fix the interest rate that will apply to either borrowing or lending a certain principal amount during a specified future time period. When an FRA is first negotiated the specified interest rate usually equals the forward rate. The contract then has zero value.

Most FRAs are based on LIBOR. A trader who will borrow a certain principal amount at LIBOR for a future period can enter into an FRA where for the specified time period LIBOR will be received on the principal amount and a predetermined fixed rate will be paid on the principal amount. This converts the uncertain floating LIBOR rate to a fixed rate. If LIBOR proves to be greater (less) than the fixed rate the payoff from the FRA is positive (negative).

A trader who will earn interest at LIBOR for a future time period can similarly lock in the rate by entering into an FRA where LIBOR is paid and a fixed rate is received. Because interest is paid in arrears on loans, the payoff from an FRA is due at the end of the specified time period. Usually however, the contract is settled at the beginning of the period by a payment of the present value of the payoff.

Example 4.3

Suppose that a company enters into an FRA that is designed to ensure it will receive a fixed rate of 4% on a principal of $100 million for a 3-month period starting in 3 years. The FRA is an exchange where LIBOR is paid and 4% is received for the 3-month period. If 3-month LIBOR proves to be 4.5% for the 3-month period, the cash flow to the lender will be

$$100{,}000{,}000 \times (0.04 - 0.045) \times 0.25 = -\$125{,}000$$

at the 3.25-year point. This is equivalent to a cash flow equal to the present value of $-\$125{,}000$ at the 3-year point. The cash flow to the party on the opposite side of the transaction will be $+\$125{,}000$ at the 3.25-year point or the present value of this at the 3-year point. (All interest rates in this example are expressed with quarterly compounding.)

Suppose company X has agreed to lend money at LIBOR to company Y for the period of time between T_1 and T_2 and enters into an FRA to fix the rate of interest it will receive. Define:

R_K: The rate of interest agreed to in the FRA

R_F: The forward LIBOR interest rate for the period between times T_1 and T_2, calculated today[4]

---

[4] The determination of LIBOR forward rates is discussed in Chapter 7.

R_M: The actual LIBOR interest rate observed in the market at time T_1 for the period between times T_1 and T_2

L: The principal underlying the contract.

We assume that the rates R_K, R_F, and R_M are all measured with a compounding frequency reflecting the length of the period they apply to. This means that, if $T_2 - T_1 = 0.5$, they are expressed with semiannual compounding; if $T_2 - T_1 = 0.25$, they are expressed with quarterly compounding; and so on. (This assumption corresponds to the usual market practices for FRAs.)

Normally company X would earn R_M from the LIBOR loan. The FRA means that it will earn R_K. The extra interest rate (which may be negative) that it earns as a result of entering into the FRA is $R_K - R_M$. The interest rate is set at time T_1 and paid at time T_2. The extra interest rate therefore leads to a cash flow to company X at time T_2 of

$$L(R_K - R_M)(T_2 - T_1) \qquad (4.7)$$

Similarly company Y's cash flow at time T_2 (which can be negative) is

$$L(R_M - R_K)(T_2 - T_1) \qquad (4.8)$$

Equations (4.7) and (4.8) make it clear that the FRA is an agreement where company X will receive interest on the principal between T_1 and T_2 at the fixed rate of R_K and pay interest at the realized LIBOR rate of R_M. Company Y will pay interest on the principal between T_1 and T_2 at the fixed rate of R_K and receive interest at R_M. This interpretation will be important when we come to consider swaps in Chapter 7.

As mentioned, FRAs are usually settled at time T_1 rather than T_2. The payoff must then be discounted from time T_2 to T_1. For company X the payoff is the present value at time T_1 of

$$L(R_K - R_M)(T_2 - T_1)$$

received at time T_2, and for company Y the payoff is the present value at time T_1 of

$$L(R_M - R_K)(T_2 - T_1)$$

received at time T_2. The discount rate should be the risk-free rate at time T_1 for the period between T_1 and T_2.

Valuation

To value an FRA, we first note that it is always worth zero when $R_K = R_F$ and usually the contract is designed so that $R_K = R_F$ at time zero. As time passes, R_K (the agreed fixed rate) remains the same but R_F is likely to change. The contract therefore no longer has a value of zero.

To determine the value of an FRA after it has been initiated, we compare two FRAs. The first promises that the current LIBOR forward rate R_F will be received on a principal of L between times T_1 and T_2; the second promises that R_K will be received on the same principal between the same two dates. In both cases the realized LIBOR, R_M, is paid. The two contracts are the same except for the interest payments received at time T_2. In the case of the first contract the interest is $L R_F(T_2 - T_1)$; in the case of the second contract it is $L R_K(T_2 - T_1)$. The excess of the value of the second contract over the first is, therefore, the present value of the difference between these interest payment, or

$$L(R_K - R_F)(T_2 - T_1)e^{-R_2 T_2}$$

where R_2 is the continuously compounded riskless zero rate for a maturity T_2.[5] Because the value of the first FRA (where R_F is received) is zero, the value of the second FRA (where R_K is received) is

$$V_{FRA} = L(R_K - R_F)(T_2 - T_1)e^{-R_2 T_2} \tag{4.9}$$

Similarly, the value of an FRA which promises that an interest rate of R_K will be paid on borrowings of L between T_1 and T_2 is

$$V_{FRA} = L(R_F - R_K)(T_2 - T_1)e^{-R_2 T_2} \tag{4.10}$$

By comparing equations (4.7) and (4.9) (or equations (4.8) and (4.10)), we see that an FRA can be valued if we:

1. Calculate the payoff on the assumption that forward rates are realized (that is, on the assumption that $R_M = R_F$)
2. Discount this payoff at the risk-free rate

We shall use this result when we come to value swaps (which are porfolios of FRAs) in Chapter 7.

Example 4.4

Suppose that the forward LIBOR rate for the period between time 1.5 years and time 2 years in the future is 5% (with semiannual compounding) and that some time ago a company entered into an FRA where it will receive 5.8% (with semi-annual compounding) and pay LIBOR on a principal of $100 million for the period. The 2-year risk-free rate is 4% (with continuous compounding). From equation (4.9), the value of the FRA is

$$100,000,000 \times (0.058 - 0.050) \times 0.5e^{-0.04 \times 2} = \$369,200$$

4.10 DURATION

The *duration* of a bond, as its name implies, is a measure of how long the holder of the bond has to wait before receiving the present value of the cash payments. A zero-coupon bond that lasts n years has a duration of n years. However, a coupon-bearing bond lasting n years has a duration of less than n years, because the holder receives some of the cash payments prior to year n.

Suppose that a bond provides the holder with cash flows c_i at time t_i ($1 \leqslant i \leqslant n$). The bond price B and bond yield y (continuously compounded) are related by

$$B = \sum_{i=1}^{n} c_i e^{-y t_i} \tag{4.11}$$

---

[5] Note that R_K, R_M, and R_F are expressed with a compounding frequency corresponding to $T_2 - T_1$, whereas R_2 is expressed with continuous compounding.

The duration of the bond, D, is defined as

$$D = \frac{\sum_{i=1}^{n} t_i c_i e^{-yt_i}}{B} \tag{4.12}$$

This can be written

$$D = \sum_{i=1}^{n} t_i \left[\frac{c_i e^{-yt_i}}{B} \right]$$

The term in square brackets is the ratio of the present value of the cash flow at time t_i to the bond price. The bond price is the present value of all payments. The duration is therefore a weighted average of the times when payments are made, with the weight applied to time t_i being equal to the proportion of the bond's total present value provided by the cash flow at time t_i. The sum of the weights is 1.0. Note that, for the purposes of the definition of duration, all discounting is done at the bond yield rate of interest, y. (We do not use a different zero rate for each cash flow in the way described in Section 4.6.)

When a small change Δy in the yield is considered, it is approximately true that

$$\Delta B = \frac{dB}{dy} \Delta y \tag{4.13}$$

From equation (4.11), this becomes

$$\Delta B = -\Delta y \sum_{i=1}^{n} c_i t_i e^{-yt_i} \tag{4.14}$$

(Note that there is a negative relationship between B and y. When bond yields increase, bond prices decrease. When bond yields decrease, bond prices increase.) From equations (4.12) and (4.14), the key duration relationship is obtained:

$$\Delta B = -BD \, \Delta y \tag{4.15}$$

This can be written

$$\frac{\Delta B}{B} = -D \, \Delta y \tag{4.16}$$

Equation (4.16) is an approximate relationship between percentage changes in a bond price and changes in its yield. It is easy to use and is the reason why duration, first suggested by Frederick Macaulay in 1938, has become such a popular measure.

Consider a 3-year 10% coupon bond with a face value of $100. Suppose that the yield on the bond is 12% per annum with continuous compounding. This means that $y = 0.12$. Coupon payments of $5 are made every 6 months. Table 4.7 shows the calculations necessary to determine the bond's duration. The present values of the bond's cash flows, using the yield as the discount rate, are shown in column 3 (e.g., the present value of the first cash flow is $5e^{-0.12 \times 0.5} = 4.709$). The sum of the numbers in column 3 gives the bond's price as 94.213. The weights are calculated by dividing the numbers in column 3 by 94.213. The sum of the numbers in column 5 gives the duration as 2.653 years.

DV01 is the price change from a 1-basis-point increase in all rates. Gamma is the change in DV01 from a 1-basis-point increase in all rates. The following example investigates the accuracy of the duration relationship in equation (4.15).

Table 4.7   Calculation of duration.

Time (years)	Cash flow ($)	Present value	Weight	Time × weight
0.5	5	4.709	0.050	0.025
1.0	5	4.435	0.047	0.047
1.5	5	4.176	0.044	0.066
2.0	5	3.933	0.042	0.083
2.5	5	3.704	0.039	0.098
3.0	105	73.256	0.778	2.333
Total:	130	94.213	1.000	2.653

Example 4.5

For the bond in Table 4.7, the bond price, B, is 94.213 and the duration, D, is 2.653, so that equation (4.15) gives

$$\Delta B = -94.213 \times 2.653 \times \Delta y$$

or

$$\Delta B = -249.95 \times \Delta y$$

When the yield on the bond increases by 10 basis points ($= 0.1\%$), $\Delta y = +0.001$. The duration relationship predicts that $\Delta B = -249.95 \times 0.001 = -0.250$, so that the bond price goes down to $94.213 - 0.250 = 93.963$. How accurate is this? Valuing the bond in terms of its yield in the usual way, we find that, when the bond yield increases by 10 basis points to 12.1%, the bond price is

$$5e^{-0.121 \times 0.5} + 5e^{-0.121 \times 1.0} + 5e^{-0.121 \times 1.5} + 5e^{-0.121 \times 2.0}$$
$$+ 5e^{-0.121 \times 2.5} + 105e^{-0.121 \times 3.0} = 93.963$$

which is (to three decimal places) the same as that predicted by the duration relationship.

Modified Duration

The preceding analysis is based on the assumption that y is expressed with continuous compounding. If y is expressed with annual compounding, it can be shown that the approximate relationship in equation (4.15) becomes

$$\Delta B = -\frac{BD \, \Delta y}{1 + y}$$

More generally, if y is expressed with a compounding frequency of m times per year, then

$$\Delta B = -\frac{BD \, \Delta y}{1 + y/m}$$

A variable D^*, defined by

$$D^* = \frac{D}{1 + y/m}$$

is sometimes referred to as the bond's *modified duration*. It allows the duration relationship to be simplified to

$$\Delta B = -BD^* \Delta y \tag{4.17}$$

when y is expressed with a compounding frequency of m times per year. The following example investigates the accuracy of the modified duration relationship.

Example 4.6

The bond in Table 4.6 has a price of 94.213 and a duration of 2.653. The yield, expressed with semiannual compounding is 12.3673%. The modified duration, D^*, is given by

$$D^* = \frac{2.653}{1 + 0.123673/2} = 2.499$$

From equation (4.17),

$$\Delta B = -94.213 \times 2.4985 \times \Delta y$$

or

$$\Delta B = -235.39 \times \Delta y$$

When the yield (semiannually compounded) increases by 10 basis points ($= 0.1\%$), we have $\Delta y = +0.001$. The duration relationship predicts that we expect ΔB to be $-235.39 \times 0.001 = -0.235$, so that the bond price goes down to $94.213 - 0.235 = 93.978$. How accurate is this? An exact calculation similar to that in the previous example shows that, when the bond yield (semiannually compounded) increases by 10 basis points to 12.4673%, the bond price becomes 93.978. This shows that the modified duration calculation gives good accuracy for small yield changes.

Another term that is sometimes used is *dollar duration*. This is the product of modified duration and bond price, so that $\Delta B = -D_\$ \Delta y$, where $D_\$$ is dollar duration.

Bond Portfolios

The duration, D, of a bond portfolio can be defined as a weighted average of the durations of the individual bonds in the portfolio, with the weights being proportional to the bond prices. Equations (4.15) to (4.17) then apply, with B being defined as the value of the bond portfolio. They estimate the change in the value of the bond portfolio for a small change Δy in the yields of all the bonds.

It is important to realize that, when duration is used for bond portfolios, there is an implicit assumption that the yields of all bonds will change by approximately the same amount. When the bonds have widely differing maturities, this happens only when there is a parallel shift in the zero-coupon yield curve. We should therefore interpret equations (4.15) to (4.17) as providing estimates of the impact on the price of a bond portfolio of a small parallel shift, Δy, in the zero curve.

By choosing a portfolio so that the duration of assets equals the duration of liabilities (i.e., the net duration is zero), a financial institution eliminates its exposure to small parallel shifts in the yield curve. But it is still exposed to shifts that are either large or nonparallel.

4.11 CONVEXITY

The duration relationship applies only to small changes in yields. This is illustrated in Figure 4.3, which shows the relationship between the percentage change in value and change in yield for two bond portfolios having the same duration. The gradients of the two curves are the same at the origin. This means that both bond portfolios change in value by the same percentage for small yield changes and is consistent with equation (4.16). For large yield changes, the portfolios behave differently. Portfolio X has more curvature in its relationship with yields than portfolio Y. A factor known as *convexity* measures this curvature and can be used to improve the relationship in equation (4.16).

A measure of convexity is

$$C = \frac{1}{B}\frac{d^2B}{dy^2} = \frac{\sum_{i=1}^{n} c_i t_i^2 e^{-yt_i}}{B}$$

From Taylor series expansions, we obtain a more accurate expression than equation (4.13), given by

$$\Delta B = \frac{dB}{dy}\Delta y + \frac{1}{2}\frac{d^2B}{dy^2}\Delta y^2 \tag{4.18}$$

This leads to

$$\frac{\Delta B}{B} = -D\,\Delta y + \frac{1}{2}C(\Delta y)^2$$

For a portfolio with a particular duration, the convexity of a bond portfolio tends to be greatest when the portfolio provides payments evenly over a long period of time. It is

---

Figure 4.3 Two bond portfolios with the same duration.

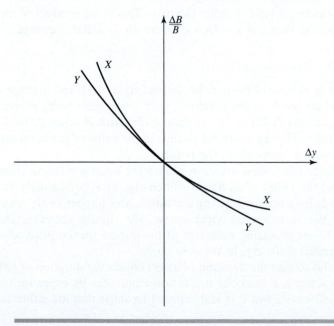

least when the payments are concentrated around one particular point in time. By choosing a portfolio of assets and liabilities with a net duration of zero and a net convexity of zero, a financial institution can make itself immune to relatively large parallel shifts in the zero curve. However, it is still exposed to nonparallel shifts.

4.12 THEORIES OF THE TERM STRUCTURE OF INTEREST RATES

It is natural to ask what determines the shape of the zero curve. Why is it sometimes downward sloping, sometimes upward sloping, and sometimes partly upward sloping and partly downward sloping? A number of different theories have been proposed. The simplest is *expectations theory*, which conjectures that long-term interest rates should reflect expected future short-term interest rates. More precisely, it argues that a forward interest rate corresponding to a certain future period is equal to the expected future zero interest rate for that period. Another idea, *market segmentation theory*, conjectures that there need be no relationship between short-, medium-, and long-term interest rates. Under the theory, a major investor such as a large pension fund or an insurance company invests in bonds of a certain maturity and does not readily switch from one maturity to another. The short-term interest rate is determined by supply and demand in the short-term bond market; the medium-term interest rate is determined by supply and demand in the medium-term bond market; and so on.

The theory that is most appealing is *liquidity preference theory*. The basic assumption underlying the theory is that investors prefer to preserve their liquidity and invest funds for short periods of time. Borrowers, on the other hand, usually prefer to borrow at fixed rates for long periods of time. This leads to a situation in which forward rates are greater than expected future zero rates. The theory is also consistent with the empirical result that yield curves tend to be upward sloping more often than they are downward sloping.

The Management of Net Interest Income

To understand liquidity preference theory, it is useful to consider the interest rate risk faced by banks when they take deposits and make loans. The *net interest income* of the bank is the excess of the interest received over the interest paid and needs to be carefully managed.

Consider a simple situation where a bank offers consumers a one-year and a five-year deposit rate as well as a one-year and five-year mortgage rate. The rates are shown in Table 4.8. We make the simplifying assumption that the expected one-year interest rate for future time periods to equal the one-year rates prevailing in the market today. Loosely speaking this means that the market considers interest rate increases to be just as likely as interest rate decreases. As a result, the rates in Table 4.8 are "fair" in that

Table 4.8 Example of rates offered by a bank to its customers.

Maturity (years)	Deposit rate	Mortgage rate
1	3%	6%
5	3%	6%

they reflect the market's expectations (i.e., they correspond to expectations theory). Investing money for one year and reinvesting for four further one-year periods give the same expected overall return as a single five-year investment. Similarly, borrowing money for one year and refinancing each year for the next four years leads to the same expected financing costs as a single five-year loan.

Suppose you have money to deposit and agree with the prevailing view that interest rate increases are just as likely as interest rate decreases. Would you choose to deposit your money for one year at 3% per annum or for five years at 3% per annum? The chances are that you would choose one year because this gives you more financial flexibility. It ties up your funds for a shorter period of time.

Now suppose that you want a mortgage. Again you agree with the prevailing view that interest rate increases are just as likely as interest rate decreases. Would you choose a one-year mortgage at 6% or a five-year mortgage at 6%? The chances are that you would choose a five-year mortgage because it fixes your borrowing rate for the next five years and subjects you to less refinancing risk.

When the bank posts the rates shown in Table 4.8, it is likely to find that the majority of its depositors opt for one-year deposits and the majority of its borrowers opt for five-year mortgages. This creates an asset/liability mismatch for the bank and subjects it to risks. There is no problem if interest rates fall. The bank will find itself financing the five-year 6% loans with deposits that cost less than 3% in the future and net interest income will increase. However, if rates rise, the deposits that are financing these 6% loans will cost more than 3% in the future and net interest income will decline. A 3% rise in interest rates would reduce the net interest income to zero.

It is the job of the asset/liability management group to ensure that the maturities of the assets on which interest is earned and the maturities of the liabilities on which interest is paid are matched. One way it can do this is by increasing the five-year rate on both deposits and mortgages. For example, it could move to the situation in Table 4.9 where the five-year deposit rate is 4% and the five-year mortgage rate 7%. This would make five-year deposits relatively more attractive and one-year mortgages relatively more attractive. Some customers who chose one-year deposits when the rates were as in Table 4.8 will switch to five-year deposits in the Table 4.9 situation. Some customers who chose five-year mortgages when the rates were as in Table 4.8 will choose one-year mortgages. This may lead to the maturities of assets and liabilities being matched. If there is still an imbalance with depositors tending to choose a one-year maturity and borrowers a five-year maturity, five-year deposit and mortgage rates could be increased even further. Eventually the imbalance will disappear.

The net result of all banks behaving in the way we have just described is liquidity preference theory. Long-term rates tend to be higher than those that would be predicted by expected future short-term rates. The yield curve is upward sloping most

Table 4.9 Five-year rates are increased in an attempt to match maturities of assets and liabilities.

Maturity (years)	Deposit rate	Mortgage rate
1	3%	6%
5	4%	7%

Business Snapshot 4.2   Liquidity and the 2007–2009 Financial Crisis

During the credit crisis that started in July 2007 there was a "flight to quality," where financial institutions and investors looked for safe investments and were less inclined than before to take credit risks. Financial institutions that relied on short-term funding experienced liquidity problems. One example is Northern Rock in the United Kingdom, which financed much of its mortgage portfolio with wholesale deposits, some lasting only 3 months. Starting in September 2007, the depositors became nervous and refused to roll over the funding they were providing to Northern Rock, i.e., at the end of a 3-month period they would refuse to deposit their funds for a further 3-month period. As a result, Northern Rock was unable to finance its assets. It was taken over by the U.K. government in early 2008. In the United States, financial institutions such as Bear Stearns and Lehman Brothers experienced similar liquidity problems because they had chosen to fund part of their operations with short-term funds.

---

of the time. It is downward sloping only when the market expects a steep decline in short-term rates.

Many banks now have sophisticated systems for monitoring the decisions being made by customers so that, when they detect small differences between the maturities of the assets and liabilities being chosen by customers they can fine tune the rates they offer. Sometimes derivatives such as interest rate swaps are also used to manage their exposure. The result of all this is that net interest income is usually very stable. This has not always been the case. In the United States, the failure of Savings and Loan companies in the 1980s and the failure of Continental Illinois in 1984 were to a large extent a result of the fact that they did not match the maturities of assets and liabilities. Both failures proved to be very expensive for U.S. taxpayers.

Liquidity

In addition to creating problems in the way that has been described, a portfolio where maturities are mismatched can lead to liquidity problems. Consider a financial institution that funds 5-year fixed rate loans with wholesale deposits that last only 3 months. It might recognize its exposure to rising interest rates and hedge its interest rate risk. (One way of doing this is by using interest rate swaps, as mentioned earlier.) However, it still has a liquidity risk. Wholesale depositors may, for some reason, lose confidence in the financial institution and refuse to continue to provide the financial institution with short-term funding. The financial institution, even if it has adequate equity capital, will then experience a severe liquidity problem that could lead to its downfall. As described in Business Snapshot 4.2, these types of liquidity problems were the root cause of some of the failures of financial institutions during the crisis that started in 2007.

SUMMARY

The compounding frequency used for an interest rate defines the units in which it is measured. The difference between an annually compounded rate and a quarterly compounded rate is analogous to the difference between a distance measured in miles and a distance measured in kilometers. Traders frequently use continuous compounding when analyzing the value of options and more complex derivatives.

Many different types of interest rates are quoted in financial markets and calculated by analysts. The n-year zero or spot rate is the rate applicable to an investment lasting for n years when all of the return is realized at the end. The par yield on a bond of a certain maturity is the coupon rate that causes the bond to sell for its par value. Forward rates are the rates applicable to future periods of time implied by today's zero rates.

The method most commonly used to calculate zero rates is known as the bootstrap method. It involves starting with short-term instruments and moving progressively to longer-term instruments, making sure that the zero rates calculated at each stage are consistent with the prices of the instruments. It is used daily by trading desks to calculate a variety of zero curves.

A forward rate agreement (FRA) is an over-the-counter agreement where an interest rate (usually LIBOR) will be exchanged for a specified interest rate with both rates being applied to a predetermined principal over a predetermined period. An FRA can be valued by assuming that forward rates are realized and discounting the resulting payoff.

An important concept in interest rate markets is *duration*. Duration measures the sensitivity of the value of a bond portfolio to a small parallel shift in the zero-coupon yield curve. Specifically,

$$\Delta B = -BD \, \Delta y$$

where B is the value of the bond portfolio, D is the duration of the portfolio, Δy is the size of a small parallel shift in the zero curve, and ΔB is the resultant effect on the value of the bond portfolio.

Liquidity preference theory can be used to explain the interest rate term structures that are observed in practice. The theory argues that most entities like to borrow long and lend short. To match the maturities of borrowers and lenders, it is necessary for financial institutions to raise long-term rates so that forward interest rates are higher than expected future spot interest rates.

FURTHER READING

Fabozzi, F. J. *Bond Markets, Analysis, and Strategies*, 8th edn. Upper Saddle River, NJ: Pearson, 2012.

Grinblatt, M., and F. A. Longstaff. "Financial Innovation and the Role of Derivatives Securities: An Empirical Analysis of the Treasury Strips Program," *Journal of Finance*, 55, 3 (2000): 1415–36.

Jorion, P. *Big Bets Gone Bad: Derivatives and Bankruptcy in Orange County*. New York: Academic Press, 1995.

Stigum, M., and A. Crescenzi. *Money Markets*, 4th edn. New York: McGraw Hill, 2007.

Practice Questions (Answers in Solutions Manual)

4.1. A bank quotes an interest rate of 7% per annum with quarterly compounding. What is the equivalent rate with (a) continuous compounding and (b) annual compounding?

4.2. Explain how LIBOR is determined.

4.3. The 6-month and 1-year zero rates are both 5% per annum. For a bond that has a life of 18 months and pays a coupon of 4% per annum (with semiannual payments and one having just been made), the yield is 5.2% per annum. What is the bond's price? What is the 18-month zero rate? All rates are quoted with semiannual compounding.

4.4. An investor receives $1,100 in one year in return for an investment of $1,000 now. Calculate the percentage return per annum with:
(a) Annual compounding
(b) Semiannual compounding
(c) Monthly compounding
(d) Continuous compounding.

4.5. Suppose that risk-free zero interest rates with continuous compounding are as follows:

Maturity (months)	Rate (% per annum)
3	3.0
6	3.2
9	3.4
12	3.5
15	3.6
18	3.7

Calculate forward interest rates for the second, third, fourth, fifth, and sixth quarters.

4.6. Assuming that risk-free zero rates are as in Problem 4.5, what is the value of an FRA where the holder will pay LIBOR and receive 4.5% (quarterly compounded) for a three-month period starting in one year on a principal of $1,000,000? The forward LIBOR rate for the three-month period is 5% (quarterly compounded).

4.7. The term structure of interest rates is upward-sloping. Put the following in order of magnitude:
(a) The 5-year zero rate
(b) The yield on a 5-year coupon-bearing bond
(c) The forward rate corresponding to the period between 4.75 and 5 years in the future.
What is the answer when the term structure of interest rates is downward-sloping?

4.8. What does duration tell you about the sensitivity of a bond portfolio to interest rates. What are the limitations of the duration measure?

4.9. What rate of interest with continuous compounding is equivalent to 8% per annum with monthly compounding?

4.10. A deposit account pays 4% per annum with continuous compounding, but interest is actually paid quarterly. How much interest will be paid each quarter on a $10,000 deposit?

4.11. Suppose that 6-month, 12-month, 18-month, 24-month, and 30-month zero rates are, respectively, 4%, 4.2%, 4.4%, 4.6%, and 4.8% per annum, with continuous compounding. Estimate the cash price of a bond with a face value of 100 that will mature in 30 months and pay a coupon of 4% per annum semiannually.

4.12. A 3-year bond provides a coupon of 8% semiannually and has a cash price of 104. What is the bond's yield?

4.13. Suppose that the 6-month, 12-month, 18-month, and 24-month zero rates are 5%, 6%, 6.5%, and 7%, respectively. What is the 2-year par yield?

4.14. Suppose that risk-free zero interest rates with continuous compounding are as follows:

Maturity (years)	Rate (% per annum)
1	2.0
2	3.0
3	3.7
4	4.2
5	4.5

Calculate forward interest rates for the second, third, fourth, and fifth years.

4.15. Use the risk-free rates in Problem 4.14 to value an FRA where you will pay 5% (annually compounded) and receive LIBOR for the third year on $1 million. The forward LIBOR rate (annually compounded) for the third year is 5.5%.

4.16. A 10-year 8% coupon bond currently sells for $90. A 10-year 4% coupon bond currently sells for $80. What is the 10-year zero rate? (*Hint*: Consider taking a long position in two of the 4% coupon bonds and a short position in one of the 8% coupon bonds.)

4.17. Explain carefully why liquidity preference theory is consistent with the observation that the term structure of interest rates tends to be upward-sloping more often than it is downward-sloping.

4.18. "When the zero curve is upward-sloping, the zero rate for a particular maturity is greater than the par yield for that maturity. When the zero curve is downward-sloping the reverse is true." Explain why this is so.

4.19. Why are U.S. Treasury rates significantly lower than other rates that are close to risk-free?

4.20. Why does a loan in the repo market involve very little credit risk?

4.21. Explain why an FRA is equivalent to the exchange of a floating rate of interest for a fixed rate of interest.

4.22. A 5-year bond with a yield of 7% (continuously compounded) pays an 8% coupon at the end of each year.
   (a) What is the bond's price?
   (b) What is the bond's duration?
   (c) Use the duration to calculate the effect on the bond's price of a 0.2% decrease in its yield.
   (d) Recalculate the bond's price on the basis of a 6.8% per annum yield and verify that the result is in agreement with your answer to (c).

4.23. The cash prices of 6-month and 1-year Treasury bills are 94.0 and 89.0. A 1.5-year Treasury bond that will pay coupons of $4 every 6 months currently sells for $94.84. A 2-year Treasury bond that will pay coupons of $5 every 6 months currently sells for $97.12. Calculate the 6-month, 1-year, 1.5-year, and 2-year Treasury zero rates.

4.24. "An interest rate swap where 6-month LIBOR is exchanged for a fixed rate of 5% on a principal of $100 million for 5 years involves a known cash flow and a portfolio of nine FRAs." Explain this statement.

Further Questions

4.25. When compounded annually an interest rate is 11%. What is the rate when expressed with (a) semiannual compounding, (b) quarterly compounding, (c) monthly compounding, (d) weekly compounding, and (e) daily compounding.

4.26. The table below gives Treasury zero rates and cash flows on a Treasury bond. Zero rates are continuously compounded.
(a) What is the bond's theoretical price?
(b) What is the bond's yield assuming it sells for its theoretical price?

Maturity (years)	Zero rate	Coupon payment	Principal
0.5	2.0%	$20	
1.0	2.3%	$20	
1.5	2.7%	$20	
2.0	3.2%	$20	$1,000

4.27. A 5-year bond provides a coupon of 5% per annum payable semiannually. Its price is 104. What is the bond's yield? You may find Excel's Solver useful.

4.28. Suppose that 3-month, 6-month, 12-month, 2-year, and 3-year OIS rates are 2.0%, 2.5%, 3.2%, 4.5%, and 5%, respectively. The 3-month, 6-month, and 12-month OISs involve a single exchange at maturity; the 2-year and 3-year OISs involve quarterly exchanges. The compounding frequencies used for expressing the rates correspond to the frequency of exchanges. Calculate the OIS zero rates using continuous compounding. Interpolate between continuously compounded rates linearly to determine rates between 6 months and 12 months, between 12 months and 2 years, and between 2 years and 3 years. You may find Excel's Solver useful.

4.29. An interest rate is quoted as 5% per annum with semiannual compounding. What is the equivalent rate with (a) annual compounding, (b) monthly compounding, and (c) continuous compounding.

4.30. The 6-month, 12-month, 18-month, and 24-month zero rates are 4%, 4.5%, 4.75%, and 5%, with semiannual compounding.
(a) What are the rates with continuous compounding?
(b) What is the forward rate for the 6-month period beginning in 18 months?
(c) What is the two-year par yield?

4.31. Suppose the risk-free rates are as in Problem 4.30. What is the value of an FRA where the holder pays LIBOR and receives 7% (semiannually compounded) for a six-month period beginning in 18 months? The current forward rate for this period is 6% (semiannually compounded) and the principal is $10 million.

4.32. The following table gives the prices of bonds:

Bond principal ($)	Time to maturity (years)	Annual coupon* ($)	Bond price ($)
100	0.50	0.0	98
100	1.00	0.0	95
100	1.50	6.2	101
100	2.00	8.0	104

* Half the stated coupon is assumed to be paid every six months.

(a) Calculate zero rates for maturities of 6 months, 12 months, 18 months, and 24 months.

(b) What are the forward rates for the following periods: 6 months to 12 months, 12 months to 18 months, and 18 months to 24 months?

(c) What are the 6-month, 12-month, 18-month, and 24-month par yields for bonds that provide semiannual coupon payments?

(d) Estimate the price and yield of a 2-year bond providing a semiannual coupon of 7% per annum.

4.33. Portfolio A consists of a 1-year zero-coupon bond with a face value of $2,000 and a 10-year zero-coupon bond with a face value of $6,000. Portfolio B consists of a 5.95-year zero-coupon bond with a face value of $5,000. The current yield on all bonds is 10% per annum.

(a) Show that both portfolios have the same duration.

(b) Show that the percentage changes in the values of the two portfolios for a 0.1% per annum increase in yields are the same.

(c) What are the percentage changes in the values of the two portfolios for a 5% per annum increase in yields?

4.34. Verify that DerivaGem agrees with the price of the bond in Section 4.6. Test how well DV01 predicts the effect of a 1-basis-point increase in all rates. Estimate the duration of the bond from DV01. Use DV01 and Gamma to predict the effect of a 200-basis-point increase in all rates. Use Gamma to estimate the bond's convexity. (*Hint*: In DerivaGem, DV01 is dB/dy, where B is the price of the bond and y is its yield measured in basis points, and Gamma is d^2B/dy^2, where y is measured in percent.)

CHAPTER 5

Determination of Forward and Futures Prices

In this chapter we examine how forward prices and futures prices are related to the spot price of the underlying asset. Forward contracts are easier to analyze than futures contracts because there is no daily settlement—only a single payment at maturity. We therefore start this chapter by considering the relationship between the forward price and the spot price. Luckily it can be shown that the forward price and futures price of an asset are usually very close when the maturities of the two contracts are the same. This is convenient because it means that results obtained for forwards can be assumed to be true for futures.

In the first part of the chapter we derive some important general results on the relationship between forward (or futures) prices and spot prices. We then use the results to examine the relationship between futures prices and spot prices for contracts on stock indices, foreign exchange, and commodities. We will consider interest rate futures contracts in the next chapter.

5.1 INVESTMENT ASSETS vs. CONSUMPTION ASSETS

When considering forward and futures contracts, it is important to distinguish between investment assets and consumption assets. An *investment asset* is an asset that is held solely for investment purposes by at least some traders. Stocks and bonds are clearly investment assets. Gold and silver are also examples of investment assets. Note that investment assets do not have to be held exclusively for investment. (Silver, for example, has a number of industrial uses.) However, they do have to satisfy the requirement that they are held by some traders solely for investment. A *consumption asset* is an asset that is held primarily for consumption. It is not normally held for investment. Examples of consumption assets are commodities such as copper, crude oil, corn, and pork bellies.

As we shall see later in this chapter, we can use arbitrage arguments to determine the forward and futures prices of an investment asset from its spot price and other observable market variables. We cannot do this for consumption assets.

107

5.2 SHORT SELLING

Some of the arbitrage strategies presented in this chapter involve *short selling*. This trade, usually simply referred to as "shorting", involves selling an asset that is not owned. It is something that is possible for some—but not all—investment assets. We will illustrate how it works by considering a short sale of shares of a stock.

Suppose an investor instructs a broker to short 500 shares of company X. The broker will carry out the instructions by borrowing the shares from someone who owns them and selling them in the market in the usual way. At some later stage, the investor will close out the position by purchasing 500 shares of company X in the market. These shares are then used to replace the borrowed shares so that the short position is closed out. The investor takes a profit if the stock price has declined and a loss if it has risen. If at any time while the contract is open the broker has to return the borrowed shares and there are no other shares that can be borrowed, the investor is forced to close out the position, even if not ready to do so. Often a fee is charged for lending the shares to the party doing the shorting.

An investor with a short position must pay to the broker any income, such as dividends or interest, that would normally be received on the securities that have been shorted. The broker will transfer this income to the account of the client from whom the securities have been borrowed. Consider the position of an investor who shorts 500 shares in April when the price per share is $120 and closes out the position by buying them back in July when the price per share is $100. Suppose that a dividend of $1 per share is paid in May. The investor receives $500 \times \$120 = \$60,000$ in April when the short position is initiated. The dividend leads to a payment by the investor of $500 \times \$1 = \$500$ in May. The investor also pays $500 \times \$100 = \$50,000$ for shares when the position is closed out in July. The net gain, therefore, is

$$\$60,000 - \$500 - \$50,000 = \$9,500$$

when any fee for borrowing the shares is ignored. Table 5.1 illustrates this example and shows that the cash flows from the short sale are the mirror image of the cash flows from purchasing the shares in April and selling them in July. (Again, the fee for borrowing the shares is not considered.)

Table 5.1 Cash flows from short sale and purchase of shares.

Purchase of shares	
April: Purchase 500 shares for $120	−$60,000
May: Receive dividend	+$500
July: Sell 500 shares for $100 per share	+$50,000
Net profit = −$9,500	

Short sale of shares	
April: Borrow 500 shares and sell them for $120	+$60,000
May: Pay dividend	−$500
July: Buy 500 shares for $100 per share	−$50,000
Replace borrowed shares to close short position	
Net profit = +$9,500	

The investor is required to maintain a *margin account* with the broker. The margin account consists of cash or marketable securities deposited by the investor with the broker to guarantee that the investor will not walk away from the short position if the share price increases. It is similar to the margin account discussed in Chapter 2 for futures contracts. An initial margin is required and if there are adverse movements (i.e., increases) in the price of the asset that is being shorted, additional margin may be required. If the additional margin is not provided, the short position is closed out. The margin account does not represent a cost to the investor. This is because interest is usually paid on the balance in margin accounts and, if the interest rate offered is unacceptable, marketable securities such as Treasury bills can be used to meet margin requirements. The proceeds of the sale of the asset belong to the investor and normally form part of the initial margin.

From time to time regulations are changed on short selling. In 1938, the uptick rule was introduced. This allowed shares to be shorted only on an "uptick"—that is, when the most recent movement in the share price was an increase. The SEC abolished the uptick rule in July 2007, but introduced an "alternative uptick" rule in February 2010. Under this rule, when the price of a stock has decreased by more than 10% in one day, there are restrictions on short selling for that day and the next. These restrictions are that the stock can be shorted only at a price that is higher than the best current bid price. Occasionally there are temporary bans on short selling. This happened in a number of countries in 2008 because it was considered that short selling contributed to the high market volatility that was being experienced.

5.3 ASSUMPTIONS AND NOTATION

In this chapter we will assume that the following are all true for some market participants:

1. The market participants are subject to no transaction costs when they trade.
2. The market participants are subject to the same tax rate on all net trading profits.
3. The market participants can borrow money at the same risk-free rate of interest as they can lend money.
4. The market participants take advantage of arbitrage opportunities as they occur.

Note that we do not require these assumptions to be true for all market participants. All that we require is that they be true—or at least approximately true—for a few key market participants such as large derivatives dealers. It is the trading activities of these key market participants and their eagerness to take advantage of arbitrage opportunities as they occur that determine the relationship between forward and spot prices.

The following notation will be used throughout this chapter:

T: Time until delivery date in a forward or futures contract (in years)

S_0: Price of the asset underlying the forward or futures contract today

F_0: Forward or futures price today

r: Zero-coupon risk-free rate of interest per annum, expressed with continuous compounding, for an investment maturing at the delivery date (i.e., in T years).

The risk-free rate, r, is the interest rate at which money is borrowed or lent when there is no credit risk, so that the borrowed money is certain to be repaid. As discussed in Chapter 4, participants in derivatives markets use the OIS rate as a proxy for the risk-free rate.

5.4 FORWARD PRICE FOR AN INVESTMENT ASSET

The easiest forward contract to value is one written on an investment asset that provides the holder with no income and for which there are no storage costs. Non-dividend-paying stocks and zero-coupon bonds are examples of such investment assets.

Consider a long forward contract to purchase a non-dividend-paying stock in 3 months.[1] Assume the current stock price is $40 and the 3-month risk-free interest rate is 5% per annum.

Suppose first that the forward price is relatively high at $43. An arbitrageur can borrow $40 at the risk-free interest rate of 5% per annum, buy one share, and short a forward contract to sell one share in 3 months. At the end of the 3 months, the arbitrageur delivers the share and receives $43. The sum of money required to pay off the loan is

$$40e^{0.05 \times 3/12} = \$40.50$$

By following this strategy, the arbitrageur locks in a profit of $43.00 - $40.50 = $2.50 at the end of the 3-month period.

Suppose next that the forward price is relatively low at $39. An arbitrageur can short one share, invest the proceeds of the short sale at 5% per annum for 3 months, and take a long position in a 3-month forward contract. The proceeds of the short sale grow to $40e^{0.05 \times 3/12}$ or $40.50 in 3 months. At the end of the 3 months, the arbitrageur pays $39, takes delivery of the share under the terms of the forward contract, and uses it to close out the short position. A net gain of

$$\$40.50 - \$39.00 = \$1.50$$

is therefore made at the end of the 3 months. The two trading strategies we have considered are summarized in Table 5.2.

Under what circumstances do arbitrage opportunities such as those in Table 5.2 not exist? The first arbitrage works when the forward price is greater than $40.50. The second arbitrage works when the forward price is less than $40.50. We deduce that for there to be no arbitrage the forward price must be exactly $40.50.

A Generalization

To generalize this example, we consider a forward contract on an investment asset with price S_0 that provides no income. Using our notation, T is the time to maturity, r is the risk-free rate, and F_0 is the forward price. The relationship between F_0 and S_0 is

$$F_0 = S_0 e^{rT} \tag{5.1}$$

---

[1] Forward contracts on individual stocks do not often arise in practice. However, they form useful examples for developing our ideas. Futures on individual stocks started trading in the United States in November 2002.

Table 5.2 Arbitrage opportunities when forward price is out of line with spot price for asset providing no income. (Asset price = $40; interest rate = 5%; maturity of forward contract = 3 months.)

Forward Price = $43	*Forward Price = $39*
Action now:	*Action now:*
Borrow $40 at 5% for 3 months	Short 1 unit of asset to realize $40
Buy one unit of asset	Invest $40 at 5% for 3 months
Enter into forward contract to sell asset in 3 months for $43	Enter into a forward contract to buy asset in 3 months for $39
Action in 3 months:	*Action in 3 months:*
Sell asset for $43	Buy asset for $39
Use $40.50 to repay loan with interest	Close short position
	Receive $40.50 from investment
Profit realized = $2.50	Profit realized = $1.50

If $F_0 > S_0 e^{rT}$, arbitrageurs can buy the asset and short forward contracts on the asset. If $F_0 < S_0 e^{rT}$, they can short the asset and enter into long forward contracts on it.[2] In our example, $S_0 = 40$, $r = 0.05$, and $T = 0.25$, so that equation (5.1) gives

$$F_0 = 40e^{0.05 \times 0.25} = \$40.50$$

which is in agreement with our earlier calculations.

A long forward contract and a spot purchase both lead to the asset being owned at time T. The forward price is higher than the spot price because of the cost of financing the spot purchase of the asset during the life of the forward contract. This point was overlooked by Kidder Peabody in 1994, much to its cost (see Business Snapshot 5.1).

Example 5.1

Consider a 4-month forward contract to buy a zero-coupon bond that will mature 1 year from today. (This means that the bond will have 8 months to go when the forward contract matures.) The current price of the bond is $930. We assume that the 4-month risk-free rate of interest (continuously compounded) is 6% per annum. Because zero-coupon bonds provide no income, we can use equation (5.1) with $T = 4/12$, $r = 0.06$, and $S_0 = 930$. The forward price, F_0, is given by

$$F_0 = 930e^{0.06 \times 4/12} = \$948.79$$

This would be the delivery price in a contract negotiated today.

---

[2] For another way of seeing that equation (5.1) is correct, consider the following strategy: buy one unit of the asset and enter into a short forward contract to sell it for F_0 at time T. This costs S_0 and is certain to lead to a cash inflow of F_0 at time T. Therefore S_0 must equal the present value of F_0; that is, $S_0 = F_0 e^{-rT}$, or equivalently $F_0 = S_0 e^{rT}$.

Business Snapshot 5.1   Kidder Peabody's Embarrassing Mistake

Investment banks have developed a way of creating a zero-coupon bond, called a *strip*, from a coupon-bearing Treasury bond by selling each of the cash flows underlying the coupon-bearing bond as a separate security. Joseph Jett, a trader working for Kidder Peabody, had a relatively simple trading strategy. He would buy strips and sell them in the forward market. As equation (5.1) shows, the forward price of a security providing no income is always higher than the spot price. Suppose, for example, that the 3-month interest rate is 4% per annum and the spot price of a strip is \$70. The 3-month forward price of the strip is $70e^{0.04 \times 3/12} = \$70.70$.

Kidder Peabody's computer system reported a profit on each of Jett's trades equal to the excess of the forward price over the spot price (\$0.70 in our example). In fact, this profit was nothing more than the cost of financing the purchase of the strip. But, by rolling his contracts forward, Jett was able to prevent this cost from accruing to him.

The result was that the system reported a profit of \$100 million on Jett's trading (and Jett received a big bonus) when in fact there was a loss in the region of \$350 million. This shows that even large financial institutions can get relatively simple things wrong!

What If Short Sales Are Not Possible?

Short sales are not possible for all investment assets and sometimes a fee is charged for borrowing assets. As it happens, this does not matter. To derive equation (5.1), we do not need to be able to short the asset. All that we require is that there be market participants who hold the asset purely for investment (and by definition this is always true of an investment asset). If the forward price is too low, they will find it attractive to sell the asset and take a long position in a forward contract.

We continue to consider the case where the underlying investment asset gives rise to no storage costs or income. If $F_0 > S_0 e^{rT}$, an investor can adopt the following strategy:

1. Borrow S_0 dollars at an interest rate r for T years.
2. Buy 1 unit of the asset.
3. Enter into a forward contract to sell 1 unit of the asset.

At time T, the asset is sold for F_0. An amount $S_0 e^{rT}$ is required to repay the loan at this time and the investor makes a profit of $F_0 - S_0 e^{rT}$.

Suppose next that $F_0 < S_0 e^{rT}$. In this case, an investor who owns the asset can:

1. Sell the asset for S_0.
2. Invest the proceeds at interest rate r for time T.
3. Enter into a forward contract to buy 1 unit of the asset.

At time T, the cash invested has grown to $S_0 e^{rT}$. The asset is repurchased for F_0 and the investor makes a profit of $S_0 e^{rT} - F_0$ relative to the position the investor would have been in if the asset had been kept.

As in the non-dividend-paying stock example considered earlier, we can expect the forward price to adjust so that neither of the two arbitrage opportunities we have considered exists. This means that the relationship in equation (5.1) must hold.

5.5   KNOWN INCOME

In this section we consider a forward contract on an investment asset that will provide a perfectly predictable cash income to the holder. Examples are stocks paying known dividends and coupon-bearing bonds. We adopt the same approach as in the previous section. We first look at a numerical example and then review the formal arguments.

Consider a forward contract to purchase a coupon-bearing bond whose current price is \$900. We will suppose that the forward contract matures in 9 months. We will also suppose that a coupon payment of \$40 is expected on the bond after 4 months. We assume that the 4-month and 9-month risk-free interest rates (continuously compounded) are, respectively, 3% and 4% per annum.

Suppose first that the forward price is relatively high at \$910. An arbitrageur can borrow \$900 to buy the bond and enter into the forward contract to sell the bond for \$910. The coupon payment has a present value of $40e^{-0.03 \times 4/12} = \$39.60$. Of the \$900, \$39.60 is therefore borrowed at 3% per annum for 4 months so that it can be repaid with the coupon payment. The remaining \$860.40 is borrowed at 4% per annum for 9 months. The amount owing at the end of the 9-month period is $860.40e^{0.04 \times 0.75} = \$886.60$. A sum of \$910 is received for the bond under the terms of the forward contract. The arbitrageur therefore makes a net profit of

$$910.00 - 886.60 = \$23.40$$

Suppose next that the forward price is relatively low at \$870. An investor can short the bond and enter into the forward contract to buy the bond for \$870. Of the \$900 realized from shorting the bond, \$39.60 is invested for 4 months at 3% per annum so that it grows into an amount sufficient to pay the coupon on the bond. The remaining \$860.40 is invested for 9 months at 4% per annum and grows to \$886.60. Under the terms of the forward contract, \$870 is paid to buy the bond and the short position is closed out. The investor therefore gains

$$886.60 - 870 = \$16.60$$

The two strategies we have considered are summarized in Table 5.3.[3] The first strategy in Table 5.3 produces a profit when the forward price is greater than \$886.60, whereas the second strategy produces a profit when the forward price is less than \$886.60. It follows that if there are no arbitrage opportunities then the forward price must be \$886.60.

A Generalization

We can generalize from this example to argue that, when an investment asset will provide income with a present value of I during the life of a forward contract, we have

$$F_0 = (S_0 - I)e^{rT} \tag{5.2}$$

---

[3] If shorting the bond is not possible, investors who already own the bond will sell it and buy a forward contract on the bond increasing the value of their position by \$16.60. This is similar to the strategy we described for the asset in the previous section.

Table 5.3 Arbitrage opportunities when 9-month forward price is out of line with spot price for asset providing known cash income. (Asset price = $900; income of $40 occurs at 4 months; 4-month and 9-month rates are, respectively, 3% and 4% per annum.)

Forward price = $910	*Forward price = $870*
Action now:	*Action now*:
Borrow $900: $39.60 for 4 months and $860.40 for 9 months	Short 1 unit of asset to realize $900
Buy 1 unit of asset	Invest $39.60 for 4 months and $860.40 for 9 months
Enter into forward contract to sell asset in 9 months for $910	Enter into a forward contract to buy asset in 9 months for $870
Action in 4 months:	*Action in 4 months*:
Receive $40 of income on asset	Receive $40 from 4-month investment
Use $40 to repay first loan with interest	Pay income of $40 on asset
Action in 9 months:	*Action in 9 months*:
Sell asset for $910	Receive $886.60 from 9-month investment
Use $886.60 to repay second loan with interest	Buy asset for $870
	Close out short position
Profit realized = $23.40	Profit realized = $16.60

In our example, $S_0 = 900.00$, $I = 40e^{-0.03 \times 4/12} = 39.60$, $r = 0.04$, and $T = 0.75$, so that

$$F_0 = (900.00 - 39.60)e^{0.04 \times 0.75} = \$886.60$$

This is in agreement with our earlier calculation. Equation (5.2) applies to any investment asset that provides a known cash income.

If $F_0 > (S_0 - I)e^{rT}$, an arbitrageur can lock in a profit by buying the asset and shorting a forward contract on the asset; if $F_0 < (S_0 - I)e^{rT}$, an arbitrageur can lock in a profit by shorting the asset and taking a long position in a forward contract. If short sales are not possible, investors who own the asset will find it profitable to sell the asset and enter into long forward contracts.[4]

Example 5.2

Consider a 10-month forward contract on a stock when the stock price is $50. We assume that the risk-free rate of interest (continuously compounded) is 8% per annum for all maturities and also that dividends of $0.75 per share are expected after 3 months, 6 months, and 9 months. The present value of the dividends, I, is

$$I = 0.75e^{-0.08 \times 3/12} + 0.75e^{-0.08 \times 6/12} + 0.75e^{-0.08 \times 9/12} = 2.162$$

The variable T is 10 months, so that the forward price, F_0, from equation (5.2), is

---

[4] For another way of seeing that equation (5.2) is correct, consider the following strategy: buy one unit of the asset and enter into a short forward contract to sell it for F_0 at time T. This costs S_0 and is certain to lead to a cash inflow of F_0 at time T and an income with a present value of I. The initial outflow is S_0. The present value of the inflows is $I + F_0e^{-rT}$. Hence, $S_0 = I + F_0e^{-rT}$, or equivalently $F_0 = (S_0 - I)e^{rT}$.

given by

$$F_0 = (50 - 2.162)e^{0.08 \times 10/12} = \$51.14$$

If the forward price were less than this, an arbitrageur would short the stock and buy forward contracts. If the forward price were greater than this, an arbitrageur would short forward contracts and buy the stock in the spot market.

5.6 KNOWN YIELD

We now consider the situation where the asset underlying a forward contract provides a known yield rather than a known cash income. This means that the income is known when expressed as a percentage of the asset's price at the time the income is paid. Suppose that an asset is expected to provide a yield of 5% per annum. This could mean that income is paid once a year and is equal to 5% of the asset price at the time it is paid, in which case the yield would be 5% with annual compounding. Alternatively, it could mean that income is paid twice a year and is equal to 2.5% of the asset price at the time it is paid, in which case the yield would be 5% per annum with semiannual compounding. In Section 4.4 we explained that we will normally measure interest rates with continuous compounding. Similarly, we will normally measure yields with continuous compounding. Formulas for translating a yield measured with one compounding frequency to a yield measured with another compounding frequency are the same as those given for interest rates in Section 4.4.

Define q as the average yield per annum on an asset during the life of a forward contract with continuous compounding. It can be shown (see Problem 5.20) that

$$F_0 = S_0 e^{(r-q)T} \tag{5.3}$$

Example 5.3

Consider a 6-month forward contract on an asset that is expected to provide income equal to 2% of the asset price once during a 6-month period. The risk-free rate of interest (with continuous compounding) is 10% per annum. The asset price is $25. In this case, $S_0 = 25$, $r = 0.10$, and $T = 0.5$. The yield is 4% per annum with semiannual compounding. From equation (4.3), this is 3.96% per annum with continuous compounding. It follows that $q = 0.0396$, so that from equation (5.3) the forward price, F_0, is given by

$$F_0 = 25e^{(0.10 - 0.0396) \times 0.5} = \$25.77$$

5.7 VALUING FORWARD CONTRACTS

The value of a forward contract at the time it is first entered into is close to zero. At a later stage, it may prove to have a positive or negative value. It is important for banks and other financial institutions to value the contract each day. (This is referred to as marking to market the contract.) Using the notation introduced earlier, we suppose K is the delivery price for a contract that was negotiated some time ago, the delivery date is T years from today, and r is the T-year risk-free interest rate. The variable F_0 is the forward price that would be applicable if we negotiated the contract today. In addition, we define f to be the value of forward contract today.

It is important to be clear about the meaning of the variables F_0, K, and f. At the beginning of the life of the forward contract, the delivery price, K, is set equal to the forward price at that time and the value of the contract, f, is 0. As time passes, K stays the same (because it is part of the definition of the contract), but the forward price changes and the value of the contract becomes either positive or negative.

A general result, applicable to all long forward contracts (both those on investment assets and those on consumption assets), is

$$f = (F_0 - K)e^{-rT} \qquad (5.4)$$

To see why equation (5.4) is correct, we use an argument analogous to the one we used for forward rate agreements in Section 4.9. We form a portfolio today consisting of (a) a forward contract to buy the underlying asset for K at time T and (b) a forward contract to sell the asset for F_0 at time T. The payoff from the portfolio at time T is $S_T - K$ from the first contract and $F_0 - S_T$ from the second contract. The total payoff is $F_0 - K$ and is known for certain today. The portfolio is therefore a risk-free investment and its value today is the payoff at time T discounted at the risk-free rate or $(F_0 - K)e^{-rT}$. The value of the forward contract to sell the asset for F_0 is worth zero because F_0 is the forward price that applies to a forward contract entered into today. It follows that the value of a (long) forward contract to buy an asset for K at time T must be $(F_0 - K)e^{-rT}$. Similarly, the value of a (short) forward contract to sell the asset for K at time T is $(K - F_0)e^{-rT}$.

Example 5.4

A long forward contract on a non-dividend-paying stock was entered into some time ago. It currently has 6 months to maturity. The risk-free rate of interest (with continuous compounding) is 10% per annum, the stock price is $25, and the delivery price is $24. In this case, $S_0 = 25$, $r = 0.10$, $T = 0.5$, and $K = 24$. From equation (5.1), the 6-month forward price, F_0, is given by

$$F_0 = 25e^{0.1 \times 0.5} = \$26.28$$

From equation (5.4), the value of the forward contract is

$$f = (26.28 - 24)e^{-0.1 \times 0.5} = \$2.17$$

Equation (5.4) shows that we can value a long forward contract on an asset by making the assumption that the price of the asset at the maturity of the forward contract equals the forward price F_0. To see this, note that when we make that assumption, a long forward contract provides a payoff at time T of $F_0 - K$. This has a present value of $(F_0 - K)e^{-rT}$, which is the value of f in equation (5.4). Similarly, we can value a short forward contract on the asset by assuming that the current forward price of the asset is realized. These results are analogous to the result in Section 4.9 that we can value a forward rate agreement on the assumption that forward rates are realized.

Using equation (5.4) in conjunction with equation (5.1) gives the following expression for the value of a forward contract on an investment asset that provides no income

$$f = S_0 - Ke^{-rT} \qquad (5.5)$$

Similarly, using equation (5.4) in conjunction with equation (5.2) gives the following

---

Business Snapshot 5.2 A Systems Error?

A foreign exchange trader working for a bank enters into a long forward contract to buy 1 million pounds sterling at an exchange rate of 1.5000 in 3 months. At the same time, another trader on the next desk takes a long position in 16 contracts for 3-month futures on sterling. The futures price is 1.5000 and each contract is on 62,500 pounds. The positions taken by the forward and futures traders are therefore the same. Within minutes of the positions being taken, the forward and the futures prices both increase to 1.5040. The bank's systems show that the futures trader has made a profit of $4,000, while the forward trader has made a profit of only $3,900. The forward trader immediately calls the bank's systems department to complain. Does the forward trader have a valid complaint?

The answer is no! The daily settlement of futures contracts ensures that the futures trader realizes an almost immediate profit corresponding to the increase in the futures price. If the forward trader closed out the position by entering into a short contract at 1.5040, the forward trader would have contracted to buy 1 million pounds at 1.5000 in 3 months and sell 1 million pounds at 1.5040 in 3 months. This would lead to a $4,000 profit—but in 3 months, not today. The forward trader's profit is the present value of $4,000. This is consistent with equation (5.4).

The forward trader can gain some consolation from the fact that gains and losses are treated symmetrically. If the forward/futures prices dropped to 1.4960 instead of rising to 1.5040, then the futures trader would take a loss of $4,000 while the forward trader would take a loss of only $3,900.

---

expression for the value of a long forward contract on an investment asset that provides a known income with present value I:

$$f = S_0 - I - Ke^{-rT} \tag{5.6}$$

Finally, using equation (5.4) in conjunction with equation (5.3) gives the following expression for the value of a long forward contract on an investment asset that provides a known yield at rate q:

$$f = S_0 e^{-qT} - Ke^{-rT} \tag{5.7}$$

When a futures price changes, the gain or loss on a futures contract is calculated as the change in the futures price multiplied by the size of the position. This gain is realized almost immediately because futures contracts are settled daily. Equation (5.4) shows that, when a forward price changes, the gain or loss is the present value of the change in the forward price multiplied by the size of the position. The difference between the gain/loss on forward and futures contracts can cause confusion on a foreign exchange trading desk (see Business Snapshot 5.2).

5.8   ARE FORWARD PRICES AND FUTURES PRICES EQUAL?

Technical Note 24 at www-2.rotman.utoronto.ca/~hull/TechnicalNotes provides an arbitrage argument to show that, when the short-term risk-free interest rate is constant, the forward price for a contract with a certain delivery date is in theory the same as the futures price for a contract with that delivery date. The argument can be extended to cover situations where the interest rate is a known function of time.

When interest rates vary unpredictably (as they do in the real world), forward and futures prices are in theory no longer the same. We can get a sense of the nature of the relationship by considering the situation where the price of the underlying asset, S, is strongly positively correlated with interest rates. When S increases, an investor who holds a long futures position makes an immediate gain because of the daily settlement procedure. The positive correlation indicates that it is likely that interest rates have also increased, thereby increasing the rate at which the gain can be invested. Similarly, when S decreases, the investor will incur an immediate loss and it is likely that interest rates have just decreased, thereby reducing the rate at which the loss has to be financed. The positive correlation therefore works in the investor's favor. An investor holding a forward contract rather than a futures contract is not affected in this way by interest rate movements. It follows that a long futures contract will be slightly more attractive than a similar long forward contract. Hence, when S is strongly positively correlated with interest rates, futures prices will tend to be slightly higher than forward prices. When S is strongly negatively correlated with interest rates, a similar argument shows that forward prices will tend to be slightly higher than futures prices.

The theoretical differences between forward and futures prices for contracts that last only a few months are in most circumstances sufficiently small to be ignored. In practice, there are a number of factors not reflected in theoretical models that may cause forward and futures prices to be different. These include taxes, transactions costs, and margin requirements. The risk that the counterparty will default may be less in the case of a futures contract because of the role of the exchange clearing house. Also, in some instances, futures contracts are more liquid and easier to trade than forward contracts. Despite all these points, for most purposes it is reasonable to assume that forward and futures prices are the same. This is the assumption we will usually make in this book. We will use the symbol F_0 to represent both the futures price and the forward price of an asset today.

One exception to the rule that futures and forward contracts can be assumed to be the same concerns Eurodollar futures. This will be discussed in Section 6.3.

5.9 FUTURES PRICES OF STOCK INDICES

We introduced futures on stock indices in Section 3.5 and showed how a stock index futures contract is a useful tool in managing equity portfolios. Table 3.3 shows futures prices for a number of different indices. We are now in a position to consider how index futures prices are determined.

A stock index can usually be regarded as the price of an investment asset that pays dividends.[5] The investment asset is the portfolio of stocks underlying the index, and the dividends paid by the investment asset are the dividends that would be received by the holder of this portfolio. It is usually assumed that the dividends provide a known yield rather than a known cash income. If q is the dividend yield rate (expressed with

---

[5] One exception here is the contract in Business Snapshot 5.3.

Business Snapshot 5.3 The CME Nikkei 225 Futures Contract

The arguments in this chapter on how index futures prices are determined require that the index be the value of an investment asset. This means that it must be the value of a portfolio of assets that can be traded. The asset underlying the Chicago Mercantile Exchange's futures contract on the Nikkei 225 Index does not qualify, and the reason why is quite subtle. Suppose S is the value of the Nikkei 225 Index. This is the value of a portfolio of 225 Japanese stocks measured in yen. The variable underlying the CME futures contract on the Nikkei 225 has a *dollar value* of $5S$. In other words, the futures contract takes a variable that is measured in yen and treats it as though it is dollars.

We cannot invest in a portfolio whose value will always be $5S$ dollars. The best we can do is to invest in one that is always worth $5S$ yen or in one that is always worth $5QS$ dollars, where Q is the dollar value of 1 yen. The variable $5S$ dollars is not, therefore, the price of an investment asset and equation (5.8) does not apply.

CME's Nikkei 225 futures contract is an example of a *quanto*. A quanto is a derivative where the underlying asset is measured in one currency and the payoff is in another currency. Quantos will be discussed further in Chapter 30.

---

continuous compounding), equation (5.3) gives the futures price, F_0, as

$$F_0 = S_0 e^{(r-q)T} \tag{5.8}$$

This shows that the futures price increases at rate $r - q$ with the maturity of the futures contract. In Table 3.3, the December futures settlement price of the S&P 500 is about 0.7% less than the June settlement price. This indicates that, at the beginning of May 2016, the short-term risk-free rate r was less than the dividend yield q by about 1.4% per year.

Example 5.5

Consider a 3-month futures contract on an index. Suppose that the stocks underlying the index provide a dividend yield of 1% per annum (continuously compounded), that the current value of the index is 1,300, and that the continuously compounded risk-free interest rate is 5% per annum. In this case, $r = 0.05$, $S_0 = 1,300$, $T = 0.25$, and $q = 0.01$. Hence, the futures price, F_0, is given by

$$F_0 = 1,300 e^{(0.05-0.01) \times 0.25} = \$1,313.07$$

In practice, the dividend yield on the portfolio underlying an index varies week by week throughout the year. For example, a large proportion of the dividends on the NYSE stocks are paid in the first week of February, May, August, and November each year. The chosen value of q should represent the average annualized dividend yield during the life of the contract. The dividends used for estimating q should be those for which the ex-dividend date is during the life of the futures contract.

Index Arbitrage

If $F_0 > S_0 e^{(r-q)T}$, profits can be made by buying the stocks underlying the index at the spot price (i.e., for immediate delivery) and shorting futures contracts. If $F_0 < S_0 e^{(r-q)T}$,

Business Snapshot 5.4   Index Arbitrage in October 1987

To do index arbitrage, a trader must be able to trade both the index futures contract and the portfolio of stocks underlying the index very quickly at the prices quoted in the market. In normal market conditions this is possible using program trading, and the relationship in equation (5.8) holds well. Examples of days when the market was anything but normal are October 19 and 20 of 1987. On what is termed "Black Monday," October 19, 1987, the market fell by more than 20%, and the 604 million shares traded on the New York Stock Exchange easily exceeded all previous records. The exchange's systems were overloaded, and orders placed to buy or sell shares on that day could be delayed by up to two hours before being executed.

For most of October 19, 1987, futures prices were at a significant discount to the underlying index. For example, at the close of trading the S&P 500 Index was at 225.06 (down 57.88 on the day), whereas the futures price for December delivery on the S&P 500 was 201.50 (down 80.75 on the day). This was largely because the delays in processing orders made index arbitrage impossible. On the next day, Tuesday, October 20, 1987, the New York Stock Exchange placed temporary restrictions on the way in which program trading could be done. This also made index arbitrage very difficult and the breakdown of the traditional linkage between stock indices and stock index futures continued. At one point the futures price for the December contract was 18% less than the S&P 500 Index. However, after a few days the market returned to normal, and the activities of arbitrageurs ensured that equation (5.8) governed the relationship between futures and spot prices of indices.

profits can be made by doing the reverse—that is, shorting or selling the stocks underlying the index and taking a long position in futures contracts. These strategies are known as *index arbitrage*. When $F_0 < S_0 e^{(r-q)T}$, index arbitrage is often done by a pension fund that owns an indexed portfolio of stocks. When $F_0 > S_0 e^{(r-q)T}$, it might be done by a bank or a corporation holding short-term money market investments. For indices involving many stocks, index arbitrage is sometimes accomplished by trading a relatively small representative sample of stocks whose movements closely mirror those of the index. Usually index arbitrage is implemented through *program trading*. This involves using a computer system to generate the trades.

Most of the time the activities of arbitrageurs ensure that equation (5.8) holds, but occasionally arbitrage is impossible and the futures price does get out of line with the spot price (see Business Snapshot 5.4).

5.10   FORWARD AND FUTURES CONTRACTS ON CURRENCIES

We now move on to consider forward and futures foreign currency contracts. For the sake of definiteness we will assume that the domestic currency is the U.S. dollar (i.e., we take the perspective of a U.S. investor). The underlying asset is one unit of the foreign currency. We will therefore define the variable S_0 as the current spot price in U.S. dollars of one unit of the foreign currency and F_0 as the forward or futures price in U.S. dollars of one unit of the foreign currency. This is consistent with the way we have

Figure 5.1 Two ways of converting 1,000 units of a foreign currency to dollars at time T. Here, S_0 is spot exchange rate, F_0 is forward exchange rate, and r and r_f are the dollar and foreign risk-free rates.

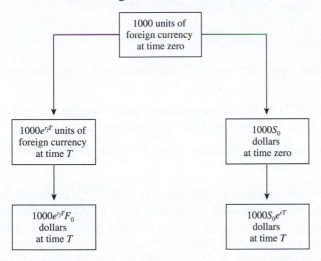

defined S_0 and F_0 for other assets underlying forward and futures contracts. However, as mentioned in Section 2.11, it does not necessarily correspond to the way spot and forward exchange rates are quoted. For major exchange rates other than the British pound, euro, Australian dollar, and New Zealand dollar, a spot or forward exchange rate is normally quoted as the number of units of the currency that are equivalent to one U.S. dollar.

A foreign currency has the property that the holder of the currency can earn interest at the risk-free interest rate prevailing in the foreign country. For example, the holder can invest the currency in a foreign-denominated bond. We define r_f as the value of the foreign risk-free interest rate when money is invested for time T. The variable r is the domestic risk-free rate when money is invested for this period of time.

The relationship between F_0 and S_0 is

$$F_0 = S_0 e^{(r-r_f)T} \tag{5.9}$$

This is the well-known interest rate parity relationship from international finance. The reason it is true is illustrated in Figure 5.1. Suppose that an individual starts with 1,000 units of the foreign currency. There are two ways it can be converted to dollars at time T. One is by investing it for T years at r_f and entering into a forward contract to sell the proceeds for dollars at time T. This generates $1,000e^{r_f T}F_0$ dollars. The other is by exchanging the foreign currency for dollars in the spot market and investing the proceeds for T years at rate r. This generates $1,000S_0e^{rT}$ dollars. In the absence of arbitrage opportunities, the two strategies must give the same result. Hence,

$$1,000e^{r_f T}F_0 = 1,000S_0e^{rT}$$

so that

$$F_0 = S_0 e^{(r-r_f)T}$$

Example 5.6

Suppose that the 2-year interest rates in Australia and the United States are 3% and 1%, respectively, and the spot exchange rate is 0.7500 USD per AUD. From equation (5.9), the 2-year forward exchange rate should be

$$0.7500e^{(0.01-0.03)\times 2} = 0.7206$$

Suppose first that the 2-year forward exchange rate is less than this, say 0.7000. An arbitrageur can:

1. Borrow 1,000 AUD at 3% per annum for 2 years, convert to 750 USD and invest the USD at 1% (both rates are continuously compounded).

2. Enter into a forward contract to buy 1,061.84 AUD for $1,061.84 \times 0.7000 = 743.29$ USD in 2 years.

The 750 USD that are invested at 1% grow to $750e^{0.01\times 2} = 765.15$ USD in 2 years. Of this, 743.29 USD are used to purchase 1,061.84 AUD under the terms of the forward contract. This is exactly enough to repay principal and interest on the 1,000 AUD that are borrowed ($1,000e^{0.03\times 2} = 1,061.84$). The strategy therefore gives rise to a riskless profit of $765.15 - 743.29 = 21.87$ USD. (If this does not sound very exciting, consider following a similar strategy where you borrow 100 million AUD!)

Suppose next that the 2-year forward rate is 0.7600 (greater than the 0.7206 value given by equation (5.9)). An arbitrageur can:

1. Borrow 1,000 USD at 1% per annum for 2 years, convert to $1,000/0.7500 = 1,333.33$ AUD, and invest the AUD at 3%.

2. Enter into a forward contract to sell 1,415.79 AUD for $1,415.79 \times 0.76 = 1,075.99$ USD in 2 years.

The 1,333.33 AUD that are invested at 3% grow to $1,333.33e^{0.03\times 2} = 1,415.79$ AUD in 2 years. The forward contract has the effect of converting this to 1,075.99 USD. The amount needed to payoff the USD borrowings is $1,000e^{0.01\times 2} = 1,020.20$ USD. The strategy therefore gives rise to a riskless profit of $1,075.99 - 1,020.20 = 55.79$ USD.

Table 5.4 shows currency futures quotes on May 3, 2016. The quotes are U.S. dollars per unit of the foreign currency. (In the case of the Japanese yen, the quote is U.S. dollars per 100 yen.) This is the usual quotation convention for futures contracts. Equation (5.9) applies with r equal to the U.S. risk-free rate and r_f equal to the foreign risk-free rate.

On May 3, 2016, the short-term interest rate on the Australian dollar was higher than the short-term interest rate on the U.S. dollar. This corresponds to the $r_f > r$ situation and explains why settlement futures prices for this currency decrease with maturity in Table 5.4. For all the other currencies considered in the table, short-term interest rates were lower than on the U.S. dollar. This corresponds to the $r > r_f$ situation and explains why the settlement futures prices of these currencies increase with maturity.

Table 5.4 Futures quotes for a selection of CME Group contracts on foreign currencies on May 3, 2016.

	Open	High	Low	Prior settlement	Last trade	Change	Volume
Australian Dollar, USD per AUD, 100,000 AUD							
June 2016	0.7651	0.7708	0.7477	0.7642	0.7479	−0.0163	163,519
Sept. 2016	0.7628	0.7670	0.7451	0.7613	0.7451	−0.0162	316
British Pound, USD per GBP, 62,500 GBP							
June 2016	1.4671	1.4771	1.4533	1.4668	1.4552	−0.0116	117,683
Sept. 2016	1.4682	1.4767	1.4548	1.4674	1.4563	−0.0111	108
Canadian Dollar, USD per CAD, 100,000 CAD							
June 2016	0.7978	0.8025	0.7870	0.7969	0.7870	−0.0099	84,828
Sept. 2016	0.7980	0.8018	0.7874	0.7969	0.7888	−0.0081	413
Dec. 2016	0.7980	0.7980	0.7875	0.7970	0.7875	−0.0095	137
Euro, USD per EUR, 125,000 EUR							
June 2016	1.15425	1.16305	1.15145	1.15370	1.15345	−0.00025	217,744
Sept. 2016	1.15855	1.16650	1.15540	1.15735	1.15755	+0.00020	744
Dec. 2016	1.16500	1.17000	1.15970	1.16135	1.16160	+0.00025	96
Japanese Yen, USD per 100 yen, 12.5 million yen							
June 2016	0.94065	0.94830	0.94015	0.94015	0.94175	+0.00160	100,707
Sept. 2016	0.94525	0.95090	0.94410	0.94320	0.94570	+0.00250	158
Swiss Franc, USD per CHF, 125,000 CHF							
June 2016	1.0489	1.0607	1.0485	1.0492	1.0506	+0.0014	29,070
Sept. 2016	1.0543	1.0650	1.0543	1.0540	1.0563	+0.0023	105

Example 5.7

In Table 5.4, the September settlement price for the Australian dollar is about 0.4% lower than the June settlement price. This indicates that the futures prices are decreasing at about $4 \times 0.4 = 1.6\%$ per year with maturity. From equation (5.9) this is an estimate of the amount by which short-term Australian interest rates exceeded short-term U.S. interest rates at the beginning of May 2016.

A Foreign Currency as an Asset Providing a Known Yield

Equation (5.9) is identical to equation (5.3) with q replaced by r_f. This is not a coincidence. A foreign currency can be regarded as an investment asset paying a known yield. The yield is the risk-free rate of interest in the foreign currency.

To understand this, we note that the value of interest paid in a foreign currency depends on the value of the foreign currency. Suppose that the interest rate on British pounds is 5% per annum. To a U.S. investor the British pound provides an income equal to 5% of the value of the British pound per annum. In other words it is an asset that provides a yield of 5% per annum.

5.11 FUTURES ON COMMODITIES

We now move on to consider futures contracts on commodities. First we look at the futures prices of commodities that are investment assets such as gold and silver.[6] We then go on to examine the futures prices of consumption assets.

Income and Storage Costs

As explained in Business Snapshot 3.1, the hedging strategies of gold producers leads to a requirement on the part of investment banks to borrow gold. Gold owners such as central banks charge interest in the form of what is known as the *gold lease rate* when they lend gold. The same is true of silver. Gold and silver can therefore provide income to the holder. Like other commodities they also have storage costs.

Equation (5.1) shows that, in the absence of storage costs and income, the forward price of a commodity that is an investment asset is given by

$$F_0 = S_0 e^{rT} \tag{5.10}$$

Storage costs can be treated as negative income. If U is the present value of all the storage costs, net of income, during the life of a forward contract, it follows from equation (5.2) that

$$F_0 = (S_0 + U)e^{rT} \tag{5.11}$$

Example 5.8

Consider a 1-year futures contract on an investment asset that provides no income. It costs \$2 per unit to store the asset, with the payment being made at the end of the year. Assume that the spot price is \$450 per unit and the risk-free rate is 7% per annum for all maturities. This corresponds to $r = 0.07$, $S_0 = 450$, $T = 1$, and

$$U = 2e^{-0.07 \times 1} = 1.865$$

From equation (5.11), the theoretical futures price, F_0, is given by

$$F_0 = (450 + 1.865)e^{0.07 \times 1} = \$484.63$$

If the actual futures price is greater than 484.63, an arbitrageur can buy the asset and short 1-year futures contracts to lock in a profit. If the actual futures price is less than 484.63, an investor who already owns the asset can improve the return by selling the asset and buying futures contracts.

If the storage costs (net of income) incurred at any time are proportional to the price of the commodity, they can be treated as negative yield. In this case, from equation (5.3),

$$F_0 = S_0 e^{(r+u)T} \tag{5.12}$$

where u denotes the storage costs per annum as a proportion of the spot price net of any yield earned on the asset.

---

[6] Recall that, for an asset to be an investment asset, it need not be held solely for investment purposes. What is required is that some individuals hold it for investment purposes and that these individuals be prepared to sell their holdings and go long forward contracts, if the latter look more attractive. This explains why silver, although it has industrial uses, is an investment asset.

Consumption Commodities

Commodities that are consumption assets rather than investment assets usually provide no income, but can be subject to significant storage costs. We now review the arbitrage strategies used to determine futures prices from spot prices carefully.[7] Suppose that, instead of equation (5.11), we have

$$F_0 > (S_0 + U)e^{rT} \qquad\qquad (5.13)$$

To take advantage of this opportunity, an arbitrageur can implement the following strategy:

1. Borrow an amount $S_0 + U$ at the risk-free rate and use it to purchase one unit of the commodity and to pay storage costs.

2. Short a futures contract on one unit of the commodity.

If we regard the futures contract as a forward contract, so that there is no daily settlement, this strategy leads to a profit of $F_0 - (S_0 + U)e^{rT}$ at time T. There is no problem in implementing the strategy for any commodity. However, as arbitrageurs do so, there will be a tendency for S_0 to increase and F_0 to decrease until equation (5.13) is no longer true. We conclude that equation (5.13) cannot hold for any significant length of time.

Suppose next that

$$F_0 < (S_0 + U)e^{rT} \qquad\qquad (5.14)$$

When the commodity is an investment asset, we can argue that many investors hold the commodity solely for investment. When they observe the inequality in equation (5.14), they will find it profitable to do the following:

1. Sell the commodity, save the storage costs, and invest the proceeds at the risk-free interest rate.

2. Take a long position in a futures contract.

The result is a riskless profit at maturity of $(S_0 + U)e^{rT} - F_0$ relative to the position the investors would have been in if they had held the commodity. It follows that equation (5.14) cannot hold for long. Because neither equation (5.13) nor (5.14) can hold for long, we must have $F_0 = (S_0 + U)e^{rT}$.

This argument cannot be used for a commodity that is a consumption asset rather than an investment asset. Individuals and companies who own a consumption commodity usually plan to use it in some way. They are reluctant to sell the commodity in the spot market and buy forward or futures contracts, because forward and futures contracts cannot be used in a manufacturing process or consumed in some other way. There is therefore nothing to stop equation (5.14) from holding, and all we can assert for a consumption commodity is

$$F_0 \leqslant (S_0 + U)e^{rT} \qquad\qquad (5.15)$$

---

[7] For some commodities the spot price depends on the delivery location. We assume that the delivery location for spot and futures are the same.

If storage costs are expressed as a proportion u of the spot price, the equivalent result is

$$F_0 \leqslant S_0 e^{(r+u)T} \tag{5.16}$$

Convenience Yields

We do not necessarily have equality in equations (5.15) and (5.16) because users of a consumption commodity may feel that ownership of the physical commodity provides benefits that are not obtained by holders of futures contracts. For example, an oil refiner is unlikely to regard a futures contract on crude oil in the same way as crude oil held in inventory. The crude oil in inventory can be an input to the refining process, whereas a futures contract cannot be used for this purpose. In general, ownership of the physical asset enables a manufacturer to keep a production process running and perhaps profit from temporary local shortages. A futures contract does not do the same. The benefits from holding the physical asset are sometimes referred to as the *convenience yield* provided by the commodity. If the dollar amount of storage costs is known and has a present value U, then the convenience yield y is defined such that

$$F_0 e^{yT} = (S_0 + U)e^{rT}$$

If the storage costs per unit are a constant proportion, u, of the spot price, then y is defined so that

$$F_0 e^{yT} = S_0 e^{(r+u)T}$$

or

$$F_0 = S_0 e^{(r+u-y)T} \tag{5.17}$$

The convenience yield simply measures the extent to which the left-hand side is less than the right-hand side in equation (5.15) or (5.16). For investment assets the convenience yield must be zero; otherwise, there are arbitrage opportunities. Table 2.2 in Chapter 2 shows that, on May 3, 2016, the futures price of live cattle decreased as the maturity of the contract increased from June 2016 to April 2017. This pattern suggests that the convenience yield, y, is greater than $r + u$ during this period.

The convenience yield reflects the market's expectations concerning the future availability of the commodity. The greater the possibility that shortages will occur, the higher the convenience yield. If users of the commodity have high inventories, there is very little chance of shortages in the near future and the convenience yield tends to be low. If inventories are low, shortages are more likely and the convenience yield is usually higher.

5.12 THE COST OF CARRY

The relationship between futures prices and spot prices can be summarized in terms of the *cost of carry*. This measures the storage cost plus the interest that is paid to finance the asset less the income earned on the asset. For a non-dividend-paying stock, the cost of carry is r, because there are no storage costs and no income is earned; for a stock index, it is $r - q$, because income is earned at rate q on the asset. For a currency, it is $r - r_f$; for a commodity that provides income at rate q and requires storage costs at rate u, it is $r - q + u$; and so on.

Define the cost of carry as c. For an investment asset, the futures price is

$$F_0 = S_0 e^{cT} \qquad (5.18)$$

For a consumption asset, it is

$$F_0 = S_0 e^{(c-y)T} \qquad (5.19)$$

where y is the convenience yield.

5.13 DELIVERY OPTIONS

Whereas a forward contract normally specifies that delivery is to take place on a particular day, a futures contract often allows the party with the short position to choose to deliver at any time during a certain period. (Typically the party has to give a few days' notice of its intention to deliver.) The choice introduces a complication into the determination of futures prices. Should the maturity of the futures contract be assumed to be the beginning, middle, or end of the delivery period? Even though most futures contracts are closed out prior to maturity, it is important to know when delivery would have taken place in order to calculate the theoretical futures price.

If the futures price is an increasing function of the time to maturity, it can be seen from equation (5.19) that $c > y$, so that the benefits from holding the asset (including convenience yield and net of storage costs) are less than the risk-free rate. It is usually optimal in such a case for the party with the short position to deliver as early as possible, because the interest earned on the cash received outweighs the benefits of holding the asset. As a rule, futures prices in these circumstances should be calculated on the basis that delivery will take place at the beginning of the delivery period. If futures prices are decreasing as time to maturity increases ($c < y$), the reverse is true. It is then usually optimal for the party with the short position to deliver as late as possible, and futures prices should, as a rule, be calculated on this assumption.

5.14 FUTURES PRICES AND EXPECTED FUTURE SPOT PRICES

We refer to the market's average opinion about what the spot price of an asset will be at a certain future time as the *expected spot price* of the asset at that time. Suppose that it is now June and the September futures price of corn is 450 cents. It is interesting to ask what the expected spot price of corn in September is. Is it less than 450 cents, greater than 450 cents, or exactly equal to 450 cents? As illustrated in Figure 2.1, the futures price converges to the spot price at maturity. If the expected spot price is less than 450 cents, the market must be expecting the September futures price to decline, so that traders with short positions gain and traders with long positions lose. If the expected spot price is greater than 450 cents, the reverse must be true. The market must be expecting the September futures price to increase, so that traders with long positions gain while those with short positions lose.

Keynes and Hicks

Economists John Maynard Keynes and John Hicks argued that, if hedgers tend to hold short positions and speculators tend to hold long positions, the futures price of an asset will be below the expected spot price.[8] This is because speculators require compensation for the risks they are bearing. They will trade only if they can expect to make money on average. Hedgers will lose money on average, but they are likely to be prepared to accept this because the futures contract reduces their risks. If hedgers tend to hold long positions while speculators hold short positions, Keynes and Hicks argued that the futures price will be above the expected spot price for a similar reason.

Risk and Return

The modern approach to explaining the relationship between futures prices and expected spot prices is based on the relationship between risk and expected return in the economy. In general, the higher the risk of an investment, the higher the expected return demanded by an investor. The capital asset pricing model, which is explained in the appendix to Chapter 3, shows that there are two types of risk in the economy: systematic and nonsystematic. Nonsystematic risk should not be important to an investor. It can be almost completely eliminated by holding a well-diversified portfolio. An investor should not therefore require a higher expected return for bearing non-systematic risk. Systematic risk, in contrast, cannot be diversified away. It arises from a correlation between returns from the investment and returns from the whole stock market. An investor generally requires a higher expected return than the risk-free interest rate for bearing positive amounts of systematic risk. Also, an investor is prepared to accept a lower expected return than the risk-free interest rate when the systematic risk in an investment is negative.

The Risk in a Futures Position

Let us consider a speculator who takes a long position in a futures contract that lasts for T years in the hope that the spot price of the asset will be above the futures price at the end of the life of the futures contract. We ignore daily settlement and assume that the futures contract can be treated as a forward contract. We suppose that the speculator puts the present value of the futures price into a risk-free investment while simultaneously taking a long futures position. The proceeds of the risk-free investment are used to buy the asset on the delivery date. The asset is then immediately sold for its market price. The cash flows to the speculator are as follows:

Today: $-F_0 e^{-rT}$

End of futures contract: $+S_T$

where F_0 is the futures price today, S_T is the price of the asset at time T at the end of the futures contract, and r is the risk-free return on funds invested for time T.

How do we value this investment? The discount rate we should use for the expected cash flow at time T equals an investor's required return on the investment. Suppose that k is an investor's required return for this investment. The present value of this investment is

$$-F_0 e^{-rT} + E(S_T)e^{-kT}$$

where E denotes expected value. We can assume that all investments in securities

---

[8] See: J. M. Keynes, *A Treatise on Money.* London: Macmillan, 1930; and J. R. Hicks, *Value and Capital.* Oxford: Clarendon Press, 1939.

Table 5.5   Relationship between futures price and expected future spot price.

Underlying asset	Relationship of expected return k from asset to risk-free rate r	Relationship of futures price F to expected future spot price $E(S_T)$
No systematic risk	$k = r$	$F_0 = E(S_T)$
Positive systematic risk	$k > r$	$F_0 < E(S_T)$
Negative systematic risk	$k < r$	$F_0 > E(S_T)$

markets are priced so that they have zero net present value. This means that

$$-F_0 e^{-rT} + E(S_T)e^{-kT} = 0$$

or

$$F_0 = E(S_T)e^{(r-k)T} \qquad (5.20)$$

As we have just discussed, the returns investors require on an investment depend on its systematic risk. The investment we have been considering is in essence an investment in the asset underlying the futures contract. If the returns from this asset are uncorrelated with the stock market, the correct discount rate to use is the risk-free rate r, so we should set $k = r$. Equation (5.20) then gives

$$F_0 = E(S_T)$$

This shows that the futures price is an unbiased estimate of the expected future spot price when the return from the underlying asset is uncorrelated with the stock market.

If the return from the asset is positively correlated with the stock market, $k > r$ and equation (5.20) leads to $F_0 < E(S_T)$. This shows that, when the asset underlying the futures contract has positive systematic risk, we should expect the futures price to understate the expected future spot price. An example of an asset that has positive systematic risk is a stock index. The expected return of investors on the stocks underlying an index is generally more than the risk-free rate, r. The dividends provide a return of q. The expected increase in the index must therefore be more than $r - q$. Equation (5.8) is therefore consistent with the prediction that the futures price understates the expected future stock price for a stock index.

If the return from the asset is negatively correlated with the stock market, $k < r$ and equation (5.20) gives $F_0 > E(S_T)$. This shows that, when the asset underlying the futures contract has negative systematic risk, we should expect the futures price to overstate the expected future spot price.

These results are summarized in Table 5.5.

Normal Backwardation and Contango

When the futures price is below the expected future spot price, the situation is known as *normal backwardation*; and when the futures price is above the expected future spot price, the situation is known as *contango*. However, it should be noted that sometimes these terms are used to refer to whether the futures price is below or above the current spot price, rather than the expected future spot price.

SUMMARY

For most purposes, the futures price of a contract with a certain delivery date can be considered to be the same as the forward price for a contract with the same delivery date. It can be shown that in theory the two should be exactly the same when interest rates are perfectly predictable.

For the purposes of understanding futures (or forward) prices, it is convenient to divide futures contracts into two categories: those in which the underlying asset is held for investment by at least some traders and those in which the underlying asset is held primarily for consumption purposes.

In the case of investment assets, we have considered three different situations:

1. The asset provides no income.
2. The asset provides a known dollar income.
3. The asset provides a known yield.

The results are summarized in Table 5.6. They enable futures prices to be obtained for contracts on stock indices, currencies, gold, and silver. Storage costs can be treated as negative income.

In the case of consumption assets, it is not possible to obtain the futures price as a function of the spot price and other observable variables. Here the parameter known as the asset's convenience yield becomes important. It measures the extent to which users of the commodity feel that ownership of the physical asset provides benefits that are not obtained by the holders of the futures contract. These benefits may include the ability to profit from temporary local shortages or the ability to keep a production process running. We can obtain an upper bound for the futures price of consumption assets using arbitrage arguments, but we cannot nail down an equality relationship between futures and spot prices.

The concept of cost of carry is sometimes useful. The cost of carry is the storage cost of the underlying asset plus the cost of financing it minus the income received from it. In the case of investment assets, the futures price is greater than the spot price by an amount reflecting the cost of carry. In the case of consumption assets, the futures price is greater than the spot price by an amount reflecting the cost of carry net of the convenience yield.

If we assume the capital asset pricing model is true, the relationship between the futures price and the expected future spot price depends on whether the return on the

Table 5.6 Summary of results for a contract with time to maturity T on an investment asset with price S_0 when the risk-free interest rate for a T-year period is r.

Asset	Forward/futures price	Value of long forward contract with delivery price K
Provides no income:	$S_0 e^{rT}$	$S_0 - Ke^{-rT}$
Provides known income with present value I:	$(S_0 - I)e^{rT}$	$S_0 - I - Ke^{-rT}$
Provides known yield q:	$S_0 e^{(r-q)T}$	$S_0 e^{-qT} - Ke^{-rT}$

asset is positively or negatively correlated with the return on the stock market. Positive correlation will tend to lead to a futures price lower than the expected future spot price, whereas negative correlation will tend to lead to a futures price higher than the expected future spot price. Only when the correlation is zero will the theoretical futures price be equal to the expected future spot price.

FURTHER READING

Cox, J. C., J. E. Ingersoll, and S. A. Ross. "The Relation between Forward Prices and Futures Prices," *Journal of Financial Economics*, 9 (December 1981): 321–46.

Jarrow, R. A., and G. S. Oldfield. "Forward Contracts and Futures Contracts," *Journal of Financial Economics*, 9 (December 1981): 373–82.

Richard, S., and S. Sundaresan. "A Continuous-Time Model of Forward and Futures Prices in a Multigood Economy," *Journal of Financial Economics*, 9 (December 1981): 347–72.

Routledge, B. R., D. J. Seppi, and C. S. Spatt. "Equilibrium Forward Curves for Commodities," *Journal of Finance*, 55, 3 (2000) 1297–1338.

Practice Questions (Answers in Solutions Manual)

5.1. Explain what happens when an investor shorts a certain share.

5.2. What is the difference between the forward price and the value of a forward contract?

5.3. Suppose that you enter into a 6-month forward contract on a non-dividend-paying stock when the stock price is $30 and the risk-free interest rate (with continuous compounding) is 5% per annum. What is the forward price?

5.4. A stock index currently stands at 350. The risk-free interest rate is 4% per annum (with continuous compounding) and the dividend yield on the index is 3% per annum. What should the futures price for a 4-month contract be?

5.5. Explain carefully why the futures price of gold can be calculated from its spot price and other observable variables whereas the futures price of copper cannot.

5.6. Explain carefully the meaning of the terms *convenience yield* and *cost of carry*. What is the relationship between futures price, spot price, convenience yield, and cost of carry?

5.7. Explain why a foreign currency can be treated as an asset providing a known yield.

5.8. Is the futures price of a stock index greater than or less than the expected future value of the index? Explain your answer.

5.9. A 1-year long forward contract on a non-dividend-paying stock is entered into when the stock price is $40 and the risk-free rate of interest is 5% per annum with continuous compounding.
(a) What are the forward price and the initial value of the forward contract?
(b) Six months later, the price of the stock is $45 and the risk-free interest rate is still 5%. What are the forward price and the value of the forward contract?

5.10. The risk-free rate of interest is 7% per annum with continuous compounding, and the dividend yield on a stock index is 3.2% per annum. The current value of the index is 150. What is the 6-month futures price?

5.11. Assume that the risk-free interest rate is 4% per annum with continuous compounding and that the dividend yield on a stock index varies throughout the year. In February, May, August, and November, dividends are paid at a rate of 5% per annum. In other months, dividends are paid at a rate of 2% per annum. Suppose that the value of the index on July 31 is 1,300. What is the futures price for a contract deliverable in December 31 of the same year?

5.12. Suppose that the risk-free interest rate is 6% per annum with continuous compounding and that the dividend yield on a stock index is 4% per annum. The index is standing at 400, and the futures price for a contract deliverable in four months is 405. What arbitrage opportunities does this create?

5.13. Estimate the difference between short-term interest rates in Japan and the United States on May 3, 2016, from the information in Table 5.4.

5.14. The 2-month interest rates in Switzerland and the United States are, respectively, 1% and 2% per annum with continuous compounding. The spot price of the Swiss franc is $1.0500. The futures price for a contract deliverable in 2 months is also $1.0500. What arbitrage opportunities does this create?

5.15. The spot price of silver is $25 per ounce. The storage costs are $0.24 per ounce per year payable quarterly in advance. Assuming that interest rates are 5% per annum for all maturities, calculate the futures price of silver for delivery in 9 months.

5.16. Suppose that F_1 and F_2 are two futures contracts on the same commodity with times to maturity, t_1 and t_2, where $t_2 > t_1$. Prove that

$$F_2 \leqslant F_1 e^{r(t_2 - t_1)}$$

where r is the interest rate (assumed constant) and there are no storage costs. For the purposes of this problem, assume that a futures contract is the same as a forward contract.

5.17. When a known future cash outflow in a foreign currency is hedged by a company using a forward contract, there is no foreign exchange risk. When it is hedged using futures contracts, the daily settlement process does leave the company exposed to some risk. Explain the nature of this risk. In particular, consider whether the company is better off using a futures contract or a forward contract when:
(a) The value of the foreign currency falls rapidly during the life of the contract.
(b) The value of the foreign currency rises rapidly during the life of the contract.
(c) The value of the foreign currency first rises and then falls back to its initial value.
(d) The value of the foreign currency first falls and then rises back to its initial value.
Assume that the forward price equals the futures price.

5.18. It is sometimes argued that a forward exchange rate is an unbiased predictor of future exchange rates. Under what circumstances is this so?

5.19. Show that the growth rate in an index futures price equals the excess return on the portfolio underlying the index over the risk-free rate. Assume that the risk-free interest rate and the dividend yield are constant.

5.20. Show that equation (5.3) is true by considering an investment in the asset combined with a short position in a futures contract. Assume that all income from the asset is reinvested in the asset. Use an argument similar to that in footnotes 2 and 4 of this chapter and explain in detail what an arbitrageur would do if equation (5.3) did not hold.

5.21. Explain carefully what is meant by the expected price of a commodity on a particular future date. Suppose that the futures price for crude oil declines with the maturity of the contract at the rate of 2% per year. Assume that speculators tend to be short crude oil futures and hedgers tend to be long. What does the Keynes and Hicks argument imply about the expected future price of oil?

5.22. The Value Line Index is designed to reflect changes in the value of a portfolio of over 1,600 equally weighted stocks. Prior to March 9, 1988, the change in the index from one day to the next was calculated as the *geometric* average of the changes in the prices of the stocks underlying the index. In these circumstances, does equation (5.8) correctly relate the futures price of the index to its cash price? If not, does the equation overstate or understate the futures price?

5.23. A U.S. company is interested in using the futures contracts traded by the CME Group to hedge its Australian dollar exposure. Define r as the interest rate (all maturities) on the U.S. dollar and r_f as the interest rate (all maturities) on the Australian dollar. Assume that r and r_f are constant and that the company uses a contract expiring at time T to hedge an exposure at time t ($T > t$).
   (a) Show that the optimal hedge ratio is $e^{(r_f - r)(T-t)}$.
   (b) Show that, when t is 1 day, the optimal hedge ratio is almost exactly S_0/F_0, where S_0 is the current spot price of the currency and F_0 is the current futures price of the currency for the contract maturing at time T.
   (c) Show that the company can take account of the daily settlement of futures contracts for a hedge that lasts longer than 1 day by adjusting the hedge ratio so that it always equals the spot price of the currency divided by the futures price of the currency.

5.24. What is meant by (a) an investment asset and (b) a consumption asset? Why is the distinction between investment and consumption assets important in the determination of forward and futures prices?

5.25. What is the cost of carry for:
   (a) a non-dividend-paying stock
   (b) a stock index
   (c) a commodity with storage costs
   (d) a foreign currency.

Further Questions

5.26. In early 2012, the spot exchange rate between the Swiss Franc and U.S. dollar was 1.0404 ($ per franc). Interest rates in the United States and Switzerland were 0.25% and 0% per annum, respectively, with continuous compounding. The 3-month forward exchange rate was 1.0300 ($ per franc). What arbitrage strategy was possible? How does your answer change if the forward exchange rate is 1.0500 ($ per franc).

5.27. An index is 1,200. The three-month risk-free rate is 3% per annum and the dividend yield over the next three months is 1.2% per annum. The six-month risk-free rate is 3.5% per annum and the dividend yield over the next six months is 1% per annum. Estimate the futures price of the index for three-month and six-month contracts. All interest rates and dividend yields are continuously compounded.

5.28. Suppose the current USD/euro exchange rate is 1.2000 dollar per euro. The six-month forward exchange rate is 1.1950. The six-month USD interest rate is 1% per annum continuously compounded. Estimate the six-month euro interest rate.

5.29. The spot price of oil is $50 per barrel and the cost of storing a barrel of oil for one year is $3, payable at the end of the year. The risk-free interest rate is 5% per annum continuously compounded. What is an upper bound for the one-year futures price of oil?

5.30. A stock is expected to pay a dividend of $1 per share in 2 months and in 5 months. The stock price is $50, and the risk-free rate of interest is 8% per annum with continuous compounding for all maturities. An investor has just taken a short position in a 6-month forward contract on the stock.

(a) What are the forward price and the initial value of the forward contract?

(b) Three months later, the price of the stock is $48 and the risk-free rate of interest is still 8% per annum. What are the forward price and the value of the short position in the forward contract?

5.31. A bank offers a corporate client a choice between borrowing cash at 11% per annum and borrowing gold at 2% per annum. (If gold is borrowed, interest must be repaid in gold. Thus, 100 ounces borrowed today would require 102 ounces to be repaid in 1 year.) The risk-free interest rate is 9.25% per annum, and storage costs are 0.5% per annum. Discuss whether the rate of interest on the gold loan is too high or too low in relation to the rate of interest on the cash loan. The interest rates on the two loans are expressed with annual compounding. The risk-free interest rate and storage costs are expressed with continuous compounding.

5.32. A company that is uncertain about the exact date when it will pay or receive a foreign currency may try to negotiate with its bank a forward contract that specifies a period during which delivery can be made. The company wants to reserve the right to choose the exact delivery date to fit in with its own cash flows. Put yourself in the position of the bank. How would you price the product that the company wants?

5.33. A trader owns a commodity that provides no income and has no storage costs as part of a long-term investment portfolio. The trader can buy the commodity for $1,250 per ounce and sell it for $1,249 per ounce. The trader can borrow funds at 6% per year and invest funds at 5.5% per year (both interest rates are expressed with annual compounding). For what range of 1-year forward prices does the trader have no arbitrage opportunities? Assume the bid and offer for a forward price are the same.

5.34. A company enters into a forward contract with a bank to sell a foreign currency for K_1 at time T_1. The exchange rate at time T_1 proves to be S_1 ($> K_1$). The company asks the bank if it can roll the contract forward until time T_2 ($> T_1$) rather than settle at time T_1. The bank agrees to a new delivery price, K_2. Explain how K_2 should be calculated.

6

C H A P T E R

Interest Rate
Futures

So far we have covered futures contracts on commodities, stock indices, and foreign currencies. We have seen how they work, how they are used for hedging, and how futures prices are determined. We now move on to consider interest rate futures.

This chapter explains the popular Treasury bond and Eurodollar futures contracts that trade in the United States. Many of the other interest rate futures contracts throughout the world have been modeled on these contracts. The chapter also shows how interest rate futures contracts, when used in conjunction with the duration measure introduced in Chapter 4, can be used to hedge a company's exposure to interest rate movements.

6.1   DAY COUNT AND QUOTATION CONVENTIONS

As a preliminary to the material in this chapter, we consider the day count and quotation conventions that apply to bonds and other instruments dependent on the interest rate.

Day Counts

The day count defines the way in which interest accrues over time. Generally, we know the interest earned over some reference period (e.g., the time between coupon payments on a bond), and we are interested in calculating the interest earned over some other period.

The day count convention is usually expressed as X/Y. When we are calculating the interest earned between two dates, X defines the way in which the number of days between the two dates is calculated, and Y defines the way in which the total number of days in the reference period is measured. The interest earned between the two dates is

$$\frac{\text{Number of days between dates}}{\text{Number of days in reference period}} \times \text{Interest earned in reference period}$$

Three day count conventions that are commonly used in the United States are:

1. Actual/actual (in period)
2. 30/360
3. Actual/360

135

Business Snapshot 6.1   Day Counts Can Be Deceptive

Between February 28, 2018, and March 1, 2018, you have a choice between owning a U.S. government bond and a U.S. corporate bond. They pay the same coupon and have the same quoted price. Assuming no risk of default, which would you prefer?

It sounds as though you should be indifferent, but in fact you should have a marked preference for the corporate bond. Under the 30/360 day count convention used for corporate bonds, there are 3 days between February 28, 2018, and March 1, 2018. Under the actual/actual (in period) day count convention used for government bonds, there is only 1 day. You would earn approximately three times as much interest by holding the corporate bond!

The actual/actual (in period) day count is used for Treasury bonds in the United States. This means that the interest earned between two dates is based on the ratio of the actual days elapsed to the actual number of days in the period between coupon payments. Assume that the bond principal is $100, coupon payment dates are March 1 and September 1, and the coupon rate is 8% per annum. (This means that $4 of interest is paid on each of March 1 and September 1.) Suppose that we wish to calculate the interest earned between March 1 and July 3. The reference period is from March 1 to September 1. There are 184 (actual) days in the reference period, and interest of $4 is earned during the period. There are 124 (actual) days between March 1 and July 3. The interest earned between March 1 and July 3 is therefore

$$\frac{124}{184} \times 4 = 2.6957$$

The 30/360 day count is used for corporate and municipal bonds in the United States. This means that we assume 30 days per month and 360 days per year when carrying out calculations. With the 30/360 day count, the total number of days between March 1 and September 1 is 180. The total number of days between March 1 and July 3 is $(4 \times 30) + 2 = 122$. In a corporate bond with the same terms as the Treasury bond just considered, the interest earned between March 1 and July 3 would therefore be

$$\frac{122}{180} \times 4 = 2.7111$$

As shown in Business Snapshot 6.1, sometimes the 30/360 day count convention has surprising consequences.

The actual/360 day count is used for money market instruments in the United States. This indicates that the reference period is 360 days. The interest earned during part of a year is calculated by dividing the actual number of elapsed days by 360 and multiplying by the rate. The interest earned in 90 days is therefore exactly one-fourth of the quoted rate, and the interest earned in a whole year of 365 days is 365/360 times the quoted rate.

Conventions vary from country to country and from instrument to instrument. For example, money market instruments are quoted on an actual/365 basis in Australia, Canada, and New Zealand. LIBOR is quoted on an actual/360 for all currencies except sterling, for which it is quoted on an actual/365 basis. Euro-denominated and sterling bonds are usually quoted on an actual/actual basis.

Price Quotations of U.S. Treasury Bills

The prices of money market instruments are sometimes quoted using a *discount rate*. This is the interest earned as a percentage of the final face value rather than as a percentage of the initial price paid for the instrument. An example is Treasury bills in the United States. If the price of a 91-day Treasury bill is quoted as 8, this means that the rate of interest earned is 8% of the face value per 360 days. Suppose that the face value is $100. Interest of $2.0222 (= $100 × 0.08 × 91/360) is earned over the 91-day life. This corresponds to a true rate of interest of 2.0222/(100 − 2.0222) = 2.064% for the 91-day period. In general, the relationship between the cash price per $100 of face value and the quoted price of a Treasury bill in the United States is

$$P = \frac{360}{n}(100 - Y)$$

where P is the quoted price, Y is the cash price, and n is the remaining life of the Treasury bill measured in calendar days. For example, when the cash price of a 90-day Treasury bill is 99, the quoted price is 4.

Price Quotations of U.S. Treasury Bonds

Treasury bond prices in the United States are quoted in dollars and thirty-seconds of a dollar. The quoted price is for a bond with a face value of $100. Thus, a quote of 120-05 or $120\frac{5}{32}$ indicates that the quoted price for a bond with a face value of $100,000 is $120,156.25.

The quoted price, which traders refer to as the *clean price*, is not the same as the cash price paid by the purchaser of the bond, which is referred to by traders as the *dirty price*. In general,

Cash price = Quoted price + Accrued interest since last coupon date

To illustrate this formula, suppose that it is March 5, 2018, and the bond under consideration is an 11% coupon bond maturing on July 10, 2038, with a quoted price of 155-16 or $155.50. Because coupons are paid semiannually on government bonds (and the final coupon is at maturity), the most recent coupon date is January 10, 2018, and the next coupon date is July 10, 2018. The (actual) number of days between January 10, 2018, and March 5, 2018, is 54, whereas the (actual) number of days between January 10, 2018, and July 10, 2018, is 181. On a bond with $100 face value, the coupon payment is $5.50 on January 10 and July 10. The accrued interest on March 5, 2018, is the share of the July 10 coupon accruing to the bondholder on March 5, 2018. Because actual/actual in period is used for Treasury bonds in the United States, this is

$$\frac{54}{181} \times \$5.50 = \$1.64$$

The cash price per $100 face value for the bond is therefore

$$\$155.50 + \$1.64 = \$157.14$$

Thus, the cash price of a $100,000 bond is $157,140.

6.2 TREASURY BOND FUTURES

Table 6.1 shows interest rate futures quotes on May 3, 2016. One of the most popular long-term interest rate futures contracts is the Treasury bond futures contract traded by the CME Group. In this contract, any government bond that has between 15 and 25 years to maturity on the first day of the delivery month can be delivered. A contract which the CME Group started trading 2010 is the ultra T-bond contract, where any bond with maturity over 25 years can be delivered.

The 10-year, 5-year, and 2-year Treasury note futures contract in the United States are also very popular. In the 10-year Treasury note futures contract, any government bond (or note) with a maturity between $6\frac{1}{2}$ and 10 years can be delivered.[1] In the 5-year and 2-year Treasury note futures contracts, the note delivered has a remaining life of about 5 years and 2 years, respectively (and the original life must be less than 5.25 years).

Table 6.1   Futures quotes for a selection of CME Group contracts on interest rates on May 3, 2016.

	Open	High	Low	Prior settlement	Last trade	Change	Volume
Ultra T-Bond, $100,000							
June 2016	169-19	171-13	169-19	169-28	171-25	+1-29	63,809
Treasury Bonds, $100,000							
June 2016	161-30	164-10	161-30	162-06	163-26	+1-20	237,430
Sept. 2016	160-28	162-29	160-28	160-26	162-13	+1-19	323
10-Year Treasury Notes, $100,000							
June 2016	129-205	130-150	129-205	129-225	130-090	+0-185	1,135,200
Sept. 2016	129-185	130-110	129-185	129-175	130-060	+0-205	6,150
5-Year Treasury Notes, $100,000							
June 2016	120-225	121-050	120-220	120-227	121-012	+0-105	603,709
Sept. 2016	120-180	120-255	120-180	120-107	120-240	+0-132	6,120
2-Year Treasury Notes, $200,000							
June 2016	109-085	109-122	109-085	109-087	109-110	+0-022	204,600
Sept. 2016	109-087	109-087	109-080	109-050	109-080	+0-030	1,546
30-Day Fed Funds Rate, $5,000,000							
Sept. 2016	99.540	99.555	99.540	99.540	99.550	+0.010	6,946
Mar. 2017	99.390	99.415	99.390	99.380	99.410	+0.030	1,589
Eurodollar, $1,000,000							
June 2016	99.325	99.335	99.325	99.325	99.330	+0.005	128,589
Sept. 2016	99.215	99.245	99.215	99.215	99.235	+0.020	166,003
Dec. 2016	99.120	99.160	99.120	99.125	99.155	+0.030	207,653
Dec. 2018	98.590	98.680	98.590	98.590	98.660	+0.070	67,736
Dec. 2020	98.055	98.175	98.055	98.070	98.150	+0.080	14,233
Dec. 2022	97.640	97.745	97.640	97.655	97.730	+0.075	120

---

[1] The CME now also trades an "ultra 10-year Treasury note" futures contract. In this, the deliverable bond has a maturity between 9 years 5 months and 10 years.

As will be explained later in this section, the exchange has developed a procedure for adjusting the price received by the party with the short position according to the particular bond or note it chooses to deliver. The remaining discussion in this section focuses on the Treasury bond futures. The Treasury note and other T-bond futures traded in the United States, and many other futures in the rest of the world, are designed in a similar way to the Treasury bond futures, so that many of the points we will make are applicable to these contracts as well.

Quotes

Treasury bond and Treasury note futures contracts are quoted in dollars and thirty-seconds of a dollar per $100 face value. This is similar to the way the bonds are quoted in the spot market. In Table 6.1, the settlement price of the June 2016 Treasury bond futures contract is specified as 162-06. This means $162\frac{6}{32}$, or 162.1875. The settlement price of the 10-year Treasury note futures contract is quoted to the nearest half of a thirty-second. Thus the settlement price of 129-175 for the September 2016 contract should be interpreted as $129\frac{17.5}{32}$, or 129.546875. The 5-year and 2-year Treasury note contracts are quoted even more precisely, to the nearest quarter of a thirty-second. Thus the settlement price of 120-227 for the June 5-year Treasury note contract should be interpreted as $120\frac{22.75}{32}$, or 120.7109375. Similarly, the last trade price of 121-012 for this contract should be interpreted as $121\frac{1.25}{32}$, or 123.0390625.

Conversion Factors

As mentioned, the Treasury bond futures contract allows the party with the short position to choose to deliver any bond that has a maturity between 15 and 25 years. When a particular bond is delivered, a parameter known as its *conversion factor* defines the price received for the bond by the party with the short position. The applicable quoted price for the bond delivered is the product of the conversion factor and the most recent settlement price for the futures contract. Taking accrued interest into account (see Section 6.1), the cash received for each $100 face value of the bond delivered is

(Most recent settlement price × Conversion factor) + Accrued interest

Each contract is for the delivery of $100,000 face value of bonds. Suppose that the most recent settlement price is 120-00, the conversion factor for the bond delivered is 1.3800, and the accrued interest on this bond at the time of delivery is $3 per $100 face value. The cash received by the party with the short position (and paid by the party with the long position) is then

$$(1.3800 \times 120.00) + 3.00 = \$168.60$$

per $100 face value. A party with the short position in one contract would deliver bonds with a face value of $100,000 and receive $168,600.

The conversion factor for a bond is set equal to the quoted price the bond would have per dollar of principal on the first day of the delivery month on the assumption that the interest rate for all maturities equals 6% per annum (with semiannual compounding). The bond maturity and the times to the coupon payment dates are rounded down to the nearest 3 months for the purposes of the calculation. The practice enables the exchange to produce comprehensive tables. If, after rounding, the bond lasts for an exact number of 6-month periods, the first coupon is assumed to be paid in 6 months. If, after rounding, the bond does not last for an exact number of 6-month periods (i.e., there are an extra 3 months), the first coupon is assumed to be paid after 3 months and accrued interest is subtracted.

As a first example of these rules, consider a 10% coupon bond with 20 years and 2 months to maturity. For the purposes of calculating the conversion factor, the bond is assumed to have exactly 20 years to maturity. The first coupon payment is assumed to be made after 6 months. Coupon payments are then assumed to be made at 6-month intervals until the end of the 20 years when the principal payment is made. Assume that the face value is $100. When the discount rate is 6% per annum with semiannual compounding (or 3% per 6 months), the value of the bond is

$$\sum_{i=1}^{40} \frac{5}{1.03^i} + \frac{100}{1.03^{40}} = \$146.23$$

Dividing by the face value gives a conversion factor of 1.4623.

As a second example of the rules, consider an 8% coupon bond with 18 years and 4 months to maturity. For the purposes of calculating the conversion factor, the bond is assumed to have exactly 18 years and 3 months to maturity. Discounting all the payments back to a point in time 3 months from today at 6% per annum (compounded semi-annually) gives a value of

$$4 + \sum_{i=1}^{36} \frac{4}{1.03^i} + \frac{100}{1.03^{36}} = \$125.8323$$

The interest rate for a 3-month period is $\sqrt{1.03} - 1$, or 1.4889%. Hence, discounting back to the present gives the bond's value as $125.8323/1.014889 = \$123.99$. Subtracting the accrued interest of 2.0, this becomes $121.99. The conversion factor is therefore 1.2199.

Cheapest-to-Deliver Bond

At any given time during the delivery month, there are many bonds that can be delivered in the Treasury bond futures contract. These vary widely as far as coupon and maturity are concerned. The party with the short position can choose which of the available bonds is "cheapest" to deliver. Because the party with the short position receives

$$(\text{Most recent settlement price} \times \text{Conversion factor}) + \text{Accrued interest}$$

and the cost of purchasing a bond is

$$\text{Quoted bond price} + \text{Accrued interest}$$

the cheapest-to-deliver bond is the one for which

$$\text{Quoted bond price} - (\text{Most recent settlement price} \times \text{Conversion factor})$$

is least. Once the party with the short position has decided to deliver, it can determine the cheapest-to-deliver bond by examining each of the deliverable bonds in turn.

Example 6.1

The party with the short position has decided to deliver and is trying to choose between the three bonds in the table below. Assume the most recent settlement price is 93-08, or 93.25.

Bond	Quoted bond price ($)	Conversion factor
1	99.50	1.0382
2	143.50	1.5188
3	119.75	1.2615

The cost of delivering each of the bonds is as follows:

Bond 1: $99.50 - (93.25 \times 1.0382) = \$2.69$

Bond 2: $143.50 - (93.25 \times 1.5188) = \$1.87$

Bond 3: $119.75 - (93.25 \times 1.2615) = \$2.12$

The cheapest-to-deliver bond is Bond 2.

A number of factors determine the cheapest-to-deliver bond. When bond yields are in excess of 6%, the conversion factor system tends to favor the delivery of low-coupon long-maturity bonds. When yields are less than 6%, the system tends to favor the delivery of high-coupon short-maturity bonds. Also, when the yield curve is upward-sloping, there is a tendency for bonds with a long time to maturity to be favored, whereas when it is downward-sloping, there is a tendency for bonds with a short time to maturity to be delivered.

In addition to the cheapest-to-deliver bond option, the party with a short position has an option known as the wild card play. This is described in Business Snapshot 6.2.

Determining the Futures Price

An exact theoretical futures price for the Treasury bond contract is difficult to determine because the short party's options concerned with the timing of delivery and choice of the bond that is delivered cannot easily be valued. However, if we assume that both the cheapest-to-deliver bond and the delivery date are known, the Treasury bond futures contract is a futures contract on a traded security (the bond) that provides the holder with known income.[2] Equation (5.2) then shows that the futures price, F_0, is related to the spot price, S_0, by

$$F_0 = (S_0 - I)e^{rT} \tag{6.1}$$

where I is the present value of the coupons during the life of the futures contract, T is the time until the futures contract matures, and r is the risk-free interest rate applicable to a time period of length T.

Example 6.2

Suppose that, in a Treasury bond futures contract, it is known that the cheapest-to-deliver bond will be a 12% coupon bond with a conversion factor of 1.6000.

---

[2] In practice, for the purposes of estimating the cheapest-to-deliver bond, analysts usually assume that zero rates at the maturity of the futures contract will equal today's forward rates.

Business Snapshot 6.2   *The Wild Card Play*

The settlement price in the CME Group's Treasury bond futures contract is the price at 2:00 p.m. Chicago time. However, Treasury bonds continue trading in the spot market beyond this time and a trader with a short position can issue to the clearing house a notice of intention to deliver later in the day. If the notice is issued, the invoice price is calculated on the basis of the settlement price that day, that is, the price at 2:00 p.m.

This practice gives rise to an option known as the *wild card play*. If bond prices decline after 2:00 p.m. on the first day of the delivery month, the party with the short position can issue a notice of intention to deliver at, say, 3:45 p.m. and proceed to buy bonds in the spot market for delivery at a price calculated from the 2:00 p.m. futures price. If the bond price does not decline, the party with the short position keeps the position open and waits until the next day when the same strategy can be used.

As with the other options open to the party with the short position, the wild card play is not free. Its value is reflected in the futures price, which is lower than it would be without the option.

Suppose also that it is known that delivery will take place in 270 days. Coupons are payable semiannually on the bond. As illustrated in Figure 6.1, the last coupon date was 60 days ago, the next coupon date is in 122 days, and the coupon date thereafter is in 305 days. The term structure is flat, and the rate of interest (with continuous compounding) is 10% per annum. Assume that the current quoted bond price is $115. The cash price of the bond is obtained by adding to this quoted price the proportion of the next coupon payment that accrues to the holder. The cash price is therefore

$$115 + \frac{60}{60 + 122} \times 6 = 116.978$$

A coupon of $6 will be received after 122 days ($= 0.3342$ years). The present value of this is

$$6e^{-0.1 \times 0.3342} = 5.803$$

The futures contract lasts for 270 days ($= 0.7397$ years). The cash futures price, if the contract were written on the 12% bond, would therefore be

$$(116.978 - 5.803)e^{0.1 \times 0.7397} = 119.711$$

Figure 6.1   Time chart for Example 6.2.

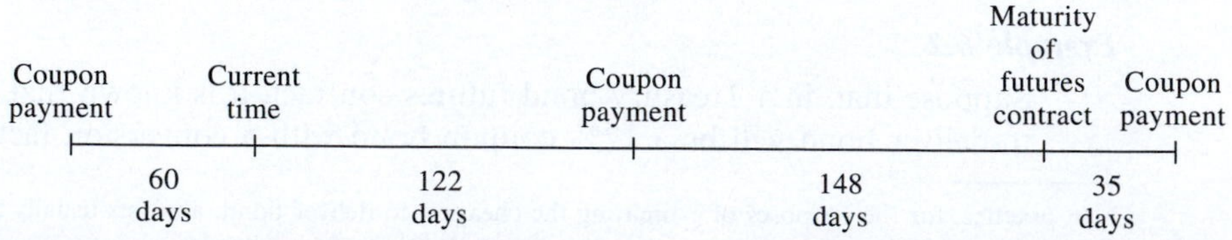

Coupon payment	Current time		Coupon payment		Maturity of futures contract	Coupon payment
60 days		122 days		148 days		35 days

At delivery, there are 148 days of accrued interest. The quoted futures price, if the contract were written on the 12% bond, is calculated by subtracting the accrued interest

$$119.711 - 6 \times \frac{148}{148 + 35} = 114.859$$

From the definition of the conversion factor, 1.6000 standard bonds are considered equivalent to each 12% bond. The quoted futures price should therefore be

$$\frac{114.859}{1.6000} = 71.79$$

6.3 EURODOLLAR FUTURES

The most popular interest rate futures contract in the United States is the three-month Eurodollar futures contract traded by the CME Group. A Eurodollar is a dollar deposited in a U.S. or foreign bank outside the United States. The Eurodollar interest rate is the rate of interest earned on Eurodollars deposited by one bank with another bank. It can be regarded as the same as the London Interbank Offered Rate (LIBOR) introduced in Chapter 4.

A three-month Eurodollar futures contract is a futures contract on the interest that will be paid (by someone who borrows at the LIBOR interest rate) on $1 million for a future three-month period. It allows a trader to speculate on a future three-month interest rate or to hedge an exposure to a future three-month interest rate. Eurodollar futures contracts have maturities in March, June, September, and December for up to 10 years into the future. This means that in 2017 a trader can use Eurodollar futures to take a position on what interest rates will be as far into the future as 2027. Short-maturity contracts trade for months other than March, June, September, and December.

To understand how Eurodollar futures contracts work, consider the June 2016 contract in Table 6.1. The last trading day is two days before the third Wednesday of the delivery month, which in the case of this contract is June 13, 2016. The contract is settled daily in the usual way until the last trading day. At 11 a.m. on the last trading day, there is a final settlement equal to $100 - R$, where R is the three-month LIBOR fixing on that day, expressed with quarterly compounding and an actual/360 day count convention. Thus, if three-month LIBOR on June 13, 2016, turned out to be 0.75% (actual/360 with quarterly compounding), the final settlement price would be 99.250. Once a final settlement has taken place, all contracts are declared closed.

The contract is designed so that a one-basis-point ($= 0.01$) move in the futures quote corresponds to a gain or loss of $25 per contract. When a Eurodollar futures quote increases by one basis point, a trader who is long one contract gains $25 and a trader who is short one contract loses $25. Similarly, when the quote decreases by one basis point a trader who is long one contract loses $25 and a trader who is short one contract gains $25. Suppose, for example, a settlement price changes from 99.325 to 99.285. Traders with long positions lose $4 \times 25 = \$100$ per contract; traders with short positions gain $100 per contract. A one-basis-point change in the futures quote corresponds to a 0.01% change in the underlying interest rate. This in turn leads to a

$$1,000,000 \times 0.0001 \times 0.25 = 25$$

Table 6.2 Possible sequence of prices for June 2016 Eurodollar futures contract.

Date	Trade price	Settlement futures price	Change	Gain per long contract
May 3, 2016	99.330			
May 3, 2016		99.325	−0.005	−12.50
May 4, 2016		99.275	−0.050	−125.00
⋮		⋮	⋮	⋮
June 13, 2016		99.220	+0.010	+25.00
Total			−0.110	−275.00

or $25 change in the interest that will be earned on $1 million in three months. The $25 per basis point rule is therefore consistent with the point made earlier that the contract locks in an interest rate on $1 million for three months.

The futures quote is 100 minus the futures interest rate. A trader who is long gains when interest rates fall and one who is short gains when interest rates rise. Table 6.2 shows a possible set of outcomes for the June 2016 contract in Table 6.1 for a trader who takes a long position on May 3, 2016, at the last trade price of 99.330.

The contract price is defined as

$$10,000 \times [100 - 0.25 \times (100 - Q)] \tag{6.2}$$

where Q is the quote. Thus, the settlement price of 99.725 for the June 2013 contract in Table 6.1 corresponds to a contract price of

$$10,000 \times [100 - 0.25 \times (100 - 99.330)] = \$998,325$$

In Table 6.2, the final contract price is

$$10,000 \times [100 - 0.25 \times (100 - 99.220)] = \$998,050$$

and the difference between the initial and final contract price is $275, This is consistent with the loss calculated in Table 6.2 using the "$25 per one-basis-point move" rule.

Example 6.3

An investor wants to lock in the interest rate for a three-month period beginning two days before the third Wednesday of September, on a principal of $100 million. We suppose that the September Eurodollar futures quote is 96.50, indicating that the investor can lock in an interest rate of $100 - 96.5$ or 3.5% per annum. The investor hedges by buying 100 contracts. Suppose that, two days before the third Wednesday of September, three-month LIBOR turns out to be 2.6%. The final settlement in the contract is then at a price of 97.40. The investor gains

$$100 \times 25 \times (9,740 - 9,650) = 225,000$$

or $225,000 on the Eurodollar futures contracts. The interest earned on the three-month investment is

$$100,000,000 \times 0.25 \times 0.026 = 650,000$$

or \$650,000. The gain on the Eurodollar futures brings this up to \$875,000, which is what the interest would be at 3.5% ($100,000,000 \times 0.25 \times 0.035 = 875,000$).

It appears that the futures trade has the effect of exactly locking an interest rate of 3.5% in all circumstances. In fact, the hedge is less than perfect because (a) futures contracts are settled daily (not all at the end) and (b) the final settlement in the futures contract happens at contract maturity, whereas the interest payment on the investment is three months later. One approximate adjustment for the second point is to reduce the size of the hedge to reflect the difference between funds received in September, and funds received three months later. In this case, we would assume an interest rate of 3.5% for the three-month period and multiply the number of contracts by $1/(1 + 0.035 \times 0.25) = 0.9913$. This would lead to 99 rather than 100 contracts being purchased.

Table 6.1 shows that the interest rate term structure in the United States was upward sloping in May 2016. Using the "Prior Settlement" column, the futures rates for three-month periods beginning June 13, 2016, September 19, 2016, December 19, 2016, December 17, 2018, December 14, 2020, and December 19, 2022, were 0.675%, 0.785%, 0.875%, 1.410%, 1.930%, and 2.345%, respectively.

Example 6.3 shows how Eurodollar futures contracts can be used by an investor who wants to hedge the interest that will be earned during a future three-month period. Note that the timing of the cash flows from the hedge does not line up exactly with the timing of the interest cash flows. This is because the futures contract is settled daily. Also, the final settlement is in September, whereas interest payments on the investment are received three months later in December. As indicated in the example, a small adjustment can be made to the hedge position to approximately allow for this second point.

Other contracts similar to the CME Group's Eurodollar futures contracts trade on interest rates in other countries. The CME Group trades Euroyen contracts. The London International Financial Futures and Options Exchange (part of Euronext) trades three-month Euribor contracts (i.e., contracts on the three-month rate for euro deposits between euro zone banks) and three-month Euroswiss futures.

Forward vs. Futures Interest Rates

The Eurodollar futures contract is similar to a forward rate agreement (FRA: see Section 4.9) in that it locks in an interest rate for a future period. For short maturities (up to a year or so), the Eurodollar futures interest rate can be assumed to be the same as the corresponding forward interest rate. For longer-dated contracts, differences between the contracts become important. Compare a Eurodollar futures contract on an interest rate for the period between times T_1 and T_2 with an FRA for the same period. The Eurodollar futures contract is settled daily. The final settlement is at time T_1 and reflects the realized interest rate for the period between times T_1 and T_2. By contrast the FRA is not settled daily and the final settlement reflecting the realized interest rate between times T_1 and T_2 is made at time T_2.[3]

There are therefore two differences between a Eurodollar futures contract and an

---

[3] As mentioned in Section 4.9, settlement may occur at time T_1, but it is then equal to the present value of what the forward contract payoff would be at time T_2.

FRA. These are:

1. The difference between a Eurodollar futures contract and a similar contract where there is no daily settlement. The latter is a hypothetical forward contract where a payoff equal to the difference between the forward interest rate and the realized interest rate is paid at time T_1.

2. The difference between the hypothetical forward contract where there is settlement at time T_1 and a true forward contract where there is settlement at time T_2 equal to the difference between the forward interest rate and the realized interest rate.

These two components to the difference between the contracts cause some confusion in practice. Both decrease the forward rate relative to the futures rate, but for long-dated contracts the reduction caused by the second difference is much smaller than that caused by the first. The reason why the first difference (daily settlement) decreases the forward rate follows from the arguments in Section 5.8. Suppose you have a contract where the payoff is $R_M - R_F$ at time T_1, where R_F is a predetermined rate for the period between T_1 and T_2 and R_M is the realized rate for this period, and you have the option to switch to daily settlement. In this case daily settlement tends to lead to cash inflows when rates are high and cash outflows when rates are low. You would therefore find switching to daily settlement to be attractive because you tend to have more money in your margin account when rates are high. As a result the market would therefore set R_F higher for the daily settlement alternative (reducing your cumulative expected payoff). To put this the other way round, switching from daily settlement to settlement at time T_1 reduces R_F.

To understand the reason why the second difference reduces the forward rate, suppose that the payoff of $R_M - R_F$ is at time T_2 instead of T_1 (as it is for a regular FRA). If R_M is high, the payoff is positive. Because rates are high, the cost to you of having the payoff that you receive at time T_2 rather than time T_1 is relatively high. If R_M is low, the payoff is negative. Because rates are low, the benefit to you of having the payoff you make at time T_2 rather than time T_1 is relatively low. Overall you would rather have the payoff at time T_1. If it is at time T_2 rather than T_1, you must be compensated by a reduction in R_F.[4]

Convexity Adjustment

Analysts make what is known as a *convexity adjustment* to account for the total difference between the two rates. One popular adjustment is[5]

$$\text{Forward rate} = \text{Futures rate} - \tfrac{1}{2}\sigma^2 T_1 T_2 \tag{6.3}$$

where, as above, T_1 is the time to maturity of the futures contract and T_2 is the time to the maturity of the rate underlying the futures contract. The variable σ is the standard deviation of the change in the short-term interest rate in 1 year. Both rates are expressed with continuous compounding.[6]

---

[4] Quantifying the effect of this type of timing difference on the value of a derivative is discussed further in Chapter 30.

[5] See Technical Note 1 at www-2.rotman.utoronto.ca/~hull/TechnicalNotes for a proof of this.

[6] This formula is based on the Ho–Lee interest rate model, which will be discussed in Chapter 32. See T. S. Y. Ho and S.-B. Lee, "Term structure movements and pricing interest rate contingent claims," *Journal of Finance*, 41 (December 1986), 1011–29.

Example 6.4

Consider the situation where $\sigma = 0.012$ and we wish to calculate the forward rate when the 8-year Eurodollar futures price quote is 94. In this case $T_1 = 8$, $T_2 = 8.25$, and the convexity adjustment is

$$\tfrac{1}{2} \times 0.012^2 \times 8 \times 8.25 = 0.00475$$

or 0.475% (47.5 basis points). The futures rate is 6% per annum on an actual/360 basis with quarterly compounding. This corresponds to 1.5% per 90 days or an annual rate of $(365/90)\ln 1.015 = 6.038\%$ with continuous compounding and an actual/365 day count. The estimate of the forward rate given by equation (6.3), therefore, is $6.038 - 0.475 = 5.563\%$ per annum with continuous compounding.

The table below shows how the size of the adjustment increases with the time to maturity.

Maturity of futures (years)	Convexity adjustments (basis points)
2	3.2
4	12.2
6	27.0
8	47.5
10	73.8

We can see from this table that the size of the adjustment is roughly proportional to the square of the time to maturity of the futures contract. For example, when the maturity doubles from 2 to 4 years, the size of the convexity approximately quadruples.

Using Eurodollar Futures to Extend the LIBOR Zero Curve

The LIBOR zero curve out to 1 year is determined by the 1-month, 3-month, 6-month, and 12-month LIBOR rates. Once the convexity adjustment just described has been made, Eurodollar futures are often used to extend the zero curve. Suppose that the ith Eurodollar futures contract matures at time T_i $(i = 1, 2, \ldots)$. It is usually assumed that the forward interest rate calculated from the ith futures contract applies to the period T_i to T_{i+1}. (In practice this is close to true.) This enables a bootstrap procedure to be used to determine zero rates. Suppose that F_i is the forward rate calculated from the ith Eurodollar futures contract and R_i is the zero rate for a maturity T_i. From equation (4.5),

$$F_i = \frac{R_{i+1}T_{i+1} - R_iT_i}{T_{i+1} - T_i}$$

so that

$$R_{i+1} = \frac{F_i(T_{i+1} - T_i) + R_iT_i}{T_{i+1}} \tag{6.4}$$

Other Euro rates such as Euroswiss, Euroyen, and Euribor are used in a similar way.

Example 6.5

The 400-day LIBOR zero rate has been calculated as 4.80% with continuous compounding and, from Eurodollar futures quotes, it has been calculated that (a) the forward rate for a 90-day period beginning in 400 days is 5.30% with continuous compounding, (b) the forward rate for a 90-day period beginning in 491 days is 5.50% with continuous compounding, and (c) the forward rate for a 90-day period beginning in 589 days is 5.60% with continuous compounding. We can use equation (6.4) to obtain the 491-day rate as

$$\frac{0.053 \times 91 + 0.048 \times 400}{491} = 0.04893$$

or 4.893%. Similarly we can use the second forward rate to obtain the 589-day rate as

$$\frac{0.055 \times 98 + 0.04893 \times 491}{589} = 0.04994$$

or 4.994%. The next forward rate of 5.60% would be used to determine the zero curve out to the maturity of the next Eurodollar futures contract. (Note that, even though the rate underlying the Eurodollar futures contract is a 90-day rate, it is assumed to apply to the 91 or 98 days elapsing between Eurodollar contract maturities.)

6.4 DURATION-BASED HEDGING STRATEGIES USING FUTURES

We discussed duration in Section 4.10. Interest rate futures can be used to hedge the yield on a bond portfolio at a future time. Define:

V_F: Contract price for one interest rate futures contract

D_F: Duration of the asset underlying the futures contract at the maturity of the futures contract

P: Forward value of the portfolio being hedged at the maturity of the hedge (in practice, this is usually assumed to be the same as the value of the portfolio today)

D_P: Duration of the portfolio at the maturity of the hedge.

If we assume that the change in the forward yield, Δy, is the same for all maturities, it is approximately true that

$$\Delta P = -PD_P \Delta y$$

It is also approximately true that

$$\Delta V_F = -V_F D_F \Delta y$$

The number of contracts required to hedge against an uncertain Δy, therefore, is

$$N^* = \frac{PD_P}{V_F D_F} \tag{6.5}$$

This is the *duration-based hedge ratio*. It is sometimes also called the *price sensitivity hedge ratio.*[7]

When the hedging instrument is a Treasury bond futures contract, the hedger must base D_F on an assumption that one particular bond will be delivered. This means that the hedger must estimate which of the available bonds is likely to be cheapest to deliver at the time the hedge is put in place. If, subsequently, the interest rate environment changes so that it looks as though a different bond will be cheapest to deliver, then the hedge has to be adjusted and as a result its performance may be worse than anticipated.

When hedges are constructed using interest rate futures, it is important to bear in mind that interest rates and futures prices move in opposite directions. When interest rates go up, an interest rate futures price goes down. When interest rates go down, the reverse happens, and the interest rate futures price goes up. Thus, a company in a position to lose money if interest rates drop should hedge by taking a long futures position. Similarly, a company in a position to lose money if interest rates rise should hedge by taking a short futures position.

The hedger tries to choose the futures contract so that the duration of the underlying asset is as close as possible to the duration of the asset being hedged. Eurodollar futures tend to be used for exposures to short-term interest rates, whereas ultra T-bond, Treasury bond, and Treasury note futures contracts are used for exposures to longer-term rates.

Example 6.6

It is August 2 and a fund manager with $10 million invested in government bonds is concerned that interest rates are expected to be highly volatile over the next 3 months. The fund manager decides to use the December T-bond futures contract to hedge the value of the portfolio. The current futures price is 93-02, or 93.0625. Because each contract is for the delivery of $100,000 face value of bonds, the futures contract price is $93,062.50.

Suppose that the duration of the bond portfolio in 3 months will be 6.80 years. The cheapest-to-deliver bond in the T-bond contract is expected to be a 20-year 12% per annum coupon bond. The yield on this bond is currently 8.80% per annum, and the duration will be 9.20 years at maturity of the futures contract.

The fund manager requires a short position in T-bond futures to hedge the bond portfolio. If interest rates go up, a gain will be made on the short futures position, but a loss will be made on the bond portfolio. If interest rates decrease, a loss will be made on the short position, but there will be a gain on the bond portfolio. The number of bond futures contracts that should be shorted can be calculated from equation (6.5) as

$$\frac{10,000,000}{93,062.50} \times \frac{6.80}{9.20} = 79.42$$

To the nearest whole number, the portfolio manager should short 79 contracts.

---

[7] For a more detailed discussion of equation (6.5), see R. J. Rendleman, "Duration-Based Hedging with Treasury Bond Futures," *Journal of Fixed Income* 9, 1 (June 1999): 84–91.

Business Snapshot 6.3 Asset–Liability Management by Banks

The asset–liability management (ALM) committees of banks now monitor their exposure to interest rates very carefully. Matching the durations of assets and liabilities is sometimes a first step, but this does not protect a bank against non-parallel shifts in the yield curve. A popular approach is known as *GAP management*. This involves dividing the zero-coupon yield curve into segments, known as *buckets*. The first bucket might be 0 to 1 month, the second 1 to 3 months, and so on. The ALM committee then investigates the effect on the value of the bank's portfolio of the zero rates corresponding to one bucket changing while those corresponding to all other buckets stay the same.

   If there is a mismatch, corrective action is usually taken. This can involve changing deposit and lending rates in the way described in Section 4.12. Alternatively, tools such as swaps, FRAs, bond futures, Eurodollar futures, and other interest rate derivatives can be used.

6.5 HEDGING PORTFOLIOS OF ASSETS AND LIABILITIES

Financial institutions sometimes attempt to hedge themselves against interest rate risk by ensuring that the average duration of their assets equals the average duration of their liabilities. (The liabilities can be regarded as short positions in bonds.) This strategy is known as *duration matching* or *portfolio immunization*. When implemented, it ensures that a small parallel shift in interest rates will have little effect on the value of the portfolio of assets and liabilities. The gain (loss) on the assets should offset the loss (gain) on the liabilities.

   Duration matching does not immunize a portfolio against nonparallel shifts in the zero curve. This is a weakness of the approach. In practice, short-term rates are usually more volatile than, and are not perfectly correlated with, long-term rates. Sometimes it even happens that short- and long-term rates move in opposite directions to each other. Duration matching is therefore only a first step and financial institutions have developed other tools to help them manage their interest rate exposure. See Business Snapshot 6.3.

SUMMARY

Two very popular interest rate contracts are the Treasury bond and Eurodollar futures contracts that trade in the United States. In the Treasury bond futures contracts, the party with the short position has a number of interesting delivery options:

1. Delivery can be made on any day during the delivery month.
2. There are a number of alternative bonds that can be delivered.
3. On any day during the delivery month, the notice of intention to deliver at the 2:00 p.m. settlement price can be made later in the day.

These options all tend to reduce the futures price.

The Eurodollar futures contract is a contract on the 3-month LIBOR interest rate two days before the third Wednesday of the delivery month. Eurodollar futures are frequently used to estimate LIBOR forward rates for the purpose of constructing a LIBOR zero curve. When long-dated contracts are used in this way, it is important to make what is termed a convexity adjustment to allow for the difference between Eurodollar futures and FRAs.

The concept of duration is important in hedging interest rate risk. It enables a hedger to assess the sensitivity of a bond portfolio to small parallel shifts in the yield curve. It also enables the hedger to assess the sensitivity of an interest rate futures price to small changes in the yield curve. The number of futures contracts necessary to protect the bond portfolio against small parallel shifts in the yield curve can therefore be calculated.

The key assumption underlying duration-based hedging is that all interest rates change by the same amount. This means that only parallel shifts in the term structure are allowed for. In practice, short-term interest rates are generally more volatile than are long-term interest rates, and hedge performance is liable to be poor if the duration of the bond underlying the futures contract differs markedly from the duration of the asset being hedged.

FURTHER READING

Burghardt, G., and W. Hoskins. "The Convexity Bias in Eurodollar Futures," *Risk*, 8, 3 (1995): 63–70.

Grinblatt, M., and N. Jegadeesh. "The Relative Price of Eurodollar Futures and Forward Contracts," *Journal of Finance*, 51, 4 (September 1996): 1499–1522.

Practice Questions (Answers in Solutions Manual)

6.1. A U.S. Treasury bond pays a 7% coupon on January 7 and July 7. How much interest accrues per $100 of principal to the bondholder between July 7, 2017, and August 8, 2017? How would your answer be different if it were a corporate bond?

6.2. It is January 9, 2018. The price of a Treasury bond with a 6% coupon that matures on October 12, 2030, is quoted as 102-07. What is the cash price?

6.3. How is the conversion factor of a bond calculated by the CME Group? How is it used?

6.4. A Eurodollar futures price changes from 96.76 to 96.82. What is the gain or loss to a trader who is long two contracts?

6.5. What is the purpose of the convexity adjustment made to Eurodollar futures rates? Why is the convexity adjustment necessary?

6.6. The 350-day LIBOR rate is 3% with continuous compounding and the forward rate calculated from a Eurodollar futures contract that matures in 350 days is 3.2% with continuous compounding. Estimate the 440-day zero rate.

6.7. It is January 30. You are managing a bond portfolio worth $6 million. The duration of the portfolio in 6 months will be 8.2 years. The September Treasury bond futures price is currently 108-15, and the cheapest-to-deliver bond will have a duration of 7.6 years in

September. How should you hedge against changes in interest rates over the next 6 months?

6.8. The price of a 90-day Treasury bill is quoted as 10.00. What continuously compounded return (on an actual/365 basis) does an investor earn on the Treasury bill for the 90-day period?

6.9. It is May 5, 2017. The quoted price of a government bond with a 12% coupon that matures on July 27, 2034, is 110-17. What is the cash price?

6.10. Suppose that the Treasury bond futures price is 101-12. Which of the following four bonds is cheapest to deliver?

Bond	Price	Conversion factor
1	125-05	1.2131
2	142-15	1.3792
3	115-31	1.1149
4	144-02	1.4026

6.11. It is July 30, 2018. The cheapest-to-deliver bond in a September 2018 Treasury bond futures contract is a 13% coupon bond, and delivery is expected to be made on September 30, 2018. Coupon payments on the bond are made on February 4 and August 4 each year. The term structure is flat, and the rate of interest with semiannual compounding is 12% per annum. The conversion factor for the bond is 1.5. The current quoted bond price is $110. Calculate the quoted futures price for the contract.

6.12. A trader is looking for arbitrage opportunities in the Treasury bond futures market. What complications are created by the fact that the party with a short position can choose to deliver any bond with a maturity between 15 and 25 years?

6.13. Suppose that the 9-month LIBOR interest rate is 8% per annum and the 6-month LIBOR interest rate is 7.5% per annum (both with actual/365 and continuous compounding). Estimate the 3-month Eurodollar futures price quote for a contract maturing in 6 months.

6.14. Suppose that the 300-day LIBOR zero rate is 4% and Eurodollar quotes for contracts maturing in 300, 398, and 489 days are 95.83, 95.62, and 95.48. Calculate 398-day and 489-day LIBOR zero rates. Assume no difference between forward and futures rates for the purposes of your calculations.

6.15. Suppose that a bond portfolio with a duration of 12 years is hedged using a futures contract in which the underlying asset has a duration of 4 years. What is likely to be the impact on the hedge of the fact that the 12-year rate is less volatile than the 4-year rate?

6.16. Suppose that it is February 20 and a treasurer realizes that on July 17 the company will have to issue $5 million of commercial paper with a maturity of 180 days. If the paper were issued today, the company would realize $4,820,000. (In other words, the company would receive $4,820,000 for its paper and have to redeem it at $5,000,000 in 180 days' time.) The September Eurodollar futures price is quoted as 92.00. How should the treasurer hedge the company's exposure?

6.17. On August 1, a portfolio manager has a bond portfolio worth $10 million. The duration of the portfolio in October will be 7.1 years. The December Treasury bond futures price is currently 91-12 and the cheapest-to-deliver bond will have a duration of 8.8 years at maturity. How should the portfolio manager immunize the portfolio against changes in interest rates over the next 2 months?

6.18. How can the portfolio manager change the duration of the portfolio to 3.0 years in Problem 6.17?

6.19. Between October 30, 2018, and November 1, 2018, you have a choice between owning a U.S. government bond paying a 12% coupon and a U.S. corporate bond paying a 12% coupon. Consider carefully the day count conventions discussed in this chapter and decide which of the two bonds you would prefer to own. Ignore the risk of default.

6.20. Suppose that a Eurodollar futures quote is 88 for a contract maturing in 60 days. What is the LIBOR forward rate for the 60- to 150-day period? Ignore the difference between futures and forwards for the purposes of this question.

6.21. The 3-month Eurodollar futures price for a contract maturing in 6 years is quoted as 95.20. The standard deviation of the change in the short-term interest rate in 1 year is 1.1%. Estimate the forward LIBOR interest rate for the period between 6.00 and 6.25 years in the future.

6.22. Explain why the forward interest rate is less than the corresponding futures interest rate calculated from a Eurodollar futures contract.

Further Questions

6.23. It is April 7, 2017. The quoted price of a U.S. government bond with a 6% per annum coupon (paid semiannually) is 120-00. The bond matures on July 27, 2033. What is the cash price? How does your answer change if it is a corporate bond?

6.24. A Treasury bond futures price is 103-12. The prices of three deliverable bonds are 115-06, 135-12, and 155-28. Their conversion factors are 1.0679, 1.2264, and 1.4169, respectively. Which bond is cheapest to deliver?

6.25. The December Eurodollar futures contract is quoted as 98.40 and a company plans to borrow $8 million for three months starting in December at LIBOR plus 0.5%.

(a) What rate can the company lock in by using the Eurodollar futures contract?
(b) What position should the company take in the contracts?
(c) If the actual three-month rate turns out to be 1.3%, what is the final settlement price on the futures contracts.

Explain why timing mismatches reduce the effectiveness of the hedge.

6.26. A Eurodollar futures quote for the period between 5.1 and 5.35 years in the future is 97.1. The standard deviation of the change in the short-term interest rate in one year is 1.4%. Estimate the forward interest rate in an FRA.

6.27. It is March 10, 2017. The cheapest-to-deliver bond in a December 2017 Treasury bond futures contract is an 8% coupon bond, and delivery is expected to be made on December 31, 2017. Coupon payments on the bond are made on March 1 and September 1 each year. The rate of interest with continuous compounding is 5% per annum for all maturities. The conversion factor for the bond is 1.2191. The current quoted bond price is $137. Calculate the quoted futures price for the contract.

6.28. Assume that a bank can borrow or lend money at the same interest rate in the LIBOR market. The 90-day rate is 10% per annum, and the 180-day rate is 10.2% per annum, both expressed with continuous compounding and actual/actual day count. The Euro-dollar futures price for a contract maturing in 91 days is quoted as 89.5. What arbitrage opportunities are open to the bank?

6.29. A Canadian company wishes to create a Canadian LIBOR futures contract from a U.S. Eurodollar futures contract and forward contracts on foreign exchange. Using an example, explain how the company should proceed. For the purposes of this problem, assume that a futures contract is the same as a forward contract.

6.30. On June 25, 2017, the futures price for the June 2017 bond futures contract is 118-23.
   (a) Calculate the conversion factor for a bond maturing on January 1, 2033, paying a coupon of 10%.
   (b) Calculate the conversion factor for a bond maturing on October 1, 2038, paying a coupon of 7%.
   (c) Suppose that the quoted prices of the bonds in (a) and (b) are 169.00 and 136.00, respectively. Which bond is cheaper to deliver?
   (d) Assuming that the cheapest-to-deliver bond is actually delivered on June 25, 2017, what is the cash price received for the bond?

6.31. A portfolio manager plans to use a Treasury bond futures contract to hedge a bond portfolio over the next 3 months. The portfolio is worth $100 million and will have a duration of 4.0 years in 3 months. The futures price is 122, and each futures contract is on $100,000 of bonds. The bond that is expected to be cheapest to deliver will have a duration of 9.0 years at the maturity of the futures contract. What position in futures contracts is required?
   (a) What adjustments to the hedge are necessary if after 1 month the bond that is expected to be cheapest to deliver changes to one with a duration of 7 years?
   (b) Suppose that all rates increase over the next 3 months, but long-term rates increase less than short-term and medium-term rates. What is the effect of this on the performance of the hedge?

CHAPTER 7

Swaps

The birth of the over-the-counter swap market can be traced to a currency swap negotiated between IBM and the World Bank in 1981. The World Bank had borrowings denominated in U.S. dollars while IBM had borrowings denominated in German deutsche marks and Swiss francs. The World Bank (which was restricted in the deutsche mark and Swiss franc borrowing it could do directly) agreed to make interest payments on IBM's borrowings while IBM in return agreed to make interest payments on the World Bank's borrowings. Since that first transaction in 1981, the swap market has seen phenomenal growth.

A swap is an over-the-counter derivatives agreement between two companies to exchange cash flows in the future. The agreement defines the dates when the cash flows are to be paid and the way in which they are to be calculated. Usually the calculation of the cash flows involves the future value of an interest rate, an exchange rate, or other market variable.

A forward contract can be viewed as a simple example of a swap. Suppose it is March 1, 2017, and a company enters into a forward contract to buy 100 ounces of gold for $1,200 per ounce in one year. The company can sell the gold in one year as soon as it is received. The forward contract is therefore equivalent to a swap where the company agrees that on March 1, 2018, it will pay $120,000 and receive $100S$, where S is the market price of one ounce of gold on that date.

Whereas a forward contract is equivalent to the exchange of cash flows on just one future date, swaps typically lead to cash-flow exchanges taking place on several future dates. In this chapter we examine how swaps are used and how they are valued. Our discussion centers on two popular swaps: plain vanilla interest rate swaps and fixed-for-fixed currency swaps. Other types of swaps are briefly reviewed at the end of this chapter and discussed in more detail in Chapter 34.

When valuing swaps, we require a "risk-free" discount rate for cash flows. The risk-free rate used by the market is discussed in Section 4.3. Prior to the 2008 crisis, LIBOR was used as a proxy for the risk-free discount rate. Since the 2008 credit crisis, the market has switched to using the OIS rate for discounting. The valuations in this chapter reflect this switch.

7.1   MECHANICS OF INTEREST RATE SWAPS

By far the most common over-the-counter derivative is a "plain vanilla" interest rate swap. In this a company agrees to pay cash flows equal to interest at a predetermined fixed rate on a notional principal for a number of years. In return, it receives interest at a floating rate on the same notional principal for the same period of time.

LIBOR

The floating rate in most interest rate swap agreements is the London Interbank Offered Rate (LIBOR), which we introduced in Chapter 4. It is the rate of interest at which a AA-rated bank can borrow money from other banks. As explained in Section 4.1, LIBOR rates are published each day for a number of different currencies. Several different borrowing periods ranging from one day to one year are considered.

Just as prime is often the reference rate of interest for floating-rate loans in the domestic financial market, LIBOR is a reference rate of interest for loans in international financial markets. To understand how it is used, consider a five-year bond with a rate of interest specified as six-month LIBOR plus 0.5% per annum. ("Six-month LIBOR" means "LIBOR for a borrowing period of six months.") The life of the bond is divided into ten periods each six-months in length. For each period the rate of interest is set at 0.5% per annum above the six-month LIBOR rate observed at the beginning of the period. Interest is paid at the end of the period.

Illustration

Consider a hypothetical three-year swap initiated on March 8, 2017, between Apple and Citigroup. We suppose Apple agrees to pay to Citigroup an interest rate of 3% per annum on a notional principal of $100 million, and in return Citigroup agrees to pay Apple the six-month LIBOR rate on the same notional principal. Apple is the *fixed-pate payer*; Citigroup is the *floating-rate payer*. We assume the agreement specifies that payments are to be exchanged every six months and that the 3% interest rate is quoted with semiannual compounding. The swap is shown in Figure 7.1.

The first exchange of payments would take place on September 8, 2017, six months after the initiation of the agreement. Apple would pay Citigroup $1.5 million. This is the interest on the $100 million principal for six months at a rate of 3% per year. Citigroup would pay Apple interest on the $100 million principal at the six-month LIBOR rate prevailing six months prior to September 8, 2017—that is, on March 8, 2017. Suppose that the six-month LIBOR rate on March 8, 2017, is 2.2%. Citigroup pays Apple $0.5 \times 0.022 \times \$100 = \$1.1$ million.[1] Note that there is no uncertainty about this first

Figure 7.1   Interest rate swap between Apple and Citigroup.

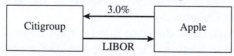

---

[1] The calculations here are simplified in that they ignore day count conventions. This point is discussed in more detail later in the chapter.

exchange of payments because it is determined by the LIBOR rate at the time the contract is agreed to.

The second exchange of payments would take place on March 8, 2018, one year after the initiation of the agreement. Apple would pay \$1.5 million to Citigroup. In return, Citigroup would pay interest on the \$100 million principal to Apple at the six-month LIBOR rate prevailing six months prior to March 8, 2018—that is, on September 8, 2017. Suppose that the six-month LIBOR rate on September 8, 2017, proves to be 2.8%. Citigroup pays $0.5 \times 0.028 \times \$100 = \$1.4$ million to Apple.

In total, there are six exchanges of payment on the swap. The fixed payments are always \$1.5 million. The floating-rate payments on a payment date are calculated using the six-month LIBOR rate prevailing six months before the payment date. An interest rate swap is generally structured so that one side remits the difference between the two payments to the other side. In our example, Apple would pay Citigroup \$0.4 million (= \$1.5 million − \$1.1 million) on September 8, 2017, and \$0.1 million (= \$1.5 million − \$1.4 million) on March 8, 2018.

Table 7.1 provides a complete example of the payments made under the swap for one particular set of LIBOR rates that could occur. The table shows the swap cash flows from the perspective of Apple. Note that the \$100 million principal is used only for the calculation of interest payments. The principal itself is not exchanged. This is why it is termed the *notional principal*.

If the principal were exchanged at the end of the life of the swap, the nature of the deal would not be changed in any way. The principal is the same for both the fixed and floating payments. Exchanging \$100 million for \$100 million at the end of the life of the swap is a transaction that would have no financial value to either Apple or Citigroup. Table 7.2 shows the cash flows in Table 7.1 with a final exchange of principal added in. This provides an interesting way of viewing the swap. The cash flows in the third column of this table are the cash flows from a long position in a floating-rate bond where the interest rate is six-month LIBOR. The cash flows in the fourth column of the table are the cash flows from a short position in a fixed-rate bond. The table shows that the swap can be regarded as the exchange of a fixed-rate bond for a floating-rate bond. Apple, whose position is described by Table 7.2, is long a floating-rate bond and short a fixed-rate bond. Citigroup is long a fixed-rate bond and short a floating-rate bond.

Table 7.1 Cash flows (\$ millions) to Apple for one possible outcome for the swap in Figure 7.1: swap lasts three years and notional principal is \$100 million.

Date	LIBOR rate (%)	Floating cash flow received	Fixed cash flow paid	Net cash flow
Mar. 8, 2017	2.20			
Sept. 8, 2017	2.80	+1.10	−1.50	−0.40
Mar. 8, 2018	3.30	+1.40	−1.50	−0.10
Sept. 8, 2018	3.50	+1.65	−1.50	+0.15
Mar. 8, 2019	3.60	+1.75	−1.50	+0.25
Sept. 8, 2019	3.90	+1.80	−1.50	+0.30
Mar. 8, 2020		+1.95	−1.50	+0.45

Table 7.2 Cash flows (millions of dollars) from Table 7.1 with a final exchange of principal included.

Date	LIBOR rate (%)	Floating cash flow received	Fixed cash flow paid	Net cash flow
Mar. 8, 2017	2.20			
Sept. 8, 2017	2.80	+1.10	−1.50	−0.40
Mar. 8, 2018	3.30	+1.40	−1.50	−0.10
Sept. 8, 2018	3.50	+1.65	−1.50	+0.15
Mar. 8, 2019	3.60	+1.75	−1.50	+0.25
Sept. 8, 2019	3.90	+1.80	−1.50	+0.30
Mar. 8, 2020		+101.95	−101.50	+0.45

This characterization of the cash flows in the swap helps to explain why the floating rate in the swap is set six months before it is paid. On a floating-rate bond, interest is generally set at the beginning of the period to which it will apply and is paid at the end of the period. The calculation of the floating-rate payments in a "plain vanilla" interest rate swap such as the one in Table 7.1 reflects this.

Using the Swap to Transform a Liability

For Apple, the swap could be used to transform a floating-rate loan into a fixed-rate loan, as indicated in Figure 7.2. Suppose that Apple has arranged to borrow $100 million for three years at LIBOR plus 10 basis points. (One basis point is 0.01%, so the rate is LIBOR plus 0.1%.) After Apple has entered into the swap, it has three sets of cash flows:

1. It pays LIBOR plus 0.1% to its outside lenders.
2. It receives LIBOR under the terms of the swap.
3. It pays 3% under the terms of the swap.

These three sets of cash flows net out to an interest rate payment of 3.1%. Thus, for Apple the swap could have the effect of transforming borrowings at a floating rate of LIBOR plus 10 basis points into borrowings at a fixed rate of 3.1%.

A company wishing to transform a fixed-rate loan into a floating-rate loan would enter into the opposite swap. Suppose that Intel has borrowed $100 million at 3.2% for three years and wishes to switch to a floating rate linked to LIBOR. Like Apple it contacts Citigroup. We assume that it agrees to enter into the swap shown in Figure 7.3. It pays LIBOR and receives 2.97%. Its position would then be as indicated Figure 7.4.

Figure 7.2 Apple uses the swap in Figure 7.1 to convert floating-rate borrowings into fixed-rate borrowings.

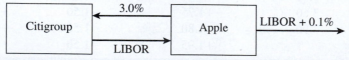

Figure 7.3 Interest rate swap between Intel and Citigtroup.

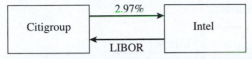

Figure 7.4 Intel uses the swap in Figure 7.3 to convert fixed-rate borrowings into floating-rate borrowings.

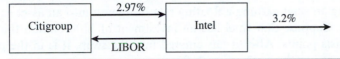

It has three sets of cash flows:

1. It pays 3.2% to its outside lenders.
2. It pays LIBOR under the terms of the swap.
3. It receives 2.97% under the terms of the swap.

These three sets of cash flows net out to an interest rate payment of LIBOR plus 0.23% (or LIBOR plus 23 basis points). Thus, for Intel the swap could have the effect of transforming borrowings at a fixed rate of 3.2% into borrowings at a floating rate of LIBOR plus 23 basis points.

Using the Swap to Transform an Asset

Swaps can also be used to transform the nature of an asset. Consider Apple in our example. The swap in Figure 7.1 could have the effect of transforming an asset earning a fixed rate of interest into an asset earning a floating rate of interest. Suppose that Apple owns $100 million in bonds that will provide interest at 2.7% per annum over the next three years. After Apple has entered into the swap, it is in the position shown in Figure 7.5. It has three sets of cash flows:

1. It receives 2.7% on the bonds.
2. It receives LIBOR under the terms of the swap.
3. It pays 3% under the terms of the swap.

These three sets of cash flows net out to an interest rate inflow of LIBOR minus 30 basis points. The swap has therefore transformed an asset earning 2.7% into an asset earning LIBOR minus 30 basis points.

Figure 7.5 Apple uses the swap in Figure 7.1 to convert a fixed-rate investment into a floating-rate investment.

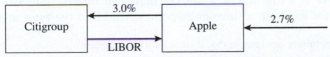

Figure 7.6   Intel uses the swap in Figure 7.3 to convert a floating-rate investment into a fixed-rate investment.

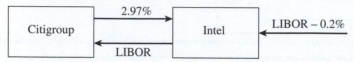

Consider next the swap entered into by Intel in Figure 7.3. The swap could have the effect of transforming an asset earning a floating rate of interest into an asset earning a fixed rate of interest. Suppose that Intel has an investment of $100 million that yields LIBOR minus 20 basis points. After it has entered into the swap, it is in the position shown in Figure 7.6. It has three sets of cash flows:

1. It receives LIBOR minus 20 basis points on its investment.
2. It pays LIBOR under the terms of the swap.
3. It receives 2.97% under the terms of the swap.

These three sets of cash flows net out to an interest rate inflow of 2.77%. Thus, one possible use of the swap for Intel is to transform an asset earning LIBOR minus 20 basis points into an asset earning 2.77%.

Organization of Trading

As discussed in Section 1.2, regulators in the United States require that standard swaps be traded on electronic platforms. As in other jurisdictions, they must then be cleared through central counterparties (CCPs). The swaps are therefore treated like futures contracts with initial and variation margin being posted by both sides.[2]

The rules do not apply when one of the parties to a swap agreement is an end user, whose main activity is not financial and who is using swaps to hedge or mitigate commercial risk.[3] In the examples in Figures 7.1 and 7.3, Apple and Intel are non-financial companies. Assuming they are using the swaps to mitigate risk, the trades could be entered into directly with Citigroup and cleared bilaterally.

Occasionally a financial institution may be lucky enough to enter into offsetting trades with two different nonfinancial companies (such as Apple and Intel) at about the same time. Usually, however, when it enters into a trade such as that in Figure 7.1, it must manage its risk by entering into the opposite trade with another financial institution. The trade with the other financial institution will be executed on an electronic platform and cleared through a CCP. The financial institution could then be in the position where the trade with the nonfinancial company is uncollateralized while the offsetting trade is fully collateralized (with both initial and variation margin being posted). This is discussed further in Section 9.2.

Note that in Figure 7.1 Citigroup received 3% in a three-year swap, whereas in Figure 7.3 it pays 2.97%. Citigroup is a market maker in interest rate swaps. The example indicates that it has built a three-basis-point spread into the rates at which it

---

[2] However, they differ from futures contracts in that there is no daily settlement.

[3] The rule does apply to insurance companies and pension plans when they use swaps to mitigate risks.

Table 7.3 Example of bid and offer fixed rates in the swap market for a swap where payments are exchanged semiannually (percent per annum).

Maturity (years)	Bid	Offer	Swap rate
2	2.55	2.58	2.565
3	2.97	3.00	2.985
4	3.15	3.19	3.170
5	3.26	3.30	3.280
7	3.40	3.44	3.420
10	3.48	3.52	3.500

transacts. This spread is to compensate it for its overheads and for potential losses in the event of a default by a counterparty.

Table 7.3 shows the full set of quotes for plain vanilla U.S. dollar swaps that might be made by a market maker such as Citigroup.[4] The bid–offer spread is three to four basis points. The average of the bid and offer fixed rates is known as the *swap rate*. This is shown in the final column of Table 7.3.

7.2 DAY COUNT ISSUES

We discussed day count conventions in Section 6.1. The day count conventions affect payments on a swap, and some of the numbers calculated in the examples we have given do not exactly reflect these day count conventions. Consider, for example, the six-month LIBOR payments in Table 7.1. Because it is a money market rate, six-month LIBOR is quoted on an actual/360 basis. The first floating payment in Table 7.1, based on the LIBOR rate of 2.2%, is shown as $1.10 million. Because there are 184 days between March 8, 2017, and September 8, 2017, it should be

$$100 \times 0.022 \times \frac{184}{360} = \$1.1244 \text{ million}$$

In general, a LIBOR-based floating-rate cash flow on a swap payment date is calculated as $LRn/360$, where L is the principal, R is the relevant LIBOR rate, and n is the number of days in the accrual period.

The fixed rate that is paid in a swap transaction is similarly quoted with a particular day count basis being specified. As a result, the fixed payments may not be exactly equal on each payment date. The fixed rate is usually quoted as actual/365 or 30/360. It is not therefore directly comparable with LIBOR because it applies to a full year. To make the rates comparable, either the six-month LIBOR rate must be multiplied by 365/360 or the fixed rate must be multiplied by 360/365.

For ease of exposition, we will ignore day count issues in our valuations of swaps in this chapter.

---

[4] The standard swap in the United States is one where fixed payments made every six months are exchanged for floating LIBOR payments made every three months. For ease of exposition, we assumed that fixed and floating payments are exchanged every six months in Table 7.1.

7.3   CONFIRMATIONS

When swaps are traded bilaterally a legal agreement, known as a confirmation, is signed by representatives of the two parties. The drafting of confirmations has been facilitated by the work of the International Swaps and Derivatives Association (ISDA) in New York. This organization has produced a number of Master Agreements that consist of clauses defining in some detail the payments required by the two sides, what happens in the event of default by either side, collateral requirements (if any), and so on. Business Snapshot 7.1 shows a possible extract from the confirmation for the swap between Apple and the Citigroup in Figure 7.1. Almost certainly, the full confirmation would state that the provisions of an ISDA Master Agreement apply to the contract.

The confirmation specifies that the following business day convention is to be used and that the U.S. calendar determines which days are business days and which days are holidays. This means that, if a payment date falls on a weekend or a U.S. holiday, the payment is made on the next business day.[5] September 8, 2018, is a Saturday. The third exchange of payments is therefore on Monday September 10, 2018.

7.4   THE COMPARATIVE-ADVANTAGE ARGUMENT

An explanation commonly put forward to explain the popularity of swaps concerns comparative advantages. In this context, a comparative advantage is advantage that leads to company being treated more favorably in one debt market than in another debt market. Consider the use of an interest rate swap to transform a liability. Some companies, it is argued, have a comparative advantage when borrowing in fixed-rate markets, whereas other companies have a comparative advantage when borrowing in floating-rate markets. To obtain a new loan, it makes sense for a company to go to the market where it has a comparative advantage. As a result, the company may borrow fixed when it wants floating, or borrow floating when it wants fixed. The swap is used to transform a fixed-rate loan into a floating-rate loan, and vice versa.

Illustration

Suppose that two companies, AAACorp and BBBCorp, both wish to borrow $10 million for five years and have been offered the rates shown in Table 7.4. AAACorp has a AAA credit rating; BBBCorp has a BBB credit rating.[6] We assume that BBBCorp wants to borrow at a fixed rate of interest, whereas AAACorp wants to borrow at a floating rate of interest linked to six-month LIBOR. Since BBBCorp has a worse credit rating than AAACorp, it pays a higher rate of interest in both fixed and floating markets.

A key feature of the rates offered to AAACorp and BBBCorp is that the difference between the two fixed rates is greater than the difference between the two floating rates.

---

[5] Another business day convention that is sometimes specified is the *modified following* business day convention, which is the same as the following business day convention except that when the next business day falls in a different month from the specified day, the payment is made on the immediately preceding business day. *Preceding* and *modified preceding* business day conventions are defined analogously.

[6] The credit ratings assigned to companies by S&P and Fitch (in order of decreasing creditworthiness) are AAA, AA, A, BBB, BB, B, and CCC. The corresponding ratings assigned by Moody's are Aaa, Aa, A, Baa, Ba, B, and Caa, respectively.

Business Snapshot 7.1 Extract from Hypothetical Swap Confirmation

Trade date	1-March-2017
Effective date	8-March-2017
Business day convention (all dates)	Following business day
Holiday calendar	U.S.
Termination date	8-March-2020

Fixed amounts

Fixed-rate payer	Apple Inc.
Fixed-rate notional principal	USD 100 million
Fixed rate	3.0% per annum
Fixed-rate day count convention	Actual/365
Fixed-rate payment dates	Each 8-March and 8-September commencing 8-September, 2017, up to and including 8-March, 2020

Floating amounts

Floating-rate payer	Citigroup Inc.
Floating-rate notional principal	USD 100 million
Floating rate	USD 6-month LIBOR
Floating-rate day count convention	Actual/360
Floating-rate payment dates	Each 8-March and 8-September commencing 8-September, 2017, up to and including 8-March, 2020

BBBCorp pays 1.2% more than AAACorp in fixed-rate markets and only 0.7% more than AAACorp in floating-rate markets. BBBCorp appears to have a comparative advantage in floating-rate markets, whereas AAACorp appears to have a comparative advantage in fixed-rate markets.[7] It is this apparent anomaly that can lead to a swap being negotiated. AAACorp borrows fixed-rate funds at 4% per annum. BBBCorp borrows floating-rate funds at LIBOR plus 0.6% per annum. They then enter into a swap agreement to ensure that AAACorp ends up with floating-rate funds and BBBCorp ends up with fixed-rate funds.

To understand how the swap might work, we first assume (somewhat unrealistically) that AAACorp and BBBCorp get in touch with each other directly. The sort of swap they might negotiate is shown in Figure 7.7. AAACorp agrees to pay BBBCorp interest

---

Table 7.4 Borrowing rates that provide a basis for the comparative-advantage argument.

	Fixed	Floating
AAACorp	4.0%	6-month LIBOR − 0.1%
BBBCorp	5.2%	6-month LIBOR + 0.6%

---

[7] Note that BBBCorp's comparative advantage in floating-rate markets does not imply that BBBCorp pays less than AAACorp in this market. It means that the extra amount that BBBCorp pays over the amount paid by AAACorp is less in this market. One of my students summarized the situation as follows: "AAACorp pays more less in fixed-rate markets; BBBCorp pays less more in floating-rate markets."

Figure 7.7 Swap agreement between AAACorp and BBBCorp when rates in Table 7.4 apply.

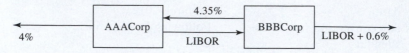

at six-month LIBOR on $10 million. In return, BBBCorp agrees to pay AAACorp interest at a fixed rate of 4.35% per annum on $10 million.

AAACorp has three sets of interest rate cash flows:

1. It pays 4% per annum to outside lenders.

2. It receives 4.35% per annum from BBBCorp.

3. It pays LIBOR to BBBCorp.

The net effect of the three cash flows is that AAACorp pays LIBOR minus 0.35% per annum. This is 0.25% per annum less than it would pay if it went directly to floating-rate markets.

BBBCorp also has three sets of interest rate cash flows:

1. It pays LIBOR + 0.6% per annum to outside lenders.

2. It receives LIBOR from AAACorp.

3. It pays 4.35% per annum to AAACorp.

The net effect of the three cash flows is that BBBCorp pays 4.95% per annum. This is 0.25% per annum less than it would pay if it went directly to fixed-rate markets.

In this example, the swap has been structured so that the net gain to both sides is the same, 0.25%. This need not be the case. However, the total apparent gain from this type of interest rate swap arrangement is always $a - b$, where a is the difference between the interest rates facing the two companies in fixed-rate markets, and b is the difference between the interest rates facing the two companies in floating-rate markets. In this case, $a = 1.2\%$ and $b = 0.7\%$, so that the total gain is 0.5%.

If the transaction between AAACorp and BBBCorp were brokered by a financial institution, an arrangement such as that shown in Figure 7.8 might result. In this case, AAACorp ends up borrowing at LIBOR − 0.33%, BBBCorp ends up borrowing at 4.97%, and the financial institution earns a spread of four basis points per year. The gain to AAACorp is 0.23%; the gain to BBBCorp is 0.23%; and the gain to the financial institution is 0.04%. The total gain to all three parties is 0.5% as before.

Figure 7.8 Swap agreement between AAACorp and BBBCorp when rates in Table 7.4 apply and swap is brokered by a financial institution.

Criticism of the Comparative-Advantage Argument

The comparative-advantage argument we have just outlined for explaining the attractiveness of interest rate swaps is open to question. Why in Table 7.4 should the spreads between the rates offered to AAACorp and BBBCorp be different in fixed and floating markets? Now that the interest rate swap market has been in existence for a long time, we might reasonably expect these types of differences to have been arbitraged away.

The reason that spread differentials appear to exist is due to the nature of the contracts available to companies in fixed and floating markets. The 4.0% and 5.2% rates available to AAACorp and BBBCorp in fixed-rate markets are five-year rates (for example, the rates at which the companies can issue five-year fixed-rate bonds). The LIBOR − 0.1% and LIBOR + 0.6% rates available to AAACorp and BBBCorp in floating-rate markets are six-month rates. In the floating-rate market, the lender usually has the opportunity to review the spread above LIBOR every time rates are reset. (In our example, rates are reset semiannually.) If the creditworthiness of AAACorp or BBBCorp has declined, the lender has the option of increasing the spread over LIBOR that is charged. In extreme circumstances, the lender can refuse to continue the loan. The providers of fixed-rate financing do not have the option to change the terms of the loan in this way.[8]

The spreads between the rates offered to AAACorp and BBBCorp are a reflection of the extent to which BBBCorp is more likely to default than AAACorp. During the next six months, there is very little chance that either AAACorp or BBBCorp will default. As we look further ahead, default statistics show that on average the probability of a default by a company with a BBB credit rating increases faster than the probability of a default by a company with a AAA credit rating. This is why the spread between the five-year rates is greater than the spread between the six-month rates.

After negotiating a floating-rate loan at LIBOR + 0.6% and entering into the swap shown in Figure 7.8, BBBCorp appears to obtain a fixed-rate loan at 4.97%. The arguments just presented show that this is not really the case. In practice, the rate paid is 4.97% only if BBBCorp can continue to borrow floating-rate funds at a spread of 0.6% over LIBOR. If, for example, the credit rating of BBBCorp declines so that the floating-rate loan is rolled over at LIBOR + 1.6%, the rate paid by BBBCorp increases to 5.97%. The market expects that BBBCorp's spread over six-month LIBOR will on average rise during the swap's life. BBBCorp's expected average borrowing rate when it enters into the swap is therefore greater than 4.97%.

The swap in Figure 7.8 locks in LIBOR − 0.33% for AAACorp for the next five years, not just for the next six months. This appears to be a good deal for AAACorp. The downside is that it is bearing the risk of a default by the financial institution. If it borrowed floating-rate funds in the usual way, it would not be bearing this risk.

7.5 VALUATION OF INTEREST RATE SWAPS

We now move on to discuss the valuation of interest rate swaps. An interest rate swap is worth close to zero when it is first initiated. After it has been in existence for some time, its value may be positive or negative.

---

[8] If the floating-rate loans are structured so that the spread over LIBOR is guaranteed in advance regardless of changes in credit rating, there is in practice little or no comparative advantage.

Each exchange of payments in an interest rate swap is a forward rate agreement (FRA) where interest at a predetermined fixed rate is exchanged for interest at the LIBOR floating rate. Consider, for example, the swap between Apple and Citigroup in Figure 7.1. The swap is a three-year deal entered into on March 8, 2017, with semiannual payments. The first exchange of payments is known at the time the swap is negotiated. The other five exchanges can be regarded as FRAs. The exchange on March 8, 2018, is an FRA where interest at 3% is exchanged for interest at the six-month LIBOR rate observed in the market on September 8, 2017; the exchange on September 8, 2018, is an FRA where interest at 3% is exchanged for interest at at the six-month LIBOR rate observed in the market on March 8, 2018; and so on.

As shown at the end of Section 4.9, an FRA can be valued by assuming that forward rates are realized. Because it is nothing more than a portfolio of FRAs, an interest rate swap can also be valued by assuming that forward rates are realized. The procedure is:

1. Calculate forward rates for each of the LIBOR rates that will determine swap cash flows.

2. Calculate the swap cash flows on the assumption that LIBOR rates will equal forward rates.

3. Discount the swap cash flows at the risk-free rate.

Example 7.1

Suppose that some time ago a financial institution entered into a swap where it agreed to make semiannual payments at a rate of 3% per annum and receive LIBOR on a notional principal of $100 million. The swap now has a remaining life of 1.25 years. Payments will therefore be made 0.25, 0.75, and 1.25 years from today. The risk-free rates with continuous compounding for maturities of 3 months, 9 months, and 15 months are 2.8%, 3.2%, and 3.4%. We suppose that the forward LIBOR rates for the 3- to 9-month and the 9- to 15-month periods are 3.4% and 3.7%, respectively, with continuous compounding. Using equation (4.4), the 3- to 9-month forward rate becomes $2 \times (e^{0.034 \times 0.5} - 1)$ or 3.429% with semiannual compounding. Similarly, the 9- to 15-month forward rate becomes 3.734% with semiannual compounding. The LIBOR rate applicable to the exchange in 0.25 years was determined 0.25 years ago. Suppose it is 2.9% with semiannual compounding.

The calculation of swap cash flows on the assumption that LIBOR rates will equal forward rates and the discounting of the cash flows are shown in the following table (all cash flows are in millions of dollars):

Time (years)	Fixed cash flow	Floating cash flow	Net cash flow	Discount factor	Present value of net cash flow
0.25	−1.5000	+1.4500	−0.0500	0.9930	−0.0497
0.75	−1.5000	+1.7145	+0.2145	0.9763	+0.2094
1.25	−1.5000	+1.8672	+0.3672	0.9584	+0.3519
Total					0.5117

Consider, for example, the 0.75 year row. The fixed cash flow is −0.5 × 0.03 × 100, or −$1.5000 million. The floating cash flow, assuming forward rates are realized, is 0.5 × 0.03429 × 100, or $1.7145 million. The net cash flow is therefore \$0.2145 million. The discount factor is $e^{-0.032 \times 0.75} = 0.9763$, so that the present value is $0.2145 \times 0.9763 = 0.2094$.

The value of the swap is obtained by summing the present values. It is \$0.5117 million. (Note that these calculations do not take account of holiday calendars and day count conventions.)

Bootstrapping LIBOR Forward Rates

The bootstrap method for calculating zero rates (such as the OIS zero rates needed for derivatives valuation) was covered in Section 4.7. We now show how a variation on that bootstrap method can be used to calculate forward LIBOR rates. FRA quotes can typically be used to obtain short-maturity forward LIBOR rates directly while swap quotes must be used for longer maturities. The latter provide information about swaps that have a value of zero.

Example 7.2

Suppose that the 6-month, 12-month, 18-month, and 24-month OIS zero rates (with continuous compounding) are 3.8%, 4.3%, 4.6%, and 4.75%, respectively. Suppose further that the six-month LIBOR rate is 4% with with semiannual compounding. The forward LIBOR rate for the period between 6 and 12 months is 5% with semiannual compounding. The forward LIBOR rate for the period between 12 and 18 months is 5.5% with semiannual compounding. We show how the forward LIBOR rate for the 18- to 24-month period can be calculated.

Suppose the two-year swap rate is 5%. The value of a two-year swap where LIBOR is paid and 5% is received is therefore zero. We know that the swap can be valued by assuming that forward rates are realized. The value of the first payment in the swap, assuming a principal of 100 is

$$0.5 \times (0.04 - 0.05) \times 100 \times e^{-0.038 \times 0.5} = -0.4906$$

The value of the second payment is

$$0.5 \times (0.05 - 0.05) \times 100 \times e^{-0.043 \times 1} = 0$$

The value of the third payments is

$$0.5 \times (0.055 - 0.05) \times 100 \times e^{-0.046 \times 1.5} = 0.2333$$

The total value of the first three payments is $-0.4906 + 0 + 0.2333 = -0.2573$. Suppose that the (assumed unknown) forward rate for the final payment is F. For the swap to be worth zero, we must have

$$0.5 \times (F - 0.05) \times 100 \times e^{-0.0475 \times 2} = 0.2573$$

This gives $F = 0.05566$, or 5.566%.

In practice, in order to value a swap such as that considered in Example 7.1, some interpolation between estimated forward rates is necessary. For example, the current 9- to 15-month forward rate might in practice be estimated as the average of the current 6- to 12-month forward rate and the current 12- to 18-month forward rates.

7.6 HOW THE VALUE CHANGES THROUGH TIME

The fixed rate in an interest rate swap is chosen so that the swap is worth zero initially. This means that the sum of the values of the FRAs underlying the swap is initially zero. It does not mean that the value of each individual FRA is zero. In general, some FRAs will have positive values while others will have negative values.

Consider the FRAs underlying the swap between Apple and Citigroup in Figure 7.1.

Value of FRA to Apple > 0 when forward interest rate > 3.0%

Value of FRA to Apple = 0 when forward interest rate = 3.0%

Value of FRA to Apple < 0 when forward interest rate < 3.0%

Suppose that the term structure of interest rates is upward sloping at the time the swap is negotiated. This means that the forward interest rates increase as the maturity of the

Figure 7.9 Value of forward rate agreements underlying a swap as a function of maturity. In (a) either the term structure of interest rates is upward sloping and fixed is received or the term structure of interest rates is downward sloping and floating is received; in (b) either the term structure of interest rates is upward sloping and floating is received or the term structure of interest rates is downward sloping and fixed is received.

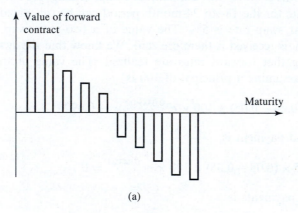

(a)

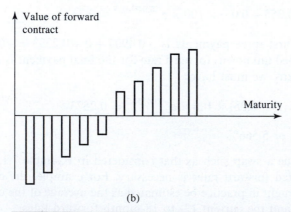

(b)

FRA increases. Because the sum of the values of the FRAs is zero, the forward interest rate must be less than 3.0% for the early payment dates and greater than 3.0% for the later payment dates. An upward-sloping term structure therefore implies that the value to Apple of the FRAs corresponding to early payment dates is negative, whereas the value of the FRAs corresponding to later payment dates is positive. The expected value of the swap at future times is therefore positive.[9] If the term structure of interest rates is downward sloping at the time the swap is negotiated, the reverse is true. The impact of the shape of the term structure of interest rates on the values of the forward contracts underlying a swap is illustrated in Figure 7.9.

7.7 FIXED-FOR-FIXED CURRENCY SWAPS

Another popular type of swap is a *fixed-for-fixed currency swap*. This involves exchanging principal and interest payments at a fixed rate in one currency for principal and interest payments at a fixed rate in another currency.

A currency swap agreement requires the principal to be specified in each of the two currencies. The principal amounts in each currency are usually exchanged at the beginning and at the end of the life of the swap. Usually the principal amounts are chosen to be approximately equivalent using the exchange rate at the swap's initiation. But when they are exchanged at the end of the life of the swap, their values may be quite different.

Illustration

Consider a hypothetical five-year currency swap agreement between British Petroleum and Barclays entered into on February 1, 2017. We suppose that British Petroleum pays a fixed rate of interest of 3% in dollars to Barclays and receives a fixed rate of interest of 4% in British pounds (sterling) from Barclays. Interest rate payments are made once a year and the principal amounts are $15 million and £10 million. This is termed a *fixed-for-fixed* currency swap because the interest rate in both currencies is fixed. The swap is shown in Figure 7.10. Initially, the principal amounts flow in the opposite direction to the arrows in Figure 7.10. The interest payments during the life of the swap and the final principal payment flow in the same direction as the arrows. Thus, at the outset of the swap, British Petroleum pays £10 million and receives $15 million. Each year during the life of the swap contract, British Petroleum receives £0.40 million (= 4% of £10 million)

Figure 7.10   A currency swap.

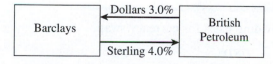

---

[9] There is no guarantee that the value will be positive. For example, if interest rates decline during the life of the swap, the value to Apple will move from being zero to becoming negative. Expected values are the values that will happen on average, not values that are certain to happen.

Table 7.5 Cash flows to British Petroleum in currency swap.

Date	Dollar cash flow (millions)	Sterling cash flow (millions)
February 1, 2017	+15.00	−10.00
February 1, 2018	−0.45	+0.40
February 1, 2019	−0.45	+0.40
February 1, 2020	−0.45	+0.40
February 1, 2021	−0.45	+0.40
February 1, 2022	−15.45	+10.40

and pays $0.45 million (= 3% of $15 million). At the end of the life of the swap, it pays $15 million and receives £10 million. These cash flows are shown in Table 7.5. The cash flows to Barclays are the opposite to those shown.

Use of a Currency Swap to Transform Liabilities and Assets

A swap such as the one just considered can be used to transform borrowings in one currency to borrowings in another currency. Suppose that British Petroleum can borrow £10 million at 4% interest. The swap has the effect of transforming this loan into one where it has borrowed $15 million at 3% interest. The initial exchange of principal converts the amount borrowed from sterling to dollars. The subsequent exchanges in the swap have the effect of swapping the interest and principal payments from sterling to dollars.

The swap can also be used to transform the nature of assets. Suppose that British Petroleum can invest $15 million to earn 3% in U.S. dollars for the next five years, but feels that sterling will strengthen (or at least not depreciate) against the dollar and prefers a U.K.-denominated investment. The swap has the effect of transforming the U.S. investment into a £10 million investment in the U.K. yielding 4%.

Comparative Advantage

Currency swaps can be motivated by comparative advantage. To illustrate this, we consider another hypothetical example. Suppose the five-year fixed-rate borrowing costs to General Electric and Qantas Airways in U.S. dollars (USD) and Australian dollars (AUD) are as shown in Table 7.6. The data in the table suggest that Australian rates are

Table 7.6 Borrowing rates providing basis for currency swap.

	USD*	AUD*
General Electric	5.0%	7.6%
Qantas Airways	7.0%	8.0%

* Quoted rates have been adjusted to reflect the differential impact of taxes.

higher than U.S. interest rates. Also, General Electric is more creditworthy than Qantas Airways, because it is offered a more favorable rate of interest in both currencies. From the viewpoint of a swap trader, the interesting aspect of Table 7.6 is that the spreads between the rates paid by General Electric and Qantas Airways in the two markets are not the same. Qantas Airways pays 2% more than General Electric in the USD market and only 0.4% more than General Electric in the AUD market.

This situation is analogous to that in Table 7.4. General Electric has a comparative advantage in the USD market, whereas Qantas Airways has a comparative advantage in the AUD market. In Table 7.4, where a plain vanilla interest rate swap was considered, we argued that comparative advantages are largely illusory. Here we are comparing the rates offered in two different currencies, and it is more likely that the comparative advantages are genuine. One possible source of comparative advantage is tax. General Electric's position might be such that USD borrowings lead to lower taxes on its worldwide income than AUD borrowings. Qantas Airways' position might be the reverse. (Note that we assume that the interest rates in Table 7.6 have been adjusted to reflect these types of tax advantages.)

We suppose that General Electric wants to borrow 20 million AUD and Qantas Airways wants to borrow 15 million USD and that the current exchange rate (USD per AUD) is 0.7500. This creates a perfect situation for a currency swap. General Electric and Qantas Airways each borrow in the market where they have a comparative advantage; that is, General Electric borrows USD whereas Qantas Airways borrows AUD. They then use a currency swap to transform General Electric's loan into a AUD loan and Qantas Airways' loan into a USD loan.

As already mentioned, the difference between the dollar interest rates is 2%, whereas the difference between the AUD interest rates is 0.4%. By analogy with the interest rate swap case, we expect the total gain to all parties to be $2.0 - 0.4 = 1.6\%$ per annum.

There are many ways in which the swap can be arranged. Figure 7.11 shows one way a swap might be brokered by a financial institution. General Electric borrows USD and Qantas Airways borrows AUD. The effect of the swap is to transform the USD interest rate of 5% per annum to an AUD interest rate of 6.9% per annum for General Electric. As a result, General Electric is 0.7% per annum better off than it would be if it went directly to AUD markets. Similarly, Qantas exchanges an AUD loan at 8% per annum for a USD loan at 6.3% per annum and ends up 0.7% per annum better off than it would be if it went directly to USD markets. The financial institution gains 1.3% per annum on its USD cash flows and loses 1.1% per annum on its AUD flows. If we ignore the difference between the two currencies, the financial institution makes a net gain of 0.2% per annum. As predicted, the total gain to all parties is 1.6% per annum.

Each year the financial institution makes a gain of USD 156,000 (= 1.3% of 12 million) and incurs a loss of AUD 220,000 (= 1.1% of 20 million). The financial

Figure 7.11 A currency swap motivated by comparative advantage.

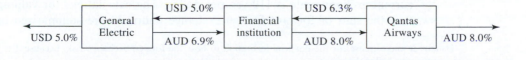

Figure 7.12   Alternative arrangement for currency swap: Qantas Airways bears some foreign exchange risk.

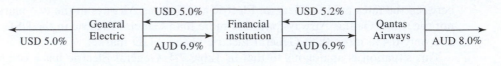

Figure 7.13   Alternative arrangement for currency swap: General Electric bears some foreign exchange risk.

institution can avoid any foreign exchange risk by buying AUD 220,000 per annum in the forward market for each year of the life of the swap, thus locking in a net gain in USD.

It is possible to redesign the swap so that the financial institution does not need to hedge. Figures 7.12 and 7.13 present two alternatives. These alternatives are unlikely to be used in practice because they do not lead to General Electric and Qantas being free of foreign exchange risk.[10] In Figure 7.12, Qantas bears some foreign exchange risk because it pays 1.1% per annum in AUD and pays 5.2% per annum in USD. In Figure 7.13, General Electric bears some foreign exchange risk because it receives 1.1% per annum in USD and pays 8% per annum in AUD.

7.8   VALUATION OF FIXED-FOR-FIXED CURRENCY SWAPS

Each exchange of payments in a fixed-for-fixed currency swap is a forward contract. As shown in Section 5.7, forward foreign exchange contracts can be valued by assuming that forward exchange rates are realized. A fixed-for-fixed currency swap can therefore be valued assuming that forward rates are realized.

Example 7.3

Suppose that the term structure of risk-free interest rates is flat in both Japan and the United States. The Japanese rate is 1.5% per annum and the U.S. rate is 2.5% per annum (both with continuous compounding). A financial institution has entered into a currency swap in which it receives 3% per annum in yen and pays 4% per annum in dollars once a year. The principals in the two currencies are $10 million and 1,200 million yen. The swap will last for another three years, and the current exchange rate is 110 yen per dollar. The calculations for valuing the swap as the sum of forward foreign exchange contracts are summarized in the

---

[10] Usually it makes sense for the financial institution to bear the foreign exchange risk, because it is in the best position to hedge the risk.

following table (all amounts are in millions):

Time (years)	Dollar cash flow	Yen cash flow	Forward exchange rate	Dollar value of yen cash flow	Net cash flow	Present value
1	−0.4	+36	0.009182	0.3306	−0.0694	−0.0677
2	−0.4	+36	0.009275	0.3339	−0.0661	−0.0629
3	−10.4	+1236	0.009368	11.5786	+1.1786	+1.0934
Total						+0.9629

The financial institution pays $0.04 \times 10 = \$0.4$ million dollars and receives $1{,}200 \times 0.03 = 36$ million yen each year. In addition, the dollar principal of $10 million is paid and the yen principal of 1,200 is received at the end of year 3. The current spot rate is $1/110 = 0.009091$ dollar per yen. In this case, $r = 2.5\%$ and $r_f = 1.5\%$ so that the one-year forward exchange rate is, from equation (5.9), $0.009091e^{(0.025-0.015)\times 1} = 0.009182$. The two- and three-year forward exchange rates in the table are calculated similarly. The forward contracts underlying the swap can be valued by assuming that the forward exchange rates are realized. If the one-year forward exchange rate is realized, the value of yen cash flow in year 1 will be $36 \times 0.009182 = 0.3306$ million dollars and the net cash flow at the end of year 1 will be $0.3306 - 0.4 = -0.0694$ million dollars. This has a present value of $-0.0.0694e^{-0.025\times 1} = -0.0677$ million dollars. This is the value of the forward contract corresponding to the exchange of cash flows at the end of year 1. The value of the other forward contracts are calculated similarly. As shown in the table, the total value of the forward contracts is $0.9629 million.

The value of a currency swap is normally zero when it is first negotiated. If the two principals are worth exactly the same using the exchange rate at the start of the swap, the value of the swap is also zero immediately after the initial exchange of principal. However, as in the case of interest rate swaps, this does not mean that each of the individual forward contracts underlying the swap has zero value. It can be shown that when interest rates in two currencies are significantly different, the payer of the high-interest-rate currency is in the position where the forward contracts corresponding to the early exchanges of cash flows have negative values, and the forward contract corresponding to final exchange of principals has a positive value. The payer of the low-interest-rate currency is likely to be in the opposite position; that is, the early exchanges of cash flows have positive values and the final exchange has a negative value.

For the payer of the low-interest-rate currency, the swap will tend to have a negative value during most of its life. The forward contracts corresponding to the early exchanges of payments have positive values, and once these exchanges have taken place, there is a tendency for the remaining forward contracts to have, in total, a negative value. For the payer of the high-interest-rate currency, the reverse is true. The value of the swap will tend to be positive during most of its life. Results of this sort are important when the credit risk in bilaterally cleared transactions is considered.

Valuation in Terms of Bond Prices

A fixed-for-fixed currency swap can also be valued in a straightforward way as the difference between two bonds. If we define V_{swap} as the value in U.S. dollars of an outstanding swap where dollars are received and a foreign currency is paid, that is,

$$V_{swap} = B_D - S_0 B_F$$

where B_F is the value, measured in the foreign currency, of the bond defined by the foreign cash flows on the swap and B_D is the value of the bond defined by the domestic cash flows on the swap, and S_0 is the spot exchange rate (expressed as number of dollars per unit of foreign currency). The value of a swap can therefore be determined from LIBOR rates in the two currencies, the term structure of interest rates in the domestic currency, and the spot exchange rate.

Similarly, the value of a swap where the foreign currency is received and dollars are paid is

$$V_{swap} = S_0 B_F - B_D$$

Example 7.4

Consider again the situation in Example 7.3. The term structure of risk-free interest rates is flat in both Japan and the United States. The Japanese rate is 1.5% per annum and the U.S. rate is 2.5% per annum (both with continuous compounding). A financial institution has entered into a currency swap in which it receives 3% per annum in yen and pays 4% per annum in dollars once a year. The principals in the two currencies are $10 million and 1,200 million yen. The swap will last for another three years, and the current exchange rate is 110 yen = $1. The calculations for valuing the swap in terms of bonds are summarized in the following table (all amounts are in millions):

Time (years)	Cash flows on dollar bond ($)	Present value ($)	Cash flows on yen bond (yen)	Present value (yen)
1	0.4	0.3901	36	35.46
2	0.4	0.3805	36	34.94
3	10.4	9.6485	1,236	1,181.61
Total		10.4191		1,252.01

The cash flows from the dollar bond underlying the swap are as shown in the second column. The present value of the cash flows using the dollar discount rate of 2.5% are shown in the third column. The cash flows from the yen bond underlying the swap are shown in the fourth column. The present value of the cash flows using the yen discount rate of 1.5% are shown in the final column of the table. The value of the dollar bond, B_D, is 10.4191 million dollars. The value of the yen bond is 1,252.01 million yen. The value of the swap in dollars is therefore $(1,252.01/110) - 10.4191 = 0.9629$ million. This is in agreement with the calculation in Example 7.3.

7.9 OTHER CURRENCY SWAPS

Two other popular currency swaps are:

1. Fixed-for-floating where a floating interest rate in one currency is exchanged for a fixed interest rate in another currency

2. Floating-for-floating where a floating interest rate in one currency is exchanged for a floating interest rate in another currency.

An example of the first type of swap would be an exchange where Sterling LIBOR on a principal of £7 million is paid and 3% on a principal of $10 million is received with payments being made semiannually for 10 years. Similarly to a fixed-for-fixed currency swap, this would involve an initial exchange of principal in the opposite direction to the interest payments and a final exchange of principal in the same direction as the interest payments at the end of the swap's life. A fixed-for-floating swap can be regarded as a portfolio consisting of a fixed-for-fixed currency swap and a fixed-for-floating interest rate swap. For instance, the swap in our example can be regarded as (a) a swap where 3% on a principal of $10 million is received and (say) 4% on a principal of £7 million is paid plus (b) an interest rate swap where 4% is received and sterling LIBOR is paid on a notional principal of £7 million.

To value the swap we are considering we can calculate the value of the dollar payments in dollars by discounting them at the dollar risk-free rate. We can calculate the value of the sterling payments by assuming that sterling LIBOR forward rates will be realized and discounting the cash flows at the sterling risk-free rate. The value of the swap is the difference between the values of the two sets of payments using current exchange rates.

An example of the second type of swap would be the exchange where sterling LIBOR on a principal of £7 million is paid and dollar LIBOR on a principal of $10 million is received. As in the other cases we have considered, this would involve an initial exchange of principal in the opposite direction to the interest payments and a final exchange of principal in the same direction as the interest payments at the end of the swap's life. A floating-for-floating swap can be regarded as a portfolio consisting of a fixed-for-fixed currency swap and two interest rate swaps, one in each currency. For instance, the swap in our example can be regarded as (a) a swap where 3% on a principal of $10 million is received and 4% on a principal of £7 million is paid plus (b) an interest rate swap where 4% is received and sterling LIBOR is paid on a notional principal of £7 million plus (c) an interest rate swap where 3% is paid and USD LIBOR is received on a notional principal of $10 million.

A floating-for-floating swap can be valued by assuming that forward interest rates in each currency will be realized and discounting the cash flows at risk-free rates. The value of the swap is the difference between the values of the two sets of payments using current exchange rates.

7.10 CREDIT RISK

When swaps and other derivatives are cleared through a central counterparty there is very little credit risk. As has been explained, standard swap transactions between a nonfinancial corporation and a derivatives dealer can be cleared bilaterally. Both sides are then potentially subject to credit risk. Consider the bilaterally cleared transaction between Intel and Citigroup in Figure 7.3. This would be netted with all other bilaterally cleared derivatives between Intel and Citigroup. If Intel defaults when the net value of the outstanding transactions to Citigroup is greater than the collateral (if

---

Business Snapshot 7.2 The Hammersmith and Fulham Story

Between 1987 to 1989 the London Borough of Hammersmith and Fulham in Great Britain entered into about 600 interest rate swaps and related instruments with a total notional principal of about 6 billion pounds. The transactions appear to have been entered into for speculative rather than hedging purposes. The two employees of Hammersmith and Fulham that were responsible for the trades had only a sketchy understanding of the risks they were taking and how the products they were trading worked.

By 1989, because of movements in sterling interest rates, Hammersmith and Fulham had lost several hundred million pounds on the swaps. To the banks on the other side of the transactions, the swaps were worth several hundred million pounds. The banks were concerned about credit risk. They had entered into offsetting swaps to hedge their interest rate risks. If Hammersmith and Fulham defaulted they would still have to honor their obligations on the offsetting swaps and would take a huge loss.

What happened was something a little different from a default. Hammersmith and Fulham's auditor asked to have the transactions declared void because Hammersmith and Fulham did not have the authority to enter into the transactions. The British courts agreed. The case was appealed and went all the way to the House of Lords, then Britain's highest court. The final decision was that Hammersmith and Fulham did not have the authority to enter into the swaps, but that they ought to have the authority to do so in the future for risk management purposes. Needless to say, banks were furious that their contracts were overturned in this way by the courts.

---

any) posted by Intel, Citigroup will incur a loss.[11] Similarly, if Citigroup defaults when the net value of the outstanding transactions to Intel is greater than the collateral (if any) posted by Citigroup, Intel will incur a loss.

It is important to distinguish between the credit risk and market risk to a financial institution in any contract. The credit risk arises from the possibility of a default by the counterparty when the value of the contract to the financial institution is positive. The market risk arises from the possibility that market variables such as interest rates and exchange rates will move in such a way that the value of a contract to the financial institution becomes negative. Market risks can be hedged by entering into offsetting contracts; credit risks are less easy to hedge.

One of the more bizarre stories in swap markets is outlined in Business Snapshot 7.2. It concerns a British Local Authority, Hammersmith and Fulham, and shows that, in addition to bearing market risk and credit risk, banks trading swaps also sometimes bear legal risk.

7.11   CREDIT DEFAULT SWAPS

A swap which has grown in importance since the year 2000 is a *credit default swap* (CDS). This is a swap that allows companies to hedge credit risks in the same way that

---

[11] The Master Agreement between Intel and Citigroup covers all oustanding derivatives and may or may not require collateral to be posted as the net value of the transactions changes.

they have hedged market risks for many years. A CDS is like an insurance contract that pays off if a particular company or country defaults. The company or country is known as the *reference entity*. The buyer of credit protection pays an insurance premium, known as the *CDS spread*, to the seller of protection for the life of the contract or until the reference entity defaults. Suppose that the notional principal of the CDS is $100 million and the CDS spread for a five-year deal is 120 basis points. The insurance premium would be 120 basis points applied to $100 million or $1.2 million per year. If the reference entity does not default during the five years, nothing is received in return for the insurance premiums. If reference entity does default and bonds issued by the reference entity are worth 40 cents per dollar of principal immediately after default, the seller of protection has to make a payment to the buyer of protection equal to $60 million. The idea here is that, if the buyer of protection owned a portfolio of bonds issued by the reference entity with a principal of $100 million, the insurance payoff would be sufficient to bring the value of the portfolio back up to $100 million.

Credit default swaps are discussed in more detail in Chapter 25.

7.12 OTHER TYPES OF SWAPS

Many other types of swaps are traded. We will discuss some of them in Chapter 34. At this stage we provide an overview.

Variations on the Standard Interest Rate Swap

In fixed-for-floating interest rate swaps, LIBOR is by far the most common reference floating interest rate. In the examples in this chapter, the tenor (i.e., payment frequency) of LIBOR has been six-months, but swaps where the tenor of LIBOR is one month, three months, and 12 months also trade regularly. The tenor on the floating side does not have to match the tenor on the fixed side. (Indeed, as pointed out in footnote 4, the standard interest rate swap in the United States is one where there are quarterly LIBOR payments and semiannual fixed payments.) Floating rates such as commercial paper (CP) rate are occasionally used. Sometimes floating-for-floating interest rates swaps (known as *basis swaps*) are negotiated. For example, the three-month CP rate plus 10 basis points might be exchanged for three-month LIBOR with both being applied to the same principal. (This deal would allow a company to hedge its exposure when assets and liabilities are subject to different floating rates.)

The principal in a swap agreement can be varied throughout the term of the swap to meet the needs of a counterparty. In an *amortizing swap*, the principal reduces in a predetermined way. (This might be designed to correspond to the amortization schedule on a loan.) In a *step-up swap*, the principal increases in a predetermined way. (This might be designed to correspond to drawdowns on a loan agreement.) Forward swaps (sometimes referred to as *deferred swaps*) where the parties do not begin to exchange interest payments until some future date are also sometimes arranged. Sometimes swaps are negotiated where the principal to which the fixed payments are applied is different from the principal to which the floating payments are applied.

A *constant maturity swap* (CMS swap) is an agreement to exchange a LIBOR rate for a swap rate. An example would be an agreement to exchange six-month LIBOR applied to a certain principal for the 10-year swap rate applied to the same principal every six months for the next five years. A *constant maturity Treasury swap* (CMT swap) is a similar agreement to exchange a LIBOR rate for a particular Treasury rate (e.g., the 10-year Treasury rate).

In a *compounding swap*, interest on one or both sides is compounded forward to the end of the life of the swap according to preagreed rules and there is only one payment date at the end of the life of the swap. In a *LIBOR-in-arrears* swap the LIBOR rate observed on a payment date is used to calculate the payment on that date. (As explained in Section 7.1, in a standard deal the LIBOR rate observed on one payment date is used to determine the payment on the next payment date.) In an *accrual swap*, the interest on one side of the swap accrues only when the floating reference rate is in a certain range.

Quantos

Sometimes a rate observed in one currency is applied to a principal amount in another currency. One such deal would be where three-month LIBOR observed in the United States is exchanged for three-month LIBOR in Britain with both principals being applied to a principal of 10 million British pounds. This type of swap is referred to as a *diff swap* or a *quanto*.

Equity Swaps

An *equity swap* is an agreement to exchange the total return (dividends and capital gains) realized on an equity index for either a fixed or a floating rate of interest. For example, the total return on the S&P 500 in successive six-month periods might be exchanged for LIBOR with both being applied to the same principal. Equity swaps can be used by portfolio managers to convert returns from a fixed or floating investment to the returns from investing in an equity index, and vice versa.

Options

Sometimes there are options embedded in a swap agreement. For example, in an *extendable swap*, one party has the option to extend the life of the swap beyond the specified period. In a *puttable swap*, one party has the option to terminate the swap early. Options on swaps, or *swaptions*, are also available. These provide one party with the right at a future time to enter into a swap where a predetermined fixed rate is exchanged for floating.

Commodity, Volatility, and Other Swaps

Commodity swaps are in essence a series of forward contracts on a commodity with different maturity dates and the same delivery prices. In a *volatility swap*, there are a series of time periods. At the end of each period, one side pays a preagreed volatility while the other side pays the historical volatility realized during the period. Both volatilities are multiplied by the same notional principal in calculating payments.

Swaps are limited only by the imagination of financial engineers and the desire of corporate treasurers and fund mangers for exotic structures. In Chapter 34 we will describe the famous 5/30 swap entered into between Procter and Gamble and Bankers Trust where payments depended in a complex way on the 30-day commercial paper rate, a 30-year Treasury bond price, and the yield on a 5-year Treasury bond.

SUMMARY

The two most common types of swaps are interest rate swaps and currency swaps. In an interest rate swap, one party agrees to pay the other party interest at a fixed rate on a notional principal for a number of years. In return, it receives interest at a floating rate on the same notional principal for the same period of time. In a currency swap, one party agrees to pay interest on a principal amount in one currency. In return, it receives interest on a principal amount in another currency.

Principal amounts are not exchanged in an interest rate swap. In a currency swap, principal amounts are usually exchanged at both the beginning and the end of the life of the swap. For a party paying interest in the foreign currency, the foreign principal is received, and the domestic principal is paid at the beginning of the life of the swap. At the end of the life of the swap, the foreign principal is paid and the domestic principal is received.

An interest rate swap can be used to transform a floating-rate loan into a fixed-rate loan, or vice versa. It can also be used to transform a floating-rate investment to a fixed-rate investment, or vice versa. A currency swap can be used to transform a loan in one currency into a loan in another currency. It can also be used to transform an investment denominated in one currency into an investment denominated in another currency.

The interest rate and currency swaps considered in main part of the chapter can be regarded portfolios of forward contracts. They can be valued by assuming the forward interest rates and exchange rates observed in the market today will occur in the future.

FURTHER READING

Alm, J., and F. Lindskog, "Foreign Currency Interest Rate Swaps in Asset-Liability Management for Insurers," *European Actuarial Journal*, 3 (2013): 133–58.

Corb, H. *Interest Rate Swaps and Other Derivatives*. New York: Columbia University Press, 2012.

Flavell, R. *Swaps and Other Derivatives*, 2nd edn. Chichester: Wiley, 2010.

Johannes, M., and S. Sundaresan, "The Impact of Collateralization on Swap Rates," *Journal of Finance*, 61, 1 (February 2007): 383–410.

Litzenberger, R. H. "Swaps: Plain and Fanciful," *Journal of Finance*, 47, 3 (1992): 831–50.

Memmel, C., and A. Schertler. "Bank Management of the Net Interest Margin: New Measures," *Financial Management and Portfolio Management*, 27, 3 (2013): 275–97.

Purnanandan, A. "Interest Rate Derivatives at Commercial Banks: An Empirical Investigation," *Journal of Monetary Economics*, 54 (2007): 1769–1808.

Practice Questions (Answers in Solutions Manual)

7.1. Companies A and B have been offered the following rates per annum on a $20 million five-year loan:

	Fixed rate	*Floating rate*
Company A	5.0%	LIBOR + 0.1%
Company B	6.4%	LIBOR + 0.6%

Company A requires a floating-rate loan; Company B requires a fixed-rate loan. Design a swap that will net a bank, acting as intermediary, 0.1% per annum and that will appear equally attractive to both companies.

7.2. A $100 million interest rate swap has a remaining life of 10 months. Under the terms of the swap, six-month LIBOR is exchanged for 4% per annum (compounded semiannually). Six-month LIBOR forward rates for all maturities are 3% (with semiannual compounding). The six-month LIBOR rate was 2.4% two months ago. OIS rates for all maturities are 2.7% with continuous compounding. What is the current value of the swap to the party paying floating? What is the value to the party paying fixed?

7.3. Company X wishes to borrow U.S. dollars at a fixed rate of interest. Company Y wishes to borrow Japanese yen at a fixed rate of interest. The amounts required by the two companies are roughly the same at the current exchange rate. The companies have been quoted the following interest rates, which have been adjusted for the impact of taxes:

	Yen	Dollars
Company X	5.0%	9.6%
Company Y	6.5%	10.0%

Design a swap that will net a bank, acting as intermediary, 50 basis points per annum. Make the swap equally attractive to the two companies and ensure that all foreign exchange risk is assumed by the bank.

7.4. Explain what a seven-year swap rate is.

7.5. A currency swap has a remaining life of 15 months. It involves exchanging interest at 10% on £20 million for interest at 6% on $30 million once a year. The term structure of risk-free interest rates in the United Kingdom is flat at 7% and the term structure of risk-free interest rates in the United States is flat at 4% (both with annual compounding). The current exchange rate (dollars per pound sterling) is 1.5500. What is the value of the swap to the party paying sterling? What is the value of the swap to the party paying dollars?

7.6. Explain the difference between the credit risk and the market risk in a financial contract.

7.7. A corporate treasurer tells you that he has just negotiated a five-year loan at a competitive fixed rate of interest of 5.2%. The treasurer explains that he achieved the 5.2% rate by borrowing at six-month LIBOR plus 150 basis points and swapping LIBOR for 3.7%. He goes on to say that this was possible because his company has a comparative advantage in the floating-rate market. What has the treasurer overlooked?

7.8. A bank enters into an interest rate swap with a nonfinancial counterparty using bilaterally clearing where it is paying a fixed rate of 3% and receiving LIBOR. No collateral is posted and no other transactions are outstanding between the bank and the counterparty. What credit risk is the bank subject to? Discuss whether the credit risk is greater when the yield curve is upward sloping or when it is downward sloping.

7.9. Companies X and Y have been offered the following rates per annum on a $5 million 10-year investment:

	Fixed rate	Floating rate
Company X	8.0%	LIBOR
Company Y	8.8%	LIBOR

Company X requires a fixed-rate investment; company Y requires a floating-rate investment. Design a swap that will net a bank, acting as intermediary, 0.2% per annum and will appear equally attractive to X and Y.

7.10. A financial institution has entered into an interest rate swap with company X. Under the terms of the swap, it receives 4% per annum and pays six-month LIBOR on a principal of $10 million for five years. Payments are made every six months. Suppose that company X defaults on the sixth payment date (end of year 3) when six-month forward LIBOR rates for all maturities are 2% per annum. What is the loss to the financial institution? Assume that six-month LIBOR was 3% per annum halfway through year 3 and that at the time of the default all OIS rates are 1.8% per annum. OIS rates are expressed with continuous compounding; other rates are expressed with semiannual compounding.

7.11. A financial institution has entered into a 10-year currency swap with company Y. Under the terms of the swap, the financial institution receives interest at 3% per annum in Swiss francs and pays interest at 8% per annum in U.S. dollars. Interest payments are exchanged once a year. The principal amounts are 7 million dollars and 10 million francs. Suppose that company Y declares bankruptcy at the end of year 6, when the exchange rate is $0.80 per franc. What is the cost to the financial institution? Assume that, at the end of year 6, risk-free interest rates are 3% per annum in Swiss francs and 8% per annum in U.S. dollars for all maturities. All interest rates are quoted with annual compounding.

7.12. Companies A and B face the following interest rates (adjusted for the differential impact of taxes):

	Company A	Company B
U.S. dollars (floating rate)	LIBOR + 0.5%	LIBOR + 1.0%
Canadian dollars (fixed rate)	5.0%	6.5%

Assume that A wants to borrow U.S. dollars at a floating rate of interest and B wants to borrow Canadian dollars at a fixed rate of interest. A financial institution is planning to arrange a swap and requires a 50-basis-point spread. If the swap is equally attractive to A and B, what rates of interest will A and B end up paying?

7.13. After it hedges its foreign exchange risk using forward contracts, is the financial institution's average spread in Figure 7.11 likely to be greater than or less than 20 basis points? Explain your answer.

7.14. "Nonfinancial companies with high credit risks are the ones that cannot access fixed-rate markets directly. They are the companies that are most likely to be paying fixed and receiving floating in an interest rate swap." Assume that this statement is true. Do you think it increases or decreases the risk of a financial institution's swap portfolio? Assume that companies are most likely to default when interest rates are high.

7.15. Why is the expected loss to a bank from a default on a swap with a counterparty less than the expected loss from the default on a loan to the counterparty when the loan and swap have the same principal? Assume that there are no other derivatives transactions between the bank and the counterparty, that the swap is cleared bilaterally, and that no collateral is provided by the counterparty in the case of either the swap or the loan.

7.16. A bank finds that its assets are not matched with its liabilities. It is taking floating-rate deposits and making fixed-rate loans. How can swaps be used to offset the risk?

7.17. Explain how you would value a swap that is the exchange of a floating rate in one currency for a fixed rate in another currency.

7.18. OIS rates have been estimated as 3.4% for all maturities. The three-month LIBOR rate is 3.5%. For a six-month swap where payments are exchanged every three months the swap rate is 3.6%. All rates are expressed with quarterly compounding. What is the LIBOR forward rate for the 3- to 6-month period.

7.19. Six-month LIBOR is 5%. LIBOR forward rates for the 6- to 12-month period and for the 12- to 18-month period are 5.5%. Swap rates for 2- and 3-year semiannual pay swaps are 5.4% and 5.6%, respectively. Estimate the LIBOR forward rates for for 18 months to 2 years, 2 to 2.5 years, and 2.5 to 3 years. Assume that the 2.5-year swap rate is the average of the 2- and 3-year swap rates and that OIS zero rates for all maturities are 4.5%. OIS rates are expressed with continuous compounding; all other rates are expressed with semiannual compounding.

Further Questions

7.20. (a) Company A has been offered the swap quotes in Table 7.3. It can borrow for three years at 3.45%. What floating rate can it swap this fixed rate into? (b) Company B has been offered the swap quotes in Table 7.3. It can borrow for five years at LIBOR plus 75 basis points. What fixed rate can it swap this rate into? (c) Explain the rollover risks that Company B is taking.

7.21. (a) Company X has been offered the swap quotes in Table 7.3. It can invest for four years at 2.8%. What floating rate can it swap this fixed rate into? (b) Company Y has been offered the swap quotes in Table 7.3. It is confident that it will be able to invest at LIBOR minus 50 basis points for the next ten years. What fixed rate can it swap this floating rate into?

7.22. The one-year LIBOR rates is 3%, and the LIBOR forward rate for the 1- to 2-year period is 3.2%, respectively. The three-year swap rate for a swap with annual payments is 3.2%. What is the LIBOR forward rate for the 2- to 3-year period if OIS zero rates for maturities of one, two, and three years are 2.5%, 2.7%, and 2.9%, respectively. What is the value of a three-year swap where 4% is received and LIBOR is paid on a principal of $100 million. All rates are annually compounded

7.23. In an interest rate swap, a financial institution has agreed to pay 3.6% per annum and to receive three-month LIBOR in return on a notional principal of $100 million with payments being exchanged every three months. The swap has a remaining life of 14 months. Three-month forward LIBOR for all maturities is currently 4% per annum. The three-month LIBOR rate one month ago was 3.2% per annum. OIS rates for all maturities are currently 3.8% with continuous compounding. All other rates are compounded quarterly. What is the value of the swap?

7.24. Company A, a British manufacturer, wishes to borrow U.S. dollars at a fixed rate of interest. Company B, a U.S. multinational, wishes to borrow sterling at a fixed rate of interest. They have been quoted the following rates per annum:

	Sterling	U.S. Dollars
Company A	11.0%	7.0%
Company B	10.6%	6.2%

(Rates have been adjusted for differential tax effects.) Design a swap that will net a bank, acting as intermediary, 10 basis points per annum and that will produce a gain of 15 basis points per annum for each of the two companies.

7.25. Suppose that the term structure of risk-free interest rates is flat in the United States and Australia. The USD interest rate is 7% per annum and the AUD rate is 9% per annum. The current value of the AUD is 0.62 USD. Under the terms of a swap agreement, a financial institution pays 8% per annum in AUD and receives 4% per annum in USD. The principals in the two currencies are $12 million USD and 20 million AUD. Payments are exchanged every year, with one exchange having just taken place. The swap will last two more years. What is the value of the swap to the financial institution? Assume all interest rates are continuously compounded.

7.26. The five-year swap rate when cash flows are exchanged semiannually is 4%. A company wants a swap where it receives payments at 4.2% per annum on a principal of $10 million. The OIS zero curve is flat at 3.6%. How much should a derivatives dealer charge the company. All rates are expressed with semiannual compounding. (Ignore bid–offer spreads.)

CHAPTER 8

Securitization and the Credit Crisis of 2007

Derivatives such as forwards, futures, swaps, and options are concerned with transferring risk from one entity in the economy to another. The first seven chapters of this book have focused on forwards, futures, and swaps. Before moving on to discuss options, we consider another important way of transferring risk in the economy: securitization.

Securitization is of particular interest because of its role in the credit crisis (sometimes referred to as the "credit crunch") that started in 2007. The crisis had its origins in financial products created from mortgages in the United States, but rapidly spread from the United States to other countries and from financial markets to the real economy. Some financial institutions failed; others had to be rescued by national governments. There can be no question that the first decade of the twenty-first century was disastrous for the financial sector.

In this chapter, we examine the nature of securitization and its role in the crisis. In the course of the chapter, we will learn about the U.S. mortgage market, asset-backed securities, collateralized debt obligations, waterfalls, and the importance of incentives in financial markets.

8.1 SECURITIZATION

Traditionally, banks have funded their loans primarily from deposits. In the 1960s, U.S. banks found that they could not keep pace with the demand for residential mortgages with this type of funding. This led to the development of the mortgage-backed security (MBS) market. Portfolios of mortgages were created and the cash flows (interest and principal payments) generated by the portfolios were packaged as securities and sold to investors. The U.S. government created the Government National Mortgage Association (GNMA, also known as Ginnie Mae) in 1968. This organization guaranteed (for a fee) interest and principal payments on qualifying mortgages and created the securities that were sold to investors.

Thus, although banks originated the mortgages, they did not keep them on their balance sheets. Securitization allowed them to increase their lending faster than their deposits were growing. GNMA's guarantee protected MBS investors against defaults by borrowers.[1]

In the 1980s, the securitization techniques developed for the mortgage market were applied to asset classes such as automobile loans and credit card receivables in the United States. Securitization also become popular in other parts of the world. As the securitization market developed, investors became comfortable with situations where they did not have a guarantee against defaults by borrowers.

ABSs

A securitization arrangement of the type used during the 2000 to 2007 period is shown in Figure 8.1. This is known as an *asset-backed security* or ABS. A portfolio of income-producing assets such as loans is sold by the originating banks to a special purpose vehicle (SPV) and the cash flows from the assets are then allocated to tranches. Figure 8.1 is simpler than the structures that were typically created because it has only three tranches (in practice, many more tranches were used). These are the senior tranche, the mezzanine tranche, and the equity tranche. The portfolio has a principal of $100 million. This is divided as follows: $80 million to the senior tranche, $15 million to the mezzanine tranche, and $5 million to the equity tranche. The senior tranche has a yield of LIBOR plus 60 basis points, the mezzanine tranche has a yield of LIBOR plus 250 basis points, and the equity tranche has a yield of LIBOR plus 2,000 basis points.

It sounds as though the equity tranche has the best deal, but this is not necessarily the

Figure 8.1 An asset-backed security (simplified); bp = basis points (1 bp = 0.01%).

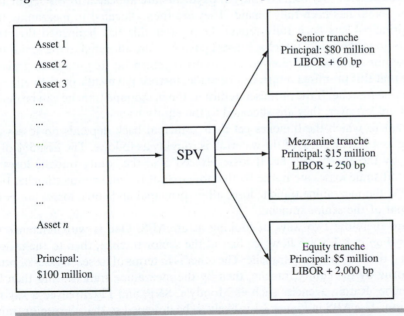

---

[1] However, MBS investors did face uncertainty about mortgage prepayments. Prepayments tend to be greatest when interest rates are low and the reinvestment opportunities open to investors are not particularly attractive. In the early days of MBSs, many MBS investors realized lower returns than they expected because they did not take this into account.

Figure 8.2   The waterfall in an asset-backed security.

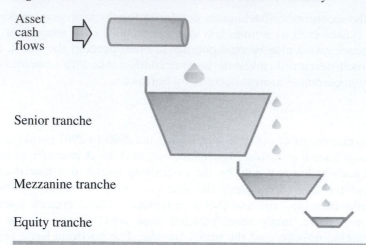

case. The payments of interest and principal are not guaranteed. The yield (like the yield on a bond) is the return that will be realized if there are no defaults affecting the tranche. The equity tranche is more likely to lose part of its principal, and less likely to receive the promised interest payments on its outstanding principal, than the other tranches. Cash flows are allocated to tranches by specifying what is known as a waterfall. The general way a waterfall works is illustrated in Figure 8.2. A separate waterfall is applied to principal and interest payments. Principal payments are allocated to the senior tranche until its principal has been fully repaid. They are then allocated to mezzanine tranche until its principal has been fully repaid. Only after this has happened do principal repayments go to the equity tranche. Interest payments are allocated to the senior tranche until the senior tranche has received its promised return on its outstanding principal. Assuming that this promised return can be made, interest payments are then allocated to the mezzanine tranche. If the promised return to the mezzanine tranche can be made and cash flows are left over, they are allocated to the equity tranche.

The extent to which the tranches get their principal back depends on losses on the underlying assets. The effect of the waterfall is roughly as follows. The first 5% of losses are borne by the equity tranche. If losses exceed 5%, the equity tranche loses all its principal and some losses are borne by the principal of the mezzanine tranche. If losses exceed 20%, the mezzanine tranche loses all its principal and some losses are borne by the principal of the senior tranche.

There are therefore two ways of looking at an ABS. One is with reference to the waterfall in Figure 8.2. Cash flows go first to the senior tranche, then to the mezzanine tranche, and then to the equity tranche. The other is in terms of losses. Losses of principal are first borne by the equity tranche, then by the mezzanine tranche, and then by the senior tranche. Rating agencies such as Moody's, S&P, and Fitch played a key role in securitization. The ABS in Figure 8.1 is likely to be designed so that the senior tranche is given the highest possible rating, AAA. The mezzanine tranche is typically rated BBB (well below AAA, but still investment grade). The equity tranche is typically unrated.

The description of ABSs that we have given so far is somewhat simplified. Typically, more than three tranches with a wide range of ratings were created. In the waterfall rules, as we have described them, the allocation of cash flows to tranches is sequential in that they always flow first to the most senior tranche, then to the next most senior tranche, and so on. In practice, the rules are somewhat more complicated than this and are described in a legal document that is several hundred pages long. Another complication is that there was often some overcollateralization where the total principal of the tranches was less than the total principal of the underlying assets. Also, the weighted average return promised to the tranches was less than the weighted average return payable on the assets.[2]

ABS CDOs

Finding investors to buy the senior AAA-rated tranches of ABSs was usually not difficult, because the tranches promised returns that were very attractive when compared with the return on AAA-rated bonds. Equity tranches were typically retained by the originator of the assets or sold to a hedge fund.

Finding investors for mezzanine tranches was more difficult. This led to the creation of ABSs of ABSs. The way this was done is shown in Figure 8.3. Many different mezzanine tranches, created in the way indicated in Figure 8.1, are put in a portfolio and the risks associated with the cash flows from the portfolio are tranched out in the same way as the risks associated with cash flows from the assets are tranched out in Figure 8.1. The resulting structure is known as an *ABS CDO* or *Mezz ABS CDO*. (CDO is short for collateralized debt obligation.) In the example in Figure 8.3, the senior tranche of the ABS CDO accounts for 65% of the principal of the ABS mezzanine tranches, the mezzanine tranche of the ABS CDO accounts for 25% of the principal, and the equity tranche accounts for the remaining 10% of the principal. The structure is designed so that the senior tranche of the ABS CDO is given the highest credit rating of AAA. This means that the total of the AAA-rated instruments created in the example that is considered here is about 90% (80% plus 65% of 15%) of the principal of the underlying portfolios. This seems high but, if the securitization were carried further with an ABS being created from tranches of ABS CDOs (and this did happen), the percentage would be pushed even higher.

In the example in Figure 8.3, the AAA-rated tranche of the ABS can expect to receive its promised return and get its principal back if losses on the underlying portfolio of

Figure 8.3   Creation of ABSs and an ABS CDO from portfolios of assets (simplified).

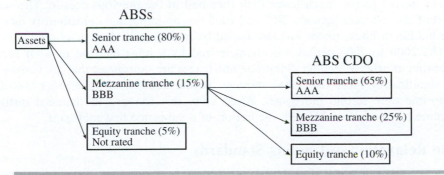

---

[2] Both this feature and overcollateralization had the potential to increase the profitability of the structure for its creator.

Table 8.1 Estimated losses to tranches of ABS CDO in Figure 8.3.

Losses on underlying assets	Losses to mezzanine tranche of ABS	Losses to equity tranche of ABS CDO	Losses to mezzanine tranche of ABS CDO	Losses to senior tranche of ABS CDO
10%	33.3%	100.0%	93.3%	0.0%
13%	53.3%	100.0%	100.0%	28.2%
17%	80.0%	100.0%	100.0%	69.2%
20%	100.0%	100.0%	100.0%	100.0%

assets is less than 20% because all losses of principal would then be absorbed by the more junior tranches. The AAA-rated tranche of the ABS CDO in Figure 8.3 is more risky. It will receive the promised return and get its principal back if losses on the underlying assets are 10.25% or less. This is because a loss of 10.25% means that mezzanine tranches of ABSs have to absorb losses equal to 5.25% of the ABS principal. As these tranches have a total principal equal to 15% of the ABS principal, they lose 5.25/15 or 35% of their principal. The equity and mezzanine tranches of the ABS CDO are then wiped out, but the senior tranche just manages to survive intact.

The senior tranche of the ABS CDO suffers losses if losses on the underlying portfolios are more than 10.25%. Consider, for example, the situation where losses are 17% on the underlying portfolios. Of the 17%, 5% is borne by the equity tranche of the ABS and 12% by the mezzanine tranche of the ABS. Losses on the mezzanine tranches are therefore 12/15 or 80% of their principal. The first 35% is absorbed by the equity and mezzanine tranches of the ABS CDO. The senior tranche of the ABS CDO therefore loses 45/65 or 69.2% of its value. These and other results are summarized in Table 8.1. Our calculations assume that all ABS portfolios have the same default rate.

8.2 THE U.S. HOUSING MARKET

Figure 8.4 gives the S&P/Case–Shiller composite-10 index for house prices in the United States between January 1987 and March 2016. This tracks house prices for ten metropolitan areas of the United States. It shows that, in about the year 2000, house prices started to rise much faster than they had in the previous decade. The very low level of interest rates between 2002 and 2005 was an important contributory factor, but the bubble in house prices was also fueled by mortgage-lending practices.

The 2000 to 2006 period was characterized by a huge increase in what is termed subprime mortgage lending. Subprime mortgages are mortgages that are considered to be significantly more risky than average. Before 2000, most mortgages classified as subprime were second mortgages. After 2000, this changed as financial institutions became more comfortable with the notion of a subprime first mortgage.

The Relaxation of Lending Standards

The relaxation of lending standards and the growth of subprime mortgages made house purchase possible for many families that had previously been considered to be not sufficiently creditworthy to qualify for a mortgage. These families increased the demand

Figure 8.4   The S&P/Case–Shiller Composite-10 index of U.S. real estate prices, 1987–2016.

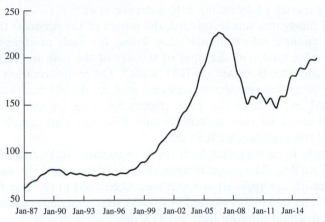

for real estate and prices rose. To mortgage brokers and mortgage lenders, it was attractive to make more loans, particularly when higher house prices resulted. More lending meant bigger profits. Higher house prices meant that the lending was well covered by the underlying collateral. If the borrower defaulted, it was less likely that the resulting foreclosure would lead to a loss.

Mortgage brokers and mortgage lenders naturally wanted to keep increasing their profits. Their problem was that, as house prices rose, it was more difficult for first-time buyers to afford a house. In order to continue to attract new entrants to the housing market, they had to find ways to relax their lending standards even more—and this is exactly what they did. The amount lent as a percentage of the house price increased. Adjustable-rate mortgages (ARMS) were developed where there was a low "teaser" rate of interest that would last for two or three years and be followed by a rate that was much higher.[3] A typical teaser rate was about 6% and the interest rate after the end of the teaser rate period was typically six-month LIBOR plus 6%.[4] However, teaser rates as low as 1% or 2% have been reported. Lenders also became more cavalier in the way they reviewed mortgage applications. Indeed, the applicant's income and other information reported on the application form were frequently not checked.

Subprime Mortgage Securitization

Subprime mortgages were frequently securitized in the way indicated in Figures 8.1 to 8.3. The investors in tranches created from subprime mortgages usually had no guarantees that interest and principal would be paid. Securitization played a part in the

---

[3] If real estate prices increased, lenders expected the borrowers to prepay and take out a new mortgage at the end of the teaser rate period. However, prepayment penalties, often zero on prime mortgages, were quite high on subprime mortgages.

[4] A "2/28" ARM, for example, is an ARM where the rate is fixed for two years and then floats for the remaining 28 years.

crisis. The behavior of mortgage originators was influenced by their knowledge that mortgages would be securitized.[5] When considering new mortgage applications, the question was not "Is this a credit risk we want to assume?" Instead it was "Is this a mortgage we can make money on by selling it to someone else?"

When a portfolio of mortgages was securitized, the buyers of the products that were created felt they had enough information if they knew, for each mortgage in the portfolio, the loan-to-value ratio (i.e., the ratio of the size of the loan to the assessed value of the house) and the borrower's FICO score.[6] Other information on the mortgage application forms was considered irrelevant and, as already mentioned, was often not even checked by lenders. The most important thing for the lender was whether the mortgage could be sold to others—and this depended largely on the loan-to-value ratio and the applicant's FICO score.

It is interesting to note in passing that both the loan-to-value ratio and the FICO score were of doubtful quality. The property assessors who determined the value of a house at the time of a mortgage application sometimes succumbed to pressure from the lenders to come up with high values. Potential borrowers were sometimes counseled to take certain actions that would improve their FICO scores.[7]

Why was the government not regulating the behavior of mortgage lenders? The answer is that the U.S. government had since the 1990s been trying to expand home ownership and had been applying pressure to mortgage lenders to increase loans to low- and moderate-income people. Some state legislators, such as those in Ohio and Georgia, were concerned about what was going on and wanted to curtail predatory lending.[8] However, the courts decided that national standards should prevail.

A number of terms have been used to describe mortgage lending during the period leading up to the credit crunch. One is "liar loans" because individuals applying for a mortgage, knowing that no checks would be carried out, sometimes chose to lie on the application form. Another term used to describe some borrowers is "NINJA" (no income, no job, no assets).

The Bubble Bursts

All bubbles burst eventually and this one was no exception. In 2007, many mortgage holders found that they could no longer afford their mortgages when the teaser rates ended. This led to foreclosures and large numbers of houses coming on the market, which in turn led to a decline in house prices. Other mortgage holders, who had borrowed 100%, or close to 100%, of the cost of a house found that they had negative equity.

One of the features of the U.S. housing market is that mortgages are nonrecourse in many states. This means that, when there is a default, the lender is able to take possession of the house, but other assets of the borrower are off-limits. Consequently, the borrower has a free American-style put option. He or she can at any time sell the

---

[5] See B. J. Keys, T. Mukherjee, A. Seru, and V. Vig, "Did Securitization Lead to Lax Screening? Evidence from Subprime Loans," *Quarterly Journal of Economics*, 125, 1 (February 2010): 307–62

[6] FICO is a credit score developed by the Fair Isaac Corporation and is widely used in the United States. It ranges from 300 to 850.

[7] One such action might be to make regular payments on a new credit card for a few months.

[8] Predatory lending describes the situation where a lender deceptively convinces borrowers to agree to unfair and abusive loan terms.

house to the lender for the principal outstanding on the mortgage. This feature encouraged speculative activity and was partly responsible for the bubble. Market participants realized belatedly how costly and destabilizing the put option could be. If the borrower had negative equity, the optimal decision was to exchange the house for the outstanding principal on the mortgage. The house was then sold by the lender, adding to the downward pressure on house prices.

It would be a mistake to assume that all mortgage defaulters were in the same position. Some were unable to meet mortgage payments and suffered greatly when they had to give up their homes. But many of the defaulters were speculators who bought multiple homes as rental properties and chose to exercise their put options. It was their tenants who suffered. There are also reports that some house owners (who were not speculators) were quite creative in extracting value from their put options. After handing the keys to their houses to the lender, they turned around and bought (sometimes at a bargain price) other houses that were in foreclosure. Imagine two people owning identical houses next to each other. Both have mortgages of $250,000. Both houses are worth $200,000 and in foreclosure can be expected to sell for $170,000. What is the owners' optimal strategy? The answer is that each person should exercise the put option and buy the neighbor's house.

The United States was not alone in having declining real estate prices. Prices declined in many other countries as well. Real estate prices in the United Kingdom were particularly badly affected. As Figure 8.4 indicates, average house prices in the United States did recover after 2012.

The Losses

As foreclosures increased, the losses on mortgages also increased. It might be thought that a 35% reduction in house prices would lead to at most a 35% loss of principal on defaulting mortgages. In fact, the losses were far greater than that. Houses in foreclosure were often in poor condition and sold for a small fraction of their value prior to the credit crisis. In 2008 and 2009, losses as high 75% of the mortgage principal were reported for mortgages on houses in foreclosure in some cases.

Investors in tranches that were formed from the mortgages incurred big losses. The value of the ABS tranches created from subprime mortgages was monitored by a series of indices known as ABX. These indices indicated that the tranches originally rated BBB had lost about 80% of their value by the end of 2007 and about 97% of their value by mid-2009. The value of the ABS CDO tranches created from BBB tranches was monitored by a series of indices known as TABX. These indices indicated that the tranches originally rated AAA lost about 80% of their value by the end of 2007 and were essentially worthless by mid-2009.

Financial institutions such as UBS, Merrill Lynch, and Citigroup had big positions in some of the tranches and incurred huge losses, as did the insurance giant AIG, which provided protection against losses on ABS CDO tranches that had originally been rated AAA. Many financial institutions had to be rescued with government funds. There have been few worse years in financial history than 2008. Bear Stearns was taken over by JP Morgan Chase; Merrill Lynch was taken over by Bank of America; Goldman Sachs and Morgan Stanley, which had formerly been investment banks, became bank holding companies with both commercial and investment banking interests; and Lehman Brothers was allowed to fail (see Business Snapshot 1.1).

The Credit Crisis

The losses on securities backed by residential mortgages led to a severe credit crisis. In 2006, banks were reasonably well capitalized, loans were relatively easy to obtain, and credit spreads (the excess of the interest rate on a loan over the risk-free interest rate) were low. By 2008, the situation was totally different. The capital of banks had been badly eroded by their losses. They had become much more risk-averse and were reluctant to lend. Creditworthy individuals and corporations found borrowing difficult. Credit spreads had increased dramatically. The world experienced its worst recession in several generations. As discussed in Section 4.3, the three-month LIBOR–OIS spread briefly reached 364 basis points in October 2008, indicating an extreme reluctance of banks to lend to each other for longer periods than overnight. Another measure of the stress in financial markets is the TED spread. This is the excess of the three-month Eurodollar deposit rate over the three-month Treasury interest. In normal market conditions, it is 30 to 50 basis points. It reached over 450 basis points in October 2008.

8.3   WHAT WENT WRONG?

"Irrational exuberance" is a phrase coined by Alan Greenspan, Chairman of the Federal Reserve Board, to describe the behavior of investors during the bull market of the 1990s. It can also be applied to the period leading up the the credit crisis. Mortgage lenders, the investors in tranches of ABSs and ABS CDOs that were created from residential mortgages, and the companies that sold protection on the tranches assumed that the good times would last for ever. They thought that U.S. house prices would continue to increase. There might be declines in one or two areas, but the possibility of the widespread decline shown in Figure 8.4 was a scenario not considered by most people.

Many factors contributed to the crisis that started in 2007. Mortgage originators used lax lending standards. Products were developed to enable mortgage originators to profitably transfer credit risk to investors. Rating agencies moved from their traditional business of rating bonds, where they had a great deal of experience, to rating structured products, which were relatively new and for which there were relatively little historical data. The products bought by investors were complex and in many instances investors and rating agencies had inaccurate or incomplete information about the quality of the underlying assets. Investors in the structured products that were created thought they had found a money machine and chose to rely on rating agencies rather than forming their own opinions about the underlying risks. The return offered by the products rated AAA was high compared with the returns on bonds rated AAA.

Structured products such as those in Figures 8.1 and 8.3 are highly dependent on the default correlation between the underlying assets. Default correlation measures the tendency for different borrowers to default at about the same time. If the default correlation between the underlying assets in Figure 8.1 is low, the AAA-rated tranches are very unlikely to experience losses. As this default correlation increases, they become more vulnerable. The tranches of ABS CDOs in Figure 8.3 are even more heavily dependent on default correlation.

If mortgages exhibit moderate default correlation (as they do in normal times), there is very little chance of a high overall default rate and the AAA-rated tranches of both ABSs and ABS CDOs that are created from mortgages are fairly safe. However, as many investors found to their cost, default correlations tend to increase in stressed market conditions. This makes very high default rates possible.

There was a tendency to assume that a tranche with a particular rating could be equated to a bond with the that rating. The rating agencies published the criteria they used for rating tranches. S&P and Fitch rated a tranche so as to ensure that the probability of the tranche experiencing a loss was the same as the probability of a similarly rated bond experiencing a loss. Moody's rated a tranche so that the expected loss from the tranche was the the same as the expected loss from a similarly rated bond.[9] The procedures used by rating agencies were therefore designed to ensure that one aspect of the loss distributions of tranches and bonds were matched. However, other aspects of the distributions were liable to be quite different.

The differences between tranches and bonds were accentuated by the fact tranches were often quite thin. The AAA tranches often accounted for about 80% of the principal as in Figure 8.1, but it was not unusual for there to be 15 to 20 other tranches. Each of these tranches would be 1% or 2% wide. Such thin tranches are likely to either incur no losses or be totally wiped out. The chance of investors recovering part of their principal (as bondholders usually do) is small. Consider, for example, a BBB tranche that is responsible for losses in the range 5% to 6%, If losses on the underlying portfolio are less than 5%, the tranche is safe. If losses are greater than 6%, the tranche is wiped out. Only in the case where losses are between 5% and 6% is a partial recovery made by investors.

The difference between a thin BBB-rated tranche and a BBB-rated bond was over-looked by many investors. The difference makes the tranches of ABS CDOs created from the BBB-rated tranches of ABSs much riskier than tranches created in a similar way from BBB bonds. Losses on a portfolio of BBB bonds can reasonably be assumed to be unlikely to exceed 25% in even the most severe market conditions. Table 8.1 shows that 100% losses on a portfolio of BBB tranches can occur relatively easily—and this is even more true when the tranches are only 1% or 2% wide.

Regulatory Arbitrage

Many of the mortgages were originated by banks and it was banks that were the main investors in the tranches that were created from the mortgages. Why would banks choose to securitize mortgages and then buy the securitized products that were created? The answer concerns what is termed *regulatory arbitrage*. The regulatory capital banks were required to keep for the tranches created from a portfolio of mortgages was much less than the regulatory capital that would be required for the mortgages themselves.

Incentives

One of the lessons from the crisis is the importance of incentives. Economists use the term "agency costs" to describe the situation where incentives are such that the interests of two parties in a business relationship are not perfectly aligned. The process by which

---

[9] For a discussion of the criteria used by rating agencies and the reasonableness of the ratings given the criteria used, see J.C. Hull and A. White, "Ratings Arbitrage and Structured Products," *Journal of Derivatives*, 20, 1 (Fall 2012): 80–86, and "The Risk of Tranches Created from Mortgages," *Financial Analysts Journal*, 66, 5 (September/October 2010): 54–67.

mortgages were originated, securitized, and sold to investors was unfortunately riddled with agency costs.

The incentive of the originators of mortgages was to make loans that would be acceptable to the creators of the ABS and ABS CDO tranches. The incentive of the individuals who valued the houses on which the mortgages were written was to please the lender by providing as high a valuation as possible so that the loan-to-value ratio was as low as possible. (Pleasing the lender was likely to lead to more business from that lender.) The main concern of the creators of tranches was how the tranches would be rated. They wanted the volume of AAA-rated tranches that they created to be as high as possible and found ways of using the published criteria of rating agencies to achieve this. The rating agencies were paid by the issuers of the securities they rated and about half their income came from structured products.

Another source of agency costs concerns the incentives of the employees of financial institutions. Employee compensation falls into three categories: regular salary, the end-of-year bonus, and stock or stock options. Many employees at all levels of seniority in financial institutions, particularly traders, receive much of their compensation in the form of end-of-year bonuses. This form of compensation is focused on short-term performance. If an employee generates huge profits one year and is responsible for severe losses the next, the employee will often receive a big bonus the first year and will not have to return it the following year. (The employee might lose his or her job as a result of the second year losses, but even that is not a disaster. Financial institutions seem to be surprisingly willing to recruit individuals with losses on their résumés.)

Imagine you are an employee of a financial institution in 2006 responsible for investing in ABS CDOs created from mortgages. Almost certainly you would have recognized that there was a bubble in the U.S. housing market and would expect that bubble to burst sooner or later. However, it is possible that you would decide to continue with your ABS CDO investments. If the bubble did not burst until after the end of 2006, you would still get a nice bonus at the end of 2006.

8.4   THE AFTERMATH

Prior to the crisis, over-the-counter derivatives markets were largely unregulated. This has changed. As mentioned in earlier chapters, there is now a requirement that most standardized over-the-counter derivatives be cleared through central counterparties (CCPs). This means that they are treated similarly to derivatives such as futures that trade on exchanges. Banks are usually members of one or more CCPs. When trading standardized derivatives, they are required to post initial margin and variation margin with the CCP and are also required to contribute to a default fund. For transactions between financial institutions that continue to be cleared bilaterally, collateral arrangements are now regulated rather than chosen by the parties involved.

The bonuses paid by banks have come under more scrutiny and in some jurisdictions there are limits on the size of the bonuses that can be paid. The way bonuses are paid is changing. Before the crisis it was common for a trader's bonus for a year to be paid in full at the end of the year with no possibility of the bonus having to be returned. It is now more common for this bonus to be spread over several years so that part of the bonus can be clawed back if results are not as good as expected.

Business Snapshot 8.1   The Basel Committee

As the activities of banks became more global in the 1980s, it became necessary for regulators in different countries to work together to determine an international regulatory framework. As a result the Basel Committee on Banking Supervision was formed. In 1988, it published a set of rules for the capital banks were required to keep for credit risk. These capital requirements have become known as Basel I. They were modified to accommodate the netting of transactions in 1995. In 1996 a new capital requirement for market risk was published. This capital requirement was implemented in 1998. In 1999 significant changes were proposed for the calculation of the capital requirements for credit risk and a capital requirement for operational risk was introduced. These rules are referred to as Basel II. Basel II is considerably more complicated than Basel I and its implementation was delayed until 2007 (later in some countries). During the credit crisis and afterwards the Basel committee introduced new regulatory requirements known as Basel II.5, which increased capital for market risk. After that came Basel III, which tightened capital requirements and introduced liquidity requirements.

The Dodd–Frank Act in the United States and similar legislation in the United Kingdom and European Union provide for more oversight of financial institutions and include much new legislation affecting financial institutions. For example, in the United States proprietary trading and other similar activities of deposit-taking institutions are being restricted. (This is known as the "Volcker rule" because it was proposed by former Federal Reserve chairman Paul Volcker.) An independent committee in the United Kingdom chaired by Sir John Vickers has proposed that the retail operations of banks be ring-fenced. The Liikanen committee in the European Union similarly recommends that proprietary trading and other high-risk activities be separated from other banking activities.

Banks throughout the world are regulated by the Basel Committee on Banking Supervision.[10] Prior to the crisis, the committee implemented regulations known as Basel I and Basel II. These are summarized in Business Snapshot 8.1. Following the crisis, it has implemented what is known as "Basel II.5." This increases the capital requirements for market risk. Basel III was published in 2010 is being implemented over a period lasting until 2019. It increases the amount of capital and quality of capital that banks are required to keep. It also requires banks to satisfy certain liquidity requirements. As discussed in Business Snapshot 4.2, one cause of problems during the crisis was the tendency of banks to place too much reliance on the use of short-term liabilities for long-term funding needs. The liquidity requirements are designed to make it more difficult for them to do this.

SUMMARY

Securitization is a process used by banks to create securities from loans and other income-producing assets. The securities are sold to investors. This removes the loans

---

[10] For more details on the work of the Basel Committee and bank regulatory requirements, see J. C. Hull, *Risk Management and Financial Institutions*, 4th edition, Wiley, 2015.

from the banks' balance sheets and enables the banks to expand their lending faster than would otherwise be possible. The first loans to be securitized were mortgages in the United States in the 1960s and 1970s. Investors who bought the mortgage-backed securities were not exposed to the risk of borrowers defaulting because the loans were backed by the Government National Mortgage Association. Later automobile loans, corporate loans, credit card receivables, and subprime mortgages were securitized. In many cases, investors in the securities created from these instruments did not have a guarantee against defaults.

Securitization played a part in the credit crisis that started in 2007. Tranches were created from subprime mortgages and new tranches were then created from these tranches. The origins of the crisis can be found in the U.S. housing market. The U.S. government was keen to encourage home ownership. Interest rates were low. Mortgage brokers and mortgage lenders found it attractive to do more business by relaxing their lending standards. Securitization meant that the investors bearing the credit risk were not usually the same as the original lenders. Rating agencies gave AAA ratings to the senior tranches that were created. There was no shortage of buyers for these AAA-rated tranches because their yields were higher than the yields on other AAA-rated securities. Banks thought the "good times" would continue and, because compensation plans focused their attention on short-term profits, chose to ignore the housing bubble and its potential impact on some very complicated products they were trading.

House prices rose as both first-time buyers and speculators entered the market. Some mortgages had included a low "teaser rate" for two or three years. After the teaser rate ended, there was a significant increase in the interest rate for some borrowers. Unable to meet the higher interest rate they had no choice but to default. This led to foreclosures and an increase in the supply of houses be sold. The price increases between 2000 and 2006 began to be reversed. Speculators and others who found that the amount owing on their mortgages was greater than the value of their houses (i.e., they had negative equity) defaulted. This accentuated the price decline.

Banks are paying a price for the crisis. New legislation and regulation will reduce their profitability. For example, capital requirements are being increased, liquidity regulations are being introduced, and OTC derivatives are being much more tightly regulated.

FURTHER READING

Gorton, G. "The Subprime Panic," *European Financial Management*, 15, 1 (January 2009): 10–46.

Hull, J. C. "The Financial Crisis of 2007: Another Case of Irrational Exuberance," in: *The Finance Crisis and Rescue: What Went Wrong? Why? What Lessons Can be Learned.* University of Toronto Press, 2008.

Hull, J. C., and A. White. "Ratings Arbitrage and Structured Products," *Journal of Derivatives*, 20, 1 (Fall 2012): 80–86.

Keys, B. J., T. Mukherjee, A. Seru, and V. Vig. "Did Securitization Lead to Lax Screening? Evidence from Subprime Loans," *Quarterly Journal of Economics*, 125, 1 (2010): 307–62.

Krinsman, A. N. "Subprime Mortgage Meltdown: How Did It Happen and How Will It End," *Journal of Structured Finance*, 13, 2 (Summer 2007): 13–19.

Mian, A., and A. Sufi. "The Consequences of Mortgage Credit Expansion: Evidence from the U.S. Mortgage Default Crisis," *Quarterly Journal of Economics*, 124, 4 (November 2009): 1449–96.

Sorkin, A. R. *Too Big to Fail.* New York: Penguin, 2009.

Tett, G. *Fool's Gold: How the Bold Dream of a Small Tribe at JP Morgan Was Corrupted by Wall Street Greed and Unleashed a Catastrophe*. New York: Free Press, 2009

Zimmerman, T. "The Great Subprime Meltdown," *Journal of Structured Finance*, Fall 2007, 7–20.

Practice Questions (Answers in Solutions Manual)

8.1. What was the role of GNMA (Ginnie Mae) in the mortgage-backed securities market of the 1970s?

8.2. Explain what is meant by (a) an ABS and (b) an ABS CDO.

8.3. What is a mezzanine tranche?

8.4. What is the waterfall in a securitization?

8.5. What are the numbers in Table 8.1 for a loss rate of (a) 12% and (b) 15%?

8.6. What is a subprime mortgage?

8.7. Why do you think the increase in house prices during the 2000 to 2007 period is referred to as a bubble?

8.8. Why did mortgage lenders frequently not check on information provided by potential borrowers on mortgage application forms during the 2000 to 2007 period?

8.9. How were the risks in ABS CDOs misjudged by the market?

8.10. What is meant by the term "agency costs"? How did agency costs play a role in the credit crisis?

8.11. How is an ABS CDO created? What was the motivation to create ABS CDOs?

8.12. Explain the impact of an increase in default correlation on the risks of the senior tranche of an ABS. What is its impact on the risks of the equity tranche?

8.13. Explain why the AAA-rated tranche of an ABS CDO is more risky than the AAA-rated tranche of an ABS.

8.14. Explain why the end-of-year bonus is sometimes referred to as "short-term compensation."

8.15. Add rows in Table 8.1 corresponding to losses on the underlying assets of (a) 2%, (b) 6%, (c) 14%, and (d) 18%.

Further Questions

8.16. Suppose that the principal assigned to the senior, mezzanine, and equity tranches is 70%, 20%, and 10% for both the ABS and the ABS CDO in Figure 8.3. What difference does this make to Table 8.1?

8.17. "Resecuritization was a badly flawed idea. AAA tranches created from the mezzanine tranches of ABSs are bound to have a higher probability of default than the AAA-rated tranches of ABSs." Discuss this point of view.

8.18. Suppose that mezzanine tranches of the ABS CDOs, similar to those in Figure 8.3, are resecuritized to form what is referred to as a "CDO squared." As in the case of tranches created from ABSs in Figure 8.3, 65% of the principal is allocated to a AAA tranche, 25% to a BBB tranche, and 10% to the equity tranche. How high does the loss percentage have to be on the underlying assets for losses to be experienced by a AAA-rated tranche that is created in this way? (Assume that every portfolio of assets that is used to create ABSs experiences the same loss rate.)

8.19. Investigate what happens as the width of the mezzanine tranche of the ABS in Figure 8.3 is decreased with the reduction of mezzanine tranche principal being divided equally between the equity and senior tranches. In particular, what is the effect on Table 8.1?

8.20. Suppose that the structure in Figure 8.1 is created in 2000 and lasts 10 years. There are no defaults on the underlying assets until the end of the eighth year when 17% of the principal is lost because of defaults during the credit crisis. No principal is lost in the final two years. There are no repayments of principal until the end. Evaluate the relative performance of the tranches. Assume a constant LIBOR rate of 3%. Consider both interest and principal payments.

9

CHAPTER

XVAs

Before moving on to discuss how options and other more complex derivatives are valued, we consider various price adjustments that have become important in derivatives markets. These are the credit valuation adjustment (CVA), the debit (or debt) valuation adjustment (DVA), the funding valuation adjustment (FVA), the margin valuation adjustment (MVA), and the capital valuation adjustment (KVA). Collectively the adjustments are known as XVAs. Some of the adjustments have a stronger theoretical basis than others. As we shall see, financial economists have no problem with CVA and DVA, but have reservations about FVA, MVA, and KVA.

9.1 CVA AND DVA

Most of this book is concerned with determining the no-default value of derivatives, that is, the value assuming that neither of the two sides will default. CVA and DVA are adjustments to the no-default value reflecting the possibility of a default by one of the two sides. Here we provide an overview of them. More details on their calculation are in Chapter 24.

Suppose that a bank and a counterparty have entered into a portfolio of derivative transactions that are cleared bilaterally. The master agreement between the bank and the counterparty will almost certainly state that *netting* applies. This means that all outstanding derivatives between the two sides are considered as a single derivative in the event of a default. When one party declares bankruptcy, fails to post collateral as required, or fails to perform as promised in some other way, the other party will declare an event of default. This leads to an early termination of the outstanding derivatives between the bank and the counterparty a few days later and a *settlement amount* is calculated. The settlement amount reflects the value of the derivatives and is adjusted to allow for the fact that the nondefaulting party will incur costs equal to half the applicable bid–offer spreads when replacing the transactions in the portfolio.

Suppose that it is the bank's counterparty that defaults and neither side posts collateral. (Later we explain the impact of collateral.) If the early termination happens when the outstanding derivatives portfolio has a positive value to the bank and a negative value to the counterparty, the bank will be an unsecured creditor for the settlement amount and is likely to incur a loss because it will fail to receive it in full. In

199

the opposite situation, where the portfolio has a negative value to the bank and a positive value to the counterparty, the settlement amount is owed by the bank to the counterparty (or to the counterparty's liquidators) and will be paid in full so that there is no loss.

The credit valuation adjustment (CVA) is the bank's estimate of the present value of the expected cost to the bank of a counterparty default. Suppose that the life of the longest outstanding derivatives transaction between the bank and the counterparty is T years. To calculate CVA, the bank divides the next T years into a number of intervals. For each interval, it calculates:

1. The probability of an early termination during the interval arising from a counterparty default; and

2. The present value of the expected loss from the derivatives portfolio if there is an early termination at the midpoint of the interval.

Suppose that there are N intervals, q_i is the probability of default by the counterparty during the ith interval, and v_i is the present value of the expected loss if there is a default at the midpoint of the ith interval. CVA is calculated as:

$$\text{CVA} = \sum_{i=1}^{N} q_i v_i \tag{9.1}$$

This formula is deceptively simple but the procedure for implementing it is quite complicated and computationally very time consuming. It will be explained in Chapter 24.

Define f_{nd} as the no-default value of the derivatives portfolio to the bank. As explained earlier, this is the value of the portfolio assuming that neither side will default. When the possibility of a counterparty default is taken into account, the value of the portfolio to the bank becomes

$$f_{\text{nd}} - \text{CVA}$$

But this is not the end of the story. The bank itself might default. This is liable to lead to a loss to the counterparty and an equal and opposite gain to the bank. The debit (or debt) valuation adjustment (DVA) is the present value of the expected gain to the bank from the possibility that it might itself default. It is calculated similarly to CVA:

$$\text{DVA} = \sum_{i=1}^{N} q_i^* v_i^* \tag{9.2}$$

where q_i^* is the probability of a default by the bank during the ith interval and v_i^* is the present value of the bank's gain (and the counterparty's loss) if the bank defaults at the midpoint of the interval. Taking both CVA and DVA into account, the value of the portfolio to the bank is

$$f_{\text{nd}} - \text{CVA} + \text{DVA}$$

The idea that a bank will gain from its own default seems strange to many people. How can there be a gain from a default? One way of thinking about this is as follows. Derivatives are what are referred to as "zero-sum games." The gain to one side always equals the loss to the other side. If the bank's counterparty is worse off because of the possibility that the bank will default on the outstanding derivatives, the bank must be better off. The reason why the bank is better off is that, in circumstances where it defaults, it avoids having to honor its contracts when the no-default value of those contracts to the bank is negative.

Without DVA, it is liable to be difficult for derivatives transactions to be agreed to. Consider two market participants, X and Y, who are negotiating a bilaterally cleared interest rate swap where X will be paying a fixed rate of interest and receiving LIBOR with no collateral being posted. For the purposes of our example we assume that there are no other trades between these two parties.[1] The two sides agree that, if there is no default risk, the fixed rate should be 2.2%. We suppose that, when X takes Y's default risk into account, it determines it should pay 2.1% rather than 2.2%. (The 0.1% per annum reduction is compensation to X for possibility that Y might default.) But when Y takes X's default risk into account, it determines that it should receive 2.35% rather than 2.2%. (The extra 0.15% is compensation to Y for the possibility that X might default.) It is easy to see that the two sides are unlikely do a deal if each side considers only the possibility of the other side defaulting. But if each side calculates a DVA (recognizing that it might itself default), the two sides will have a better chance of doing a deal because they will value the expected cash flows from the swap similarly.

DVA has a counterintuitive effect. As the bank's creditworthiness declines, q_i^* in equation (9.2) increases and DVA increases. This makes the derivatives portfolio more valuable to the bank. As the bank's creditworthiness improves, q_i^* decreases and DVA decreases so that the portfolio is less valuable. Why should the bank gain from a worsening of its credit quality? The reason is that as the bank becomes more likely to default it is more likely that it will not have to honor its derivatives obligations.

Collateral

When the agreement between the two parties requires collateral to be posted, the situation is more complicated. A *credit support annex* (CSA) to the master agreement specifies how the required amount of collateral is calculated and what form the collateral can take. Interest is normally paid on cash collateral at close to the fed funds rate, or similar overnight rate. When the collateral takes the form of securities, a haircut is usually applied to the market value of the securities.

If a bank's counterparty defaults, the bank is entitled to keep any collateral that has been posted by the counterparty if it is less than any settlement amount it is owed. Similarly, if the bank defaults, the counterparty can use any collateral posted by the bank to cover any settlement amount it is owed. Any collateral in excess of the settlement amount must be returned.

Equations (9.1) and (9.2) are still correct when collateral is posted, but the calculation of v_i and v_i^* is more complicated. The calculation must take into account the collateral that would be provided by the bank or by the counterparty at the time of an early termination. Usually the calculation involves an assumption that the defaulting party will stop posting collateral, and will stop returning excess collateral, several days before the early termination. The number of days assumed here is known as the *cure period* or *margin period of risk*. For example, if the cure period is 10 days, the collateral at the time of the early termination would be assumed to be that specified in the CSA 10 days earlier.

---

[1] When there are other trades and a master agreement covering them is in place, each side should assess expected incremental losses arising from the new trade on the portfolio of trades between the two sides.

9.2   FVA AND MVA

The funding valuation adjustment (FVA) and margin valuation adjustment (MVA) are adjustments to the value of a derivatives portfolio for the cost of funding derivative positions. To illustrate how they might arise, suppose that a derivatives dealer, Bank A, is in the situation illustrated in Figure 9.1. It has entered into a five-year interest rate swap with a corporate end user and has hedged its risk by entering into an exactly offsetting swap with another dealer, Bank B. It appears that Bank A has locked in a profit of 0.1% per year because it receives 3% from Bank B and pays 2.9% to the end user. We suppose that the transaction between Bank A and Bank B is cleared through a CCP with both sides posting initial margin and variation margin. (As explained in earlier chapters, this is required under post-crisis regulations for a standard swap such as this.)

If the transaction with the end user in Figure 9.1 were cleared through the same CCP as the transaction between the banks, Bank A's situation is straightforward. The CCP will net off the two transactions so that they do not lead to any incremental initial margin requirement for Bank A. Indeed, because the transactions always give a net positive value to the bank, margin requirements should be slightly less than they would be without the two transactions.

But let us assume that the transaction between Bank A and the end user is cleared bilaterally with no collateral being required while, as already mentioned, the transaction between Bank A and Bank B is cleared through a CCP. The transactions do then have some funding implications. First, the swap with Bank B is liable to lead the CCP requiring additional initial margin from Bank A during the life of the transaction. If we assume that the cost of funding initial margin is greater than the interest paid by the CCP on initial margin there is a cost to Bank A in funding the incremental initial margin attributable to the transaction. This is referred to as a margin valuation adjustment (MVA) and reduces the value to the bank of its transaction with the end user.[2]

The CCP's variation margin can also lead to funding requirements. Suppose that the transaction with Bank B has a negative value to Bank A so that the transaction with the end user has a positive value to Bank A. Bank A will have funds tied up in the variation margin it has posted with the CCP.[3] It will not receive any collateral to offset this initial margin from the end user. This gives rise to a funding need because Bank A has to increase its funding from external sources. In the opposite situation, where the transaction with Bank B has a positive value and the transaction with the end user has a negative value, it receives variation margin from the CCP and does not have to provide any collateral or margin to the end user. This gives rise to a source of funding.

We continue to assume that the cost of funding margin is greater than the interest paid on it. There is a cost in the first case just considered (Bank A has to increase its funding from external sources) and a benefit in the second case (Bank A can reduce its

---

[2] The initial margin required by the CCP does not necessarily increase as a result of the transaction. In determining initial margin the CCP will look at all the transactions Bank A has that are cleared with the CCP. It can be the case that the swap with Bank B partially offsets other transactions that Bank A is clearing through the CCP and the initial margin decreases as a result. The incremental MVA for the transaction is then negative.

[3] Remember that, although a CCP is in many ways similar to a futures clearing house, swaps are different from futures in that they are not settled daily. Therefore, when Bank A pays variation margin, it receives interest on it and when it receives variation margin it must pay interest on it. In the case of futures, the daily settlement means that the variation margin belongs to the recipient and there is no interest paid on it.

Figure 9.1 Swaps entered into by Bank A. The transaction with Bank B is cleared through a CCP. The transaction with the end user is cleared bilaterally.

funding from external sources). FVA is an adjustment to the value of derivatives that reflects these costs and benefits. The present value of the expected future funding cost is referred to as the funding cost adjustment (FCA) and the present value of the expected future funding benefit is referred to as the funding benefit adjustment (FBA). The funding value adjustment, FVA, reduces the value of derivatives by the excess of FCA over FBA. Whether there is a positive or negative adjustment to the value of the swaps in Figure 9.1 depends on whether the swap with Bank B is more likely to have a positive or negative value as time passes. This depends on the shape of the term structure of interest rates, as discussed in Section 7.6.

The situation in Figure 9.1 is not the only way FVA and MVA can arise. An FVA potentially arises whenever a bank enters into an uncollateralized derivative transaction with a counterparty. When the uncollateralized derivative has a positive value, there is a funding cost. When it has a negative value, there is a funding benefit.[4] For example, if the bank buys an uncollateralized option from a counterparty, the option has a positive value and there is a funding cost equal to the excess of the assumed cost of funding over the risk-free rate assumed in the pricing of the option. If the bank sells an uncollateralized option to the counterparty, the option has a negative value and there is a funding benefit. MVA can arise whenever a transaction gives rise to incremental initial margin requirements. As explained in earlier chapters, rules are being implemented requiring initial margin for bilaterally cleared transactions between financial institutions as well as for those cleared through CCPs.[5]

To calculate the MVA or FVA it is necessary to answer the question: "What is the cost of funding the margin in a situation such as Figure 9.1?" This is where there is often a disagreement between theory and practice. Many banks argue that the cost of funding margin is equal to their average debt funding cost. Suppose the margin is provided in U.S. dollars.[6] If the interest received by a bank on U.S. dollar margin is the federal funds rate minus 20 basis points and a bank's average funding cost is the federal funds rate plus 100 basis points, FVA and MVA would be calculated by these banks on the assumption of a funding cost of 120 basis points per year.

Financial economics argues that the way an investment is funded should not affect the required return on the investment. The required return should reflect the riskiness of

---

[4] To see how this works in Figure 9.1, note that the swap with the end user is uncollateralized. When it has a positive value (and the offsetting deal with the CCP has a negative value), there is a funding cost. When it has a negative value (and the offsetting deal with the CCP has a positive value), there is a funding benefit.

[5] Also default fund contributions to CCPs can be considered to be akin to initial margin from a funding perspective.

[6] In practice a bank can choose which currency to post margin in and can in some circumstances post securities such as Treasury bills instead of cash. (Securities are typically subject to a haircut in determining their value for collateral purposes.) Choosing what is best can involve complex calculations.

the investment. An investment in initial margin or variation margin usually has very low risk.[7] As such, the bank should be comfortable with a return that is close to the risk-free rate. If the return requirement on margin in our example is assumed to be the fed funds rate plus 10 basis points and the interest paid on margin is the federal funds rate minus 20 basis points, then the funding cost (or benefit) is 30 basis points, not the 120 basis points calculated earlier.

To explain why the average funding cost of the fed funds rate plus 100 basis points should not be used, Hull and White (2012) use two arguments.[8] The first argument is that there is a gain to the bank from the 100 basis points credit spread because it might default of the debt it issues. This is similar to the DVA discussed earlier and is referred to as DVA2 by Hull and White. Because of this benefit, the bank does not have to pass the funding cost on to the derivatives desk.[9]

For the second argument, suppose that the risk-free rate is 2% and the bank's funding cost is 3.5%. If a project comes along that is risk-free and provides a return of 3%, should the bank undertake it? The answer is that the project should be undertaken. The appropriate discount rate for the project's cash flows is 2% and the project has a positive present value when this discount rate is used. It is not correct to argue that the bank is funding itself at 3.5% and should therefore only undertake projects earning more than 3.5%.

Consider what happens as the bank enters into projects that are risk-free (or nearly risk-free). Its funding costs should come down in such a way that the incremental costs of funding a risk-free project should be 2%, not 3.5%. To take an extreme example, suppose that the bank we are considering were to double in size by undertaking entirely risk-free projects. The bank's funding cost should change to 2.75% (an average of 3.5% for the old projects and 2% for the new projects). If the average funding cost of 3.5% is used as the required return for all projects, low-risk projects will tend to seem unattractive and high-risk projects will tend to seem attractive.

Andersen *et al.* (2016) also question the use of average funding costs in calculating FVA. They consider the situation where debtholders do not anticipate the investment in margin that will be made by the bank and are pleasantly surprised because it leads to the bank becoming less risky.[10] There is then a transfer of wealth from the shareholders to the debtholders.

The XVA debate has an interesting analogy. In a first corporate finance course, students learn how to calculate a weighted average cost of capital (WACC) for a (nonfinancial) corporation and how the discount rate used for the expected cash flows of a capital investment project should be calculated. They learn that the discount rate should depend on the risk of the project, not how it is financed. For projects that are more risky than average, the discount rate should be higher than the WACC. For projects that are less risky than average, the discount rate should be lower than the WACC.

---

[7] For instance, in the example in Figure 9.1 there might be a very small chance of margin being lost because of a failure of the CCP.

[8] See J. C. Hull and A. White, "The FVA Debate," *Risk*, 25th anniversary edition (July 2012): 83–85.

[9] However, if part of the 100 basis points is for liquidity or other things that are not reflective of the default risk of the bank, this is a deadweight cost of doing business and could be a valid source of FVA.

[10] See L. B. G. Andersen, D. Duffie, and Y. Song, "Funding Value Adjustments," Working Paper, ssrn 2746010.

But many companies use a single WACC for all projects. This tends to make risky projects more attractive than they should be and safe projects less attractive than they should be. With all else equal, the use of a single discount rate leads to companies becoming more risky over time.

The XVA analogy is that many of a bank's investments that we are concerned with when considering FVA and MVA are lower-than-average-risk investments. An investment in initial margin or variation margin is usually low risk compared with other things the bank does. As such, its marginal effect is to lower the average cost of the bank's funding.

The difference between the views of some financial engineers and financial economists on FVA and MVA is that financial economists work with marginal funding costs while the financial engineers work with average costs. The essence of the debate can be summarized by the following imaginary dialogue:

Financial Economist:	The cost you should use for funding a project should reflect the risk of the project. By using average funding costs you are assuming that all the bank's projects are equally risky.
Financial Engineer:	But tying up funds in initial margin or a low-risk hedged derivatives position prevents me from using the funds elsewhere. On average the bank gets a much higher return than it does on things like initial margin. There is a cost to low-risk, low-return projects.
Financial Economist:	You talk as though funds for your business are in short supply. If you have good projects, whether they are low risk or high risk, the market will provide funding for you.
Financial Engineer:	I am not sure that is how things work in practice.

9.3 KVA

KVA, capital valuation adjustment, is a charge to a derivatives transaction for the incremental capital requirements that the transaction gives rise to. Suppose that as a result of entering into a particular transaction a bank calculates that regulations require it to hold an extra \$1 million of equity capital throughout the life of the transaction.[11] What is the cost of this?

Again there is a divergence between between financial economics theory and the opinions of many practitioners. Many practitioners would argue that if equity shareholders require a return of 15% per annum and a bank invests in a low-risk project that will require additional equity capital, the return on the additional capital should be at least 15%. (This is similar to nonfinancial companies using WACC as a hurdle rate for all projects, as discussed earlier.) In the derivatives context this means that there should be a price adjustment, a KVA, to ensure that the return on the incremental equity capital is 15%. Financial economists argue that how a company is financed should not affect how it evaluates projects (except possibly for tax effects). As a bank uses more

---

[11] In practice, capital requirements (like margin requirements) vary through time. Also, the expected incremental capital required at any given time has a number of components: credit risk capital, market risk capital, and operational risk capital. These must be estimated separately.

equity to finance itself, it becomes less risky and the providers of both debt and equity capital require a lower return. This argument is over 50 years old in the finance literature and so its theoretical validity has stood the test of time.[12] Many practitioners disagree with the theory. As in the case of MVA and FVA the difference between the two sides is whether average or marginal capital costs should be used. We can imagine the following dialogue:

Financial Economist:	You do not need to make a KVA. As long as a derivatives book provides a return reflecting its risk your investors will be happy.
Practitioner:	Equity capital requirements for derivatives have gone up since the crisis. My equity investors require a 15% per annum return. If I enter into a derivatives transaction that requires additional capital under the new regulations, I need to make sure that the return on that capital is at least 15%.
Financial Economist:	But as more of the bank is financed by equity capital it becomes less risky and the return required by equity investors goes down. This is true even if the average risk of the whole bank does not change. So the marginal return required on new equity capital is low.
Practitioner:	I am not sure that is how things work in practice.

9.4   CALCULATION ISSUES

All of the XVAs are computationally time-consuming to calculate. Monte Carlo simulations are necessary to determine expected credit exposures, expected funding costs, and expected capital requirements at future times. CVA is often actively managed by banks. They sometimes buy protection against their counterparties defaulting using credit default swaps (see Section 7.11) or similar instruments. This reduces their expected losses from defaults.

As discussed in Section 9.1, CVA and DVA must be calculated on the whole portfolio of derivatives that a bank has with a counterparty. It cannot be calculated on a transaction-by-transaction basis. This is because of the impact of netting. A new bilaterally cleared transaction with a counterparty will increase or decrease CVA and DVA depending on what happens when it is netted with other transactions that have been entered into with the counterparty. If it tends to increase credit exposure for the bank in the future, the incremental CVA will be positive; if it tends to decrease credit exposure in the future the incremental CVA will decrease. Similarly for DVA.

The incremental FVA can be calculated on a transaction-by-transaction basis. This is because the net funding required for a portfolio of transactions at any future time is the sum of that for the individual transactions.[13] MVA for transactions cleared through a

---

[12] See F. Modigliani and M. H. Miller, "The Cost of Capital, Corporation Finance, and the Theory of Investment," *American Economic Review*, 48, 3 (1958): 261–297; and F. Modigliani and M. H. Miller, "Corporate Income Taxes and the Cost of Capital: A Correction," *American Economic Review*, 53, 3 (1963): 433–443.

[13] This is only approximately true when the impact of a default on funding requirements is considered.

CCP has to be calculated on a portfolio basis. In the case of the example in Figure 9.1, it is the impact of a new transaction on the initial margin required by the CCP for portfolio that Bank A is clearing through the CCP that determines the incremental initial margin requirements and therefore MVA. KVA is even more complicated. The rules used by regulators are such that a bank must in theory sometimes model the bank's whole portfolio when calculating incremental capital requirements.

SUMMARY

Banks and other derivatives market participants have for many years been concerned about counterparty credit risk. Two adjustments are the credit valuation adjustment (CVA) and debt or debit valuation adjustment (DVA). CVA is an adjustment by a bank for the possibility that its counterparty will default and it reduces the value of the derivatives portfolio it has with the counterparty. DVA is an adjustment for the possibility that the bank will default and it increases the value of the derivatives portfolio. There is no real argument about whether these adjustments should be made, but many people are less comfortable with DVA than CVA. Why should a bank benefit from the possibility that it will itself default? As the probability of a default increases, the benefit increases.

The funding valuation adjustment (FVA) is an adjustment to the value of a derivatives position arising from the funding required (or the funding generated) by a derivatives transaction. The margin valuation adjustment (MVA) quantifies the cost of funding initial margin. The capital valuation adjustment (KVA) is a valuation adjustment reflecting the impact of a derivatives position on capital requirements. Finance theory argues that the way a project is funded should not influence its valuation. In particular, the current average debt and equity costs should not be assumed to be the same as the incremental effect of a new transaction on funding costs. In spite of this, many banks do calculate MVA, FVA, and KVA based on these average costs.

FURTHER READING

Andersen, L. B. G., D. Duffie, and Y. Song. "Funding Value Adjustments," Working Paper, ssrn 2746010.

Gregory, J. *The XVA Challenge: Counterparty Credit Risk, Funding, Collateral, and Capital.* Chichester: Wiley, 2015.

Hull, J. C., and A. White, "The FVA Debate," *Risk*, 25th anniversary edition (July 2012): 83–85.

Hull, J. C., and A. White. "Valuing Derivatives: Funding Value Adjustments and Fair Value," *Financial Analysts Journal*, 70, 3 (May/June 2014): 46–56.

Hull, J. C., and A. White. "Collateral and Credit Issues in Derivatives Pricing," *Journal of Credit Risk*, 10, 3 (2014): 3–28.

Hull, J. C., and A. White. "XVAs: A Gap Between Theory and Practice," *Risk*, 29, 5 (May 2016): 50–52.

Kenyon, C., and Green, A. D. (eds.) *Landmarks in XVA.* London: Risk Books, 2016.

Practice Questions (Answers in Solutions Manual)

9.1. Explain what CVA and DVA measure.

9.2. If the market considers that the default probability for a bank has increased, what happens to its DVA? What happens to the income it reports?

9.3. "The impact of DVA on earnings volatility is generally greater than that of CVA." Explain this statement.

9.4. Explain what MVA and FVA measure.

9.5. Explain the difference between the views of financial economists and most practitioners on how MVA and FVA should be calculated.

9.6. Explain what KVA measures.

9.7. Explain the difference between the views of financial economists and most practitioners on how KVA should be calculated.

9.8. Explain why FVA can be calculated for a transaction without considering the portfolio to which the transaction belongs, but that the same is not true of MVA.

9.9. Suppose that a bank buys an option from a client. The option is uncollateralized and there are no other transactions outstanding with the client. The expected values of the option at the midpoint of years 1, 2, and 3 are 6, 5, and 4. The probability of the counterparty defaulting in each of the three years is 3%. The probability of the bank defaulting in each of the three years is 2%. Estimate the bank's CVA and DVA for the transaction. Assume no recovery in the event of a default and zero interest rates.

9.10. Explain how the "cure period" is used in the calculation of CVA.

9.11. A company is trying to decide between issuing debt and equity to fulfill a funding need. What in theory should happen to the return required by equity holders if it chooses (a) debt and (b) equity?

9.12. Explain the meaning of "netting". Suppose no collateral is posted. Why does a netting agreement usually reduce credit risks to both sides? Under what circumstances does netting have no effect on credit risk?

Further Questions

9.13. The average funding cost for a company is 5% per annum when the risk-free rate is 3%. The company is currently undertaking projects worth $9 million. It plans to increase its size by undertaking $1 million of risk-free projects. What would you expect to happen to its average funding cost?

9.14. Suppose that, for a particular three-year derivative entered into by a bank, two outcomes, A and B, are equally likely. Under outcome A, the values of the derivative at the midpoint of the first, second, and third years are 3, 5, and 7, respectively. Under outcome B, the values of the derivative at the midpoints of the first, second, and third years are −2, −4, and −6. The probability of the counterparty defaulting each year is 1% and the probability of the bank defaulting each year is 0.5%. Calculate the bank's CVA and DVA. Assume that interest rates are zero, no collateral is posted, and there are no other transactions between the two parties.

CHAPTER 10

Mechanics of Options Markets

We introduced options in Chapter 1. This chapter explains how options markets are organized, what terminology is used, how the contracts are traded, how margin requirements are set, and so on. Later chapters will examine such topics as trading strategies involving options, the determination of option prices, and the ways in which portfolios of options can be hedged. This chapter is concerned primarily with stock options. It also presents some introductory material on currency options, index options, and futures options. More details concerning these instruments can be found in Chapters 17 and 18.

Options are fundamentally different from forward and futures contracts. An option gives the holder of the option the right to do something, but the holder does not have to exercise this right. By contrast, in a forward or futures contract, the two parties have committed themselves to some action. It costs a trader nothing (except for the margin/collateral requirements) to enter into a forward or futures contract, whereas the purchase of an option requires an up-front payment.

When charts showing the gain or loss from options trading are produced, the usual practice is to ignore the time value of money, so that the profit is the final payoff minus the initial cost. This chapter follows this practice.

10.1 TYPES OF OPTIONS

As mentioned in Chapter 1, there are two types of options. A *call option* gives the holder of the option the right to buy an asset by a certain date for a certain price. A *put option* gives the holder the right to sell an asset by a certain date for a certain price. The date specified in the contract is known as the *expiration date* or the *maturity date*. The price specified in the contract is known as the *exercise price* or the *strike price*.

Options can be either American or European, a distinction that has nothing to do with geographical location. *American options* can be exercised at any time up to the expiration date, whereas *European options* can be exercised only on the expiration date itself. Most of the options that are traded on exchanges are American. However, European options are generally easier to analyze than American options, and some of the properties of an American option are frequently deduced from those of its European counterpart.

Figure 10.1   Profit from buying a European call option on one share of a stock. Option price = \$5; strike price = \$100.

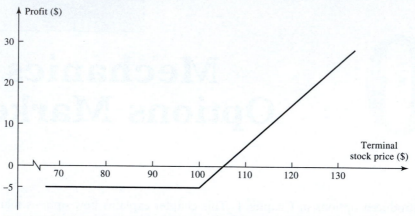

Call Options

Consider the situation of an investor who buys a European call option with a strike price of \$100 to purchase 100 shares of a certain stock. Suppose that the current stock price is \$98, the expiration date of the option is in 4 months, and the price of an option to purchase one share is \$5. The initial investment is \$500. Because the option is European, the investor can exercise only on the expiration date. If the stock price on this date is less than \$100, the investor will clearly choose not to exercise. (There is no point in buying for \$100 a share that has a market value of less than \$100.) In these circumstances, the investor loses the whole of the initial investment of \$500. If the stock price is above \$100 on the expiration date, the option will be exercised. Suppose, for example, that the stock price is \$115. By exercising the option, the investor is able to buy 100 shares for \$100 per share. If the shares are sold immediately, the investor makes a gain of \$15 per share, or \$1,500, ignoring transaction costs. When the initial cost of the option is taken into account, the net profit to the investor is \$1,000.

Figure 10.1 shows how the investor's net profit or loss on an option to purchase one share varies with the final stock price in this example. For instance, when the final stock price is \$120 the profit from an option to purchase one share is \$15. It is important to realize that an investor sometimes exercises an option and makes a loss overall. Suppose that, in the example, the stock price is \$102 at the expiration of the option. The investor would exercise for a gain of $102 - \$100 = \$2$ per option and realize a loss overall of \$3 when the initial cost of the option is taken into account. It is tempting to argue that the investor should not exercise the option in these circumstances. However, not exercising would lead to a loss of \$5, which is worse than the \$3 loss when the investor exercises. In general, call options should always be exercised at the expiration date if the stock price is above the strike price.

Put Options

Whereas the purchaser of a call option is hoping that the stock price will increase, the purchaser of a put option is hoping that it will decrease. Consider an investor who

Figure 10.2 Profit from buying a European put option on one share of a stock. Option price = \$7; strike price = \$70.

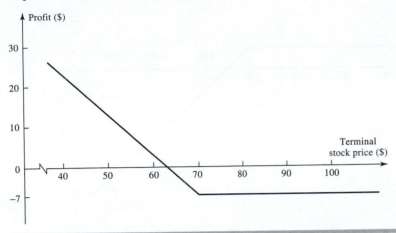

buys a European put option with a strike price of \$70 to sell 100 shares of a certain stock. Suppose that the current stock price is \$65, the expiration date of the option is in 3 months, and the price of an option to sell one share is \$7. The initial investment is \$700. Because the option is European, it will be exercised only if the stock price is below \$70 on the expiration date. Suppose that the stock price is \$55 on this date. The investor can buy 100 shares for \$55 per share and, under the terms of the put option, sell the same shares for \$70 to realize a gain of \$15 per share, or \$1,500. (Again, transaction costs are ignored.) When the \$700 initial cost of the option is taken into account, the investor's net profit is \$800. There is no guarantee that the investor will make a gain. If the final stock price is above \$70, the put option expires worthless, and the investor loses \$700. Figure 10.2 shows the way in which the investor's profit or loss on an option to sell one share varies with the terminal stock price in this example.

Early Exercise

As mentioned earlier, exchange-traded stock options are usually American rather than European. This means that the investor in the foregoing examples would not have to wait until the expiration date before exercising the option. We will see later that there are some circumstances when it is optimal to exercise American options before the expiration date.

10.2 OPTION POSITIONS

There are two sides to every option contract. On one side is the investor who has taken the long position (i.e., has bought the option). On the other side is the investor who has taken a short position (i.e., has sold or *written* the option). The writer of an option receives cash up front, but has potential liabilities later. The writer's profit or loss is the reverse of that for the purchaser of the option. Figures 10.3 and 10.4 show the variation of the profit or loss with the final stock price for writers of the options considered in Figures 10.1 and 10.2.

Figure 10.3 Profit from writing a European call option on one share of a stock. Option price = \$5; strike price = \$100.

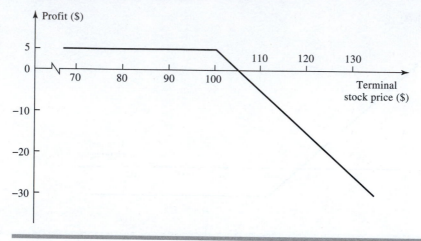

There are four types of option positions:

1. A long position in a call option
2. A long position in a put option
3. A short position in a call option
4. A short position in a put option.

It is often useful to characterize a European option in terms of its payoff to the purchaser of the option. The initial cost of the option is then not included in the calculation. If K is the strike price and S_T is the final price of the underlying asset, the

Figure 10.4 Profit from writing a European put option on one share of a stock. Option price = \$7; strike price = \$70.

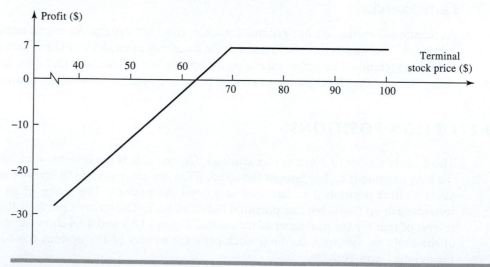

Figure 10.5   Payoffs from positions in European options: (a) long call; (b) short call; (c) long put; (d) short put. Strike price $= K$; price of asset at maturity $= S_T$.

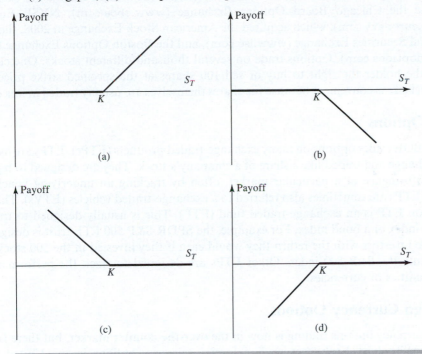

payoff from a long position in a European call option is

$$\max(S_T - K, 0)$$

This reflects the fact that the option will be exercised if $S_T > K$ and will not be exercised if $S_T \leqslant K$. The payoff to the holder of a short position in the European call option is

$$-\max(S_T - K, 0) = \min(K - S_T, 0)$$

The payoff to the holder of a long position in a European put option is

$$\max(K - S_T, 0)$$

and the payoff from a short position in a European put option is

$$-\max(K - S_T, 0) = \min(S_T - K, 0)$$

Figure 10.5 illustrates these payoffs.

10.3   UNDERLYING ASSETS

This section provides a first look at how options on stocks, currencies, stock indices, and futures are traded on exchanges.

Stock Options

Most trading in stock options is on exchanges. In the United States, the exchanges include the Chicago Board Options Exchange (www.cboe.com), NYSE Euronext (www.euronext.com), which acquired the American Stock Exchange in 2008, the International Securities Exchange (www.ise.com), and the Boston Options Exchange (www.bostonoptions.com). Options trade on several thousand different stocks. One contract gives the holder the right to buy or sell 100 shares at the specified strike price. This contract size is convenient because the shares themselves are usually traded in lots of 100.

ETP Options

The CBOE trades options on many exchange-traded products (ETPs). ETPs are listed on an exchange and traded like a share of a company's stock. They are designed to replicate the performance of a particular market, often by tracking an underlying benchmark index. ETPs are sometimes also referred to a exchange-traded vehicles (ETVs). The most common ETP is an exchange-traded fund (ETF). This is usually designed to track an equity index or a bond index. For example, the SPDR S&P 500 ETF trust is designed to provide investors with the return they would earn if they invested in the 500 stocks that constitute the S&P 500 index. Other ETPs are designed to track the performance of commodities or currencies.

Foreign Currency Options

Most currency options trading is now in the over-the-counter market, but there is some exchange trading. Exchanges trading foreign currency options in the United States include NASDAQ OMX (www.nasdaqtrader.com), which acquired the Philadelphia Stock Exchange in 2008. This exchange offers European-style contracts on a variety of different currencies. One contract is to buy or sell 10,000 units of a foreign currency (1,000,000 units in the case of the Japanese yen) for U.S. dollars. Foreign currency options contracts are discussed further in Chapter 17.

Index Options

Many different index options currently trade throughout the world in both the over-the-counter market and the exchange-traded market. The most popular exchange-traded contracts in the United States are those on the S&P 500 Index (SPX), the S&P 100 Index (OEX), the Nasdaq-100 Index (NDX), and the Dow Jones Industrial Index (DJX). All of these trade on the Chicago Board Options Exchange. Most of the contracts are European. An exception is the OEX contract on the S&P 100, which is American. One contract is usually to buy or sell 100 times the index at the specified strike price. Settlement is always in cash, rather than by delivering the portfolio underlying the index. Consider, for example, one call contract on an index with a strike price of 980. If it is exercised when the value of the index is 992, the writer of the contract pays the holder $(992 - 980) \times 100 = \$1,200$. Index options are discussed further in Chapter 17.

Futures Options

When an exchange trades a particular futures contract, it often also trades American options on that contract. The life of a futures option normally ends a short period of time before the expiration of trading in the underlying futures contract. When a call option is exercised, the holder's gain equals the excess of the futures price over the strike price. When a put option is exercised, the holder's gain equals the excess of the strike price over the futures price. Futures options contracts are discussed further in Chapter 18.

10.4 SPECIFICATION OF STOCK OPTIONS

In the rest of this chapter, we will focus on stock options. As already mentioned, a standard exchange-traded stock option in the United States is an American-style option contract to buy or sell 100 shares of the stock. Details of the contract (the expiration date, the strike price, what happens when dividends are declared, how large a position investors can hold, and so on) are specified by the exchange.

Expiration Dates

One of the items used to describe a stock option is the month in which the expiration date occurs. Thus, a January call trading on IBM is a call option on IBM with an expiration date in January. The precise expiration date is the third Friday of the expiration month and trading takes place every business day (8:30 a.m. to 3:00 p.m., Chicago time) until the expiration date.

Stock options in the United States are on a January, February, or March cycle. The January cycle consists of the months of January, April, July, and October. The February cycle consists of the months of February, May, August, and November. The March cycle consists of the months of March, June, September, and December. If the expiration date for the current month has not yet been reached, options trade with expiration dates in the current month, the following month, and the next two months in the cycle. If the expiration date of the current month has passed, options trade with expiration dates in the next month, the next-but-one month, and the next two months of the expiration cycle. For example, IBM is on a January cycle. At the beginning of January, options are traded with expiration dates in January, February, April, and July; at the end of January, they are traded with expiration dates in February, March, April, and July; at the beginning of May, they are traded with expiration dates in May, June, July, and October; and so on. When one option reaches expiration, trading in another is started.

Longer-term options, known as LEAPS (long-term equity anticipation securities), also trade on many stocks in the United States. These have expiration dates up to 39 months into the future. The expiration dates for LEAPS on stocks are always the third Friday of a January.

Strike Prices

The exchange normally chooses the strike prices at which options can be written so that they are spaced $2.50, $5, or $10 apart. Typically the spacing is $2.50 when the stock price is between $5 and $25, $5 when the stock price is between $25 and $200, and $10 for stock prices above $200. As will be explained shortly, stock splits and stock dividends can lead to nonstandard strike prices.

When a new expiration date is introduced, the two or three strike prices closest to the current stock price are usually selected by the exchange. If the stock price moves outside the range defined by the highest and lowest strike price, trading is usually introduced in an option with a new strike price. To illustrate these rules, suppose that the stock price is $84 when trading begins in the October options. Call and put options would probably first be offered with strike prices of $80, $85, and $90. If the stock price rose above $90, it is likely that a strike price of $95 would be offered; if it fell below $80, it is likely that a strike price of $75 would be offered; and so on.

Terminology

For any given asset at any given time, many different option contracts may be trading. Suppose there are four expiration dates and five strike prices for options on a particular stock. If call and put options trade with every expiration date and every strike price, there are a total of 40 different contracts. All options of the same type (calls or puts) on a stock are referred to as an *option class*. For example, IBM calls are one class, whereas IBM puts are another class. An *option series* consists of all the options of a given class with the same expiration date and strike price. In other words, it refers to a particular contract that is traded. For example, IBM 160 October 2017 calls would constitute an option series.

Options are referred to as *in the money*, *at the money*, or *out of the money*. If S is the stock price and K is the strike price, a call option is in the money when $S > K$, at the money when $S = K$, and out of the money when $S < K$. A put option is in the money when $S < K$, at the money when $S = K$, and out of the money when $S > K$. Clearly, an option will be exercised only when it is in the money. In the absence of transaction costs, an in-the-money option will always be exercised on the expiration date if it has not been exercised previously.[1]

The *intrinsic value* of an option is defined as the value it would have if there were no time to maturity, so that the exercise decision had to be made immediately. For a call option, the intrinsic value is therefore $\max(S - K, 0)$. For a put option, it is $\max(K - S, 0)$. An in-the-money American option must be worth at least as much as its intrinsic value because the holder has the right to exercise it immediately. Often it is optimal for the holder of an in-the-money American option to wait rather than exercise immediately. The excess of an option's value over its intrinsic value is the option's *time value*. The total value of an option is therefore the sum of its intrinsic value and its time value.

FLEX Options

The Chicago Board Options Exchange offers FLEX (short for flexible) options on equities and equity indices. These are options where the traders agree to nonstandard terms. These nonstandard terms can involve a strike price or an expiration date that is different from what is usually offered by the exchange. They can also involve the option being European when they are normally American or vice versa. FLEX options are an attempt by option exchanges to regain business from the over-the-counter markets. The exchange specifies a minimum size (e.g., 100 contracts) for FLEX option trades.

---

[1] Section 20.4 provides alternative definitions, often used by traders, for in the money, out of the money, and at the money.

Other Nonstandard Products

In addition to flex options, the CBOE trades a number of other nonstandard products. Examples are:

1. *Weeklys*. These are options that are created on a Thursday and expire on Friday of the following week.

2. *Binary options*. These are options that provide a fixed payoff of $100 if the strike price is reached. For example, a binary call with a strike price of $50 provides a payoff of $100 if the price of the underlying stock exceeds $50 on the expiry date and zero otherwise; a binary put with a strike price of $50 provides a payoff of $100 if the price of the stock is below $50 on the expiry date and zero otherwise. Binary options are discussed further in Chapter 26.

3. *Credit event binary options* (CEBOs). These are options that provide a fixed payoff if a particular company (known as the reference entity) suffers a "credit event" by the maturity date. Credit events are defined as bankruptcy, failure to pay interest or principal on debt, and a restructuring of debt. Maturity dates are in December of a particular year and payoffs, if any, are made on the maturity date. A CEBO is a type of credit default swap (see Section 7.11 for an introduction to credit default swaps and Chapter 25 for more details).

4. *DOOM options*. These are deep-out-of-the-money put options. Because they have a low strike price, they cost very little. They provide a payoff only if the price of the underlying asset plunges. DOOM options provide the same sort of protection as CEBOs, which have just been described.

Dividends and Stock Splits

The early over-the-counter options were dividend protected. If a company declared a cash dividend, the strike price for options on the company's stock was reduced on the ex-dividend day by the amount of the dividend. Exchange-traded options are not usually adjusted for cash dividends. In other words, when a cash dividend occurs, there are no adjustments to the terms of the option contract. An exception is sometimes made for large cash dividends (see Business Snapshot 10.1).

Exchange-traded options are adjusted for stock splits. A stock split occurs when the existing shares are "split" into more shares. For example, in a 3-for-1 stock split, three new shares are issued to replace each existing share. Because a stock split does not change the assets or the earning ability of a company, we should not expect it to have any effect on the wealth of the company's shareholders. All else being equal, the 3-for-1 stock split should cause the stock price to go down to one-third of its previous value. In general, an n-for-m stock split should cause the stock price to go down to m/n of its previous value. The terms of option contracts are adjusted to reflect expected changes in a stock price arising from a stock split. After an n-for-m stock split, the strike price is reduced to m/n of its previous value, and the number of shares covered by one contract is increased to n/m of its previous value. If the stock price declines in the way expected, the positions of both the writer and the purchaser of a contract remain unchanged.

Example 10.1

Consider a call option to buy 100 shares of a company for $30 per share. Suppose the company makes a 2-for-1 stock split. The terms of the option contract are

---

Business Snapshot 10.1   Gucci Group's Large Dividend

When there is a large cash dividend (typically one that is more than 10% of the stock price), a committee of the Options Clearing Corporation (OCC) at the Chicago Board Options Exchange can decide to adjust the terms of options traded on the exchange.

On May 28, 2003, Gucci Group NV (GUC) declared a cash dividend of 13.50 euros (approximately $15.88) per common share and this was approved at the annual shareholders' meeting on July 16, 2003. The dividend was about 16% of the share price at the time it was declared. In this case, the OCC committee decided to adjust the terms of options. The result was that the holder of a call contract paid 100 times the strike price on exercise and received $1,588 of cash in addition to 100 shares; the holder of a put contract received 100 times the strike price on exercise and delivered $1,588 of cash in addition to 100 shares. These adjustments had the effect of reducing the strike price by $15.88.

Adjustments for large dividends are not always made. For example, Deutsche Terminbörse chose not to adjust the terms of options traded on that exchange when Daimler-Benz surprised the market on March 10, 1998, with a dividend equal to about 12% of its stock price.

---

then changed so that it gives the holder the right to purchase 200 shares for $15 per share.

Stock options are adjusted for stock dividends. A stock dividend involves a company issuing more shares to its existing shareholders. For example, a 20% stock dividend means that investors receive one new share for each five already owned. A stock dividend, like a stock split, has no effect on either the assets or the earning power of a company. The stock price can be expected to go down as a result of a stock dividend. The 20% stock dividend referred to is essentially the same as a 6-for-5 stock split. All else being equal, it should cause the stock price to decline to 5/6 of its previous value. The terms of an option are adjusted to reflect the expected price decline arising from a stock dividend in the same way as they are for that arising from a stock split.

Example 10.2

Consider a put option to sell 100 shares of a company for $15 per share. Suppose the company declares a 25% stock dividend. This is equivalent to a 5-for-4 stock split. The terms of the option contract are changed so that it gives the holder the right to sell 125 shares for $12.

Adjustments are also made for rights issues. The basic procedure is to calculate the theoretical price of the rights and then to reduce the strike price by this amount.

Position Limits and Exercise Limits

The Chicago Board Options Exchange often specifies a *position limit* for option contracts. This defines the maximum number of option contracts that an investor can hold on one side of the market. For this purpose, long calls and short puts are considered to be on the same side of the market. Also considered to be on the same side are short calls and long puts. The *exercise limit* usually equals the position limit. It defines the maximum number of contracts that can be exercised by any individual (or group of individuals acting together) in any period of five consecutive business days. Options on the largest and most frequently traded stocks have positions limits of 250,000 contracts. Smaller capitalization stocks have position limits of 200,000, 75,000, 50,000, or 25,000 contracts.

Position limits and exercise limits are designed to prevent the market from being unduly influenced by the activities of an individual investor or group of investors. However, whether the limits are really necessary is a controversial issue.

10.5 TRADING

Traditionally, exchanges have had to provide a large open area for individuals to meet and trade options. This has changed. Most derivatives exchanges are fully electronic, so traders do not have to physically meet. The International Securities Exchange (www.ise.com) launched the first all-electronic options market for equities in the United States in May 2000. Over 95% of the orders at the Chicago Board Options Exchange are handled electronically. The remainder are mostly large or complex institutional orders that require the skills of traders.

Market Makers

Most options exchanges use market makers to facilitate trading. A market maker for a certain option is an individual who, when asked to do so, will quote both a bid and an offer price on the option. The bid is the price at which the market maker is prepared to buy, and the offer or asked is the price at which the market maker is prepared to sell. At the time the bid and offer prices are quoted, the market maker does not know whether the trader who asked for the quotes wants to buy or sell the option. The offer is always higher than the bid, and the amount by which the offer exceeds the bid is referred to as the *bid–offer* spread. The exchange sets upper limits for the bid–offer spread. For example, it might specify that the spread be no more than $0.25 for options priced at less than $0.50, $0.50 for options priced between $0.50 and $10, $0.75 for options priced between $10 and $20, and $1 for options priced over $20.

The existence of the market maker ensures that buy and sell orders can always be executed at some price without any delays. Market makers therefore add liquidity to the market. The market makers themselves make their profits from the bid–offer spread. They use methods such as those that will be discussed in Chapter 19 to hedge their risks.

Offsetting Orders

An investor who has purchased options can close out the position by issuing an offsetting order to sell the same number of options. Similarly, an investor who has written options can close out the position by issuing an offsetting order to buy the same number of options. (In this respect options markets are similar to futures markets.) If, when an option contract is traded, neither investor is closing an existing position, the open interest increases by one contract. If one investor is closing an existing position and the other is not, the open interest stays the same. If both investors are closing existing positions, the open interest goes down by one contract.

10.6 COMMISSIONS

The types of orders that can be placed with a broker for options trading are similar to those for futures trading (see Section 2.8). A market order is executed immediately, a limit order specifies the least favorable price at which the order can be executed, and so on.

For a retail investor, commissions vary significantly from broker to broker. Discount brokers generally charge lower commissions than full-service brokers. The actual amount charged is often calculated as a fixed cost plus a proportion of the dollar amount of the trade. Table 10.1 shows the sort of schedule that might be offered by a discount broker. Using this schedule, the purchase of eight contracts when the option price is $3 would cost $20 + (0.02 × $2,400) = $68 in commissions.

If an option position is closed out by entering into an offsetting trade, the commission must be paid again. If the option is exercised, the commission is the same as it would be if the investor placed an order to buy or sell the underlying stock.

Consider an investor who buys one call contract with a strike price of $50 when the stock price is $49. We suppose the option price is $4.50, so that the cost of the contract is $450. Under the schedule in Table 10.1, the purchase or sale of one contract always costs $30 (both the maximum and minimum commission is $30 for the first contract). Suppose that the stock price rises and the option is exercised when the stock reaches $60. Assuming that the investor pays 0.75% commission to exercise the option and a further 0.75% commission to sell the stock, there is an additional cost of

$$2 \times 0.0075 \times \$60 \times 100 = \$90$$

The total commission paid is therefore $120, and the net profit to the investor is

$$\$1,000 - \$450 - \$120 = \$430$$

Note that selling the option for $10 instead of exercising it would save the investor $60 in commissions. (The commission payable when an option is sold is only $30 in our example.) As this example indicates, the commission system can push retail investors in the direction of selling options rather than exercising them.

A hidden cost in option trading (and in stock trading) is the market maker's bid–offer spread. Suppose that, in the example just considered, the bid price was $4.00 and the offer price was $4.50 at the time the option was purchased. We can reasonably assume that a "fair" price for the option is halfway between the bid and the offer price, or

Table 10.1 Sample commission schedule for a discount broker.

Dollar amount of trade	Commission*
< $2,500	$20 + 2% of dollar amount
$2,500 to $10,000	$45 + 1% of dollar amount
> $10,000	$120 + 0.25% of dollar amount

* Maximum commission is $30 per contract for the first five contracts plus $20 per contract for each additional contract. Minimum commission is $30 per contract for the first contract plus $2 per contract for each additional contract.

$4.25. The cost to the buyer and to the seller of the market maker system is the difference between the fair price and the price paid. This is $0.25 per option, or $25 per contract.

10.7 MARGIN REQUIREMENTS

We discussed margin requirements for futures contracts in Chapter 2. The purpose of margin is to provide a guarantee that the entity providing margin will live up to its obligations. If a trader buys an asset such as a stock or an option for cash there is no margin requirement. This is because the trade does not give rise to future obligations. As discussed in Section 5.2, if the trader shorts a stock, margin is required because the trader then has the obligation to close out the position by buying the stock at some future time. Similarly, when the trader sells (i.e., writes) an option, margin is required because the trader has obligations in the event that the option is exercised.

Assets are not always purchased for cash. For example, when shares are purchased in the United States, an investor can borrow up to 50% of the price from the broker. This is known as *buying on margin*. If the share price declines so that the loan is substantially more than 50% of the stock's current value, there is a "margin call", where the broker requests that cash be deposited by the investor. If the margin call is not met, the broker sells the stock.

When call and put options with maturities less than 9 months are purchased, the option price must be paid in full. Investors are not allowed to buy these options on margin because options already contain substantial leverage and buying on margin would raise this leverage to an unacceptable level. For options with maturities greater than 9 months investors can buy on margin, borrowing up to 25% of the option value.

Writing Naked Options

As mentioned, a trader who writes options is required to maintain funds in a margin account. Both the trader's broker and the exchange want to be satisfied that the trader will not default if the option is exercised. The amount of margin required depends on the trader's position.

A *naked option* is an option that is not combined with an offsetting position in the underlying stock. The initial and maintenance margin required by the CBOE for a written naked call option is the greater of the following two calculations:

1. A total of 100% of the proceeds of the sale plus 20% of the underlying share price less the amount, if any, by which the option is out of the money
2. A total of 100% of the option proceeds plus 10% of the underlying share price.

For a written naked put option, it is the greater of

1. A total of 100% of the proceeds of the sale plus 20% of the underlying share price less the amount, if any, by which the option is out of the money
2. A total of 100% of the option proceeds plus 10% of the exercise price.

The 20% in the preceding calculations is replaced by 15% for options on a broadly based stock index because a stock index is usually less volatile than the price of an individual stock.

Example 10.3

An investor writes four naked call option contracts on a stock. The option price is $5, the strike price is $40, and the stock price is $38. Because the option is $2 out of the money, the first calculation gives

$$400 \times (5 + 0.2 \times 38 - 2) = \$4,240$$

The second calculation gives

$$400 \times (5 + 0.1 \times 38) = \$3,520$$

The initial margin requirement is therefore $4,240. Note that, if the option had been a put, it would be $2 in the money and the margin requirement would be

$$400 \times (5 + 0.2 \times 38) = \$5,040$$

In both cases, the proceeds of the sale can be used to form part of the margin account.

A calculation similar to the initial margin calculation (but with the current market price of the contract replacing the proceeds of sale) is repeated every day. Funds can be withdrawn from the margin account when the calculation indicates that the margin required is less than the current balance in the margin account. When the calculation indicates that a greater margin is required, a margin call will be made.

Other Rules

In Chapter 12, we will examine option trading strategies such as covered calls, protective puts, spreads, combinations, straddles, and strangles. The CBOE has special rules for determining the margin requirements when these trading strategies are used. These are described in the *CBOE Margin Manual*, which is available on the CBOE website (www.cboe. com).

As an example of the rules, consider an investor who writes a covered call. This is a written call option when the shares that might have to be delivered are already owned. Covered calls are far less risky than naked calls, because the worst that can happen is that the investor is required to sell shares already owned at below their market value. No margin is required on the written option. However, the investor can borrow an amount equal to $0.5 \min(S, K)$, rather than the usual $0.5S$, on the stock position.

10.8 THE OPTIONS CLEARING CORPORATION

The Options Clearing Corporation (OCC) performs much the same function for options markets as the clearing house does for futures markets (see Chapter 2). It guarantees that options writers will fulfill their obligations under the terms of options contracts and keeps a record of all long and short positions. The OCC has a number of members, and all option trades must be cleared through a member. If a broker is not itself a member of an exchange's OCC, it must arrange to clear its trades with a member. Members are required to have a certain minimum amount of capital and to contribute to a special fund that can be used if any member defaults on an option obligation.

The funds used to purchase an option must be deposited with the OCC by the morning of the business day following the trade. The writer of the option maintains a margin account with a broker, as described earlier.[2] The broker maintains a margin account with the OCC member that clears its trades. The OCC member in turn maintains a margin account with the OCC.

Exercising an Option

When an investor instructs a broker to exercise an option, the broker notifies the OCC member that clears its trades. This member then places an exercise order with the OCC. The OCC randomly selects a member with an outstanding short position in the same option. The member, using a procedure established in advance, selects a particular investor who has written the option. If the option is a call, this investor is required to sell stock at the strike price. If it is a put, the investor is required to buy stock at the strike price. The investor is said to be *assigned*. The buy/sell transaction takes place on the third business day following the exercise order. When an option is exercised, the open interest goes down by one.

At the expiration of the option, all in-the-money options should be exercised unless the transaction costs are so high as to wipe out the payoff from the option. Some brokers will automatically exercise options for a client at expiration when it is in their client's interest to do so. Many exchanges also have rules for exercising options that are in the money at expiration.

10.9 REGULATION

Exchange-traded options markets are regulated in a number of different ways. Both the exchange and Options Clearing Corporations have rules governing the behavior of traders. In addition, there are both federal and state regulatory authorities. In general, options markets have demonstrated a willingness to regulate themselves. There have been no major scandals or defaults by OCC members. Investors can have a high level of confidence in the way the market is run.

The Securities and Exchange Commission is responsible for regulating options markets in stocks, stock indices, currencies, and bonds at the federal level. The Commodity Futures Trading Commission is responsible for regulating markets for options on futures. The major options markets are in the states of Illinois and New York. These states actively enforce their own laws on unacceptable trading practices.

10.10 TAXATION

Determining the tax implications of option trading strategies can be tricky, and an investor who is in doubt about this should consult a tax specialist. In the United States,

---

[2] The margin requirements described in the previous section are the minimum requirements specified by the OCC. A broker may require a higher margin from its clients. However, it cannot require a lower margin. Some brokers do not allow their retail clients to write uncovered options at all.

the general rule is that (unless the taxpayer is a professional trader) gains and losses from the trading of stock options are taxed as capital gains or losses. The way that capital gains and losses are taxed in the United States was discussed in Section 2.10. For both the holder and the writer of a stock option, a gain or loss is recognized when (a) the option expires unexercised or (b) the option position is closed out. If the option is exercised, the gain or loss from the option is rolled into the position taken in the stock and recognized when the stock position is closed out. For example, when a call option is exercised, the party with a long position is deemed to have purchased the stock at the strike price plus the call price. This is then used as a basis for calculating this party's gain or loss when the stock is eventually sold. Similarly, the party with the short call position is deemed to have sold the stock at the strike price plus the call price. When a put option is exercised, the seller of the option is deemed to have bought the stock for the strike price less the original put price and the purchaser of the option is deemed to have sold the stock for the strike price less the original put price.

Wash Sale Rule

One tax consideration in option trading in the United States is the wash sale rule. To understand this rule, imagine an investor who buys a stock when the price is $60 and plans to keep it for the long term. If the stock price drops to $40, the investor might be tempted to sell the stock and then immediately repurchase it, so that the $20 loss is realized for tax purposes. To prevent this practice, the tax authorities have ruled that when the repurchase is within 30 days of the sale (i.e., between 30 days before the sale and 30 days after the sale), any loss on the sale is not deductible. The disallowance also applies where, within the 61-day period, the taxpayer enters into an option or similar contract to acquire the stock. Thus, selling a stock at a loss and buying a call option within a 30-day period will lead to the loss being disallowed.

Constructive Sales

Prior to 1997, if a United States taxpayer shorted a security while holding a long position in a substantially identical security, no gain or loss was recognized until the short position was closed out. This means that short positions could be used to defer recognition of a gain for tax purposes. The situation was changed by the Tax Relief Act of 1997. An appreciated property is now treated as "constructively sold" when the owner does one of the following:

1. Enters into a short sale of the same or substantially identical property
2. Enters into a futures or forward contract to deliver the same or substantially identical property
3. Enters into one or more positions that eliminate substantially all of the loss and opportunity for gain.

It should be noted that transactions reducing only the risk of loss or only the opportunity for gain should not result in constructive sales. Therefore an investor holding a long position in a stock can buy in-the-money put options on the stock without triggering a constructive sale.

Tax practitioners sometimes use options to minimize tax costs or maximize tax benefits (see Business Snapshot 10.2). Tax authorities in many jurisdictions have

---

Business Snapshot 10.2   Tax Planning Using Options

As a simple example of a possible tax planning strategy using options, suppose that Country A has a tax regime where the tax is low on interest and dividends and high on capital gains, while Country B has a tax regime where tax is high on interest and dividends and low on capital gains. It is advantageous for a company to receive the income from a security in Country A and the capital gain, if there is one, in Country B. The company would like to keep capital losses in Country A, where they can be used to offset capital gains on other items. All of this can be accomplished by arranging for a subsidiary company in Country A to have legal ownership of the security and for a subsidiary company in Country B to buy a call option on the security from the company in Country A, with the strike price of the option equal to the current value of the security. During the life of the option, income from the security is earned in Country A. If the security price rises sharply, the option will be exercised and the capital gain will be realized in Country B. If it falls sharply, the option will not be exercised and the capital loss will be realized in Country A.

---

proposed legislation designed to combat the use of derivatives for tax purposes. Before entering into any tax-motivated transaction, a corporate treasurer or private individual should explore in detail how the structure could be unwound in the event of legislative change and how costly this process could be.

10.11 WARRANTS, EMPLOYEE STOCK OPTIONS, AND CONVERTIBLES

Warrants are options issued by a financial institution or nonfinancial corporation. For example, a financial institution might issue 1 million put warrants on gold, each warrant giving the holder the right to sell 10 ounces of gold for $1,000 per ounce. It could then proceed to create a market for the warrants. To exercise the warrant, the holder would contact the financial institution. A common use of warrants by a nonfinancial corporation is at the time of a bond issue. The corporation issues call warrants giving the holder the right to buy its own stock for a certain price at a certain future time and then attaches them to the bonds to make the bonds more attractive to investors.

Employee stock options are call options issued to employees by their company to motivate them to act in the best interests of the company's shareholders (see Chapter 16). They are usually at the money at the time of issue. Accounting standards now require them to be expensed at fair market value on the income statement of the company.

Convertible bonds, often referred to as *convertibles*, are bonds issued by a company that can be converted into equity at certain times using a predetermined exchange ratio. They are therefore bonds with an embedded call option on the company's stock.

One feature of warrants, employee stock options, and convertibles is that a predetermined number of options are issued. By contrast, the number of options on a particular stock that trade on the CBOE or another exchange is not predetermined. (As people take positions in a particular option series, the number of options outstanding increases; as people close out positions, it declines.) Warrants issued by a company on its own stock, employee stock options, and convertibles are different from exchange-traded options in another important way. When these instruments are exercised, the company issues more shares of its own stock and sells them to the option holder for the strike price. The exercise of the instruments therefore leads to an increase in the number of shares of the company's stock that are outstanding. By contrast, when an exchange-traded call option is exercised, the party with the short position buys in the market shares that have already been issued and sells them to the party with the long position for the strike price. The company whose stock underlies the option is not involved in any way.

10.12 OVER-THE-COUNTER OPTIONS MARKETS

Most of this chapter has focused on exchange-traded options markets. The over-the-counter market for options has become increasingly important since the early 1980s and is now larger than the exchange-traded market. As explained in Chapter 1, the main participants in over-the-counter markets are financial institutions, corporate treasurers, and fund managers. There is a wide range of assets underlying the options. Over-the-counter options on foreign exchange and interest rates are particularly popular. The chief potential disadvantage of the over-the-counter market is that the option writer may default. This means that the purchaser is subject to some credit risk. In an attempt to overcome this disadvantage, market participants (and regulators) often require counterparties to post collateral. This was discussed in Section 2.5.

The instruments traded in the over-the-counter market are often structured by financial institutions to meet the precise needs of their clients. Sometimes this involves choosing exercise dates, strike prices, and contract sizes that are different from those offered by an exchange. In other cases the structure of the option is different from standard calls and puts. The option is then referred to as an *exotic option*. Chapter 26 describes a number of different types of exotic options.

SUMMARY

There are two types of options: calls and puts. A call option gives the holder the right to buy the underlying asset for a certain price by a certain date. A put option gives the holder the right to sell the underlying asset by a certain date for a certain price. There are four possible positions in options markets: a long position in a call, a short position in a call, a long position in a put, and a short position in a put. Taking a short position in an option is known as writing it. Options are currently traded on stocks, stock indices, foreign currencies, futures contracts, and other assets.

An exchange must specify the terms of the option contracts it trades. In particular, it must specify the size of the contract, the precise expiration time, and the strike price. In the United States one stock option contract gives the holder the right to buy or sell 100 shares. The expiration of a stock option contract is the third Friday of the expiration month. Options with several different expiration months trade at any given time. Strike prices are at $2\frac{1}{2}$, $5, or $10 intervals, depending on the stock price. The strike price is generally fairly close to the stock price when trading in an option begins.

The terms of a stock option are not normally adjusted for cash dividends. However, they are adjusted for stock dividends, stock splits, and rights issues. The aim of the adjustment is to keep the positions of both the writer and the buyer of a contract unchanged.

Most option exchanges use market makers. A market maker is an individual who is prepared to quote both a bid price (at which he or she is prepared to buy) and an offer price (at which he or she is prepared to sell). Market makers improve the liquidity of the market and ensure that there is never any delay in executing market orders. They themselves make a profit from the difference between their bid and offer prices (known as their bid–offer spread). The exchange has rules specifying upper limits for the bid–offer spread.

Writers of options have potential liabilities and are required to maintain a margin account with their brokers. If it is not a member of the Options Clearing Corporation, the broker will maintain a margin account with a firm that is a member. This firm will in turn maintain a margin account with the Options Clearing Corporation. The Options Clearing Corporation is responsible for keeping a record of all outstanding contracts, handling exercise orders, and so on.

Not all options are traded on exchanges. Many options are traded in the over-the-counter (OTC) market. An advantage of over-the-counter options is that they can be tailored by a financial institution to meet the particular needs of a corporate treasurer or fund manager.

FURTHER READING

Chicago Board Options Exchange. *Margin Manual*. Available online at the CBOE website: www.cboe.com.

Practice Questions (Answers in Solutions Manual)

10.1. An investor buys a European put on a share for $3. The stock price is $42 and the strike price is $40. Under what circumstances does the investor make a profit? Under what circumstances will the option be exercised? Draw a diagram showing the variation of the investor's profit with the stock price at the maturity of the option.

10.2. An investor sells a European call on a share for $4. The stock price is $47 and the strike price is $50. Under what circumstances does the investor make a profit? Under what circumstances will the option be exercised? Draw a diagram showing the variation of the investor's profit with the stock price at the maturity of the option.

10.3. An investor sells a European call option with strike price of K and maturity T and buys a put with the same strike price and maturity. Describe the investor's position.

10.4. Explain why margin accounts are required when clients write options but not when they buy options.

10.5. A stock option is on a February, May, August, and November cycle. What options trade on (a) April 1 and (b) May 30?

10.6. A company declares a 2-for-1 stock split. Explain how the terms change for a call option with a strike price of $60.

10.7. "Employee stock options issued by a company are different from regular exchange-traded call options on the company's stock because they can affect the capital structure of the company." Explain this statement.

10.8. A corporate treasurer is designing a hedging program involving foreign currency options. What are the pros and cons of using (a) NASDAQ OMX and (b) the over-the-counter market for trading?

10.9. Suppose that a European call option to buy a share for $100.00 costs $5.00 and is held until maturity. Under what circumstances will the holder of the option make a profit? Under what circumstances will the option be exercised? Draw a diagram illustrating how the profit from a long position in the option depends on the stock price at maturity of the option.

10.10. Suppose that a European put option to sell a share for $60 costs $8 and is held until maturity. Under what circumstances will the seller of the option (the party with the short position) make a profit? Under what circumstances will the option be exercised? Draw a diagram illustrating how the profit from a short position in the option depends on the stock price at maturity of the option.

10.11. Describe the terminal value of the following portfolio: a newly entered-into long forward contract on an asset and a long position in a European put option on the asset with the same maturity as the forward contract and a strike price that is equal to the forward price of the asset at the time the portfolio is set up. Show that the European put option has the same value as a European call option with the same strike price and maturity.

10.12. A trader buys a call option with a strike price of $45 and a put option with a strike price of $40. Both options have the same maturity. The call costs $3 and the put costs $4. Draw a diagram showing the variation of the trader's profit with the asset price.

10.13. Explain why an American option is always worth at least as much as a European option on the same asset with the same strike price and exercise date.

10.14. Explain why an American option is always worth at least as much as its intrinsic value.

10.15. Explain carefully the difference between writing a put option and buying a call option.

10.16. The treasurer of a corporation is trying to choose between options and forward contracts to hedge the corporation's foreign exchange risk. Discuss the advantages and disadvantages of each.

10.17. Consider an exchange-traded call option contract to buy 500 shares with a strike price of $40 and maturity in 4 months. Explain how the terms of the option contract change when there is: (a) a 10% stock dividend; (b) a 10% cash dividend; and (c) a 4-for-1 stock split.

10.18. "If most of the call options on a stock are in the money, it is likely that the stock price has risen rapidly in the last few months." Discuss this statement.

10.19. What is the effect of an unexpected cash dividend on (a) a call option price and (b) a put option price?

10.20. Options on General Motors stock are on a March, June, September, and December cycle. What options trade on (a) March 1, (b) June 30, and (c) August 5?

10.21. Explain why the market maker's bid–offer spread represents a real cost to options investors.

10.22. A U.S. investor writes five naked call option contracts. The option price is $3.50, the strike price is $60.00, and the stock price is $57.00. What is the initial margin requirement?

Further Questions

10.23. Calculate the intrinsic value and time value from the mid market (average of bid and offer) prices for the September call options in Table 1.2. Do the same for the September put options in Table 1.3. Assume in each case that the current mid market stock price is $696.00.

10.24. A trader has a put option contract to sell 100 shares of a stock for a strike price of $60. What is the effect on the terms of the contract of
(a) A $2 dividend being declared
(b) A $2 dividend being paid
(c) A 5-for-2 stock split
(d) A 5% stock dividend being paid.

10.25. A trader writes 5 naked put option contracts with each contract being on 100 shares. The option price is $10, the time to maturity is 6 months, and the strike price is $64.
(a) What is the margin requirement if the stock price is $58?
(b) How would the answer to (a) change if the rules for index options applied?
(c) How would the answer to (a) change if the stock price were $70?
(d) How would the answer to (a) change if the trader is buying instead of selling the options?

10.26. The price of a stock is $40. The price of a 1-year European put option on the stock with a strike price of $30 is quoted as $7 and the price of a 1-year European call option on the stock with a strike price of $50 is quoted as $5. Suppose that an investor buys 100 shares, shorts 100 call options, and buys 100 put options. Draw a diagram illustrating how the investor's profit or loss varies with the stock price over the next year. How does your answer change if the investor buys 100 shares, shorts 200 call options, and buys 200 put options?

10.27. "If a company does not do better than its competitors but the stock market goes up, executives do very well from their stock options. This makes no sense." Discuss this viewpoint. Can you think of alternatives to the usual employee stock option plan that take the viewpoint into account.

10.28. Use DerivaGem to calculate the value of an American put option on a non-dividend-paying stock when the stock price is $30, the strike price is $32, the risk-free rate is 5%, the volatility is 30%, and the time to maturity is 1.5 years. (Choose "Binomial American" for the "option type" and 50 time steps.)
(a) What is the option's intrinsic value?
(b) What is the option's time value?
(c) What would a time value of zero indicate? What is the value of an option with zero time value?
(d) Using a trial and error approach, calculate how low the stock price would have to be for the time value of the option to be zero.

10.29. On July 20, 2004, Microsoft surprised the market by announcing a $3 dividend. The ex-dividend date was November 17, 2004, and the payment date was December 2, 2004. Its stock price at the time was about $28. It also changed the terms of its employee stock options so that each exercise price was adjusted downward to

$$\text{Predividend exercise price} \times \frac{\text{Closing price} - \$3.00}{\text{Closing price}}$$

The number of shares covered by each stock option outstanding was adjusted upward to

$$\text{Number of shares predividend} \times \frac{\text{Closing price}}{\text{Closing price} - \$3.00}$$

"Closing Price" means the official NASDAQ closing price of a share of Microsoft common stock on the last trading day before the ex-dividend date. Evaluate this adjustment. Compare it with the system used by exchanges to adjust for extraordinary dividends (see Business Snapshot 10.1).

CHAPTER 11

Properties of Stock Options

In this chapter, we look at the factors affecting stock option prices. We use a number of different arbitrage arguments to explore the relationships between European option prices, American option prices, and the underlying stock price. The most important of these relationships is put–call parity, which is a relationship between the price of a European call option, the price of a European put option, and the underlying stock price.

The chapter examines whether American options should be exercised early. It shows that it is never optimal to exercise an American call option on a non-dividend-paying stock prior to the option's expiration, but that under some circumstances the early exercise of an American put option on such a stock is optimal. When there are dividends, it can be optimal to exercise either calls or puts early.

11.1 FACTORS AFFECTING OPTION PRICES

There are six factors affecting the price of a stock option:

1. The current stock price, S_0
2. The strike price, K
3. The time to expiration, T
4. The volatility of the stock price, σ
5. The risk-free interest rate, r
6. The dividends that are expected to be paid.

In this section, we consider what happens to option prices when there is a change to one of these factors, with all the other factors remaining fixed. The results are summarized in Table 11.1.

Figures 11.1 and 11.2 show how European call and put prices depend on the first five factors in the situation where $S_0 = 50$, $K = 50$, $r = 5\%$ per annum, $\sigma = 30\%$ per annum, $T = 1$ year, and there are no dividends. In this case the call price is 7.116 and the put price is 4.677.

Table 11.1 Summary of the effect on the price of a stock option of
increasing one variable while keeping all others fixed.

Variable	European call	European put	American call	American put
Current stock price	+	−	+	−
Strike price	−	+	−	+
Time to expiration	?	?	+	+
Volatility	+	+	+	+
Risk-free rate	+	−	+	−
Amount of future dividends	−	+	−	+

+ indicates that an increase in the variable causes the option price to increase or stay the same;
− indicates that an increase in the variable causes the option price to decrease or stay the same;
? indicates that the relationship is uncertain.

Stock Price and Strike Price

If a call option is exercised at some future time, the payoff will be the amount by which
the stock price exceeds the strike price. Call options therefore become more valuable as
the stock price increases and less valuable as the strike price increases. For a put option,
the payoff on exercise is the amount by which the strike price exceeds the stock price.
Put options therefore behave in the opposite way from call options: they become less
valuable as the stock price increases and more valuable as the strike price increases.
Figure 11.1a–d illustrate the way in which put and call prices depend on the stock price
and strike price.

Time to Expiration

Now consider the effect of the expiration date. Both put and call American options
become more valuable (or at least do not decrease in value) as the time to expiration
increases. Consider two American options that differ only as far as the expiration date is
concerned. The owner of the long-life option has all the exercise opportunities open to
the owner of the short-life option—and more. The long-life option must therefore
always be worth at least as much as the short-life option.

Although European put and call options usually become more valuable as the time
to expiration increases (see Figure 11.1e, f), this is not always the case. Consider two
European call options on a stock: one with an expiration date in 1 month, the other
with an expiration date in 2 months. Suppose that a very large dividend is expected in
6 weeks. The dividend will cause the stock price to decline, so that the short-life option
could be worth more than the long-life option.[1]

Volatility

The precise way in which volatility is defined is explained in Chapter 15. Roughly
speaking, the *volatility* of a stock price is a measure of how uncertain we are about

---

[1] We assume that, when the life of the option is changed, the dividends on the stock and their timing remain
unchanged.

future stock price movements. As volatility increases, the chance that the stock will do very well or very poorly increases. For the owner of a stock, these two outcomes tend to offset each other. However, this is not so for the owner of a call or put. The owner of a call benefits from price increases but has limited downside risk in the event of price decreases because the most the owner can lose is the price of the option. Similarly, the owner of a put benefits from price decreases, but has limited downside risk in the event of price increases. The values of both calls and puts therefore increase as volatility increases (see Figure 11.2a, b).

Figure 11.1   Effect of changes in stock price, strike price, and expiration date on option prices when $S_0 = 50$, $K = 50$, $r = 5\%$, $\sigma = 30\%$, and $T = 1$.

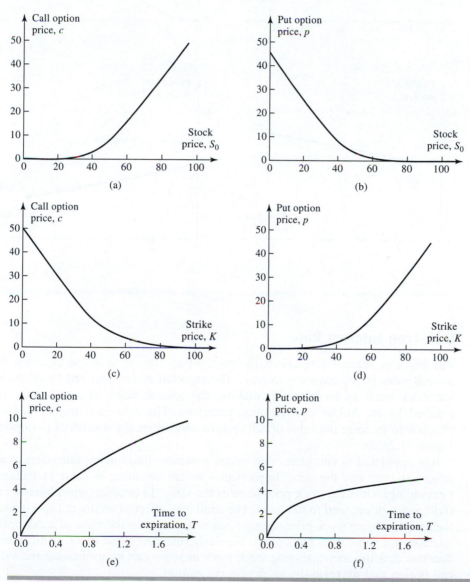

Figure 11.2 Effect of changes in volatility and risk-free interest rate on option prices when $S_0 = 50$, $K = 50$, $r = 5\%$, $\sigma = 30\%$, and $T = 1$.

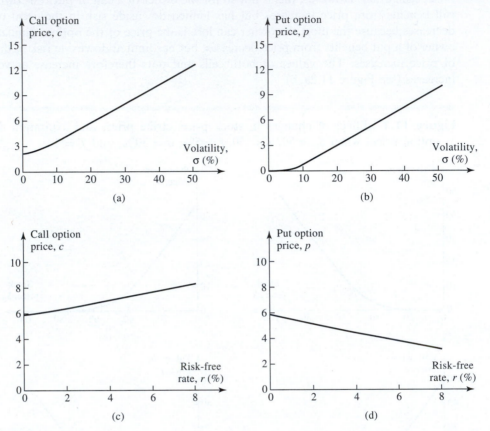

(a)

(b)

(c)

(d)

Risk-Free Interest Rate

The risk-free interest rate affects the price of an option in a less clear-cut way. As interest rates in the economy increase, the expected return required by investors from the stock tends to increase. In addition, the present value of any future cash flow received by the holder of the option decreases. The combined impact of these two effects is to increase the value of call options and decrease the value of put options (see Figure 11.2c, d).

It is important to emphasize that we are assuming that interest rates change while all other variables stay the same. In particular we are assuming in Table 11.1 that interest rates change while the stock price remains the same. In practice, when interest rates rise (fall), stock prices tend to fall (rise). The combined effect of an interest rate increase and the accompanying stock price decrease can be to decrease the value of a call option and increase the value of a put option. Similarly, the combined effect of an interest rate decrease and the accompanying stock price increase can be to increase the value of a call option and decrease the value of a put option.

Amount of Future Dividends

Dividends have the effect of reducing the stock price on the ex-dividend date. This is bad news for the value of call options and good news for the value of put options. Consider a dividend whose ex-dividend date is during the life of an option. The value of the option is negatively related to the size of the dividend if the option is a call and positively related to the size of the dividend if the option is a put.

11.2 ASSUMPTIONS AND NOTATION

In this chapter, we will make assumptions similar to those made when deriving forward and futures prices in Chapter 5. We assume that there are some market participants, such as large investment banks, for which the following statements are true:

1. There are no transaction costs.
2. All trading profits (net of trading losses) are subject to the same tax rate.
3. Borrowing and lending are possible at the risk-free interest rate.

We assume that these market participants are prepared to take advantage of arbitrage opportunities as they arise. As discussed in Chapters 1 and 5, this means that any available arbitrage opportunities disappear very quickly. For the purposes of our analysis, it is therefore reasonable to assume that there are no arbitrage opportunities.

We will use the following notation:

S_0: Current stock price

K: Strike price of option

T: Time to expiration of option

S_T: Stock price on the expiration date

r: Continuously compounded risk-free rate of interest for an investment maturing in time T

C: Value of American call option to buy one share

P: Value of American put option to sell one share

c: Value of European call option to buy one share

p: Value of European put option to sell one share

It should be noted that r is the nominal risk-free rate of interest, not the real risk-free rate of interest.[2] The proxies used by the market for the risk-free rate of interest were discussed in Section 4.3. A simple arbitrage argument suggests that $r > 0$ and this is the assumption we make in deriving results in this chapter.[3] However, during some periods the monetary policies of governments have led to interest rates being negative in some currencies such as the euro, Swiss franc, and Japanese yen. Problem 11.22 considers the impact of negative interest rates on the results in this chapter.

---

[2] The real rate of interest is the rate of interest earned after adjustment for the effects of inflation. For example, if the nominal rate of interest is 3% and inflation is 2%, the real rate of interest is approximately 1%.

[3] If r is not greater than zero, there is no advantage to investing spare funds over keeping the funds as (uninvested) cash. To put this another way, why would anyone buy a bond providing a zero or negative yield?

11.3 UPPER AND LOWER BOUNDS FOR OPTION PRICES

In this section, we derive upper and lower bounds for option prices. These bounds do not depend on any particular assumptions about the factors mentioned in Section 11.1 (except $r > 0$). If an option price is above the upper bound or below the lower bound, then there are profitable opportunities for arbitrageurs.

Upper Bounds

An American or European call option gives the holder the right to buy one share of a stock for a certain price. No matter what happens, the option can never be worth more than the stock. Hence, the stock price is an upper bound to the option price:

$$c \leqslant S_0 \quad \text{and} \quad C \leqslant S_0 \tag{11.1}$$

If these relationships were not true, an arbitrageur could easily make a riskless profit by buying the stock and selling the call option.

An American put option gives the holder the right to sell one share of a stock for K. No matter how low the stock price becomes, the option can never be worth more than K. Hence,

$$P \leqslant K \tag{11.2}$$

For European options, we know that at maturity the option cannot be worth more than K. It follows that it cannot be worth more than the present value of K today:

$$p \leqslant Ke^{-rT} \tag{11.3}$$

If this were not true, an arbitrageur could make a riskless profit by writing the option and investing the proceeds of the sale at the risk-free interest rate.

Lower Bound for Calls on Non-Dividend-Paying Stocks

A lower bound for the price of a European call option on a non-dividend-paying stock is

$$S_0 - Ke^{-rT}$$

We first look at a numerical example and then consider a more formal argument.

Suppose that $S_0 = \$20$, $K = \$18$, $r = 10\%$ per annum, and $T = 1$ year. In this case,

$$S_0 - Ke^{-rT} = 20 - 18e^{-0.1} = 3.71$$

or \$3.71. Consider the situation where the European call price is \$3.00, which is less than the theoretical minimum of \$3.71. An arbitrageur can short the stock and buy the call to provide a cash inflow of $\$20.00 - \$3.00 = \$17.00$. If invested for 1 year at 10% per annum, the \$17.00 grows to $17e^{0.1 \times 1} = \$18.79$. At the end of the year, the option expires. If the stock price is greater than \$18.00, the arbitrageur exercises the option paying \$18.00 for the stock and uses the stock to close out the short position. This leads to a profit of

$$\$18.79 - \$18.00 = \$0.79$$

If the stock price is less than \$18.00, the stock is bought in the market and the short position is closed out. The arbitrageur then makes an even greater profit. For example, if the stock price is $17.00, the arbitrageur's profit is

$$\$18.79 - \$17.00 = \$1.79$$

For a more formal argument, we consider the following two portfolios:

> *Portfolio A*: one European call option plus a zero-coupon bond that provides a payoff of K at time T
>
> *Portfolio B*: one share of the stock.

In portfolio A, the zero-coupon bond will be worth K at time T. If $S_T > K$, the call option is exercised at maturity and portfolio A is worth S_T. If $S_T < K$, the call option expires worthless and the portfolio is worth K. Hence, at time T, portfolio A is worth

$$\max(S_T, \, K)$$

Portfolio B is worth S_T at time T. Hence, portfolio A is always worth as much as, and can be worth more than, portfolio B at the option's maturity. It follows that in the absence of arbitrage opportunities this must also be true today. The zero-coupon bond is worth Ke^{-rT} today. Hence,

$$c + Ke^{-rT} \geqslant S_0$$

or

$$c \geqslant S_0 - Ke^{-rT}$$

Because the worst that can happen to a call option is that it expires worthless, its value cannot be negative. This means that $c \geqslant 0$, so that

$$c \geqslant \max(S_0 - Ke^{-rT}, \, 0) \tag{11.4}$$

Example 11.1

Consider a European call option on a non-dividend-paying stock when the stock price is $51, the strike price is $50, the time to maturity is 6 months, and the risk-free interest rate is 12% per annum. In this case, $S_0 = 51$, $K = 50$, $T = 0.5$, and $r = 0.12$. From equation (11.4), a lower bound for the option price is $S_0 - Ke^{-rT}$, or

$$51 - 50e^{-0.12 \times 0.5} = \$3.91$$

Lower Bound for European Puts on Non-Dividend-Paying Stocks

For a European put option on a non-dividend-paying stock, a lower bound for the price is

$$Ke^{-rT} - S_0$$

Again, we first consider a numerical example and then look at a more formal argument. Suppose that $S_0 = \$37$, $K = \$40$, $r = 5\%$ per annum, and $T = 0.5$ years. In this case,

$$Ke^{-rT} - S_0 = 40e^{-0.05 \times 0.5} - 37 = \$2.01$$

Consider the situation where the European put price is $1.00, which is less than the theoretical minimum of $2.01. An arbitrageur can borrow $38.00 for 6 months to buy both the put and the stock. At the end of the 6 months, the arbitrageur will be required to repay $38e^{0.05 \times 0.5} = \$38.96$. If the stock price is below $40.00, the arbitrageur exercises the option to sell the stock for $40.00, repays the loan, and makes a profit of

$$\$40.00 - \$38.96 = \$1.04$$

If the stock price is greater than $40.00, the arbitrageur discards the option, sells the stock, and repays the loan for an even greater profit. For example, if the stock price is $42.00, the arbitrageur's profit is

$$\$42.00 - \$38.96 = \$3.04$$

For a more formal argument, we consider the following two portfolios:

Portfolio C: one European put option plus one share

Portfolio D: a zero-coupon bond paying off K at time T.

If $S_T < K$, then the option in portfolio C is exercised at option maturity and the portfolio becomes worth K. If $S_T > K$, then the put option expires worthless and the portfolio is worth S_T at this time. Hence, portfolio C is worth

$$\max(S_T, K)$$

in time T. Portfolio D is worth K in time T. Hence, portfolio C is always worth as much as, and can sometimes be worth more than, portfolio D in time T. It follows that in the absence of arbitrage opportunities portfolio C must be worth at least as much as portfolio D today. Hence,

$$p + S_0 \geqslant Ke^{-rT}$$

or

$$p \geqslant Ke^{-rT} - S_0$$

Because the worst that can happen to a put option is that it expires worthless, its value cannot be negative. This means that

$$p \geqslant \max(Ke^{-rT} - S_0, 0) \tag{11.5}$$

Example 11.2

Consider a European put option on a non-dividend-paying stock when the stock price is $38, the strike price is $40, the time to maturity is 3 months, and the risk-free rate of interest is 10% per annum. In this case $S_0 = 38$, $K = 40$, $T = 0.25$, and $r = 0.10$. From equation (11.5), a lower bound for the option price is $Ke^{-rT} - S_0$, or

$$40e^{-0.1 \times 0.25} - 38 = \$1.01$$

11.4 PUT–CALL PARITY

We now derive an important relationship between the prices of European put and call options that have the same strike price and time to maturity. Consider the following two portfolios that were used in the previous section:

Portfolio A: one European call option plus a zero-coupon bond that provides a payoff of K at time T

Portfolio C: one European put option plus one share of the stock.

Table 11.2 Portfolios illustrating put–call parity.

		$S_T > K$	$S_T < K$
Portfolio A	Call option	$S_T - K$	0
	Zero-coupon bond	K	K
	Total	S_T	K
Portfolio C	Put Option	0	$K - S_T$
	Share	S_T	S_T
	Total	S_T	K

We continue to assume that the stock pays no dividends. The call and put options have the same strike price K and the same time to maturity T.

As discussed in the previous section, the zero-coupon bond in portfolio A will be worth K at time T. If the stock price S_T at time T proves to be above K, then the call option in portfolio A will be exercised. This means that portfolio A is worth $(S_T - K) + K = S_T$ at time T in these circumstances. If S_T proves to be less than K, then the call option in portfolio A will expire worthless and the portfolio will be worth K at time T.

In portfolio C, the share will be worth S_T at time T. If S_T proves to be below K, then the put option in portfolio C will be exercised. This means that portfolio C is worth $(K - S_T) + S_T = K$ at time T in these circumstances. If S_T proves to be greater than K, then the put option in portfolio C will expire worthless and the portfolio will be worth S_T at time T.

The situation is summarized in Table 11.2. If $S_T > K$, both portfolios are worth S_T at time T; if $S_T < K$, both portfolios are worth K at time T. In other words, both are worth

$$\max(S_T, K)$$

when the options expire at time T. Because they are European, the options cannot be exercised prior to time T. Since the portfolios have identical values at time T, they must have identical values today. If this were not the case, an arbitrageur could buy the less expensive portfolio and sell the more expensive one. Because the portfolios are guaranteed to cancel each other out at time T, this trading strategy would lock in an arbitrage profit equal to the difference in the values of the two portfolios.

The components of portfolio A are worth c and Ke^{-rT} today, and the components of portfolio C are worth p and S_0 today. Hence,

$$c + Ke^{-rT} = p + S_0 \tag{11.6}$$

This relationship is known as *put–call parity*. It shows that the value of a European call with a certain exercise price and exercise date can be deduced from the value of a European put with the same exercise price and exercise date, and vice versa.

To illustrate the arbitrage opportunities when equation (11.6) does not hold, suppose that the stock price is \$31, the exercise price is \$30, the risk-free interest rate is 10% per annum, the price of a three-month European call option is \$3, and the price of a

3-month European put option is $2.25. In this case,

$$c + Ke^{-rT} = 3 + 30e^{-0.1 \times 3/12} = \$32.26$$
$$p + S_0 = 2.25 + 31 = \$33.25$$

Portfolio C is overpriced relative to portfolio A. An arbitrageur can buy the securities in portfolio A and short the securities in portfolio C. The strategy involves buying the call and shorting both the put and the stock, generating a positive cash flow of

$$-3 + 2.25 + 31 = \$30.25$$

up front. When invested at the risk-free interest rate, this amount grows to

$$30.25e^{0.1 \times 0.25} = \$31.02$$

in three months. If the stock price at expiration of the option is greater than $30, the call will be exercised. If it is less than $30, the put will be exercised. In either case, the arbitrageur ends up buying one share for $30. This share can be used to close out the short position. The net profit is therefore

$$\$31.02 - \$30.00 = \$1.02$$

For an alternative situation, suppose that the call price is $3 and the put price is $1. In this case,

$$c + Ke^{-rT} = 3 + 30e^{-0.1 \times 3/12} = \$32.26$$
$$p + S_0 = 1 + 31 = \$32.00$$

Portfolio A is overpriced relative to portfolio C. An arbitrageur can short the securities in portfolio A and buy the securities in portfolio C to lock in a profit. The strategy involves shorting the call and buying both the put and the stock with an initial investment of

$$\$31 + \$1 - \$3 = \$29$$

When the investment is financed at the risk-free interest rate, a repayment of $29e^{0.1 \times 0.25} = \$29.73$ is required at the end of the three months. As in the previous case, either the call or the put will be exercised. The short call and long put option position therefore leads to the stock being sold for $30.00. The net profit is therefore

$$\$30.00 - \$29.73 = \$0.27$$

These examples are illustrated in Table 11.3. Business Snapshot 11.1 shows how options and put–call parity can help us understand the positions of the debt holders and equity holders in a company.

American Options

Put–call parity holds only for European options. However, it is possible to derive some results for American option prices. It can be shown (see Problem 11.18) that, when there are no dividends,

$$S_0 - K \leqslant C - P \leqslant S_0 - Ke^{-rT} \tag{11.7}$$

Example 11.3

An American call option on a non-dividend-paying stock with strike price $20.00 and maturity in 5 months is worth $1.50. Suppose that the current stock price is

Table 11.3 Arbitrage opportunities when put–call parity does not hold. Stock price = \$31; interest rate = 10%; call price = \$3. Both put and call have strike price of \$30 and three months to maturity.

Three-month put price = \$2.25	*Three-month put price = \$1*
Action now:	*Action now*:
Buy call for \$3	Borrow \$29 for 3 months
Short put to realize \$2.25	Short call to realize \$3
Short the stock to realize \$31	Buy put for \$1
Invest \$30.25 for 3 months	Buy the stock for \$31
Action in 3 months if $S_T > 30$:	*Action in 3 months if $S_T > 30$:*
Receive \$31.02 from investment	Call exercised: sell stock for \$30
Exercise call to buy stock for \$30	Use \$29.73 to repay loan
Net profit = \$1.02	Net profit = \$0.27
Action in 3 months if $S_T < 30$:	*Action in 3 months if $S_T < 30$:*
Receive \$31.02 from investment	Exercise put to sell stock for \$30
Put exercised: buy stock for \$30	Use \$29.73 to repay loan
Net profit = \$1.02	Net profit = \$0.27

\$19.00 and the risk-free interest rate is 10% per annum. From equation (11.7), we have

$$19 - 20 \leqslant C - P \leqslant 19 - 20e^{-0.1 \times 5/12}$$

or

$$1 \geqslant P - C \geqslant 0.18$$

showing that $P - C$ lies between \$1.00 and \$0.18. With C at \$1.50, P must lie between \$1.68 and \$2.50. In other words, upper and lower bounds for the price of an American put with the same strike price and expiration date as the American call are \$2.50 and \$1.68.

11.5 CALLS ON A NON-DIVIDEND-PAYING STOCK

In this section, we first show that it is never optimal to exercise an American call option on a non-dividend-paying stock before the expiration date.

To illustrate the general nature of the argument, consider an American call option on a non-dividend-paying stock with one month to expiration when the stock price is \$70 and the strike price is \$40. The option is deep in the money, and the investor who owns the option might well be tempted to exercise it immediately. However, if the investor plans to hold the stock obtained by exercising the option for more than one month, this is not the best strategy. A better course of action is to keep the option and exercise it at the end of the month. The \$40 strike price is then paid out one month later than it would be if the option were exercised immediately, so that interest is earned on the \$40 for one month. Because the stock pays no dividends, no income from the stock is sacrificed. A further advantage of waiting rather than exercising immediately is that there is some chance (however remote) that the stock price will fall below \$40 in one

---

Business Snapshot 11.1 Put–Call Parity and Capital Structure

Fischer Black, Myron Scholes, and Robert Merton were the pioneers of option pricing. In the early 1970s, they also showed that options can be used to characterize the capital structure of a company. Today this analysis is widely used by financial institutions to assess a company's credit risk.

To illustrate the analysis, consider a simple situation where a company has assets that are financed with zero-coupon bonds and equity. The bonds mature in five years at which time a principal payment of K is required. The company pays no dividends. If the assets are worth more than K in five years, the equity holders choose to repay the bond holders. If the assets are worth less than K, the equity holders choose to declare bankruptcy and the bond holders end up owning the company.

The value of the equity in five years is therefore $\max(A_T - K, 0)$, where A_T is the value of the company's assets at that time. This shows that the equity holders have a five-year European call option on the assets of the company with a strike price of K. What about the bondholders? They get $\min(A_T, K)$ in five years. This is the same as $K - \max(K - A_T, 0)$. This shows that today the bonds are worth the present value of K minus the value of a five-year European put option on the assets with a strike price of K.

To summarize, if c and p are the values, respectively, of five-year call and put options on the company's assets with strike price K, then

$$\text{Value of company's equity} = c$$

$$\text{Value of company's debt} = PV(K) - p$$

Denote the value of the assets of the company today by A_0. The value of the assets must equal the total value of the instruments used to finance the assets. This means that it must equal the sum of the value of the equity and the value of the debt, so that

$$A_0 = c + [PV(K) - p]$$

Rearranging this equation, we have

$$c + PV(K) = p + A_0$$

This is the put–call parity result in equation (11.6) for call and put options on the assets of the company.

---

month. In this case the investor will not exercise in one month and will be glad that the decision to exercise early was not taken!

This argument shows that there are no advantages to exercising early if the investor plans to keep the stock for the remaining life of the option (one month, in this case). What if the investor thinks the stock is currently overpriced and is wondering whether to exercise the option and sell the stock? In this case, the investor is better off selling the option than exercising it.[4] The option will be bought by another investor who does want to hold the stock. Such investors must exist. Otherwise the current stock price would not be $70. The price obtained for the option will be greater than its intrinsic value of $30, for the reasons mentioned earlier.

---

[4] As an alternative strategy, the investor can keep the option and short the stock to lock in a better profit than $30.

For a more formal argument, we can use equation (11.4):

$$c \geqslant S_0 - Ke^{-rT}$$

Because the owner of an American call has all the exercise opportunities open to the owner of the corresponding European call, we must have $C \geqslant c$. Hence,

$$C \geqslant S_0 - Ke^{-rT}$$

Given $r > 0$, it follows that $C > S_0 - K$ when $T > 0$. This means that C is always greater than the option's intrinsic value prior to maturity. If it were optimal to exercise at a particular time prior to maturity, C would equal the option's intrinsic value at that time. It follows that it can never be optimal to exercise early.

To summarize, there are two reasons an American call on a non-dividend-paying stock should not be exercised early. One relates to the insurance that it provides. A call option, when held instead of the stock itself, in effect insures the holder against the stock price falling below the strike price. Once the option has been exercised and the strike price has been exchanged for the stock price, this insurance vanishes. The other reason concerns the time value of money. From the perspective of the option holder, the later the strike price is paid out the better.

Bounds

Because American call options are never exercised early when there are no dividends, they are equivalent to European call options, so that $C = c$. From equations (11.1) and (11.4), it follows that lower and upper bounds for both c and C are given by

$$\max(S_0 - Ke^{-rT}, 0) \quad \text{and} \quad S_0$$

respectively. These bounds are illustrated in Figure 11.3.

The general way in which the call price varies with the stock price, S_0, is shown in Figure 11.4. As r or T or the stock price volatility increases, the line relating the call price to the stock price moves in the direction indicated by the arrows.

Figure 11.3 Bounds for European and American call options when there are no dividends.

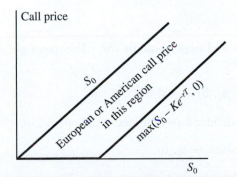

Figure 11.4   Variation of price of an American or European call option on a non-dividend-paying stock with the stock price. Curve moves in the direction of the arrows when there is an increase in the interest rate, time to maturity, or stock price volatility.

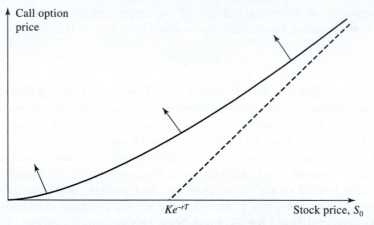

11.6 PUTS ON A NON-DIVIDEND-PAYING STOCK

It can be optimal to exercise an American put option on a non-dividend-paying stock early. Indeed, at any given time during its life, the put option should always be exercised early if it is sufficiently deep in the money.

To illustrate, consider an extreme situation. Suppose that the strike price is $10 and the stock price is virtually zero. By exercising immediately, an investor makes an immediate gain of $10. If the investor waits, the gain from exercise might be less than $10, but it cannot be more than $10, because negative stock prices are impossible. Furthermore, receiving $10 now is preferable to receiving $10 in the future. It follows that the option should be exercised immediately.

Like a call option, a put option can be viewed as providing insurance. A put option, when held in conjunction with the stock, insures the holder against the stock price falling below a certain level. However, a put option is different from a call option in that it may be optimal for an investor to forgo this insurance and exercise early in order to realize the strike price immediately. In general, the early exercise of a put option becomes more attractive as S_0 decreases, as r increases, and as the volatility decreases.

Bounds

From equations (11.3) and (11.5), lower and upper bounds for a European put option when there are no dividends are given by

$$\max(Ke^{-rT} - S_0, 0) \leqslant p \leqslant Ke^{-rT}$$

For an American put option on a non-dividend-paying stock, the condition

$$P \geqslant \max(K - S_0, 0)$$

must apply because the option can be exercised at any time. This is a stronger

Figure 11.5 Bounds for European and American put options when there are no dividends.

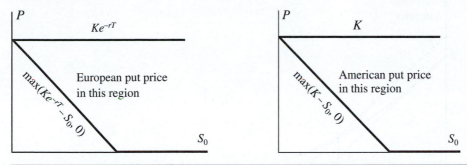

condition than the one for a European put option in equation (11.5). Using the result in equation (11.2), bounds for an American put option on a non-dividend-paying stock are

$$\max(K - S_0, 0) \leqslant P \leqslant K$$

Figure 11.5 illustrates the bounds.

Figure 11.6 shows the general way in which the price of an American put option varies with S_0. As we argued earlier, provided that $r > 0$, it is always optimal to exercise an American put immediately when the stock price is sufficiently low. When early exercise is optimal, the value of the option is $K - S_0$. The curve representing the value of the put therefore merges into the put's intrinsic value, $K - S_0$, for a sufficiently small value of S_0. In Figure 11.6, this value of S_0 is shown as point A. The line relating the put price to the stock price moves in the direction indicated by the arrows when r decreases, when the volatility increases, and when T increases.

Because there are some circumstances when it is desirable to exercise an American put option early, it follows that an American put option is always worth more than the

Figure 11.6 Variation of price of an American put option with stock price. Curve moves in the direction of the arrows when the time to maturity or stock price volatility increases or when the interest rate decreases.

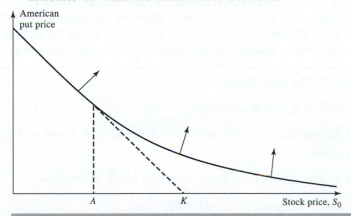

Figure 11.7   Variation of price of a European put option with the stock price.

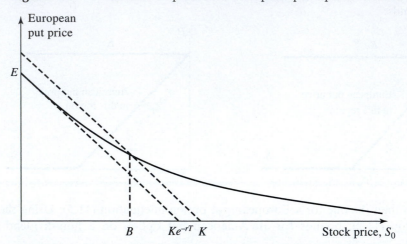

corresponding European put option. Furthermore, because an American put is sometimes worth its intrinsic value (see Figure 11.6), it follows that a European put option must sometimes be worth less than its intrinsic value. This means that the curve representing the relationship between the put price and the stock price for a European option must be below the corresponding curve for an American option.

Figure 11.7 shows the variation of the European put price with the stock price. Note that point B in Figure 11.7, at which the price of the option is equal to its intrinsic value, must represent a higher value of the stock price than point A in Figure 11.6 because the curve in Figure 11.7 is below that in Figure 11.6. Point E in Figure 11.7 is where $S_0 = 0$ and the European put price is Ke^{-rT}.

11.7   EFFECT OF DIVIDENDS

The results produced so far in this chapter have assumed that we are dealing with options on a non-dividend-paying stock. In this section, we examine the impact of dividends. We assume that the dividends that will be paid during the life of the option are known. In many situations, this assumption is often not too unreasonable. We will use D to denote the present value of the dividends during the life of the option. In the calculation of D, a dividend is assumed to occur at the time of its ex-dividend date.

Lower Bound for Calls and Puts

We can redefine portfolios A and B as follows:

Portfolio A: one European call option plus an amount of cash equal to $D + Ke^{-rT}$

Portfolio B: one share

A similar argument to the one used to derive equation (11.4) shows that

$$c \geqslant \max(S_0 - D - Ke^{-rT}, 0) \tag{11.8}$$

We can also redefine portfolios C and D as follows:

Portfolio C: one European put option plus one share
Portfolio D: an amount of cash equal to $D + Ke^{-rT}$

A similar argument to the one used to derive equation (11.5) shows that

$$p \geqslant \max(D + Ke^{-rT} - S_0, 0) \qquad (11.9)$$

Early Exercise

When dividends are expected, we can no longer assert that an American call option will not be exercised early. Sometimes it is optimal to exercise an American call immediately prior to an ex-dividend date. It is never optimal to exercise a call at other times. This point is discussed further in Section 15.12.

Put–Call Parity

Comparing the value at option maturity of the redefined portfolios A and C shows that, with dividends, the put–call parity result in equation (11.6) becomes

$$c + D + Ke^{-rT} = p + S_0 \qquad (11.10)$$

Dividends cause equation (11.7) to be modified (see Problem 11.19) to

$$S_0 - D - K \leqslant C - P \leqslant S_0 - Ke^{-rT} \qquad (11.11)$$

SUMMARY

There are six factors affecting the value of a stock option: the current stock price, the strike price, the time to expiration, the stock price volatility, the risk-free interest rate, and the dividends expected during the life of the option. The value of a call usually increases as the current stock price, the time to expiration, the volatility, and the risk-free interest rate increase. The value of a call decreases as the strike price and expected dividends increase. The value of a put usually increases as the strike price, the time to expiration, the volatility, and the expected dividends increase. The value of a put decreases as the current stock price and the risk-free interest rate increase.

It is possible to reach some conclusions about the value of stock options without making any assumptions about the volatility of stock prices. For example, the price of a call option on a stock must always be worth less than the price of the stock itself. Similarly, the price of a put option on a stock must always be worth less than the option's strike price.

A European call option on a non-dividend-paying stock must be worth more than

$$\max(S_0 - Ke^{-rT}, 0)$$

where S_0 is the stock price, K is the strike price, r is the risk-free interest rate, and T is the time to expiration. A European put option on a non-dividend-paying stock must be worth more than

$$\max(Ke^{-rT} - S_0, 0)$$

When dividends with present value D will be paid, the lower bound for a European call option becomes

$$\max(S_0 - D - Ke^{-rT}, 0)$$

and the lower bound for a European put option becomes

$$\max(Ke^{-rT} + D - S_0, 0)$$

Put–call parity is a relationship between the price, c, of a European call option on a stock and the price, p, of a European put option on a stock. For a non-dividend-paying stock, it is

$$c + Ke^{-rT} = p + S_0$$

For a dividend-paying stock, the put–call parity relationship is

$$c + D + Ke^{-rT} = p + S_0$$

Put–call parity does not hold for American options. However, it is possible to use arbitrage arguments to obtain upper and lower bounds for the difference between the price of an American call and the price of an American put.

In Chapter 15, we will carry the analyses in this chapter further by making specific assumptions about the probabilistic behavior of stock prices. The analysis will enable us to derive exact pricing formulas for European stock options. In Chapters 13 and 21, we will see how numerical procedures can be used to price American options.

FURTHER READING

Broadie, M., and J. Detemple. "American Option Valuation: New Bounds, Approximations, and a Comparison of Existing Methods," *Review of Financial Studies*, 9, 4 (1996): 1211–50.

Merton, R.C.. "On the Pricing of Corporate Debt: The Risk Structure of Interest Rates," *Journal of Finance*, 29, 2 (1974): 449–70.

Merton, R.C. "The Relationship between Put and Call Prices: Comment," *Journal of Finance*, 28 (March 1973): 183–84.

Stoll, H.R. "The Relationship between Put and Call Option Prices," *Journal of Finance*, 24 (December 1969): 801–24.

Practice Questions (Answers in Solutions Manual)

11.1. List the six factors that affect stock option prices.

11.2. What is a lower bound for the price of a 4-month call option on a non-dividend-paying stock when the stock price is $28, the strike price is $25, and the risk-free interest rate is 8% per annum?

11.3. What is a lower bound for the price of a 1-month European put option on a non-dividend-paying stock when the stock price is $12, the strike price is $15, and the risk-free interest rate is 6% per annum?

11.4. Give two reasons why the early exercise of an American call option on a non-dividend-paying stock is not optimal. The first reason should involve the time value of money. The second should apply even if interest rates are zero.

11.5. "The early exercise of an American put is a trade-off between the time value of money and the insurance value of a put." Explain this statement.

11.6. Why is an American call option on a dividend-paying stock always worth at least as much as its intrinsic value. Is the same true of a European call option? Explain your answer.

11.7. The price of a non-dividend-paying stock is $19 and the price of a 3-month European call option on the stock with a strike price of $20 is $1. The risk-free rate is 4% per annum. What is the price of a 3-month European put option with a strike price of $20?

11.8. Explain why the arguments leading to put–call parity for European options cannot be used to give a similar result for American options.

11.9. What is a lower bound for the price of a 6-month call option on a non-dividend-paying stock when the stock price is $80, the strike price is $75, and the risk-free interest rate is 10% per annum?

11.10. What is a lower bound for the price of a 2-month European put option on a non-dividend-paying stock when the stock price is $58, the strike price is $65, and the risk-free interest rate is 5% per annum?

11.11. A 4-month European call option on a dividend-paying stock is currently selling for $5. The stock price is $64, the strike price is $60, and a dividend of $0.80 is expected in 1 month. The risk-free interest rate is 12% per annum for all maturities. What opportunities are there for an arbitrageur?

11.12. A 1-month European put option on a non-dividend-paying stock is currently selling for $2.50. The stock price is $47, the strike price is $50, and the risk-free interest rate is 6% per annum. What opportunities are there for an arbitrageur?

11.13. Give an intuitive explanation of why the early exercise of an American put becomes more attractive as the risk-free rate increases and volatility decreases.

11.14. The price of a European call that expires in 6 months and has a strike price of $30 is $2. The underlying stock price is $29, and a dividend of $0.50 is expected in 2 months and again in 5 months. Risk-free interest rates (all maturities) are 10%. What is the price of a European put option that expires in 6 months and has a strike price of $30?

11.15. Explain the arbitrage opportunities in Problem 11.14 if the European put price is $3.

11.16. The price of an American call on a non-dividend-paying stock is $4. The stock price is $31, the strike price is $30, and the expiration date is in 3 months. The risk-free interest rate is 8%. Derive upper and lower bounds for the price of an American put on the same stock with the same strike price and expiration date.

11.17. Explain carefully the arbitrage opportunities in Problem 11.16 if the American put price is greater than the calculated upper bound.

11.18. Prove the result in equation (11.7). (*Hint*: For the first part of the relationship, consider (a) a portfolio consisting of a European call plus an amount of cash equal to K, and (b) a portfolio consisting of an American put option plus one share.)

11.19. Prove the result in equation (11.11). (*Hint*: For the first part of the relationship, consider (a) a portfolio consisting of a European call plus an amount of cash equal to $D + K$, and (b) a portfolio consisting of an American put option plus one share.)

11.20. Consider a 5-year call option on a non-dividend-paying stock granted to employees. The option can be exercised at any time after the end of the first year. Unlike a regular exchange-traded call option, the employee stock option cannot be sold. What is the likely impact of this restriction on the early-exercise decision?

11.21. Use the software DerivaGem to verify that Figures 11.1 and 11.2 are correct.

11.22. What is the impact (if any) of negative interest rates on:
(a) The put–call parity result for European options
(b) The result that American call options on non-dividend-paying stocks should never be exercised early
(c) The result that American put options on non-dividend-paying stocks should sometimes be exercised early.
Assume that holding cash earning zero interest is not possible.

Further Questions

11.23. Calls were traded on exchanges before puts. During the period of time when calls were traded but puts were not traded, how would you create a European put option on a non-dividend-paying stock synthetically.

11.24. The prices of European call and put options on a non-dividend-paying stock with an expiration date in 12 months and a strike price of $120 are $20 and $5, respectively. The current stock price is $130. What is the implied risk-free rate?

11.25. A European call option and put option on a stock both have a strike price of $20 and an expiration date in 3 months. Both sell for $3. The risk-free interest rate is 10% per annum, the current stock price is $19, and a $1 dividend is expected in 1 month. Identify the arbitrage opportunity open to a trader.

11.26. Suppose that c_1, c_2, and c_3 are the prices of European call options with strike prices K_1, K_2, and K_3, respectively, where $K_3 > K_2 > K_1$ and $K_3 - K_2 = K_2 - K_1$. All options have the same maturity. Show that

$$c_2 \leqslant 0.5(c_1 + c_3)$$

(*Hint*: Consider a portfolio that is long one option with strike price K_1, long one option with strike price K_3, and short two options with strike price K_2.)

11.27. What is the result corresponding to that in Problem 11.26 for European put options?

11.28. You are the manager and sole owner of a highly leveraged company. All the debt will mature in 1 year. If at that time the value of the company is greater than the face value of the debt, you will pay off the debt. If the value of the company is less than the face value of the debt, you will declare bankruptcy and the debt holders will own the company.
(a) Express your position as an option on the value of the company.
(b) Express the position of the debt holders in terms of options on the value of the company.
(c) What can you do to increase the value of your position?

11.29. Consider an option on a stock when the stock price is $41, the strike price is $40, the risk-free rate is 6%, the volatility is 35%, and the time to maturity is 1 year. Assume that a dividend of $0.50 is expected after 6 months.

   (a) Use DerivaGem to value the option assuming it is a European call.

   (b) Use DerivaGem to value the option assuming it is a European put.

   (c) Verify that put–call parity holds.

   (d) Explore using DerivaGem what happens to the price of the options as the time to maturity becomes very large and there are no dividends. Explain your results.

11.30. Consider a put option on a non-dividend-paying stock when the stock price is $40, the strike price is $42, the risk-free interest rate is 2%, the volatility is 25% per annum, and the time to maturity is three months. Use DerivaGem to determine the following:

   (a) The price of the option if it is European (use Black–Scholes: European)

   (b) The price of the option if it is American (use Binomial: American with 100 tree steps)

   (c) Point B in Figure 11.7.

11.31. Section 11.1 gives an example of a situation where the value of a European call option decreases as the time to maturity is increased. Give an example of a situation where the same thing happens for a European put option.

CHAPTER 12

Trading Strategies Involving Options

We discussed the profit pattern from an investment in a single option in Chapter 10. In this chapter we look at what can be achieved when an option is traded in conjunction with other assets. In particular, we examine the properties of portfolios consisting of (a) an option and a zero-coupon bond, (b) an option and the asset underlying the option, and (c) two or more options on the same asset.

A natural question is why a trader would want the profit patterns discussed here. The answer is that the choices a trader makes depend on the trader's judgment about how prices will move and the trader's willingness to take risks. Principal-protected notes, discussed in Section 12.1 appeal to individuals who are risk-averse. They do not want to risk losing their principal, but have an opinion about whether a particular asset will increase or decrease in value and are prepared to let the return they earn on this principal depend on whether they are right. If a trader is willing to take rather more risk than this, he or she could choose a bull or bear spread, discussed in Section 12.3. Yet more risk would be taken with a straightforward long position in a call or put option.

Suppose that a trader feels there will be a big move in price of an asset, but does not know whether this will be up or down. There are a number of alternative trading strategies. A risk-averse trader might choose a reverse butterfly spread, discussed in Section 12.3, where there will be a small gain if the trader's hunch is correct and a small loss if it is not. A more aggressive investor might choose a straddle or strangle, discussed in Section 12.4, where potential gains and losses are larger.

Further trading strategies involving options are considered in later chapters. For example, Chapter 17 shows how options on stock indices can be used to manage the risks in a stock portfolio and explains how range forward contracts can be used to hedge a foreign exchange exposure; Chapter 19 covers the way in which Greek letters are used to manage the risks when derivatives are traded; Chapter 26 covers exotic options and what is known as static options replication.

12.1 PRINCIPAL-PROTECTED NOTES

Options are often used to create what are termed *principal-protected notes* for the retail market. These are products that appeal to conservative investors. The return earned by the investor depends on the performance of a stock, a stock index, or other risky asset, but the initial principal amount invested is not at risk. An example will illustrate how a simple principal-protected note can be created.

Example 12.1

Suppose that the 3-year interest rate is 6% with continuous compounding. This means that $1,000e^{-0.06\times3} = \$835.27$ will grow to $1,000 in 3 years. The difference between $1,000 and $835.27 is $164.73. Suppose that a stock portfolio is worth $1,000 and provides a dividend yield of 1.5% per annum. Suppose further that a 3-year at-the-money European call option on the stock portfolio can be purchased for less than $164.73. (From DerivaGem, it can be verified that this will be the case if the volatility of the value of the portfolio is less than about 15%.) A bank can offer clients a $1,000 investment opportunity consisting of:

1. A 3-year zero-coupon bond with a principal of $1,000
2. A 3-year at-the-money European call option on the stock portfolio.

If the value of the porfolio increases the investor gets whatever $1,000 invested in the portfolio would have grown to. (This is because the zero-coupon bond pays off $1,000 and this equals the strike price of the option.) If the value of the portfolio goes down, the option has no value, but payoff from the zero-coupon bond ensures that the investor receives the original $1,000 principal invested.

The attraction of a principal-protected note is that an investor is able to take a risky position without risking any principal. The worst that can happen is that the investor loses the chance to earn interest, or other income such as dividends, on the initial investment for the life of the note.

There are many variations on the product in Example 12.1. An investor who thinks that the price of an asset will decline can buy a principal-protected note consisting of a zero-coupon bond plus a put option. The investor's payoff in 3 years is then $1,000 plus the payoff (if any) from the put option.

Is a principal-protected note a good deal from the retail investor's perspective? A bank will always build in a profit for itself when it creates a principal-protected note. This means that, in Example 12.1, the zero-coupon bond plus the call option will always cost the bank less than $1,000. In addition, investors are taking the risk that the bank will not be in a position to make the payoff on the principal-protected note at maturity. (Some retail investors lost money on principal-protected notes created by Lehman Brothers when it failed in 2008.) In some situations, therefore, an investor will be better off if he or she buys the underlying option in the usual way and invests the remaining principal in a risk-free investment. However, this is not always the case. The investor is likely to face wider bid–offer spreads on the option than the bank and is likely to earn lower interest rates than the bank. It is therefore possible that the bank can add value for the investor while making a profit itself.

Now let us look at the principal-protected notes from the perspective of the bank. The economic viability of the structure in Example 12.1 depends critically on the level of interest rates and the volatility of the portfolio. If the interest rate is 3% instead of 6%, the bank has only $1,000 - 1,000e^{-0.03\times3} = \$86.07$ with which to buy the call option. If interest rates are 6%, but the volatility is 25% instead of 15%, the price of the option would be about $221. In either of these circumstances, the product described in Example 12.1 cannot be profitably created by the bank. However, there are a number of ways the bank can still create a viable 3-year product. For example, the strike price of the option can be increased so that the value of the portfolio has to rise by, say, 15% before the investor makes a gain; the investor's return could be capped; the return of the investor could depend on the average price of the asset instead of the final price; a knockout barrier could be specified. The derivatives involved in some of these alternatives will be discussed later in the book. (Capping the option corresponds to the creation of a bull spread for the investor and will be discussed later in this chapter.)

One way in which a bank can sometimes create a profitable principal-protected note when interest rates are low or volatilities are high is by increasing its life. Consider the situation in Example 12.1 when (a) the interest rate is 3% rather than 6% and (b) the stock portfolio has a volatility of 15% and provides a dividend yield of 1.5%. DerivaGem shows that a 3-year at-the-money European option costs about $119. This is more than the funds available to purchase it ($1,000 - 1,000e^{-0.03 \times 3} = \$86.07$). A 10-year at-the-money option costs about $217. This is less than the funds available to purchase it ($1,000 - 1,000e^{-0.03 \times 10} = \$259.18$), making the structure profitable. When the life is increased to 20 years, the option cost is about $281, which is much less than the funds available to purchase it ($1,000 - 1,000e^{-0.03 \times 20} = \$451.19$), so that the structure is even more profitable.

A critical variable for the bank in our example is the dividend yield. The higher it is, the more profitable the product is for the bank. If the dividend yield were zero, the principal-protected note in Example 12.1 cannot be profitable for the bank no matter how long it lasts. (This follows from equation (11.4).)

12.2 TRADING AN OPTION AND THE UNDERLYING ASSET

For convenience, we will assume that the asset underlying the options considered in the rest of the chapter is a stock. (Similar trading strategies can be developed for other underlying assets.) We will also follow the usual practice of calculating the profit from a trading strategy as the final payoff minus the initial cost without any discounting.

There are a number of different trading strategies involving a single option on a stock and the stock itself. The profits from these are illustrated in Figure 12.1. In this figure and in other figures throughout this chapter, the dashed line shows the relationship between profit and the stock price for the individual securities constituting the portfolio, whereas the solid line shows the relationship between profit and the stock price for the whole portfolio.

In Figure 12.1a, the portfolio consists of a long position in a stock plus a short position in a European call option. This is known as *writing a covered call*. The long stock position "covers" or protects the investor from the payoff on the short call that becomes necessary if there is a sharp rise in the stock price. In Figure 12.1b, a short position in a stock is combined with a long position in a call option. This is the reverse of writing a covered call. In Figure 12.1c, the investment strategy involves buying a European put option on a stock and the stock itself. This is referred to as a *protective put* strategy. In Figure 12.1d, a short position in a put option is combined with a short position in the stock. This is the reverse of a protective put.

The profit patterns in Figures 12.1a, b, c, and d have the same general shape as the profit patterns discussed in Chapter 10 for short put, long put, long call, and short call,

Figure 12 .1 Profit patterns (a) long position in a stock combined with short position in a call; (b) short position in a stock combined with long position in a call; (c) long position in a put combined with long position in a stock; (d) short position in a put combined with short position in a stock.

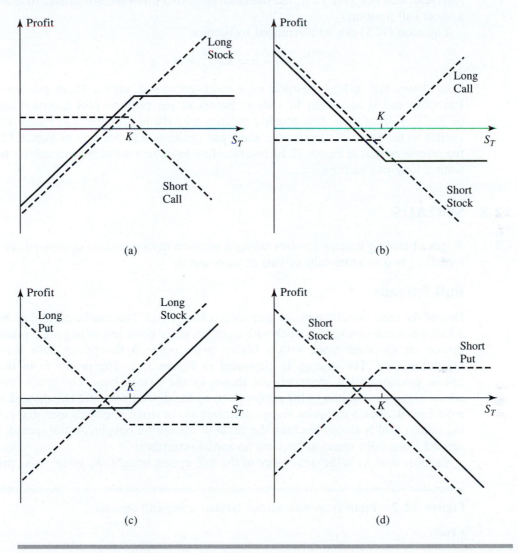

respectively. Put–call parity provides a way of understanding why this is so. From Chapter 11, the put–call parity relationship is

$$p + S_0 = c + Ke^{-rT} + D \tag{12.1}$$

where p is the price of a European put, S_0 is the stock price, c is the price of a European call, K is the strike price of both call and put, r is the risk-free interest rate, T is the time to maturity of both call and put, and D is the present value of the dividends anticipated during the life of the options.

Equation (12.1) shows that a long position in a European put combined with a long position in the stock is equivalent to a long European call position plus a certain amount ($= Ke^{-rT} + D$) of cash. This explains why the profit pattern in Figure 12.1c is similar to the profit pattern from a long call position. The position in Figure 12.1d is the reverse of that in Figure 12.1c and therefore leads to a profit pattern similar to that from a short call position.

Equation (12.1) can be rearranged to become

$$S_0 - c = Ke^{-rT} + D - p$$

This shows that a long position in a stock combined with a short position in a European call is equivalent to a short European put position plus a certain amount ($= Ke^{-rT} + D$) of cash. This equality explains why the profit pattern in Figure 12.1a is similar to the profit pattern from a short put position. The position in Figure 12.1b is the reverse of that in Figure 12.1a and therefore leads to a profit pattern similar to that from a long put position.

12.3 SPREADS

A spread trading strategy involves taking a position in two or more options of the same type (i.e., two or more calls or two or more puts).

Bull Spreads

One of the most popular types of spreads is a *bull spread.* This can be created by buying a European call option on a stock with a certain strike price and selling a European call option on the same stock with a higher strike price. Both options have the same expiration date. The strategy is illustrated in Figure 12.2. The profits from the two option positions taken separately are shown by the dashed lines. The profit from the whole strategy is the sum of the profits given by the dashed lines and is indicated by the solid line. Because a call price always decreases as the strike price increases, the value of the option sold is always less than the value of the option bought. A bull spread, when created from calls, therefore requires an initial investment.

Suppose that K_1 is the strike price of the call option bought, K_2 is the strike price of

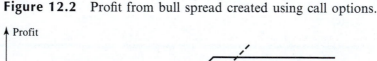

Figure 12.2   Profit from bull spread created using call options.

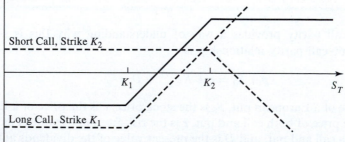

Table 12.1 Payoff from a bull spread created using calls.

Stock price range	Payoff from long call option	Payoff from short call option	Total payoff
$S_T \leqslant K_1$	0	0	0
$K_1 < S_T < K_2$	$S_T - K_1$	0	$S_T - K_1$
$S_T \geqslant K_2$	$S_T - K_1$	$-(S_T - K_2)$	$K_2 - K_1$

the call option sold, and S_T is the stock price on the expiration date of the options. Table 12.1 shows the total payoff that will be realized from a bull spread in different circumstances. If the stock price does well and is greater than the higher strike price, the payoff is the difference between the two strike prices, or $K_2 - K_1$. If the stock price on the expiration date lies between the two strike prices, the payoff is $S_T - K_1$. If the stock price on the expiration date is below the lower strike price, the payoff is zero. The profit in Figure 12.2 is calculated by subtracting the initial investment from the payoff.

A bull spread strategy limits the investor's upside as well as downside risk. The strategy can be described by saying that the investor has a call option with a strike price equal to K_1 and has chosen to give up some upside potential by selling a call option with strike price K_2 ($K_2 > K_1$). In return for giving up the upside potential, the investor gets the price of the option with strike price K_2. Three types of bull spreads can be distinguished:

1. Both calls are initially out of the money.
2. One call is initially in the money; the other call is initially out of the money.
3. Both calls are initially in the money.

The most aggressive bull spreads are those of type 1. They cost very little to set up and have a small probability of giving a relatively high payoff ($= K_2 - K_1$). As we move from type 1 to type 2 and from type 2 to type 3, the spreads become more conservative.

Example 12.2

An investor buys for $3 a 3-month European call with a strike price of $30 and sells for $1 a 3-month European call with a strike price of $35. The payoff from this bull spread strategy is $5 if the stock price is above $35, and zero if it is below $30. If the stock price is between $30 and $35, the payoff is the amount by which the stock price exceeds $30. The cost of the strategy is $3 − $1 = $2. So the profit is:

Stock price range	Profit
$S_T \leqslant 30$	−2
$30 < S_T < 35$	$S_T - 32$
$S_T \geqslant 35$	3

Bull spreads can also be created by buying a European put with a low strike price and selling a European put with a high strike price, as illustrated in Figure 12.3. Unlike bull spreads created from calls, those created from puts involve a positive up-front cash flow to the investor, but have margin requirements and a payoff that is either negative or zero.

Figure 12.3   Profit from bull spread created using put options.

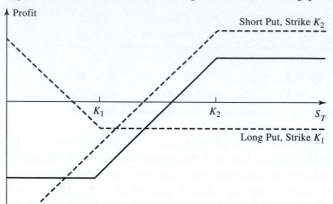

Bear Spreads

An investor who enters into a bull spread is hoping that the stock price will increase. By contrast, an investor who enters into a *bear spread* is hoping that the stock price will decline. Bear spreads can be created by buying a European put with one strike price and selling a European put with another strike price. The strike price of the option purchased is greater than the strike price of the option sold. (This is in contrast to a bull spread, where the strike price of the option purchased is always less than the strike price of the option sold.) In Figure 12.4, the profit from the spread is shown by the solid line. A bear spread created from puts involves an initial cash outflow because the price of the put sold is less than the price of the put purchased. In essence, the investor has bought a put with a certain strike price and chosen to give up some of the profit potential by selling a put with a lower strike price. In return for the profit given up, the investor gets the price of the option sold.

Assume that the strike prices are K_1 and K_2, with $K_1 < K_2$. Table 12.2 shows the payoff that will be realized from a bear spread in different circumstances. If the stock

Figure 12.4   Profit from bear spread created using put options.

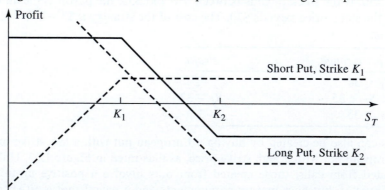

Table 12.2 Payoff from a bear spread created with put options.

Stock price range	Payoff from long put option	Payoff from short put option	Total payoff
$S_T \leqslant K_1$	$K_2 - S_T$	$-(K_1 - S_T)$	$K_2 - K_1$
$K_1 < S_T < K_2$	$K_2 - S_T$	0	$K_2 - S_T$
$S_T \geqslant K_2$	0	0	0

---

price is greater than K_2, the payoff is zero. If the stock price is less than K_1, the payoff is $K_2 - K_1$. If the stock price is between K_1 and K_2, the payoff is $K_2 - S_T$. The profit is calculated by subtracting the initial cost from the payoff.

Example 12.3

An investor buys for $3 a 3-month European put with a strike price of $35 and sells for $1 a 3-month European put with a strike price of $30. The payoff from this bear spread strategy is zero if the stock price is above $35, and $5 if it is below $30. If the stock price is between $30 and $35, the payoff is $35 - S_T$. The options cost $3 - $1 = $2 up front. So the profit is:

Stock price range	Profit
$S_T \leqslant 30$	$+3$
$30 < S_T < 35$	$33 - S_T$
$S_T \geqslant 35$	-2

Like bull spreads, bear spreads limit both the upside profit potential and the downside risk. Bear spreads can be created using calls instead of puts. The investor buys a call with a high strike price and sells a call with a low strike price, as illustrated in Figure 12.5. Bear spreads created with calls involve an initial cash inflow, but have margin requirements and a payoff that is either negative or zero.

Figure 12.5 Profit from bear spread created using call options.

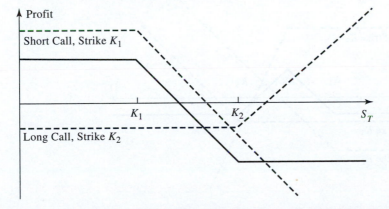

Table 12.3 Payoff from a box spread.

Stock price range	Payoff from bull call spread	Payoff from bear put spread	Total payoff
$S_T \leqslant K_1$	0	$K_2 - K_1$	$K_2 - K_1$
$K_1 < S_T < K_2$	$S_T - K_1$	$K_2 - S_T$	$K_2 - K_1$
$S_T \geqslant K_2$	$K_2 - K_1$	0	$K_2 - K_1$

Box Spreads

A box spread is a combination of a bull call spread with strike prices K_1 and K_2 and a bear put spread with the same two strike prices. As shown in Table 12.3, the payoff from a box spread is always $K_2 - K_1$. The value of a box spread is therefore always the present value of this payoff or $(K_2 - K_1)e^{-rT}$. If it has a different value there is an arbitrage opportunity. If the market price of the box spread is too low, it is profitable to buy the box. This involves buying a call with strike price K_1, buying a put with strike price K_2, selling a call with strike price K_2, and selling a put with strike price K_1. If the market price of the box spread is too high, it is profitable to sell the box. This involves buying a call with strike price K_2, buying a put with strike price K_1, selling a call with strike price K_1, and selling a put with strike price K_2.

It is important to realize that a box-spread arbitrage only works with European options. Many of the options that trade on exchanges are American. As shown in Business Snapshot 12.1, inexperienced traders who treat American options as European are liable to lose money.

Butterfly Spreads

A *butterfly spread* involves positions in options with three different strike prices. It can be created by buying a European call option with a relatively low strike price K_1,

Figure 12.6 Profit from butterfly spread using call options.

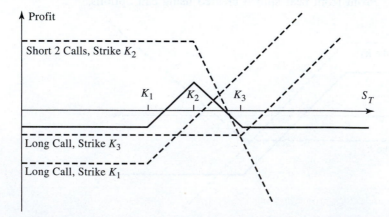

Business Snapshot 12.1 Losing Money with Box Spreads

Suppose that a stock has a price of $50 and a volatility of 30%. No dividends are expected and the risk-free rate is 8%. A trader offers you the chance to sell on the CBOE a 2-month box spread where the strike prices are $55 and $60 for $5.10. Should you do the trade?

The trade certainly sounds attractive. In this case $K_1 = 55$, $K_2 = 60$, and the payoff is certain to be $5 in 2 months. By selling the box spread for $5.10 and investing the funds for 2 months you would have more than enough funds to meet the $5 payoff in 2 months. The theoretical value of the box spread today is $5 \times e^{-0.08 \times 2/12} = \$4.93$.

Unfortunately there is a snag. CBOE stock options are American and the $5 payoff from the box spread is calculated on the assumption that the options comprising the box are European. Option prices for this example (calculated using DerivaGem) are shown in the table below. A bull call spread where the strike prices are $55 and $60 costs $0.96 - 0.26 = \$0.70$. (This is the same for both European and American options because, as we saw in Chapter 11, the price of a European call is the same as the price of an American call when there are no dividends.) A bear put spread with the same strike prices costs $9.46 - 5.23 = \$4.23$ if the options are European and $10.00 - 5.44 = \$4.56$ if they are American. The combined value of both spreads if they are created with European options is $0.70 + 4.23 = \$4.93$. This is the theoretical box spread price calculated above. The combined value of buying both spreads if they are American is $0.70 + 4.56 = \$5.26$. Selling a box spread created with American options for $5.10 would not be a good trade. You would realize this almost immediately as the trade involves selling a $60 strike put and this would be exercised against you almost as soon as you sold it!

Option type	Strike price	European option price	American option price
Call	60	0.26	0.26
Call	55	0.96	0.96
Put	60	9.46	10.00
Put	55	5.23	5.44

Table 12.4 Payoff from a butterfly spread.

Stock price range	Payoff from first long call	Payoff from second long call	Payoff from short calls	Total payoff*
$S_T \leqslant K_1$	0	0	0	0
$K_1 < S_T \leqslant K_2$	$S_T - K_1$	0	0	$S_T - K_1$
$K_2 < S_T < K_3$	$S_T - K_1$	0	$-2(S_T - K_2)$	$K_3 - S_T$
$S_T \geqslant K_3$	$S_T - K_1$	$S_T - K_3$	$-2(S_T - K_2)$	0

* These payoffs are calculated using the relationship $K_2 = 0.5(K_1 + K_3)$.

buying a European call option with a relatively high strike price K_3, and selling two European call options with a strike price K_2 that is halfway between K_1 and K_3. Generally, K_2 is close to the current stock price. The pattern of profits from the strategy is shown in Figure 12.6. A butterfly spread leads to a profit if the stock price stays close to K_2, but gives rise to a small loss if there is a significant stock price move in either direction. It is therefore an appropriate strategy for an investor who feels that large stock price moves are unlikely. The strategy requires a small investment initially. The payoff from a butterfly spread is shown in Table 12.4.

Suppose that a certain stock is currently worth $61. Consider an investor who feels that a significant price move in the next 6 months is unlikely. Suppose that the market prices of 6-month European calls are as follows:

Strike price ($)	Call price ($)
55	10
60	7
65	5

The investor could create a butterfly spread by buying one call with a $55 strike price, buying one call with a $65 strike price, and selling two calls with a $60 strike price. It costs $10 + $5 − (2 × $7) = $1 to create the spread. If the stock price in 6 months is greater than $65 or less than $55, the total payoff is zero, and the investor incurs a net loss of $1. If the stock price is between $56 and $64, a profit is made. The maximum profit, $4, occurs when the stock price in 6 months is $60.

Butterfly spreads can be created using put options. The investor buys two European puts, one with a low strike price and one with a high strike price, and sells two European puts with an intermediate strike price, as illustrated in Figure 12.7. The butterfly spread in the example considered above would be created by buying one put with a strike price of $55, another with a strike price of $65, and selling two puts with a strike price of $60. The use of put options results in exactly the same spread as the use of call options. Put–call parity can be used to show that the initial investment is the same in both cases.

Figure 12.7   Profit from butterfly spread using put options.

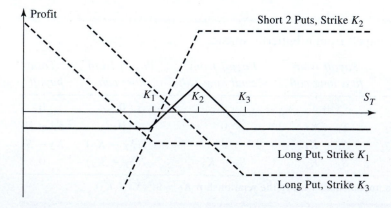

A butterfly spread can be sold or shorted by following the reverse strategy. Options are sold with strike prices of K_1 and K_3, and two options with the middle strike price K_2 are purchased. This strategy produces a modest profit if there is a significant movement in the stock price.

Calendar Spreads

Up to now we have assumed that the options used to create a spread all expire at the same time. We now move on to *calendar spreads* in which the options have the same strike price and different expiration dates.

A calendar spread can be created by selling a European call option with a certain strike price and buying a longer-maturity European call option with the same strike price. The longer the maturity of an option, the more expensive it usually is. A calendar spread therefore usually requires an initial investment. Profit diagrams for calendar spreads are usually produced so that they show the profit when the short-maturity option expires on the assumption that the long-maturity option is closed out at that time. The profit pattern for a calendar spread produced from call options is shown in Figure 12.8. The pattern is similar to the profit from the butterfly spread in Figure 12.6. The investor makes a profit if the stock price at the expiration of the short-maturity option is close to the strike price of the short-maturity option. However, a loss is incurred when the stock price is significantly above or significantly below this strike price.

To understand the profit pattern from a calendar spread, first consider what happens if the stock price is very low when the short-maturity option expires. The short-maturity option is worthless and the value of the long-maturity option is close to zero. The investor therefore incurs a loss that is close to the cost of setting up the spread initially. Consider next what happens if the stock price, S_T, is very high when the short-maturity option expires. The short-maturity option costs the investor $S_T - K$, and the long-maturity option is worth close to $S_T - K$, where K is the strike price of the options. Again, the investor makes a net loss that is close to the cost of setting up the spread

Figure 12.8 Profit from calendar spread created using two call options, calculated at the time when the short-maturity call option expires.

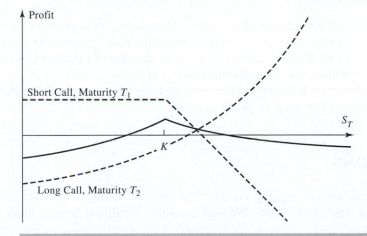

Figure 12.9   Profit from calendar spread created using two put options, calculated at the time when the short-maturity put option expires.

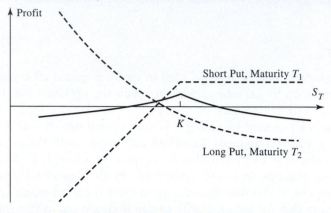

initially. If S_T is close to K, the short-maturity option costs the investor either a small amount or nothing at all. However, the long-maturity option is still quite valuable. In this case a net profit is made.

In a *neutral calendar spread*, a strike price close to the current stock price is chosen. A *bullish calendar spread* involves a higher strike price, whereas a *bearish calendar spread* involves a lower strike price.

Calendar spreads can be created with put options as well as call options. The investor buys a long-maturity put option and sells a short-maturity put option. As shown in Figure 12.9, the profit pattern is similar to that obtained from using calls.

A *reverse calendar spread* is the opposite to that in Figures 12.8 and 12.9. The investor buys a short-maturity option and sells a long-maturity option. A small profit arises if the stock price at the expiration of the short-maturity option is well above or well below the strike price of the short-maturity option. However, a loss results if it is close to the strike price.

Diagonal Spreads

Bull, bear, and calendar spreads can all be created from a long position in one call and a short position in another call. In the case of bull and bear spreads, the calls have different strike prices and the same expiration date. In the case of calendar spreads, the calls have the same strike price and different expiration dates.

In a *diagonal spread* both the expiration date and the strike price of the calls are different. This increases the range of profit patterns that are possible.

12.4   COMBINATIONS

A *combination* is an option trading strategy that involves taking a position in both calls and puts on the same stock. We will consider straddles, strips, straps, and strangles.

Straddle

One popular combination is a *straddle*, which involves buying a European call and put with the same strike price and expiration date. The profit pattern is shown in Figure 12.10. The strike price is denoted by K. If the stock price is close to this strike price at expiration of the options, the straddle leads to a loss. However, if there is a sufficiently large move in either direction, a significant profit will result. The payoff from a straddle is calculated in Table 12.5.

A straddle is appropriate when an investor is expecting a large move in a stock price but does not know in which direction the move will be. Consider an investor who feels that the price of a certain stock, currently valued at $69 by the market, will move significantly in the next 3 months. The investor could create a straddle by buying both a put and a call with a strike price of $70 and an expiration date in 3 months. Suppose that the call costs $4 and the put costs $3. If the stock price stays at $69, it is easy to see that the strategy costs the investor $6. (An up-front investment of $7 is required, the call expires worthless, and the put expires worth $1.) If the stock price moves to $70, a loss of $7 is experienced. (This is the worst that can happen.) However, if the stock price jumps up to $90, a profit of $13 is made; if the stock moves down to $55, a profit of $8 is made; and so on. As discussed in Business Snapshot 12.2 an investor should carefully consider whether the jump that he or she anticipates is already reflected in option prices before putting on a straddle trade.

The straddle in Figure 12.10 is sometimes referred to as a *bottom straddle* or *straddle purchase*. A *top straddle* or *straddle write* is the reverse position. It is created by selling a call and a put with the same exercise price and expiration date. It is a highly risky strategy.

Figure 12.10   Profit from a straddle.

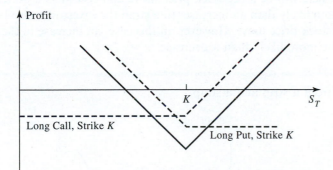

Table 12.5   Payoff from a straddle.

Range of stock price	Payoff from call	Payoff from put	Total payoff
$S_T \leqslant K$	0	$K - S_T$	$K - S_T$
$S_T > K$	$S_T - K$	0	$S_T - K$

Business Snapshot 12.2   How to Make Money from Trading Straddles

Suppose that a big move is expected in a company's stock price because there is a takeover bid for the company or the outcome of a major lawsuit involving the company is about to be announced. Should you trade a straddle?

A straddle seems a natural trading strategy in this case. However, if your view of the company's situation is much the same as that of other market participants, this view will be reflected in the prices of options. Options on the stock will be significantly more expensive than options on a similar stock for which no jump is expected. The V-shaped profit pattern from the straddle in Figure 12.10 will have moved downward, so that a bigger move in the stock price is necessary for you to make a profit.

For a straddle to be an effective strategy, you must believe that there are likely to be big movements in the stock price and these beliefs must be different from those of most other investors. Market prices incorporate the beliefs of market participants. To make money from any investment strategy, you must take a view that is different from most of the rest of the market—and you must be right!

If the stock price on the expiration date is close to the strike price, a profit results. However, the loss arising from a large move is unlimited.

Strips and Straps

A *strip* consists of a long position in one European call and two European puts with the same strike price and expiration date. A *strap* consists of a long position in two European calls and one European put with the same strike price and expiration date. The profit patterns from strips and straps are shown in Figure 12.11. In a strip the investor is betting that there will be a big stock price move and considers a decrease in the stock price to be more likely than an increase. In a strap the investor is also betting that there will be a big stock price move. However, in this case, an increase in the stock price is considered to be more likely than a decrease.

Figure 12.11   Profit from a strip and a strap.

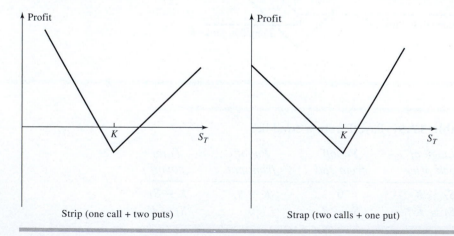

Strip (one call + two puts)   Strap (two calls + one put)

Strangles

In a *strangle*, sometimes called a *bottom vertical combination*, an investor buys a European put and a European call with the same expiration date and different strike prices. The profit pattern is shown in Figure 12.12. The call strike price, K_2, is higher than the put strike price, K_1. The payoff function for a strangle is calculated in Table 12.6.

A strangle is a similar strategy to a straddle. The investor is betting that there will be a large price move, but is uncertain whether it will be an increase or a decrease. Comparing Figures 12.12 and 12.10, we see that the stock price has to move farther in a strangle than in a straddle for the investor to make a profit. However, the downside risk if the stock price ends up at a central value is less with a strangle.

The profit pattern obtained with a strangle depends on how close together the strike prices are. The farther they are apart, the less the downside risk and the farther the stock price has to move for a profit to be realized.

The sale of a strangle is sometimes referred to as a *top vertical combination*. It can be appropriate for an investor who feels that large stock price moves are unlikely. However, as with sale of a straddle, it is a risky strategy involving unlimited potential loss to the investor.

12.5 OTHER PAYOFFS

This chapter has demonstrated just a few of the ways in which options can be used to produce an interesting relationship between profit and stock price. If European options

Figure 12.12   Profit from a strangle.

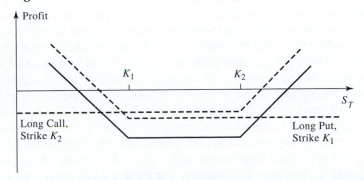

Table 12.6   Payoff from a strangle.

Range of stock price	Payoff from call	Payoff from put	Total payoff
$S_T \leqslant K_1$	0	$K_1 - S_T$	$K_1 - S_T$
$K_1 < S_T < K_2$	0	0	0
$S_T \geqslant K_2$	$S_T - K_2$	0	$S_T - K_2$

Figure 12.13 "Spike payoff" from a butterfly spread that can be used as a building block to create other payoffs.

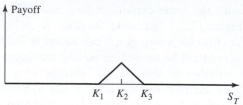

expiring at time T were available with every single possible strike price, any payoff function at time T could in theory be obtained. The easiest illustration of this involves butterfly spreads. Recall that a butterfly spread is created by buying options with strike prices K_1 and K_3 and selling two options with strike price K_2, where $K_1 < K_2 < K_3$ and $K_3 - K_2 = K_2 - K_1$. Figure 12.13 shows the payoff from a butterfly spread. The pattern could be described as a spike. As K_1 and K_3 move closer together, the spike becomes smaller. Through the judicious combination of a large number of very small spikes, any payoff function can in theory be approximated as accurately as desired.

SUMMARY

Principal-protected notes can be created from a zero-coupon bond and a European call option. They are attractive to some investors because the issuer of the product guarantees that the purchaser will receive his or her principal back regardless of the performance of the asset underlying the option.

A number of common trading strategies involve a single option and the underlying stock. For example, writing a covered call involves buying the stock and selling a call option on the stock; a protective put involves buying a put option and buying the stock. The former is similar to selling a put option; the latter is similar to buying a call option.

Spreads involve either taking a position in two or more calls or taking a position in two or more puts. A bull spread can be created by buying a call (put) with a low strike price and selling a call (put) with a high strike price. A bear spread can be created by buying a put (call) with a high strike price and selling a put (call) with a low strike price. A butterfly spread involves buying calls (puts) with a low and high strike price and selling two calls (puts) with some intermediate strike price. A calendar spread involves selling a call (put) with a short time to expiration and buying a call (put) with a longer time to expiration. A diagonal spread involves a long position in one option and a short position in another option such that both the strike price and the expiration date are different.

Combinations involve taking a position in both calls and puts on the same stock. A straddle combination involves taking a long position in a call and a long position in a put with the same strike price and expiration date. A strip consists of a long position in one call and two puts with the same strike price and expiration date. A strap consists of a long position in two calls and one put with the same strike price and expiration date. A strangle consists of a long position in a call and a put with different strike prices and the same expiration date. There are many other ways in which options can be used to produce interesting payoffs. It is not surprising that option trading has steadily increased in popularity and continues to fascinate investors.

FURTHER READING

Bharadwaj, A. and J. B. Wiggins. "Box Spread and Put–Call Parity Tests for the S&P Index LEAPS Markets," *Journal of Derivatives*, 8, 4 (Summer 2001): 62–71.

Chaput, J. S., and L. H. Ederington, "Option Spread and Combination Trading," *Journal of Derivatives*, 10, 4 (Summer 2003): 70–88.

McMillan, L. G. *Options as a Strategic Investment*, 5th edn. Upper Saddle River, NJ: Prentice Hall, 2012.

Rendleman, R. J. "Covered Call Writing from an Expected Utility Perspective," *Journal of Derivatives*, 8, 3 (Spring 2001): 63–75.

Ronn, A. G. and E. I. Ronn. "The Box–Spread Arbitrage Conditions," *Review of Financial Studies*, 2, 1 (1989): 91–108.

Practice Questions (Answers in Solutions Manual)

12.1. What is meant by a protective put? What position in call options is equivalent to a protective put?

12.2. Explain two ways in which a bear spread can be created.

12.3. When is it appropriate for an investor to purchase a butterfly spread?

12.4. Call options on a stock are available with strike prices of $15, $17\frac{1}{2}$, and $20, and expiration dates in 3 months. Their prices are $4, $2, and $\frac{1}{2}$, respectively. Explain how the options can be used to create a butterfly spread. Construct a table showing how profit varies with stock price for the butterfly spread.

12.5. What trading strategy creates a reverse calendar spread?

12.6. What is the difference between a strangle and a straddle?

12.7. A call option with a strike price of $50 costs $2. A put option with a strike price of $45 costs $3. Explain how a strangle can be created from these two options. What is the pattern of profits from the strangle?

12.8. Use put–call parity to relate the initial investment for a bull spread created using calls to the initial investment for a bull spread created using puts.

12.9. Explain how an aggressive bear spread can be created using put options.

12.10. Suppose that put options on a stock with strike prices $30 and $35 cost $4 and $7, respectively. How can the options be used to create (a) a bull spread and (b) a bear spread? Construct a table that shows the profit and payoff for both spreads.

12.11. Use put–call parity to show that the cost of a butterfly spread created from European puts is identical to the cost of a butterfly spread created from European calls.

12.12. A call with a strike price of $60 costs $6. A put with the same strike price and expiration date costs $4. Construct a table that shows the profit from a straddle. For what range of stock prices would the straddle lead to a loss?

12.13. Construct a table showing the payoff from a bull spread when puts with strike prices K_1 and K_2, with $K_2 > K_1$, are used.

12.14. An investor believes that there will be a big jump in a stock price, but is uncertain as to the direction. Identify six different strategies the investor can follow and explain the differences among them.

12.15. How can a forward contract on a stock with a particular delivery price and delivery date be created from options?

12.16. "A box spread comprises four options. Two can be combined to create a long forward position and two to create a short forward position." Explain this statement.

12.17. What is the result if the strike price of the put is higher than the strike price of the call in a strangle?

12.18. A foreign currency is currently worth $0.64. A 1-year butterfly spread is set up using European call options with strike prices of $0.60, $0.65, and $0.70. The risk-free interest rates in the United States and the foreign country are 5% and 4% respectively, and the volatility of the exchange rate is 15%. Use the DerivaGem software to calculate the cost of setting up the butterfly spread position. Show that the cost is the same if European put options are used instead of European call options.

12.19. An index provides a dividend yield of 1% and has a volatility of 20%. The risk-free interest rate is 4%. How long does a principal-protected note, created as in Example 12.1, have to last for it to be profitable for the bank issuing it? Use DerivaGem.

12.20. Explain the statement at the end of Section 12.1 that, when dividends are zero, the principal protected note cannot be profitable for the bank no matter how long it lasts.

Further Questions

12.21. A trader creates a bear spread by selling a 6-month put option with a $25 strike price for $2.15 and buying a 6-month put option with a $29 strike price for $4.75. What is the initial investment? What is the total payoff (excluding the initial investment) when the stock price in 6 months is (a) $23, (b) $28, and (c) $33.

12.22. A trader sells a strangle by selling a 6-month European call option with a strike price of $50 for $3 and selling a 6-month European put option with a strike price of $40 for $4. For what range of prices of the underlying asset in 6 months does the trader make a profit?

12.23. Three put options on a stock have the same expiration date and strike prices of $55, $60, and $65. The market prices are $3, $5, and $8, respectively. Explain how a butterfly spread can be created. Construct a table showing the profit from the strategy. For what range of stock prices would the butterfly spread lead to a loss?

12.24. A diagonal spread is created by buying a call with strike price K_2 and exercise date T_2 and selling a call with strike price K_1 and exercise date T_1, where $T_2 > T_1$. Draw a diagram showing the profit from the spread at time T_1 when (a) $K_2 > K_1$ and (b) $K_2 < K_1$.

12.25. Draw a diagram showing the variation of an investor's profit and loss with the terminal stock price for a portfolio consisting of:
(a) One share and a short position in one call option
(b) Two shares and a short position in one call option
(c) One share and a short position in two call options
(d) One share and a short position in four call options.
In each case, assume that the call option has an exercise price equal to the current stock price.

12.26. Suppose that the price of a non-dividend-paying stock is $32, its volatility is 30%, and the risk-free rate for all maturities is 5% per annum. Use DerivaGem to calculate the cost of setting up the following positions:

(a) A bull spread using European call options with strike prices of $25 and $30 and a maturity of 6 months

(b) A bear spread using European put options with strike prices of $25 and $30 and a maturity of 6 months

(c) A butterfly spread using European call options with strike prices of $25, $30, and $35 and a maturity of 1 year

(d) A butterfly spread using European put options with strike prices of $25, $30, and $35 and a maturity of 1 year

(e) A straddle using options with a strike price of $30 and a 6-month maturity

(f) A strangle using options with strike prices of $25 and $35 and a 6-month maturity.

In each case provide a table showing the relationship between profit and final stock price. Ignore the impact of discounting.

12.27. What trading position is created from a long strangle and a short straddle when both have the same time to maturity? Assume that the strike price in the straddle is halfway between the two strike prices of the strangle.

12.28. Describe the trading position created in which a call option is bought with strike price K_2 and a put option is sold with strike price K_1 when both have the same time to maturity and $K_2 > K_1$. What does the position become when $K_1 = K_2$?

12.29. A bank decides to create a five-year principal-protected note on a non-dividend-paying stock by offering investors a zero-coupon bond plus a bull spread created from calls. The risk-free rate is 4% and the stock price volatility is 25%. The low-strike-price option in the bull spread is at the money. What is the maximum ratio of the high strike price to the low strike price in the bull spread. Use DerivaGem.

CHAPTER 13

Binomial Trees

A useful and very popular technique for pricing an option involves constructing a *binomial tree*. This is a diagram representing different possible paths that might be followed by the stock price over the life of an option. The underlying assumption is that the stock price follows a *random walk*. In each time step, it has a certain probability of moving up by a certain percentage amount and a certain probability of moving down by a certain percentage amount. In the limit, as the time step becomes smaller, this model is the same as the Black–Scholes–Merton model we will be discussing in Chapter 15. Indeed, in the appendix to this chapter, we show that the European option price given by the binomial tree converges to the Black–Scholes–Merton price as the time step becomes smaller.

The material in this chapter is important for a number of reasons. First, it explains the nature of the no-arbitrage arguments that are used for valuing options. Second, it explains the binomial tree numerical procedure that is widely used for valuing American options and other derivatives. Third, it introduces a very important principle known as risk-neutral valuation.

The general approach to constructing trees in this chapter is the one used in an important paper published by Cox, Ross, and Rubinstein in 1979. More details on numerical procedures using binomial trees are given in Chapter 21.

13.1 A ONE-STEP BINOMIAL MODEL AND A NO-ARBITRAGE ARGUMENT

We start by considering a very simple situation. A stock price is currently $20, and it is known that at the end of 3 months it will be either $22 or $18. We are interested in valuing a European call option to buy the stock for $21 in 3 months. This option will have one of two values at the end of the 3 months. If the stock price turns out to be $22, the value of the option will be $1; if the stock price turns out to be $18, the value of the option will be zero. The situation is illustrated in Figure 13.1.

It turns out that a relatively simple argument can be used to price the option in this example. The only assumption needed is that arbitrage opportunities do not exist. We set up a portfolio of the stock and the option in such a way that there is no uncertainty

Figure 13.1 Stock price movements for numerical example in Section 13.1.

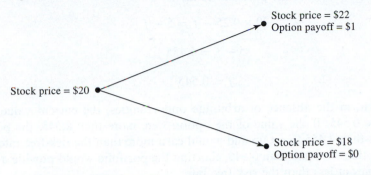

Stock price = $22
Option payoff = $1

Stock price = $20

Stock price = $18
Option payoff = $0

about the value of the portfolio at the end of the 3 months. We then argue that, because the portfolio has no risk, the return it earns must equal the risk-free interest rate. This enables us to work out the cost of setting up the portfolio and therefore the option's price. Because there are two securities (the stock and the stock option) and only two possible outcomes, it is always possible to set up the riskless portfolio.

Consider a portfolio consisting of a long position in Δ shares of the stock and a short position in one call option (Δ is the Greek capital letter "delta"). We calculate the value of Δ that makes the portfolio riskless. If the stock price moves up from $20 to $22, the value of the shares is 22Δ and the value of the option is 1, so that the total value of the portfolio is $22\Delta - 1$. If the stock price moves down from $20 to $18, the value of the shares is 18Δ and the value of the option is zero, so that the total value of the portfolio is 18Δ. The portfolio is riskless if the value of Δ is chosen so that the final value of the portfolio is the same for both alternatives. This means that

$$22\Delta - 1 = 18\Delta$$

or

$$\Delta = 0.25$$

A riskless portfolio is therefore

Long: 0.25 shares

Short: 1 option.

If the stock price moves up to $22, the value of the portfolio is

$$22 \times 0.25 - 1 = 4.5$$

If the stock price moves down to $18, the value of the portfolio is

$$18 \times 0.25 = 4.5$$

Regardless of whether the stock price moves up or down, the value of the portfolio is always 4.5 at the end of the life of the option.

Riskless portfolios must, in the absence of arbitrage opportunities, earn the risk-free rate of interest. Suppose that, in this case, the risk-free rate is 4% per annum (continuously compounded). It follows that the value of the portfolio today must be the present value of 4.5, or

$$4.5e^{-0.04 \times 3/12} = 4.455$$

The value of the stock price today is known to be $20. Suppose the option price is denoted by f. The value of the portfolio today is

$$20 \times 0.25 - f = 5 - f$$

It follows that

$$5 - f = 4.455$$

or

$$f = 0.545$$

This shows that, in the absence of arbitrage opportunities, the current value of the option must be 0.545. If the value of the option were more than 0.545, the portfolio would cost less than 4.455 to set up and would earn more than the risk-free rate. If the value of the option were less than 0.545, shorting the portfolio would provide a way of borrowing money at less than the risk-free rate.

Trading 0.25 shares is, of course, not possible. However, the argument is the same if we imagine selling 400 options and buying 100 shares. In general, it is necessary to buy Δ shares for each option sold to form a riskless portfolio. The parameter Δ (delta) is important in the hedging of options. It is discussed further later in this chapter and in Chapter 19.

A Generalization

We can generalize the no-arbitrage argument just presented by considering a stock whose price is S_0 and an option on the stock (or any derivative dependent on the stock) whose current price is f. We suppose that the option lasts for time T and that during the life of the option the stock price can either move up from S_0 to a new level, $S_0 u$, where $u > 1$, or down from S_0 to a new level, $S_0 d$, where $d < 1$. The percentage increase in the stock price when there is an up movement is $u - 1$; the percentage decrease when there is a down movement is $1 - d$. If the stock price moves up to $S_0 u$, we suppose that the payoff from the option is f_u; if the stock price moves down to $S_0 d$, we suppose the payoff from the option is f_d. The situation is illustrated in Figure 13.2.

As before, we imagine a portfolio consisting of a long position in Δ shares and a short position in one option. We calculate the value of Δ that makes the portfolio riskless. If there is an up movement in the stock price, the value of the portfolio at the end of the life of the option is

$$S_0 u \Delta - f_u$$

Figure 13.2   Stock and option prices in a general one-step tree.

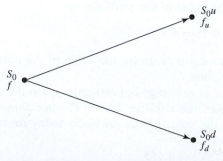

If there is a down movement in the stock price, the value becomes

$$S_0 d\Delta - f_d$$

The two are equal when

$$S_0 u\Delta - f_u = S_0 d\Delta - f_d$$

or

$$\Delta = \frac{f_u - f_d}{S_0 u - S_0 d} \tag{13.1}$$

In this case, the portfolio is riskless and, for there to be no arbitrage opportunities, it must earn the risk-free interest rate. Equation (13.1) shows that Δ is the ratio of the change in the option price to the change in the stock price as we move between the nodes at time T.

If we denote the risk-free interest rate by r, the present value of the portfolio is

$$(S_0 u\Delta - f_u)e^{-rT}$$

The cost of setting up the portfolio is

$$S_0\Delta - f$$

It follows that

$$S_0\Delta - f = (S_0 u\Delta - f_u)e^{-rT}$$

or

$$f = S_0\Delta(1 - ue^{-rT}) + f_u e^{-rT}$$

Substituting from equation (13.1) for Δ, we obtain

$$f = S_0\left(\frac{f_u - f_d}{S_0 u - S_0 d}\right)(1 - ue^{-rT}) + f_u e^{-rT}$$

or

$$f = \frac{f_u(1 - de^{-rT}) + f_d(ue^{-rT} - 1)}{u - d}$$

or

$$f = e^{-rT}[pf_u + (1 - p)f_d] \tag{13.2}$$

where

$$p = \frac{e^{rT} - d}{u - d} \tag{13.3}$$

Equations (13.2) and (13.3) enable an option to be priced when stock price movements are given by a one-step binomial tree. The only assumption needed for the equation is that there are no arbitrage opportunities in the market.

In the numerical example considered previously (see Figure 13.1), $u = 1.1$, $d = 0.9$, $r = 0.04$, $T = 0.25$, $f_u = 1$, and $f_d = 0$. From equation (13.3), we have

$$p = \frac{e^{0.04 \times 3/12} - 0.9}{1.1 - 0.9} = 0.5503$$

and, from equation (13.2), we have

$$f = e^{-0.04 \times 0.25}(0.5503 \times 1 + 0.4497 \times 0) = 0.545$$

The result agrees with the answer obtained earlier in this section.

Irrelevance of the Stock's Expected Return

The option pricing formula in equation (13.2) does not involve the probabilities of the stock price moving up or down. For example, we get the same option price when the probability of an upward movement is 0.5 as we do when it is 0.9. This is surprising and seems counterintuitive. It is natural to assume that, as the probability of an upward movement in the stock price increases, the value of a call option on the stock increases and the value of a put option on the stock decreases. This is not the case.

The key reason is that we are not valuing the option in absolute terms. We are calculating its value in terms of the price of the underlying stock. The probabilities of future up or down movements are already incorporated into the stock price: we do not need to take them into account again when valuing the option in terms of the stock price.

13.2 RISK-NEUTRAL VALUATION

We are now in a position to introduce a very important principle in the pricing of derivatives known as *risk-neutral valuation*. This states that, when valuing a derivative, we can make the assumption that investors are *risk-neutral*. This assumption means investors do not increase the expected return they require from an investment to compensate for increased risk. A world where investors are risk-neutral is referred to as a *risk-neutral world*. The world we live in is, of course, not a risk-neutral world. The higher the risks investors take, the higher the expected returns they require. However, it turns out that assuming a risk-neutral world gives us the right option price for the world we live in, as well as for a risk-neutral world. Almost miraculously, it finesses the problem that we know hardly anything about the risk aversion of the buyers and sellers of options.

Risk-neutral valuation seems a surprising result when it is first encountered. Options are risky investments. Should not a person's risk preferences affect how they are priced? The answer is that, when we are pricing an option in terms of the price of the underlying stock, risk preferences are unimportant. As investors become more risk-averse, stock prices decline, but the formulas relating option prices to stock prices remain the same.

A risk-neutral world has two features that simplify the pricing of derivatives:

1. The expected return on a stock (or any other investment) is the risk-free rate.
2. The discount rate used for the expected payoff on an option (or any other instrument) is the risk-free rate.

Returning to equation (13.2), the parameter p should be interpreted as the probability of an up movement in a risk-neutral world, so that $1 - p$ is the probability of a down movement in this world. (We assume $u > e^{rT}$, so that $0 < p < 1$.) The expression

$$p f_u + (1 - p) f_d$$

is the expected future payoff from the option in a risk-neutral world and equation (13.2) states that the value of the option today is its expected future payoff in a risk-neutral world discounted at the risk-free rate. This is an application of risk-neutral valuation.

To prove the validity of our interpretation of p, we note that, when p is the probability of an up movement, the expected stock price $E(S_T)$ at time T is given by

$$E(S_T) = pS_0u + (1-p)S_0d$$

or

$$E(S_T) = pS_0(u-d) + S_0d$$

Substituting from equation (13.3) for p gives

$$E(S_T) = S_0e^{rT} \tag{13.4}$$

This shows that the stock price grows, on average, at the risk-free rate when p is the probability of an up movement. In other words, the stock price behaves exactly as we would expect it to behave in a risk-neutral world when p is the probability of an up movement.

Risk-neutral valuation is a very important general result in the pricing of derivatives. It states that, when we assume the world is risk-neutral, we get the right price for a derivative in all worlds, not just in a risk-neutral one. We have shown that risk-neutral valuation is correct when a simple binomial model is assumed for how the price of the the stock evolves. It can be shown that the result is true regardless of the assumptions we make about the evolution of the stock price.

To apply risk-neutral valuation to the pricing of a derivative, we first calculate what the probabilities of different outcomes would be if the world were risk-neutral. We then calculate the expected payoff from the derivative and discount that expected payoff at the risk-free rate of interest.

The One-Step Binomial Example Revisited

We now return to the example in Figure 13.1 and illustrate that risk-neutral valuation gives the same answer as no-arbitrage arguments. In Figure 13.1, the stock price is currently $20 and will move either up to $22 or down to $18 at the end of 3 months. The option considered is a European call option with a strike price of $21 and an expiration date in 3 months. The risk-free interest rate is 4% per annum.

We define p as the probability of an upward movement in the stock price in a risk-neutral world. We can calculate p from equation (13.3). Alternatively, we can argue that the expected return on the stock in a risk-neutral world must be the risk-free rate of 4%. This means that p must satisfy

$$22p + 18(1-p) = 20e^{0.04 \times 3/12}$$

or

$$4p = 20e^{0.04 \times 3/12} - 18$$

That is, p must be 0.5503.

At the end of the 3 months, the call option has a 0.5503 probability of being worth 1 and a 0.4497 probability of being worth zero. Its expected value is therefore

$$0.5503 \times 1 + 0.4497 \times 0 = 0.5503$$

In a risk-neutral world this should be discounted at the risk-free rate. The value of the option today is therefore

$$0.5503e^{-0.04 \times 3/12}$$

or \$0.545. This is the same as the value obtained earlier, demonstrating that no-arbitrage arguments and risk-neutral valuation give the same answer.

Real World vs. Risk-Neutral World

It should be emphasized that p is the probability of an up movement in a risk-neutral world. In general, this is not the same as the probability of an up movement in the real world. In our example $p = 0.5503$. When the probability of an up movement is 0.5503, the expected return on both the stock and the option is the risk-free rate of 4%. Suppose that, in the real world, the expected return on the stock is 10% and p^* is the probability of an up movement in this world. It follows that

$$22p^* + 18(1 - p^*) = 20e^{0.10 \times 3/12}$$

so that $p^* = 0.6266$.

The expected payoff from the option in the real world is then given by

$$p^* \times 1 + (1 - p^*) \times 0$$

or 0.6266. Unfortunately, it is not easy to know the correct discount rate to apply to the expected payoff in the real world. The return the market requires on the stock is 10% and this is the discount rate that would be used for the expected cash flows from an investment in the stock. A position in a call option is riskier than a position in the stock. As a result the discount rate to be applied to the payoff from a call option is greater than 10%, but we do not have a direct measure of how much greater than 10% it should be.[1] Using risk-neutral valuation solves this problem because we know that in a risk-neutral world the expected return on all assets (and therefore the discount rate to use for all expected payoffs) is the risk-free rate.

13.3 TWO-STEP BINOMIAL TREES

We can extend the analysis to a two-step binomial tree such as that shown in Figure 13.3. Here the stock price starts at \$20 and in each of two time steps may go up by 10% or down by 10%. Each time step is 3 months long and the risk-free interest rate is 4% per annum. We consider a 6-month option with a strike price of \$21.

The objective of the analysis is to calculate the option price at the initial node of the tree. This can be done by repeatedly applying the principles established earlier in the chapter. Figure 13.4 shows the same tree as Figure 13.3, but with both the stock price and the option price at each node. (The stock price is the upper number and the option price is the lower number.) The option prices at the final nodes of the tree are easily calculated. They are the payoffs from the option. At node D the stock price is 24.2 and the option price is $24.2 - 21 = 3.2$; at nodes E and F the option is out of the money and its value is zero.

At node C the option price is zero, because node C leads to either node E or node F and at both of those nodes the option price is zero. We calculate the option price at node B by focusing our attention on the part of the tree shown in Figure 13.5. Using the

---

[1] Since we know the correct value of the option is 0.545, we can deduce that the correct real-world discount rate is 55.96%. This is because $0.545 = 0.6266e^{-0.5596 \times 3/12}$.

Figure 13.3 Stock prices in a two-step tree.

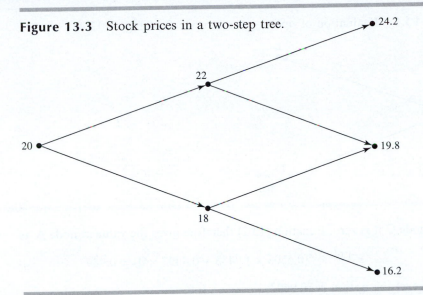

notation introduced earlier in the chapter, $u = 1.1$, $d = 0.9$, $r = 0.04$, and $T = 0.25$, so that $p = 0.5503$, and equation (13.2) gives the value of the option at node B as

$$e^{-0.04 \times 3/12}(0.5503 \times 3.2 + 0.4497 \times 0) = 1.7433$$

It remains for us to calculate the option price at the initial node A. We do so by focusing on the first step of the tree. We know that the value of the option at node B is 1.7433 and

Figure 13.4 Stock and option prices in a two-step tree. The upper number at each node is the stock price and the lower number is the option price.

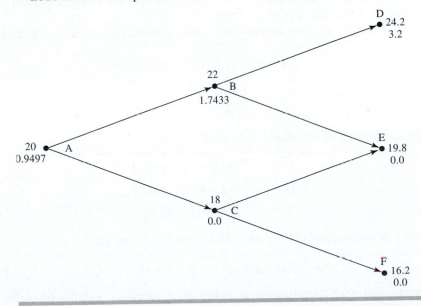

Figure 13.5   Evaluation of option price at node B of Figure 13.4.

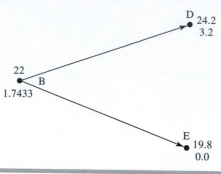

that at node C it is zero. Equation (13.2) therefore gives the value at node A as

$$e^{-0.04 \times 3/12}(0.5503 \times 1.7433 + 0.4497 \times 0) = 0.9497$$

The value of the option is \$0.9497.

Note that this example was constructed so that u and d (the proportional up and down movements) were the same at each node of the tree and so that the time steps were of the same length. As a result, the risk-neutral probability, p, as calculated by equation (13.3) is the same at each node.

A Generalization

We can generalize the case of two time steps by considering the situation in Figure 13.6. The stock price is initially S_0. During each time step, it either moves up to u times its value at the beginning of the time step or moves down to d times this value. The notation for the value of the option is shown on the tree. (For example, after two up movements the value of the option is f_{uu}.) We suppose that the risk-free interest rate is r and the length of the time step is Δt years.

Because the length of a time step is now Δt rather than T, equations (13.2) and (13.3) become

$$f = e^{-r\Delta t}[pf_u + (1-p)f_d] \tag{13.5}$$

$$p = \frac{e^{r\Delta t} - d}{u - d} \tag{13.6}$$

Repeated application of equation (13.5) gives

$$f_u = e^{-r\Delta t}[pf_{uu} + (1-p)f_{ud}] \tag{13.7}$$

$$f_d = e^{-r\Delta t}[pf_{ud} + (1-p)f_{dd}] \tag{13.8}$$

$$f = e^{-r\Delta t}[pf_u + (1-p)f_d] \tag{13.9}$$

Substituting from equations (13.7) and (13.8) into (13.9), we get

$$f = e^{-2r\Delta t}[p^2 f_{uu} + 2p(1-p)f_{ud} + (1-p)^2 f_{dd}] \tag{13.10}$$

This is consistent with the principle of risk-neutral valuation mentioned earlier. The

Figure 13.6 Stock and option prices in general two-step tree.

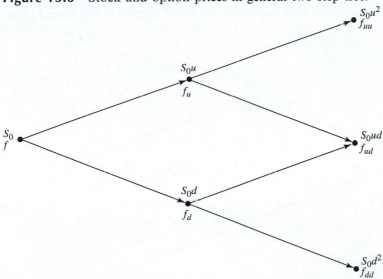

variables p^2, $2p(1-p)$, and $(1-p)^2$ are the probabilities that the upper, middle, and lower final nodes will be reached. The option price is equal to its expected payoff in a risk-neutral world discounted at the risk-free interest rate.

As we add more steps to the binomial tree, the risk-neutral valuation principle continues to hold. The option price is always equal to its expected payoff in a risk-neutral world discounted at the risk-free interest rate.

13.4 A PUT EXAMPLE

The procedures described in this chapter can be used to price puts as well as calls. Consider a 2-year European put with a strike price of $52 on a stock whose current price is $50. We suppose that there are two time steps of 1 year, and in each time step the stock price either moves up by 20% or moves down by 20%. We also suppose that the risk-free interest rate is 5%.

The tree is shown in Figure 13.7. In this case $u = 1.2$, $d = 0.8$, $\Delta t = 1$, and $r = 0.05$. From equation (13.6) the value of the risk-neutral probability, p, is given by

$$p = \frac{e^{0.05 \times 1} - 0.8}{1.2 - 0.8} = 0.6282$$

The possible final stock prices are: $72, $48, and $32. In this case, $f_{uu} = 0$, $f_{ud} = 4$, and $f_{dd} = 20$. From equation (13.10),

$$f = e^{-2 \times 0.05 \times 1}(0.6282^2 \times 0 + 2 \times 0.6282 \times 0.3718 \times 4 + 0.3718^2 \times 20) = 4.1923$$

The value of the put is $4.1923. This result can also be obtained using equation (13.5)

Figure 13.7   Using a two-step tree to value a European put option. At each node, the upper number is the stock price and the lower number is the option price.

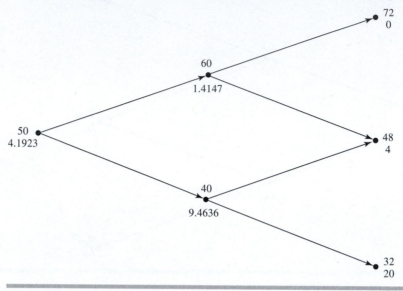

and working back through the tree one step at a time. Figure 13.7 shows the intermediate option prices that are calculated.

13.5 AMERICAN OPTIONS

Up to now all the options we have considered have been European. We now move on to consider how American options can be valued using a binomial tree such as that in Figure 13.4 or 13.7. The procedure is to work back through the tree from the end to the beginning, testing at each node to see whether early exercise is optimal. The value of the option at the final nodes is the same as for the European option. At earlier nodes the value of the option is the greater of

1. The value given by equation (13.5)
2. The payoff from early exercise.

Figure 13.8 shows how Figure 13.7 is affected if the option under consideration is American rather than European. The stock prices and their probabilities are unchanged. The values for the option at the final nodes are also unchanged. At node B, equation (13.5) gives the value of the option as 1.4147, whereas the payoff from early exercise is negative (= −8). Clearly early exercise is not optimal at node B, and the value of the option at this node is 1.4147. At node C, equation (13.5) gives the value of the option as 9.4636, whereas the payoff from early exercise is 12. In this case, early exercise is optimal and the value of the option at the node is 12. At the initial node A, the value given by equation (13.5) is

$$e^{-0.05 \times 1}(0.6282 \times 1.4147 + 0.3718 \times 12.0) = 5.0894$$

Figure 13.8 Using a two-step tree to value an American put option. At each node, the upper number is the stock price and the lower number is the option price.

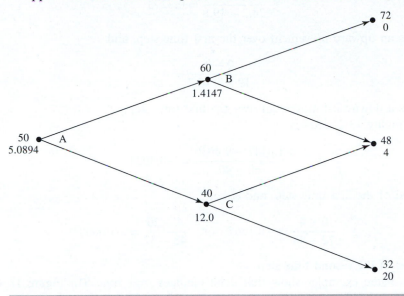

and the payoff from early exercise is 2. In this case early exercise is not optimal. The value of the option is therefore $5.0894.

13.6 DELTA

At this stage, it is appropriate to introduce *delta*, an important parameter (sometimes referred to as a "Greek letter" or simply a "Greek") in the pricing and hedging of options.

The delta (Δ) of a stock option is the ratio of the change in the price of the stock option to the change in the price of the underlying stock. It is the number of units of the stock we should hold for each option shorted in order to create a riskless portfolio. It is the same as the Δ introduced earlier in this chapter. The construction of a riskless portfolio is sometimes referred to as *delta hedging*. The delta of a call option is positive, whereas the delta of a put option is negative.

From Figure 13.1, we can calculate the value of the delta of the call option being considered as

$$\frac{1 - 0}{22 - 18} = 0.25$$

This is because when the stock price changes from $18 to $22, the option price changes from $0 to $1. (This is also the value of Δ calculated in Section 13.1.)

In Figure 13.4 the delta corresponding to stock price movements over the first time step is

$$\frac{1.7433 - 0}{22 - 18} = 0.4358$$

The delta for stock price movements over the second time step is

$$\frac{3.2 - 0}{24.2 - 19.8} = 0.7273$$

if there is an upward movement over the first time step, and

$$\frac{0 - 0}{19.8 - 16.2} = 0$$

if there is a downward movement over the first time step.
From Figure 13.7, delta is

$$\frac{1.4147 - 9.4636}{60 - 40} = -0.4024$$

at the end of the first time step, and either

$$\frac{0 - 4}{72 - 48} = -0.1667 \quad \text{or} \quad \frac{4 - 20}{48 - 32} = -1.0000$$

at the end of the second time step.

The two-step examples show that delta changes over time. (In Figure 13.4, delta changes from 0.4358 to either 0.7273 or 0; and, in Figure 13.7, it changes from −0.4024 to either −0.1667 or −1.0000.) Thus, in order to maintain a riskless hedge using an option and the underlying stock, we need to adjust our holdings in the stock periodically. We will return to this feature of options in Chapter 19.

13.7 MATCHING VOLATILITY WITH u AND d

The three parameters necessary to construct a binomial tree with time step Δt are u, d, and p. Once u and d have been specified, p must be chosen so that the expected return is the risk-free rate r. We have already shown that

$$p = \frac{e^{r\Delta t} - d}{u - d} \tag{13.11}$$

The parameters u and d should be chosen to match volatility. The volatility of a stock (or any other asset), σ, is defined so that the standard deviation of its return in a short period of time Δt is $\sigma\sqrt{\Delta t}$ (see Chapter 15 for a further discussion of this). Equivalently the variance of the return in time Δt is $\sigma^2 \Delta t$. The variance of a variable X is defined as $E(X^2) - [E(X)]^2$, where E denotes expected value. During a time step of length Δt, there is a probability p that the stock will provide a return of $u - 1$ and a probability $1 - p$ that it will provide a return of $d - 1$. It follows that volatility is matched if

$$p(u - 1)^2 + (1 - p)(d - 1)^2 - [p(u - 1) + (1 - p)(d - 1)]^2 = \sigma^2 \Delta t \tag{13.12}$$

Substituting for p from equation (13.11), this simplifies to

$$e^{r\Delta t}(u + d) - ud - e^{2r\Delta t} = \sigma^2 \Delta t \tag{13.13}$$

Figure 13.9 Change in stock price in time Δt in (a) the real world and (b) the risk-neutral world.

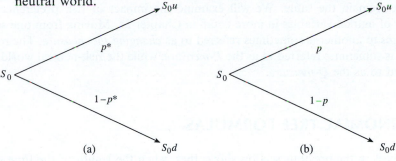

(a)   (b)

When terms in Δt^2 and higher powers of Δt are ignored, a solution to equation (13.13) is[2]

$$u = e^{\sigma\sqrt{\Delta t}} \quad \text{and} \quad d = e^{-\sigma\sqrt{\Delta t}}$$

These are the values of u and d used by Cox, Ross, and Rubinstein (1979).

In the analysis just given we chose u and d to match volatility in the risk-neutral world. What happens if instead we match volatility in the real world? As we will now show, the formulas for u and d are the same.

Suppose that p^* is the probability of an up-movement in the real world while p is as before the probability of an up-movement in a risk-neutral world. This is illustrated in Figure 13.9. Define μ as the expected return in the real world. We must have

$$p^* u + (1 - p^*)d = e^{\mu\Delta t}$$

or

$$p^* = \frac{e^{\mu\Delta t} - d}{u - d} \tag{13.14}$$

Suppose that σ is the volatility in the real world. The equation matching the variance is the same as equation (13.12) except that p is replaced by p^*. When this equation is combined with equation (13.14), we obtain

$$e^{\mu\Delta t}(u + d) - ud - e^{2\mu\Delta t} = \sigma^2 \Delta t$$

This is the same as equation (13.13) except the r is replaced by μ. When terms in Δt^2 and higher powers of Δt are ignored, it has the same solution as equation (13.13):

$$u = e^{\sigma\sqrt{\Delta t}} \quad \text{and} \quad d = e^{-\sigma\sqrt{\Delta t}}$$

Girsanov's Theorem

The results we have just produced are closely related to an important result known as *Girsanov's theorem*. When we move from the risk-neutral world to the real world, the expected return from the stock price changes, but its volatility remains the same. More

---

[2] We are here using the series expansion

$$e^x = 1 + x + \frac{x^2}{2!} + \frac{x^3}{3!} + \cdots$$

generally, when we move from a world with one set of risk preferences to a world with another set of risk preferences, the expected growth rates in variables change, but their volatilities remain the same. We will examine the impact of risk preferences on the behavior of market variables in more detail in Chapter 28. Moving from one set of risk preferences to another is sometimes referred to as *changing the measure*. The real-world measure is sometimes referred to as the *P-measure*, while the risk-neutral world measure is referred to as the *Q-measure*.[3]

13.8 THE BINOMIAL TREE FORMULAS

The analysis in the previous section shows that, when the length of the time step on a binomial tree is Δt, we should match volatility by setting

$$u = e^{\sigma\sqrt{\Delta t}} \tag{13.15}$$

and

$$d = e^{-\sigma\sqrt{\Delta t}} \tag{13.16}$$

Also, from equation (13.6),

$$p = \frac{a - d}{u - d} \tag{13.17}$$

where

$$a = e^{r\Delta t} \tag{13.18}$$

Equations (13.15) to (13.18) define the tree.

Consider again the American put option in Figure 13.8, where the stock price is $50, the strike price is $52, the risk-free rate is 5%, the life of the option is 2 years, and there are two time steps. In this case, $\Delta t = 1$. Suppose that the volatility σ is 30%. Then, from equations (13.15) to (13.18), we have

$$u = e^{0.3 \times 1} = 1.3499, \qquad d = \frac{1}{1.3499} = 0.7408, \qquad a = e^{0.05 \times 1} = 1.0513$$

and

$$p = \frac{1.0513 - 0.7408}{1.3499 - 0.7408} = 0.5097$$

The tree is shown in Figure 13.10. The value of the put option is 7.43. (This is different from the value obtained in Figure 13.8 by assuming $u = 1.2$ and $d = 0.8$.) Note that the option is exercised at the end of the first time step if the lower node is reached.

13.9 INCREASING THE NUMBER OF STEPS

The binomial model presented above is unrealistically simple. Clearly, an analyst can expect to obtain only a very rough approximation to an option price by assuming that

---

[3] With the notation we have been using, p is the probability under the Q-measure, while p^* is the probability under the P-measure.

Figure 13.10 Two-step tree to value a 2-year American put option when the stock price is 50, strike price is 52, risk-free rate is 5%, and volatility is 30%.

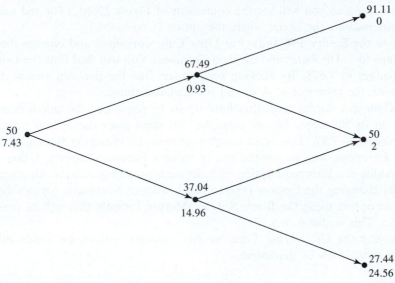

stock price movements during the life of the option consist of one or two binomial steps.

When binomial trees are used in practice, the life of the option is typically divided into 30 or more time steps. In each time step there is a binomial stock price movement. With 30 time steps there are 31 terminal stock prices and 2^{30}, or about 1 billion, possible stock price paths are implicitly considered.

The equations defining the tree are equations (13.15) to (13.18), regardless of the number of time steps. Suppose, for example, that there are five steps instead of two in the example we considered in Figure 13.10. The parameters would be $\Delta t = 2/5 = 0.4$, $r = 0.05$, and $\sigma = 0.3$. These values give $u = e^{0.3 \times \sqrt{0.4}} = 1.2089$, $d = 1/1.2089 = 0.8272$, $a = e^{0.05 \times 0.4} = 1.0202$, and $p = (1.0202 - 0.8272)/(1.2089 - 0.8272) = 0.5056$.

As the number of time steps is increased (so that Δt becomes smaller), the binomial tree model makes the same assumptions about stock price behavior as the Black–Scholes–Merton model, which will be presented in Chapter 15. When the binomial tree is used to price a European option, the price converges to the Black–Scholes–Merton price, as expected, as the number of time steps is increased. This is proved in the appendix to this chapter.

13.10 USING DerivaGem

The software accompanying this book, DerivaGem, is a useful tool for becoming comfortable with binomial trees. After loading the software in the way described at the end of this book, go to the Equity_FX_Indx_Fut_Opts_Calc worksheet. Choose Equity as the Underlying Type and select Binomial American as the Option Type.

Enter the stock price, volatility, risk-free rate, time to expiration, exercise price, and tree steps, as 50, 30%, 5%, 2, 52, and 2, respectively. Click on the *Put* button and then on *Calculate*. The price of the option is shown as 7.428 in the box labeled Price. Now click on *Display Tree* and you will see the equivalent of Figure 13.10. (The red numbers in the software indicate the nodes where the option is exercised.)

Return to the Equity_FX_Indx_Fut_Opts_Calc worksheet and change the number of time steps to 5. Hit *Enter* and click on *Calculate*. You will find that the value of the option changes to 7.671. By clicking on *Display Tree* the five-step tree is displayed, together with the values of u, d, a, and p calculated above.

DerivaGem can display trees that have up to 10 steps, but the calculations can be done for up to 500 steps. In our example, 500 steps gives the option price (to two decimal places) as 7.47. This is an accurate answer. By changing the Option Type to Binomial European, we can use the tree to value a European option. Using 500 time steps, the value of a European option with the same parameters as the American option is 6.76. (By changing the Option Type to Black–Scholes European, we can display the value of the option using the Black–Scholes–Merton formula that will be presented in Chapter 15. This is also 6.76.)

By changing the Underlying Type, we can consider options on assets other than stocks. These will now be discussed.

13.11 OPTIONS ON OTHER ASSETS

We introduced options on indices, currencies, and futures contracts in Chapter 10 and will cover them in more detail in Chapters 17 and 18. It turns out that we can construct and use binomial trees for these options in exactly the same way as for options on stocks except that the equation for p changes. As in the case of options on stocks, equation (13.2) applies so that the value at a node (before the possibility of early exercise is considered) is p times the value if there is an up movement plus $1 - p$ times the value if there is a down movement, discounted at the risk-free rate.

Options on Stocks Paying a Continuous Dividend Yield

Consider a stock paying a known dividend yield at rate q. The total return from dividends and capital gains in a risk-neutral world is r. The dividends provide a return of q. Capital gains must therefore provide a return of $r - q$. If the stock starts at S_0, its expected value after one time step of length Δt must be $S_0 e^{(r-q)\Delta t}$. This means that

$$pS_0 u + (1 - p)S_0 d = S_0 e^{(r-q)\Delta t}$$

so that

$$p = \frac{e^{(r-q)\Delta t} - d}{u - d}$$

As in the case of options on non-dividend-paying stocks, we match volatility by setting $u = e^{\sigma\sqrt{\Delta t}}$ and $d = 1/u$. This means that we can use equations (13.15) to (13.18), except that we set $a = e^{(r-q)\Delta t}$ instead of $a = e^{r\Delta t}$.

Options on Stock Indices

When calculating a futures price for a stock index in Chapter 5 we assumed that the stocks underlying the index provided a dividend yield at rate q. We make a similar assumption here. The valuation of an option on a stock index is therefore very similar to the valuation of an option on a stock paying a known dividend yield.

Example 13.1

A stock index is currently 810 and has a volatility of 20% and a dividend yield of 2%. The risk-free rate is 5%. Figure 13.11 shows the output from DerivaGem for valuing a European 6-month call option with a strike price of 800 using a two-step tree. In this case,

$$\Delta t = 0.25, \qquad u = e^{0.20 \times \sqrt{0.25}} = 1.1052,$$

$$d = 1/u = 0.9048, \qquad a = e^{(0.05-0.02) \times 0.25} = 1.0075$$

$$p = (1.0075 - 0.9048)/(1.1052 - 0.9048) = 0.5126$$

The value of the option is 53.39.

Figure 13.11   Two-step tree to value a European 6-month call option on an index when the index level is 810, strike price is 800, risk-free rate is 5%, volatility is 20%, and dividend yield is 2% (DerivaGem output).

At each node:
 Upper value = Underlying Asset Price
 Lower value = Option Price
Shading indicates where option is exercised

Strike price = 800
Discount factor per step = 0.9876
Time step, dt = 0.2500 years, 91.25 days
Growth factor per step, a = 1.0075
Probability of up move, p = 0.5126
Up step size, u = 1.1052
Down step size, d = 0.9048

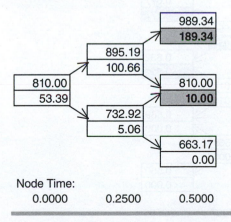

Node Time:
   0.0000   0.2500   0.5000

Options on Currencies

As pointed out in Section 5.10, a foreign currency can be regarded as an asset providing a yield at the foreign risk-free rate of interest, r_f. By analogy with the stock index case we can construct a tree for options on a currency by using equations (13.15) to (13.18) and setting $a = e^{(r-r_f)\Delta t}$.

Example 13.2

A foreign currency is currently worth 0.6100 U.S. dollars and this exchange rate has a volatility of 12%. The foreign risk-free rate is 7% and the U.S. risk-free rate is 5%. Figure 13.12 shows the output from DerivaGem for valuing a 3-month American call option with a strike price of 0.6000 using a three-step tree. In this case,

$$\Delta t = 0.08333, \quad u = e^{0.12 \times \sqrt{0.08333}} = 1.0352$$

$$d = 1/u = 0.9660, \quad a = e^{(0.05-0.07)\times 0.08333} = 0.9983$$

$$p = (0.9983 - 0.9660)/(1.0352 - 0.9660) = 0.4673$$

The value of the option is 0.019.

Figure 13.12   Three-step tree to value an American 3-month call option on a currency when the value of the currency is 0.6100, strike price is 0.6000, risk-free rate is 5%, volatility is 12%, and foreign risk-free rate is 7% (DerivaGem output).

At each node:
 Upper value = Underlying Asset Price
 Lower value = Option Price
Shading indicates where option is exercised

Strike price = 0.6
Discount factor per step = 0.9958
Time step, dt = 0.0833 years, 30.42 days
Growth factor per step, a = 0.9983
Probability of up move, p = 0.4673
Up step size, u = 1.0352
Down step size, d = 0.9660

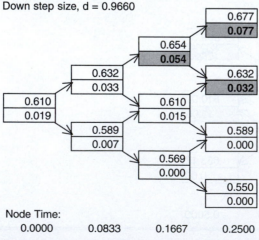

Node Time:
   0.0000   0.0833   0.1667   0.2500

Options on Futures

It costs nothing to take a long or a short position in a futures contract. It follows that in a risk-neutral world a futures price should have an expected growth rate of zero. (We discuss this point in more detail in Section 18.6.) As above, we define p as the probability of an up movement in the futures price, u as the percentage up movement, and d as the percentage down movement. If F_0 is the initial futures price, the expected futures price at the end of one time step of length Δt should also be F_0. This means that

$$pF_0 u + (1 - p)F_0 d = F_0$$

so that

$$p = \frac{1 - d}{u - d}$$

and we can use equations (13.15) to (13.18) with $a = 1$.

Example 13.3

A futures price is currently 31 and has a volatility of 30%. The risk-free rate is 5%. Figure 13.13 shows the output from DerivaGem for valuing a 9-month American put option with a strike price of 30 using a three-step tree. In this case,

$$\Delta t = 0.25, \quad u = e^{0.3\sqrt{0.25}} = 1.1618$$

$$d = 1/u = 1/1.1618 = 0.8607, \quad a = 1,$$

$$p = (1 - 0.8607)/(1.1618 - 0.8607) = 0.4626$$

The value of the option is 2.84.

SUMMARY

This chapter has provided a first look at the valuation of options on stocks and other assets using trees. In the simple situation where movements in the price of a stock during the life of an option are governed by a one-step binomial tree, it is possible to set up a riskless portfolio consisting of a position in the stock option and a position in the stock. In a world with no arbitrage opportunities, riskless portfolios must earn the risk-free interest. This enables the stock option to be priced in terms of the stock. It is interesting to note that no assumptions are required about the actual (real-world) probabilities of up and down movements in the stock price.

When stock price movements are governed by a multistep binomial tree, we can treat each binomial step separately and work back from the end of the life of the option to the beginning to obtain the current value of the option. Again only no-arbitrage arguments are used, and no assumptions are required about the actual (real-world) probabilities of up and down movements in the stock price.

A very important principle states that we can assume the world is risk-neutral when valuing an option. This chapter has shown, through both numerical examples and algebra, that no-arbitrage arguments and risk-neutral valuation are equivalent and lead to the same option prices.

The delta of a stock option, Δ, considers the effect of a small change in the underlying stock price on the change in the option price. It is the ratio of the change in the option

Figure 13.13 Three-step tree to value an American 9-month put option on a futures contract when the futures price is 31, strike price is 30, risk-free rate is 5%, and volatility is 30% (DerivaGem output).

At each node:
 Upper value = Underlying Asset Price
 Lower value = Option Price
Shading indicates where option is exercised

Strike price = 30
Discount factor per step = 0.9876
Time step, dt = 0.2500 years, 91.25 days
Growth factor per step, a = 1.000
Probability of up move, p = 0.4626
Up step size, u = 1.1618
Down step size, d = 0.8607

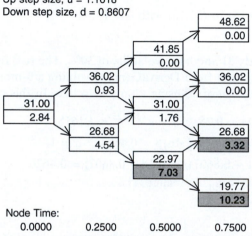

Node Time:
 0.0000   0.2500   0.5000   0.7500

price to the change in the stock price. For a riskless position, an investor should buy Δ shares for each option sold. An inspection of a typical binomial tree shows that delta changes during the life of an option. This means that to hedge a particular option position, we must change our holding in the underlying stock periodically.

Constructing binomial trees for valuing options on stock indices, currencies, and futures contracts is very similar to doing so for valuing options on stocks. In Chapter 21, we will return to binomial trees and provide more details on how they are used in practice.

FURTHER READING

Coval, J. D. and T. Shumway. "Expected Option Returns," *Journal of Finance*, 56, 3 (2001): 983–1009.

Cox, J. C., S. A. Ross, and M. Rubinstein. "Option Pricing: A Simplified Approach," *Journal of Financial Economics* 7 (October 1979): 229–64.

Rendleman, R., and B. Bartter. "Two State Option Pricing," *Journal of Finance* 34 (1979): 1092–1110.

Shreve, S. E. *Stochastic Calculus for Finance I: The Binomial Asset Pricing Model*. New York: Springer, 2005.

Practice Questions (Answers in Solutions Manual)

13.1. A stock price is currently $40. It is known that at the end of 1 month it will be either $42 or $38. The risk-free interest rate is 8% per annum with continuous compounding. What is the value of a 1-month European call option with a strike price of $39?

13.2. Explain the no-arbitrage and risk-neutral valuation approaches to valuing a European option using a one-step binomial tree.

13.3. What is meant by the "delta" of a stock option?

13.4. A stock price is currently $50. It is known that at the end of 6 months it will be either $45 or $55. The risk-free interest rate is 10% per annum with continuous compounding. What is the value of a 6-month European put option with a strike price of $50?

13.5. A stock price is currently $100. Over each of the next two 6-month periods it is expected to go up by 10% or down by 10%. The risk-free interest rate is 8% per annum with continuous compounding. What is the value of a 1-year European call option with a strike price of $100?

13.6. For the situation considered in Problem 13.5, what is the value of a 1-year European put option with a strike price of $100? Verify that the European call and European put prices satisfy put–call parity.

13.7. What are the formulas for u and d in terms of volatility?

13.8. Consider the situation in which stock price movements during the life of a European option are governed by a two-step binomial tree. Explain why it is not possible to set up a position in the stock and the option that remains riskless for the whole of the life of the option.

13.9. A stock price is currently $50. It is known that at the end of 2 months it will be either $53 or $48. The risk-free interest rate is 10% per annum with continuous compounding. What is the value of a 2-month European call option with a strike price of $49? Use no-arbitrage arguments.

13.10. A stock price is currently $80. It is known that at the end of 4 months it will be either $75 or $85. The risk-free interest rate is 5% per annum with continuous compounding. What is the value of a 4-month European put option with a strike price of $80? Use no-arbitrage arguments.

13.11. A stock price is currently $40. It is known that at the end of 3 months it will be either $45 or $35. The risk-free rate of interest with quarterly compounding is 8% per annum. Calculate the value of a 3-month European put option on the stock with an exercise price of $40. Verify that no-arbitrage arguments and risk-neutral valuation arguments give the same answers.

13.12. A stock price is currently $50. Over each of the next two 3-month periods it is expected to go up by 6% or down by 5%. The risk-free interest rate is 5% per annum with continuous compounding. What is the value of a 6-month European call option with a strike price of $51?

13.13. For the situation considered in Problem 13.12, what is the value of a 6-month European put option with a strike price of $51? Verify that the European call and European put prices satisfy put–call parity. If the put option were American, would it ever be optimal to exercise it early at any of the nodes on the tree?

13.14. A stock price is currently $25. It is known that at the end of 2 months it will be either $23 or $27. The risk-free interest rate is 10% per annum with continuous compounding. Suppose S_T is the stock price at the end of 2 months. What is the value of a derivative that pays off S_T^2 at this time?

13.15. Calculate u, d, and p when a binomial tree is constructed to value an option on a foreign currency. The tree step size is 1 month, the domestic interest rate is 5% per annum, the foreign interest rate is 8% per annum, and the volatility is 12% per annum.

13.16. The volatility of a non-dividend-paying stock whose price is $78, is 30%. The risk-free rate is 3% per annum (continuously compounded) for all maturities. Calculate values for u, d, and p when a 2-month time step is used. What is the value a 4-month European call option with a strike price of $80 given by a two-step binomial tree. Suppose a trader sells 1,000 options (10 contracts). What position in the stock is necessary to hedge the trader's position at the time of the trade?

13.17. A stock index is currently 1,500. Its volatility is 18%. The risk-free rate is 4% per annum (continuously compounded) for all maturities and the dividend yield on the index is 2.5%. Calculate values for u, d, and p when a 6-month time step is used. What is the value a 12-month American put option with a strike price of 1,480 given by a two-step binomial tree.

13.18. The futures price of a commodity is $90. Use a three-step tree to value (a) a 9-month American call option with strike price $93 and (b) a 9-month American put option with strike price $93. The volatility is 28% and the risk-free rate (all maturities) is 3% with continuous compounding.

Further Questions

13.19. The current price of a non-dividend-paying biotech stock is $140 with a volatility of 25%. The risk-free rate is 4%. For a 3-month time step:
(a) What is the percentage up movement?
(b) What is the percentage down movement?
(c) What is the probability of an up movement in a risk-neutral world?
(d) What is the probability of a down movement in a risk-neutral world?
Use a two-step tree to value a 6-month European call option and a 6-month European put option. In both cases the strike price is $150.

13.20. In Problem 13.19, suppose a trader sells 10,000 European call options and the two-step tree describes the behavior of the stock. How many shares of the stock are needed to hedge the 6-month European call for the first and second 3-month period? For the second time period, consider both the case where the stock price moves up during the first period and the case where it moves down during the first period.

13.21. A stock price is currently $50. It is known that at the end of 6 months it will be either $60 or $42. The risk-free rate of interest with continuous compounding is 12% per annum. Calculate the value of a 6-month European call option on the stock with an exercise price of $48. Verify that no-arbitrage arguments and risk-neutral valuation arguments give the same answers.

13.22. A stock price is currently $40. Over each of the next two 3-month periods it is expected to go up by 10% or down by 10%. The risk-free interest rate is 12% per annum with continuous compounding. (a) What is the value of a 6-month European put option with a strike price of $42? (b) What is the value of a 6-month American put option with a strike price of $42?

13.23. Using a "trial-and-error" approach, estimate how high the strike price has to be in Problem 13.22 for it to be optimal to exercise the option immediately.

13.24. A stock price is currently $30. During each 2-month period for the next 4 months it will increase by 8% or reduce by 10%. The risk-free interest rate is 5%. Use a two-step tree to calculate the value of a derivative that pays off $[\max(30 - S_T, 0)]^2$, where S_T is the stock price in 4 months. If the derivative is American-style, should it be exercised early?

13.25. Consider a European call option on a non-dividend-paying stock where the stock price is $40, the strike price is $40, the risk-free rate is 4% per annum, the volatility is 30% per annum, and the time to maturity is 6 months.
(a) Calculate u, d, and p for a two-step tree.
(b) Value the option using a two-step tree.
(c) Verify that DerivaGem gives the same answer.
(d) Use DerivaGem to value the option with 5, 50, 100, and 500 time steps.

13.26. Repeat Problem 13.25 for an American put option on a futures contract. The strike price and the futures price are $50, the risk-free rate is 10%, the time to maturity is 6 months, and the volatility is 40% per annum.

13.27. Footnote 1 of this chapter shows that the correct discount rate to use for the real-world expected payoff in the case of the call option considered in Figure 13.1 is 55.96%. Show that if the option is a put rather than a call the discount rate is -70.4%. Explain why the two real-world discount rates are so different.

13.28. A stock index is currently 990, the risk-free rate is 5%, and the dividend yield on the index is 2%. Use a three-step tree to value an 18-month American put option with a strike price of 1,000 when the volatility is 20% per annum. How much does the option holder gain by being able to exercise early? When is the gain made?

13.29. Calculate the value of 9-month American call option to buy 1 million units of a foreign currency using a three-step binomial tree. The current exchange rate is 0.79 and the strike price is 0.80 (both expressed as dollars per unit of the foreign currency). The volatility of the exchange rate is 12% per annum. The domestic and foreign risk-free rates are 2% and 5%, respectively. What position in the foreign currency is initially necessary to hedge the risk?

APPENDIX

DERIVATION OF THE BLACK–SCHOLES–MERTON OPTION-PRICING FORMULA FROM A BINOMIAL TREE

One way of deriving the famous Black–Scholes–Merton result for valuing a European option on a non-dividend-paying stock is by allowing the number of time steps in a binomial tree to approach infinity.

Suppose that a tree with n time steps is used to value a European call option with strike price K and life T. Each step is of length T/n. If there have been j upward movements and $n - j$ downward movements on the tree, the final stock price is $S_0 u^j d^{n-j}$, where u is the proportional up movement, d is the proportional down movement, and S_0 is the initial stock price. The payoff from a European call option is then

$$\max(S_0 u^j d^{n-j} - K, 0)$$

From the properties of the binomial distribution, the probability of exactly j upward and $n - j$ downward movements is given by

$$\frac{n!}{(n - j)! \, j!} p^j (1 - p)^{n-j}$$

It follows that the expected payoff from the call option is

$$\sum_{j=0}^{n} \frac{n!}{(n - j)! \, j!} p^j (1 - p)^{n-j} \max(S_0 u^j d^{n-j} - K, 0)$$

As the tree represents movements in a risk-neutral world, we can discount this at the risk-free rate r to obtain the option price:

$$c = e^{-rT} \sum_{j=0}^{n} \frac{n!}{(n - j)! \, j!} p^j (1 - p)^{n-j} \max(S_0 u^j d^{n-j} - K, 0) \qquad \text{(13A.1)}$$

The terms in equation (13A.1) are nonzero when the final stock price is greater than the strike price, that is, when

$$S_0 u^j d^{n-j} > K$$

or

$$\ln(S_0/K) > -j \ln(u) - (n - j) \ln(d)$$

Since $u = e^{\sigma \sqrt{T/n}}$ and $d = e^{-\sigma \sqrt{T/n}}$, this condition becomes

$$\ln(S_0/K) > n\sigma \sqrt{T/n} - 2j\sigma \sqrt{T/n}$$

or

$$j > \frac{n}{2} - \frac{\ln(S_0/K)}{2\sigma \sqrt{T/n}}$$

Equation (13A.1) can therefore be written

$$c = e^{-rT} \sum_{j>\alpha} \frac{n!}{(n - j)! \, j!} p^j (1 - p)^{n-j} (S_0 u^j d^{n-j} - K)$$

where

$$\alpha = \frac{n}{2} - \frac{\ln(S_0/K)}{2\sigma\sqrt{T/n}}$$

For convenience, we define

$$U_1 = \sum_{j>\alpha} \frac{n!}{(n-j)!\,j!} p^j(1-p)^{n-j} u^j d^{n-j} \tag{13A.2}$$

and

$$U_2 = \sum_{j>\alpha} \frac{n!}{(n-j)!\,j!} p^j(1-p)^{n-j} \tag{13A.3}$$

so that

$$c = e^{-rT}(S_0 U_1 - K U_2) \tag{13A.4}$$

Consider first U_2. As is well known, the binomial distribution approaches a normal distribution as the number of trials approaches infinity. Specifically, when there are n trials and p is the probability of success, the probability distribution of the number of successes is approximately normal with mean np and standard deviation $\sqrt{np(1-p)}$. The variable U_2 in equation (13A.3) is the probability of the number of successes being more than α. From the properties of the normal distribution, it follows that, for large n,

$$U_2 = N\left(\frac{np-\alpha}{\sqrt{np(1-p)}}\right) \tag{13A.5}$$

where N is the cumulative probability distribution function for a standard normal variable. Substituting for α, we obtain

$$U_2 = N\left(\frac{\ln(S_0/K)}{2\sigma\sqrt{T}\sqrt{p(1-p)}} + \frac{\sqrt{n}\,(p-\frac{1}{2})}{\sqrt{p(1-p)}}\right) \tag{13A.6}$$

From equations (13.15) to (13.18), we have

$$p = \frac{e^{rT/n} - e^{-\sigma\sqrt{T/n}}}{e^{\sigma\sqrt{T/n}} - e^{-\sigma\sqrt{T/n}}}$$

By expanding the exponential functions in a series, we see that, as n tends to infinity, $p(1-p)$ tends to $\frac{1}{4}$ and $\sqrt{n}(p-\frac{1}{2})$ tends to

$$\frac{(r-\sigma^2/2)\sqrt{T}}{2\sigma}$$

so that in the limit, as n tends to infinity, equation (13A.6) becomes

$$U_2 = N\left(\frac{\ln(S_0/K) + (r-\sigma^2/2)T}{\sigma\sqrt{T}}\right) \tag{13A.7}$$

We now move on to evaluate U_1. From equation (13A.2), we have

$$U_1 = \sum_{j>\alpha} \frac{n!}{(n-j)!\, j!} (pu)^j [(1-p)d]^{n-j} \qquad \text{(13A.8)}$$

Define

$$p^* = \frac{pu}{pu + (1-p)d} \qquad \text{(13A.9)}$$

It then follows that

$$1 - p^* = \frac{(1-p)d}{pu + (1-p)d}$$

and we can write equation (13A.8) as

$$U_1 = [pu + (1-p)d]^n \sum_{j>\alpha} \frac{n!}{(n-j)!\, j!} (p^*)^j (1-p^*)^{n-j}$$

Since the expected rate of return in the risk-neutral world is the risk-free rate r, it follows that $pu + (1-p)d = e^{rT/n}$ and

$$U_1 = e^{rT} \sum_{j>\alpha} \frac{n!}{(n-j)!\, j!} (p^*)^j (1-p^*)^{n-j}$$

This shows that U_1 involves a binomial distribution where the probability of an up movement is p^* rather than p. Approximating the binomial distribution with a normal distribution, we obtain, similarly to equation (13A.5),

$$U_1 = e^{rT} N \left(\frac{np^* - \alpha}{\sqrt{np^*(1-p^*)}} \right)$$

and substituting for α gives, as with equation (13A.6),

$$U_1 = e^{rT} N \left(\frac{\ln(S_0/K)}{2\sigma\sqrt{T}\sqrt{p^*(1-p^*)}} + \frac{\sqrt{n}(p^* - \frac{1}{2})}{\sqrt{p^*(1-p^*)}} \right)$$

Substituting for u and d in equation (13A.9) gives

$$p^* = \left(\frac{e^{rT/n} - e^{-\sigma\sqrt{T/n}}}{e^{\sigma\sqrt{T/n}} - e^{-\sigma\sqrt{T/n}}} \right) \left(\frac{e^{\sigma\sqrt{T/n}}}{e^{rT/n}} \right)$$

By expanding the exponential functions in a series we see that, as n tends to infinity, $p^*(1-p^*)$ tends to $\frac{1}{4}$ and $\sqrt{n}(p^* - \frac{1}{2})$ tends to

$$\frac{(r + \sigma^2/2)\sqrt{T}}{2\sigma}$$

with the result that

$$U_1 = e^{rT} N \left(\frac{\ln(S_0/K) + (r + \sigma^2/2)T}{\sigma\sqrt{T}} \right) \qquad \text{(13A.10)}$$

From equations (13A.4), (13A.7), and (13A.10), we have

$$c = S_0 N(d_1) - Ke^{-rT} N(d_2)$$

where

$$d_1 = \frac{\ln(S_0/K) + (r + \sigma^2/2)T}{\sigma\sqrt{T}}$$

and

$$d_2 = \frac{\ln(S_0/K) + (r - \sigma^2/2)T}{\sigma\sqrt{T}} = d_1 - \sigma\sqrt{T}$$

This is the Black–Scholes–Merton formula for the valuation of a European call option. It will be discussed in Chapter 15. An alternative derivation is given in the appendix to that chapter.

CHAPTER 14

Wiener Processes and Itô's Lemma

Any variable whose value changes over time in an uncertain way is said to follow a *stochastic process*. Stochastic processes can be classified as *discrete time* or *continuous time*. A discrete-time stochastic process is one where the value of the variable can change only at certain fixed points in time, whereas a continuous-time stochastic process is one where changes can take place at any time. Stochastic processes can also be classified as *continuous variable* or *discrete variable*. In a continuous-variable process, the underlying variable can take any value within a certain range, whereas in a discrete-variable process, only certain discrete values are possible.

This chapter develops a continuous-variable, continuous-time stochastic process for stock prices. A similar process is often assumed for the prices of other assets. Learning about this process is the first step to understanding the pricing of options and other more complicated derivatives. It should be noted that, in practice, we do not observe stock prices following continuous-variable, continuous-time processes. Stock prices are restricted to discrete values (e.g., multiples of a cent) and changes can be observed only when the exchange is open for trading. Nevertheless, the continuous-variable, continuous-time process proves to be a useful model for many purposes.

Many people feel that continuous-time stochastic processes are so complicated that they should be left entirely to "rocket scientists." This is not so. The biggest hurdle to understanding these processes is the notation. Here we present a step-by-step approach aimed at getting the reader over this hurdle. We also explain an important result known as *Itô's lemma* that is central to the pricing of derivatives.

14.1 THE MARKOV PROPERTY

A *Markov process* is a particular type of stochastic process where only the current value of a variable is relevant for predicting the future. The past history of the variable and the way that the present has emerged from the past are irrelevant.

Stock prices are usually assumed to follow a Markov process. Suppose that the price of a stock is $100 now. If the stock price follows a Markov process, our predictions for the future should be unaffected by the price one week ago, one month ago, or one year ago. The only relevant piece of information is that the price is now \$100.[1] Predictions for the future are uncertain and must be expressed in terms of probability distributions. The Markov property implies that the probability distribution of the price at any particular future time is not dependent on the particular path followed by the price in the past.

The Markov property of stock prices is consistent with the weak form of market efficiency. This states that the present price of a stock impounds all the information contained in a record of past prices. If the weak form of market efficiency were not true, technical analysts could make above-average returns by interpreting charts of the past history of stock prices. There is very little evidence that they are in fact able to do this.

It is competition in the marketplace that tends to ensure that weak-form market efficiency and the Markov property hold. There are many investors watching the stock market closely. This leads to a situation where a stock price, at any given time, reflects the information in past prices. Suppose that it was discovered that a particular pattern in a stock price always gave a 65% chance of subsequent steep price rises. Investors would attempt to buy a stock as soon as the pattern was observed, and demand for the stock would immediately rise. This would lead to an immediate rise in its price and the observed effect would be eliminated, as would any profitable trading opportunities.

14.2 CONTINUOUS-TIME STOCHASTIC PROCESSES

Consider a variable that follows a Markov stochastic process. Suppose that its current value is 10 and that the change in its value during a year is $\phi(0, 1)$, where $\phi(m, v)$ denotes a probability distribution that is normally distributed with mean m and variance v.[2] What is the probability distribution of the change in the value of the variable during 2 years?

The change in 2 years is the sum of two normal distributions, each of which has a mean of zero and variance of 1.0. Because the variable is Markov, the two probability distributions are independent. When we add two independent normal distributions, the result is a normal distribution where the mean is the sum of the means and the variance is the sum of the variances. The mean of the change during 2 years in the variable we are considering is, therefore, zero and the variance of this change is 2.0. Hence, the change in the variable over 2 years has the distribution $\phi(0, 2)$. The standard deviation of the change is $\sqrt{2}$.

Consider next the change in the variable during 6 months. The variance of the change in the value of the variable during 1 year equals the variance of the change during the first 6 months plus the variance of the change during the second 6 months. We assume these are the same. It follows that the variance of the change during a 6-month period must be 0.5. Equivalently, the standard deviation of the change is $\sqrt{0.5}$. The probability distribution for the change in the value of the variable during 6 months is $\phi(0, 0.5)$.

---

[1] Statistical properties of the stock price history may be useful in determining the characteristics of the stochastic process followed by the stock price (e.g., its volatility). The point being made here is that the particular path followed by the stock in the past is irrelevant.

[2] Variance is the square of standard deviation. The standard deviation of a 1-year change in the value of the variable we are considering is therefore 1.0.

A similar argument shows that the probability distribution for the change in the value of the variable during 3 months is $\phi(0, 0.25)$. More generally, the change during any time period of length T is $\phi(0, T)$. In particular, the change during a very short time period of length Δt is $\phi(0, \Delta t)$.

Note that, when Markov processes are considered, the variances of the changes in successive time periods are additive. The standard deviations of the changes in successive time periods are not additive. The variance of the change in the variable in our example is 1.0 per year, so that the variance of the change in 2 years is 2.0 and the variance of the change in 3 years is 3.0. The standard deviations of the changes in 2 and 3 years are $\sqrt{2}$ and $\sqrt{3}$, respectively. Uncertainty is often measured by standard deviation. These results therefore explain why uncertainty is sometimes referred to as being proportional to the square root of time.

Wiener Process

The process followed by the variable we have been considering is known as a *Wiener process*. It is a particular type of Markov stochastic process with a mean change of zero and a variance rate of 1.0 per year. It has been used in physics to describe the motion of a particle that is subject to a large number of small molecular shocks and is sometimes referred to as *Brownian motion*.

Expressed formally, a variable z follows a Wiener process if it has the following two properties:

Property 1. *The change Δz during a small period of time Δt is*

$$\Delta z = \epsilon\sqrt{\Delta t} \tag{14.1}$$

where ϵ has a standard normal distribution $\phi(0, 1)$.

Property 2. *The values of Δz for any two different short intervals of time, Δt, are independent.*

It follows from the first property that Δz itself has a normal distribution with

$$\text{mean of } \Delta z = 0$$
$$\text{standard deviation of } \Delta z = \sqrt{\Delta t}$$
$$\text{variance of } \Delta z = \Delta t$$

The second property implies that z follows a Markov process.

Consider the change in the value of z during a relatively long period of time, T. This can be denoted by $z(T) - z(0)$. It can be regarded as the sum of the changes in z in N small time intervals of length Δt, where

$$N = \frac{T}{\Delta t}$$

Thus,

$$z(T) - z(0) = \sum_{i=1}^{N} \epsilon_i \sqrt{\Delta t} \tag{14.2}$$

where the ϵ_i $(i = 1, 2, \ldots, N)$ are distributed $\phi(0, 1)$. We know from the second property of Wiener processes that the ϵ_i are independent of each other. It follows from equation (14.2) that $z(T) - z(0)$ is normally distributed, with

$$\text{mean of } [z(T) - z(0)] = 0$$
$$\text{variance of} [z(T) - z(0)] = N\,\Delta t = T$$
$$\text{standard deviation of } [z(T) - z(0)] = \sqrt{T}$$

This is consistent with the discussion earlier in this section.

Example 14.1

Suppose that the value, z, of a variable that follows a Wiener process is initially 25 and that time is measured in years. At the end of 1 year, the value of the variable is normally distributed with a mean of 25 and a standard deviation of 1.0. At the end of 5 years, it is normally distributed with a mean of 25 and a standard deviation of $\sqrt{5}$, or 2.236. Our uncertainty about the value of the variable at a certain time in the future, as measured by its standard deviation, increases as the square root of how far we are looking ahead.

In ordinary calculus, it is usual to proceed from small changes to the limit as the small changes become closer to zero. Thus, $dx = a\,dt$ is the notation used to indicate that $\Delta x = a\,\Delta t$ in the limit as $\Delta t \to 0$. We use similar notational conventions in stochastic calculus. So, when we refer to dz as a Wiener process, we mean that it has the properties for Δz given above in the limit as $\Delta t \to 0$.

Figure 14.1 illustrates what happens to the path followed by z as the limit $\Delta t \to 0$ is approached. Note that the path is quite "jagged." This is because the standard deviation of the movement in z in time Δt equals $\sqrt{\Delta t}$ and, when Δt is small, $\sqrt{\Delta t}$ is much bigger than Δt. Two intriguing properties of Wiener processes, related to this $\sqrt{\Delta t}$ property, are as follows:

1. The expected length of the path followed by z in any time interval is infinite.

2. The expected number of times z equals any particular value in any time interval is infinite.[3]

Generalized Wiener Process

The mean change per unit time for a stochastic process is known as the *drift rate* and the variance per unit time is known as the *variance rate*. The basic Wiener process, dz, that has been developed so far has a drift rate of zero and a variance rate of 1.0. The drift rate of zero means that the expected value of z at any future time is equal to its current value. The variance rate of 1.0 means that the variance of the change in z in a time interval of length T equals T. A *generalized Wiener process* for a variable x can be defined in terms of dz as

$$dx = a\,dt + b\,dz \tag{14.3}$$

where a and b are constants.

To understand equation (14.3), it is useful to consider the two components on the right-hand side separately. The $a\,dt$ term implies that x has an expected drift rate of a per unit of time. Without the $b\,dz$ term, the equation is $dx = a\,dt$, which implies that

---

[3] This is because z has some nonzero probability of equaling any value v in the time interval. If it equals v in time t, the expected number of times it equals v in the immediate vicinity of t is infinite.

Figure 14.1 How a Wiener process is obtained when $\Delta t \to 0$ in equation (14.1).

Relatively large value of Δt

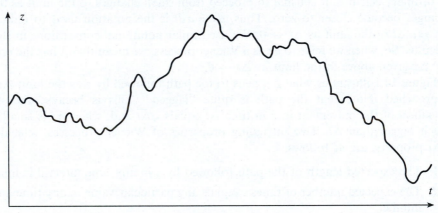

Smaller value of Δt

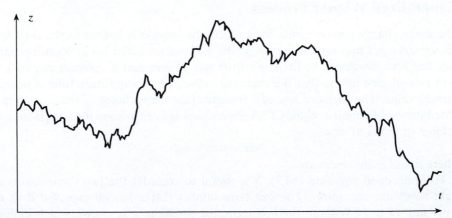

The true process obtained as $\Delta t \to 0$

$dx/dt = a$. Integrating with respect to time, we get

$$x = x_0 + at$$

where x_0 is the value of x at time 0. In a period of time of length T, the variable x increases by an amount aT. The $b\,dz$ term on the right-hand side of equation (14.3) can be regarded as adding noise or variability to the path followed by x. The amount of this noise or variability is b times a Wiener process. A Wiener process has a variance rate per unit time of 1.0. It follows that b times a Wiener process has a variance rate per unit time of b^2. In a small time interval Δt, the change Δx in the value of x is given by equations (14.1) and (14.3) as

$$\Delta x = a\,\Delta t + b\epsilon\sqrt{\Delta t}$$

where, as before, ϵ has a standard normal distribution $\phi(0, 1)$. Thus Δx has a normal distribution with

$$\text{mean of } \Delta x = a\,\Delta t$$

$$\text{standard deviation of } \Delta x = b\sqrt{\Delta t}$$

$$\text{variance of } \Delta x = b^2\,\Delta t$$

Similar arguments to those given for a Wiener process show that the change in the value of x in any time interval T is normally distributed with

$$\text{mean of change in } x = aT$$

$$\text{standard deviation of change in } x = b\sqrt{T}$$

$$\text{variance of change in } x = b^2 T$$

To summarize, the generalized Wiener process given in equation (14.3) has an expected drift rate (i.e., average drift per unit of time) of a and a variance rate (i.e., variance per unit of time) of b^2. It is illustrated in Figure 14.2.

Figure 14.2 Generalized Wiener process with $a = 0.3$ and $b = 1.5$.

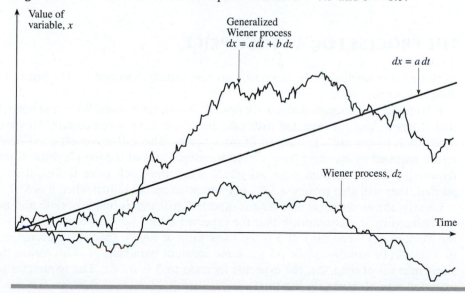

Example 14.2

    Consider the situation where the cash position of a company, measured in thousands of dollars, follows a generalized Wiener process with a drift of 20 per year and a variance rate of 900 per year. Initially, the cash position is 50. At the end of 1 year the cash position will have a normal distribution with a mean of 70 and a standard deviation of $\sqrt{900}$, or 30. At the end of 6 months it will have a normal distribution with a mean of 60 and a standard deviation of $30\sqrt{0.5} = 21.21$. Our uncertainty about the cash position at some time in the future, as measured by its standard deviation, increases as the square root of how far ahead we are looking. (Note that the cash position can become negative. We can interpret this as a situation where the company is borrowing funds.)

Itô Process

A further type of stochastic process, known as an *Itô process*, can be defined. This is a generalized Wiener process in which the parameters a and b are functions of the value of the underlying variable x and time t. An Itô process can therefore be written as

$$dx = a(x, t)\, dt + b(x, t)\, dz \tag{14.4}$$

Both the expected drift rate and variance rate of an Itô process are liable to change over time. They are functions of the current value of x and the current time, t. In a small time interval between t and $t + \Delta t$, the variable changes from x to $x + \Delta x$, where

$$\Delta x = a(x, t)\Delta t + b(x, t)\epsilon\sqrt{\Delta t}$$

This equation involves a small approximation. It assumes that the drift and variance rate of x remain constant, equal to their values at time t, in the time interval between t and $t + \Delta t$.

    Note that the process in equation (14.4) is Markov because the change in x at time t depends only on the value of x at time t, not on its history. A non-Markov process could be defined by letting a and b in equation (14.4) depend on values of x prior to time t.

14.3 THE PROCESS FOR A STOCK PRICE

In this section we discuss the stochastic process usually assumed for the price of a non-dividend-paying stock.

    It is tempting to suggest that a stock price follows a generalized Wiener process; that is, that it has a constant expected drift rate and a constant variance rate. However, this model fails to capture a key aspect of stock prices. This is that the expected percentage return required by investors from a stock is independent of the stock's price. If investors require a 14% per annum expected return when the stock price is \$10, then, *ceteris paribus*, they will also require a 14% per annum expected return when it is \$50.

    Clearly, the assumption of constant expected drift rate is inappropriate and needs to be replaced by the assumption that the expected return (i.e., expected drift divided by the stock price) is constant. If S is the stock price at time t, then the expected drift rate in S should be assumed to be μS for some constant parameter μ. This means that in a short interval of time, Δt, the expected increase in S is $\mu S\,\Delta t$. The parameter μ is the expected rate of return on the stock.

If the coefficient of dz is zero, so that there is no uncertainty, then this model implies that

$$\Delta S = \mu S \, \Delta t$$

in the limit, as $\Delta t \to 0$, so that:

$$dS = \mu S \, dt$$

or

$$\frac{dS}{S} = \mu \, dt$$

Integrating between time 0 and time T, we get

$$S_T = S_0 e^{\mu T} \tag{14.5}$$

where S_0 and S_T are the stock price at time 0 and time T. Equation (14.5) shows that, when there is no uncertainty, the stock price grows at a continuously compounded rate of μ per unit of time.

In practice, of course, there is uncertainty. A reasonable assumption is that the variability of the return in a short period of time, Δt, is the same regardless of the stock price. In other words, an investor is just as uncertain about the return when the stock price is \$50 as when it is \$10. This suggests that the standard deviation of the change in a short period of time Δt should be proportional to the stock price and leads to the model

$$dS = \mu S \, dt + \sigma S \, dz$$

or

$$\frac{dS}{S} = \mu \, dt + \sigma \, dz \tag{14.6}$$

Equation (14.6) is the most widely used model of stock price behavior. The variable μ is the stock's expected rate of return. The variable σ is the volatility of the stock price. The variable σ^2 is referred to as its variance rate. The model in equation (14.6) represents the stock price process in the real world. In a risk-neutral world, μ equals the risk-free rate r.

Discrete-Time Model

The model of stock price behavior we have developed is known as *geometric Brownian motion*. The discrete-time version of the model is

$$\frac{\Delta S}{S} = \mu \, \Delta t + \sigma \epsilon \sqrt{\Delta t} \tag{14.7}$$

or

$$\Delta S = \mu S \, \Delta t + \sigma S \epsilon \sqrt{\Delta t} \tag{14.8}$$

The variable ΔS is the change in the stock price S in a small time interval Δt, and as before ϵ has a standard normal distribution (i.e., a normal distribution with a mean of zero and standard deviation of 1.0). The parameter μ is the expected rate of return per unit of time from the stock. The parameter σ is the stock price volatility. In this chapter we will assume these parameters are constant.

The left-hand side of equation (14.7) is the discrete approximation to the return provided by the stock in a short period of time, Δt. The term $\mu \, \Delta t$ is the expected value of this return, and the term $\sigma \epsilon \sqrt{\Delta t}$ is the stochastic component of the return. The variance of the stochastic component (and, therefore, of the whole return) is $\sigma^2 \Delta t$. This is consistent with the definition of the volatility σ given in Section 13.7; that is, σ is such that $\sigma\sqrt{\Delta t}$ is the standard deviation of the return in a short time period Δt.

Equation (14.7) shows that $\Delta S/S$ is approximately normally distributed with mean $\mu \Delta t$ and standard deviation $\sigma\sqrt{\Delta t}$. In other words,

$$\frac{\Delta S}{S} \sim \phi(\mu\,\Delta t,\ \sigma^2\Delta t) \tag{14.9}$$

Example 14.3

Consider a stock that pays no dividends, has a volatility of 30% per annum, and provides an expected return of 15% per annum with continuous compounding. In this case, $\mu = 0.15$ and $\sigma = 0.30$. The process for the stock price is

$$\frac{dS}{S} = 0.15\,dt + 0.30\,dz$$

If S is the stock price at a particular time and ΔS is the increase in the stock price in the next small interval of time, the discrete approximation to the process is

$$\frac{\Delta S}{S} = 0.15\Delta t + 0.30\epsilon\sqrt{\Delta t}$$

where ϵ has a standard normal distribution. Consider a time interval of 1 week, or 0.0192 year, so that $\Delta t = 0.0192$. Then the approximation gives

$$\frac{\Delta S}{S} = 0.15 \times 0.0192 + 0.30 \times \sqrt{0.0192}\,\epsilon$$

or

$$\Delta S = 0.00288S + 0.0416S\epsilon$$

Monte Carlo Simulation

A Monte Carlo simulation of a stochastic process is a procedure for sampling random outcomes for the process. We will use it as a way of developing some understanding of the nature of the stock price process in equation (14.6).

Consider the situation in Example 14.3 where the expected return from a stock is 15% per annum and the volatility is 30% per annum. The stock price change over 1 week was shown to be approximately

$$\Delta S = 0.00288S + 0.0416S\epsilon \tag{14.10}$$

A path for the stock price over 10 weeks can be simulated by sampling repeatedly for ϵ from $\phi(0, 1)$ and substituting into equation (14.10). The expression =RAND() in Excel produces a random sample between 0 and 1. The inverse cumulative normal distribution is NORMSINV. The instruction to produce a random sample from a standard normal distribution in Excel is therefore =NORMSINV(RAND()). Table 14.1 shows one path for a stock price that was sampled in this way. The initial stock price is assumed to be $100. For the first period, ϵ is sampled as 0.52. From equation (14.10), the change during the first time period is

$$\Delta S = 0.00288 \times 100 + 0.0416 \times 100 \times 0.52 = 2.45$$

Therefore, at the beginning of the second time period, the stock price is $102.45. The

Table 14.1 Simulation of stock price when $\mu = 0.15$ and $\sigma = 0.30$ during 1-week periods.

Stock price at start of period	Random sample for ϵ	Change in stock price during period
100.00	0.52	2.45
102.45	1.44	6.43
108.88	−0.86	−3.58
105.30	1.46	6.70
112.00	−0.69	−2.89
109.11	−0.74	−3.04
106.06	0.21	1.23
107.30	−1.10	−4.60
102.69	0.73	3.41
106.11	1.16	5.43
111.54	2.56	12.20

value of ϵ sampled for the next period is 1.44. From equation (14.10), the change during the second time period is

$$\Delta S = 0.00288 \times 102.45 + 0.0416 \times 102.45 \times 1.44 = 6.43$$

So, at the beginning of the next period, the stock price is \$108.88, and so on.[4] Note that, because the process we are simulating is Markov, the samples for ϵ should be independent of each other.

Table 14.1 assumes that stock prices are measured to the nearest cent. It is important to realize that the table shows only one possible pattern of stock price movements. Different random samples would lead to different price movements. Any small time interval Δt can be used in the simulation. In the limit as $\Delta t \to 0$, a perfect description of the stochastic process is obtained. The final stock price of 111.54 in Table 14.1 can be regarded as a random sample from the distribution of stock prices at the end of 10 weeks. By repeatedly simulating movements in the stock price, a complete probability distribution of the stock price at the end of this time is obtained. Monte Carlo simulation is discussed in more detail in Chapter 21.

14.4 THE PARAMETERS

The process for a stock price developed in this chapter involves two parameters, μ and σ. The parameter μ is the expected return (annualized) earned by an investor in a short period of time. Most investors require higher expected returns to induce them to take higher risks. It follows that the value of μ should depend on the risk of the return from the stock.[5] It should also depend on the level of interest rates in the economy. The higher the level of interest rates, the higher the expected return required on any given stock.

---

[4] In practice, it is more efficient to sample $\ln S$ rather than S, as will be discussed in Section 21.6.

[5] More precisely, μ depends on that part of the risk that cannot be diversified away by the investor.

Fortunately, we do not have to concern ourselves with the determinants of μ in any detail because the value of a derivative dependent on a stock is, in general, independent of μ. The parameter σ, the stock price volatility, is, by contrast, critically important to the determination of the value of many derivatives. We will discuss procedures for estimating σ in Chapter 15. Typical values of σ for a stock are in the range 0.15 to 0.60 (i.e., 15% to 60%).

The standard deviation of the proportional change in the stock price in a small interval of time Δt is $\sigma\sqrt{\Delta t}$. As a rough approximation, the standard deviation of the proportional change in the stock price over a relatively long period of time T is $\sigma\sqrt{T}$. This means that, as an approximation, volatility can be interpreted as the standard deviation of the change in the stock price in 1 year. In Chapter 15, we will show that the volatility of a stock price is exactly equal to the standard deviation of the continuously compounded return provided by the stock in 1 year.

14.5 CORRELATED PROCESSES

So far we have considered how the stochastic process for a single variable can be represented. We now extend the analysis to the situation where there are two or more variables following correlated stochastic processes. Suppose that the processes followed by two variables x_1 and x_2 are

$$dx_1 = a_1\,dt + b_1\,dz_1 \quad \text{and} \quad dx_2 = a_2\,dt + b_2\,dz_2$$

where dz_1 and dz_2 are Wiener processes.

As has been explained, the discrete-time approximations for these processes are

$$\Delta x_1 = a_1\,\Delta t + b_1\,\epsilon_1\sqrt{\Delta t} \quad \text{and} \quad \Delta x_2 = a_2\,\Delta t + b_2\,\epsilon_2\sqrt{\Delta t}$$

where ϵ_1 and ϵ_2 are samples from a standard normal distribution $\phi(0, 1)$.

The variables x_1 and x_2 can be simulated in the way described in Section 14.3. If they are uncorrelated with each other, the random samples ϵ_1 and ϵ_2 that are used to obtain movements in a particular period of time Δt should be independent of each other.

If x_1 and x_2 have a nonzero correlation ρ, then the ϵ_1 and ϵ_2 that are used to obtain movements in a particular period of time should be sampled from a bivariate normal distribution. Each variable in the bivariate normal distribution has a standard normal distribution and the correlation between the variables is ρ. In this situation, we would refer to the Wiener processes dz_1 and dz_2 as having a correlation ρ.

Obtaining samples for uncorrelated standard normal variables in cells in Excel involves putting the instruction "=NORMSINV(RAND())" in each of the cells. To sample standard normal variables ϵ_1 and ϵ_2 with correlation ρ, we can set

$$\epsilon_1 = u \quad \text{and} \quad \epsilon_2 = \rho u + \sqrt{1 - \rho^2}\,v$$

where u and v are sampled as uncorrelated variables with standard normal distributions.

Note that, in the processes we have assumed for x_1 and x_2, the parameters a_1, a_2, b_1, and b_2 can be functions of x_1, x_2, and t. In particular, a_1 and b_1 can be functions of x_2 as well as x_1 and t; and a_2 and b_2 can be functions of x_1 as well as x_2 and t.

The results here can be generalized. When there are three different variables following correlated stochastic processes, we have to sample three different ϵ's. These have a trivariate normal distribution. When there are n correlated variables, we have n different ϵ's and these must be sampled from an appropriate multivariate normal distribution. The way this is done is explained in Chapter 21.

14.6 ITÔ'S LEMMA

The price of a stock option is a function of the underlying stock's price and time. More generally, we can say that the price of any derivative is a function of the stochastic variables underlying the derivative and time. A serious student of derivatives must, therefore, acquire some understanding of the behavior of functions of stochastic variables. An important result in this area was discovered by the mathematician K. Itô in 1951,[6] and is known as *Itô's lemma*.

Suppose that the value of a variable x follows the Itô process

$$dx = a(x, t)\,dt + b(x, t)\,dz \qquad (14.11)$$

where dz is a Wiener process and a and b are functions of x and t. The variable x has a drift rate of a and a variance rate of b^2. Itô's lemma shows that a function G of x and t follows the process

$$dG = \left(\frac{\partial G}{\partial x}a + \frac{\partial G}{\partial t} + \tfrac{1}{2}\frac{\partial^2 G}{\partial x^2}b^2\right)dt + \frac{\partial G}{\partial x}b\,dz \qquad (14.12)$$

where the dz is the same Wiener process as in equation (14.11). Thus, G also follows an Itô process, with a drift rate of

$$\frac{\partial G}{\partial x}a + \frac{\partial G}{\partial t} + \tfrac{1}{2}\frac{\partial^2 G}{\partial x^2}b^2$$

and a variance rate of

$$\left(\frac{\partial G}{\partial x}\right)^2 b^2$$

A completely rigorous proof of Itô's lemma is beyond the scope of this book. In the appendix to this chapter, we show that the lemma can be viewed as an extension of well-known results in differential calculus.

Earlier, we argued that

$$dS = \mu S\,dt + \sigma S\,dz \qquad (14.13)$$

with μ and σ constant, is a reasonable model of stock price movements. From Itô's lemma, it follows that the process followed by a function G of S and t is

$$dG = \left(\frac{\partial G}{\partial S}\mu S + \frac{\partial G}{\partial t} + \tfrac{1}{2}\frac{\partial^2 G}{\partial S^2}\sigma^2 S^2\right)dt + \frac{\partial G}{\partial S}\sigma S\,dz \qquad (14.14)$$

Note that both S and G are affected by the same underlying source of uncertainty, dz. This proves to be very important in the derivation of the Black–Scholes–Merton results.

---

[6] See K. Itô, "On Stochastic Differential Equations," *Memoirs of the American Mathematical Society*, 4 (1951): 1–51.

Application to Forward Contracts

To illustrate Itô's lemma, consider a forward contract on a non-dividend-paying stock. Assume that the risk-free rate of interest is constant and equal to r for all maturities. From equation (5.1),

$$F_0 = S_0 e^{rT}$$

where F_0 is the forward price at time zero, S_0 is the spot price at time zero, and T is the time to maturity of the forward contract.

We are interested in what happens to the forward price as time passes. We define F as the forward price at a general time t, and S as the stock price at time t, with $t < T$. The relationship between F and S is given by

$$F = Se^{r(T-t)} \tag{14.15}$$

Assuming that the process for S is given by equation (14.13), we can use Itô's lemma to determine the process for F. From equation (14.15),

$$\frac{\partial F}{\partial S} = e^{r(T-t)}, \qquad \frac{\partial^2 F}{\partial S^2} = 0, \qquad \frac{\partial F}{\partial t} = -rSe^{r(T-t)}$$

From equation (14.14), the process for F is given by

$$dF = \left[e^{r(T-t)}\mu S - rSe^{r(T-t)} \right] dt + e^{r(T-t)}\sigma S\, dz$$

Substituting F for $Se^{r(T-t)}$ gives

$$dF = (\mu - r)F\, dt + \sigma F\, dz \tag{14.16}$$

Like S, the forward price F follows geometric Brownian motion. It has the same volatility as S and an expected growth rate of $\mu - r$ rather than μ.

14.7 THE LOGNORMAL PROPERTY

We now use Itô's lemma to derive the process followed by $\ln S$ when S follows the process in equation (14.13). We define

$$G = \ln S$$

Since

$$\frac{\partial G}{\partial S} = \frac{1}{S}, \qquad \frac{\partial^2 G}{\partial S^2} = -\frac{1}{S^2}, \qquad \frac{\partial G}{\partial t} = 0$$

it follows from equation (14.14) that the process followed by G is

$$dG = \left(\mu - \frac{\sigma^2}{2} \right) dt + \sigma\, dz \tag{14.17}$$

Since μ and σ are constant, this equation indicates that $G = \ln S$ follows a generalized Wiener process. It has constant drift rate $\mu - \sigma^2/2$ and constant variance rate σ^2. The change in ln S between time 0 and some future time T is therefore normally distributed, with mean $(\mu - \sigma^2/2)T$ and variance $\sigma^2 T$. This means that

$$\ln S_T - \ln S_0 \sim \phi\left[\left(\mu - \frac{\sigma^2}{2}\right)T, \, \sigma^2 T\right] \qquad \textbf{(14.18)}$$

or

$$\ln S_T \sim \phi\left[\ln S_0 + \left(\mu - \frac{\sigma^2}{2}\right)T, \, \sigma^2 T\right] \qquad \textbf{(14.19)}$$

where S_T is the stock price at time T, S_0 is the stock price at time 0, and as before $\phi(m, v)$ denotes a normal distribution with mean m and variance v.

Equation (14.19) shows that ln S_T is normally distributed. A variable has a lognormal distribution if the natural logarithm of the variable is normally distributed. The model of stock price behavior we have developed in this chapter therefore implies that a stock's price at time T, given its price today, is lognormally distributed. The standard deviation of the logarithm of the stock price is $\sigma\sqrt{T}$. It is proportional to the square root of how far ahead we are looking.

SUMMARY

Stochastic processes describe the probabilistic evolution of the value of a variable through time. A Markov process is one where only the present value of the variable is relevant for predicting the future. The past history of the variable and the way in which the present has emerged from the past is irrelevant.

A Wiener process dz is a Markov process describing the evolution of a normally distributed variable. The drift of the process is zero and the variance rate is 1.0 per unit time. This means that, if the value of the variable is x_0 at time 0, then at time T it is normally distributed with mean x_0 and standard deviation $\sqrt{T}$.

A generalized Wiener process describes the evolution of a normally distributed variable with a drift of a per unit time and a variance rate of b^2 per unit time, where a and b are constants. This means that if, as before, the value of the variable is x_0 at time 0, it is normally distributed with a mean of $x_0 + aT$ and a standard deviation of $b\sqrt{T}$ at time T.

An Itô process is a process where the drift and variance rate of x can be a function of both x itself and time. The change in x in a very short period of time is, to a good approximation, normally distributed, but its change over longer periods of time is liable to be nonnormal.

One way of gaining an intuitive understanding of a stochastic process for a variable is to use Monte Carlo simulation. This involves dividing a time interval into many small time steps and randomly sampling possible paths for the variable. The future probability distribution for the variable can then be calculated. Monte Carlo simulation is discussed further in Chapter 21.

Itô's lemma is a way of calculating the stochastic process followed by a function of a variable from the stochastic process followed by the variable itself. As we shall see in Chapter 15, Itô's lemma plays a very important part in the pricing of derivatives. A key point is that the Wiener process dz underlying the stochastic process for the variable is exactly the same as the Wiener process underlying the stochastic process for the function of the variable. Both are subject to the same underlying source of uncertainty.

The stochastic process usually assumed for a stock price is geometric Brownian motion. Under this process the return to the holder of the stock in a small period of time is normally distributed and the returns in two nonoverlapping periods are independent. The value of the stock price at a future time has a lognormal distribution. The Black–Scholes–Merton model, which we cover in the next chapter, is based on the geometric Brownian motion assumption.

FURTHER READING

On Efficient Markets and the Markov Property of Stock Prices

Brealey, R. A. *An Introduction to Risk and Return from Common Stock*, 2nd edn. Cambridge, MA: MIT Press, 1986.

Cootner, P. H. (ed.) *The Random Character of Stock Market Prices*. Cambridge, MA: MIT Press, 1964.

On Stochastic Processes

Cox, D. R., and H. D. Miller. *The Theory of Stochastic Processes*. London: Chapman & Hall, 1977.

Feller, W. *Introduction to Probability Theory and Its Applications*. New York: Wiley, 1968.

Karlin, S., and H. M. Taylor. *A First Course in Stochastic Processes*, 2nd edn. New York: Academic Press, 1975.

Shreve, S. E. *Stochastic Calculus for Finance II: Continuous-Time Models*. New York: Springer, 2008.

Practice Questions (Answers in Solutions Manual)

14.1. What would it mean to assert that the temperature at a certain place follows a Markov process? Do you think that temperatures do, in fact, follow a Markov process?

14.2. Can a trading rule based on the past history of a stock's price ever produce returns that are consistently above average? Discuss.

14.3. A company's cash position, measured in millions of dollars, follows a generalized Wiener process with a drift rate of 0.5 per quarter and a variance rate of 4.0 per quarter. How high does the company's initial cash position have to be for the company to have a less than 5% chance of a negative cash position by the end of 1 year?

14.4. Variables X_1 and X_2 follow generalized Wiener processes, with drift rates μ_1 and μ_2 and variances σ_1^2 and σ_2^2. What process does $X_1 + X_2$ follow if:
(a) The changes in X_1 and X_2 in any short interval of time are uncorrelated?
(b) There is a correlation ρ between the changes in X_1 and X_2 in any short time interval?

14.5. Consider a variable S that follows the process

$$dS = \mu\, dt + \sigma\, dz$$

For the first three years, $\mu = 2$ and $\sigma = 3$; for the next three years, $\mu = 3$ and $\sigma = 4$. If the initial value of the variable is 5, what is the probability distribution of the value of the variable at the end of year 6?

14.6. Suppose that G is a function of a stock price S and time. Suppose that σ_S and σ_G are the volatilities of S and G. Show that, when the expected return of S increases by $\lambda\sigma_S$, the growth rate of G increases by $\lambda\sigma_G$, where λ is a constant.

14.7. Stock A and stock B both follow geometric Brownian motion. Changes in any short interval of time are uncorrelated with each other. Does the value of a portfolio consisting of one of stock A and one of stock B follow geometric Brownian motion? Explain your answer.

14.8. The process for the stock price in equation (14.8) is

$$\Delta S = \mu S\,\Delta t + \sigma S \epsilon \sqrt{\Delta t}$$

where μ and σ are constant. Explain carefully the difference between this model and each of the following:

$$\Delta S = \mu\,\Delta t + \sigma \epsilon \sqrt{\Delta t}$$
$$\Delta S = \mu S\,\Delta t + \sigma \epsilon \sqrt{\Delta t}$$
$$\Delta S = \mu\,\Delta t + \sigma S \epsilon \sqrt{\Delta t}$$

Why is the model in equation (14.8) a more appropriate model of stock price behavior than any of these three alternatives?

14.9. It has been suggested that the short-term interest rate r follows the stochastic process

$$dr = a(b - r)\,dt + rc\,dz$$

where a, b, c are positive constants and dz is a Wiener process. Describe the nature of this process.

14.10. Suppose that a stock price S follows geometric Brownian motion with expected return μ and volatility σ:

$$dS = \mu S\,dt + \sigma S\,dz$$

What is the process followed by the variable S^n? Show that S^n also follows geometric Brownian motion.

14.11. Suppose that x is the yield to maturity with continuous compounding on a zero-coupon bond that pays off \$1 at time T. Assume that x follows the process

$$dx = a(x_0 - x)\,dt + sx\,dz$$

where a, x_0, and s are positive constants and dz is a Wiener process. What is the process followed by the bond price?

Further Questions

14.12. A stock whose price is \$30 has an expected return of 9% and a volatility of 20%. In Excel, simulate the stock price path over 5 years using monthly time steps and random samples from a normal distribution. Chart the simulated stock price path. By hitting F9, observe how the path changes as the random samples change.

14.13. Suppose that a stock price has an expected return of 16% per annum and a volatility of 30% per annum. When the stock price at the end of a certain day is \$50, calculate the following:
   (a) The expected stock price at the end of the next day
   (b) The standard deviation of the stock price at the end of the next day
   (c) The 95% confidence limits for the stock price at the end of the next day.

14.14. A company's cash position, measured in millions of dollars, follows a generalized Wiener process with a drift rate of 0.1 per month and a variance rate of 0.16 per month. The initial cash position is 2.0.
   (a) What are the probability distributions of the cash position after 1 month, 6 months, and 1 year?
   (b) What are the probabilities of a negative cash position at the end of 6 months and 1 year?
   (c) At what time in the future is the probability of a negative cash position greatest?

14.15. Suppose that x is the yield on a perpetual government bond that pays interest at the rate of $1 per annum. Assume that x is expressed with continuous compounding, that interest is paid continuously on the bond, and that x follows the process

$$dx = a(x_0 - x)\,dt + sx\,dz$$

where a, x_0, and s are positive constants, and dz is a Wiener process. What is the process followed by the bond price? What is the expected instantaneous return (including interest and capital gains) to the holder of the bond?

14.16. If S follows the geometric Brownian motion process in equation (14.6), what is the process followed by
   (a) $y = 2S$
   (b) $y = S^2$
   (c) $y = e^S$
   (d) $y = e^{r(T-t)}/S$.
   In each case express the coefficients of dt and dz in terms of y rather than S.

14.17. A stock price is currently 50. Its expected return and volatility are 12% and 30%, respectively. What is the probability that the stock price will be greater than 80 in 2 years? (*Hint*: $S_T > 80$ when $\ln S_T > \ln 80$.)

14.18. Stock A, whose price is $30, has an expected return of 11% and a volatility of 25%. Stock B, whose price is $40, has an expected return of 15% and a volatility of 30%. The processes driving the returns are correlated with correlation parameter ρ. In Excel, simulate the two stock price paths over 3 months using daily time steps and random samples from normal distributions. Chart the results and by hitting F9 observe how the paths change as the random samples change. Consider values for ρ equal to 0.25, 0.75, and 0.95.

APPENDIX

A NONRIGOROUS DERIVATION OF ITÔ'S LEMMA

In this appendix, we show how Itô's lemma can be regarded as a natural extension of other, simpler results. Consider a continuous and differentiable function G of a variable x. If Δx is a small change in x and ΔG is the resulting small change in G, a well-known result from ordinary calculus is

$$\Delta G \approx \frac{dG}{dx} \Delta x \tag{14A.1}$$

In other words, ΔG is approximately equal to the rate of change of G with respect to x multiplied by Δx. The error involves terms of order Δx^2. If more precision is required, a Taylor series expansion of ΔG can be used:

$$\Delta G = \frac{dG}{dx} \Delta x + \frac{1}{2} \frac{d^2 G}{dx^2} \Delta x^2 + \frac{1}{6} \frac{d^3 G}{dx^3} \Delta x^3 + \cdots$$

For a continuous and differentiable function G of two variables x and y, the result analogous to equation (14A.1) is

$$\Delta G \approx \frac{\partial G}{\partial x} \Delta x + \frac{\partial G}{\partial y} \Delta y \tag{14A.2}$$

and the Taylor series expansion of ΔG is

$$\Delta G = \frac{\partial G}{\partial x} \Delta x + \frac{\partial G}{\partial y} \Delta y + \frac{1}{2} \frac{\partial^2 G}{\partial x^2} \Delta x^2 + \frac{\partial^2 G}{\partial x \, \partial y} \Delta x \, \Delta y + \frac{1}{2} \frac{\partial^2 G}{\partial y^2} \Delta y^2 + \cdots \tag{14A.3}$$

In the limit, as Δx and Δy tend to zero, equation (14A.3) becomes

$$dG = \frac{\partial G}{\partial x} dx + \frac{\partial G}{\partial y} dy \tag{14A.4}$$

We now extend equation (14A.4) to cover functions of variables following Itô processes. Suppose that a variable x follows the Itô process

$$dx = a(x, t) \, dt + b(x, t) \, dz \tag{14A.5}$$

and that G is some function of x and of time t. By analogy with equation (14A.3), we can write

$$\Delta G = \frac{\partial G}{\partial x} \Delta x + \frac{\partial G}{\partial t} \Delta t + \frac{1}{2} \frac{\partial^2 G}{\partial x^2} \Delta x^2 + \frac{\partial^2 G}{\partial x \, \partial t} \Delta x \, \Delta t + \frac{1}{2} \frac{\partial^2 G}{\partial t^2} \Delta t^2 + \cdots \tag{14A.6}$$

Equation (14A.5) can be discretized to

$$\Delta x = a(x, t) \, \Delta t + b(x, t) \epsilon \sqrt{\Delta t}$$

or, if arguments are dropped,

$$\Delta x = a \, \Delta t + b \epsilon \sqrt{\Delta t} \tag{14A.7}$$

This equation reveals an important difference between the situation in equation (14A.6) and the situation in equation (14A.3). When limiting arguments were used to move from equation (14A.3) to equation (14A.4), terms in Δx^2 were ignored because they were second-order terms. From equation (14A.7), we have

$$\Delta x^2 = b^2 \epsilon^2 \Delta t + \text{terms of higher order in } \Delta t \qquad \textbf{(14A.8)}$$

This shows that the term involving Δx^2 in equation (14A.6) has a component that is of order Δt and cannot be ignored.

The variance of a standard normal distribution is 1.0. This means that

$$E(\epsilon^2) - [E(\epsilon)]^2 = 1$$

where E denotes expected value. Since $E(\epsilon) = 0$, it follows that $E(\epsilon^2) = 1$. The expected value of $\epsilon^2 \Delta t$, therefore, is Δt. The variance of $\epsilon^2 \Delta t$ is, from the properties of the standard normal distribution, $2\Delta t^2$. We know that the variance of the change in a stochastic variable in time Δt is proportional to Δt, not Δt^2. The variance of $\epsilon^2 \Delta t$ is therefore too small for it to have a stochastic component. As a result, we can treat $\epsilon^2 \Delta t$ as nonstochastic and equal to its expected value, Δt, as Δt tends to zero. It follows from equation (14A.8) that Δx^2 becomes nonstochastic and equal to $b^2 dt$ as Δt tends to zero. Taking limits as Δx and Δt tend to zero in equation (14A.6), and using this last result, we obtain

$$dG = \frac{\partial G}{\partial x} dx + \frac{\partial G}{\partial t} dt + \frac{1}{2} \frac{\partial^2 G}{\partial x^2} b^2 dt \qquad \textbf{(14A.9)}$$

This is Itô's lemma. If we substitute for dx from equation (14A.5), equation (14A.9) becomes

$$dG = \left(\frac{\partial G}{\partial x} a + \frac{\partial G}{\partial t} + \frac{1}{2} \frac{\partial^2 G}{\partial x^2} b^2 \right) dt + \frac{\partial G}{\partial x} b \, dz.$$

Technical Note 29 at www-2.rotman.utoronto.ca/~hull/TechnicalNotes provides proofs of extensions to Itô's lemma. When G is a function of variables $x_1, x_2, \ldots, x_n$ and

$$dx_i = a_i \, dt + b_i \, dz_i$$

we have

$$dG = \left(\sum_{i=1}^{n} \frac{\partial G}{\partial x_i} a_i + \frac{\partial G}{\partial t} + \frac{1}{2} \sum_{i=1}^{n} \sum_{j=1}^{n} \frac{\partial^2 G}{\partial x_i \, \partial x_j} b_i b_j \rho_{ij} \right) dt + \sum_{i=1}^{n} \frac{\partial G}{\partial x_i} b_i \, dz_i \qquad \textbf{(14A.10)}$$

Also, when G is a function of a variable x with several sources of uncertainty so that

$$dx = a \, dt + \sum_{i=1}^{m} b_i \, dz_i$$

we have

$$dG = \left(\frac{\partial G}{\partial x} a + \frac{\partial G}{\partial t} + \frac{1}{2} \frac{\partial^2 G}{\partial x^2} \sum_{i=1}^{m} \sum_{j=1}^{m} b_i b_j \rho_{ij} \right) dt + \frac{\partial G}{\partial x} \sum_{i=1}^{m} b_i \, dz_i \qquad \textbf{(14A.11)}$$

In these equations, ρ_{ij} is the correlation between dz_i and dz_j (see Section 14.5).

CHAPTER 15

The Black–Scholes–Merton Model

In the early 1970s, Fischer Black, Myron Scholes, and Robert Merton achieved a major breakthrough in the pricing of European stock options.[1] This was the development of what has become known as the Black–Scholes–Merton (or Black–Scholes) model. The model has had a huge influence on the way that traders price and hedge derivatives. In 1997, the importance of the model was recognized when Robert Merton and Myron Scholes were awarded the Nobel prize for economics. Sadly, Fischer Black died in 1995; otherwise he too would undoubtedly have been one of the recipients of this prize.

How did Black, Scholes, and Merton make their breakthrough? Previous researchers had made similar assumptions and had correctly calculated the expected payoff from a European option. However, as explained in Section 13.2, it is difficult to know the correct discount rate to use for this payoff. Black and Scholes used the capital asset pricing model (see the appendix to Chapter 3) to determine a relationship between the market's required return on the option and the required return on the stock. This was not easy because the relationship depends on both the stock price and time. Merton's approach was different from that of Black and Scholes. It involved setting up a riskless portfolio consisting of the option and the underlying stock and arguing that the return on the portfolio over a short period of time must be the risk-free return. This is similar to what we did in Section 13.1—but more complicated because the portfolio changes continuously through time. Merton's approach was more general than that of Black and Scholes because it did not rely on the assumptions of the capital asset pricing model.

This chapter covers Merton's approach to deriving the Black–Scholes–Merton model. It explains how volatility can be either estimated from historical data or implied from option prices using the model. It shows how the risk-neutral valuation argument introduced in Chapter 13 can be used. It also shows how the Black–Scholes–Merton model can be extended to deal with European call and put options on dividend-paying stocks and presents some results on the pricing of American call options on dividend-paying stocks.

[1] See F. Black and M. Scholes, "The Pricing of Options and Corporate Liabilities," *Journal of Political Economy*, 81 (May/June 1973): 637–59; R.C. Merton, "Theory of Rational Option Pricing," *Bell Journal of Economics and Management Science*, 4 (Spring 1973): 141–83.

15.1 LOGNORMAL PROPERTY OF STOCK PRICES

The model of stock price behavior used by Black, Scholes, and Merton is the model we developed in Chapter 14. It assumes that percentage changes in the stock price in a very short period of time are normally distributed. Define

μ: Expected return in a short period of time (annualized)

σ: Volatility of the stock price.

The mean and standard deviation of the return in time Δt are approximately $\mu \Delta t$ and $\sigma\sqrt{\Delta t}$, so that

$$\frac{\Delta S}{S} \sim \phi(\mu \Delta t, \sigma^2 \Delta t) \tag{15.1}$$

where ΔS is the change in the stock price S in time Δt, and $\phi(m, v)$ denotes a normal distribution with mean m and variance v. (This is equation (14.9).)

As shown in Section 14.7, the model implies that

$$\ln S_T - \ln S_0 \sim \phi\left[\left(\mu - \frac{\sigma^2}{2}\right)T, \sigma^2 T\right]$$

so that

$$\ln \frac{S_T}{S_0} \sim \phi\left[\left(\mu - \frac{\sigma^2}{2}\right)T, \sigma^2 T\right] \tag{15.2}$$

and

$$\ln S_T \sim \phi\left[\ln S_0 + \left(\mu - \frac{\sigma^2}{2}\right)T, \sigma^2 T\right] \tag{15.3}$$

where S_T is the stock price at a future time T and S_0 is the stock price at time 0. There is no approximation here. The variable $\ln S_T$ is normally distributed, so that S_T has a lognormal distribution. The mean of $\ln S_T$ is $\ln S_0 + (\mu - \sigma^2/2)T$ and the standard deviation of $\ln S_T$ is $\sigma\sqrt{T}$.

Example 15.1

Consider a stock with an initial price of \$40, an expected return of 16% per annum, and a volatility of 20% per annum. From equation (15.3), the probability distribution of the stock price S_T in 6 months' time is given by

$$\ln S_T \sim \phi[\ln 40 + (0.16 - 0.2^2/2) \times 0.5, 0.2^2 \times 0.5]$$
$$\ln S_T \sim \phi(3.759, 0.02)$$

There is a 95% probability that a normally distributed variable has a value within 1.96 standard deviations of its mean. In this case, the standard deviation is $\sqrt{0.02} = 0.141$. Hence, with 95% confidence,

$$3.759 - 1.96 \times 0.141 < \ln S_T < 3.759 + 1.96 \times 0.141$$

This can be written

$$e^{3.759-1.96\times0.141} < S_T < e^{3.759+1.96\times0.141}$$

or

$$32.55 < S_T < 56.56$$

Thus, there is a 95% probability that the stock price in 6 months will lie between 32.55 and 56.56.

Figure 15.1 Lognormal distribution.

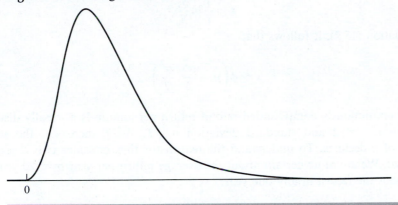

A variable that has a lognormal distribution can take any value between zero and infinity. Figure 15.1 illustrates the shape of a lognormal distribution. Unlike the normal distribution, it is skewed so that the mean, median, and mode are all different. From equation (15.3) and the properties of the lognormal distribution, it can be shown that the expected value $E(S_T)$ of S_T is given by

$$E(S_T) = S_0 e^{\mu T} \tag{15.4}$$

The variance var(S_T) of S_T, can be shown to be given by[2]

$$\text{var}(S_T) = S_0^2 e^{2\mu T}(e^{\sigma^2 T} - 1) \tag{15.5}$$

Example 15.2

Consider a stock where the current price is \$20, the expected return is 20% per annum, and the volatility is 40% per annum. The expected stock price, $E(S_T)$, and the variance of the stock price, var(S_T), in 1 year are given by

$$E(S_T) = 20e^{0.2 \times 1} = 24.43 \quad \text{and} \quad \text{var}(S_T) = 400e^{2 \times 0.2 \times 1}(e^{0.4^2 \times 1} - 1) = 103.54$$

The standard deviation of the stock price in 1 year is $\sqrt{103.54}$, or 10.18.

15.2 THE DISTRIBUTION OF THE RATE OF RETURN

The lognormal property of stock prices can be used to provide information on the probability distribution of the continuously compounded rate of return earned on a stock between times 0 and T. If we define the continuously compounded rate of return per annum realized between times 0 and T as x, then

$$S_T = S_0 e^{xT}$$

---

[2] See Technical Note 2 at www-2.rotman.utoronto.ca/~hull/TechnicalNotes for a proof of the results in equations (15.4) and (15.5). For a more extensive discussion of the properties of the lognormal distribution, see J. Aitchison and J. A. C. Brown, *The Lognormal Distribution*. Cambridge University Press, 1966.

so that

$$x = \frac{1}{T} \ln \frac{S_T}{S_0} \tag{15.6}$$

From equation (15.2), it follows that

$$x \sim \phi\left(\mu - \frac{\sigma^2}{2}, \frac{\sigma^2}{T}\right) \tag{15.7}$$

Thus, the continuously compounded rate of return per annum is normally distributed with mean $\mu - \sigma^2/2$ and standard deviation $\sigma/\sqrt{T}$. As T increases, the standard deviation of x declines. To understand the reason for this, consider two cases: $T = 1$ and $T = 20$. We are more certain about the average return per year over 20 years than we are about the return in any one year.

Example 15.3

Consider a stock with an expected return of 17% per annum and a volatility of 20% per annum. The probability distribution for the average rate of return (continuously compounded) realized over 3 years is normal, with mean

$$0.17 - \frac{0.2^2}{2} = 0.15$$

or 15% per annum, and standard deviation

$$\sqrt{\frac{0.2^2}{3}} = 0.1155$$

or 11.55% per annum. Because there is a 95% chance that a normally distributed variable will lie within 1.96 standard deviations of its mean, we can be 95% confident that the average continuously compounded return realized over 3 years will be between $15 - 1.96 \times 11.55 = -7.6\%$ and $15 + 1.96 \times 11.55 = +37.6\%$ per annum.

15.3   THE EXPECTED RETURN

The expected return, μ, required by investors from a stock depends on the riskiness of the stock. The higher the risk, the higher the expected return. It also depends on the level of interest rates in the economy. The higher the level of interest rates, the higher the expected return required on any given stock. Fortunately, we do not have to concern ourselves with the determinants of μ in any detail. It turns out that the value of a stock option, when expressed in terms of the value of the underlying stock, does not depend on μ at all. Nevertheless, there is one aspect of the expected return from a stock that frequently causes confusion and needs to be explained.

Our model of stock price behavior implies that, in a very short period of time Δt, the mean return is $\mu \Delta t$. It is natural to assume from this that μ is the expected continuously compounded return on the stock. However, this is not the case. The continuously compounded return, x, actually realized over a period of time of length T

is given by equation (15.6) as

$$x = \frac{1}{T} \ln \frac{S_T}{S_0}$$

and, as indicated in equation (15.7), the expected value $E(x)$ of x is $\mu - \sigma^2/2$.

The reason why the expected continuously compounded return is different from μ is subtle, but important. Suppose we consider a very large number of very short periods of time of length Δt. Define S_i as the stock price at the end of the ith interval and ΔS_i as $S_{i+1} - S_i$. Under the assumptions we are making for stock price behavior, the arithmetic average of the returns on the stock in each interval is close to μ. In other words, $\mu \, \Delta t$ is close to the arithmetic mean of the $\Delta S_i/S_i$. However, the expected return over the whole period covered by the data, expressed with a compounding interval of Δt, is a geometric average and is close to $\mu - \sigma^2/2$, not μ.[3] Business Snapshot 15.1 provides a numerical example concerning the mutual fund industry to illustrate why this is so.

For another explanation of what is going on, we start with equation (15.4):

$$E(S_T) = S_0 e^{\mu T}$$

Taking logarithms, we get

$$\ln[E(S_T)] = \ln(S_0) + \mu T$$

It is now tempting to set $\ln[E(S_T)] = E[\ln(S_T)]$, so that $E[\ln(S_T)] - \ln(S_0) = \mu T$, or $E[\ln(S_T/S_0)] = \mu T$, which leads to $E(x) = \mu$. However, we cannot do this because ln is a nonlinear function. In fact, $\ln[E(S_T)] > E[\ln(S_T)]$, so that $E[\ln(S_T/S_0)] < \mu T$, which leads to $E(x) < \mu$. (As shown above, $E(x) = \mu - \sigma^2/2$.)

15.4 VOLATILITY

The volatility, σ, of a stock is a measure of our uncertainty about the returns provided by the stock. Stocks typically have a volatility between 15% and 60%.

From equation (15.7), the volatility of a stock price can be defined as the standard deviation of the return provided by the stock in 1 year when the return is expressed using continuous compounding.

When Δt is small, equation (15.1) shows that $\sigma^2 \Delta t$ is approximately equal to the variance of the percentage change in the stock price in time Δt. This means that $\sigma \sqrt{\Delta t}$ is approximately equal to the standard deviation of the percentage change in the stock price in time Δt. Suppose that $\sigma = 0.3$, or 30%, per annum and the current stock price is \$50. The standard deviation of the percentage change in the stock price in 1 week is approximately

$$30 \times \sqrt{\frac{1}{52}} = 4.16\%$$

A 1-standard-deviation move in the stock price in 1 week is therefore $50 \times 0.0416 = 2.08$.

Uncertainty about a future stock price, as measured by its standard deviation, increases—at least approximately—with the square root of how far ahead we are looking. For example, the standard deviation of the stock price in 4 weeks is approximately twice the standard deviation in 1 week.

---

[3] The arguments in this section show that the term "expected return" is ambiguous. It can refer either to μ or to $\mu - \sigma^2/2$. Unless otherwise stated, it will be used to refer to μ throughout this book.

Business Snapshot 15.1 Mutual Fund Returns Can Be Misleading

The difference between μ and $\mu - \sigma^2/2$ is closely related to an issue in the reporting of mutual fund returns. Suppose that the following is a sequence of returns per annum reported by a mutual fund manager over the last five years (measured using annual compounding): 15%, 20%, 30%, −20%, 25%.

The arithmetic mean of the returns, calculated by taking the sum of the returns and dividing by 5, is 14%. However, an investor would actually earn less than 14% per annum by leaving the money invested in the fund for 5 years. The dollar value of $100 at the end of the 5 years would be

$$100 \times 1.15 \times 1.20 \times 1.30 \times 0.80 \times 1.25 = \$179.40$$

By contrast, a 14% return with annual compounding would give

$$100 \times 1.14^5 = \$192.54$$

The return that gives $179.40 at the end of five years is 12.4%. This is because

$$100 \times (1.124)^5 = 179.40$$

What average return should the fund manager report? It is tempting for the manager to make a statement such as: "The average of the returns per year that we have realized in the last 5 years is 14%." Although true, this is misleading. It is much less misleading to say: "The average return realized by someone who invested with us for the last 5 years is 12.4% per year." In some jurisdictions, regulations require fund managers to report returns the second way.

This phenomenon is an example of a result that is well known in mathematics. The geometric mean of a set of numbers is always less than the arithmetic mean. In our example, the return multipliers each year are 1.15, 1.20, 1.30, 0.80, and 1.25. The arithmetic mean of these numbers is 1.140, but the geometric mean is only 1.124 and it is the geometric mean that equals 1 plus the return realized over the 5 years.

Estimating Volatility from Historical Data

To estimate the volatility of a stock price empirically, the stock price is usually observed at fixed intervals of time (e.g., every day, week, or month). Define:

$n + 1$: Number of observations

S_i: Stock price at end of ith interval, with $i = 0, 1, \ldots, n$

τ: Length of time interval in years

and let

$$u_i = \ln\left(\frac{S_i}{S_{i-1}}\right) \quad \text{for } i = 1, 2, \ldots, n$$

The usual estimate, s, of the standard deviation of the u_i is given by

$$s = \sqrt{\frac{1}{n-1} \sum_{i=1}^{n} (u_i - \bar{u})^2}$$

or

$$s = \sqrt{\frac{1}{n-1}\sum_{i=1}^{n} u_i^2 - \frac{1}{n(n-1)}\left(\sum_{i=1}^{n} u_i\right)^2}$$

where $\bar{u}$ is the mean of the u_i.[4]

From equation (15.2), the standard deviation of the u_i is $\sigma\sqrt{\tau}$. The variable s is therefore an estimate of $\sigma\sqrt{\tau}$. It follows that σ itself can be estimated as $\hat{\sigma}$, where

$$\hat{\sigma} = \frac{s}{\sqrt{\tau}}$$

The standard error of this estimate can be shown to be approximately $\hat{\sigma}/\sqrt{2n}$.

Choosing an appropriate value for n is not easy. More data generally lead to more accuracy, but σ does change over time and data that are too old may not be relevant for predicting the future volatility. A compromise that seems to work reasonably well is to use closing prices from daily data over the most recent 90 to 180 days. Alternatively, as a rule of thumb, n can be set equal to the number of days to which the volatility is to be applied. Thus, if the volatility estimate is to be used to value a 2-year option, daily data for the last 2 years are used. More sophisticated approaches to estimating volatility involving GARCH models are discussed in Chapter 23.

Example 15.4

Table 15.1 shows a possible sequence of stock prices during 21 consecutive trading days. In this case, $n = 20$, so that

$$\sum_{i=1}^{n} u_i = 0.09531 \quad \text{and} \quad \sum_{i=1}^{n} u_i^2 = 0.00326$$

and the estimate of the standard deviation of the daily return is

$$\sqrt{\frac{0.00326}{19} - \frac{0.09531^2}{20 \times 19}} = 0.01216$$

or 1.216%. Assuming that there are 252 trading days per year, $\tau = 1/252$ and the data give an estimate for the volatility per annum of $0.01216\sqrt{252} = 0.193$, or 19.3%. The standard error of this estimate is

$$\frac{0.193}{\sqrt{2 \times 20}} = 0.031$$

or 3.1% per annum.

The foregoing analysis assumes that the stock pays no dividends, but it can be adapted to accommodate dividend-paying stocks. The return, u_i, during a time interval that includes an ex-dividend day is given by

$$u_i = \ln\frac{S_i + D}{S_{i-1}}$$

where D is the amount of the dividend. The return in other time intervals is still

$$u_i = \ln\frac{S_i}{S_{i-1}}$$

---

[4] The mean $\bar{u}$ is often assumed to be zero when estimates of historical volatilities are made.

Table 15.1   Computation of volatility.

Day i	Closing stock price (dollars), S_i	Price relative S_i/S_{i-1}	Daily return $u_i = \ln(S_i/S_{i-1})$
0	20.00		
1	20.10	1.00500	0.00499
2	19.90	0.99005	−0.01000
3	20.00	1.00503	0.00501
4	20.50	1.02500	0.02469
5	20.25	0.98780	−0.01227
6	20.90	1.03210	0.03159
7	20.90	1.00000	0.00000
8	20.90	1.00000	0.00000
9	20.75	0.99282	−0.00720
10	20.75	1.00000	0.00000
11	21.00	1.01205	0.01198
12	21.10	1.00476	0.00475
13	20.90	0.99052	−0.00952
14	20.90	1.00000	0.00000
15	21.25	1.01675	0.01661
16	21.40	1.00706	0.00703
17	21.40	1.00000	0.00000
18	21.25	0.99299	−0.00703
19	21.75	1.02353	0.02326
20	22.00	1.01149	0.01143

However, as tax factors play a part in determining returns around an ex-dividend date, it is probably best to discard altogether data for intervals that include an ex-dividend date.

Trading Days vs. Calendar Days

An important issue is whether time should be measured in calendar days or trading days when volatility parameters are being estimated and used. As shown in Business Snapshot 15.2, research shows that volatility is much higher when the exchange is open for trading than when it is closed. As a result, practitioners tend to ignore days when the exchange is closed when estimating volatility from historical data and when calculating the life of an option. The volatility per annum is calculated from the volatility per trading day using the formula

$$\text{Volatility} \atop \text{per annum} = {\text{Volatility} \atop \text{per trading day}} \times \sqrt{\text{Number of trading days} \atop \text{per annum}}$$

This is what we did in Example 15.4 when calculating volatility from the data in Table 15.1. The number of trading days in a year is usually assumed to be 252 for stocks.

Business Snapshot 15.2 What Causes Volatility?

It is natural to assume that the volatility of a stock is caused by new information reaching the market. This new information causes people to revise their opinions about the value of the stock. The price of the stock changes and volatility results. This view of what causes volatility is not supported by research. With several years of daily stock price data, researchers can calculate:

1. The variance of stock price returns between the close of trading on one day and the close of trading on the next day when there are no intervening nontrading days

2. The variance of the stock price returns between the close of trading on Friday and the close of trading on Monday

The second of these is the variance of returns over a 3-day period. The first is a variance over a 1-day period. We might reasonably expect the second variance to be three times as great as the first variance. Fama (1965), French (1980), and French and Roll (1986) show that this is not the case. These three research studies estimate the second variance to be, respectively, 22%, 19%, and 10.7% higher than the first variance.

At this stage one might be tempted to argue that these results are explained by more news reaching the market when the market is open for trading. But research by Roll (1984) does not support this explanation. Roll looked at the prices of orange juice futures. By far the most important news for orange juice futures prices is news about the weather and this is equally likely to arrive at any time. When Roll did a similar analysis to that just described for stocks, he found that the second (Friday-to-Monday) variance for orange juice futures is only 1.54 times the first variance.

The only reasonable conclusion from all this is that volatility is to a large extent caused by trading itself. (Traders usually have no difficulty accepting this conclusion!)

The life of an option is also usually measured using trading days rather than calendar days. It is calculated as T years, where

$$T = \frac{\text{Number of trading days until option maturity}}{252}$$

15.5 THE IDEA UNDERLYING THE BLACK–SCHOLES–MERTON DIFFERENTIAL EQUATION

The Black–Scholes–Merton differential equation is an equation that must be satisfied by the price of any derivative dependent on a non-dividend-paying stock. The equation is derived in the next section. Here we consider the nature of the arguments we will use.

These are similar to the no-arbitrage arguments we used to value stock options in Chapter 13 for the situation where stock price movements were assumed to be binomial. They involve setting up a riskless portfolio consisting of a position in the derivative and a position in the stock. In the absence of arbitrage opportunities, the return from the portfolio must be the risk-free interest rate, r. This leads to the Black-Scholes-Merton differential equation.

Figure 15.2   Relationship between call price and stock price. Current stock price is S_0.

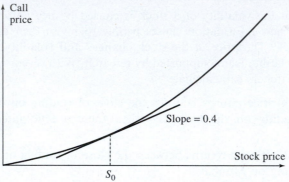

The reason a riskless portfolio can be set up is that the stock price and the derivative price are both affected by the same underlying source of uncertainty: stock price movements. In any short period of time, the price of the derivative is perfectly correlated with the price of the underlying stock. When an appropriate portfolio of the stock and the derivative is established, the gain or loss from the stock position always offsets the gain or loss from the derivative position so that the overall value of the portfolio at the end of the short period of time is known with certainty.

Suppose, for example, that at a particular point in time the relationship between a small change ΔS in the stock price and the resultant small change Δc in the price of a European call option is given by

$$\Delta c = 0.4 \, \Delta S$$

This means that the slope of the line representing the relationship between c and S is 0.4, as indicated in Figure 15.2. A riskless portfolio would consist of:

1. A long position in 40 shares

2. A short position in 100 call options.

Suppose, for example, that the stock price increases by 10 cents. The option price will increase by 4 cents and the $40 \times 0.1 = \$4$ gain on the shares is equal to the $100 \times 0.04 = \$4$ loss on the short option position.

There is one important difference between the Black–Scholes–Merton analysis and our analysis using a binomial model in Chapter 13. In Black–Scholes–Merton, the position in the stock and the derivative is riskless for only a very short period of time. (Theoretically, it remains riskless only for an instantaneously short period of time.) To remain riskless, it must be adjusted, or *rebalanced*, frequently.[5] For example, the relationship between Δc and ΔS in our example might change from $\Delta c = 0.4 \, \Delta S$ today to $\Delta c = 0.5 \, \Delta S$ tomorrow. This would mean that, in order to maintain the riskless position, an extra 10 shares would have to be purchased for each 100 call options sold. It is nevertheless true that the return from the riskless portfolio in any very short period of time must be the risk-free interest rate. This is the key element in the Black–Scholes–Merton analysis and leads to their pricing formulas.

---

[5] We discuss the rebalancing of portfolios in more detail in Chapter 19.

Assumptions

The assumptions we use to derive the Black–Scholes–Merton differential equation are as follows:

1. The stock price follows the process developed in Chapter 14 with μ and σ constant.
2. The short selling of securities with full use of proceeds is permitted.
3. There are no transaction costs or taxes. All securities are perfectly divisible.
4. There are no dividends during the life of the derivative.
5. There are no riskless arbitrage opportunities.
6. Security trading is continuous.
7. The risk-free rate of interest, r, is constant and the same for all maturities.

As we discuss in later chapters, some of these assumptions can be relaxed. For example, σ and r can be known functions of t. We can even allow interest rates to be stochastic provided that the stock price distribution at maturity of the option is still lognormal.

15.6 DERIVATION OF THE BLACK–SCHOLES–MERTON DIFFERENTIAL EQUATION

In this section, the notation is different from elsewhere in the book. We consider a derivative's price at a general time t (not at time zero). If T is the maturity date, the time to maturity is $T - t$.

The stock price process we are assuming is the one we developed in Section 14.3:

$$dS = \mu S\,dt + \sigma S\,dz \tag{15.8}$$

Suppose that f is the price of a call option or other derivative contingent on S. The variable f must be some function of S and t. Hence, from equation (14.14),

$$df = \left(\frac{\partial f}{\partial S}\mu S + \frac{\partial f}{\partial t} + \frac{1}{2}\frac{\partial^2 f}{\partial S^2}\sigma^2 S^2\right)dt + \frac{\partial f}{\partial S}\sigma S\,dz \tag{15.9}$$

The discrete versions of equations (15.8) and (15.9) are

$$\Delta S = \mu S\,\Delta t + \sigma S\,\Delta z \tag{15.10}$$

and

$$\Delta f = \left(\frac{\partial f}{\partial S}\mu S + \frac{\partial f}{\partial t} + \frac{1}{2}\frac{\partial^2 f}{\partial S^2}\sigma^2 S^2\right)\Delta t + \frac{\partial f}{\partial S}\sigma S\,\Delta z \tag{15.11}$$

where Δf and ΔS are the changes in f and S in a small time interval Δt. Recall from the discussion of Itô's lemma in Section 14.6 that the Wiener processes underlying f and S are the same. In other words, the $\Delta z \ (= \epsilon\sqrt{\Delta t})$ in equations (15.10) and (15.11) are the same. It follows that a portfolio of the stock and the derivative can be constructed so that the Wiener process is eliminated. The portfolio is

-1: derivative

$+\partial f/\partial S$: shares.

The holder of this portfolio is short one derivative and long an amount $\partial f / \partial S$ of shares. Define Π as the value of the portfolio. By definition

$$\Pi = -f + \frac{\partial f}{\partial S} S \tag{15.12}$$

The change $\Delta \Pi$ in the value of the portfolio in the time interval Δt is given by[6]

$$\Delta \Pi = -\Delta f + \frac{\partial f}{\partial S} \Delta S \tag{15.13}$$

Substituting equations (15.10) and (15.11) into equation (15.13) yields

$$\Delta \Pi = \left(-\frac{\partial f}{\partial t} - \frac{1}{2} \frac{\partial^2 f}{\partial S^2} \sigma^2 S^2 \right) \Delta t \tag{15.14}$$

Because this equation does not involve Δz, the portfolio must be riskless during time Δt. The assumptions listed in the preceding section imply that the portfolio must instantaneously earn the same rate of return as other short-term risk-free securities. If it earned more than this return, arbitrageurs could make a riskless profit by borrowing money to buy the portfolio; if it earned less, they could make a riskless profit by shorting the portfolio and buying risk-free securities. It follows that

$$\Delta \Pi = r \Pi \, \Delta t \tag{15.15}$$

where r is the risk-free interest rate. Substituting from equations (15.12) and (15.14) into (15.15), we obtain

$$\left(\frac{\partial f}{\partial t} + \frac{1}{2} \frac{\partial^2 f}{\partial S^2} \sigma^2 S^2 \right) \Delta t = r \left(f - \frac{\partial f}{\partial S} S \right) \Delta t$$

so that

$$\frac{\partial f}{\partial t} + rS \frac{\partial f}{\partial S} + \frac{1}{2} \sigma^2 S^2 \frac{\partial^2 f}{\partial S^2} = rf \tag{15.16}$$

Equation (15.16) is the Black–Scholes–Merton differential equation. It has many solutions, corresponding to all the different derivatives that can be defined with S as the underlying variable. The particular derivative that is obtained when the equation is solved depends on the *boundary conditions* that are used. These specify the values of the derivative at the boundaries of possible values of S and t. In the case of a European call option, the key boundary condition is

$$f = \max(S - K, 0) \quad \text{when } t = T$$

In the case of a European put option, it is

$$f = \max(K - S, 0) \quad \text{when } t = T$$

Example 15.5

A forward contract on a non-dividend-paying stock is a derivative dependent on the stock. As such, it should satisfy equation (15.16). From equation (5.5), we

---

[6] This derivation of equation (15.16) is not completely rigorous. We need to justify ignoring changes in $\partial f / \partial S$ in time Δt in equation (15.13). A more rigorous derivation involves setting up a self-financing portfolio (i.e., a portfolio that requires no infusion or withdrawal of money).

know that the value of the forward contract, f, at a general time t is given in terms of the stock price S at this time by

$$f = S - Ke^{-r(T-t)}$$

where K is the delivery price. This means that

$$\frac{\partial f}{\partial t} = -rKe^{-r(T-t)}, \qquad \frac{\partial f}{\partial S} = 1, \qquad \frac{\partial^2 f}{\partial S^2} = 0$$

When these are substituted into the left-hand side of equation (15.16), we obtain

$$-rKe^{-r(T-t)} + rS$$

This equals rf, showing that equation (15.16) is indeed satisfied.

A Perpetual Derivative

Consider a perpetual derivative that pays off a fixed amount Q when the stock price equals H for the first time. In this case, the value of the derivative for a particular S has no dependence on t, so the $\partial f/\partial t$ term vanishes and the partial differential equation (15.16) becomes an ordinary differential equation.

Suppose first that $S < H$. The boundary conditions for the derivative are $f = 0$ when $S = 0$ and $f = Q$ when $S = H$. The simple solution $f = QS/H$ satisfies both the boundary conditions and the differential equation. It must therefore be the value of the derivative.

Suppose next that $S > H$. The boundary conditions are now $f = 0$ as S tends to infinity and $f = Q$ when $S = H$. The derivative price

$$f = Q\left(\frac{S}{H}\right)^{-\alpha}$$

where α is positive, satisfies the boundary conditions. It also satisfies the differential equation when

$$-r\alpha + \tfrac{1}{2}\sigma^2\alpha(\alpha + 1) - r = 0$$

or $\alpha = 2r/\sigma^2$. The value of the derivative is therefore

$$f = Q\left(\frac{S}{H}\right)^{-2r/\sigma^2} \tag{15.17}$$

Problem 15.23 shows how equation (15.17) can be used to price a perpetual American put option. Section 26.2 extends the analysis to show how perpetual American call and put options can be priced when the underlying asset provides a yield at rate q.

The Prices of Tradeable Derivatives

Any function $f(S, t)$ that is a solution of the differential equation (15.16) is the theoretical price of a derivative that could be traded. If a derivative with that price existed, it would not create any arbitrage opportunities. Conversely, if a function $f(S, t)$ does not satisfy the differential equation (15.16), it cannot be the price of a derivative without creating arbitrage opportunities for traders.

To illustrate this point, consider first the function e^S. This does not satisfy the differential equation (15.16). It is therefore not a candidate for being the price of a derivative dependent on the stock price. If an instrument whose price was always e^S existed, there would be an arbitrage opportunity. As a second example, consider the function

$$\frac{e^{(\sigma^2 - 2r)(T-t)}}{S}$$

This does satisfy the differential equation, and so is, in theory, the price of a tradeable security. (It is the price of a derivative that pays off $1/S_T$ at time T.) For other examples of tradeable derivatives, see Problems 15.11, 15.12, 15.23, and 15.29.

15.7 RISK-NEUTRAL VALUATION

We introduced risk-neutral valuation in connection with the binomial model in Chapter 13. It is without doubt the single most important tool for the analysis of derivatives. It arises from one key property of the Black–Scholes–Merton differential equation (15.16). This property is that the equation does not involve any variables that are affected by the risk preferences of investors. The variables that do appear in the equation are the current stock price, time, stock price volatility, and the risk-free rate of interest. All are independent of risk preferences.

The Black–Scholes–Merton differential equation would not be independent of risk preferences if it involved the expected return, μ, on the stock. This is because the value of μ does depend on risk preferences. The higher the level of risk aversion by investors, the higher μ will be for any given stock. It is fortunate that μ happens to drop out in the derivation of the differential equation.

Because the Black–Scholes–Merton differential equation is independent of risk preferences, an ingenious argument can be used. If risk preferences do not enter the equation, they cannot affect its solution. Any set of risk preferences can, therefore, be used when evaluating f. In particular, the very simple assumption that all investors are risk neutral can be made.

In a world where investors are risk neutral, the expected return on all investment assets is the risk-free rate of interest, r. The reason is that risk-neutral investors do not require a premium to induce them to take risks. It is also true that the present value of any cash flow in a risk-neutral world can be obtained by discounting its expected value at the risk-free rate. The assumption that the world is risk neutral does, therefore, considerably simplify the analysis of derivatives.

Consider a derivative that provides a payoff at one particular time. It can be valued using risk-neutral valuation by using the following procedure:

1. Assume that the expected return from the underlying asset is the risk-free interest rate, r (i.e., assume $\mu = r$).
2. Calculate the expected payoff from the derivative.
3. Discount the expected payoff at the risk-free interest rate.

It is important to appreciate that risk-neutral valuation (or the assumption that all investors are risk neutral) is merely an artificial device for obtaining solutions to the

Black–Scholes–Merton differential equation. The solutions that are obtained are valid in all worlds, not just those where investors are risk neutral. When we move from a risk-neutral world to a risk-averse world, two things happen. The expected payoff from the derivative changes and the discount rate that must be used for this payoff changes. It happens that these two changes always offset each other exactly.

Application to Forward Contracts on a Stock

We valued forward contracts on a non-dividend-paying stock in Section 5.7. In Example 15.5, we verified that the pricing formula satisfies the Black–Scholes–Merton differential equation. In this section we derive the pricing formula from risk-neutral valuation. We make the assumption that interest rates are constant and equal to r. This is somewhat more restrictive than the assumption in Chapter 5.

Consider a long forward contract that matures at time T with delivery price, K. As indicated in Figure 1.2, the value of the contract at maturity is

$$S_T - K$$

where S_T is the stock price at time T. From the risk-neutral valuation argument, the value of the forward contract at time 0 is its expected value at time T in a risk-neutral world discounted at the risk-free rate of interest. Denoting the value of the forward contract at time zero by f, this means that

$$f = e^{-rT} \hat{E}(S_T - K)$$

where $\hat{E}$ denotes the expected value in a risk-neutral world. Since K is a constant, this equation becomes

$$f = e^{-rT} \hat{E}(S_T) - Ke^{-rT} \qquad (15.18)$$

The expected return μ on the stock becomes r in a risk-neutral world. Hence, from equation (15.4), we have

$$\hat{E}(S_T) = S_0 e^{rT} \qquad (15.19)$$

Substituting equation (15.19) into equation (15.18) gives

$$f = S_0 - Ke^{-rT}$$

This is in agreement with equation (5.5).

15.8 BLACK–SCHOLES–MERTON PRICING FORMULAS

The most famous solutions to the differential equation (15.16) are the Black–Scholes–Merton formulas for the prices of European call and put options. These formulas are:

$$c = S_0 N(d_1) - Ke^{-rT} N(d_2) \qquad (15.20)$$

and

$$p = Ke^{-rT} N(-d_2) - S_0 N(-d_1) \qquad (15.21)$$

Figure 15.3   Shaded area represents $N(x)$.

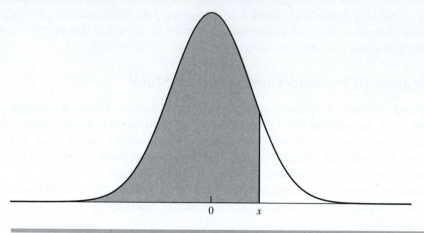

where

$$d_1 = \frac{\ln(S_0/K) + (r + \sigma^2/2)T}{\sigma\sqrt{T}}$$

$$d_2 = \frac{\ln(S_0/K) + (r - \sigma^2/2)T}{\sigma\sqrt{T}} = d_1 - \sigma\sqrt{T}$$

The function $N(x)$ is the cumulative probability distribution function for a variable with a standard normal distribution. In other words, it is the probability that a variable with a standard normal distribution will be less than x. It is illustrated in Figure 15.3. The remaining variables should be familiar. The variables c and p are the European call and European put price, S_0 is the stock price at time zero, K is the strike price, r is the continuously compounded risk-free rate, σ is the stock price volatility, and T is the time to maturity of the option.

One way of deriving the Black–Scholes–Merton formulas is by solving the differential equation (15.16) subject to the boundary condition mentioned in Section 15.6.[7] (See Problem 15.17 to prove that the call price in equation (15.20) satisfies the differential equation.) Another approach is to use risk-neutral valuation. Consider a European call option. The expected value of the option at maturity in a risk-neutral world is

$$\hat{E}[\max(S_T - K, 0)]$$

where, as before, $\hat{E}$ denotes the expected value in a risk-neutral world. From the risk-neutral valuation argument, the European call option price c is this expected value discounted at the risk-free rate of interest, that is,

$$c = e^{-rT}\hat{E}[\max(S_T - K, 0)] \tag{15.22}$$

---

[7] The differential equation gives the call and put prices at a general time t. For example, the call price that satisfies the differential equation is $c = SN(d_1) - Ke^{-r(T-t)}N(d_2)$, where

$$d_1 = \frac{\ln(S/K) + (r + \sigma^2/2)(T - t)}{\sigma\sqrt{T - t}}$$

and $d_2 = d_1 - \sigma\sqrt{T - t}$.

The appendix at the end of this chapter shows that this equation leads to the result in equation (15.20).

Since it is never optimal to exercise early an American call option on a non-dividend-paying stock (see Section 11.5), equation (15.20) is the value of an American call option on a non-dividend-paying stock. Unfortunately, no exact analytic formula for the value of an American put option on a non-dividend-paying stock has been produced. Numerical procedures for calculating American put values are discussed in Chapter 21.

When the Black–Scholes–Merton formula is used in practice the interest rate r is set equal to the zero-coupon risk-free interest rate for a maturity T. As we show in later chapters, this is theoretically correct when r is a known function of time. It is also theoretically correct when the interest rate is stochastic provided that the stock price at time T is lognormal and the volatility parameter is chosen appropriately. As mentioned earlier, time is normally measured as the number of trading days left in the life of the option divided by the number of trading days in 1 year.

Understanding $N(d_1)$ and $N(d_2)$

The term $N(d_2)$ in equation (15.20) has a fairly simple interpretation. It is the probability that a call option will be exercised in a risk-neutral world. The $N(d_1)$ term is not quite so easy to interpret. The expression $S_0 N(d_1) e^{rT}$ is the expected stock price at time T in a risk-neutral world when stock prices less than the strike price are counted as zero. The strike price is only paid if the stock price is greater than K and as just mentioned this has a probability of $N(d_2)$. The expected payoff in a risk-neutral world is therefore

$$S_0 N(d_1) e^{rT} - K N(d_2)$$

Present-valuing this from time T to time zero gives the Black–Scholes–Merton equation for a European call option:

$$c = S_0 N(d_1) - K e^{-rT} N(d_2)$$

For another way of looking at the Black–Scholes–Merton equation for the value of a European call option, note that it can be written as

$$c = e^{-rT} N(d_2)[S_0 e^{rT} N(d_1)/N(d_2) - K]$$

The terms here have the following interpretation:

$$
\begin{aligned}
e^{-rT}: &\ \text{Present value factor} \\
N(d_2): &\ \text{Probability of exercise} \\
S_0 e^{rT} N(d_1)/N(d_2): &\ \text{Expected stock price in a risk-neutral world if option is exercised} \\
K: &\ \text{Strike price paid if option is exercised.}
\end{aligned}
$$

Properties of the Black–Scholes–Merton Formulas

We now show that the Black–Scholes–Merton formulas have the right general properties by considering what happens when some of the parameters take extreme values.

When the stock price, S_0, becomes very large, a call option is almost certain to be exercised. It then becomes very similar to a forward contract with delivery price K.

From equation (5.5), we expect the call price to be

$$S_0 - Ke^{-rT}$$

This is, in fact, the call price given by equation (15.20) because, when S_0 becomes very large, both d_1 and d_2 become very large, and $N(d_1)$ and $N(d_2)$ become close to 1.0. When the stock price becomes very large, the price of a European put option, p, approaches zero. This is consistent with equation (15.21) because $N(-d_1)$ and $N(-d_2)$ are both close to zero in this case.

Consider next what happens when the volatility σ approaches zero. Because the stock is virtually riskless, its price will grow at rate r to $S_0 e^{rT}$ at time T and the payoff from a call option is

$$\max(S_0 e^{rT} - K,\ 0)$$

Discounting at rate r, the value of the call today is

$$e^{-rT} \max(S_0 e^{rT} - K,\ 0) = \max(S_0 - Ke^{-rT},\ 0)$$

To show that this is consistent with equation (15.20), consider first the case where $S_0 > Ke^{-rT}$. This implies that $\ln(S_0/K) + rT > 0$. As σ tends to zero, d_1 and d_2 tend to $+\infty$, so that $N(d_1)$ and $N(d_2)$ tend to 1.0 and equation (15.20) becomes

$$c = S_0 - Ke^{-rT}$$

When $S_0 < Ke^{-rT}$, it follows that $\ln(S_0/K) + rT < 0$. As σ tends to zero, d_1 and d_2 tend to $-\infty$, so that $N(d_1)$ and $N(d_2)$ tend to zero and equation (15.20) gives a call price of zero. The call price is therefore always $\max(S_0 - Ke^{-rT},\ 0)$ as σ tends to zero. Similarly, it can be shown that the put price is always $\max(Ke^{-rT} - S_0,\ 0)$ as σ tends to zero.

15.9 CUMULATIVE NORMAL DISTRIBUTION FUNCTION

When implementing equations (15.20) and (15.21), it is necessary to evaluate the cumulative normal distribution function $N(x)$. Tables for $N(x)$ are provided at the end of this book. The NORMSDIST function in Excel also provides a convenient way of calculating $N(x)$.

Example 15.6

The stock price 6 months from the expiration of an option is $42, the exercise price of the option is $40, the risk-free interest rate is 10% per annum, and the volatility is 20% per annum. This means that $S_0 = 42$, $K = 40$, $r = 0.1$, $\sigma = 0.2$, $T = 0.5$,

$$d_1 = \frac{\ln(42/40) + (0.1 + 0.2^2/2) \times 0.5}{0.2\sqrt{0.5}} = 0.7693$$

$$d_2 = \frac{\ln(42/40) + (0.1 - 0.2^2/2) \times 0.5}{0.2\sqrt{0.5}} = 0.6278$$

and

$$Ke^{-rT} = 40e^{-0.05} = 38.049$$

Hence, if the option is a European call, its value c is given by

$$c = 42N(0.7693) - 38.049N(0.6278)$$

If the option is a European put, its value p is given by

$$p = 38.049N(-0.6278) - 42N(-0.7693)$$

Using the NORMSDIST function in Excel gives

$$N(0.7693) = 0.7791, \qquad N(-0.7693) = 0.2209$$
$$N(0.6278) = 0.7349, \qquad N(-0.6278) = 0.2651$$

so that

$$c = 4.76, \qquad p = 0.81$$

Ignoring the time value of money, the stock price has to rise by \$2.76 for the purchaser of the call to break even. Similarly, the stock price has to fall by \$2.81 for the purchaser of the put to break even.

15.10 WARRANTS AND EMPLOYEE STOCK OPTIONS

The exercise of a regular call option on a company has no effect on the number of the company's shares outstanding. If the writer of the option does not own the company's shares, he or she must buy them in the market in the usual way and then sell them to the option holder for the strike price. As explained in Chapter 10, warrants and employee stock options are different from regular call options in that exercise leads to the company issuing more shares and then selling them to the option holder for the strike price. As the strike price is less than the market price, this dilutes the interest of the existing shareholders.

How should potential dilution affect the way we value outstanding warrants and employee stock options? The answer is that it should not! Assuming markets are efficient the stock price will reflect potential dilution from all outstanding warrants and employee stock options. This is explained in Business Snapshot 15.3.[8]

Consider next the situation a company is in when it is contemplating a new issue of warrants (or employee stock options). We suppose that the company is interested in calculating the cost of the issue assuming that there are no compensating benefits. We assume that the company has N shares worth S_0 each and the number of new options contemplated is M, with each option giving the holder the right to buy one share for K. The value of the company today is NS_0. This value does not change as a result of the warrant issue. Suppose that without the warrant issue the share price will be S_T at the warrant's maturity. This means that (with or without the warrant issue) the total value of the equity and the warrants at time T will NS_T. If the warrants are exercised, there is a cash inflow from the strike price increasing this to $NS_T + MK$. This value is distributed

---

[8] Analysts sometimes assume that the sum of the values of the warrants and the equity (rather than just the value of the equity) is lognormal. The result is a Black–Scholes type of equation for the value of the warrant in terms of the value of the warrant. See Technical Note 3 at www-2.rotman.utoronto.ca/~hull/TechnicalNotes for an explanation of this model.

> **Business Snapshot 15.3**   Warrants, Employee Stock Options, and Dilution
>
> Consider a company with 100,000 shares each worth $50. It surprises the market with
> an announcement that it is granting 100,000 stock options to its employees with a
> strike price of $50. If the market sees little benefit to the shareholders from the
> employee stock options in the form of reduced salaries and more highly motivated
> managers, the stock price will decline immediately after the announcement of the
> employee stock options. If the stock price declines to $45, the dilution cost to the
> current shareholders is $5 per share or $500,000 in total.
>
>   Suppose that the company does well so that by the end of three years the share
> price is $100. Suppose further that all the options are exercised at this point. The
> payoff to the employees is $50 per option. It is tempting to argue that there will be
> further dilution in that 100,000 shares worth $100 per share are now merged with
> 100,000 shares for which only $50 is paid, so that (a) the share price reduces to $75
> and (b) the payoff to the option holders is only $25 per option. However, this
> argument is flawed. The exercise of the options is anticipated by the market and
> already reflected in the share price. The payoff from each option exercised is $50.
>
>   This example illustrates the general point that when markets are efficient the
> impact of dilution from executive stock options or warrants is reflected in the stock
> price as soon as they are announced and does not need to be taken into account
> again when the options are valued.

among $N + M$ shares, so that the share price immediately after exercise becomes

$$\frac{NS_T + MK}{N + M}$$

Therefore the payoff to an option holder if the option is exercised is

$$\frac{NS_T + MK}{N + M} - K$$

or

$$\frac{N}{N + M}(S_T - K)$$

This shows that the value of each option is the value of

$$\frac{N}{N + M}$$

regular call options on the company's stock. Therefore the total cost of the options is
M times this. Since we are assuming that there are no benefits to the company from the
warrant issue, the total value of the company's equity will decline by the total cost of
the options as soon as the decision to issue the warrants becomes generally known. This
means that the reduction in the stock price is

$$\frac{M}{N + M}$$

times the value of a regular call option with strike price K and maturity T.

Example 15.7

A company with 1 million shares worth $40 each is considering issuing 200,000 warrants each giving the holder the right to buy one share with a strike price of $60 in 5 years. It wants to know the cost of this. The interest rate is 3% per annum, and the volatility is 30% per annum. The company pays no dividends. From equation (15.20), the value of a 5-year European call option on the stock is $7.04. In this case, $N = 1,000,000$ and $M = 200,000$, so that the value of each warrant is

$$\frac{1,000,000}{1,000,000 + 200,000} \times 7.04 = 5.87$$

or $5.87. The total cost of the warrant issue is $200,000 \times 5.87 = \$1.17$ million. Assuming the market perceives no benefits from the warrant issue, we expect the stock price to decline by $1.17 to $38.83.

15.11 IMPLIED VOLATILITIES

The one parameter in the Black–Scholes–Merton pricing formulas that cannot be directly observed is the volatility of the stock price. In Section 15.4, we discussed how this can be estimated from a history of the stock price. In practice, traders usually work with what are known as *implied volatilities*. These are the volatilities implied by option prices observed in the market.[9]

To illustrate how implied volatilities are calculated, suppose that the market price of a European call option on a non-dividend-paying stock is 1.875 when $S_0 = 21$, $K = 20$, $r = 0.1$, and $T = 0.25$. The implied volatility is the value of σ that, when substituted into equation (15.20), gives $c = 1.875$. Unfortunately, it is not possible to invert equation (15.20) so that σ is expressed as a function of S_0, K, r, T, and c. However, an iterative search procedure can be used to find the implied σ. For example, we can start by trying $\sigma = 0.20$. This gives a value of c equal to 1.76, which is too low. Because c is an increasing function of σ, a higher value of σ is required. We can next try a value of 0.30 for σ. This gives a value of c equal to 2.10, which is too high and means that σ must lie between 0.20 and 0.30. Next, a value of 0.25 can be tried for σ. This also proves to be too high, showing that σ lies between 0.20 and 0.25. Proceeding in this way, we can halve the range for σ at each iteration and the correct value of σ can be calculated to any required accuracy.[10] In this example, the implied volatility is 0.235, or 23.5%, per annum. A similar procedure can be used in conjunction with binomial trees to find implied volatilities for American options.

Implied volatilities are used to monitor the market's opinion about the volatility of a particular stock. Whereas historical volatilities (see Section 15.4) are backward looking, implied volatilities are forward looking. Traders often quote the implied volatility of an option rather than its price. This is convenient because the implied volatility tends to be less variable than the option price. The implied volatilities of actively traded options on an asset are often used by traders to estimate appropriate implied volatilities for other options on the asset.

---

[9] Implied volatilities for European and American options can be calculated using DerivaGem.

[10] This method is presented for illustration. Other more powerful methods, such as the Newton–Raphson method, are often used in practice (see footnote 3 of Chapter 4).

The VIX Index

The CBOE publishes indices of implied volatility. The most popular index, the SPX VIX, is an index of the implied volatility of 30-day options on the S&P 500 calculated from a wide range of calls and puts. It is sometimes referred to as the "fear factor." An index value of 15 indicates that the implied volatility of 30-day options on the S&P 500 is estimated as 15%. Information on the way the index is calculated is in Section 26.15. Trading in futures on the VIX started in 2004 and trading in options on the VIX started in 2006. One contract is on 1,000 times the index.

Example 15.8

Suppose that a trader buys an April futures contract on the VIX when the futures price is 18.5 (corresponding to a 30-day S&P 500 volatility of 18.5%) and closes out the contract when the futures price is 19.3 (corresponding to an S&P 500 volatility of 19.3%). The trader makes a gain of $800.

A trade involving options on the S&P 500 is a bet on the future level of the S&P 500, which depends on the volatility of the S&P 500. By contrast, a futures or options contract on the VIX is a bet only on volatility. Figure 15.4 shows the VIX index between January 2004 and July 2016. Between 2004 and mid-2007 it tended to stay between 10 and 20. It reached 30 during the second half of 2007 and a record 80 in October and November 2008 after Lehman's bankruptcy. By early 2010, it had declined to a more normal levels, but it spiked again in May 2010 and the second half of 2011 because of stresses and uncertainties in financial markets.

VIX monitors the volatility of the S&P 500. The CBOE publishes a range of other volatility indices. These are on other stock indices, commodity indices, interest rates, currencies, and some individual stocks (for example, Amazon and Goldman Sachs). There is even a volatility index of the VIX index (VVIX).

Figure 15.4 The VIX index, January 2004 to July 2016.

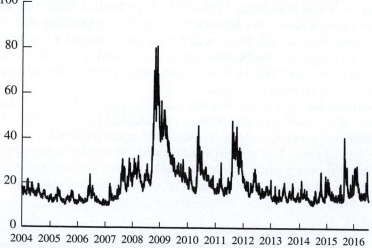

15.12 DIVIDENDS

Up to now, we have assumed that the stock on which the option is written pays no dividends. In this section, we modify the Black–Scholes–Merton model to take account of dividends. We assume that the amount and timing of the dividends during the life of an option can be predicted with certainty. When options last for relatively short periods of time, this assumption is not too unreasonable. (For long-life options it is usual to assume that the dividend yield rather the dollar dividend payments are known. Options can then be valued as will be described in the Chapter 17.) The date on which the dividend is paid should be assumed to be the ex-dividend date. On this date the stock price declines by the amount of the dividend.[11]

European Options

European options can be analyzed by assuming that the stock price is the sum of two components: a riskless component that corresponds to the known dividends during the life of the option and a risky component. The riskless component, at any given time, is the present value of all the dividends during the life of the option discounted from the ex-dividend dates to the present at the risk-free rate. By the time the option matures, the dividends will have been paid and the riskless component will no longer exist. The Black–Scholes–Merton formula is therefore correct if S_0 is equal to the risky component of the stock price and σ is the volatility of the process followed by the risky component.[12]

Operationally, this means that the Black–Scholes–Merton formulas can be used provided that the stock price is reduced by the present value of all the dividends during the life of the option, the discounting being done from the ex-dividend dates at the risk-free rate. As already mentioned, a dividend is counted as being during the life of the option only if its ex-dividend date occurs during the life of the option.

Example 15.9

Consider a European call option on a stock when there are ex-dividend dates in two months and five months. The dividend on each ex-dividend date is expected to be $0.50. The current share price is $40, the exercise price is $40, the stock price volatility is 30% per annum, the risk-free rate of interest is 9% per annum, and the time to maturity is six months. The present value of the dividends is

$$0.5e^{-0.09 \times 2/12} + 0.5e^{-0.09 \times 5/12} = 0.9742$$

The option price can therefore be calculated from the Black–Scholes–Merton

---

[11] For tax reasons the stock price may go down by somewhat less than the cash amount of the dividend. To take account of this phenomenon, we need to interpret the word 'dividend' in the context of option pricing as the reduction in the stock price on the ex-dividend date caused by the dividend. Thus, if a dividend of $1 per share is anticipated and the share price normally goes down by 80% of the dividend on the ex-dividend date, the dividend should be assumed to be $0.80 for the purpose of the analysis.

[12] This is not quite the same as the volatility of the whole stock price. (In theory, they cannot both follow geometric Brownian motion.) At time zero, the volatility of the risky component is approximately equal to the volatility of the whole stock price multiplied by $S_0/(S_0 - D)$, where D is the present value of the dividends.

formula, with $S_0 = 40 - 0.9742 = 39.0258$, $K = 40$, $r = 0.09$, $\sigma = 0.3$, and $T = 0.5$:

$$d_1 = \frac{\ln(39.0258/40) + (0.09 + 0.3^2/2) \times 0.5}{0.3\sqrt{0.5}} = 0.2020$$

$$d_2 = \frac{\ln(39.0258/40) + (0.09 - 0.3^2/2) \times 0.5}{0.3\sqrt{0.5}} = -0.0102$$

Using the NORMSDIST function in Excel gives

$$N(d_1) = 0.5800, \quad N(d_2) = 0.4959$$

and, from equation (15.20), the call price is

$$39.0258 \times 0.5800 - 40e^{-0.09 \times 0.5} \times 0.4959 = 3.67$$

or $3.67.

Some researchers have criticized the approach just described for calculating the value of a European option on a dividend-paying stock. They argue that volatility should be applied to the stock price, not to the stock price less the present value of dividends. A number of different numerical procedures have been suggested for doing this.[13] When volatility is calculated from historical data, it might make sense to use one of these procedures. However, in practice the volatility used to price an option is nearly always implied from the prices of other options using procedures we will outline in Chapter 20. If an analyst uses the same model for both implying and applying volatilities, the resulting prices should be accurate and not highly model dependent. Another important point is that in practice, as will be explained in Chapter 18, practitioners usually value a European option in terms of the forward price of the underlying asset. This avoids the need to estimate explicitly the income that is expected from the asset. The volatility of the forward stock price is the same as the volatility of a variable equal to the stock price minus the present value of dividends.

The model we have proposed where the stock price is divided into two components is internally consistent and widely used in practice. We will use the same model when valuing American options in Chapter 21.

American Call Options

Consider next American call options. Chapter 11 showed that in the absence of dividends American options should never be exercised early. An extension to the argument shows that, when there are dividends, it can only be optimal to exercise at a time immediately before the stock goes ex-dividend. We assume that n ex-dividend dates are anticipated and that they are at times $t_1, t_2, \ldots, t_n$, with $t_1 < t_2 < \cdots < t_n$. The dividends corresponding to these times will be denoted by $D_1, D_2, \ldots, D_n$, respectively.

We start by considering the possibility of early exercise just prior to the final ex-dividend date (i.e., at time t_n). If the option is exercised at time t_n, the investor receives

$$S(t_n) - K$$

---

[13] See, for example, N. Areal and A. Rodrigues, "Fast Trees for Options with Discrete Dividends," *Journal of Derivatives*, 21, 1 (Fall 2013), 49–63.

where $S(t)$ denotes the stock price at time t. If the option is not exercised, the stock price drops to $S(t_n) - D_n$. As shown by equation (11.4), the value of the option is then greater than

$$S(t_n) - D_n - Ke^{-r(T-t_n)}$$

It follows that, if

$$S(t_n) - D_n - Ke^{-r(T-t_n)} \geqslant S(t_n) - K$$

that is,

$$D_n \leqslant K\left[1 - e^{-r(T-t_n)}\right] \tag{15.23}$$

it cannot be optimal to exercise at time t_n. On the other hand, if

$$D_n > K\left[1 - e^{-r(T-t_n)}\right] \tag{15.24}$$

for any reasonable assumption about the stochastic process followed by the stock price, it can be shown that it is always optimal to exercise at time t_n for a sufficiently high value of $S(t_n)$. The inequality in (15.24) will tend to be satisfied when the final ex-dividend date is fairly close to the maturity of the option (i.e., $T - t_n$ is small) and the dividend is large.

Consider next time t_{n-1}, the penultimate ex-dividend date. If the option is exercised immediately prior to time t_{n-1}, the investor receives $S(t_{n-1}) - K$. If the option is not exercised at time t_{n-1}, the stock price drops to $S(t_{n-1}) - D_{n-1}$ and the earliest subsequent time at which exercise could take place is t_n. Hence, from equation (11.4), a lower bound to the option price if it is not exercised at time t_{n-1} is

$$S(t_{n-1}) - D_{n-1} - Ke^{-r(t_n-t_{n-1})}$$

It follows that if

$$S(t_{n-1}) - D_{n-1} - Ke^{-r(t_n-t_{n-1})} \geqslant S(t_{n-1}) - K$$

or

$$D_{n-1} \leqslant K\left[1 - e^{-r(t_n-t_{n-1})}\right]$$

it is not optimal to exercise immediately prior to time t_{n-1}. Similarly, for any $i < n$, if

$$D_i \leqslant K\left[1 - e^{-r(t_{i+1}-t_i)}\right] \tag{15.25}$$

it is not optimal to exercise immediately prior to time t_i.

The inequality in (15.25) is approximately equivalent to

$$D_i \leqslant Kr(t_{i+1} - t_i)$$

Assuming that K is fairly close to the current stock price, this inequality is satisfied when the dividend yield on the stock is less than the risk-free rate of interest. This is often the case.

We can conclude from this analysis that, in many circumstances, the most likely time for the early exercise of an American call is immediately before the final ex-dividend date, t_n. Furthermore, if inequality (15.25) holds for $i = 1, 2, \ldots, n - 1$ and inequality (15.23) holds, we can be certain that early exercise is never optimal, and the American option can be treated as a European option.

Black's Approximation

Black suggests an approximate procedure for taking account of early exercise in call options.[14] This involves calculating, as described earlier in this section, the prices of European options that mature at times T and t_n, and then setting the American price equal to the greater of the two.[15] This is an approximation because it in effect assumes the option holder has to decide at time zero whether the option will be exercised at time T or t_n.

SUMMARY

We started this chapter by examining the properties of the process for stock prices introduced in Chapter 14. The process implies that the price of a stock at some future time, given its price today, is lognormal. It also implies that the continuously compounded return from the stock in a period of time is normally distributed. Our uncertainty about future stock prices increases as we look further ahead. The standard deviation of the logarithm of the stock price is proportional to the square root of how far ahead we are looking.

To estimate the volatility σ of a stock price empirically, the stock price is observed at fixed intervals of time (e.g., every day, every week, or every month). For each time period, the natural logarithm of the ratio of the stock price at the end of the time period to the stock price at the beginning of the time period is calculated. The volatility is estimated as the standard deviation of these numbers divided by the square root of the length of the time period in years. Usually, days when the exchanges are closed are ignored in measuring time for the purposes of volatility calculations.

The differential equation for the price of any derivative dependent on a stock can be obtained by creating a riskless portfolio of the derivative and the stock. Because the derivative's price and the stock price both depend on the same underlying source of uncertainty, this can always be done. The portfolio that is created remains riskless for only a very short period of time. However, the return on a riskless porfolio must always be the risk-free interest rate if there are to be no arbitrage opportunities.

The expected return on the stock does not enter into the Black–Scholes–Merton differential equation. This leads to an extremely useful result known as risk-neutral valuation. This result states that when valuing a derivative dependent on a stock price, we can assume that the world is risk neutral. This means that we can assume that the expected return from the stock is the risk-free interest rate, and then discount expected payoffs at the risk-free interest rate. The Black–Scholes–Merton equations for European call and put options can be derived by either solving their differential equation or by using risk-neutral valuation.

An implied volatility is the volatility that, when used in conjunction with the Black–Scholes–Merton option pricing formula, gives the market price of the option. Traders

---

[14] See F. Black, "Fact and Fantasy in the Use of Options," *Financial Analysts Journal*, 31 (July/August 1975): 36–41, 61–72.

[15] For an exact formula, suggested by Roll, Geske, and Whaley, for valuing American calls when there is only one ex-dividend date, see Technical Note 4 at www-2.rotman.utoronto.ca/~hull/TechnicalNotes. This involves the cumulative bivariate normal distribution function. A procedure for calculating this function is given in Technical Note 5 and a worksheet for calculating the cumulative bivariate normal distribution can be found on the author's website.

monitor implied volatilities. They often quote the implied volatility of an option rather than its price. They have developed procedures for using the volatilities implied by the prices of actively traded options to estimate volatilities for other options on the same asset.

The Black–Scholes–Merton results can be extended to cover European call and put options on dividend-paying stocks. The procedure is to use the Black–Scholes–Merton formula with the stock price reduced by the present value of the dividends anticipated during the life of the option, and the volatility equal to the volatility of the stock price net of the present value of these dividends.

In theory, it can be optimal to exercise American call options immediately before any ex-dividend date. In practice, it is often only necessary to consider the final ex-dividend date. Fischer Black has suggested an approximation. This involves setting the American call option price equal to the greater of two European call option prices. The first European call option expires at the same time as the American call option; the second expires immediately prior to the final ex-dividend date.

FURTHER READING

On the Distribution of Stock Price Changes

Blattberg, R., and N. Gonedes, "A Comparison of the Stable and Student Distributions as Statistical Models for Stock Prices," *Journal of Business*, 47 (April 1974): 244–80.

Fama, E. F., "The Behavior of Stock Market Prices," *Journal of Business*, 38 (January 1965): 34–105.

Kon, S. J., "Models of Stock Returns—A Comparison," *Journal of Finance*, 39 (March 1984): 147–65.

Richardson, M., and T. Smith, "A Test for Multivariate Normality in Stock Returns," *Journal of Business*, 66 (1993): 295–321.

On the Black–Scholes–Merton Analysis

Black, F. "Fact and Fantasy in the Use of Options and Corporate Liabilities," *Financial Analysts Journal*, 31 (July/August 1975): 36–41, 61–72.

Black, F. "How We Came Up with the Option Pricing Formula," *Journal of Portfolio Management*, 15, 2 (1989): 4–8.

Black, F., and M. Scholes, "The Pricing of Options and Corporate Liabilities," *Journal of Political Economy*, 81 (May/June 1973): 637–59.

Merton, R. C., "Theory of Rational Option Pricing," *Bell Journal of Economics and Management Science*, 4 (Spring 1973): 141–83.

On Risk-Neutral Valuation

Cox, J. C., and S. A. Ross, "The Valuation of Options for Alternative Stochastic Processes," *Journal of Financial Economics*, 3 (1976): 145–66.

Smith, C. W., "Option Pricing: A Review," *Journal of Financial Economics*, 3 (1976): 3–54.

On the Causes of Volatility

Fama, E. F. "The Behavior of Stock Market Prices." *Journal of Business*, 38 (January 1965): 34–105.

French, K. R. "Stock Returns and the Weekend Effect." *Journal of Financial Economics*, 8 (March 1980): 55–69.

French, K. R., and R. Roll "Stock Return Variances: The Arrival of Information and the Reaction of Traders." *Journal of Financial Economics*, 17 (September 1986): 5–26.

Roll R. "Orange Juice and Weather," *American Economic Review*, 74, 5 (December 1984): 861–80.

Practice Questions (Answers in Solutions Manual)

15.1. What does the Black–Scholes–Merton stock option pricing model assume about the probability distribution of the stock price in one year? What does it assume about the probability distribution of the continuously compounded rate of return on the stock during the year?

15.2. The volatility of a stock price is 30% per annum. What is the standard deviation of the percentage price change in one trading day?

15.3. Explain the principle of risk-neutral valuation.

15.4. Calculate the price of a 3-month European put option on a non-dividend-paying stock with a strike price of $50 when the current stock price is $50, the risk-free interest rate is 10% per annum, and the volatility is 30% per annum.

15.5. What difference does it make to your calculations in Problem 15.4 if a dividend of $1.50 is expected in 2 months?

15.6. What is *implied volatility*? How can it be calculated?

15.7. A stock price is currently $40. Assume that the expected return from the stock is 15% and that its volatility is 25%. What is the probability distribution for the rate of return (with continuous compounding) earned over a 2-year period?

15.8. A stock price follows geometric Brownian motion with an expected return of 16% and a volatility of 35%. The current price is $38.
   (a) What is the probability that a European call option on the stock with an exercise price of $40 and a maturity date in 6 months will be exercised?
   (b) What is the probability that a European put option on the stock with the same exercise price and maturity will be exercised?

15.9. Using the notation in this chapter, prove that a 95% confidence interval for S_T is between $S_0 e^{(\mu - \sigma^2/2)T - 1.96\sigma\sqrt{T}}$ and $S_0 e^{(\mu - \sigma^2/2)T + 1.96\sigma\sqrt{T}}$.

15.10. A portfolio manager announces that the average of the returns realized in each year of the last 10 years is 20% per annum. In what respect is this statement misleading?

15.11. Assume that a non-dividend-paying stock has an expected return of μ and a volatility of σ. An innovative financial institution has just announced that it will trade a security that pays off a dollar amount equal to $\ln S_T$ at time T, where S_T denotes the value of the stock price at time T.
   (a) Use risk-neutral valuation to calculate the price of the security at time t in terms of the stock price, S, at time t. The risk-free rate is r.
   (b) Confirm that your price satisfies the differential equation (15.16).

15.12. Consider a derivative that pays off S_T^n at time T, where S_T is the stock price at that time. When the stock pays no dividends and its price follows geometric Brownian motion, it can be shown that its price at time t ($t \leqslant T$) has the form $h(t, T)S^n$, where S is the stock price at time t and h is a function only of t and T.
   (a) By substituting into the Black–Scholes–Merton partial differential equation, derive an ordinary differential equation satisfied by $h(t, T)$.
   (b) What is the boundary condition for the differential equation for $h(t, T)$?
   (c) Show that $h(t, T) = e^{[0.5\sigma^2 n(n-1) + r(n-1)](T-t)}$, where r is the risk-free interest rate and σ is the stock price volatility.

15.13. What is the price of a European call option on a non-dividend-paying stock when the stock price is $52, the strike price is $50, the risk-free interest rate is 12% per annum, the volatility is 30% per annum, and the time to maturity is 3 months?

15.14. What is the price of a European put option on a non-dividend-paying stock when the stock price is $69, the strike price is $70, the risk-free interest rate is 5% per annum, the volatility is 35% per annum, and the time to maturity is 6 months?

15.15. Consider an American call option on a stock. The stock price is $70, the time to maturity is 8 months, the risk-free rate of interest is 10% per annum, the exercise price is $65, and the volatility is 32%. A dividend of $1 is expected after 3 months and again after 6 months. Show that it can never be optimal to exercise the option on either of the two dividend dates. Use DerivaGem to calculate the price of the option.

15.16. A call option on a non-dividend-paying stock has a market price of $2\frac{1}{2}$. The stock price is $15, the exercise price is $13, the time to maturity is 3 months, and the risk-free interest rate is 5% per annum. What is the implied volatility?

15.17. With the notation used in this chapter:
   (a) What is $N'(x)$?
   (b) Show that $SN'(d_1) = Ke^{-r(T-t)}N'(d_2)$, where S is the stock price at time t and

$$d_1 = \frac{\ln(S/K) + (r + \sigma^2/2)(T - t)}{\sigma\sqrt{T - t}}, \quad d_2 = \frac{\ln(S/K) + (r - \sigma^2/2)(T - t)}{\sigma\sqrt{T - t}}$$

   (c) Calculate $\partial d_1/\partial S$ and $\partial d_2/\partial S$.
   (d) Show that when $c = SN(d_1) - Ke^{-r(T-t)}N(d_2)$, it follows that

$$\frac{\partial c}{\partial t} = -rKe^{-r(T-t)}N(d_2) - SN'(d_1)\frac{\sigma}{2\sqrt{T - t}}$$

   where c is the price of a call option on a non-dividend-paying stock.
   (e) Show that $\partial c/\partial S = N(d_1)$.
   (f) Show that c satisfies the Black–Scholes–Merton differential equation.
   (g) Show that c satisfies the boundary condition for a European call option, i.e., that $c = \max(S - K, 0)$ as $t \to T$.

15.18. Show that the Black–Scholes–Merton formulas for call and put options satisfy put–call parity.

15.19. A stock price is currently $50 and the risk-free interest rate is 5%. Use the DerivaGem software to translate the following table of European call options on the stock into a table of implied volatilities, assuming no dividends. Are the option prices consistent with the assumptions underlying Black–Scholes–Merton?

Strike price ($)	*Maturity (months)*		
	3	*6*	*12*
45	7.0	8.3	10.5
50	3.7	5.2	7.5
55	1.6	2.9	5.1

15.20. Explain carefully why Black's approach to evaluating an American call option on a dividend-paying stock may give an approximate answer even when only one dividend is anticipated. Does the answer given by Black's approach understate or overstate the true option value? Explain your answer.

15.21. Consider an American call option on a stock. The stock price is $50, the time to maturity is 15 months, the risk-free rate of interest is 8% per annum, the exercise price is $55, and the volatility is 25%. Dividends of $1.50 are expected in 4 months and 10 months. Show that it can never be optimal to exercise the option on either of the two dividend dates. Calculate the price of the option.

15.22. Show that the probability that a European call option will be exercised in a risk-neutral world is, with the notation introduced in this chapter, $N(d_2)$. What is an expression for the value of a derivative that pays off $100 if the price of a stock at time T is greater than K?

15.23. Use the result in equation (15.17) to determine the value of a perpetual American put option on a non-dividend-paying stock with strike price K if it is exercised when the stock price equals H where $H < K$. Assume that the current stock price S is greater than H. What is the value of H that maximizes the option value? Deduce the value of a perpetual American put with strike price K.

15.24. A company has an issue of executive stock options outstanding. Should dilution be taken into account when the options are valued? Explain your answer.

15.25. A company's stock price is $50 and 10 million shares are outstanding. The company is considering giving its employees 3 million at-the-money 5-year call options. Option exercises will be handled by issuing more shares. The stock price volatility is 25%, the 5-year risk-free rate is 5%, and the company does not pay dividends. Estimate the cost to the company of the employee stock option issue.

Further Questions

15.26. If the volatility of a stock is 18% per annum, estimate the standard deviation of the percentage price change in (a) 1 day, (b) 1 week, and (c) 1 month.

15.27. A stock price is currently $50. Assume that the expected return from the stock is 18% and its volatility is 30%. What is the probability distribution for the stock price in 2 years? Calculate the mean and standard deviation of the distribution. Determine the 95% confidence interval.

15.28. Suppose that observations on a stock price (in dollars) at the end of each of 15 consecutive weeks are as follows:

30.2, 32.0, 31.1, 30.1, 30.2, 30.3, 30.6, 33.0, 32.9, 33.0, 33.5, 33.5, 33.7, 33.5, 33.2

Estimate the stock price volatility. What is the standard error of your estimate?

15.29. A financial institution plans to offer a security that pays off a dollar amount equal to S_T^2 at time T, where S_T is the price at time T of a stock that pays no dividends.
 (a) Use risk-neutral valuation to calculate the price of the security at time t in terms of the stock price S at time t and other variables. (*Hint*: The expected value of S_T^2 can be calculated from the mean and variance of S_T given in Section 15.1.)
 (b) Confirm that your price satisfies the differential equation (15.16).

15.30. Consider an option on a non-dividend-paying stock when the stock price is $30, the exercise price is $29, the risk-free interest rate is 5%, the volatility is 25% per annum, and the time to maturity is 4 months.
 (a) What is the price of the option if it is a European call?
 (b) What is the price of the option if it is an American call?

    (c) What is the price of the option if it is a European put?

    (d) Verify that put–call parity holds.

15.31. Assume that the stock in Problem 15.30 is due to go ex-dividend in $1\frac{1}{2}$ months. The expected dividend is 50 cents.

    (a) What is the price of the option if it is a European call?

    (b) What is the price of the option if it is a European put?

    (c) If the option is an American call, are there any circumstances under which it will be exercised early?

15.32. Consider an American call option when the stock price is \$18, the exercise price is \$20, the time to maturity is 6 months, the volatility is 30% per annum, and the risk-free interest rate is 10% per annum. Two equal dividends are expected during the life of the option with ex-dividend dates at the end of 2 months and 5 months. Assume the dividends are 40 cents. Use Black's approximation and the DerivaGem software to value the option. How high can the dividends be without the American option being worth more than the corresponding European option?

15.33. The appendix derives the key result

$$E[\max(V - K, 0)] = E(V)N(d_1) - KN(d_2)$$

Show that

$$E[\max(K - V, 0)] = KN(-d_1) - E(V)N(-d_2)$$

and use this to derive the Black–Scholes–Merton formula for the price of a European put option on a non-dividend-paying stock.

APPENDIX

PROOF OF THE BLACK–SCHOLES–MERTON FORMULA USING RISK-NEUTRAL VALUATION

We will prove the Black–Scholes result by first proving another key result that will also be useful in future chapters.

Key Result

If V is lognormally distributed and the standard deviation of $\ln V$ is w, then

$$E[\max(V - K, 0)] = E(V)N(d_1) - KN(d_2) \qquad (15A.1)$$

where

$$d_1 = \frac{\ln[E(V)/K] + w^2/2}{w}$$

$$d_2 = \frac{\ln[E(V)/K] - w^2/2}{w}$$

and E denotes the expected value. (See Problem 15.33 for a similar result for puts.)

Proof of Key Result

Define $g(V)$ as the probability density function of V. It follows that

$$E[\max(V - K, 0)] = \int_K^\infty (V - K)g(V)\,dV \qquad (15A.2)$$

The variable $\ln V$ is normally distributed with standard deviation w. From the properties of the lognormal distribution, the mean of $\ln V$ is m, where [16]

$$m = \ln[E(V)] - w^2/2 \qquad (15A.3)$$

Define a new variable

$$Q = \frac{\ln V - m}{w} \qquad (15A.4)$$

This variable is normally distributed with a mean of zero and a standard deviation of 1.0. Denote the density function for Q by $h(Q)$ so that

$$h(Q) = \frac{1}{\sqrt{2\pi}}e^{-Q^2/2}$$

Using equation (15A.4) to convert the expression on the right-hand side of equation (15A.2) from an integral over V to an integral over Q, we get

$$E[\max(V - K, 0)] = \int_{(\ln K - m)/w}^\infty (e^{Qw+m} - K)\,h(Q)\,dQ$$

or

$$E[\max(V - K, 0)] = \int_{(\ln K - m)/w}^\infty e^{Qw+m}h(Q)dQ - K\int_{(\ln K - m)/w}^\infty h(Q)dQ \qquad (15A.5)$$

---

[16] For a proof of this, see Technical Note 2 at www-2.rotman.utoronto.ca/~hull/TechnicalNotes.

Now

$$e^{Qw+m}h(Q) = \frac{1}{\sqrt{2\pi}}e^{(-Q^2+2Qw+2m)/2} = \frac{1}{\sqrt{2\pi}}e^{[-(Q-w)^2+2m+w^2]/2}$$

$$= \frac{e^{m+w^2/2}}{\sqrt{2\pi}}e^{[-(Q-w)^2]/2} = e^{m+w^2/2}h(Q-w)$$

This means that equation (15A.5) becomes

$$E[\max(V-K, 0)] = e^{m+w^2/2}\int_{(\ln K-m)/w}^{\infty} h(Q-w)dQ - K\int_{(\ln K-m)/w}^{\infty} h(Q)dQ \quad \textbf{(15A.6)}$$

If we define $N(x)$ as the probability that a variable with a mean of zero and a standard deviation of 1.0 is less than x, the first integral in equation (15A.6) is

$$1 - N[(\ln K - m)/w - w] = N[(-\ln K + m)/w + w]$$

Substituting for m from equation (15A.3) leads to

$$N\left(\frac{\ln[E(V)/K] + w^2/2}{w}\right) = N(d_1)$$

Similarly the second integral in equation (15A.6) is $N(d_2)$. Equation (15A.6), therefore, becomes

$$E[\max(V-K, 0)] = e^{m+w^2/2}N(d_1) - KN(d_2)$$

Substituting for m from equation (15A.3) gives the key result.

The Black–Scholes–Merton Result

We now consider a call option on a non-dividend-paying stock maturing at time T. The strike price is K, the risk-free rate is r, the current stock price is S_0, and the volatility is σ. As shown in equation (15.22), the call price c is given by

$$c = e^{-rT}\hat{E}[\max(S_T - K, 0)] \quad \textbf{(15A.7)}$$

where S_T is the stock price at time T and $\hat{E}$ denotes the expectation in a risk-neutral world. Under the stochastic process assumed by Black–Scholes–Merton, S_T is log-normal. Also, from equations (15.3) and (15.4), $\hat{E}(S_T) = S_0 e^{rT}$ and the standard deviation of $\ln S_T$ is $\sigma\sqrt{T}$.

From the key result just proved, equation (15A.7) implies

$$c = e^{-rT}[S_0 e^{rT}N(d_1) - KN(d_2)] = S_0 N(d_1) - Ke^{-rT}N(d_2)$$

where

$$d_1 = \frac{\ln[\hat{E}(S_T)/K] + \sigma^2 T/2}{\sigma\sqrt{T}} = \frac{\ln(S_0/K) + (r + \sigma^2/2)T}{\sigma\sqrt{T}}$$

$$d_2 = \frac{\ln[\hat{E}(S_T)/K] - \sigma^2 T/2}{\sigma\sqrt{T}} = \frac{\ln(S_0/K) + (r - \sigma^2/2)T}{\sigma\sqrt{T}}$$

This is the Black–Scholes–Merton result.

16

Employee Stock Options

Employee stock options are call options on a company's stock granted by the company to its employees. The options give the employees a stake in the fortunes of the company. If the company does well so that the company's stock price moves above the strike price, employees gain by exercising the options and then selling the stock they acquire at the market price.

Many companies, particularly technology companies, feel that the only way they can attract and keep the best employees is to offer them attractive stock option packages. Some companies grant options only to senior management; others grant them to people at all levels in the organization. Microsoft was one of the first companies to use employee stock options. All Microsoft employees were granted options and, as the company's stock price rose, it is estimated that over 10,000 of them became millionaires. Employee stock options have become less popular in recent years for reasons we will explain in this chapter. (Microsoft, for example, announced in 2003 that it would discontinue the use of options and award shares of Microsoft to employees instead.) But many companies throughout the world continue to be enthusiastic users of employee stock options.

Employee stock options are popular with start-up companies. Often these companies do not have the resources to pay key employees as much as they could earn with an established company and they solve this problem by supplementing the salaries of the employees with stock options. If the company does well and shares are sold to the public in an initial public offering (IPO), the options are likely to prove to be very valuable. Some newly formed companies have even granted options to students who worked for just a few months during their summer break—and in some cases this has led to windfalls of hundreds of thousands of dollars for the students.

This chapter explains how stock option plans work and how their popularity has been influenced by their accounting treatment. It discusses whether employee stock options help to align the interests of shareholders with those of top executives running a company. It also describes how these options are valued and looks at backdating scandals.

16.1 CONTRACTUAL ARRANGEMENTS

Employee stock options often last as long as 10 to 15 years. Very often the strike price is set equal to the stock price on the grant date so that the option is initially at the money.

The following are common features of employee stock option plans:

1. There is a vesting period during which the options cannot be exercised. This vesting period can be as long as four years.

2. When employees leave their jobs (voluntarily or involuntarily) during the vesting period, they forfeit their options.

3. When employees leave (voluntarily or involuntarily) after the vesting period, they forfeit options that are out of the money and they have to exercise vested options that are in the money almost immediately.

4. Employees are not permitted to sell the options.

5. When an employee exercises options, the company issues new shares and sells them to the employee for the strike price.

The Early Exercise Decision

The fourth feature of employee stock option plans noted above has important implications. If employees, for whatever reason, want to realize a cash benefit from options that have vested, they must exercise the options and sell the underlying shares. They cannot sell the options to someone else. This leads to a tendency for employee stock options to be exercised earlier than similar exchange-traded or over-the-counter call options.

Consider a call option on a stock paying no dividends. In Section 11.5 we showed that, if it is a regular call option, it should never be exercised early. The holder of the option will always do better by selling the option rather than exercising it before the end of its life. However, the arguments we used in Section 11.5 are not applicable to employee stock options because they cannot be sold. The only way employees can realize a cash benefit from the options (or diversify their holdings) is by exercising the options and selling the stock. It is therefore not unusual for an employee stock option to be exercised well before it would be optimal to exercise the option if it were a regular exchange-traded or over-the-counter option.

Should an employee ever exercise his or her options before maturity and then keep the stock rather than selling it? Assume that the option's strike price is constant during the life of the option and the option can be exercised at any time. To answer the question we consider two options: the employee stock option and an otherwise identical regular option that can be sold in the market. We refer to the first option as option A and the second as option B. If the stock pays no dividends, we know that option B should never be exercised early. It follows that it is not optimal to exercise option A and keep the stock. If the employee wants to maintain a stake in his or her company, a better strategy is to keep the option. This delays paying the strike price and maintains the insurance value of the option, as described in Section 11.5. Only when it is optimal to exercise option B can it be a rational strategy for an employee to exercise option A before maturity and keep the stock.[1] As discussed in Section 15.12, it is optimal to exercise option B only when a relatively high dividend is imminent.

In practice the early exercise behavior of employees varies widely from company to company. In some companies, there is a culture of not exercising early; in others, employees tend to exercise options and sell the stock soon after the end of the vesting period, even if the options are only slightly in the money.

---

[1] The only exception to this could be when an executive wants to own the stock for its voting rights.

16.2 DO OPTIONS ALIGN THE INTERESTS OF SHAREHOLDERS AND MANAGERS?

For investors to have confidence in capital markets, it is important that the interests of shareholders and managers are reasonably well aligned. This means that managers should be motivated to make decisions that are in the best interests of shareholders. Managers are the agents of the shareholders and, as mentioned in Chapter 8, economists use the term *agency costs* to describe the losses experienced when the interests of agents and principals are not aligned.

Do employee stock options help align the interests of employees and shareholders? The answer to this question is not straightforward. There can be little doubt that they serve a useful purpose for a start-up company. The options are an excellent way for the main shareholders, who are usually also senior executives, to motivate employees to work long hours. If the company is successful and there is an IPO, the employees will do very well; but if the company is unsuccessful, the options will be worthless.

It is the options granted to the senior executives of publicly traded companies that are most controversial. Executive stock options are sometimes referred to as an executive's "pay for performance." If the company's stock price goes up, so that shareholders make gains, the executive is rewarded. However, this overlooks the asymmetric payoffs of options. If the company does badly then the shareholders lose money, but all that happens to the executives is that they fail to make a gain. Unlike the shareholders, they do not experience a loss.[2] Many people think that a better type of pay for performance is a *restricted stock unit*. This entitles the executive to own a share of the company's stock at a particular future time (the vesting date). The gains and losses of the executives then mirror those of other shareholders. It is sometimes argued that the asymmetric payoffs of options can lead to senior executives taking risks they would not otherwise take. This may or may not be in the interests of the company's shareholders.

What temptations do stock options create for a senior executive? Suppose an executive plans to exercise a large number of stock options in three months and sell the stock. He or she might be tempted to time announcements of good news—or even move earnings from one quarter to another—so that the stock price increases just before the options are exercised. Alternatively, if at-the-money options are due to be granted to the executive in three months, the executive might be tempted to take actions that reduce the stock price just before the grant date. The type of behavior we are talking about here is of course totally unacceptable—and may well be illegal. But the backdating scandals, which are discussed later in this chapter, show that the way some executives have handled issues related to stock options leaves much to be desired.

Even when there is no impropriety of the type we have just mentioned, executive stock options are liable to have the effect of motivating executives to focus on short-term profits at the expense of longer-term performance. Managers of large funds worry that, because stock options are such a huge component of an executive's compensation, they are liable to be a big source of distraction. Senior management may spend too

---

[2] When options have moved out of the money, companies have sometimes replaced them with new at-the-money options. This practice known as "repricing" leads to the executive's gains and losses being even less closely tied to those of the shareholders.

much time thinking about all the different aspects of their compensation and not enough time running the company.

A manager's inside knowledge and ability to affect outcomes and announcements is always liable to interact with his or her trading in a way that is to the disadvantage of other shareholders. One radical suggestion for mitigating this problem is to require executives to give notice to the market—perhaps one week's notice—of an intention to buy or sell their company's stock.[3] (Once the notice of an intention to trade had been given, it would be binding on the executive.) This allows the market to form its own conclusions about why the executive is trading. As a result, the price may increase before the executive buys and decrease before the executive sells.

16.3 ACCOUNTING ISSUES

An employee stock option represents a cost to the company and a benefit to the employee just like any other form of compensation. This point, which for many is self-evident, is actually quite controversial. Many corporate executives appear to believe that an option has no value unless it is in the money. As a result, they argue that an at-the-money option issued by the company is not a cost to the company. The reality is that, if options are valuable to employees, they must represent a cost to the company's shareholders—and therefore to the company. There is no free lunch. The cost to the company of the options arises from the fact that the company has agreed that, if its stock does well, it will sell shares to employees at a price less than that which would apply in the open market.

Prior to 1995, the cost charged to the income statement of a company when it issued stock options was the intrinsic value. Most options were at the money when they were first issued, so that this cost was zero. In 1995, accounting standard FAS 123 was issued. Many people expected it to require the expensing of options at their fair value. However, as a result of intense lobbying, the 1995 version of FAS 123 only encouraged companies to expense the fair value of the options they granted on the income statement. It did not require them to do so. If fair value was not expensed on the income statement, it had to be reported in a footnote to the company's accounts.

Accounting standards have now changed to require the expensing of all stock-based compensation at its fair value on the income statement. In February 2004, the International Accounting Standards Board issued IAS 2 requiring companies to start expensing stock options in 2005. In December 2004, FAS 123 was revised to require the expensing of employee stock options in the United States starting in 2005.

The effect of the new accounting standards is to require options to be valued on the grant date and the amount to be recorded as an expense in the income statement for the year in which the grant is made. Valuation at a time later than the grant date is not required. It can be argued that options should be revalued at financial year ends (or every quarter) until they are exercised or reach the end of their lives.[4] This would treat them in the same way as other derivative transactions entered into by the company. If the option became more valuable from one year to the next, there would then be an

---

[3] This would apply to the exercise of options because, if an executive wants to exercise options and sell the stock that is acquired, then he or she would have to give notice of intention to sell.

[4] See J. C. Hull and A. White, "Accounting for Employee Stock Options: A Practical Approach to Handling the Valuation Issues," *Journal of Derivatives Accounting*, 1, 1 (2004): 3–9.

additional amount to be expensed. However, if it declined in value, there would be a positive impact on income.

This approach would have a number of advantages. The cumulative charge to the company would reflect the actual cost of the options (either zero if the options are not exercised or the option payoff if they are exercised). Although the charge in any year would depend on the option pricing model used, the cumulative charge over the life of the option would not.[5] Arguably there would be much less incentive for the company to engage in the backdating practices described later in the chapter. The disadvantage usually cited for accounting in this way is that it is undesirable because it introduces volatility into the income statement.[6]

Alternatives to Stock Options

The accounting rules which came into effect in 2005 have led companies to consider alternatives to traditional compensation plans where at-the-money stock options are granted. We have already mentioned restricted stock units (RSUs), which are shares that will be owned by the employee at a future time (the vesting date). Many companies have replaced stock options by RSUs. A variation on an RSU is a market-leveraged stock unit (MSU), in which the number of shares that will be owned on the vesting date is equal to S_T/S_0, where S_0 is the stock price on the grant date and S_T is the stock price on the vesting date.[7]

If the stock market as a whole goes up, employees with stock options tend to do well, even if their own company's stock price underperforms the market. One way of overcoming this problem is to tie the strike price of the options to the performance of an index such as the S&P 500. Suppose that on the option grant date the stock price is $30 and the S&P 500 is 2,000. The strike price would initially be set at $30. If the S&P 500 increased by 10% to 2,200, then the strike price would also increase by 10% to $33. If the S&P 500 moved down by 15% to 1,700, then the strike price would also move down by 15% to $25.50. The effect of this is that the company's stock price performance has to beat that of the S&P 500 to become in the money. As an alternative to using the S&P 500 as the reference index, the company could use an index of the prices of stocks in the same industrial sector as the company.

16.4 VALUATION

Accounting standards give companies quite a bit of latitude in choosing a method for valuing employee stock options. In this section we review some of the alternatives.

---

[5] Interestingly, if an option is settled in cash rather than by the company issuing new shares, it is subject to the accounting treatment proposed here. (However, there is no economic difference between an option that is settled in cash and one that is settled by selling new shares to the employee.)

[6] In fact the income statement is likely be less volatile if stock options are revalued. When the company does well, income is reduced by revaluing the executive stock options. When the company does badly, it is increased.

[7] Sometimes there is an upper and lower bound to the number of shares which will vest and sometimes S_0 and S_T are defined as average stock prices over a number of days preceding the grant data and vesting date, respectively. For an analysis of MSUs, see J. C. Hull and A. White, "The Valuation of Market-Leveraged Stock Units," *Journal of Derivatives*, 21, 3 (Spring 2014): 85–90.

The "Quick and Dirty" Approach

A frequently used approach is based on what is known as the option's *expected life*. This is the average time for which employees hold the option before it is exercised or expires. The expected life can be approximately estimated from historical data on the early exercise behavior of employees and reflects the vesting period, the impact of employees leaving the company, and the tendency we mentioned in Section 16.1 for employee stock options to be exercised earlier than regular options. The Black–Scholes–Merton model is used with the life of the option, T, set equal to the expected life. The volatility is usually estimated from several years of historical data as described in Section 15.4.

It should be emphasized that using the Black–Scholes–Merton formula in this way has no theoretical validity. There is no reason why the value of a European stock option with the time to maturity, T, set equal to the expected life should be approximately the same as the value of the American-style employee stock option that we are interested in. However, the results given by the model are not unreasonable in many situations. Companies, when reporting their employee stock option expense, will frequently mention the volatility and expected life used in their Black–Scholes–Merton computations.

Example 16.1

A company grants 1,000,000 options to its executives on November 1, 2014. The stock price on that date is $30 and the strike price of the options is also $30. The options last for 10 years and vest after three years. The company has issued similar at-the-money options for the last 10 years. The average time to exercise or expiry of these options is 4.5 years. The company therefore decides to use an "expected life" of 4.5 years. It estimates the long-term volatility of the stock price, using 5 years of historical data, to be 25%. The present value of dividends during the next 4.5 years is estimated to be $4. The 4.5-year zero-coupon risk-free interest rate is 5%. The option is therefore valued using the Black–Scholes–Merton model (adjusted for dividends in the way described in Section 15.12) with $S_0 = 30 - 4 = 26$, $K = 30$, $r = 5\%$, $\sigma = 25\%$, and $T = 4.5$. The Black–Scholes–Merton formula gives the value of one option as $6.31. Hence, the income statement expense is $1,000,000 \times 6.31$, or $6,310,000.

Binomial Tree Approach

A more sophisticated approach to valuing employee stock options involves building a binomial tree as outlined in Chapter 13 and adjusting the rules used when rolling back through the tree to reflect (a) whether the option has vested, (b) the probability of the employee leaving the company, and (c) the probability of the employee choosing to exercise the option. The terms of the option define whether the option has vested at different nodes of the tree. Historical data on turnover rates for employees can be used to estimate the probability of the option being either prematurely exercised or forfeited at a node because the employee leaves the company. The probability of an employee choosing to exercise the option at different nodes of the tree is more difficult to quantify. Clearly this probability increases as the ratio of the stock price to the strike price increases and as the time to the option's maturity declines. If enough historical data is available, the probability of exercise as a function of these two variables can be estimated—at least approximately.

Example 16.2

Suppose a company grants stock options that last 8 years and vest after 3 years. The stock price and strike price are both $40. The stock price volatility is 30%, the risk-free rate is 5%, and the company pays no dividends. Figure 16.1 shows how a four-step tree could be used to value the option. (This is for illustration; in practice more time steps would be used.) In this case, $\sigma = 0.3$, $\Delta t = 2$, and $r = 0.05$, so that, with the notation of Chapter 13, $a = e^{0.05 \times 2} = 1.1052$, $u = e^{0.3\sqrt{2}} = 1.5285$, $d = 1/u = 0.6543$, and $p = (a - d)/(u - d) = 0.5158$. The probability on the "up branches" is 0.5158 and the probability on the "down branches" is 0.4842. There are three nodes where early exercise could be desirable: D, G, and H. (The option has not vested at node B and is not in the money at the other nodes prior to maturity.) We assume that the probabilities that the holder will choose to exercise at nodes D, G, and H (conditional on no earlier exercise) have been estimated as 40%, 80%, and 30%, respectively. We suppose that the probability of an employee leaving the company during each time step is 5%. (This corresponds to an employee turnover rate of approximately 2.5% per year.) For the purposes of the calculation, it is assumed that employees always leave at the end of a time period. If an employee leaves the company before an option has vested or when the option is out of the money, the option is forfeited. In other cases the option must be exercised immediately.

Figure 16.1   Valuation of employee stock option in Example 16.2.

At each node:
Upper value = Underlying asset price
Lower value = Option price
Values in bold are a result of early exercise.

Strike price = 40
Discount factor per step = 0.9048
Time step, dt = 2.0000 years, 730.00 days
Growth factor per step, a = 1.1052
Probability of up move, p = 0.5158
Up step size, u = 1.5285
Down step size, d = 0.6543

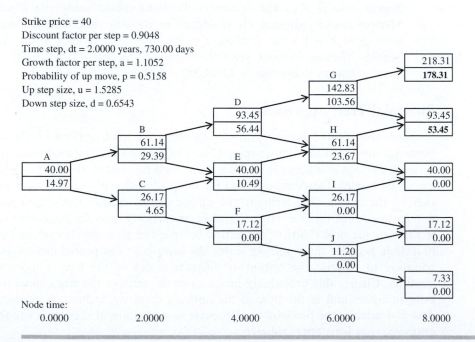

Node time:
0.0000   2.0000   4.0000   6.0000   8.0000

The value of the option at the final nodes is its intrinsic value. Consider the nodes at time 6 years. Nodes I and J are easy. Since these nodes are certain to lead to nodes where the option is worth nothing, the value of the option is zero at these nodes. At node H there is a 30% chance that the employee will choose to exercise the option. In cases where the employee does not choose to exercise, there is a 5% chance that the employee leaves the company and has to exercise. The total probability of exercise is therefore $0.3 + 0.7 \times 0.05 = 0.335$. If the option is exercised, its value is $61.14 - 40 = 21.14$. If it is not exercised, its value is

$$e^{-0.05 \times 2}(0.5158 \times 53.45 + 0.4842 \times 0) = 24.95$$

The value of the option at node H is therefore

$$0.335 \times 21.14 + 0.665 \times 24.95 = 23.67$$

The value at node G is similarly

$$0.81 \times 102.83 + 0.19 \times 106.64 = 103.56$$

We now move on to the nodes at time 4 years. At node F the option is clearly worth zero. At node E there is a 5% chance that the employee will forfeit the option because he or she leaves the company and a 95% chance that the option will be retained. In the latter case the option is worth

$$e^{-0.05 \times 2}(0.5158 \times 23.67 + 0.4842 \times 0) = 11.05$$

The option is therefore worth $0.95 \times 11.05 = 10.49$. At node D there is a 0.43 probability that the option will be exercised and a 0.57 chance that it will be retained. The value of the option is 56.44.

Consider next the initial node and the nodes at time 2 years. The option has not vested at these nodes. There is a 5% chance that the option will be forfeited and a 95% chance that it will be retained for a further 2 years. This leads to the valuations shown in Figure 16.1. The valuation of the option at the initial node is 14.97. (This compares with a valuation of 17.98 for a regular option using the same tree.)

The Exercise Multiple Approach

Hull and White suggest a simple model where an employee exercises as soon as the option has vested and the ratio of the stock price to the strike price is above a certain level.[8] They refer to the ratio of stock price to strike price that triggers exercise as the "exercise multiple". The option can be valued using a binomial or trinomial tree. As outlined in Section 27.6, it is important to construct a binomial or trinomial tree where nodes lie on the stock prices that will lead to exercise. For example, if the strike price is $30 and the assumption is that employees exercise when the ratio of the stock price to the strike price is 1.5, the tree should be constructed so that there are nodes at a stock price level of $45. The tree calculations are similar to those for Example 16.2 and take account of the probability of an employee leaving the company.[9] To estimate the exercise multiple, it is necessary to calculate from historical data the average ratio of

---

[8] See J. C. Hull and A. White, "How to value employee stock options," *Financial Analysts Journal*, 60, 1 (January/February 2004): 3–9.

[9] Software implementing this approach is on www-2.rotman.utoronto.ca/~hull.

stock price to strike price at the time of exercise. (Exercises at maturity and those arising from the termination of the employee's job are not included in the calculation of the average.) This may be easier to estimate from historical data than the expected life because the latter is quite heavily dependent on the particular path that has been followed by the stock's price.

A Market-Based Approach

One way of valuing an employee stock option is to see what the market would pay for it. Cisco was the first to try this in 2006. It proposed selling options with the exact terms of its employee stock options to institutional investors. This approach was rejected by the SEC on the grounds that the range of investors bidding for the options was not wide enough.

Zions Bancorp has suggested an alternative approach. It proposed that securities providing payoffs mirroring those actually realized by its employees be sold. Suppose that the strike price for a particular grant to employees is $40 and it turns out that 1% of employees exercise after exactly 5 years when the stock price is $60, 2% exercise after exactly 6 years when the stock price is $65, and so on. Then 1% of the securities owned by an investor will provide a $20 payoff after 5 years, 2% will provide a payoff of $25 after 6 years, and so on.

Zions Bancorp tested the idea using its own stock option grant to its employees. It sold the securities using a Dutch auction process. In this individuals or companies can submit a bid indicating the price they are prepared to pay and the number of options they are prepared to buy. The clearing price is the highest bid such that the aggregate number of options sought at that price or a higher price equals or exceeds the number of options for sale. Buyers who have bid more than the clearing price get their orders filled at the clearing price and the buyer who bid the clearing price gets the remainder. Zions Bancorp announced that it had received SEC approval for its market-based approach in October 2007, but the approach has not been used to any great extent.

Dilution

The fact that a company issues new stock when an employee stock option is exercised leads to some dilution for existing stock holders because new shares are being sold to employees at below the current stock price. It is natural to assume that this dilution takes place at the time the option is exercised. However, this is not the case. As explained in Section 15.10, stock prices are diluted when the market first hears about a stock option grant. The possible exercise of options is anticipated and immediately reflected in the stock price. This point is emphasized by the example in Business Snapshot 15.3.

The stock price immediately after a grant is announced to the public reflects any dilution. Provided that this stock price is used in the valuation of the option, it is not necessary to adjust the option price for dilution. In many instances the market expects a company to make regular stock option grants and so the market price of the stock anticipates dilution even before the announcement is made.

If a company is contemplating a stock option grant that will surprise the market, the cost can be calculated as described in Example 15.7. This cost can be compared with benefits such as lower regular employee remuneration and less employee turnover.

16.5 BACKDATING SCANDALS

No discussion of employee stock options would be complete without mentioning backdating scandals. Backdating is the practice of marking a document with a date that precedes the current date.

Suppose that a company decides to grant at-the-money options to its executives on April 30 when the stock price is $50. If the stock price was $42 on April 3, it is tempting to behave as if those the options were granted on April 3 and use a strike price of $42. This is legal provided that the company reports the options as $8 in the money on the date when the decision to grant the options is made, April 30. But it is illegal for the company to report the options as at-the-money and granted on April 3. The value on April 3 of an option with a strike price of $42 is much less than its value on April 30. Shareholders are misled about the true cost of the decision to grant options if the company reports the options as granted on April 3.

How prevalent is backdating? To answer this question, researchers have investigated whether a company's stock price has, on average, a tendency to be low at the time of the grant date that the company reports. Early research by Yermack shows that stock prices tend to increase after reported grant dates.[10] Lie extended Yermack's work, showing that stock prices also tended to decrease before reported grant dates.[11] The period covered by this research was 1993 to 2002. The research clearly shows that stock prices tended to be at a low point on reported grant dates. The stock price on a reported grant date was on average lower than that on each of the 30 days before the grant date and lower than that on each of the 30 days after the grant date. Statistical tests carried out by the researchers showed that this could not have happened by chance. The research led regulators to conclude that backdating was occurring. In August 2002, the SEC required option grants by public companies to be reported within two business days. Heron and Lie showed that this led to a dramatic change in the stock price patterns around the grant date—particularly for those companies that complied with the SEC rule.[12] Reported grant dates were no longer low-stock-price dates. It might be argued that the patterns observed by Yermack and Lie can be explained by managers choosing grant dates after bad news or before good news, but Heron and Lie's research shows that, although there might been a tendency for this to happen, it is not the major explanation of the Yermack and Lie results.

Estimates of the number of companies that illegally backdated stock option grants in the United States vary widely. Tens and maybe hundreds of companies seem to have engaged in the practice. Many companies seem to have adopted the view that it was acceptable to backdate up to one month. Some CEOs resigned when their backdating practices came to light. In August 2007, Gregory Reyes of Brocade Communications Systems, Inc., became the first CEO to be tried for backdating stock option grants. Allegedly, Mr. Reyes said to a human resources employee: "It is not illegal if you do not get caught." In June 2010, he was sentenced to 18 months in prison and fined $15 million.

---

[10] See D. Yermack, "Good timing: CEO stock option awards and company news announcements," *Journal of Finance*, 52 (1997), 449–476.

[11] See E. Lie, "On the timing of CEO stock option awards," *Management Science*, 51, 5 (May 2005), 802–12.

[12] See R. Heron and E. Lie, "Does backdating explain the stock price pattern around executive stock option grants," *Journal of Financial Economics*, 83, 2 (February 2007), 271–95.

Companies involved in backdating have had to restate past financial statements and have been defendants in class action suits brought by shareholders who claim to have lost money as a result of backdating. For example, McAfee announced in December 2007 that it would restate earnings between 1995 and 2005 by $137.4 million. In 2006, it set aside $13.8 million to cover lawsuits.

SUMMARY

Until 2005, at-the-money stock option grants were a very attractive form of compensation. They had no impact on the income statement and were very valuable to employees. Accounting standards now require options to be expensed.

There are a number of different approaches to valuing employee stock options. A common approach is to use the Black–Scholes–Merton model with the life of the option set equal to the expected time to exercise or expiry of the option. Another approach is to assume that options are exercised as soon as the ratio of the stock price to the strike price reaches a certain barrier. A third approach is to try and estimate the relationship between the probability of exercise, the ratio of the stock price to the strike price, and the time to option maturity. A fourth approach is to create a market for securities that replicate the payoffs on the options.

Academic research has shown beyond doubt that many companies have engaged in the illegal practice of backdating stock option grants in order to reduce the strike price, while still contending that the options were at the money. The first prosecutions for this illegal practice were in 2007.

FURTHER READING

Carpenter, J., "The Exercise and Valuation of Executive Stock Options," *Journal of Financial Economics*, 48, 2 (May 1998): 127–58.

Core, J. E., and W. R. Guay, "Stock Option Plans for Non-Executive Employees," *Journal of Financial Economics*, 61, 2 (2001): 253–87.

Heron, R., and E. Lie, "Does Backdating Explain the Stock Price Pattern around Executive Stock Option Grants," *Journal of Financial Economics*, 83, 2 (February 2007): 271–95.

Huddart, S., and M. Lang, "Employee Stock Option Exercises: An Empirical Analysis," *Journal of Accounting and Economics*, 21, 1 (February): 5–43.

Hull, J. C., and A. White, "How to Value Employee Stock Options," *Financial Analysts Journal*, 60, 1 (January/February 2004): 3–9.

Lie, E., "On the Timing of CEO Stock Option Awards," *Management Science*, 51, 5 (May 2005): 802–12.

Yermack, D., "Good Timing: CEO Stock Option Awards and Company News Announcements," *Journal of Finance*, 52 (1997): 449–76.

Practice Questions (Answers in Solutions Manual)

16.1. Why was it attractive for companies to grant at-the-money stock options prior to 2005? What changed in 2005?

16.2. What are the main differences between a typical employee stock option and an American call option traded on an exchange or in the over-the-counter market?

16.3. Explain why employee stock options on a non-dividend-paying stock are frequently exercised before the end of their lives, whereas an exchange-traded call option on such a stock is never exercised early.

16.4. "Stock option grants are good because they motivate executives to act in the best interests of shareholders." Discuss this viewpoint.

16.5. "Granting stock options to executives is like allowing a professional footballer to bet on the outcome of games." Discuss this viewpoint.

16.6. Why did some companies backdate stock option grants in the United States prior to 2002? What changed in 2002?

16.7. In what way would the benefits of backdating be reduced if a stock option grant had to be revalued at the end of each quarter?

16.8. Explain how you would do an analysis similar to that of Yermack and Lie to determine whether the backdating of stock option grants was happening.

16.9. On May 31 a company's stock price is $70. One million shares are outstanding. An executive exercises 100,000 stock options with a strike price of $50. What is the impact of this on the stock price?

16.10. The notes accompanying a company's financial statements say: "Our executive stock options last 10 years and vest after 4 years. We valued the options granted this year using the Black–Scholes–Merton model with an expected life of 5 years and a volatility of 20%." What does this mean? Discuss the modeling approach used by the company.

16.11. In a Dutch auction of 10,000 options, bids are as follows: A bids $30 for 3,000; B bids $33 for 2,500; C bids $29 for 5,000; D bids $40 for 1,000; E bids $22 for 8,000; and F bids $35 for 6,000. What is the result of the auction? Who buys how many at what price?

16.12. A company has granted 500,000 options to its executives. The stock price and strike price are both $40. The options last for 12 years and vest after 4 years. The company decides to value the options using an expected life of 5 years and a volatility of 30% per annum. The company pays no dividends and the risk-free rate is 4%. What will the company report as an expense for the options on its income statement?

16.13. A company's CFO says: "The accounting treatment of stock options is crazy. We granted 10,000,000 at-the-money stock options to our employees last year when the stock price was $30. We estimated the value of each option on the grant date to be $5. At our year-end the stock price had fallen to $4, but we were still stuck with a $50 million charge to the P&L." Discuss.

Further Questions

16.14. What is the (risk-neutral) expected life for the employee stock option in Example 16.2? What is the value of the option obtained by using this expected life in Black–Scholes–Merton?

16.15. A company has granted 2,000,000 options to its employees. The stock price and strike price are both $60. The options last for 8 years and vest after 2 years. The company decides to value the options using an expected life of 6 years and a volatility of 22% per annum. Dividends on the stock are $1 per year, payable halfway through each year, and the risk-free rate is 5%. What will the company report as an expense for the options on its income statement?

16.16. A company has granted 1,000,000 options to its employees. The stock price and strike price are both \$20. The options last 10 years and vest after 3 years. The stock price volatility is 30%, the risk-free rate is 5%, and the company pays no dividends. Use a four-step tree to value the options. Assume that there is a probability of 4% that an employee leaves the company at the end of each of the time steps on your tree. Assume also that the probability of voluntary early exercise at a node, conditional on no prior exercise, when (a) the option has vested and (b) the option is in the money, is

$$1 - \exp[-a(S/K - 1)/T]$$

where S is the stock price, K is the strike price, T is the time to maturity, and $a = 2$.

16.17. (a) Hedge funds earn a management fee plus an incentive fee that is a percentage of the profits, if any, that they generate (see Business Snapshot 1.3). How is a fund manager motivated to behave with this type of compensation package?

   (b) "Granting options to an executive gives the executive the same type of compensation package as a hedge fund manager and motivates him or her to behave in the same way as a hedge fund manager." Discuss this statement.

CHAPTER 17

Options on Stock Indices and Currencies

Options on stock indices and currencies were introduced in Chapter 10. This chapter discusses them in more detail. It explains how they work and reviews some of the ways they can be used. In the second half of the chapter, the valuation results in Chapter 15 are extended to cover European options on a stock paying a known dividend yield. It is then argued that both stock indices and currencies are analogous to stocks paying dividend yields. This enables the results for options on a stock paying a dividend yield to be applied to these types of options as well.

17.1 OPTIONS ON STOCK INDICES

Several exchanges trade options on stock indices. Some of the indices track the movement of the market as a whole. Others are based on the performance of a particular sector (e.g., computer technology, oil and gas, transportation, or telecoms). Among the index options traded on the Chicago Board Options Exchange (CBOE) are American and European options on the S&P 100 (OEX and XEO), European options on the S&P 500 (SPX), European options on the Dow Jones Industrial Average (DJX), and European options on the Nasdaq 100 (NDX). In Chapter 10, we explained that the CBOE trades LEAPS and flex options on individual stocks. It also offers these option products on indices.

One index option contract is usually on 100 times the index. (Note that the Dow Jones index used for index options is 0.01 times the usually quoted Dow Jones index.) Index options are settled in cash. This means that, on exercise of the option, the holder of a call option contract receives $(S - K) \times 100$ in cash and the writer of the option pays this amount in cash, where S is the value of the index at the close of trading on the day of the exercise and K is the strike price. Similarly, the holder of a put option contract receives $(K - S) \times 100$ in cash and the writer of the option pays this amount in cash.

Portfolio Insurance

Portfolio managers can use options on a well-diversified index to limit their downside risk. Suppose that the value of the index today is S_0. Consider a manager in charge of a well-diversified portfolio whose beta is 1.0. A beta of 1.0 implies that the returns from the portfolio mirror those from the index. Assuming the dividend yield from the portfolio is the same as the dividend yield from the index, the percentage changes in the value of the portfolio can be expected to be approximately the same as the percentage changes in the value of the index. Since each contract is on 100 times the index, it follows that the value of the portfolio is protected against the possibility of the index falling below K if, for each $100S_0$ dollars in the portfolio, the manager buys one put option contract with strike price K. Suppose that the manager's portfolio is worth $500,000 and the value of the index is currently 1,000. The portfolio is worth 500 times the index. The manager can obtain insurance against the value of the portfolio dropping below $450,000 in the next three months by buying five three-month put option contracts on the index with a strike price of 900.

To illustrate how the insurance works, consider the situation where the index drops to 880 in three months. The portfolio will be worth about $440,000. The payoff from the options will be $5 \times (900 - 880) \times 100 = \$10,000$, bringing the total value of the portfolio up to the insured value of $450,000.

When the Portfolio's Beta Is Not 1.0

If the portfolio's beta (β) is not 1.0, β put options must be purchased for each $100S_0$ dollars in the portfolio, where S_0 is the current value of the index. Suppose that the $500,000 portfolio just considered has a beta of 2.0 instead of 1.0. We continue to assume that the index is 1,000. The number of put options required is

$$2.0 \times \frac{500,000}{1,000 \times 100} = 10$$

rather than 5 as before.

To calculate the appropriate strike price, the capital asset pricing model can be used (see the appendix to Chapter 3). Suppose that the risk free rate is 12%, the dividend yield on both the index and the portfolio is 4%, and protection is required against the value of the portfolio dropping below $450,000 in the next three months. Under the

---

Table 17.1 Calculation of expected value of portfolio when the index is 1,040 in three months and $\beta = 2.0$.

Value of index in three months:	1,040
Return from change in index:	40/1,000, or 4% per three months
Dividends from index:	$0.25 \times 4 = 1\%$ per three months
Total return from index:	$4 + 1 = 5\%$ per three months
Risk-free interest rate:	$0.25 \times 12 = 3\%$ per three months
Excess return from index over risk-free interest rate:	$5 - 3 = 2\%$ per three months
Expected excess return from portfolio over risk-free interest rate:	$2 \times 2 = 4\%$ per three months
Expected return from portfolio:	$3 + 4 = 7\%$ per three months
Dividends from portfolio:	$0.25 \times 4 = 1\%$ per three months
Expected increase in value of portfolio:	$7 - 1 = 6\%$ per three months
Expected value of portfolio:	$\$500,000 \times 1.06 = \$530,000$

Table 17.2   Relationship between value of index
and value of portfolio for $\beta = 2.0$.

Value of index in three months	Value of portfolio in three months ($)
1,080	570,000
1,040	530,000
1,000	490,000
960	450,000
920	410,000
880	370,000

capital asset pricing model, the expected excess return of a portfolio over the risk-free rate is assumed to equal beta times the excess return of the index portfolio over the risk-free rate. The model enables the expected value of the portfolio to be calculated for different values of the index at the end of three months. Table 17.1 shows the calculations for the case where the index is 1,040. In this case, the expected value of the portfolio at the end of the three months is $530,000. Similar calculations can be carried out for other values of the index at the end of the three months. The results are shown in Table 17.2. The strike price for the options that are purchased should be the index level corresponding to the protection level required on the portfolio. In this case, the protection level is $450,000 and so the correct strike price for the 10 put option contracts that are purchased is 960.[1]

To illustrate how the insurance works, consider what happens if the value of the index falls to 880. As shown in Table 17.2, the value of the portfolio is then about $370,000. The put options pay off $(960 - 880) \times 10 \times 100 = \$80,000$, and this is exactly what is necessary to move the total value of the portfolio manager's position up from $370,000 to the required level of $450,000.

The examples in this section show that there are two reasons why the cost of hedging increases as the beta of a portfolio increases. More put options are required and they have a higher strike price.

17.2 CURRENCY OPTIONS

Currency options are primarily traded in the over-the-counter market. The advantage of this market is that large trades are possible, with strike prices, expiration dates, and other features tailored to meet the needs of corporate treasurers. Although currency options do trade on NASDAQ OMX in the United States, the exchange-traded market for these options is much smaller than the over-the-counter market.

An example of a European call option is a contract that gives the holder the right to buy one million euros with U.S. dollars at an exchange rate of 1.1000 U.S. dollars per euro. If the actual exchange rate at the maturity of the option is 1.1500, the payoff is

---

[1] Approximately 1% of $500,000, or $5,000, will be earned in dividends over the next three months. If we want the insured level of $450,000 to include dividends, we can choose a strike price corresponding to $445,000 rather than $450,000. This is 955.

$1,000,000 \times (1.1500 - 1.1000) = \$50,000$. Similarly, an example of a European put option is a contract that gives the holder the right to sell ten million Australian dollars for U.S. dollars at an exchange rate of 0.7000 U.S. dollars per Australian dollar. If the actual exchange rate at the maturity of the option is 0.6700, the payoff is $10,000,000 \times (0.7000 - 0.6700) = \$300,000$.

For a corporation wishing to hedge a foreign exchange exposure, foreign currency options are an alternative to forward contracts. A U.S. company due to receive sterling at a known time in the future can hedge its risk by buying put options on sterling that mature at that time. The hedging strategy guarantees that the exchange rate applicable to the sterling will not be less than the strike price, while allowing the company to benefit from any favorable exchange-rate movements. Similarly, a U.S. company due to pay sterling at a known time in the future can hedge by buying calls on sterling that mature at that time. This hedging strategy guarantees that the cost of the sterling will not be greater than a certain amount while allowing the company to benefit from favorable exchange-rate movements. Whereas a forward contract locks in the exchange rate for a future transaction, an option provides a type of insurance. This is not free. It costs nothing to enter into a forward transaction, but options require a premium to be paid up front.

Range Forwards

A *range forward contract* is a variation on a standard forward contract for hedging foreign exchange risk. Consider a U.S. company that knows it will receive one million pounds sterling in three months. Suppose that the three-month forward exchange rate is 1.3200 dollars per pound. The company could lock in this exchange rate for the dollars it receives by entering into a short forward contract to sell one million pounds sterling in three months. This would ensure that the amount received for the one million pounds is $1,320,000.

An alternative is to buy a European put option with a strike price of K_1 and sell a European call option with a strike price K_2, where $K_1 < 1.3200 < K_2$. This is known as a short position in a range forward contract. The payoff is shown in Figure 17.1a. Both options are on one million pounds. If the exchange rate in three months proves to be less than K_1, the put option is exercised and as a result the company is able to sell the

Figure 17.1 Payoffs from (a) short and (b) long position in a range forward contract.

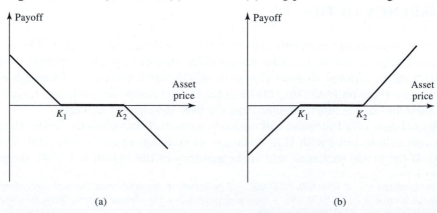

(a) (b)

Figure 17.2 Exchange rate realized when a range forward contract is used to hedge either a future foreign currency inflow or a future foreign currency outflow.

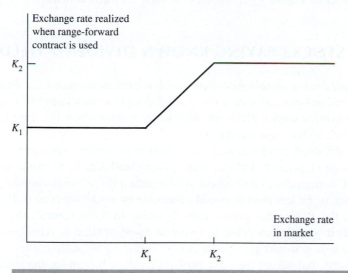

one million pounds at an exchange rate of K_1. If the exchange rate is between K_1 and K_2, neither option is exercised and the company gets the current exchange rate for the one million pounds. If the exchange rate is greater than K_2, the call option is exercised against the company and the one million pounds is sold at an exchange rate of K_2. The exchange rate realized for the one million pounds is shown in Figure 17.2.

If the company knew it was due to pay rather than receive one million pounds in three months, it could sell a European put option with strike price K_1 and buy a European call option with strike price K_2. This is a long position in a range forward contract and the payoff is shown in Figure 17.1b. If the exchange rate in three months proves to be less than K_1, the put option is exercised against the company and as a result the company buys the one million pounds it needs at an exchange rate of K_1. If the exchange rate is between K_1 and K_2, neither option is exercised and the company buys the one million pounds at the current exchange rate. If the exchange rate is greater than K_2, the call option is exercised and the company is able to buy the one million pounds at an exchange rate of K_2. The exchange rate paid for the one million pounds is the same as that received for the one million pounds in the earlier example and is shown in Figure 17.2.

In practice, a range forward contract is set up so that the price of the put option equals the price of the call option. This means that it costs nothing to set up the range forward contract, just as it costs nothing to set up a regular forward contract. Suppose that the U.S. and British interest rates are both 2%, so that the spot exchange rate is 1.3200 (the same as the forward exchange rate). Suppose further that the exchange rate volatility is 14%. We can use DerivaGem to show that a European put with strike price 1.3000 to sell one pound has the same price as a European call option with a strike price of 1.3414 to buy one pound. (Both are worth 0.0273.) Setting $K_1 = 1.3000$ and $K_2 = 1.3414$ therefore leads to a contract with zero cost in our example.

As the strike prices of the call and put options in a range forward contract are moved together, the range forward contract becomes a regular forward contract. The (short) range forward contract in Figure 17.1a becomes a short forward contract and the (long) range forward contract in Figure 17.1b becomes a long forward contract.

17.3 OPTIONS ON STOCKS PAYING KNOWN DIVIDEND YIELDS

In this section we produce a simple rule that enables valuation results for European options on a non-dividend-paying stock to be extended so that they apply to European options on a stock paying a known dividend yield. Later we show how this enables us to value options on stock indices and currencies.

Suppose that the dividend yield per year (measured with continuous compounding) is q. Dividends cause stock prices to reduce on the ex-dividend date by the amount of the dividend payment. The payment of a dividend yield at rate q therefore causes the growth rate in the stock price to be less than it would otherwise be by an amount q. If, with a dividend yield of q, the stock price grows from S_0 today to S_T at time T, then in the absence of dividends it would grow from S_0 today to $S_T e^{qT}$ at time T. Alternatively, in the absence of dividends it would grow from $S_0 e^{-qT}$ today to S_T at time T.

This argument shows that we get the same probability distribution for the stock price at time T in each of the following two cases:

1. The stock starts at price S_0 and provides a dividend yield at rate q.
2. The stock starts at price $S_0 e^{-qT}$ and pays no dividends.

This leads to a simple rule. When valuing a European option lasting for time T on a stock paying a known dividend yield at rate q, we reduce the current stock price from S_0 to $S_0 e^{-qT}$ and then value the option as though the stock pays no dividends.[2]

Lower Bounds for Option Prices

As a first application of this rule, consider the problem of determining bounds for the price of a European option on a stock paying a dividend yield at rate q. Substituting $S_0 e^{-qT}$ for S_0 in equation (11.4), we see that a lower bound for the European call option price, c, is given by

$$c \geqslant \max\left(S_0 e^{-qT} - Ke^{-rT}, 0\right) \tag{17.1}$$

We can also prove this directly by considering the following two portfolios:

Portfolio A: one European call option plus an amount of cash equal to Ke^{-rT}

Portfolio B: e^{-qT} shares with dividends being reinvested in additional shares.

To obtain a lower bound for a European put option, we can similarly replace S_0 by $S_0 e^{-qT}$ in equation (11.5) to get

$$p \geqslant \max\left(Ke^{-rT} - S_0 e^{-qT}, 0\right) \tag{17.2}$$

---

[2] This rule is analogous to the one developed in Section 15.12 for valuing a European option on a stock paying known cash dividends. (In that case we concluded that it is correct to reduce the stock price by the present value of the dividends; in this case we discount the stock price at the dividend yield rate.)

This result can also be proved directly by considering the following portfolios:

> *Portfolio C*: one European put option plus e^{-qT} shares with dividends on the shares being reinvested in additional shares
>
> *Portfolio D*: an amount of cash equal to Ke^{-rT}.

Put–Call Parity

Replacing S_0 by S_0e^{-qT} in equation (11.6) we obtain put–call parity for an option on a stock paying a dividend yield at rate q:

$$c + Ke^{-rT} = p + S_0e^{-qT} \tag{17.3}$$

This result can also be proved directly by considering the following two portfolios:

> *Portfolio A*: one European call option plus an amount of cash equal to Ke^{-rT}
>
> *Portfolio C*: one European put option plus e^{-qT} shares with dividends on the shares being reinvested in additional shares.

Both portfolios are both worth $\max(S_T, K)$ at time T. They must therefore be worth the same today, and the put–call parity result in equation (17.3) follows. For American options, the put–call parity relationship is (see Problem 17.12)

$$S_0e^{-qT} - K \leqslant C - P \leqslant S_0 - Ke^{-rT}$$

Pricing Formulas

By replacing S_0 by S_0e^{-qT} in the Black–Scholes–Merton formulas, equations (15.20) and (15.21), we obtain the price, c, of a European call and the price, p, of a European put on a stock paying a dividend yield at rate q as

$$c = S_0e^{-qT}N(d_1) - Ke^{-rT}N(d_2) \tag{17.4}$$
$$p = Ke^{-rT}N(-d_2) - S_0e^{-qT}N(-d_1) \tag{17.5}$$

Since

$$\ln\frac{S_0e^{-qT}}{K} = \ln\frac{S_0}{K} - qT$$

it follows that d_1 and d_2 are given by

$$d_1 = \frac{\ln(S_0/K) + (r - q + \sigma^2/2)T}{\sigma\sqrt{T}}$$
$$d_2 = \frac{\ln(S_0/K) + (r - q - \sigma^2/2)T}{\sigma\sqrt{T}} = d_1 - \sigma\sqrt{T}$$

These results were first derived by Merton.[3] As discussed in Chapter 15, the word *dividend* should, for the purposes of option valuation, be defined as the reduction in the stock price on the ex-dividend date arising from any dividends declared. If the dividend yield rate is known but not constant during the life of the option, equations (17.4)

---

[3] See R.C. Merton, "Theory of Rational Option Pricing," *Bell Journal of Economics and Management Science*, 4 (Spring 1973): 141–83.

and (17.5) are still true, with q equal to the average annualized dividend yield during the option's life.

Differential Equation and Risk-Neutral Valuation

To prove the results in equations (17.4) and (17.5) more formally, we can either solve the differential equation that the option price must satisfy or use risk-neutral valuation.

When we include a dividend yield of q in the analysis in Section 15.6, the differential equation (15.16) becomes[4]

$$\frac{\partial f}{\partial t} + (r - q)S\frac{\partial f}{\partial S} + \frac{1}{2}\sigma^2 S^2 \frac{\partial^2 f}{\partial S^2} = rf \qquad (17.6)$$

Like equation (15.16), this does not involve any variable affected by risk preferences. Therefore the risk-neutral valuation procedure described in Section 15.7 can be used.

In a risk-neutral world, the total return from the stock must be r. The dividends provide a return of q. The expected growth rate in the stock price must therefore be $r - q$. It follows that the risk-neutral process for the stock price is

$$dS = (r - q)S\,dt + \sigma S\,dz \qquad (17.7)$$

To value a derivative dependent on a stock that provides a dividend yield equal to q, we set the expected growth rate of the stock equal to $r - q$ and discount the expected payoff at rate r. When the expected growth rate in the stock price is $r - q$, the expected stock price at time T is $S_0 e^{(r-q)T}$. A similar analysis to that in the appendix to Chapter 15 gives the expected payoff for a call option in a risk-neutral world as

$$e^{(r-q)T} S_0 N(d_1) - KN(d_2)$$

where d_1 and d_2 are defined as above. Discounting at rate r for time T leads to equation (17.4).

17.4 VALUATION OF EUROPEAN STOCK INDEX OPTIONS

In valuing index futures in Chapter 5, we assumed that the index could be treated as an asset paying a known yield. In valuing index options, we make similar assumptions. This means that equations (17.1) and (17.2) provide a lower bound for European index options; equation (17.3) is the put–call parity result for European index options; equations (17.4) and (17.5) can be used to value European options on an index; and the binomial tree approach can be used for American options. In all cases, S_0 is equal to the current value of the index, σ is equal to the volatility of the index, and q is equal to the average annualized dividend yield on the index during the life of the option expressed with continuous compounding.

Example 17.1

Consider a European call option on an index that is two months from maturity. The current value of the index is 930, the exercise price is 900, the risk-free interest rate is

---

[4] See Technical Note 6 at www-2.rotman.utoronto.ca/~hull/TechnicalNotes for a proof of this.

8% per annum, and the volatility of the index is 20% per annum. Dividend yields of 0.2% and 0.3% (expressed with continuous compounding) are expected in the first month and the second month, respectively. In this case $S_0 = 930$, $K = 900$, $r = 0.08$, $\sigma = 0.2$, and $T = 2/12$. The total dividend yield during the option's life is $0.2\% + 0.3\% = 0.5\%$. This corresponds to 3% per annum. Hence, $q = 0.03$ and

$$d_1 = \frac{\ln(930/900) + (0.08 - 0.03 + 0.2^2/2) \times 2/12}{0.2\sqrt{2/12}} = 0.5444$$

$$d_2 = \frac{\ln(930/900) + (0.08 - 0.03 - 0.2^2/2) \times 2/12}{0.2\sqrt{2/12}} = 0.4628$$

$$N(d_1) = 0.7069, \qquad N(d_2) = 0.6782$$

so that the call price, c, is given by equation (17.4) as

$$c = 930 \times 0.7069 e^{-0.03 \times 2/12} - 900 \times 0.6782 e^{-0.08 \times 2/12} = 51.83$$

One contract, if on 100 times the index, would cost $5,183.

The calculation of q should include only dividends for which the ex-dividend dates occur during the life of the option. In the United States ex-dividend dates tend to occur during the first week of February, May, August, and November. At any given time the correct value of q is therefore likely to depend on the life of the option. This is even more true for indices in other countries. In Japan, for example, all companies tend to use the same ex-dividend dates.

If the absolute amount of the dividend that will be paid on the stocks underlying the index (rather than the dividend yield) is assumed to be known, the basic Black–Scholes–Merton formulas can be used with the initial stock price being reduced by the present value of the dividends. This is the approach recommended in Chapter 15 for a stock paying known dividends. However, it may be difficult to implement for a broadly based stock index because it requires a knowledge of the dividends expected on every stock underlying the index.

It is sometimes argued that, in the long run, the return from investing a certain amount of money in a well-diversified stock portfolio is almost certain to beat the return from investing the same amount of money in a bond portfolio. If this were so, a long-dated put option allowing the stock portfolio to be sold for the value of the bond portfolio should not cost very much. In fact, as indicated by Business Snapshot 17.1, it is quite expensive.

Forward Prices

Define F_0 as the forward price of the index for a contract with maturity T. As shown by equation (5.3), $F_0 = S_0 e^{(r-q)T}$. This means that the equations for the European call price c and the European put price p in equations (17.4) and (17.5) can be written

$$c = F_0 e^{-rT} N(d_1) - K e^{-rT} N(d_2) \tag{17.8}$$

$$p = K e^{-rT} N(-d_2) - F_0 e^{-rT} N(-d_1) \tag{17.9}$$

where

$$d_1 = \frac{\ln(F_0/K) + \sigma^2 T/2}{\sigma\sqrt{T}} \quad \text{and} \quad d_2 = \frac{\ln(F_0/K) - \sigma^2 T/2}{\sigma\sqrt{T}}$$

Business Snapshot 17.1 Can We Guarantee that Stocks Will Beat Bonds in the Long Run?

It is often said that if you are a long-term investor you should buy stocks rather than bonds. Consider a U.S. fund manager who is trying to persuade investors to buy, as a long-term investment, an equity fund that is expected to mirror the S&P 500. The manager might be tempted to offer purchasers of the fund a guarantee that their return will be at least as good as the return on risk-free bonds over the next 10 years. Historically stocks have outperformed bonds in the United States over almost any 10-year period. It appears that the fund manager would not be giving much away.

In fact, this type of guarantee is surprisingly expensive. Suppose that an equity index is 1,000 today, the dividend yield on the index is 1% per annum, the volatility of the index is 15% per annum, and the 10-year risk-free rate is 5% per annum. To outperform bonds, the stocks underlying the index must earn more than 5% per annum. The dividend yield will provide 1% per annum. The capital gains on the stocks must therefore provide 4% per annum. This means that we require the index level to be at least $1,000e^{0.04 \times 10} = 1,492$ in 10 years.

A guarantee that the return on $1,000 invested in the index will be greater than the return on $1,000 invested in bonds over the next 10 years is therefore equivalent to the right to sell the index for 1,492 in 10 years. This is a European put option on the index and can be valued from equation (17.5) with $S_0 = 1,000$, $K = 1,492$, $r = 5\%$, $\sigma = 15\%$, $T = 10$, and $q = 1\%$. The value of the put option is 169.7. This shows that the guarantee contemplated by the fund manager is worth about 17% of the fund—hardly something that should be given away!

The put–call parity relationship in equation (17.3) can be written

$$c + Ke^{-rT} = p + F_0 e^{-rT}$$

or

$$F_0 = K + (c - p)e^{rT} \tag{17.10}$$

If, as is not uncommon in the exchange-traded markets, pairs of puts and calls with the same strike price are traded actively for a particular maturity date, this equation can be used to estimate the forward price of the index for that maturity date. Once the forward prices of the index for a number of different maturity dates have been obtained, the term structure of forward prices can be estimated, and other options can be valued using equations (17.8) and (17.9). The advantage of this approach is that the dividend yield on the index does not have to be estimated explicitly.

Implied Dividend Yields

If estimates of the dividend yield are required (e.g., because an American option is being valued), European calls and puts with the same strike price and time to maturity can be used. From equation (17.3),

$$q = -\frac{1}{T} \ln \frac{c - p + Ke^{-rT}}{S_0}$$

For a particular strike price and time to maturity, the estimates of q calculated from this equation are liable to be unreliable. But when the results from many matched pairs of calls and puts are combined, a clearer picture of the term structure of dividend yields being assumed by the market emerges.

17.5 VALUATION OF EUROPEAN CURRENCY OPTIONS

To value currency options, we define S_0 as the spot exchange rate. To be precise, S_0 is the value of one unit of the foreign currency in U.S. dollars. As explained in Section 5.10, a foreign currency is analogous to a stock paying a known dividend yield. The owner of foreign currency receives a yield equal to the risk-free interest rate, r_f, in the foreign currency. Equations (17.1) and (17.2), with q replaced by r_f, provide bounds for the European call price, c, and the European put price, p:

$$c \geqslant \max\left(S_0 e^{-r_f T} - K e^{-rT}, 0\right)$$
$$p \geqslant \max\left(K e^{-rT} - S_0 e^{-r_f T}, 0\right)$$

Equation (17.3), with q replaced by r_f, provides the put–call parity result for European currency options:

$$c + K e^{-rT} = p + S_0 e^{-r_f T}$$

Finally, equations (17.4) and (17.5) provide the pricing formulas for European currency options when q is replaced by r_f:

$$c = S_0 e^{-r_f T} N(d_1) - K e^{-rT} N(d_2) \qquad (17.11)$$
$$p = K e^{-rT} N(-d_2) - S_0 e^{-r_f T} N(-d_1) \qquad (17.12)$$

where

$$d_1 = \frac{\ln(S_0/K) + (r - r_f + \sigma^2/2)T}{\sigma\sqrt{T}}$$
$$d_2 = \frac{\ln(S_0/K) + (r - r_f - \sigma^2/2)T}{\sigma\sqrt{T}} = d_1 - \sigma\sqrt{T}$$

Both the domestic interest rate, r, and the foreign interest rate, r_f, are the rates for a maturity T.

Example 17.2

Consider a 4-month European call option on the British pound. Suppose that the current exchange rate is 1.6000, the exercise price is 1.6000, the risk-free interest rate in the United States is 8% per annum, the risk-free interest rate in Britain is 11% per annum, and the option price is 4.3 cents. In this case, $S_0 = 1.6$, $K = 1.6$, $r = 0.08$, $r_f = 0.11$, $T = 0.3333$, and $c = 0.043$. The implied volatility can be calculated by trial and error. A volatility of 20% gives an option price of 0.0639; a volatility of 10% gives an option price of 0.0285; and so on. The implied volatility is 14.1%.

Put and call options on a currency are symmetrical in that a put option to sell one unit of currency A for currency B at strike price K is the same as a call option to buy K units of B with currency A at strike price $1/K$ (see Problem 17.8).

Using Forward Exchange Rates

Because banks and other financial institutions trade forward contracts on foreign exchange rates actively, forward exchange rates are often used for valuing options. From equation (5.9), the forward exchange rate, F_0, for a maturity T is given by

$$F_0 = S_0 e^{(r-r_f)T}$$

This relationship allows equations (17.11) and (17.12) to be simplified to

$$c = e^{-rT}[F_0 N(d_1) - K N(d_2)] \tag{17.13}$$

$$p = e^{-rT}[K N(-d_2) - F_0 N(-d_1)] \tag{17.14}$$

where

$$d_1 = \frac{\ln(F_0/K) + \sigma^2 T/2}{\sigma\sqrt{T}}$$

$$d_2 = \frac{\ln(F_0/K) - \sigma^2 T/2}{\sigma\sqrt{T}} = d_1 - \sigma\sqrt{T}$$

Equations (17.13) and (17.14) are the same as equations (17.8) and (17.9). As we shall see in Chapter 18, a European option on the spot price of any asset can be valued in terms of the price of a forward or futures contract on the asset using equations (17.13) and (17.14). The maturity of the forward or futures contract must be the same as the maturity of the European option.

17.6 AMERICAN OPTIONS

As described in Chapter 13, binomial trees can be used to value American options on indices and currencies. As in the case of American options on a non-dividend-paying stock, the parameter determining the size of up movements, u, is set equal to $e^{\sigma\sqrt{\Delta t}}$, where σ is the volatility and Δt is the length of time steps. The parameter determining the size of down movements, d, is set equal to $1/u$, or $e^{-\sigma\sqrt{\Delta t}}$. For a non-dividend-paying stock, the probability of an up movement is

$$p = \frac{a - d}{u - d}$$

where $a = e^{r\Delta t}$. For options on indices and currencies, the formula for p is the same, but a is defined differently. In the case of options on an index,

$$a = e^{(r-q)\Delta t} \tag{17.15}$$

where q is the dividend yield on the index. In the case of options on a currency,

$$a = e^{(r-r_f)\Delta t} \tag{17.16}$$

where r_f is the foreign risk-free rate. Example 13.1 in Section 13.11 shows how a two-step tree can be constructed to value an option on an index. Example 13.2 shows how a three-step tree can be constructed to value an option on a currency. Further examples of the use of binomial trees to value options on indices and currencies are given in Chapter 21.

In some circumstances, it is optimal to exercise American currency and index options prior to maturity. Thus, American currency and index options are worth more than their European counterparts. In general, call options on high-interest currencies and put options on low-interest currencies are the most likely to be exercised prior to maturity. The reason is that a high-interest currency is expected to depreciate and a low-interest currency is expected to appreciate. Similarly, call options on indices with high-dividend yields and put options on indices with low-dividend yields are most likely to be exercised early.

SUMMARY

The index options trading on exchanges are settled in cash. On exercise of an index call option contract, the holder typically receives 100 times the amount by which the index exceeds the strike price. Similarly, on exercise of an index put option contract, the holder receives 100 times the amount by which the strike price exceeds the index. Index options can be used for portfolio insurance. If the value of the portfolio mirrors the index, it is appropriate to buy one put option contract for each $100S_0$ dollars in the portfolio, where S_0 is the value of the index. If the portfolio does not mirror the index, β put option contracts should be purchased for each $100S_0$ dollars in the portfolio, where β is the beta of the portfolio from the capital asset pricing model. The strike price of the put options purchased should reflect the level of insurance required.

Most currency options are traded in the over-the-counter market. They can be used by corporate treasurers to hedge a foreign exchange exposure. For example, a U.S. corporate treasurer who knows that the company will be receiving sterling at a certain time in the future can hedge by buying put options that mature at that time. Similarly, a U.S. corporate treasurer who knows that the company will be paying sterling at a certain time in the future can hedge by buying call options that mature at that time. Currency options can also be used to create a range forward contract. This is a zero-cost contract that can be used to provide downside protection while giving up some of the upside for a company with a known foreign exchange exposure.

The Black–Scholes–Merton formula for valuing European options on a non-dividend-paying stock can be extended to cover European options on a stock paying a known dividend yield. The extension can be used to value European options on stock indices and currencies because:

1. A stock index is analogous to a stock paying a dividend yield. The dividend yield is the dividend yield on the stocks that make up the index.

2. A foreign currency is analogous to a stock paying a dividend yield. The foreign risk-free interest rate plays the role of the dividend yield.

Binomial trees can be used to value American options on stock indices and currencies.

FURTHER READING

Biger, N., and J.C. Hull. "The Valuation of Currency Options," *Financial Management*, 12 (Spring 1983): 24–28.

Bodie, Z. "On the Risk of Stocks in the Long Run," *Financial Analysts Journal*, 51, 3 (1995): 18–22.

Garman, M.B., and S.W. Kohlhagen. "Foreign Currency Option Values," *Journal of International Money and Finance*, 2 (December 1983): 231–37.

Giddy, I.H., and G. Dufey. "Uses and Abuses of Currency Options," *Journal of Applied Corporate Finance*, 8, 3 (1995): 49–57.

Grabbe, J.O. "The Pricing of Call and Put Options on Foreign Exchange," *Journal of International Money and Finance*, 2 (December 1983): 239–53.

Merton, R.C. "Theory of Rational Option Pricing," *Bell Journal of Economics and Management Science*, 4 (Spring 1973): 141–83.

Practice Questions (Answers in Solutions Manual)

17.1. A portfolio is currently worth $10 million and has a beta of 1.0. An index is currently standing at 800. Explain how a put option on the index with a strike price of 700 can be used to provide portfolio insurance.

17.2. "Once we know how to value options on a stock paying a dividend yield, we know how to value options on stock indices and currencies." Explain this statement.

17.3. A stock index is currently 300, the dividend yield on the index is 3% per annum, and the risk-free interest rate is 8% per annum. What is a lower bound for the price of a six-month European call option on the index when the strike price is 290?

17.4. A currency is currently worth $0.80 and has a volatility of 12%. The domestic and foreign risk-free interest rates are 6% and 8%, respectively. Use a two-step binomial tree to value (a) a European four-month call option with a strike price of 0.79 and (b) an American four-month call option with the same strike price.

17.5. Explain how corporations can use range forward contracts to hedge their foreign exchange risk when they are due to receive a certain amount of a foreign currency in the future.

17.6. Calculate the value of a three-month at-the-money European call option on a stock index when the index is at 250, the risk-free interest rate is 10% per annum, the volatility of the index is 18% per annum, and the dividend yield on the index is 3% per annum.

17.7. Calculate the value of an eight-month European put option on a currency with a strike price of 0.50. The current exchange rate is 0.52, the volatility of the exchange rate is 12%, the domestic risk-free interest rate is 4% per annum, and the foreign risk-free interest rate is 8% per annum.

17.8. Show that the formula in equation (17.12) for a put option to sell one unit of currency A for currency B at strike price K gives the same value as equation (17.11) for a call option to buy K units of currency B for currency A at strike price $1/K$.

17.9. A foreign currency is currently worth $1.50. The domestic and foreign risk-free interest rates are 5% and 9%, respectively. Calculate a lower bound for the value of a six-month call option on the currency with a strike price of $1.40 if it is (a) European and (b) American.

17.10. Consider a stock index currently standing at 250. The dividend yield on the index is 4% per annum, and the risk-free rate is 6% per annum. A three-month European call option on the index with a strike price of 245 is currently worth $10. What is the value of a three-month put option on the index with a strike price of 245?

17.11. An index currently stands at 696 and has a volatility of 30% per annum. The risk-free rate of interest is 7% per annum and the index provides a dividend yield of 4% per annum. Calculate the value of a three-month European put with an exercise price of 700.

17.12. Show that, if C is the price of an American call with exercise price K and maturity T on a stock paying a dividend yield of q, and P is the price of an American put on the same stock with the same strike price and exercise date, then

$$S_0 e^{-qT} - K < C - P < S_0 - Ke^{-rT},$$

where S_0 is the stock price, r is the risk-free rate, and $r > 0$. (*Hint*: To obtain the first half of the inequality, consider possible values of:

Portfolio A: a European call option plus an amount K invested at the risk-free rate
Portfolio B: an American put option plus e^{-qT} of stock with dividends being re-invested in the stock.

To obtain the second half of the inequality, consider possible values of:

Portfolio C: an American call option plus an amount Ke^{-rT} invested at the risk-free rate
Portfolio D: a European put option plus one stock with dividends being reinvested in the stock.)

17.13. Show that a European call option on a currency has the same price as the corresponding European put option on the currency when the forward price equals the strike price.

17.14. Would you expect the volatility of a stock index to be greater or less than the volatility of a typical stock? Explain your answer.

17.15. Does the cost of portfolio insurance increase or decrease as the beta of a portfolio increases? Explain your answer.

17.16. Suppose that a portfolio is worth $60 million and a stock index stands at 1,200. If the value of the portfolio mirrors the value of the index, what options should be purchased to provide protection against the value of the portfolio falling below $54 million in one year's time?

17.17. Consider again the situation in Problem 17.16. Suppose that the portfolio has a beta of 2.0, the risk-free interest rate is 5% per annum, and the dividend yield on both the portfolio and the index is 3% per annum. What options should be purchased to provide protection against the value of the portfolio falling below $54 million in one year's time?

17.18. An index currently stands at 1,500. European call and put options with a strike price of 1,400 and time to maturity of six months have market prices of 154.00 and 34.25, respectively. The six-month risk-free rate is 5%. What is the implied dividend yield?

17.19. A total return index tracks the return, including dividends, on a certain portfolio. Explain how you would value (a) forward contracts and (b) European options on the index.

17.20. What is the put–call parity relationship for European currency options?

17.21. Prove the results in equations (17.1), (17.2), and (17.3) using the portfolios indicated.

17.22. Can an option on the yen/euro exchange rate be created from two options, one on the dollar/euro exchange rate, and the other on the dollar/yen exchange rate? Explain your answer.

Further Questions

17.23. The Dow Jones Industrial Average on July 20, 2016, was 18,580 and the price of a September 185 (European) call option on the index was $3.35. Use the DerivaGem software to calculate the implied volatility of this option. Assume the risk-free rate was 0.7% and the dividend yield was 2.75%. The option expires on September 16, 2016. Estimate the price of a September 185 put option. What is the volatility implied by the price you estimate for this option? (Note that options are on the Dow Jones index divided by 100.)

17.24. A stock index currently stands at 300 and has a volatility of 20%. The risk-free interest rate is 8% and the dividend yield on the index is 3%. Use a three-step binomial tree to value a six-month put option on the index with a strike price of 300 if it is (a) European and (b) American?

17.25. Suppose that the spot price of the Canadian dollar is U.S. $0.95 and that the Canadian dollar/U.S. dollar exchange rate has a volatility of 8% per annum. The risk-free rates of interest in Canada and the United States are 4% and 5% per annum, respectively. Calculate the value of a European call option to buy one Canadian dollar for U.S. $0.95 in nine months. Use put–call parity to calculate the price of a European put option to sell one Canadian dollar for U.S. $0.95 in nine months. What is the price of a call option to buy U.S. $0.95 with one Canadian dollar in nine months?

17.26. The spot price of an index is 1,000 and the risk-free rate is 4%. The prices of 3-month European call and put options when the strike price is 950 are 78 and 26. Estimate (a) the dividend yield and (b) the implied volatility.

17.27. Assume that the price of currency A expressed in terms of the price of currency B follows the process $dS = (r_B - r_A)S\,dt + \sigma S\,dz$, where r_A is the risk-free interest rate in currency A and r_B is the risk-free interest rate in currency B. What is the process followed by the price of currency B expressed in terms of currency A?

17.28. Suppose the USD/euro exchange rate is 1.3000. The exchange rate volatility is 15%. A U.S. company will receive 1 million euros in three months. The euro and USD risk-free rates are 5% and 4%, respectively. The company decides to use a range forward contract with the lower strike price equal to 1.2500.
    (a) What should the higher strike price be to create a zero-cost contract?
    (b) What position in calls and puts should the company take?
    (c) Show that your answer to (a) does not depend on interest rates provided that the interest rate differential between the two currencies, $r - r_f$, remains the same.

17.29. In Business Snapshot 17.1, what is the cost of a guarantee that the return on the fund will not be negative over the next 10 years?

17.30. The one-year forward price of the Mexican peso is $0.0750 per MXN. The U.S. risk-free rate is 1.25% and the Mexican risk-free rate is 4.5%. The exchange rate volatility is 13%. What are the values of one-year European and American put options with a strike price of $0.0800.

18

Futures Options and Black's Model

The options we have considered so far provide the holder with the right to buy or sell a certain asset by a certain date for a certain price. They are sometimes termed *options on spot* or *spot options* because, when the options are exercised, the sale or purchase of the asset at the agreed-on price takes place immediately. In this chapter we move on to consider *options on futures*, also known as *futures options*. In these contracts, exercise of the option gives the holder a position in a futures contract.

The Commodity Futures Trading Commission in the U.S. authorized the trading of options on futures on an experimental basis in 1982. Permanent trading was approved in 1987, and since then the popularity of the contract has grown very fast.

In this chapter we consider how futures options work and the differences between these options and spot options. We examine how futures options can be priced, explore the relative pricing of futures options and spot options, and discuss what are known as futures-style options.

In 1976, Fischer Black proposed a model, now known as Black's model, for valuing European options on futures.[1] As this chapter will show, the model has proved to be an important alternative to the Black–Scholes–Merton model for valuing a wide range of European spot options.

18.1 NATURE OF FUTURES OPTIONS

A futures option is the right, but not the obligation, to enter into a futures contract at a certain futures price by a certain date. Specifically, a futures call option is the right to enter into a long futures contract at a certain price; a futures put option is the right to enter into a short futures contract at a certain price. Futures options are generally American; that is, they can be exercised any time during the life of the contract.

If a futures call option is exercised, the holder acquires a long position in the underlying futures contract plus a cash amount equal to the most recent settlement futures price minus the strike price. If a futures put option is exercised, the holder acquires a short position in the underlying futures contract plus a cash amount equal to the strike price minus the most recent settlement futures price. As the following examples show, the effective payoff from a futures call option is $\max(F - K, 0)$ and

---

[1] See F. Black, "The Pricing of Commodity Contracts," *Journal of Financial Economics*, 3 (1976), 167–79.

the effective payoff from a futures put option is $\max(K - F, 0)$, where F is the futures price at the time of exercise and K is the strike price.

Example 18.1

Suppose it is August 15 and a trader has one September futures call option contract on copper with a strike price of 320 cents per pound. One futures contract is on 25,000 pounds of copper. Suppose that the futures price of copper for delivery in September is currently 331 cents, and at the close of trading on August 14 (the last settlement) it was 330 cents. If the option is exercised, the trader receives a cash amount of

$$25,000 \times (330 - 320)\,\text{cents} = \$2,500$$

plus a long position in a futures contract to buy 25,000 pounds of copper in September. If desired, the position in the futures contract can be closed out immediately. This would leave the trader with the $2,500 cash payoff plus an amount

$$25,000 \times (331 - 330)\,\text{cents} = \$250$$

reflecting the change in the futures price since the last settlement. The total payoff from exercising the option on August 15 is $2,750, which equals $25,000(F - K)$, where F is the futures price at the time of exercise and K is the strike price.

Example 18.2

A trader has one December futures put option on corn with a strike price of 600 cents per bushel. One futures contract is on 5,000 bushels of corn. Suppose that the current futures price of corn for delivery in December is 580, and the most recent settlement price is 579 cents. If the option is exercised, the trader receives a cash amount of

$$5,000 \times (600 - 579)\,\text{cents} = \$1,050$$

plus a short position in a futures contract to sell 5,000 bushels of corn in December. If desired, the position in the futures contract can be closed out. This would leave the trader with the $1,050 cash payoff minus an amount

$$5,000 \times (580 - 579)\,\text{cents} = \$50$$

reflecting the change in the futures price since the last settlement. The net payoff from exercise is $1,000, which equals $5,000(K - F)$, where F is the futures price at the time of exercise and K is the strike price.

Expiration Months

Futures options are referred to by the delivery month of the underlying futures contract —not by the expiration month of the option. As mentioned earlier, most futures options are American. The expiration date of a futures option contract is usually a short period of time before the last trading day of the underlying futures contract. (For example, the CME Group Treasury bond futures option expires on the latest Friday that precedes by at least two business days the end of the month before the futures delivery month.) An exception is the CME Group mid-curve Eurodollar contract where the futures contract expires much later than the options contract.

Popular contracts trading in the United States are those on corn, soybeans, cotton, sugar-world, crude oil, natural gas, gold, Treasury bonds, Treasury notes, five-year Treasury notes, 30-day federal funds, Eurodollars, one-year and two-year mid-curve Eurodollars, Euribor, Eurobunds, and the S&P 500.

Options on Interest Rate Futures

The most actively traded interest rate options offered by exchanges in the United States are those on Treasury bond futures, Treasury note futures, and Eurodollar futures.

A Treasury bond futures option, which is traded by the CME Group, is an option to enter a Treasury bond futures contract. As mentioned in Chapter 6, one Treasury bond futures contract is for the delivery of $100,000 of Treasury bonds. The price of a Treasury bond futures option is quoted as a percentage of the face value of the underlying Treasury bonds to the nearest sixty-fourth of 1%.

An option on Eurodollar futures, which is traded by the CME Group, is an option to enter into a Eurodollar futures contract. As explained in Chapter 6, when the Eurodollar futures quote changes by 1 basis point, or 0.01%, there is a gain or loss on a Eurodollar futures contract of $25. Similarly, in the pricing of options on Eurodollar futures, 1 basis point represents $25.

Interest rate futures option contracts work in the same way as the other futures options contracts discussed in this chapter. For example, in addition to the cash payoff, the holder of a call option obtains a long position in the futures contract when the option is exercised and the option writer obtains a corresponding short position. The total payoff from the call, including the value of the futures position, is $\max(F - K, 0)$, where F is the futures price at the time of exercise and K is the strike price.

Interest rate futures prices increase when bond prices increase (i.e., when interest rates fall). They decrease when bond prices decrease (i.e., when interest rates rise). An investor who thinks that short-term interest rates will rise can speculate by buying put options on Eurodollar futures, whereas an investor who thinks the rates will fall can speculate by buying call options on Eurodollar futures. An investor who thinks that long-term interest rates will rise can speculate by buying put options on Treasury note futures or Treasury bond futures, whereas an investor who thinks the rates will fall can speculate by buying call options on these instruments.

Example 18.3

It is February and the futures price for the June Eurodollar contract is 96.82 (corresponding to a 3-month Eurodollar interest rate of 3.18% per annum). The price of a call option on the contract with a strike price of 97.00 is quoted as 0.1, or 10 basis points. This option could be attractive to an investor who feels that interest rates are likely to come down. Suppose that short-term interest rates do drop by about 100 basis points and the investor exercises the call when the Eurodollar futures price is 97.78 (corresponding to a 3-month Eurodollar interest rate of 3.22% per annum). The payoff is $25 \times (97.78 - 97.00) \times 100 = \$1,950$. The cost of the contract is $10 \times 25 = \$250$. The investor's profit is therefore $1,700.

Example 18.4

It is August and the futures price for the December Treasury bond contract is 96-09 (or $96\frac{9}{32} = 96.28125$). The yield on long-term government bonds is about 6.4% per annum. An investor who feels that this yield will fall by December might choose to buy December calls with a strike price of 98. Assume that the price of these calls is 1-04 (or $1\frac{4}{64} = 1.0625\%$ of the principal). If long-term rates fall to 6% per annum and the Treasury bond futures price rises to 100-00, the investor will make a net profit per $100 of bond futures of

$$100.00 - 98.00 - 1.0625 = 0.9375$$

Since one option contract is for the purchase or sale of instruments with a face value of $100,000, the investor's profit is $937.50 per option contract bought.

18.2 REASONS FOR THE POPULARITY OF FUTURES OPTIONS

It is natural to ask why people choose to trade options on futures rather than options on the underlying asset. The main reason appears to be that a futures contract is, in many circumstances, more liquid and easier to trade than the underlying asset. Furthermore, a futures price is known immediately from trading on the futures exchange, whereas the spot price of the underlying asset may not be so readily available.

Consider Treasury bonds. The market for Treasury bond futures is much more active than the market for any particular Treasury bond. Also, a Treasury bond futures price is known immediately from exchange trading. By contrast, the current market price of a bond can be obtained only by contacting one or more dealers. It is not surprising that investors would rather take delivery of a Treasury bond futures contract than Treasury bonds.

Futures on commodities are also often easier to trade than the commodities themselves. For example, it is much easier and more convenient to make or take delivery of a live-cattle futures contract than it is to make or take delivery of the cattle.

An important point about a futures option is that exercising it does not usually lead to delivery of the underlying asset, as in most circumstances the underlying futures contract is closed out prior to delivery. Futures options are therefore normally eventually settled in cash. This is appealing to many investors, particularly those with limited capital who may find it difficult to come up with the funds to buy the underlying asset when an option on spot is exercised. Another advantage sometimes cited for futures options is that futures and futures options are traded on the same exchange. This facilitates hedging, arbitrage, and speculation. It also tends to make the markets more efficient. A final point is that futures options entail lower transaction costs than spot options in many situations.

18.3 EUROPEAN SPOT AND FUTURES OPTIONS

The payoff from a European call option with strike price K on the spot price of an asset is

$$\max(S_T - K, 0)$$

where S_T is the spot price at the option's maturity. The payoff from a European call option with the same strike price on the futures price of the asset is

$$\max(F_T - K, 0)$$

where F_T is the futures price at the option's maturity. If the futures contract matures at the same time as the option, then $F_T = S_T$ and the two options are equivalent. Similarly, a European futures put option is worth the same as its spot put option counterpart when the futures contract matures at the same time as the option.

Most of the futures options that trade are American-style. However, as we shall see, it is useful to study European futures options because the results that are obtained can be used to value the corresponding European spot options.

18.4 PUT–CALL PARITY

In Chapter 11, we derived a put–call parity relationship for European stock options. We now consider a similar argument to derive a put–call parity relationship for European futures options. Consider European futures call and put options, both with strike price K and time to expiration T. We can form two portfolios:

> *Portfolio A*: a European futures call option plus an amount of cash equal to Ke^{-rT}
> *Portfolio B*: a European futures put option plus a long futures contract plus an amount of cash equal to F_0e^{-rT}, where F_0 is the futures price

In portfolio A, the cash can be invested at the risk-free rate, r, and grows to K at time T. Let F_T be the futures price at maturity of the option. If $F_T > K$, the call option in portfolio A is exercised and portfolio A is worth F_T. If $F_T \leqslant K$, the call is not exercised and portfolio A is worth K. The value of portfolio A at time T is therefore

$$\max(F_T, K)$$

In portfolio B, the cash can be invested at the risk-free rate to grow to F_0 at time T. The put option provides a payoff of $\max(K - F_T, 0)$. The futures contract provides a payoff of $F_T - F_0$.[2] The value of portfolio B at time T is therefore

$$F_0 + (F_T - F_0) + \max(K - F_T, 0) = \max(F_T, K)$$

Because the two portfolios have the same value at time T and European options cannot be exercised early, it follows that they are worth the same today. The value of portfolio A today is

$$c + Ke^{-rT}$$

where c is the price of the futures call option. The daily settlement process ensures that the futures contract in portfolio B is worth zero today. Portfolio B is therefore worth

$$p + F_0e^{-rT}$$

where p is the price of the futures put option. Hence

$$c + Ke^{-rT} = p + F_0e^{-rT} \qquad (18.1)$$

The difference between this put–call parity relationship and the one for a non-dividend-paying stock in equation (11.6) is that the stock price, S_0, is replaced by the discounted futures price, F_0e^{-rT}.

---

[2] This analysis assumes that a futures contract is like a forward contract and settled at the end of its life rather than on a day-to-day basis.

As shown in Section 18.3, when the underlying futures contract matures at the same time as the option, European futures and spot options are the same. Equation (18.1) therefore gives a relationship between the price of a call option on the spot price, the price of a put option on the spot price, and the futures price when both options mature at the same time as the futures contract.

Example 18.5

Suppose that the price of a European call option on a commodity for delivery in six months is $0.56 per ounce when the strike price is $8.50. Assume that the futures price for delivery in six months is currently $8.00, and the risk-free interest rate for an investment that matures in six months is 10% per annum. From a rearrangement of equation (18.1), the price of a European put option on the spot price with the same maturity and exercise date as the call option is

$$0.56 + 8.50e^{-0.1 \times 6/12} - 8.00e^{-0.1 \times 6/12} = 1.04$$

For American futures options, the put–call relationship is (see Problem 18.19)

$$F_0 e^{-rT} - K < C - P < F_0 - K e^{-rT} \tag{18.2}$$

18.5 BOUNDS FOR FUTURES OPTIONS

The put–call parity relationship in equation (18.1) provides bounds for European call and put options. Because the price of a put, p, cannot be negative, it follows from equation (18.1) that

$$c + K e^{-rT} \geqslant F_0 e^{-rT}$$

so that

$$c \geqslant \max\big((F_0 - K)e^{-rT},\, 0\big) \tag{18.3}$$

Similarly, because the price of a call option cannot be negative, it follows from equation (18.1) that

$$K e^{-rT} \leqslant F_0 e^{-rT} + p$$

so that

$$p \geqslant \max\big((K - F_0)e^{-rT},\, 0\big) \tag{18.4}$$

These bounds are analogous to the ones derived for European stock options in Chapter 11. The prices of European call and put options are very close to their lower bounds when the options are deep in the money. To see why this is so, we return to the put–call parity relationship in equation (18.1). When a call option is deep in the money, a put option with the same strike price is deep out of the money. This means that p is very close to zero. The difference between c and its lower bound equals p, so that the price of the call option must be very close to its lower bound. A similar argument applies to put options.

Because American futures options can be exercised at any time, we must have

$$C \geqslant \max(F_0 - K,\, 0)$$

and

$$P \geqslant \max(K - F_0,\, 0)$$

Thus, assuming interest rates are positive, the lower bound for an American option price is always higher than the lower bound for the corresponding European option price. There is always some chance that an American futures option will be exercised early.

18.6 DRIFT OF A FUTURES PRICE IN A RISK-NEUTRAL WORLD

There is a general result that allows us to use the analysis in Section 17.3 for futures options. This result is that in a risk-neutral world a futures price behaves in the same way as a stock paying a dividend yield at the domestic risk-free interest rate r.

One clue that this might be so is given by noting that the put–call parity relationship for futures options prices is the same as that for options on a stock paying a dividend yield at rate q when the stock price is replaced by the futures price and $q = r$ (compare equations (18.1) and (17.3)).

To prove the result formally, we calculate the drift of a futures price in a risk-neutral world. We define F_t as the futures price at time t and suppose the settlement dates are at times $0, \Delta t, 2\Delta t, \ldots$ If we enter into a long futures contract at time 0, its value is zero. At time Δt, it provides a payoff of $F_{\Delta t} - F_0$. If r is the very-short-term (Δt-period) interest rate at time 0, risk-neutral valuation gives the value of the contract at time 0 as

$$e^{-r\Delta t}\hat{E}[F_{\Delta t} - F_0]$$

where $\hat{E}$ denotes expectations in a risk-neutral world. We must therefore have

$$e^{-r\Delta t}\hat{E}(F_{\Delta t} - F_0) = 0$$

showing that

$$\hat{E}(F_{\Delta t}) = F_0$$

Similarly, $\hat{E}(F_{2\Delta t}) = F_{\Delta t}$, $\hat{E}(F_{3\Delta t}) = F_{2\Delta t}$, and so on. Putting many results like this together, we see that

$$\hat{E}(F_T) = F_0$$

for any time T.

The drift of the futures price in a risk-neutral world is therefore zero. From equation (17.7), the futures price behaves like a stock providing a dividend yield q equal to r. This result is a very general one. It is true for all futures prices and does not depend on any assumptions about interest rates, volatilities, etc.[3]

The usual assumption made for the process followed by a futures price F in the risk-neutral world is

$$dF = \sigma F\,dz \tag{18.5}$$

where σ is a constant.

Differential Equation

For another way of seeing that a futures price behaves like a stock paying a dividend yield at rate q, we can derive the differential equation satisfied by a derivative dependent

---

[3] As we will discover in Chapter 28, a more precise statement of the result is: "A futures price has zero drift in the traditional risk-neutral world where the numeraire is the money market account." A zero-drift stochastic process is known as a martingale. A forward price is a martingale in a different risk-neutral world. This is one where the numeraire is a zero-coupon bond maturing at time T.

on a futures price in the same way as we derived the differential equation for a derivative dependent on a non-dividend-paying stock in Section 15.6. This is[4]

$$\frac{\partial f}{\partial t} + \frac{1}{2}\frac{\partial^2 f}{\partial F^2}\sigma^2 F^2 = rf \tag{18.6}$$

It has the same form as equation (17.6) with q set equal to r. This confirms that, for the purpose of valuing derivatives, a futures price can be treated in the same way as a stock providing a dividend yield at rate r.

18.7 BLACK'S MODEL FOR VALUING FUTURES OPTIONS

European futures options can be valued by extending the results we have produced. Fischer Black was the first to show this in a paper published in 1976.[5] Assuming that the futures price follows the (lognormal) process in equation (18.5), the European call price c and the European put price p for a futures option are given by equations (17.4) and (17.5) with S_0 replaced by F_0 and $q = r$:

$$c = e^{-rT}[F_0 N(d_1) - KN(d_2)] \tag{18.7}$$
$$p = e^{-rT}[KN(-d_2) - F_0 N(-d_1)] \tag{18.8}$$

where

$$d_1 = \frac{\ln(F_0/K) + \sigma^2 T/2}{\sigma\sqrt{T}}$$
$$d_2 = \frac{\ln(F_0/K) - \sigma^2 T/2}{\sigma\sqrt{T}} = d_1 - \sigma\sqrt{T}$$

and σ is the volatility of the futures price. When the cost of carry and the convenience yield are functions only of time, it can be shown that the volatility of the futures price is the same as the volatility of the underlying asset.

Example 18.6

Consider a European put futures option on a commodity. The time to the option's maturity is 4 months, the current futures price is $20, the exercise price is $20, the risk-free interest rate is 9% per annum, and the volatility of the futures price is 25% per annum. In this case, $F_0 = 20$, $K = 20$, $r = 0.09$, $T = 4/12$, $\sigma = 0.25$, and $\ln(F_0/K) = 0$, so that

$$d_1 = \frac{\sigma\sqrt{T}}{2} = 0.07216$$
$$d_2 = -\frac{\sigma\sqrt{T}}{2} = -0.07216$$
$$N(-d_1) = 0.4712, \quad N(-d_2) = 0.5288$$

[4] See Technical Note 7 at www-2.rotman.utoronto.ca/~hull/TechnicalNotes for a proof of this.
[5] See F. Black, "The Pricing of Commodity Contracts," *Journal of Financial Economics*, 3 (March 1976): 167–79.

and the put price p is given by

$$p = e^{-0.09 \times 4/12}(20 \times 0.5288 - 20 \times 0.4712) = 1.12$$

or $1.12.

18.8 USING BLACK'S MODEL INSTEAD OF BLACK–SCHOLES–MERTON

The results in Section 18.3 show that European futures options and European spot options are equivalent when the option contract matures at the same time as the futures contract. Specifically, equations (18.7) and (18.8) provide the price of a European option on the spot price of a asset where F_0 is the futures price of the asset for a contract maturing at the same time as the option.

Example 18.7

Consider a six-month European call option on the spot price of gold, that is, an option to buy one ounce of gold in the spot market in six months. The strike price is $1,200, the six-month futures price of gold is $1,240, the risk-free rate of interest is 5% per annum, and the volatility of the futures price is 20%. The option is the same as a six-month European option on the six-month futures price. The value of the option is therefore given by equation (18.7) as

$$e^{-0.05 \times 0.5}[1,240N(d_1) - 1,200N(d_2)]$$

where

$$d_1 = \frac{\ln(1,240/1,200) + 0.2^2 \times 0.5/2}{0.2 \times \sqrt{0.5}} = 0.3026$$

$$d_2 = \frac{\ln(1,240/1,200) - 0.2^2 \times 0.5/2}{0.2 \times \sqrt{0.5}} = 0.1611$$

It is $88.37.

Traders like to use Black's model rather than Black–Scholes–Merton to value European spot options. It has a fairly general applicability. The underlying asset can be a consumption or investment asset and it can provide income to the holder. Often F_0 is set equal to the forward price rather than the futures price. When interest rates are assumed to be deterministic, forward and futures prices are equal and so this is valid. As we will see later in the book, when interest rates are stochastic it is valid to set F_0 equal to the forward price provided that r is the risk-free rate for maturity T.

The big advantage of Black's model is that it avoids the need to estimate the income (or convenience yield) on the underlying asset. The futures or forward price that is used in the model incorporate the market's estimate of this income.

Equations (17.13) and (17.14) show Black's model being used to value European options on the spot value of a currency. In this case, Black's model avoids the need to estimate the foreign risk-free rate explicit because all information needed about this rate is captured by F_0. Equations (17.8) and (17.9) show Black's model being used to value European options on the spot value of an index. In this case, dividends on the underlying portfolio of stocks do not have to be estimated explicitly because all information needed about dividends is captured by F_0.

When considering stock indices in Section 17.4, we explained that put–call parity is used to imply the forward prices for maturities for which there are actively traded options. Interpolation is then used to estimate forward prices for other maturities. The same approach can be used for a wide range of other underlying assets.

18.9 VALUATION OF FUTURES OPTIONS USING BINOMIAL TREES

This section examines, more formally than in Chapter 13, how binomial trees can be used to price futures options. A key difference between futures options and stock options is that there are no up-front costs when a futures contract is entered into.

Suppose that the current futures price is 30 and that it will move either up to 33 or down to 28 over the next month. We consider a one-month call option on the futures with a strike price of 29 and ignore daily settlement. The situation is as indicated in Figure 18.1. If the futures price proves to be 33, the payoff from the option is 4 and the value of the futures contract is 3. If the futures price proves to be 28, the payoff from the option is zero and the value of the futures contract is −2.[6]

To set up a riskless hedge, we consider a portfolio consisting of a short position in one option contract and a long position in Δ futures contracts. If the futures price moves up to 33, the value of the portfolio is $3\Delta - 4$; if it moves down to 28, the value of the portfolio is -2Δ. The portfolio is riskless when these are the same, that is, when

$$3\Delta - 4 = -2\Delta$$

or $\Delta = 0.8$.

For this value of Δ, we know the portfolio will be worth $3 \times 0.8 - 4 = -1.6$ in one month. Assume a risk-free interest rate of 6%. The value of the portfolio today must be

$$-1.6e^{-0.06 \times 1/12} = -1.592$$

Figure 18.1   Futures price movements in numerical example.

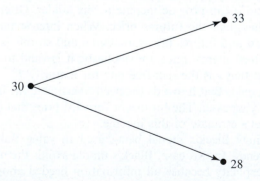

---

[6] There is an approximation here in that the gain or loss on the futures contract is not realized at time T. It is realized day by day between time 0 and time T. However, as the length of the time step in a multistep binomial tree becomes shorter, the approximation becomes better.

The portfolio consists of one short option and Δ futures contracts. Because the value of the futures contract today is zero, the value of the option today must be 1.592.

A Generalization

We can generalize this analysis by considering a futures price that starts at F_0 and is anticipated to rise to $F_0 u$ or move down to $F_0 d$ over the time period T. We consider an option maturing at time T and suppose that its payoff is f_u if the futures price moves up and f_d if it moves down. The situation is summarized in Figure 18.2.

The riskless portfolio in this case consists of a short position in one option combined with a long position in Δ futures contracts, where

$$\Delta = \frac{f_u - f_d}{F_0 u - F_0 d}$$

The value of the portfolio at time T is then always

$$(F_0 u - F_0)\Delta - f_u$$

Denoting the risk-free interest rate by r, we obtain the value of the portfolio today as

$$[(F_0 u - F_0)\Delta - f_u]e^{-rT}$$

Another expression for the present value of the portfolio is $-f$, where f is the value of the option today. It follows that

$$-f = [(F_0 u - F_0)\Delta - f_u]e^{-rT}$$

Substituting for Δ and simplifying reduces this equation to

$$f = e^{-rT}[pf_u + (1 - p)f_d] \qquad \textbf{(18.9)}$$

where

$$p = \frac{1 - d}{u - d} \qquad \textbf{(18.10)}$$

This agrees with the result in Section 13.9. Equation (18.10) gives the risk-neutral probability of an up movement.

Figure 18.2 Futures price and option price in a general situation.

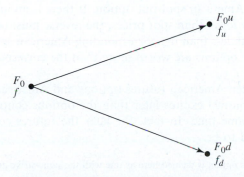

In the numerical example considered previously (see Figure 18.1), $u = 1.1$, $d = 0.9333$, $r = 0.06$, $T = 1/12$, $f_u = 4$, and $f_d = 0$. From equation (18.10),

$$p = \frac{1 - 0.9333}{1.1 - 0.9333} = 0.4$$

and, from equation (18.9),

$$f = e^{-0.06 \times 1/12}[0.4 \times 4 + 0.6 \times 0] = 1.592$$

This result agrees with the answer obtained for this example earlier.

Multistep Trees

Multistep binomial trees are used to value American-style futures options in much the same way that they are used to value options on stocks. This is explained in Section 13.9. The parameter u defining up movements in the futures price is $e^{\sigma\sqrt{\Delta t}}$, where σ is the volatility of the futures price and Δt is the length of one time step. The probability of an up movement in the future price is that in equation (18.10):

$$p = \frac{1 - d}{u - d}$$

Example 13.3 illustrates the use of multistep binomial trees for valuing a futures option. Example 21.3 in Chapter 21 provides a further illustration.

18.10 AMERICAN FUTURES OPTIONS vs. AMERICAN SPOT OPTIONS

Traded futures options are in practice usually American. Assuming that the risk-free rate of interest, r, is positive, there is always some chance that it will be optimal to exercise an American futures option early. American futures options are therefore worth more than their European counterparts.

It is not generally true that an American futures option is worth the same as the corresponding American spot option when the futures and options contracts have the same maturity.[7] Suppose, for example, that there is a normal market with futures prices consistently higher than spot prices prior to maturity. An American futures call option must be worth more than the corresponding American spot call option. The reason is that in some situations the futures option will be exercised early, in which case it will provide a greater profit to the holder. Similarly, an American futures put option must be worth less than the corresponding American spot put option. If there is an inverted market with futures prices consistently lower than spot prices, the reverse must be true. American futures call options are worth less than the corresponding American spot call option, whereas American futures put options are worth more than the corresponding American spot put option.

The differences just described between American futures options and American spot options hold true when the futures contract expires later than the options contract as well as when the two expire at the same time. In fact, the later the futures contract expires the greater the differences tend to be.

---

[7] The spot option "corresponding" to a futures option is defined here as one with the same strike price and the same expiration date.

18.11 FUTURES-STYLE OPTIONS

Some exchanges, particularly those in Europe, trade what are termed *futures-style options*. These are futures contracts on the payoff from an option. Normally a trader who buys (sells) an option, whether on the spot price of an asset or on the futures price of an asset, pays (receives) cash up front. By contrast, traders who buy or sell a futures-style option post margin in the same way that they do on a regular futures contract (see Chapter 2). The contract is settled daily as with any other futures contract and the final settlement price is the payoff from the option. Just as a futures contract is a bet on what the future price of an asset will be, a futures-style option is a bet on what the payoff from an option will be.[8] If interest rates are constant, the futures price in a futures-style option is the same as the forward price in a forward contract on the option payoff. Our analysis of forward contracts in Chapter 5 shows that this is the current option price compounded forward at the risk-free rate.

Black's model in equations (18.7) and (18.8) gives the current European option price. The futures price in a futures-style call option is therefore

$$F_0 N(d_1) - K N(d_2)$$

and the futures price in a futures-style put option is

$$K N(-d_2) - F_0 N(-d_1)$$

where d_1 and d_2 are as defined in equations (18.7) and (18.8). These formulas do not depend on the level of interest rates. They are correct for a futures-style option on a futures contract and a futures-style option on the spot value of an asset. In the first case, F_0 is the current futures price for the contract underlying the option; in the second case, it is the current futures price for a futures contract on the underlying asset maturing at the same time as the option.

The put–call parity relationship for a futures-style options is

$$p + F_0 = c + K$$

An American futures-style option can be exercised early, in which case there is an immediate final settlement at the option's intrinsic value. As it turns out, it is never optimal to exercise an American futures-style option early because the futures price of the option is always greater than the intrinsic value. This type of American futures-style option can therefore be treated as though it is European.

SUMMARY

Futures options require delivery of the underlying futures contract on exercise. When a call is exercised, the holder acquires a long futures position plus a cash amount equal to the excess of the futures price over the strike price. Similarly, when a put is exercised the holder acquires a short position plus a cash amount equal to the excess of the strike

---

[8] For a more detailed discussion of futures-style options, see D. Lieu, "Option Pricing with Futures-Style Margining," *Journal of Futures Markets*, 10, 4 (1990), 327–38. For pricing when interest rates are stochastic, see R.-R. Chen and L. Scott, "Pricing Interest Rate Futures Options with Futures-Style Margining." *Journal of Futures Markets*, 13, 1 (1993) 15–22.

price over the futures price. The futures contract that is delivered usually expires slightly later than the option.

A futures price behaves in the same way as a stock that provides a dividend yield equal to the risk-free rate, r. This means that the results produced in Chapter 17 for options on a stock paying a dividend yield apply to futures options if we replace the stock price by the futures price and set the dividend yield equal to the risk-free interest rate. Pricing formulas for European futures options were first produced by Fischer Black in 1976. They assume that the futures price is lognormally distributed at the option's expiration.

If the expiration dates for the option and futures contracts are the same, a European futures option is worth exactly the same as the corresponding European spot option. This result is often used to value European spot options. The result is not true for American options. If the futures market is normal, an American futures call is worth more than the corresponding American spot call option, while an American futures put is worth less than the corresponding American spot put option. If the futures market is inverted, the reverse is true.

FURTHER READING

Black, F. "The Pricing of Commodity Contracts," *Journal of Financial Economics*, 3 (1976): 167–79.

Practice Questions (Answers in Solutions Manual)

18.1. Explain the difference between a call option on yen and a call option on yen futures.

18.2. Why are options on bond futures more actively traded than options on bonds?

18.3. "A futures price is like a stock paying a dividend yield." What is the dividend yield?

18.4. A futures price is currently 50. At the end of six months it will be either 56 or 46. The risk-free interest rate is 6% per annum. What is the value of a six-month European call option on the futures with a strike price of 50?

18.5. How does the put–call parity formula for a futures option differ from put–call parity for an option on a non-dividend-paying stock?

18.6. Consider an American futures call option where the futures contract and the option contract expire at the same time. Under what circumstances is the futures option worth more than the corresponding American option on the underlying asset?

18.7. Calculate the value of a five-month European futures put option when the futures price is $19, the strike price is $20, the risk-free interest rate is 12% per annum, and the volatility of the futures price is 20% per annum.

18.8. Suppose you buy a put option contract on October gold futures with a strike price of $1,400 per ounce. Each contract is for the delivery of 100 ounces. What happens if you exercise when the October futures price is $1,380?

18.9. Suppose you sell a call option contract on April live cattle futures with a strike price of 130 cents per pound. Each contract is for the delivery of 40,000 pounds. What happens if the contract is exercised when the futures price is 135 cents?

18.10. Consider a two-month futures call option with a strike price of 40 when the risk-free interest rate is 10% per annum. The current futures price is 47. What is a lower bound for the value of the futures option if it is (a) European and (b) American?

18.11. Consider a four-month futures put option with a strike price of 50 when the risk-free interest rate is 10% per annum. The current futures price is 47. What is a lower bound for the value of the futures option if it is (a) European and (b) American?

18.12. A futures price is currently 60 and its volatility is 30%. The risk-free interest rate is 8% per annum. Use a two-step binomial tree to calculate the value of a six-month European call option on the futures with a strike price of 60. If the call were American, would it ever be worth exercising it early?

18.13. In Problem 18.12, what does the binomial tree give for the value of a six-month European put option on futures with a strike price of 60? If the put were American, would it ever be worth exercising it early? Verify that the call prices calculated in Problem 18.12 and the put prices calculated here satisfy put–call parity relationships.

18.14. A futures price is currently 25, its volatility is 30% per annum, and the risk-free interest rate is 10% per annum. What is the value of a nine-month European call on the futures with a strike price of 26?

18.15. A futures price is currently 70, its volatility is 20% per annum, and the risk-free interest rate is 6% per annum. What is the value of a five-month European put on the futures with a strike price of 65?

18.16. Suppose that a one-year futures price is currently 35. A one-year European call option and a one-year European put option on the futures with a strike price of 34 are both priced at 2 in the market. The risk-free interest rate is 10% per annum. Identify an arbitrage opportunity.

18.17. "The price of an at-the-money European futures call option always equals the price of a similar at-the-money European futures put option." Explain why this statement is true.

18.18. Suppose that a futures price is currently 30. The risk-free interest rate is 5% per annum. A three-month American futures call option with a strike price of 28 is worth 4. Calculate bounds for the price of a three-month American futures put option with a strike price of 28.

18.19. Show that, if C is the price of an American call option on a futures contract when the strike price is K and the maturity is T, and P is the price of an American put on the same futures contract with the same strike price and exercise date, then

$$F_0 e^{-rT} - K < C - P < F_0 - Ke^{-rT}$$

where F_0 is the futures price and r is the risk-free rate. Assume that $r > 0$ and that there is no difference between forward and futures contracts. (*Hint*: Use an analogous approach to that indicated for Problem 17.12.)

18.20. Calculate the price of a three-month European call option on the spot value of silver. The three-month futures price is $12, the strike price is $13, the risk-free rate is 4% and the volatility of the price of silver is 25%.

18.21. A corporation knows that in three months it will have $5 million to invest for 90 days at LIBOR minus 50 basis points and wishes to ensure that the rate obtained will be at least 6.5%. What position in exchange-traded options should it take to hedge?

Further Questions

18.22. A futures price is currently 40. It is known that at the end of three months the price will be either 35 or 45. What is the value of a three-month European call option on the futures with a strike price of 42 if the risk-free interest rate is 7% per annum?

18.23. The futures price of an asset is currently 78 and the risk-free rate is 3%. A six-month put on the futures with a strike price of 80 is currently worth 6.5. What is the value of a six-month call on the futures with a strike price of 80 if both the put and call are European? What is the range of possible values of the six-month call with a strike price of 80 if both put and call are American?

18.24. Use a three-step tree to value an American futures put option when the futures price is 50, the life of the option is 9 months, the strike price is 50, the risk-free rate is 3%, and the volatility is 25%.

18.25. It is February 4. July call options on corn futures with strike prices of 260, 270, 280, 290, and 300 cost 26.75, 21.25, 17.25, 14.00, and 11.375, respectively. July put options with these strike prices cost 8.50, 13.50, 19.00, 25.625, and 32.625, respectively. The options mature on June 19, the current July corn futures price is 278.25, and the risk-free interest rate is 1.1%. Calculate implied volatilities for the options using DerivaGem. Comment on the results you get.

18.26. Calculate the implied volatility of soybean futures prices from the following information concerning a European put on soybean futures:

Current futures price	525
Exercise price	525
Risk-free rate	6% per annum
Time to maturity	5 months
Put price	20

18.27. Calculate the price of a six-month European put option on the spot value of the S&P 500. The six-month forward price of the index is 1,400, the strike price is 1,450, the risk-free rate is 5%, and the volatility of the index is 15%.

18.28. The strike price of a futures option is 550 cents, the risk-free interest rate is 3%, the volatility of the futures price is 20%, and the time to maturity of the option is 9 months. The futures price is 500 cents.
    (a) What is the price of the option if it is a European call?
    (b) What is the price of the option if it is a European put?
    (c) Verify that put–call parity holds.
    (d) What is the futures price for a futures-style option if it is a call?
    (e) What is the futures price for a futures-style option if it is a put?

CHAPTER 19

The Greek Letters

A financial institution that sells an option to a client in the over-the-counter markets is faced with the problem of managing its risk. If the option happens to be the same as one that is traded actively on an exchange or in the OTC market, the financial institution can neutralize its exposure by buying the same option as it has sold. But when the option has been tailored to the needs of a client and does not correspond to the standardized products traded by exchanges, hedging the exposure is far more difficult.

In this chapter we discuss some of the alternative approaches to this problem. We cover what are commonly referred to as the "Greek letters", or simply the "Greeks". Each Greek letter measures a different dimension to the risk in an option position and the aim of a trader is to manage the Greeks so that all risks are acceptable. The analysis presented in this chapter is applicable to market makers in options on an exchange as well as to traders working in the over-the-counter market for financial institutions.

Toward the end of the chapter, we will consider the creation of options synthetically. This turns out to be very closely related to the hedging of options. Creating an option position synthetically is essentially the same task as hedging the opposite option position. For example, creating a long call option synthetically is the same as hedging a short position in the call option.

19.1 ILLUSTRATION

In the next few sections we use as an example the position of a financial institution that has sold for $300,000 a European call option on 100,000 shares of a non-dividend-paying stock. We assume that the stock price is $49, the strike price is $50, the risk-free interest rate is 5% per annum, the stock price volatility is 20% per annum, the time to maturity is 20 weeks (0.3846 years), and the expected return from the stock is 13% per annum.[1] With our usual notation, this means that

$$S_0 = 49, \quad K = 50, \quad r = 0.05, \quad \sigma = 0.20, \quad T = 0.3846, \quad \mu = 0.13$$

The Black–Scholes–Merton price of the option is about $240,000. (This is because the

---

[1] As shown in Chapters 13 and 15, the expected return is irrelevant to the pricing of an option. It is given here because it can have some bearing on the effectiveness of a hedging procedure.

value of an option to buy one share is \$2.40.) The financial institution has therefore sold a product for \$60,000 more than its theoretical value. But it is faced with the problem of hedging the risks.[2]

19.2 NAKED AND COVERED POSITIONS

One strategy open to the financial institution is to do nothing. This is sometimes referred to as a *naked position*. It is a strategy that works well if the stock price is below \$50 at the end of the 20 weeks. The option then costs the financial institution nothing and it makes a profit of \$300,000. A naked position works less well if the call is exercised because the financial institution then has to buy 100,000 shares at the market price prevailing in 20 weeks to cover the call. The cost to the financial institution is 100,000 times the amount by which the stock price exceeds the strike price. For example, if after 20 weeks the stock price is \$60, the option costs the financial institution \$1,000,000. This is considerably greater than the \$300,000 charged for the option.

As an alternative to a naked position, the financial institution can adopt a *covered position*. This involves buying 100,000 shares as soon as the option has been sold. If the option is exercised, this strategy works well, but in other circumstances it could lead to a significant loss. For example, if the stock price drops to \$40, the financial institution loses \$900,000 on its stock position. This is also considerably greater than the \$300,000 charged for the option.[3]

Neither a naked position nor a covered position provides a good hedge. If the assumptions underlying the Black–Scholes–Merton formula hold, the cost to the financial institution should always be \$240,000 on average for both approaches.[4] But on any one occasion the cost is liable to range from zero to over \$1,000,000. A good hedge would ensure that the cost is always close to \$240,000.

A Stop-Loss Strategy

One interesting hedging procedure that is sometimes proposed involves a *stop-loss strategy*. To illustrate the basic idea, consider an institution that has written a call option with strike price K to buy one unit of a stock. The hedging procedure involves buying one unit of the stock as soon as its price rises above K and selling it as soon as its price falls below K. The objective is to hold a naked position whenever the stock price is less than K and a covered position whenever the stock price is greater than K. The procedure is designed to ensure that at time T the institution owns the stock if the option closes in the money and does not own it if the option closes out of the money. In the situation illustrated in Figure 19.1, it involves buying the stock at time t_1, selling it at time t_2, buying it at time t_3, selling it at time t_4, buying it at time t_5, and delivering it at time T.

---

[2] A call option on a non-dividend-paying stock is a convenient example with which to develop our ideas. The points that will be made apply to other types of options and to other derivatives.

[3] Put–call parity shows that the exposure from writing a covered call is the same as the exposure from writing a naked put.

[4] More precisely, the present value of the expected cost is \$240,000 for both approaches assuming that appropriate risk-adjusted discount rates are used.

Figure 19.1 A stop-loss strategy.

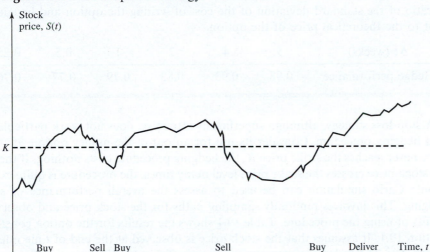

As usual, we denote the initial stock price by S_0. The cost of setting up the hedge initially is S_0 if $S_0 > K$ and zero otherwise. It seems as though the total cost, Q, of writing and hedging the option is the option's initial intrinsic value:

$$Q = \max(S_0 - K, 0) \tag{19.1}$$

This is because all purchases and sales subsequent to time 0 are made at price K. If this were in fact correct, the hedging procedure would work perfectly in the absence of transaction costs. Furthermore, the cost of hedging the option would always be less than its Black–Scholes–Merton price. Thus, a trader could earn riskless profits by writing options and hedging them.

There are two key reasons why equation (19.1) is incorrect. The first is that the cash flows to the hedger occur at different times and must be discounted. The second is that purchases and sales cannot be made at exactly the same price K. This second point is critical. If we assume a risk-neutral world with zero interest rates, we can justify ignoring the time value of money. But we cannot legitimately assume that both purchases and sales are made at the same price. If markets are efficient, the hedger cannot know whether, when the stock price equals K, it will continue above or below K.

As a practical matter, purchases must be made at a price $K + \epsilon$ and sales must be made at a price $K - \epsilon$, for some small positive number ϵ. Thus, every purchase and subsequent sale involves a cost (apart from transaction costs) of 2ϵ. A natural response on the part of the hedger is to monitor price movements more closely, so that ϵ is reduced. Assuming that stock prices change continuously, ϵ can be made arbitrarily small by monitoring the stock prices closely. But as ϵ is made smaller, trades tend to occur more frequently. Thus, the lower cost per trade is offset by the increased frequency of trading. As $\epsilon \to 0$, the expected number of trades tends to infinity.[5]

---

[5] As mentioned in Section 14.2, the expected number of times a Wiener process equals any particular value in a given time interval is infinite.

Table 19.1 Performance of stop-loss strategy. The performance measure is the ratio of the standard deviation of the cost of writing the option and hedging it to the theoretical price of the option.

Δt (weeks)	5	4	2	1	0.5	0.25
Hedge performance	0.98	0.93	0.83	0.79	0.77	0.76

A stop-loss strategy, although superficially attractive, does not work particularly well as a hedging procedure. Consider its use for an out-of-the-money option. If the stock price never reaches the strike price K, the hedging procedure costs nothing. If the path of the stock price crosses the strike price level many times, the procedure is quite expensive. Monte Carlo simulation can be used to assess the overall performance of stop-loss hedging. This involves randomly sampling paths for the stock price and observing the results of using the procedure. Table 19.1 shows the results for the option considered in Section 19.1. It assumes that the stock price is observed at the end of time intervals of length Δt.[6] The hedge performance measure in Table 19.1 is the ratio of the standard deviation of the cost of hedging the option to the Black–Scholes–Merton price. (The cost of hedging was calculated as the cumulative cost excluding the impact of interest payments and discounting.) Each result is based on one million sample paths for the stock price. An effective hedging scheme should have a hedge performance measure close to zero. In this case, it seems to stay above 0.7 regardless of how small Δt is. This emphasizes that the stop-loss strategy is not a good hedging procedure.

19.3 GREEK LETTER CALCULATION

Most traders use more sophisticated hedging procedures than those mentioned so far. These hedging procedures involve calculating measures such as delta, gamma, and vega. The measures are collectively referred to as *Greek letters*. They quantify different aspects of the risk in an option position. This chapter considers the properties of some of most important Greek letters.

In order to calculate a Greek letter, it is necessary to assume an option pricing model. Traders usually assume the Black–Scholes–Merton model (or its extensions in Chapters 17 and 18) for European options and the binomial tree model (introduced in Chapter 13) for American options. (As has been pointed out, the latter makes the same assumptions as Black–Scholes–Merton model.) When calculating Greek letters, traders normally set the volatility equal to the current implied volatility. This approach, which is sometimes referred to as using the "practitioner Black–Scholes model," is appealing. When volatility is set equal to the implied volatility, the model gives the option price at a particular time as an exact function of the price of the underlying asset, the implied volatility, interest rates, and (possibly) dividends. The only way the option price can change in a short time period is if one of these variables changes. A trader naturally feels confident if the risks of changes in all these variables have been adequately hedged.

---

[6] The precise hedging rule used was as follows. If the stock price moves from below K to above K in a time interval of length Δt, it is bought at the end of the interval. If it moves from above K to below K in the time interval, it is sold at the end of the interval; otherwise, no action is taken.

In this chapter, we first consider the calculation of Greek letters for a European option on a non-dividend-paying stock. We then present results for other European options. Chapter 21 will show how Greek letters can be calculated for American-style options.

19.4 DELTA HEDGING

The *delta* (Δ) of an option was introduced in Chapter 13. It is defined as the rate of change of the option price with respect to the price of the underlying asset. It is the slope of the curve that relates the option price to the underlying asset price. Suppose that the delta of a call option on a stock is 0.6. This means that when the stock price changes by a small amount, the option price changes by about 60% of that amount. Figure 19.2 shows the relationship between a call price and the underlying stock price. When the stock price corresponds to point A, the option price corresponds to point B, and Δ is the slope of the line indicated. In general,

$$\Delta = \frac{\partial c}{\partial S}$$

where c is the price of the call option and S is the stock price.

Suppose that, in Figure 19.2, the stock price is $100 and the option price is $10. Imagine an investor who has sold call options to buy 2,000 shares of a stock. The investor's position could be hedged by buying $0.6 \times 2,000 = 1,200$ shares. The gain (loss) on the stock position would then tend to offset the loss (gain) on the option position. For example, if the stock price goes up by $1 (producing a gain of $1,200 on the shares purchased), the option price will tend to go up by $0.6 \times \$1 = \$0.60$ (producing a loss of $1,200 on the options written); if the stock price goes down by $1 (producing a loss of $1,200 on the shares purchased), the option price will tend to go down by $0.60 (producing a gain of $1,200 on the options written).

In this example, the delta of the trader's short position in 2,000 options is

$$0.6 \times (-2,000) = -1,200$$

This means that the trader loses $1,200\Delta S$ on the option position when the stock price

---

Figure 19.2 Calculation of delta.

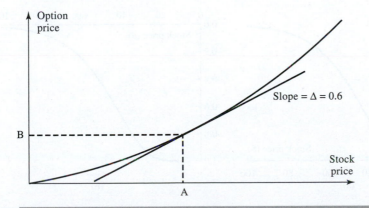

increases by ΔS. The delta of one share of the stock is 1.0, so that the long position in 1,200 shares has a delta of +1,200. The delta of the trader's overall position in our example is, therefore, zero. The delta of the stock position offsets the delta of the option position. A position with a delta of zero is referred to as *delta neutral*.

It is important to realize that, since the delta of an option does not remain constant, the trader's position remains delta hedged (or delta neutral) for only a relatively short period of time. The hedge has to be adjusted periodically. This is known as *rebalancing*. In our example, by the end of 1 day the stock price might have increased to $110. As indicated by Figure 19.2, an increase in the stock price leads to an increase in delta. Suppose that delta rises from 0.60 to 0.65. An extra $0.05 \times 2,000 = 100$ shares would then have to be purchased to maintain the hedge. A procedure such as this, where the hedge is adjusted on a regular basis, is referred to as *dynamic hedging*. It can be contrasted with *static hedging*, where a hedge is set up initially and never adjusted. Static hedging is sometimes also referred to as "hedge-and-forget."

Delta is closely related to the Black–Scholes–Merton analysis. As explained in Chapter 15, the Black–Scholes–Merton differential equation can be derived by setting up a riskless portfolio consisting of a position in an option on a stock and a position in the stock. Expressed in terms of Δ, the portfolio is

-1: option

$+\Delta$: shares of the stock.

Using our new terminology, we can say that options can be valued by setting up a delta-neutral position and arguing that the return on the position should (instantaneously) be the risk-free interest rate.

Delta of European Stock Options

For a European call option on a non-dividend-paying stock, it can be shown (see Problem 15.17) that the Black–Scholes–Merton model gives

$$\Delta(\text{call}) = N(d_1)$$

Figure 19.3 Variation of delta with stock price for (a) a call option and (b) a put option on a non-dividend-paying stock ($K = 50$, $r = 0$, $\sigma = 25\%$, $T = 2$).

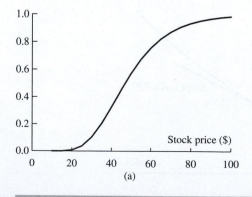

(a)

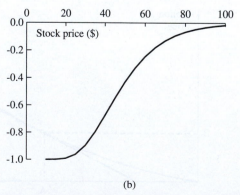

(b)

Figure 19.4 Typical patterns for variation of delta with time to maturity for a call option ($S_0 = 50$, $r = 0$, $\sigma = 25\%$).

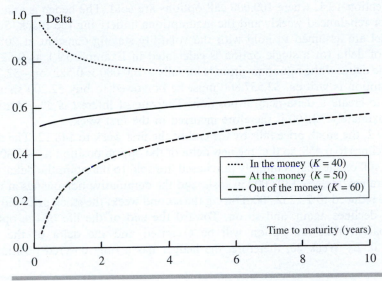

where d_1 is defined as in equation (15.20) and $N(x)$ is the cumulative distribution function for a standard normal distribution. The formula gives the delta of a long position in one call option. The delta of a short position in one call option is $-N(d_1)$. Using delta hedging for a short position in a European call option involves maintaining a long position of $N(d_1)$ for each option sold. Similarly, using delta hedging for a long position in a European call option involves maintaining a short position of $N(d_1)$ shares for each option purchased.

For a European put option on a non-dividend-paying stock, delta is given by

$$\Delta(\text{put}) = N(d_1) - 1$$

Delta is negative, which means that a long position in a put option should be hedged with a long position in the underlying stock, and a short position in a put option should be hedged with a short position in the underlying stock. Figure 19.3 shows the variation of the delta of a call option and a put option with the stock price. Figure 19.4 shows the variation of delta with the time to maturity for in-the-money, at-the-money, and out-of-the-money call options.

Example 19.1

Consider again the call option on a non-dividend-paying stock in Section 19.1 where the stock price is $49, the strike price is $50, the risk-free rate is 5%, the time to maturity is 20 weeks (= 0.3846 years), and the volatility is 20%. In this case,

$$d_1 = \frac{\ln(49/50) + (0.05 + 0.2^2/2) \times 0.3846}{0.2 \times \sqrt{0.3846}} = 0.0542$$

Delta is $N(d_1)$, or 0.522. When the stock price changes by ΔS, the option price changes by $0.522 \Delta S$.

Dynamic Aspects of Delta Hedging

Tables 19.2 and 19.3 provide two examples of the operation of delta hedging for the example in Section 19.1, where 100,000 call options are sold. The hedge is assumed to be adjusted or rebalanced weekly and the assumptions underlying the Black–Scholes–Merton model are assumed to hold with the volatility staying constant at 20%. The initial value of delta for a single option is calculated in Example 19.1 as 0.522. This means that the delta of the option position is initially $-100,000 \times 0.522$, or $-52,200$. As soon as the option is written, $2,557,800 must be borrowed to buy 52,200 shares at a price of $49 to create a delta-neutral position. The rate of interest is 5%. An interest cost of approximately $2,500 is therefore incurred in the first week.

In Table 19.2, the stock price falls by the end of the first week to $48.12. The delta of the option declines to 0.458, so that the new delta of the option position is $-45,800$. This means that 6,400 of the shares initially purchased are sold to maintain the delta-neutral hedge. The strategy realizes $308,000 in cash, and the cumulative borrowings at the end of Week 1 are reduced to $2,252,300. During the second week, the stock price reduces to $47.37, delta declines again, and so on. Toward the end of the life of the option, it becomes apparent that the option will be exercised and the delta of the option approaches 1.0. By Week 20, therefore, the hedger has a fully covered position. The

Table 19.2 Simulation of delta hedging. Option closes in the money and cost of hedging is $263,300.

Week	Stock price	Delta	Shares purchased	Cost of shares purchased ($000)	Cumulative cost including interest ($000)	Interest cost ($000)
0	49.00	0.522	52,200	2,557.8	2,557.8	2.5
1	48.12	0.458	(6,400)	(308.0)	2,252.3	2.2
2	47.37	0.400	(5,800)	(274.7)	1,979.8	1.9
3	50.25	0.596	19,600	984.9	2,966.6	2.9
4	51.75	0.693	9,700	502.0	3,471.5	3.3
5	53.12	0.774	8,100	430.3	3,905.1	3.8
6	53.00	0.771	(300)	(15.9)	3,893.0	3.7
7	51.87	0.706	(6,500)	(337.2)	3,559.5	3.4
8	51.38	0.674	(3,200)	(164.4)	3,398.5	3.3
9	53.00	0.787	11,300	598.9	4,000.7	3.8
10	49.88	0.550	(23,700)	(1,182.2)	2,822.3	2.7
11	48.50	0.413	(13,700)	(664.4)	2,160.6	2.1
12	49.88	0.542	12,900	643.5	2,806.2	2.7
13	50.37	0.591	4,900	246.8	3,055.7	2.9
14	52.13	0.768	17,700	922.7	3,981.3	3.8
15	51.88	0.759	(900)	(46.7)	3,938.4	3.8
16	52.87	0.865	10,600	560.4	4,502.6	4.3
17	54.87	0.978	11,300	620.0	5,126.9	4.9
18	54.62	0.990	1,200	65.5	5,197.3	5.0
19	55.87	1.000	1,000	55.9	5,258.2	5.1
20	57.25	1.000	0	0.0	5,263.3	

Table 19.3 Simulation of delta hedging. Option closes out of the money and cost of hedging is $256,600.

Week	Stock price	Delta	Shares purchased	Cost of shares purchased ($000)	Cumulative cost including interest ($000)	Interest cost ($000)
0	49.00	0.522	52,200	2,557.8	2,557.8	2.5
1	49.75	0.568	4,600	228.9	2,789.2	2.7
2	52.00	0.705	13,700	712.4	3,504.3	3.4
3	50.00	0.579	(12,600)	(630.0)	2,877.7	2.8
4	48.38	0.459	(12,000)	(580.6)	2,299.9	2.2
5	48.25	0.443	(1,600)	(77.2)	2,224.9	2.1
6	48.75	0.475	3,200	156.0	2,383.0	2.3
7	49.63	0.540	6,500	322.6	2,707.9	2.6
8	48.25	0.420	(12,000)	(579.0)	2,131.5	2.1
9	48.25	0.410	(1,000)	(48.2)	2,085.4	2.0
10	51.12	0.658	24,800	1,267.8	3,355.2	3.2
11	51.50	0.692	3,400	175.1	3,533.5	3.4
12	49.88	0.542	(15,000)	(748.2)	2,788.7	2.7
13	49.88	0.538	(400)	(20.0)	2,771.4	2.7
14	48.75	0.400	(13,800)	(672.7)	2,101.4	2.0
15	47.50	0.236	(16,400)	(779.0)	1,324.4	1.3
16	48.00	0.261	2,500	120.0	1,445.7	1.4
17	46.25	0.062	(19,900)	(920.4)	526.7	0.5
18	48.13	0.183	12,100	582.4	1,109.6	1.1
19	46.63	0.007	(17,600)	(820.7)	290.0	0.3
20	48.12	0.000	(700)	(33.7)	256.6	

hedger receives $5 million for the stock held, so that the total cost of writing the option and hedging it is $263,300.

Table 19.3 illustrates an alternative sequence of events such that the option closes out of the money. As it becomes clear that the option will not be exercised, delta approaches zero. By Week 20 the hedger has a naked position and has incurred costs totaling $256,600.

In Tables 19.2 and 19.3, the costs of hedging the option, when discounted to the beginning of the period, are close to but not exactly the same as the Black–Scholes–Merton price of $240,000. If the hedging worked perfectly, the cost of hedging would, after discounting, be exactly equal to the Black–Scholes–Merton price for every simulated stock price path. The reason for the variation in the hedging cost is that the hedge is rebalanced only once a week. As rebalancing takes place more frequently, the variation in the hedging cost is reduced. Of course, the examples in Tables 19.2 and 19.3 are idealized in that they assume that the volatility is constant and there are no transaction costs.

Table 19.4 shows statistics on the performance of delta hedging obtained from one million random stock price paths in our example. The performance measure is calculated, similarly to Table 19.1, as the ratio of the standard deviation of the cost of hedging the option to the Black–Scholes–Merton price of the option. It is clear that delta hedging is a

Table 19.4   Performance of delta hedging. The performance measure is the ratio of the standard deviation of the cost of writing the option and hedging it to the theoretical price of the option.

Time between hedge rebalancing (weeks):	5	4	2	1	0.5	0.25
Performance measure:	0.42	0.38	0.28	0.21	0.16	0.13

great improvement over a stop-loss strategy. Unlike a stop-loss strategy, the performance of delta-hedging gets steadily better as the hedge is monitored more frequently.

Delta hedging aims to keep the value of the financial institution's position as close to unchanged as possible. Initially, the value of the written option is $240,000. In the situation depicted in Table 19.2, the value of the option can be calculated as $414,500 in Week 9. (This value is obtained from the Black–Scholes–Merton model by setting the stock price equal to $53 and the time to maturity equal to 11 weeks.) Thus, the financial institution has lost $174,500 on its short option position. Its cash position, as measured by the cumulative cost, is $1,442,900 worse in Week 9 than in Week 0. The value of the shares held has increased from $2,557,800 to $4,171,100. The net effect of all this is that the value of the financial institution's position has changed by only $4,100 between Week 0 and Week 9.

Where the Cost Comes From

The delta-hedging procedure in Tables 19.2 and 19.3 creates the equivalent of a long position in the option. This neutralizes the short position the financial institution created by writing the option. As the tables illustrate, delta hedging a short position generally involves selling stock just after the price has gone down and buying stock just after the price has gone up. It might be termed a buy-high, sell-low trading strategy! The average cost of $240,000 comes from the present value of the difference between the price at which stock is purchased and the price at which it is sold.

Delta of a Portfolio

The delta of a portfolio of options or other derivatives dependent on a single asset whose price is S is

$$\frac{\partial \Pi}{\partial S}$$

where Π is the value of the portfolio.

The delta of the portfolio can be calculated from the deltas of the individual options in the portfolio. If a portfolio consists of a quantity w_i of option i ($1 \leqslant i \leqslant n$), the delta of the portfolio is given by

$$\Delta = \sum_{i=1}^{n} w_i \Delta_i$$

where Δ_i is the delta of the ith option. The formula can be used to calculate the position in the underlying asset necessary to make the delta of the portfolio zero. When this position has been taken, the portfolio is delta neutral.

Suppose a financial institution has the following three positions in options on a stock:

1. A long position in 100,000 call options with strike price $55 and an expiration date in 3 months. The delta of each option is 0.533.

2. A short position in 200,000 call options with strike price $56 and an expiration date in 5 months. The delta of each option is 0.468.

3. A short position in 50,000 put options with strike price $56 and an expiration date in 2 months. The delta of each option is −0.508.

The delta of the whole portfolio is

$$100{,}000 \times 0.533 - 200{,}000 \times 0.468 - 50{,}000 \times (-0.508) = -14{,}900$$

This means that the portfolio can be made delta neutral by buying 14,900 shares.

Transaction Costs

Derivatives dealers usually rebalance their positions once a day to maintain delta neutrality. When the dealer has a small number of options on a particular asset, this is liable to be prohibitively expensive because of the bid–offer spreads the dealer is subject to on trades. For a large portfolio of options, it is more feasible. Only one trade in the underlying asset is necessary to zero out delta for the whole portfolio. The bid–offer spread transaction costs are absorbed by the profits on many different trades.

19.5 THETA

The *theta* (Θ) of a portfolio of options is the rate of change of the value of the portfolio with respect to the passage of time with all else remaining the same. Theta is sometimes referred to as the *time decay* of the portfolio. For a European call option on a non-dividend-paying stock, it can be shown from the Black–Scholes–Merton formula (see Problem 15.17) that

$$\Theta(\text{call}) = -\frac{S_0 N'(d_1)\sigma}{2\sqrt{T}} - rKe^{-rT}N(d_2)$$

where d_1 and d_2 are defined as in equation (15.20) and

$$N'(x) = \frac{1}{\sqrt{2\pi}}e^{-x^2/2} \tag{19.2}$$

is the probability density function for a standard normal distribution.

For a European put option on the stock,

$$\Theta(\text{put}) = -\frac{S_0 N'(d_1)\sigma}{2\sqrt{T}} + rKe^{-rT}N(-d_2)$$

Because $N(-d_2) = 1 - N(d_2)$, the theta of a put exceeds the theta of the corresponding call by rKe^{-rT}.

In these formulas, time is measured in years. Usually, when theta is quoted, time is measured in days, so that theta is the change in the portfolio value when 1 day passes with all else remaining the same. We can measure theta either "per calendar day" or "per trading day." To obtain the theta per calendar day, the formula for theta must be divided by 365; to obtain theta per trading day, it must be divided by 252. (DerivaGem measures theta per calendar day.)

Example 19.2

As in Example 19.1, consider a call option on a non-dividend-paying stock where the stock price is $49, the strike price is $50, the risk-free rate is 5%, the time to maturity is 20 weeks ($= 0.3846$ years), and the volatility is 20%. In this case, $S_0 = 49$, $K = 50$, $r = 0.05$, $\sigma = 0.2$, and $T = 0.3846$.

The option's theta is

$$-\frac{S_0 N'(d_1)\sigma}{2\sqrt{T}} - rKe^{-rT}N(d_2) = -4.31$$

The theta is $-4.31/365 = -0.0118$ per calendar day, or $-4.31/252 = -0.0171$ per trading day.

Theta is usually negative for an option.[7] This is because, as time passes with all else remaining the same, the option tends to become less valuable. The variation of Θ with stock price for a call option on a stock is shown in Figure 19.5. When the stock price is very low, theta is close to zero. For an at-the-money call option, theta is large and negative. As the stock price becomes larger, theta tends to $-rKe^{-rT}$. (In our example, $r = 0$.) Figure 19.6 shows typical patterns for the variation of Θ with the time to maturity for in-the-money, at-the-money, and out-of-the-money call options.

Figure 19.5 Variation of theta of a European call option with stock price ($K = 50$, $r = 0$, $\sigma = 0.25$, $T = 2$).

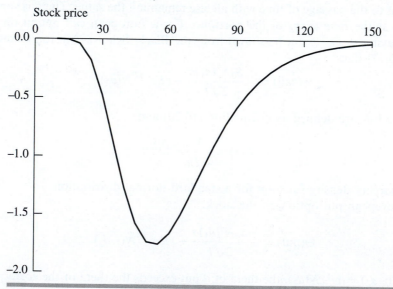

---

[7] An exception to this could be an in-the-money European put option on a non-dividend-paying stock or an in-the-money European call option on a currency with a very high interest rate.

Figure 19.6   Typical patterns for variation of theta of a European call option with time to maturity ($S_0 = 50$, $K = 50$, $r = 0$, $\sigma = 25\%$).

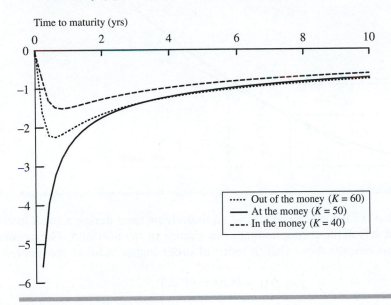

Theta is not the same type of hedge parameter as delta. There is uncertainty about the future stock price, but there is no uncertainty about the passage of time. It makes sense to hedge against changes in the price of the underlying asset, but it does not make any sense to hedge against the passage of time. In spite of this, many traders regard theta as a useful descriptive statistic for a portfolio. This is because, as we shall see later, in a delta-neutral portfolio theta is a proxy for gamma.

19.6   GAMMA

The *gamma* (Γ) of a portfolio of options on an underlying asset is the rate of change of the portfolio's delta with respect to the price of the underlying asset. It is the second partial derivative of the portfolio with respect to asset price:

$$\Gamma = \frac{\partial^2 \Pi}{\partial S^2}$$

If gamma is small, delta changes slowly, and adjustments to keep a portfolio delta neutral need to be made only relatively infrequently. However, if gamma is highly negative or highly positive, delta is very sensitive to the price of the underlying asset. It is then quite risky to leave a delta-neutral portfolio unchanged for any length of time. Figure 19.7 illustrates this point. When the stock price moves from S to S', delta hedging assumes that the option price moves from C to C', when in fact it moves from C to C''. The difference between C' and C'' leads to a hedging error. The size of the error depends on the curvature of the relationship between the option price and the stock price. Gamma measures this curvature.

Figure 19.7   Hedging error introduced by nonlinearity.

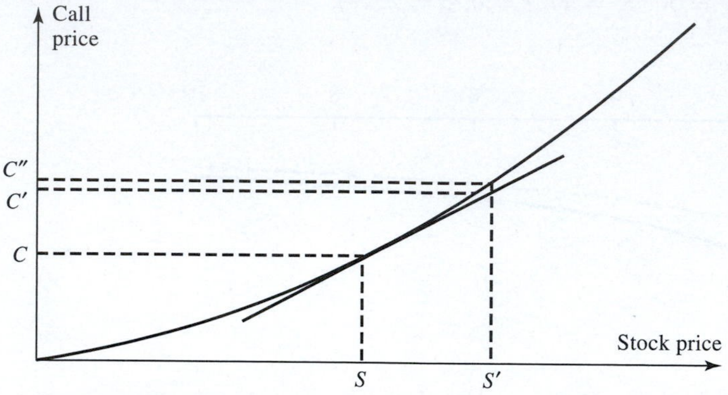

Suppose that ΔS is the price change of an underlying asset during a small interval of time, Δt, and $\Delta \Pi$ is the corresponding price change in the portfolio. The appendix at the end of this chapter shows that, if terms of order higher than Δt are ignored,

$$\Delta \Pi = \Theta \, \Delta t + \tfrac{1}{2} \Gamma \, \Delta S^2 \qquad\qquad \textbf{(19.3)}$$

for a delta-neutral portfolio, where Θ is the theta of the portfolio. Figure 19.8 shows the nature of the relationship between $\Delta \Pi$ and ΔS. When gamma is positive, theta tends to be negative. The portfolio declines in value if there is no change in S, but increases in value if there is a large positive or negative change in S. When gamma is negative, theta tends to be positive and the reverse is true: the portfolio increases in value if there is no change in S but decreases in value if there is a large positive or negative change in S. As the absolute value of gamma increases, the sensitivity of the value of the portfolio to S increases.

Example 19.3

Suppose that the gamma of a delta-neutral portfolio of options on an asset is $-10,000$. Equation (19.3) shows that, if a change of $+2$ or -2 in the price of the asset occurs over a short period of time, there is an unexpected decrease in the value of the portfolio of approximately $0.5 \times 10,000 \times 2^2 = \$20,000$.

Making a Portfolio Gamma Neutral

A position in the underlying asset has zero gamma and cannot be used to change the gamma of a portfolio. What is required is a position in an instrument such as an option that is not linearly dependent on the underlying asset.

Suppose that a delta-neutral portfolio has a gamma equal to Γ, and a traded option has a gamma equal to Γ_T. If the number of traded options added to the portfolio is w_T, the gamma of the portfolio is

$$w_T \Gamma_T + \Gamma$$

Hence, the position in the traded option necessary to make the portfolio gamma neutral is $-\Gamma / \Gamma_T$. Including the traded option is likely to change the delta of the portfolio, so

Figure 19.8   Relationship between $\Delta\Pi$ and ΔS in time Δt for a delta-neutral portfolio with (a) slightly positive gamma, (b) large positive gamma, (c) slightly negative gamma, and (d) large negative gamma.

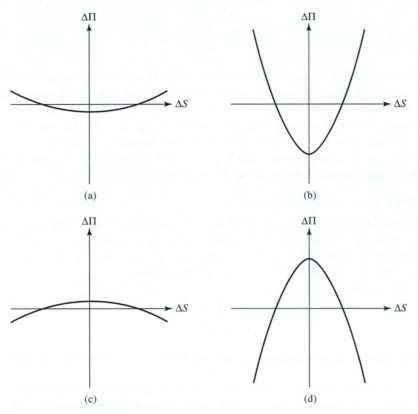

the position in the underlying asset then has to be changed to maintain delta neutrality. Note that the portfolio is gamma neutral only for a short period of time. As time passes, gamma neutrality can be maintained only if the position in the traded option is adjusted so that it is always equal to $-\Gamma/\Gamma_T$.

Making a portfolio gamma neutral as well as delta-neutral can be regarded as a correction for the hedging error illustrated in Figure 19.7. Delta neutrality provides protection against relatively small stock price moves between rebalancing. Gamma neutrality provides protection against larger movements in this stock price between hedge rebalancing. Suppose that a portfolio is delta neutral and has a gamma of $-3,000$. The delta and gamma of a particular traded call option are 0.62 and 1.50, respectively. The portfolio can be made gamma neutral by including in the portfolio a long position of

$$\frac{3,000}{1.5} = 2,000$$

in the call option. However, the delta of the portfolio will then change from zero to $2,000 \times 0.62 = 1,240$. Therefore 1,240 units of the underlying asset must be sold from the portfolio to keep it delta neutral.

Calculation of Gamma

For a European call or put option on a non-dividend-paying stock, the gamma given by the Black–Scholes–Merton model is

$$\Gamma = \frac{N'(d_1)}{S_0 \sigma \sqrt{T}}$$

where d_1 is defined as in equation (15.20) and $N'(x)$ is as given by equation (19.2). The gamma of a long position is always positive and varies with S_0 in the way indicated in Figure 19.9. The variation of gamma with time to maturity for out-of-the-money, at-the-money, and in-the-money options is shown in Figure 19.10. For an at-the-money option, gamma increases as the time to maturity decreases. Short-life at-the-money options have very high gammas, which means that the value of the option holder's position is highly sensitive to jumps in the stock price.

Example 19.4

As in Example 19.1, consider a call option on a non-dividend-paying stock where the stock price is $49, the strike price is $50, the risk-free rate is 5%, the time to maturity is 20 weeks ($= 0.3846$ years), and the volatility is 20%. In this case, $S_0 = 49$, $K = 50$, $r = 0.05$, $\sigma = 0.2$, and $T = 0.3846$.

The option's gamma is

$$\frac{N'(d_1)}{S_0 \sigma \sqrt{T}} = 0.066$$

When the stock price changes by ΔS, the delta of the option changes by $0.066\Delta S$.

Figure 19.9 Variation of gamma with stock price for an option ($K = 50$, $r = 0$, $\sigma = 25\%$, $T = 2$).

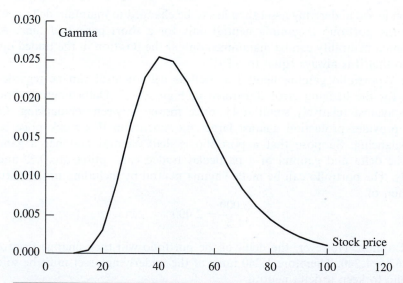

Figure 19.10   Variation of gamma with time to maturity for a stock option ($S_0 = 50$,
   $K = 50$, $r = 0$, $\sigma = 25\%$).

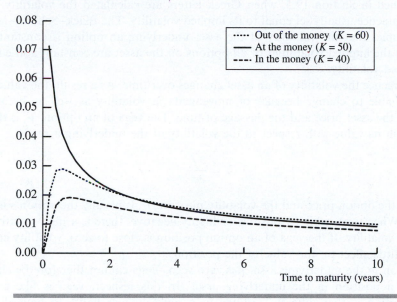

19.7   RELATIONSHIP BETWEEN DELTA, THETA, AND GAMMA

The price of a single derivative dependent on a non-dividend-paying stock must satisfy
the differential equation (15.16). It follows that the value of Π of a portfolio of such
derivatives also satisfies the differential equation

$$\frac{\partial \Pi}{\partial t} + rS\frac{\partial \Pi}{\partial S} + \tfrac{1}{2}\sigma^2 S^2 \frac{\partial^2 \Pi}{\partial S^2} = r\Pi$$

Since

$$\Theta = \frac{\partial \Pi}{\partial t}, \qquad \Delta = \frac{\partial \Pi}{\partial S}, \qquad \Gamma = \frac{\partial^2 \Pi}{\partial S^2}$$

it follows that

$$\Theta + rS\Delta + \tfrac{1}{2}\sigma^2 S^2 \Gamma = r\Pi \tag{19.4}$$

Similar results can be produced for other underlying assets (see Problem 19.19).
   For a delta-neutral portfolio, $\Delta = 0$ and

$$\Theta + \tfrac{1}{2}\sigma^2 S^2 \Gamma = r\Pi$$

This shows that, when Θ is large and positive, gamma of a portfolio tends to be large
and negative, and vice versa. This is consistent with the way in which Figure 19.8 has
been drawn and explains why theta can to some extent be regarded as a proxy for
gamma in a delta-neutral portfolio.

19.8 VEGA

As mentioned in Section 19.3, when Greek letters are calculated the volatility of the asset is in practice usually set equal to its implied volatility. The Black–Scholes–Merton model assumes that the volatility of the asset underlying an option is constant. This means that the implied volatilities of all options on the asset are constant and equal to this assumed volatility.

But in practice the volatility of an asset changes over time. As a result, the value of an option is liable to change because of movements in volatility as well as because of changes in the asset price and the passage of time. The vega of an option, $\mathcal{V}$, is the rate of change in its value with respect to the volatility of the underlying asset:[8]

$$\mathcal{V} = \frac{\partial f}{\partial \sigma}$$

where f is the option price and the volatility measure, σ, is usually the option's implied volatility. When vega is highly positive or highly negative, there is a high sensitivity to changes in volatility. If the vega of an option position is close to zero, volatility changes have very little effect on the value of the position.

A position in the underlying asset has zero vega. Vega cannot therefore be changed by taking a position in the underlying asset. In this respect, vega is like gamma. A complication is that different options in a portfolio are liable to have different implied volatilities. If all implied volatilities are assumed to change by the same amount during any short period of time, vega can be treated like gamma and the vega risk in a portfolio of options can be hedged by taking a position in a single option. If $\mathcal{V}$ is the vega of a portfolio and $\mathcal{V}_T$ is the vega of a traded option, a position of $-\mathcal{V}/\mathcal{V}_T$ in the traded option makes the portfolio instantaneously vega neutral. Unfortunately, a portfolio that is gamma neutral will not in general be vega neutral, and vice versa. If a hedger requires a portfolio to be both gamma and vega neutral, at least two traded options dependent on the underlying asset must be used.

Example 19.5

Consider a portfolio that is delta neutral, with a gamma of $-5,000$ and a vega (measuring sensitivity to implied volatility) of $-8,000$. The options shown in the following table can be traded. The portfolio can be made vega neutral by including a long position in 4,000 of Option 1. This would increase delta to 2,400 and require that 2,400 units of the asset be sold to maintain delta neutrality. The gamma of the portfolio would change from $-5,000$ to $-3,000$.

	Delta	Gamma	Vega
Portfolio	0	−5000	−8000
Option 1	0.6	0.5	2.0
Option 2	0.5	0.8	1.2

To make the portfolio gamma and vega neutral, both Option 1 and Option 2 can be used. If w_1 and w_2 are the quantities of Option 1 and Option 2 that are

---

[8] Vega is the name given to one of the "Greek letters" in option pricing, but it is not one of the letters in the Greek alphabet.

added to the portfolio, we require that

$$-5{,}000 + 0.5w_1 + 0.8w_2 = 0$$

and

$$-8{,}000 + 2.0w_1 + 1.2w_2 = 0$$

The solution to these equations is $w_1 = 400$, $w_2 = 6{,}000$. The portfolio can therefore be made gamma and vega neutral by including 400 of Option 1 and 6,000 of Option 2. The delta of the portfolio, after the addition of the positions in the two traded options, is $400 \times 0.6 + 6{,}000 \times 0.5 = 3{,}240$. Hence, 3,240 units of the asset would have to be sold to maintain delta neutrality.

Hedging in the way indicated in Example 19.5 assumes that the implied volatilities of all options in a portfolio will change by the same amount during a short period of time. In practice, this is not necessarily true and a trader's hedging problem is more complex. As we will see in the next chapter, for any given underlying asset a trader monitors a "volatility surface" that describes the implied volatilities of options with different strike prices and times to maturity. The trader's total vega risk for a portfolio is related to the different ways in which the volatility surface can change.

For a European call or put option on a non-dividend-paying stock, vega given by the Black–Scholes–Merton model is

$$\mathcal{V} = S_0 \sqrt{T}\, N'(d_1)$$

where d_1 is defined as in equation (15.20). The formula for $N'(x)$ is given in equation (19.2). The vega of a long position in a European or American option is always positive. The general way in which vega varies with S_0 is shown in Figure 19.11.

Figure 19.11 Variation of vega with stock price for an option ($K = 50$, $r = 0$, $\sigma = 25\%$, $T = 2$).

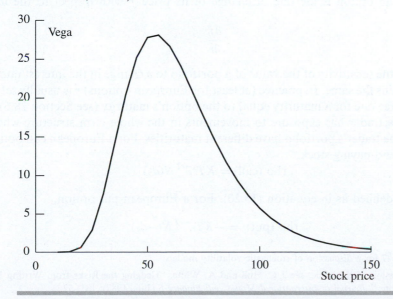

Example 19.6

As in Example 19.1, consider a call option on a non-dividend-paying stock where the stock price is $49, the strike price is $50, the risk-free rate is 5%, the time to maturity is 20 weeks ($= 0.3846$ years), and the implied volatility is 20%. In this case, $S_0 = 49$, $K = 50$, $r = 0.05$, $\sigma = 0.2$, and $T = 0.3846$.

The option's vega is

$$S_0\sqrt{T}N'(d_1) = 12.1$$

Thus a 1% (0.01) increase in the implied volatility from (20% to 21%) increases the value of the option by approximately $0.01 \times 12.1 = 0.121$.

Calculating vega from the Black–Scholes–Merton model and its extensions may seem strange because one of the assumptions underlying the model is that volatility is constant. It would be theoretically more correct to calculate vega from a model in which volatility is assumed to be stochastic.[9] However, traders prefer the simpler approach of measuring vega in terms of potential movements in the Black–Scholes–Merton implied volatility.

Gamma neutrality protects against large changes in the price of the underlying asset between hedge rebalancing. Vega neutrality protects against changes in volatility. As might be expected, whether it is best to use an available traded option for vega or gamma hedging depends on the time between hedge rebalancing and the volatility of the volatility.[10]

When volatilities change, the implied volatilities of short-dated options tend to change by more than the implied volatilities of long-dated options. The vega of a portfolio is therefore often calculated by changing the volatilities of long-dated options by less than that of short-dated options. One way of doing this is discussed in Section 23.6.

19.9 RHO

The *rho* of an option is the rate of change of its price f with respect to the interest rate r:

$$\frac{\partial f}{\partial r}$$

It measures the sensitivity of the value of a portfolio to a change in the interest rate when all else remains the same. In practice (at least for European options) r is usually set equal to the risk-free rate for a maturity equal to the option's maturity (see Section 28.6). This means that a trader has exposure to movements in the whole term structure when the options in the trader's portfolio have different maturities. For a European call option on a non-dividend-paying stock,

$$\text{rho (call)} = KTe^{-rT}N(d_2)$$

where d_2 is defined as in equation (15.20). For a European put option,

$$\text{rho (put)} = -KTe^{-rT}N(-d_2)$$

---

[9] See Chapter 27 for a discussion of stochastic volatility models.

[10] For a discussion of this issue, see J. C. Hull and A. White, "Hedging the Risks from Writing Foreign Currency Options," *Journal of International Money and Finance* 6 (June 1987): 131–52.

Example 19.7

As in Example 19.1, consider a call option on a non-dividend-paying stock where the stock price is $49, the strike price is $50, the risk-free rate is 5%, the time to maturity is 20 weeks (= 0.3846 years), and the volatility is 20%. In this case, $S_0 = 49$, $K = 50$, $r = 0.05$, $\sigma = 0.2$, and $T = 0.3846$.

The option's rho is

$$KTe^{-rT}N(d_2) = 8.91$$

This means that a 1% (0.01) increase in the risk-free rate (from 5% to 6%) increases the value of the option by approximately $0.01 \times 8.91 = 0.0891$.

19.10 THE REALITIES OF HEDGING

In an ideal world, traders working for financial institutions would be able to rebalance their portfolios very frequently in order to maintain all Greeks equal to zero. In practice, this is not possible. When managing a large portfolio dependent on a single underlying asset, traders usually make delta zero, or close to zero, at least once a day by trading the underlying asset. Unfortunately, a zero gamma and a zero vega are less easy to achieve because it is difficult to find options or other nonlinear derivatives that can be traded in the volume required at competitive prices. Business Snapshot 19.1 provides a discussion of how dynamic hedging is organized at financial institutions.

As already mentioned, there are big economies of scale in trading derivatives. Maintaining delta neutrality for a small number of options on an asset by trading daily is usually not economically feasible because the trading costs per option hedged are high.[11] But when a derivatives dealer maintains delta neutrality for a large portfolio of options on an asset, the trading costs per option hedged are more reasonable.

19.11 SCENARIO ANALYSIS

In addition to monitoring risks such as delta, gamma, and vega, option traders often also carry out a scenario analysis. The analysis involves calculating the gain or loss on their portfolio over a specified period under a variety of different scenarios. The time period chosen is likely to depend on the liquidity of the instruments. The scenarios can be either chosen by management or generated by a model.

Consider a bank with a portfolio of options dependent on the USD/EUR exchange rate. The two key variables on which the value of the portfolio depends are the exchange rate and the exchange-rate volatility. The bank could calculate a table such as Table 19.5 showing the profit or loss experienced during a 2-week period under different scenarios. This table considers seven different exchange rate movements and three different implied volatility movements. The table makes the simplifying assumption that the implied volatilities of all options in the portfolio change by the same amount. (Note: +2% would indicate a volatility change from 10% to 12%, not 10% to 10.2%.)

---

[11] The trading costs arise from the fact that each day the hedger buys some of the underlying asset at the offer price or sells some of the underlying asset at the bid price.

Business Snapshot 19.1   Dynamic Hedging in Practice

In a typical arrangement at a financial institution, the responsibility for a portfolio of derivatives dependent on a particular underlying asset is assigned to one trader or to a group of traders working together. For example, one trader at Goldman Sachs might be assigned responsibility for all derivatives dependent on the value of the Australian dollar. A computer system calculates the value of the portfolio and Greek letters for the portfolio. Limits are defined for each Greek letter and special permission is required if a trader wants to exceed a limit at the end of a trading day.

The delta limit is often expressed as the equivalent maximum position in the underlying asset. For example, the delta limit for a stock at a particular bank might be $1 million. If the stock price is $50, this means that the absolute value of delta as we have calculated it can be no more than 20,000. The vega limit is usually expressed as a maximum dollar exposure per 1% change in implied volatilities.

As a matter of course, options traders make themselves delta neutral—or close to delta neutral—at the end of each day. Gamma and vega are monitored, but are not usually managed on a daily basis. Financial institutions often find that their business with clients involves writing options and that as a result they accumulate negative gamma and vega. They are then always looking out for opportunities to manage their gamma and vega risks by buying options at competitive prices.

There is one aspect of an options portfolio that mitigates problems of managing gamma and vega somewhat. Options are often close to the money when they are first sold, so that they have relatively high gammas and vegas. But after some time has elapsed, the underlying asset price has often changed enough for them to become deep out of the money or deep in the money. Their gammas and vegas are then very small and of little consequence. A nightmare scenario for an options trader is where written options remain very close to the money as the maturity date is approached.

In Table 19.5, the greatest loss is in the lower right corner of the table. The loss corresponds to implied volatilities increasing by 2% and the exchange rate moving up by 0.06. Usually the greatest loss in a table such as Table 19.5 occurs at one of the corners, but this is not always so. Consider, for example, the situation where a bank's portfolio consists of a short position in a butterfly spread (see Section 12.3). The greatest loss will be experienced if the exchange rate stays where it is.

Table 19.5   Profit or loss realized in 2 weeks under different scenarios ($ million).

Implied volatility changes	Exchange rate change						
	−0.06	−0.04	−0.02	0.00	+0.02	+0.04	+0.06
−2%	+102	+55	+25	+6	−10	−34	−80
0%	+80	+40	+17	+2	−14	−38	−85
+2%	+60	+25	+9	−2	−18	−42	−90

19.12 EXTENSION OF FORMULAS

The formulas produced so far for delta, theta, gamma, vega, and rho have been for a European option on a non-dividend-paying stock. Table 19.6 shows how they change when the stock pays a continuous dividend yield at rate q. The expressions for d_1 and d_2 are as for equations (17.4) and (17.5). By setting q equal to the dividend yield on an index, we obtain the Greek letters for European options on indices. By setting q equal to the foreign risk-free rate, we obtain the Greek letters for European options on a currency. By setting $q = r$, we obtain delta, gamma, theta, and vega for European options on a futures contract. The rho for a call futures option is $-cT$ and the rho for a European put futures option is $-pT$.

In the case of currency options, there are two rhos corresponding to the two interest rates. The rho corresponding to the domestic interest rate is given by the formula in Table 19.6 (with d_2 as in equation (17.11)). The rho corresponding to the foreign interest rate for a European call on a currency is

$$\text{rho(call, foreign rate)} = -Te^{-r_f T}S_0 N(d_1)$$

For a European put, it is

$$\text{rho(put, foreign rate)} = Te^{-r_f T}S_0 N(-d_1)$$

with d_1 as in equation (17.11).

The calculation of Greek letters for American options is discussed in Chapter 21.

Delta of Forward Contracts

The concept of delta can be applied to financial instruments other than options. Consider a forward contract on a non-dividend-paying stock. Equation (5.5) shows that the value of a forward contract is $S_0 - Ke^{-rT}$, where K is the delivery price and T is the forward contract's time to maturity. When the price of the stock changes by ΔS, with all else remaining the same, the value of a forward contract on the stock also changes by ΔS. The

---

Table 19.6 Greek letters for European options on an asset providing a yield at rate q.

Greek letter	Call option	Put option
Delta	$e^{-qT}N(d_1)$	$e^{-qT}[N(d_1) - 1]$
Gamma	$\dfrac{N'(d_1)e^{-qT}}{S_0\sigma\sqrt{T}}$	$\dfrac{N'(d_1)e^{-qT}}{S_0\sigma\sqrt{T}}$
Theta	$-S_0 N'(d_1)\sigma e^{-qT}/(2\sqrt{T})$ $+ qS_0 N(d_1)e^{-qT} - rKe^{-rT}N(d_2)$	$-S_0 N'(d_1)\sigma e^{-qT}/(2\sqrt{T})$ $- qS_0 N(-d_1)e^{-qT} + rKe^{-rT}N(-d_2)$
Vega	$S_0\sqrt{T}N'(d_1)e^{-qT}$	$S_0\sqrt{T}N'(d_1)e^{-qT}$
Rho	$KTe^{-rT}N(d_2)$	$-KTe^{-rT}N(-d_2)$

delta of a long forward contract on one share of the stock is therefore always 1.0. This means that a long forward contract on one share can be hedged by shorting one share; a short forward contract on one share can be hedged by purchasing one share.[12]

For an asset providing a dividend yield at rate q, equation (5.7) shows that the forward contract's delta is e^{-qT}. For the delta of a forward contract on a stock index, q is set equal to the dividend yield on the index in this expression. For the delta of a forward foreign exchange contract, it is set equal to the foreign risk-free rate, r_f.

Delta of a Futures Contract

From equation (5.1), the futures price for a contract on a non-dividend-paying stock is $S_0 e^{rT}$, where T is the time to maturity of the futures contract. This shows that when the price of the stock changes by ΔS, with all else remaining the same, the futures price changes by $\Delta S\, e^{rT}$. Since futures contracts are settled daily, the holder of a long futures position makes an almost immediate gain of this amount. The delta of a futures contract is therefore e^{rT}. For a futures position on an asset providing a dividend yield at rate q, equation (5.3) shows similarly that delta is $e^{(r-q)T}$.

It is interesting that daily settlement makes the deltas of futures and forward contracts slightly different. This is true even when interest rates are constant and the forward price equals the futures price. (A related point is made in Business Snapshot 5.2.)

Sometimes a futures contract is used to achieve a delta-neutral position. Define:

T: Maturity of futures contract

H_A: Required position in asset for delta hedging

H_F: Alternative required position in futures contracts for delta hedging.

If the underlying asset is a non-dividend-paying stock, the analysis we have just given shows that

$$H_F = e^{-rT} H_A \tag{19.5}$$

When the underlying asset pays a dividend yield q,

$$H_F = e^{-(r-q)T} H_A \tag{19.6}$$

For a stock index, we set q equal to the dividend yield on the index; for a currency, we set it equal to the foreign risk-free rate, r_f, so that

$$H_F = e^{-(r-r_f)T} H_A \tag{19.7}$$

Example 19.8

Suppose that a portfolio of currency options held by a U.S. bank can be made delta neutral with a short position of 458,000 pounds sterling. Risk-free rates are 4% in the United States and 7% in the United Kingdom. From equation (19.7), hedging using 9-month currency futures requires a short futures position

$$e^{-(0.04-0.07)\times 9/12} \times 458{,}000$$

or £468,442. Since each futures contract is for the purchase or sale of £62,500, seven contracts would be shorted. (Seven is the nearest whole number to 468,442/62,500.)

---

[12] These are hedge-and-forget schemes. Since delta is always 1.0, no changes need to be made to the position in the stock during the life of the contract.

19.13 PORTFOLIO INSURANCE

A portfolio manager is often interested in acquiring a put option on his or her portfolio. This provides protection against market declines while preserving the potential for a gain if the market does well. One approach (discussed in Section 17.1) is to buy put options on a market index such as the S&P 500. An alternative is to create the options synthetically.

Creating an option synthetically involves maintaining a position in the underlying asset (or futures on the underlying asset) so that the delta of the position is equal to the delta of the required option. The position necessary to create an option synthetically is the reverse of that necessary to hedge it. This is because the procedure for hedging an option involves the creation of an equal and opposite option synthetically.

There are two reasons why it may be more attractive for the portfolio manager to create the required put option synthetically than to buy it in the market. First, option markets do not always have the liquidity to absorb the trades required by managers of large funds. Second, fund managers often require strike prices and exercise dates that are different from those available in exchange-traded options markets.

The synthetic option can be created from trading the portfolio or from trading in index futures contracts. We first examine the creation of a put option by trading the portfolio. From Table 19.6, the delta of a European put on the portfolio is

$$\Delta = e^{-qT}[N(d_1) - 1] \qquad (19.8)$$

where, with our usual notation,

$$d_1 = \frac{\ln(S_0/K) + (r - q + \sigma^2/2)T}{\sigma\sqrt{T}}$$

The other variables are defined as usual: S_0 is the value of the portfolio, K is the strike price, r is the risk-free rate, q is the dividend yield on the portfolio, σ is the volatility of the portfolio, and T is the life of the option. The volatility of the portfolio can usually be assumed to be its beta times the volatility of a well-diversified market index.

To create the put option synthetically, the fund manager should ensure that at any given time a proportion

$$e^{-qT}[1 - N(d_1)]$$

of the stocks in the original portfolio has been sold and the proceeds invested in riskless assets. As the value of the original portfolio declines, the delta of the put given by equation (19.8) becomes more negative and the proportion of the original portfolio sold must be increased. As the value of the original portfolio increases, the delta of the put becomes less negative and the proportion of the original portfolio sold must be decreased (i.e., some of the original portfolio must be repurchased).

Using this strategy to create portfolio insurance means that at any given time funds are divided between the stock portfolio on which insurance is required and riskless assets. As the value of the stock portfolio increases, riskless assets are sold and the position in the stock portfolio is increased. As the value of the stock portfolio declines, the position in the stock portfolio is decreased and riskless assets are purchased. The cost of the insurance arises from the fact that the portfolio manager is always selling after a decline in the market and buying after a rise in the market.

Example 19.9

A portfolio is worth $90 million. To protect against market downturns the managers of the portfolio require a 6-month European put option on the portfolio with a strike price of $87 million. The risk-free rate is 9% per annum, the dividend yield is 3% per annum, and the volatility of the portfolio is estimated as 25% per annum. The S&P 500 index stands at 900. As the portfolio is considered to mimic the S&P 500 fairly closely, one alternative, discussed in Section 17.1, is to buy 1,000 put option contracts on the S&P 500 with a strike price of 870. Another alternative is to create the required option synthetically. In this case, $S_0 = 90$ million, $K = 87$ million, $r = 0.09$, $q = 0.03$, $\sigma = 0.25$, and $T = 0.5$, so that

$$d_1 = \frac{\ln(90/87) + (0.09 - 0.03 + 0.25^2/2)0.5}{0.25\sqrt{0.5}} = 0.4499$$

and the delta of the required option is

$$e^{-qT}[N(d_1) - 1] = -0.3215$$

This shows that 32.15% of the portfolio should be sold initially and invested in risk-free assets to match the delta of the required option. The amount of the portfolio sold must be monitored frequently. For example, if the value of the original portfolio reduces to $88 million after 1 day, the delta of the required option changes to 0.3679 and a further 4.64% of the original portfolio should be sold and invested in risk-free assets. If the value of the portfolio increases to $92 million, the delta of the required option changes to -0.2787 and 4.28% of the original portfolio should be repurchased.

Use of Index Futures

Using index futures to create options synthetically can be preferable to using the underlying stocks because the transaction costs associated with trades in index futures are generally lower than those associated with the corresponding trades in the underlying stocks. The dollar amount of the futures contracts shorted as a proportion of the value of the portfolio should from equations (19.6) and (19.8) be

$$e^{-qT}e^{-(r-q)T^*}[1 - N(d_1)] = e^{q(T^*-T)}e^{-rT^*}[1 - N(d_1)]$$

where T^* is the maturity of the futures contract. If the portfolio is worth A_1 times the index and each index futures contract is on A_2 times the index, the number of futures contracts shorted at any given time should be

$$e^{q(T^*-T)}e^{-rT^*}[1 - N(d_1)]A_1/A_2$$

Example 19.10

Suppose that in the previous example futures contracts on the S&P 500 maturing in 9 months are used to create the option synthetically. In this case initially $T = 0.5$, $T^* = 0.75$, $A_1 = 100{,}000$, and $d_1 = 0.4499$. Each index futures contract is on 250 times the index, so that $A_2 = 250$. The number of futures contracts shorted should be

$$e^{q(T^*-T)}e^{-rT^*}[1 - N(d_1)]A_1/A_2 = 122.96$$

or 123, rounding to the nearest whole number. As time passes and the index changes, the position in futures contracts must be adjusted.

This analysis assumes that the portfolio mirrors the index. When this is not the case, it is necessary to (a) calculate the portfolio's beta, (b) find the position in options on the index that gives the required protection, and (c) choose a position in index futures to create the options synthetically. As discussed in Section 17.1, the strike price for the options should be the expected level of the market index when the portfolio reaches its insured value. The number of options required is beta times the number that would be required if the portfolio had a beta of 1.0.

19.14 STOCK MARKET VOLATILITY

We discussed in Chapter 15 the issue of whether volatility is caused solely by the arrival of new information or whether trading itself generates volatility. Portfolio insurance strategies such as those just described have the potential to increase volatility. When the market declines, they cause portfolio managers either to sell stock or to sell index futures contracts. Either action may accentuate the decline (see Business Snapshot 19.2). The sale of stock is liable to drive down the market index further in a direct way. The sale of index futures contracts is liable to drive down futures prices. This creates selling pressure on stocks via the mechanism of index arbitrage (see Chapter 5), so that the market index is liable to be driven down in this case as well. Similarly, when the market rises, the portfolio insurance strategies cause portfolio managers either to buy stock or to buy futures contracts. This may accentuate the rise.

In addition to formal portfolio trading strategies, we can speculate that many investors consciously or subconsciously follow portfolio insurance rules of their own. For example, an investor may choose to sell when the market is falling to limit the downside risk.

Whether portfolio insurance trading strategies (formal or informal) affect volatility depends on how easily the market can absorb the trades that are generated by portfolio insurance. If portfolio insurance trades are a very small fraction of all trades, there is likely to be no effect. But if portfolio insurance becomes very popular, it is liable to have a destabilizing effect on the market, as it did in 1987.

SUMMARY

Financial institutions offer a variety of option products to their clients. Often the options do not correspond to the standardized products traded by exchanges. The financial institutions are then faced with the problem of hedging their exposure. Naked and covered positions leave them subject to an unacceptable level of risk. One course of action that is sometimes proposed is a stop-loss strategy. This involves holding a naked position when an option is out of the money and converting it to a covered position as soon as the option moves into the money. Although superficially attractive, the strategy does not provide a good hedge.

The delta (Δ) of an option is the rate of change of its price with respect to the price of the underlying asset. Delta hedging involves creating a position with zero delta (sometimes referred to as a delta-neutral position). Because the delta of the underlying asset

---

Business Snapshot 19.2   Was Portfolio Insurance to Blame for the Crash of 1987?

On Monday, October 19, 1987, the Dow Jones Industrial Average dropped by more than 20%. Many people feel that portfolio insurance played a major role in this crash. In October 1987 between $60 billion and $90 billion of equity assets were subject to portfolio insurance trading rules where put options were created synthetically in the way discussed in Section 19.13. During the period Wednesday, October 14, 1987, to Friday, October 16, 1987, the market declined by about 10%, with much of this decline taking place on Friday afternoon. The portfolio trading rules should have generated at least $12 billion of equity or index futures sales as a result of this decline. In fact, portfolio insurers had time to sell only $4 billion and they approached the following week with huge amounts of selling already dictated by their models. It is estimated that on Monday, October 19, sell programs by three portfolio insurers accounted for almost 10% of the sales on the New York Stock Exchange, and that portfolio insurance sales amounted to 21.3% of all sales in index futures markets. It is likely that the decline in equity prices was exacerbated by investors other than portfolio insurers selling heavily because they anticipated the actions of portfolio insurers.

Because the market declined so fast and the stock exchange systems were overloaded, many portfolio insurers were unable to execute the trades generated by their models and failed to obtain the protection they required. Needless to say, the popularity of portfolio insurance schemes has declined significantly since 1987. One of the morals of this story is that it is dangerous to follow a particular trading strategy—even a hedging strategy—when many other market participants are doing the same thing.

---

is 1.0, one way of hedging is to take a position of $-\Delta$ in the underlying asset for each long option being hedged. The delta of an option changes over time. This means that the position in the underlying asset has to be frequently adjusted.

Once an option position has been made delta neutral, the next stage is often to look at its gamma (Γ). The gamma of an option is the rate of change of its delta with respect to the price of the underlying asset. It is a measure of the curvature of the relationship between the option price and the asset price. The impact of this curvature on the performance of delta hedging can be reduced by making an option position gamma neutral. If Γ is the gamma of the position being hedged, this reduction is usually achieved by taking a position in a traded option that has a gamma of $-\Gamma$.

Delta and gamma hedging are both based on the assumption that the volatility of the underlying asset is constant. In practice, volatilities do change over time. The vega of an option or an option portfolio measures the rate of change of its value with respect to volatility, often implied volatility. Sometimes the same change is assumed to apply to all volatilities. A trader who wishes to hedge an option position against volatility changes can make the position vega neutral. As with the procedure for creating gamma neutrality, this usually involves taking an offsetting position in a traded option. If the trader wishes to achieve both gamma and vega neutrality, at least two traded options are usually required.

Two other measures of the risk of an option position are theta and rho. Theta measures the rate of change of the value of the position with respect to the passage of time, with all else remaining constant. Rho measures the rate of change of the value of the position with respect to the interest rate, with all else remaining constant.

In practice, option traders usually rebalance their portfolios at least once a day to maintain delta neutrality. It is usually not feasible to maintain gamma and vega neutrality on a regular basis. Typically a trader monitors these measures. If they get too large, either corrective action is taken or trading is curtailed.

Portfolio managers are sometimes interested in creating put options synthetically for the purposes of insuring an equity portfolio. They can do so either by trading the portfolio or by trading index futures on the portfolio. Trading the portfolio involves splitting the portfolio between equities and risk-free securities. As the market declines, more is invested in risk-free securities. As the market increases, more is invested in equities. Trading index futures involves keeping the equity portfolio intact and selling index futures. As the market declines, more index futures are sold; as it rises, fewer are sold. This type of portfolio insurance works well in normal market conditions. On Monday, October 19, 1987, when the Dow Jones Industrial Average dropped very sharply, it worked badly. Portfolio insurers were unable to sell either stocks or index futures fast enough to protect their positions.

FURTHER READING

Passarelli, D. *Trading Option Greeks: How Time, Volatility, and Other Factors Drive Profits*, 2nd edn. Hoboken, NJ: Wiley, 2012.

Taleb, N. N., *Dynamic Hedging: Managing Vanilla and Exotic Options*. New York: Wiley, 1996.

Practice Questions (Answers in Solutions Manual)

19.1. Explain how a stop-loss trading rule can be implemented for the writer of an out-of-the-money call option. Why does it provide a relatively poor hedge?

19.2. What does it mean to assert that the delta of a call option is 0.7? How can a short position in 1,000 options be made delta neutral when the delta of each option is 0.7?

19.3. Calculate the delta of an at-the-money six-month European call option on a non-dividend-paying stock when the risk-free interest rate is 10% per annum and the stock price volatility is 25% per annum.

19.4. What does it mean to assert that the theta of an option position is −0.1 when time is measured in years? If a trader feels that neither a stock price nor its implied volatility will change, what type of option position is appropriate?

19.5. What is meant by the gamma of an option position? What are the risks in the situation where the gamma of a position is highly negative and the delta is zero?

19.6. "The procedure for creating an option position synthetically is the reverse of the procedure for hedging the option position." Explain this statement.

19.7. Why did portfolio insurance not work well on October 19, 1987?

19.8. The Black–Scholes–Merton price of an out-of-the-money call option with an exercise price of $40 is $4. A trader who has written the option plans to use a stop-loss strategy. The trader's plan is to buy at $40.10 and to sell at $39.90. Estimate the expected number of times the stock will be bought or sold.

19.9. Suppose that a stock price is currently $20 and that a call option with an exercise price of $25 is created synthetically using a continually changing position in the stock. Consider the following two scenarios: (a) Stock price increases steadily from $20 to $35 during the life of the option; (b) Stock price oscillates wildly, ending up at $35. Which scenario would make the synthetically created option more expensive? Explain your answer.

19.10. What is the delta of a short position in 1,000 European call options on silver futures? The options mature in 8 months, and the futures contract underlying the option matures in 9 months. The current 9-month futures price is $8 per ounce, the exercise price of the options is $8, the risk-free interest rate is 12% per annum, and the volatility of silver futures prices is 18% per annum.

19.11. In Problem 19.10, what initial position in 9-month silver futures is necessary for delta hedging? If silver itself is used, what is the initial position? If 1-year silver futures are used, what is the initial position? Assume no storage costs for silver.

19.12. A company uses delta hedging to hedge a portfolio of long positions in put and call options on a currency. Which of the following would give the most favorable result?
(a) A virtually constant spot rate
(b) Wild movements in the spot rate
Explain your answer.

19.13. Repeat Problem 19.12 for a financial institution with a portfolio of short positions in put and call options on a currency.

19.14. A financial institution has just sold 1,000 7-month European call options on the Japanese yen. Suppose that the spot exchange rate is 0.80 cent per yen, the exercise price is 0.81 cent per yen, the risk-free interest rate in the United States is 8% per annum, the risk-free interest rate in Japan is 5% per annum, and the volatility of the yen is 15% per annum. Calculate the delta, gamma, vega, theta, and rho of the financial institution's position. Interpret each number.

19.15. Under what circumstances is it possible to make a European option on a stock index both gamma neutral and vega neutral by adding a position in one other European option?

19.16. A fund manager has a well-diversified portfolio that mirrors the performance of the S&P 500 and is worth $360 million. The value of the S&P 500 is 1,200, and the portfolio manager would like to buy insurance against a reduction of more than 5% in the value of the portfolio over the next 6 months. The risk-free interest rate is 6% per annum. The dividend yield on both the portfolio and the S&P 500 is 3%, and the volatility of the index is 30% per annum.
(a) If the fund manager buys traded European put options, how much would the insurance cost?
(b) Explain carefully alternative strategies open to the fund manager involving traded European call options, and show that they lead to the same result.
(c) If the fund manager decides to provide insurance by keeping part of the portfolio in risk-free securities, what should the initial position be?
(d) If the fund manager decides to provide insurance by using 9-month index futures, what should the initial position be?

19.17. Repeat Problem 19.16 on the assumption that the portfolio has a beta of 1.5. Assume that the dividend yield on the portfolio is 4% per annum.

19.18. Show by substituting for the various terms in equation (19.4) that the equation is true for:
   (a) A single European call option on a non-dividend-paying stock
   (b) A single European put option on a non-dividend-paying stock
   (c) Any portfolio of European put and call options on a non-dividend-paying stock.

19.19. What is the equation corresponding to equation (19.4) for (a) a portfolio of derivatives on a currency and (b) a portfolio of derivatives on a futures price?

19.20. Suppose that $70 billion of equity assets are the subject of portfolio insurance schemes. Assume that the schemes are designed to provide insurance against the value of the assets declining by more than 5% within 1 year. Making whatever estimates you find necessary, use the DerivaGem software to calculate the value of the stock or futures contracts that the administrators of the portfolio insurance schemes will attempt to sell if the market falls by 23% in a single day.

19.21. Does a forward contract on a stock index have the same delta as the corresponding futures contract? Explain your answer.

19.22. A bank's position in options on the dollar/euro exchange rate has a delta of 30,000 and a gamma of −80,000. Explain how these numbers can be interpreted. The exchange rate (dollars per euro) is 0.90. What position would you take to make the position delta neutral? After a short period of time, the exchange rate moves to 0.93. Estimate the new delta. What additional trade is necessary to keep the position delta neutral? Assuming the bank did set up a delta-neutral position originally, has it gained or lost money from the exchange-rate movement?

19.23. Use the put–call parity relationship to derive, for a non-dividend-paying stock, the relationship between:
   (a) The delta of a European call and the delta of a European put
   (b) The gamma of a European call and the gamma of a European put
   (c) The vega of a European call and the vega of a European put
   (d) The theta of a European call and the theta of a European put.

Further Questions

19.24. A financial institution has the following portfolio of over-the-counter options on sterling:

Type	Position	Delta of option	Gamma of option	Vega of option
Call	−1,000	0.50	2.2	1.8
Call	−500	0.80	0.6	0.2
Put	−2,000	−0.40	1.3	0.7
Call	−500	0.70	1.8	1.4

A traded option is available with a delta of 0.6, a gamma of 1.5, and a vega of 0.8.
   (a) What position in the traded option and in sterling would make the portfolio both gamma neutral and delta neutral?
   (b) What position in the traded option and in sterling would make the portfolio both vega neutral and delta neutral? Assume that all implied volatilities change by the same amount so that vegas can be aggregated.

19.25. Consider again the situation in Problem 19.24. Suppose that a second traded option with a delta of 0.1, a gamma of 0.5, and a vega of 0.6 is available. How could the portfolio be made delta, gamma, and vega neutral?

19.26. Consider a 1-year European call option on a stock when the stock price is $30, the strike price is $30, the risk-free rate is 5%, and the volatility is 25% per annum. Use the DerivaGem software to calculate the price, delta, gamma, vega, theta, and rho of the option. Verify that delta is correct by changing the stock price to $30.1 and recomputing the option price. Verify that gamma is correct by recomputing the delta for the situation where the stock price is $30.1. Carry out similar calculations to verify that vega, theta, and rho are correct. Use the DerivaGem Applications Builder functions to plot the option price, delta, gamma, vega, theta, and rho against the stock price for the stock option.

19.27. A deposit instrument offered by a bank guarantees that investors will receive a return during a 6-month period that is the greater of (a) zero and (b) 40% of the return provided by a market index. An investor is planning to put $100,000 in the instrument. Describe the payoff as an option on the index. Assuming that the risk-free rate of interest is 8% per annum, the dividend yield on the index is 3% per annum, and the volatility of the index is 25% per annum, is the product a good deal for the investor?

19.28. The formula for the price c of a European call futures option in terms of the futures price F_0 is given in Chapter 18 as

$$c = e^{-rT}[F_0 N(d_1) - KN(d_2)]$$

where

$$d_1 = \frac{\ln(F_0/K) + \sigma^2 T/2}{\sigma\sqrt{T}} \quad \text{and} \quad d_2 = d_1 - \sigma\sqrt{T}$$

and K, r, T, and σ are the strike price, interest rate, time to maturity, and volatility, respectively.

(a) Prove that $F_0 N'(d_1) = KN'(d_2)$.
(b) Prove that the delta of the call price with respect to the futures price is $e^{-rT}N(d_1)$.
(c) Prove that the vega of the call price is $F_0\sqrt{T}N'(d_1)e^{-rT}$.
(d) Prove the formula for the rho of a call futures option given in Section 19.12.
The delta, gamma, theta, and vega of a call futures option are the same as those for a call option on a stock paying dividends at rate q, with q replaced by r and S_0 replaced by F_0. Explain why the same is not true of the rho of a call futures option.

19.29. Use DerivaGem to check that equation (19.4) is satisfied for the option considered in Section 19.1. (*Note*: DerivaGem produces a value of theta "per calendar day." The theta in equation (19.4) is "per year.")

19.30. Use the DerivaGem Application Builder functions to reproduce Table 19.2. (In Table 19.2 the stock position is rounded to the nearest 100 shares.) Calculate the gamma and theta of the position each week. Calculate the change in the value of the portfolio each week and check whether equation (19.3) is approximately satisfied. (*Note*: DerivaGem produces a value of theta "per calendar day." The theta in equation (19.3) is "per year.")

APPENDIX

TAYLOR SERIES EXPANSIONS AND GREEK LETTERS

A Taylor series expansion of the change in the portfolio value in a short period of time shows the role played by different Greek letters. If the volatility of the underlying asset is assumed to be constant, the value Π of the portfolio is a function of the asset price S, and time t. The Taylor series expansion gives

$$\Delta\Pi = \frac{\partial\Pi}{\partial S}\Delta S + \frac{\partial\Pi}{\partial t}\Delta t + \frac{1}{2}\frac{\partial^2\Pi}{\partial S^2}\Delta S^2 + \frac{1}{2}\frac{\partial^2\Pi}{\partial t^2}\Delta t^2 + \frac{\partial^2\Pi}{\partial S\,\partial t}\Delta S\,\Delta t + \cdots \qquad \textbf{(19A.1)}$$

where $\Delta\Pi$ and ΔS are the change in Π and S in a small time interval Δt. Delta hedging eliminates the first term on the right-hand side. The second term is nonstochastic. The third term (which is of order Δt) can be made zero by ensuring that the portfolio is gamma neutral as well as delta neutral. Other terms are of order higher than Δt.

For a delta-neutral portfolio, the first term on the right-hand side of equation (19A.1) is zero, so that

$$\Delta\Pi = \Theta\,\Delta t + \frac{1}{2}\Gamma\,\Delta S^2$$

when terms of order higher than Δt are ignored. This is equation (19.3).

The Practitioner Black–Scholes Model

In practice, volatility is not constant. As explained in this chapter, practitioners usually set volatility equal to implied volatility when calculating Greek letters. From the definition of implied volatility, the option price is an exact function of the asset price, implied volatility, time, interest rates, and dividends. As an approximation, we can ignore changes in interest rates and dividends and assume that an option price, f, is at any given time a function of only two variables: the asset price, S, and the implied volatility, σ_{imp}. The change in the option price over a short period of time is then given by

$$\Delta f = \frac{\partial f}{\partial S}\Delta S + \frac{\partial f}{\partial\sigma_{\mathrm{imp}}}\Delta\sigma_{\mathrm{imp}} + \frac{1}{2}\frac{\partial^2 f}{\partial S^2}(\Delta S)^2 + \frac{1}{2}\frac{\partial^2 f}{\partial\sigma_{\mathrm{imp}}^2}(\Delta\sigma_{\mathrm{imp}})^2 + \frac{\partial^2 f}{\partial S\,\partial\sigma_{\mathrm{imp}}}\Delta S\,\Delta\sigma_{\mathrm{imp}} + \cdots$$

Delta, vega, and gamma hedging deal with the first three terms in this expansion (which are the most important ones). Traders sometimes define other Greek letters such as $\partial^2 f/\partial\sigma_{\mathrm{imp}}^2$ and $\partial^2 f/\partial S\,\partial\sigma_{\mathrm{imp}}$ to explore their exposure to later terms in the Taylor series.

When portfolios of options are considered, the trader's problem is more complicated because the implied volatility of an option on a particular asset depends on the option's strike price and time to maturity. The trader must consider the portfolio's exposure to the different ways the volatility surface can change over a short period of time. Volatility surfaces are discussed in the next chapter.

20

Volatility Smiles

How close are the market prices of options to those predicted by the Black–Scholes–Merton model? Do traders really use the Black–Scholes–Merton model when determining a price for an option? Are the probability distributions of asset prices really lognormal? This chapter answers these questions. It explains that traders do use the Black–Scholes–Merton model—but not in exactly the way that Black, Scholes, and Merton originally intended. This is because they allow the volatility used to price an option to depend on its strike price and time to maturity.

A plot of the implied volatility of an option with a certain life as a function of its strike price is known as a *volatility smile*. This chapter describes the volatility smiles that traders use in equity and foreign currency markets. It explains the relationship between a volatility smile and the risk-neutral probability distribution being assumed for the future asset price. It also discusses how option traders use volatility surfaces as pricing tools.

20.1 WHY THE VOLATILITY SMILE IS THE SAME FOR CALLS AND PUTS

This section shows that the implied volatility of a European call option is the same as that of a European put option when they have the same strike price and time to maturity. This means that the volatility smile for European calls with a certain maturity is the same as that for European puts with the same maturity. This is a particularly convenient result. It shows that when talking about a volatility smile we do not have to worry about whether the options are calls or puts.

As explained in earlier chapters, put–call parity provides a relationship between the prices of European call and put options when they have the same strike price and time to maturity. With a dividend yield on the underlying asset of q, the relationship is

$$p + S_0 e^{-qT} = c + Ke^{-rT} \tag{20.1}$$

As usual, c and p are the European call and put price. They have the same strike price, K, and time to maturity, T. The variable S_0 is the price of the underlying asset today, and r is the risk-free interest rate for maturity T.

A key feature of the put–call parity relationship is that it is based on a relatively simple no-arbitrage argument. It does not require any assumption about the probability distribution of the asset price in the future. It is true both when the asset price distribution is lognormal and when it is not lognormal.

Suppose that, for a particular value of the volatility, p_{BS} and c_{BS} are the values of European put and call options calculated using the Black–Scholes–Merton model. Suppose further that p_{mkt} and c_{mkt} are the market values of these options. Because put–call parity holds for the Black–Scholes–Merton model, we must have

$$p_{BS} + S_0 e^{-qT} = c_{BS} + K e^{-rT}$$

In the absence of arbitrage opportunities, put–call parity also holds for the market prices, so that

$$p_{mkt} + S_0 e^{-qT} = c_{mkt} + K e^{-rT}$$

Subtracting these two equations, we get

$$p_{BS} - p_{mkt} = c_{BS} - c_{mkt} \tag{20.2}$$

This shows that the dollar pricing error when the Black–Scholes–Merton model is used to price a European put option should be exactly the same as the dollar pricing error when it is used to price a European call option with the same strike price and time to maturity.

Suppose that the implied volatility of the put option is 22%. This means that $p_{BS} = p_{mkt}$ when a volatility of 22% is used in the Black–Scholes–Merton model. From equation (20.2), it follows that $c_{BS} = c_{mkt}$ when this volatility is used. The implied volatility of the call is, therefore, also 22%. This argument shows that the implied volatility of a European call option is always the same as the implied volatility of a European put option when the two have the same strike price and maturity date. To put this another way, for a given strike price and maturity, the correct volatility to use in conjunction with the Black–Scholes–Merton model to price a European call should always be the same as that used to price a European put. This means that the volatility smile (i.e., the relationship between implied volatility and strike price for a particular maturity) is the same for European calls and European puts. More generally, it means that the volatility surface (i.e., the implied volatility as a function of strike price and time to maturity) is the same for European calls and European puts. These results are also true to a good approximation for American options.

Example 20.1

The value of a foreign currency is $0.60. The risk-free interest rate is 5% per annum in the United States and 10% per annum in the foreign country. The market price of a European call option on the foreign currency with a maturity of 1 year and a strike price of $0.59 is 0.0236. DerivaGem shows that the implied volatility of the call is 14.5%. For there to be no arbitrage, the put–call parity relationship in equation (20.1) must apply with q equal to the foreign risk-free rate. The price p of a European put option with a strike price of $0.59 and maturity of 1 year therefore satisfies

$$p + 0.60 e^{-0.10 \times 1} = 0.0236 + 0.59 e^{-0.05 \times 1}$$

so that $p = 0.0419$. DerivaGem shows that, when the put has this price, its implied volatility is also 14.5%. This is what we expect from the analysis just given.

20.2 FOREIGN CURRENCY OPTIONS

The volatility smile used by traders to price foreign currency options has the general form shown in Figure 20.1. The implied volatility is relatively low for at-the-money options. It becomes progressively higher as an option moves either into the money or out of the money.

In the appendix at the end of this chapter, we show how to determine the risk-neutral probability distribution for an asset price at a future time from the volatility smile given by options maturing at that time. We refer to this as the *implied distribution*. The volatility smile in Figure 20.1 corresponds to the implied distribution shown by the solid line in Figure 20.2. A lognormal distribution with the same mean and standard deviation as the implied distribution is shown by the dashed line in Figure 20.2. It can be seen that the implied distribution has heavier tails than the lognormal distribution.[1]

To see that Figures 20.1 and 20.2 are consistent with each other, consider first a deep-out-of-the-money call option with a high strike price of K_2 (K_2/S_0 well above 1.0). This option pays off only if the exchange rate proves to be above K_2. Figure 20.2 shows that the probability of this is higher for the implied probability distribution than for the lognormal distribution. We therefore expect the implied distribution to give a relatively high price for the option. A relatively high price leads to a relatively high implied volatility—and this is exactly what we observe in Figure 20.1 for the option. The two figures are therefore consistent with each other for high strike prices. Consider next a deep-out-of-the-money put option with a low strike price of K_1 (K_1/S_0 well below 1.0). This option pays off only if the exchange rate proves to be below K_1. Figure 20.2 shows that the probability of this is also higher for the implied probability distribution than for the lognormal distribution. We therefore expect the implied distribution to give a relatively high price, and a relatively high implied volatility, for this option as well. Again, this is exactly what we observe in Figure 20.1.

Figure 20.1 Volatility smile for foreign currency options (K = strike price, S_0 = current exchange rate).

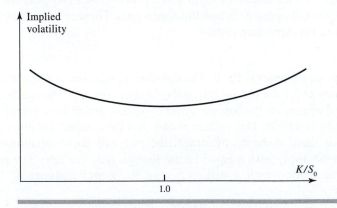

---

[1] This is known as *kurtosis*. Note that, in addition to having a heavier tail, the implied distribution is more "peaked." Both small and large movements in the exchange rate are more likely than with the lognormal distribution. Intermediate movements are less likely.

Figure 20.2   Implied and lognormal distribution for foreign currency options.

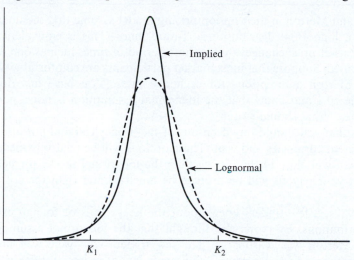

Empirical Results

We have just shown that the volatility smile used by traders for foreign currency options implies that they consider that the lognormal distribution understates the probability of extreme movements in exchange rates. To test whether they are right, Table 20.1 examines the daily movements in 10 different exchange rates over a 10-year period between 2005 and 2015. The exchange rates are those between the U.S. dollar and the following currencies: Australian dollar, British pound, Canadian dollar, Danish krone, euro, Japanese yen, Mexican peso, New Zealand dollar, Swedish krona, and Swiss franc. The first step in the production of the table is to calculate the standard deviation of daily percentage change in each exchange rate. The next stage is to note how often the actual percentage change exceeded 1 standard deviation, 2 standard deviations, and so on. The final stage is to calculate how often this would have happened if the percentage changes had been normally distributed. (The lognormal model implies that percentage changes are almost exactly normally distributed over a one-day time period.)

Table 20.1   Percentage of days when daily exchange rate moves are greater than 1, 2, ..., 6 standard deviations (SD = standard deviation of daily change).

	Real world	Lognormal model
>1 SD	23.32	31.73
>2 SD	4.67	4.55
>3 SD	1.30	0.27
>4 SD	0.49	0.01
>5 SD	0.24	0.00
>6 SD	0.13	0.00

Business Snapshot 20.1   Making Money from Foreign Currency Options

Black, Scholes, and Merton in their option pricing model assume that the underlying asset price has a lognormal distribution at future times. This is equivalent to the assumption that asset price changes over a short period of time, such as one day, are normally distributed. Suppose that most market participants are comfortable with the Black–Scholes–Merton assumptions for exchange rates. You have just done the analysis in Table 20.1 and know that the lognormal assumption is not a good one for exchange rates. What should you do?

The answer is that you should buy deep-out-of-the-money call and put options on a variety of different currencies and wait. These options will be relatively inexpensive and more of them will close in the money than the lognormal model predicts. The present value of your payoffs will on average be much greater than the cost of the options.

In the mid-1980s, a few traders knew about the heavy tails of foreign exchange probability distributions. Everyone else thought that the lognormal assumption of Black–Scholes–Merton was reasonable. The few traders who were well informed followed the strategy we have described—and made lots of money. By the late 1980s everyone realized that foreign currency options should be priced with a volatility smile and the trading opportunity disappeared.

Daily changes exceed 3 standard deviations on 1.30% of days. The lognormal model predicts that this should happen on only 0.27% of days. Daily changes exceed 4, 5, and 6 standard deviations on 0.49%, 0.24%, and 0.13% of days, respectively. The lognormal model predicts that we should hardly ever observe this happening. The table therefore provides evidence to support the existence of heavy tails (Figure 20.2) and the volatility smile used by traders (Figure 20.1). Business Snapshot 20.1 shows how you could have made money if you had done the analysis in Table 20.1 ahead of the rest of the market.

Reasons for the Smile in Foreign Currency Options

Why are exchange rates not lognormally distributed? Two of the conditions for an asset price to have a lognormal distribution are:

1. The volatility of the asset is constant.
2. The price of the asset changes smoothly with no jumps.

In practice, neither of these conditions is satisfied for an exchange rate. The volatility of an exchange rate is far from constant, and exchange rates frequently exhibit jumps, sometimes in response to the actions of central banks. It turns out that both a nonconstant volatility and jumps will have the effect of making extreme outcomes more likely.

The impact of jumps and nonconstant volatility depends on the option maturity. As the maturity of the option is increased, the percentage impact of a nonconstant volatility on prices becomes more pronounced, but its percentage impact on implied volatility usually becomes less pronounced. The percentage impact of jumps on both prices and the implied volatility becomes less pronounced as the maturity of the option is increased.[2] The result of all this is that the volatility smile becomes less pronounced as option maturity increases.

20.3 EQUITY OPTIONS

Prior to the crash of 1987, there was no marked volatility smile for equity options. Since 1987, the volatility smile used by traders to price equity options (both on individual stocks and on stock indices) has had the general form shown in Figure 20.3. This is sometimes referred to as a *volatility skew*. The volatility decreases as the strike price increases. The volatility used to price a low-strike-price option (i.e., a deep-out-of-the-money put or a deep-in-the-money call) is significantly higher than that used to price a high-strike-price option (i.e., a deep-in-the-money put or a deep-out-of-the-money call).

The volatility smile for equity options corresponds to the implied probability distribution given by the solid line in Figure 20.4. A lognormal distribution with the same mean and standard deviation as the implied distribution is shown by the dotted line. It can be seen that the implied distribution has a heavier left tail and a less heavy right tail than the lognormal distribution.

To see that Figures 20.3 and 20.4 are consistent with each other, we proceed as for Figures 20.1 and 20.2 and consider options that are deep out of the money. From

Figure 20.3   Volatility smile for equities (K = strike price, S_0 = current equity price).

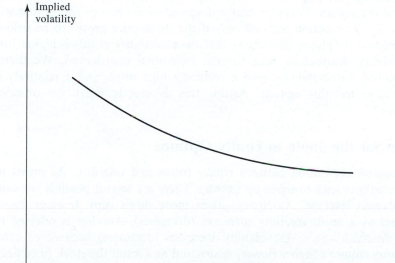

---

[2] When we look at sufficiently long-dated options, jumps tend to get "averaged out," so that the exchange rate distribution when there are jumps is almost indistinguishable from the one obtained when the exchange rate changes smoothly.

Figure 20.4   Implied distribution and lognormal distribution for equity options.

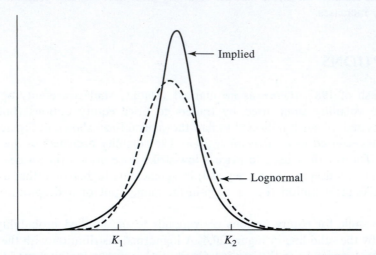

Figure 20.4, a deep-out-of-the-money call with a strike price of K_2 (K_2/S_0 well above 1.0) has a lower price when the implied distribution is used than when the lognormal distribution is used. This is because the option pays off only if the stock price proves to be above K_2, and the probability of this is lower for the implied probability distribution than for the lognormal distribution. Therefore, we expect the implied distribution to give a relatively low price for the option. A relatively low price leads to a relatively low implied volatility—and this is exactly what we observe in Figure 20.3 for the option. Consider next a deep-out-of-the-money put option with a strike price of K_1. This option pays off only if the stock price proves to be below K_1 (K_1/S_0 well below 1.0). Figure 20.4 shows that the probability of this is higher for the implied probability distribution than for the lognormal distribution. We therefore expect the implied distribution to give a relatively high price, and a relatively high implied volatility, for this option. Again, this is exactly what we observe in Figure 20.3.

The Reason for the Smile in Equity Options

There is a negative correlation between equity prices and volatility. As prices move down (up), volatilities tend to move up (down). There are several possible reasons for this. One concerns leverage. As equity prices move down (up), leverage increases (decreases) and as a result volatility increases (decreases). Another is referred to as the *volatility feedback effect*. As volatility increases (decreases) because of external factors, investors require a higher (lower) return and as a result the stock price declines (increases). A further explanation is crashophobia (see Business Snapshot 20.2).

Whatever the reason for the negative correlation, it means that stock price declines are accompanied by increases in volatility, making even greater declines possible. Stock price increases are accompanied by decreases in volatility, making further stock price increases less likely. This explains the heavy left tail and thin right tail of the implied distribution in Figure 20.4.

Business Snapshot 20.2   Crashophobia

It is interesting that the pattern in Figure 20.3 for equities has existed only since the stock market crash of October 1987. Prior to October 1987, implied volatilities were much less dependent on strike price. This has led Mark Rubinstein to suggest that one reason for the equity volatility smile may be "crashophobia." Traders are concerned about the possibility of another crash similar to October 1987, and they price options accordingly.

  There is some empirical support for this explanation. Declines in the S&P 500 tend to be accompanied by a steepening of the volatility skew. When the S&P increases, the skew tends to become less steep.

20.4 ALTERNATIVE WAYS OF CHARACTERIZING THE VOLATILITY SMILE

There are a number of ways of characterizing the volatility smile. Sometimes it is shown as the relationship between implied volatility and strike price K. However, this relationship depends on the price of the asset. As the price of the asset increases (decreases), the central at-the-money strike price increases (decreases) so that the curve relating the implied volatility to the strike price moves to right (left).[3] For this reason the implied volatility is often plotted as a function of the strike price divided by the current asset price, K/S_0. This is what we have done Figures 20.1 and 20.3.

  A refinement of this is to calculate the volatility smile as the relationship between the implied volatility and K/F_0, where F_0 is the forward price of the asset for a contract maturing at the same time as the options that are considered. Traders also often define an "at-the-money" option as an option where $K = F_0$, not as an option where $K = S_0$. The argument for this is that F_0, not S_0, is the expected stock price on the option's maturity date in a risk-neutral world.

  Yet another approach to defining the volatility smile is as the relationship between the implied volatility and the delta of the option (where delta is defined as in Chapter 19). This approach sometimes makes it possible to apply volatility smiles to options other than European and American calls and puts. When the approach is used, an at-the-money option is then defined as a call option with a delta of 0.5 or a put option with a delta of -0.5. These are referred to as "50-delta options."

20.5 THE VOLATILITY TERM STRUCTURE AND VOLATILITY SURFACES

Traders allow the implied volatility to depend on time to maturity as well as strike price. Implied volatility tends to be an increasing function of maturity when short-dated volatilities are historically low. This is because there is then an expectation that volatilities will increase. Similarly, volatility tends to be a decreasing function of

---

[3] Research by Derman suggests that this adjustment is sometimes "sticky" in the case of exchange-traded options. See E. Derman, "Regimes of Volatility," *Risk*, April 1999: 55–59.

Table 20.2 Volatility surface.

| | K/S₀ | | | | |
	0.90	0.95	1.00	1.05	1.10
1 month	14.2	13.0	12.0	13.1	14.5
3 month	14.0	13.0	12.0	13.1	14.2
6 month	14.1	13.3	12.5	13.4	14.3
1 year	14.7	14.0	13.5	14.0	14.8
2 year	15.0	14.4	14.0	14.5	15.1
5 year	14.8	14.6	14.4	14.7	15.0

maturity when short-dated volatilities are historically high. This is because there is then an expectation that volatilities will decrease.

Volatility surfaces combine volatility smiles with the volatility term structure to tabulate the volatilities appropriate for pricing an option with any strike price and any maturity. An example of a volatility surface that might be used for foreign currency options is given in Table 20.2.

One dimension of Table 20.2 is K/S_0; the other is time to maturity. The main body of the table shows implied volatilities calculated from the Black–Scholes–Merton model. At any given time, some of the entries in the table are likely to correspond to options for which reliable market data are available. The implied volatilities for these options are calculated directly from their market prices and entered into the table. The rest of the table is typically determined using interpolation. The table shows that the volatility smile becomes less pronounced as the option maturity increases. As mentioned earlier, this is what is observed for currency options. (It is also what is observed for options on most other assets.)

When a new option has to be valued, financial engineers look up the appropriate volatility in the table. For example, when valuing a 9-month option with a K/S_0 ratio of 1.05, a financial engineer would interpolate between 13.4 and 14.0 in Table 20.2 to obtain a volatility of 13.7%. This is the volatility that would be used in the Black–Scholes–Merton formula or a binomial tree. When valuing a 1.5-year option with a K/S_0 ratio of 0.925, a two-dimensional (bilinear) interpolation would be used to give an implied volatility of 14.525%.

The shape of the volatility smile depends on the option maturity. As illustrated in Table 20.2, the smile tends to become less pronounced as the option maturity increases. Define T as the time to maturity and F_0 as the forward price of the asset for a contract maturing at the same time as the option. Some financial engineers choose to define the volatility smile as the relationship between implied volatility and

$$\frac{1}{\sqrt{T}} \ln\left(\frac{K}{F_0}\right)$$

rather than as the relationship between the implied volatility and K. The smile is then usually much less dependent on the time to maturity.

20.6 MINIMUM VARIANCE DELTA

The formulas for delta and other Greek letters in Chapter 19 assume that the implied volatility remains the same when the asset price changes. This is not what is usually expected to happen. Consider, for example, a stock or stock index option. The volatility smile has the shape shown in Figure 20.3. Two phenomenon can be identified:

1. As the equity price increases (decreases), K/S_0 decreases (increases) and the volatility increases (decreases). In other words, the option moves up the curve in Figure 20.3 when the equity price increases and down the curve when the equity price decreases.

2. There is a negative correlation between equity prices and their volatilities. When the equity price increases, the whole curve in Figure 20.3 tends to move down; when the equity price decreases, the whole curve in Figure 20.3 tends to move up.

It turns out that the second effect dominates the first, so that implied volatilities tend to move down (up) when the equity price moves up (down) The delta that takes this relationship between implied volatilities and equity prices into account is referred to as the *minimum variance delta*. It is:

$$\Delta_{MV} = \frac{\partial f_{BSM}}{\partial S} + \frac{\partial f_{BSM}}{\partial \sigma_{imp}} \frac{\partial E(\sigma_{imp})}{\partial S}$$

where f_{BSM} is the Black–Scholes–Merton price of the option, σ_{imp} is the option's implied volatility, $E(\sigma_{imp})$ denotes the expectation of σ_{imp} as a function of the equity price, S. This gives

$$\Delta_{MV} = \Delta_{BSM} + \mathcal{V}_{BSM} \frac{\partial E(\sigma_{imp})}{\partial S}$$

where Δ_{BSM} and $\mathcal{V}_{BSM}$ are the delta and vega calculated from the Black–Scholes–Merton (constant volatility) model. Because $\mathcal{V}_{BSM}$ is positive and, as we have just explained $\partial E(\sigma_{imp})/\partial S$ is negative, the minimum variance delta is less than the Black–Scholes–Merton delta.[4]

20.7 THE ROLE OF THE MODEL

How important is the option-pricing model if traders are prepared to use a different volatility for every option? It can be argued that the Black–Scholes–Merton model is no more than a sophisticated interpolation tool used by traders for ensuring that an option is priced consistently with the market prices of other actively traded options. If traders stopped using Black–Scholes–Merton and switched to another plausible model, then the volatility surface and the shape of the smile would change, but arguably the dollar prices quoted in the market would not change appreciably. Greek letters and therefore hedging strategies do depend on the model used. An unrealistic model is liable to lead to poor hedging.

---

[4] For a further discussion of this, see, for example, J. C. Hull and A. White, "Optimal Delta Hedging of Options," Working paper, University of Toronto, 2016.

Models have most effect on the pricing of derivatives when similar derivatives do not trade actively in the market. For example, the pricing of many of the nonstandard exotic derivatives we will discuss in later chapters is model-dependent.

20.8 WHEN A SINGLE LARGE JUMP IS ANTICIPATED

Let us now consider an example of how an unusual volatility smile might arise in equity markets. Suppose that a stock price is currently $50 and an important news announcement due in a few days is expected either to increase the stock price by $8 or to reduce it by $8. (This announcement could concern the outcome of a takeover attempt or the verdict in an important lawsuit.) The probability distribution of the stock price in, say, 1 month might then consist of a mixture of two lognormal distributions, the first corresponding to favorable news, the second to unfavorable news. The situation is illustrated in Figure 20.5. The solid line shows the mixture-of-lognormals distribution for the stock price in 1 month; the dashed line shows a lognormal distribution with the same mean and standard deviation as this distribution.

The true probability distribution is bimodal (certainly not lognormal). One easy way to investigate the general effect of a bimodal stock price distribution is to consider the extreme case where there are only two possible future stock prices. This is what we will now do.

Suppose that the stock price is currently $50 and that it is known that in 1 month it will be either $42 or $58. Suppose further that the risk-free rate is 12% per annum. The situation is illustrated in Figure 20.6. Options can be valued using the binomial model from Chapter 13. In this case $u = 1.16$, $d = 0.84$, $a = 1.0101$, and $p = 0.5314$. The results from valuing a range of different options are shown in Table 20.3. The first column shows alternative strike prices; the second column shows prices of 1-month European call options; the third column shows the prices of one-month European put option prices; the fourth column shows implied volatilities. (As shown in Section 20.1,

---

Figure 20.5 Effect of a single large jump. The solid line is the true distribution; the dashed line is the lognormal distribution.

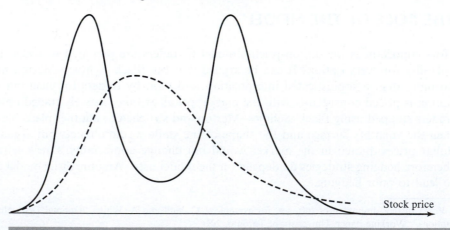

Stock price

Figure 20.6 Change in stock price in 1 month.

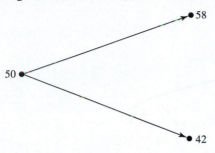

the implied volatility of a European put option is the same as that of a European call option when they have the same strike price and maturity.) Figure 20.7 displays the volatility smile from Table 20.3. It is actually a "frown" (the opposite of that observed for currencies) with volatilities declining as we move out of or into the money. The volatility implied from an option with a strike price of 50 will overprice an option with a strike price of 44 or 56.

SUMMARY

The Black–Scholes–Merton model and its extensions assume that the probability distribution of the underlying asset at any given future time is lognormal. This assumption is not the one made by traders. They assume the probability distribution of an equity price has a heavier left tail and a less heavy right tail than the lognormal distribution. They also assume that the probability distribution of an exchange rate has a heavier right tail and a heavier left tail than the lognormal distribution.

Traders use volatility smiles to allow for nonlognormality. The volatility smile defines the relationship between the implied volatility of an option and its strike price. For

Table 20.3 Implied volatilities in situation where it is known that the stock price will move from $50 to either $42 or $58.

Strike price ($)	Call price ($)	Put price ($)	Implied volatility (%)
42	8.42	0.00	0.0
44	7.37	0.93	58.8
46	6.31	1.86	66.6
48	5.26	2.78	69.5
50	4.21	3.71	69.2
52	3.16	4.64	66.1
54	2.10	5.57	60.0
56	1.05	6.50	49.0
58	0.00	7.42	0.0

Figure 20.7   Volatility smile for situation in Table 20.3.

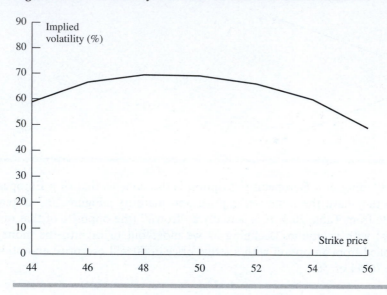

equity options, the volatility smile tends to be downward sloping. This means that out-of-the-money puts and in-the-money calls tend to have high implied volatilities whereas out-of-the-money calls and in-the-money puts tend to have low implied volatilities. For foreign currency options, the volatility smile is U-shaped. Both out-of-the-money and in-the-money options have higher implied volatilities than at-the-money options.

Often traders also use a volatility term structure. The implied volatility of an option then depends on its life. When volatility smiles and volatility term structures are combined, they produce a volatility surface. This defines implied volatility as a function of both the strike price and the time to maturity.

FURTHER READING

Bakshi, G., C. Cao, and Z. Chen. "Empirical Performance of Alternative Option Pricing Models," *Journal of Finance*, 52, No. 5 (December 1997): 2004–49.

Bates, D. S. "Post-'87 Crash Fears in the S&P Futures Market," *Journal of Econometrics*, 94 (January/February 2000): 181–238.

Daglish, T., J. C. Hull, and W. Suo. "Volatility Surfaces: Theory, Rules of Thumb, and Empirical Evidence," *Quantitative Finance*, 7, 5 (2007), 507–24.

Derman, E. "Regimes of Volatility," *Risk*, April 1999: 55–59.

Ederington, L. H., and W. Guan. "Why Are Those Options Smiling," *Journal of Derivatives*, 10, 2 (2002): 9–34.

Jackwerth, J. C., and M. Rubinstein. "Recovering Probability Distributions from Option Prices," *Journal of Finance*, 51 (December 1996): 1611–31.

Melick, W. R., and C. P. Thomas. "Recovering an Asset's Implied Probability Density Function from Option Prices: An Application to Crude Oil during the Gulf Crisis," *Journal of Financial and Quantitative Analysis*, 32, 1 (March 1997): 91–115.

Reiswich, D., and U. Wystup. "FX Volatility Smile Construction," Working Paper, Frankfurt School of Finance and Management, April 2010.

Rubinstein, M. "Nonparametric Tests of Alternative Option Pricing Models Using All Reported Trades and Quotes on the 30 Most Active CBOE Option Classes from August 23, 1976, through August 31, 1978," *Journal of Finance*, 40 (June 1985): 455–80.

Practice Questions (Answers in Solutions Manual)

20.1. What volatility smile is likely to be observed when:
  (a) Both tails of the stock price distribution are less heavy than those of the lognormal distribution?
  (b) The right tail is heavier, and the left tail is less heavy, than that of a lognormal distribution?

20.2. What volatility smile is observed for equities?

20.3. What volatility smile is likely to be caused by jumps in the underlying asset price? Is the pattern likely to be more pronounced for a 2-year option than for a 3-month option?

20.4. A European call and put option have the same strike price and time to maturity. The call has an implied volatility of 30% and the put has an implied volatility of 25%. What trades would you do?

20.5. Explain carefully why a distribution with a heavier left tail and less heavy right tail than the lognormal distribution gives rise to a downward sloping volatility smile.

20.6. The market price of a European call is $3.00 and its price given by Black–Scholes–Merton model with a volatility of 30% is $3.50. The price given by this Black–Scholes–Merton model for a European put option with the same strike price and time to maturity is $1.00. What should the market price of the put option be? Explain the reasons for your answer.

20.7. Explain what is meant by "crashophobia."

20.8. A stock price is currently $20. Tomorrow, news is expected to be announced that will either increase the price by $5 or decrease the price by $5. What are the problems in using Black–Scholes–Merton to value 1-month options on the stock?

20.9. What volatility smile is likely to be observed for 6-month options when the volatility is uncertain and positively correlated to the stock price?

20.10. Explain the problems in testing a stock option pricing model empirically.

20.11. Suppose that a central bank's policy is to allow an exchange rate to fluctuate between 0.97 and 1.03. What pattern of implied volatilities for options on the exchange rate would you expect to see?

20.12. Option traders sometimes refer to deep-out-of-the-money options as being options on volatility. Why do you think they do this?

20.13. A European call option on a certain stock has a strike price of $30, a time to maturity of 1 year, and an implied volatility of 30%. A European put option on the same stock has a strike price of $30, a time to maturity of 1 year, and an implied volatility of 33%. What is the arbitrage opportunity open to a trader? Does the arbitrage work only when the lognormal assumption underlying Black–Scholes–Merton holds? Explain carefully the reasons for your answer.

20.14. Suppose that the result of a major lawsuit affecting a company is due to be announced tomorrow. The company's stock price is currently $60. If the ruling is favorable to the company, the stock price is expected to jump to $75. If it is unfavorable, the stock is expected to jump to $50. What is the risk-neutral probability of a favorable ruling? Assume that the volatility of the company's stock will be 25% for 6 months after the ruling if the ruling is favorable and 40% if it is unfavorable. Use DerivaGem to calculate the relationship between implied volatility and strike price for 6-month European options on the company today. The company does not pay dividends. Assume that the 6-month risk-free rate is 6%. Consider call options with strike prices of $30, $40, $50, $60, $70, and $80.

20.15. An exchange rate is currently 0.8000. The volatility of the exchange rate is quoted as 12% and interest rates in the two countries are the same. Using the lognormal assumption, estimate the probability that the exchange rate in 3 months will be (a) less than 0.7000, (b) between 0.7000 and 0.7500, (c) between 0.7500 and 0.8000, (d) between 0.8000 and 0.8500, (e) between 0.8500 and 0.9000, and (f) greater than 0.9000. Based on the volatility smile usually observed in the market for exchange rates, which of these estimates would you expect to be too low and which would you expect to be too high?

20.16. A stock price is $40. A 6-month European call option on the stock with a strike price of $30 has an implied volatility of 35%. A 6-month European call option on the stock with a strike price of $50 has an implied volatility of 28%. The 6-month risk-free rate is 5% and no dividends are expected. Explain why the two implied volatilities are different. Use DerivaGem to calculate the prices of the two options. Use put–call parity to calculate the prices of 6-month European put options with strike prices of $30 and $50. Use DerivaGem to calculate the implied volatilities of these two put options.

20.17. "The Black–Scholes–Merton model is used by traders as an interpolation tool." Discuss this view.

20.18. Using Table 20.2, calculate the implied volatility a trader would use for an 8-month option with $K/S_0 = 1.04$.

Further Questions

20.19. A company's stock is selling for $4. The company has no outstanding debt. Analysts consider the liquidation value of the company to be at least $300,000 and there are 100,000 shares outstanding. What volatility smile would you expect to see?

20.20. A company is currently awaiting the outcome of a major lawsuit. This is expected to be known within 1 month. The stock price is currently $20. If the outcome is positive, the stock price is expected to be $24 at the end of 1 month. If the outcome is negative, it is expected to be $18 at this time. The 1-month risk-free interest rate is 8% per annum.
(a) What is the risk-neutral probability of a positive outcome?
(b) What are the values of 1-month call options with strike prices of $19, $20, $21, $22, and $23?
(c) Use DerivaGem to calculate a volatility smile for 1-month call options.
(d) Verify that the same volatility smile is obtained for 1-month put options.

20.21. A futures price is currently $40. The risk-free interest rate is 5%. Some news is expected tomorrow that will cause the volatility over the next 3 months to be either 10% or 30%. There is a 60% chance of the first outcome and a 40% chance of the second outcome. Use DerivaGem to calculate a volatility smile for 3-month futures options.

20.22. Data for a number of foreign currencies are provided on the author's website:

http://www-2.rotman.utoronto.ca/~hull/data

Choose a currency and use the data to produce a table similar to Table 20.1.

20.23. Data for a number of stock indices are provided on the author's website:

http://www-2.rotman.utoronto.ca/~hull/data

Choose an index and test whether a three-standard-deviation down movement happens more often than a three-standard-deviation up movement.

20.24. Consider a European call and a European put with the same strike price and time to maturity. Show that they change in value by the same amount when the volatility increases from a level σ_1 to a new level σ_2 within a short period of time. (*Hint*: Use put–call parity.)

20.25. An exchange rate is currently 1.0 and the implied volatilities of 6-month European options with strike prices 0.7, 0.8, 0.9, 1.0, 1.1, 1.2, 1.3 are 13%, 12%, 11%, 10%, 11%, 12%, 13%. The domestic and foreign risk-free rates are both 2.5%. Calculate the implied probability distribution using an approach similar to that used for Example 20A.1 in the appendix to this chapter. Compare it with the implied distribution where all the implied volatilities are 11.5%.

20.26. Using Table 20.2, calculate the implied volatility a trader would use for an 11-month option with $K/S_0 = 0.98$.

APPENDIX

DETERMINING IMPLIED RISK-NEUTRAL DISTRIBUTIONS FROM VOLATILITY SMILES

The price of a European call option on an asset with strike price K and maturity T is given by

$$c = e^{-rT} \int_{S_T=K}^{\infty} (S_T - K) \, g(S_T) \, dS_T$$

where r is the interest rate (assumed constant), S_T is the asset price at time T, and g is the risk-neutral probability density function of S_T. Differentiating once with respect to K gives

$$\frac{\partial c}{\partial K} = -e^{-rT} \int_{S_T=K}^{\infty} g(S_T) \, dS_T$$

Differentiating again with respect to K gives

$$\frac{\partial^2 c}{\partial K^2} = e^{-rT} \, g(K)$$

This shows that the probability density function g is given by

$$g(K) = e^{rT} \frac{\partial^2 c}{\partial K^2} \tag{20A.1}$$

This result, which is from Breeden and Litzenberger (1978), allows risk-neutral probability distributions to be estimated from volatility smiles.[5] Suppose that c_1, c_2, and c_3 are the prices of T-year European call options with strike prices of $K - \delta$, K, and $K + \delta$, respectively. Assuming δ is small, an estimate of $g(K)$, obtained by approximating the partial derivative in equation (20A.1), is

$$e^{rT} \frac{c_1 + c_3 - 2c_2}{\delta^2}$$

For another way of understanding this formula, suppose you set up a butterfly spread with strike prices $K - \delta$, K, and $K + \delta$, and maturity T. This means that you buy a call with strike price $K - \delta$, buy a call with strike price $K + \delta$, and sell two calls with strike price K. The value of your position is $c_1 + c_3 - 2c_2$. The value of the position can also be calculated by integrating the payoff over the risk-neutral probability distribution, $g(S_T)$, and discounting at the risk-free rate. The payoff is shown in Figure 20A.1. Since δ is small, we can assume that $g(S_T) = g(K)$ in the whole of the range $K - \delta < S_T < K + \delta$, where the payoff is nonzero. The area under the "spike" in Figure 20A.1 is $0.5 \times 2\delta \times \delta = \delta^2$. The value of the payoff (when δ is small) is therefore $e^{-rT} g(K)\delta^2$. It follows that

$$e^{-rT} g(K)\delta^2 = c_1 + c_3 - 2c_2$$

---

[5] See D. T. Breeden and R. H. Litzenberger, "Prices of State-Contingent Claims Implicit in Option Prices," *Journal of Business*, 51 (1978), 621–51.

Figure 20A.1 Payoff from butterfly spread.

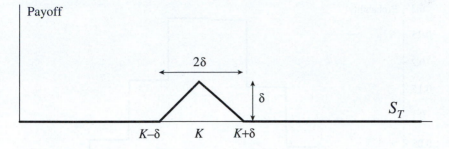

which leads directly to

$$g(K) = e^{rT} \frac{c_1 + c_3 - 2c_2}{\delta^2} \tag{20A.2}$$

Example 20A.1

Suppose that the price of a non-dividend-paying stock is $10, the risk-free interest rate is 3%, and the implied volatilities of 3-month European options with strike prices of $6, $7, $8, $9, $10, $11, $12, $13, $14 are 30%, 29%, 28%, 27%, 26%, 25%, 24%, 23%, 22%, respectively. One way of applying the above results is as follows. Assume that $g(S_T)$ is constant between $S_T = 6$ and $S_T = 7$, constant between $S_T = 7$ and $S_T = 8$, and so on. Define:

$$g(S_T) = g_1 \quad \text{for} \quad 6 \leqslant S_T < 7$$
$$g(S_T) = g_2 \quad \text{for} \quad 7 \leqslant S_T < 8$$
$$g(S_T) = g_3 \quad \text{for} \quad 8 \leqslant S_T < 9$$
$$g(S_T) = g_4 \quad \text{for} \quad 9 \leqslant S_T < 10$$
$$g(S_T) = g_5 \quad \text{for} \quad 10 \leqslant S_T < 11$$
$$g(S_T) = g_6 \quad \text{for} \quad 11 \leqslant S_T < 12$$
$$g(S_T) = g_7 \quad \text{for} \quad 12 \leqslant S_T < 13$$
$$g(S_T) = g_8 \quad \text{for} \quad 13 \leqslant S_T < 14$$

The value of g_1 can be calculated by interpolating to get the implied volatility for a 3-month option with a strike price of $6.5 as 29.5%. This means that options with strike prices of $6, $6.5, and $7 have implied volatilities of 30%, 29.5%, and 29%, respectively. From DerivaGem their prices are $4.045, $3.549, and $3.055, respectively. Using equation (20A.2), with $K = 6.5$ and $\delta = 0.5$, gives

$$g_1 = \frac{e^{0.03 \times 0.25}(4.045 + 3.055 - 2 \times 3.549)}{0.5^2} = 0.0057$$

Similar calculations show that

$$g_2 = 0.0444, \quad g_3 = 0.1545, \quad g_4 = 0.2781$$
$$g_5 = 0.2813, \quad g_6 = 0.1659, \quad g_7 = 0.0573, \quad g_8 = 0.0113$$

Figure 20A.2   Implied probability distribution for Example 20A.1.

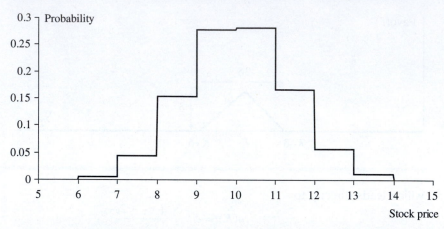

Figure 20A.2 displays the implied distribution. (Note that the area under the probability distribution is 0.9985. The probability that $S_T < 6$ or $S_T > 14$ is therefore 0.0015.) Although not obvious from Figure 20A.2, the implied distribution does have a heavier left tail and less heavy right tail than a lognormal distribution. For the lognormal distribution based on a single volatility of 26%, the probability of a stock price between \$6 and \$7 is 0.0031 (compared with 0.0057 in Figure 20A.2) and the probability of a stock price between \$13 and \$14 is 0.0167 (compared with 0.0113 in Figure 20A.2).

CHAPTER 21

Basic Numerical Procedures

This chapter discusses three numerical procedures for valuing derivatives when analytic results such as the Black–Scholes–Merton formulas do not exist. The first represents the asset price movements in the form of a tree and was introduced in Chapter 13. The second is Monte Carlo simulation, which we encountered briefly in Chapter 14 when stochastic processes were explained. The third involves finite difference methods.

Monte Carlo simulation is usually used for derivatives where the payoff is dependent on the history of the underlying variable or where there are several underlying variables. Trees and finite difference methods are usually used for American options and other derivatives where the holder has decisions to make prior to maturity. In addition to valuing a derivative, all the procedures can be used to calculate Greek letters such as delta, gamma, and vega.

The basic procedures discussed in this chapter can be used to handle most of the derivatives valuation problems encountered in practice. However, sometimes they have to be adapted to cope with particular situations, as will be explained in Chapter 27.

21.1 BINOMIAL TREES

Binomial trees were introduced in Chapter 13. They can be used to value either European or American options. The Black–Scholes–Merton formulas and their extensions that were presented in Chapters 15, 17, and 18 provide analytic valuations for European options.[1] There are no analytic valuations for American options. Binomial trees are therefore most useful for valuing these types of options.[2]

As explained in Chapter 13, the binomial tree valuation approach involves dividing the life of the option into a large number of small time intervals of length Δt. It assumes that in each time interval the price of the underlying asset moves from its initial value of S to one of two new values, Su and Sd. The approach is illustrated in Figure 21.1. In

---

[1] The Black–Scholes–Merton formulas are based on the same set of assumptions as binomial trees. As shown in the appendix to Chapter 13, in the limit as the number of time steps is increased, the price given by a binomial tree for a European option converges to the Black–Scholes–Merton price.

[2] Some analytic approximations for valuing American options have been suggested. See, for example, Technical Note 8 at www-2.rotman.utoronto.ca/~hull/TechnicalNotes for a description of the quadratic approximation approach.

Figure 21.1 Asset price movements in time Δt under the binomial model.

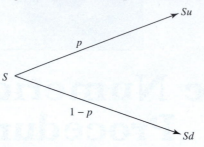

general, $u > 1$ and $d < 1$. The movement from S to Su, therefore, is an "up" movement and the movement from S to Sd is a "down" movement. The probability of an up movement will be denoted by p. The probability of a down movement is $1 - p$.

Risk-Neutral Valuation

The risk-neutral valuation principle, explained in Chapters 13 and 15, states that an option (or other derivative) can be valued on the assumption that the world is risk neutral. This means that for valuation purposes we can use the following procedure:

1. Assume that the expected return from all traded assets is the risk-free interest rate.
2. Value payoffs from the derivative by calculating their expected values and discounting at the risk-free interest rate.

This principle underlies the way trees are used.

Determination of p, u, and d

The parameters p, u, and d must give correct values for the mean and variance of asset price changes during a time interval of length Δt. Because we are working in a risk-neutral world, the expected return from the asset is the risk-free interest rate, r. Suppose that the asset provides a yield of q. The expected return in the form of capital gains must be $r - q$. This means that the expected value of the asset price at the end of a time interval of length Δt must be $Se^{(r-q)\Delta t}$, where S is the asset price at the beginning of the time interval. To match the mean return with the tree, we therefore need

$$Se^{(r-q)\Delta t} = pSu + (1 - p)Sd$$

or

$$e^{(r-q)\Delta t} = pu + (1 - p)d \tag{21.1}$$

The variance of a variable Q is defined as $E(Q^2) - [E(Q)]^2$. Defining R as the percentage change in the asset price in time Δt, there is a probability p that $1 + R$ is u and a probability $1 - p$ that it is d. Using equation (21.1), it follows that the variance of $1 + R$ is

$$pu^2 + (1 - p)d^2 - e^{2(r-q)\Delta t}$$

Since adding a constant to a variable makes no difference to its variance, the variance of $1 + R$ is the same as the variance of R. As explained in Section 15.4, this is $\sigma^2 \Delta t$.

Hence,

$$pu^2 + (1 - p)d^2 - e^{2(r-q)\Delta t} = \sigma^2 \Delta t$$

From equation (21.1), $e^{(r-q)\Delta t}(u + d) = pu^2 + (1 - p)d^2 + ud$, so that

$$e^{(r-q)\Delta t}(u + d) - ud - e^{2(r-q)\Delta t} = \sigma^2 \Delta t \tag{21.2}$$

Equations (21.1) and (21.2) impose two conditions on p, u, and d. A third condition used by Cox, Ross, and Rubinstein (1979) is[3]

$$u = 1/d \tag{21.3}$$

A solution to equations (21.1) to (21.3), when terms of higher order than Δt are ignored, is[4]

$$p = \frac{a - d}{u - d} \tag{21.4}$$

$$u = e^{\sigma\sqrt{\Delta t}} \tag{21.5}$$

$$d = e^{-\sigma\sqrt{\Delta t}} \tag{21.6}$$

where

$$a = e^{(r-q)\Delta t} \tag{21.7}$$

The variable a is sometimes referred to as the *growth factor*. Equations (21.4) to (21.7) are the same as those in Sections 13.8 and 13.11.

Tree of Asset Prices

Figure 21.2 shows the complete tree of asset prices that is considered when the binomial model is used with four time steps. At time zero, the asset price, S_0, is known. At time Δt, there are two possible asset prices, $S_0 u$ and $S_0 d$; at time $2\Delta t$, there are three possible asset prices, $S_0 u^2$, S_0, and $S_0 d^2$; and so on. In general, at time $i \Delta t$, we consider $i + 1$ asset prices. These are

$$S_0 u^j d^{i-j}, \quad j = 0, 1, \ldots, i$$

Note that the relationship $u = 1/d$ is used in computing the asset price at each node of the tree in Figure 21.2. For example, the asset price when $j = 2$ and $i = 3$ is $S_0 u^2 d = S_0 u$. Note also that the tree recombines in the sense that an up movement followed by a down movement leads to the same asset price as a down movement followed by an up movement.

Working Backward through the Tree

Options are evaluated by starting at the end of the tree (time T) and working backward. This is known as *backward induction*. The value of the option is known at time T. For example, a put option is worth $\max(K - S_T, 0)$ and a call option is worth $\max(S_T - K, 0)$,

---

[3] See J.C. Cox, S.A. Ross, and M. Rubinstein, "Option Pricing: A Simplified Approach," *Journal of Financial Economics*, 7 (October 1979), 229–63.

[4] To see this, we note that equations (21.4) and (21.7) satisfy the conditions in equations (21.1) and (21.3) exactly. The exponential function e^x can be expanded as $1 + x + x^2/2 + \cdots$. When terms of higher order than Δt are ignored, equation (21.5) implies that $u = 1 + \sigma\sqrt{\Delta t} + \frac{1}{2}\sigma^2 \Delta t$ and equation (21.6) implies that $d = 1 - \sigma\sqrt{\Delta t} + \frac{1}{2}\sigma^2 \Delta t$. Also, $e^{(r-q)\Delta t} = 1 + (r - q)\Delta t$ and $e^{2(r-q)\Delta t} = 1 + 2(r - q)\Delta t$. By substitution, we see that equation (21.2) is satisfied when terms of higher order than Δt are ignored.

Figure 21.2   Tree used to value an option.

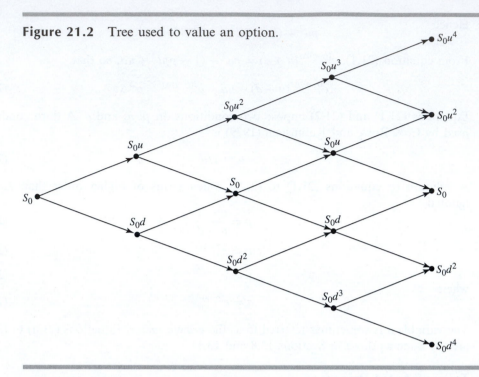

where S_T is the asset price at time T and K is the strike price. Because a risk-neutral world is being assumed, the value at each node at time $T - \Delta t$ can be calculated as the expected value at time T discounted at rate r for a time period Δt. Similarly, the value at each node at time $T - 2\Delta t$ can be calculated as the expected value at time $T - \Delta t$ discounted for a time period Δt at rate r, and so on. If the option is American, it is necessary to check at each node to see whether early exercise is preferable to holding the option for a further time period Δt. Eventually, by working back through all the nodes, we are able to obtain the value of the option at time zero.

Example 21.1

Consider a 5-month American put option on a non-dividend-paying stock when the stock price is $50, the strike price is $50, the risk-free interest rate is 10% per annum, and the volatility is 40% per annum. With our usual notation, this means that $S_0 = 50$, $K = 50$, $r = 0.10$, $\sigma = 0.40$, $T = 0.4167$, and $q = 0$. Suppose that we divide the life of the option into five intervals of length 1 month ($= 0.0833$ year) for the purposes of constructing a binomial tree. Then $\Delta t = 0.0833$ and using equations (21.4) to (21.7) gives

$$u = e^{\sigma\sqrt{\Delta t}} = 1.1224, \qquad d = e^{-\sigma\sqrt{\Delta t}} = 0.8909, \qquad a = e^{r\Delta t} = 1.0084$$

$$p = \frac{a - d}{u - d} = 0.5073, \qquad 1 - p = 0.4927$$

Figure 21.3 shows the binomial tree produced by DerivaGem. At each node there are two numbers. The top one shows the stock price at the node; the lower one shows the value of the option at the node. The probability of an up movement is always 0.5073; the probability of a down movement is always 0.4927.

Figure 21.3 Binomial tree from DerivaGem for American put on non-dividend-paying stock (Example 21.1).

At each node:
 Upper value = Underlying Asset Price
 Lower value = Option Price
 Shading indicates where option is exercised

Strike price = 50
Discount factor per step = 0.9917
Time step, dt = 0.0833 years, 30.42 days
Growth factor per step, a = 1.0084
Probability of up move, p = 0.5073
Up step size, u = 1.1224
Down step size, d = 0.8909

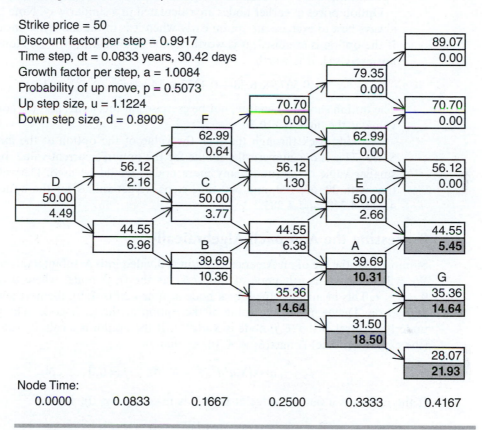

Node Time:
0.0000   0.0833   0.1667   0.2500   0.3333   0.4167

The stock price at the jth node ($j = 0, 1, \ldots, i$) at time $i \, \Delta t$ ($i = 0, 1, \ldots, 5$) is calculated as $S_0 u^j d^{i-j}$. For example, the stock price at node A ($i = 4$, $j = 1$) (i.e., the second node up at the end of the fourth time step) is $50 \times 1.1224 \times 0.8909^3 = \$39.69$. The option prices at the final nodes are calculated as $\max(K - S_T, 0)$. For example, the option price at node G is $50.00 - 35.36 = 14.64$. The option prices at the penultimate nodes are calculated from the option prices at the final nodes. First, we assume no exercise of the option at the nodes. This means that the option price is calculated as the present value of the expected option price one time step later. For example, at node E, the option price is calculated as

$$(0.5073 \times 0 + 0.4927 \times 5.45)e^{-0.10 \times 0.0833} = 2.66$$

whereas at node A it is calculated as

$$(0.5073 \times 5.45 + 0.4927 \times 14.64)e^{-0.10 \times 0.0833} = 9.90$$

We then check to see if early exercise is preferable to waiting. At node E, early exercise would give a value for the option of zero because both the stock price and strike price are $50. Clearly it is best to wait. The correct value for the option at node E is therefore $2.66. At node A, it is a different story. If the option is exercised, it is worth $50.00 − $39.69, or $10.31. This is more than $9.90. If node A is reached, then the option should be exercised and the correct value for the option at node A is $10.31.

Option prices at earlier nodes are calculated in a similar way. Note that it is not always best to exercise an option early when it is in the money. Consider node B. If the option is exercised, it is worth $50.00 − $39.69, or $10.31. However, if it is not exercised, it is worth

$$(0.5073 \times 6.38 + 0.4927 \times 14.64)e^{-0.10\times0.0833} = 10.36$$

The option should, therefore, not be exercised at this node, and the correct option value at the node is $10.36.

Working back through the tree, the value of the option at the initial node is $4.49. This is our numerical estimate for the option's current value. In practice, a smaller value of Δt, and many more nodes, would be used. DerivaGem shows that with 30, 50, 100, and 500 time steps we get values for the option of 4.263, 4.272, 4.278, and 4.283.

Expressing the Approach Algebraically

Suppose that the life of an American option is divided into N subintervals of length Δt. We will refer to the jth node at time $i\,\Delta t$ as the (i, j) node, where $0 \leqslant i \leqslant N$ and $0 \leqslant j \leqslant i$. This means that the lowest node at time $i\,\Delta t$ is $(i, 0)$, the next lowest is $(i, 1)$, and so on. Define $f_{i,j}$ as the value of the option at the (i, j) node. The price of the underlying asset at the (i, j) node is $S_0 u^j d^{i-j}$. If the option is a call, its value at time T (the expiration date) is $\max(S_T - K, 0)$, so that

$$f_{N,j} = \max(S_0 u^j d^{N-j} - K,\ 0), \quad j = 0, 1, \dots, N$$

If the option is a put, its value at time T is $\max(K - S_T, 0)$, so that

$$f_{N,j} = \max(K - S_0 u^j d^{N-j},\ 0), \quad j = 0, 1, \dots, N$$

There is a probability p of moving from the (i, j) node at time $i\,\Delta t$ to the $(i+1, j+1)$ node at time $(i+1)\,\Delta t$, and a probability $1 - p$ of moving from the (i, j) node at time $i\,\Delta t$ to the $(i+1, j)$ node at time $(i+1)\,\Delta t$. Assuming no early exercise, risk-neutral valuation gives

$$f_{i,j} = e^{-r\Delta t}[p f_{i+1,j+1} + (1 - p)f_{i+1,j}]$$

for $0 \leqslant i \leqslant N - 1$ and $0 \leqslant j \leqslant i$. When early exercise is possible, this value for $f_{i,j}$ must be compared with the option's intrinsic value, so that for a call

$$f_{i,j} = \max\{S_0 u^j d^{i-j} - K,\ e^{-r\Delta t}[p f_{i+1,j+1} + (1 - p)f_{i+1,j}]\}$$

and for a put

$$f_{i,j} = \max\{K - S_0 u^j d^{i-j},\ e^{-r\Delta t}[p f_{i+1,j+1} + (1 - p)f_{i+1,j}]\}$$

Note that, because the calculations start at time T and work backward, the value at

Figure 21.4 Convergence of the price of the option in Example 21.1 calculated from the DerivaGem Application Builder functions.

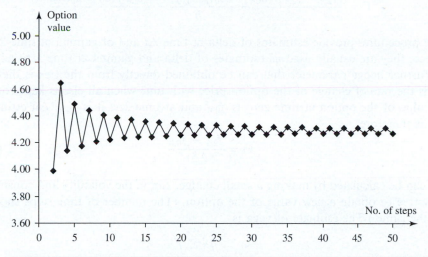

time $i\,\Delta t$ captures not only the effect of early exercise possibilities at time $i\,\Delta t$, but also the effect of early exercise at subsequent times.

In the limit as Δt tends to zero, an exact value for the American put is obtained. In practice, $N = 30$ usually gives reasonable results. Figure 21.4 shows the convergence of the option price in Example 21.1. This figure was calculated using the Application Builder functions provided with the DerivaGem software (see Sample Application A).

Estimating Delta and Other Greek Letters

It will be recalled that the delta (Δ) of an option is the rate of change of its price with respect to the underlying stock price. It can be calculated as

$$\frac{\Delta f}{\Delta S}$$

where ΔS is a small change in the asset price and Δf is the corresponding small change in the option price. At time Δt, we have an estimate $f_{1,1}$ for the option price when the asset price is $S_0 u$ and an estimate $f_{1,0}$ for the option price when the asset price is $S_0 d$. This means that, when $\Delta S = S_0 u - S_0 d$, $\Delta f = f_{1,1} - f_{1,0}$. Therefore an estimate of delta at time Δt is

$$\Delta = \frac{f_{1,1} - f_{1,0}}{S_0 u - S_0 d} \tag{21.8}$$

To determine gamma (Γ), note that we have two estimates of Δ at time $2\Delta t$. When $S = (S_0 u^2 + S_0)/2$ (halfway between the second and third node), delta is $(f_{2,2} - f_{2,1})/(S_0 u^2 - S_0)$; when $S = (S_0 + S_0 d^2)/2$ (halfway between the first and second node), delta is $(f_{2,1} - f_{2,0})/(S_0 - S_0 d^2)$. The difference between the two values of S is h, where

$$h = 0.5(S_0 u^2 - S_0 d^2)$$

Gamma is the change in delta divided by h:

$$\Gamma = \frac{[(f_{2,2} - f_{2,1})/(S_0 u^2 - S_0)] - [(f_{2,1} - f_{2,0})/(S_0 - S_0 d^2)]}{h} \tag{21.9}$$

These procedures provide estimates of delta at time Δt and of gamma at time $2\Delta t$. In practice, they are usually used as estimates of delta and gamma at time zero as well.[5]

A further hedge parameter that can be obtained directly from the tree is theta (Θ). This is the rate of change of the option price with time when all else is kept constant. The value of the option at time zero is $f_{0,0}$ and at time $2\Delta t$ it is $f_{2,1}$. An estimate of theta is therefore

$$\Theta = \frac{f_{2,1} - f_{0,0}}{2\Delta t} \tag{21.10}$$

Vega can be calculated by making a small change, $\Delta\sigma$, in the volatility and constructing a new tree to obtain a new value of the option. (The number of time steps should be kept the same.) The estimate of vega is

$$\mathcal{V} = \frac{f^* - f}{\Delta\sigma}$$

where f and f^* are the estimates of the option price from the original and the new tree, respectively. Rho can be calculated similarly.

Example 21.2

Consider again Example 21.1. From Figure 21.3, $f_{1,0} = 6.96$ and $f_{1,1} = 2.16$. Equation (21.8) gives an estimate for delta of

$$\frac{2.16 - 6.96}{56.12 - 44.55} = -0.41$$

From equation (21.9), an estimate of the gamma of the option can be obtained from the values at nodes B, C, and F as

$$\frac{[(0.64 - 3.77)/(62.99 - 50.00)] - [(3.77 - 10.36)/(50.00 - 39.69)]}{11.65} = 0.03$$

From equation (21.10), an estimate of the theta of the option can be obtained from the values at nodes D and C as

$$\frac{3.77 - 4.49}{0.1667} = -4.3 \quad \text{per year}$$

or -0.012 per calendar day. These are only rough estimates. They become progressively better as the number of time steps on the tree is increased. Using 50 time steps, DerivaGem provides estimates of -0.415, 0.034, and -0.0117 for delta, gamma, and theta, respectively. By making small changes to parameters and recomputing values, vega and rho are estimated as 0.123 and -0.072, respectively.

---

[5] If slightly more accuracy is required for delta and gamma, we can start the binomial tree at time $-2\Delta t$ and assume that the stock price is S_0 at this time. This leads to the option price being calculated for three different stock prices at time zero.

21.2 USING THE BINOMIAL TREE FOR OPTIONS ON INDICES, CURRENCIES, AND FUTURES CONTRACTS

As explained in Chapters 13, 17 and 18, stock indices, currencies, and futures contracts can, for the purposes of option valuation, be considered as assets providing known yields. For a stock index, the relevant yield is the dividend yield on the stock portfolio underlying the index; in the case of a currency, it is the foreign risk-free interest rate; in the case of a futures contract, it is the domestic risk-free interest rate. The binomial tree approach can therefore be used to value options on stock indices, currencies, and futures contracts provided that q in equation (21.7) is interpreted appropriately.

Example 21.3

Consider a 4-month American call option on index futures where the current futures price is 300, the exercise price is 300, the risk-free interest rate is 8% per

Figure 21.5 Binomial tree produced by DerivaGem for American call option on an index futures contract (Example 21.3).

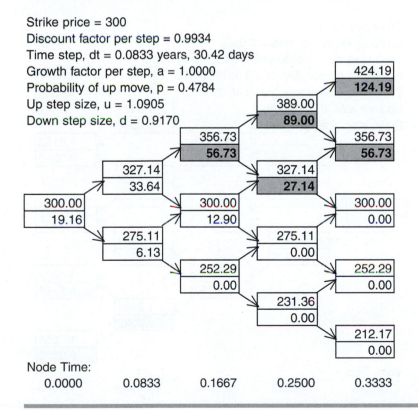

At each node:
 Upper value = Underlying Asset Price
 Lower value = Option Price
Shading indicates where option is exercised

Strike price = 300
Discount factor per step = 0.9934
Time step, dt = 0.0833 years, 30.42 days
Growth factor per step, a = 1.0000
Probability of up move, p = 0.4784
Up step size, u = 1.0905
Down step size, d = 0.9170

	424.19
	124.19
389.00	
89.00	
356.73	356.73
56.73	**56.73**
327.14	327.14
33.64	**27.14**
300.00	300.00	300.00
19.16	12.90	0.00
275.11	275.11	
6.13	0.00	
252.29	252.29
0.00	0.00
231.36	
0.00	
212.17
0.00

Node Time:
   0.0000   0.0833   0.1667   0.2500   0.3333

annum, and the volatility of the index is 30% per annum. The life of the option is divided into four 1-month periods for the purposes of constructing the tree. In this case, $F_0 = 300$, $K = 300$, $r = 0.08$, $\sigma = 0.3$, $T = 0.3333$, and $\Delta t = 0.0833$. Because a futures contract is analogous to a stock paying dividends at a rate r, q should be set equal to r in equation (21.7). This gives $a = 1$. The other parameters necessary to construct the tree are

$$u = e^{\sigma\sqrt{\Delta t}} = 1.0905, \qquad d = 1/u = 0.9170$$
$$p = \frac{a - d}{u - d} = 0.4784, \qquad 1 - p = 0.5216$$

The tree, as produced by DerivaGem, is shown in Figure 21.5. (The upper number is the futures price; the lower number is the option price.) The estimated value of the option is 19.16. More accuracy is obtained using more steps. With 50 time steps, DerivaGem gives a value of 20.18; with 100 time steps it gives 20.22.

Figure 21.6   Binomial tree produced by DerivaGem for American put option on a currency (Example 21.4).

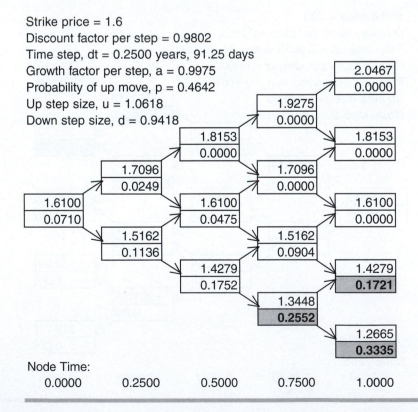

At each node:
 Upper value = Underlying Asset Price
 Lower value = Option Price
Shading indicates where option is exercised

Strike price = 1.6
Discount factor per step = 0.9802
Time step, dt = 0.2500 years, 91.25 days
Growth factor per step, a = 0.9975
Probability of up move, p = 0.4642
Up step size, u = 1.0618
Down step size, d = 0.9418

Node Time:
   0.0000   0.2500   0.5000   0.7500   1.0000

Example 21.4

Consider a 1-year American put option on the British pound (GBP). The current exchange rate (USD per GBP) is 1.6100, the strike price is 1.6000, the U.S. risk-free interest rate is 8% per annum, the sterling risk-free interest rate is 9% per annum, and the volatility of the sterling exchange rate is 12% per annum. In this case, $S_0 = 1.61$, $K = 1.60$, $r = 0.08$, $r_f = 0.09$, $\sigma = 0.12$, and $T = 1.0$. The life of the option is divided into four 3-month periods for the purposes of constructing the tree, so that $\Delta t = 0.25$. In this case, $q = r_f$ and equation (21.7) gives

$$a = e^{(0.08-0.09)\times 0.25} = 0.9975$$

The other parameters necessary to construct the tree are

$$u = e^{\sigma\sqrt{\Delta t}} = 1.0618, \quad d = 1/u = 0.9418 \quad p = \frac{a-d}{u-d} = 0.4642, \quad 1 - p = 0.5358$$

The tree, as produced by DerivaGem, is shown in Figure 21.6. (The upper number is the exchange rate; the lower number is the option price.) The estimated value of the option is $0.0710. (Using 50 time steps, DerivaGem gives the value of the option as 0.0738; with 100 time steps it also gives 0.0738.)

21.3 BINOMIAL MODEL FOR A DIVIDEND-PAYING STOCK

We now move on to the more tricky issue of how the binomial model can be used for a dividend-paying stock. As in Chapter 15, the word "dividend" will, for the purposes of our discussion, be used to refer to the reduction in the stock price on the ex-dividend date as a result of the dividend.

Known Dividend Yield

For long-life stock options, it is sometimes assumed for convenience that there is a known continuous dividend yield of q on the stock. The options can then be valued in the same way as options on a stock index.

For more accuracy, known dividend yields can be assumed to be paid discretely. Suppose that there is a single dividend, and the dividend yield (i.e., the dividend as a percentage of the stock price) is known. The parameters u, d, and p can be calculated as though no dividends are expected. If the time $i\,\Delta t$ is prior to the stock going ex-dividend, the nodes on the tree correspond to stock prices

$$S_0 u^j d^{i-j}, \quad j = 0, 1, \ldots, i$$

If the time $i\,\Delta t$ is after the stock goes ex-dividend, the nodes correspond to stock prices

$$S_0(1-\delta)u^j d^{i-j}, \quad j = 0, 1, \ldots, i$$

where δ is the dividend yield. The tree has the form shown in Figure 21.7. Several known dividend yields during the life of an option can be dealt with similarly. If δ_i is the total dividend yield associated with all ex-dividend dates between time zero and time $i\,\Delta t$, the nodes at time $i\,\Delta t$ correspond to stock prices

$$S_0(1-\delta_i)u^j d^{i-j}$$

Figure 21.7   Tree when stock pays a known dividend yield at one particular time.

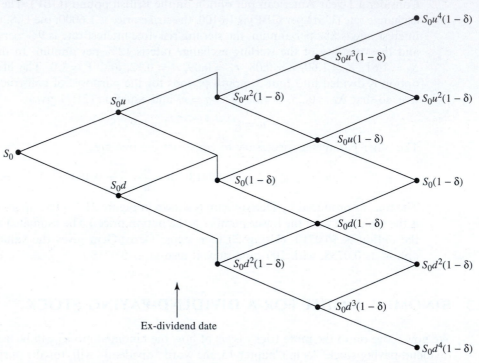

Ex-dividend date

Known Dollar Dividend

In some situations, particularly when the life of the option is short, the most realistic assumption is that the dollar amount of the dividend rather than the dividend yield is known in advance. If the volatility of the stock, σ, is assumed constant, the tree then takes the form shown in Figure 21.8. It does not recombine, which means that the number of nodes that have to be evaluated is liable to become very large. Suppose that there is only one dividend, that the ex-dividend date, τ, is between $k \, \Delta t$ and $(k+1) \, \Delta t$, and that the dollar amount of the dividend is D. When $i \leqslant k$, the nodes on the tree at time $i \, \Delta t$ correspond to stock prices

$$S_0 u^j d^{i-j}, \quad j = 0, 1, 2, \ldots, i$$

as before. When $i = k + 1$, the nodes on the tree correspond to stock prices

$$S_0 u^j d^{i-j} - D, \quad j = 0, 1, 2, \ldots, i$$

When $i = k + 2$, the nodes on the tree correspond to stock prices

$$(S_0 u^j d^{i-1-j} - D)u \quad \text{and} \quad (S_0 u^j d^{i-1-j} - D)d$$

for $j = 0, 1, 2, \ldots, i - 1$, so that there are $2i$ rather than $i + 1$ nodes. When $i = k + m$, there are $m(k + 2)$ rather than $k + m + 1$ nodes. The number of nodes expands even faster when there are several ex-dividend dates during the option's life.

Figure 21.8 Tree when dollar amount of dividend is assumed known and volatility is assumed constant.

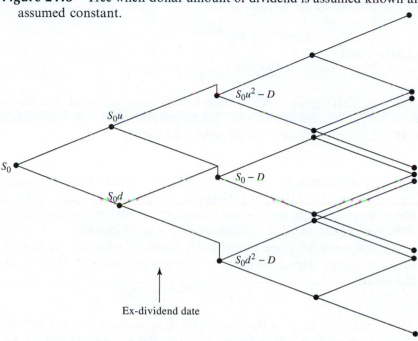

Section 15.12 explained that European options on dividend-paying stocks are valued by assuming that the stock price has two components: a part that is uncertain and a part that is the present value of dividends paid during the life of the option. It outlined a number of reasons why practitioners find this a sensible assumption. American options clearly have to be valued using the same model as European options. (Otherwise the prices of American options that should never be exercised early will not be the same as the prices of European options.) American options on stocks paying known dividends are therefore in practice valued using the approach in Section 15.12. As it happens, this solves the node-proliferation problem in Figure 21.8.

Suppose that there is only one ex-dividend date, τ, during the life of the option and that $k\,\Delta t \leqslant \tau \leqslant (k+1)\,\Delta t$. The value S^* of the uncertain component (i.e., the component not used to pay dividends) at time $i\,\Delta t$ is given by

$$S^* = S \quad \text{when } i\,\Delta t > \tau$$

and

$$S^* = S - De^{-r(\tau - i\Delta t)} \quad \text{when } i\,\Delta t \leqslant \tau$$

where D is the dividend. Define σ^* as the volatility of S^*. The parameters p, u, and d can be calculated from equations (21.4) to (21.7) with σ replaced by σ^* and a tree can be constructed in the usual way to model S^*.[6] By adding to the stock price at each node, the present value of future dividends (if any), the tree can be converted into another tree

---

[6] As discussed in Section 15.12, the difference between σ and σ^* does not usually have to be considered explicitly because in practice analysts normally work with volatilities implied from market prices using their models and these are σ^*-volatilities.

that models S. Suppose that S_0^* is the value of S^* at time zero. At time $i\,\Delta t$, the nodes on this tree correspond to the stock prices

$$S_0^* u^j d^{i-j} + De^{-r(\tau - i\,\Delta t)}, \quad j = 0, 1, \dots, i$$

when $i\,\Delta t < \tau$ and

$$S_0^* u^j d^{i-j}, \quad j = 0, 1, \dots, i$$

when $i\,\Delta t > \tau$. This approach, which leads to a situation where the tree recombines so that there are $i + 1$ nodes at time $i\,\Delta t$, can be generalized in a straightforward way to deal with the situation where there are several dividends.

Example 21.5

Consider a 5-month American put option on a stock that is expected to pay a single dividend of \$2.06 during the life of the option. The initial stock price is \$52, the strike price is \$50, the risk-free interest rate is 10% per annum, the volatility is 40% per annum, and the ex-dividend date is in $3\frac{1}{2}$ months.

We first construct a tree to model S^*, the stock price less the present value of future dividends during the life of the option. At time zero, the present value of the dividend is

$$2.06 \times e^{-0.2917 \times 0.1} = 2.00$$

The initial value of S^* is therefore 50.00. If we assume that the 40% per annum volatility refers to S^*, then Figure 21.3 provides a binomial tree for S^*. (This is because S^* has the same initial value and volatility as the stock price that Figure 21.3 was based upon.) Adding the present value of the dividend at each node leads to Figure 21.9, which is a binomial model for S. The probabilities at each node are, as in Figure 21.3, 0.5073 for an up movement and 0.4927 for a down movement. Working back through the tree in the usual way gives the option price as \$4.44. (Using 50 time steps, DerivaGem gives a value for the option of 4.208; using 100 steps it gives 4.214.)

Control Variate Technique

A technique known as the *control variate technique* can improve the accuracy of the pricing of an American option.[7] This involves using the same tree to calculate the value of both the American option, f_A, and the corresponding European option, f_E. The Black–Scholes–Merton price of the European option, f_{BSM}, is also calculated. The error when the tree is used to price the European option, $f_{BSM} - f_E$, is assumed equal to the error when the tree is used to price the American option. This gives the estimate of the price of the American option as

$$f_A + (f_{BSM} - f_E)$$

To illustrate this approach, Figure 21.10 values the option in Figure 21.3 on the assumption that it is European. The price obtained, f_E, is \$4.32. From the Black–Scholes–Merton formula, the true European price of the option, f_{BSM}, is \$4.08. The

---

[7] See J. C. Hull and A. White, "The Use of the Control Variate Technique in Option Pricing," *Journal of Financial and Quantitative Analysis*, 23 (September 1988): 237–51.

Figure 21.9 Tree produced by DerivaGem for Example 21.5.

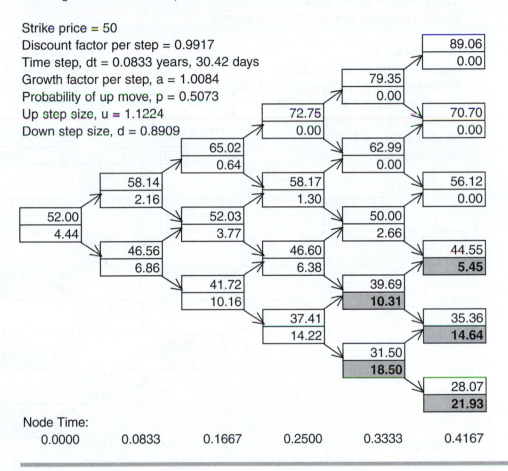

At each node:
Upper value = Underlying Asset Price
Lower value = Option Price
Shading indicates where option is exercised

Strike price = 50
Discount factor per step = 0.9917
Time step, dt = 0.0833 years, 30.42 days
Growth factor per step, a = 1.0084
Probability of up move, p = 0.5073
Up step size, u = 1.1224
Down step size, d = 0.8909

					89.06
					0.00
				79.35	
				0.00	
			72.75		70.70
			0.00		0.00
		65.02		62.99	
		0.64		0.00	
	58.14		58.17		56.12
	2.16		1.30		0.00
52.00		52.03		50.00	
4.44		3.77		2.66	
	46.56		46.60		44.55
	6.86		6.38		**5.45**
		41.72		39.69	
		10.16		**10.31**	
			37.41		35.36
			14.22		**14.64**
				31.50	
				18.50	
					28.07
					21.93

Node Time:
0.0000   0.0833   0.1667   0.2500   0.3333   0.4167

estimate of the American price in Figure 21.3, f_A, is \$4.49. The control variate estimate of the American price, therefore, is

$$4.49 + (4.08 - 4.32) = 4.25$$

A good estimate of the American price, calculated using 100 steps, is 4.278. The control variate approach does, therefore, produce a considerable improvement over the basic tree estimate of 4.49 in this case.

The control variate technique in effect involves using the tree to calculate the difference between the European and the American price rather than the American price itself. We give a further application of the control variate technique when we discuss Monte Carlo simulation later in the chapter.

Figure 21.10 Tree, as produced by DerivaGem, for European version of option in Figure 21.3. At each node, the upper number is the stock price, and the lower number is the option price.

At each node:
 Upper value = Underlying Asset Price
 Lower value = Option Price
Shading indicates where option is exercised

Strike price = 50
Discount factor per step = 0.9917
Time step, dt = 0.0833 years, 30.42 days
Growth factor per step, a = 1.0084
Probability of up move, p = 0.5073
Up step size, u = 1.1224
Down step size, d = 0.8909

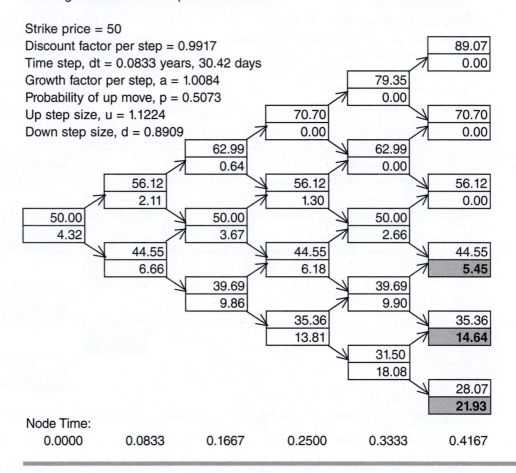

Node Time:					
0.0000	0.0833	0.1667	0.2500	0.3333	0.4167

21.4 ALTERNATIVE PROCEDURES FOR CONSTRUCTING TREES

The Cox, Ross, and Rubinstein approach described so far is not the only way of building a binomial tree. The change in $\ln S$ in time Δt in a risk-neutral world has mean $(r - q - \sigma^2/2)\Delta t$ and standard deviation $\sigma\sqrt{\Delta t}$. These can be matched by setting $p = 0.5$ and

$$u = e^{(r-q-\sigma^2/2)\Delta t + \sigma\sqrt{\Delta t}}, \qquad d = e^{(r-q-\sigma^2/2)\Delta t - \sigma\sqrt{\Delta t}}$$

This alternative tree-building procedure has the advantage over the Cox, Ross, and

Rubinstein approach that the probabilities are always 0.5 regardless of the value of σ or the number of time steps.[8] Its disadvantage is that it is not quite as straightforward to calculate delta, gamma, and theta from the tree because the tree is no longer centered at the initial stock price.

Example 21.6

Consider a 9-month American call option on a foreign currency. The foreign currency is worth 0.7900 when measured in the domestic currency, the strike price is 0.7950, the domestic risk-free interest rate is 6% per annum, the foreign risk-free interest rate is 10% per annum, and the volatility of the exchange rate is 4% per annum. In this case, $S_0 = 0.79$, $K = 0.795$, $r = 0.06$, $r_f = 0.10$, $\sigma = 0.04$, and

Figure 21.11 Binomial tree for American call option on a foreign currency. At each node, upper number is spot exchange rate and lower number is option price. All probabilities are 0.5.

At each node:
 Upper value = Underlying Asset Price
 Lower value = Option Price
Shading indicates where option is exercised

Strike price = 0.795
Discount factor per step = 0.9851
Time step, dt = 0.2500 years, 91.25 days

Probability of up move, p = 0.5000

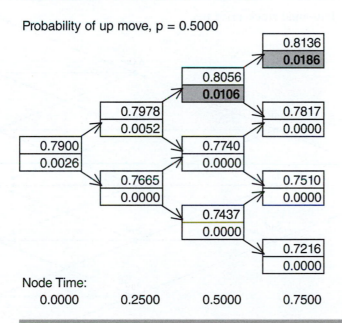

Node Time:
   0.0000   0.2500   0.5000   0.7500

---

[8] When time steps are so large that $\sigma < |(r - q)\sqrt{\Delta t}|$, the Cox, Ross, and Rubinstein tree gives negative probabilities. The alternative procedure described here does not have that drawback.

$T = 0.75$. Using the alternative tree-building procedure, we set $\Delta t = 0.25$ (3 steps) and the probabilities on each branch to 0.5, so that

$$u = e^{(0.06-0.10-0.0016/2)0.25+0.04\sqrt{0.25}} = 1.0098$$
$$d = e^{(0.06-0.10-0.0016/2)0.25-0.04\sqrt{0.25}} = 0.9703$$

The tree for the exchange rate is shown in Figure 21.11. The tree gives the value of the option as $0.0026.

Trinomial Trees

Trinomial trees can be used as an alternative to binomial trees. The general form of the tree is as shown in Figure 21.12. Suppose that p_u, p_m, and p_d are the probabilities of up, middle, and down movements at each node and Δt is the length of the time step. For an asset paying dividends at a rate q, parameter values that match the mean and standard deviation of changes in $\ln S$ are

$$u = e^{\sigma\sqrt{3\Delta t}}, \quad d = 1/u$$

$$p_d = -\sqrt{\frac{\Delta t}{12\sigma^2}}\left(r - q - \frac{\sigma^2}{2}\right) + \frac{1}{6}, \quad p_m = \frac{2}{3}, \quad p_u = \sqrt{\frac{\Delta t}{12\sigma^2}}\left(r - q - \frac{\sigma^2}{2}\right) + \frac{1}{6}$$

Calculations for a trinomial tree are analogous to those for a binomial tree. We work from the end of the tree to the beginning. At each node we calculate the value of

Figure 21.12 Trinomial stock price tree.

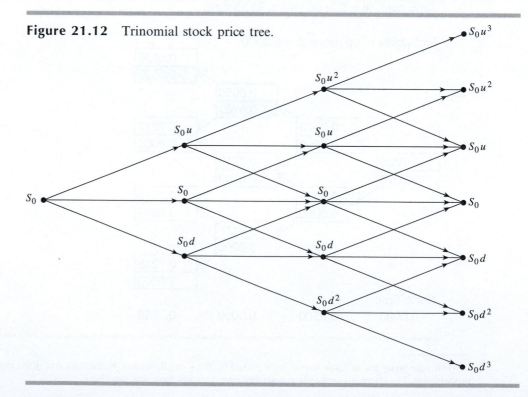

exercising and the value of continuing. The value of continuing is

$$e^{-r\Delta t}(p_u f_u + p_m f_m + p_d f_d)$$

where f_u, f_m, and f_d are the values of the option at the subsequent up, middle, and down nodes, respectively. The trinomial tree approach proves to be equivalent to the explicit finite difference method, which will be described in Section 21.8.

Figlewski and Gao have proposed an enhancement of the trinomial tree method, which they call the *adaptive mesh model*. In this, a high-resolution (small-Δt) tree is grafted onto a low-resolution (large-Δt) tree.[9] When valuing a regular American option, high resolution is most useful for the parts of the tree close to the strike price at the end of the life of the option.

21.5 TIME-DEPENDENT PARAMETERS

Up to now we have assumed that r, q, r_f, and σ are constants. In practice, they are usually assumed to be time dependent. The values of these variables between times t and $t + \Delta t$ are assumed to be equal to their forward values.[10]

To make r and q (or r_f) a function of time in a Cox–Ross–Rubinstein binomial tree, we set

$$a = e^{[f(t)-g(t)]\Delta t} \tag{21.11}$$

for nodes at time t, where $f(t)$ is the forward interest rate between times t and $t + \Delta t$ and $g(t)$ is the forward value of q (or r_f) between these times. This does not change the geometry of the tree because u and d do not depend on a. The probabilities on the branches emanating from nodes at time t are:[11]

$$p = \frac{e^{[f(t)-g(t)]\Delta t} - d}{u - d} \tag{21.12}$$

$$1 - p = \frac{u - e^{[f(t)-g(t)]\Delta t}}{u - d}$$

The rest of the way that we use the tree is the same as before, except that when discounting between times t and $t + \Delta t$ we use $f(t)$.

Making the volatility, σ, a function of time in a binomial tree is more difficult. Suppose $\sigma(t)$ is the volatility used to price an option with maturity t. One approach is to make the length of each time step inversely proportional to the average variance rate during the time step. The values of u and d are then the same everywhere and the tree recombines. Define the $V = o(T)^2 T$, where T is the life of the tree, and define t_i as the end of the ith time step. For N time steps, we choose t_i to satisfy $\sigma(t_i)^2 t_i = iV/N$ and set $u = e^{\sqrt{V/N}}$ with $d = 1/u$. The parameter p is defined in terms of u, d, r, and q as for a constant volatility. This procedure can be combined with the procedure just mentioned for dealing

---

[9] See S. Figlewski and B. Gao, "The Adaptive Mesh Model: A New Approach to Efficient Option Pricing," *Journal of Financial Economics*, 53 (1999): 313–51.

[10] The forward dividend yield and forward variance rate are calculated in the same way as the forward interest rate. (The variance rate is the square of the volatility.)

[11] For a sufficiently large number of time steps, these probabilities are always positive.

Business Snapshot 21.1   Calculating Pi with Monte Carlo Simulation

Suppose the sides of the square in Figure 21.13 are one unit in length. Imagine that you fire darts randomly at the square and calculate the percentage that lie in the circle. What should you find? The square has an area of 1.0 and the circle has a radius of 0.5 The area of the circle is π times the radius squared or $\pi/4$. It follows that the proportion of darts that lie in the circle should be $\pi/4$. We can estimate π by multiplying the proportion that lie in the circle by 4.

We can use an Excel spreadsheet to simulate the dart throwing as illustrated in Table 21.1. We define both cell A1 and cell B1 as =RAND( ). A1 and B1 are random numbers between 0 and 1 and define how far to the right and how high up the dart lands in the square in Figure 21.13. We then define cell C1 as

=IF((A1−0.5)^2+(B1−0.5)^2<0.5^2,4,0)

This has the effect of setting C1 equal to 4 if the dart lies in the circle and 0 otherwise.

Define the next 99 rows of the spreadsheet similarly to the first one. (This is a "select and drag" operation in Excel.) Define C102 as =AVERAGE(C1:C100) and C103 as =STDEV(C1:C100). C102 (which is 3.04 in Table 21.1) is an estimate of π calculated from 100 random trials. C103 is the standard deviation of our results and as we will see in Example 21.7 can be used to assess the accuracy of the estimate. Increasing the number of trials improves accuracy—but convergence to the correct value of 3.14159 is slow.

---

with nonconstant interest rates so that both interest rates and volatilities are time-dependent.

21.6 MONTE CARLO SIMULATION

We now explain Monte Carlo simulation, a quite different approach for valuing derivatives from binomial trees. Business Snapshot 21.1 illustrates the random sampling idea underlying Monte Carlo simulation by showing how a simple Excel program can be constructed to estimate π.

When used to value an option, Monte Carlo simulation uses the risk-neutral valuation result. We sample paths to obtain the expected payoff in a risk-neutral world

Figure 21.13   Calculation of π by throwing darts.

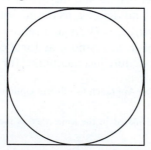

Table 21.1 Sample spreadsheet calculations in Business Snapshot 21.1.

	A	B	C
1	0.207	0.690	4
2	0.271	0.520	4
3	0.007	0.221	0
⋮	⋮	⋮	⋮
100	0.198	0.403	4
101			
102		Mean:	3.04
103		SD:	1.69

and then discount this payoff at the risk-free rate. Consider a derivative dependent on a single market variable S that provides a payoff at time T. Assuming that interest rates are constant, we can value the derivative as follows:

1. Sample a random path for S in a risk-neutral world.
2. Calculate the payoff from the derivative.
3. Repeat steps 1 and 2 to get many sample values of the payoff from the derivative in a risk-neutral world.
4. Calculate the mean of the sample payoffs to get an estimate of the expected payoff in a risk-neutral world.
5. Discount this expected payoff at the risk-free rate to get an estimate of the value of the derivative.

This is illustrated by the Monte Carlo worksheet in DerivaGem 3.00.

Suppose that the process followed by the underlying market variable in a risk-neutral world is

$$dS = \hat{\mu} S \, dt + \sigma S \, dz \tag{21.13}$$

where dz is a Wiener process, $\hat{\mu}$ is the expected return in a risk-neutral world, and σ is the volatility.[12] To simulate the path followed by S, we can divide the life of the derivative into N short intervals of length Δt and approximate equation (21.13) as

$$S(t + \Delta t) - S(t) = \hat{\mu} S(t) \, \Delta t + \sigma S(t) \epsilon \sqrt{\Delta t} \tag{21.14}$$

where $S(t)$ denotes the value of S at time t, ϵ is a random sample from a normal distribution with mean zero and standard deviation of 1.0. This enables the value of S at time Δt to be calculated from the initial value of S, the value at time $2 \Delta t$ to be calculated from the value at time Δt, and so on. An illustration of the procedure is in Section 14.3. One simulation trial involves constructing a complete path for S using N random samples from a normal distribution.

---

[12] If S is the price of a non-dividend-paying stock then $\hat{\mu} = r$, if it is an exchange rate then $\hat{\mu} = r - r_f$, and so on. Note that the volatility is the same in a risk-neutral world as in the real world, as explained in Section 13.7.

In practice, it is usually more accurate to simulate $\ln S$ rather than S. From Itô's lemma the process followed by $\ln S$ is

$$d \ln S = \left(\hat{\mu} - \frac{\sigma^2}{2} \right) dt + \sigma \, dz \tag{21.15}$$

so that

$$\ln S(t + \Delta t) - \ln S(t) = \left(\hat{\mu} - \frac{\sigma^2}{2} \right) \Delta t + \sigma \epsilon \sqrt{\Delta t}$$

or equivalently

$$S(t + \Delta t) = S(t) \exp\left[\left(\hat{\mu} - \frac{\sigma^2}{2} \right) \Delta t + \sigma \epsilon \sqrt{\Delta t} \right] \tag{21.16}$$

This equation is used to construct a path for S.

Working with $\ln S$ rather than S gives more accuracy. Also, if $\hat{\mu}$ and σ are constant, then

$$\ln S(T) - \ln S(0) = \left(\hat{\mu} - \frac{\sigma^2}{2} \right) T + \sigma \epsilon \sqrt{T}$$

is true for all T.[13] It follows that

$$S(T) = S(0) \exp\left[\left(\hat{\mu} - \frac{\sigma^2}{2} \right) T + \sigma \epsilon \sqrt{T} \right] \tag{21.17}$$

This equation can be used to value derivatives that provide a nonstandard payoff at time T. As shown in Business Snapshot 21.2, it can also be used to check the Black–Scholes–Merton formulas.

The key advantage of Monte Carlo simulation is that it can be used when the payoff depends on the path followed by the underlying variable S as well as when it depends only on the final value of S. (For example, it can be used when payoffs depend on the average value of S between time 0 and time T.) Payoffs can occur at several times during the life of the derivative rather than all at the end. Any stochastic process for S can be accommodated. As will be shown shortly, the procedure can also be extended to accommodate situations where the payoff from the derivative depends on several underlying market variables. The drawbacks of Monte Carlo simulation are that it is computationally very time consuming and cannot easily handle situations where there are early exercise opportunities.[14]

Derivatives Dependent on More than One Market Variable

We discussed correlated stochastic processes in Section 14.5. Consider the situation where the payoff from a derivative depends on n variables θ_i ($1 \leq i \leq n$). Define s_i as the volatility of θ_i, $\hat{m}_i$ as the expected growth rate of θ_i in a risk-neutral world, and ρ_{ik} as the correlation between the Wiener processes driving θ_i and θ_k.[15] As in the single-variable case, the life of the derivative must be divided into N subintervals of length Δt. The

[13] By contrast, equation (21.14) is exactly true only in the limit as Δt tends to zero.

[14] As discussed in Chapter 27, a number of researchers have suggested ways Monte Carlo simulation can be extended to value American options.

[15] Note that s_i, $\hat{m}_i$, and ρ_{ik} are not necessarily constant; they may depend on the θ_i.

Business Snapshot 21.2 Checking Black–Scholes–Merton in Excel

The Black–Scholes–Merton formula for a European call option can be checked by using a binomial tree with a very large number of time steps. An alternative way of checking it is to use Monte Carlo simulation. Table 21.2 shows a spreadsheet that can be constructed. The cells C2, D2, E2, F2, and G2 contain S_0, K, r, σ, and T, respectively. Cells D4, E4, and F4 calculate d_1, d_2, and the Black–Scholes–Merton price, respectively. (The Black–Scholes–Merton price is 4.817 in the sample spreadsheet.)

NORMSINV is the inverse cumulative function for the standard normal distribution. It follows that NORMSINV(RAND()) gives a random sample from a standard normal distribution. We set cell A1 as

=$C$2*EXP(($E$2−$F$2*$F$2/2)*$G$2+$F$2*NORMSINV(RAND( ))*SQRT($G$2))

This corresponds to equation (21.17) and is a random sample from the set of all stock prices at time T. We set cell B1 as

=EXP(−$E$2*$G$2)*MAX(A1−$D$2,0)

This is the present value of the payoff from a call option. We define the next 999 rows of the spreadsheet similarly to the first one. (This is a "select and drag" operation in Excel.) Define B1002 as AVERAGE(B1:B1000), which is 4.98 in the sample spreadsheet. This is an estimate of the value of the option and should be not too far from the Black–Scholes–Merton price. B1003 is defined as STDEV(B1:B1000). As we shall see in Example 21.8, it can be used to assess the accuracy of the estimate.

---

discrete version of the process for θ_i is then

$$\theta_i(t + \Delta t) - \theta_i(t) = \hat{m}_i \theta_i(t)\, \Delta t + s_i \theta_i(t) \epsilon_i \sqrt{\Delta t} \tag{21.18}$$

where ϵ_i is a random sample from a standard normal distribution. The coefficient of correlation between ϵ_i and ϵ_k is ρ_{ik} ($1 \leqslant i; k \leqslant n$). One simulation trial involves obtaining N samples of the ϵ_i ($1 \leqslant i \leqslant n$) from a multivariate standardized normal distribution. These are substituted into equation (21.18) to produce simulated paths for each θ_i, thereby enabling a sample value for the derivative to be calculated.

Table 21.2 Monte Carlo simulation to check Black–Scholes–Merton.

	A	*B*	*C*	*D*	*E*	*F*	*G*
1	45.95	0	S_0	K	r	σ	T
2	54.49	4.38	50	50	0.05	0.3	0.5
3	50.09	0.09		d_1	d_2	BSM price	
4	47.46	0		0.2239	0.0118	4.817	
5	44.93	0					
⋮	⋮	⋮					
1000	68.27	17.82					
1001							
1002	Mean:	4.98					
1003	SD:	7.68					

Generating the Random Samples from Normal Distributions

The instruction =NORMSINV(RAND()) in Excel can be used to generate a random sample from a standard normal distribution, as in Business Snapshot 21.2. When two correlated samples ϵ_1 and ϵ_2 from standard normal distributions are required, an appropriate procedure is as follows. Independent samples x_1 and x_2 from a univariate standardized normal distribution are obtained as just described. The required samples ϵ_1 and ϵ_2 are then calculated as follows:

$$\epsilon_1 = x_1$$
$$\epsilon_2 = \rho x_1 + x_2\sqrt{1 - \rho^2}$$

where ρ is the coefficient of correlation.

More generally, consider the situation where we require n correlated samples from normal distributions with the correlation between sample i and sample j being ρ_{ij}. We first sample n independent variables x_i $(1 \leqslant i \leqslant n)$, from univariate standardized normal distributions. The required samples, ϵ_i $(1 \leqslant i \leqslant n)$, are then defined as follows:

$$\left. \begin{array}{l} \epsilon_1 = \alpha_{11}x_1 \\ \epsilon_2 = \alpha_{21}x_1 + \alpha_{22}x_2 \\ \epsilon_3 = \alpha_{31}x_1 + \alpha_{32}x_2 + \alpha_{33}x_3 \end{array} \right\} \qquad \textbf{(21.19)}$$

and so on. We choose the coefficients α_{ij} so that the correlations and variances are correct. This can be done step by step as follows. Set $\alpha_{11} = 1$; choose α_{21} so that $\alpha_{21}\alpha_{11} = \rho_{21}$; choose α_{22} so that $\alpha_{21}^2 + \alpha_{22}^2 = 1$; choose α_{31} so that $\alpha_{31}\alpha_{11} = \rho_{31}$; choose α_{32} so that $\alpha_{31}\alpha_{21} + \alpha_{32}\alpha_{22} = \rho_{32}$; choose α_{33} so that $\alpha_{31}^2 + \alpha_{32}^2 + \alpha_{33}^2 = 1$; and so on.[16] This procedure is known as the *Cholesky decomposition*.

Number of Trials

The accuracy of the result given by Monte Carlo simulation depends on the number of trials. It is usual to calculate the standard deviation as well as the mean of the discounted payoffs given by the simulation trials. Denote the mean by μ and the standard deviation by ω. The variable μ is the simulation's estimate of the value of the derivative. The standard error of the estimate is

$$\frac{\omega}{\sqrt{M}}$$

where M is the number of trials. A 95% confidence interval for the price f of the derivative is therefore given by

$$\mu - \frac{1.96\omega}{\sqrt{M}} < f < \mu + \frac{1.96\omega}{\sqrt{M}}$$

This shows that uncertainty about the value of the derivative is inversely proportional to the square root of the number of trials. To double the accuracy of a simulation, we

---

[16] If the equations for the α's do not have real solutions, the assumed correlation structure is internally inconsistent This will be discussed further in Section 23.7.

must quadruple the number of trials; to increase the accuracy by a factor of 10, the number of trials must increase by a factor of 100; and so on.

Example 21.7

In Table 21.1, π is calculated as the average of 100 numbers. The standard deviation of the numbers is 1.69. In this case, $\omega = 1.69$ and $M = 100$, so that the standard error of the estimate is $1.69/\sqrt{100} = 0.169$. The spreadsheet therefore gives a 95% confidence interval for π as $(3.04 - 1.96 \times 0.169)$ to $(3.04 + 1.96 \times 0.169)$ or 2.71 to 3.37. (The correct value of 3.14159 lies within this confidence interval.)

Example 21.8

In Table 21.2, the value of the option is calculated as the average of 1000 numbers. The standard deviation of the numbers is 7.68. In this case, $\omega = 7.68$ and $M = 1000$. The standard error of the estimate is $7.68/\sqrt{1000} = 0.24$. The spreadsheet therefore gives a 95% confidence interval for the option value as $(4.98 - 1.96 \times 0.24)$ to $(4.98 + 1.96 \times 0.24)$, or 4.51 to 5.45. (The Black–Scholes–Merton price, 4.817, lies within this confidence interval.)

Sampling through a Tree

Instead of implementing Monte Carlo simulation by randomly sampling from the stochastic process for an underlying variable, we can use an N-step binomial tree and sample from the 2^N paths that are possible. Suppose we have a binomial tree where the probability of an "up" movement is 0.6. The procedure for sampling a random path through the tree is as follows. At each node, we sample a random number between 0 and 1. If the number is less than 0.4, we take the down branch. If it is greater than 0.4, we take the up branch. Once we have a complete path from the initial node to the end of the tree, we can calculate a payoff. This completes the first trial. A similar procedure is used to complete more trials. The mean of the payoffs is discounted at the risk-free rate to get an estimate of the value of the derivative.[17]

Example 21.9

Suppose that the tree in Figure 21.3 is used to value an option that pays off $\max(S_{ave} - 50, 0)$, where S_{ave} is the average stock price during the 5 months (with the first and last stock price being included in the average). This is known as an Asian option. When ten simulation trials are used one possible result is shown in Table 21.3. The value of the option is calculated as the average payoff discounted at the risk-free rate. In this case, the average payoff is $7.08 and the risk-free rate is 10% and so the calculated value is $7.08e^{-0.1 \times 5/12} = 6.79$. (This illustrates the methodology. In practice, we would have to use more time steps on the tree and many more simulation trials to get an accurate answer.)

Calculating the Greek Letters

The Greek letters discussed in Chapter 19 can be calculated using Monte Carlo simulation. Suppose that we are interested in the partial derivative of f with respect

---

[17] See D. Mintz, "Less is More," *Risk*, July 1997: 42–45, for a discussion of how sampling through a tree can be made efficient.

Table 21.3 Monte Carlo simulation to value Asian option from the tree in Figure 21.3. Payoff is amount by which average stock price exceeds $50. U = up movement; D = down movement.

Trial	Path	Average stock price	Option payoff
1	UUUUD	64.98	14.98
2	UUUDD	59.82	9.82
3	DDDUU	42.31	0.00
4	UUUUU	68.04	18.04
5	UUDDU	55.22	5.22
6	UDUUD	55.22	5.22
7	DDUDD	42.31	0.00
8	UUDDU	55.22	5.22
9	UUUDU	62.25	12.25
10	DDUUD	45.56	0.00
Average			7.08

to x, where f is the value of the derivative and x is the value of an underlying variable or a parameter. First, Monte Carlo simulation is used in the usual way to calculate an estimate $\hat{f}$ for the value of the derivative. A small increase Δx is then made in the value of x, and a new value for the derivative, $\hat{f}^*$, is calculated in the same way as $\hat{f}$. An estimate for the hedge parameter is given by

$$\frac{\hat{f}^* - \hat{f}}{\Delta x}$$

In order to minimize the standard error of the estimate, the number of time intervals, N, the random samples that are used, and the number of trials, M, should be the same for calculating both $\hat{f}$ and $\hat{f}^*$.

Applications

Monte Carlo simulation tends to be numerically more efficient than other procedures when there are three or more stochastic variables. This is because the time taken to carry out a Monte Carlo simulation increases approximately linearly with the number of variables, whereas the time taken for most other procedures increases exponentially with the number of variables. One advantage of Monte Carlo simulation is that it can provide a standard error for the estimates that it makes. Another is that it is an approach that can accommodate complex payoffs and complex stochastic processes. Also, it can be used when the payoff depends on some function of the whole path followed by a variable, not just its terminal value.

21.7 VARIANCE REDUCTION PROCEDURES

If the stochastic processes for the variables underlying a derivative are simulated as indicated in equations (21.13) to (21.18), a very large number of trials is usually necessary to estimate the value of the derivative with reasonable accuracy. This is very expensive in terms of computation time. In this section, we examine a number of variance reduction procedures that can lead to dramatic savings in computation time.

Antithetic Variable Technique

In the antithetic variable technique, a simulation trial involves calculating two values of the derivative. The first value f_1 is calculated in the usual way; the second value f_2 is calculated by changing the sign of all the random samples from standard normal distributions. (If ϵ is a sample used to calculate f_1, then $-\epsilon$ is the corresponding sample used to calculate f_2.) The sample value of the derivative calculated from a simulation trial is the average of f_1 and f_2. This works well because when f_1 is above the true value, f_2 tends to be below, and vice versa.

Denote $\bar{f}$ as the average of f_1 and f_2:

$$\bar{f} = \frac{f_1 + f_2}{2}$$

The final estimate of the value of the derivative is the average of the $\bar{f}$'s. If $\bar{\omega}$ is the standard deviation of the $\bar{f}$'s, and M is the number of simulation trials (i.e., the number of pairs of values calculated), then the standard error of the estimate is

$$\bar{\omega}/\sqrt{M}$$

This is usually much less than the standard error calculated using $2M$ random trials.

Control Variate Technique

We have already given one example of the control variate technique in connection with the use of trees to value American options (see Section 21.3). The control variate technique is applicable when there are two similar derivatives, A and B. Derivative A is the one being valued; derivative B is similar to derivative A and has an analytic solution available. Two simulations using the same random number streams and the same Δt are carried out in parallel. The first is used to obtain an estimate f_A^* of the value of A; the second is used to obtain an estimate f_B^*, of the value of B. A better estimate f_A of the value of A is then obtained using the formula

$$f_A = f_A^* - f_B^* + f_B \tag{21.20}$$

where f_B is the known true value of B calculated analytically. Hull and White provide an example of the use of the control variate technique when evaluating the effect of stochastic volatility on the price of a European call option.[18] In this case, A is the option assuming stochastic volatility and B is the option assuming constant volatility.

Importance Sampling

Importance sampling is best explained with an example. Suppose that we wish to calculate the price of a deep-out-of-the-money European call option with strike

---

[18] See J.C. Hull and A. White, "The Pricing of Options on Assets with Stochastic Volatilities," *Journal of Finance*, 42 (June 1987): 281–300.

price K and maturity T. If we sample values for the underlying asset price at time T in the usual way, most of the paths will lead to zero payoff. This is a waste of computation time because the zero-payoff paths contribute very little to the determination of the value of the option. We therefore try to choose only important paths, that is, paths where the stock price is above K at maturity.

Suppose F is the unconditional probability distribution function for the stock price at time T and q, the probability of the stock price being greater than K at maturity, is known analytically. Then $G = F/q$ is the probability distribution of the stock price conditional on the stock price being greater than K. To implement importance sampling, we sample from G rather than F. The estimate of the value of the option is the average discounted payoff multiplied by q.

Stratified Sampling

Sampling representative values rather than random values from a probability distribution usually gives more accuracy. Stratified sampling is a way of doing this. Suppose we wish to take 1000 samples from a probability distribution. We would divide the distribution into 1000 equally likely intervals and choose a representative value (typically the mean or median) for each interval.

In the case of a standard normal distribution when there are n intervals, we can calculate the representative value for the ith interval as

$$N^{-1}\left(\frac{i - 0.5}{n}\right)$$

where N^{-1} is the inverse cumulative normal distribution. For example, when $n = 4$ the representative values corresponding to the four intervals are $N^{-1}(0.125)$, $N^{-1}(0.375)$, $N^{-1}(0.625)$, $N^{-1}(0.875)$. The function N^{-1} can be calculated using the NORMSINV function in Excel.

Moment Matching

Moment matching involves adjusting the samples taken from a standardized normal distribution so that the first, second, and possibly higher moments are matched. Suppose that we sample from a normal distribution with mean 0 and standard deviation 1 to calculate the change in the value of a particular variable over a particular time period. Suppose that the samples are ϵ_i ($1 \leqslant i \leqslant n$). To match the first two moments, we calculate the mean of the samples, m, and the standard deviation of the samples, s. We then define adjusted samples ϵ_i^* ($1 \leqslant i \leqslant n$) as

$$\epsilon_i^* = \frac{\epsilon_i - m}{s}$$

These adjusted samples have the correct mean of 0 and the correct standard deviation of 1.0. We use the adjusted samples for all calculations.

Moment matching saves computation time, but can lead to memory problems because every number sampled must be stored until the end of the simulation. Moment matching is sometimes termed *quadratic resampling*. It is often used in conjunction with the antithetic variable technique. Because the latter automatically matches all odd moments, the goal of moment matching then becomes that of matching the second moment and, possibly, the fourth moment.

Using Quasi-Random Sequences

A quasi-random sequence (also called a *low-discrepancy* sequence) is a sequence of representative samples from a probability distribution.[19] Descriptions of the use of quasi-random sequences appear in Brotherton-Ratcliffe, and Press *et al.*[20] Quasi-random sequences can have the desirable property that they lead to the standard error of an estimate being proportional to $1/M$ rather than $1/\sqrt{M}$, where M is the sample size.

Quasi-random sampling is similar to stratified sampling. The objective is to sample representative values for the underlying variables. In stratified sampling, it is assumed that we know in advance how many samples will be taken. A quasi-random sampling procedure is more flexible. The samples are taken in such a way that we are always "filling in" gaps between existing samples. At each stage of the simulation, the sampled points are roughly evenly spaced throughout the probability space.

Figure 21.14 shows points generated in two dimensions using a procedure by Sobol'.[21] It can be seen that successive points do tend to fill in the gaps left by previous points.

21.8 FINITE DIFFERENCE METHODS

Finite difference methods value a derivative by solving the differential equation that the derivative satisfies. The differential equation is converted into a set of difference equations, and the difference equations are solved iteratively.

To illustrate the approach, we consider how it might be used to value an American put option on a stock paying a dividend yield of q. The differential equation that the option must satisfy is, from equation (17.6),

$$\frac{\partial f}{\partial t} + (r - q)S\frac{\partial f}{\partial S} + \tfrac{1}{2}\sigma^2 S^2 \frac{\partial^2 f}{\partial S^2} = rf \tag{21.21}$$

Suppose that the life of the option is T. We divide this into N equally spaced intervals of length $\Delta t = T/N$. A total of $N + 1$ times are therefore considered

$$0, \ \Delta t, \ 2\Delta t, \ \ldots, \ T$$

Suppose that S_{max} is a stock price sufficiently high that, when it is reached, the put has virtually no value. We define $\Delta S = S_{max}/M$ and consider a total of $M + 1$ equally spaced stock prices:

$$0, \ \Delta S, \ 2\Delta S, \ \ldots, \ S_{max}$$

The level S_{max} is chosen so that one of these is the current stock price.

---

[19] The term *quasi-random* is a misnomer. A quasi-random sequence is totally deterministic.

[20] See R. Brotherton-Ratcliffe, "Monte Carlo Motoring," *Risk*, December 1994: 53–58; W. H. Press, S. A. Teukolsky, W. T. Vetterling, and B. P. Flannery, *Numerical Recipes in C: The Art of Scientific Computing*, 2nd edn. Cambridge University Press, 1992.

[21] See I. M. Sobol', *USSR Computational Mathematics and Mathematical Physics*, 7, 4 (1967): 86–112. A description of Sobol's procedure is in W. H. Press, S. A. Teukolsky, W. T. Vetterling, and B. P. Flannery, *Numerical Recipes in C: The Art of Scientific Computing*, 2nd edn. Cambridge University Press, 1992.

Figure 21.14   First 1,024 points of a Sobol' sequence.

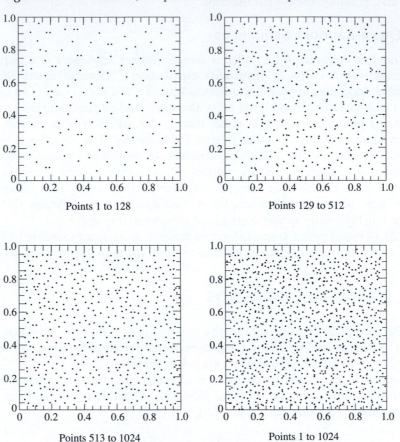

The time points and stock price points define a grid consisting of a total of $(M + 1)(N + 1)$ points, as shown in Figure 21.15. We define the (i, j) point on the grid as the point that corresponds to time $i \Delta t$ and stock price $j \Delta S$. We will use the variable $f_{i,j}$ to denote the value of the option at the (i, j) point.

Implicit Finite Difference Method

For an interior point (i, j) on the grid, $\partial f / \partial S$ can be approximated as

$$\frac{\partial f}{\partial S} = \frac{f_{i,j+1} - f_{i,j}}{\Delta S} \tag{21.22}$$

or as

$$\frac{\partial f}{\partial S} = \frac{f_{i,j} - f_{i,j-1}}{\Delta S} \tag{21.23}$$

Equation (21.22) is known as the *forward difference approximation*; equation (21.23) is known as the *backward difference approximation*. We use a more symmetrical approximation by averaging the two:

$$\frac{\partial f}{\partial S} = \frac{f_{i,j+1} - f_{i,j-1}}{2\,\Delta S} \tag{21.24}$$

For $\partial f/\partial t$, we will use a forward difference approximation so that the value at time $i\,\Delta t$ is related to the value at time $(i+1)\,\Delta t$:

$$\frac{\partial f}{\partial t} = \frac{f_{i+1,j} - f_{i,j}}{\Delta t} \tag{21.25}$$

Consider next $\partial^2 f/\partial S^2$. The backward difference approximation for $\partial f/\partial S$ at the (i, j) point is given by equation (21.23). The backward difference at the $(i, j+1)$ point is

$$\frac{f_{i,j+1} - f_{i,j}}{\Delta S}$$

Hence a finite difference approximation for $\partial^2 f/\partial S^2$ at the (i, j) point is

$$\frac{\partial^2 f}{\partial S^2} = \left(\frac{f_{i,j+1} - f_{i,j}}{\Delta S} - \frac{f_{i,j} - f_{i,j-1}}{\Delta S} \right) \bigg/ \Delta S$$

or

$$\frac{\partial^2 f}{\partial S^2} = \frac{f_{i,j+1} + f_{i,j-1} - 2f_{i,j}}{\Delta S^2} \tag{21.26}$$

Figure 21.15   Grid for finite difference approach.

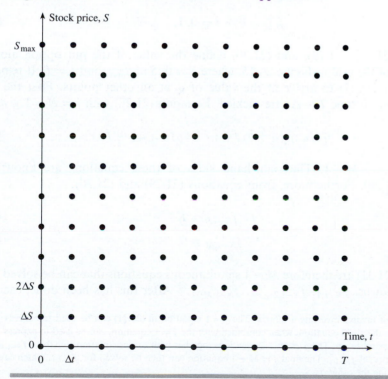

Substituting equations (21.24), (21.25), and (21.26) into the differential equation (21.21) and noting that $S = j \Delta S$ gives

$$\frac{f_{i+1,j} - f_{i,j}}{\Delta t} + (r - q)j \Delta S \frac{f_{i,j+1} - f_{i,j-1}}{2 \Delta S} + \frac{1}{2}\sigma^2 j^2 \Delta S^2 \frac{f_{i,j+1} + f_{i,j-1} - 2f_{i,j}}{\Delta S^2} = r f_{i,j}$$

for $j = 1, 2, \ldots, M - 1$ and $i = 0, 1, \ldots, N - 1$. Rearranging terms, we obtain

$$a_j f_{i,j-1} + b_j f_{i,j} + c_j f_{i,j+1} = f_{i+1,j} \qquad (21.27)$$

where

$$a_j = \tfrac{1}{2}(r - q)j \Delta t - \tfrac{1}{2}\sigma^2 j^2 \Delta t$$

$$b_j = 1 + \sigma^2 j^2 \Delta t + r \Delta t$$

$$c_j = -\tfrac{1}{2}(r - q)j \Delta t - \tfrac{1}{2}\sigma^2 j^2 \Delta t$$

The value of the put at time T is $\max(K - S_T, 0)$, where S_T is the stock price at time T. Hence,

$$f_{N,j} = \max(K - j \Delta S, 0), \quad j = 0, 1, \ldots, M \qquad (21.28)$$

The value of the put option when the stock price is zero is K. Hence,

$$f_{i,0} = K, \quad i = 0, 1, \ldots, N \qquad (21.29)$$

We assume that the put option is worth zero when $S = S_{\max}$, so that

$$f_{i,M} = 0, \quad i = 0, 1, \ldots, N \qquad (21.30)$$

Equations (21.28), (21.29), and (21.30) define the value of the put option along the three edges of the grid in Figure 21.15, where $S = 0$, $S = S_{\max}$, and $t = T$. It remains to use equation (21.27) to arrive at the value of f at all other points. First the points corresponding to time $T - \Delta t$ are tackled. Equation (21.27) with $i = N - 1$ gives

$$a_j f_{N-1,j-1} + b_j f_{N-1,j} + c_j f_{N-1,j+1} = f_{N,j} \qquad (21.31)$$

for $j = 1, 2, \ldots, M - 1$. The right-hand sides of these equations are known from equation (21.28). Furthermore, from equations (21.29) and (21.30),

$$f_{N-1,0} = K \qquad (21.32)$$

$$f_{N-1,M} = 0 \qquad (21.33)$$

Equations (21.31) are therefore $M - 1$ simultaneous equations that can be solved for the $M - 1$ unknowns: $f_{N-1,1}, f_{N-1,2}, \ldots, f_{N-1,M-1}$.[22] After this has been done, each value

---

[22] This does not involve inverting a matrix. The $j = 1$ equation in (21.31) can be used to express $f_{N-1,2}$ in terms of $f_{N-1,1}$; the $j = 2$ equation, when combined with the $j = 1$ equation, can be used to express $f_{N-1,3}$ in terms of $f_{N-1,1}$; and so on. The $j = M - 2$ equation, together with earlier equations, enables $f_{N-1,M-1}$ to be expressed in terms of $f_{N-1,1}$. The final $j = M - 1$ equation can then be solved for $f_{N-1,1}$, which can then be used to determine the other $f_{N-1,j}$.

of $f_{N-1,j}$ is compared with $K - j \Delta S$. If $f_{N-1,j} < K - j \Delta S$, early exercise at time $T - \Delta t$ is optimal and $f_{N-1,j}$ is set equal to $K - j \Delta S$. The nodes corresponding to time $T - 2 \Delta t$ are handled in a similar way, and so on. Eventually, $f_{0,1}, f_{0,2}, f_{0,3}, \ldots,$ $f_{0,M-1}$ are obtained. One of these is the option price of interest.

The control variate technique can be used in conjunction with finite difference methods. The same grid is used to value an option similar to the one under consideration but for which an analytic valuation is available. Equation (21.20) is then used.

Example 21.10

Table 21.4 shows the result of using the implicit finite difference method as just described for pricing the American put option in Example 21.1. Values of 20, 10, and 5 were chosen for M, N, and ΔS, respectively. Thus, the option price is evaluated at \$5 stock price intervals between \$0 and \$100 and at half-month time intervals throughout the life of the option. The option price given by the grid is \$4.07. The same grid gives the price of the corresponding European option as \$3.91. The true European price given by the Black–Scholes–Merton formula is \$4.08. The control variate estimate of the American price is therefore

$$4.07 + (4.08 - 3.91) = \$4.24$$

Explicit Finite Difference Method

The implicit finite difference method has the advantage of being very robust. It always converges to the solution of the differential equation as ΔS and Δt approach zero.[23] One of the disadvantages of the implicit finite difference method is that $M - 1$ simultaneous equations have to be solved in order to calculate the $f_{i,j}$ from the $f_{i+1,j}$. The method can be simplified if the values of $\partial f / \partial S$ and $\partial^2 f / \partial S^2$ at point (i, j) on the grid are assumed to be the same as at point $(i + 1, j)$. Equations (21.24) and (21.26) then become

$$\frac{\partial f}{\partial S} = \frac{f_{i+1,j+1} - f_{i+1,j-1}}{2 \Delta S}$$

$$\frac{\partial^2 f}{\partial S^2} = \frac{f_{i+1,j+1} + f_{i+1,j-1} - 2 f_{i+1,j}}{\Delta S^2}$$

The difference equation is

$$\frac{f_{i+1,j} - f_{i,j}}{\Delta t} + (r - q) j \Delta S \frac{f_{i+1,j+1} - f_{i+1,j-1}}{2 \Delta S}$$

$$+ \tfrac{1}{2} \sigma^2 j^2 \Delta S^2 \frac{f_{i+1,j+1} + f_{i+1,j-1} - 2 f_{i+1,j}}{\Delta S^2} = r f_{i,j}$$

or

$$f_{i,j} = a_j^* f_{i+1,j-1} + b_j^* f_{i+1,j} + c_j^* f_{i+1,j+1} \qquad \textbf{(21.34)}$$

---

[23] A general rule in finite difference methods is that ΔS should be kept proportional to $\sqrt{\Delta t}$ as they approach zero.

Table 21.4   Grid to value American option in Example 21.1 using implicit finite difference methods.

Stock price (dollars)	Time to maturity (months)										
	5	4.5	4	3.5	3	2.5	2	1.5	1	0.5	0
100	0.00	0.00	0.00	0.00	0.00	0.00	0.00	0.00	0.00	0.00	0.00
95	0.02	0.02	0.01	0.01	0.00	0.00	0.00	0.00	0.00	0.00	0.00
90	0.05	0.04	0.03	0.02	0.01	0.01	0.00	0.00	0.00	0.00	0.00
85	0.09	0.07	0.05	0.03	0.02	0.01	0.01	0.00	0.00	0.00	0.00
80	0.16	0.12	0.09	0.07	0.04	0.03	0.02	0.01	0.00	0.00	0.00
75	0.27	0.22	0.17	0.13	0.09	0.06	0.03	0.02	0.01	0.00	0.00
70	0.47	0.39	0.32	0.25	0.18	0.13	0.08	0.04	0.02	0.00	0.00
65	0.82	0.71	0.60	0.49	0.38	0.28	0.19	0.11	0.05	0.02	0.00
60	1.42	1.27	1.11	0.95	0.78	0.62	0.45	0.30	0.16	0.05	0.00
55	2.43	2.24	2.05	1.83	1.61	1.36	1.09	0.81	0.51	0.22	0.00
50	4.07	3.88	3.67	3.45	3.19	2.91	2.57	2.17	1.66	0.99	0.00
45	6.58	6.44	6.29	6.13	5.96	5.77	5.57	5.36	5.17	5.02	5.00
40	10.15	10.10	10.05	10.01	10.00	10.00	10.00	10.00	10.00	10.00	10.00
35	15.00	15.00	15.00	15.00	15.00	15.00	15.00	15.00	15.00	15.00	15.00
30	20.00	20.00	20.00	20.00	20.00	20.00	20.00	20.00	20.00	20.00	20.00
25	25.00	25.00	25.00	25.00	25.00	25.00	25.00	25.00	25.00	25.00	25.00
20	30.00	30.00	30.00	30.00	30.00	30.00	30.00	30.00	30.00	30.00	30.00
15	35.00	35.00	35.00	35.00	35.00	35.00	35.00	35.00	35.00	35.00	35.00
10	40.00	40.00	40.00	40.00	40.00	40.00	40.00	40.00	40.00	40.00	40.00
5	45.00	45.00	45.00	45.00	45.00	45.00	45.00	45.00	45.00	45.00	45.00
0	50.00	50.00	50.00	50.00	50.00	50.00	50.00	50.00	50.00	50.00	50.00

where

$$a_j^* = \frac{1}{1 + r\,\Delta t}\left(-\tfrac{1}{2}(r - q)j\,\Delta t + \tfrac{1}{2}\sigma^2 j^2 \Delta t\right)$$

$$b_j^* = \frac{1}{1 + r\,\Delta t}\left(1 - \sigma^2 j^2 \Delta t\right)$$

$$c_j^* = \frac{1}{1 + r\,\Delta t}\left(\tfrac{1}{2}(r - q)j\,\Delta t + \tfrac{1}{2}\sigma^2 j^2 \Delta t\right)$$

This creates what is known as the *explicit finite difference method*.[24] Figure 21.16 shows the difference between the implicit and explicit methods. The implicit method leads to equation (21.27), which gives a relationship between three different values of the option at time $i\,\Delta t$ (i.e., $f_{i,j-1}$, $f_{i,j}$, and $f_{i,j+1}$) and one value of the option at time $(i + 1)\,\Delta t$ (i.e., $f_{i+1,j}$). The explicit method leads to equation (21.34), which gives a relationship

---

[24] We also obtain the explicit finite difference method if we use the backward difference approximation instead of the forward difference approximation for $\partial f/\partial t$.

Figure 21.16   Difference between implicit and explicit finite difference methods.

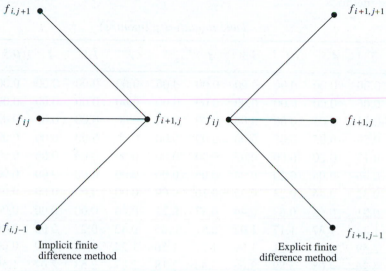

Implicit finite
difference method

Explicit finite
difference method

between one value of the option at time $i\,\Delta t$ (i.e., $f_{i,j}$) and three different values of the option at time $(i+1)\,\Delta t$ (i.e., $f_{i+1,j-1}$, $f_{i+1,j}$, $f_{i+1,j+1}$).

Example 21.11

Table 21.5 shows the result of using the explicit version of the finite difference method for pricing the American put option described in Example 21.1. As in Example 21.10, values of 20, 10, and 5 were chosen for M, N, and ΔS, respectively. The option price given by the grid is \$4.26.[25]

Change of Variable

When geometric Brownian motion is used for the underlying asset price, it is computationally more efficient to use finite difference methods with $\ln S$ rather than S as the underlying variable. Define $Z = \ln S$. Equation (21.21) becomes

$$\frac{\partial f}{\partial t} + \left(r - q - \frac{\sigma^2}{2}\right)\frac{\partial f}{\partial Z} + \tfrac{1}{2}\sigma^2\frac{\partial^2 f}{\partial Z^2} = rf$$

The grid then evaluates the derivative for equally spaced values of Z rather than for equally spaced values of S. The difference equation for the implicit method becomes

$$\frac{f_{i+1,j} - f_{i,j}}{\Delta t} + (r - q - \sigma^2/2)\frac{f_{i,j+1} - f_{i,j-1}}{2\Delta Z} + \tfrac{1}{2}\sigma^2\frac{f_{i,j+1} + f_{i,j-1} - 2f_{i,j}}{\Delta Z^2} = rf_{i,j}$$

or

$$\alpha_j\,f_{i,j-1} + \beta_j\,f_{i,j} + \gamma_j\,f_{i,j+1} = f_{i+1,j} \qquad (21.35)$$

---

[25] The negative numbers and other inconsistencies in the top left-hand part of the grid will be explained later.

Table 21.5 Grid to value American option in Example 21.1 using explicit finite difference methods.

Stock price (dollars)	Time to maturity (months)										
	5	4.5	4	3.5	3	2.5	2	1.5	1	0.5	0
100	0.00	0.00	0.00	0.00	0.00	0.00	0.00	0.00	0.00	0.00	0.00
95	0.06	0.00	0.00	0.00	0.00	0.00	0.00	0.00	0.00	0.00	0.00
90	−0.11	0.05	0.00	0.00	0.00	0.00	0.00	0.00	0.00	0.00	0.00
85	0.28	−0.05	0.05	0.00	0.00	0.00	0.00	0.00	0.00	0.00	0.00
80	−0.13	0.20	0.00	0.05	0.00	0.00	0.00	0.00	0.00	0.00	0.00
75	0.46	0.06	0.20	0.04	0.06	0.00	0.00	0.00	0.00	0.00	0.00
70	0.32	0.46	0.23	0.25	0.10	0.09	0.00	0.00	0.00	0.00	0.00
65	0.91	0.68	0.63	0.44	0.37	0.21	0.14	0.00	0.00	0.00	0.00
60	1.48	1.37	1.17	1.02	0.81	0.65	0.42	0.27	0.00	0.00	0.00
55	2.59	2.39	2.21	1.99	1.77	1.50	1.24	0.90	0.59	0.00	0.00
50	4.26	4.08	3.89	3.68	3.44	3.18	2.87	2.53	2.07	1.56	0.00
45	6.76	6.61	6.47	6.31	6.15	5.96	5.75	5.50	5.24	5.00	5.00
40	10.28	10.20	10.13	10.06	10.01	10.00	10.00	10.00	10.00	10.00	10.00
35	15.00	15.00	15.00	15.00	15.00	15.00	15.00	15.00	15.00	15.00	15.00
30	20.00	20.00	20.00	20.00	20.00	20.00	20.00	20.00	20.00	20.00	20.00
25	25.00	25.00	25.00	25.00	25.00	25.00	25.00	25.00	25.00	25.00	25.00
20	30.00	30.00	30.00	30.00	30.00	30.00	30.00	30.00	30.00	30.00	30.00
15	35.00	35.00	35.00	35.00	35.00	35.00	35.00	35.00	35.00	35.00	35.00
10	40.00	40.00	40.00	40.00	40.00	40.00	40.00	40.00	40.00	40.00	40.00
5	45.00	45.00	45.00	45.00	45.00	45.00	45.00	45.00	45.00	45.00	45.00
0	50.00	50.00	50.00	50.00	50.00	50.00	50.00	50.00	50.00	50.00	50.00

where

$$\alpha_j = \frac{\Delta t}{2\Delta Z}(r - q - \sigma^2/2) - \frac{\Delta t}{2\Delta Z^2}\sigma^2$$

$$\beta_j = 1 + \frac{\Delta t}{\Delta Z^2}\sigma^2 + r\,\Delta t$$

$$\gamma_j = -\frac{\Delta t}{2\Delta Z}(r - q - \sigma^2/2) - \frac{\Delta t}{2\Delta Z^2}\sigma^2$$

The difference equation for the explicit method becomes

$$\frac{f_{i+1,j} - f_{i,j}}{\Delta t} + (r - q - \sigma^2/2)\frac{f_{i+1,j+1} - f_{i+1,j-1}}{2\Delta Z} + \frac{1}{2}\sigma^2\frac{f_{i+1,j+1} + f_{i+1,j-1} - 2f_{i+1,j}}{\Delta Z^2} = rf_{i,j}$$

or

$$\alpha_j^* f_{i+1,j-1} + \beta_j^* f_{i+1,j} + \gamma_j^* f_{i+1,j+1} = f_{i,j} \tag{21.36}$$

where

$$\alpha_j^* = \frac{1}{1 + r\Delta t}\left[-\frac{\Delta t}{2\Delta Z}(r - q - \sigma^2/2) + \frac{\Delta t}{2\Delta Z^2}\sigma^2 \right] \qquad (21.37)$$

$$\beta_j^* = \frac{1}{1 + r\Delta t}\left(1 - \frac{\Delta t}{\Delta Z^2}\sigma^2 \right) \qquad (21.38)$$

$$\gamma_j^* = \frac{1}{1 + r\Delta t}\left[\frac{\Delta t}{2\Delta Z}(r - q - \sigma^2/2) + \frac{\Delta t}{2\Delta Z^2}\sigma^2 \right] \qquad (21.39)$$

The change of variable approach has the property that α_j, β_j, and γ_j as well as α_j^*, β_j^*, and γ_j^* are independent of j. In most cases, a good choice for ΔZ is $\sigma\sqrt{3\Delta t}$.

Relation to Trinomial Tree Approaches

The explicit finite difference method is equivalent to the trinomial tree approach.[26] In the expressions for a_j^*, b_j^*, and c_j^* in equation (21.34), we can interpret terms as follows:

$-\frac{1}{2}(r - q)j\,\Delta t + \frac{1}{2}\sigma^2 j^2\Delta t$:   Probability of stock price decreasing from $j\,\Delta S$ to $(j - 1)\Delta S$ in time Δt.

$1 - \sigma^2 j^2 \Delta t$:   Probability of stock price remaining unchanged at $j\,\Delta S$ in time Δt.

$\frac{1}{2}(r - q)j\,\Delta t + \frac{1}{2}\sigma^2 j^2 \Delta t$:   Probability of stock price increasing from $j\,\Delta S$ to $(j + 1)\Delta S$ in time Δt.

This interpretation is illustrated in Figure 21.17. The three probabilities sum to unity. They give the expected increase in the stock price in time Δt as $(r - q)j\,\Delta S\,\Delta t = (r - q)S\,\Delta t$. This is the expected increase in a risk-neutral world. For small values

Figure 21.17   Interpretation of explicit finite difference method as a trinomial tree.

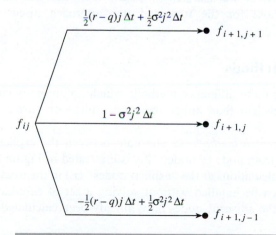

[26] It can also be shown that the implicit finite difference method is equivalent to a multinomial tree approach where there are $M + 1$ branches emanating from each node.

of Δt, they also give the variance of the change in the stock price in time Δt as $\sigma^2 j^2 \Delta S^2 \Delta t = \sigma^2 S^2 \Delta t$. This corresponds to the stochastic process followed by S. The value of f at time $i\,\Delta t$ is calculated as the expected value of f at time $(i+1)\,\Delta t$ in a risk-neutral world discounted at the risk-free rate.

For the explicit version of the finite difference method to work well, the three "probabilities"

$$-\tfrac{1}{2}(r-q)j\,\Delta t + \tfrac{1}{2}\sigma^2 j^2 \Delta t,$$

$$1 - \sigma^2 j^2 \Delta t$$

$$\tfrac{1}{2}(r-q)j\,\Delta t + \tfrac{1}{2}\sigma^2 j^2 \Delta t$$

should all be positive. In Example 21.11, $1 - \sigma^2 j^2 \Delta t$ is negative when $j \geqslant 13$ (i.e., when $S \geqslant 65$). This explains the negative option prices and other inconsistencies in the top left-hand part of Table 21.5. This example illustrates the main problem associated with the explicit finite difference method. Because the probabilities in the associated tree may be negative, it does not necessarily produce results that converge to the solution of the differential equation.[27]

When the change-of-variable approach is used (see equations (21.36) to (21.39)), the probability that $Z = \ln S$ will decrease by ΔZ, stay the same, and increase by ΔZ are

$$-\frac{\Delta t}{2\Delta Z}(r - q - \sigma^2/2) + \frac{\Delta t}{2\Delta Z^2}\sigma^2$$

$$1 - \frac{\Delta t}{\Delta Z^2}\sigma^2$$

$$\frac{\Delta t}{2\Delta Z}(r - q - \sigma^2/2) + \frac{\Delta t}{2\Delta Z^2}\sigma^2$$

respectively. These movements in Z correspond to the stock price changing from S to $Se^{-\Delta Z}$, S, and $Se^{\Delta Z}$, respectively. If we set $\Delta Z = \sigma\sqrt{3\Delta t}$, then the tree and the probabilities are identical to those for the trinomial tree approach discussed in Section 21.4.

Other Finite Difference Methods

Researchers have proposed other finite difference methods which are in many circumstances more computationally efficient than either the pure explicit or pure implicit method.

In what is known as the *hopscotch method*, we alternate between the explicit and implicit calculations as we move from node to node. This is illustrated in Figure 21.18. At each time, we first do all the calculations at the "explicit nodes" (E) in the usual way. The "implicit nodes" (I) can then be handled without solving a set of simultaneous equations because the values at the adjacent nodes have already been calculated.

---

[27] J.C. Hull and A. White, "Valuing Derivative Securities Using the Explicit Finite Difference Method," *Journal of Financial and Quantitative Analysis*, 25 (March 1990): 87–100, show how this problem can be overcome. In the situation considered here it is sufficient to construct the grid in $\ln S$ rather than S to ensure convergence.

Figure 21.18 The hopscotch method. I indicates node at which implicit calculations are done; E indicates node at which explicit calculations are done.

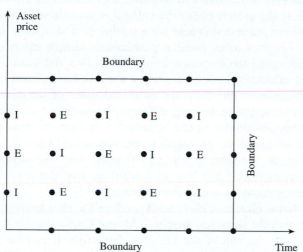

In the *Crank–Nicolson* method, the estimate of

$$\frac{f_{i+1,j} - f_{i,j}}{\Delta t}$$

is set equal to an average of that given by the implicit and the explicit methods.

Applications of Finite Difference Methods

Finite difference methods can be used for the same types of derivative pricing problems as tree approaches. They can handle American-style as well as European-style derivatives but cannot easily be used in situations where the payoff from a derivative depends on the past history of the underlying variable. Finite difference methods can, at the expense of a considerable increase in computer time, be used when there are several state variables. The grid in Figure 21.15 then becomes multidimensional.

The method for calculating Greek letters is similar to that used for trees. Delta, gamma, and theta can be calculated directly from the $f_{i,j}$ values on the grid. For vega, it is necessary to make a small change to volatility and recalculate the value of the derivative using the same grid.

SUMMARY

We have presented three different numerical procedures for valuing derivatives when no analytic solution is available. These involve the use of trees, Monte Carlo simulation, and finite difference methods.

Binomial trees assume that, in each short interval of time Δt, a stock price either moves up by a multiplicative amount u or down by a multiplicative amount d. The sizes of u

and d and their associated probabilities are chosen so that the change in the stock price has the correct mean and standard deviation in a risk-neutral world. Derivative prices are calculated by starting at the end of the tree and working backward. For an American option, the value at a node is the greater of (a) the value if it is exercised immediately and (b) the discounted expected value if it is held for a further period of time Δt.

Monte Carlo simulation involves using random numbers to sample many different paths that the variables underlying the derivative could follow in a risk-neutral world. For each path, the payoff is calculated and discounted at the risk-free interest rate. The arithmetic average of the discounted payoffs is the estimated value of the derivative.

Finite difference methods solve the underlying differential equation by converting it to a difference equation. They are similar to tree approaches in that the computations work back from the end of the life of the derivative to the beginning. The explicit finite difference method is functionally the same as using a trinomial tree. The implicit finite difference method is more complicated but has the advantage that the user does not have to take any special precautions to ensure convergence.

In practice, the method that is chosen is likely to depend on the characteristics of the derivative being evaluated and the accuracy required. Monte Carlo simulation works forward from the beginning to the end of the life of a derivative. It can be used for European-style derivatives and can cope with a great deal of complexity as far as the payoffs are concerned. It becomes relatively more efficient as the number of underlying variables increases. Tree approaches and finite difference methods work from the end of the life of a security to the beginning and can accommodate American-style as well as European-style derivatives. However, they are difficult to apply when the payoffs depend on the past history of the state variables as well as on their current values. Also, they are liable to become computationally very time consuming when three or more variables are involved.

FURTHER READING

General

Clewlow, L., and C. Strickland, *Implementing Derivatives Models*. Chichester: Wiley, 1998.

Press, W. H., S. A. Teukolsky, W. T. Vetterling, and B. P. Flannery, *Numerical Recipes in C: The Art of Scientific Computing*, 3rd edn. Cambridge University Press, 2007.

On Tree Approaches

Cox, J. C, S. A. Ross, and M. Rubinstein. "Option Pricing: A Simplified Approach," *Journal of Financial Economics*, 7 (October 1979): 229–64.

Figlewski, S., and B. Gao. "The Adaptive Mesh Model: A New Approach to Efficient Option Pricing," *Journal of Financial Economics*, 53 (1999): 313–51.

Hull, J. C., and A. White, "The Use of the Control Variate Technique in Option Pricing," *Journal of Financial and Quantitative Analysis*, 23 (September 1988): 237–51.

Rendleman, R., and B. Bartter, "Two State Option Pricing," *Journal of Finance*, 34 (1979): 1092–1110.

On Monte Carlo Simulation

Boyle, P. P., "Options: A Monte Carlo Approach," *Journal of Financial Economics*, 4 (1977): 323–38.

Boyle, P. P., M. Broadie, and P. Glasserman. "Monte Carlo Methods for Security Pricing," *Journal of Economic Dynamics and Control*, 21 (1997): 1267–1322.

Broadie, M., P. Glasserman, and G. Jain. "Enhanced Monte Carlo Estimates for American Option Prices," *Journal of Derivatives*, 5 (Fall 1997): 25–44.

On Finite Difference Methods

Hull, J. C., and A. White, "Valuing Derivative Securities Using the Explicit Finite Difference Method," *Journal of Financial and Quantitative Analysis*, 25 (March 1990): 87–100.

Wilmott, P., *Derivatives: The Theory and Practice of Financial Engineering*. Chichester: Wiley, 1998.

Practice Questions (Answers in Solutions Manual)

21.1. Which of the following can be estimated for an American option by constructing a single binomial tree: delta, gamma, vega, theta, rho?

21.2. Calculate the price of a 3-month American put option on a non-dividend-paying stock when the stock price is $60, the strike price is $60, the risk-free interest rate is 10% per annum, and the volatility is 45% per annum. Use a binomial tree with a time interval of 1 month.

21.3. Explain how the control variate technique is implemented when a tree is used to value American options.

21.4. Calculate the price of a 9-month American call option on corn futures when the current futures price is 198 cents, the strike price is 200 cents, the risk-free interest rate is 8% per annum, and the volatility is 30% per annum. Use a binomial tree with a time interval of 3 months.

21.5. Consider an option that pays off the amount by which the final stock price exceeds the average stock price achieved during the life of the option. Can this be valued using the binomial tree approach? Explain your answer.

21.6. "For a dividend-paying stock, the tree for the stock price does not recombine; but the tree for the stock price less the present value of future dividends does recombine." Explain this statement.

21.7. Show that the probabilities in a Cox, Ross, and Rubinstein binomial tree are negative when the condition in footnote 8 holds.

21.8. Use stratified sampling with 100 trials to improve the estimate of π in Business Snapshot 21.1 and Table 21.1.

21.9. Explain why the Monte Carlo simulation approach cannot easily be used for American-style derivatives.

21.10. A 9-month American put option on a non-dividend-paying stock has a strike price of $49. The stock price is $50, the risk-free rate is 5% per annum, and the volatility is 30% per annum. Use a three-step binomial tree to calculate the option price.

21.11. Use a three-time-step binomial tree to value a 9-month American call option on wheat futures. The current futures price is 400 cents, the strike price is 420 cents, the risk-free rate is 6%, and the volatility is 35% per annum. Estimate the delta of the option from your tree.

21.12. A 3-month American call option on a stock has a strike price of $20. The stock price is $20, the risk-free rate is 3% per annum, and the volatility is 25% per annum. A dividend of $2 is expected in 1.5 months. Use a three-step binomial tree to calculate the option price.

21.13. A 1-year American put option on a non-dividend-paying stock has an exercise price of $18. The current stock price is $20, the risk-free interest rate is 15% per annum, and the volatility of the stock price is 40% per annum. Use the DerivaGem software with four 3-month time steps to estimate the value of the option. Display the tree and verify that the option prices at the final and penultimate nodes are correct. Use DerivaGem to value the European version of the option. Use the control variate technique to improve your estimate of the price of the American option.

21.14. A 2-month American put option on a stock index has an exercise price of 480. The current level of the index is 484, the risk-free interest rate is 10% per annum, the dividend yield on the index is 3% per annum, and the volatility of the index is 25% per annum. Divide the life of the option into four half-month periods and use the tree approach to estimate the value of the option.

21.15. How can the control variate approach improve the estimate of the delta of an American option when the tree approach is used?

21.16. Suppose that Monte Carlo simulation is being used to evaluate a European call option on a non-dividend-paying stock when the volatility is stochastic. How could the control variate and antithetic variable technique be used to improve numerical efficiency? Explain why it is necessary to calculate six values of the option in each simulation trial when both the control variate and the antithetic variable technique are used.

21.17. How do equations (21.27) to (21.30) change when the implicit finite difference method is being used to evaluate an American call option on a currency?

21.18. An American put option on a non-dividend-paying stock has 4 months to maturity. The exercise price is $21, the stock price is $20, the risk-free rate of interest is 10% per annum, and the volatility is 30% per annum. Use the explicit version of the finite difference approach to value the option. Use stock price intervals of $4 and time intervals of 1 month.

21.19. The spot price of copper is $0.60 per pound. Suppose that the futures prices (dollars per pound) are as follows:

3 months	0.59
6 months	0.57
9 months	0.54
12 months	0.50

The volatility of the price of copper is 40% per annum and the risk-free rate is 6% per annum. Use a binomial tree to value an American call option on copper with an exercise price of $0.60 and a time to maturity of 1 year. Divide the life of the option into four 3-month periods for the purposes of constructing the tree. (*Hint*: As explained in Section 18.7, the futures price of a variable is its expected future price in a risk-neutral world.)

21.20. Use the binomial tree in Problem 21.19 to value a security that pays off x^2 in 1 year where x is the price of copper.

21.21. When do the boundary conditions for $S = 0$ and $S \to \infty$ affect the estimates of derivative prices in the explicit finite difference method?

21.22. How would you use the antithetic variable method to improve the estimate of the European option in Business Snapshot 21.2 and Table 21.2?

21.23. A company has issued a 3-year convertible bond that has a face value of $25 and can be exchanged for two of the company's shares at any time. The company can call the issue, forcing conversion, when the share price is greater than or equal to $18. Assuming that the company will force conversion at the earliest opportunity, what are the boundary conditions for the price of the convertible? Describe how you would use finite difference methods to value the convertible assuming constant interest rates. Assume there is no risk of the company defaulting.

21.24. Provide formulas that can be used for obtaining three random samples from standard normal distributions when the correlation between sample i and sample j is $\rho_{i,j}$.

Further Questions

21.25. An American put option to sell a Swiss franc for dollars has a strike price of $0.80 and a time to maturity of 1 year. The Swiss franc's volatility is 10%, the dollar interest rate is 6%, the Swiss franc interest rate is 3%, and the current exchange rate is 0.81. Use a three-step binomial tree to value the option. Estimate the delta of the option from your tree.

21.26. A 1-year American call option on silver futures has an exercise price of $9.00. The current futures price is $8.50, the risk-free rate of interest is 12% per annum, and the volatility of the futures price is 25% per annum. Use the DerivaGem software with four 3-month time steps to estimate the value of the option. Display the tree and verify that the option prices at the final and penultimate nodes are correct. Use DerivaGem to value the European version of the option. Use the control variate technique to improve your estimate of the price of the American option.

21.27. A 6-month American call option on a stock is expected to pay dividends of $1 per share at the end of the second month and the fifth month. The current stock price is $30, the exercise price is $34, the risk-free interest rate is 10% per annum, and the volatility of the part of the stock price that will not be used to pay the dividends is 30% per annum. Use the DerivaGem software with the life of the option divided into six time steps to estimate the value of the option. Compare your answer with that given by Black's approximation (see Section 15.12).

21.28. The current value of the British pound is $1.60 and the volatility of the pound/dollar exchange rate is 15% per annum. An American call option has an exercise price of $1.62 and a time to maturity of 1 year. The risk-free rates of interest in the United States and the United Kingdom are 6% per annum and 9% per annum, respectively. Use the explicit finite difference method to value the option. Consider exchange rates at intervals of 0.20 between 0.80 and 2.40 and time intervals of 3 months.

21.29. Answer the following questions concerned with the alternative procedures for constructing trees in Section 21.4:

(a) Show that the binomial model in Section 21.4 is exactly consistent with the mean and variance of the change in the logarithm of the stock price in time Δt.

(b) Show that the trinomial model in Section 21.4 is consistent with the mean and variance of the change in the logarithm of the stock price in time Δt when terms of order $(\Delta t)^2$ and higher are ignored.

(c) Construct an alternative to the trinomial model in Section 21.4 so that the probabilities are 1/6, 2/3, and 1/6 on the upper, middle, and lower branches emanating from each node. Assume that the branching is from S to Su, Sm, or Sd with $m^2 = ud$. Match the mean and variance of the change in the logarithm of the stock price exactly.

21.30. The DerivaGem Application Builder functions enable you to investigate how the prices of options calculated from a binomial tree converge to the correct value as the number of time steps increases. (See Figure 21.4 and Sample Application A in DerivaGem.) Consider a put option on a stock index where the index level is 900, the strike price is 900, the risk-free rate is 5%, the dividend yield is 2%, and the time to maturity is 2 years.

(a) Produce results similar to Sample Application A on convergence for the situation where the option is European and the volatility of the index is 20%.

(b) Produce results similar to Sample Application A on convergence for the situation where the option is American and the volatility of the index is 20%.

(c) Produce a chart showing the pricing of the American option when the volatility is 20% as a function of the number of time steps when the control variate technique is used.

(d) Suppose that the price of the American option in the market is 85.0. Produce a chart showing the implied volatility estimate as a function of the number of time steps.

21.31. Estimate delta, gamma, and theta from the tree in Example 21.3. Explain how each can be interpreted.

21.32. How much is gained from exercising early at the lowest node at the 9-month point in Example 21.4?

21.33. A four-step Cox–Ross–Rubinstein binomial tree is used to price a one-year American put option on an index when the index level is 500, the strike price is 500, the dividend yield is 2%, the risk-free rate is 5%, and the volatility is 25% per annum. What is the option price, delta, gamma, and theta? Explain how you would calculate vega and rho.

22

Value at Risk and Expected Shortfall

Chapter 19 examined measures such as delta, gamma, and vega for describing different aspects of the risk in a portfolio of derivatives. A financial institution usually calculates each of these measures each day for every market variable to which it is exposed. Often there are hundreds, or even thousands, of these market variables. A delta–gamma–vega analysis, therefore, leads to a very large number of different risk measures being produced each day. These risk measures provide valuable information for the financial institution's traders. However, they do not provide a way of measuring the total risk to which the financial institution is exposed.

Value at risk (VaR) and expected shortfall (ES) are attempts to provide a single number summarizing the total risk in a portfolio of financial assets. They have become widely used by corporate treasurers and fund managers as well as by financial institutions. Bank regulators have traditionally used VaR in determining the capital a bank is required to keep for the risks it is bearing, but they are switching to ES for market risks.

This chapter explains the VaR and ES measures and describes the two main approaches for calculating them. These are known as the *historical simulation* approach and the *model-building* approach.

22.1 THE VaR AND ES MEASURES

When using the value-at-risk measure, an analyst is interested in making a statement of the following form: "I am X percent certain there will not be a loss of more than V dollars in the next N days." The variable V is the VaR of the portfolio. It is a function of two parameters: the time horizon (N days) and the confidence level ($X\%$). It is the loss level over N days that has a probability of only $(100 - X)\%$ of being exceeded.

Bank regulators have traditionally required banks to calculate VaR for market risk with $N = 10$ and $X = 99$ (see the discussion in Business Snapshot 22.1). If VaR with these parameters is \$20 million for a bank, it is 99% certain that it will not lose more than \$20 million over the next 10 days. The 99th percentile of the 10-day loss distribution is \$20 million. Alternatively we can say that the first percentile of the gain distribution is −\$20 million. VaR is illustrated in Figures 22.1 and 22.2.

VaR is an attractive measure because it is easy to understand. In essence, it asks the simple question "How bad can things get?" This is the question all senior managers

---

Business Snapshot 22.1   How Bank Regulators Use VaR

The Basel Committee on Bank Supervision is a committee of the world's bank regulators that meets regularly in Basel, Switzerland. In 1988 it published what has become known as Basel I. This is an agreement between the regulators on how the capital a bank is required to hold for credit risk should be calculated. Later the Basel Committee published *The 1996 Amendment* which was implemented in 1998 and required banks to hold capital for market risk as well as credit risk. The Amendment distinguishes between a bank's trading book and its banking book. The banking book consists primarily of loans and is not usually revalued on a regular basis for managerial and accounting purposes. The trading book consists of the myriad of different instruments that are traded by the bank (stocks, bonds, swaps, forward contracts, options, etc.) and is normally revalued daily.

The 1996 Amendment calculates capital for the trading book using the VaR measure with $N = 10$ and $X = 99$. This means that it focuses on the revaluation loss over a 10-day period that is expected to be exceeded only 1% of the time. The capital the bank is required to hold is k times this VaR measure (with an adjustment for what are termed specific risks). The multiplier k is chosen on a bank-by-bank basis by the regulators and must be at least 3.0. For a bank with excellent well-tested VaR estimation procedures, it is likely that k will be set equal to the minimum value of 3.0. For other banks it may be higher.

Basel I has been followed by Basel II, Basel II.5, and Basel III. Basel II (which was implemented in most parts of the world in about 2007) uses VaR with a one-year time horizon and a 99.9% confidence level for calculating capital for credit risk and operational risk. Basel II.5 (which was implemented in 2012) revised the way market risk capital is calculated. One of the changes involves what is known as *stressed VaR*. This is a VaR measure based on how market variables have moved during a particularly adverse time period. Basel III is increasing the amount of capital that banks are required to hold and the proportion of that capital that must be equity. Another change being made by regulators, known as the *Fundamental Review of the Trading Book*, involves basing the capital for market risk on expected shortfall with a 97.5% confidence level rather than VaR with a 99% confidence level.

---

want answered. They are very comfortable with the idea of compressing all the Greek letters for all the market variables underlying a portfolio into a single number.

If we accept that it is useful to have a single number to describe the risk of a portfolio, an interesting question is whether VaR is the best alternative. Some researchers have argued that VaR may tempt traders to choose a portfolio with a return distribution similar to that in Figure 22.2. The portfolios in Figures 22.1 and 22.2 have the same VaR, but the portfolio in Figure 22.2 is much riskier because big losses are more likely.

A measure that deals with the problem we have just mentioned is *expected shortfall* (ES).[1] VaR asks the question: "How bad can things get?" ES asks: "If things do get bad,

---

[1] This measure is also known as *C-VaR* or *expected tail loss*. In P. Artzner, F. Delbaen, J.-M. Eber, and D. Heath, "Coherent Measures of Risk," *Mathematical Finance*, 9 (1999): 203–28, the authors define certain properties that a good risk measure should have and show that the standard VaR measure does not have all of them whereas ES does. For more details, see J. C. Hull, *Risk Management and Financial Institutions*, 4th edn. Hoboken, NJ: Wiley, 2015.

Figure 22.1 Calculation of VaR from the probability distribution of the change in the portfolio value; confidence level is $X\%$. Gains in portfolio value are positive; losses are negative.

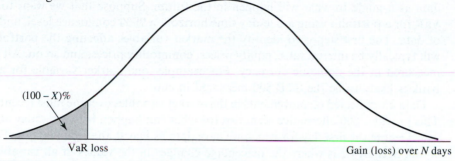

Figure 22.2 Alternative situation to Figure 22.1. VaR is the same, but the potential loss is larger.

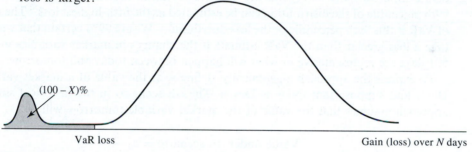

how much can the company expect to lose?" ES is the expected loss during an N-day period conditional on the loss being worse than the VaR loss. For example, with $X = 99$ and $N = 10$, the expected shortfall is the average amount the company loses over a 10-day period when the loss is worse than the 10-day 99% VaR. As mentioned in Business Snapshot 22.1, bank regulation is changing so that the capital for market risk is based on ES, not VaR. The confidence level is changing from 99% to 97.5%.

The Time Horizon

VaR and ES each have two parameters: the time horizon N, measured in days, and the confidence level X. In practice, analysts often set $N = 1$ in the first instance when VaR or ES is estimated for market risk. This is because there is not usually enough data available to estimate directly the behavior of market variables over periods of time longer than 1 day. The usual assumptions are

$$N\text{-day VaR} = 1\text{-day VaR} \times \sqrt{N}$$
$$N\text{-day ES} = 1\text{-day ES} \times \sqrt{N}$$

These formulas are exactly true when the changes in the value of the portfolio on successive days have independent identical normal distributions with mean zero. In other cases they are approximations.

22.2 HISTORICAL SIMULATION

Historical simulation is one popular way of estimating VaR or ES. It involves using past data as a guide to what will happen in the future. Suppose that we want to calculate VaR for a portfolio using a one-day time horizon, a 99% confidence level, and 501 days of data. The first step is to identify the market variables affecting the portfolio. These will typically be interest rates, equity prices, commodity prices, and so on. All prices are measured in the domestic currency. For example, one market variable for a German bank is likely to be the S&P 500 measured in euros.

Data are collected on movements in the market variables over the most recent 501 days. This provides 500 alternative scenarios for what can happen between today and tomorrow. Denote the first day for which we have data as Day 0, the second day as Day 1, and so on. Scenario 1 is where the percentage changes in the values of all variables are the same as they were between Day 0 and Day 1, Scenario 2 is where they are the same as between Day 1 and Day 2, and so on. For each scenario, the dollar change in the value of the portfolio between today and tomorrow is calculated. This defines a probability distribution for daily loss (gains are negative losses) in the value of the portfolio. The 99th percentile of the distribution can be estimated as the fifth-highest loss.[2] The estimate of VaR is this 99th percentile of the loss distribution. We are 99% certain that we will not take a loss greater than the VaR estimate if the changes in market variables in the last 501 days are representative of what will happen between today and tomorrow.

To express the approach algebraically, define v_i as the value of a market variable on Day i and suppose that today is Day n. The ith scenario in the historical simulation approach assumes that the value of the market variable tomorrow will be

$$\text{Value under } i\text{th scenario} = v_n \frac{v_i}{v_{i-1}}$$

Illustration: Investment in Four Stock Indices

To illustrate the calculations underlying the approach, suppose that an investor in the United States owns, on September 25, 2008, a portfolio worth $10 million consisting of investments in four stock indices: the Dow Jones Industrial Average (DJIA) in the United States, the FTSE 100 in the United Kingdom, the CAC 40 in France, and the Nikkei 225 in Japan. The value of the investment in each index on September 25, 2008, is shown in Table 22.1. An Excel spreadsheet containing 501 days of historical data on the closing prices of the four indices, together with exchange rates and a complete set of VaR and ES calculations are on the author's website:[3]

www-2.rotman.utoronto.ca/~hull/OFOD/VaRExample

Because we are considering a U.S. investor, the value of the FTSE 100, CAC 40, and Nikkei 225 must be measured in U.S. dollars. For example, the FTSE 100 was 5,823.40 on August 10, 2006, when the exchange rate was 1.8918 USD per GBP. This means

---

[2] There are alternatives here. A case can be made for using the fifth-highest loss, the sixth-highest loss, or an average of the two. In Excel's PERCENTILE function, when there are n observations and k is an integer, the $k/(n-1)$ percentile is the observation ranked $k+1$. Other percentiles are calculated using linear interpolation.

[3] To keep the example as straightforward as possible, only days when all four indices traded were included in the compilation of the data and dividends are not considered.

Table 22.1   Investment portfolio used for VaR calculations.

Index	Portfolio value ($000s)
DJIA	4,000
FTSE 100	3,000
CAC 40	1,000
Nikkei 225	2,000
Total	10,000

that, measured in U.S. dollars, it was $5,823.40 \times 1.8918 = 11,016.71$. An extract from the data with all indices measured in U.S. dollars is in Table 22.2.

September 25, 2008, is an interesting date to choose in evaluating an equity investment. The turmoil in credit markets, which started in August 2007, was over a year old. Equity prices had been declining for several months. Volatilities were increasing. Lehman Brothers had filed for bankruptcy ten days earlier. The Treasury Secretary's $700 billion Troubled Asset Relief Program (TARP) had not yet been passed by the United States Congress.

Table 22.3 shows the values of the indices (measured in U.S. dollars) on September 26, 2008, for the scenarios considered. Scenario 1 (the first row in Table 22.3) shows the values of indices on September 26, 2008, assuming that their percentage changes between September 25 and September 26, 2008, are the same as they were between August 7 and August 8, 2006; Scenario 2 (the second row in Table 22.3) shows the values of market variables on September 26, 2008, assuming these percentage changes are the same as those between August 8 and August 9, 2006; and so on. In general, Scenario i assumes that the percentage changes in the indices between September 25 and September 26 are the same as they were between Day $i - 1$ and Day i for $1 \leqslant i \leqslant 500$. The 500 rows in Table 22.3 are the 500 scenarios considered.

The DJIA was 11,022.06 on September 25, 2008. On August 8, 2006, it was 11,173.59, down from 11,219.38 on August 7, 2006. Therefore the value of the DJIA under Scenario 1 is

$$11,022.06 \times \frac{11,173.59}{11,219.38} = 10,977.08$$

Table 22.2   U.S. dollar equivalent of stock indices for historical simulation (equals index value multiplied by exchange rate).

Day	Date	DJIA	FTSE 100	CAC 40	Nikkei 225
0	Aug. 7, 2006	11,219.38	11,131.84	6,373.89	131.77
1	Aug. 8, 2006	11,173.59	11,096.28	6,378.16	134.38
2	Aug. 9, 2006	11,076.18	11,185.35	6,474.04	135.94
3	Aug. 10, 2006	11,124.37	11,016.71	6,357.49	135.44
⋮	⋮	⋮	⋮	⋮	⋮
499	Sept. 24, 2008	10,825.17	9,438.58	6,033.93	114.26
500	Sept. 25, 2008	11,022.06	9,599.90	6,200.40	112.82

Table 22.3   Scenarios generated for September 26, 2008, using data in Table 22.2.

Scenario number	DJIA	FTSE 100	CAC 40	Nikkei 225	Portfolio value ($000s)	Loss ($000s)
1	10,977.08	9,569.23	6,204.55	115.05	10,014.334	−14.334
2	10,925.97	9,676.96	6,293.60	114.13	10,027.481	−27.481
3	11,070.01	9,455.16	6,088.77	112.40	9,946.736	53.264
⋮	⋮	⋮	⋮	⋮	⋮	
499	10,831.43	9,383.49	6,051.94	113.85	9,857.465	142.535
500	11,222.53	9,763.97	6,371.45	111.40	10,126.439	−126.439

Similarly, the values of the FTSE 100, the CAC 40, and the Nikkei 225 are 9,569.23, 6,204.55, and 115.05, respectively. Therefore the value of the portfolio under Scenario 1 is (in $000s)

$$4,000 \times \frac{10,977.08}{11,022.06} + 3,000 \times \frac{9,569.23}{9,599.90}$$
$$+ 1,000 \times \frac{6,204.55}{6,200.40} + 2,000 \times \frac{115.05}{112.82} = 10,014.334$$

The portfolio therefore has a gain of $14,334 under Scenario 1. A similar calculation is carried out for the other scenarios. A histogram for the losses is shown in Figure 22.3 (with gains being recorded as negative losses). The bars on the histogram represent losses ($000s) in the ranges 450 to 550, 350 to 450, 250 to 350, and so on.

Figure 22.3   Histogram of losses for the scenarios considered between September 25 and September 26, 2008.

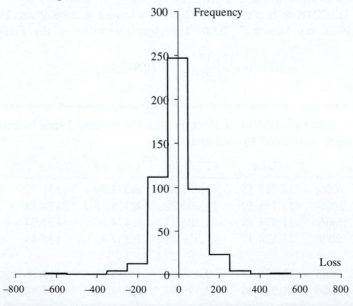

Table 22.4 Losses ranked from highest to lowest for 500 scenarios.

Scenario number	Loss ($000s)
494	477.841
339	345.435
349	282.204
329	277.041
487	253.385
227	217.974
131	202.256
238	201.389
473	191.269
306	191.050
477	185.127
495	184.450
376	182.707
237	180.105
365	172.224
⋮	⋮

The losses for the 500 different scenarios are then ranked. An extract from the results of doing this is shown in Table 22.4. The worst scenario is number 494 (where indices are assumed to change in the same way that they did at the time of the bankruptcy of Lehman Brothers). The one-day 99% value at risk can be estimated as the fifth worst loss. This is $253,385.

As explained in Section 22.1, the ten-day 99% VaR is usually calculated as $\sqrt{10}$ times the one-day 99% VaR. In this case the ten-day VaR would therefore be

$$\sqrt{10} \times 253,385 = 801,274$$

or $801,274.

Each day the VaR estimate in our example would be updated using the most recent 501 days of data. Consider, for example, what happens on September 26, 2008 (Day 501). We find out new values for all the market variables and are able to calculate a new value for the portfolio. We then go through the procedure we have outlined to calculate a new VaR. Data on the market variables from August 8, 2006, to September 26, 2008 (Day 1 to Day 501) are used in the calculation. (This gives us the required 500 observations on the percentage changes in market variables; the August 7, 2006, Day 0, values of the market variables are no longer used.) Similarly, on the next trading day September 29, 2008 (Day 502), data from August 9, 2006, to September 29, 2008 (Day 2 to Day 502) are used to determine VaR, and so on.

In practice, a financial institution's portfolio is, of course, considerably more complicated than the one we have considered here. It is likely to consist of thousands or tens of thousands of positions (involving exchange rates, commodity prices, interest rates, and so on). Some of the bank's positions are typically in forward contracts, options, and other derivatives. Also, the portfolio itself is likely to change from day to day. If a bank's trading leads to a riskier porfolio, VaR typically increases; if it leads to a less risky porfolio, VaR typically decreases. The VaR is calculated on any given day on the assumption that the portfolio will remain unchanged over the next business day.

In the case of interest rates, a bank typically needs several term structures of zero-coupon interest rates in a number of different currencies in order to value its portfolio. The market variables that are considered are the ones from which these term structures are calculated (see Chapter 4 for the calculation of the term structure of zero rates). There might be as many as ten market variables for each zero curve to which the bank is exposed.

Expected Shortfall

To calculate expected shortfall using historical simulation we average the observations in the tail of the distribution of losses. In the case of our example, the five worst losses ($000s) are from scenarios 494, 339, 349, 329, and 487 (see Table 22.4). The average of the losses for these scenarios is $327,181. This is the expected shortfall estimate.

Stressed VaR and Stressed ES

The calculations given so far assume that the most recent data is used for the historical simulation on any given day. For example, when calculating VaR and ES for the four-index example, we used data from the immediately preceding 501 days. However, historical simulations can be based on data from any period in the past. Periods of high volatility will tend to give high values for VaR and ES, while periods of low volatility will tend to give low values.

Regulators have introduced measures known as *stressed VaR* and *stressed ES*. To calculate these measures, a financial institution must search for a 251-day period of extreme stress for their current portfolio. The data for that 251-day period then plays the same role as the 501-day period in our example. The changes in market variables between Day 0 and Day 1 of the 251-day period are used to create the first scenario; the changes in market variables between Day 1 and Day 2 of the 251-day period are used to create the second scenario; and so on. In total, 250 scenarios are created. The one-day 99% stressed VaR can be calculated as the loss that is midway between the loss for the second worst scenario and the loss for the third worst scenario. The one-day 99% ES can be calculated as $0.4c_1 + 0.4c_2 + 0.2c_3$, where c_1, c_2, and c_3 are the three worst losses with $c_1 > c_2 > c_3$.

22.3 MODEL-BUILDING APPROACH

The main alternative to historical simulation is the model-building approach. Before getting into the details of the approach, it is appropriate to mention one issue concerned with the units for measuring volatility.

Daily Volatilities

In option pricing, time is usually measured in years, and the volatility of an asset is usually quoted as a "volatility per year". When using the model-building approach to calculate VaR or ES for market risk, time is usually measured in days and the volatility of an asset is usually quoted as a "volatility per day."

What is the relationship between the volatility per year used in option pricing and the volatility per day used in VaR or ES calculations? Let us define σ_{year} as the volatility per year of a certain asset and σ_{day} as the equivalent volatility per day of the asset. Assuming 252 trading days in a year, equation (15.2) gives the standard deviation of the continuously compounded return on the asset in 1 year as either σ_{year} or $\sigma_{day}\sqrt{252}$. It follows that

$$\sigma_{year} = \sigma_{day}\sqrt{252}$$

or

$$\sigma_{day} = \frac{\sigma_{year}}{\sqrt{252}}$$

so that daily volatility is about 6% of annual volatility.

As pointed out in Section 15.4, σ_{day} is approximately equal to the standard deviation of the percentage change in the asset price in one day. For the purposes of calculating VaR or ES we assume exact equality. The daily volatility of an asset price (or any other variable) is therefore defined as equal to the standard deviation of the percentage change in one day.

Our discussion in the next few sections assumes that estimates of daily volatilities and correlations are available. Chapter 23 discusses how the estimates can be produced.

Single-Asset Case

Consider how VaR is calculated using the model-building approach in a very simple situation where the portfolio consists of a position in a single stock: $10 million in shares of Microsoft. We suppose that $N = 10$ and $X = 99$, so that we are interested in the loss level over 10 days that we are 99% confident will not be exceeded. Initially, we consider a 1-day time horizon.

Assume that the volatility of Microsoft is 2% per day (corresponding to about 32% per year). Because the size of the position is $10 million, the standard deviation of daily changes in the value of the position is 2% of $10 million, or $200,000.

It is customary in the model-building approach to assume that the expected change in a market variable over the time period considered is zero. This is not exactly true, but it is a reasonable assumption. The expected change in the price of a market variable over a short time period is generally small when compared with the standard deviation of the change. Suppose, for example, that Microsoft has an expected return of 20% per annum. Over a 1-day period, the expected return is 0.20/252, or about 0.08%, whereas the standard deviation of the return is 2%. Over a 10-day period, the expected return is 0.08×10, or about 0.8%, whereas the standard deviation of the return is $2\sqrt{10}$, or about 6.3%.

So far, we have established that the change in the value of the portfolio of Microsoft shares over a 1-day period has a standard deviation of $200,000 and (at least approximately) a mean of zero. We assume that the change is normally distributed.[4] From the

---

[4] To be consistent with the option pricing assumption in Chapter 15, we could assume that the price of Microsoft is lognormal tomorrow. Because 1 day is such a short period of time, this is almost indistinguishable from the assumption we do make—that the change in the stock price between today and tomorrow is normal.

Excel NORMSINV function, $N^{-1}(0.01) = -2.326$. This means that there is a 1% probability that a normally distributed variable will decrease in value by more than 2.326 standard deviations. Equivalently, it means that we are 99% certain that a normally distributed variable will not decrease in value by more than 2.326 standard deviations. The 1-day 99% VaR for our portfolio consisting of a $10 million position in Microsoft is therefore

$$2.326 \times 200{,}000 = \$465{,}300$$

As discussed earlier, the N-day VaR is calculated as $\sqrt{N}$ times the 1-day VaR. The 10-day 99% VaR for Microsoft is therefore

$$465{,}300 \times \sqrt{10} = \$1{,}471{,}300$$

Consider next a portfolio consisting of a $5 million position in AT&T, and suppose the daily volatility of AT&T is 1% (approximately 16% per year). A similar calculation to that for Microsoft shows that the standard deviation of the change in the value of the portfolio in 1 day is

$$5{,}000{,}000 \times 0.01 = 50{,}000$$

Assuming the change is normally distributed, the 1-day 99% VaR is

$$50{,}000 \times 2.326 = \$116{,}300$$

and the 10-day 99% VaR is

$$116{,}300 \times \sqrt{10} = \$367{,}800$$

Two-Asset Case

Now consider a portfolio consisting of both $10 million of Microsoft shares and $5 million of AT&T shares. We suppose that the returns on the two shares have a bivariate normal distribution with a correlation of 0.3. A standard result in statistics tells us that, if two variables X and Y have standard deviations equal to σ_X and σ_Y with the coefficient of correlation between them equal to ρ, the standard deviation of $X + Y$ is given by

$$\sigma_{X+Y} = \sqrt{\sigma_X^2 + \sigma_Y^2 + 2\rho\sigma_X\sigma_Y}$$

To apply this result, we set X equal to the change in the value of the position in Microsoft over a 1-day period and Y equal to the change in the value of the position in AT&T over a 1-day period, so that

$$\sigma_X = 200{,}000 \quad \text{and} \quad \sigma_Y = 50{,}000$$

The standard deviation of the change in the value of the portfolio consisting of both stocks over a 1-day period is therefore

$$\sqrt{200{,}000^2 + 50{,}000^2 + 2 \times 0.3 \times 200{,}000 \times 50{,}000} = 220{,}200$$

The mean change is assumed to be zero and the change is normally distributed. So the 1-day 99% VaR is therefore

$$220{,}200 \times 2.326 = \$512{,}300$$

The 10-day 99% VaR is $\sqrt{10}$ times this, or $1,620,100.

The Benefits of Diversification

In the example we have just considered:

1. The 10-day 99% VaR for the portfolio of Microsoft shares is $1,471,300.
2. The 10-day 99% VaR for the portfolio of AT&T shares is $367,800.
3. The 10-day 99% VaR for the portfolio of both Microsoft and AT&T shares is $1,620,100.

The amount

$$(1,471,300 + 367,800) - 1,620,100 = \$219,000$$

represents the benefits of diversification. If Microsoft and AT&T were perfectly correlated, the VaR for the portfolio of both Microsoft and AT&T would equal the VaR for the Microsoft portfolio plus the VaR for the AT&T portfolio. Less than perfect correlation leads to some of the risk being "diversified away."[5]

ES Calculation

When the loss is normally distributed with mean μ and standard deviation σ, it can be shown that ES with a confidence level of X is given by

$$\text{ES} = \mu + \sigma \frac{e^{-Y^2/2}}{\sqrt{2\pi}(1-X)} \tag{22.1}$$

where Y is the Xth percentile point of the standard normal distribution (i.e., it is the point on a normal distribution with mean zero and standard deviation one that has a probability $1 - X$ of being exceeded). This shows that, when μ is assumed to be zero, ES like VaR is proportional to σ.

The formula shows that in our example the ten-day ES for the Microsoft portfolio with 99% confidence ($X = 0.99$ and $Y = 2.326$) is $1,687,000; the ten-day ES for the AT&T portfolio with 99% confidence is $421,400; and the ten-day ES for the combined portfolio with 99% confidence is $1,856,100.

22.4 THE LINEAR MODEL

The examples we have just considered are simple illustrations of the use of the linear model for calculating VaR or ES. Suppose that we have a portfolio worth P consisting of n assets with an amount α_i being invested in asset i ($1 \leqslant i \leqslant n$). Define Δx_i as the return on asset i in one day. The dollar change in the value of the investment in asset i in one day is $\alpha_i \Delta x_i$ and

$$\Delta P = \sum_{i=1}^{n} \alpha_i \Delta x_i \tag{22.2}$$

where ΔP is the dollar change in the value of the whole portfolio in one day.

---

[5] Harry Markowitz was one of the first researchers to study the benefits of diversification to a portfolio manager. He was awarded a Nobel prize for this research in 1990. See H. Markowitz, "Portfolio Selection," *Journal of Finance*, 7, 1 (March 1952): 77–91.

In the example considered in the previous section, \$10 million was invested in the first asset (Microsoft) and \$5 million was invested in the second asset (AT&T), so that (in millions of dollars) $\alpha_1 = 10$, $\alpha_2 = 5$, and

$$\Delta P = 10\Delta x_1 + 5\Delta x_2$$

If we assume that the Δx_i in equation (22.2) are multivariate normal, then ΔP is normally distributed. To calculate VaR or ES, we therefore need to calculate only the mean and standard deviation of ΔP. We assume, as discussed in the previous section, that the expected value of each Δx_i is zero. This implies that the mean of ΔP is zero.

To calculate the standard deviation of ΔP, we define σ_i as the daily volatility of the ith asset and ρ_{ij} as the coefficient of correlation between returns on asset i and asset j. This means that σ_i is the standard deviation of Δx_i, and ρ_{ij} is the coefficient of correlation between Δx_i and Δx_j. The variance of ΔP, which we will denote by σ_P^2, is given by

$$\sigma_P^2 = \sum_{i=1}^{n} \sum_{j=1}^{n} \rho_{ij} \alpha_i \alpha_j \sigma_i \sigma_j \qquad (22.3)$$

This equation can also be written as

$$\sigma_P^2 = \sum_{i=1}^{n} \alpha_i^2 \sigma_i^2 + 2 \sum_{i=1}^{n} \sum_{j<i} \rho_{ij} \alpha_i \alpha_j \sigma_i \sigma_j$$

The standard deviation of the change over N days is $\sigma_P \sqrt{N}$, and the 99% VaR for an N-day time horizon is $2.326 \sigma_P \sqrt{N}$.

The portfolio return in one day is $\Delta P/P$. From equation (22.3), the variance of this is

$$\sum_{i=1}^{n} \sum_{j=1}^{n} \rho_{ij} w_i w_j \sigma_i \sigma_j$$

where $w_i = \alpha_i/P$ is the weight of the ith investment in the portfolio. This version of equation (22.3) is the one usually used by portfolio managers.

In the example considered in the previous section, $\sigma_1 = 0.02$, $\sigma_2 = 0.01$, and $\rho_{12} = 0.3$. As already noted, $\alpha_1 = 10$ and $\alpha_2 = 5$, so that from equation (22.3)

$$\sigma_P^2 = 10^2 \times 0.02^2 + 5^2 \times 0.01^2 + 2 \times 10 \times 5 \times 0.3 \times 0.02 \times 0.01 = 0.0485$$

and $\sigma_P = 0.2202$. This is the standard deviation of the change in the portfolio value per day (in millions of dollars). The ten-day 99% VaR is $2.326 \times 0.2202 \times \sqrt{10} = \$1.62$ million. This agrees with the calculation in the previous section.

Correlation and Covariance Matrices

A correlation matrix is a matrix where the entry in the ith row and jth column is the correlation ρ_{ij} between variable i and j. It is shown in Table 22.5. Since a variable is always perfectly correlated with itself, the diagonal elements of the correlation matrix are 1. Furthermore, because $\rho_{ij} = \rho_{ji}$, the correlation matrix is symmetric. The

Table 22.5 A correlation matrix: ρ_{ij} is the correlation between variable i and variable j.

$$
\begin{bmatrix}
1 & \rho_{12} & \rho_{13} & \cdots & \rho_{1n} \\
\rho_{21} & 1 & \rho_{23} & \cdots & \rho_{2n} \\
\rho_{31} & \rho_{32} & 1 & \cdots & \rho_{3n} \\
\vdots & \vdots & \vdots & \vdots & \vdots \\
\rho_{n1} & \rho_{n2} & \rho_{n3} & \cdots & 1
\end{bmatrix}
$$

correlation matrix, together with the daily standard deviations of the variables, enables the portfolio variance to be calculated using equation (22.3).

Instead of working with correlations and volatilities, analysts often use variances and covariances. The daily variance var_i of variable i is the square of its daily volatility:

$$
\text{var}_i = \sigma_i^2
$$

The covariance cov_{ij} between variable i and variable j is the product of the daily volatility of variable i, the daily volatility of variable j, and the correlation between i and j:

$$
\text{cov}_{ij} = \sigma_i \sigma_j \rho_{ij}
$$

The equation for the variance of the portfolio in equation (22.3) can be written

$$
\sigma_P^2 = \sum_{i=1}^{n} \sum_{j=1}^{n} \text{cov}_{ij}\, \alpha_i \alpha_j \tag{22.4}
$$

In a *covariance matrix*, the entry in the ith row and jth column is the covariance between variable i and variable j. As just mentioned, the covariance between a variable and itself is its variance. The diagonal entries in the matrix are therefore variances (see Table 22.6). For this reason, the covariance matrix is sometimes called the *variance–covariance matrix*. (Like the correlation matrix, it is symmetric.) Using matrix notation, the equation for the variance of the portfolio just given becomes

$$
\sigma_P^2 = \alpha^{\mathsf{T}} C \alpha
$$

Table 22.6 A variance–covariance matrix: cov_{ij} is the covariance between variable i and variable j. Diagonal entries are variance: $\text{cov}_{ii} = \text{var}_i$

$$
\begin{bmatrix}
\text{var}_1 & \text{cov}_{12} & \text{cov}_{13} & \cdots & \text{cov}_{1n} \\
\text{cov}_{21} & \text{var}_2 & \text{cov}_{23} & \cdots & \text{cov}_{2n} \\
\text{cov}_{31} & \text{cov}_{32} & \text{var}_3 & \cdots & \text{cov}_{3n} \\
\vdots & \vdots & \vdots & \vdots & \vdots \\
\text{cov}_{n1} & \text{cov}_{n2} & \text{cov}_{n3} & \cdots & \text{var}_n
\end{bmatrix}
$$

where α is the (column) vector whose ith element is α_i, C is the variance–covariance matrix, and α^{T} is the transpose of α.

The variances and covariances are generally calculated from historical data. We will illustrate this in Section 23.8 for the four-index example introduced in Section 22.2.

Handling Interest Rates

It is out of the question in the model-building approach to define a separate market variable for every single bond price or interest rate to which a company is exposed. Some simplifications are necessary when the model-building approach is used. One possibility is to assume that only parallel shifts in the yield curve occur. It is then necessary to define only one market variable: the size of the parallel shift. The changes in the value of a bond portfolio can then be calculated using the duration relationship

$$\Delta P = -DP\Delta y$$

where P is the value of the portfolio, ΔP is the change in P in one day, D is the modified duration of the portfolio, and Δy is the parallel shift in 1 day.

This approach does not usually give enough accuracy. The procedure usually followed is to choose as market variables the prices of zero-coupon bonds with standard maturities: 1 month, 3 months, 6 months, 1 year, 2 years, 5 years, 7 years, 10 years, and 30 years. For the purposes of calculating VaR or ES, the cash flows from instruments in the portfolio are mapped into cash flows occurring on the standard maturity dates. Consider a $1 million position in a Treasury bond lasting 1.2 years that pays a coupon of 6% semiannually. Coupons are paid in 0.2, 0.7, and 1.2 years, and the principal is paid in 1.2 years. This bond is, therefore, in the first instance regarded as a $30,000 position in 0.2-year zero-coupon bond plus a $30,000 position in a 0.7-year zero-coupon bond plus a $1.03 million position in a 1.2-year zero-coupon bond. The position in the 0.2-year bond is then replaced by an approximately equivalent position in 1-month and 3-month zero-coupon bonds; the position in the 0.7-year bond is replaced by an approximately equivalent position in 6-month and 1-year zero-coupon bonds; and the position in the 1.2-year bond is replaced by an approximately equivalent position in 1-year and 2-year zero-coupon bonds. The result is that the position in the 1.2-year coupon-bearing bond is regarded as a position in zero-coupon bonds having maturities of 1 month, 3 months, 6 months, 1 year, and 2 years.

This procedure is known as *cash-flow mapping*. One way of doing it is explained in Technical Note 25 at www-2.rotman.utoronto.ca/~hull/TechnicalNotes. Note that cash-flow mapping is not necessary when the historical simulation approach is used. This is because the complete term structure of interest rates can be calculated from the variables that are considered for each of the scenarios generated by using the bootstrap method in Chapter 4.

Applications of the Linear Model

The simplest application of the linear model is to a portfolio with no derivatives consisting of positions in stocks and bonds. Cash-flow mapping converts the bonds to zero-coupon bonds with standard maturities. The change in the value of the portfolio is linearly dependent on the returns on the stocks and these zero-coupon bonds.

As explained in Chapter 4, OIS discounting is normally used when derivatives are valued. It is therefore necessary for the cash-flow mapping procedure to be such that mapped cash flows are equivalent to the original cash flows under OIS discounting when derivatives are considered. Suppose a forward contract to buy foreign exchange matures at time T. The contract can be regarded as the exchange of a foreign zero-coupon bond maturing at time T for a domestic zero-coupon bond maturing at time T. For the purposes of calculating VaR or ES, the forward contract is therefore treated as a long position in the foreign bond combined with a short position in the domestic bond. Each bond is handled using a cash-flow mapping procedure.

An interest rate swap where OIS is exchanged for a fixed rate is equivalent to the exchange of a bond providing fixed cash flows for a bond providing floating (OIS) cash flows. We can use the result that the floating-rate bond is worth the bond principal immediately after a payment date to collapse the structure into an exchange of zero-coupon bonds. When the floating rate is LIBOR, we can assume that the future spread between LIBOR and OIS rates is equal to the forward spreads calculated today. These forward spreads can then be subtracted from the fixed side so that the structure becomes an OIS-for-fixed swap.

The Linear Model and Options

We now consider how we might try to use the linear model when there are options. Consider first a portfolio consisting of options on a single stock whose current price is S. Suppose that the delta of the position (calculated in the way described in Chapter 19) is δ.[6] Since δ is the rate of change of the value of the portfolio with S, it is approximately true that

$$\delta = \frac{\Delta P}{\Delta S}$$

or

$$\Delta P = \delta \, \Delta S \tag{22.5}$$

where ΔS is the dollar change in the stock price in 1 day and ΔP is, as usual, the dollar change in the portfolio in 1 day. Define Δx as the percentage change in the stock price in 1 day, so that

$$\Delta x = \frac{\Delta S}{S}$$

It follows that an approximate relationship between ΔP and Δx is

$$\Delta P = S\delta \, \Delta x$$

When we have a position in several underlying market variables that includes options, we can derive an approximate linear relationship between ΔP and the Δx_i similarly. This relationship is

$$\Delta P = \sum_{i=1}^{n} S_i \delta_i \, \Delta x_i \tag{22.6}$$

---

[6] Normally we denote the delta and gamma of a portfolio by Δ and Γ. In this section and the next, we use the lower case Greek letters δ and γ to avoid overworking Δ.

where S_i is the value of the ith market variable and δ_i is the delta of the portfolio with respect to the ith market variable. This corresponds to equation (22.2):

$$\Delta P = \sum_{i=1}^{n} \alpha_i \, \Delta x_i$$

with $\alpha_i = S_i \delta_i$. Equation (22.3) or (22.4) can therefore be used to calculate the standard deviation of ΔP.

Example 22.1

A portfolio consists of options on Microsoft and AT&T. The options on Microsoft have a delta of 1,000, and the options on AT&T have a delta of 20,000. The Microsoft share price is $120, and the AT&T share price is $30. From equation (22.6), it is approximately true that

$$\Delta P = 120 \times 1,000 \times \Delta x_1 + 30 \times 20,000 \times \Delta x_2$$

or

$$\Delta P = 120,000 \Delta x_1 + 600,000 \Delta x_2$$

where Δx_1 and Δx_2 are the returns from Microsoft and AT&T in 1 day and ΔP is the resultant change in the value of the portfolio. (The portfolio is assumed to be equivalent to an investment of $120,000 in Microsoft and $600,000 in AT&T.) Assuming that the daily volatility of Microsoft is 2% and the daily volatility of AT&T is 1% and the correlation between the daily changes is 0.3, the standard deviation of ΔP (in thousands of dollars) is

$$\sqrt{(120 \times 0.02)^2 + (600 \times 0.01)^2 + 2 \times 120 \times 0.02 \times 600 \times 0.01 \times 0.3} = 7.099$$

22.5 THE QUADRATIC MODEL

When a portfolio includes options, the linear model is an approximation. It does not take account of the gamma of the portfolio. As discussed in Chapter 19, delta is defined as the rate of change of the portfolio value with respect to an underlying market variable and gamma is defined as the rate of change of the delta with respect to the market variable. Gamma measures the curvature of the relationship between the portfolio value and an underlying market variable.

Figure 22.4 shows the impact of a nonzero gamma on the probability distribution of the value of the portfolio. When gamma is positive, the probability distribution tends to be positively skewed; when gamma is negative, it tends to be negatively skewed. Figures 22.5 and 22.6 illustrate the reason for this result. Figure 22.5 shows the relationship between the value of a long call option and the price of the underlying asset. A long call is an example of an option position with positive gamma. The figure shows that, when the probability distribution for the price of the underlying asset at the end of 1 day is normal, the probability distribution for the option price is positively skewed.[7] Figure 22.6 shows the relationship between the value of a short call position and the

---

[7] As mentioned in footnote 4, we can use the normal distribution as an approximation to the lognormal distribution in VaR calculations.

Figure 22.4 Probability distribution for value of portfolio: (a) positive gamma; (b) negative gamma.

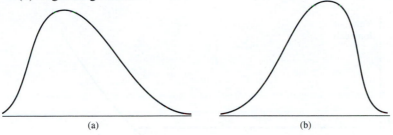

(a)   (b)

price of the underlying asset. A short call position has a negative gamma. In this case, we see that a normal distribution for the price of the underlying asset at the end of 1 day gets mapped into a negatively skewed distribution for the value of the option position.

The VaR or ES for a portfolio is critically dependent on the left tail of the probability distribution of the portfolio value. For example, when the confidence level used is 99%, the VaR is the value in the left tail below which there is only 1% of the distribution. As indicated in Figures 22.4a and 22.5, a positive gamma portfolio tends to have a less heavy left tail than the normal distribution. If the distribution of ΔP is normal, the calculated VaR tends to be too high. Similarly, as indicated in Figures 22.4b and 22.6, a negative gamma portfolio tends to have a heavier left tail than the normal distribution. If the distribution of ΔP is normal, the calculated VaR tends to be too low.

For a more accurate estimate of VaR than that given by the linear model, both delta and gamma measures can be used to relate ΔP to the Δx_i. Consider a portfolio dependent on a single asset whose price is S. Suppose δ and γ are the delta and gamma of the portfolio. From the appendix to Chapter 19, the equation

$$\Delta P = \delta \, \Delta S + \tfrac{1}{2}\gamma(\Delta S)^2$$

is an improvement over the approximation in equation (22.5).[8] Setting

$$\Delta x = \frac{\Delta S}{S}$$

reduces this to

$$\Delta P = S\delta \, \Delta x + \tfrac{1}{2}S^2\gamma(\Delta x)^2 \tag{22.7}$$

More generally for a portfolio with n underlying market variables, with each instrument in the portfolio being dependent on only one of the market variables, equation (22.7) becomes

$$\Delta P = \sum_{i=1}^{n} S_i\delta_i \, \Delta x_i + \sum_{i=1}^{n} \tfrac{1}{2}S_i^2\gamma_i \, (\Delta x_i)^2$$

where S_i is the value of the ith market variable, and δ_i and γ_i are the delta and gamma of the portfolio with respect to the ith market variable. When individual instruments in the

---

[8] The Taylor series expansion in the appendix to Chapter 19 suggests the approximation $\Delta P = \Theta \, \Delta t + \delta \, \Delta S + \tfrac{1}{2}\gamma(\Delta S)^2$ when terms of higher order than Δt are ignored. In practice, the $\Theta \, \Delta t$ term is so small that it is usually ignored.

Figure 22.5   Translation of normal probability distribution for asset into probability distribution for value of a long call on asset.

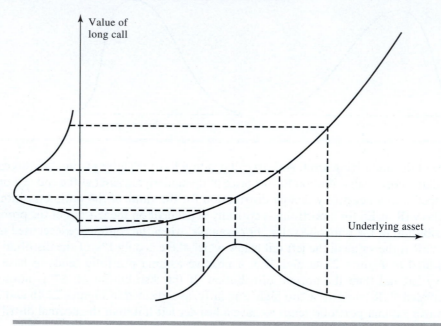

Figure 22.6   Translation of normal probability distribution for asset into probability distribution for value of a short call on asset.

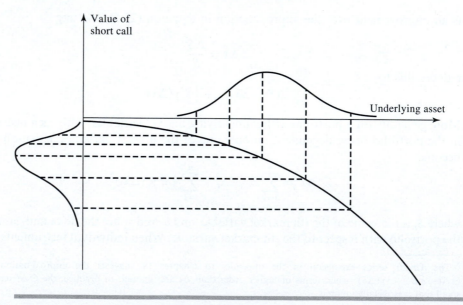

portfolio may be dependent on more than one market variable, this equation takes the more general form

$$\Delta P = \sum_{i=1}^{n} S_i \delta_i \, \Delta x_i + \sum_{i=1}^{n} \sum_{j=1}^{n} \frac{1}{2} S_i S_j \gamma_{ij} \, \Delta x_i \, \Delta x_j \qquad (22.8)$$

where γ_{ij} is a "cross gamma" defined as

$$\gamma_{ij} = \frac{\partial^2 P}{\partial S_i \, \partial S_j}$$

Equation (22.8) is not as easy to work with as equation (22.2) because ΔP is not normally distributed. If there are only a small number of variables, equation (22.8) can be used to calculate moments for ΔP. A result in statistics known as the Cornish–Fisher expansion can be used to estimate percentiles of the probability distribution from the moments.[9]

22.6 MONTE CARLO SIMULATION

As an alternative to the procedure described so far, the model-building approach can be implemented using Monte Carlo simulation to generate the probability distribution for ΔP. Suppose we wish to calculate a 1-day VaR for a portfolio. The procedure is as follows:

1. Value the portfolio today in the usual way using the current values of market variables.
2. Sample once from the multivariate normal probability distribution of the Δx_i.[10]
3. Use the values of the Δx_i that are sampled to determine the value of each market variable at the end of one day.
4. Revalue the portfolio at the end of the day in the usual way.
5. Subtract the value calculated in Step 1 from the value in Step 4 to determine a sample ΔP.
6. Repeat Steps 2 to 5 many times to build up a probability distribution for ΔP.

The VaR is calculated as the appropriate percentile of the probability distribution of ΔP. Suppose, for example, that we calculate 5,000 different sample values of ΔP in the way just described. The 1-day 99% VaR is the value of ΔP for the 50th worst outcome; the 1-day VaR 95% is the value of ΔP for the 250th worst outcome; and so on.[11] The N-day VaR is usually assumed to be the 1-day VaR multiplied by $\sqrt{N}$.[12]

---

[9] See Technical Note 10 at www-2.rotman.utoronto.ca/~hull/TechnicalNotes for details of the calculation of moments and the use of Cornish–Fisher expansions. When there is a single underlying variable, $E(\Delta P) = 0.5S^2\gamma\sigma^2$, $E(\Delta P^2) = S^2\delta^2\sigma^2 + 0.75S^4\gamma^2\sigma^4$, and $E(\Delta P^3) = 4.5S^4\delta^2\gamma\sigma^4 + 1.875S^6\gamma^3\sigma^6$, where S is the value of the variable and σ is its daily volatility. Sample Application E in the DerivaGem Applications implements the Cornish–Fisher expansion method for this case.

[10] One way of doing so is given in Section 21.6.

[11] As in the case of historical simulation, extreme value theory can be used to "smooth the tails" so that better estimates of extreme percentiles are obtained.

[12] This is only approximately true when the portfolio includes options, but it is the assumption that is made in practice for most VaR calculation methods.

The drawback of Monte Carlo simulation is that it tends to be slow because a company's complete portfolio (which might consist of hundreds of thousands of different instruments) has to be revalued many times.[13] One way of speeding things up is to assume that equation (22.8) describes the relationship between ΔP and the Δx_i. We can then jump straight from Step 2 to Step 5 in the Monte Carlo simulation and avoid the need for a complete revaluation of the portfolio. This is sometimes referred to as the *partial simulation approach*. A similar approach is sometimes used when implementing historical simulation.

22.7 COMPARISON OF APPROACHES

We have discussed two methods for estimating VaR: the historical simulation approach and the model-building approach. The basic model-building approach in Sections 22.3 and 22.4 assumes that changes in the portfolio's value are linearly dependent on the underlying market variables. This means that it is not accurate when the portfolio contains derivatives. Monte Carlo simulation can be used to avoid the linearity assumption, but the speed advantages of the model-building approach are then lost. The model-building approach is most appropriate for portfolios consisting of long and short positions in assets without any derivatives. Results can be produced speedily and it can be used in conjunction with volatility updating procedures such as those we will describe in the next chapter. It has the disadvantage that it assumes a multivariate normal distribution for the asset returns. (Often these returns have heavier tails than the normal distribution, as illustrated in Table 20.1.)

The historical simulation approach has the advantage that historical data determine the joint probability distribution of the market variables. It also avoids the need for cash-flow mapping. The main disadvantages of historical simulation are that it is computationally slow and does not easily allow volatility updating schemes to be used.[14]

22.8 BACK TESTING

Once a model for calculating VaR has been developed, an important reality check is *back testing*. This involves testing how well the VaR estimates would have performed in the past. Suppose that we are calculating a 1-day 99% VaR. Back testing would involve looking at how often the loss in a day exceeded the 1-day 99% VaR that would have been calculated for that day. If this happened on about 1% of the days, we can feel reasonably comfortable with the methodology for calculating VaR. If it happened on, say, 7% of days, the methodology is suspect. Unfortunately ES is more difficult to back test than VaR.

---

[13] An approach for limiting the number of portfolio revaluations is proposed in F. Jamshidian and Y. Zhu, "Scenario Simulation Model: Theory and Methodology," *Finance and Stochastics*, 1 (1997), 43–67.

[14] For a way of adapting the historical simulation approach to incorporate volatility updating, see J. C. Hull and A. White, "Incorporating Volatility Updating into the Historical Simulation Method for Value-at-Risk," *Journal of Risk* 1, No. 1 (1998): 5–19.

22.9 PRINCIPAL COMPONENTS ANALYSIS

One approach to handling the risk arising from groups of highly correlated market variables is principal components analysis. This is a standard statistical tool with many applications in risk management. It takes historical data on movements in the market variables and attempts to define a set of components or factors that explain the movements.

The approach is best illustrated with an example. The market variables we will consider are swap rates with maturities 1 year, 2 years 3 years, 4 years, 5 years, 7 years, 10 years, and 30 years. Tables 22.7 and 22.8 show results produced for these market variables using 2,780 daily observations between 2000 and 2011. The first column in Table 22.7 shows the maturities of the rates that were considered. The remaining eight columns in the table show the eight factors (or principal components) describing the rate moves. The first factor, shown in the column labeled PC1, corresponds to a roughly parallel shift in the yield curve. When we have one unit of that factor, the 1-year rate increases by 0.216 basis points, the 2-year rate increases by 0.331 basis points, and so on. The second factor is shown in the column labeled PC2. It corresponds to a "twist" or change of slope of the yield curve. Rates between 1 year and 4 years move in one direction; rates between 5 years and 30 years move in the other direction. The third factor corresponds to a "bowing" of the yield curve. Relatively short rates (1 year and 2 year) and relatively long rates (10 year and 30 year) move in one direction; the intermediate rates move in the other direction. The interest rate move for a particular factor is known as *factor loading*. In our example, the first factor's loading for the 1-year rate is 0.216.[15] (Note that the signs for factor loadings are somewhat arbitrary. We can change the signs for all factor loadings corresponding to a particular factor without changing the model. For example, if we did so for the first factor, −1 unit of that factor would result in the same yield curve changes as +1 unit does in Table 22.7.)

Because there are eight rates and eight factors, the interest rate changes observed on any given day can always be expressed as a linear sum of the factors by solving a set of eight simultaneous equations. The quantity of a particular factor in the interest rate changes on a particular day is known as the *factor score* for that day.

Table 22.7 Factor loadings for swap data.

	PC1	*PC2*	*PC3*	*PC4*	*PC5*	*PC6*	*PC7*	*PC8*
1y	0.216	−0.501	0.627	−0.487	0.122	0.237	0.011	−0.034
2y	0.331	−0.429	0.129	0.354	−0.212	−0.674	−0.100	0.236
3y	0.372	−0.267	−0.157	0.414	−0.096	0.311	0.413	−0.564
4y	0.392	−0.110	−0.256	0.174	−0.019	0.551	−0.416	0.512
5y	0.404	0.019	−0.355	−0.269	0.595	−0.278	−0.316	−0.327
7y	0.394	0.194	−0.195	−0.336	0.007	−0.100	0.685	0.422
10y	0.376	0.371	0.068	−0.305	−0.684	−0.039	−0.278	−0.279
30y	0.305	0.554	0.575	0.398	0.331	0.022	0.007	0.032

[15] The factor loadings have the property that the sum of their squares for each factor is 1.0. Also, note that a factor is not changed if the signs of all its factor loadings are reversed.

Table 22.8   Standard deviation of factor scores (basis points).

PC1	PC2	PC3	PC4	PC5	PC6	PC7	PC8
17.55	4.77	2.08	1.29	0.91	0.73	0.56	0.53

The importance of a factor is measured by the standard deviation of its factor score. The standard deviations of the factor scores in our example are shown in Table 22.8 and the factors are listed in order of their importance. The numbers in Table 22.8 are measured in basis points. A quantity of the first factor equal to 1 standard deviation, therefore, corresponds to the 1-year rate moving by $0.216 \times 17.55 = 3.78$ basis points, the 2-year rate moving by $0.331 \times 17.55 = 5.81$ basis points, and so on.

Software for carrying out the calculations underlying Tables 22.7 and 22.8 is on the author's website (www-2.rotman.utoronto.ca/~hull/ofod). The factors have the property that the factor scores are uncorrelated across the data. For instance, in our example, the first factor score (amount of parallel shift) is uncorrelated with the second factor score (amount of twist) across the 2,780 days. The variances of the factor scores have the property that they add up to the total variance of the data. From Table 22.8, the total variance of the original data (that is, sum of the variance of the observations on the 1-year rate, the variance of the observations on the 2-year rate, and so on) is

$$17.55^2 + 4.77^2 + 2.08^2 + \cdots + 0.53^2 = 338.8$$

From this it can be seen that the first factor accounts for $17.55^2/338.8 = 90.9\%$ of the variance in the original data; the first two factors account for

$$(17.55^2 + 4.77^2)/338.8 = 97.7\%$$

Figure 22.7   The three most important factors driving movements in swap rates.

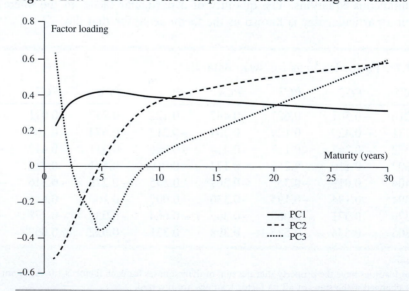

of the variance in the data; the third factor accounts for a further 1.3% of the variance. This shows that most of the risk in interest rate moves is accounted for by the first two or three factors. It suggests that we can relate the risks in a portfolio of interest rate dependent instruments to movements in these factors instead of considering all eight interest rates.

The three most important factors from Table 22.7 are plotted in Figure 22.7.[16]

Using Principal Components Analysis to Calculate VaR

To illustrate how a principal components analysis can be used to calculate VaR, consider a portfolio with the exposures to interest rate moves shown in Table 22.9. A 1-basis-point change in the 3-year rate causes the portfolio value to increase by $10 million, a 1-basis-point change in the 4-year rate causes it to increase by $4 million, and so on. Suppose the first two factors are used to model rate moves. (As mentioned above, this captures 97.7% of the variance in rate moves.) Using the data in Table 22.7, the exposure to the first factor (measured in millions of dollars per factor score basis point) is

$$10 \times 0.372 + 4 \times 0.392 - 8 \times 0.404 - 7 \times 0.394 + 2 \times 0.376 = +0.05$$

and the exposure to the second factor is

$$10 \times (-0.267) + 4 \times (-0.110) - 8 \times 0.019 - 7 \times 0.194 + 2 \times 0.371 = -3.88$$

Suppose that f_1 and f_2 are the factor scores (measured in basis points). The change in the portfolio value is, to a good approximation, given by

$$\Delta P = -0.05 f_1 - 3.88 f_2$$

The factor scores are uncorrelated and have the standard deviations given in Table 22.8. The standard deviation of ΔP is therefore

$$\sqrt{0.05^2 \times 17.55^2 + 3.88^2 \times 4.77^2} = 18.48$$

Assuming normally distributed factors, the 1-day 99% VaR is $18.48 \times 2.326 = 43.08$. Note that the data in Table 22.9 are such that there is very little exposure to the first factor and significant exposure to the second factor. Using only one factor would significantly understate VaR (see Problem 22.11). (The duration-based method for

Table 22.9 Change in portfolio value for a 1-basis-point rate move ($ millions).

3-year rate	4-year rate	5-year rate	7-year rate	10-year rate
+10	+4	−8	−7	+2

---

[16] Results similar to those described here, concerning the nature of the factors and the amount of the total risk they account for, are obtained when a principal components analysis is used to explain the movements in almost any yield curve in any country.

handling interest rates, mentioned in Section 22.4, would also significantly understate VaR as it considers only parallel shifts in the yield curve.)

A principal components analysis can in theory be used for market variables other than interest rates. Suppose that a financial institution has exposures to a number of different stock indices. A principal components analysis can be used to identify factors describing movements in the indices and the most important of these can be used to replace the market indices in a VaR analysis. How effective a principal components analysis is for a group of market variables depends on how closely correlated they are.

As explained earlier in the chapter, VaR is usually calculated by relating the actual changes in a portfolio to percentage changes in market variables (the Δx_i). For a VaR calculation, it may therefore be most appropriate to carry out a principal components analysis on percentage changes in market variables rather than actual changes.

SUMMARY

A value at risk (VaR) calculation is aimed at making a statement of the form: "We are X percent certain that we will not lose more than V dollars in the next N days." The variable V is the VaR, $X\%$ is the confidence level, and N days is the time horizon. Expected shortfall (ES) is the expected loss conditional on the loss being greater than the VaR level.

One approach to calculating VaR or ES is historical simulation. This involves creating a database consisting of the daily movements in all market variables over a period of time. The first simulation trial assumes that the percentage changes in each market variable are the same as those on the first day covered by the database; the second simulation trial assumes that the percentage changes are the same as those on the second day; and so on. The change in the portfolio value, ΔP, is calculated for each simulation trial, and the VaR is calculated as the appropriate percentile of the probability distribution of ΔP. ES is the average of the observations in the VaR tail.

An alternative is the model-building approach. This is relatively straightforward if two assumptions can be made:

1. The change in the value of the portfolio (ΔP) is linearly dependent on percentage changes in market variables.

2. The percentage changes in market variables are multivariate normally distributed.

The probability distribution of ΔP is then normal, and there are analytic formulas for relating the standard deviation of ΔP to the volatilities and correlations of the underlying market variables. The VaR or ES can be calculated from well-known properties of the normal distribution.

When a portfolio includes options, ΔP is not linearly related to the percentage changes in market variables. From knowledge of the gamma of the portfolio, we can derive an approximate quadratic relationship between ΔP and percentage changes in market variables. Monte Carlo simulation can then be used to estimate VaR.

In the next chapter we discuss how volatilities and correlations can be estimated and monitored.

FURTHER READING

Artzner P., F. Delbaen, J.-M. Eber, and D. Heath. "Coherent Measures of Risk," *Mathematical Finance*, 9 (1999): 203–28.

Basak, S., and A. Shapiro. "Value-at-Risk-Based Risk Management: Optimal Policies and Asset Prices," *Review of Financial Studies*, 14, 2 (2001): 371–405.

Boudoukh, J., M. Richardson, and R. Whitelaw. "The Best of Both Worlds," *Risk*, May 1998: 64–67.

Dowd, K. *Beyond Value at Risk: The New Science of Risk Management*. New York: Wiley, 1998.

Duffie, D., and J. Pan. "An Overview of Value at Risk," *Journal of Derivatives*, 4, 3 (Spring 1997): 7–49.

Embrechts, P., C. Kluppelberg, and T. Mikosch. *Modeling Extremal Events for Insurance and Finance*. New York: Springer, 1997.

Hull, J.C., and A. White. "Value at Risk When Daily Changes in Market Variables Are Not Normally Distributed," *Journal of Derivatives*, 5 (Spring 1998): 9–19.

Hull, J.C., and A. White. "Incorporating Volatility Updating into the Historical Simulation Method for Value at Risk," *Journal of Risk*, 1, 1 (1998): 5–19.

Jackson, P., D.J. Maude, and W. Perraudin. "Bank Capital and Value at Risk." *Journal of Derivatives*, 4, 3 (Spring 1997): 73–90.

Jamshidian, F., and Y. Zhu. "Scenario Simulation Model: Theory and Methodology," *Finance and Stochastics*, 1 (1997): 43–67.

Jorion, P. *Value at Risk*, 3rd edn. McGraw-Hill, 2007.

Longin, F.M. "Beyond the VaR," *Journal of Derivatives*, 8, 4 (Summer 2001): 36–48.

Marshall, C., and M. Siegel. "Value at Risk: Implementing a Risk Measurement Standard," *Journal of Derivatives* 4, 3 (Spring 1997): 91–111.

Neftci, S. "Value at Risk Calculations, Extreme Events and Tail Estimation," *Journal of Derivatives*, 7, 3 (Spring 2000): 23–38.

Rich, D. "Second Generation VaR and Risk-Adjusted Return on Capital," *Journal of Derivatives*, 10, 4 (Summer 2003): 51–61.

Practice Questions (Answers in Solutions Manual)

22.1. Consider a position consisting of a $100,000 investment in asset A and a $100,000 investment in asset B. Assume that the daily volatilities of both assets are 1% and that the coefficient of correlation between their returns is 0.3. Estimate the 5-day 99% VaR and ES for the portfolio assuming normally distributed returns.

22.2. Describe three ways of handling instruments that are dependent on interest rates when the model-building approach is used to calculate VaR. How would you handle these instruments when historical simulation is used to calculate VaR?

22.3. A financial institution owns a portfolio of options on the U.S. dollar–sterling exchange rate. The delta of the portfolio is 56.0. The current exchange rate is 1.5000. Derive an approximate linear relationship between the change in the portfolio value and the percentage change in the exchange rate. If the daily volatility of the exchange rate is 0.7%, estimate the 10-day 99% VaR.

22.4. Suppose you know that the gamma of the portfolio in the previous question is 16.2. How does this change your estimate of the relationship between the change in the portfolio value and the percentage change in the exchange rate?

22.5. Suppose that the daily change in the value of a portfolio is, to a good approximation, linearly dependent on two factors, calculated from a principal components analysis. The delta of a portfolio with respect to the first factor is 6 and the delta with respect to the second factor is −4. The standard deviations of the factors are 20 and 8, respectively. What is the 5-day 90% VaR?

22.6. Suppose that a company has a portfolio consisting of positions in stocks and bonds. Assume that there are no derivatives. Explain the assumptions underlying (a) the linear model and (b) the historical simulation model for calculating VaR.

22.7. Explain how a forward contract to sell foreign currency is mapped into a portfolio of zero-coupon bonds with standard maturities for the purposes of a VaR calculation.

22.8. Explain the difference between value at risk and expected shortfall.

22.9. Explain why the linear model can provide only approximate estimates of VaR for a portfolio containing options.

22.10. Some time ago a company entered into a forward contract to buy £1 million for $1.5 million. The contract now has 6 months to maturity. The daily volatility of a 6-month zero-coupon sterling bond (when its price is translated to dollars) is 0.06% and the daily volatility of a 6-month zero-coupon dollar bond is 0.05%. The correlation between returns from the two bonds is 0.8. The current exchange rate is 1.53. Calculate the standard deviation of the change in the dollar value of the forward contract in 1 day. What is the 10-day 99% VaR? Assume that the 6-month interest rate in both sterling and dollars is 5% per annum with continuous compounding.

22.11. The text calculates a VaR estimate for the example in Table 22.9 assuming two factors. How does the estimate change if you assume (a) one factor and (b) three factors.

22.12. A bank has a portfolio of options on an asset. The delta of the options is −30 and the gamma is −5. Explain how these numbers can be interpreted. The asset price is 20 and its volatility is 1% per day. Adapt Sample Application E in the DerivaGem Application Builder software to calculate VaR.

22.13. Suppose that in Problem 22.12 the vega of the portfolio is −2 per 1% change in the annual volatility. Derive a model relating the change in the portfolio value in 1 day to delta, gamma, and vega. Explain without doing detailed calculations how you would use the model to calculate a VaR estimate.

22.14. The one-day 99% VaR is calculated for the four-index example in Section 22.2 as $253,385. Look at the underlying spreadsheets on the author's website and calculate: (a) the one-day 95% VaR, (b) the one-day 95% ES, (c) the one-day 97% VaR, and (d) the one-day 97% ES.

22.15. Use the spreadsheets on the author's website to calculate the one-day 99% VaR and ES, employing the basic methodology in Section 22.2, if the four-index portfolio considered in Section 22.2 is equally divided between the four indices.

Further Questions

22.16. A company has a position in bonds worth $6 million. The modified duration of the portfolio is 5.2 years. Assume that only parallel shifts in the yield curve can take place and that the standard deviation of the daily yield change (when yield is measured in percent) is 0.09. Use the duration model to estimate the 20-day 90% VaR for the portfolio. Explain carefully the weaknesses of this approach to calculating VaR. Explain two alternatives that give more accuracy.

22.17. Consider a position consisting of a $300,000 investment in gold and a $500,000 investment in silver. Suppose that the daily volatilities of these two assets are 1.8% and 1.2%, respectively, and that the coefficient of correlation between their returns is 0.6. What is the 10-day 97.5% VaR and ES for the portfolio? By how much does diversification reduce the VaR? Assume normally distributed returns.

22.18. Consider a portfolio of options on a single asset. Suppose that the delta of the portfolio is 12, the value of the asset is $10, and the daily volatility of the asset is 2%. Estimate the 1-day 95% VaR for the portfolio from the delta. Suppose next that the gamma of the portfolio is −2.6. Derive a quadratic relationship between the change in the portfolio value and the percentage change in the underlying asset price in one day. How would you use this in a Monte Carlo simulation?

22.19. A company has a long position in a 2-year bond and a 3-year bond, as well as a short position in a 5-year bond. Each bond has a principal of $100 and pays a 5% coupon annually. Calculate the company's exposure to the 1-year, 2-year, 3-year, 4-year, and 5-year rates. Use the data in Tables 22.7 and 22.8 to calculate a 20-day 95% VaR on the assumption that rate changes are explained by (a) one factor, (b) two factors, and (c) three factors. Assume that the zero-coupon yield curve is flat at 5%.

22.20. A bank has written a call option on one stock and a put option on another stock. For the first option the stock price is 50, the strike price is 51, the volatility is 28% per annum, and the time to maturity is 9 months. For the second option the stock price is 20, the strike price is 19, the volatility is 25% per annum, and the time to maturity is 1 year. Neither stock pays a dividend, the risk-free rate is 6% per annum, and the correlation between stock price returns is 0.4. Calculate a 10-day 99% VaR:
(a) Using only deltas
(b) Using the partial simulation approach
(c) Using the full simulation approach.

22.21. Use equation (22.1) to show that when the loss distribution is normal, VaR with 99% confidence is almost exactly the same as ES with 97.5% confidence.

22.22. Suppose that the portfolio considered in Section 22.2 has (in $000s) 3,000 in DJIA, 3,000 in FTSE, 1,000 in CAC 40 and 3,000 in Nikkei 225. Use the spreadsheet on the author's website to calculate what difference this makes to the one-day 99% VaR and ES that is calculated in Section 22.2.

23

Estimating Volatilities and Correlations

In this chapter we explain how historical data can be used to produce estimates of the current and future levels of volatilities and correlations. The chapter is relevant both to the calculation of value at risk using the model-building approach and to the valuation of derivatives. When calculating value at risk, we are most interested in the current levels of volatilities and correlations because we are assessing possible changes in the value of a portfolio over a very short period of time. When valuing derivatives, forecasts of volatilities and correlations over the whole life of the derivative are usually required.

The chapter considers models with imposing names such as exponentially weighted moving average (EWMA), autoregressive conditional heteroscedasticity (ARCH), and generalized autoregressive conditional heteroscedasticity (GARCH). The distinctive feature of the models is that they recognize that volatilities and correlations are not constant. During some periods, a particular volatility or correlation may be relatively low, whereas during other periods it may be relatively high. The models attempt to keep track of the variations in the volatility or correlation through time.

23.1 ESTIMATING VOLATILITY

Define σ_n as the volatility of a market variable on day n, as estimated at the end of day $n-1$. The square of the volatility, σ_n^2, on day n is the *variance rate*. We described the standard approach to estimating σ_n from historical data in Section 15.4. Suppose that the value of the market variable at the end of day i is S_i. The variable u_i is defined as the continuously compounded return during day i (between the end of day $i-1$ and the end of day i):

$$u_i = \ln \frac{S_i}{S_{i-1}}$$

An unbiased estimate of the variance rate per day, σ_n^2, using the most recent m observations on the u_i is

$$\sigma_n^2 = \frac{1}{m-1} \sum_{i=1}^{m} (u_{n-i} - \bar{u})^2 \qquad (23.1)$$

where $\bar{u}$ is the mean of the u_is:

$$\bar{u} = \frac{1}{m}\sum_{i=1}^{m} u_{n-i}$$

For the purposes of monitoring daily volatility, the formula in equation (23.1) is usually changed in a number of ways:

1. u_i is defined as the percentage change in the market variable between the end of day $i-1$ and the end of day i, so that:[1]

$$u_i = \frac{S_i - S_{i-1}}{S_{i-1}} \qquad (23.2)$$

2. $\bar{u}$ is assumed to be zero.[2]
3. $m-1$ is replaced by m.[3]

These three changes make very little difference to the estimates that are calculated, but they allow us to simplify the formula for the variance rate to

$$\sigma_n^2 = \frac{1}{m}\sum_{i=1}^{m} u_{n-i}^2 \qquad (23.3)$$

where u_i is given by equation (23.2).[4]

Weighting Schemes

Equation (23.3) gives equal weight to $u_{n-1}^2, u_{n-2}^2, \ldots, u_{n-m}^2$. Our objective is to estimate the current level of volatility, σ_n. It therefore makes sense to give more weight to recent data. A model that does this is

$$\sigma_n^2 = \sum_{i=1}^{m} \alpha_i u_{n-i}^2 \qquad (23.4)$$

The variable α_i is the amount of weight given to the observation i days ago. The α's are positive. If we choose them so that $\alpha_i < \alpha_j$ when $i > j$, less weight is given to older observations. The weights must sum to unity, so that

$$\sum_{i=1}^{m} \alpha_i = 1$$

An extension of the idea in equation (23.4) is to assume that there is a long-run average

---

[1] This is consistent with the point made in Section 22.3 about the way that volatility is defined for the purposes of VaR calculations.

[2] As explained in Section 22.3, this assumption is reasonable because the expected change in a variable in one day is very small when compared with the standard deviation of changes.

[3] Replacing $m-1$ by m moves us from an unbiased estimate of the variance to a maximum likelihood estimate. Maximum likelihood estimates are discussed later in this chapter.

[4] Note that the u's in this chapter play the same role as the Δx's in Chapter 22. Both are daily percentage changes in market variables. In the case of the u's, the subscripts count observations made on different days on the same market variable. In the case of the Δx's, they count observations made on the same day on different market variables. The use of subscripts for σ is similarly different between the two chapters. In this chapter, the subscripts refer to days; in Chapter 22 they referred to market variables.

variance rate and that this should be given some weight. This leads to the model that takes the form

$$\sigma_n^2 = \gamma V_L + \sum_{i=1}^{m} \alpha_i u_{n-i}^2 \tag{23.5}$$

where V_L is the long-run variance rate and γ is the weight assigned to V_L. Since the weights must sum to unity, we have

$$\gamma + \sum_{i=1}^{m} \alpha_i = 1$$

This is known as an ARCH(m) model. It was first suggested by Engle.[5] The estimate of the variance is based on a long-run average variance and m observations. The older an observation, the less weight it is given. Defining $\omega = \gamma V_L$, the model in equation (23.5) can be written

$$\sigma_n^2 = \omega + \sum_{i=1}^{m} \alpha_i u_{n-i}^2 \tag{23.6}$$

In the next two sections we discuss two important approaches to monitoring volatility using the ideas in equations (23.4) and (23.5).

23.2   THE EXPONENTIALLY WEIGHTED MOVING AVERAGE MODEL

The exponentially weighted moving average (EWMA) model is a particular case of the model in equation (23.4) where the weights α_i decrease exponentially as we move back through time. Specifically, $\alpha_{i+1} = \lambda \alpha_i$, where λ is a constant between 0 and 1.

It turns out that this weighting scheme leads to a particularly simple formula for updating volatility estimates. The formula is

$$\sigma_n^2 = \lambda \sigma_{n-1}^2 + (1 - \lambda) u_{n-1}^2 \tag{23.7}$$

The estimate, σ_n, of the volatility of a variable for day n (made at the end of day $n - 1$) is calculated from σ_{n-1} (the estimate that was made at the end of day $n - 2$ of the volatility for day $n - 1$) and u_{n-1} (the most recent daily percentage change in the variable).

To understand why equation (23.7) corresponds to weights that decrease exponentially, we substitute for σ_{n-1}^2 to get

$$\sigma_n^2 = \lambda [\lambda \sigma_{n-2}^2 + (1 - \lambda) u_{n-2}^2] + (1 - \lambda) u_{n-1}^2$$

or

$$\sigma_n^2 = (1 - \lambda)(u_{n-1}^2 + \lambda u_{n-2}^2) + \lambda^2 \sigma_{n-2}^2$$

Substituting in a similar way for σ_{n-2}^2 gives

$$\sigma_n^2 = (1 - \lambda)(u_{n-1}^2 + \lambda u_{n-2}^2 + \lambda^2 u_{n-3}^2) + \lambda^3 \sigma_{n-3}^2$$

[5] See R. Engle "Autoregressive Conditional Heteroscedasticity with Estimates of the Variance of U.K. Inflation," *Econometrica*, 50 (1982): 987–1008.

Continuing in this way gives

$$\sigma_n^2 = (1 - \lambda) \sum_{i=1}^{m} \lambda^{i-1} u_{n-i}^2 + \lambda^m \sigma_{n-m}^2$$

For large m, the term $\lambda^m \sigma_{n-m}^2$ is sufficiently small to be ignored, so that equation (23.7) is the same as equation (23.4) with $\alpha_i = (1 - \lambda)\lambda^{i-1}$. The weights for the u_i decline at rate λ as we move back through time. Each weight is λ times the previous weight.

Example 23.1

Suppose that λ is 0.90, the volatility estimated for a market variable for day $n - 1$ is 1% per day, and during day $n - 1$ the market variable increased by 2%. This means that $\sigma_{n-1}^2 = 0.01^2 = 0.0001$ and $u_{n-1}^2 = 0.02^2 = 0.0004$. Equation (23.7) gives

$$\sigma_n^2 = 0.9 \times 0.0001 + 0.1 \times 0.0004 = 0.00013$$

The estimate of the volatility, σ_n, for day n is therefore $\sqrt{0.00013}$, or 1.14%, per day. Note that the expected value of u_{n-1}^2 is σ_{n-1}^2, or 0.0001. In this example, the realized value of u_{n-1}^2 is greater than the expected value, and as a result our volatility estimate increases. If the realized value of u_{n-1}^2 had been less than its expected value, our estimate of the volatility would have decreased.

The EWMA approach has the attractive feature that relatively little data need be stored. At any given time, only the current estimate of the variance rate and the most recent observation on the value of the market variable need be remembered. When a new observation on the market variable is obtained, a new daily percentage change is calculated and equation (23.7) is used to update the estimate of the variance rate. The old estimate of the variance rate and the old value of the market variable can then be discarded.

The EWMA approach is designed to track changes in the volatility. Suppose there is a big move in the market variable on day $n - 1$, so that u_{n-1}^2 is large. From equation (23.7) this causes the estimate of the current volatility to move upward. The value of λ governs how responsive the estimate of the daily volatility is to the most recent daily percentage change. A low value of λ leads to a great deal of weight being given to the u_{n-1}^2 when σ_n is calculated. In this case, the estimates produced for the volatility on successive days are themselves highly volatile. A high value of λ (i.e., a value close to 1.0) produces estimates of the daily volatility that respond relatively slowly to new information provided by the daily percentage change.

The RiskMetrics database, which was originally created by JP Morgan and made publicly available in 1994, used the EWMA model with $\lambda = 0.94$ for updating daily volatility estimates. This is because the company found that, across a range of different market variables, this value of λ gives forecasts of the variance rate that come closest to the realized variance rate.[6] The realized variance rate on a particular day was calculated as an equally weighted average of the u_i^2 on the subsequent 25 days (see Problem 23.19).

---

[6] See JP Morgan, *RiskMetrics Monitor*, Fourth Quarter, 1995. We will explain an alternative (maximum likelihood) approach to estimating parameters later in the chapter.

23.3 THE GARCH(1,1) MODEL

We now move on to discuss what is known as the GARCH(1,1) model, proposed by Bollerslev in 1986.[7] The difference between the GARCH(1,1) model and the EWMA model is analogous to the difference between equation (23.4) and equation (23.5). In GARCH(1,1), σ_n^2 is calculated from a long-run average variance rate, V_L, as well as from σ_{n-1} and u_{n-1}. The equation for GARCH(1,1) is

$$\sigma_n^2 = \gamma V_L + \alpha u_{n-1}^2 + \beta \sigma_{n-1}^2 \tag{23.8}$$

where γ is the weight assigned to V_L, α is the weight assigned to u_{n-1}^2, and β is the weight assigned to σ_{n-1}^2. Since the weights must sum to unity, it follows that

$$\gamma + \alpha + \beta = 1$$

The EWMA model is a particular case of GARCH(1,1) where $\gamma = 0$, $\alpha = 1 - \lambda$, and $\beta = \lambda$.

The "(1,1)" in GARCH(1,1) indicates that σ_n^2 is based on the most recent observation of u^2 and the most recent estimate of the variance rate. The more general GARCH(p,q) model calculates σ_n^2 from the most recent p observations on u^2 and the most recent q estimates of the variance rate.[8] GARCH(1,1) is by far the most popular of the GARCH models.

Setting $\omega = \gamma V_L$, the GARCH(1,1) model can also be written

$$\sigma_n^2 = \omega + \alpha u_{n-1}^2 + \beta \sigma_{n-1}^2 \tag{23.9}$$

This is the form of the model that is usually used for the purposes of estimating the parameters. Once ω, α, and β have been estimated, we can calculate γ as $1 - \alpha - \beta$. The long-term variance V_L can then be calculated as ω/γ. For a stable GARCH(1,1) process we require $\alpha + \beta < 1$. Otherwise the weight applied to the long-term variance is negative.

Example 23.2

Suppose that a GARCH(1,1) model is estimated from daily data as

$$\sigma_n^2 = 0.000002 + 0.13u_{n-1}^2 + 0.86\sigma_{n-1}^2$$

This corresponds to $\alpha = 0.13$, $\beta = 0.86$, and $\omega = 0.000002$. Because $\gamma = 1 - \alpha - \beta$, it follows that $\gamma = 0.01$. Because $\omega = \gamma V_L$, it follows that $V_L = 0.0002$. In other words, the long-run average variance per day implied by the model is 0.0002. This corresponds to a volatility of $\sqrt{0.0002} = 0.014$, or 1.4%, per day.

[7] See T. Bollerslev, "Generalized Autoregressive Conditional Heteroscedasticity," *Journal of Econometrics*, 31 (1986): 307–27.

[8] Other GARCH models have been proposed that incorporate asymmetric news. These models are designed so that σ_n depends on the sign of u_{n-1}. Arguably, the models are more appropriate for equities than GARCH(1,1). As mentioned in Chapter 20, the volatility of an equity's price tends to be inversely related to the price so that a negative u_{n-1} should have a bigger effect on σ_n than the same positive u_{n-1}. For a discussion of models for handling asymmetric news, see D. Nelson, "Conditional Heteroscedasticity and Asset Returns: A New Approach," *Econometrica*, 59 (1990): 347–70; R. F. Engle and V. Ng, "Measuring and Testing the Impact of News on Volatility," *Journal of Finance*, 48 (1993): 1749–78.

Suppose that the estimate of the volatility on day $n - 1$ is 1.6% per day, so that $\sigma_{n-1}^2 = 0.016^2 = 0.000256$, and that on day $n - 1$ the market variable decreased by 1%, so that $u_{n-1}^2 = 0.01^2 = 0.0001$. Then

$$\sigma_n^2 = 0.000002 + 0.13 \times 0.0001 + 0.86 \times 0.000256 = 0.00023516$$

The new estimate of the volatility is therefore $\sqrt{0.00023516} = 0.0153$, or 1.53%, per day.

The Weights

Substituting for σ_{n-1}^2 in equation (23.9) gives

$$\sigma_n^2 = \omega + \alpha u_{n-1}^2 + \beta(\omega + \alpha u_{n-2}^2 + \beta \sigma_{n-2}^2)$$

or

$$\sigma_n^2 = \omega + \beta\omega + \alpha u_{n-1}^2 + \alpha\beta u_{n-2}^2 + \beta^2 \sigma_{n-2}^2$$

Substituting for σ_{n-2}^2 gives

$$\sigma_n^2 = \omega + \beta\omega + \beta^2\omega + \alpha u_{n-1}^2 + \alpha\beta u_{n-2}^2 + \alpha\beta^2 u_{n-3}^2 + \beta^3 \sigma_{n-3}^2$$

Continuing in this way, we see that the weight applied to u_{n-i}^2 is $\alpha\beta^{i-1}$. The weights decline exponentially at rate β. The parameter β can be interpreted as a "decay rate". It is similar to λ in the EWMA model. It defines the relative importance of the observations on the u's in determining the current variance rate. For example, if $\beta = 0.9$, then u_{n-2}^2 is only 90% as important as u_{n-1}^2; u_{n-3}^2 is 81% as important as u_{n-1}^2; and so on. The GARCH(1,1) model is similar to the EWMA model except that, in addition to assigning weights that decline exponentially to past u^2, it also assigns some weight to the long-run average volatility.

Mean Reversion

The GARCH (1,1) model recognizes that over time the variance tends to get pulled back to a long-run average level of V_L. The amount of weight assigned to V_L is $\gamma = 1 - \alpha - \beta$. The GARCH(1,1) is equivalent to a model where the variance V follows the stochastic process

$$dV = a(V_L - V)\,dt + \xi V\,dz$$

where time is measured in days, $a = 1 - \alpha - \beta$, and $\xi = \alpha\sqrt{2}$ (see Problem 23.14). This is a mean-reverting model. The variance has a drift that pulls it back to V_L at rate a. When $V > V_L$, the variance has a negative drift; when $V < V_L$, it has a positive drift. Superimposed on the drift is a volatility ξ. Chapter 27 discusses this type of model further.

23.4 CHOOSING BETWEEN THE MODELS

In practice, variance rates do tend to be mean reverting. The GARCH(1,1) model incorporates mean reversion, whereas the EWMA model does not. GARCH (1,1) is therefore theoretically more appealing than the EWMA model.

In the next section, we will discuss how best-fit parameters ω, α, and β in GARCH(1,1) can be estimated. When the parameter ω is zero, the GARCH(1,1) reduces to EWMA. In circumstances where the best-fit value of ω turns out to be negative, the GARCH(1,1) model is not stable and it makes sense to switch to the EWMA model.

23.5 MAXIMUM LIKELIHOOD METHODS

It is now appropriate to discuss how the parameters in the models we have been considering are estimated from historical data. The approach used is known as the *maximum likelihood method*. It involves choosing values for the parameters that maximize the chance (or likelihood) of the data occurring.

To illustrate the method, we start with a very simple example. Suppose that we sample 10 stocks at random on a certain day and find that the price of one of them declined on that day and the prices of the other nine either remained the same or increased. What is the best estimate of the probability of a randomly chosen stock's price declining on the day? The natural answer is 0.1. Let us see if this is what the maximum likelihood method gives.

Suppose that the probability of a price decline is p. The probability that one particular stock declines in price and the other nine do not is $p(1-p)^9$. Using the maximum likelihood approach, the best estimate of p is the one that maximizes $p(1-p)^9$. Differentiating this expression with respect to p and setting the result equal to zero, we find that $p = 0.1$ maximizes the expression. This shows that the maximum likelihood estimate of p is 0.1, as expected.

Estimating a Constant Variance

Our next example of maximum likelihood methods considers the problem of estimating the variance of a variable X from m observations on X when the underlying distribution is normal with zero mean. Assume that the observations are $u_1, u_2, \ldots, u_m$. Denote the variance by v. The likelihood of u_i being observed is defined as the probability density function for X when $X = u_i$. This is

$$\frac{1}{\sqrt{2\pi v}} \exp\left(\frac{-u_i^2}{2v}\right)$$

The likelihood of m observations occurring in the order in which they are observed is

$$\prod_{i=1}^{m}\left[\frac{1}{\sqrt{2\pi v}} \exp\left(\frac{-u_i^2}{2v}\right)\right] \qquad (23.10)$$

Using the maximum likelihood method, the best estimate of v is the value that maximizes this expression.

Maximizing an expression is equivalent to maximizing the logarithm of the expression. Taking logarithms of the expression in equation (23.10) and ignoring constant multiplicative factors, it can be seen that we wish to maximize

$$\sum_{i=1}^{m}\left[-\ln(v) - \frac{u_i^2}{v}\right] \qquad (23.11)$$

or

$$-m \ln(v) - \sum_{i=1}^{m} \frac{u_i^2}{v}$$

Differentiating this expression with respect to v and setting the resulting equation to zero, we see that the maximum likelihood estimator of v is[9]

$$\frac{1}{m} \sum_{i=1}^{m} u_i^2$$

Estimating EWMA or GARCH (1,1) Parameters

We now consider how the maximum likelihood method can be used to estimate the parameters when EWMA, GARCH (1,1), or some other volatility updating scheme is used. Define $v_i = \sigma_i^2$ as the variance estimated for day i. Assume that the probability distribution of u_i conditional on the variance is normal. A similar analysis to the one just given shows the best parameters are the ones that maximize

$$\prod_{i=1}^{m} \left[\frac{1}{\sqrt{2\pi v_i}} \exp\left(\frac{-u_i^2}{2v_i}\right) \right]$$

Taking logarithms, we see that this is equivalent to maximizing

$$\sum_{i=1}^{m} \left[-\ln(v_i) - \frac{u_i^2}{v_i} \right] \tag{23.12}$$

This is the same as the expression in equation (23.11), except that v is replaced by v_i. It is necessary to search iteratively to find the parameters in the model that maximize the expression in equation (23.12).

The spreadsheet in Table 23.1 indicates how the calculations could be organized for the GARCH(1,1) model. The table analyzes data on the S&P 500 between July 18, 2005, and August 13, 2010.[10] The first column in the table records the date. The second column counts the days. The third column shows the S&P 500, S_i, at the end of day i. The fourth column shows the proportional change in the S&P 500 between the end of day $i - 1$ and the end of day i. This is $u_i = (S_i - S_{i-1})/S_{i-1}$.

We start by storing trial values for ω, α, and β in cells of the spreadsheet. We use an iterative procedure to move from these values to optimal values. The fifth column shows the estimate of the variance rate, $v_i = \sigma_i^2$, for day i made at the end of day $i - 1$. On day 3, we start things off by setting the variance equal to u_2^2. On subsequent days, equation (23.9) is used with the current values of ω, α, and β. The sixth column tabulates the likelihood measure, $-\ln(v_i) - u_i^2/v_i$. The iterative search procedure chooses ω, α, and β to maximize the sum of the numbers in the sixth column.[11]

---

[9] This confirms the point made in footnote 3.

[10] The data and calculations can be found at www-2.rotman.utoronto.ca/~hull/OFOD/GarchExample.

[11] As discussed later, a general purpose algorithm such as Solver in Microsoft's Excel can be used. Alternatively, a special purpose algorithm, such as Levenberg–Marquardt, can be used. See, e.g., W. H. Press, B. P. Flannery, S. A. Teukolsky, and W. T. Vetterling. *Numerical Recipes in C: The Art of Scientific Computing*, Cambridge University Press, 1988.

Table 23.1 Estimation of Parameters in GARCH(1,1) Model for S&P 500 between July 18, 2005, and August 13, 2010.

Date	Day i	S_i	u_i	$v_i = \sigma_i^2$	$-\ln(v_i) - u_i^2/v_i$
18-Jul-2005	1	1221.13			
19-Jul-2005	2	1229.35	0.006731		
20-Jul-2005	3	1235.20	0.004759	0.00004531	9.5022
21-Jul-2005	4	1227.04	−0.006606	0.00004447	9.0393
22-Jul-2005	5	1233.68	0.005411	0.00004546	9.3545
25-Jul-2005	6	1229.03	−0.003769	0.00004517	9.6906
⋮	⋮	⋮	⋮	⋮	⋮
11-Aug-2010	1277	1089.47	−0.028179	0.00011834	2.3322
12-Aug-2010	1278	1083.61	−0.005379	0.00017527	8.4841
13-Aug-2010	1279	1079.25	−0.004024	0.00016327	8.6209
					10,228.2349

Trial estimates of GARCH parameters

$\omega = 0.0000013465 \quad \alpha = 0.083394 \quad \beta = 0.910116$

In our example, the optimal values of the parameters turn out to be

$$\omega = 0.0000013465, \quad \alpha = 0.083394, \quad \beta = 0.910116$$

and the maximum value of the function in equation (23.12) is 10,228.2349. The numbers shown in Table 23.1 were calculated on the final iteration of the search for the optimal ω, α, and β.

The long-term variance rate, V_L, in our example is

$$\frac{\omega}{1 - \alpha - \beta} = \frac{0.0000013465}{0.006490} = 0.0002075$$

The long-term volatility is $\sqrt{0.0002075}$, or 1.4404%, per day.

Figures 23.1 and 23.2 show the S&P 500 index and its GARCH(1,1) volatility during the 5-year period covered by the data. Most of the time, the volatility was less than 2% per day, but volatilities as high as 5% per day were experienced during the credit crisis. (Very high volatilities are also indicated by the VIX index—see Section 15.11.)

An alternative approach to estimating parameters in GARCH(1,1), which is sometimes more robust, is known as *variance targeting*.[12] This involves setting the long-run average variance rate, V_L, equal to the sample variance calculated from the data (or to some other value that is believed to be reasonable). The value of ω then equals $V_L(1 - \alpha - \beta)$ and only two parameters (α and β) have to be estimated. For the data in Table 23.1, the sample variance is 0.0002412, which gives a daily volatility of 1.5531%. Setting V_L equal to the sample variance, the values of α and β that maximize the objective function in equation (23.12) are 0.08445 and 0.9101, respectively. The value of the objective function is 10,228.1941, only marginally below the value of 10,228.2349 obtained using the earlier procedure.

---

[12] See R. Engle and J. Mezrich, "GARCH for Groups," *Risk*, August 1996: 36–40.

Figure 23.1 S&P 500 index: July 18, 2005, to August 13, 2010.

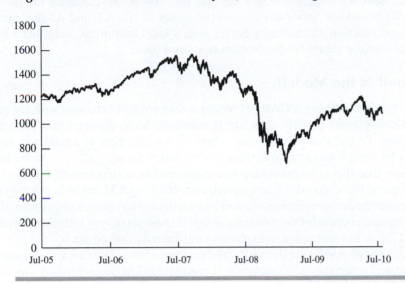

When the EWMA model is used, the estimation procedure is relatively simple. We set $\omega = 0$, $\alpha = 1 - \lambda$, and $\beta = \lambda$, and only one parameter has to be estimated. In the data in Table 23.1, the value of λ that maximizes the objective function in equation (23.12) is 0.9374 and the value of the objective function is 10,192.5104.

For both GARCH (1,1) and EWMA, we can use the Solver routine in Excel to search for the values of the parameters that maximize the likelihood function. The routine works well provided that the spreadsheet is structured so that the parameters being searched for have roughly equal values. For example, in GARCH (1,1) we could let cells

Figure 23.2 Daily volatility of S&P 500 index: July 18, 2005, to August 13, 2010.

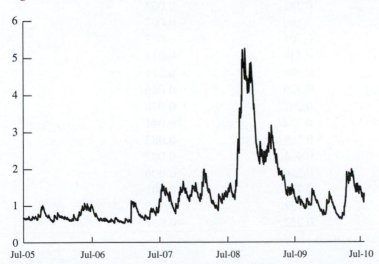

A1, A2, and A3 contain $\omega \times 10^5$, 10α, and β. We could then set B1 = A1/100,000, B2 = A2/10, and B3 = A3. We would use B1, B2, and B3 to calculate the likelihood function. We would ask Solver to calculate the values of A1, A2, and A3 that maximize the likelihood function. Occasionally Solver gives a local maximum, so testing a number of different starting values for parameters is a good idea.

How Good Is the Model?

The assumption underlying a GARCH model is that volatility changes with the passage of time. During some periods volatility is relatively high; during other periods it is relatively low. To put this another way, when u_i^2 is high, there is a tendency for u_{i+1}^2, $u_{i+2}^2, \ldots$ to be high; when u_i^2 is low, there is a tendency for u_{i+1}^2, $u_{i+2}^2, \ldots$ to be low. We can test how true this is by examining the autocorrelation structure of the u_i^2.

Let us assume the u_i^2 do exhibit autocorrelation. If a GARCH model is working well, it should remove the autocorrelation. We can test whether it has done so by considering the autocorrelation structure for the variables u_i^2 / σ_i^2. If these show very little autocorrelation, our model for σ_i has succeeded in explaining autocorrelations in the u_i^2.

Table 23.2 shows results for the S&P 500 data used above. The first column shows the lags considered when the autocorrelation is calculated. The second shows autocorrelations for u_i^2; the third shows autocorrelations for u_i^2 / σ_i^2.[13] The table shows that the autocorrelations are positive for u_i^2 for all lags between 1 and 15. In the case of u_i^2 / σ_i^2, some of the autocorrelations are positive and some are negative. They are all much smaller in magnitude than the autocorrelations for u_i^2.

Table 23.2   Autocorrelations before and after the use of a GARCH model for S&P 500 data.

Time lag	Autocorrelation for u_i^2	Autocorrelation for u_i^2 / σ_i^2
1	0.183	−0.063
2	0.385	−0.004
3	0.160	−0.007
4	0.301	0.022
5	0.339	0.014
6	0.308	−0.011
7	0.329	0.026
8	0.207	0.038
9	0.324	0.041
10	0.269	0.083
11	0.431	−0.007
12	0.286	0.006
13	0.224	0.001
14	0.121	0.017
15	0.222	−0.031

[13] For a series x_i, the autocorrelation with a lag of k is the coefficient of correlation between x_i and x_{i+k}.

The GARCH model appears to have done a good job in explaining the data. For a more scientific test, we can use what is known as the Ljung–Box statistic.[14] If a certain series has m observations the Ljung–Box statistic is

$$m \sum_{k=1}^{K} w_k \eta_k^2$$

where η_k is the autocorrelation for a lag of k, K is the number of lags considered, and

$$w_k = \frac{m+2}{m-k}$$

For $K = 15$, zero autocorrelation can be rejected with 95% confidence when the Ljung–Box statistic is greater than 25.

From Table 23.2, the Ljung–Box statistic for the u_i^2 series is about 1,566. This is strong evidence of autocorrelation. For the u_i^2/σ_i^2 series, the Ljung–Box statistic is 21.7, suggesting that the autocorrelation has been largely removed by the GARCH model.

23.6 USING GARCH(1,1) TO FORECAST FUTURE VOLATILITY

The variance rate estimated at the end of day $n-1$ for day n, when GARCH(1,1) is used, is

$$\sigma_n^2 = (1 - \alpha - \beta)V_L + \alpha u_{n-1}^2 + \beta \sigma_{n-1}^2$$

so that

$$\sigma_n^2 - V_L = \alpha(u_{n-1}^2 - V_L) + \beta(\sigma_{n-1}^2 - V_L)$$

On day $n+t$ in the future,

$$\sigma_{n+t}^2 - V_L = \alpha(u_{n+t-1}^2 - V_L) + \beta(\sigma_{n+t-1}^2 - V_L)$$

The expected value of u_{n+t-1}^2 is σ_{n+t-1}^2. Hence,

$$E[\sigma_{n+t}^2 - V_L] = (\alpha + \beta)E[\sigma_{n+t-1}^2 - V_L]$$

where E denotes expected value. Using this equation repeatedly yields

$$E[\sigma_{n+t}^2 - V_L] = (\alpha + \beta)^t (\sigma_n^2 - V_L)$$

or

$$E[\sigma_{n+t}^2] = V_L + (\alpha + \beta)^t (\sigma_n^2 - V_L) \tag{23.13}$$

This equation forecasts the volatility on day $n+t$ using the information available at the end of day $n-1$. In the EWMA model, $\alpha + \beta = 1$ and equation (23.13) shows that the expected future variance rate equals the current variance rate. When $\alpha + \beta < 1$, the final term in the equation becomes progressively smaller as t increases. Figure 23.3 shows the expected path followed by the variance rate for situations where the current variance rate is different from V_L. As mentioned earlier, the variance rate exhibits mean reversion with a reversion level of V_L and a reversion rate of $1 - \alpha - \beta$. Our forecast of the future

---

[14] See G. M. Ljung and G. E. P. Box, "On a Measure of Lack of Fit in Time Series Models," *Biometrica*, 65 (1978): 297–303.

Figure 23.3 Expected path for the variance rate when (a) current variance rate is above long-term variance rate and (b) current variance rate is below long-term variance rate.

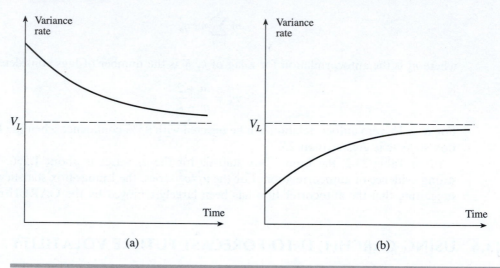

(a)   (b)

variance rate tends towards V_L as we look further and further ahead. This analysis emphasizes the point that we must have $\alpha + \beta < 1$ for a stable GARCH(1,1) process. When $\alpha + \beta > 1$, the weight given to the long-term average variance is negative and the process is "mean fleeing" rather than "mean reverting".

For the S&P 500 data considered earlier, $\alpha + \beta = 0.9935$ and $V_L = 0.0002075$. Suppose that the estimate of the current variance rate per day is 0.0003. (This corresponds to a volatility of 1.732% per day.) In 10 days, the expected variance rate is

$$0.0002075 + 0.9935^{10}(0.0003 - 0.0002075) = 0.0002942$$

The expected volatility per day is 1.72%, still well above the long-term volatility of 1.44% per day. However, the expected variance rate in 500 days is

$$0.0002075 + 0.9935^{500}(0.0003 - 0.0002075) = 0.0002110$$

and the expected volatility per day is 1.45%, very close to the long-term volatility.

Volatility Term Structures

Suppose it is day n. Define:

$$V(t) = E(\sigma_{n+t}^2)$$

and

$$a = \ln\frac{1}{\alpha + \beta}$$

so that equation (23.13) becomes

$$V(t) = V_L + e^{-at}[V(0) - V_L]$$

Here, $V(t)$ is an estimate of the instantaneous variance rate in t days. The average

Table 23.3 S&P 500 volatility term structure predicted from GARCH(1,1).

Option life (days)	10	30	50	100	500
Option volatility (% per annum)	27.36	27.10	26.87	26.35	24.32

variance rate per day between today and time T is given by

$$\frac{1}{T}\int_0^T V(t)\,dt = V_L + \frac{1-e^{-aT}}{aT}[V(0)-V_L]$$

The larger T is, the closer this is to V_L. Define $\sigma(T)$ as the volatility per annum that should be used to price a T-day option under GARCH(1,1). Assuming 252 days per year, $\sigma(T)^2$ is 252 times the average variance rate per day, so that

$$\sigma(T)^2 = 252\left(V_L + \frac{1-e^{-aT}}{aT}[V(0)-V_L]\right) \tag{23.14}$$

As discussed in Chapter 20, the market prices of different options on the same asset are often used to calculate a *volatility term structure*. This is the relationship between the implied volatilities of the options and their maturities. Equation (23.14) can be used to estimate a volatility term structure based on the GARCH(1,1) model. The estimated volatility term structure is not usually the same as the implied volatility term structure. However, as we will show, it is often used to predict the way that the implied volatility term structure will respond to volatility changes.

When the current volatility is above the long-term volatility, the GARCH(1,1) model estimates a downward-sloping volatility term structure. When the current volatility is below the long-term volatility, it estimates an upward-sloping volatility term structure. In the case of the S&P 500 data, $a = \ln(1/0.99351) = 0.006511$ and $V_L = 0.0002075$. Suppose that the current variance rate per day, $V(0)$, is estimated as 0.0003 per day. It follows from equation (23.14) that

$$\sigma(T)^2 = 252\left(0.0002075 + \frac{1-e^{-0.006511T}}{0.006511T}(0.0003 - 0.0002075)\right)$$

where T is measured in days. Table 23.3 shows the volatility per year for different values of T.

Impact of Volatility Changes

Equation (23.14) can be written

$$\sigma(T)^2 = 252\left[V_L + \frac{1-e^{-aT}}{aT}\left(\frac{\sigma(0)^2}{252} - V_L\right)\right]$$

When $\sigma(0)$ changes by $\Delta\sigma(0)$, $\sigma(T)$ changes by approximately

$$\frac{1-e^{-aT}}{aT}\frac{\sigma(0)}{\sigma(T)}\Delta\sigma(0) \tag{23.15}$$

Table 23.4   Impact of 1% change in the instantaneous volatility predicted
from GARCH(1,1).

Option life (days)	10	30	50	100	500
Increase in volatility (%)	0.97	0.92	0.87	0.77	0.33

Table 23.4 shows the effect of a volatility change on options of varying maturities for
the S&P 500 data considered above. We assume as before that $V(0) = 0.0003$, so that
$\sigma(0) = \sqrt{252} \times \sqrt{0.0003} = 27.50\%$. The table considers a 100-basis-point change in the
instantaneous volatility from 27.50% per year to 28.50% per year. This means that
$\Delta\sigma(0) = 0.01$, or 1%.

Many financial institutions use analyses such as this when determining the exposure
of their books to volatility changes. Rather than consider an across-the-board increase
of 1% in implied volatilities when calculating vega, they relate the size of the volatility
increase that is considered to the maturity of the option. Based on Table 23.4, a 0.97%
volatility increase would be considered for a 10-day option, a 0.92% increase for a
30-day option, a 0.87% increase for a 50-day option, and so on.

23.7 CORRELATIONS

The discussion so far has centered on the estimation and forecasting of volatility. As
explained in Chapter 22, correlations also play a key role in the calculation of VaR. In
this section, we show how correlation estimates can be updated in a similar way to
volatility estimates.

The correlation between two variables X and Y can be defined as

$$\frac{\mathrm{cov}(X, Y)}{\sigma_X \sigma_Y}$$

where σ_X and σ_Y are the standard deviations of X and Y and $\mathrm{cov}(X, Y)$ is the covariance
between X and Y. The covariance between X and Y is defined as

$$E[(X - \mu_X)(Y - \mu_Y)]$$

where μ_X and μ_Y are the means of X and Y, and E denotes the expected value.
Although it is easier to develop intuition about the meaning of a correlation than it
is for a covariance, it is covariances that are the fundamental variables of our analysis.[15]

Define x_i and y_i as the percentage changes in X and Y between the end of day $i - 1$
and the end of day i:

$$x_i = \frac{X_i - X_{i-1}}{X_{i-1}}, \qquad y_i = \frac{Y_i - Y_{i-1}}{Y_{i-1}}$$

where X_i and Y_i are the values of X and Y at the end of day i. We also define the

---

[15] An analogy here is that variance rates were the fundamental variables for the EWMA and GARCH
procedures in the first part of this chapter, even though volatilities are easier to understand.

following:

$\sigma_{x,n}$: Daily volatility of variable X, estimated for day n

$\sigma_{y,n}$: Daily volatility of variable Y, estimated for day n

cov_n: Estimate of covariance between daily changes in X and Y, calculated on day n.

The estimate of the correlation between X and Y on day n is

$$\frac{\text{cov}_n}{\sigma_{x,n}\,\sigma_{y,n}}$$

Using equal weighting and assuming that the means of x_i and y_i are zero, equation (23.3) shows that the variance rates of X and Y can be estimated from the most recent m observations as

$$\sigma_{x,n}^2 = \frac{1}{m}\sum_{i=1}^{m} x_{n-i}^2, \qquad \sigma_{y,n}^2 = \frac{1}{m}\sum_{i=1}^{m} y_{n-i}^2$$

A similar estimate for the covariance between X and Y is

$$\text{cov}_n = \frac{1}{m}\sum_{i=1}^{m} x_{n-i}\,y_{n-i} \tag{23.16}$$

One alternative for updating covariances is an EWMA model similar to equation (23.7). The formula for updating the covariance estimate is then

$$\text{cov}_n = \lambda\,\text{cov}_{n-1} + (1-\lambda)x_{n-1}\,y_{n-1}$$

A similar analysis to that presented for the EWMA volatility model shows that the weights given to observations on the $x_i\,y_i$ decline as we move back through time. The lower the value of λ, the greater the weight that is given to recent observations.

Example 23.3

Suppose that $\lambda = 0.95$ and that the estimate of the correlation between two variables X and Y on day $n-1$ is 0.6. Suppose further that the estimate of the volatilities for the X and Y on day $n-1$ are 1% and 2%, respectively. From the relationship between correlation and covariance, the estimate of the covariance between the X and Y on day $n-1$ is

$$0.6 \times 0.01 \times 0.02 = 0.00012$$

Suppose that the percentage changes in X and Y on day $n-1$ are 0.5% and 2.5%, respectively. The variance and covariance for day n would be updated as follows:

$$\sigma_{x,n}^2 = 0.95 \times 0.01^2 + 0.05 \times 0.005^2 = 0.00009625$$
$$\sigma_{y,n}^2 = 0.95 \times 0.02^2 + 0.05 \times 0.025^2 = 0.00041125$$
$$\text{cov}_n = 0.95 \times 0.00012 + 0.05 \times 0.005 \times 0.025 = 0.00012025$$

The new volatility of X is $\sqrt{0.00009625} = 0.981\%$ and the new volatility of Y is $\sqrt{0.00041125} = 2.028\%$. The new coefficient of correlation between X and Y is

$$\frac{0.00012025}{0.00981 \times 0.02028} = 0.6044$$

GARCH models can also be used for updating covariance estimates and forecasting the future level of covariances. For example, the GARCH(1,1) model for updating a covariance is

$$\text{cov}_n = \omega + \alpha x_{n-1} y_{n-1} + \beta \text{cov}_{n-1}$$

and the long-term average covariance is $\omega/(1 - \alpha - \beta)$. Formulas similar to those in equations (23.13) and (23.14) can be developed for forecasting future covariances and calculating the average covariance during the life of an option.[16]

Consistency Condition for Covariances

Once all the variances and covariances have been calculated, a variance–covariance matrix can be constructed. As explained in Section 22.4, when $i \neq j$, the (i, j)th element of this matrix shows the covariance between variable i and variable j. When $i = j$, it shows the variance of variable i.

Not all symmetric variance–covariance matrices are internally consistent. The condition for an $N \times N$ variance–covariance matrix Ω to be internally consistent is

$$\boldsymbol{w}^\mathsf{T} \Omega \boldsymbol{w} \geqslant 0 \tag{23.17}$$

for all $N \times 1$ vectors $\boldsymbol{w}$, where $\boldsymbol{w}^\mathsf{T}$ is the transpose of $\boldsymbol{w}$. A matrix that satisfies this property is known as *positive-semidefinite*.

To understand why the condition in equation (23.17) must hold, suppose that $\boldsymbol{w}^\mathsf{T}$ is $[w_1, w_2, \ldots, w_n]$. The expression $\boldsymbol{w}^\mathsf{T} \Omega \boldsymbol{w}$ is the variance of $w_1 x_1 + w_2 x_2 + \cdots + w_n x_n$, where x_i is the value of variable i. As such, it cannot be negative.

To ensure that a positive-semidefinite matrix is produced, variances and covariances should be calculated consistently. For example, if variances are calculated by giving equal weight to the last m data items, the same should be done for covariances. If variances are updated using an EWMA model with $\lambda = 0.94$, the same should be done for covariances.

An example of a variance–covariance matrix that is not internally consistent is

$$\begin{bmatrix} 1 & 0 & 0.9 \\ 0 & 1 & 0.9 \\ 0.9 & 0.9 & 1 \end{bmatrix}$$

The variance of each variable is 1.0, and so the covariances are also coefficients of correlation. The first variable is highly correlated with the third variable and the second variable is highly correlated with the third variable. However, there is no correlation at all between the first and second variables. This seems strange. When $\boldsymbol{w}$ is set equal to $(1, 1, -1)$, the condition in equation (23.17) is not satisfied, proving that the matrix is not positive-semidefinite.[17]

---

[16] The ideas in this chapter can be extended to multivariate GARCH models, where an entire variance–covariance matrix is updated in a consistent way. For a discussion of alternative approaches, see R. Engle and J. Mezrich, "GARCH for Groups," *Risk*, August 1996: 36–40.

[17] It can be shown that the condition for a 3×3 matrix of correlations to be internally consistent is

$$\rho_{12}^2 + \rho_{13}^2 + \rho_{23}^2 - 2\rho_{12}\rho_{13}\rho_{23} \leqslant 1$$

where ρ_{ij} is the coefficient of correlation between variables i and j.

23.8 APPLICATION OF EWMA TO FOUR-INDEX EXAMPLE

We now return to the example considered in Section 22.2. This involved a portfolio on September 25, 2008, consisting of a \$4 million investment in the Dow Jones Industrial Average, a \$3 million investment in the FTSE 100, a \$1 million investment in the CAC 40, and a \$2 million investment in the Nikkei 225. Daily returns were collected over 500 days ending on September 25, 2008. Data and all calculations presented here can be found at: www-2.rotman.utoronto.ca/~hull/OFOD/VaRExample.

The correlation matrix that would be calculated on September 25, 2008, by giving equal weight to the last 500 returns is shown in Table 23.5. The FTSE 100 and CAC 40 are very highly correlated. The Dow Jones Industrial Average is moderately highly correlated with both the FTSE 100 and the CAC 40. The correlation of the Nikkei 225 with other indices is less high.

The covariance matrix for the equal-weight case is shown in Table 23.6. From equation (22.4), this matrix gives the variance of the portfolio losses (\$000s) as 8,761.833. The standard deviation is the square root of this, or 93.60. The one-day 99% VaR in \$000s is therefore $2.326 \times 93.60 = 217.757$, or \$217,757, and the one-day 99% ES is \$249,476 from equation (22.1). This compares with a VaR of \$253,385 and an ES of \$327,181, calculated using the historical simulation approach in Section 22.2.

Instead of calculating variances and covariances by giving equal weight to all observed returns, we now use the exponentially weighted moving average method with $\lambda = 0.94$. This gives the variance–covariance matrix in Table 23.7.[18] From equation (22.4), the

Table 23.5 Correlation matrix on September 25, 2008, calculated by giving equal weight to the last 500 daily returns: variable 1 is DJIA; variable 2 is FTSE 100; variable 3 is CAC 40; variable 4 is Nikkei 225.

$$
\begin{bmatrix}
1 & 0.489 & 0.496 & -0.062 \\
0.489 & 1 & 0.918 & 0.201 \\
0.496 & 0.918 & 1 & 0.211 \\
-0.062 & 0.201 & 0.211 & 1
\end{bmatrix}
$$

Table 23.6 Covariance matrix on September 25, 2008, calculated by giving equal weight to the last 500 daily returns: variable 1 is DJIA; variable 2 is FTSE 100; variable 3 is CAC 40; variable 4 is Nikkei 225.

$$
\begin{bmatrix}
0.0001227 & 0.0000768 & 0.0000767 & -0.0000095 \\
0.0000768 & 0.0002010 & 0.0001817 & 0.0000394 \\
0.0000767 & 0.0001817 & 0.0001950 & 0.0000407 \\
-0.0000095 & 0.0000394 & 0.0000407 & 0.0001909
\end{bmatrix}
$$

[18] In the EWMA calculations, the variance was initially set equal to the population variance. This is an alternative to setting it equal to the first squared return as in Table 23.1. The two approaches give similar final variances, and the final variance is all we are interested in.

Table 23.7 Covariance matrix on September 25, 2008, calculated using the EWMA method with $\lambda = 0.94$: variable 1 is DJIA; variable 2 is FTSE 100; variable 3 is CAC 40; variable 4 is Nikkei 225.

$$\begin{bmatrix} 0.0004801 & 0.0004303 & 0.0004257 & -0.0000396 \\ 0.0004303 & 0.0010314 & 0.0009630 & 0.0002095 \\ 0.0004257 & 0.0009630 & 0.0009535 & 0.0001681 \\ -0.0000396 & 0.0002095 & 0.0001681 & 0.0002541 \end{bmatrix}$$

variance of portfolio losses ($000s) is 40,995.765. The standard deviation is the square root of this, or 202.474. The one-day 99% VaR is therefore

$$2.326 \times 202.474 = 471.025$$

This is $471,025, and the one-day ES is $539,637 from equation (22.1). These are over twice as high as the values given when returns are equally weighted. Tables 23.8 and 23.9 show the reasons. The standard deviation of a portfolio consisting of long positions in securities increases with the standard deviations of security returns and also with the correlations between security returns. Table 23.8 shows that the estimated daily standard deviations are much higher when EWMA is used than when data are equally weighted. This is because volatilities were much higher during the period immediately preceding September 25, 2008, than during the rest of the 500 days covered by the data. Comparing Table 23.9 with Table 23.5, we see that correlations had also increased.[19]

Table 23.8 Volatilities (% per day) using equal weighting and EWMA.

	DJIA	FTSE 100	CAC 40	Nikkei 225
Equal weighting:	1.11	1.42	1.40	1.38
EWMA:	2.19	3.21	3.09	1.59

Table 23.9 Correlation matrix on September 25, 2008, calculated using the EWMA method: variable 1 is DJIA; variable 2 is FTSE 100; variable 3 is CAC 40; variable 4 is Nikkei 225.

$$\begin{bmatrix} 1 & 0.611 & 0.629 & -0.113 \\ 0.611 & 1 & 0.971 & 0.409 \\ 0.629 & 0.971 & 1 & 0.342 \\ -0.113 & 0.409 & 0.342 & 1 \end{bmatrix}$$

[19] This is an example of the phenomenon that correlations tend to increase in adverse market conditions.

SUMMARY

Most popular option pricing models, such as Black–Scholes–Merton, assume that the volatility of the underlying asset is constant. This assumption is far from perfect. In practice, the volatility of an asset, like the asset's price, is a stochastic variable. Unlike the asset price, it is not directly observable. This chapter has discussed procedures for attempting to keep track of the current level of volatility.

We define u_i as the percentage change in a market variable between the end of day $i - 1$ and the end of day i. The variance rate of the market variable (that is, the square of its volatility) is calculated as a weighted average of the u_i^2. The key feature of the procedures that have been discussed here is that they do not give equal weight to the observations on the u_i^2. The more recent an observation, the greater the weight assigned to it. In the EWMA and the GARCH(1,1) models, the weights assigned to observations decrease exponentially as the observations become older. The GARCH(1,1) model differs from the EWMA model in that some weight is also assigned to the long-run average variance rate. It has a structure that enables forecasts of the future level of variance rate to be produced relatively easily.

Maximum likelihood methods are usually used to estimate parameters from historical data in the EWMA, GARCH(1,1), and similar models. These methods involve using an iterative procedure to determine the parameter values that maximize the chance or likelihood that the historical data will occur. Once its parameters have been determined, a GARCH(1,1) model can be judged by how well it removes autocorrelation from the u_i^2.

For every model that is developed to track variances, there is a corresponding model that can be developed to track covariances. The procedures described here can therefore be used to update the complete variance–covariance matrix used in value at risk calculations.

FURTHER READING

Bollerslev, T. "Generalized Autoregressive Conditional Heteroscedasticity," *Journal of Econometrics*, 31 (1986): 307–27.

Cumby, R., S. Figlewski, and J. Hasbrook. "Forecasting Volatilities and Correlations with EGARCH Models," *Journal of Derivatives*, 1, 2 (Winter 1993): 51–63.

Engle, R. F. "Autoregressive Conditional Heteroscedasticity with Estimates of the Variance of U.K. Inflation," *Econometrica* 50 (1982): 987–1008.

Engle R. F., and J. Mezrich. "Grappling with GARCH," *Risk*, September 1995: 112–117.

Engle, R. F., and J. Mezrich, "GARCH for Groups," *Risk*, August 1996: 36–40.

Engle, R. F., and V. Ng, "Measuring and Testing the Impact of News on Volatility," *Journal of Finance*, 48 (1993): 1749–78.

Noh, J., R. F. Engle, and A. Kane. "Forecasting Volatility and Option Prices of the S&P 500 Index," *Journal of Derivatives*, 2 (1994): 17–30.

Practice Questions (Answers in Solutions Manual)

23.1. Explain the exponentially weighted moving average (EWMA) model for estimating volatility from historical data.

23.2. What is the difference between the exponentially weighted moving average model and the GARCH(1,1) model for updating volatilities?

23.3. The most recent estimate of the daily volatility of an asset is 1.5% and the price of the asset at the close of trading yesterday was $30.00. The parameter λ in the EWMA model is 0.94. Suppose that the price of the asset at the close of trading today is $30.50. How will this cause the volatility to be updated by the EWMA model?

23.4. A company uses an EWMA model for forecasting volatility. It decides to change the parameter λ from 0.95 to 0.85. Explain the likely impact on the forecasts.

23.5. The volatility of a certain market variable is 30% per annum. Calculate a 99% confidence interval for the size of the percentage daily change in the variable.

23.6. A company uses the GARCH(1,1) model for updating volatility. The three parameters are ω, α, and β. Describe the impact of making a small increase in each of the parameters while keeping the others fixed.

23.7. The most recent estimate of the daily volatility of the U.S. dollar/sterling exchange rate is 0.6% and the exchange rate at 4 p.m. yesterday was 1.5000. The parameter λ in the EWMA model is 0.9. Suppose that the exchange rate at 4 p.m. today proves to be 1.4950. How would the estimate of the daily volatility be updated?

23.8. Assume that S&P 500 at close of trading yesterday was 1,040 and the daily volatility of the index was estimated as 1% per day at that time. The parameters in a GARCH(1,1) model are $\omega = 0.000002$, $\alpha = 0.06$, and $\beta = 0.92$. If the level of the index at close of trading today is 1,060, what is the new volatility estimate?

23.9. Suppose that the daily volatilities of asset A and asset B, calculated at the close of trading yesterday, are 1.6% and 2.5%, respectively. The prices of the assets at close of trading yesterday were $20 and $40 and the estimate of the coefficient of correlation between the returns on the two assets was 0.25. The parameter λ used in the EWMA model is 0.95.
   (a) Calculate the current estimate of the covariance between the assets.
   (b) On the assumption that the prices of the assets at close of trading today are $20.5 and $40.5, update the correlation estimate.

23.10. The parameters of a GARCH(1,1) model are estimated as $\omega = 0.000004$, $\alpha = 0.05$, and $\beta = 0.92$. What is the long-run average volatility and what is the equation describing the way that the variance rate reverts to its long-run average? If the current volatility is 20% per year, what is the expected volatility in 20 days?

23.11. Suppose that the current daily volatilities of asset X and asset Y are 1.0% and 1.2%, respectively. The prices of the assets at close of trading yesterday were $30 and $50 and the estimate of the coefficient of correlation between the returns on the two assets made at this time was 0.50. Correlations and volatilities are updated using a GARCH(1,1) model. The estimates of the model's parameters are $\alpha = 0.04$ and $\beta = 0.94$. For the correlation $\omega = 0.000001$, and for the volatilities $\omega = 0.000003$. If the prices of the two assets at close of trading today are $31 and $51, how is the correlation estimate updated?

23.12. Suppose that the daily volatility of the FTSE 100 stock index (measured in pounds sterling) is 1.8% and the daily volatility of the dollar/sterling exchange rate is 0.9%. Suppose further that the correlation between the FTSE 100 and the dollar/sterling exchange rate is 0.4. What is the volatility of the FTSE 100 when it is translated to U.S. dollars? Assume that the dollar/sterling exchange rate is expressed as the number of U.S. dollars per pound sterling. (*Hint*: When $Z = XY$, the percentage daily change in Z

is approximately equal to the percentage daily change in X plus the percentage daily change in Y.)

23.13. Suppose that in Problem 23.12 the correlation between the S&P 500 Index (measured in dollars) and the FTSE 100 Index (measured in sterling) is 0.7, the correlation between the S&P 500 Index (measured in dollars) and the dollar/sterling exchange rate is 0.3, and the daily volatility of the S&P 500 index is 1.6%. What is the correlation between the S&P 500 index (measured in dollars) and the FTSE 100 index when it is translated to dollars? (*Hint*: For three variables X, Y, and Z, the covariance between $X + Y$ and Z equals the covariance between X and Z plus the covariance between Y and Z.)

23.14. Show that the GARCH (1,1) model $\sigma_n^2 = \omega + \alpha u_{n-1}^2 + \beta \sigma_{n-1}^2$ in equation (23.9) is equivalent to the stochastic volatility model $dV = a(V_L - V)\,dt + \xi V\,dz$, where time is measured in days, V is the square of the volatility of the asset price, and

$$a = 1 - \alpha - \beta, \qquad V_L = \frac{\omega}{1 - \alpha - \beta}, \qquad \xi = \alpha\sqrt{2}$$

What is the stochastic volatility model when time is measured in years? (*Hint*: The variable u_{n-1} is the return on the asset price in time Δt. It can be assumed to be normally distributed with mean zero and standard deviation σ_{n-1}. It follows from the moments of the normal distribution that the mean and variance of u_{n-1}^2 are σ_{n-1}^2 and $2\sigma_{n-1}^4$, respectively.)

23.15. At the end of Section 23.8, the VaR and ES for the four-index example were calculated using the model-building approach. How do the VaR and ES estimates change if the investment is $2.5 million in each index? Carry out calculations when (a) volatilities and correlations are estimated using the equally weighted model and (b) when they are estimated using the EWMA model with $\lambda = 0.94$. Use the spreadsheets on the author's website.

23.16. What is the effect of changing λ from 0.94 to 0.97 in the EWMA calculations in the four-index example at the end of Section 23.8. Use the spreadsheets on the author's website.

Further Questions

23.17. Suppose that the price of gold at close of trading yesterday was $600 and its volatility was estimated as 1.3% per day. The price at the close of trading today is $596. Update the volatility estimate using
(a) The EWMA model with $\lambda = 0.94$
(b) The GARCH(1,1) model with $\omega = 0.000002$, $\alpha = 0.04$, and $\beta = 0.94$.

23.18. Suppose that in Problem 23.17 the price of silver at the close of trading yesterday was $16, its volatility was estimated as 1.5% per day, and its correlation with gold was estimated as 0.8. The price of silver at the close of trading today is unchanged at $16. Update the volatility of silver and the correlation between silver and gold using the two models in Problem 23.17. In practice, is the ω parameter likely to be the same for gold and silver?

23.19. An Excel spreadsheet containing over 900 days of daily data on a number of different exchange rates and stock indices can be downloaded from the author's website:

www-2.rotman.utoronto.ca/~hull/data.

Choose one exchange rate and one stock index. Estimate the value of λ in the EWMA model that minimizes the value of $\sum_i (v_i - \beta_i)^2$, where v_i is the variance forecast made at the end of day $i - 1$ and β_i is the variance calculated from data between day i and day $i + 25$. Use the Solver tool in Excel. Set the variance forecast at the end of the first day equal to the square of the return on that day to start the EWMA calculations.

23.20. Suppose that the parameters in a GARCH (1,1) model are $\alpha = 0.03$, $\beta = 0.95$, and $\omega = 0.000002$.
   (a) What is the long-run average volatility?
   (b) If the current volatility is 1.5% per day, what is your estimate of the volatility in 20, 40, and 60 days?
   (c) What volatility should be used to price 20-, 40-, and 60-day options?
   (d) Suppose that there is an event that increases the current volatility by 0.5% to 2% per day. Estimate the effect on the volatility in 20, 40, and 60 days.
   (e) Estimate by how much the event increases the volatilities used to price 20-, 40-, and 60-day options.

23.21. The calculations for the four-index example at the end of Section 23.8 assume that the investments in the DJIA, FTSE 100, CAC 40, and Nikkei 225 are $4 million, $3 million, $1 million, and $2 million, respectively. How do the VaR and ES estimates change if the investments are $3 million, $3 million, $1 million, and $3 million, respectively? Carry out calculations when (a) volatilities and correlations are estimated using the equally weighted model and (b) when they are estimated using the EWMA model. What is the effect of changing λ from 0.94 to 0.90 in the EWMA calculations? Use the spreadsheets on the author's website.

23.22. Estimate parameters for EWMA and GARCH(1, 1) from data on the euro–USD exchange rate between July 27, 2005, and July 27, 2010. This data can be found on the author's website:
                                www-2.rotman.utoronto.ca/~hull/data.

CHAPTER 24

Credit Risk

Most of the derivatives considered so far in this book have been concerned with market risk. In this chapter we consider another important risk for financial institutions: credit risk. Most financial institutions devote considerable resources to the measurement and management of credit risk. Regulators have for many years required banks to keep capital to reflect the credit risks they are bearing.

Credit risk arises from the possibility that borrowers and counterparties in derivatives transactions may default. This chapter discusses a number of different approaches to estimating the probability that a company will default and explains the key difference between risk-neutral and real-world probabilities of default. It examines the nature of the credit risk in over-the-counter derivatives transactions and discusses the clauses derivatives dealers write into their derivatives agreements to reduce credit risk. It also covers default correlation, Gaussian copula models, and the estimation of credit value at risk.

Chapter 25 will discuss credit derivatives and show how ideas introduced in this chapter can be used to value these instruments.

24.1 CREDIT RATINGS

Rating agencies, such as Moody's, S&P, and Fitch, are in the business of providing ratings describing the creditworthiness of corporate bonds. The best rating assigned by Moody's is Aaa. Bonds with this rating are considered to have almost no chance of defaulting. The next best rating is Aa. Following that comes A, Baa, Ba, B, Caa, Ca, and C. Only bonds with ratings of Baa or above are considered to be *investment grade*. The S&P and Fitch ratings corresponding to Moody's Aaa, Aa, A, Baa, Ba, B, Caa, Ca, and C are AAA, AA, A, BBB, BB, B, CCC, CC, and C, respectively. To create finer rating measures, Moody's divides its Aa rating category into Aa1, Aa2, and Aa3, its A category into A1, A2, and A3, and so on. Similarly, S&P and Fitch divide their AA rating category into AA+, AA, and AA−, their A rating category into A+, A, and A−, and so on. Moody's Aaa category and the S&P/Fitch AAA category are not subdivided, nor usually are the two lowest rating categories.

24.2 HISTORICAL DEFAULT PROBABILITIES

Table 24.1 is typical of the data produced by rating agencies. It shows the default experience during a 20-year period of bonds that had a particular rating at the beginning of the period. For example, a bond with a credit rating of Baa has a 0.185% chance of defaulting by the end of the first year, a 0.480% chance of defaulting by the end of the second year, and so on. The probability of a bond defaulting during a particular year can be calculated from the table. For example, the probability that a bond initially rated Baa will default during the second year is $0.480\% - 0.185\% = 0.295\%$.

Table 24.1 shows that, for investment-grade bonds, the probability of default in a year tends to be an increasing function of time (e.g., the probabilities of an A-rated bond defaulting during years 0–5, 5–10, 10–15, and 15–20 are 0.794%, 1.519%, 1.737%, and 2.037%, respectively). This is because the bond issuer is initially considered to be creditworthy, and the more time that elapses, the greater the possibility that its financial health will decline. For bonds with a poor credit rating, the probability of default is often a decreasing function of time (e.g., the probabilities that a B-rated bond will default during years 0–5, 5–10, 10–15, and 15–20 are 22.071%, 14.227%, 7.070%, and 4.703%, respectively). The reason here is that, for a bond with a poor credit rating, the next year or two may be critical. The longer the issuer survives, the greater the chance that its financial health improves.

Hazard Rates

From Table 24.1 we can calculate the probability of a bond rated Caa or below defaulting during the third year as $25.639\% - 18.857\% = 6.782\%$. We will refer to this as the *unconditional default probability*. It is the probability of default during the third year as seen today. The probability that the bond will survive until the end of year 2 is $100\% - 18.857\% = 81.143\%$. The probability that it will default during the third year conditional on no earlier default is therefore 0.06782/0.81143, or 8.36%.

The 8.36% we have just calculated is a conditional probability for a 1-year time period. Suppose instead that we consider a short time period of length Δt. The *hazard rate* $\lambda(t)$ at time t is defined so that $\lambda(t) \Delta t$ is the probability of default between time t and $t + \Delta t$ conditional on no earlier default.

If $V(t)$ is the cumulative probability of the company surviving to time t (i.e., no default by time t), the conditional probability of default between time t and $t + \Delta t$

Table 24.1 Average cumulative default rates (%), 1970–2015 (*Source*: Moody's).

Term (years):	1	2	3	4	5	7	10	15	20
Aaa	0.000	0.011	0.011	0.031	0.087	0.198	0.396	0.725	0.849
Aa	0.022	0.061	0.112	0.196	0.305	0.540	0.807	1.394	2.266
A	0.056	0.170	0.357	0.555	0.794	1.345	2.313	4.050	6.087
Baa	0.185	0.480	0.831	1.252	1.668	2.525	4.033	7.273	10.734
Ba	0.959	2.587	4.501	6.538	8.442	11.788	16.455	23.930	30.164
B	3.632	8.529	13.515	17.999	22.071	29.028	36.298	43.368	48.071
Caa–C	10.671	18.857	25.639	31.075	35.638	41.812	47.843	50.601	51.319

is $[V(t) - V(t + \Delta t)]/V(t)$. Since this equals $\lambda(t)\,\Delta t$, it follows that

$$V(t + \Delta t) - V(t) = -\lambda(t)V(t)\,\Delta t$$

Taking limits

$$\frac{dV(t)}{dt} = -\lambda(t)V(t)$$

from which

$$V(t) = e^{-\int_0^t \lambda(\tau)d\tau}$$

Defining $Q(t)$ as the probability of default by time t, so that $Q(t) = 1 - V(t)$, gives

$$Q(t) = 1 - e^{-\int_0^t \lambda(\tau)d\tau}$$

or

$$Q(t) = 1 - e^{-\bar{\lambda}(t)t} \tag{24.1}$$

where $\bar{\lambda}(t)$ is the average hazard rate between time 0 and time t. Another term used for the hazard rate is *default intensity*.

24.3 RECOVERY RATES

When a company goes bankrupt, those that are owed money by the company file claims against the assets of the company.[1] Sometimes there is a reorganization in which these creditors agree to a partial payment of their claims. In other cases the assets are sold by the liquidator and the proceeds are used to meet the claims as far as possible. Some claims typically have priority over other claims and are met more fully.

The recovery rate for a bond is normally defined as the bond's market value shortly after default, as a percent of its face value. Table 24.2 provides historical data on average recovery rates for different categories of bonds. The average recovery rate ranges from 53.4% for first lien bonds (which are both senior to other lenders and secured) to 24.2% for bonds that rank after all other lenders.

Table 24.2   Recovery rates on corporate bonds as a percentage of face value, 1983–2015 (*Source*: Moody's).

Class	Average recovery rate (%)
1st lien bond	53.4
2nd lien bond	49.7
Senior unsecured bond	37.6
Senior subordinated bond	31.1
Subordinated bond	31.9
Junior subordinated bond	24.2

---

[1] In the United States, the claim made by a bond holder is the bond's face value plus accrued interest.

The Dependence of Recovery Rates on Default Rates

In Chapter 8, we saw that one of the lessons from the credit crisis of 2007 is that the average recovery rate on mortgages is negatively related to the mortgage default rate. As the mortgage default rate increases, foreclosures lead to more houses being offered for sale and a decline in house prices. This in turn results in a decline in recovery rates.

The average recovery rate on corporate bonds exhibits a similar negative dependence on default rates.[2] In a year when the number of bonds defaulting is low, economic conditions are usually good and the average recovery rate on those bonds that do default might be as high as 60%; in a year when the default rate on corporate bonds is high, economic conditions are usually poor and the average recovery rate on the defaulting bonds might be as low as 30%. The result of the negative dependence is that a bad year for defaults is doubly bad for a lender because it is usually accompanied by a low recovery rate.

24.4 ESTIMATING DEFAULT PROBABILITIES FROM BOND YIELD SPREADS

Tables such as Table 24.1 provide one way of estimating default probabilities. Another approach is to look at bond yield spreads. A bond's yield spread is the excess of the promised yield on the bond over the risk-free rate. The usual assumption is that the excess yield is compensation for the possibility of default.[3]

Suppose that the bond yield spread for a T-year bond is $s(T)$ per annum. This means that the average loss rate on the bond between time 0 and time T should be approximately $s(T)$ per annum. Suppose that the average hazard rate during this time is $\bar{\lambda}(T)$. Another expression for the average loss rate is $\bar{\lambda}(T)(1 - R)$, where R is the estimated recovery rate. This means that it is approximately true that

$$\bar{\lambda}(T)(1 - R) = s(T)$$

or

$$\bar{\lambda}(T) = \frac{s(T)}{1 - R} \tag{24.2}$$

The approximation works very well in a wide range of situations.

Example 24.1

Suppose that 1-year, 2-year, and 3-year bonds issued by a corporation yield 150, 180, and 195 basis points more than the risk-free rate, respectively. If the recovery rate is estimated at 40%, the average hazard rate for year 1 given by equation (24.2) is $0.0150/(1 - 0.4) = 0.025$ or 2.5% per annum. Similarly, the average hazard rate for years 1 and 2 is $0.0180/(1 - 0.4) = 0.030$ or 3.0% per annum, and the average hazard rate for all three years is $0.0195/(1 - 0.4) = 0.0325$ or 3.25%. These results imply that the average hazard rate for the second year is

---

[2] See E. I. Altman, B. Brady, A. Resti, and A. Sironi, "The Link between Default and Recovery Rates: Theory, Empirical Evidence, and Implications," *Journal of Business*, 78, 6 (2005): 2203–28.

[3] This assumption is not perfect, as we discuss later. For example, the price of a corporate bond is affected by its liquidity. The lower the liquidity, the lower its price.

$2 \times 0.03 - 1 \times 0.025 = 0.035$ or 3.5% and that the average hazard rate for the third year is $3 \times 0.0325 - 2 \times 0.03 = 0.0375$ or 3.75%.

Matching Bond Prices

For a more precise calculation we can choose hazard rates so that they match bond prices. The approach is similar to the bootstrap method for calculating a zero-coupon yield curve described in Section 4.7. Suppose that bonds with maturities t_i are used, where $t_1 < t_2 < t_3 \cdots$. The shortest maturity bond is used to calculate the hazard rate out to time t_1. The next shortest maturity bond is used to calculate the hazard rate between times t_1 and t_2, and so on.

Example 24.2

Suppose that the risk-free rate is 5% per annum (continuously compounded) for all maturities and 1-year, 2-year, and 3-year bonds have yields of 6.5%, 6.8%, and 6.95%, respectively (also continuously compounded). (This is consistent with the data in Example 24.1.) We suppose that each bond has a face value of $100 and provides semiannual coupons at the rate of 8% per year (with a coupon having just been paid). The values of the bonds can be calculated from their yields as $101.33, $101.99, and $102.47. If the bonds were risk-free the bond values (obtained by discounting cash flows at 5%) would be $102.83, $105.52, and $108.08, respectively. This means that the present value of expected default losses on the 1-year bond must be $102.83 − $101.33 = $1.50. Similarly, the present value of expected default losses on the 2-year and 3-year bonds must be $3.53 and $5.61. Suppose that the hazard rate in year i is λ_i ($1 \leqslant i \leqslant 3$) and the recovery rate is 40%.

  Consider the 1-year bond. The probability of a default in the first 6 months is $1 - e^{-0.5\lambda_1}$ and the probability of a default during the following 6 months is $e^{-0.5\lambda_1} - e^{-\lambda_1}$. We assume that defaults can happen only at the midpoints of these 6-month intervals. The possible default times are therefore in 3 months and 9 months. The (forward) risk-free value of the bond at the 3-month point is

$$4e^{-0.05 \times 0.25} + 104e^{-0.05 \times 0.75} = \$104.12$$

Given the definition of recovery rate in the previous section, if there is a default the bond will be worth $40. The present value of the loss if there is a default at the 3-month point is therefore

$$(104.12 - 40)e^{-0.05 \times 0.25} = \$63.33$$

The risk-free value of the bond at the 9-month point is $104e^{-0.05 \times 0.25} = \$102.71$. If there is a default, the bond will be worth $40. The present value of a loss if there is a default at the 9-month point is therefore

$$(102.71 - 40)e^{-0.05 \times 0.75} = \$60.40$$

The hazard rate λ_1 must therefore satisfy

$$(1 - e^{-0.5\lambda_1}) \times 63.33 + (e^{-0.5\lambda_1} - e^{-\lambda_1}) \times 60.40 = 1.50$$

The solution to this (e.g., by using Solver in Excel) is $\lambda_1 = 2.46\%$.

The 2-year bond is considered next. Its default probabilities at times 3 months and 9 months are known from the analysis of the 1-year bond. The hazard rate for the second year is calculated so that the present value of the expected loss on the bond is $3.53. The 3-year bond is treated similarly. The hazard rate for the second and third years prove to be 3.48% and 3.74%. (Note that the three estimated hazard rates are very similar to those calculated in Example 24.1 using equation (24.2).) A worksheet showing the calculations is on the author's website: www-2.rotman.utoronto.ca/~hull/ofod.

The Risk-Free Rate

The methods we have just presented for calculating default probabilities are critically dependent on the choice of a risk-free rate. The spreads in Example 24.1 are differences between bond yields and risk-free rates. The calculation of the expected losses from default implied by bond prices in Example 24.2 depends on calculating the prices of risk-free bonds. The benchmark risk-free rate used by bond traders is usually a Treasury rate. For example, a bond trader might quote the yield on a bond as being a spread of 250 basis points over Treasuries. However, as discussed in Section 4.3, Treasury rates are too low to be useful proxies for risk-free rates.

Credit default swap (CDS) spreads, which were briefly explained in Section 7.11 and will be discussed in more detail in Chapter 25, provide a credit spread estimate that does not depend on the risk-free rate. A number of researchers have attempted to imply risk-free rates by comparing bond yields to CDS spreads. The evidence is that the implied risk-free rate is, in normal market conditions, about 10 basis points below the corresponding LIBOR/swap rate, or close to the OIS rate.[4]

Asset Swap Spreads

In practice, the LIBOR/swap rate is often used as the risk-free benchmark when credit calculations are carried out. Asset swap spreads provide a useful direct estimate of the spread of bond yields over the LIBOR/swap curve.

To explain how asset swaps work, consider the situation where an asset swap spread for a particular bond is quoted as 150 basis points. There are three possible situations:

1. The bond sells for its par value of 100. The swap then involves one side (company A) paying the coupon on the bond and the other side (company B) paying LIBOR plus 150 basis points. Note that it is the promised coupons that are exchanged. The exchanges take place regardless of whether the bond defaults.

2. The bond sells below its par value, say, for 95. The swap is then structured so that, in addition to the coupons, company A pays $5 per $100 of notional principal at the outset. Company B pays LIBOR plus 150 basis points.

3. The underlying bond sells above par, say, for 108. The swap is then structured so that, in addition to LIBOR plus 150 basis points, company B makes a payment of $8 per $100 of principal at the outset. Company A pays the coupons.

The effect of all this is that the present value of the asset swap spread is the amount by

---

[4] See J. C. Hull, M. Predescu, and A. White, "The Relationship between Credit Default Swap Spreads, Bond Yields, and Credit Rating Announcements," *Journal of Banking and Finance*, 28 (November 2004): 2789–2811.

which the price of the corporate bond is exceeded by the price of a similar risk-free bond where the risk-free rate is assumed to be given by the LIBOR/swap curve (see Problem 24.20). This result is useful for calculations such as those in Example 24.2.

24.5 COMPARISON OF DEFAULT PROBABILITY ESTIMATES

The default probabilities estimated from historical data are usually much less than those derived from bond yield spreads. The difference between the two was particularly large during the credit crisis which started in mid-2007. This is because there was what is termed a "flight to quality" during the crisis, where all investors wanted to hold safe securities such as Treasury bonds. The prices of corporate bonds declined, thereby increasing their yields. The credit spread on these bonds increased and calculations such as the one in equation (24.2) gave very high hazard rate estimates.

Table 24.3 shows the difference between default probability estimates calculated from historical data and those implied from credit spreads. To avoid results being heavily influenced by the crisis period, it uses only pre-crisis data in calculating estimates from bond yield spreads.

The second column of Table 24.3 is based on the 7-year column of Table 24.1. (We use the 7-year column because the bonds we will look at later have a life of about 7 years.) To explain the calculations, note that equation (24.1) gives

$$\bar{\lambda}(7) = -\tfrac{1}{7}\ln[1 - Q(7)]$$

where $\bar{\lambda}(t)$ is the average hazard rate by time t and $Q(t)$ is the cumulative probability of default by time t taken from the data in Table 24.1, which shows default rates for companies with different credit ratings. For example, for an A-rated company, $Q(7)$ is 0.01441. The average 7-year hazard rate is therefore

$$\bar{\lambda}(7) = -\tfrac{1}{7}\ln(1 - 0.01345) = 0.00193$$

or 0.193%.

To calculate average hazard rates from bond yields in the third column of Table 24.3, we use equation (24.2) and bond yields published by Merrill Lynch. The results shown are averages between December 1996 and June 2007. The recovery rate is assumed to be 40%. The Merrill Lynch bonds have a life of about seven years. (This explains why we

Table 24.3 Seven-year average hazard rates (% per annum).

Rating	Historical hazard rate	Hazard rate from bonds	Ratio	Difference
Aaa	0.028	0.596	21.0	0.568
Aa	0.077	0.728	9.4	0.651
A	0.193	1.145	5.9	0.952
Baa	0.365	2.126	5.8	1.761
Ba	1.792	4.671	2.6	2.879
B	4.898	8.017	1.6	3.119
Caa and lower	7.736	18.395	2.4	10.659

Table 24.4 Expected excess return on bonds (basis points).

Rating	Bond yield spread over Treasuries	Spread of risk-free rate over Treasuries	Spread for historical defaults	Excess return
Aaa	78	42	2	34
Aa	86	42	5	39
A	111	42	12	57
Baa	169	42	22	105
Ba	322	42	108	172
B	523	42	294	187
Caa	1146	42	464	640

focused on the 7-year column in Table 24.1 when calculating historical default probabilities.) To calculate the bond yield spread, we assume, as discussed in the previous section, that the risk-free interest rate is the 7-year swap rate minus 10 basis points. For example, for A-rated bonds, the average Merrill Lynch yield was 5.995%. The average 7-year swap rate was 5.408%, so that the average risk-free rate was 5.308%. This gives the average 7-year hazard rate as

$$\frac{0.05995 - 0.05308}{1 - 0.4} = 0.01145$$

or 1.145%.

Table 24.3 shows that the ratio of the hazard rate backed out from bond prices to the hazard rate calculated from historical data is very high for investment-grade companies and tends to decline as a company's credit rating declines.[5] The difference between the two hazard rates tends to increase as the credit rating declines.

Table 24.4 provides another way of looking at these results. It shows the expected excess return over the risk-free rate (which is still assumed to be the 7-year swap rate minus 10 basis points) earned by investors in bonds with different credit rating. Consider again an A-rated bond. The average spread over 7-year Treasuries is 111 basis points. Of this, 42 basis points are accounted for by the average spread between 7-year Treasuries and our proxy for the risk-free rate. A spread of 12 basis points is necessary to cover expected defaults. (This equals the historical hazard rate from Table 24.3 multiplied by 0.6 to allow for recoveries.) This leaves an expected excess return (after expected defaults have been taken into account) of 57 basis points.[6]

Tables 24.3 and 24.4 show that a large percentage difference between hazard rate estimates translates into a small expected excess return on the bond. For Aaa-rated bonds, the ratio of the two hazard rates is 21.0, but the expected excess return is only 34 basis points. The expected excess return tends to increase as credit quality declines.

The expected excess return in Table 24.4 does not remain constant through time. Credit spreads, and therefore expected excess returns, were high in 2001, 2002, and the first half of 2003. After that they were fairly low until the credit crisis.

---

[5] The results in Tables 24.3 and 24.4 are updates of the results in J. C. Hull, M. Predescu, and A. White, "Bond Prices, Default Probabilities, and Risk Premiums," *Journal of Credit Risk*, 1, 2 (Spring 2005): 53–60.

[6] To keep calculations as intuitive as possible, no adjustments have been made for the impact of compounding frequency issues on spreads, returns, and hazard rates.

Real-World vs. Risk-Neutral Probabilities

The default probabilities or hazard rates implied from credit spreads are risk-neutral estimates. They can be used to calculate expected cash flows in a risk-neutral world when there is credit risk. The value of the cash flows is obtained using risk-neutral valuation by discounting the expected cash flows at a risk-free rate. Example 24.2 shows an application of this to the calculation of the cost of defaults. We will see more applications in the next chapter.

Default probabilities or hazard rates calculated from historical data are real-world (sometimes termed *physical*) default probabilities. Table 24.3 shows that risk-neutral default probabilities are much higher than real-world default probabilities. The expected excess return in Table 24.4 arises directly from the difference between real-world and risk-neutral default probabilities. If there were no expected excess return, then the real-world and risk-neutral default probabilities would be the same, and vice versa.

Why do we see such big differences between real-world and risk-neutral default probabilities? As we have just argued, this is the same as asking why corporate bond traders earn more than the risk-free rate on average.

One reason often advanced for the results is that corporate bonds are relatively illiquid and the returns on bonds are higher than they would otherwise be to compensate for this. This is true, but research shows that it does not fully explain the results in Table 24.4.[7] Another possible reason for the results is that the subjective default probabilities of bond traders may be much higher than the those given in Table 24.1. Bond traders may be allowing for depression scenarios much worse than anything seen during the period covered by historical data. However, it is difficult to see how this can explain a large part of the excess return that is observed.

By far the most important reason for the results in Tables 24.3 and 24.4 is that bonds do not default independently of each other. There are periods of time when default rates are very low and periods of time when they are very high. Evidence for this can be obtained by looking at the default rates in different years. Moody's statistics show that since 1970 the default rate per year for all rated companies has ranged from a low of 0.09% in 1979 to highs of 3.97% and 5.35% in 2001 and 2009, respectively. The year-to-year variation in default rates gives rise to systematic risk (i.e., risk that cannot be diversified away) and bond traders earn an excess expected return for bearing the risk. (This is similar to the excess expected return earned by equity holders that is calculated by the capital asset pricing model—see the appendix to Chapter 3.) The variation in default rates from year to year may be because of overall economic conditions and it may be because a default by one company has a ripple effect resulting in defaults by other companies. (The latter is referred to by researchers as *credit contagion*.)

In addition to the systematic risk we have just talked about, there is nonsystematic (or idiosyncratic) risk associated with each bond. If we were talking about stocks, we would argue that investors can to a large extent diversify away the nonsystematic risk by choosing a portfolio of, say, 30 stocks. They should not therefore demand a risk premium for bearing nonsystematic risk. For bonds, the arguments are not so clear-cut. Bond returns are highly skewed with limited upside. (For example, on an individual bond, there

---

[7] For example, J. Dick-Nielsen, P. Feldhütter, and D. Lando, "Corporate Bond Liquidity before and after the Onset of the Subprime Crisis," *Journal of Financial Economics*, 103, 3 (2012), 471–92, uses a number of different liquidity measures and a large database of bond trades. It shows that the liquidity component of credit spreads is relatively small.

might be a 99.75% chance of a 7% return in a year, and a 0.25% chance of a −60% return in the year, the first outcome corresponding to no default and the second to default.) This type of risk is difficult to "diversify away".[8] It would require tens of thousands of different bonds. In practice, many bond portfolios are far from fully diversified. As a result, bond traders may earn an extra return for bearing nonsystematic risk as well as for bearing the systematic risk mentioned in the previous paragraph.

Which Default Probability Estimate Should Be Used?

At this stage it is natural to ask whether we should use real-world or risk-neutral default probabilities in the analysis of credit risk. The answer depends on the purpose of the analysis. When valuing credit derivatives or estimating the impact of default risk on the pricing of instruments, risk-neutral default probabilities should be used. This is because the analysis calculates the present value of expected future cash flows and almost invariably (implicitly or explicitly) involves using risk-neutral valuation. When carrying out scenario analyses to calculate potential future losses from defaults, real-world default probabilities should be used.

24.6 USING EQUITY PRICES TO ESTIMATE DEFAULT PROBABILITIES

When we use a table such as Table 24.1 to estimate a company's real-world probability of default, we are relying on the company's credit rating. Unfortunately, credit ratings are revised relatively infrequently. This has led some analysts to argue that equity prices can provide more up-to-date information for estimating default probabilities.

In 1974, Merton proposed a model where a company's equity is an option on the assets of the company.[9] Suppose, for simplicity, that a firm has one zero-coupon bond outstanding and that the bond matures at time T. Define:

V_0: Value of company's assets today

V_T: Value of company's assets at time T

E_0: Value of company's equity today

E_T: Value of company's equity at time T

D: Debt repayment due at time T

σ_V: Volatility of assets (assumed constant)

σ_E: Instantaneous volatility of equity.

If $V_T < D$, it is (at least in theory) rational for the company to default on the debt at time T. The value of the equity is then zero. If $V_T > D$, the company should make the debt repayment at time T and the value of the equity at this time is $V_T - D$. Merton's model, therefore, gives the value of the firm's equity at time T as

$$E_T = \max(V_T - D, 0)$$

This shows that the equity is a call option on the value of the assets with a strike price

---

[8] See J. D. Amato and E. M. Remolona, "The Credit Spread Puzzle," *BIS Quarterly Review*, 5 (Dec. 2003): 51–63.

[9] See R. Merton "On the Pricing of Corporate Debt: The Risk Structure of Interest Rates," *Journal of Finance*, 29 (1974): 449–70.

equal to the repayment required on the debt. The Black–Scholes–Merton formula gives the value of the equity today as

$$E_0 = V_0 N(d_1) - De^{-rT} N(d_2) \qquad (24.3)$$

where

$$d_1 = \frac{\ln(V_0/D) + (r + \sigma_V^2/2)T}{\sigma_V \sqrt{T}} \quad \text{and} \quad d_2 = d_1 - \sigma_V \sqrt{T}$$

The value of the debt today is $V_0 - E_0$.

The risk-neutral probability that the company will default on the debt is $N(-d_2)$. To calculate this, we require V_0 and σ_V. Neither of these are directly observable. However, if the company is publicly traded, we can observe E_0. This means that equation (24.3) provides one condition that must be satisfied by V_0 and σ_V. We can also estimate σ_E from historical data or options. From Itô's lemma,

$$\sigma_E E_0 = \frac{\partial E}{\partial V} \sigma_V V_0 = N(d_1) \sigma_V V_0 \qquad (24.4)$$

This provides another equation that must be satisfied by V_0 and σ_V. Equations (24.3) and (24.4) provide a pair of simultaneous equations that can be solved for V_0 and σ_V.[10]

Example 24.3

The value of a company's equity is \$3 million and the volatility of the equity is 80%. The debt that will have to be paid in 1 year is \$10 million. The risk-free rate is 5% per annum. In this case $E_0 = 3$, $\sigma_E = 0.80$, $r = 0.05$, $T = 1$, and $D = 10$. Solving equations (24.3) and (24.4) as indicated in footnote 10 yields $V_0 = 12.40$ and $\sigma_V = 0.2123$. The parameter d_2 is 1.1408, so that the probability of default is $N(-d_2) = 0.127$, or 12.7%. The market value of the debt is $V_0 - E_0$, or 9.40. The present value of the promised payment on the debt is $10e^{-0.05 \times 1} = 9.51$. The expected loss on the debt is therefore $(9.51 - 9.40)/9.51$, or about 1.2% of its no-default value.

The basic Merton model we have just presented has been extended in a number of ways. For example, one version of the model assumes that a default occurs whenever the value of the assets falls below a barrier level. Another allows payments on debt instruments to be required at more than one time.

How well do the default probabilities produced by Merton's model and its extensions correspond to actual default experience? The answer is that Merton's model and its extensions produce a good ranking of default probabilities (risk-neutral or real-world). This means that a monotonic transformation can be used to convert the probability of default output from Merton's model into a good estimate of either the real-world or risk-neutral default probability.[11] It may seem strange to take a default probability $N(-d_2)$ that is in theory a risk-neutral default probability (because it is calculated from an option-pricing model) and use it to estimate a real-world default probability. Given

---

[10] To solve two nonlinear equations of the form $F(x, y) = 0$ and $G(x, y) = 0$, the Solver routine in Excel can be asked to find the values of x and y that minimize $[F(x, y)]^2 + [G(x, y)]^2$.

[11] Moody's KMV provides a service that transforms a default probability produced by Merton's model into a real-world default probability (which it refers to as an expected default frequency, or EDF). CreditGrades use Merton's model to estimate credit spreads, which are closely linked to risk-neutral default probabilities.

the nature of the calibration process we have just described, the underlying assumption is that the ranking of the risk-neutral default probabilities of different companies is the same as the ranking of their real-world default probabilities.

24.7 CREDIT RISK IN DERIVATIVES TRANSACTIONS

In this section we consider how credit risk is quantified for bilaterally cleared derivatives transactions. This topic was introduced in Chapter 9. Typically, bilaterally cleared derivatives between two companies are governed by an International Swaps and Derivatives Association (ISDA) Master Agreement. For transactions between financial institutions, it must state that initial margin and variation margin will be posted. Transactions are netted for the purpose of calculating claims in the event of default and for calculating variation margin, but not for calculating initial margin.

The Master Agreement defines the circumstances when an *event of default* occurs. For example, when one side fails to make payments on outstanding derivatives transactions as required or fails to post margin (i.e., collateral) as required or declares bankruptcy, there is an event of default. The other side then has the right to terminate all outstanding transactions. There are two circumstances when this is likely to lead to a loss for the nondefaulting party:

1. The total value of the transactions to the nondefaulting party is positive and greater than the collateral (if any) posted by the defaulting party. The nondefaulting party is then an unsecured creditor for the value of the transactions minus the value of the collateral.

2. The total value of the transactions is positive to the defaulting party and the collateral posted by the nondefaulting party is greater than this value. The nondefaulting party is then an unsecured creditor for the return of the excess collateral it has posted.

For the purposes of our discussion, we ignore the bid–offer spread costs incurred by the nondefaulting party when it replaces the transactions it had with the defaulting party.

CVA and DVA

CVA and DVA were introduced in Chapter 9. A bank's credit valuation adjustment (CVA) for a counterparty is the present value of the expected cost to the bank of a default by the counterparty. Its debit (or debt) valuation adjustment (DVA) is the present value of the expected cost to the counterparty of a default by the bank. The possibility of the bank defaulting is a benefit to the bank because it means that there is some possibility that the bank will not have to make payments as required on its derivatives. DVA, a cost to the counterparty, therefore increases the value of its derivatives portfolio to the bank.

The no-default value of outstanding transactions is their value assuming neither side will default. (Derivatives pricing models such as Black–Scholes–Merton provide no-default values.) If f_{nd} is the no-default value to the bank of its outstanding derivatives transactions with the counterparty, the value the outstanding transactions when possible defaults are taken into account is

$$f_{nd} - \text{CVA} + \text{DVA}$$

Suppose that the life of the longest outstanding derivative between the bank and the counterparty is T years. As explained in Chapter 9, the interval between time 0 and time T is divided into N subintervals and CVA and DVA are estimated as

$$\text{CVA} = \sum_{i=1}^{N} q_i v_i, \quad \text{DVA} = \sum_{i=1}^{N} q_i^* v_i^*$$

Here q_i is the risk-neutral probability of the counterparty defaulting during the ith interval, v_i is the present value of the expected loss to the bank if the counterparty defaults at the midpoint of the ith interval, q_i^* is the risk-neutral probability of the bank defaulting during the ith interval, and v_i^* is the present value of the expected loss to the counterparty (gain to the bank) if the bank defaults at the midpoint of the ith interval.

Consider first the calculation of q_i. Note that q_i should be a risk-neutral default probability because we are valuing future cash flows and (implicitly) using risk-neutral valuation (see Section 24.5). Suppose that t_i is the end point of the ith interval, so that q_i is the risk-neutral probability of a counterparty default between times t_{i-1} and t_i. We first estimate credit spreads for the counterparty for a number of different maturities. Using interpolation, we then obtain an estimate, $s(t_i)$, of the counterparty's credit spread for maturity t_i $(1 \leqslant i \leqslant N)$. From equation (24.2), an estimate of the counterparty's average hazard rate between times 0 and t_i is $s(t_i)/(1 - R)$, where R is the recovery rate expected in the event of a counterparty default. From equation (24.1), the probability that the counterparty will not default by time t_i is

$$\exp\left(-\frac{s(t_i)t_i}{1 - R}\right)$$

This means that

$$q_i = \exp\left(-\frac{s(t_{i-1})t_{i-1}}{1 - R}\right) - \exp\left(-\frac{s(t_i)t_i}{1 - R}\right)$$

is the probability of the counterparty defaulting during the ith interval. The probability q_i^* is similarly calculated from the bank's credit spreads.

Consider next the calculation of the v_i assuming that no collateral is posted. This usually requires a computationally very time consuming Monte Carlo simulation. The market variables determining the no-default value of the outstanding transactions between the bank and the counterparty are simulated in a risk-neutral world between time 0 and time T. On each simulation trial, the exposure of the bank to the counterparty at the midpoint of each interval is calculated. The exposure is equal to $\max(V, 0)$, where V is the total value of the transactions to the bank. (If the transactions in total have a negative value to the bank, there is no exposure; if they have a positive value, the exposure is equal to this positive value.) The variable v_i is set equal to the present value of the average exposure across all simulation trials multiplied by one minus the recovery rate. The variable v_i^* is calculated similarly from the counterparty's exposure to the bank.

When there is a collateral agreement between the bank and the counterparty, the calculation of v_i is more complicated. It is necessary to estimate on each simulation trial the amount of collateral held by each side at the midpoint of the ith interval in the event of a default. In this calculation, it is usually assumed that the counterparty stops posting collateral and stops returning any excess collateral held c days before a default. The parameter c, which is typically 10 or 20 days, is referred to as the *cure period* or *margin period of risk*. In order to know what collateral is held at the midpoint of an interval in the event of a default, it is necessary to calculate the value of transactions c days earlier. The way exposure is calculated is illustrated with the following example. The present value of the expected loss v_i is calculated from the average exposure across all simulation trials as in the no-collateral case. A similar analysis of the average exposure of the counterparty to the bank leads to v_i^*.

Example 24.4

There is a two-way zero-threshold collateral agreement between a bank and its (nonfinancial) counterparty. This means that each side is required to post collateral worth $\max(V, 0)$ with the other side, where V is the value of the outstanding transactions to the other side. The cure period is 20 days. Suppose that time τ is the midpoint of one of the intervals used in the bank's CVA calculation.

1. On a particular simulation trial, the value of outstanding transactions to the bank at time τ is 50 and their value 20 days earlier is 45. In this case, the calculation assumes that the bank has collateral worth 45 in the event of a default at time τ. The bank's exposure is the uncollateralized value it has in the derivatives transactions, or 5.

2. On a particular simulation trial the value of outstanding transactions to the bank at time τ is 50 and their value 20 days earlier is 55. In this case, it is assumed that the bank will have adequate collateral and its exposure is zero.

3. On a particular simulation trial the value of outstanding transactions to the bank at time τ is -50 and the value 20 days earlier is -45. In this case, the bank is assumed to have posted less than 50 of collateral in the event of a default at time τ and its exposure is zero.

4. On a particular simulation trial the value of outstanding transactions to the bank at time τ is -50 and the value 20 days earlier is -55. In this case, it is assumed that 55 of collateral is held by the counterparty 20 days before time τ and, in the event of a default at time τ, none of it is returned. The bank's exposure is therefore 5, the excess collateral it has posted.

In addition to calculating CVA, banks usually calculate peak exposure at the midpoint of each interval. This is a high percentile of the exposures given by the Monte Carlo simulation trials. For example, if the percentile is 97.5% and there are 10,000 Monte Carlo trials, the peak exposure at a particular midpoint is the 250th highest exposure at that point. The maximum peak exposure is the maximum of the peak exposures at all midpoints.[12]

Banks usually store all the paths sampled for all market variables and all the valuations calculated on each path. This enables the impact of a new transaction on CVA and DVA to be calculated relatively quickly. Only the value of the new transaction for each sample path needs to be calculated in order to determine its incremental effect on CVA and DVA. If the value of the new transaction is positively correlated to existing transactions, it is likely to increase CVA and DVA. If it is negatively correlated to existing transactions (e.g., because it is wholly or partially unwinding those transactions), it is likely to decrease CVA and DVA.

---

[12] There is a theoretical issue here (which is usually ignored). The peak exposure is a scenario analysis measure and should be calculated using real-world default estimates rather than risk-neutral estimates.

The method for calculating CVA that we have presented assumes that the probability of default by the counterparty is independent of the bank's exposure. This is a reasonable assumption in many situations. Traders use the term *wrong-way risk* to describe the situation where the probability of default is positively correlated with exposure and the term *right-way risk* to describe the situation where the probability of default is negatively correlated with exposure. More complicated models than those we describe have been developed to describe dependence between default probability and exposure.

A bank has one CVA and one DVA for each of its counterparties. The CVAs and DVAs can be regarded as derivatives which change in value as market variables change, counterparty credit spreads change, and bank credit spreads change. The risks in CVA (and occasionally DVA) are managed in the same way as the risks in other derivatives using Greek letter calculations, scenario analyses, etc.

Credit Risk Mitigation

There are a number of ways banks try to reduce credit risk in bilaterally cleared transactions. One, which we have already mentioned, is netting. Suppose a bank has three uncollateralized transactions with a counterparty worth +$10 million, +$30 million, and −$25 million. If they are regarded as independent transactions, the bank's exposure on the transactions is $10 million, $30 million, and $0 for a total exposure of $40 million. With netting, the transactions are regarded as a single transaction worth $15 million and the exposure is reduced from $40 million to $15 million.

Collateral agreements are an important way of reducing credit risk. Collateral can be either cash (which usually earns interest) or marketable securities. (The latter may be subject to a haircut to calculate their cash equivalent for collateral purposes.) Collateral agreements between financial institutions are now determined by regulation. Derivatives transactions receive favorable treatment in the event of a default. The nondefaulting party is entitled to keep any collateral posted by the other side. Expensive and time-consuming legal proceedings are not usually necessary.

Another credit risk mitigation technique used by financial institutions is known as a *downgrade trigger*. This is a clause in the Master Agreement between a bank and a nonfinancial counterparty stating that if the credit rating of the counterparty falls below a certain level, say BBB, the bank has the option to require collateral or close out all outstanding derivatives transactions at market value. Downgrade triggers do not provide protection against a relatively big jump in a counterparty's credit rating (e.g., from A to default). Moreover, they work well only if relatively little use is made of them. If the counterparty has many downgrade triggers with different derivatives dealers, they are likely to provide little protection to those dealers (see Business Snapshot 24.1).

Special Cases

In this section we consider two special cases where CVA can be calculated without Monte Carlo simulation.

The first special case is where the portfolio between the bank and the counterparty consists of a single uncollateralized derivative that provides a payoff to the bank at time T. (The bank could for instance have bought a European option with remaining life T from the counterparty.) The bank's exposure at a future time is the no-default value of the derivative at that time. The present value of the exposure is therefore the

---

Business Snapshot 24.1   Downgrade Triggers and AIG

AIG provides an example of the operation of downgrade triggers. By 2008, AIG had entered into many derivatives transactions where it guaranteed the performance of the AAA-rated tranches of ABS CDOs. (See Chapter 8 for a description of ABS CDOs.) Many of AIG's transactions had downgrade triggers stating that AIG did not have to post collateral provided its credit rating remained above AA. On September 15, 2008, it was downgraded below AA by Moody's, S&P, and Fitch. The tranches it had guaranteed were performing badly and it immediately received collateral calls from many counterparties. It was unable to meet the collateral calls and bankruptcy was avoided only by a massive government bailout.

---

present value of the derivative's future value. This is the no-default value of the derivative today. Hence

$$v_i = f_{nd}(1 - R)$$

for all i, where f_{nd} is the no-default value of the derivative today and R is the recovery rate. This implies

$$\text{CVA} = (1 - R)f_{nd}\sum_{i=1}^{N}q_i$$

In this case $\text{DVA} = 0$, so that the value f of the derivative today after allowing for credit risk is

$$f = f_{nd} - (1 - R)f_{nd}\sum_{i=1}^{N}q_i \tag{24.5}$$

One particular derivative of the type we are considering is a T-year zero-coupon bond issued by the counterparty. Assuming recoveries on the bond and the derivative are the same, the value of the bond, B, is

$$B = B_{nd} - (1 - R)B_{nd}\sum_{i=1}^{N}q_i \tag{24.6}$$

where B_{nd} is the no-default value of the bond. From equations (24.5) and (24.6),

$$\frac{f}{f_{nd}} = \frac{B}{B_{nd}}$$

If y is the yield on the T-year bond issued by the counterparty and y_{nd} is the yield on a similar riskless bond, $B = e^{-yT}$ and $B_{nd} = e^{-y_{nd}T}$, so that this equation gives

$$f = f_{nd}e^{-(y-y_{nd})T}$$

This shows that the derivative can be valued by increasing the discount rate that is applied to the expected payoff in a risk-neutral world by the counterparty's T-year credit spread.

Example 24.5

> The Black–Scholes–Merton price of a 2-year uncollateralized option is $3. Two-year zero-coupon bonds issued by the company selling the option have a yield 1.5% greater than the risk-free rate. The value of the option after default risk is considered is $3e^{-0.015 \times 2} = \$2.91$. (This assumes that the option stands alone and is not netted with other derivatives in the event of default.)

For the second special case, we consider a bank that has entered into an uncollateralized forward transaction with a counterparty where it has agreed to buy an asset for price K at time T. The bank has no other transactions with the counterparty. Define F_t as the forward price at time t for delivery of the asset at time T. The value of the transaction at time t is, from Section 5.7,

$$(F_t - K)e^{-r(T-t)}$$

where r is the risk-free interest rate (assumed constant).

The bank's exposure at time t is therefore

$$\max[(F_t - K)e^{-r(T-t)}, \ 0] = e^{-r(T-t)}\max[F_t - K, \ 0]$$

The expected value of F_t in a risk-neutral world is F_0. The standard deviation of $\ln F_t$ is $\sigma\sqrt{t}$, where σ is the volatility of F_t. From equation (15A.1) the expected exposure at time t is therefore

$$w(t) = e^{-r(T-t)}\big[F_0 N(d_1(t)) - KN(d_2(t))\big]$$

where

$$d_1(t) = \frac{\ln(F_0/K) + \sigma^2 t/2}{\sigma\sqrt{t}}, \qquad d_2(t) = d_1(t) - \sigma\sqrt{t}$$

It follows that

$$v_i = w(t_i)e^{-rt_i}(1 - R) = e^{-rT}(1 - R)\big[F_0 N(d_1(t_i)) - KN(d_2(t_i))\big]$$

Example 24.6

> A bank has entered into a forward contract to buy 1 million ounces of gold from a mining company in 2 years for $1,500 per ounce. The current 2-year forward price is $1,600 per ounce. We suppose that only two intervals each 1-year long are considered in the calculation of CVA. The probability of the company defaulting during the first year is 2% and the probability that it will default during the second year is 3%. The risk-free rate is 5% per annum. A 30% recovery in the event of default is anticipated. The volatility of the forward price of gold is 20%.
>
> In this case, $q_1 = 0.02$, $q_2 = 0.03$, $F_0 = 1,600$, $K = 1,500$, $\sigma = 0.2$, $r = 0.05$, $R = 0.3$, $t_1 = 0.5$, and $t_2 = 1.5$.
>
> $$d_1(t_1) = \frac{\ln(1600/1500) + 0.2^2 \times 0.5/2}{0.2\sqrt{0.5}} = 0.5271$$
>
> $$d_2(t_1) = d_1 - 0.2\sqrt{0.5} = 0.3856$$
>
> so that
>
> $$v_1 = e^{-0.05 \times 2.0} \times (1 - 0.3)[1600N(0.5271) - 1500N(0.3856)] = 92.67$$
>
> Similarly $v_2 = 130.65$.

The expected cost of defaults is

$$q_1 v_1 + q_2 v_2 = 0.02 \times 92.67 + 0.03 \times 130.65 = 5.77$$

The no-default value of the forward contract is $(1600 - 1500)e^{-0.05 \times 2} = 90.48$. When counterparty defaults are considered, the value drops to $90.48 - 5.77 = 84.71$. The calculation can be extended to allow the times when the mining company can default to be more frequent (see Problem 24.29). DVA, which increases the value of the derivative, can be calculated in a similar way to CVA (see Problem 24.30).

24.8   DEFAULT CORRELATION

The term *default correlation* is used to describe the tendency for two companies to default at about the same time. There are a number of reasons why default correlation exists. Companies in the same industry or the same geographic region tend to be affected similarly by external events and as a result may experience financial difficulties at the same time. Economic conditions generally cause average default rates to be higher in some years than in other years. A default by one company may cause a default by another—the credit contagion effect. Default correlation means that credit risk cannot be completely diversified away and is the major reason why risk-neutral default probabilities are greater than real-world default probabilities (see Section 24.5).

Default correlation is important in the determination of probability distributions for default losses from a portfolio of exposures to different counterparties.[13] Two types of default correlation models that have been suggested by researchers are referred to as *reduced form models* and *structural models*.

Reduced form models assume that the hazard rates for different companies follow stochastic processes and are correlated with macroeconomic variables. When the hazard rate for company A is high there is a tendency for the hazard rate for company B to be high. This induces a default correlation between the two companies.

Reduced form models are mathematically attractive and reflect the tendency for economic cycles to generate default correlations. Their main disadvantage is that the range of default correlations that can be achieved is limited. Even when there is a perfect correlation between the hazard rates of the two companies, the probability that they will both default during the same short period of time is usually very low. This is liable to be a problem in some circumstances. For example, when two companies operate in the same industry and the same country or when the financial health of one company is for some reason heavily dependent on the financial health of another company, a relatively high default correlation may be warranted. One approach to solving this problem is by extending the model so that the hazard rate exhibits large jumps.

Structural models are based on a model similar to Merton's model (see Section 24.6). A company defaults if the value of its assets is below a certain level. Default correlation between companies A and B is introduced into the model by assuming that the stochastic process followed by the assets of company A is correlated with the stochastic process followed by the assets of company B. Structural models have the advantage over

---

[13] A binomial correlation measure that has been used by rating agencies is described in Technical Note 26 at www-2.rotman.utoronto.ca/~hull/TechnicalNotes.

reduced form models that the correlation can be made as high as desired. Their main disadvantage is that they are liable to be computationally quite slow.

The Gaussian Copula Model for Time to Default

A model that has become a popular practical tool is the Gaussian copula model for the time to default. It can be shown to be similar to Merton's structural model. It assumes that all companies will default eventually and attempts to quantify the correlation between the probability distributions of the times to default for two or more different companies.

The model can be used in conjunction with either real-world or risk-neutral default probabilities. The left tail of the real-world probability distribution for the time to default of a company can be estimated from data produced by rating agencies such as that in Table 24.1. The left tail of the risk-neutral probability distribution of the time to default can be estimated from bond prices using the approach in Section 24.4.

Define t_1 as the time to default of company 1 and t_2 as the time to default of company 2. If the probability distributions of t_1 and t_2 were normal, we could assume that the joint probability distribution of t_1 and t_2 is bivariate normal. As it happens, the probability distribution of a company's time to default is not even approximately normal. This is where a Gaussian copula model comes in. We transform t_1 and t_2 into new variables x_1 and x_2 using

$$x_1 = N^{-1}[Q_1(t_1)], \qquad x_2 = N^{-1}[Q_2(t_2)]$$

where Q_1 and Q_2 are the cumulative probability distributions for t_1 and t_2, and N^{-1} is the inverse of the cumulative normal distribution ($u = N^{-1}(v)$ when $v = N(u)$). These are "percentile-to-percentile" transformations. The 5-percentile point in the probability distribution for t_1 is transformed to $x_1 = -1.645$, which is the 5-percentile point in the standard normal distribution; the 10-percentile point in the probability distribution for t_1 is transformed to $x_1 = -1.282$, which is the 10-percentile point in the standard normal distribution; and so on. The t_2-to-x_2 transformation is similar.

By construction, x_1 and x_2 have normal distributions with mean zero and unit standard deviation. The model assumes that the joint distribution of x_1 and x_2 is bivariate normal. This assumption is referred to as using a *Gaussian copula*. The assumption is convenient because it means that the joint probability distribution of t_1 and t_2 is fully defined by the cumulative default probability distributions Q_1 and Q_2 for t_1 and t_2, together with a single correlation parameter that defines the correlation between x_1 and x_2.

The attraction of the Gaussian copula model is that it can be extended to many companies. Suppose that we are considering n companies and that t_i is the time to default of the ith company. We transform each t_i into a new variable, x_i, that has a standard normal distribution. The transformation is the percentile-to-percentile transformation

$$x_i = N^{-1}[Q_i(t_i)]$$

where Q_i is the cumulative probability distribution for t_i. It is then assumed that the x_i are multivariate normal. The default correlation between t_i and t_j is measured as the correlation between x_i and x_j. This is referred to as the *copula correlation*.[14]

---

[14] As an approximation, the copula correlation between t_i and t_j is often assumed to be the correlation between the equity returns for companies i and j.

The Gaussian copula is a useful way of representing the correlation structure between variables that are not normally distributed. It allows the correlation structure of the variables to be estimated separately from their marginal (unconditional) distributions. Although the variables themselves are not multivariate normal, the approach assumes that after a transformation is applied to each variable they are multivariate normal.

Example 24.7

Suppose that we wish to simulate defaults during the next 5 years in 10 companies. The copula default correlations between each pair of companies is 0.2. For each company the cumulative probability of a default during the next 1, 2, 3, 4, 5 years is 1%, 3%, 6%, 10%, 15%, respectively. When a Gaussian copula is used we sample from a multivariate normal distribution to obtain the x_i ($1 \leqslant i \leqslant 10$) with the pairwise correlation between the x_i being 0.2. We then convert the x_i to t_i, a time to default. When the sample from the normal distribution is less than $N^{-1}(0.01) = -2.33$, a default takes place within the first year; when the sample is between -2.33 and $N^{-1}(0.03) = -1.88$, a default takes place during the second year; when the sample is between -1.88 and $N^{-1}(0.06) = -1.55$, a default takes place during the third year; when the sample is between -1.55 and $N^{-1}(0.10) = -1.28$, a default takes place during the fourth year; when the sample is between -1.28 and $N^{-1}(0.15) = -1.04$, a default takes place during the fifth year. When the sample is greater than -1.04, there is no default during the 5 years.

A Factor-Based Correlation Structure

To avoid defining a different correlation between x_i and x_j for each pair of companies i and j in the Gaussian copula model, a one-factor model is often used. The assumption is that

$$x_i = a_i F + \sqrt{1 - a_i^2}\, Z_i \tag{24.7}$$

In this equation, F is a common factor affecting defaults for all companies and Z_i is a factor affecting only company i. The variable F and the variables Z_i have independent standard normal distributions. The a_i are constant parameters between -1 and $+1$. The correlation between x_i and x_j is $a_i a_j$.[15]

Suppose that the probability that company i will default by a particular time T is $Q_i(T)$. Under the Gaussian copula model, a default happens by time T when $N(x_i) < Q_i(T)$ or $x_i < N^{-1}[Q_i(T)]$. From equation (24.7), this condition is

$$a_i F + \sqrt{1 - a_i^2}\, Z_i < N^{-1}[Q_i(T)]$$

or

$$Z_i < \frac{N^{-1}[Q_i(T)] - a_i F}{\sqrt{1 - a_i^2}}$$

Conditional on the value of the factor F, the probability of default is therefore

$$Q_i(T \mid F) = N\left(\frac{N^{-1}[Q_i(T)] - a_i F}{\sqrt{1 - a_i^2}}\right) \tag{24.8}$$

---

[15] The parameter a_i is sometimes approximated as the correlation of company i's equity returns with a well-diversified market index.

A particular case of the one-factor Gaussian copula model is where the probability distributions of default are the same for all i and the correlation between x_i and x_j is the same for all i and j. Suppose that $Q_i(T) = Q(T)$ for all i and that the common correlation is ρ, so that $a_i = \sqrt{\rho}$ for all i. Equation (24.8) becomes

$$Q(T \mid F) = N\left(\frac{N^{-1}[Q(T)] - \sqrt{\rho}\, F}{\sqrt{1-\rho}}\right) \tag{24.9}$$

24.9 CREDIT VaR

Credit value at risk can be defined analogously to the way value at risk is defined for market risks (see Chapter 22). For example, a credit VaR with a confidence level of 99.9% and a 1-year time horizon is the credit loss that we are 99.9% confident will not be exceeded over 1 year.

Consider a bank with a very large portfolio of similar loans. As an approximation, assume that the probability of default is the same for each loan and the correlation between each pair of loans is the same. When the Gaussian copula model for time to default is used, the right-hand side of equation (24.9) is to a good approximation equal to the percentage of defaults by time T as a function of F. The factor F has a standard normal distribution. We are $X\%$ certain that its value will be greater than $N^{-1}(1 - X) = -N^{-1}(X)$. We are therefore $X\%$ certain that the percentage of losses over T years on a large portfolio will be less than $V(X, T)$, where

$$V(X, T) = N\left(\frac{N^{-1}[Q(T)] + \sqrt{\rho}\, N^{-1}(X)}{\sqrt{1-\rho}}\right) \tag{24.10}$$

This result was first produced by Vasicek.[16] As in equation (24.9), $Q(T)$ is the probability of default by time T and ρ is the copula correlation between any pair of loans.

A rough estimate of the credit VaR when an $X\%$ confidence level is used and the time horizon is T is therefore $L(1 - R)V(X, T)$, where L is the size of the loan portfolio and R is the recovery rate. The contribution of a particular loan of size L_i to the credit VaR is $L_i(1 - R)V(X, T)$. This model underlies some of the formulas that regulators use for credit risk capital.[17]

Example 24.8

Suppose that a bank has a total of $100 million of retail exposures. The 1-year probability of default averages 2% and the recovery rate averages 60%. The copula correlation parameter is estimated as 0.1. In this case,

$$V(0.999, 1) = N\left(\frac{N^{-1}(0.02) + \sqrt{0.1}\, N^{-1}(0.999)}{\sqrt{1-0.1}}\right) = 0.128$$

showing that the 99.9% worst case default rate is 12.8%. The 1-year 99.9% credit VaR is therefore $100 \times 0.128 \times (1 - 0.6)$ or $5.13 million.

[16] See O. Vasicek, "Probability of Loss on a Loan Portfolio," Working Paper, KMV, 1987. Vasicek's results were published in *Risk* magazine in December 2002 under the title "Loan Portfolio Value".

[17] For further details, see J.C. Hull, *Risk Management and Financial Institutions*, 4th edn. Hoboken, NJ: Wiley, 2015.

CreditMetrics

Many banks have developed other procedures for calculating credit VaR. One popular approach is known as CreditMetrics. This involves estimating a probability distribution of credit losses by carrying out a Monte Carlo simulation of the credit rating changes of all counterparties. Suppose we are interested in determining the probability distribution of losses over a 1-year period. On each simulation trial, we sample to determine the credit rating changes and defaults of all counterparties during the year. We then revalue our outstanding contracts to determine the total of credit losses for the year. After a large number of simulation trials, a probability distribution for credit losses is obtained. This can be used to calculate credit VaR.

This approach is liable to be computationally quite time intensive. However, it has the advantage that credit losses are defined as those arising from credit downgrades as well as defaults (with credit upgrades being counted as negative losses). Also the impact of credit mitigation clauses such as those described in Section 24.7 can be approximately incorporated into the analysis.

Table 24.5 is typical of the historical data provided by rating agencies on credit rating changes and could be used as a basis for a CreditMetrics Monte Carlo simulation. It shows the percentage probability of a bond moving from one rating category to another during a 1-year period. For example, a bond that starts with an A credit rating has a 90.85% chance of still having an A rating at the end of 1 year. It has a 0.06% chance of defaulting during the year, a 0.12% chance of dropping to B, and so on.[18]

In sampling to determine credit losses, the credit rating changes for different counterparties should not be assumed to be independent. A Gaussian copula model is typically used to construct a joint probability distribution of rating changes similarly to the way it is used in the model in the previous section to describe the joint probability distribution of times to default. The copula correlation between the rating transitions

Table 24.5 One-year ratings transition matrix, 1970–2015, with probabilities expressed as percentages and transitions to the WR (without rating) category being allocated proportionally to other categories, calculated from Moody's data.

Initial rating	Rating at year-end								
	Aaa	Aa	A	Baa	Ba	B	Caa	Ca–C	Default
Aaa	90.85	8.45	0.61	0.06	0.02	0.00	0.00	0.00	0.00
Aa	0.88	89.62	8.89	0.46	0.07	0.04	0.02	0.00	0.02
A	0.06	2.70	90.85	5.63	0.54	0.12	0.05	0.01	0.06
Baa	0.04	0.17	4.53	90.19	3.95	0.73	0.17	0.02	0.19
Ba	0.01	0.05	0.51	6.73	83.02	7.82	0.74	0.14	1.00
B	0.01	0.04	0.17	0.50	5.35	82.24	7.26	0.63	3.82
Caa	0.00	0.01	0.03	0.13	0.49	8.19	77.93	3.28	9.95
Ca–C	0.00	0.00	0.07	0.00	0.82	3.23	12.41	51.90	31.58
Default	0.00	0.00	0.00	0.00	0.00	0.00	0.00	0.00	100.00

---

[18] Technical Note 11 at www-2.rotman.utoronto.ca/~hull/TechnicalNotes explains how a table such as Table 24.5 can be used to calculate transition matrices for periods other than 1 year.

for two companies is usually set equal to the correlation between their equity returns using a factor model similar to that in Section 24.8.

As an illustration of the CreditMetrics approach suppose that we are simulating the rating change of a Aaa and a Baa company over a 1-year period using the transition matrix in Table 24.5. Suppose that the correlation between the equities of the two companies is 0.2. On each simulation trial, we would sample two variables x_A and x_B from normal distributions so that their correlation is 0.2. The variable x_A determines the new rating of the Aaa company and variable x_B determines the new rating of the Baa company. Since $N^{-1}(0.9085) = 1.3316$, the Aaa company stays Aaa if $x_A < 1.3316$; since $N^{-1}(0.9085 + 0.0845) = 2.4573$, it becomes Aa if $1.3316 \leqslant x_A < 2.4593$; since $N^{-1}(0.9085 + 0.0845 + 0.0061) = 3.1214$, it becomes A if $2.4593 \leqslant x_A < 3.1214$; and so on. Consider next the Baa company. Since $N^{-1}(0.0004) = -3.3528$, the Baa company becomes Aaa if $x_B < -3.3528$; since $N^{-1}(0.0004 + 0.0017) = -2.8627$, it becomes Aa if $-3.3528 \leqslant x_B < -2.8627$; since $N^{-1}(0.0004 + 0.0017 + 0.0453) = -1.6706$, it becomes A if $-2.8627 \leqslant x_B < -1.6706$; and so on. The Aaa never defaults during the year. The Baa defaults when $x_B > N^{-1}(0.9981)$, that is, when $x_B > 2.8943$.

SUMMARY

The probability that a company will default during a particular period of time in the future can be estimated from historical data, bond prices, or equity prices. The default probabilities calculated from bond prices are risk-neutral probabilities; those calculated from historical data are real-world probabilities; equity prices can be used to estimate either real-world or risk-neutral probabilities. Real-world probabilities should be used for scenario analysis and the calculation of credit VaR. Risk-neutral probabilities should be used for valuing credit-sensitive instruments. Risk-neutral default probabilities are often significantly higher than real-world default probabilities.

The credit valuation adjustment (CVA) is the amount by which a bank reduces the value of a derivatives portfolio with a counterparty because of the possibility of the counterparty defaulting. The debt (or debit) valuation adjustment is the amount by which it increases the value of a portfolio because it might itself default. The calculation of CVA and DVA involves a time-consuming Monte Carlo simulation to determine the expected future exposures of the two sides of the portfolio.

Credit VaR can be defined similarly to the way VaR is defined for market risk. One approach to calculating it is the Gaussian copula model of time to default. This is used by regulators in the calculation of capital for credit risk. Another popular approach for calculating credit VaR is CreditMetrics. This uses a Gaussian copula model for credit rating changes.

FURTHER READING

Altman, E. I. "Measuring Corporate Bond Mortality and Performance," *Journal of Finance*, 44 (1989): 902–22.

Altman, E. I., B. Brady, A. Resti, and A. Sironi. "The Link Between Default and Recovery Rates: Theory, Empirical Evidence, and Implications," *Journal of Business*, 78, 6 (2005), 2203–28.

Duffie, D., and K. Singleton "Modeling Term Structures of Defaultable Bonds," *Review of Financial Studies*, 12 (1999): 687–720.

Finger, C. C. "A Comparison of Stochastic Default Rate Models," *RiskMetrics Journal*, 1 (November 2000): 49–73.

Gregory, J. *Counterparty Credit Risk and Credit Value Adjustment: A Continuing Challenge for Global Financial Markets*, 2nd edn. Chichester, U.K.: Wiley, 2012.

Hull, J. C., M. Predescu, and A. White. "Relationship between Credit Default Swap Spreads, Bond Yields, and Credit Rating Announcements," *Journal of Banking and Finance*, 28 (November 2004): 2789–2811.

Kealhofer, S. "Quantifying Credit Risk I: Default Prediction," *Financial Analysts Journal*, 59, 1 (2003a): 30–44.

Kealhofer, S. "Quantifying Credit Risk II: Debt Valuation," *Financial Analysts Journal*, 59, 3 (2003b): 78–92.

Li, D. X. "On Default Correlation: A Copula Approach," *Journal of Fixed Income*, March 2000: 43–54.

Merton, R. C. "On the Pricing of Corporate Debt: The Risk Structure of Interest Rates," *Journal of Finance*, 29 (1974): 449–70.

Vasicek, O. "Loan Portfolio Value," *Risk* (December 2002), 160–62.

Practice Questions (Answers in the Solutions Manual)

24.1. The spread between the yield on a 3-year corporate bond and the yield on a similar risk-free bond is 50 basis points. The recovery rate is 30%. Estimate the average hazard rate per year over the 3-year period.

24.2. Suppose that in Problem 24.1 the spread between the yield on a 5-year bond issued by the same company and the yield on a similar risk-free bond is 60 basis points. Assume the same recovery rate of 30%. Estimate the average hazard rate per year over the 5-year period. What do your results indicate about the average hazard rate in years 4 and 5?

24.3. Should researchers use real-world or risk-neutral default probabilities for (a) calculating credit value at risk and (b) adjusting the price of a derivative for defaults?

24.4. How are recovery rates usually defined?

24.5. Explain the difference between an unconditional default probability density and a hazard rate.

24.6. Verify (a) that the numbers in the second column of Table 24.3 are consistent with the numbers in Table 24.1 and (b) that the numbers in the fourth column of Table 24.4 are consistent with the numbers in Table 24.3 and a recovery rate of 40%.

24.7. Describe how netting works. A bank already has one transaction with a counterparty on its books. Explain why a new transaction by a bank with a counterparty can have the effect of increasing or reducing the bank's credit exposure to the counterparty.

24.8. "DVA can improve the bottom line when a bank is experiencing financial difficulties." Explain why this statement is true.

24.9. Explain the difference between the Gaussian copula model for the time to default and CreditMetrics as far as the following are concerned: (a) the definition of a credit loss and (b) the way in which default correlation is modeled.

24.10. Suppose that the LIBOR/swap curve is flat at 6% with continuous compounding and a 5-year bond with a coupon of 5% (paid semiannually) sells for 90.00. How would an asset swap on the bond be structured? What is the asset swap spread that would be calculated in this situation?

24.11. Show that the value of a coupon-bearing corporate bond is the sum of the values of its constituent zero-coupon bonds when the amount claimed in the event of default is the no-default value of the bond, but that this is not so when the claim amount is the face value of the bond plus accrued interest.

24.12. A 4-year corporate bond provides a coupon of 4% per year payable semiannually and has a yield of 5% expressed with continuous compounding. The risk-free yield curve is flat at 3% with continuous compounding. Assume that defaults can take place at the end of each year (immediately before a coupon or principal payment) and that the recovery rate is 30%. Estimate the risk-neutral default probability on the assumption that it is the same each year.

24.13. A company has issued 3- and 5-year bonds with a coupon of 4% per annum payable annually. The yields on the bonds (expressed with continuous compounding) are 4.5% and 4.75%, respectively. Risk-free rates are 3.5% with continuous compounding for all maturities. The recovery rate is 40%. Defaults can take place halfway through each year. The risk-neutral default rates per year are Q_1 for years 1 to 3 and Q_2 for years 4 and 5. Estimate Q_1 and Q_2.

24.14. Suppose that a financial institution has entered into a swap dependent on the sterling interest rate with counterparty X and an exactly offsetting swap with counterparty Y. Which of the following statements are true and which are false? Explain your answers.

   (a) The total present value of the cost of defaults is the sum of the present value of the cost of defaults on the contract with X plus the present value of the cost of defaults on the contract with Y.
   (b) The expected exposure in 1 year on both contracts is the sum of the expected exposure on the contract with X and the expected exposure on the contract with Y.
   (c) The 95% upper confidence limit for the exposure in 1 year on both contracts is the sum of the 95% upper confidence limit for the exposure in 1 year on the contract with X and the 95% upper confidence limit for the exposure in 1 year on the contract with Y.

24.15. "A long forward contract subject to credit risk is a combination of a short position in a no-default put and a long position in a call subject to credit risk." Explain this statement.

24.16. Why does the credit exposure on a matched pair of forward contracts resemble a straddle?

24.17. Explain why the impact of credit risk on a matched pair of interest rate swaps tends to be less than that on a matched pair of currency swaps.

24.18. "When a bank is negotiating currency swaps, it should try to ensure that it is receiving the lower interest rate currency from companies with low credit risk." Explain why.

24.19. Does put–call parity hold when there is default risk? Explain your answer.

24.20. Suppose that in an asset swap B is the market price of the bond per dollar of principal, B^* is the default-free value of the bond per dollar of principal, and V is the present value of the asset swap spread per dollar of principal. Show that $V = B^* - B$.

24.21. Show that under Merton's model in Section 24.6 the credit spread on a T-year zero-coupon bond is $-\ln[N(d_2) + N(-d_1)/L]/T$, where $L = De^{-rT}/V_0$.

24.22. Suppose that the spread between the yield on a 3-year zero-coupon riskless bond and a 3-year zero-coupon bond issued by a corporation is 1%. By how much does Black–Scholes–Merton overstate the value of a 3-year European option sold by the corporation.

24.23. Give an example of (a) right-way risk and (b) wrong-way risk.

Further Questions

24.24. The credit spreads for 1-, 2-, 3-, 4-, and 5-year zero-coupon bonds are 50, 60, 70, 80, and 87 basis points, respectively. The recovery rate is 35%. Estimate the average hazard rate each year.

24.25. The LIBOR/swap curve is flat at 3% with continuous compounding and a 4-year bond with a coupon of 4% per annum (paid semiannually) sells for 101. How would an asset swap on the bond be structured? What is the asset swap spread?

24.26. Suppose a 3-year corporate bond provides a coupon of 7% per year payable semiannually and has a yield of 5% (expressed with semiannual compounding). The yields for all maturities on risk-free bonds is 4% per annum (expressed with semiannual compounding). Assume that defaults can take place every 6 months (immediately before a coupon payment) and the recovery rate is 45%. Estimate the hazard rate (assumed constant) for the three years. Assume that the probability of default immediately before a coupon payment is the default probability given by the hazard rate for the previous six months.

24.27. A company has 1- and 2-year bonds outstanding, each providing a coupon of 8% per year payable annually. The yields on the bonds (expressed with continuous compounding) are 6.0% and 6.6%, respectively. Risk-free rates are 4.5% for all maturities. The recovery rate is 35%. Defaults can take place halfway through each year. Estimate the risk-neutral default probability each year.

24.28. Explain carefully the distinction between real-world and risk-neutral default probabilities. Which is higher? A bank enters into a credit derivative where it agrees to pay $100 at the end of 1 year if a certain company's credit rating falls from A to Baa or lower during the year. The 1-year risk-free rate is 5%. Using Table 24.5, estimate a value for the derivative. What assumptions are you making? Do they tend to overstate or understate the value of the derivative.

24.29. The value of a company's equity is $4 million and the volatility of its equity is 60%. The debt that will have to be repaid in 2 years is $15 million. The risk-free interest rate is 6% per annum. Use Merton's model to estimate the expected loss from default, the probability of default, and the recovery rate in the event of default. (*Hint*: The Solver function in Excel can be used for this question, as indicated in footnote 10.)

24.30. Suppose that a bank has a total of $10 million of exposures of a certain type. The 1-year probability of default averages 1% and the recovery rate averages 40%. The copula correlation parameter is 0.2. Estimate the 99.5% 1-year credit VaR.

24.31. Extend Example 24.6 to calculate CVA when default can happen in the middle of each month. Assume that the default probability per month during the first year is 0.001667 and the default probability per month during the second year is 0.0025.

24.32. Calculate DVA in Example 24.6. Assume that default can happen in the middle of each month. The default probability of the bank is 0.001 per month for the two years and the recovery rate in the event of a bank default is 40%.

CHAPTER 25

Credit Derivatives

An important development in derivatives markets since the late 1990s has been the growth of credit derivatives. In 2000, the total notional principal for outstanding credit derivatives contracts was about $800 billion. By the credit crisis of 2007, this had become $50 trillion. After the crisis, the size of the market declined. The total notional principal was about $12 trillion in December 2015. Credit derivatives are contracts where the payoff depends on the creditworthiness of one or more companies or countries. This chapter explains how credit derivatives work and how they are valued.

Credit derivatives allow companies to trade credit risks in much the same way that they trade market risks. Banks and other financial institutions used to be in the position where they could do little once they had assumed a credit risk except wait (and hope for the best). Now they can actively manage their portfolios of credit risks, keeping some and entering into credit derivative contracts to protect themselves from others (see Business Snapshot 25.1). Banks have historically been the biggest buyers of credit protection and insurance companies have been the biggest sellers.

Credit derivatives can be categorized as "single-name" or "multi-name." The most popular single-name credit derivative is a credit default swap. The payoff from this instrument depends on the creditworthiness of one company or country. There are two sides to the contract: the buyer and seller of protection. There is a payoff from the seller of protection to the buyer of protection if the specified entity (company or country) defaults on its obligations. One multi-name credit derivative is a collateralized debt obligation. In this, a portfolio of debt instruments is specified and a complex structure is created where the cash flows from the portfolio are channelled to different categories of investors. Chapter 8 describes how multi-name credit derivatives were created from residential mortgages during the period leading up to the credit crisis. This chapter focuses on the situation where the underlying credit risks are those of corporations or countries.

This chapter starts by explaining how credit default swaps work and how they are valued. It then explains credit indices and the way in which traders can use them to buy protection on a portfolio. After that it moves on to cover basket credit default swaps, asset-backed securities, and collateralized debt obligations. It expands on the material in Chapter 24 to show how the Gaussian copula model of default correlation can be used to value tranches of collateralized debt obligations.

569

> **Business Snapshot 25.1**   Who Bears the Credit Risk?
>
> Traditionally banks have been in the business of making loans and then bearing the credit risk that the borrower will default. However, banks have for some time been reluctant to keep loans on their balance sheets. This is because, after the capital required by regulators has been accounted for, the average return earned on loans is often less attractive than that on other assets. As discussed in Section 8.1, banks created asset-backed securities to pass loans (and their credit risk) on to investors. In the late 1990s and early 2000s, banks also made extensive use of credit derivatives to shift the credit risk in their loans to other parts of the financial system.
>
>   The result of all this is that the financial institution bearing the credit risk of a loan is often different from the financial institution that did the original credit checks. As the credit crisis starting in 2007 has shown, this is not always good for the overall health of the financial system.

25.1   CREDIT DEFAULT SWAPS

The most popular credit derivative is a *credit default swap* (CDS). This was introduced in Section 7.11. It is a contract that provides insurance against the risk of a default by particular company. The company is known as the *reference entity* and a default by the company is known as a *credit event*. The buyer of the insurance obtains the right to sell bonds issued by the company for their face value when a credit event occurs and the seller of the insurance agrees to buy the bonds for their face value when a credit event occurs.[1] The total face value of the bonds that can be sold is known as the credit default swap's *notional principal*.

   The buyer of the CDS makes periodic payments to the seller until the end of the life of the CDS or until a credit event occurs. In a standard contract, payments are made in arrears every quarter, but deals where payments are made every month, 6 months, or 12 months or where payments are made in advance occasionally also occur. The settlement in the event of a default usually involves a cash payment.

   An example will help to illustrate how a typical deal is structured. Suppose that two parties enter into a 5-year credit default swap on March 20, 2015. Assume that the notional principal is $100 million and the buyer agrees to pay 90 basis points per annum for protection against default by the reference entity, with payments being made quarterly in arrears.

   The CDS is shown in Figure 25.1. If the reference entity does not default (i.e., there is no credit event), the buyer receives no payoff and pays 22.5 basis points (a quarter of 90 basis points) on $100 million on June 20, 2015, and every quarter thereafter until March 20, 2020. The amount paid each quarter is $0.00225 \times 100,000,000$, or $225,000.[2] If there is a credit event, a substantial payoff is likely. Suppose that the buyer notifies the seller of a credit event on May 20, 2018 (2 months into the fourth year). If the contract

---

[1] The face value (or par value) of a coupon-bearing bond is the principal amount that the issuer repays at maturity if it does not default.

[2] The quarterly payments are liable to be slightly different from $225,000 because of the application of the day count conventions described in Chapter 6.

Figure 25.1 Credit default swap.

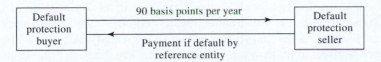

specifies physical settlement, the buyer has the right to sell bonds issued by the reference entity with a face value of $100 million for $100 million. If, as is now usual, there is cash settlement, an ISDA-organized auction process is used to determine the mid-market value of the cheapest deliverable bond several days after the credit event. Suppose the auction indicates that the bond is worth $35 per $100 of face value. The cash payoff would be $65 million.

The regular payments from the buyer of protection to the seller of protection cease when there is a credit event. However, because these payments are made in arrears, a final accrual payment by the buyer is usually required. In our example, where there is a default on May 20, 2018, the buyer would be required to pay to the seller the amount of the annual payment accrued between March 20, 2018, and May 20, 2018 (approximately $150,000), but no further payments would be required.

The total amount paid per year, as a percent of the notional principal, to buy protection (90 basis points in our example) is known as the *CDS spread*. Several large banks are market makers in the credit default swap market. When quoting on a new 5-year credit default swap on a company, a market maker might bid 250 basis points and offer 260 basis points. This means that the market maker is prepared to buy protection by paying 250 basis points per year (i.e., 2.5% of the principal per year) and to sell protection for 260 basis points per year (i.e., 2.6% of the principal per year).

Many different companies and countries are reference entities for the CDS contracts that trade. As mentioned, payments are usually made quarterly in arrears. Contracts with maturities of 5 years are most popular, but other maturities such as 1, 2, 3, 7, and 10 years are also sometimes used. Usually contracts mature on one of the following standard dates: March 20, June 20, September 20, and December 20. The effect of this is that the actual time to maturity of a contract when it is initiated is close to, but not necessarily the same as, the number of years to maturity that is specified. Suppose you call a dealer on November 15, 2015, to buy 5-year protection on a company. The contract would probably last until December 20, 2020. Your first payment would be due on December 20, 2015, and would equal an amount covering the November 15, 2015, to December 20, 2015, period.[3] A key aspect of a CDS contract is the definition of a credit event (i.e., a default). Usually a credit event is defined as a failure to make a payment as it becomes due, a restructuring of debt, or a bankruptcy. Restructuring is sometimes excluded in North American contracts, particularly in situations where the yield on the reference entity's debt is high. More information on the CDS market is given in Business Snapshot 25.2.

---

[3] If the time to the first standard date is less than 1 month, then the first payment is typically made on the second standard payment date; otherwise it is made on the first standard payment date.

Business Snapshot 25.2   The CDS Market

In 1998 and 1999, the International Swaps and Derivatives Association (ISDA) developed a standard contract for trading credit default swaps in the over-the-counter market. Since then the market has grown in popularity. A CDS contract is like an insurance contract in many ways, but there is one key difference. An insurance contract provides protection against losses on an asset that is owned by the protection buyer. In the case of a CDS, the underlying asset does not have to be owned.

During the credit turmoil of 2007 and 2008, regulators became very concerned about systemic risk (see Business Snapshot 1.2). They felt that credit default swaps were a source of vulnerability for financial markets. The danger is that a default by one financial institution might lead to big losses by its counterparties in CDS transactions and further defaults by other financial institutions. Regulatory concerns were fueled by troubles at insurance giant AIG. This was a big seller of protection on the AAA-rated tranches created from mortgages (see Business Snapshot 24.1). The protection proved very costly to AIG and the company was bailed out by the U.S. government.

During 2007 and 2008, trading ceased in many types of credit derivatives, but CDSs continued to trade actively (although the cost of protection increased dramatically). The advantage of CDSs over some other credit derivatives is that the way they work is straightforward. Other credit derivatives, such as those created from the securitization of household mortgages (see Chapter 8), lack this transparency.

It is not uncommon for the volume of CDSs on a company to be greater than its debt. Cash settlement of contracts is then clearly necessary. When Lehman defaulted in September 2008, there was about \$400 billion of CDS contracts and \$155 billion of Lehman debt outstanding. The cash payout to the buyers of protection (determined by an ISDA auction process) was 91.375% of principal.

There is one important difference between credit default swaps and the other over-the-counter derivatives that we have considered in this book. The other over-the-counter derivatives depend on interest rates, exchange rates, equity indices, commodity prices, and so on. There is no reason to assume that any one market participant has better information than any other market participant about these variables.

Credit default swaps spreads depend on the probability that a particular company will default during a particular period of time. Arguably some market participants have more information to estimate this probability than others. A financial institution that works closely with a particular company by providing advice, making loans, and handling new issues of securities is likely to have more information about the creditworthiness of the company than another financial institution that has no dealings with the company. Economists refer to this as an *asymmetric information* problem. Financial institutions emphasize that the decision to buy protection against the risk of default by a company is normally made by a risk manager and is not based on any special information that may exist elsewhere in the financial institution about the company.

Credit Default Swaps and Bond Yields

A CDS can be used to hedge a position in a corporate bond. Suppose that an investor buys a 5-year corporate bond yielding 7% per year for its face value and at the same time enters into a 5-year CDS to buy protection against the issuer of the bond defaulting. Suppose that the CDS spread is 200 basis points, or 2%, per annum. The effect of the CDS is to convert the corporate bond to a risk-free bond (at least approximately). If the bond issuer does not default, the investor earns 5% per year when the CDS spread is netted against the corporate bond yield. If the bond does default, the investor earns 5% up to the time of the default. Under the terms of the CDS, the investor is then able to exchange the bond for its face value. This face value can be invested at the risk-free rate for the remainder of the 5 years.

This shows that the spread of the yield on an n-year bond issued by a company over the risk-free rate should approximately equal the company's n-year CDS spread. If it is markedly more than this, an investor can earn more than the risk-free rate by buying the corporate bond and buying protection. If it is markedly less than this, an investor can borrow at less than the risk-free rate by shorting the bond and selling CDS protection.

The *CDS–bond basis* is defined as

$$\text{CDS–bond basis} = \text{CDS spread} - \text{Bond yield spread}$$

The bond yield spread is calculated using the LIBOR/swap rate as the risk-free rate. Usually the bond yield spread is set equal to the asset swap spread.

The arbitrage argument given above suggests that the CDS–bond basis should be close to zero. In fact it tends to be positive during some periods (e.g., pre-2007) and negative during other periods (e.g., the 2007–2009 credit crisis). The sign of the CDS–bond basis since the credit crisis has depended on the reference entity and has been sometimes positive and sometimes negative.

The Cheapest-to-Deliver Bond

As explained in Section 24.3, the recovery rate on a bond is defined as the value of the bond immediately after default as a percent of face value. This means that the payoff from a CDS is $L(1 - R)$, where L is the notional principal and R is the recovery rate.

Usually a CDS specifies that a number of different bonds can be delivered in the event of a default. The bonds typically have the same seniority, but they may not sell for the same percentage of face value immediately after a default.[4] This gives the holder of a CDS a cheapest-to-deliver bond option. As already mentioned, an auction process, organized by ISDA, is usually used to determine the value of the cheapest-to-deliver bond and, therefore, the payoff to the buyer of protection.

25.2 VALUATION OF CREDIT DEFAULT SWAPS

The CDS spread for a particular reference entity can be calculated from default probability estimates. We will illustrate how this is done for a 5-year CDS.

Suppose that the hazard rate of the reference entity is 2% per annum for the whole of the 5-year life of the CDS. Table 25.1 shows survival probabilities and unconditional probabilities of default. From equation (24.1), the probability of survival to time t

---

[4] There are a number of reasons for this. The claim that is made in the event of a default is typically equal to the bond's face value plus accrued interest. Bonds with high accrued interest at the time of default therefore tend to have higher prices immediately after default. Also the market may judge that in the event of a reorganization of the company some bond holders will fare better than others.

Table 25.1 Unconditional default probabilities
and survival probabilities.

Year	Probability of surviving to year end	Probability of default during year
1	0.9802	0.0198
2	0.9608	0.0194
3	0.9418	0.0190
4	0.9231	0.0186
5	0.9048	0.0183

is $e^{-0.02t}$. The probability of default during a year is the probability of survival to the beginning of the year minus the probability of survival to the end of the year. For example, the probability of survival to time 2 years is $e^{-0.02 \times 2} = 0.9608$ and the probability of survival to time 3 years is $e^{-0.02 \times 3} = 0.9418$. The probability of default during the third year is $0.9608 - 0.9418 = 0.0190$.

We will assume that defaults always happen halfway through a year and that payments on the credit default swap are made once a year, at the end of each year. We also assume that the risk-free interest rate is 5% per annum with continuous compounding and the recovery rate is 40%. There are three parts to the calculation. These are shown in Tables 25.2, 25.3, and 25.4.

Table 25.2 shows the calculation of the present value of the expected payments made on the CDS assuming that payments are made at the rate of s per year and the notional principal is $1. For example, there is a 0.9418 probability that the third payment of s is made. The expected payment is therefore $0.9418s$ and its present value is $0.9418se^{-0.05 \times 3} = 0.8106s$. The total present value of the expected payments is $4.0728s$.

Table 25.3 shows the calculation of the present value of the expected payoff assuming a notional principal of $1. As mentioned earlier, we are assuming that defaults always happen halfway through a year. For example, there is a 0.0190 probability of a payoff halfway through the third year. Given that the recovery rate is 40%, the expected payoff at this time is $0.0190 \times 0.6 \times 1 = 0.0114$. The present value of the expected payoff is $0.0114e^{-0.05 \times 2.5} = 0.0101$. The total present value of the expected payoffs is $0.0506.

Table 25.2 Calculation of the present value of expected payments.
Payment $= s$ per annum.

Time (years)	Probability of survival	Expected payment	Discount factor	PV of expected payment
1	0.9802	0.9802s	0.9512	0.9324s
2	0.9608	0.9608s	0.9048	0.8694s
3	0.9418	0.9418s	0.8607	0.8106s
4	0.9231	0.9231s	0.8187	0.7558s
5	0.9048	0.9048s	0.7788	0.7047s
Total				4.0728s

Table 25.3 Calculation of the present value of expected payoff.
   Notional principal = $1.

Time (years)	Probability of default	Recovery rate	Expected payoff ($)	Discount factor	PV of expected payoff ($)
0.5	0.0198	0.4	0.0119	0.9753	0.0116
1.5	0.0194	0.4	0.0116	0.9277	0.0108
2.5	0.0190	0.4	0.0114	0.8825	0.0101
3.5	0.0186	0.4	0.0112	0.8395	0.0094
4.5	0.0183	0.4	0.0110	0.7985	0.0088
Total					0.0506

As a final step, Table 25.4 considers the accrual payment made in the event of a default. For example, there is a 0.0190 probability that there will be a final accrual payment halfway through the third year. The accrual payment is $0.5s$. The expected accrual payment at this time is therefore $0.0190 \times 0.5s = 0.0095s$. Its present value is $0.0095se^{-0.05 \times 2.5} = 0.0084s$. The total present value of the expected accrual payments is $0.0422s$.

From Tables 25.2 and 25.4, the present value of the expected payments is

$$4.0728s + 0.0422s = 4.1150s$$

From Table 25.3, the present value of the expected payoff is 0.0506. Equating the two gives

$$4.1150s = 0.0506$$

or $s = 0.0123$. The mid-market CDS spread for the 5-year deal we have considered should be 0.0123 times the principal or 123 basis points per year. This result can also be produced using the DerivaGem CDS worksheet.

The calculations assume that defaults happen only at points midway between payment dates. This simple assumption usually gives good results, but can easily be relaxed so that more default times are considered.

Table 25.4 Calculation of the present value of accrual payment.

Time (years)	Probability of default	Expected accrual payment	Discount factor	PV of expected accrual payment
0.5	0.0198	0.0099s	0.9753	0.0097s
1.5	0.0194	0.0097s	0.9277	0.0090s
2.5	0.0190	0.0095s	0.8825	0.0084s
3.5	0.0186	0.0093s	0.8395	0.0078s
4.5	0.0183	0.0091s	0.7985	0.0073s
Total				0.0422s

Marking to Market a CDS

A CDS, like most other derivatives, is revalued (i.e., marked to market) daily. It may have a positive or negative value. Suppose, for example the credit default swap in our example had been negotiated some time ago for a spread of 150 basis points, the present value of the payments by the buyer would be $4.1150 \times 0.0150 = 0.0617$ and the present value of the payoff would be 0.0506 as above. The value of swap to the seller would therefore be $0.0617 - 0.0506$, or 0.0111 times the principal. Similarly the marked-to-market value of the swap to the buyer of protection would be -0.0111 times the principal.

Estimating Default Probabilities

The default probabilities used to value a CDS should be risk-neutral default probabilities, not real-world default probabilities (see Section 24.5 for the difference between the two). Risk-neutral default probabilities can be estimated from bond prices or asset swaps as explained in Chapter 24. An alternative is to imply them from CDS quotes. The latter approach is similar to the practice in options markets of implying volatilities from the prices of actively traded options and using them to value other options.

Suppose we change the example in Tables 25.2, 25.3, and 25.4 so that we do not know the default probabilities. Instead we know that the mid-market CDS spread for a newly issued 5-year CDS is 100 basis points per year. We can reverse-engineer our calculations (using Excel in conjunction with Solver) to conclude that the implied hazard rate is 1.63% per year.

The DerivaGem software can be used to calculate a term structure of hazard rates from a term structure of CDS spreads or vice versa.

Binary Credit Default Swaps

A binary credit default swap is structured similarly to a regular credit default swap except that the payoff is a fixed dollar amount. Suppose that, in the example we considered in Tables 25.1 to 25.4, the payoff is \$1 instead of $1 - R$ dollars and the swap spread is s. Tables 25.1, 25.2 and 25.4 are the same, but Table 25.3 is replaced by Table 25.5. The CDS spread for a new binary CDS is given by $4.1150s = 0.0844$, so that the CDS spread s is 0.0205, or 205 basis points.

Table 25.5 Calculation of the present value of expected payoff from a binary credit default swap. Principal $= \$1$.

Time (years)	Probability of default	Expected payoff (\$)	Discount factor	PV of expected payoff (\$)
0.5	0.0198	0.0198	0.9753	0.0193
1.5	0.0194	0.0194	0.9277	0.0180
2.5	0.0190	0.0190	0.8825	0.0168
3.5	0.0186	0.0186	0.8395	0.0157
4.5	0.0183	0.0183	0.7985	0.0146
Total				0.0844

How Important Is the Recovery Rate?

Whether we use CDS spreads or bond prices to estimate default probabilities we need an estimate of the recovery rate. However, provided that we use the same recovery rate for (a) estimating risk-neutral default probabilities and (b) valuing a CDS, the value of the CDS (or the estimate of the CDS spread) is not very sensitive to the recovery rate. This is because the implied probabilities of default approximately proportional to $1/(1 - R)$ and the payoffs from a CDS are proportional to $1 - R$.

This argument does not apply to the valuation of binary CDS. Implied probabilities of default are still approximately proportional to $1/(1 - R)$. However, for a binary CDS, the payoffs from the CDS are independent of R. If we have a CDS spread for both a plain vanilla CDS and a binary CDS, we can estimate both the recovery rate and the default probability (see Problem 25.25).

25.3 CREDIT INDICES

Participants in credit markets have developed indices to track credit default swap spreads. In 2004 there were agreements between different producers of indices that led to some consolidation. Two important standard portfolios used by index providers are:

1. CDX NA IG, a portfolio of 125 investment grade companies in North America
2. iTraxx Europe, a portfolio of 125 investment grade names in Europe

These portfolios are updated on March 20 and September 20 each year. Companies that are no longer investment grade are dropped from the portfolios and new investment grade companies are added.[5]

Suppose that the 5-year CDX NA IG index is quoted by a market maker as bid 65 basis points, offer 66 basis points per dollar of notional principal. (This is referred to as the index spread.) Roughly speaking, this means that a trader can buy CDS protection on all 125 companies in the index for 66 basis points per company. Suppose a trader wants $800,000 of protection on each company. The total cost is $0.0066 \times 800,000 \times 125$, or $660,000 per year. The trader can similarly sell $800,000 of protection on each of the 125 companies for a total of $650,000 per annum. When a company defaults, the protection buyer receives the usual CDS payoff and the annual payment is reduced by $660,000/125 = \$5,280$. The most common maturity for an index CDS is 5 years, but contracts also trade with maturities of 3, 7, and 10 years. The maturity dates for these types of contracts on the index are usually December 20 and June 20. (This means that a "5-year" contract actually lasts between $4\frac{3}{4}$ and $5\frac{1}{4}$ years.) Roughly speaking, the index is the average of the CDS spreads on the companies in the underlying portfolio.[6]

---

[5] On September 20, 2016, the Series 26 iTraxx Europe portfolio and the Series 27 CDX NA IG portfolio were defined. The series numbers indicate that, by the end of September 2016, the iTraxx Europe portfolio had been updated 25 times and the CDX NA IG portfolio had been updated 26 times.

[6] More precisely, the index is slightly lower than the average of the credit default swap spreads for the companies in the portfolio. To understand the reason for this consider a portfolio consisting of two companies, one with a spread of 1,000 basis points and the other with a spread of 10 basis points. To buy protection on the companies would cost slightly less than 505 basis points per company. This is because the 1,000 basis points is not expected to be paid for as long as the 10 basis points and should therefore carry less weight. Another complication for CDX NA IG, but not iTraxx Europe, is that the definition of default applicable to the index includes restructuring, whereas the definition for CDS contracts on the underlying companies may not.

25.4 THE USE OF FIXED COUPONS

The precise way in which CDS and CDS index transactions work is a little more complicated than has been described up to now. For each underlying and each maturity, a coupon and a recovery rate are specified. A price is calculated from the quoted spread using the following procedure:

1. Assume four payments per year, made in arrears.

2. Imply a hazard rate from the quoted spread. This involves calculations similar to those in Section 25.2. An iterative search is used to determine the hazard rate that leads to the quoted spread.

3. Calculate a "duration" D for the CDS payments. This is the number that the spread is multiplied by to get the present value of the spread payments. (In the example in Section 25.2, it is 4.1150.)[7]

4. The price P is given by $P = 100 - 100 \times D \times (s - c)$, where s is the spread and c is the coupon expressed in decimal form.

When a trader buys protection the trader pays $100 - P$ per $100 of the total remaining notional and the seller of protection receives this amount. (If $100 - P$ is negative, the buyer of protection receives money and the seller of protection pays money.) The buyer of protection then pays the coupon times the remaining notional on each payment date. (On a CDS, the remaining notional is the original notional until default and zero thereafter. For a CDS index, the remaining notional is the number of names in the index that have not yet defaulted multiplied by the principal per name.) The payoff when there is a default is calculated in the usual way. This arrangement facilitates trading because the instruments trade like bonds. The regular quarterly payments made by the buyer of protection are independent of the spread at the time the buyer enters into the contract.

Example 25.1

Suppose that the iTraxx Europe index quote is 34 basis points and the coupon is 40 basis points for a contract lasting exactly 5 years, with both quotes being expressed using an actual/360 day count. (This is the usual day count convention in CDS and CDS index markets.) The equivalent actual/actual quotes are 0.345% for the index and 0.406% for the coupon. Suppose that the yield curve is flat at 4% per year (actual/actual, continuously compounded). The specified recovery rate is 40%. With four payments per year in arrears, the implied hazard rate is 0.5717%. The duration is 4.447 years. The price is therefore

$$100 - 100 \times 4.447 \times (0.00345 - 0.00406) = 100.27$$

Consider a contract where protection is $1 million per name. Initially, the seller of protection would pay the buyer $1,000,000 \times 125 \times 0.0027$. Thereafter, the buyer of protection would make quarterly payments in arrears at an annual rate of $1,000,000 \times 0.00406 \times n$, where n is the number of companies that have not defaulted. When a company defaults, the payoff is calculated in the usual way and there is an accrual payment from the buyer to the seller calculated at the rate of 0.406% per year on $1 million.

---

[7] This use of the term "duration" is different from that in Chapter 4.

25.5 CDS FORWARDS AND OPTIONS

Once the CDS market was well established, it was natural for derivatives dealers to trade forwards and options on credit default swap spreads.[8]

A forward credit default swap is the obligation to buy or sell a particular credit default swap on a particular reference entity at a particular future time T. If the reference entity defaults before time T, the forward contract ceases to exist. Thus a bank could enter into a forward contract to sell 5-year protection on a company for 280 basis points starting in 1 year. If the company defaulted before the 1-year point, the forward contract would cease to exist.

A credit default swap option is an option to buy or sell a particular credit default swap on a particular reference entity at a particular future time T. For example, a trader could negotiate the right to buy 5-year protection on a company starting in 1 year for 280 basis points. This is a call option. If the 5-year CDS spread for the company in 1 year turns out to be more than 280 basis points, the option will be exercised; otherwise it will not be exercised. The cost of the option would be paid up front. Similarly an investor might negotiate the right to sell 5-year protection on a company for 280 basis points starting in 1 year. This is a put option. If the 5-year CDS spread for the company in 1 year turns out to be less than 280 basis points, the option will be exercised; otherwise it will not be exercised. Again the cost of the option would be paid up front. Like CDS forwards, CDS options are usually structured so that they cease to exist if the reference entity defaults before option maturity.

25.6 BASKET CREDIT DEFAULT SWAPS

In what is referred to as a *basket credit default swap* there are a number of reference entities. An *add-up basket* CDS provides a payoff when any of the reference entities default. A *first-to-default* CDS provides a payoff only when the first default occurs. A *second-to-default* CDS provides a payoff only when the second default occurs. More generally, a *kth-to-default* CDS provides a payoff only when the *k*th default occurs. Payoffs are calculated in the same way as for a regular CDS. After the relevant default has occurred, there is a settlement. The swap then terminates and there are no further payments by either party.

25.7 TOTAL RETURN SWAPS

A *total return swap* is a type of credit derivative. It is an agreement to exchange the total return on a bond (or any portfolio of assets) for LIBOR plus a spread. The total return includes coupons, interest, and the gain or loss on the asset over the life of the swap.

An example of a total return swap is a 5-year agreement with a notional principal of $100 million to exchange the total return on a corporate bond for LIBOR plus 25 basis points. This is illustrated in Figure 25.2. On coupon payment dates the payer pays the

---

[8] The valuation of these instruments is discussed in J. C. Hull and A. White, "The Valuation of Credit Default Swap Options," *Journal of Derivatives*, 10, 5 (Spring 2003): 40–50.

Figure 25.2   Total return swap.

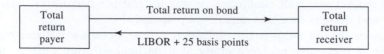

coupons earned on an investment of $100 million in the bond. The receiver pays interest at a rate of LIBOR plus 25 basis points on a principal of $100 million. (LIBOR is set on one coupon date and paid on the next as in a plain vanilla interest rate swap.) At the end of the life of the swap there is a payment reflecting the change in value of the bond. For example, if the bond increases in value by 10% over the life of the swap, the payer is required to pay $10 million (= 10% of $100 million) at the end of the 5 years. Similarly, if the bond decreases in value by 15%, the receiver is required to pay $15 million at the end of the 5 years. If there is a default on the bond, the swap is usually terminated and the receiver makes a final payment equal to the excess of $100 million over the market value of the bond.

If the notional principal is added to both sides at the end of the life of the swap, the total return swap can be characterized as follows. The payer pays the cash flows on an investment of $100 million in the corporate bond. The receiver pays the cash flows on a $100 million bond paying LIBOR plus 25 basis points. If the payer owns the corporate bond, the total return swap allows it to pass the credit risk on the bond to the receiver. If it does not own the bond, the total return swap allows it to take a short position in the bond.

Total return swaps are often used as a financing tool. One scenario that could lead to the swap in Figure 25.2 is as follows. The receiver wants financing to invest $100 million in the reference bond. It approaches the payer (which is likely to be a financial institution) and agrees to the swap. The payer then invests $100 million in the bond. This leaves the receiver in the same position as it would have been if it had borrowed money at LIBOR plus 25 basis points to buy the bond. The payer retains ownership of the bond for the life of the swap and faces less credit risk than it would have done if it had lent money to the receiver to finance the purchase of the bond, with the bond being used as collateral for the loan. If the receiver defaults the payer does not have the legal problem of trying to realize on the collateral. Total return swaps are similar to repos (see Section 4.1) in that they are structured to minimize credit risk when securities are being financed.

The spread over LIBOR received by the payer is compensation for bearing the risk that the receiver will default. The payer will lose money if the receiver defaults at a time when the reference bond's price has declined. The spread therefore depends on the credit quality of the receiver, the credit quality of the bond issuer, and the correlation between the two.

There are a number of variations on the standard deal we have described. Sometimes, instead of there being a cash payment for the change in value of the bond, there is physical settlement where the payer exchanges the underlying asset for the notional principal at the end of the life of the swap. Sometimes the change-in-value payments are made periodically rather than all at the end.

25.8 COLLATERALIZED DEBT OBLIGATIONS

We discussed asset-backed securities (ABSs) in Chapter 8. Figure 8.1 shows a simple structure. An ABS where the underlying assets are bonds is known as a *collateralized debt obligation*, or *CDO*. A waterfall similar to that indicated in Figure 8.2 is defined for the interest and principal payments on the bonds. The precise rules underlying the waterfall are complicated, but they are designed to ensure that, if one tranche is more senior than another, it is more likely to receive promised interest payments and repayments of principal.

Synthetic CDOs

When a CDO is created from a bond portfolio, as just described, the resulting structure is known as a *cash CDO*. In an important market development, it was recognized that a long position in a corporate bond has a similar risk to a short position in a CDS when the reference entity in the CDS is the company issuing the bond. This led to an alternative structure known as a *synthetic CDO*.

The originator of a synthetic CDO chooses a portfolio of companies and a maturity (e.g., 5 years) for the structure. It sells CDS protection on each company in the portfolio with the CDS maturities equaling the maturity of the structure. The synthetic CDO principal is the total of the notional principals underlying the CDSs. The originator has cash inflows equal to the CDS spreads and cash outflows when companies in the portfolio default. Tranches are formed and the cash inflows and outflows are distributed to tranches. The rules for determining the cash inflows and outflows of tranches are more straightforward for a synthetic CDO than for a cash CDO. Suppose that there are only three tranches: equity, mezzanine, and senior. The rules might be as follows:

1. The equity tranche is responsible for the payouts on the CDSs until they reach 5% of the synthetic CDO principal. It earns a spread of 1,000 basis points per year on the outstanding tranche principal.

2. The mezzanine tranche is responsible for payouts in excess of 5% up to a maximum of 20% of the synthetic CDO principal. It earns a spread of 100 basis points per year on the outstanding tranche principal.

3. The senior tranche is responsible for payouts in excess of 20%. It earns a spread of 10 basis points per year on the outstanding tranche principal.

To understand how the synthetic CDO would work, suppose that its principal is $100 million. The equity, mezzanine, and senior tranche principals are $5 million, $15 million, and $80 million, respectively. The tranches initially earn the specified spreads on these notional principals. Suppose that after 1 year defaults by companies in the portfolio lead to payouts of $2 million on the CDSs. The equity tranche holders are responsible for these payouts. The equity tranche principal reduces to $3 million and its spread (1,000 basis points) is then earned on $3 million instead of $5 million. If, later during the life of the CDO, there are further payouts of $4 million on the CDSs, the cumulative of the payments required by the equity tranche is $5 million, so that its outstanding principal becomes zero. The mezzanine tranche holders have to pay $1 million. This reduces their outstanding principal to $14 million.

Cash CDOs require an initial investment by the tranche holders (to finance the underlying bonds). By contrast, the holders of synthetic CDOs do not have to make an initial investment. They just have to agree to the way cash inflows and outflows will be calculated. In practice, they are almost invariably required to post the initial tranche principal as collateral. When the tranche becomes responsible for a payoff on a CDS, the money is taken out of the collateral. The balance in the collateral account usually earns interest at LIBOR.

Standard Portfolios and Single-Tranche Trading

In the synthetic CDO we have described, CDSs on individual companies were sold to create a portfolio of instruments equivalent to a portfolio of bonds. In a further market development, it was recognized that tranches can be traded without any underlying portfolio being created. An imaginary reference portfolio is used to define the cash flows on tranches. The buyer of protection pays the tranche spread to the seller of protection, and the seller of protection pays amounts to the buyer that correspond to those losses on the reference portfolio of CDSs that the tranche is responsible for. This is sometimes referred to as *single-tranche trading* because one tranche can be traded without there being any trading in other tranches.

In Section 25.3, we discussed CDS indices such as CDX NA IG and iTraxx Europe. The market has used the portfolios underlying these indices to define standard synthetic CDO tranches. These trade very actively. The six standard tranches of iTraxx Europe cover losses in the ranges 0–3%, 3–6%, 6–9%, 9–12%, 12–22%, and 22–100%. The six standard tranches of CDX NA IG cover losses in the ranges 0–3%, 3–7%, 7–10%, 10–15%, 15–30%, and 30–100%.

Table 25.6 shows the quotes for 5-year iTraxx tranches at the end of January of three successive years. The index spread is the cost in basis points of buying protection on all the companies in the index, as described in Section 25.3. The quotes for all tranches except the 0–3% tranche is the cost in basis point per year of buying tranche protection. (As explained earlier, this is paid on a principal that declines as the tranche experiences losses.) In the case of the 0–3% (equity) tranche, the protection buyer makes an initial payment and then pays 500 basis points per year on the outstanding tranche principal. The quote is for the initial payment as a percentage of the initial tranche principal.

What a difference two years makes in the credit markets! Table 25.6 shows that the credit crisis led to a huge increase in credit spreads. The iTraxx index rose from 23 basis

Table 25.6 Mid-market quotes, from the Creditex Group, for 5-year tranches of iTraxx Europe. Quotes are in basis points except for the 0–3% tranche where the quote equals the percent of the tranche principal that must be paid up front in addition to 500 basis points per year.

Date	Tranche					iTraxx index
	0–3%	3–6%	6–9%	9–12%	12–22%	
January 31, 2007	10.34%	41.59	11.95	5.60	2.00	23
January 31, 2008	30.98%	316.90	212.40	140.00	73.60	77
January 30, 2009	64.28%	1185.63	606.69	315.63	97.13	165

points in January 2007 to 165 basis points in January 2009. The individual tranche quotes have also shown huge increases. One reason for the changes is that the default probabilities assessed by the market for investment-grade corporations increased. However, it is also the case that protection sellers were in many cases experiencing liquidity problems. They became more averse to risk and increased the risk premiums they required.

25.9 ROLE OF CORRELATION IN A BASKET CDS AND CDO

The cost of protection in a kth-to-default CDS or a tranche of a CDO is critically dependent on default correlation. Suppose that a basket of 100 reference entities is used to define a 5-year kth-to-default CDS and that each reference entity has a risk-neutral probability of 2% of defaulting during the 5 years. When the default correlation between the reference entities is zero the binomial distribution shows that the probability of one or more defaults during the 5 years is 86.74% and the probability of 10 or more defaults is 0.0034%. A first-to-default CDS is therefore quite valuable whereas a tenth-to-default CDS is worth almost nothing.

As the default correlation increases the probability of one or more defaults declines and the probability of 10 or more defaults increases. In the limit where the default correlation between the reference entities is perfect the probability of one or more defaults equals the probability of ten or more defaults and is 2%. This is because in this extreme situation the reference entities are essentially the same. Either they all default (with probability 2%) or none of them default (with probability 98%).

The valuation of a tranche of a CDO is similarly dependent on default correlation. If the correlation is low, the junior equity tranche is very risky and the senior tranches are very safe. As the default correlation increases, the junior tranches become less risky and the senior tranches become more risky. In the limit where the default correlation is perfect and the recovery rate is zero, the tranches are equally risky.

25.10 VALUATION OF A SYNTHETIC CDO

Synthetic CDOs can be valued using the DerivaGem software. To explain the calculations, suppose that the payment dates on a synthetic CDO tranche are at times $\tau_1, \tau_2, \ldots, \tau_m$ and $\tau_0 = 0$. Define E_j as the expected tranche principal at time τ_j and $v(\tau)$ as the present value of \$1 received at time τ. Suppose that the spread on a particular tranche (i.e., the number of basis points paid for protection) is s per year. This spread is paid on the remaining tranche principal. The present value of the expected regular spread payments on the CDO is therefore given by sA, where

$$A = \sum_{j=1}^{m} (\tau_j - \tau_{j-1}) E_j v(\tau_j) \tag{25.1}$$

The expected loss between times τ_{j-1} and τ_j is $E_{j-1} - E_j$. Assume that the loss occurs at the midpoint of the time interval (i.e., at time $0.5\tau_{j-1} + 0.5\tau_j$). The present value of the expected payoffs on the CDO tranche is

$$C = \sum_{j=1}^{m}(E_{j-1} - E_j)v(0.5\tau_{j-1} + 0.5\tau_j) \tag{25.2}$$

The accrual payment due on the losses is given by sB, where

$$B = \sum_{j=1}^{m}0.5(\tau_j - \tau_{j-1})(E_{j-1} - E_j)v(0.5\tau_{j-1} + 0.5\tau_j) \tag{25.3}$$

The value of the tranche to the protection buyer is $C - sA - sB$. The breakeven spread on the tranche occurs when the present value of the payments equals the present value of the payoffs or

$$C = sA + sB$$

The breakeven spread is therefore

$$s = \frac{C}{A + B} \tag{25.4}$$

Equations (25.1) to (25.3) show the key role played by the expected tranche principal in calculating the breakeven spread for a tranche. If we know the expected principal for a tranche on all payment dates and we also know the zero-coupon yield curve, the breakeven tranche spread can be calculated from equation (25.4).

If there is an upfront payment and a fixed spread of s^* (as is the case in Table 25.6 for the 0–3% tranche where s^* is 500 basis points), the upfront payment as a percent of the principal is $C - s^*(A + B)$.

Using the Gaussian Copula Model of Time to Default

The one-factor Gaussian copula model of time to default was introduced in Section 24.8. This is the standard market model for valuing synthetic CDOs. All companies are assumed to have the same probability $Q(t)$ of defaulting by time t. Equation (24.9) converts this unconditional probability of default by time t to the probability of default by time t conditional on the factor F:

$$Q(t \mid F) = N\left(\frac{N^{-1}[Q(t)] - \sqrt{\rho}\,F}{\sqrt{1 - \rho}}\right) \tag{25.5}$$

Here ρ is the copula correlation, assumed to be the same for any pair of companies.

In the calculation of $Q(t)$, it is usually assumed that the hazard rate for a company is constant and consistent with the index spread. The hazard rate that is assumed can be calculated by using the CDS valuation approach in Section 25.2 and searching for the hazard rate that gives the index spread. Suppose that this hazard rate is λ. Then, from equation (24.1),

$$Q(t) = 1 - e^{-\lambda t} \tag{25.6}$$

From the properties of the binomial distribution, the standard market model gives the probability of exactly k defaults by time t, conditional on F, as

$$P(k, t \mid F) = \frac{n!}{(n - k)!\,k!}Q(t \mid F)^k[1 - Q(t \mid F)]^{n-k} \tag{25.7}$$

where n is the number of reference entities in the portfolio. Suppose that the tranche under consideration covers losses on the portfolio between α_L and α_H. The parameter α_L is known as the *attachment point* and the parameter α_H is known as the *detachment point*. Define

$$n_L = \frac{\alpha_L n}{1 - R} \quad \text{and} \quad n_H = \frac{\alpha_H n}{1 - R}$$

where R is the recovery rate. Also, define $m(x)$ as the smallest integer greater than x. Without loss of generality, we assume that the initial tranche principal is 1. The tranche principal stays 1 while the number of defaults, k, is less than $m(n_L)$. It is zero when the number of defaults is greater than or equal to $m(n_H)$. Otherwise, the tranche principal is

$$\frac{\alpha_H - k(1 - R)/n}{\alpha_H - \alpha_L}$$

Define $E_j(F)$ as the expected tranche principal at time τ_j conditional on the value of the factor F. It follows that

$$E_j(F) = \sum_{k=0}^{m(n_L)-1} P(k, \tau_j \mid F) + \sum_{k=m(n_L)}^{m(n_H)-1} P(k, \tau_j \mid F)\frac{\alpha_H - k(1 - R)/n}{\alpha_H - \alpha_L} \tag{25.8}$$

Define $A(F)$, $B(F)$, and $C(F)$ as the values of A, B, and C conditional on F. Similarly to equations (25.1) to (25.3),

$$A(F) = \sum_{j=1}^{m}(\tau_j - \tau_{j-1})E_j(F)v(\tau_j) \tag{25.9}$$

$$B(F) = \sum_{j=1}^{m} 0.5(\tau_j - \tau_{j-1})(E_{j-1}(F) - E_j(F))v(0.5\tau_{j-1} + 0.5\tau_j) \tag{25.10}$$

$$C(F) = \sum_{j=1}^{m}(E_{j-1}(F) - E_j(F))v(0.5\tau_{j-1} + 0.5\tau_j) \tag{25.11}$$

The variable F has a standard normal distribution. To calculate the unconditional values of A, B, and C, it is necessary to integrate $A(F)$, $B(F)$, and $C(F)$ over a standard normal distribution. Once the unconditional values have been calculated, the breakeven spread on the tranche can be calculated as $C/(A + B)$ or the upfront payment can be calculated as $C - s^*(A + B)$.

The integration is best accomplished with a procedure known as Gaussian quadrature. It involves the following approximation:

$$\int_{-\infty}^{\infty} \frac{1}{\sqrt{2\pi}} e^{-F^2/2}g(F)\,dF \approx \sum_{k=1}^{M} w_k g(F_k) \tag{25.12}$$

As M increases, accuracy increases. The values of w_k and F_k for different values of M are given on the author's website.[9] The value of M is twice the "number of integration

---

[9] The parameters w_k and F_k are calculated from the roots of Hermite polynomials. For more information on Gaussian quadrature, see Technical Note 21 at www-2.rotman.utoronto.ca/~hull/TechnicalNotes.

points" variable in DerivaGem. Setting the number of integration points equal to 20 usually gives good results.

Example 25.2

Consider the mezzanine tranche of iTraxx Europe (5-year maturity) when the copula correlation is 0.15 and the recovery rate is 40%. In this case, $\alpha_L = 0.03$, $\alpha_H = 0.06$, $n = 125$, $n_L = 6.25$, and $n_H = 12.5$. We suppose that the term structure of interest rates is flat at 3.5%, payments are made quarterly, and the CDS spread on the index is 50 basis points. A calculation similar to that in Section 25.2 shows that the constant hazard rate corresponding to the CDS spread is 0.83% (with continuous compounding). An extract from the remaining calculations is shown in Table 25.7. A value of $M = 60$ is used in equation (25.12). The factor values, F_k, and their weights, w_k, are shown in the first segment of the table. The expected

Table 25.7   Valuation of CDO in Example 25.2: principal $= 1$; payments are per unit of spread.

Weights and values for factors

w_k	$\cdots$	0.1579	0.1579	0.1342	0.0969	$\cdots$
F_k	$\cdots$	0.2020	-0.2020	-0.6060	-1.0104	$\cdots$

Expected principal, $E_j(F_k)$

Time					
$j = 1$	$\cdots$	1.0000	1.0000	1.0000	1.0000	$\cdots$
$\vdots$	$\vdots$	$\vdots$	$\vdots$	$\vdots$	$\vdots$	$\vdots$
$j = 19$	$\cdots$	0.9953	0.9687	0.8636	0.6134	$\cdots$
$j = 20$	$\cdots$	0.9936	0.9600	0.8364	0.5648	$\cdots$

PV expected payment, $A(F_k)$

$j = 1$	$\cdots$	0.2478	0.2478	0.2478	0.2478	$\cdots$
$\vdots$	$\vdots$	$\vdots$	$\vdots$	$\vdots$	$\vdots$	$\vdots$
$j = 19$	$\cdots$	0.2107	0.2051	0.1828	0.1299	$\cdots$
$j = 20$	$\cdots$	0.2085	0.2015	0.1755	0.1185	$\cdots$
Total	$\cdots$	4.5624	4.5345	4.4080	4.0361	$\cdots$

PV expected accrual payment, $B(F_k)$

$j = 1$	$\cdots$	0.0000	0.0000	0.0000	0.0000	$\cdots$
$\vdots$	$\vdots$	$\vdots$	$\vdots$	$\vdots$	$\vdots$	$\vdots$
$j = 19$	$\cdots$	0.0001	0.0008	0.0026	0.0051	$\cdots$
$j = 20$	$\cdots$	0.0002	0.0009	0.0029	0.0051	$\cdots$
Total	$\cdots$	0.0007	0.0043	0.0178	0.0478	$\cdots$

PV expected payoff, $C(F_k)$

$j = 1$	$\cdots$	0.0000	0.0000	0.0000	0.0000	$\cdots$
$\vdots$	$\vdots$	$\vdots$	$\vdots$	$\vdots$	$\vdots$	$\vdots$
$j = 19$	$\cdots$	0.0011	0.0062	0.0211	0.0412	$\cdots$
$j = 20$	$\cdots$	0.0014	0.0074	0.0230	0.0410	$\cdots$
Total	$\cdots$	0.0055	0.0346	0.1423	0.3823	$\cdots$

tranche principals on payment dates conditional on the factor values are calculated from equations (25.5) to (25.8) and shown in the second segment of the table. The values of A, B, and C conditional on the factor values are calculated in the last three segments of the table using equations (25.9) to (25.11). The unconditional values of A, B, and C are calculated by integrating $A(F)$, $B(F)$, and $C(F)$ over the probability distribution of F. This is done by setting $g(F)$ equal in turn to $A(F)$, $B(F)$, and $C(F)$ in equation (25.12). The result is

$$A = 4.2846, \quad B = 0.0187, \quad C = 0.1496$$

The breakeven tranche spread is $0.1496/(4.2846 + 0.0187) = 0.0348$, or 348 basis points.

This result can be obtained from DerivaGem. The CDS worksheet is used to convert the 50-basis-point spread to a hazard rate of 0.83%. The CDO worksheet is then used with this hazard rate and 30 integration points.

Valuation of kth-to-Default CDS

A kth-to-default CDS (see Section 25.6) can also be valued using the standard market model by conditioning on the factor F. The conditional probability that the kth default happens between times τ_{j-1} and τ_j is the conditional probability that there are k or more defaults by time τ_j minus the conditional probability that there are k or more defaults by time τ_{j-1}. This can be calculated from equations (25.5) to (25.7) as

$$\sum_{q=k}^{n} P(q, \tau_j \mid F) - \sum_{q=k}^{n} P(q, \tau_{j-1} \mid F)$$

Defaults between time τ_{j-1} and τ_j can be assumed to happen at time $0.5\tau_{j-1} + 0.5\tau_j$. This allows the present value of payments and of payoffs, conditional on F, to be calculated in the same way as for regular CDS payoffs (see Section 25.2). By integrating over F, the unconditional present values of payments and payoffs can be calculated.

Example 25.3

Consider a portfolio consisting of 10 bonds each with a hazard rate of 2% per annum. Suppose we are interested in valuing a third-to-default CDS where payments are made annually in arrears. Assume that the copula correlation is 0.3, the recovery rate is 40%, and all risk-free rates are 5%. As in Table 25.7, we consider $M = 60$ different factor values. The unconditional cumulative probability of each bond defaulting by years 1, 2, 3, 4, 5 is 0.0198, 0.0392, 0.0582, 0.0769, 0.0952, respectively. Equation (25.5) shows that, conditional on $F = -1.0104$, these default probabilities are 0.0361, 0.0746, 0.1122, 0.1484, 0.1830, respectively. From the binomial distribution, the conditional probability of three or more defaults by times 1, 2, 3, 4, 5 years is 0.0047, 0.0335, 0.0928, 0.1757, 0.2717, respectively. The conditional probability of the third default happening during years 1, 2, 3, 4, 5 is therefore 0.0047, 0.0289, 0.0593, 0.0829, 0.0960, respectively. An analysis similar to that in Section 25.2 shows that the present values of payoffs, regular payments, and accrual payments conditional on $F = -1.0104$ are 0.1379, $3.8443s$, and $0.1149s$, where s is the spread. Similar calculations are carried out for the other 59 factor values and equation (25.12) is used to integrate over F. The unconditional present values of payoffs, regular payments, and accrual payments are 0.0629, 4.0580s, and 0.0524s. The breakeven CDS spread is therefore $0.0629/(4.0580 + 0.0524) = 0.0153$, or 153 basis points.

Implied Correlation

In the standard market model, the recovery rate R is usually assumed to be 40%. This leaves the copula correlation ρ as the only unknown parameter. This makes the model similar to Black–Scholes–Merton, where there is only one unknown parameter, the volatility. Market participants like to imply a correlation from the market quotes for tranches in the same way that they imply a volatility from the market prices of options.

Suppose that the values of $\{\alpha_L, \alpha_H\}$ for successively more senior tranches are $\{\alpha_0, \alpha_1\}$, $\{\alpha_1, \alpha_2\}$, $\{\alpha_2, \alpha_3\}, \ldots$, with $\alpha_0 = 0$. (For example, in the case of iTraxx Europe, $\alpha_0 = 0$, $\alpha_1 = 0.03$, $\alpha_2 = 0.06$, $\alpha_3 = 0.09$, $\alpha_4 = 0.12$, $\alpha_5 = 0.22$, $\alpha_6 = 1.00$.) There are two alternative implied correlation measures. One is *compound correlation* or *tranche correlation*. For a tranche $\{\alpha_{q-1}, \alpha_q\}$, this is the value of the correlation, ρ, that leads to the spread calculated from the model being the same as the spread in the market. It is found using an iterative search. The other is *base correlation*. For a particular value of α_q ($q \geqslant 1$), this is the value of ρ that leads to the $\{0, \alpha_q\}$ tranche being priced consistently with the market. It is obtained using the following steps:

1. Calculate the compound correlation for each tranche.

2. Use the compound correlation to calculate the present value of the expected loss on each tranche during the life of the CDO as a percent of the initial tranche principal. This is the variable we have defined as C above. Suppose that the value of C for the $\{\alpha_{q-1}, \alpha_q\}$ tranche is C_q.

3. Calculate the present value of the expected loss on the $\{0, \alpha_q\}$ tranche as a percent of the total principal of the underlying portfolio. This is $\sum_{p=1}^{q} C_p(\alpha_p - \alpha_{p-1})$.

Figure 25.3   Vertical axis gives present value of expected loss on 0 to X% tranche as a percent of total underlying principal for iTraxx Europe on January 31, 2007.

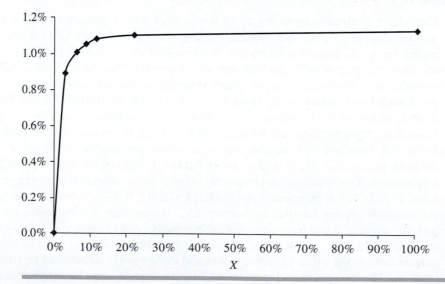

Table 25.8 Implied correlations for 5-year iTraxx Europe tranches on January 31, 2007.

Compound correlations

Tranche	0–3%	3–6%	6–9%	9–12%	12–22%
Implied correlation	17.7%	7.8%	14.0%	18.2%	23.3%

Base correlations

Tranche	0–3%	0–6%	0–9%	0–12%	0–22%
Implied correlation	17.7%	28.4%	36.5%	43.2%	60.5%

4. The C-value for the $\{0, \alpha_q\}$ tranche is the value calculated in Step 3 divided by α_q. The base correlation is the value of the correlation parameter, ρ, that is consistent with this C-value. It is found using an iterative search.

The present value of the loss as a percent of underlying portfolio that would be calculated in Step 3 for the iTraxx Europe quotes for January 31, 2007, given in Table 25.6 are shown in Figure 25.3. The implied correlations for these quotes are shown in Table 25.8. The calculations were carried out using DerivaGem assuming that the term structure of interest rates is flat at 3% and the recovery rate is 40%. The CDSs worksheet shows that the 23-basis-point spread implies a hazard rate of 0.382%. The implied correlations are calculated using the CDOs worksheet. The values underlying Figure 25.3 can also be calculated with this worksheet using the expression in Step 3 above.

The correlation patterns in Table 25.8 exhibit a "correlation smile". As the tranche becomes more senior, the implied correlation first decreases and then increases. The base correlations exhibit a correlation skew where the implied correlation is an increasing function of the tranche detachment point.

If market prices were consistent with the one-factor Gaussian copula model, then the implied correlations (both compound and base) would be the same for all tranches. From the pronounced smiles and skews that are observed in practice, we can infer that market prices are not consistent with this model.

Valuing Nonstandard Tranches

We do not need a model to value the standard tranches of a standard portfolio such as iTraxx Europe because the spreads for these tranches can be observed in the market. Sometimes quotes need to be produced for nonstandard tranches of a standard portfolio. Suppose that you need a quote for the 4–8% iTraxx Europe tranche. One approach is to interpolate base correlations so as to estimate the base correlation for the 0–4% tranche and the 0–8% tranche. These two base correlations allow the present value of expected loss (as a percent of the underlying portfolio principal) to be estimated for these tranches. The present value of the expected loss for the 4–8% tranche (as a percent of the underlying principal) can be estimated as the difference between the present value of expected losses for the 0–8% and 0–4% tranches. This can be used to imply a compound correlation and a breakeven spread for the tranche.

It is now recognized that this is not the best way to proceed. A better approach is to calculate expected losses for each of the standard tranches and produce a chart such as

Figure 25.3 showing the variation of expected loss for the $0-X\%$ tranche with X. Values on this chart can be interpolated to give the expected loss for the 0–4% and the 0–8% tranches. The difference between these expected losses is a better estimate of the expected loss on the 4–8% tranche than that obtained from the base correlation approach.

It can be shown that for no arbitrage the expected losses when calculated as in Figure 25.3 must increase with X at a decreasing rate. If base correlations are interpolated and then used to calculate expected losses, this no-arbitrage condition is often not satisfied. (The problem here is that the base correlation for the $0-X\%$ tranche is a nonlinear function of the expected loss on the $0-X\%$ tranche.) The direct approach of interpolating expected losses is therefore much better than the indirect approach of interpolating base correlations. What is more, it can be done so as to ensure that the no-arbitrage condition just mentioned is satisfied.

25.11 ALTERNATIVES TO THE STANDARD MARKET MODEL

This section outlines a number of alternatives to the one-factor Gaussian copula model that has become the market standard.

Heterogeneous Model

The standard market model is a homogeneous model in the sense that the time-to-default probability distributions are assumed to be the same for all companies and the copula correlations for any pair of companies are the same. The homogeneity assumption can be relaxed so that a more general model is used. However, this model is more complicated to implement because each company has a different probability of defaulting by any given time and $P(k, t \mid F)$ can no longer be calculated using the binomial formula in equation (25.7). It is necessary to use a numerical procedure such as that described in Andersen et al. (2003) and Hull and White (2004).[10]

Other Copulas

The one-factor Gaussian copula model is a particular model of the correlation between times to default. Many other one-factor copula models have been proposed. These include the Student t copula, the Clayton copula, Archimedean copula, and Marshall–Olkin copula. We can also create new one-factor copulas by assuming that F and the Z_i in equation (24.7) have nonnormal distributions with mean 0 and standard deviation 1. Hull and White show that a good fit to the market is obtained when F and the Z_i have Student t distributions with four degrees of freedom.[11] They call this the *double t copula*.

Another approach is to increase the number of factors in the model. Unfortunately, the model is then much slower to run because it is necessary to integrate over several normal distributions instead of just one.

---

[10] See L. Andersen, J. Sidenius, and S. Basu, "All Your Hedges in One Basket," *Risk*, November 2003; and J. C. Hull and A. White, "Valuation of a CDO and nth-to-Default Swap without Monte Carlo Simulation," *Journal of Derivatives*, 12, 2 (Winter 2004), 8–23.

[11] See J. C. Hull and A. White, "Valuation of a CDO and nth-to-Default Swap without Monte Carlo Simulation," *Journal of Derivatives*, 12, 2 (Winter 2004), 8–23.

Random Recovery and Factor Loadings

Andersen and Sidenius have suggested a model where the copula correlation ρ in equation (25.5) is a function of F and the recovery rate is negatively related to the default rate.[12]

In general, ρ increases as F decreases. This means that in states of the world where the default rate is high (i.e., states of the world where F is low) the default correlation is also high. There is empirical evidence suggesting that this is the case.[13] Andersen and Sidenius find that this model fits market quotes much better than the standard market model.

The Implied Copula Model

Hull and White show how a copula can be implied from market quotes.[14] The simplest version of the model assumes that a certain average hazard rate applies to all companies in a portfolio over the life of a CDO. That average hazard rate has a probability distribution that can be implied from the pricing of tranches. The calculation of the implied copula is similar in concept to the idea, discussed in Chapter 20, of calculating an implied probability distribution for a stock price from option prices.

Dynamic Models

The models discussed so far can be characterized as static models. In essence they model the average default environment over the life of the CDO. The model constructed for a 5-year CDO is different from the model constructed for a 7-year CDO, which is in turn different from the model constructed for a 10-year CDO. Dynamic models are different from static models in that they attempt to model the evolution of the loss on a portfolio through time. There are three different types of dynamic models:

1. *Structural Models*: These are similar to the models described in Section 24.6 except that the stochastic processes for the asset prices of many companies are modeled simultaneously. When the asset price for a company reaches a barrier, there is a default. The processes followed by the assets are correlated. The problem with these types of models is that they have to be implemented with Monte Carlo simulation and calibration is therefore difficult.

2. *Reduced Form Models*: In these models the hazard rates of companies are modeled. In order to build in a realistic amount of correlation, it is necessary to assume that there are jumps in the hazard rates.

[12] See L. B. G. Andersen and J. Sidenius, "Extension of the Gaussian Copula Model: Random Recovery and Random Factor Loadings," *Journal of Credit Risk*, 1, 1 (Winter 2004), 29–70.

[13] See, for example, A. Sevigny and O. Renault, "Default Correlation: Empirical Evidence," Working Paper, Standard and Poors, 2002; S. R. Das, L. Freed, G. Geng, and N. Kapadia, "Correlated Default Risk," *Journal of Fixed Income*, 16 (2006), 2, 7–32, J. C. Hull, M. Predescu, and A. White, "The Valuation of Correlation-Dependent Credit Derivatives Using a Structural Model," *Journal of Credit Risk*, 6 (2010), 99–132; and A. Ang and J. Chen, "Asymmetric Correlation of Equity Portfolios," *Journal of Financial Economics*, 63 (2002), 443–494.

[14] See J. C. Hull and A. White, "Valuing Credit Derivatives Using an Implied Copula Approach," *Journal of Derivatives*, 14 (2006), 8–28; and J. C. Hull and A. White, "An Improved Implied Copula Model and its Application to the Valuation of Bespoke CDO Tranches," *Journal of Investment Management*, 8, 3 (2010), 11–31.

3. *Top Down Models*: These are models where the total loss on a portfolio is modeled directly. The models do not consider what happens to individual companies.

SUMMARY

Credit derivatives enable banks and other financial institutions to actively manage their credit risks. They can be used to transfer credit risk from one company to another and to diversify credit risk by swapping one type of exposure for another.

The most common credit derivative is a credit default swap. This is a contract where one company buys insurance from another company against a third company (the reference entity) defaulting on its obligations. The payoff is designed to equal the difference between the face value of a bond issued by the reference entity and its value immediately after a default. Credit default swaps can be analyzed by calculating the present value of the expected payments and the present value of the expected payoff in a risk-neutral world.

A forward credit default swap is an obligation to enter into a particular credit default swap on a particular date. A credit default swap option is the right to enter into a particular credit default swap on a particular date. Both instruments cease to exist if the reference entity defaults before the date. A kth-to-default CDS is defined as a CDS that pays off when the kth default occurs in a portfolio of companies.

A total return swap is an instrument where the total return on a portfolio of credit-sensitive assets is exchanged for LIBOR plus a spread. Total return swaps are often used as financing vehicles. A company wanting to purchase a portfolio of assets will approach a financial institution to buy the assets on its behalf. The financial institution then enters into a total return swap with the company where it pays the return on the assets to the company and receives LIBOR plus a spread. The advantage of this type of arrangement is that the financial institution has less exposure than if it had lent the company money to buy the portfolio.

In a collateralized debt obligation a number of different securities are created from a portfolio of corporate bonds or commercial loans. There are rules for determining how credit losses are allocated. The result of the rules is that securities with both very high and very low credit ratings are created from the portfolio. In a synthetic collateralized debt obligation, cash flows on tranches are defined from a reference portfolio of credit default swaps. The standard market model for pricing both a kth-to-default CDS and tranches of a synthetic CDO is the one-factor Gaussian copula model for time to default.

FURTHER READING

Andersen, L. B. G., and J. Sidenius, "Extensions to the Gaussian Copula: Random Recovery and Random Factor Loadings," *Journal of Credit Risk*, 1, No. 1 (Winter 2004): 29–70.

Andersen, L. B. G., J. Sidenius, and S. Basu, "All Your Hedges in One Basket," *Risk*, 16, 10 (November 2003): 67–72.

Das, S., *Credit Derivatives: Trading & Management of Credit & Default Risk*, 3rd edn. New York: Wiley, 2005.

Hull, J. C., and A. White, "Valuation of a CDO and nth to Default Swap without Monte Carlo Simulation," *Journal of Derivatives*, 12, No. 2 (Winter 2004): 8–23.

Hull, J.C., and A. White, "Valuing Credit Derivatives Using an Implied Copula Approach," *Journal of Derivatives*, 14, 2 (Winter 2006), 8–28.

Hull, J.C., and A. White, "An Improved Implied Copula Model and its Application to the Valuation of Bespoke CDO Tranches," *Journal of Investment Management*, 8, 3 (2010), 11–31.

Laurent, J.-P., and J. Gregory, "Basket Default Swaps, CDOs and Factor Copulas," *Journal of Risk*, 7, 4 (2005), 8–23.

Li, D.X., "On Default Correlation: A Copula Approach," *Journal of Fixed Income*, March 2000: 43–54.

Schönbucher, P.J., *Credit Derivatives Pricing Models*. New York: Wiley, 2003.

Tavakoli, J.M., *Credit Derivatives & Synthetic Structures: A Guide to Instruments and Applications*, 2nd edn. New York: Wiley, 1998.

Practice Questions (Answers in Solutions Manual)

25.1. Explain the difference between a regular credit default swap and a binary credit default swap.

25.2. A 5-year credit default swap requires a quarterly payment at the rate of 60 basis points per year. The principal is $300 million and the credit default swap is settled in cash. A default occurs after 4 years and 2 months, and the price of the cheapest deliverable bond is estimated as 40% of its face value shortly after the default. List the cash flows and their timing for the seller of the credit default swap.

25.3. Explain the difference between a cash CDO and a synthetic CDO.

25.4. Explain the term "single-tranche trading."

25.5. What is a first-to-default credit default swap? Does its value increase or decrease as the default correlation between the companies in the basket increases? Explain your answer.

25.6. Explain the difference between risk-neutral and real-world default probabilities. Which should be used for valuing CDSs?

25.7. Explain why a total return swap can be useful as a financing tool.

25.8. Suppose that the risk-free zero curve is flat at 7% per annum with continuous compounding and that defaults can occur halfway through each year in a new 5-year credit default swap. Suppose that the recovery rate is 30% and the hazard rate is 3%. Estimate the credit default swap spread. Assume payments are made annually.

25.9. What is the value of the swap in Problem 25.8 per dollar of notional principal to the protection buyer if the credit default swap spread is 150 basis points?

25.10. What is the credit default swap spread in Problem 25.8 if it is a binary CDS?

25.11. How does a 5-year nth-to-default credit default swap work? Consider a basket of 100 reference entities where each reference entity has a probability of defaulting in each year of 1%. As the default correlation between the reference entities increases what would you expect to happen to the value of the swap when (a) $n = 1$ and (b) $n = 25$. Explain your answer.

25.12. What is the formula relating the payoff on a CDS to the notional principal and the recovery rate?

25.13. Show that the spread for a new plain vanilla CDS should be $(1 - R)$ times the spread for a similar new binary CDS, where R is the recovery rate.

25.14. Verify that, if the CDS spread for the example in Tables 25.1 to 25.4 is 100 basis points, the hazard rate must be 1.63% per year. How does the hazard rate change when the recovery rate is 20% instead of 40%? Verify that your answer is consistent with the implied hazard rate being approximately proportional to $1/(1 - R)$, where R is the recovery rate.

25.15. A company enters into a total return swap where it receives the return on a corporate bond paying a coupon of 5% and pays LIBOR. Explain the difference between this and a regular swap where 5% is exchanged for LIBOR.

25.16. Explain how forward contracts and options on credit default swaps are structured.

25.17. "The position of a buyer of a credit default swap is similar to the position of someone who is long a risk-free bond and short a corporate bond." Explain this statement.

25.18. Why is there a potential asymmetric information problem in credit default swaps?

25.19. Does valuing a CDS using real-world default probabilities rather than risk-neutral default probabilities overstate or understate its value? Explain your answer.

25.20. What is the difference between a total return swap and an asset swap?

25.21. Suppose that in a one-factor Gaussian copula model the 5-year probability of default for each of 125 names is 3% and the pairwise copula correlation is 0.2. Calculate, for factor values of -2, -1, 0, 1, and 2: (a) the default probability conditional on the factor value and (b) the probability of more than 10 defaults conditional on the factor value.

25.22. Explain the difference between base correlation and compound correlation.

25.23. In Example 25.2, what is the tranche spread for the 9% to 12% tranche assuming a tranche correlation of 0.15?

Further Questions

25.24. Suppose that the risk-free zero curve is flat at 6% per annum with continuous compounding and that defaults can occur at times 0.25 years, 0.75 years, 1.25 years, and 1.75 years in a 2-year plain vanilla credit default swap with semiannual payments. Suppose that the recovery rate is 20% and the unconditional probabilities of default (as seen at time zero) are 1% at times 0.25 years and 0.75 years, and 1.5% at times 1.25 years and 1.75 years. What is the credit default swap spread? What would the credit default spread be if the instrument were a binary credit default swap?

25.25. Assume that the hazard rate for a company is λ and the recovery rate is R. The risk-free interest rate is 5% per annum. Default always occurs halfway through a year. The spread for a 5-year plain vanilla CDS where payments are made annually is 120 basis points and the spread for a 5-year binary CDS where payments are made annually is 160 basis points. Estimate R and λ.

25.26. Explain how you would expect the returns offered on the various tranches in a synthetic CDO to change when the correlation between the bonds in the portfolio increases.

25.27. Suppose that:
(a) The yield on a 5-year risk-free bond is 7%.
(b) The yield on a 5-year corporate bond issued by company X is 9.5%.
(c) A 5-year credit default swap providing insurance against company X defaulting costs 150 basis points per year.

What arbitrage opportunity is there in this situation? What arbitrage opportunity would there be if the credit default spread were 300 basis points instead of 150 basis points?

25.28. In Example 25.3, what is the spread for (a) a first-to-default CDS and (b) a second-to-default CDS?

25.29. In Example 25.2, what is the tranche spread for the 6% to 9% tranche assuming a tranche correlation of 0.15?

25.30. The 1-, 2-, 3-, 4-, and 5-year CDS spreads are 100, 120, 135, 145, and 152 basis points, respectively. The risk-free rate is 3% for all maturities, the recovery rate is 35%, and payments are quarterly. Use DerivaGem to calculate the hazard rate each year. What is the probability of default in year 1? What is the probability of default in year 2?

25.31. Table 25.6 shows the 5-year iTraxx index was 77 basis points on January 31, 2008. Assume the risk-free rate is 5% for all maturities, the recovery rate is 40%, and payments are quarterly. Assume also that the spread of 77 basis points applies to all maturities. Use the DerivaGem CDS worksheet to calculate a hazard rate consistent with the spread. Use this in the CDO worksheet with 10 integration points to imply base correlations for each tranche from the quotes for January 31, 2008.

26

Exotic Options

Derivatives such as European and American call and put options are what are termed *plain vanilla products*. They have standard well-defined properties and trade actively. Their prices or implied volatilities are quoted by exchanges or by interdealer brokers on a regular basis. One of the exciting aspects of the over-the-counter derivatives market is the number of nonstandard products that have been created by financial engineers. These products are termed *exotic options*, or simply *exotics*. Although they usually constitute a relatively small part of its portfolio, exotics are important to a derivatives dealer because they are generally much more profitable than plain vanilla products.

Exotic products are developed for a number of reasons. Sometimes they meet a genuine hedging need in the market; sometimes there are tax, accounting, legal, or regulatory reasons why corporate treasurers, fund managers, and financial institutions find exotic products attractive; sometimes the products are designed to reflect a view on potential future movements in particular market variables; occasionally an exotic product is designed by a derivatives dealer to appear more attractive than it is to an unwary corporate treasurer or fund manager.

In this chapter, we describe some of the more commonly occurring exotic options and discuss their valuation. We assume that the underlying asset provides a yield at rate q. As discussed in Chapters 17 and 18, for an option on a stock index q should be set equal to the dividend yield on the index, for an option on a currency it should be set equal to the foreign risk-free rate, and for an option on a futures contract it should be set equal to the domestic risk-free rate. Many of the options discussed in this chapter can be valued using the DerivaGem software.

26.1 PACKAGES

A *package* is a portfolio consisting of standard European calls, standard European puts, forward contracts, cash, and the underlying asset itself. We discussed a number of different types of packages in Chapter 12: bull spreads, bear spreads, butterfly spreads, calendar spreads, straddles, strangles, and so on.

Often a package is structured by traders so that it has zero cost initially. An example is a *range forward contract*.[1] This was discussed in Section 17.2. It consists of a long call and a short put or a short call and a long put. The call strike price is greater than the put strike price and the strike prices are chosen so that the value of the call equals the value of the put.

It is worth noting that any derivative can be converted into a zero-cost product by deferring payment until maturity. Consider a European call option. If c is the cost of the option when payment is made at time zero, then $A = ce^{rT}$ is the cost when payment is made at time T, the maturity of the option. The payoff is then $\max(S_T - K, 0) - A$ or $\max(S_T - K - A, -A)$. When the strike price, K, equals the forward price, other names for a deferred payment option are break forward, Boston option, forward with optional exit, and cancelable forward.

26.2 PERPETUAL AMERICAN CALL AND PUT OPTIONS

The differential equation that must be satisfied by the price of a derivative when there is a dividend at rate q is equation (17.6):

$$\frac{\partial f}{\partial t} + (r - q)S\frac{\partial f}{\partial S} + \frac{1}{2}\sigma^2 S^2 \frac{\partial^2 f}{\partial S^2} = rf$$

Consider a derivative that pays off a fixed amount Q when $S = H$ for the first time. If $S < H$, the boundary conditions for the differential equation are that $f = Q$ when $S = H$ and $f = 0$ when $S = 0$. The solution $f = Q(S/H)^\alpha$ satisfies the boundary conditions when $\alpha > 0$. Furthermore, it satisfies the differential equation when

$$(r - q)\alpha + \tfrac{1}{2}\alpha(\alpha - 1)\sigma^2 = r$$

The positive solution to this equation is $\alpha = \alpha_1$, where

$$\alpha_1 = \frac{-w + \sqrt{w^2 + 2\sigma^2 r}}{\sigma^2}$$

and $w = r - q - \sigma^2/2$. It follows that the value of the derivative must be $Q(S/H)^{\alpha_1}$ because this satisfies the boundary conditions and the differential equation.

Consider next a perpetual American call option with strike price K. If the option is exercised when $S = H$, the payoff is $H - K$ and from the result just proved the value of the option is $(H - K)(S/H)^{\alpha_1}$. The holder of the call option can choose the asset price, H, at which the option is exercised. The optimal H is the one that maximizes the value we have just calculated. Using standard calculus methods, it is $H = H_1$, where

$$H_1 = K\frac{\alpha_1}{\alpha_1 - 1}$$

---

[1] Other names used for a range forward contract are zero-cost collar, flexible forward, cylinder option, option fence, min–max, and forward band.

The price of a perpetual call if $S < H_1$ is therefore

$$(H_1 - K)\left(\frac{S_0}{H_1}\right)^{\alpha_1} = \frac{K}{\alpha_1 - 1}\left(\frac{\alpha_1 - 1}{\alpha_1}\frac{S}{K}\right)^{\alpha_1}$$

If $S > H_1$, the call should be exercised immediately and is worth $S - K$.

To value an American put, we consider a derivative that pays off Q when $S = H$ in the situation where $S > H$ (so that the barrier H is reached from above). In this case, the boundary conditions for the differential equation are that $f = Q$ when $S = H$ and $f = 0$ as S tends to infinity. In this case, the solution $f = Q(S/H)^{-\alpha}$ satisfies the boundary conditions when $\alpha > 0$. As above, we can show that it also satisfies the differential equation when $\alpha = \alpha_2$, where

$$\alpha_2 = \frac{w + \sqrt{w^2 + 2\sigma^2 r}}{\sigma^2}$$

If the holder of the American put chooses to exercise when $S = H$, the value of the put is $(K - H)(S/H)^{-\alpha_2}$. The holder of the put will choose the exercise level $H = H_2$ to maximize this. This is

$$H_2 = K\frac{\alpha_2}{\alpha_2 + 1}$$

The price of a perpetual put if $S > H_2$ is therefore

$$(K - H_2)\left(\frac{S_0}{H_2}\right)^{-\alpha_2} = \frac{K}{\alpha_2 + 1}\left(\frac{\alpha_2 + 1}{\alpha_2}\frac{S}{K}\right)^{-\alpha_2}$$

If $S < H_2$, the put should be exercised immediately and is worth $K - S$.

Section 15.6 and Problem 15.23 give particular cases of the results here for $q = 0$.

26.3 NONSTANDARD AMERICAN OPTIONS

In a standard American option, exercise can take place at any time during the life of the option and the exercise price is always the same. The American options that are traded in the over-the-counter market sometimes have nonstandard features. For example:

1. Early exercise may be restricted to certain dates. The instrument is then known as a *Bermudan option*. (Bermuda is between Europe and America!)

2. Early exercise may be allowed during only part of the life of the option. For example, there may be an initial "lock out" period with no early exercise.

3. The strike price may change during the life of the option.

The warrants issued by corporations on their own stock often have some or all of these features. For example, in a 7-year warrant, exercise might be possible on particular dates during years 3 to 7, with the strike price being $30 during years 3 and 4, $32 during the next 2 years, and $33 during the final year.

Nonstandard American options can usually be valued using a binomial tree. At each node, the test (if any) for early exercise is adjusted to reflect the terms of the option.

26.4 GAP OPTIONS

A gap call option is a European call options that pays off $S_T - K_1$ when $S_T > K_2$. The difference between a gap call option and a regular call option with a strike price of K_2 is that the payoff when $S_T > K_2$ is increased by $K_2 - K_1$. (This increase is positive or negative depending on whether $K_2 > K_1$ or $K_1 > K_2$.)

A gap call option can be valued by a small modification to the Black–Scholes–Merton formula. With our usual notation, the value is

$$S_0 e^{-qT} N(d_1) - K_1 e^{-rT} N(d_2) \tag{26.1}$$

where

$$d_1 = \frac{\ln(S_0/K_2) + (r - q + \sigma^2/2)T}{\sigma\sqrt{T}}$$

$$d_2 = d_1 - \sigma\sqrt{T}$$

The price in this formula is greater than the price given by the Black–Scholes–Merton formula for a regular call option with strike price K_2 by

$$(K_2 - K_1)e^{-rT} N(d_2)$$

To understand this difference, note that the probability that the option will be exercised is $N(d_2)$ and, when it is exercised, the payoff to the holder of the gap option is greater than that to the holder of the regular option by $K_2 - K_1$.

For a gap put option, the payoff is $K_1 - S_T$ when $S_T < K_2$. The value of the option is

$$K_1 e^{-rT} N(-d_2) - S_0 e^{-qT} N(-d_1) \tag{26.2}$$

where d_1 and d_2 are defined as for equation (26.1).

Example 26.1

An asset is currently worth \$500,000. Over the next year, its price is expected to have a volatility of 20%. The risk-free rate is 5%, and no income is expected. Suppose that an insurance company agrees to buy the asset for \$400,000 if its value has fallen below \$400,000 at the end of one year. The payout will be $400,000 - S_T$ whenever the value of the asset is less than \$400,000. The insurance company has provided a regular put option where the policyholder has the right to sell the asset to the insurance company for \$400,000 in one year. This can be valued using equation (15.21), with $S_0 = 500,000$, $K = 400,000$, $r = 0.05$, $\sigma = 0.2$, $T = 1$. The value is \$3,436.

Suppose next that the cost of transferring the asset is \$50,000 and this cost is borne by the policyholder. The option is then exercised only if the value of the asset is less than \$350,000. In this case, the cost to the insurance company is $K_1 - S_T$ when $S_T < K_2$, where $K_2 = 350,000$, $K_1 = 400,000$, and S_T is the price of the asset in one year. This is a gap put option. The value is given by equation (26.2), with $S_0 = 500,000$, $K_1 = 400,000$, $K_2 = 350,000$, $r = 0.05$, $q = 0$, $\sigma = 0.2$, $T = 1$. It is \$1,896. Recognizing the costs to the policyholder of making a claim reduces the cost of the policy to the insurance company by about 45% in this case.

26.5 FORWARD START OPTIONS

Forward start options are options that will start at some time in the future. Sometimes employee stock options, which were discussed in Chapter 16, can be viewed as forward start options. This is because the company commits (implicitly or explicitly) to granting at-the-money options to employees in the future.

Consider a forward start at-the-money European call option that will start at time T_1 and mature at time T_2. Suppose that the asset price is S_0 at time zero and S_1 at time T_1. To value the option, we note from the European option pricing formulas in Chapters 15 and 17 that the value of an at-the-money call option on an asset is proportional to the asset price. The value of the forward start option at time T_1 is therefore cS_1/S_0, where c is the value at time zero of an at-the-money option that lasts for $T_2 - T_1$. Using risk-neutral valuation, the value of the forward start option at time zero is

$$e^{-rT_1} \hat{E}\left[c \frac{S_1}{S_0} \right]$$

where $\hat{E}$ denotes the expected value in a risk-neutral world. Since c and S_0 are known and $\hat{E}[S_1] = S_0 e^{(r-q)T_1}$, the value of the forward start option is ce^{-qT_1}. For a non-dividend-paying stock, $q = 0$ and the value of the forward start option is exactly the same as the value of a regular at-the-money option with the same life as the forward start option.

26.6 CLIQUET OPTIONS

A cliquet option (which is also called a ratchet or strike reset option) is a series of call or put options with rules for determining the strike price. Suppose that the reset dates are at times $t_1, t_2, \ldots, t_{n-1}$, with t_n being the end of the cliquet's life. A simple structure would be as follows. The first option has a strike price K equal to the initial asset price and lasts between times 0 and t_1; the second option provides a payoff at time t_2 with a strike price equal to the value of the asset at time t_1; the third option provides a payoff at time t_3 with a strike price equal to the value of the asset at time t_2; and so on. This is a regular option plus $n - 1$ forward start options. The latter can be valued as described in Section 26.5.

Some cliquet options are much more complicated than the one described here. For example, sometimes there are upper and lower limits on the total payoff over the whole period; sometimes cliquets terminate at the end of a period if the asset price is in a certain range. When analytic results are not available, Monte Carlo simulation is often the best approach for valuation.

26.7 COMPOUND OPTIONS

Compound options are options on options. There are four main types of compound options: a call on a call, a put on a call, a call on a put, and a put on a put. Compound options have two strike prices and two exercise dates. Consider, for example, a call on a call. On the first exercise date, T_1, the holder of the compound option is entitled to pay the first strike price, K_1, and receive a call option. The call option gives the holder the right to buy the underlying asset for the second strike price, K_2, on the second exercise date, T_2. The compound option will be exercised on the first exercise date only if the value of the option on that date is greater than the first strike price.

When the usual geometric Brownian motion assumption is made, European-style compound options can be valued analytically in terms of integrals of the bivariate normal distribution.[2] With our usual notation, the value at time zero of a European call option on a call option is

$$S_0 e^{-qT_2} M(a_1, b_1; \sqrt{T_1/T_2}) - K_2 e^{-rT_2} M(a_2, b_2; \sqrt{T_1/T_2}) - e^{-rT_1} K_1 N(a_2)$$

where

$$a_1 = \frac{\ln(S_0/S^*) + (r - q + \sigma^2/2)T_1}{\sigma\sqrt{T_1}}, \quad a_2 = a_1 - \sigma\sqrt{T_1}$$

$$b_1 = \frac{\ln(S_0/K_2) + (r - q + \sigma^2/2)T_2}{\sigma\sqrt{T_2}}, \quad b_2 = b_1 - \sigma\sqrt{T_2}$$

The function $M(a, b : \rho)$ is the cumulative bivariate normal distribution function that the first variable will be less than a and the second will be less than b when the coefficient of correlation between the two is ρ.[3] The variable S^* is the asset price at time T_1 for which the option price at time T_1 equals K_1. If the actual asset price is above S^* at time T_1, the first option will be exercised; if it is not above S^*, the option expires worthless.

With similar notation, the value of a European put on a call is

$$K_2 e^{-rT_2} M(-a_2, b_2; -\sqrt{T_1/T_2}) - S_0 e^{-qT_2} M(-a_1, b_1; -\sqrt{T_1/T_2}) + e^{-rT_1} K_1 N(-a_2)$$

The value of a European call on a put is

$$K_2 e^{-rT_2} M(-a_2, -b_2; \sqrt{T_1/T_2}) - S_0 e^{-qT_2} M(-a_1, -b_1; \sqrt{T_1/T_2}) - e^{-rT_1} K_1 N(-a_2)$$

The value of a European put on a put is

$$S_0 e^{-qT_2} M(a_1, -b_1; -\sqrt{T_1/T_2}) - K_2 e^{-rT_2} M(a_2, -b_2; -\sqrt{T_1/T_2}) + e^{-rT_1} K_1 N(a_2)$$

26.8 CHOOSER OPTIONS

A *chooser* option (sometimes referred to as an *as you like it* option) has the feature that, after a specified period of time, the holder can choose whether the option is a call or a put. Suppose that the time when the choice is made is T_1. The value of the chooser option at this time is

$$\max(c, p)$$

where c is the value of the call underlying the option and p is the value of the put underlying the option.

If the options underlying the chooser option are both European and have the same strike price, put–call parity can be used to provide a valuation formula. Suppose that S_1

---

[2] See R. Geske, "The Valuation of Compound Options," *Journal of Financial Economics*, 7 (1979): 63–81; M. Rubinstein, "Double Trouble," *Risk*, December 1991/January 1992: 53–56.

[3] See Technical Note 5 at www-2.rotman.utoronto.ca/~hull/TechnicalNotes for a numerical procedure for calculating M. A function for calculating M is also on the website.

is the asset price at time T_1, K is the strike price, T_2 is the maturity of the options, and r is the risk-free interest rate. Put–call parity implies that

$$\max(c, p) = \max(c, c + Ke^{-r(T_2-T_1)} - S_1 e^{-q(T_2-T_1)})$$
$$= c + e^{-q(T_2-T_1)} \max(0, Ke^{-(r-q)(T_2-T_1)} - S_1)$$

This shows that the chooser option is a package consisting of:

1. A call option with strike price K and maturity T_2
2. $e^{-q(T_2-T_1)}$ put options with strike price $Ke^{-(r-q)(T_2-T_1)}$ and maturity T_1

As such, it can readily be valued.

More complex chooser options can be defined where the call and the put do not have the same strike price and time to maturity. They are then not packages and have features that are somewhat similar to compound options.

26.9 BARRIER OPTIONS

Barrier options are options where the payoff depends on whether the underlying asset's price reaches a certain level during a certain period of time.

A number of different types of barrier options regularly trade in the over-the-counter market. They are attractive to some market participants because they are less expensive than the corresponding regular options. These barrier options can be classified as either *knock-out options* or *knock-in options*. A knock-out option ceases to exist when the underlying asset price reaches a certain barrier; a knock-in option comes into existence only when the underlying asset price reaches a barrier.

Equations (17.4) and (17.5) show that the values at time zero of a regular call and put option are

$$c = S_0 e^{-qT} N(d_1) - Ke^{-rT} N(d_2)$$
$$p = Ke^{-rT} N(-d_2) - S_0 e^{-qT} N(-d_1)$$

where

$$d_1 = \frac{\ln(S_0/K) + (r - q + \sigma^2/2)T}{\sigma\sqrt{T}}$$

$$d_2 = \frac{\ln(S_0/K) + (r - q - \sigma^2/2)T}{\sigma\sqrt{T}} = d_1 - \sigma\sqrt{T}$$

A *down-and-out call* is one type of knock-out option. It is a regular call option that ceases to exist if the asset price reaches a certain barrier level H. The barrier level is below the initial asset price. The corresponding knock-in option is a *down-and-in call*. This is a regular call that comes into existence only if the asset price reaches the barrier level.

If H is less than or equal to the strike price, K, the value of a down-and-in call at time zero is

$$c_{di} = S_0 e^{-qT}(H/S_0)^{2\lambda} N(y) - Ke^{-rT}(H/S_0)^{2\lambda-2} N(y - \sigma\sqrt{T})$$

where

$$\lambda = \frac{r - q + \sigma^2/2}{\sigma^2}$$

$$y = \frac{\ln[H^2/(S_0 K)]}{\sigma\sqrt{T}} + \lambda\sigma\sqrt{T}$$

Because the value of a regular call equals the value of a down-and-in call plus the value of a down-and-out call, the value of a down-and-out call is given by

$$c_{do} = c - c_{di}$$

If $H \geqslant K$, then

$$c_{do} = S_0 N(x_1)e^{-qT} - Ke^{-rT}N(x_1 - \sigma\sqrt{T})$$
$$- S_0 e^{-qT}(H/S_0)^{2\lambda}N(y_1) + Ke^{-rT}(H/S_0)^{2\lambda-2}N(y_1 - \sigma\sqrt{T})$$

and

$$c_{di} = c - c_{do}$$

where

$$x_1 = \frac{\ln(S_0/H)}{\sigma\sqrt{T}} + \lambda\sigma\sqrt{T}, \quad y_1 = \frac{\ln(H/S_0)}{\sigma\sqrt{T}} + \lambda\sigma\sqrt{T}$$

An *up-and-out call* is a regular call option that ceases to exist if the asset price reaches a barrier level, H, that is higher than the current asset price. An *up-and-in call* is a regular call option that comes into existence only if the barrier is reached. When H is less than or equal to K, the value of the up-and-out call, c_{uo}, is zero and the value of the up-and-in call, c_{ui}, is c. When H is greater than K,

$$c_{ui} = S_0 N(x_1)e^{-qT} - Ke^{-rT}N(x_1 - \sigma\sqrt{T}) - S_0 e^{-qT}(H/S_0)^{2\lambda}[N(-y) - N(-y_1)]$$
$$+ Ke^{-rT}(H/S_0)^{2\lambda-2}[N(-y + \sigma\sqrt{T}) - N(-y_1 + \sigma\sqrt{T})]$$

and

$$c_{uo} = c - c_{ui}$$

Put barrier options are defined similarly to call barrier options. An *up-and-out put* is a put option that ceases to exist when a barrier, H, that is greater than the current asset price is reached. An *up-and-in put* is a put that comes into existence only if the barrier is reached. When the barrier, H, is greater than or equal to the strike price, K, their prices are

$$p_{ui} = -S_0 e^{-qT}(H/S_0)^{2\lambda}N(-y) + Ke^{-rT}(H/S_0)^{2\lambda-2}N(-y + \sigma\sqrt{T})$$

and

$$p_{uo} = p - p_{ui}$$

When H is less than or equal to K,

$$p_{uo} = -S_0 N(-x_1)e^{-qT} + Ke^{-rT}N(-x_1 + \sigma\sqrt{T})$$
$$+ S_0 e^{-qT}(H/S_0)^{2\lambda}N(-y_1) - Ke^{-rT}(H/S_0)^{2\lambda-2}N(-y_1 + \sigma\sqrt{T})$$

and

$$p_{ui} = p - p_{uo}$$

A *down-and-out put* is a put option that ceases to exist when a barrier less than the current asset price is reached. A *down-and-in put* is a put option that comes into existence only when the barrier is reached. When the barrier is greater than the strike price, $p_{do} = 0$ and $p_{di} = p$. When the barrier is less than the strike price,

$$p_{di} = -S_0 N(-x_1)e^{-qT} + Ke^{-rT}N(-x_1 + \sigma\sqrt{T}) + S_0 e^{-qT}(H/S_0)^{2\lambda}[N(y) - N(y_1)]$$
$$- Ke^{-rT}(H/S_0)^{2\lambda-2}[N(y - \sigma\sqrt{T}) - N(y_1 - \sigma\sqrt{T})]$$

and

$$p_{do} = p - p_{di}$$

All of these valuations make the usual assumption that the probability distribution for the asset price at a future time is lognormal. An important issue for barrier options is the frequency with which the asset price, S, is observed for purposes of determining whether the barrier has been reached. The analytic formulas given in this section assume that S is observed continuously and sometimes this is the case.[4] Often, the terms of a contract state that S is observed periodically; for example, once a day at 3 p.m. Broadie, Glasserman, and Kou provide a way of adjusting the formulas we have just given for the situation where the price of the underlying is observed discretely.[5] The barrier level H is replaced by $He^{0.5826\sigma\sqrt{T/m}}$ for an up-and-in or up-and-out option and by $He^{-0.5826\sigma\sqrt{T/m}}$ for a down-and-in or down-and-out option, where m is the number of times the asset price is observed (so that T/m is the time interval between observations).

Barrier options often have quite different properties from regular options. For example, sometimes vega is negative. Consider an up-and-out call option when the asset price is close to the barrier level. As volatility increases, the probability that the barrier will be hit increases. As a result, a volatility increase can cause the price of the barrier option to decrease in these circumstances.

One disadvantage of the barrier options we have considered so far is that a "spike" in the asset price can cause the option to be knocked in or out. An alternative structure is a *Parisian option*, where the asset price has to be above or below the barrier for a period of time for the option to be knocked in or out. For example, a down-and-out Parisian put option with a strike price equal to 90% of the initial asset price and a barrier at 75% of the initial asset price might specify that the option is knocked out if the asset price is below the barrier for 50 days. The confirmation might specify that the 50 days are a "continuous period of 50 days" or "any 50 days during the option's life." Parisian options are more difficult to value than regular barrier options.[6] Monte Carlo simulation and binomial trees can be used with the enhancements discussed in Sections 27.5 and 27.6.

26.10 BINARY OPTIONS

Binary or digital options are options with discontinuous payoffs. A simple example of a binary option is a *cash-or-nothing call*. This pays off nothing if the asset price ends up

---

[4] One way to track whether a barrier has been reached from below (above) is to send a limit order to the exchange to sell (buy) the asset at the barrier price and see whether the order is filled.

[5] M. Broadie, P. Glasserman, and S. G. Kou, "A Continuity Correction for Discrete Barrier Options," *Mathematical Finance* 7, 4 (October 1997): 325–49.

[6] See, for example, M. Chesney, J. Cornwall, M. Jeanblanc-Picqué, G. Kentwell, and M. Yor, "Parisian pricing," *Risk*, 10, 1 (1997), 77–79.

below the strike price at time T and pays a fixed amount, Q, if it ends up above the strike price. In a risk-neutral world, the probability of the asset price being above the strike price at the maturity of an option is, with our usual notation, $N(d_2)$. The value of a cash-or-nothing call is therefore $Qe^{-rT}N(d_2)$. A *cash-or-nothing put* is defined analogously to a cash-or-nothing call. It pays off Q if the asset price is below the strike price and nothing if it is above the strike price. The value of a cash-or-nothing put is $Qe^{-rT}N(-d_2)$.

Another type of binary option is an *asset-or-nothing call*. This pays off nothing if the underlying asset price ends up below the strike price and pays the asset price if it ends up above the strike price. With our usual notation, the value of an asset-or-nothing call is $S_0e^{-qT}N(d_1)$. An *asset-or-nothing put* pays off nothing if the underlying asset price ends up above the strike price and the asset price if it ends up below the strike price. The value of an asset-or-nothing put is $S_0e^{-qT}N(-d_1)$.

Binary options have discontinuous payoffs. This can create problems if the underlying asset is thinly traded so that relatively small buy or sell trades move the price. Consider a cash-or-nothing call with a strike price of $20 and a payoff of $1 million. If the final asset price is $19.99, there is no payoff; if it is $20 or more, the payoff is $1 million. If there is one day left in the life of the option and the price a little below $20, it would be tempting for the holder of the cash-or-nothing call to place buy orders for the underlying asset to tip the price over $20. A similar issue can arise with barrier options on thinly traded assets. If the price of the underlying asset is close to the barrier, one side is likely to be tempted to place buy or sell orders to ensure that the barrier is reached.

A regular European call option is equivalent to a long position in an asset-or-nothing call and a short position in a cash-or-nothing call where the cash payoff in the cash-or-nothing call equals the strike price. Similarly, a regular European put option is equivalent to a long position in a cash-or-nothing put and a short position in an asset-or-nothing put where the cash payoff on the cash-or-nothing put equals the strike price.

26.11 LOOKBACK OPTIONS

The payoffs from lookback options depend on the maximum or minimum asset price reached during the life of the option. The payoff from a *floating lookback call* is the amount that the final asset price exceeds the minimum asset price achieved during the life of the option. The payoff from a *floating lookback put* is the amount by which the maximum asset price achieved during the life of the option exceeds the final asset price.

Valuation formulas have been produced for floating lookbacks.[7] The value of a floating lookback call at time zero is

$$c_{fl} = S_0e^{-qT}N(a_1) - S_0e^{-qT}\frac{\sigma^2}{2(r-q)}N(-a_1) - S_{min}e^{-rT}\left[N(a_2) - \frac{\sigma^2}{2(r-q)}e^{Y_1}N(-a_3)\right]$$

---

[7] See B. Goldman, H. Sosin, and M. A. Gatto, "Path-Dependent Options: Buy at the Low, Sell at the High," *Journal of Finance*, 34 (December 1979): 1111–27.; M. Garman, "Recollection in Tranquility," *Risk*, March (1989): 16–19.

where

$$a_1 = \frac{\ln(S_0/S_{min}) + (r - q + \sigma^2/2)T}{\sigma\sqrt{T}}$$

$$a_2 = a_1 - \sigma\sqrt{T},$$

$$a_3 = \frac{\ln(S_0/S_{min}) + (-r + q + \sigma^2/2)T}{\sigma\sqrt{T}}$$

$$Y_1 = -\frac{2(r - q - \sigma^2/2)\ln(S_0/S_{min})}{\sigma^2}$$

and S_{min} is the minimum asset price achieved to date. (If the lookback has just been originated, $S_{min} = S_0$.) See Problem 26.23 for the $r = q$ case.

The value of a floating lookback put is

$$p_{fl} = S_{max}e^{-rT}\left[N(b_1) - \frac{\sigma^2}{2(r - q)}e^{Y_2}N(-b_3)\right] + S_0e^{-qT}\frac{\sigma^2}{2(r - q)}N(-b_2) - S_0e^{-qT}N(b_2)$$

where

$$b_1 = \frac{\ln(S_{max}/S_0) + (-r + q + \sigma^2/2)T}{\sigma\sqrt{T}}$$

$$b_2 = b_1 - \sigma\sqrt{T}$$

$$b_3 = \frac{\ln(S_{max}/S_0) + (r - q - \sigma^2/2)T}{\sigma\sqrt{T}}$$

$$Y_2 = \frac{2(r - q - \sigma^2/2)\ln(S_{max}/S_0)}{\sigma^2}$$

and S_{max} is the maximum asset price achieved to date. (If the lookback has just been originated, then $S_{max} = S_0$.)

A floating lookback call is a way that the holder can buy the underlying asset at the lowest price achieved during the life of the option. Similarly, a floating lookback put is a way that the holder can sell the underlying asset at the highest price achieved during the life of the option.

Example 26.2

Consider a newly issued floating lookback put on a non-dividend-paying stock where the stock price is 50, the stock price volatility is 40% per annum, the risk-free rate is 10% per annum, and the time to maturity is 3 months. In this case, $S_{max} = 50$, $S_0 = 50$, $r = 0.1$, $q = 0$, $\sigma = 0.4$, and $T = 0.25$, $b_1 = -0.025$, $b_2 = -0.225$, $b_3 = 0.025$, and $Y_2 = 0$, so that the value of the lookback put is 7.79. A newly issued floating lookback call on the same stock is worth 8.04.

In a fixed lookback option, a strike price is specified. For a *fixed lookback call option*, the payoff is the same as a regular European call option except that the final asset price is replaced by the maximum asset price achieved during the life of the option. For a *fixed lookback put option*, the payoff is the same as a regular European put option except that the the final asset price is replaced by the minimum asset price achieved during the life of the option. Define $S^*_{max} = \max(S_{max}, K)$, where as before S_{max} is the maximum asset price achieved to date and K is the strike price. Also, define p^*_{fl} as the value of a floating lookback put which lasts for the same period as the fixed lookback call when the actual maximum asset price so far, S_{max}, is replaced by S^*_{max}. A put–call parity type of argument shows that the value of the fixed lookback call option, c_{fix} is given by[8]

$$c_{fix} = p^*_{fl} + S_0 e^{-qT} - K e^{-rT}$$

Similarly, if $S^*_{min} = \min(S_{min}, K)$, then the value of a fixed lookback put option, p_{fix}, is given by

$$p_{fix} = c^*_{fl} + K e^{-rT} - S_0 e^{-qT}$$

where c^*_{fl} is the value of a floating lookback call that lasts for the same period as the fixed lookback put when the actual minimum asset price so far, S_{min}, is replaced by S^*_{min}. This shows that the equations given above for floating lookbacks can be modified to price fixed lookbacks.

Lookbacks are appealing to investors, but very expensive when compared with regular options. As with barrier options, the value of a lookback option is liable to be sensitive to the frequency with which the asset price is observed for the purposes of computing the maximum or minimum. The formulas above assume that the asset price is observed continuously. Broadie, Glasserman, and Kou provide a way of adjusting the formulas we have just given for the situation where the asset price is observed discretely.[9]

26.12 SHOUT OPTIONS

A *shout option* is a European option where the holder can "shout" to the writer at one time during its life. At the end of the life of the option, the option holder receives either the usual payoff from a European option or the intrinsic value at the time of the shout, whichever is greater. Suppose the strike price is $50 and the holder of a call shouts when the price of the underlying asset is $60. If the final asset price is less than $60, the holder receives a payoff of $10. If it is greater than $60, the holder receives the excess of the asset price over $50.

A shout option has some of the same features as a lookback option, but is considerably less expensive. It can be valued by noting that if the holder shouts at a time τ when the asset price is S_τ the payoff from the option is

$$\max(0, \, S_T - S_\tau) + (S_\tau - K)$$

where, as usual, K is the strike price and S_T is the asset price at time T. The value at time τ if the holder shouts is therefore the present value of $S_\tau - K$ (received at time T) plus the value of a European option with strike price S_τ. The latter can be calculated using Black–Scholes–Merton formulas.

A shout option is valued by constructing a binomial or trinomial tree for the underlying asset in the usual way. Working back through the tree, the value of the option if the holder shouts and the value if the holder does not shout can be calculated at each node.

---

[8] The argument was proposed by H. Y. Wong and Y. K. Kwok, "Sub-replication and Replenishing Premium: Efficient Pricing of Multi-state Lookbacks," *Review of Derivatives Research*, 6 (2003), 83–106.

[9] M. Broadie, P. Glasserman, and S. G. Kou, "Connecting Discrete and Continuous Path-Dependent Options," *Finance and Stochastics*, 2 (1998): 1–28.

The option's price at the node is the greater of the two. The procedure for valuing a shout option is therefore similar to the procedure for valuing a regular American option.

26.13 ASIAN OPTIONS

Asian options are options where the payoff depends on the arithmetic average of the price of the underlying asset during the life of the option. The payoff from an *average price call* is $\max(0, S_{ave} - K)$ and that from an *average price put* is $\max(0, K - S_{ave})$, where S_{ave} is the average price of the underlying asset. Average price options tend to be less expensive than regular options and are arguably more appropriate than regular options for meeting some of the needs of corporate treasurers. Suppose that a U.S. corporate treasurer expects to receive a cash flow of 100 million Australian dollars spread evenly over the next year from the company's Australian subsidiary. The treasurer is likely to be interested in an option that guarantees that the average exchange rate realized during the year is above some level. An average price put option can achieve this more effectively than regular put options.

Average price options can be valued using similar formulas to those used for regular options if it is assumed that S_{ave} is lognomal. As it happens, when the usual assumption is made for the process followed by the asset price, this is a reasonable assumption.[10] A popular approach is to fit a lognormal distribution to the first two moments of S_{ave} and use Black's model.[11] Suppose that M_1 and M_2 are the first two moments of S_{ave}. The value of average price calls and puts are given by equations (18.9) and (18.10), with

$$F_0 = M_1 \tag{26.3}$$

and

$$\sigma^2 = \frac{1}{T} \ln\left(\frac{M_2}{M_1^2}\right) \tag{26.4}$$

When the average is calculated continuously, and r, q, and σ are constant (as in DerivaGem):

$$M_1 = \frac{e^{(r-q)T} - 1}{(r-q)T} S_0$$

and

$$M_2 = \frac{2e^{[2(r-q)+\sigma^2]T} S_0^2}{(r-q+\sigma^2)(2r-2q+\sigma^2)T^2} + \frac{2S_0^2}{(r-q)T^2}\left(\frac{1}{2(r-q)+\sigma^2} - \frac{e^{(r-q)T}}{r-q+\sigma^2}\right)$$

More generally, when the average is calculated from observations at times T_i ($1 \leqslant i \leqslant m$),

$$M_1 = \frac{1}{m}\sum_{i=1}^{m} F_i \quad \text{and} \quad M_2 = \frac{1}{m^2}\left(\sum_{i=1}^{m} F_i^2 e^{\sigma_i^2 T_i} + 2\sum_{j=1}^{m}\sum_{i=1}^{j-1} F_i F_j e^{\sigma_i^2 T_i}\right)$$

where F_i and σ_i are the forward price and implied volatility for maturity T_i. See Technical Note 27 on www-2.rotman.utoronto.ca/~hull/TechnicalNotes for a proof of this.

---

[10] When the asset price follows geometric Brownian motion, the geometric average of the price is exactly lognormal and the arithmetic average is approximately lognormal.

[11] See S. M. Turnbull and L. M. Wakeman, "A Quick Algorithm for Pricing European Average Options," *Journal of Financial and Quantitative Analysis*, 26 (September 1991): 377–89.

Example 26.3

Consider a newly issued average price call option on a non-dividend-paying stock where the stock price is 50, the strike price is 50, the stock price volatility is 40% per annum, the risk-free rate is 10% per annum, and the time to maturity is 1 year. In this case, $S_0 = 50$, $K = 50$, $r = 0.1$, $q = 0$, $\sigma = 0.4$, and $T = 1$. If the average is calculated continuously, $M_1 = 52.59$ and $M_2 = 2{,}922.76$. From equations (26.3) and (26.4), $F_0 = 52.59$ and $\sigma = 23.54\%$. Equation (18.9), with $K = 50$, $T = 1$, and $r = 0.1$, gives the value of the option as 5.62. When 12, 52, and 250 observations are used for the average, the price is 6.00, 5.70, and 5.63, respectively.

We can modify the analysis to accommodate the situation where the option is not newly issued and some prices used to determine the average have already been observed. Suppose that the averaging period is composed of a period of length t_1 over which prices have already been observed and a future period of length t_2 (the remaining life of the option). Suppose that the average asset price during the first time period is $\bar{S}$. The payoff from an average price call is

$$\max\left(\frac{\bar{S}t_1 + S_{\text{ave}}t_2}{t_1 + t_2} - K, 0\right)$$

where S_{ave} is the average asset price during the remaining part of the averaging period. This is the same as

$$\frac{t_2}{t_1 + t_2}\max(S_{\text{ave}} - K^*, 0)$$

where

$$K^* = \frac{t_1 + t_2}{t_2}K - \frac{t_1}{t_2}\bar{S}$$

When $K^* > 0$, the option can be valued in the same way as a newly issued Asian option provided that we change the strike price from K to K^* and multiply the result by $t_2/(t_1 + t_2)$. When $K^* < 0$ the option is certain to be exercised and can be valued as a forward contract. The value is

$$\frac{t_2}{t_1 + t_2}[M_1 e^{-rt_2} - K^* e^{-rt_2}]$$

Another type of Asian option is an average strike option. An *average strike call* pays off $\max(0, S_T - S_{\text{ave}})$ and an *average strike put* pays off $\max(0, S_{\text{ave}} - S_T)$. Average strike options can guarantee that the average price paid for an asset in frequent trading over a period of time is not greater than the final price. Alternatively, it can guarantee that the average price received for an asset in frequent trading over a period of time is not less than the final price. It can be valued as an option to exchange one asset for another when S_{ave} is assumed to be lognormal.

26.14 OPTIONS TO EXCHANGE ONE ASSET FOR ANOTHER

Options to exchange one asset for another (sometimes referred to as *exchange options*) arise in various contexts. An option to buy yen with Australian dollars is, from the point of view of a U.S. investor, an option to exchange one foreign currency asset for another foreign currency asset. A stock tender offer is an option to exchange shares in one stock for shares in another stock.

Consider a European option to give up an asset worth U_T at time T and receive in return an asset worth V_T. The payoff from the option is

$$\max(V_T - U_T, 0)$$

A formula for valuing this option was first produced by Margrabe.[12] Suppose that the asset prices, U and V, both follow geometric Brownian motion with volatilities σ_U and σ_V. Suppose further that the instantaneous correlation between U and V is ρ, and the yields provided by U and V are q_U and q_V, respectively. The value of the option at time zero is

$$V_0 e^{-q_V T} N(d_1) - U_0 e^{-q_U T} N(d_2) \tag{26.5}$$

where

$$d_1 = \frac{\ln(V_0/U_0) + (q_U - q_V + \hat{\sigma}^2/2)T}{\hat{\sigma}\sqrt{T}}, \quad d_2 = d_1 - \hat{\sigma}\sqrt{T}$$

and

$$\hat{\sigma} = \sqrt{\sigma_U^2 + \sigma_V^2 - 2\rho\sigma_U\sigma_V}$$

and U_0 and V_0 are the values of U and V at times zero.

This result will be proved in Chapter 28. It is interesting to note that equation (26.5) is independent of the risk-free rate r. This is because, as r increases, the growth rate of both asset prices in a risk-neutral world increases, but this is exactly offset by an increase in the discount rate. The variable $\hat{\sigma}$ is the volatility of V/U. Comparisons with equation (17.4) show that the option price is the same as the price of U_0 European call options on an asset worth V/U when the strike price is 1.0, the risk-free interest rate is q_U, and the dividend yield on the asset is q_V. Mark Rubinstein shows that the American version of this option can be characterized similarly for valuation purposes.[13] It can be regarded as U_0 American options to buy an asset worth V/U for 1.0 when the risk-free interest rate is q_U and the dividend yield on the asset is q_V. The option can therefore be valued as described in Chapter 21 using a binomial tree.

An option to obtain the better or worse of two assets can be regarded as a position in one of the assets combined with an option to exchange it for the other asset:

$$\min(U_T, V_T) = V_T - \max(V_T - U_T, 0)$$
$$\max(U_T, V_T) = U_T + \max(V_T - U_T, 0)$$

26.15 OPTIONS INVOLVING SEVERAL ASSETS

Options involving two or more risky assets are sometimes referred to as *rainbow options*. One example is the bond futures contract traded on the CBOT described in Chapter 6. The party with the short position is allowed to choose between a large number of different bonds when making delivery.

---

[12] See W. Margrabe, "The Value of an Option to Exchange One Asset for Another," *Journal of Finance*, 33 (March 1978): 177–86.

[13] See M. Rubinstein, "One for Another," *Risk*, July/August 1991: 30–32

Probably the most popular option involving several assets is a European *basket option*. This is an option where the payoff is dependent on the value of a portfolio (or basket) of assets. The assets are usually either individual stocks or stock indices or currencies. A European basket option can be valued with Monte Carlo simulation, by assuming that the assets follow correlated geometric Brownian motion processes. A much faster approach is to calculate the first two moments of the basket at the maturity of the option in a risk-neutral world, and then assume that value of the basket is lognormally distributed at that time. The option can then be valued using Black's model with the parameters shown in equations (26.3) and (26.4). In this case,

$$M_1 = \sum_{i=1}^{n} F_i \quad \text{and} \quad M_2 = \sum_{i=1}^{n} \sum_{j=1}^{n} F_i F_j e^{\rho_{ij}\sigma_i\sigma_j T}$$

where n is the number of assets, T is the option maturity, F_i and σ_i are the forward price and volatility of the ith asset, and ρ_{ij} is the correlation between the ith and jth asset. See Technical Note 28 at www-2.rotman.utoronto.ca/~hull/TechnicalNotes.

26.16 VOLATILITY AND VARIANCE SWAPS

A volatility swap is an agreement to exchange the realized volatility of an asset between time 0 and time T for a prespecifed fixed volatility. The realized volatility is usually calculated as described in Section 15.4 but with the assumption that the mean daily return is zero. Suppose that there are n daily observations on the asset price during the period between time 0 and time T. The realized volatility is

$$\bar{\sigma} = \sqrt{\frac{252}{n-2} \sum_{i=1}^{n-1} \left[\ln\left(\frac{S_{i+1}}{S_i}\right) \right]^2}$$

where S_i is the ith observation on the asset price. (Sometimes $n-1$ might replace $n-2$ in this formula.)

The payoff from the volatility swap at time T to the payer of the fixed volatility is $L_{\text{vol}}(\bar{\sigma} - \sigma_K)$, where L_{vol} is the notional principal and σ_K is the fixed volatility. Whereas an option provides a complex exposure to the asset price and volatility, a volatility swap is simpler in that it has exposure only to volatility.

A variance swap is an agreement to exchange the realized variance rate $\bar{V}$ between time 0 and time T for a prespecified variance rate. The variance rate is the square of the volatility ($\bar{V} = \bar{\sigma}^2$). Variance swaps are easier to value than volatility swaps. This is because the variance rate between time 0 and time T can be replicated using a portfolio of put and call options. The payoff from a variance swap at time T to the payer of the fixed variance rate is $L_{\text{var}}(\bar{V} - V_K)$, where L_{var} is the notional principal and V_K is the fixed variance rate. Often the notional principal for a variance swap is expressed in terms of the corresponding notional principal for a volatility swap using $L_{\text{var}} = L_{\text{vol}}/(2\sigma_K)$.

Valuation of Variance Swap

Technical Note 22 at www-2.rotman.utoronto.ca/~hull/TechnicalNotes shows that, for any value S^* of the asset price, the expected average variance between times 0 and T is

$$\hat{E}(\bar{V}) = \frac{2}{T}\ln\frac{F_0}{S^*} - \frac{2}{T}\left[\frac{F_0}{S^*} - 1\right] + \frac{2}{T}\left[\int_{K=0}^{S^*}\frac{1}{K^2}e^{rT}p(K)\,dK + \int_{K=S^*}^{\infty}\frac{1}{K^2}e^{rT}c(K)\,dK\right] \quad (26.6)$$

where F_0 is the forward price of the asset for a contract maturing at time T, $c(K)$ is the price of a European call option with strike price K and time to maturity T, and $p(K)$ is the price of a European put option with strike price K and time to maturity T.

This provides a way of valuing a variance swap.[14] The value of an agreement to receive the realized variance between time 0 and time T and pay a variance rate of V_K, with both being applied to a principal of L_{var}, is

$$L_{var}[\hat{E}(\bar{V}) - V_K]e^{-rT} \quad (26.7)$$

Suppose that the prices of European options with strike prices K_i ($1 \leqslant i \leqslant n$) are known, where $K_1 < K_2 < \cdots < K_n$. A standard approach for implementing equation (26.6) is to set S^* equal to the first strike price below F_0 and then approximate the integrals as

$$\int_{K=0}^{S^*}\frac{1}{K^2}e^{rT}p(K)\,dK + \int_{K=S^*}^{\infty}\frac{1}{K^2}e^{rT}c(K)\,dK = \sum_{i=1}^{n}\frac{\Delta K_i}{K_i^2}e^{rT}Q(K_i) \quad (26.8)$$

where $\Delta K_i = 0.5(K_{i+1} - K_{i-1})$ for $2 \leqslant i \leqslant n-1$, $\Delta K_1 = K_2 - K_1$, $\Delta K_n = K_n - K_{n-1}$. The function $Q(K_i)$ is the price of a European put option with strike price K_i if $K_i < S^*$ and the price of a European call option with strike price K_i if $K_i > S^*$. When $K_i = S^*$, the function $Q(K_i)$ is equal to the average of the prices of a European call and a European put with strike price K_i.

Example 26.4

Consider a 3-month contract to receive the realized variance rate of an index over the 3 months and pay a variance rate of 0.045 on a principal of \$100 million. The risk-free rate is 4% and the dividend yield on the index is 1%. The current level of the index is 1020. Suppose that, for strike prices of 800, 850, 900, 950, 1,000, 1,050, 1,100, 1,150, 1,200, the 3-month implied volatilities of the index are 29%, 28%, 27%, 26%, 25%, 24%, 23%, 22%, 21%, respectively. In this case, $n = 9$, $K_1 = 800$, $K_2 = 850, \ldots$, $K_9 = 1,200$, $F_0 = 1,020e^{(0.04-0.01)\times0.25} = 1,027.68$, and $S^* = 1,000$. DerivaGem shows that $Q(K_1) = 2.22$, $Q(K_2) = 5.22$, $Q(K_3) = 11.05$, $Q(K_4) = 21.27$, $Q(K_5) = 51.21$, $Q(K_6) = 38.94$, $Q(K_7) = 20.69$, $Q(K_8) = 9.44$, $Q(K_9) = 3.57$. Also, $\Delta K_i = 50$ for all i. Hence,

$$\sum_{i}^{n}\frac{\Delta K_i}{K_i^2}e^{rT}Q(K_i) = 0.008139$$

From equations (26.6) and (26.8), it follows that

$$\hat{E}(\bar{V}) = \frac{2}{0.25}\ln\left(\frac{1027.68}{1,000}\right) - \frac{2}{0.25}\left(\frac{1027.68}{1,000} - 1\right) + \frac{2}{0.25} \times 0.008139 = 0.0621$$

---

[14] See also K. Demeterfi, E. Derman, M. Kamal, and J. Zou, "A Guide to Volatility and Variance Swaps," *The Journal of Derivatives*, 6, 4 (Summer 1999), 9–32. For options on variance and volatility, see P. Carr and R. Lee, "Realized Volatility and Variance: Options via Swaps," *Risk*, May 2007, 76–83.

From equation (26.7), the value of the variance swap (in millions of dollars) is $100 \times (0.0621 - 0.045)e^{-0.04 \times 0.25} = 1.69$.

Valuation of a Volatility Swap

To value a volatility swap, we require $\hat{E}(\bar{\sigma})$, where $\bar{\sigma}$ is the average value of volatility between time 0 and time T. We can write

$$\bar{\sigma} = \sqrt{\hat{E}(\bar{V})}\sqrt{1 + \frac{\bar{V} - \hat{E}(\bar{V})}{\hat{E}(\bar{V})}}$$

Expanding the second term on the right-hand side in a series gives the approximation:

$$\bar{\sigma} = \sqrt{\hat{E}(\bar{V})}\left\{1 + \frac{\bar{V} - \hat{E}(\bar{V})}{2\hat{E}(\bar{V})} - \frac{1}{8}\left[\frac{\bar{V} - \hat{E}(\bar{V})}{\hat{E}(\bar{V})}\right]^2\right\}$$

Taking expectations,

$$\hat{E}(\bar{\sigma}) = \sqrt{\hat{E}(\bar{V})}\left\{1 - \frac{1}{8}\left[\frac{\text{var}(\bar{V})}{\hat{E}(\bar{V})^2}\right]\right\} \tag{26.9}$$

where $\text{var}(\bar{V})$ is the variance of $\bar{V}$. The valuation of a volatility swap therefore requires an estimate of the variance of the average variance rate during the life of the contract. The value of an agreement to receive the realized volatility between time 0 and time T and pay a volatility of σ_K, with both being applied to a principal of L_{vol}, is

$$L_{\text{vol}}[\hat{E}(\bar{\sigma}) - \sigma_K]e^{-rT}$$

Example 26.5

For the situation in Example 26.4, consider a volatility swap where the realized volatility is received and a volatility of 23% is paid on a principal of $100 million. In this case $\hat{E}(\bar{V}) = 0.0621$. Suppose that the standard deviation of the average variance over 3 months has been estimated as 0.01. This means that $\text{var}(\bar{V}) = 0.0001$. Equation (26.9) gives

$$\hat{E}(\bar{\sigma}) = \sqrt{0.0621}\left(1 - \frac{1}{8} \times \frac{0.0001}{0.0621^2}\right) = 0.2484$$

The value of the swap in (millions of dollars) is

$$100 \times (0.2484 - 0.23)e^{-0.04 \times 0.25} = 1.82$$

The VIX Index

In equation (26.6), the ln function can be approximated by the first two terms in a series expansion:

$$\ln\left(\frac{F_0}{S^*}\right) = \left(\frac{F_0}{S^*} - 1\right) - \frac{1}{2}\left(\frac{F_0}{S^*} - 1\right)^2$$

This means that the risk-neutral expected cumulative variance is calculated as

$$\hat{E}(\bar{V})T = -\left(\frac{F_0}{S^*} - 1\right)^2 + 2\sum_{i=1}^{n}\frac{\Delta K_i}{K_i^2}e^{rT}Q(K_i) \tag{26.10}$$

Since 2004 the VIX volatility index (see Section 15.11) has been based on equation (26.10). The procedure used on any given day is to calculate $\hat{E}(\bar{V})T$ for options that trade in the market and have maturities immediately above and below 30 days. The 30-day risk-neutral expected cumulative variance is calculated from these two numbers using interpolation. This is then multiplied by 365/30 and the index is set equal to the square root of the result. More details on the calculation can be found on the CBOE website.

26.17 STATIC OPTIONS REPLICATION

If the procedures described in Chapter 19 are used for hedging exotic options, some are easy to handle, but others are very difficult because of discontinuities (see Business Snapshot 26.1). For the difficult cases, a technique known as static options replication is sometimes useful.[15] This involves searching for a portfolio of actively traded options that approximately replicates the exotic option. Shorting this position provides the hedge.[16]

The basic principle underlying static options replication is as follows. If two portfolios are worth the same on a certain boundary, they are also worth the same at all interior points of the boundary. Consider as an example a 9-month up-and-out call option on a non-dividend-paying stock where the stock price is 50, the strike price is 50, the barrier is 60, the risk-free interest rate is 10% per annum, and the volatility is 30% per annum. Suppose that $f(S, t)$ is the value of the option at time t for a stock price of S. Any boundary in (S, t) space can be used for the purposes of producing the replicating portfolio. A convenient one to choose is shown in Figure 26.1. It is defined by $S = 60$ and $t = 0.75$. The values of the up-and-out option on the boundary are given by

$$f(S, 0.75) = \max(S - 50, 0) \quad \text{when } S < 60$$
$$f(60, t) = 0 \quad \text{when } 0 \leqslant t \leqslant 0.75$$

There are many ways that these boundary values can be approximately matched using regular options. The natural option to match the first boundary is a 9-month European call with a strike price of 50. The first component of the replicating portfolio is therefore one unit of this option. (We refer to this option as option A.)

One way of matching the $f(60, t)$ boundary is to proceed as follows:

1. Divide the life of the option into N steps of length Δt

2. Choose a European call option with a strike price of 60 and maturity at time $N \Delta t$ $(= 9 \text{ months})$ to match the boundary at the $\{60, (N - 1)\Delta t\}$ point

3. Choose a European call option with a strike price of 60 and maturity at time $(N - 1)\Delta t$ to match the boundary at the $\{60, (N - 2)\Delta t\}$ point

and so on. Note that the options are chosen in sequence so that they have zero value on the parts of the boundary matched by earlier options.[17] The option with a strike price

---

[15] See E. Derman, D. Ergener, and I. Kani, "Static Options Replication," *Journal of Derivatives* 2, 4 (Summer 1995): 78–95.

[16] Technical Note 22 at www-2.rotman.utoronto.ca/~hull/TechnicalNotes provides an example of static replication. It shows that the variance rate of an asset can be replicated by a position in the asset and out-of-the-money options on the asset. This result, which leads to equation (26.6), can be used to hedge variance swaps.

[17] This is not a requirement. If K points on the boundary are to be matched, we can choose K options and solve a set of K linear equations to determine required positions in the options.

Business Snapshot 26.1 Is Delta Hedging Easier or More Difficult
 for Exotics?

As described in Chapter 19, we can approach the hedging of exotic options by
creating a delta neutral position and rebalancing frequently to maintain delta
neutrality. When we do this we find some exotic options are easier to hedge than
plain vanilla options and some are more difficult.

An example of an exotic option that is relatively easy to hedge is an average price
option where the averaging period is the whole life of the option. As time passes, we
observe more of the asset prices that will be used in calculating the final average. This
means that our uncertainty about the payoff decreases with the passage of time. As a
result, the option becomes progressively easier to hedge. In the final few days, the
delta of the option always approaches zero because price movements during this time
have very little impact on the payoff.

By contrast barrier options are relatively difficult to hedge. Consider a down-and-
out call option on a currency when the exchange rate is 0.0005 above the barrier. If
the barrier is hit, the option is worth nothing. If the barrier is not hit, the option may
prove to be quite valuable. The delta of the option is discontinuous at the barrier
making conventional hedging very difficult.

---

of 60 that matures in 9 months has zero value on the vertical boundary that is matched
by option A. The option maturing at time $i \, \Delta t$ has zero value at the point $\{60, i \, \Delta t\}$ that
is matched by the option maturing at time $(i + 1)\Delta t$ for $1 \leqslant i \leqslant N - 1$.

Suppose that $\Delta t = 0.25$. In addition to option A, the replicating portfolio consists of
positions in European options with strike price 60 that mature in 9, 6, and 3 months.
We will refer to these as options B, C, and D, respectively. Given our assumptions

---

Figure 26.1 Boundary points used for static options replication example.

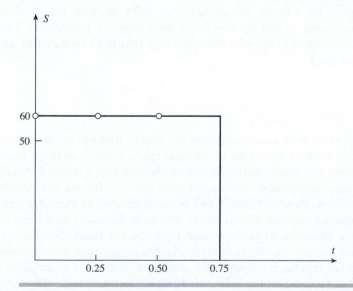

Table 26.1   The portfolio of European call options used to replicate an up-and-out option.

Option	Strike price	Maturity (years)	Position	Initial value
A	50	0.75	1.00	+6.99
B	60	0.75	−2.66	−8.21
C	60	0.50	0.97	+1.78
D	60	0.25	0.28	+0.17

about volatility and interest rates, option B is worth 4.33 at the {60, 0.5} point. Option A is worth 11.54 at this point. The position in option B necessary to match the boundary at the {60, 0.5} point is therefore $-11.54/4.33 = -2.66$. Option C is worth 4.33 at the {60, 0.25} point. The position taken in options A and B is worth −4.21 at this point. The position in option C necessary to match the boundary at the {60, 0.25} point is therefore $4.21/4.33 = 0.97$. Similar calculations show that the position in option D necessary to match the boundary at the {60, 0} point is 0.28.

The portfolio chosen is summarized in Table 26.1. (See also Sample Application F of the DerivaGem Applications.) It is worth 0.73 initially (i.e., at time zero when the stock price is 50). This compares with 0.31 given by the analytic formula for the up-and-out call earlier in this chapter. The replicating portfolio is not exactly the same as the up-and-out option because it matches the latter at only three points on the second boundary. If we use the same procedure, but match at 18 points on the second boundary (using options that mature every half month), the value of the replicating portfolio reduces to 0.38. If 100 points are matched, the value reduces further to 0.32.

To hedge a derivative, the portfolio that replicates its boundary conditions must be shorted. The hedge lasts until the end of the life of the derivative or until the boundary is reached, whichever happens first. If the boundary is reached, the hedge portfolio must be unwound and a new hedge portfolio set up.

Static options replication has the advantage over delta hedging that it does not require frequent rebalancing. It can be used for a wide range of derivatives. The user has a great deal of flexibility in choosing the boundary that is to be matched and the options that are to be used.

SUMMARY

Exotic options are options with rules governing the payoff that are more complicated than standard options. We have discussed 15 different types of exotic options: packages, perpetual American options, nonstandard American options, gap options, forward start options, cliquet options, compound options, chooser options, barrier options, binary options, lookback options, shout options, Asian options, options to exchange one asset for another, and options involving several assets. We have discussed how these can be valued using the same assumptions as those used to derive the Black–Scholes–Merton model in Chapter 15. Some can be valued analytically, but using much more complicated formulas than those for regular European calls and puts, some can be handled using analytic approximations, and some can be valued using extensions of the numerical procedures in Chapter 21. We will present more numerical procedures for valuing exotic options in Chapter 27.

Some exotic options are easier to hedge than the corresponding regular options; others are more difficult. In general, Asian options are easier to hedge because the payoff becomes progressively more certain as we approach maturity. Barrier options can be more difficult to hedge because delta is discontinuous at the barrier. One approach to hedging an exotic option, known as static options replication, is to find a portfolio of regular options whose value matches the value of the exotic option on some boundary. The exotic option is hedged by shorting this portfolio.

FURTHER READING

Carr, P., and R. Lee, "Realized Volatility and Variance: Options via Swaps," *Risk*, May 2007, 76–83.

Clewlow, L., and C. Strickland, *Exotic Options: The State of the Art*. London: Thomson Business Press, 1997.

Demeterfi, K., E. Derman, M. Kamal, and J. Zou, "More than You Ever Wanted to Know about Volatility Swaps," *Journal of Derivatives*, 6, 4 (Summer, 1999), 9–32.

Derman, E., D. Ergener, and I. Kani, "Static Options Replication," *Journal of Derivatives*, 2, 4 (Summer 1995): 78–95.

Geske, R., "The Valuation of Compound Options," *Journal of Financial Economics*, 7 (1979): 63–81.

Goldman, B., H. Sosin, and M. A. Gatto, "Path Dependent Options: Buy at the Low, Sell at the High," *Journal of Finance*, 34 (December 1979); 1111–27.

Margrabe, W., "The Value of an Option to Exchange One Asset for Another," *Journal of Finance*, 33 (March 1978): 177–86.

Rubinstein, M., and E. Reiner, "Breaking Down the Barriers," *Risk*, September (1991): 28–35.

Rubinstein, M., "Double Trouble," *Risk*, December/January (1991/1992): 53–56.

Rubinstein, M., "One for Another," *Risk*, July/August (1991): 30–32.

Rubinstein, M., "Options for the Undecided," *Risk*, April (1991): 70–73.

Rubinstein, M., "Pay Now, Choose Later," *Risk*, February (1991): 44–47.

Rubinstein, M., "Somewhere Over the Rainbow," *Risk*, November (1991): 63–66.

Rubinstein, M., "Two in One," *Risk* May (1991): 49.

Rubinstein, M., and E. Reiner, "Unscrambling the Binary Code," *Risk*, October 1991: 75–83.

Stulz, R. M., "Options on the Minimum or Maximum of Two Assets," *Journal of Financial Economics*, 10 (1982): 161–85.

Turnbull, S. M., and L. M. Wakeman, "A Quick Algorithm for Pricing European Average Options," *Journal of Financial and Quantitative Analysis*, 26 (September 1991): 377–89.

Practice Questions (Answers in Solutions Manual)

26.1. Explain the difference between a forward start option and a chooser option.

26.2. Describe the payoff from a portfolio consisting of a floating lookback call and a floating lookback put with the same maturity.

26.3. Consider a chooser option where the holder has the right to choose between a European call and a European put at any time during a 2-year period. The maturity dates and strike prices for the calls and puts are the same regardless of when the choice is made. Is it ever optimal to make the choice before the end of the 2-year period? Explain your answer.

26.4. Suppose that c_1 and p_1 are the prices of a European average price call and a European average price put with strike price K and maturity T, c_2 and p_2 are the prices of a European average strike call and European average strike put with maturity T, and c_3 and p_3 are the prices of a regular European call and a regular European put with strike price K and maturity T. Show that $c_1 + c_2 - c_3 = p_1 + p_2 - p_3$.

26.5. The text derives a decomposition of a particular type of chooser option into a call maturing at time T_2 and a put maturing at time T_1. Derive an alternative decomposition into a call maturing at time T_1 and a put maturing at time T_2.

26.6. Section 26.9 gives two formulas for a down-and-out call. The first applies to the situation where the barrier, H, is less than or equal to the strike price, K. The second applies to the situation where $H \geqslant K$. Show that the two formulas are the same when $H = K$.

26.7. Explain why a down-and-out put is worth zero when the barrier is greater than the strike price.

26.8. Suppose that the strike price of an American call option on a non-dividend-paying stock grows at rate g. Show that if g is less than the risk-free rate, r, it is never optimal to exercise the call early.

26.9. How can the value of a forward start put option on a non-dividend-paying stock be calculated if it is agreed that the strike price will be 10% greater than the stock price at the time the option starts?

26.10. If a stock price follows geometric Brownian motion, what process does $A(t)$ follow where $A(t)$ is the arithmetic average stock price between time zero and time t?

26.11. Explain why delta hedging is easier for Asian options than for regular options.

26.12. Calculate the price of a 1-year European option to give up 100 ounces of silver in exchange for 1 ounce of gold. The current prices of gold and silver are \$1,520 and \$16, respectively; the risk-free interest rate is 10% per annum; the volatility of each commodity price is 20%; and the correlation between the two prices is 0.7. Ignore storage costs.

26.13. Is a European down-and-out option on an asset worth the same as a European down-and-out option on the asset's futures price for a futures contract maturing at the same time as the option?

26.14. Answer the following questions about compound options:
   (a) What put–call parity relationship exists between the price of a European call on a call and a European put on a call? Show that the formulas given in the text satisfy the relationship.
   (b) What put–call parity relationship exists between the price of a European call on a put and a European put on a put? Show that the formulas given in the text satisfy the relationship.

26.15. Does a floating lookback call become more valuable or less valuable as we increase the frequency with which we observe the asset price in calculating the minimum?

26.16. Does a down-and-out call become more valuable or less valuable as we increase the frequency with which we observe the asset price in determining whether the barrier has been crossed? What is the answer to the same question for a down-and-in call?

26.17. Explain why a regular European call option is the sum of a down-and-out European call and a down-and-in European call. Is the same true for American call options?

26.18. What is the value of a derivative that pays off $100 in 6 months if an index is greater than 1,000 and zero otherwise? Assume that the current level of the index is 960, the risk-free rate is 8% per annum, the dividend yield on the index is 3% per annum, and the volatility of the index is 20%.

26.19. In a 3-month down-and-out call option on silver futures the strike price is $20 per ounce and the barrier is $18. The current futures price is $19, the risk-free interest rate is 5%, and the volatility of silver futures is 40% per annum. Explain how the option works and calculate its value. What is the value of a regular call option on silver futures with the same terms? What is the value of a down-and-in call option on silver futures with the same terms?

26.20. A new European-style floating lookback call option on a stock index has a maturity of 9 months. The current level of the index is 400, the risk-free rate is 6% per annum, the dividend yield on the index is 4% per annum, and the volatility of the index is 20%. Use DerivaGem to value the option.

26.21. Estimate the value of a new 6-month European-style average price call option on a non-dividend-paying stock. The initial stock price is $30, the strike price is $30, the risk-free interest rate is 5%, and the stock price volatility is 30%.

26.22. Use DerivaGem to calculate the value of:
   (a) A regular European call option on a non-dividend-paying stock where the stock price is $50, the strike price is $50, the risk-free rate is 5% per annum, the volatility is 30%, and the time to maturity is one year
   (b) A down-and-out European call which is as in (a) with the barrier at $45
   (c) A down-and-in European call which is as in (a) with the barrier at $45.

   Show that the option in (a) is worth the sum of the values of the options in (b) and (c).

26.23. Explain adjustments that have to be made when $r = q$ for (a) the valuation formulas for floating lookback call options in Section 26.11 and (b) the formulas for M_1 and M_2 in Section 26.13.

26.24. Value the variance swap in Example 26.4 of Section 26.16 assuming that the implied volatilities for options with strike prices 800, 850, 900, 950, 1,000, 1,050, 1,100, 1,150, 1,200 are 20%, 20.5%, 21%, 21.5%, 22%, 22.5%, 23%, 23.5%, 24%, respectively.

26.25. Verify that the results in Section 26.2 for the value of a derivative that pays Q when $S = H$ are consistent with those in Section 15.6.

Further Questions

26.26. What is the value in dollars of a derivative that pays off £10,000 in 1 year provided that the dollar/sterling exchange rate is greater than 1.5000 at that time? The current exchange rate is 1.4800. The dollar and sterling interest rates are 4% and 8% per annum, respectively. The volatility of the exchange rate is 12% per annum.

26.27. Consider an up-and-out barrier call option on a non-dividend-paying stock when the stock price is 50, the strike price is 50, the volatility is 30%, the risk-free rate is 5%, the time to maturity is 1 year, and the barrier at $80. Use the DerivaGem software to value the option and graph the relationship between (a) the option price and the stock price, (b) the delta and the stock price, (c) the option price and the time to maturity, and

(d) the option price and the volatility. Provide an intuitive explanation for the results you get. Show that the delta, gamma, theta, and vega for an up-and-out barrier call option can be either positive or negative.

26.28. Sample Application F in the DerivaGem Application Builder Software considers the static options replication example in Section 26.17. It shows the way a hedge can be constructed using four options (as in Section 26.17) and two ways a hedge can be constructed using 16 options.
(a) Explain the difference between the two ways a hedge can be constructed using 16 options. Explain intuitively why the second method works better.
(b) Improve on the four-option hedge by changing Tmat for the third and fourth options.
(c) Check how well the 16-option portfolios match the delta, gamma, and vega of the barrier option.

26.29. Consider a down-and-out call option on a foreign currency. The initial exchange rate is 0.90, the time to maturity is 2 years, the strike price is 1.00, the barrier is 0.80, the domestic risk-free interest rate is 5%, the foreign risk-free interest rate is 6%, and the volatility is 25% per annum. Use DerivaGem to develop a static option replication strategy involving five options.

26.30. Suppose that a stock index is currently 900. The dividend yield is 2%, the risk-free rate is 5%, and the volatility is 40%. Use the results in Technical Note 27 on the author's website to calculate the value of a 1-year average price call where the strike price is 900 and the index level is observed at the end of each quarter for the purposes of the averaging. Compare this with the price calculated by DerivaGem for a 1-year average price option where the price is observed continuously. Provide an intuitive explanation for any differences between the prices.

26.31. Use the DerivaGem Application Builder software to compare the effectiveness of daily delta hedging for (a) the option considered in Tables 19.2 and 19.3 and (b) an average price call with the same parameters. Use Sample Application C. For the average price option you will find it necessary to change the calculation of the option price in cell C16, the payoffs in cells H15 and H16, and the deltas (cells G46 to G186 and N46 to N186). Carry out 20 Monte Carlo simulation runs for each option by repeatedly pressing F9. On each run record the cost of writing and hedging the option, the volume of trading over the whole 20 weeks and the volume of trading between weeks 11 and 20. Comment on the results.

26.32. In the DerivaGem Application Builder Software modify Sample Application D to test the effectiveness of delta and gamma hedging for a call on call compound option on a 100,000 units of a foreign currency where the exchange rate is 0.67, the domestic risk-free rate is 5%, the foreign risk-free rate is 6%, the volatility is 12%. The time to maturity of the first option is 20 weeks, and the strike price of the first option is 0.015. The second option matures 40 weeks from today and has a strike price of 0.68. Explain how you modified the cells. Comment on hedge effectiveness.

26.33. Outperformance certificates (also called "sprint certificates," "accelerator certificates," or "speeders") are offered to investors by many European banks as a way of investing in a company's stock. The initial investment equals the stock price, S_0. If the stock price goes up between time 0 and time T, the investor gains k times the increase at time T, where k is a constant greater than 1.0. However, the stock price used to calculate the gain at time T is capped at some maximum level M. If the stock price goes down, the investor's loss is equal to the decrease. The investor does not receive dividends.

(a) Show that an outperformance certificate is a package.

(b) Calculate using DerivaGem the value of a one-year outperformance certificate when the stock price is 50 euros, $k = 1.5$, $M = 70$ euros, the risk-free rate is 5%, and the stock price volatility is 25%. Dividends equal to 0.5 euros are expected in 2 months, 5 months, 8 months, and 11 months.

26.34. Carry out the analysis in Example 26.4 of Section 26.16 to value the variance swap on the assumption that the life of the swap is 1 month rather than 3 months.

26.35. What is the relationship between a regular call option, a binary call option, and a gap call option?

26.36. Produce a formula for valuing a cliquet option where an amount Q is invested to produce a payoff at the end of n periods. The return earned each period is the greater of the return on an index (excluding dividends) and zero.

CHAPTER 27

More on Models and Numerical Procedures

Up to now the models we have used to value options have been based on the geometric Brownian motion model of asset price behavior that underlies the Black–Scholes–Merton formulas and the numerical procedures we have used have been relatively straightforward. In this chapter we introduce a number of new models and explain how the numerical procedures can be adapted to cope with particular situations.

Chapter 20 explained how traders overcome the weaknesses in the geometric Brownian motion model by using volatility surfaces. A volatility surface determines an appropriate volatility to substitute into Black–Scholes–Merton when pricing plain vanilla options. Unfortunately it says little about the volatility that should be used for exotic options when the pricing formulas of Chapter 26 are used. Suppose the volatility surface shows that the correct volatility to use when pricing a one-year plain vanilla option with a strike price of $40 is 27%. This is liable to be totally inappropriate for pricing a barrier option (or some other exotic option) that has a strike price of $40 and a life of one year.

The first part of this chapter discusses a number of alternatives to geometric Brownian motion that are designed to deal with the problem of pricing exotic options consistently with plain vanilla options. These alternative asset price processes fit the market prices of plain vanilla options better than geometric Brownian motion. As a result, we can have more confidence in using them to value exotic options.

The second part of the chapter extends the discussion of numerical procedures. It explains how convertible bonds and some types of path-dependent derivatives can be valued using trees. It discusses the special problems associated with valuing barrier options numerically and how these problems can be handled. Finally, it outlines alternative ways of constructing trees for two correlated variables and shows how Monte Carlo simulation can be used to value derivatives when there are early exercise opportunities.

As in earlier chapters, results are presented for derivatives dependent on an asset providing a yield at rate q. For an option on a stock index, q should be set equal to the dividend yield on the index; for an option on a currency, it should be set equal to the foreign risk-free rate; for an option on a futures contract, it should be set equal to the domestic risk-free rate.

27.1 ALTERNATIVES TO BLACK–SCHOLES–MERTON

The Black–Scholes–Merton model assumes that an asset's price changes continously in a way that produces a lognormal distribution for the price at any future time. There are many alternative processes that can be assumed. One possibility is to retain the property that the asset price changes continuously, but assume a process other than geometric Brownian motion. Another alternative is to overlay continuous asset price changes with jumps. Yet another alternative is to assume a process where all the asset price changes that take place are jumps. We will consider examples of all three types of processes in this section. In particular, we will consider the constant elasticity of variance model, Merton's mixed jump–diffusion model, and the variance-gamma model. All three models are implemented in DerivaGem. The types of processes we consider in this section are known collectively as *Levy processes*.[1]

The Constant Elasticity of Variance Model

One alternative to Black–Scholes–Merton is the *constant elasticity of variance* (CEV) model. This is a diffusion model where the risk-neutral process for a stock price S is

$$dS = (r - q)S\,dt + \sigma S^\beta\,dz$$

where r is the risk-free rate, q is the dividend yield, dz is a Wiener process, σ is a volatility parameter, and β is a positive constant.[2] The parameter σ is roughly equivalent to the volatility in the usual lognormal model multiplied by $F_0^{1-\beta}$.

When $\beta = 1$, the CEV model is the geometric Brownian motion model we have been using up to now. When $\beta < 1$, the volatility increases as the stock price decreases. This creates a probability distribution similar to that observed for equities with a heavy left tail and less heavy right tail (see Figure 20.4).[3] When $\beta > 1$, the volatility increases as the stock price increases. This creates a probability distribution with a heavy right tail and a less heavy left tail. This corresponds to a volatility smile where the implied volatility is an increasing function of the strike price. This type of volatility smile is sometimes observed for options on futures.

The valuation formulas for European call and put options under the CEV model are

$$c = S_0 e^{-qT}[1 - \chi^2(a, b + 2, c)] - K e^{-rT}\chi^2(c, b, a)$$

$$p = K e^{-rT}[1 - \chi^2(c, b, a)] - S_0 e^{-qT}\chi^2(a, b + 2, c)$$

when $0 < \beta < 1$, and

$$c = S_0 e^{-qT}[1 - \chi^2(c, -b, a)] - K e^{-rT}\chi^2(a, 2 - b, c)$$

$$p = K e^{-rT}[1 - \chi^2(a, 2 - b, c)] - S_0 e^{-qT}\chi^2(c, -b, a)$$

---

[1] Roughly speaking, a Levy process is a continuous-time stochastic process with stationary independent increments.

[2] See J. C. Cox and S. A. Ross, "The Valuation of Options for Alternative Stochastic Processes," *Journal of Financial Economics*, 3 (March 1976): 145–66.

[3] The reason is as follows. As the stock price decreases, the volatility increases making even lower stock price more likely; when the stock price increases, the volatility decreases making higher stock prices less likely.

when $\beta > 1$, with

$$a = \frac{[Ke^{-(r-q)T}]^{2(1-\beta)}}{(1-\beta)^2 v}, \qquad b = \frac{1}{1-\beta}, \qquad c = \frac{S^{2(1-\beta)}}{(1-\beta)^2 v}$$

where

$$v = \frac{\sigma^2}{2(r-q)(\beta-1)}[e^{2(r-q)(\beta-1)T} - 1]$$

and $\chi^2(z, k, v)$ is the cumulative probability that a variable with a noncentral χ^2 distribution with noncentrality parameter v and k degrees of freedom is less than z. A procedure for computing $\chi^2(z, k, v)$ is provided in Technical Note 12 on the author's website: www-2.rotman.utoronto.ca/~hull/TechnicalNotes.

The CEV model is useful for valuing exotic equity options. The parameters of the model can be chosen to fit the prices of plain vanilla options as closely as possible by minimizing the sum of the squared differences between model prices and market prices.

Merton's Mixed Jump–Diffusion Model

Merton has suggested a model where jumps are combined with continuous changes.[4] Define:

   λ: Average number of jumps per year

   k: Average jump size, measured as a percentage of the asset price

The percentage jump size is assumed to be drawn from a probability distribution in the model.

The probability of a jump in time Δt is $\lambda \, \Delta t$. The average growth rate in the asset price from the jumps is therefore λk. The risk-neutral process for the asset price is

$$\frac{dS}{S} = (r - q - \lambda k) \, dt + \sigma \, dz + dp$$

where dz is a Wiener process, dp is the Poisson process generating the jumps, and σ is the volatility of the geometric Brownian motion. The processes dz and dp are assumed to be independent.

An important particular case of Merton's model is where the logarithm of one plus the size of the percentage jump is normal. Assume that the standard deviation of the normal distribution is s. Merton shows that a European option price can then be written

$$\sum_{n=0}^{\infty} \frac{e^{-\lambda'T}(\lambda'T)^n}{n!} f_n$$

where $\lambda' = \lambda(1 + k)$. The variable f_n is the Black–Scholes–Merton option price when the dividend yield is q, the variance rate is

$$\sigma^2 + \frac{ns^2}{T}$$

---

[4] See R. C. Merton, "Option Pricing When Underlying Stock Returns Are Discontinuous," *Journal of Financial Economics*, 3 (March 1976): 125–44.

and the risk-free rate is

$$r - \lambda k + \frac{n\gamma}{T}$$

where $\gamma = \ln(1 + k)$.

This model gives rise to heavier left and heavier right tails than Black–Scholes–Merton. It can be used for pricing currency options. As in the case of the CEV model, the model parameters are chosen by minimizing the sum of the squared differences between model prices and market prices.

Simulating Jumps

Models that involve jumps can be implemented with Monte Carlo simulation. When jumps are generated by a Poisson process, the probability of exactly m jumps in time t is

$$\frac{e^{-\lambda t}(\lambda t)^m}{m!}$$

where λ is the average number of jumps per year. Equivalently, λt is the average number of jumps in time t.

Suppose that on average 0.5 jumps happen per year. The probability of m jumps in 2 years is

$$\frac{e^{-0.5 \times 2}(0.5 \times 2)^m}{m!}$$

Table 27.1 gives the probability and cumulative probability of 0, 1, 2, 3, 4, 5, 6, 7, and 8 jumps in 2 years. (The numbers in a table such as this can be calculated using the POISSON function in Excel.)

To simulate a process following jumps over 2 years, it is necessary to determine on each simulation trial:

1. The number of jumps

2. The size of each jump.

To determine the number of jumps, on each simulation trial we sample a random number between 0 and 1 and use Table 27.1 as a look-up table. If the random number is between 0 and 0.3679, no jumps occur; if the random number is between 0.3679 and

Table 27.1 Probabilities for number of jumps in 2 years.

Number of jumps, m	Probability of exactly m jumps	Probability of m jumps or less
0	0.3679	0.3679
1	0.3679	0.7358
2	0.1839	0.9197
3	0.0613	0.9810
4	0.0153	0.9963
5	0.0031	0.9994
6	0.0005	0.9999
7	0.0001	1.0000
8	0.0000	1.0000

0.7358, one jump occurs; if the random number is between 0.7358 and 0.9197, two jumps occur; and so on. To determine the size of each jump, it is necessary on each simulation trial to sample from the probability distribution for the jump size once for each jump that occurs. Once the number of jumps and the jump sizes have been determined, the final value of the variable being simulated is known for the simulation trial.

In a mixed jump–diffusion model, jumps are superimposed upon the usual lognormal diffusion process that is assumed for stock prices. The process then has two components (the usual diffusion component and the jump component) and each must be sampled separately. The diffusion component is sampled as described in Sections 21.6 and 21.7 while the jump component is sampled as just described. When derivatives are valued, it is important to ensure that the overall expected return from the asset (from both components) is the risk-free rate.

The Variance-Gamma Model

An example of a pure jump model that is proving quite popular is the *variance-gamma model*.[5] Define a variable g as the change over time T in a variable that follows a gamma process with mean rate of 1 and variance rate of v. A gamma process is a pure jump process where small jumps occur very frequently and large jumps occur only occasionally. The probability density for g is

$$\frac{g^{T/v-1}e^{-g/v}}{v^{T/v}\Gamma(T/v)}$$

where $\Gamma(\cdot)$ denotes the gamma function. This probability density can be computed in Excel using the GAMMADIST($\cdot,\cdot,\cdot,\cdot$) function. The first argument of the function is g, the second is T/v, the third is v, and the fourth is TRUE or FALSE, where TRUE returns the cumulative probability distribution function and FALSE returns the probability density function we have just given.

As usual, we define S_T as the asset price at time T, S_0 as the asset price today, r as the risk-free interest rate, and q as the dividend yield. Conditional on g, $\ln S_T$ has a risk-neutral probability distribution under the variance-gamma model that is normal. The conditional mean is

$$\ln S_0 + (r-q)T + \omega + \theta g$$

and the conditional standard deviation is

$$\sigma\sqrt{g}$$

where

$$\omega = (T/v)\ln(1 - \theta v - \sigma^2 v/2)$$

The variance-gamma model has three parameters: v, σ, and θ.[6] The parameter v is the variance rate of the gamma process, σ is the volatility, and θ is a parameter defining skewness. When $\theta = 0$, $\ln S_T$ is symmetric; when $\theta < 0$, it is negatively skewed (as for equities); and when $\theta > 0$, it is positively skewed.

---

[5] See D. B. Madan, P. P. Carr, and E. C. Chang, "The Variance-Gamma Process and Option Pricing," *European Finance Review*, 2 (1998): 79–105.

[6] Note that all these parameters are liable to change when we move from the real world to the risk-neutral world. This is in contrast to pure diffusion models where the volatility remains the same.

Suppose that we are interested in using Excel to obtain 10,000 random samples of the change in an asset price between time 0 and time T using the variance-gamma model. As a preliminary, we could set cells E1, E2, E3, E4, E5, E6, and E7 equal to $T, v, \theta, \sigma, r, q$, and S_0, respectively. We could also set E8 equal to ω by defining it as

$$= \$E\$1 * LN(1 - \$E\$3 * \$E\$2 - \$E\$4 * \$E\$4 * \$E\$2/2)/\$E\$2$$

We could then proceed as follows:

1. Sample values for g using the GAMMAINV function. Set the contents of cells A1, A2, ..., A10000 as

$$= GAMMAINV(RAND(), \ \$E\$1/\$E\$2, \ \$E\$2)$$

2. For each value of g we sample a value z for a variable that is normally distributed with mean θg and standard deviation $\sigma\sqrt{g}$. This can be done by defining cell B1 as

$$= A1 * \$E\$3 + SQRT(A1) * \$E\$4 * NORMSINV(RAND())$$

and cells B2, B3, ..., B10000 similarly.

3. The stock price S_T is given by

$$S_T = S_0 \exp[(r - q)T + \omega + z]$$

By defining C1 as

$$= \$E\$7 * EXP((\$E\$5 - \$E\$6) * \$E\$1 + B1 + \$E\$8)$$

and C2, C3, ..., C10000 similarly, random samples from the distribution of S_T are created in these cells.

Figure 27.1 Distributions obtained with variance-gamma process and geometric Brownian motion.

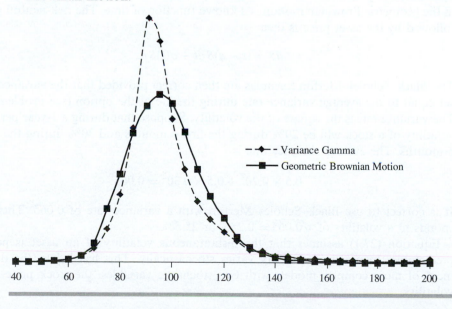

Figure 27.1 shows the probability distribution that is obtained using the variance-gamma model for S_T when $S_0 = 100$, $T = 0.5$, $v = 0.5$, $\theta = 0.1$, $\sigma = 0.2$, and $r = q = 0$. For comparison it also shows the distribution given by geometric Brownian motion when the volatility, σ is 0.2 (or 20%). Although not clear in Figure 27.1, the variance-gamma distribution has heavier tails than the lognormal distribution given by geometric Brownian motion.

One way of characterizing the variance-gamma distribution is that g defines the rate at which information arrives during time T. If g is large, a great deal of information arrives and the sample we take from a normal distribution in step 2 above has a relatively large mean and variance. If g is small, relatively little information arrives and the sample we take has a relatively small mean and variance. The parameter T is the usual time measure, and g is sometimes referred to as measuring economic time or time adjusted for the flow of information.

Semi-analytic European option valuation formulas are provided by Madan *et al.* (1998). The variance-gamma model tends to produce a U-shaped volatility smile. The smile is not necessarily symmetrical. It is very pronounced for short maturities and "dies away" for long maturities. The model can be fitted to either equity or foreign currency plain vanilla option prices.

27.2 STOCHASTIC VOLATILITY MODELS

The Black–Scholes–Merton model assumes that volatility is constant. In practice, as discussed in Chapter 23, volatility varies through time. The variance-gamma model reflects this with its g variable. Low values of g correspond to a low arrival rate for information and a low volatility; high values of g correspond to a high arrival rate for information and a high volatility.

An alternative to the variance-gamma model is a model where the process followed by the volatility variable is specified explicitly. Suppose first that the volatility parameter in the geometric Brownian motion is a known function of time. The risk-neutral process followed by the asset price is then

$$dS = (r - q)S \, dt + \sigma(t)S \, dz \qquad (27.1)$$

The Black–Scholes–Merton formulas are then correct provided that the variance rate is set equal to the average variance rate during the life of the option (see Problem 27.6). The variance rate is the square of the volatility. Suppose that during a 1-year period the volatility of a stock will be 20% during the first 6 months and 30% during the second 6 months. The average variance rate is

$$0.5 \times 0.20^2 + 0.5 \times 0.30^2 = 0.065$$

It is correct to use Black–Scholes–Merton with a variance rate of 0.065. This corresponds to a volatility of $\sqrt{0.065} = 0.255$, or 25.5%.

Equation (27.1) assumes that the instantaneous volatility of an asset is perfectly predictable. In practice, volatility varies stochastically. This has led to the development of more complex models with two stochastic variables: the stock price and its volatility.

One model that has been used by researchers is

$$dS/S = (r - q)\,dt + \sqrt{V}\,dz_S \tag{27.2}$$

$$dV = a(V_L - V)\,dt + \xi V^\alpha\,dz_V \tag{27.3}$$

where a, V_L, ξ, and α are constants, and dz_S and dz_V are Wiener processes. The variable V in this model is the asset's variance rate. The variance rate has a drift that pulls it back to a level V_L at rate a.

Hull and White show that, when volatility is stochastic but uncorrelated with the asset price, the price of a European option is the Black–Scholes–Merton price integrated over the probability distribution of the average variance rate during the life of the option.[7] Thus, a European call price is

$$\int_0^\infty c(\bar{V})\,g(\bar{V})\,d\bar{V}$$

where $\bar{V}$ is the average value of the variance rate, c is the Black–Scholes–Merton price expressed as a function of $\bar{V}$, and g is the probability density function of $\bar{V}$ in a risk-neutral world. This result can be used to show that Black–Scholes–Merton overprices options that are at the money or close to the money, and underprices options that are deep-in- or deep-out-of-the-money. The model is consistent with the pattern of implied volatilities observed for currency options (see Section 20.2).

The case where the asset price and volatility are correlated is more complicated. Option prices can be obtained using Monte Carlo simulation. In the particular case where $\alpha = 0.5$, Hull and White provide a series expansion and Heston provides an analytic result.[8] The pattern of implied volatilities obtained when the volatility is negatively correlated with the asset price is similar to that observed for equities (see Section 20.3).[9]

Chapter 23 discusses exponentially weighted moving average (EWMA) and GARCH(1,1) models. These are alternative approaches to characterizing a stochastic volatility model. Duan shows that it is possible to use GARCH(1,1) as the basis for an internally consistent option pricing model.[10] (See Problem 23.14 for the equivalence of GARCH(1,1) and stochastic volatility models.)

The SABR Model

A stochastic volatility model that has become very popular with practitioners for valuing European options (particularly interest rate options) maturing at a particular time T is the SABR model developed by Hagan *et al.* (2002).[11] The advantage of the

---

[7] See J.C. Hull and A. White, "The Pricing of Options on Assets with Stochastic Volatilities," *Journal of Finance*, 42 (June 1987): 281–300. This result is independent of the process followed by the variance rate.

[8] See J.C. Hull and A. White, "An Analysis of the Bias in Option Pricing Caused by a Stochastic Volatility," *Advances in Futures and Options Research*, 3 (1988): 27–61; S.L. Heston, "A Closed Form Solution for Options with Stochastic Volatility with Applications to Bonds and Currency Options," *Review of Financial Studies*, 6, 2 (1993): 327–43. The Heston model is implemented in DerivaGem 4.00.

[9] The reason is given in footnote 3.

[10] See J.-C. Duan, "The GARCH Option Pricing Model," *Mathematical Finance*, vol. 5 (1995), 13–32; and J.-C. Duan, "Cracking the Smile" *RISK*, vol. 9 (December 1996), 55-59.

[11] See P. Hagan, D. Kumar, A. Lesniewski, and D. Woodward, "Managing Smile Risk," *Wilmott*, September 2002: 84–108, and also www.math.ku.dk/~rolf/SABR.pdf. SABR is short for "stochastic alpha, beta, and rho." We use σ instead of Hagan *et al.*'s α.

model is that it can fit the volatility smiles observed in practice reasonably well and is useful for managing risks associated with movements in the smile through time.

The model is

$$dF = \sigma F^\beta \, dz$$

$$\frac{d\sigma}{\sigma} = v \, dw$$

where F is a forward interest rate or the forward price of an asset, dz and dw are Wiener processes, σ is the stochastic volatility, and β and v are constants.[12] Three other parameters are ρ, the correlation between dz and dw, σ_0, the initial value of σ, and F_0, the initial value of F.

Hagan *et al.* derive an approximate formula for the Black-model implied volatility given by SABR for a European option with strike price K (see Sections 18.7 and 18.8 for Black's model). Define

$$x = (F_0 K)^{(1-\beta)/2}, \qquad y = (1-\beta)\ln(F_0/K)$$

$$A = \frac{\sigma_0}{x(1 + y^2/24 + y^4/1920)}, \qquad B = 1 + \left(\frac{(1-\beta)^2 \sigma_0^2}{24x^2} + \frac{\rho\beta v \sigma_0}{4x} + \frac{2-3\rho^2}{24} v^2\right) T$$

$$\phi = \frac{vx}{\sigma_0} \ln\left(\frac{F_0}{K}\right), \qquad \chi = \ln\left(\frac{\sqrt{1 - 2\rho\phi + \phi^2} + \phi - \rho}{1 - \rho}\right)$$

The implied volatility is $AB\phi/\chi$. If $F = K$, this becomes $\sigma_0 B/(F_0^{1-\beta})$.[13]

The parameter σ_0 defines the level of the volatility. (It is roughly equivalent to the volatility estimate in the usual lognormal model multiplied by $F_0^{1-\beta}$.) The parameter ρ defines the shape of the smile. For a large positive ρ, the smile is upward sloping; for a large negative ρ, it is downward sloping; and for intermediate values of ρ, it is U-shaped. As the parameter v increases, the smile become more accentuated. (See Problem 27.24.) The SABR model is implemented in DerivaGem 4.00.

Often β is chosen equal to 0.5 in interest rate applications of the SABR model. The parameters ρ, σ_0, and v that fit the smile typically depend on the maturity T being considered. However, as mentioned earlier, the model has proved a useful way of managing the risks in smile movements.

27.3 THE IVF MODEL

The parameters of the models we have discussed so far can be chosen so that they provide an approximate fit to the prices of plain vanilla options on any given day. Financial institutions sometimes want to go one stage further and use a model that provides an exact fit to the prices of these options.[14] In 1994 Derman and Kani, Dupire,

---

[12] This is the process for F in a world where F has zero drift. When interest rates are stochastic, it is correct to discount the expected payoff from the derivative in this world from time T to time zero at the T-year rate. This is explained in the next chapter.

[13] Other researchers have come up with slightly more accurate formulas, but this is the one that is most widely used.

[14] There is a practical reason for this. If the bank does not use a model with this property, there is a danger that traders working for the bank will spend their time arbitraging the bank's internal models.

and Rubinstein developed a model that is designed to do this. It has become known as the *implied volatility function* (IVF) model or the *local volatility* model.[15] It provides an exact fit to the European option prices observed on any given day, regardless of the shape of the volatility surface.

The risk-neutral process for the asset price in the model has the form

$$dS = [r(t) - q(t)]S\,dt + \sigma(S, t)S\,dz$$

where $r(t)$ is the instantaneous forward interest rate for a contract maturing at time t and $q(t)$ is the dividend yield as a function of time. The volatility $\sigma(S, t)$ is a function of both S and t and is chosen so that the model prices all European options consistently with the market. It is shown both by Dupire and by Andersen and Brotherton-Ratcliffe that $\sigma(S, t)$ can be calculated analytically:[16]

$$[\sigma(K, T)]^2 = 2\frac{\partial c_{\mathrm{mkt}}/\partial T + q(T)c_{\mathrm{mkt}} + K[r(T) - q(T)]\partial c_{\mathrm{mkt}}/\partial K}{K^2(\partial^2 c_{\mathrm{mkt}}/\partial K^2)} \tag{27.4}$$

where $c_{\mathrm{mkt}}(K, T)$ is the market price of a European call option with strike price K and maturity T. If a sufficiently large number of European call prices are available in the market, this equation can be used to estimate the $\sigma(S, t)$ function.[17]

Andersen and Brotherton-Ratcliffe implement the model by using equation (27.4) together with the implicit finite difference method. An alternative approach, the *implied tree* methodology suggested by Derman and Kani and Rubinstein, involves constructing a tree for the asset price that is consistent with option prices in the market.

When it is used in practice the IVF model is recalibrated daily to the prices of plain vanilla options. It is a tool to price exotic options consistently with plain vanilla options. As discussed in Chapter 20 plain vanilla options define the risk-neutral probability distribution of the asset price at all future times. It follows that the IVF model gets the risk-neutral probability distribution of the asset price at all future times correct. This means that options providing payoffs at just one time (e.g., all-or-nothing and asset-or-nothing options) are priced correctly by the IVF model. However, the model does not necessarily get the joint distribution of the asset price at two or more times correct. This means that exotic options such as compound options and barrier options may be priced incorrectly.[18]

---

[15] See B. Dupire, "Pricing with a Smile," *Risk*, February (1994): 18–20; E. Derman and I. Kani, "Riding on a Smile," *Risk*, February (1994): 32–39; M. Rubinstein, "Implied Binomial Trees" *Journal of Finance*, 49, 3 (July 1994), 771–818.

[16] See B. Dupire, "Pricing with a Smile," *Risk*, February (1994), 18–20; L. B. G. Andersen and R. Brotherton-Ratcliffe "The Equity Option Volatility Smile: An Implicit Finite Difference Approach," *Journal of Computation Finance* 1, No. 2 (Winter 1997/98): 5–37. Dupire considers the case where r and q are zero; Andersen and Brotherton-Ratcliffe consider the more general situation.

[17] Some smoothing of the observed volatility surface is typically necessary.

[18] Hull and Suo test the IVF model by assuming that all derivative prices are determined by a stochastic volatility model. They found that the model works reasonably well for compound options, but sometimes gives serious errors for barrier options. See J. C. Hull and W. Suo, "A Methodology for the Assessment of Model Risk and its Application to the Implied Volatility Function Model," *Journal of Financial and Quantitative Analysis*, 37, 2 (June 2002): 297–318

27.4 CONVERTIBLE BONDS

We now move on to discuss how the numerical procedures presented in Chapter 21 can be modified to handle particular valuation problems. We start by considering convertible bonds.

Convertible bonds are bonds issued by a company where the holder has the option to exchange the bonds for the company's stock at certain times in the future. The *conversion ratio* is the number of shares of stock obtained for one bond (this can be a function of time). The bonds are almost always callable (i.e., the issuer has the right to buy them back at certain times at a predetermined prices). The holder always has the right to convert the bond once it has been called. The call feature is therefore usually a way of forcing conversion earlier than the holder would otherwise choose. Sometimes the holder's call option is conditional on the price of the company's stock being above a certain level.

Credit risk plays an important role in the valuation of convertibles. If credit risk is ignored, poor prices are obtained because the coupons and principal payments on the bond are overvalued. Ingersoll provides a way of valuing convertibles using a model similar to Merton's (1974) model discussed in Section 24.6.[19] He assumes geometric Brownian motion for the issuer's total assets and models the company's equity, its convertible debt, and its other debt as claims contingent on the value of the assets. Credit risk is taken into account because the debt holders get repaid in full only if the value of the assets exceeds the amount owing to them.

A simpler model that is widely used in practice involves modeling the issuer's stock price. It is assumed that the stock follows geometric Brownian motion except that there is a probability $\lambda \Delta t$ that there will be a default in each short period of time Δt. In the event of a default the stock price falls to zero and there is a recovery on the bond. The variable λ is the risk-neutral hazard rate defined in Section 24.2.

The stock price process can be represented by varying the usual binomial tree so that at each node there is:

1. A probability p_u of a percentage up movement of size u over the next time period of length Δt
2. A probability p_d of a percentage down movement of size d over the next time period of length Δt
3. A probability $\lambda \Delta t$, or more accurately $1 - e^{-\lambda \Delta t}$, that there will be a default with the stock price moving to zero over the next time period of length Δt

Assume that σ is the volatility of the stock price conditional on no default and p_{def} is the probability of default. Parameter values that match σ and give an overall expected return for the stock of $r - q$ are:

$$p_u = \frac{a - de^{-\lambda \Delta t}}{u - d}, \quad p_d = \frac{ue^{-\lambda \Delta t} - a}{u - d}, \quad p_{\text{def}} = 1 - e^{-\lambda \Delta t}, \quad u = e^{\sigma \sqrt{\Delta t}}, \quad d = \frac{1}{u}$$

where $a = e^{(r-q)\Delta t}$, r is the risk-free rate, and q is the dividend yield on the stock.

The life of the tree is set equal to the life of the convertible bond. The value of the convertible at the final nodes of the tree is calculated based on any conversion options

---

[19] See J.E. Ingersoll, "A Contingent Claims Valuation of Convertible Securities," *Journal of Financial Economics*, 4, (May 1977), 289–322.

that the holder has at that time. We then roll back through the tree. At nodes where the terms of the instrument allow conversion we test whether conversion is optimal. We also test whether the position of the issuer can be improved by calling the bonds. If so, we assume that the bonds are called and retest whether conversion is optimal.

Example 27.1

Consider a 9-month zero-coupon bond issued by company XYZ with a face value of $100. Suppose that it can be exchanged for two shares of company XYZ's stock at any time during the 9 months. Assume also that it is callable for $113 at any time. The initial stock price is $50, its volatility is 30% per annum, and there are no dividends. The hazard rate λ is 1% per year, and all risk-free rates for all maturities are 5%. Suppose that in the event of a default the bond is worth $40 (i.e., the recovery rate, as it is usually defined, is 40%).

Figure 27.2 shows the stock price tree that can be used to value the convertible when there are three time steps ($\Delta t = 0.25$). The upper number at each node is the stock price; the lower number is the price of the convertible bond. The tree parameters are:

$$u = e^{0.3\sqrt{0.25}} = 1.1618, \quad d = 1/u = 0.8607$$

$$a = e^{0.05 \times 0.25} = 1.0126, \quad p_u = 0.5115, \quad p_d = 0.4860, \quad p_{\text{def}} = 0.0025$$

At the three default nodes the stock price is zero and the bond price is 40.

Consider first the final nodes. At nodes G and H the bond should be converted and is worth twice the stock price. At nodes I and J the bond should not be converted and is worth 100.

Moving back through the tree enables the value to be calculated at earlier nodes. Consider, for example, node E. The value, if the bond is converted,

---

Figure 27.2 Tree for valuing convertible. Upper number at each node is stock price; lower number is convertible bond price.

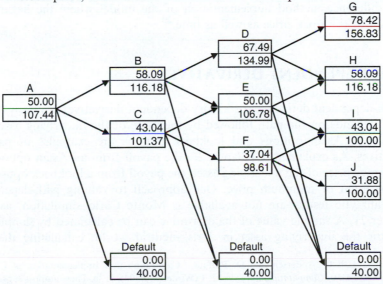

is $2 \times 50 = \$100$. If it is not converted, then there is (a) a probability 0.5115 that it will move to node H, where the bond is worth 116.18, (b) a 0.4860 probability that it will move down to node I, where the bond is worth 100, and (c) a 0.0025 probability that it will default and be worth 40. The value of the bond if it is not converted is therefore

$$(0.5115 \times 116.18 + 0.4860 \times 100 + 0.0025 \times 40) \times e^{-0.05 \times 0.25} = 106.78$$

This is more than the value of 100 that it would have if converted. We deduce that it is not worth converting the bond at node E. Finally, we note that the bond issuer would not call the bond at node E because this would be offering 113 for a bond worth 106.78.

As another example consider node B. The value of the bond if it is converted is $2 \times 58.09 = 116.18$. If it is not converted a similar calculation to that just given for node E gives its value as 119.54. The convertible bond holder will therefore choose not to convert. However, at this stage the bond issuer will call the bond for 113 and the bond holder will then decide that converting is better than being called. The value of the bond at node B is therefore 116.18. A similar argument is used to arrive at the value at node D. With no conversion the value is 135.08. However, the bond is called, forcing conversion and reducing the value at the node to 134.99.

The value of the convertible is its value at the initial node A, or 107.44.

When interest is paid on the debt, it must be taken into account. At each node, when valuing the bond on the assumption that it is not converted, the present value of any interest payable on the bond in the next time step should be included. The risk-neutral hazard rate λ can be estimated from either bond prices or credit default swap spreads. In a more general implementation, λ, σ, and r are functions of time. This can be handled using a trinomial rather than a binomial tree (see Section 21.4).

One disadvantage of the model we have presented is that the probability of default is independent of the stock price. This has led some researchers to suggest an implicit finite difference method implementation of the model where the hazard rate λ is a function of the stock price as well as time.[20]

27.5 PATH-DEPENDENT DERIVATIVES

A path-dependent derivative (or history-dependent derivative) is a derivative where the payoff depends on the path followed by the price of the underlying asset, not just its final value. Asian options and lookback options are examples of path-dependent derivatives. As explained in Chapter 26, the payoff from an Asian option depends on the average price of the underlying asset; the payoff from a lookback option depends on its maximum or minimum price. One approach to valuing path-dependent options when analytic results are not available is Monte Carlo simulation, as discussed in Chapter 21. A sample value of the derivative can be calculated by sampling a random path for the underlying asset in a risk-neutral world, calculating the payoff, and

---

[20] See, e.g., L. B. G. Andersen and D. Buffum, "Calibration and Implementation of Convertible Bond Models," *Journal of Computational Finance*, 7, 1 (Winter 2003/04), 1–34. These authors suggest assuming that the hazard rate is inversely proportional to S^{α}, where S is the stock price and α is a positive constant.

discounting the payoff at the risk-free interest rate. An estimate of the value of the derivative is found by obtaining many sample values of the derivative in this way and calculating their mean.

The main problem with Monte Carlo simulation is that the computation time necessary to achieve the required level of accuracy can be unacceptably high. Also, American-style path-dependent derivatives (i.e., path-dependent derivatives where one side has exercise opportunities or other decisions to make) cannot easily be handled. In this section, we show how the binomial tree methods presented in Chapter 21 can be extended to cope with some path-dependent derivatives.[21] The procedure can handle American-style path-dependent derivatives and is computationally more efficient than Monte Carlo simulation for European-style path-dependent derivatives.

For the procedure to work, two conditions must be satisfied:

1. The payoff from the derivative must depend on a single function, F, of the path followed by the underlying asset.

2. It must be possible to calculate the value of F at time $\tau + \Delta t$ from the value of F at time τ and the value of the underlying asset at time $\tau + \Delta t$.

First we construct a tree for the underlying asset's price in the usual way. The next step is to work forward through the tree establishing the maximum and minimum values of the path function at each node. Because the value of the path function at time $\tau + \Delta t$ depends only on the value of the path function at time τ and the value of the underlying variable at time $\tau + \Delta t$, the maximum and minimum values of the path function for the nodes at time $\tau + \Delta t$ can be calculated in a straightforward way from those for the nodes at time τ. The second stage is to choose representative values of the path function at each node. There are a number of approaches. A simple rule is to choose the representative values as the maximum value, the minimum value, and a number of other values that are equally spaced between the maximum and the minimum. As we roll back through the tree, we value the derivative for each of the representative values of the path function. When the value of the derivative is needed for other values of the path function, it is calculated by interpolation.

To illustrate the nature of the calculation, consider the problem of valuing the average price call option in Example 26.3 of Section 26.13 when the payoff depends on the arithmetic average stock price. The initial stock price is 50, the strike price is 50, the risk-free interest rate is 10%, the stock price volatility is 40%, and the time to maturity is 1 year. For 20 time steps, the binomial tree parameters are $\Delta t = 0.05$, $u = 1.0936$, $d = 0.9144$, $p = 0.5056$, and $1 - p = 0.4944$. The path function is the arithmetic average of the stock price.

Figure 27.3 shows the calculations that are carried out in one small part of the tree. Node X is the central node at time 0.2 year (at the end of the fourth time step). Nodes Y and Z are the two nodes at time 0.25 year that are reachable from node X. The stock price at node X is 50. Forward induction shows that the maximum average stock price that is achievable in reaching node X is 53.83. The minimum is 46.65. (The initial and final stock prices are included when calculating the average.) From node X, the tree branches to one of the two nodes Y and Z. At node Y, the stock price is 54.68 and the bounds for the average are 47.99 and 57.39. At node Z, the stock price is 45.72 and the bounds for the average stock price are 43.88 and 52.48.

---

[21] This approach was suggested in J. C. Hull and A. White, "Efficient Procedures for Valuing European and American Path-Dependent Options," *Journal of Derivatives*, 1, 1 (Fall 1993): 21–31.

Figure 27.3   Part of tree for valuing option on the arithmetic average.

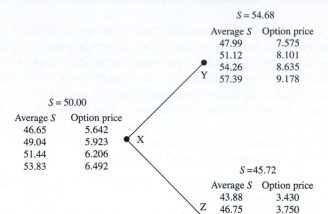

Suppose that the representative values of the average are chosen to be four equally spaced values at each node. This means that, at node X, averages of 46.65, 49.04, 51.44, and 53.83 are considered. At node Y, the averages 47.99, 51.12, 54.26, and 57.39 are considered. At node Z, the averages 43.88, 46.75, 49.61, and 52.48 are considered. Assume that backward induction has already been used to calculate the value of the option for each of the alternative values of the average at nodes Y and Z. Values are shown in Figure 27.3 (e.g., at node Y when the average is 51.12, the value of the option is 8.101).

Consider the calculations at node X for the case where the average is 51.44. If the stock price moves up to node Y, the new average will be

$$\frac{5 \times 51.44 + 54.68}{6} = 51.98$$

The value of the derivative at node Y for this average can be found by interpolating between the values when the average is 51.12 and when it is 54.26. It is

$$\frac{(51.98 - 51.12) \times 8.635 + (54.26 - 51.98) \times 8.101}{54.26 - 51.12} = 8.247$$

Similarly, if the stock price moves down to node Z, the new average will be

$$\frac{5 \times 51.44 + 45.72}{6} = 50.49$$

and by interpolation the value of the derivative is 4.182.

The value of the derivative at node X when the average is 51.44 is, therefore,

$$(0.5056 \times 8.247 + 0.4944 \times 4.182)e^{-0.1 \times 0.05} = 6.206$$

The other values at node X are calculated similarly. Once the values at all nodes at time 0.2 year have been calculated, the nodes at time 0.15 year can be considered.

The value given by the full tree for the option at time zero is 7.17. As the number of time steps and the number of averages considered at each node is increased, the value of the option converges to the correct answer. With 60 time steps and 100 averages at each node, the value of the option is 5.58. The analytic approximation for the value of the option, as calculated in Example 26.3, with continuous averaging is 5.62.

A key advantage of the method described here is that it can handle American options. The calculations are as we have described them except that we test for early exercise at each node for each of the alternative values of the path function at the node. (In practice, the early exercise decision is liable to depend on both the value of the path function and the value of the underlying asset.) Consider the American version of the average price call considered here. The value calculated using the 20-step tree and four averages at each node is 7.77; with 60 time steps and 100 averages, the value is 6.17.

The approach just described can be used in a wide range of different situations. The two conditions that must be satisfied were listed at the beginning of this section. Efficiency is improved somewhat if quadratic rather than linear interpolation is used at each node.

27.6 BARRIER OPTIONS

Chapter 26 presented analytic results for standard barrier options. This section considers numerical procedures that can be used for barrier options when there are no analytic results.

In principle, many barrier options can be valued using the binomial and trinomial trees discussed in Chapter 21. Consider an up-and-out option. A simple approach is to value this in the same way as a regular option except that, when a node above the barrier is encountered, the value of the option is set equal to zero.

Trinomial trees work better than binomial trees, but even for them convergence is very slow when the simple approach is used. A large number of time steps are required to obtain a reasonably accurate result. The reason for this is that the barrier being assumed by the tree is different from the true barrier.[22] Define the *inner barrier* as the barrier formed by nodes just on the inside of the true barrier (i.e., closer to the center of the tree) and *the outer barrier* as the barrier formed by nodes just outside the true barrier (i.e., farther away from the center of the tree). Figure 27.4 shows the inner and outer barrier for a trinomial tree on the assumption that the true barrier is horizontal. The usual tree calculations implicitly assume that the outer barrier is the true barrier because the barrier conditions are first used at nodes on this barrier. When the time step is Δt, the vertical spacing between the nodes is of order $\sqrt{\Delta t}$. This means that errors created by the difference between the true barrier and the outer barrier also tend to be of order $\sqrt{\Delta t}$.

One approach to overcoming this problem is to:

1. Calculate the price of the derivative on the assumption that the inner barrier is the true barrier.

---

[22] For a discussion of this, see P.P. Boyle and S.H. Lau, "Bumping Up Against the Barrier with the Binomial Method," *Journal of Derivatives*, 1, 4 (Summer 1994): 6–14.

Figure 27.4 Barriers assumed by trinomial trees.

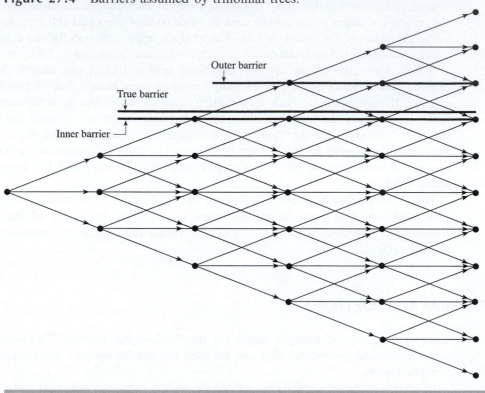

2. Calculate the value of the derivative on the assumption that the outer barrier is the true barrier.

3. Interpolate between the two prices.

Another approach is to ensure that nodes lie on the barrier. Suppose that the initial stock price is S_0 and that the barrier is at H. In a trinomial tree, there are three possible movements in the asset's price at each node: up by a proportional amount u; stay the same; and down by a proportional amount d, where $d = 1/u$. We can always choose u so that nodes lie on the barrier. The condition that must be satisfied by u is

$$H = S_0 u^N$$

or

$$\ln H = \ln S_0 + N \ln u$$

for some positive or negative N.

When discussing trinomial trees in Section 21.4, the value suggested for u was $e^{\sigma\sqrt{3\Delta t}}$, so that $\ln u = \sigma\sqrt{3\Delta t}$. In the situation considered here, a good rule is to choose $\ln u$ as close as possible to this value, consistent with the condition given above. This means that

$$\ln u = \frac{\ln H - \ln S_0}{N}$$

Figure 27.5   Tree with nodes lying on barrier.

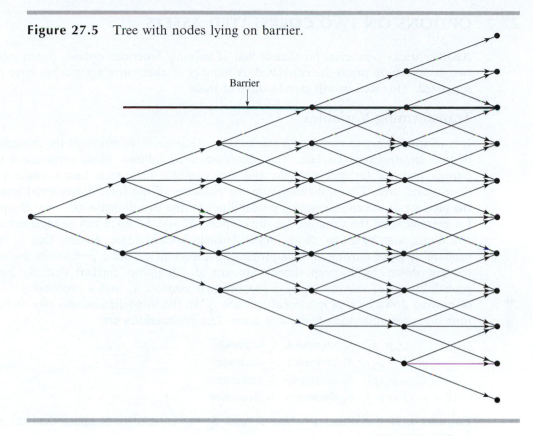

where

$$N = \text{int}\left[\frac{\ln H - \ln S_0}{\sigma\sqrt{3\Delta t}} + 0.5\right]$$

and int(x) is the integral part of x.

This leads to a tree of the form shown in Figure 27.5. The probabilities p_u, p_m, and p_d on the upper, middle, and lower branches of the tree are chosen to match the first two moments of the return, so that

$$p_d = -\frac{(r - q - \sigma^2/2)\Delta t}{2\ln u} + \frac{\sigma^2\Delta t}{2(\ln u)^2}, \quad p_m = 1 - \frac{\sigma^2\Delta t}{(\ln u)^2}, \quad p_u = \frac{(r - q - \sigma^2/2)\Delta t}{2\ln u} + \frac{\sigma^2\Delta t}{2(\ln u)^2}$$

The methods presented so far work reasonably well when the initial asset price is not close to the barrier. When the initial asset price is close to a barrier, the adaptive mesh model, which was introduced in Section 21.4, can be used.[23] The idea behind the model is that computational efficiency can be improved by grafting a fine tree onto a coarse tree to achieve a more detailed modeling of the asset price in the regions of the tree where it is needed most. To value a barrier option, it is computationally efficient to have a fine tree close to barriers with nodes on the barriers.

---

[23] See S. Figlewski and B. Gao, "The Adaptive Mesh Model: A New Approach to Efficient Option Pricing," *Journal of Financial Economics*, 53 (1999): 313–51.

27.7   OPTIONS ON TWO CORRELATED ASSETS

Another tricky numerical problem is that of valuing American options dependent on two assets whose prices are correlated. A number of alternative approaches have been suggested. This section will explain three of these.

Transforming Variables

It is relatively easy to construct a tree in three dimensions to represent the movements of two *uncorrelated* variables. The procedure is as follows. First, construct a two-dimensional tree for each variable, and then combine these trees into a single three-dimensional tree. The probabilities on the branches of the three-dimensional tree are the product of the corresponding probabilities on the two-dimensional trees. Suppose, for example, that the variables are stock prices, S_1 and S_2. Each can be represented in two dimensions by a Cox, Ross, and Rubinstein binomial tree. Assume that S_1 has a probability p_1 of moving up by a proportional amount u_1 and a probability $1 - p_1$ of moving down by a proportional amount d_1. Suppose further that S_2 has a probability p_2 of moving up by a proportional amount u_2 and a probability $1 - p_2$ of moving down by a proportional amount d_2. In the three-dimensional tree there are four branches emanating from each node. The probabilities are:

$$p_1 p_2 : \quad S_1 \text{ increases; } S_2 \text{ increases}$$
$$p_1(1 - p_2) : \quad S_1 \text{ increases; } S_2 \text{ decreases}$$
$$(1 - p_1)p_2 : \quad S_1 \text{ decreases; } S_2 \text{ increases}$$
$$(1 - p_1)(1 - p_2) : \quad S_1 \text{ decreases; } S_2 \text{ decreases}$$

Consider next the situation where S_1 and S_2 are correlated. Suppose that the risk-neutral processes are:

$$dS_1 = (r - q_1)S_1\,dt + \sigma_1 S_1\,dz_1$$
$$dS_2 = (r - q_2)S_2\,dt + \sigma_2 S_2\,dz_2$$

and the instantaneous correlation between the Wiener processes, dz_1 and dz_2, is ρ. This means that

$$d\ln S_1 = (r - q_1 - \sigma_1^2/2)\,dt + \sigma_1\,dz_1$$
$$d\ln S_2 = (r - q_2 - \sigma_2^2/2)\,dt + \sigma_2\,dz_2$$

Two new uncorrelated variables can be defined:[24]

$$x_1 = \sigma_2 \ln S_1 + \sigma_1 \ln S_2$$
$$x_2 = \sigma_2 \ln S_1 - \sigma_1 \ln S_2$$

These variables follow the processes

$$dx_1 = [\sigma_2(r - q_1 - \sigma_1^2/2) + \sigma_1(r - q_2 - \sigma_2^2/2)]\,dt + \sigma_1\sigma_2\sqrt{2(1 + \rho)}\,dz_A$$
$$dx_2 = [\sigma_2(r - q_1 - \sigma_1^2/2) - \sigma_1(r - q_2 - \sigma_2^2/2)]\,dt + \sigma_1\sigma_2\sqrt{2(1 - \rho)}\,dz_B$$

where dz_A and dz_B are uncorrelated Wiener processes.

---

[24] This idea was suggested in J.C. Hull and A. White, "Valuing Derivative Securities Using the Explicit Finite Difference Method," *Journal of Financial and Quantitative Analysis*, 25 (1990): 87–100.

The variables x_1 and x_2 can be modeled using two separate binomial trees. In time Δt, x_i has a probability p_i of increasing by h_i and a probability $1 - p_i$ of decreasing by h_i. The variables h_i and p_i are chosen so that the tree gives correct values for the first two moments of the distribution of x_1 and x_2. Because they are uncorrelated, the two trees can be combined into a single three-dimensional tree, as already described. At each node of the tree, S_1 and S_2 can be calculated from x_1 and x_2 using the inverse relationships

$$S_1 = \exp\left[\frac{x_1 + x_2}{2\sigma_2}\right] \quad \text{and} \quad S_2 = \exp\left[\frac{x_1 - x_2}{2\sigma_1}\right]$$

The procedure for rolling back through a three-dimensional tree to value a derivative is analogous to that for a two-dimensional tree.

Using a Nonrectangular Tree

Rubinstein has suggested a way of building a three-dimensional tree for two correlated stock prices by using a nonrectangular arrangement of the nodes.[25] From a node (S_1, S_2), where the first stock price is S_1 and the second stock price is S_2, there is a 0.25 chance of moving to each of the following:

$$(S_1u_1, S_2A), \quad (S_1u_1, S_2B), \quad (S_1d_1, S_2C), \quad (S_1d_1, S_2D)$$

where

$$u_1 = \exp[(r - q_1 - \sigma_1^2/2)\,\Delta t + \sigma_1\sqrt{\Delta t}\,]$$

$$d_1 = \exp[(r - q_1 - \sigma_1^2/2)\,\Delta t - \sigma_1\sqrt{\Delta t}\,]$$

and

$$A = \exp[(r - q_2 - \sigma_2^2/2)\Delta t + \sigma_2\sqrt{\Delta t}\,(\rho + \sqrt{1 - \rho^2}\,)]$$

$$B = \exp[(r - q_2 - \sigma_2^2/2)\Delta t + \sigma_2\sqrt{\Delta t}\,(\rho - \sqrt{1 - \rho^2}\,)]$$

$$C = \exp[(r - q_2 - \sigma_2^2/2)\Delta t - \sigma_2\sqrt{\Delta t}\,(\rho - \sqrt{1 - \rho^2}\,)]$$

$$D = \exp[(r - q_2 - \sigma_2^2/2)\Delta t - \sigma_2\sqrt{\Delta t}\,(\rho + \sqrt{1 - \rho^2}\,)]$$

When the correlation is zero, this method is equivalent to constructing separate trees for S_1 and S_2 using the alternative binomial tree construction method in Section 21.4.

Adjusting the Probabilities

A third approach to building a three-dimensional tree for S_1 and S_2 involves first assuming no correlation and then adjusting the probabilities at each node to reflect the correlation.[26] The alternative binomial tree construction method for each of S_1 and S_2 in Section 21.4 is used. This method has the property that all probabilities are 0.5. When the two binomial trees are combined on the assumption that there is no correlation, the

[25] See M. Rubinstein, "Return to Oz," *Risk*, November (1994): 67–70.

[26] This approach was suggested in the context of interest rate trees in J. C. Hull and A. White, "Numerical Procedures for Implementing Term Structure Models II: Two-Factor Models," *Journal of Derivatives*, Winter (1994): 37–48.

Table 27.2 Combination of binomials assuming
no correlation.

S_2-move	S_1-move	
	Down	Up
Up	0.25	0.25
Down	0.25	0.25

Table 27.3 Combination of binomials assuming
correlation of ρ.

S_2-move	S_1-move	
	Down	Up
Up	$0.25(1 - \rho)$	$0.25(1 + \rho)$
Down	$0.25(1 + \rho)$	$0.25(1 - \rho)$

probabilities are as shown in Table 27.2. When the probabilities are adjusted to reflect the correlation, they become those shown in Table 27.3.

27.8 MONTE CARLO SIMULATION AND AMERICAN OPTIONS

Monte Carlo simulation is well suited to valuing path-dependent options and options where there are many stochastic variables. Trees and finite difference methods are well suited to valuing American-style options. What happens if an option is both path dependent and American? What happens if an American option depends on several stochastic variables? Section 27.5 explained a way in which the binomial tree approach can be modified to value path-dependent options in some situations. A number of researchers have adopted a different approach by searching for a way in which Monte Carlo simulation can be used to value American-style options.[27] This section explains two alternative ways of proceeding.

The Least-Squares Approach

In order to value an American-style option it is necessary to choose between exercising and continuing at each early exercise point. The value of exercising is normally easy to determine. A number of researchers including Longstaff and Schwartz provide a way of determining the value of continuing when Monte Carlo simulation is used.[28] Their approach involves using a least-squares analysis to determine the best-fit relationship between the value of continuing and the values of relevant variables at each time an early exercise decision has to be made. The approach is best illustrated with a numerical example. We use the one in the Longstaff–Schwartz paper.

---

[27] Tilley was the first researcher to publish a solution to the problem. See J. A. Tilley, "Valuing American Options in a Path Simulation Model," *Transactions of the Society of Actuaries*, 45 (1993): 83–104.

[28] See F. A. Longstaff and E. S. Schwartz, "Valuing American Options by Simulation: A Simple Least-Squares Approach," *Review of Financial Studies*, 14, 1 (Spring 2001): 113–47.

Table 27.4 Sample paths for put option example.

Path	$t = 0$	$t = 1$	$t = 2$	$t = 3$
1	1.00	1.09	1.08	1.34
2	1.00	1.16	1.26	1.54
3	1.00	1.22	1.07	1.03
4	1.00	0.93	0.97	0.92
5	1.00	1.11	1.56	1.52
6	1.00	0.76	0.77	0.90
7	1.00	0.92	0.84	1.01
8	1.00	0.88	1.22	1.34

Consider a 3-year American put option on a non-dividend-paying stock that can be exercised at the end of year 1, the end of year 2, and the end of year 3. The risk-free rate is 6% per annum (continuously compounded). The current stock price is 1.00 and the strike price is 1.10. Assume that the eight paths shown in Table 27.4 are sampled for the stock price. (This example is for illustration only; in practice many more paths would be sampled.) If the option can be exercised only at the 3-year point, it provides a cash flow equal to its intrinsic value at that point. This is shown in the last column of Table 27.5.

If the put option is in the money at the 2-year point, the option holder must decide whether to exercise. Table 27.4 shows that the option is in the money at the 2-year point for paths 1, 3, 4, 6, and 7. For these paths, we assume an approximate relationship:

$$V = a + bS + cS^2$$

where S is the stock price at the 2-year point and V is the value of continuing, discounted back to the 2-year point. Our five observations on S are: 1.08, 1.07, 0.97, 0.77, and 0.84. From Table 27.5 the corresponding values for V are: 0.00, $0.07e^{-0.06\times1}$, $0.18e^{-0.06\times1}$, $0.20e^{-0.06\times1}$, and $0.09e^{-0.06\times1}$. The values of a, b, and c that minimize

$$\sum_{i=1}^{5}(V_i - a - bS_i - cS_i^2)^2$$

where S_i and V_i are the ith observation on S and V, respectively, are $a = -1.070$,

Table 27.5 Cash flows if exercise only possible at 3-year point.

Path	$t = 1$	$t = 2$	$t = 3$
1	0.00	0.00	0.00
2	0.00	0.00	0.00
3	0.00	0.00	0.07
4	0.00	0.00	0.18
5	0.00	0.00	0.00
6	0.00	0.00	0.20
7	0.00	0.00	0.09
8	0.00	0.00	0.00

Table 27.6 Cash flows if exercise only possible at 2- and 3-year point.

Path	$t = 1$	$t = 2$	$t = 3$
1	0.00	0.00	0.00
2	0.00	0.00	0.00
3	0.00	0.00	0.07
4	0.00	0.13	0.00
5	0.00	0.00	0.00
6	0.00	0.33	0.00
7	0.00	0.26	0.00
8	0.00	0.00	0.00

$b = 2.983$ and $c = -1.813$, so that the best-fit relationship is

$$V = -1.070 + 2.983S - 1.813S^2$$

This gives the value at the 2-year point of continuing for paths 1, 3, 4, 6, and 7 of 0.0369, 0.0461, 0.1176, 0.1520, and 0.1565, respectively. From Table 27.4 the value of exercising is 0.02, 0.03, 0.13, 0.33, and 0.26. This means that we should exercise at the 2-year point for paths 4, 6, and 7. Table 27.6 summarizes the cash flows assuming exercise at either the 2-year point or the 3-year point for the eight paths.

Consider next the paths that are in the money at the 1-year point. These are paths 1, 4, 6, 7, and 8. From Table 27.4 the values of S for the paths are 1.09, 0.93, 0.76, 0.92, and 0.88, respectively. From Table 27.6, the corresponding continuation values discounted back to $t = 1$ are 0.00, $0.13e^{-0.06 \times 1}$, $0.33e^{-0.06 \times 1}$, $0.26e^{-0.06 \times 1}$, and 0.00, respectively. The least-squares relationship is

$$V = 2.038 - 3.335S + 1.356S^2$$

This gives the value of continuing at the 1-year point for paths 1, 4, 6, 7, 8 as 0.0139, 0.1092, 0.2866, 0.1175, and 0.1533, respectively. From Table 27.4 the value of exercising is 0.01, 0.17, 0.34, 0.18, and 0.22, respectively. This means that we should exercise at the 1-year point for paths 4, 6, 7, and 8. Table 27.7 summarizes the cash flows assuming that early exercise is possible at all three times. The value of the option is determined by

Table 27.7 Cash flows from option.

Path	$t = 1$	$t = 2$	$t = 3$
1	0.00	0.00	0.00
2	0.00	0.00	0.00
3	0.00	0.00	0.07
4	0.17	0.00	0.00
5	0.00	0.00	0.00
6	0.34	0.00	0.00
7	0.18	0.00	0.00
8	0.22	0.00	0.00

discounting each cash flow back to time zero at the risk-free rate and calculating the mean of the results. It is

$$\tfrac{1}{8}(0.07e^{-0.06\times3} + 0.17e^{-0.06\times1} + 0.34e^{-0.06\times1} + 0.18e^{-0.06\times1} + 0.22e^{-0.06\times1}) = 0.1144$$

Since this is greater than 0.10, it is not optimal to exercise the option immediately.

This method can be extended in a number of ways. If the option can be exercised at any time we can approximate its value by considering a large number of exercise points (just as a binomial tree does). The relationship between V and S can be assumed to be more complicated. For example we could assume that V is a cubic rather than a quadratic function of S. The method can be used where the early exercise decision depends on several state variables. A functional form for the relationship between V and the variables is assumed and the parameters are estimated using the least-squares approach, as in the example just considered.

The Exercise Boundary Parameterization Approach

A number of researchers, such as Andersen, have proposed an alternative approach where the early exercise boundary is parameterized and the optimal values of the parameters are determined iteratively by starting at the end of the life of the option and working backward.[29] To illustrate the approach, we continue with the put option example and assume that the eight paths shown in Table 27.4 have been sampled. In this case, the early exercise boundary at time t can be parameterized by a critical value of S, $S^*(t)$. If the asset price at time t is below $S^*(t)$ we exercise at time t; if it is above $S^*(t)$ we do not exercise at time t. The value of $S^*(3)$ is 1.10. If the stock price is above 1.10 when $t = 3$ (the end of the option's life) we do not exercise; if it is below 1.10 we exercise. We now consider the determination of $S^*(2)$.

Suppose that we choose a value of $S^*(2)$ less than 0.77. The option is not exercised at the 2-year point for any of the paths. The value of the option at the 2-year point for the eight paths is then 0.00, 0.00, $0.07e^{-0.06\times1}$, $0.18e^{-0.06\times1}$, 0.00, $0.20e^{-0.06\times1}$, $0.09e^{-0.06\times1}$, and 0.00, respectively. The average of these is 0.0636. Suppose next that $S^*(2) = 0.77$. The value of the option at the 2-year point for the eight paths is then 0.00, 0.00, $0.07e^{-0.06\times1}$, $0.18e^{-0.06\times1}$, 0.00, 0.33, $0.09e^{-0.06\times1}$, and 0.00, respectively. The average of these is 0.0813. Similarly when $S^*(2)$ equals 0.84, 0.97, 1.07, and 1.08, the average value of the option at the 2-year point is 0.1032, 0.0982, 0.0938, and 0.0963, respectively. This analysis shows that the optimal value of $S^*(2)$ (i.e., the one that maximizes the average value of the option) is 0.84. (More precisely, it is optimal to choose $0.84 \leqslant S^*(2) < 0.97$.) When we choose this optimal value for $S^*(2)$, the value of the option at the 2-year point for the eight paths is 0.00, 0.00, 0.0659, 0.1695, 0.00, 0.33, 0.26, and 0.00, respectively. The average value is 0.1032.

We now move on to calculate $S^*(1)$. If $S^*(1) < 0.76$ the option is not exercised at the 1-year point for any of the paths and the value at the option at the 1-year point is $0.1032e^{-0.06\times1} = 0.0972$. If $S^*(1) = 0.76$, the value of the option for each of the eight paths at the 1-year point is 0.00, 0.00, $0.0659e^{-0.06\times1}$, $0.1695e^{-0.06\times1}$, 0.0, 0.34, $0.26e^{-0.06\times1}$, and 0.00, respectively. The average value of the option is 0.1008. Similarly when $S^*(1)$ equals 0.88, 0.92, 0.93, and 1.09 the average value of the option is 0.1283,

---

[29] See L. B. G. Andersen, "A Simple Approach to the Pricing of Bermudan Swaptions in the Multifactor LIBOR Market Model," *Journal of Computational Finance*, 3, 2 (Winter 2000): 1–32.

0.1202, 0.1215, and 0.1228, respectively. The analysis therefore shows that the optimal value of $S^*(1)$ is 0.88. (More precisely, it is optimal to choose $0.88 \leqslant S^*(1) < 0.92$.) The value of the option at time zero with no early exercise is $0.1283e^{-0.06 \times 1} = 0.1208$. This is greater than the value of 0.10 obtained by exercising at time zero.

In practice, tens of thousands of simulations are carried out to determine the early exercise boundary in the way we have described. Once the early exercise boundary has been obtained, the paths for the variables are discarded and a new Monte Carlo simulation using the early exercise boundary is carried out to value the option. Our American put option example is simple in that we know that the early exercise boundary at a time can be defined entirely in terms of the value of the stock price at that time. In more complicated situations it is necessary to make assumptions about how the early exercise boundary should be parameterized.

Upper Bounds

The two approaches we have outlined tend to underprice American-style options because they assume a suboptimal early exercise boundary. This has led Andersen and Broadie to propose a procedure that provides an upper bound to the price.[30] This procedure can be used in conjunction with any algorithm that generates a lower bound and pinpoints the true value of an American-style option more precisely than the algorithm does by itself.

SUMMARY

A number of models have been developed to fit the volatility smiles that are observed in practice. The constant elasticity of variance model leads to a volatility smile similar to that observed for equity options. The jump–diffusion model leads to a volatility smile similar to that observed for currency options. Variance-gamma and stochastic volatility models are more flexible in that they can lead to either the type of volatility smile observed for equity options or the type of volatility smile observed for currency options. The implied volatility function model provides even more flexibility than this. It is designed to provide an exact fit to any pattern of European option prices observed in the market.

The natural technique to use for valuing path-dependent options is Monte Carlo simulation. This has the disadvantage that it is fairly slow and unable to handle American-style derivatives easily. Luckily, trees can be used to value many types of path-dependent derivatives. The approach is to choose representative values for the underlying path function at each node of the tree and calculate the value of the derivative for each of these values as we roll back through the tree.

The binomial tree methodology can be extended to value convertible bonds. Extra branches corresponding to a default by the company are added to the tree. The roll-back calculations then reflect the holder's option to convert and the issuer's option to call.

Trees can be used to value many types of barrier options, but the convergence of the option value to the correct value as the number of time steps is increased tends to be slow. One approach for improving convergence is to arrange the geometry of the tree so

---

[30] See L. B. G. Andersen and M. Broadie, "A Primal-Dual Simulation Algorithm for Pricing Multi-Dimensional American Options," *Management Science*, 50, 9 (2004), 1222–34.

that nodes always lie on the barriers. Another is to use an interpolation scheme to adjust for the fact that the barrier being assumed by the tree is different from the true barrier. A third is to design the tree so that it provides a finer representation of movements in the underlying asset price near the barrier.

One way of valuing options dependent on the prices of two correlated assets is to apply a transformation to the asset price to create two new uncorrelated variables. These two variables are each modeled with trees and the trees are then combined to form a single three-dimensional tree. At each node of the tree, the inverse of the transformation gives the asset prices. A second approach is to arrange the positions of nodes on the three-dimensional tree to reflect the correlation. A third approach is to start with a tree that assumes no correlation between the variables and then adjust the probabilities on the tree to reflect the correlation.

Monte Carlo simulation is not naturally suited to valuing American-style options, but there are two ways it can be adapted to handle them. The first uses a least-squares analysis to relate the value of continuing (i.e, not exercising) to the values of relevant variables. The second involves parameterizing the early exercise boundary and determining it iteratively by working back from the end of the life of the option to the beginning.

FURTHER READING

Andersen, L. B. G., "A Simple Approach to the Pricing of Bermudan Swaptions in the Multifactor LIBOR Market Model," *Journal of Computational Finance*, 3, 2 (Winter 2000): 1–32.

Andersen, L. B. G., and R. Brotherton-Ratcliffe, "The Equity Option Volatility Smile: An Implicit Finite Difference Approach," *Journal of Computational Finance*, 1, 2 (Winter 1997/98): 3–37.

Bodurtha, J. N., and M. Jermakyan, "Non-Parametric Estimation of an Implied Volatility Surface," *Journal of Computational Finance*, 2, 4 (Summer 1999): 29–61.

Boyle, P. P., and S. H. Lau, "Bumping Up Against the Barrier with the Binomial Method," *Journal of Derivatives*, 1, 4 (Summer 1994): 6–14.

Cox, J. C. and S. A. Ross, "The Valuation of Options for Alternative Stochastic Processes," *Journal of Financial Economics*, 3 (March 1976), 145–66.

Derman, E., and I. Kani, "Riding on a Smile," *Risk*, February (1994): 32–39.

Duan, J.-C., "The GARCH Option Pricing Model," *Mathematical Finance*, 5 (1995): 13–32.

Duan, J.-C., "Cracking the Smile," *Risk*, December (1996): 55–59.

Dupire, B., "Pricing with a Smile," *Risk*, February (1994): 18–20.

Figlewski, S., and B. Gao, "The Adaptive Mesh Model: A New Approach to Efficient Option Pricing," *Journal of Financial Economics*, 53 (1999): 313–51.

Hagan, P., D. Kumar, A. Lesniewski, and D. Woodward, "Managing Smile Risk," *Wilmott*, September 2002: 84–108. Also www.math.ku.dk/~rolf/SABR.pdf.

Heston, S. L., "A Closed Form Solution for Options with Stochastic Volatility with Applications to Bonds and Currency Options," *Review of Financial Studies*, 6, 2 (1993): 327–43.

Hull, J. C., and A. White, "Efficient Procedures for Valuing European and American Path-Dependent Options," *Journal of Derivatives*, 1, 1 (Fall 1993): 21–31.

Hull J. C., and A. White, "The Pricing of Options on Assets with Stochastic Volatilities," *Journal of Finance*, 42 (June 1987): 281–300.

Hull, J. C. and W. Suo, "A Methodology for the Assessment of Model Risk and its Application to the Implied Volatility Function Model," *Journal of Financial and Quantitative Analysis*, 37, 2 (2002): 297–318.

Longstaff, F. A. and E. S. Schwartz, "Valuing American Options by Simulation: A Simple Least-Squares Approach," *Review of Financial Studies*, 14, 1 (Spring 2001): 113–47.

Madan D. B., P. P. Carr, and E. C. Chang, "The Variance-Gamma Process and Option Pricing" *European Finance Review*, 2 (1998): 79–105.

Merton, R. C., "Option Pricing When Underlying Stock Returns Are Discontinuous," *Journal of Financial Economics*, 3 (March 1976): 125–44.

Milanov, K., O. Kounchev, F. J. Fabozzi, S. Kim, and S. T. Rachev, "A Binomial Tree Model for Convertible Bond Pricing," 22, 3 (Winter 2013): 79–94.

Rebonato, R., '*Volatility and Correlation: The Perfect Hedger and the Fox*, 2nd edn. Chichester: Wiley, 2004.

Ritchken, P, and R. Trevor, "Pricing Options Under Generalized GARCH and Stochastic Volatility Processes," *Journal of Finance* 54, 1 (February 1999): 377–402

Rubinstein, M., "Implied Binomial Trees," *Journal of Finance*, 49, 3 (July 1994): 771–818.

Rubinstein, M., "Return to Oz," *Risk*, November (1994): 67–70.

Stutzer, M., "A Simple Nonparametric Approach to Derivative Security Valuation," *Journal of Finance*, 51 (December 1996): 1633–52.

Tilley, J. A., "Valuing American Options in a Path Simulation Model," *Transactions of the Society of Actuaries*, 45 (1993): 83–104.

Practice Questions (Answers in Solutions Manual)

27.1. Confirm that the CEV model formulas satisfy put–call parity.

27.2. What is Merton's mixed jump–diffusion model price for a European call option when $r = 5\%$, $q = 0$, $\lambda = 0.3$, $k = 50\%$, $\sigma = 25\%$, $S_0 = 30$, $K = 30$, $s = 50\%$, and $T = 1$. Use DerivaGem to check your price.

27.3. Confirm that Merton's jump–diffusion model satisfies put–call parity when the jump size is lognormal.

27.4. Suppose that the volatility of an asset will be 20% from month 0 to month 6, 22% from month 6 to month 12, and 24% from month 12 to month 24. What volatility should be used in Black–Scholes–Merton to value a 2-year option?

27.5. Consider the case of Merton's jump–diffusion model where jumps always reduce the asset price to zero. Assume that the average number of jumps per year is λ. Show that the price of a European call option is the same as in a world with no jumps except that the risk-free rate is $r + \lambda$ rather than r. Does the possibility of jumps increase or reduce the value of the call option in this case? (*Hint*: Value the option assuming no jumps and assuming one or more jumps. The probability of no jumps in time T is $e^{-\lambda T}$).

27.6. At time 0 the price of a non-dividend-paying stock is S_0. Suppose that the time interval between 0 and T is divided into two subintervals of length t_1 and t_2. During the first subinterval, the risk-free interest rate and volatility are r_1 and σ_1, respectively. During the second subinterval, they are r_2 and σ_2, respectively. Assume that the world is risk neutral.
(a) Use the results in Chapter 15 to determine the stock price distribution at time T in terms of r_1, r_2, σ_1, σ_2, t_1, t_2, and S_0.

(b) Suppose that $\bar{r}$ is the average interest rate between time zero and T and that $\bar{V}$ is the average variance rate between times zero and T. What is the stock price distribution as a function of T in terms of $\bar{r}$, $\bar{V}$, T, and S_0?

(c) What are the results corresponding to (a) and (b) when there are three subintervals with different interest rates and volatilities?

(d) Show that if the risk-free rate, r, and the volatility, σ, are known functions of time, the stock price distribution at time T in a risk-neutral world is

$$\ln S_T \sim \phi[\ln S_0 + (\bar{r} - \tfrac{1}{2}\bar{V})T, \ VT]$$

where $\bar{r}$ is the average value of r, $\bar{V}$ is equal to the average value of σ^2, and S_0 is the stock price today and $\phi(m, v)$ is a normal distribution with mean m and variance v.

27.7. Write down the equations for simulating the path followed by the asset price in the stochastic volatility model in equations (27.2) and (27.3).

27.8. "The IVF model does not necessarily get the evolution of the volatility surface correct." Explain this statement.

27.9. "The IVF model correctly values any derivative whose payoff depends on the value of the underlying asset at only one time." Explain why.

27.10. Use a three-time-step tree to value an American floating lookback call option on a currency when the initial exchange rate is 1.6, the domestic risk-free rate is 5% per annum, the foreign risk-free interest rate is 8% per annum, the exchange rate volatility is 15%, and the time to maturity is 18 months. Use the approach in Section 27.5.

27.11. What happens to the variance-gamma model as the parameter v tends to zero?

27.12. Use a three-time-step tree to value an American put option on the geometric average of the price of a non-dividend-paying stock when the stock price is $40, the strike price is $40, the risk-free interest rate is 10% per annum, the volatility is 35% per annum, and the time to maturity is three months. The geometric average is measured from today until the option matures.

27.13. Can the approach for valuing path-dependent options in Section 27.5 be used for a 2-year American-style option that provides a payoff equal to $\max(S_{ave} - K, 0)$, where S_{ave} is the average asset price over the three months preceding exercise? Explain your answer.

27.14. Verify that the 6.492 number in Figure 27.3 is correct.

27.15. Examine the early exercise policy for the eight paths considered in the example in Section 27.8. What is the difference between the early exercise policy given by the least squares approach and the exercise boundary parameterization approach? Which gives a higher option price for the paths sampled?

27.16. Consider a European put option on a non-dividend paying stock when the stock price is $100, the strike price is $110, the risk-free rate is 5% per annum, and the time to maturity is one year. Suppose that the average variance rate during the life of an option has a 0.20 probability of being 0.06, a 0.5 probability of being 0.09, and a 0.3 probability of being 0.12. The volatility is uncorrelated with the stock price. Estimate the value of the option. Use DerivaGem.

27.17. When there are two barriers how can a tree be designed so that nodes lie on both barriers?

27.18. Consider an 18-month zero-coupon bond with a face value of $100 that can be converted into five shares of the company's stock at any time during its life. Suppose that the current share price is $20, no dividends are paid on the stock, the risk-free rate for all maturities is 6% per annum with continuous compounding, and the share price volatility conditional on no default is 25% per annum. Assume that the hazard rate is 3% per year and the recovery rate is 35%. The bond is callable at $110. Use a three-time-step tree to calculate the value of the bond. What is the value of the conversion option (net of the issuer's call option)?

Further Questions

27.19. A new European-style floating lookback call option on a stock index has a maturity of 9 months. The current level of the index is 400, the risk-free rate is 6% per annum, the dividend yield on the index is 4% per annum, and the volatility of the index is 20%. Use the approach in Section 27.5 to value the option and compare your answer to the result given by DerivaGem using the analytic valuation formula.

27.20. Technical Note 13 at www-2.rotman.utoronto.ca/~hull/TechnicalNotes provides a different approach to valuing lookbacks. Value the lookback in Problem 27.19 using this approach. Show that it gives the same answer as the approach in Section 27.5.

27.21. Suppose that the volatilities used to price a 6-month currency option are as in Table 20.2. Assume that the domestic and foreign risk-free rates are 5% per annum and the current exchange rate is 1.00. Consider a bull spread that consists of a long position in a 6-month call option with strike price 1.05 and a short position in a 6-month call option with a strike price 1.10.
   (a) What is the value of the spread?
   (b) What single volatility if used for both options gives the correct value of the bull spread? (Use the DerivaGem Application Builder in conjunction with Goal Seek or Solver.)
   (c) Does your answer support the assertion at the beginning of the chapter that the correct volatility to use when pricing exotic options can be counterintuitive?
   (d) Does the IVF model give the correct price for the bull spread?

27.22. Repeat the analysis in Section 27.8 for the put option example on the assumption that the strike price is 1.13. Use both the least squares approach and the exercise boundary parameterization approach.

27.23. In the SABR model, suppose that $F_0 = 5$, $\beta = 0.5$, $\sigma_0 = 0.447$ (equivalent to a lognormal volatility of 20%), and $T = 1$. Show how the volatility smile varies with ρ for (a) $v = 0.6$ and (b) $v = 1.2$. Consider value of ρ equal to 0.4, 0.2, 0, −0.2, −0.4 and values of the strike price equal to 4.0, 4.5, 5.0, 5.5, 6.0.

27.24. A European call option on a non-dividend-paying stock has a time to maturity of 6 months and a strike price of $100. The stock price is $100 and the risk-free rate is 5%. Use DerivaGem to answer the following questions:
   (a) What is the Black–Scholes–Merton price of the option if the volatility is 30%?
   (b) What is the CEV volatility parameter that gives the same price for the option as you calculated in (a) when $\alpha = 0.5$?
   (c) In Merton's mixed jump–diffusion model, the average frequency of jumps is 1 per

year, the average percentage jump size is 2%, and the standard deviation of the logarithm of 1 plus the percentage jump size is 20%. What is the volatility of the diffusion part of the process that gives the same price for the option as you calculated in (a)?

(d) In the variance-gamma model, $\theta = 0$ and $v = 40\%$. What value of the volatility gives the same price for the option as you calculated in (a)?

(e) For the models you have developed in (b), (c), and (d), calculate the volatility smile by considering European call options with strike prices between 80 and 120. Describe the nature of the probability distributions implied by the smiles.

27.25. A 3-year convertible bond with a face value of $100 has been issued by company ABC. It pays a coupon of $5 at the end of each year. It can be converted into ABC's equity at the end of the first year or at the end of the second year. At the end of the first year, it can be exchanged for 3.6 shares immediately after the coupon date. At the end of the second year, it can be exchanged for 3.5 shares immediately after the coupon date. The current stock price is $25 and the stock price volatility conditional on no default is 25%. No dividends are paid on the stock. The risk-free interest rate is 5% with continuous compounding. The yield on bonds issued by ABC is 7% with continuous compounding and the recovery rate is 30%.

(a) Use a three-step tree to calculate the value of the bond.

(b) How much is the conversion option worth?

(c) What difference does it make to the value of the bond if the bond is callable for $115 immediately before the coupon payment at the end of years 1 and 2?

(d) Explain how your analysis would change if there were a dividend payment of $1 on the equity at the 6-month, 18-month, and 30-month points. Detailed calculations are not required.

(*Hint*: Use equation (24.2) to estimate the average hazard rate.)

27.26. Show that, if there is no recovery from the bond in the event of default, a convertible bond can be valued by assuming that (a) both the expected return and discount rate are $r + \lambda$ and (b) there is no chance of default.

CHAPTER 28

Martingales and Measures

Up to now interest rates have been assumed to be constant when valuing options. In this chapter, this assumption is relaxed in preparation for valuing interest rate derivatives in Chapters 29 to 34.

The risk-neutral valuation principle states that a derivative can be valued by (a) calculating the expected payoff on the assumption that the expected return from the underlying asset equals the risk-free interest rate and (b) discounting the expected payoff at the risk-free interest rate. When interest rates are constant, risk-neutral valuation provides a well-defined and unambiguous valuation tool. When interest rates are stochastic, it is less clear-cut. What does it mean to assume that the expected return on the underlying asset equals to the risk-free rate? Does it mean (a) that each day the expected return is the one-day risk-free rate, or (b) that each year the expected return is the 1-year risk-free rate, or (c) that over a 5-year period the expected return is the 5-year rate at the beginning of the period? What does it mean to discount expected payoffs at the risk-free rate? Can we, for example, discount an expected payoff realized in year 5 at today's 5-year risk-free rate?

In this chapter we explain the theoretical underpinnings of risk-neutral valuation when interest rates are stochastic and show that there are many different risk-neutral worlds that can be assumed in any given situation. We first define a parameter known as the *market price of risk* and show that the excess return over the risk-free interest rate earned by any derivative in a short period of time is linearly related to the market prices of risk of the underlying stochastic variables. What we will refer to as the *traditional risk-neutral world* assumes that all market prices of risk are zero, but we will find that other assumptions about the market price of risk are useful in some situations.

Martingales and *measures* are critical to a full understanding of risk neutral valuation. A martingale is a zero-drift stochastic process. A measure is the unit in which we value security prices. A key result in this chapter will be the *equivalent martingale measure result*. This states that if we use the price of a traded security as the unit of measurement then there is a market price of risk for which all security prices follow martingales.

This chapter illustrates the power of the equivalent martingale measure result by using it to extend Black's model (see Section 18.7) to the situation where interest rates are stochastic and to value options to exchange one asset for another. Chapter 29 uses the result to understand the standard market models for valuing interest rate derivatives,

Chapter 30 uses it to value some nonstandard derivatives, and Chapter 33 uses it to develop the LIBOR market model.

28.1 THE MARKET PRICE OF RISK

We start by considering the properties of derivatives dependent on the value of a single variable θ. Assume that the process followed by θ is

$$\frac{d\theta}{\theta} = m\,dt + s\,dz \tag{28.1}$$

where dz is a Wiener process. The parameters m and s are the expected growth rate in θ and the volatility of θ, respectively. We assume that they depend only on θ and time t. The variable θ need not be the price of an investment asset. It could be something as far removed from financial markets as the temperature in the center of New Orleans.

Suppose that f_1 and f_2 are the prices of two derivatives dependent only on θ and t. These can be options or other instruments that provide a payoff in the future equal to some function of θ. Assume that during the time period under consideration f_1 and f_2 provide no income.[1]

Suppose that the processes followed by f_1 and f_2 are

$$\frac{df_1}{f_1} = \mu_1\,dt + \sigma_1\,dz$$

and

$$\frac{df_2}{f_2} = \mu_2\,dt + \sigma_2\,dz$$

where μ_1, μ_2, σ_1, and σ_2 are functions of θ and t. The "dz" in these processes must be the same dz as in equation (28.1) because it is the only source of the uncertainty in the prices of f_1 and f_2.

The prices f_1 and f_2 can be related using an analysis similar to the Black–Scholes analysis described in Section 15.6. The discrete versions of the processes for f_1 and f_2 are

$$\Delta f_1 = \mu_1 f_1\,\Delta t + \sigma_1 f_1\,\Delta z \tag{28.2}$$

$$\Delta f_2 = \mu_2 f_2\,\Delta t + \sigma_2 f_2\,\Delta z \tag{28.3}$$

We can eliminate the Δz by forming an instantaneously riskless portfolio consisting of $\sigma_2 f_2$ of the first derivative and $-\sigma_1 f_1$ of the second derivative. If Π is the value of the portfolio, then

$$\Pi = (\sigma_2 f_2)f_1 - (\sigma_1 f_1)f_2 \tag{28.4}$$

and

$$\Delta \Pi = \sigma_2 f_2\,\Delta f_1 - \sigma_1 f_1\,\Delta f_2$$

Substituting from equations (28.2) and (28.3), this becomes

$$\Delta \Pi = (\mu_1 \sigma_2 f_1 f_2 - \mu_2 \sigma_1 f_1 f_2)\Delta t \tag{28.5}$$

---

[1] The analysis can be extended to derivatives that provide income (see Problem 28.7).

Because the portfolio is instantaneously riskless, it must earn the risk-free rate. Hence,

$$\Delta \Pi = r \Pi \, \Delta t$$

Substituting into this equation from equations (28.4) and (28.5) gives

$$\mu_1 \sigma_2 - \mu_2 \sigma_1 = r \sigma_2 - r \sigma_1$$

or

$$\frac{\mu_1 - r}{\sigma_1} = \frac{\mu_2 - r}{\sigma_2} \tag{28.6}$$

Note that the left-hand side of equation (28.6) depends only on the parameters of the process followed by f_1 and the right-hand side depends only on the parameters of the process followed by f_2. Define λ as the value of each side in equation (28.6), so that

$$\frac{\mu_1 - r}{\sigma_1} = \frac{\mu_2 - r}{\sigma_2} = \lambda$$

Dropping subscripts, equation (28.6) shows that if f is the price of a derivative dependent only on θ and t with

$$\frac{df}{f} = \mu \, dt + \sigma \, dz \tag{28.7}$$

then

$$\frac{\mu - r}{\sigma} = \lambda \tag{28.8}$$

The parameter λ is known as the *market price of risk* of θ. (In the context of portfolio performance measurement, it is known as the *Sharpe ratio*.) It can be dependent on both θ and t, but it is not dependent on the nature of the derivative f. Our analysis shows that, for no arbitrage, $(\mu - r)/\sigma$ must at any given time be the same for all derivatives that are dependent only on θ and t.

The market price of risk of θ measures the trade-offs between risk and return that are made for securities dependent on θ. Equation (28.8) can be written

$$\mu - r = \lambda \sigma \tag{28.9}$$

The variable σ can be loosely interpreted as the quantity of θ-risk present in f. On the right-hand side of the equation, the quantity of θ-risk is multiplied by the price of θ-risk. The left-hand side is the expected return, in excess of the risk-free interest rate, that is required to compensate for this risk. Equation (28.9) is analogous to the capital asset pricing model, which relates the expected excess return on a stock to its risk. This chapter will not be concerned with the measurement of the market price of risk. This will be discussed in Chapter 36 when the evaluation of real options is considered.

It is natural to assume that σ, the coefficient of dz, in equation (28.7) is the volatility of f. In fact, σ can be negative. This will be the case when f is negatively related to θ (so that $\partial f / \partial \theta$ is negative). It is the absolute value $|\sigma|$ of σ that is the volatility of f. One way of understanding this is to note that the process for f has the same statistical properties when we replace dz by $-dz$.

Chapter 5 distinguished between investment assets and consumption assets. An investment asset is an asset that is bought or sold purely for investment purposes by some investors. Consumption assets are held primarily for consumption. Equation (28.8) is true for all investment assets that provide no income and depend only on θ. If the variable θ itself happens to be such an asset, then

$$\frac{m - r}{s} = \lambda$$

But, in other circumstances, this relationship is not necessarily true.

Example 28.1

Consider a derivative whose price is positively related to the price of oil and depends on no other stochastic variables. Suppose that it provides an expected return of 12% per annum and has a volatility of 20% per annum. Assume that the risk-free interest rate is 8% per annum. It follows that the market price of risk of oil is

$$\frac{0.12 - 0.08}{0.2} = 0.2$$

Note that oil is a consumption asset rather than an investment asset, so its market price of risk cannot be calculated from equation (28.8) by setting μ equal to the expected return from an investment in oil and σ equal to the volatility of oil prices.

Example 28.2

Consider two securities, both of which are positively dependent on the 90-day interest rate. Suppose that the first one has an expected return of 3% per annum and a volatility of 20% per annum, and the second one has a volatility of 30% per annum. Assume that the instantaneous risk-free rate of interest is 6% per annum. The market price of interest rate risk is, using the expected return and volatility for the first security,

$$\frac{0.03 - 0.06}{0.2} = -0.15$$

From a rearrangement of equation (28.9), the expected return from the second security is, therefore,

$$0.06 - 0.15 \times 0.3 = 0.015$$

or 1.5% per annum.

Alternative Worlds

The process followed by derivative price f is

$$df = \mu f\, dt + \sigma f\, dz$$

The value of μ depends on the risk preferences of investors. In a world where the market price of risk is zero, λ equals zero. From equation (28.9) $\mu = r$, so that the process followed by f is

$$df = r f\, dt + \sigma f\, dz$$

We will refer to this as the *traditional risk-neutral world*.

Other assumptions about the market price of risk, λ, enable other worlds that are internally consistent to be defined. From equation (28.9),

$$\mu = r + \lambda\sigma$$

so that

$$df = (r + \lambda\sigma)f\,dt + \sigma f\,dz \tag{28.10}$$

The market price of risk of a variable determines the growth rates of all securities dependent on the variable. As we move from one market price of risk to another, the expected growth rates of security prices change, but their volatilities remain the same. This is Girsanov's theorem, which we illustrated for the binomial model in Section 13.7. Choosing a particular market price of risk is also referred to as defining the *probability measure*. Some value of the market price of risk corresponds to the "real world" and the growth rates of security prices that are observed in practice.

28.2 SEVERAL STATE VARIABLES

Suppose that n variables, $\theta_1, \theta_2, \ldots, \theta_n$, follow stochastic processes of the form

$$\frac{d\theta_i}{\theta_i} = m_i\,dt + s_i\,dz_i \tag{28.11}$$

for $i = 1, 2, \ldots, n$, where the dz_i are Wiener processes. The parameters m_i and s_i are expected growth rates and volatilities and may be functions of the θ_i and time. Equation (14A.10) in the appendix to Chapter 14 provides a version of Itô's lemma that covers functions of several variables. It shows that the process for the price f of a security that is dependent on the θ_i has n stochastic components. It can be written

$$\frac{df}{f} = \mu\,dt + \sum_{i=1}^{n} \sigma_i\,dz_i \tag{28.12}$$

In this equation, μ is the expected return from the security and $\sigma_i\,dz_i$ is the component of the risk of this return attributable to θ_i. Both μ and the σ_i are potentially dependent on the θ_i and time.

Technical Note 30 at www-2.rotman.utoronto.ca/~hull/TechnicalNotes shows that

$$\mu - r = \sum_{i=1}^{n} \lambda_i \sigma_i \tag{28.13}$$

where λ_i is the market price of risk for θ_i. This equation relates the expected excess return that investors require on the security to the λ_i and σ_i. Equation (28.9) is the particular case of this equation when $n = 1$. The term $\lambda_i \sigma_i$ on the right-hand side measures the extent that the excess return required by investors on a security is affected by the dependence of the security on θ_i. If $\lambda_i \sigma_i = 0$, there is no effect; if $\lambda_i \sigma_i > 0$, investors require a higher return to compensate them for the risk arising from θ_i; if $\lambda_i \sigma_i < 0$, the dependence of the security on θ_i causes investors to require a lower return than would otherwise be the case. The $\lambda_i \sigma_i < 0$ situation occurs when the variable has the effect of reducing rather than increasing the risks in the portfolio of a typical investor.

Example 28.3

A stock price depends on three underlying variables: the price of oil, the price of gold, and the performance of a stock index. Suppose that the market prices of risk for these variables are 0.2, −0.1, and 0.4, respectively. Suppose also that the σ_i in equation (28.12) corresponding to the three variables have been estimated as 0.05, 0.1, and 0.15, respectively. The excess return on the stock over the risk-free rate is

$$0.2 \times 0.05 - 0.1 \times 0.1 + 0.4 \times 0.15 = 0.06$$

or 6.0% per annum. If variables other than those considered affect the stock price, this result is still true provided that the market price of risk for each of these other variables is zero.

Equation (28.13) is closely related to arbitrage pricing theory, developed by Stephen Ross in 1976.[2] The continuous-time version of the capital asset pricing model (CAPM) can be regarded as a particular case of the equation. CAPM (see appendix to Chapter 3) argues that an investor requires excess returns to compensate for any risk that is correlated to the risk in the return from the stock market, but requires no excess return for other risks. Risks that are correlated with the return from the stock market are referred to as *systematic*; other risks are referred to as *nonsystematic*. If CAPM is true, then λ_i is proportional to the correlation between changes in θ_i and the return from the market. When θ_i is uncorrelated with the return from the market, λ_i is zero.

28.3 MARTINGALES

A *martingale* is a zero-drift stochastic process.[3] A variable θ follows a martingale if its process has the form

$$d\theta = \sigma \, dz$$

where dz is a Wiener process. The variable σ may itself be stochastic. It can depend on θ and other stochastic variables. A martingale has the convenient property that its expected value at any future time is equal to its value today. This means that

$$E(\theta_T) = \theta_0$$

where θ_0 and θ_T denote the values of θ at times zero and T, respectively. To understand this result, note that over a very small time interval the change in θ is normally distributed with zero mean. The expected change in θ over any very small time interval is therefore zero. The change in θ between time 0 and time T is the sum of its changes over many small time intervals. It follows that the expected change in θ between time 0 and time T must also be zero.

The Equivalent Martingale Measure Result

Suppose that f and g are the prices of traded securities dependent on a single source of uncertainty. Assume that the securities provide no income during the time period under consideration and define $\phi = f/g$.[4] The variable ϕ is the relative price of f with respect to g. It can be thought of as measuring the price of f in units of g rather than dollars. The security price g is referred to as the *numeraire*.

---

[2] See S. A. Ross, "The Arbitrage Theory of Capital Asset Pricing," *Journal of Economic Theory*, 13 (December 1976): 343–62.

[3] More formally, a sequence of random variables $X_0, X_1, \ldots$ is a martingale if $E(X_i \mid X_{i-1}, X_{i-2}, \ldots, X_0) = X_{i-1}$, for all $i > 0$, where E denotes expectation.

[4] Problem 28.8 extends the analysis to situations where the securities provide income.

The *equivalent martingale measure* result shows that, when there are no arbitrage opportunities, ϕ is a martingale for some choice of the market price of risk. What is more, for a given numeraire security g, the same choice of the market price of risk makes ϕ a martingale for all securities f. This choice of the market price of risk is the volatility of g. In other words, when the market price of risk is set equal to the volatility of g, the ratio f/g is a martingale for all security prices f. (Note that the market price of risk has the same dimension as volatility. Both are "per square root of time." Setting the market price of risk equal to a volatility is therefore dimensionally valid.)

To prove this result, suppose that the volatilities of f and g are σ_f and σ_g and r is the instantaneous risk-free rate. (These variables can depend on the single source of uncertainty that is being assumed.) From equation (28.10), in a world where the market price of risk is σ_g,

$$df = (r + \sigma_g \sigma_f) f \, dt + \sigma_f f \, dz$$

$$dg = (r + \sigma_g^2) g \, dt + \sigma_g g \, dz$$

Using Itô's lemma gives

$$d \ln f = (r + \sigma_g \sigma_f - \sigma_f^2/2) \, dt + \sigma_f \, dz$$

$$d \ln g = (r + \sigma_g^2/2) \, dt + \sigma_g \, dz$$

so that

$$d(\ln f - \ln g) = (\sigma_g \sigma_f - \sigma_f^2/2 - \sigma_g^2/2) \, dt + (\sigma_f - \sigma_g) \, dz$$

or

$$d\left(\ln \frac{f}{g} \right) = -\frac{(\sigma_f - \sigma_g)^2}{2} \, dt + (\sigma_f - \sigma_g) \, dz$$

Itô's lemma can be used to determine the process for f/g from the process for $\ln(f/g)$:

$$d\left(\frac{f}{g} \right) = (\sigma_f - \sigma_g) \frac{f}{g} \, dz \tag{28.14}$$

This shows that f/g is a martingale and proves the equivalent martingale measure result.

From now on, we will use the phrase "world defined by numeraire g" to mean a world where σ_g, the volatility of g, is the market price of risk. Because f/g is a martingale in this world, it follows from the result at the beginning of this section that

$$\frac{f_0}{g_0} = E_g\left(\frac{f_T}{g_T} \right)$$

or

$$f_0 = g_0 E_g\left(\frac{f_T}{g_T} \right) \tag{28.15}$$

where E_g denotes the expected value in a world defined by numeraire g.

28.4 ALTERNATIVE CHOICES FOR THE NUMERAIRE

We now present a number of examples of the equivalent martingale measure result. The first example shows that it is consistent with the traditional risk-neutral valuation result used in earlier chapters. The other examples prepare the way for the valuation of bond options, interest rate caps, and swap options in Chapter 29.

Money Market Account as the Numeraire

The dollar money market account is a security that is worth $1 at time zero and earns the instantaneous risk-free rate r at any given time.[5] The variable r may be stochastic. If we set g equal to the money market account, it grows at rate r so that

$$dg = rg\,dt \tag{28.16}$$

The drift of g is stochastic, but the volatility of g is zero. It follows from the results in Section 28.3 that f/g is a martingale in a world where the market price of risk is zero. This is the world we defined earlier as the traditional risk-neutral world. From equation (28.15),

$$f_0 = g_0 \hat{E}\left(\frac{f_T}{g_T}\right) \tag{28.17}$$

where $\hat{E}$ denotes expectations in the traditional risk-neutral world.

In this case, $g_0 = 1$ and

$$g_T = e^{\int_0^T r\,dt}$$

so that equation (28.17) reduces to

$$f_0 = \hat{E}\left(e^{-\int_0^T r\,dt} f_T\right) \tag{28.18}$$

or

$$f_0 = \hat{E}\left(e^{-\bar{r}T} f_T\right) \tag{28.19}$$

where $\bar{r}$ is the average value of r between time 0 and time T. This equation shows that one way of valuing an interest rate derivative is to simulate the short-term interest rate r in the traditional risk-neutral world. On each trial the payoff is calculated and discounted at the average value of the short rate on the sampled path.

When the short-term interest rate r is assumed to be constant, equation (28.19) reduces to

$$f_0 = e^{-rT} \hat{E}(f_T)$$

or the risk-neutral valuation relationship used in earlier chapters.

Zero-Coupon Bond Price as the Numeraire

Define $P(t, T)$ as the price at time t of a risk-free zero-coupon bond that pays off $1 at time T. We now explore the implications of setting the numeraire g equal to $P(t, T)$. Let E_T denote expectations in a world defined by this numeraire. Because $g_T = P(T, T) = 1$ and $g_0 = P(0, T)$, equation (28.15) gives

$$f_0 = P(0, T)E_T(f_T) \tag{28.20}$$

Notice the difference between equations (28.20) and (28.19). In equation (28.19), the discounting is inside the expectations operator. In equation (28.20), the discounting, as

---

[5] The money market account is the limit as Δt approaches zero of the following security. For the first short period of time of length Δt, it is invested at the initial Δt period rate; at time Δt, it is reinvested for a further period of time Δt at the new Δt period rate; at time $2\Delta t$, it is again reinvested for a further period of time Δt at the new Δt period rate; and so on. The money market accounts in other currencies are defined analogously to the dollar money market account.

represented by the $P(0, T)$ term, is outside the expectations operator. The use of $P(t, T)$ as the numeraire therefore considerably simplifies things for a security that provides a payoff solely at time T.

Consider any variable θ that is not an interest rate.[6] A forward contract on θ with maturity T is defined as a contract that pays off $\theta_T - K$ at time T, where θ_T is the value θ at time T. Define f as the value of this forward contract. From equation (28.20),

$$f_0 = P(0, T)[E_T(\theta_T) - K]$$

The forward price, F, of θ is the value of K for which f_0 equals zero. It therefore follows that

$$P(0, T)[E_T(\theta_T) - F] = 0$$

or

$$F = E_T(\theta_T) \tag{28.21}$$

Equation (28.21) shows that the forward price of any variable (except an interest rate) is its expected future spot price in a world defined by the numeraire $P(t, T)$. Note the difference here between forward prices and futures prices. The argument in Section 18.6 shows that the futures price of a variable is the expected future spot price in the traditional risk-neutral world.

To summarize, equation (28.20) shows that any security that provides a payoff at time T can be valued by calculating its expected payoff in a world defined by the numeraire that is a bond maturing at time T and discounting at the current risk-free rate for maturity T. Equation (28.21) shows that it is correct to assume that the expected value of the underlying variables equal their forward values when computing the expected payoff.

Forward Interest Rates

For the next result, define $F(t)$ as the forward interest rate as seen at time t for the period between T and T^* expressed with a compounding period of $T^* - T$. (For example, if $T^* - T = 0.5$, the interest rate is expressed with semiannual compounding; if $T^* - T = 0.25$, it is expressed with quarterly compounding; and so on.)

Define R as the realized rate between T and T^* expressed with the same compounding frequency. From the definition of a forward interest rate, a forward rate agreement paying off $F(t) - R$ at time T^* is worth zero at time t. From the result in equation (28.21), it follows that

$$P(0, T^*)E_{T^*}(F(t) - R) = 0$$

so that

$$E_{T^*}(R) = F(t) \tag{28.22}$$

Note that in this result $F(t)$ and R can be calculated from any yield curve. They do not have to be calculated from the risk-free zero curve used to define $P(0, T^*)$. In particular, $F(t)$ and R can be calculated from LIBOR rates when the risk-free rate comes from the OIS zero curve. The results we just have produced will be useful in explaining the valuation of interest rate caps and floors in the next chapter.

---

[6] The analysis given here does not apply to interest rates because forward contracts for interest rates are defined slightly differently from forward contracts for other variables, as will be seen shortly.

Annuity Factor as the Numeraire

For the next application of equivalent martingale measure arguments, consider a floating-for-fixed swap starting at a future time T with payment dates at times T_1, $T_2, \ldots, T_N$. In the swap, a fixed rate of interest is exchanged for the floating rate. Define $T_0 = T$. Assume that the notional principal is \$1. Suppose that the forward swap rate (i.e., the interest rate on the fixed side that makes the forward swap have a value of zero) is $s(t)$ at time t $(t \leqslant T)$. The value of the fixed side of the swap is

$$s(t)A(t)$$

where

$$A(t) = \sum_{i=0}^{N-1}(T_{i+1} - T_i)P(t, T_{i+1})$$

Define the value of the floating side as $V(t)$. Equating the values of the fixed and floating sides gives

$$s(t)A(t) = V(t)$$

or

$$s(t) = \frac{V(t)}{A(t)} \tag{28.23}$$

The equivalent martingale measure result can be applied by setting f equal to $V(t)$ and g equal to $A(t)$. This leads to

$$s(t) = E_A[s(T)] \tag{28.24}$$

where E_A denotes expectations in a world that is defined by the numeraire $A(t)$. Therefore, in a world defined by this numeraire, the expected future swap rate is the current swap rate.

The result in equation (28.15) shows that

$$V(0) = A(0)E_A\left[\frac{V(T)}{A(T)}\right] \tag{28.25}$$

This result, when combined with the result in equation (28.24), will be critical to an understanding of the standard market model for European swap options in the next chapter. Note that in this result $V(t)$ can be calculated from any yield curve, whereas $A(t)$ is calculated from the risk-free zero curve. In particular, the swap can be a LIBOR-for-fixed swap, while the risk-free rate is calculated from the OIS zero curve.

28.5 EXTENSION TO SEVERAL FACTORS

The results presented in Sections 28.3 and 28.4 can be extended to cover the situation when there are many independent factors.[7] Assume that there are n independent factors

---

[7] The independence condition is not critical. If factors are not independent they can be orthogonalized.

and that the processes for f and g in the traditional risk-neutral world are

$$df = rf\,dt + \sum_{i=1}^{n} \sigma_{f,i} f\,dz_i$$

and

$$dg = rg\,dt + \sum_{i=1}^{n} \sigma_{g,i} g\,dz_i$$

It follows from Section 28.2 that other internally consistent worlds can be defined by setting

$$df = \left[r + \sum_{i=1}^{n} \lambda_i \sigma_{f,i} \right] f\,dt + \sum_{i=1}^{n} \sigma_{f,i} f\,dz_i$$

and

$$dg = \left[r + \sum_{i=1}^{n} \lambda_i \sigma_{g,i} \right] g\,dt + \sum_{i=1}^{n} \sigma_{g,i} g\,dz_i$$

where the λ_i ($1 \leqslant i \leqslant n$) are the n market prices of risk. One of these other worlds is the real world.

We now extend our earlier terminology. A "world defined by numeraire g" is a world where $\lambda_i = \sigma_{g,i}$ for all i. It can be shown from Itô's lemma, using the fact that the dz_i are uncorrelated, that the process followed by f/g in this world has zero drift (see Problem 28.12). The rest of the results in the last two sections (from equation (28.15) onward) are therefore still true.

28.6 BLACK'S MODEL REVISITED

Section 18.8 explained that Black's model is a popular tool for pricing European options in terms of the forward or futures price of the underlying asset when interest rates are constant. We are now in a position to relax the constant interest rate assumption and show that Black's model can be used to price European options in terms of the forward price of the underlying asset when interest rates are stochastic.

Consider a European call option on an asset with strike price K that lasts until time T. From equation (28.20), the option's price is given by

$$c = P(0, T)E_T[\max(S_T - K, 0)] \tag{28.26}$$

where S_T is the asset price at time T and E_T denotes expectations in a world defined by numeraire $P(t, T)$. Define F_0 and F_T as the forward price of the asset at time 0 and time T for a contract maturing at time T. Because $S_T = F_T$,

$$c = P(0, T)E_T[\max(F_T - K, 0)]$$

Assume that F_T is lognormal in the world being considered, with the standard deviation of $\ln(F_T)$ equal to $\sigma_F \sqrt{T}$. This could be because the forward price follows a stochastic process with volatility σ_F. Equation(15A.1) shows that

$$E_T[\max(F_T - K, 0)] = E_T(F_T)N(d_1) - KN(d_2) \tag{28.27}$$

where

$$d_1 = \frac{\ln[E_T(F_T)/K] + \sigma_F^2 T/2}{\sigma_F \sqrt{T}}$$

$$d_2 = \frac{\ln[E_T(F_T)/K] - \sigma_F^2 T/2}{\sigma_F \sqrt{T}}$$

From equation (28.21), $E_T(F_T) = E_T(S_T) = F_0$. Hence,

$$c = P(0, T)[F_0 N(d_1) - K N(d_2)] \tag{28.28}$$

where

$$d_1 = \frac{\ln[F_0/K] + \sigma_F^2 T/2}{\sigma_F \sqrt{T}}$$

$$d_2 = \frac{\ln[F_0/K] - \sigma_F^2 T/2}{\sigma_F \sqrt{T}}$$

Similarly,

$$p = P(0, T)[K N(-d_2) - F_0 N(-d_1)] \tag{28.29}$$

where p is the price of a European put option on the asset with strike price K and time to maturity T. This is Black's model. It applies to both investment and consumption assets and, as we have just shown, is true when interest rates are stochastic provided that F_0 is the forward asset price for a contract with the same maturity as the option. The variable σ_F can be interpreted as the volatility of the forward asset price.

28.7 OPTION TO EXCHANGE ONE ASSET FOR ANOTHER

Consider next an option to exchange an investment asset worth U for an investment asset worth V. This has already been discussed in Section 26.14. Suppose that the volatilities of U and V are σ_U and σ_V and the coefficient of correlation between them is ρ.

Assume first that the assets provide no income and choose the numeraire security to be U. Setting $f = V$ in equation (28.15) gives

$$V_0 = U_0 E_U\left(\frac{V_T}{U_T}\right) \tag{28.30}$$

where E_U denotes expectations in a world defined by the numeraire U. (We are here using the multifactor extension of equation (28.15) because V and U may depend on different Wiener processes.)

The variable f in equation (28.15) can be set equal to the value of the option under consideration, so that $f_T = \max(V_T - U_T, 0)$. It follows that

$$f_0 = U_0 E_U\left[\frac{\max(V_T - U_T, 0)}{U_T}\right]$$

or

$$f_0 = U_0 E_U\left[\max\left(\frac{V_T}{U_T} - 1, 0\right)\right] \tag{28.31}$$

The volatility of V/U is $\hat{\sigma}$ (see Problem 28.13), where

$$\hat{\sigma}^2 = \sigma_U^2 + \sigma_V^2 - 2\rho\sigma_U\sigma_V$$

From equation (15A.1), equation (28.31) becomes

$$f_0 = U_0\left[E_U\left(\frac{V_T}{U_T}\right)N(d_1) - N(d_2)\right]$$

where

$$d_1 = \frac{\ln(V_0/U_0) + \hat{\sigma}^2 T/2}{\hat{\sigma}\sqrt{T}} \quad \text{and} \quad d_2 = d_1 - \hat{\sigma}\sqrt{T}$$

Substituting from equation (28.30) gives

$$f_0 = V_0 N(d_1) - U_0 N(d_2) \tag{28.32}$$

This is the value of an option to exchange one asset for another when the assets provide no income.

Problem 28.8 shows that, when f and g provide income at rate q_f and q_g, equation (28.15) becomes

$$f_0 = g_0 e^{(q_f - q_g)T} E_g\left(\frac{f_T}{g_T}\right)$$

This means that equations (28.30) and (28.31) become

$$E_U\left(\frac{V_T}{U_T}\right) = e^{(q_U - q_V)T}\frac{V_0}{U_0}$$

and

$$f_0 = e^{-q_U T} U_0 E_U\left[\max\left(\frac{V_T}{U_T} - 1,\, 0\right)\right]$$

and equation (28.32) becomes

$$f_0 = e^{-q_V T} V_0 N(d_1) - e^{-q_U T} U_0 N(d_2)$$

with d_1 and d_2 being redefined as

$$d_1 = \frac{\ln(V_0/U_0) + (q_U - q_V + \hat{\sigma}^2/2)T}{\hat{\sigma}\sqrt{T}} \quad \text{and} \quad d_2 = d_1 - \hat{\sigma}\sqrt{T}$$

This is the result given in equation (26.5) for the value of an option to exchange one asset for another.

28.8 CHANGE OF NUMERAIRE

In this section, we consider the impact of a change in numeraire on the process followed by a market variable. Suppose first that the variable is the price of a traded security, f.

In a world where the market price of dz_i risk is λ_i,

$$df = \left[r + \sum_{i=1}^{n} \lambda_i \sigma_{f,i}\right] f\, dt + \sum_{i=1}^{n} \sigma_{f,i} f\, dz_i$$

Similarly, when it is λ_i^*,

$$df = \left[r + \sum_{i=1}^{n} \lambda_i^* \sigma_{f,i}\right] f\, dt + \sum_{i=1}^{n} \sigma_{f,i} f\, dz_i$$

The effect of moving from the first world to the second is therefore to increase the expected growth rate of the price of any traded security f by

$$\sum_{i=1}^{n} (\lambda_i^* - \lambda_i) \sigma_{f,i}$$

Consider next a variable v that is not the price of a traded security. As shown in Technical Note 20 at www-2.rotman.utoronto.ca/~hull/TechnicalNotes, the expected growth rate of v responds to a change in the market price of risk in the same way as the expected growth rate of the prices of traded securities. It increases by

$$\alpha_v = \sum_{i=1}^{n} (\lambda_i^* - \lambda_i) \sigma_{v,i} \tag{28.33}$$

where $\sigma_{v,i}$ is the ith component of the volatility of v.

When we move from a numeraire of g to a numeraire of h, $\lambda_i = \sigma_{g,i}$ and $\lambda_i^* = \sigma_{h,i}$. Define $w = h/g$ and $\sigma_{w,i}$ as the ith component of the volatility of w. From Itô's lemma (see Problem 28.13),

$$\sigma_{w,i} = \sigma_{h,i} - \sigma_{g,i}$$

so that equation (28.33) becomes

$$\alpha_v = \sum_{i=1}^{n} \sigma_{w,i}\, \sigma_{v,i} \tag{28.34}$$

We will refer to w as the *numeraire ratio*. Equation (28.34) is equivalent to

$$\alpha_v = \rho \sigma_v \sigma_w \tag{28.35}$$

where σ_v is the total volatility of v, σ_w is the total volatility of w, and ρ is the instantaneous correlation between changes in v and w.[8]

This is a surprisingly simple result. The adjustment to the expected growth rate of a variable v when we change from one numeraire to another is the instantaneous covariance between the percentage change in v and the percentage change in the

---

[8] To see this, note that the changes Δv and Δw in v and w in a short period of time Δt are given by

$$\Delta v = \cdots + \sum \sigma_{v,i}\, v \epsilon_i \sqrt{\Delta t}$$
$$\Delta w = \cdots + \sum \sigma_{w,i}\, w \epsilon_i \sqrt{\Delta t}$$

Since the dz_i are uncorrelated, it follows that $E(\epsilon_i \epsilon_j) = 0$ when $i \neq j$. Also, from the definition of ρ, we have

$$\rho v \sigma_v w \sigma_w = E(\Delta v\, \Delta w) - E(\Delta v)\, E(\Delta w)$$

When terms of higher order than Δt are ignored this leads to

$$\rho \sigma_v \sigma_w = \sum \sigma_{w,i}\, \sigma_{v,i}$$

numeraire ratio. This result will be used when timing and quanto adjustments are considered in Chapter 30.

A particular case of the results in this section is when we move from the real world to the traditional risk-neutral world (where all the market prices of risk are zero). From equation (28.33), the growth rate of v changes by $-\sum_{i=1}^{n} \lambda_i \sigma_{v,i}$. This corresponds to the result in equation (28.13) when v is the price of a traded security. We have shown that it is also true when v is not the price of a traded security. In general, the way that we move from one world to another for variables that are not the prices of traded securities is the same as for those that are.

A Final Point

In this chapter we have expressed the processes for variables in terms of their expected returns and volatilities. The results if we use drifts and standard deviations are much the same. Suppose

$$df = \mu f \, dt + \sigma f \, dz$$

and we write the process as

$$df = \mu^* \, dt + \sigma^* \, dz$$

(so that $\mu^* = \mu f$ and $\sigma^* = \sigma f$). Suppose further that these processes reflect a market price of risk of λ_1. The impact of changing the market price to λ_2 is, as we have explained, to change the process to

$$df = (\mu + \lambda_2 \sigma - \lambda_1 \sigma) f \, dt + \sigma f \, dz$$

This is the same as

$$df = (\mu^* + \lambda_2 \sigma^* - \lambda_1 \sigma^*) \, dt + \sigma^* \, dz$$

SUMMARY

The market price of risk of a variable defines the trade-offs between risk and return for traded securities dependent on the variable. When there is one underlying variable, a derivative's excess return over the risk-free rate equals the market price of risk multiplied by the derivative's volatility. When there are many underlying variables, the excess return is the sum of the market price of risk multiplied by the volatility for each variable.

A powerful tool in the valuation of derivatives is risk-neutral valuation. This was introduced in Chapters 13 and 15. The principle of risk-neutral valuation shows that, if we assume that the world is risk neutral when valuing derivatives, we get the right answer—not just in a risk-neutral world, but in all other worlds as well. In the traditional risk-neutral world, the market price of risk of all variables is zero. This chapter has extended the principle of risk-neutral valuation. It has shown that, when interest rates are stochastic, there are many interesting and useful alternatives to the traditional risk-neutral world.

A martingale is a zero drift stochastic process. Any variable following a martingale has the simplifying property that its expected value at any future time equals its value today. The equivalent martingale measure result shows that, if g is a security price, there is a world in which the ratio f/g is a martingale for all security prices f. It turns out that, by appropriately choosing the numeraire security g, the valuation of many interest rate dependent derivatives can be simplified.

This chapter has used the equivalent martingale measure result to extend Black's model to the situation where interest rates are stochastic and to value an option to exchange one asset for another. In Chapters 29 to 34, it will be useful in valuing interest rate derivatives.

FURTHER READING

Baxter, M., and A. Rennie, *Financial Calculus*. Cambridge University Press, 1996.

Cox, J. C., J. E. Ingersoll, and S. A. Ross, "An Intertemporal General Equilibrium Model of Asset Prices," *Econometrica*, 53 (1985): 363–84.

Duffie, D., *Dynamic Asset Pricing Theory*, 3rd edn. Princeton University Press, 2001.

Harrison, J. M., and D. M. Kreps, "Martingales and Arbitrage in Multiperiod Securities Markets," *Journal of Economic Theory*, 20 (1979): 381–408.

Harrison, J. M., and S. R. Pliska, "Martingales and Stochastic Integrals in the Theory of Continuous Trading," *Stochastic Processes and Their Applications*, 11 (1981): 215–60.

Practice Questions (Answers in the Solutions Manual)

28.1. How is the market price of risk defined for a variable that is not the price of an investment asset?

28.2. Suppose that the market price of risk for gold is zero. If the storage costs are 1% per annum and the risk-free rate of interest is 6% per annum, what is the expected growth rate in the price of gold? Assume that gold provides no income.

28.3. Consider two securities both of which are dependent on the same market variable. The expected returns from the securities are 8% and 12%. The volatility of the first security is 15%. The instantaneous risk-free rate is 4%. What is the volatility of the second security?

28.4. An oil company is set up solely for the purpose of exploring for oil in a certain small area of Texas. Its value depends primarily on two stochastic variables: the price of oil and the quantity of proven oil reserves. Discuss whether the market price of risk for the second of these two variables is likely to be positive, negative, or zero.

28.5. Deduce the differential equation for a derivative dependent on the prices of two non-dividend-paying traded securities by forming a riskless portfolio consisting of the derivative and the two traded securities.

28.6. Suppose that an interest rate x follows the process

$$dx = a(x_0 - x)\,dt + c\sqrt{x}\,dz$$

where a, x_0, and c are positive constants. Suppose further that the market price of risk for x is λ. What is the process for x in the traditional risk-neutral world?

28.7. Prove that, when the security f provides income at rate q, equation (28.9) becomes $\mu + q - r = \lambda\sigma$. (*Hint*: Form a new security f^* that provides no income by assuming that all the income from f is reinvested in f.)

28.8. Show that when f and g provide income at rates q_f and q_g, respectively, equation (28.15) becomes

$$f_0 = g_0 e^{(q_f - q_g)T} E_g\left(\frac{f_T}{g_T}\right)$$

(*Hint*: Form new securities f^* and g^* that provide no income by assuming that all the income from f is reinvested in f and all the income in g is reinvested in g.)

28.9. "The expected future value of an interest rate in a risk-neutral world is greater than it is in the real world." What does this statement imply about the market price of risk for (a) an interest rate and (b) a bond price. Do you think the statement is likely to be true? Give reasons.

28.10. The variable S is an investment asset providing income at rate q measured in currency A. It follows the process

$$dS = \mu_S S \, dt + \sigma_S S \, dz$$

in the real world. Defining new variables as necessary, give the process followed by S, and the corresponding market price of risk, in:
(a) A world that is the traditional risk-neutral world for currency A
(b) A world that is the traditional risk-neutral world for currency B
(c) A world defined by a numeraire equal to a zero-coupon currency A bond maturing at time T
(d) A world defined by a numeraire equal to a zero-coupon currency B bond maturing at time T.

28.11. Explain the difference between the way a forward interest rate is defined and the way the forward values of other variables such as stock prices, commodity prices, and exchange rates are defined.

28.12. Prove the result in Section 28.5 that when

$$df = \left[r + \sum_{i=1}^{n} \lambda_i \sigma_{f,i} \right] f \, dt + \sum_{i=1}^{n} \sigma_{f,i} f \, dz_i$$

and

$$dg = \left[r + \sum_{i=1}^{n} \lambda_i \sigma_{g,i} \right] g \, dt + \sum_{i=1}^{n} \sigma_{g,i} g \, dz_i$$

with the dz_i uncorrelated, f/g is a martingale for $\lambda_i = \sigma_{g,i}$. (*Hint*: Start by using equation (14A.11) to get the processes for $\ln f$ and $\ln g$.)

28.13. Show that when $w = h/g$ and h and g are each dependent on n Wiener processes, the ith component of the volatility of w is the ith component of the volatility of h minus the ith component of the volatility of g. (*Hint*: Start by using equation (14A.11) to get the processes for $\ln g$ and $\ln h$.)

28.14. "If X is the expected value of a variable, X follows a martingale." Explain this statement.

Further Questions

28.15. A security's price is positively dependent on two variables: the price of copper and the yen/dollar exchange rate. Suppose that the market price of risk for these variables is 0.5 and 0.1, respectively. If the price of copper were held fixed, the volatility of the security would be 8% per annum; if the yen/dollar exchange rate were held fixed, the volatility of the security would be 12% per annum. The risk-free interest rate is 7% per annum. What is the expected rate of return from the security? If the two variables are uncorrelated with each other, what is the volatility of the security?

28.16. Suppose that the price of a zero-coupon bond maturing at time T follows the process

$$dP(t, T) = \mu_P P(t, T)\, dt + \sigma_P P(t, T)\, dz$$

and the price of a derivative dependent on the bond follows the process

$$df = \mu_f f\, dt + \sigma_f f\, dz$$

Assume only one source of uncertainty and that f provides no income.
(a) What is the forward price F of f for a contract maturing at time T?
(b) What is the process followed by F in a world defined by the numeraire $P(t, T)$?
(c) What is the process followed by F in the traditional risk-neutral world?
(d) What is the process followed by f in a world defined by a numeraire equal to a bond maturing at time T^*, where $T^* \neq T$? Assume that σ_P^* is the volatility of this bond.

28.17. Consider a variable that is not an interest rate:
(a) In what world is the futures price of the variable a martingale?
(b) In what world is the forward price of the variable a martingale?
(c) Defining variables as necessary, derive an expression for the difference between the drift of the futures price and the drift of the forward price in the traditional risk-neutral world.
(d) Show that your result is consistent with the points made in Section 5.8 about the circumstances when the futures price is above the forward price.

CHAPTER 29

Interest Rate Derivatives: The Standard Market Models

Interest rate derivatives are instruments whose payoffs are dependent in some way on the level of interest rates. In the 1980s and 1990s, the volume of trading in interest rate derivatives in both the over-the-counter and exchange-traded markets increased rapidly. Many new products were developed to meet particular needs of end users. A key challenge for derivatives traders was to find good, robust procedures for pricing and hedging these products. Interest rate derivatives are more difficult to value than equity and foreign exchange derivatives for the following reasons:

1. The behavior of an individual interest rate is more complicated than that of a stock price or an exchange rate.
2. For the valuation of many products it is necessary to develop a model describing the behavior of the entire zero-coupon yield curve.
3. The volatilities of different points on the yield curve are different.
4. Interest rates are used for discounting the derivative as well as defining its payoff.

This chapter considers the three most popular over-the-counter interest rate option products: bond options, interest rate caps/floors, and swap options. It explains how the products work and the standard market models used to value them.

29.1 BOND OPTIONS

A bond option is an option to buy or sell a particular bond by a particular date for a particular price. In addition to trading in the over-the-counter market, bond options are frequently embedded in bonds when they are issued to make them more attractive to either the issuer or potential purchasers.

Embedded Bond Options

One example of a bond with an embedded bond option is a *callable bond*. This is a bond that contains provisions allowing the issuing firm to buy back the bond at a predetermined price at certain times in the future. The holder of such a bond has sold a call option to the issuer. The strike price or call price in the option is the predetermined price that must be paid by the issuer to the holder. Callable bonds cannot usually be called for the first few years of their life. (This is known as the lock-out period.) After that, the call price is usually a decreasing function of time. For example, in a 10-year callable bond, there might be no call privileges for the first 2 years. After that, the issuer might have the right to buy the bond back at a price of 110 in years 3 and 4 of its life, at a price of 107.5 in years 5 and 6, at a price of 106 in years 7 and 8, and at a price of 103 in years 9 and 10. The value of the call option is reflected in the quoted yields on bonds. Bonds with call features generally offer higher yields than bonds with no call features.

Another type of bond with an embedded option is a *puttable bond*. This contains provisions that allow the holder to demand early redemption at a predetermined price at certain times in the future. The holder of such a bond has purchased a put option on the bond as well as the bond itself. Because the put option increases the value of the bond to the holder, bonds with put features provide lower yields than bonds with no put features. A simple example of a puttable bond is a 10-year bond where the holder has the right to be repaid at the end of 5 years. (This is sometimes referred to as a *retractable bond*.)

Loan and deposit instruments also often contain embedded bond options. For example, a 5-year fixed-rate deposit with a financial institution that can be redeemed without penalty at any time contains an American put option on a bond. (The deposit instrument is a bond that the investor has the right to put back to the financial institution at its face value at any time.) Prepayment privileges on loans and mortgages are similarly call options on bonds.

Finally, a loan commitment made by a bank or other financial institution is a put option on a bond. Consider, for example, the situation where a bank quotes a 5-year interest rate of 3% per annum to a potential borrower and states that the rate is good for the next 2 months. The client has, in effect, obtained the right to sell a 5-year bond with a 3% coupon to the financial institution for its face value any time within the next 2 months. The option will be exercised if rates increase.

European Bond Options

Many over-the-counter bond options and some embedded bond options are European. The assumption made in the standard market model for valuing European bond options is that the forward bond price has a volatility σ_B. This allows Black's model in Section 28.6 to be used. In equations (28.28) and (28.29), σ_F is set equal to σ_B and F_0 is set equal to the forward bond price F_B, so that

$$c = P(0, T)[F_B N(d_1) - K N(d_2)] \tag{29.1}$$

$$p = P(0, T)[K N(-d_2) - F_B N(-d_1)] \tag{29.2}$$

where

$$d_1 = \frac{\ln(F_B/K) + \sigma_B^2 T/2}{\sigma_B \sqrt{T}} \quad \text{and} \quad d_2 = d_1 - \sigma_B \sqrt{T}$$

In these equations, K is the strike price of the bond option, T is its time to maturity, and $P(0, T)$ is the (risk-free) discount factor for maturity T.

From Section 5.5, F_B can be calculated using the formula

$$F_B = \frac{B_0 - I}{P(0, T)} \tag{29.3}$$

where B_0 is the bond price at time zero and I is the present value of the coupons that will be paid during the life of the option. In this formula, both the spot bond price and the forward bond price are cash prices rather than quoted prices. The relationship between cash and quoted bond prices is explained in Section 6.1.

The strike price K in equations (29.1) and (29.2) should be the cash strike price. In choosing the correct value for K, the precise terms of the option are therefore important. If the strike price is defined as the cash amount that is exchanged for the bond when the option is exercised, K should be set equal to this strike price. If, as is more common, the strike price is the quoted price applicable when the option is exercised, K should be set equal to the strike price plus accrued interest at the expiration date of the option. Traders refer to the quoted price of a bond as the *clean price* and the cash price as the *dirty price*.

Example 29.1

Consider a 10-month European call option on a 9.75-year bond with a face value of $1,000. (When the option matures, the bond will have 8 years and 11 months remaining.) Suppose that the current cash bond price is $960, the strike price is $1,000, the 10-month risk-free interest rate is 10% per annum, and the volatility of the forward bond price for a contract maturing in 10 months is 9% per annum. The bond pays a coupon of 10% per year (with payments made semiannually). Coupon payments of $50 are expected in 3 months and 9 months. (This means that the accrued interest is $25 and the quoted bond price is $935.) We suppose that the 3-month and 9-month risk-free interest rates are 9.0% and 9.5% per annum, respectively. The present value of the coupon payments is, therefore,

$$50e^{-0.25 \times 0.09} + 50e^{-0.75 \times 0.095} = 95.45$$

or $95.45. The bond forward price is from equation (29.3) given by

$$F_B = (960 - 95.45)e^{0.1 \times 0.8333} = 939.68$$

(a) If the strike price is the cash price that would be paid for the bond on exercise, the parameters for equation (29.1) are $F_B = 939.68$, $K = 1000$, $P(0, T) = e^{-0.1 \times (10/12)} = 0.9200$, $\sigma_B = 0.09$, and $T = 10/12$. The price of the call option is $9.49.

(b) If the strike price is the quoted price that would be paid for the bond on exercise, 1 month's accrued interest must be added to K because the maturity of the option is 1 month after a coupon date. This produces a value for K of

$$1,000 + 100 \times 0.08333 = 1,008.33$$

The values for the other parameters in equation (29.1) are unchanged (i.e., $F_B = 939.68$, $P(0, T) = 0.9200$, $\sigma_B = 0.09$, and $T = 0.8333$). The price of the option is $7.97.

Figure 29.1 shows how the standard deviation of the logarithm of a bond's price

Figure 29.1 Standard deviation of logarithm of bond price at future times.

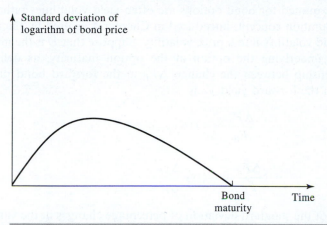

changes as we look further ahead. The standard deviation is zero today because there is no uncertainty about the bond's price today. It is also zero at the bond's maturity because we know that the bond's price will equal its face value at maturity. Between today and the maturity of the bond, the standard deviation first increases and then decreases.

The volatility σ_B that should be used when a European option on the bond is valued is

$$\frac{\text{Standard deviation of logarithm of bond price at maturity of option}}{\sqrt{\text{Time to maturity of option}}}$$

What happens when, for a particular underlying bond, the life of the option is increased? Figure 29.2 shows a typical pattern for σ_B as a function of the life of the option, with σ_B declining as the life of the option increases.

Figure 29.2 Variation of forward bond price volatility σ_B with life of option when bond is kept fixed.

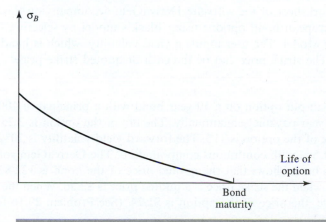

Yield Volatilities

The volatilities that are quoted for bond options are often yield volatilities rather than price volatilities. The duration concept, introduced in Chapter 4, is used by the market to convert a quoted yield volatility into a price volatility. Suppose that D is the modified duration of the bond underlying the option at the option maturity, as defined in Chapter 4. The relationship between the change ΔF_B in the forward bond price F_B and the change Δy_F in the forward yield y_F is

$$\frac{\Delta F_B}{F_B} \approx -D \Delta y_F$$

or

$$\frac{\Delta F_B}{F_B} \approx -D y_F \frac{\Delta y_F}{y_F}$$

Volatility is a measure of the standard deviation of percentage changes in the value of a variable. This equation therefore suggests that the volatility of the forward bond price σ_B used in Black's model can be approximately related to the volatility of the forward bond yield σ_y by

$$\sigma_B = D y_0 \sigma_y \tag{29.4}$$

where y_0 is the initial value of y_F. When a yield volatility is quoted for a European bond option, the implicit assumption is usually that it will be converted to a price volatility using equation (29.4), and that this volatility will then be used in conjunction with equation (29.1) or (29.2) to obtain the option's price. Suppose that the bond underlying a call option will have a modified duration of 5 years at option maturity, the forward yield is 8%, and the forward yield volatility quoted by a broker is 20%. This means that the market price of the option corresponding to the broker quote is the price given by equation (29.1) when the volatility variable σ_B is

$$5 \times 0.08 \times 0.2 = 0.08$$

or 8% per annum. Figure 29.2 shows that forward bond volatilities depend on the option considered. Forward yield volatilities as we have just defined them are more constant. This is why traders prefer them.

The Bond_Options worksheet of the software DerivaGem accompanying this book can be used to price European bond options using Black's model by selecting Black-European as the Pricing Model. The user inputs a yield volatility, which is handled in the way just described. The strike price can be the cash or quoted strike price.

Example 29.2

Consider a European put option on a 10-year bond with a principal of 100. The coupon is 8% per year payable semiannually. The life of the option is 2.25 years and the strike price of the option is 115. The forward yield volatility is 20%. The zero curve is flat at 5% with continuous compounding. The DerivaGem software accompanying this book shows that the quoted price of the bond is 122.82. The price of the option when the strike price is a quoted price is $2.36. When the strike price is a cash price, the price of the option is $1.74. (See Problem 29.16 for the manual calculation.)

29.2 INTEREST RATE CAPS AND FLOORS

A popular interest rate option offered by financial institutions in the over-the-counter market is an *interest rate cap*. Interest rate caps can best be understood by first considering a floating-rate note where the interest rate is reset periodically equal to LIBOR. The time between resets is known as the *tenor*. Suppose the tenor is 3 months. The interest rate on the note for the first 3 months is the initial 3-month LIBOR rate; the interest rate for the next 3 months is set equal to the 3-month LIBOR rate prevailing in the market at the 3-month point; and so on.

An interest rate cap is designed to provide insurance against the rate of interest on the floating-rate note rising above a certain level. This level is known as the *cap rate*. Suppose that the principal amount is $10 million, the tenor is 3 months, the life of the cap is 5 years, and the cap rate is 4%. (Because the payments are made quarterly, this cap rate is expressed with quarterly compounding.) The cap provides insurance against the interest on the floating rate note rising above 4%.

For the moment we ignore day count issues and assume that there is exactly 0.25 year between each payment date. (We will cover day count issues at the end of this section.) Suppose that on a particular reset date the 3-month LIBOR interest rate is 5%. The floating rate note would require

$$0.25 \times 0.05 \times \$10,000,000 = \$125,000$$

of interest to be paid 3 months later. With a 3-month LIBOR rate of 4% the interest payment would be

$$0.25 \times 0.04 \times \$10,000,000 = \$100,000$$

The cap therefore provides a payoff of $25,000. The payoff does not occur on the reset date when the 5% is observed: it occurs 3 months later. This reflects the usual time lag between an interest rate being observed and the corresponding payment being required.

At each reset date during the life of the cap, LIBOR is observed. If LIBOR is less than 4%, there is no payoff from the cap three months later. If LIBOR is greater than 4%, the payoff is one quarter of the excess applied to the principal of $10 million. Note that caps are usually defined so that the initial LIBOR rate, even if it is greater than the cap rate, does not lead to a payoff on the first reset date. In our example, the cap lasts for 5 years. There are, therefore, a total of 19 reset dates (at times 0.25, 0.50, 0.75, . . . , 4.75 years) and 19 potential payoffs from the caps (at times 0.50, 0.75, 1.00, . . . , 5.00 years).

The Cap as a Portfolio of Interest Rate Options

Consider a cap with a total life of T, a principal of L, and a cap rate of R_K. Suppose that the reset dates are $t_1, t_2, \ldots, t_n$ and define $t_{n+1} = T$. Define R_k as the LIBOR interest rate for the period between time t_k and t_{k+1} observed at time t_k ($1 \leqslant k \leqslant n$). The cap leads to a payoff at time t_{k+1} ($k = 1, 2, \ldots, n$) of

$$L\delta_k \max(R_k - R_K, 0) \tag{29.5}$$

where $\delta_k = t_{k+1} - t_k$.[1] Both R_k and R_K are expressed with a compounding frequency equal to the frequency of resets.

---

[1] Day count issues are discussed at the end of this section.

Expression (29.5) is the payoff from a call option on the LIBOR rate observed at time t_k with the payoff occurring at time t_{k+1}. The cap is a portfolio of n such options. LIBOR rates are observed at times $t_1, t_2, t_3, \ldots, t_n$ and the corresponding payoffs occur at times $t_2, t_3, t_4, \ldots, t_{n+1}$. The n call options underlying the cap are known as *caplets*.

A Cap as a Portfolio of Bond Options

An interest rate cap can also be characterized as a portfolio of put options on zero-coupon bonds with payoffs on the puts occurring at the time they are calculated. The payoff in expression (29.5) at time t_{k+1} is equivalent to

$$\frac{L\delta_k}{1 + R_k\delta_k}\max(R_k - R_K, 0)$$

at time t_k. A few lines of algebra show that this reduces to

$$\max\left[L - \frac{L(1 + R_K\delta_k)}{1 + R_k\delta_k}, 0\right] \tag{29.6}$$

The expression

$$\frac{L(1 + R_K\delta_k)}{1 + R_k\delta_k}$$

is the value at time t_k of a zero-coupon bond that pays off $L(1 + R_K\delta_k)$ at time t_{k+1}. The expression in (29.6) is therefore the payoff from a put option with maturity t_k on a zero-coupon bond with maturity t_{k+1} when the face value of the bond is $L(1 + R_K\delta_k)$ and the strike price is L. It follows that an interest rate cap can be regarded as a portfolio of European put options on zero-coupon bonds.

Floors and Collars

Interest rate floors and interest rate collars (sometimes called floor–ceiling agreements) are defined analogously to caps. A *floor* provides a payoff when the interest rate on the underlying floating-rate note falls below a certain rate. With the notation already introduced, a floor provides a payoff at time t_{k+1} ($k = 1, 2, \ldots, n$) of

$$L\delta_k\max(R_K - R_k, 0)$$

Analogously to an interest rate cap, an interest rate floor is a portfolio of put options on interest rates or a portfolio of call options on zero-coupon bonds. Each of the individual options comprising a floor is known as a *floorlet*. A *collar* is an instrument designed to guarantee that the interest rate on the underlying LIBOR floating-rate note always lies between two levels. A collar is a combination of a long position in a cap and a short position in a floor. It is usually constructed so that the price of the cap is initially equal to the price of the floor. The cost of entering into the collar is then zero.

Business Snapshot 29.1 gives the put–call parity relationship between caps and floors.

Valuation of Caps and Floors

As shown in equation (29.5), the caplet corresponding to the rate observed at time t_k provides a payoff at time t_{k+1} of

$$L\delta_k\max(R_k - R_K, 0)$$

Business Snapshot 29.1 Put–Call Parity for Caps and Floors

There is a put–call parity relationship between the prices of caps and floors. This is

$$\text{Value of cap} = \text{Value of floor} + \text{Value of swap}$$

In this relationship, the cap and floor have the same strike price, R_K. The swap is an agreement to receive LIBOR and pay a fixed rate of R_K with no exchange of payments on the first reset date. All three instruments have the same life and the same frequency of payments.

To see that the result is true, consider a long position in the cap combined with a short position in the floor. The cap provides a cash flow of $\text{LIBOR} - R_K$ for periods when LIBOR is greater than R_K. The short floor provides a cash flow of $-(R_K - \text{LIBOR}) = \text{LIBOR} - R_K$ for periods when LIBOR is less than R_K. There is therefore a cash flow of $\text{LIBOR} - R_K$ in all circumstances. This is the cash flow on the swap. It follows that the value of the cap minus the value of the floor must equal the value of the swap.

Note that swaps are usually structured so that LIBOR at time zero determines a payment on the first reset date. Caps and floors are usually structured so that there is no payoff on the first reset date. This is why put–call parity involves a nonstandard swap where there is no payment on the first reset date.

Under the standard market model, the value of the caplet is

$$L\delta_k P(0, t_{k+1})[F_k N(d_1) - R_K N(d_2)] \tag{29.7}$$

where

$$d_1 = \frac{\ln(F_k/R_K) + \sigma_k^2 t_k/2}{\sigma_k \sqrt{t_k}}$$

$$d_2 = \frac{\ln(F_k/R_K) - \sigma_k^2 t_k/2}{\sigma_k \sqrt{t_k}} = d_1 - \sigma_k \sqrt{t_k}$$

Here, F_k is the forward interest rate at time 0 for the period between time t_k and t_{k+1}, and σ_k is the volatility of this forward interest rate. This is a natural extension of Black's model. The volatility σ_k is multiplied by $\sqrt{t_k}$ because the interest rate R_k is observed at time t_k, but the risk-free discount factor $P(0, t_{k+1})$ reflects the fact that the payoff is at time t_{k+1}, not time t_k. The value of the corresponding floorlet is

$$L\delta_k P(0, t_{k+1})[R_K N(-d_2) - F_k N(-d_1)] \tag{29.8}$$

Example 29.3

Consider a contract that caps the LIBOR interest rate on $10 million at 8% per annum (with quarterly compounding) for 3 months starting in 1 year. This is a caplet and could be one element of a cap. Suppose that the forward LIBOR rate for the period covered by the caplet is 7% per annum with quarterly compounding and the volatility of this forward rate is 20% per annum. The continuously compounded risk-free zero rate for all maturities is 6.5%. In equation (29.7), $F_k = 0.07$, $\delta_k = 0.25$, $L = 10$, $R_K = 0.08$, $t_k = 1.0$, $t_{k+1} = 1.25$, $P(0, t_{k+1}) =$

$e^{-0.065 \times 1.25} = 0.9220$, and $\sigma_k = 0.20$. Also,

$$d_1 = \frac{\ln(0.07/0.08) + 0.2^2 \times 1/2}{0.20 \times 1} = -0.5677$$

$$d_2 = d_1 - 0.20 = -0.7677$$

so that the caplet price (in $ millions) is

$$0.25 \times 10 \times 0.9220[0.07N(-0.5677) - 0.08N(-0.7677)] = 0.00519$$

This result can also be obtained using the DerivaGem software accompanying this book.

Each caplet of a cap must be valued separately using equation (29.7). Similarly, each floorlet of a floor must be valued separately using equation (29.8). One approach is to use a different volatility for each caplet (or floorlet). The volatilities are then referred to as *spot volatilities*. An alternative approach is to use the same volatility for all the caplets (floorlets) comprising any particular cap (floor) but to vary this volatility according to the life of the cap (floor). The volatilities used are then referred to as *flat volatilities*.[2] Flat volatilities are akin to cumulative averages of spot volatilities and are therefore less variable as a function of maturity. The volatilities quoted in the market are usually flat volatilities. However, many traders like to estimate spot volatilities because this allows them to identify underpriced and overpriced caplets (floorlets). The put (call) options on Eurodollar futures are very similar to caplets (floorlets) and the spot volatilities used for caplets and floorlets on 3-month LIBOR are frequently compared with those calculated from the prices of Eurodollar futures options.

There is a smile or skew in the implied volatilities calculated from caplet/floorlet prices. Some analysts choose to model this with the SABR model which was introduced in Section 27.2. This can be useful in managing the risks associated with smile movements.

Theoretical Justification for the Model

The extension of Black's model used to value a caplet can be shown to be internally consistent by considering a world defined by a numeraire equal to a risk-free zero-coupon bond maturing at time t_{k+1}. Section 28.4 shows that:

1. The current value of any security is its expected value at time t_{k+1} in this world multiplied by the price of a zero-coupon bond maturing at time t_{k+1} (see equation (28.20)).

2. The expected value of a risk-free interest rate lasting between times t_k and t_{k+1} equals the forward interest rate in this world (see equation (28.22)).

The first of these results shows that, with the notation introduced earlier, the price of a caplet that provides a payoff at time t_{k+1} is

$$L\delta_k P(0, t_{k+1}) E_{k+1}[\max(R_k - R_K, 0)] \tag{29.9}$$

where E_{k+1} denotes expected value in a world defined by a numeraire equal to to a zero-coupon bond maturing at time t_{k+1}. When the forward interest rate underlying the cap (initially F_k) is assumed to have a constant volatility σ_k, R_k is lognormal in the world we

---

[2] Flat volatilities can be calculated from spot volatilities and vice versa (see Problem 29.20).

are considering, with the standard deviation of $\ln(R_k)$ equal to $\sigma_k\sqrt{t_k}$. From equation (15A.1), the caplet price in equation (29.9) becomes

$$L\delta_k P(0, t_{k+1})[E_{k+1}(R_k)N(d_1) - R_K N(d_2)]$$

where

$$d_1 = \frac{\ln[E_{k+1}(R_k)/R_K] + \sigma_k^2 t_k/2}{\sigma_k\sqrt{t_k}}$$

$$d_2 = \frac{\ln[E_{k+1}(R_k)/R_K] - \sigma_k^2 t_k/2}{\sigma_k\sqrt{t_k}} = d_1 - \sigma_k\sqrt{t_k}$$

The second result implies that

$$E_{k+1}(R_k) = F_k$$

which leads to the result in equation (29.7). Note that the results we have used from Section 28.4 are correct when any yield curve is used to define R_k and F_k. (It does not have to be the risk-free yield curve underlying $P(0, t_{k+1})$.) Equation (29.7) therefore has valid theoretical underpinnings in the usual situation where the rate used to define the payoff is LIBOR and the OIS term structure defines risk-free rates.

Use of DerivaGem

The software DerivaGem accompanying this book can be used to price interest rate caps and floors using Black's model. In the Cap_and_Swap_Options worksheet select Cap/Floor as the Underlying Type and Black-European as the Pricing Model. LIBOR forward rates are input with a compounding frequency corresponding to the tenor. These are used to determine the F_k. Continuously compounded OIS rates are input to determine the discount factor $P(0, t_{k+1})$. The inputs include the start and end date of the period covered by the cap, the flat volatility, and the cap settlement frequency (i.e., the tenor). The software calculates the payment dates by working back from the end of period covered by the cap to the beginning. The initial caplet/floorlet is assumed to cover a period of length between 0.5 and 1.5 times a regular period. Suppose, for example, that the period covered by the cap is 1.22 years to 2.80 years and the settlement frequency is quarterly. There are six caplets covering the periods 2.55 to 2.80 years, 2.30 to 2.55 years, 2.05 to 2.30 years, 1.80 to 2.05 years, 1.55 to 1.80 years, and 1.22 to 1.55 years.

The Impact of Day Count Conventions

The formulas we have presented so far in this section do not reflect day count conventions (see Section 6.1 for an explanation of day count conventions). Suppose that the cap rate R_K is expressed with an actual/360 day count (as would be normal in the United States). This means that the time interval δ_k in the formulas should be replaced by a_k, the *accrual fraction* for the time period between t_k and t_{k+1}. Suppose, for example, that t_k is May 1 and t_{k+1} is August 1. Under actual/360 there are 92 days between these payment dates so that $a_k = 92/360 = 0.2556$. The forward rate F_k must be expressed with an actual/360 day count. This means that we must set it by solving

$$1 + a_k F_k = \frac{P(0, t_k)}{P(0, t_{k+1})}$$

The impact of all this is much the same as calculating δ_k on an actual/actual basis converting R_K from actual/360 to actual/actual, and calculating F_k on an actual/actual basis by solving

$$1 + \delta_k F_k = \frac{P(0, t_k)}{P(0, t_{k+1})}$$

Negative Rates

Negative interest rates became a feature of financial markets in 2014. By the end of the first half of 2016, interest rates were negative for the Swedish krona, Danish krone, Japanese yen, euro, and Swiss franc. It was then estimated that more than \$10 trillion of government bonds worldwide had negative yields.

From an economics perspective, negative rates make no sense. (Why pay an entity to have use of your funds?) They also present a challenge to modelers. The standard market model for valuing caps and floors assumes that the relevant future interest rate is lognormal so that it cannot become negative. One quick fix is to use what is known as the *shifted lognormal model*. In this, a future interest rate plus a spread, α, is assumed to be lognormal. Caps and floors can then be valued using equations (29.7) and (29.8) with F_k replaced by $F_k + \alpha$ and R_K replaced by $R_K + \alpha$. The shift α, when used with flat volatilities, sometimes depends on the cap/floor maturity. The SABR model can be adjusted in a similar way to become a shifted SABR model.

An alternative is to use the *Bachelier normal model*. In a world defined by the numeraire $P(0, t_{k+1})$, the process for the forward rate underlying a caplet on the (t_k, t_{k+1}) rate in the standard market model is assumed to be

$$dF_k = \sigma_k F_k \, dz$$

where dz is a Wiener process. In the Bachelier normal model, it is

$$dF_k = \sigma_k^* \, dz$$

Consistent with the equivalent martingale measure results in Chapter 27, both processes are martingales. The Bachelier model leads to a normal rather than lognormal distribution for the underlying rate and so allows rates to become negative. Equation (29.7) for a caplet becomes

$$L\delta_k P(0, t_{k+1})\big[(F_k - R_K)N(d) + \sigma_k^* \sqrt{t_k} N'(d)\big]$$

and equation (29.8) for a floorlet becomes

$$L\delta_k P(0, t_{k+1})\big[(R_K - F_k)N(-d) + \sigma_k^* \sqrt{t_k} N'(d)\big]$$

where

$$d = \frac{F_k - R_K}{\sigma_k^* \sqrt{t_k}}$$

and $N'(x)$ is the normal distribution's density function (see equation (19.2)). Note that the volatility parameters, σ_k and σ_k^*, in the two models are quite different. For example, when the forward interest rate is 3%, σ_k might be 33% while σ_k^* is about 1%. Both the Bachelier normal and shifted lognormal models are implemented for caps, floors, and swaptions in DerivaGem 4.00.

29.3 EUROPEAN SWAP OPTIONS

Swap options, or *swaptions*, are options on interest rate swaps and are another popular type of interest rate option. They give the holder the right to enter into a certain interest rate swap at a certain time in the future. (The holder does not, of course, have to exercise this right.) Many large financial institutions that offer interest rate swap contracts to their corporate clients are also prepared to sell them swaptions or buy swaptions from them. As shown in Business Snapshot 29.2, a swaption can be viewed as a type of bond option.

To give an example of how a swaption might be used, consider a company that knows that in 6 months it will enter into a 5-year floating-rate loan agreement where the rate is tied to LIBOR and knows that it will wish to swap the floating interest payments for fixed interest payments to convert the loan into a fixed-rate loan (see Chapter 7 for a discussion of how swaps can be used in this way). At a cost, the company could enter into a swaption giving it the right to receive 6-month LIBOR and pay a certain fixed rate of interest, say 3% per annum, for a 5-year period starting in 6 months. If the fixed rate exchanged for floating on a regular 5-year swap in 6 months turns out to be less than 3% per annum, the company will choose not to exercise the swaption and will enter into a swap agreement in the usual way. However, if it turns out to be greater than 3% per annum, the company will choose to exercise the swaption and will obtain a swap at more favorable terms than those available in the market.

Swaptions, when used in the way just described, provide companies with a guarantee that the fixed rate of interest they will pay on a loan at some future time will not exceed some level. They are an alternative to forward swaps (sometimes called *deferred swaps*). Forward swaps involve no up-front cost but have the disadvantage of obligating the company to enter into a swap agreement. With a swaption, the company is able to benefit from favorable interest rate movements while acquiring protection from unfavorable interest rate movements. The difference between a swaption and a forward swap is analogous to the difference between an option on a foreign currency and a forward contract on the currency.

Valuation of European Swaptions

As explained in Chapter 7, the swap rate for a particular maturity at a particular time is the (mid-market) fixed rate that would be exchanged for LIBOR in a newly issued swap with that maturity. The model usually used to value a European option on a swap assumes that the underlying swap rate at the maturity of the option is lognormal. Consider a swaption where the holder has the right to pay a rate s_K and receive LIBOR on a swap that will last n years starting in T years. We suppose that there are m payments per year under the swap and that the notional principal is L.

Chapter 7 showed that day count conventions may lead to the fixed payments under a swap being slightly different on each payment date. For now we will ignore the effect of day count conventions and assume that each fixed payment on the swap is the fixed rate times L/m. The impact of day count conventions is considered at the end of this section.

Suppose that the swap rate for an n-year swap starting at time T proves to be s_T. By comparing the cash flows on a swap where the fixed rate is s_T to the cash flows on a swap where the fixed rate is s_K, it can be seen that the payoff from the swaption consists of a

---

Business Snapshot 29.2   Swaptions and Bond Options

As explained in Chapter 7, an interest rate swap can be regarded as an agreement to exchange a fixed-rate bond for a floating-rate bond. At the start of a swap, the value of the floating-rate bond always equals the principal amount of the swap. A swaption can therefore be regarded as an option to exchange a fixed-rate bond for the principal amount of the swap—that is, a type of bond option.

If a swaption gives the holder the right to pay fixed and receive floating, it is a put option on the fixed-rate bond with strike price equal to the principal. If a swaption gives the holder the right to pay floating and receive fixed, it is a call option on the fixed-rate bond with a strike price equal to the principal.

---

series of cash flows equal to

$$\frac{L}{m}\max(s_T - s_K, 0)$$

The cash flows are received m times per year for the n years of the life of the swap. Suppose that the swap payment dates are $T_1, T_2, \ldots, T_{mn}$, measured in years from today. (It is approximately true that $T_i = T + i/m$.) Each cash flow is the payoff from a call option on s_T with strike price s_K.

Whereas a cap is a portfolio of options on interest rates, a swaption is a single option on the swap rate with repeated payoffs. The standard market model gives the value of a swaption where the holder has the right to pay s_K as

$$\sum_{i=1}^{mn}\frac{L}{m}P(0, T_i)[s_F N(d_1) - s_K N(d_2)]$$

where

$$d_1 = \frac{\ln(s_F/s_K) + \sigma^2 T/2}{\sigma\sqrt{T}}$$

$$d_2 = \frac{\ln(s_F/s_K) - \sigma^2 T/2}{\sigma\sqrt{T}} = d_1 - \sigma\sqrt{T}$$

s_F is the forward swap rate at time zero, and σ is the volatility of the forward swap rate (so that $\sigma\sqrt{T}$ is the standard deviation of $\ln s_T$).

This is a natural extension of Black's model. The volatility σ is multiplied by $\sqrt{T}$. The $\sum_{i=1}^{mn}P(0, T_i)$ term is the discount factor for the mn payoffs. Defining A as the value of a contract that pays $1/m$ at times T_i ($1 \leqslant i \leqslant mn$), the value of the swaption becomes

$$LA[s_F N(d_1) - s_K N(d_2)] \tag{29.10}$$

where

$$A = \frac{1}{m}\sum_{i=1}^{mn}P(0, T_i)$$

If the swaption gives the holder the right to receive a fixed rate of s_K instead of paying it, the payoff from the swaption is

$$\frac{L}{m}\max(s_K - s_T, 0)$$

This is a put option on s_T. As before, the payoffs are received at times T_i ($1 \leqslant i \leqslant mn$). The standard market model gives the value of the swaption as

$$LA[s_K N(-d_2) - s_F N(-d_1)] \tag{29.11}$$

DerivaGem can be used to value swaptions using Black's model. In the Cap_and_Swap_Options worksheet, select Swap Options as the Underlying Type and Black-European as the pricing model. Inputs are similar to those for caps. LIBOR forward rates are used to determine the LIBOR forward swap rate. If this forward swap rate is known, the LIBOR forward rate can be input as flat and equal to the known value.

Example 29.4

Suppose that the risk-free zero curve is flat at 6% per annum with continuous compounding. Consider a swaption that gives the holder the right to pay 6.2% in a 3-year swap starting in 5 years. Payments are made semiannually and the principal is $100 million. The forward swap rate is 6.1% with continuous compounding, which translates as 6.194% with semiannual compounding. The volatility of the forward swap rate is 20%. In this case,

$$A = \tfrac{1}{2}(e^{-0.06 \times 5.5} + e^{-0.06 \times 6} + e^{-0.06 \times 6.5} + e^{-0.06 \times 7} + e^{-0.06 \times 7.5} + e^{-0.06 \times 8}) = 2.0035$$

Also, $s_F = 0.06194$, $s_K = 0.062$, $T = 5$, and $\sigma = 0.2$, so that

$$d_1 = \frac{\ln(0.06194/0.062) + 0.2^2 \times 5/2}{0.2\sqrt{5}} = 0.2214$$

$$d_2 = d_1 - 0.2\sqrt{5} = -0.2258$$

From equation (29.10), the value of the swaption (in $ millions) is

$$100 \times 2.0035 \times [0.06194 \times N(0.2214) - 0.062 \times N(-0.2258)] = 2.19$$

(This is in agreement with the price given by DerivaGem.)

Theoretical Justification for the Swaption Model

The extension of Black's model used for swaptions can be shown to be internally consistent by considering a world defined by a numeraire equal to the annuity A. The analysis in Section 28.4 shows that:

1. The current value of any security is the current value of the annuity multiplied by the expected value of

$$\frac{\text{Security price at time } T}{\text{Value of the annuity at time } T}$$

in this world (see equation (28.25)).

2. The expected value of the swap rate at time T in this world equals the forward swap rate (see equation (28.24)).

The first result shows that the value of the swaption is

$$LAE_A[\max(s_T - s_K, 0)]$$

From equation (15A.1), this is

$$LA[E_A(s_T)N(d_1) - s_K N(d_2)]$$

where

$$d_1 = \frac{\ln[E_A(s_T)/s_K] + \sigma^2 T/2}{\sigma\sqrt{T}}$$

$$d_2 = \frac{\ln[E_A(s_T)/s_K] - \sigma^2 T/2}{\sigma\sqrt{T}} = d_1 - \sigma\sqrt{T}$$

The second result shows that $E_A(s_T)$ equals s_F. The results lead to the swap option pricing formula in equation (29.10). They show that interest rates can be treated as constant for the purposes of discounting provided that the expected swap rate is set equal to the forward swap rate. Note that the results in Section 28.4 show that this theoretical result is valid when the floating rate in the underlying swap is not the same as the risk-free rate.

The Impact of Day Count Conventions

The above formulas can be made more precise by considering day count conventions. The fixed rate for the swap underlying the swap option is expressed with a day count convention such as actual/365 or 30/360. Suppose that $T_0 = T$ and that, for the applicable day count convention, the accrual fraction corresponding to the time period between T_{i-1} and T_i is a_i. (For example, if T_{i-1} corresponds to March 1 and T_i corresponds to September 1 and the day count is actual/365, $a_i = 184/365 = 0.5041$.) The formulas that have been presented are then correct with the annuity factor A being defined as

$$A = \sum_{i=1}^{mn} a_i P(0, T_i)$$

Negative Rates

The shifted lognormal model can be used to handle the possibility of negative interest rates when swaptions are valued. Equations (29.10) and (29.11) are used with with s_F replaced by $s_F + \alpha$ and R_K replaced by $R_K + \alpha$. The shift, α, in practice often depends on both the life of the option and the life of the underlying swap. The Bachelier normal model can also be used. When the holder has the right to pay s_K, equation (29.10) becomes

$$LA\big[(s_F - s_K)N(d) + \sigma^*\sqrt{T}N'(d)\big]$$

and when the holder has the right to receive s_K, equation (29.11) becomes

$$LA\big[(s_K - s_F)N(-d) + \sigma^*\sqrt{T}N'(d)\big]$$

where $\sigma^*\sqrt{T}$ is the standard deviation of s_T and

$$d = \frac{s_F - s_K}{\sigma^*\sqrt{T}}$$

29.4 HEDGING INTEREST RATE DERIVATIVES

This section discusses how the material on Greek letters in Chapter 19 can be extended to cover interest rate derivatives.

In the context of interest rate derivatives, delta risk is the risk associated with a shift in the zero curve. Because there are many ways in which the zero curve can shift, many deltas can be calculated. Some alternatives are:

1. Calculate the impact of a 1-basis-point parallel shift in the zero curve. This is sometimes termed a DV01.

2. Calculate the impact of small changes in the quotes for each of the instruments used to construct the zero curve.

3. Divide the zero curve (or the forward curve) into a number of sections (or buckets). Calculate the impact of shifting the rates in one bucket by 1 basis point, keeping the rest of the initial term structure unchanged. (This is described in Business Snapshot 6.3.)

4. Carry out a principal components analysis as outlined in Section 22.9. Calculate a delta with respect to the changes in each of the first few factors. The first delta then measures the impact of a small, approximately parallel, shift in the zero curve; the second delta measures the impact of a small twist in the zero curve; and so on.

In practice, traders tend to prefer the second approach. They argue that the only way the zero curve can change is if the quote for one of the instruments used to compute the zero curve changes. They therefore feel that it makes sense to focus on the exposures arising from changes in the prices of these instruments.

When several delta measures are calculated, there are many possible gamma measures. Suppose that 10 instruments are used to compute the zero curve and that deltas are calculated by considering the impact of changes in the quotes for each of these. Gamma is a second partial derivative of the form $\partial^2 \Pi / \partial x_i \, \partial x_j$, where Π is the portfolio value. There are 10 choices for x_i and 10 choices for x_j and a total of 55 different gamma measures. This may be "information overload". One approach is ignore cross-gammas and focus on the 10 partial derivatives where $i = j$. Another is to calculate a single gamma measure as the second partial derivative of the value of the portfolio with respect to a parallel shift in the zero curve. A further possibility is to calculate gammas with respect to the first two factors in a principal components analysis.

The vega of a portfolio of interest rate derivatives measures its exposure to volatility changes. One approach is to calculate the impact on the portfolio of making the same small change to the Black volatilities of all caps and European swap options. However, this assumes that one factor drives all volatilities and may be too simplistic. A better idea is to carry out a principal components analysis on the volatilities of caps and swap options and calculate vega measures corresponding to the first two or three factors.

SUMMARY

Black's model and its extensions provide a popular approach for valuing European-style interest rate options. The essence of Black's model is that the value of the variable underlying the option is assumed to be lognormal at the maturity of the option. In the case of a European bond option, Black's model assumes that the underlying bond price is lognormal at the option's maturity. For a cap, the model assumes that the interest rates underlying each of the constituent caplets are lognormally distributed. In the case of a swap option, the model assumes that the underlying swap rate is lognormally distributed.

Each of the models we have presented in this chapter is internally consistent even when the interest rate underlying the instrument being valued is not the risk-free rate. They are therefore internally consistent when OIS discounting is used instead of LIBOR discounting. However, the models are not consistent with each other. For example, when future bond prices are lognormal, future interest rates and swap rates are not lognormal; when future interest rates are lognormal, future bond prices and swap rates are not lognormal. The models cannot easily be extended to value instruments such as American swap options. Chapters 32 and 33 present more general interest rate models, which, although more complex, can be used for a much wider range of products.

Black's model involves calculating the expected payoff based on the assumption that the expected value of a variable equals its forward value and then discounting the expected payoff at the zero rate observed in the market today. This is the correct procedure for the "plain vanilla" instruments we have considered in this chapter. However, as we shall see in the next chapter, it is not correct in all situations.

FURTHER READING

Black, F. "The Pricing of Commodity Contracts," *Journal of Financial Economics*, 3 (March 1976): 167–79.

Hull, J.C., and A. White. "OIS Discounting, Interest Rate Derivatives, and the Modeling of Stochastic Interest Rate Spreads," *Journal of Investment Management*, 13, 1 (2015): 64–83.

Practice Questions (Answers in Solutions Manual)

29.1. A company caps 3-month LIBOR at 2% per annum. The principal amount is $20 million. On a reset date, 3-month LIBOR is 4% per annum. What payment would this lead to under the cap? When would the payment be made?

29.2. Explain why a swap option can be regarded as a type of bond option.

29.3. Use the Black's model to value a 1-year European put option on a 10-year bond. Assume that the current cash price of the bond is $125, the strike price is $110, the 1-year risk-free interest rate is 10% per annum, the bond's forward price volatility is 8% per annum, and the present value of the coupons to be paid during the life of the option is $10.

29.4. Explain carefully how you would use (a) spot volatilities and (b) flat volatilities to value a 5-year cap.

29.5. Calculate the price of an option that caps the 3-month rate, starting in 15 months' time, at 13% (quoted with quarterly compounding) on a principal amount of $1,000. The forward interest rate for the period in question is 12% per annum (quoted with quarterly compounding), the 18-month risk-free interest rate (continuously compounded) is 11.5% per annum, and the volatility of the forward rate is 12% per annum.

29.6. A bank uses Black's model to price European bond options. Suppose that an implied price volatility for a 5-year option on a bond maturing in 10 years is used to price a 9-year option on the bond. Would you expect the resultant price to be too high or too low? Explain your answer.

29.7. Calculate the value of a 4-year European call option on bond that will mature 5 years from today using Black's model. The 5-year cash bond price is $105, the cash price of a

4-year bond with the same coupon is $102 and both bonds have a principal of $100. The strike price of the option is $100, the 4-year risk-free interest rate is 10% per annum with continuous compounding, and the forward bond price volatility for the bond underlying the option is 2% per annum.

29.8. If the yield volatility for a 5-year put option on a bond maturing in 10 years time is specified as 22%, how should the option be valued? Assume that, based on today's interest rates the modified duration of the bond at the maturity of the option will be 4.2 years and the forward yield on the bond is 7%.

29.9. What other instrument is the same as a 5-year zero-cost collar where the strike price of the cap equals the strike price of the floor? What does the common strike price equal?

29.10. Derive a put–call parity relationship for European bond options.

29.11. Derive a put–call parity relationship for European swap options.

29.12. Explain why there is an arbitrage opportunity if the implied Black (flat) volatility of a cap is different from that of a floor.

29.13. When a bond's price is lognormal can the bond's yield be negative? Explain your answer.

29.14. What is the value of a European swap option that gives the holder the right to enter into a 3-year annual-pay swap in 4 years where a fixed rate of 5% is paid and LIBOR is received? The swap principal is $10 million. Assume that the LIBOR/swap yield curve is used for discounting and is flat at 5% per annum with annual compounding and that the volatility of the swap rate is 20%. How does the value change if all swap rates are are 5% and all OIS rates are 4.7%. Compare your answer with that given by DerivaGem.

29.15. Suppose that the yield R on a zero-coupon bond follows the process

$$dR = \mu \, dt + \sigma \, dz$$

where μ and σ are functions of R and t, and dz is a Wiener process. Use Itô's lemma to show that the volatility of the zero-coupon bond price declines to zero as it approaches maturity.

29.16. Carry out a manual calculation to verify the option prices in Example 29.2.

29.17. Suppose that all risk-free (OIS) zero rates are 6.5% (continuously compounded). The price of a 5-year semiannual cap with a principal of $100 and a cap rate of 8% (semiannually compounded) is $3. Use DerivaGem to determine:
(a) The implied 5-year flat volatility for caps and floors
(b) The floor rate in a zero-cost 5-year collar when the cap rate is 8%.
Assume that all 6-month LIBOR forward rates are 6.7% with semiannual compounding.

29.18. Show that $V_1 + f = V_2$, where V_1 is the value of a swaption to pay a fixed rate of s_K and receive LIBOR between times T_1 and T_2, f is the value of a forward swap to receive a fixed rate of s_K and pay LIBOR between times T_1 and T_2, and V_2 is the value of a swaption to receive a fixed rate of s_K between times T_1 and T_2. Deduce that $V_1 = V_2$ when s_K equals the current forward swap rate.

29.19. Suppose that risk-free zero rates and LIBOR forward rates are as in Problem 29.17. Use DerivaGem to determine the value of an option to pay a fixed rate of 6% and receive LIBOR on a 5-year swap starting in 1 year. Assume that the principal is $100 million, payments are exchanged semiannually, and the swap rate volatility is 21%.

29.20. Describe how you would (a) calculate cap flat volatilities from cap spot volatilities and (b) calculate cap spot volatilities from cap flat volatilities.

Further Questions

29.21. Consider an 8-month European put option on a Treasury bond that currently has 14.25 years to maturity. The current cash bond price is $910, the exercise price is $900, and the volatility for the bond price is 10% per annum. A coupon of $35 will be paid by the bond in 3 months. The risk-free interest rate is 8% for all maturities up to 1 year. Use Black's model to determine the price of the option. Consider both the case where the strike price corresponds to the cash price of the bond and the case where it corresponds to the quoted price.

29.22. Calculate the price of a cap on the 90-day LIBOR rate in 9 months' time when the principal amount is $1,000. Use Black's model with LIBOR discounting and the following information:

(a) The quoted 9-month Eurodollar futures price = 92. (Ignore differences between futures and forward rates.)

(b) The interest rate volatility implied by a 9-month Eurodollar option = 15% per annum.

(c) The current 12-month risk-free interest rate with continuous compounding = 7.5% per annum.

(d) The cap rate = 8% per annum. (Assume an actual/360 day count.)

29.23. A swaption gives the holder the right to receive 7.6% in a 5-year swap starting in 4 years. Payments are made annually. The forward swap rate is 8% with annual compounding and its volatility is 25% per annum. The principal is $1 million and risk-free (OIS) rates for all maturities are 7.8% (with continuous compounding). Use Black's model to price the swaption. Compare your answer to that given by DerivaGem.

29.24. Use the DerivaGem software to value a 5-year collar that guarantees that the maximum and minimum interest rates on a LIBOR-based loan (with quarterly resets) are 7% and 5%, respectively. All 3-month LIBOR forward rates are 6% per annum (with quarterly compounding). The flat volatility is 20%. Assume that the principal is $100 and the risk-free (OIS) term structure is flat at 5.8%.

29.25. Use the DerivaGem software to value a European swaption that gives you the right in 2 years to enter into a 5-year swap in which you pay a fixed rate of 6% and receive floating. Cash flows are exchanged semiannually on the swap. The continuously compounded 1-year, 2-year, 5-year, and 10-year risk-free (OIS) zero rates are 5%, 6%, 6.5%, and 7%, respectively. Assume a principal of $100. The forward swap rate is 7% (compounded semiannually) and its volatility is 15% per annum. Give an example of how the swaption might be used by a corporation. What bond option is equivalent to the swaption?

CHAPTER 30

Convexity, Timing, and Quanto Adjustments

A popular two-step procedure for valuing a European-style derivative is:

1. Calculate the expected payoff by assuming that the expected value of each underlying variable equals its forward value
2. Discount the expected payoff at the risk-free rate applicable for the time period between the valuation date and the payoff date.

We first used this procedure when valuing FRAs and swaps. Chapter 4 shows that an FRA can be valued by calculating the payoff on the assumption that the forward interest rate will be realized and then discounting the payoff at the risk-free rate. Similarly, Chapter 7 extends this, showing that swaps can be valued by calculating cash flows on the assumption that forward rates will be realized and discounting the cash flows at risk-free rates. Chapters 18 and 28 show that Black's model provides a general approach to valuing a wide range of European options—and Black's model is an application of the two-step procedure. The models presented in Chapter 29 for bond options, caps/floors, and swap options are all examples of the two-step procedure.

This raises the issue of whether it is always correct to value European-style interest rate derivatives by using the two-step procedure. The answer is no! For nonstandard interest rate derivatives, it is sometimes necessary to modify the two-step procedure so that an adjustment is made to the forward value of the variable in the first step. This chapter considers three types of adjustments: convexity adjustments, timing adjustments, and quanto adjustments.

30.1 CONVEXITY ADJUSTMENTS

Consider first an instrument that provides a payoff dependent on a bond yield observed at the time of the payoff.

Usually the forward value of a variable S is calculated with reference to a forward contract that pays off $S_T - K$ at time T. It is the value of K that causes the contract to have zero value. Forward interest rates and forward yields are defined differently.

A forward interest rate is the rate implied by a forward zero-coupon bond. More generally, a forward bond yield is the yield implied by the forward bond price.

Suppose that B_T is the price of a bond at time T, y_T is its yield, and the (bond pricing) relationship between B_T and y_T is

$$B_T = G(y_T)$$

Define B_F as the forward bond price at time zero for a transaction maturing at time T and y_F as the forward bond yield at time zero. The definition of a forward bond yield means that

$$B_F = G(y_F)$$

The function G is nonlinear. This means that, when the expected future bond price equals the forward bond price (so that we are in a world defined by a numeraire equal to a zero-coupon bond maturing at time T), the expected future bond yield does not equal the forward bond yield.

This is illustrated in Figure 30.1, which shows the relationship between bond prices and bond yields at time T. For simplicity, suppose that there are only three possible bond prices, B_1, B_2, and B_3 and that they are equally likely in a world defined by numeraire $P(t, T)$. Assume that the bond prices are equally spaced, so that $B_2 - B_1 = B_3 - B_2$. The forward bond price is the expected bond price B_2. The bond prices translate into three equally likely bond yields: y_1, y_2, and y_3. These are not equally spaced. The variable y_2 is the forward bond yield because it is the yield corresponding to the forward bond price. The expected bond yield is the average of y_1, y_2, and y_3 and is clearly greater than y_2.

Consider a derivative that provides a payoff dependent on the bond yield at time T. From equation (28.20), it can be valued by (a) calculating the expected payoff in a world defined by a numeraire equal to a zero-coupon bond maturing at time T and (b) discounting at the current risk-free rate for maturity T. We know that the expected bond price equals the forward price in the world being considered. We therefore need to know the value of the expected bond yield when the expected bond price equals the

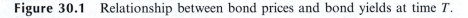

Figure 30.1   Relationship between bond prices and bond yields at time T.

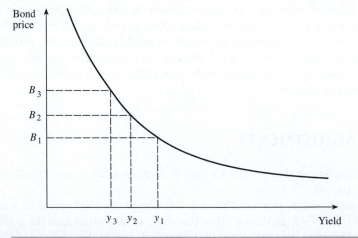

forward bond price. The analysis in the appendix at the end of this chapter shows that an approximate expression for the required expected bond yield is

$$E_T(y_T) = y_F - \frac{1}{2} y_F^2 \sigma_y^2 T \frac{G''(y_F)}{G'(y_F)}$$ (30.1)

where G' and G'' denote the first and second partial derivatives of G, E_T denotes expectations in a world that is defined by numeraire $P(t, T)$, and σ_y is the forward yield volatility. It follows that the expected payoff can be discounted at the current risk-free rate for maturity T provided the expected bond yield is assumed to be

$$y_F - \frac{1}{2} y_F^2 \sigma_y^2 T \frac{G''(y_F)}{G'(y_F)}$$

rather than y_F. The difference between the expected bond yield and the forward bond yield

$$-\frac{1}{2} y_F^2 \sigma_y^2 T \frac{G''(y_F)}{G'(y_F)}$$

is known as a *convexity adjustment*. It corresponds to the difference between y_2 and the expected yield in Figure 30.1. (The convexity adjustment is positive because $G'(y_F) < 0$ and $G''(y_F) > 0$.)

Application 1: Interest Rates

For a first application of equation (30.1), consider an instrument that provides a cash flow at time T equal to an interest rate between times T and T^* applied to a principal of L. (This example will be useful when we consider LIBOR-in-arrears swaps in Chapter 34.) Note that the interest rate applicable to the time period between times T and T^* is normally paid at time T^*; here it is assumed that it is paid early, at time T.

The cash flow at time T is $LR_T \tau$, where $\tau = T^* - T$ and R_T is the zero-coupon interest rate applicable to the period between T and T^* (expressed with a compounding period of τ).[1] The variable R_T can be viewed as the yield at time T on a zero-coupon bond maturing at time T^*. The relationship between the price of this bond and its yield is

$$G(y) = \frac{1}{1 + y\tau}$$

From equation (30.1),

$$E_T(R_T) = R_F - \frac{1}{2} R_F^2 \sigma_R^2 T \frac{G''(R_F)}{G'(R_F)}$$

or

$$E_T(R_T) = R_F + \frac{R_F^2 \sigma_R^2 \tau T}{1 + R_F \tau}$$ (30.2)

where R_F is the forward rate applicable to the period between T and T^* and σ_R is the volatility of the forward rate.

---

[1] As usual, for ease of exposition we assume actual/actual day counts in our examples.

The value of the instrument is therefore

$$P(0, T)L\tau\left[R_F + \frac{R_F^2\sigma_R^2\tau T}{1 + R_F\tau}\right]$$

Example 30.1

Consider a derivative that provides a payoff in 10 years equal to the 1-year risk-free rate (annually compounded) at that time multiplied by $1,000. Suppose that risk-free rates are 4% per annum with annual compounding for all maturities. The volatility of the forward rate corresponding to the period between 10 and 11 years is 20%. In this case, $R_F = 0.04$, $\sigma_R = 0.20$, $T = 10$, $\tau = 1$, and $P(0, T) = 1/1.04^3 = 0.6756$. The value of the derivative is

$$0.6756 \times 1000 \times 1 \times \left[0.04 + \frac{0.04^2 \times 0.20^2 \times 1 \times 10}{1 + 0.04 \times 1}\right]$$

or $27.44. (This compares with a price of $27.02 when no convexity adjustment is made.)

Application 2: Swap Rates

Consider next a derivative providing a payoff at time T equal to a swap rate observed at that time. For the purposes of calculating a convexity adjustment we can make an approximation and assume that the N-year swap rate at time T equals the yield at that time on an N-year bond with a coupon equal to today's forward swap rate. This enables equation (30.1) to be used.

Example 30.2

Consider an instrument that provides a payoff in 3 years equal to the 3-year swap rate at that time multiplied by $100. Suppose that payments are made annually on the swap, the swap rate for all maturities is 6% per annum with annual compounding, the volatility for the forward swap rate (implied from swap option prices) is 22%. The 3-year risk-free zero rate is 5% with annual compounding. When the swap rate is approximated as the yield on a 6% bond, the relevant function $G(y)$ is

$$G(y) = \frac{0.06}{1 + y} + \frac{0.06}{(1 + y)^2} + \frac{1.06}{(1 + y)^3}$$

$$G'(y) = -\frac{0.06}{(1 + y)^2} - \frac{0.12}{(1 + y)^3} - \frac{3.18}{(1 + y)^4}$$

$$G''(y) = \frac{0.12}{(1 + y)^3} + \frac{0.36}{(1 + y)^4} + \frac{12.72}{(1 + y)^5}$$

In this case the forward yield y_F is 0.06, so that $G'(y_F) = -2.6730$ and $G''(y_F) = 9.8710$. From equation (30.1),

$$E_T(y_T) = 0.06 + \frac{1}{2} \times 0.06^2 \times 0.22^2 \times 3 \times \frac{9.8710}{2.6730} = 0.06097$$

A forward swap rate of 6.097% rather than 6% should therefore be assumed when valuing the instrument. The instrument is worth

$$\frac{100 \times 0.06097}{1.05^3} = 5.27$$

or $5.27. (This compares with a price of $5.18 obtained without any convexity adjustment.)

30.2 TIMING ADJUSTMENTS

In this section consider the situation where a market variable V is observed at time T and its value is used to calculate a payoff that occurs at a later time T^*. Define:

$\quad V_T$: Value of V at time T

$E_T(V_T)$: Expected value of V_T in a world defined by numeraire $P(t, T)$

$E_{T^*}(V_T)$: Expected value of V_T in a world defined by numeraire $P(t, T^*)$.

The numeraire ratio when we move from the $P(t, T)$ numeraire to the $P(t, T^*)$ numeraire (see Section 28.8) is

$$W = \frac{P(t, T^*)}{P(t, T)}$$

This is the forward price of a zero-coupon bond lasting between times T and T^*. Define:

$\quad \sigma_V$: Volatility of V

$\quad \sigma_W$: Volatility of W

$\quad \rho_{VW}$: Correlation between V and W.

From equation (28.35), the change of numeraire increases the growth rate of V by α_V, where

$$\alpha_V = \rho_{VW}\sigma_V\sigma_W \qquad (30.3)$$

This result can be expressed in terms of the forward interest rate between times T and T^*. Define:

$\quad R_F$: Forward interest rate for period between T and T^*, expressed with a compounding frequency of m

$\quad \sigma_R$: Volatility of R_F.

The relationship between W and R_F is

$$W = \frac{1}{(1 + R_F/m)^{m(T^*-T)}}$$

The relationship between the volatility of W and the volatility of R_F can be calculated from Itô's lemma as

$$\sigma_W W = \sigma_R R_F \frac{\partial W}{\partial R_F} = -\frac{\sigma_R R_F (T^* - T)}{(1 + R_F/m)^{m(T^*-T)+1}}$$

so that

$$\sigma_W = -\frac{\sigma_R R_F (T^* - T)}{1 + R_F/m}$$

Hence equation (30.3) becomes[2]

$$\alpha_V = -\frac{\rho_{VR} \sigma_V \sigma_R R_F (T^* - T)}{1 + R_F/m}$$

where $\rho_{VR} = -\rho_{VW}$ is the instantaneous correlation between V and R_F. As an approximation, it can be assumed that R_F remains constant at its initial value and that the volatilities and correlation in this expression are constant to get, at time zero,

$$E_{T^*}(V_T) = E_T(V_T) \exp\left[-\frac{\rho_{VR} \sigma_V \sigma_R R_F (T^* - T)}{1 + R_F/m} T\right] \tag{30.4}$$

Example 30.3

Consider a derivative that provides a payoff in 6 years equal to the value of a stock index observed in 5 years. Suppose that 1,200 is the forward value of the stock index for a contract maturing in 5 years. Suppose that the volatility of the index is 20%, the volatility of the forward risk-free interest rate between years 5 and 6 is 18%, and the correlation between the two is −0.4. Suppose further that the risk-free zero curve is flat at 8% with annual compounding. The results just produced can be used with V defined as the value of the index, $T = 5$, $T^* = 6$, $m = 1$, $R_F = 0.08$, $\rho_{VR} = -0.4$, $\sigma_V = 0.20$, and $\sigma_R = 0.18$, so that

$$E_{T^*}(V_T) = E_T(V_T) \exp\left[-\frac{-0.4 \times 0.20 \times 0.18 \times 0.08 \times 1}{1 + 0.08} \times 5\right]$$

or $E_{T^*}(V_T) = 1.00535 E_T(V_T)$. From the arguments in Chapter 28, $E_T(V_T)$ is the forward price of the index, or 1,200. It follows that $E_{T^*}(V_T) = 1,200 \times 1.00535 = 1,206.42$. Using again the arguments in Chapter 28, it follows from equation (28.20) that the value of the derivative is $1,206.42 \times P(0, 6)$. In this case, $P(0, 6) = 1/1.08^6 = 0.6302$, so that the value of the derivative is 760.25.

Application 1 Revisited

The analysis just given provides a different way of producing the result in Application 1 of Section 30.1. Define R_T as the risk-free rate between times T and T^*. We know that $E_{T^*}(R_T) = R_F$ and want to calculate $E_T(R_T)$. We can apply equation (30.4). In this case, V and R_F are the same, so that $\rho_{VR} = 1$ and

$$E_{T^*}(R_T) = E_T(R_T) \exp\left[-\frac{\sigma_R^2 R_F \tau}{1 + R_F \tau} T\right]$$

---

[2] Variables R_F and W are negatively correlated. We can reflect this by setting $\sigma_W = -\sigma_R R_F(T^*-T)/(1+R_F/m)$, which is a negative number, and setting $\rho_{VW} = \rho_{VR}$. Alternatively we can change the sign of σ_W so that it is positive and set $\rho_{VW} = -\rho_{VR}$. In either case, we end up with the same formula for α_V.

where $\tau = T^* - T$ (note that $m = 1/\tau$). It follows that

$$R_F = E_T(R_T) \exp\left[-\frac{\sigma_R^2 R_F T \tau}{1 + R_F \tau}\right]$$

or

$$E_T(R_T) = R_F \exp\left[\frac{\sigma_R^2 R_F T \tau}{1 + R_F \tau}\right]$$

Approximating the exponential function gives

$$E_T(R_T) = R_F + \frac{R_F^2 \sigma_R^2 \tau T}{1 + R_F \tau}$$

This is the same result as equation (30.2).

30.3 QUANTOS

A *quanto* or *cross-currency derivative* is an instrument where two currencies are involved. The payoff is defined in terms of a variable that is measured in one of the currencies and the payoff is made in the other currency. One example of a quanto is the CME futures contract on the Nikkei discussed in Business Snapshot 5.3. The market variable underlying this contract is the Nikkei 225 index (which is measured in yen), but the contract is settled in U.S. dollars.

Consider a quanto that provides a payoff in currency X at time T. Assume that the payoff depends on the value V of a variable that is observed in currency Y at time T. Define:

$P_X(t, T)$: Value at time t in currency X of a zero-coupon bond paying off 1 unit of currency X at time T

$P_Y(t, T)$: Value at time t in currency Y of a zero-coupon bond paying off 1 unit of currency Y at time T

V_T: Value of V at time T

$E_X(V_T)$: Expected value of V_T in a world defined by numeraire $P_X(t, T)$

$E_Y(V_T)$: Expected value of V_T in a world defined by numeraire $P_Y(t, T)$.

The numeraire ratio when we move from the $P_Y(t, T)$ numeraire to the $P_X(t, T)$ numeraire is

$$W(t) = \frac{P_X(t, T)}{P_Y(t, T)} S(t)$$

where $S(t)$ is the spot exchange rate (units of Y per unit of X) at time t. It follows from this that the numeraire ratio $W(t)$ is the forward exchange rate (units of Y per unit of X) for a contract maturing at time T. Define:

σ_W: Volatility of W

σ_V: Volatility of V

ρ_{VW}: Instantaneous correlation between V and W.

From equation (28.35), the change of numeraire increases the growth rate of V by α_V, where

$$\alpha_V = \rho_{VW}\sigma_V\sigma_W \tag{30.5}$$

If it is assumed that the volatilities and correlation are constant, this means that

$$E_X(V_T) = E_Y(V_T)e^{\rho_{VW}\sigma_V\sigma_W T}$$

or as an approximation

$$E_X(V_T) = E_Y(V_T)(1 + \rho_{VW}\sigma_V\sigma_W T) \tag{30.6}$$

This equation will be used for the valuation of what are known as diff swaps in Chapter 34.

Example 30.4

Suppose that the current value of the Nikkei stock index is 15,000 yen, the 1-year dollar risk-free rate is 5%, the 1-year yen risk-free rate is 2%, and the Nikkei dividend yield is 1%. The forward price of the Nikkei for a 1-year contract denominated in yen can be calculated in the usual way from equation (5.8) as

$$15,000e^{(0.02-0.01)\times 1} = 15,150.75$$

Suppose that the volatility of the index is 20%, the volatility of the 1-year forward yen per dollar exchange rate is 12%, and the correlation between the two is 0.3. In this case $E_Y(V_T) = 15,150.75$, $\sigma_V = 0.20$, $\sigma_W = 0.12$ and $\rho = 0.3$. From equation (30.6), the expected value of the Nikkei in a world defined by a numeraire equal to a dollar bond maturing in 1 year is

$$15,150.75e^{0.3\times0.2\times0.12\times1} = 15,260.23$$

This is the forward price of the Nikkei for a contract that provides a payoff in dollars rather than yen. (As an approximation, it is also the futures price of such a contract.)

Using Traditional Risk-Neutral Measures

The numeraire-based measures we have been using work well when payoffs occur at only one time. In other situations, it is often more appropriate to use the traditional risk-neutral measure. Suppose the process followed by a variable V in the traditional currency-Y risk-neutral world is known and we wish to estimate its process in the traditional currency-X risk-neutral world. Define:

S: Spot exchange rate (units of Y per unit of X)

σ_S: Volatility of S

σ_V: Volatility of V

ρ: Instantaneous correlation between S and V.

In this case, the change of numeraire is from the money market account in currency Y to the money market account in currency X (with both money market accounts being denominated in currency X). Define g_X as the value of the money market account in currency X and g_Y as the value of the money market account in currency Y. The numeraire ratio is

$$g_X S/g_Y$$

Business Snapshot 30.1 Siegel's Paradox

Consider two currencies, X and Y. Suppose that the interest rates in the two currencies, r_X and r_Y, are constant. Define S as the number of units of currency Y per unit of currency X. As explained in Chapter 5, a currency is an asset that provides a yield at the foreign risk-free rate. The traditional risk-neutral process for S is therefore

$$dS = (r_Y - r_X)S\,dt + \sigma_S S\,dz$$

From Itô's lemma, this implies that the process for $1/S$ is

$$d(1/S) = (r_X - r_Y + \sigma_S^2)(1/S)\,dt - \sigma_S(1/S)\,dz$$

This leads to what is known as *Siegel's paradox*. Since the expected growth rate of S is $r_Y - r_X$ in a risk-neutral world, symmetry suggests that the expected growth rate of $1/S$ should be $r_X - r_Y$ rather than $r_X - r_Y + \sigma_S^2$.

To understand Siegel's paradox it is necessary to appreciate that the process we have given for S is the risk-neutral process for S in a world where the numeraire is the money market account in currency Y. The process for $1/S$, because it is deduced from the process for S, therefore also assumes that this is the numeraire. Because $1/S$ is the number of units of X per unit of Y, to be symmetrical we should measure the process for $1/S$ in a world where the numeraire is the money market account in currency X. Equation (30.7) shows that when we change the numeraire, from the money market account in currency Y to the money market account in currency X, the growth rate of a variable V increases by $\rho\sigma_V\sigma_S$, where ρ is the correlation between S and V. In this case, $V = 1/S$, so that $\rho = -1$ and $\sigma_V = \sigma_S$. It follows that the change of numeraire causes the growth rate of $1/S$ to increase by $-\sigma_S^2$. This neutralizes the $+\sigma_S^2$ in the process given above for $1/S$. The process for $1/S$ in a world where the numeraire is the money market account in currency X is therefore

$$d(1/S) = (r_X - r_Y)(1/S)\,dt - \sigma_S(1/S)\,dz$$

This is symmetrical with the process we started with for S. The paradox is resolved!

The variables $g_X(t)$ and $g_Y(t)$ have a stochastic drift but zero volatility as explained in Section 28.4. From Itô's lemma it follows that the volatility of the numeraire ratio is σ_S. The change of numeraire therefore involves increasing the expected growth rate of V by

$$\rho\sigma_V\sigma_S \tag{30.7}$$

The market price of risk changes from zero to $\rho\sigma_S$. This result enables what is known as Siegel's paradox to be understood (see Business Snapshot 30.1).

Example 30.5

A 2-year American option provides a payoff of $S - K$ pounds sterling where S is the level of the S&P 500 at the time of exercise and K is the strike price. The current level of the S&P 500 is 1,200. The risk-free interest rates in sterling and dollars are both constant at 5% and 3%, respectively, the correlation between the dollars/sterling exchange rate and the S&P 500 is 0.2, the volatility of the S&P 500 is 25%, and the volatility of the exchange rate is 12%. The dividend yield on the S&P 500 is 1.5%.

This option can be valued by constructing a binomial tree for the S&P 500 using as the numeraire the money market account in the U.K. (i.e., using the traditional risk-neutral world as seen from the perspective of a U.K. investor). From equation (30.7), the change in numeraire from the U.S. to U.K. money market account leads to an increase in the expected growth rate in the S&P 500 of

$$0.2 \times 0.25 \times 0.12 = 0.006$$

or 0.6%. The growth rate of the S&P 500 using a U.S. dollar numeraire is $3\% - 1.5\% = 1.5\%$. The growth rate using the sterling numeraire is therefore 2.1%. The risk-free interest rate in sterling is 5%. The S&P 500 therefore behaves like an asset providing a dividend yield of $5\% - 2.1\% = 2.9\%$ under the sterling numeraire. Using the parameter values of $S = 1,200$, $K = 1,200$, $r = 0.05$, $q = 0.029$, $\sigma = 0.25$, and $T = 2$ with 100 time steps, DerivaGem estimates the value of the option as £179.83.

SUMMARY

When valuing a derivative providing a payoff at a particular future time it is natural to assume that the variables underlying the derivative equal their forward values and discount at the rate of interest applicable from the valuation date to the payoff date. This chapter has shown that this is not always the correct procedure.

When a payoff depends on a bond yield y observed at time T the expected yield should be assumed to be higher than the forward yield as indicated by equation (30.1). This result can be adapted for situations where a payoff depends on a swap rate. When a variable is observed at time T but the payoff occurs at a later time T^* the forward value of the variable should be adjusted as indicated by equation (30.4). When a variable is observed in one currency but leads to a payoff in another currency the forward value of the variable should also be adjusted. In this case the adjustment is shown in equation (30.6).

These results will be used when nonstandard swaps are considered in Chapter 34.

FURTHER READING

Brotherton-Ratcliffe, R., and B. Iben, "Yield Curve Applications of Swap Products," in *Advanced Strategies in Financial Risk Management* (R. Schwartz and C. Smith, eds.). New York Institute of Finance, 1993.

Jamshidian, F., "Corralling Quantos," *Risk*, March (1994): 71–75.

Reiner, E., "Quanto Mechanics," *Risk*, March (1992), 59–63.

Practice Questions (Answers in Solutions Manual)

30.1. Explain how you would value a derivative that pays off $100R$ in 5 years, where R is the 1-year interest rate (annually compounded) observed in 4 years. What difference would it make if the payoff were in (a) 4 years and (b) 6 years?

30.2. Explain whether any convexity or timing adjustments are necessary when:
   (a) We wish to value a spread option that pays off every quarter the excess (if any) of the 5-year swap rate over the 3-month LIBOR rate applied to a principal of $100. The payoff occurs 90 days after the rates are observed.
   (b) We wish to value a derivative that pays off every quarter the 3-month LIBOR rate minus the 3-month Treasury bill rate. The payoff occurs 90 days after the rates are observed.

30.3. Suppose that in Example 29.3 of Section 29.2 the payoff occurs after 1 year (i.e., when the interest rate is observed) rather than in 15 months. What difference does this make to the inputs to Black's model?

30.4. The OIS zero curve is flat at 10% per annum with annual compounding. Calculate the value of an instrument where, in 5 years' time, the 2-year swap rate (with annual compounding) is received and a fixed rate of 10% is paid. Both are applied to a notional principal of $100. Assume that the volatility of the forward swap rate is 20% per annum and that the 12-month LIBOR–OIS spread is zero. Explain why the value of the instrument is different from zero.

30.5. What difference does it make in Problem 30.4 if the swap rate is observed in 5 years, but the exchange of payments takes place in (a) 6 years, and (b) 7 years? Assume that the volatilities of all forward rates are 20%. Assume also that the forward swap rate for the period between years 5 and 7 has a correlation of 0.8 with the forward interest rate between years 5 and 6 and a correlation of 0.95 with the forward interest rate between years 5 and 7.

30.6. The price of a bond at time T, measured in terms of its yield, is $G(y_T)$. Assume geometric Brownian motion for the forward bond yield y in a world that is defined by a numeraire equal to a bond maturing at time T. Suppose that the growth rate of the forward bond yield is α and its volatility σ_y.
   (a) Use Itô's lemma to calculate the process for the forward bond price in terms of α, σ_y, y, and $G(y)$.
   (b) The forward bond price should follow a martingale in the world considered. Use this fact to calculate an expression for α.
   (c) Show that the expression for α is, to a first approximation, consistent with equation (30.1).

30.7. The variable S is an investment asset providing income at rate q measured in currency A. It follows the process

$$dS = \mu_S S \, dt + \sigma_S S \, dz$$

in the real world. Defining new variables as necessary, give the process followed by S, and the corresponding market price of risk, in:
   (a) A world that is the traditional risk-neutral world for currency A
   (b) A world that is the traditional risk-neutral world for currency B
   (c) A world that is defined by a numeraire equal to a zero-coupon currency A bond maturing at time T.
   (d) A world that is defined by a numeraire equal to a zero-coupon currency B bond maturing at time T.

30.8. A call option provides a payoff at time T of $\max(S_T - K, 0)$ yen, where S_T is the dollar price of gold at time T and K is the strike price. Assuming that the storage costs of gold are zero and defining other variables as necessary, calculate the value of the contract.

30.9. A Canadian equity index is 400. The Canadian dollar is currently worth 0.70 U.S. dollars. The risk-free interest rates in Canada and the U.S. are constant at 6% and 4%, respectively. The dividend yield on the index is 3%. Define Q as the number of Canadian dollars per U.S. dollar and S as the value of the index. The volatility of S is 20%, the volatility of Q is 6%, and the correlation between S and Q is 0.4. Use DerivaGem to determine the value of a 2-year American-style call option on the index if:
(a) It pays off in Canadian dollars the amount by which the index exceeds 400.
(b) It pays off in U.S. dollars the amount by which the index exceeds 400.

Further Questions

30.10. Consider an instrument that will pay off S dollars in 2 years, where S is the value of the Nikkei index. The index is currently 20,000. The yen/dollar exchange rate is 100 (yen per dollar). The correlation between the exchange rate and the index is 0.3 and the dividend yield on the index is 1% per annum. The volatility of the Nikkei index is 20% and the volatility of the yen/dollar exchange rate is 12%. The interest rates (assumed constant) in the U.S. and Japan are 4% and 2%, respectively.
(a) What is the value of the instrument?
(b) Suppose that the exchange rate at some point during the life of the instrument is Q and the level of the index is S. Show that a U.S. investor can create a portfolio that changes in value by approximately ΔS dollar when the index changes in value by ΔS yen by investing S dollars in the Nikkei and shorting SQ yen.
(c) Confirm that this is correct by supposing that the index changes from 20,000 to 20,050 and the exchange rate changes from 100 to 99.7.
(d) How would you delta hedge the instrument under consideration?

30.11. Suppose that the risk-free yield curve is flat at 8% (with continuous compounding). The payoff from a derivative occurs in 4 years. It is equal to the 5-year rate minus the 2-year rate at this time, applied to a principal of $100 with both rates being continuously compounded. (The payoff can be positive or negative.) Calculate the value of the derivative. Assume that the volatility for all rates is 25%. What difference does it make if the payoff occurs in 5 years instead of 4 years? Assume all rates are perfectly correlated.

30.12. Suppose that the payoff from a derivative will occur in 10 years and will equal the 3-year U.S. dollar swap rate for a semiannual-pay swap observed at that time applied to a certain principal. Assume that the swap yield curve is flat at 8% (semiannually compounded) per annum in dollars and 3% (semiannually compounded) in yen. The forward swap rate volatility is 18%, the volatility of the 10-year "yen per dollar" forward exchange rate is 12%, and the correlation between this exchange rate and U.S. dollar interest rates is 0.25. What is the value of the derivative if the swap rate is applied to a principal of (a) $100 million with a dollar payoff and (b) 100 million yen with a yen payoff? Assume that risk-free rates are 2% in yen and 6% in dollars (both semiannually compounded).

30.13. The payoff from a derivative will occur in 8 years. It will equal the average of the 1-year risk-free interest rates observed at times 5, 6, 7, and 8 years applied to a principal of $1,000. The risk-free yield curve is flat at 6% with annual compounding and the volatilities of all rates are 16%. Assume perfect correlation between all rates. What is the value of the derivative?

APPENDIX

PROOF OF THE CONVEXITY ADJUSTMENT FORMULA

This appendix calculates a convexity adjustment for forward bond yields. Suppose that the payoff from a derivative at time T depends on a bond yield observed at that time. Define:

y_F: Forward bond yield observed today for a forward contract with maturity T

y_T: Bond yield at time T

B_T: Price of the bond at time T

σ_y: Volatility of the forward bond yield.

Suppose that the relationship between a bond price and its yield is

$$B_T = G(y_T)$$

Expanding $G(y_T)$ in a Taylor series about $y_T = y_F$ yields the following approximation:

$$B_T = G(y_F) + (y_T - y_F)G'(y_F) + 0.5(y_T - y_F)^2 G''(y_F)$$

where G' and G'' are the first and second partial derivatives of G. Taking expectations in a world defined by a numeraire equal to a zero-coupon bond maturing at time T gives

$$E_T(B_T) = G(y_F) + E_T(y_T - y_F)G'(y_F) + \tfrac{1}{2}E_T[(y_T - y_F)^2]G''(y_F)$$

where E_T denotes expectations in this world. The expression $G(y_F)$ is by definition the forward bond price. Also, because of the particular world we are working in, $E_T(B_T)$ equals the forward bond price. Hence $E_T(B_T) = G(y_F)$, so that

$$E_T(y_T - y_F)G'(y_F) + \tfrac{1}{2}E_T[(y_T - y_F)^2]G''(y_F) = 0$$

The expression $E_T[(y_T - y_F)^2]$ is approximately $\sigma_y^2 y_F^2 T$. Hence it is approximately true that

$$E_T(y_T) = y_F - \tfrac{1}{2}y_F^2 \sigma_y^2 T \frac{G''(y_F)}{G'(y_F)}$$

This shows that, to obtain the expected bond yield in a world defined by a numeraire equal to a zero-coupon bond maturing at time T, the term

$$-\tfrac{1}{2}y_F^2 \sigma_y^2 T \frac{G''(y_F)}{G'(y_F)}$$

should be added to the forward bond yield. This is the result in equation (30.1). For an alternative proof, see Problem 30.6.

31

Equilibrium Models of the Short Rate

In this chapter, we consider how models of the term structure of risk-free interest rates can be constructed in both the real world and the risk-neutral world. We first show that when a Markov process for the instantaneous short rate has been specified in the traditional risk-neutral world all rates can, at least in theory, be calculated at all times as a function of the short rate. We will spend some time studying two popular one-factor Markov models of the short rate: the Vasicek model and the Cox, Ingersoll, and Ross model. These are relatively simple models which have the convenient property that there are analytic formulas for determining bond prices.

The difference between the behavior of the short rate in the real world and the risk-neutral world is determined by the market price of interest rate risk. We explained the meaning of the term "market price of risk" in Section 28.1. The market price of risk for a bond is positive. Since interest rates and bond prices are negatively related, the market price of risk for an interest rate is negative. This means that the drift of an interest rate is greater in the risk-neutral world than in the real world. The expected future value of an interest rate is therefore greater in the risk-neutral world than in the real world.

The equilibrium models considered in this chapter can approximately match the today's term structure of interest rates, but they do not provide an exact match. However, when Monte Carlo simulation is being carried out over a long period of time for the purposes of scenario analysis, the models can be useful tools. For example, a pension fund or an insurance company that is interested in the performance of its investments over the next 20 years is likely to feel that an approximate fit to today's term structure is adequate.

In the next chapter, we extend the material in this chapter to consider short-rate models that are designed to exactly fit today's term structure of interest rates. These are used to value interest rate derivatives. In Chapter 33, we consider models of forward rates that also provide an exact fit to today's term structure.

31.1 BACKGROUND

The risk-free short rate, r, at time t is the rate that applies to an infinitesimally short period of time at time t. It is sometimes referred to as the *instantaneous short rate*. Bond prices, option prices, and other derivative prices depend only on the process followed by r

in the traditional risk-neutral world. As explained in Chapter 28, the traditional risk-neutral world is a world where, in a very short time period between t and $t + \Delta t$, investors earn on average $r(t)\Delta t$. All risk-neutral processes for r that will be considered in this chapter are processes in this traditional risk-neutral world.

From equation (28.19), the value at time t of an interest rate derivative that provides a payoff of f_T at time T is

$$\hat{E}[e^{-\bar{r}(T-t)} f_T] \tag{31.1}$$

where $\bar{r}$ is the average value of r in the time interval between t and T, and $\hat{E}$ denotes expected value in the traditional risk-neutral world.

As usual, define $P(t, T)$ as the price at time t of a risk-free zero-coupon bond that pays off \$1 at time T. From equation (31.1),

$$P(t, T) = \hat{E}[e^{-\bar{r}(T-t)}] \tag{31.2}$$

If $R(t, T)$ is the continuously compounded risk-free interest rate at time t for a term of $T - t$, then

$$P(t, T) = e^{-R(t,T)(T-t)}$$

so that

$$R(t, T) = -\frac{1}{T - t} \ln P(t, T) \tag{31.3}$$

and, from equation (31.2),

$$R(t, T) = -\frac{1}{T - t} \ln \hat{E}[e^{-\bar{r}(T-t)}] \tag{31.4}$$

This equation enables the term structure of interest rates at any given time to be obtained from the risk-neutral process for r. It shows that, once the process for r has been defined, everything about the initial zero curve and its evolution through time can be determined.

Suppose the risk-neutral process for r is Markov with one factor:

$$dr = m(r, t)\, dt + s(r, t)\, dz$$

From Itô's lemma, any derivative dependent on r follows the process

$$df = \left(\frac{\partial f}{\partial t} + m\frac{\partial f}{\partial r} + \tfrac{1}{2}s^2\frac{\partial^2 f}{\partial r^2}\right) dt + s\frac{\partial f}{\partial r}\, dz$$

Because we are working in the traditional risk-neutral world, if the derivative provides no income, this process must have the form

$$df = rf\, dt + \cdots$$

so that

$$\frac{\partial f}{\partial t} + m\frac{\partial f}{\partial r} + \tfrac{1}{2}s^2\frac{\partial^2 f}{\partial r^2} = rf$$

This is the equivalent of the Black–Scholes–Merton differential equation for interest rate derivatives. One particular solution to the equation must be the zero-coupon bond price $P(t, T)$.

Hence

$$\frac{\partial P(t, T)}{\partial t} + m \frac{\partial P(t, T)}{\partial r} + \tfrac{1}{2} s^2 \frac{\partial^2 P(t, T)}{\partial r^2} = r P(t, T) \tag{31.5}$$

It is tempting to suggest a simple model where the term structure is always flat. All zero-coupon interest rates are then r, so that $P(t, T) = e^{-r(t)(T-t)}$ at all times. However, this is not a valid stochastic model for bond prices because it cannot satisfy equation (31.5) for all T unless m and s are both zero.

31.2 ONE-FACTOR MODELS

Equilibrium models usually start with assumptions about economic variables and derive a process for the short rate, r. They then explore what the process for r implies about bond prices and option prices.

In a one-factor equilibrium model, the process for r involves only one source of uncertainty. Usually the process for the short rate is assumed to be stationary in the sense that the parameters of the process are not functions of time. This means that the process we considered earlier can be written as

$$dr = m(r)\, dt + s(r)\, dz$$

The assumption of a single factor is not as restrictive as it might appear. A one-factor model implies that all rates move in the same direction over any short time interval, but not that they all move by the same amount. The shape of the zero curve can therefore change with the passage of time.

This section considers three one-factor equilibrium models:

$m(r) = \mu r; \ \ s(r) = \sigma r$ (Rendleman and Bartter model)

$m(r) = a(b - r); \ \ s(r) = \sigma$ (Vasicek model)

$m(r) = a(b - r); \ \ s(r) = \sigma\sqrt{r}$ (Cox, Ingersoll, and Ross model)

The Rendleman and Bartter Model

In Rendleman and Bartter's model, the risk-neutral process for r is[1]

$$dr = \mu r\, dt + \sigma r\, dz$$

where μ and σ are constants. This means that r follows geometric Brownian motion. The process for r is of the same type as that assumed for a stock price in Chapter 15. It can be represented using a binomial tree similar to the one used for stocks in Chapter 13.

The assumption that the short-term interest rate behaves like a stock price is a natural starting point but is less than ideal. One important difference between interest rates and stock prices is that interest rates appear to be pulled back to some long-run average level over time. This phenomenon is known as *mean reversion*. When r is high, mean reversion tends to cause it to have a negative drift; when r is low, mean reversion tends to cause it to have a positive drift. Mean reversion is illustrated in Figure 31.1. The Rendleman and Bartter model does not incorporate mean reversion.

---

[1] See R. Rendleman and B. Bartter, "The Pricing of Options on Debt Securities," *Journal of Financial and Quantitative Analysis*, 15 (March 1980): 11–24.

Figure 31.1 Mean reversion.

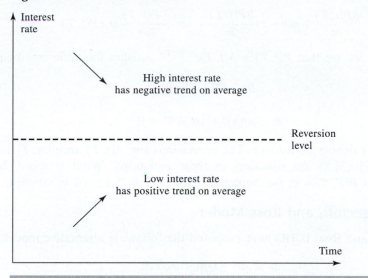

There are compelling economic arguments in favor of mean reversion. When rates are high, the economy tends to slow down and there is low demand for funds from borrowers. As a result, rates decline. When rates are low, there tends to be a high demand for funds on the part of borrowers and rates tend to rise.

The Vasicek Model

In Vasicek's model, the risk-neutral process for r is

$$dr = a(b - r)\,dt + \sigma\,dz$$

where a, b, and σ are nonnegative constants.[2] This model incorporates mean reversion. The short rate is pulled to a "reversion level" b at "reversion rate" a. Superimposed upon this pull is a normally distributed stochastic term $\sigma\,dz$.

Zero-coupon bond prices in Vasicek's model are given by

$$P(t, T) = A(t, T)e^{-B(t,T)r(t)} \tag{31.6}$$

where

$$B(t, T) = \frac{1 - e^{-a(T-t)}}{a} \tag{31.7}$$

and

$$A(t, T) = \exp\left[\frac{(B(t, T) - T + t)(a^2 b - \sigma^2/2)}{a^2} - \frac{\sigma^2 B(t, T)^2}{4a}\right] \tag{31.8}$$

(When $a = 0$, these equations become $B(t, T) = T - t$ and $A(t, T) = \exp[\sigma^2(T - t)^3/6]$.)

---

[2] See O.A. Vasicek, "An Equilibrium Characterization of the Term Structure," *Journal of Financial Economics*, 5 (1977): 177–88.

To see this, note that $m = a(b - r)$ and $s = \sigma$ in differential equation (31.5), so that

$$\frac{\partial P(t, T)}{\partial t} + a(b - r)\frac{\partial P(t, T)}{\partial r} + \tfrac{1}{2}\sigma^2\frac{\partial^2 P(t, T)}{\partial r^2} = rP(t, T)$$

By substitution, we see that $P(t, T) = A(t, T)e^{-B(t,T)r}$ satisfies this differential equation when

$$B_t - aB + 1 = 0$$

and

$$A_t - abAB + \tfrac{1}{2}\sigma^2 AB^2 = 0$$

where subscripts denote derivatives. The expressions for $A(t, T)$ and $B(t, T)$ in equations (31.7) and (31.8) are solutions to these equations. What is more, because $A(T, T) = 1$ and $B(T, T) = 0$, the boundary condition $P(T, T) = 1$ is satisfied.

The Cox, Ingersoll, and Ross Model

Cox, Ingersoll, and Ross (CIR) have proposed the following alternative model:[3]

$$dr = a(b - r)\,dt + \sigma\sqrt{r}\,dz$$

where a, b, and σ are nonnegative constants. This has the same mean-reverting drift as Vasicek, but the standard deviation of the change in the short rate in a short period of time is proportional to $\sqrt{r}$. This means that, as the short-term interest rate increases, the standard deviation increases.

Bond prices in the CIR model have the same general form as those in Vasicek's model,

$$P(t, T) = A(t, T)e^{-B(t,T)r(t)}$$

but the functions $B(t, T)$ and $A(t, T)$ are different:

$$B(t, T) = \frac{2(e^{\gamma(T-t)} - 1)}{(\gamma + a)(e^{\gamma(T-t)} - 1) + 2\gamma}$$

and

$$A(t, T) = \left[\frac{2\gamma e^{(a+\gamma)(T-t)/2}}{(\gamma + a)(e^{\gamma(T-t)} - 1) + 2\gamma}\right]^{2ab/\sigma^2}$$

with $\gamma = \sqrt{a^2 + 2\sigma^2}$.

To see this result, substitute $m = a(b - r)$ and $s = \sigma\sqrt{r}$ into differential equation (31.5) to get

$$\frac{\partial P(t, T)}{\partial t} + a(b - r)\frac{\partial P(t, T)}{\partial r} + \tfrac{1}{2}\sigma^2 r\frac{\partial^2 P(t, T)}{\partial r^2} = rP(t, T)$$

As in the case of Vasicek's model, we can prove the bond-pricing result by substituting $P(t, T) = A(t, T)e^{-B(t,T)r}$ into the differential equation. In this case, $A(t, T)$ and $B(t, T)$ are solutions of

$$B_t - aB - \tfrac{1}{2}\sigma^2 B^2 + 1 = 0, \quad A_t - abAB = 0$$

Furthermore, the boundary condition $P(T, T) = 1$ is satisfied.

---

[3] See J.C. Cox, J.E. Ingersoll, and S.A. Ross, "A Theory of the Term Structure of Interest Rates," *Econometrica*, 53 (1985): 385–407.

Properties of Vasicek and CIR

The $A(t, T)$ and $B(t, T)$ functions are different for Vasicek and CIR, but for both models

$$P(t, T) = A(t, T)e^{-B(t,T)r(t)}$$

so that

$$\frac{\partial P(t, T)}{\partial r(t)} = -B(t, T)P(t, T) \qquad (31.9)$$

From equation (31.3), the zero rate at time t for a period of $T - t$ is

$$R(t, T) = -\frac{1}{T - t}\ln A(t, T) + \frac{1}{T - t}B(t, T)r(t) \qquad (30.10)$$

This shows that the entire term structure at time t can be determined as a function of $r(t)$ once a, b, and σ have been chosen. The rate $R(t, T)$ is linearly dependent on $r(t)$. This means that the value of $r(t)$ determines the level of the term structure at time t. As shown in Figure 31.2, the shape at a particular time can be upward sloping, downward sloping, or slightly "humped."

One difference between Vasicek and CIR is that in Vasicek the short rate, $r(t)$, can become negative whereas in CIR this is not possible. If $2ab \geqslant \sigma^2$ in CIR, $r(t)$ is never zero; otherwise it occasionally touches zero.

Figure 31.2   Possible shapes of term structure in the Vasicek and CIR models.

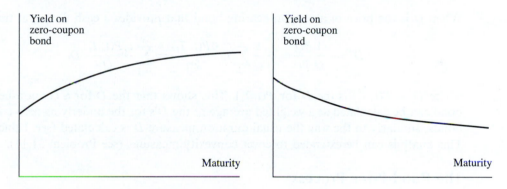

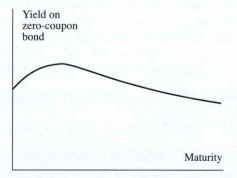

From Chapter 4, the duration D of a bond that has a price of Q is given by

$$D = -\frac{1}{Q}\frac{\partial Q}{\partial y} \quad \text{so that} \quad \frac{\Delta Q}{Q} = -D\,\Delta y$$

where y is the continuously compounded bond yield. An alternative duration measure $\hat{D}$, which can be used in conjunction with Vasicek or CIR, is defined as follows:

$$\hat{D} = -\frac{1}{Q}\frac{\partial Q}{\partial r} \quad \text{so that} \quad \frac{\Delta Q}{Q} = -\hat{D}\,\Delta r$$

Here we are measuring the sensitivity of the bond price to the short rate rather than to its yield. Equation (31.9) shows that $\hat{D} = B(t, T)$ for a T-maturity zero-coupon bond.

Example 31.1

Consider a zero-coupon bond lasting 4 years. In this case, $D = 4$, so that a 10-basis-point (0.1% or 0.001) increase in the bond's yield leads to a decrease of approximately 0.4% in the bond price. If Vasicek's model is used with $a = 0.1$,

$$\hat{D} = B(0, 4) = \frac{(1 - e^{-0.1\times 4})}{0.1} = 3.30$$

This means that a 10-basis-point increase in the short rate leads to a decrease in the bond price that is approximately 0.33%. The change in the bond price from a certain movement in the short rate is less than that from the same movement in its yield because of the impact of mean reversion.

When Q is the price of a coupon-bearing bond that provides a cash flow c_i at time T_i,

$$\hat{D} = -\frac{1}{Q}\frac{\partial Q}{\partial r} = -\frac{1}{Q}\sum_{i=1}^{n}c_i\frac{\partial P(t, T_i)}{\partial r} = \sum_{i=1}^{n}\frac{c_i P(t, T_i)}{Q}\hat{D}_i$$

where $\hat{D}_i = B(t, T_i)$ is the $\hat{D}$ for $P(t, T_i)$. This shows that the $\hat{D}$ for a coupon-bearing bond can be calculated as a weighted average of the $\hat{D}$'s for the underlying zero-coupon bonds, similarly to the way the usual duration measure D is calculated (see Table 4.6). This analysis can be extended to cover convexity measures (see Problem 31.11).

The Bond Price Process

The expected growth rate of $P(t, T)$ in the traditional risk-neutral world at time t is $r(t)$ because $P(t, T)$ is the price of a traded security that provides no income. Since $P(t, T)$ is a function of $r(t)$, the coefficient of $dz(t)$ in the process for $P(t, T)$ can be calculated from Itô's lemma as $\sigma\,\partial P(t, T)/\partial r(t)$ for Vasicek and $\sigma\sqrt{r(t)}\,\partial P(t, T)/\partial r(t)$ for CIR. Substituting from equation (31.9), the processes for $P(t, T)$ in a risk-neutral world are therefore

$$\text{Vasicek:} \quad dP(t, T) = r(t)P(t, T)\,dt - \sigma B_{\text{vas}}(t, T)P(t, T)\,dz(t) \qquad \textbf{(31.11)}$$

$$\text{CIR:} \quad dP(t, T) = r(t)P(t, T)\,dt - \sigma\sqrt{r(t)}\,B_{\text{cir}}(t, T)P(t, T)\,dz(t) \qquad \textbf{(31.12)}$$

where the subscripts to B indicate the model it applies to.

To compare the term structure of interest rates given by Vasicek and CIR for a particular value of r, it makes sense to use the same a and b. However, the Vasicek σ

should be chosen to be approximately equal to the CIR σ times $\sqrt{r(t)}$. For example, if r is 4% and σ is 0.01 in Vasicek, an appropriate value for σ in CIR would be $0.01/\sqrt{0.04} = 0.05$. Software for experimenting with the models can be found at www-2.rotman.utoronto.ca/~hull/VasicekCIR.

31.3 REAL-WORLD VS. RISK-NEUTRAL PROCESSES

Bonds have a positive market price of risk (i.e., positive systematic risk), so investors require an extra return over the risk-free rate for investing in bonds. Interest rates are negatively related to bond prices and therefore have negative market prices of risk.

Suppose that λ is the (negative) market price of risk of the short rate, r. If the risk-neutral process for r is

$$dr = m(r)\,dt + s(r)\,dz$$

the real-world process, from Chapter 28, is

$$dr = [m(r) + \lambda s(r)]\,dt + s(r)\,dz$$

In the case of Vasicek's model, the risk-neutral process is

$$dr = a(b - r)\,dt + \sigma\,dz$$

so that the real-world process is

$$dr = [a(b - r) + \lambda\sigma]\,dt + \sigma\,dz$$

Assuming λ is constant, this process is

$$dr = [a(b^* - r)]\,dt + \sigma\,dz \tag{31.13}$$

where $b^* = b + \lambda\sigma/a$. The real-world process is therefore the same as the risk-neutral process except that the reversion level is lower (because λ is negative).

In the case of CIR, the risk-neutral process is

$$dr = a(b - r)\,dt + \sigma\sqrt{r}\,dz$$

It is convenient to assume that $\lambda = \kappa\sqrt{r}$, where κ is a (negative) constant, so that the real-world process is

$$dr = [a(b - r) + \kappa\sigma r]\,dt + \sigma\sqrt{r}\,dz$$

In this case,

$$dr = a^*(b^* - r)\,dt + \sigma\sqrt{r}\,dz$$

where $a^* = a - \kappa\sigma$ and $b^* = ab/a^*$. The real-world process is therefore the same as the risk-neutral process except that the reversion rate is higher and the reversion level is lower.

Next, consider bonds. Equation (31.11) gives the risk-neutral process in Vasicek's model for a zero-coupon bond. When the market price of risk of the short rate is λ, the real-world process is

$$dP(t, T) = [r(t) - \lambda\sigma B_{vas}(t, T)]P(t, T)\,dt - \sigma B_{vas}(t, T)P(t, T)\,dz(t)$$

Equation (31.12) gives the risk-neutral process in the CIR model for a zero-coupon bond. When the market price of risk is $\kappa\sqrt{r}$, the real-world process is

$$dP(t, T) = [r(t) - \kappa\sigma B_{\text{cir}}(t, T)r(t)]P(t, T)\, dt - \sigma\sqrt{r(t)}\, B_{\text{cir}}(t, T)P(t, T)\, dz(t)$$

31.4 ESTIMATING PARAMETERS

We will illustrate the estimation of parameters with Vasicek's model. The discrete version of the model in the real world is, from equation (31.13),

$$\Delta r = a(b^* - r)\Delta t + \sigma\epsilon\sqrt{\Delta t}$$

where ϵ is a random sample from a standard normal distribution. Define r_i as the rate on day i. Daily data on 3-month Treasury rates in the United States between January 4, 1982, and August 23, 2016, together with a worksheet for the analysis in this section, is on www-2.rotman.utoronto.ca/~hull/VasicekCIR. When we use this data to regress $r_{i+1} - r_i$ against r_i, we obtain

$$r_{i+1} - r_i = 0.00000915 - 0.000545r_i$$

with a standard error of 0.000754.

We have about 250 observations per year, so that $\Delta t = 1/250$. Because $0.00000915 = 0.00229/250$, $0.000545 = 0.136/250$, and $0.000754 = 0.0119/\sqrt{250}$, the regression result is equivalent to

$$\Delta r = (0.00229 - 0.136r)\Delta t + 0.0119\epsilon\sqrt{\Delta t}$$

or

$$\Delta r = 0.136(0.0168 - r)\Delta t + 0.0119\epsilon\sqrt{\Delta t}$$

indicating that the best-fit parameters are $a = 0.136$, $b^* = 0.0168$ (or 1.68%), and $\sigma = 0.0119$ (or 1.19%). Problem 31.16 shows that the same results are obtained using maximum-likelihood methods.

So far we have estimated the parameters for Vasicek's model in the real world. If the market price of risk is λ, the previous section shows that in the risk-neutral world the parameters are $a = 0.136$, $b = 0.168 - 0.0119\lambda/a$, and $\sigma = 0.0119$. For a trial value of λ, we can use equations (31.7), (31.8), and (31.10) to estimate zero-coupon rates as a function of maturity. Solver can then be used to determine the value of λ that minimizes the sum of squared errors between the zero-coupon rates given by the model and those in the market. This best-fit value of λ turns out to be -0.175.[4] Table 31.1 compares the zero-coupon rates given by the model when this best-fit value of λ is used with those in the market. Problem 31.17 uses the same data for the CIR model.

The two-step estimation procedure we have used is a simple procedure and there has been no attempt to fit the term structure of interest rates at times other than today. In practice, researchers use more sophisticated econometric procedures. The parameters we have estimated for Vasicek's model are reasonable, but this will not always be the case.[5]

---

[4] Research such as R. Stanton, "A Nonparametric Model of Term Structure Dynamics and the Market Price of Interest Rate Risk," *Journal of Finance*, 52, 5 (December): 1973–2002, has tried to estimate the market price of risk from the average slope of the term structure of interest rates at the short end. As explained in J. C. Hull, A. Sokol, and A. White, "Short-Rate Joint-Measure Models," *Risk*, 15, 3 (2015): 59–63, this tends to produce values for the market price of risk that are much too negative (typically -1.0 or less).

[5] As Problem 31.16 shows, the results using the same data for the CIR model are not as reasonable.

Table 31.1 Best fit of model rates to those in the market, August 23, 2016.

Maturity (years)	Model rate (%)	Market Rate (%)
0.5	0.40	0.45
1.0	0.49	0.58
2.0	0.65	0.74
3.0	0.80	0.86
5.0	1.06	1.15
7.0	1.27	1.40
10.0	1.52	1.55
20.0	2.02	1.88
30.0	2.26	2.24

The period of time over which parameters are estimated and the current shape of the term structure can have a big effect on the results obtained. Some judgment is necessary to determine the most appropriate data to use when a model such as Vasicek or CIR is estimated in practice.

31.5 MORE SOPHISTICATED MODELS

The Vasicek and CIR models are simple one-factor Markov models of the short rate. A two-factor Markov model of the short rate that is an extension of Vasicek is

$$dr = (u - ar)\,dt + \sigma_1\,dz_1$$
$$du = -bu\,dt + \sigma_2\,dz_2$$

In this model, the reversion level ($= u/a$) is not constant. It follows a stochastic process. However, bond prices are analytic:

$$P(t, T) = A(t, T)e^{-B(t,T)r - C(t,T)u}$$

where $B(t, T)$ is the same as in the Vasicek model and

$$C(t, T) = \frac{1}{a(a - b)}e^{-a(T-t)} - \frac{1}{b(a - b)}e^{-b(T-t)} + \frac{1}{ab} \tag{31.14}$$

The function $A(t, T)$ is more complex (see Technical Note 14 on the author's website).

Another two-factor model which has analytic bond prices and involves similar processes to CIR was developed by Longstaff and Schwartz.[6] Other multifactor models are sometimes used in practice to describe the real-world evolution of the term structure. In Chapter 33, we will describe how general risk-neutral models can be developed in terms of forward rates.

---

[6] See F. A. Longstaff and E. S. Schwartz, "Interest Rate Volatility and the Term Structure: A Two-Factor General Equilibrium Model," *Journal of Finance*, 47, 4 (September 1992): 1259–82.

SUMMARY

When a Markov model of the (instantaneous) short rate has been specified, the current value of the short rate determines all future rates. It is therefore tempting to model the term structure of interest rates by specifying a process for the short rate. Two popular models are the Vasicek and Cox, Ingersoll, and Ross (CIR) models. In both models the short rate follows a mean-reverting process (i.e., it is pulled back toward a central value) and has some uncertainty superimposed on the mean reversion. In the case of Vasicek, the uncertain component of the change over a short period of time of length Δt always has zero mean and a constant standard deviation; in CIR, the uncertain component has zero mean and a standard deviation proportional to the square root of the short rate. In Vasicek, rates can become negative; in CIR, this is not possible. In both models the bond price $P(t, T)$ has the form $A(t, T)e^{-B(t,T)r}$, but the $A(t, T)$ and $B(t, T)$ functions in the two models are not the same.

The market price of interest rate risk is negative. If the market price of risk in Vasicek is constant, the process followed by the short rate in the real world is the same as that in the risk-neutral world except that the reversion level is lower. If the market price of risk in CIR is proportional to the square root of the short rate, the process in the real world has the same form as that in the risk-neutral world except that the reversion rate is higher and the reversion level is lower.

The models we have considered in this chapter do not provide an exact fit to the current term structure of interest rates but are useful for simulating the behavior of interest rates in some situations. When derivatives are being valued it is usually necessary to use a model that provides an exact fit to the current term structure of interest rates. Short-rate models that do this are considered in the next chapter and more general models that describe the behavior of forward rates are in Chapter 33.

FURTHER READING

Cox, J. C., J. E. Ingersoll, and S. A. Ross, "A Theory of the Term Structure of Interest Rates," *Econometrica*, 53 (1985): 385–407.

Longstaff, F. A.. and E. S. Schwartz, "Interest Rate Volatility and the Term Structure: A Two-Factor General Equilibrium Model," *Journal of Finance*, 47, 4 (September 1992): 1259–82.

Vasicek, O. A., "An Equilibrium Characterization of the Term Structure," *Journal of Financial Economics*, 5 (1977): 177–88.

Practice Questions (Answers in Solutions Manual)

31.1. Suppose that the short rate is currently 4% and its standard deviation in a short period of time Δt is $0.01\sqrt{\Delta t}$. What happens to this standard deviation when the short rate increases to 8% in (a) Vasicek's model, (b) Rendleman and Bartter's model, and (c) the Cox, Ingersoll, and Ross model?

31.2. If a stock price were mean reverting or followed a path-dependent process there would be market inefficiency. Why is there not a market inefficiency when the short-term interest rate does so?

31.3. Explain the difference between a one-factor and a two-factor model.

31.4. Suppose that in a risk-neutral world the Vasicek parameters are $a = 0.1$, $b = 0.03$, and $\sigma = 0.01$. What is the price of a 5-year zero-coupon bond with a principal of $1 when the short rate is 2%.

31.5. Suppose that in a risk-neutral world the CIR parameters are $a = 0.1$, $b = 0.03$, and $\sigma = 0.07$. The market price of interest rate risk is -1 times the square root of the short rate. What are the risk-neutral and real-world processes for (a) the short rate and (b) a zero-coupon bond with a current maturity of 4 years.

31.6. Suppose that the market price of risk of the short rate is $\lambda_1 + \lambda_2 r$ (with λ_1 and λ_2 negative). Show that if the real-world process for the short rate is the one assumed by Vasicek, the risk-neutral process has the same functional form as the real-world process. Derive the relationship between (a) the real-world reversion rate and the risk-neutral reversion rate and (b) the real-world reversion level and the risk-neutral reversion level.

31.7. Observations spaced at intervals Δt are taken on the short rate. The ith observation is r_i ($0 \leqslant i \leqslant m$). Show that the maximum-likelihood estimates of a, b^*, and σ in Vasicek's model are given by maximizing

$$\sum_{i=1}^{m}\left(-\ln(\sigma^2 \Delta t) - \frac{[r_i - r_{i-1} - a(b^* - r_{i-1})\Delta t]^2}{\sigma^2 \Delta t}\right)$$

31.8. Calculate the alternative duration measure explained in Section 31.2 for a 2-year bond with a principal of $100 paying coupons semiannually at the rate of $3 per year when Vasicek's model is used with $a = 0.13$, $b = 0.012$, $\sigma = 0.01$, and $r = 1\%$. Show that it correctly predicts the effect of an increase in r to 1.05%.

31.9. Suppose that $a = 0.1$ and $b = 0.1$ and in both the Vasicek and the Cox, Ingersoll, Ross model. In both models, the initial short rate is 10% and the initial standard deviation of the short-rate change in a short time Δt is $0.02\sqrt{\Delta t}$. Compare the prices given by the models for a zero-coupon bond that matures in year 10.

31.10. Suppose the short rate r is 4% and its real-world process is $dr = 0.1(0.05 - r)\,dt + 0.01\,dz$, while the risk-neutral process is $dr = 0.1(0.11 - r)\,dt + 0.01\,dz$:
   (a) What is the market price of interest rate risk?
   (b) What is the expected return and volatility for a 5-year zero-coupon bond in the risk-neutral world?
   (c) What is the expected return and volatility for a 5-year zero-coupon bond in the real world?

31.11. (a) What is the second partial derivative of $P(t, T)$ with respect to r in the Vasicek and CIR models?
   (b) In Section 31.2, $\hat{D}$ is presented as an alternative to the usual duration measure, D. What is a similar alternative, $\hat{C}$, to the convexity measure in Section 4.11?
   (c) What is $\hat{C}$ for $P(t, T)$? How would you calculate $\hat{C}$ for a coupon-bearing bond?
   (d) Give a Taylor series expansion for $\Delta P(t, T)$ in terms of Δr annd $(\Delta r)^2$ for Vasicek and CIR.

Further Questions

31.12. Suppose that in the risk-neutral Vasicek process $a = 0.15$, $b = 0.025$, and $\sigma = 0.012$. The market price of interest rate risk is -0.2. What are the risk-neutral and real-world processes for (a) the short rate and (b) a zero-coupon bond with a current maturity of 3 years.

31.13. Suppose that in a risk-neutral world the CIR parameters are $a = 0.15$, $b = 0.025$, and $\sigma = 0.075$. What is the price of a 5-year zero-coupon bond with a principal of \$1 when the short rate is 2.5%?

31.14. Suppose that the market price of risk of the short rate is $\lambda_1/\sqrt{r} + \lambda_2\sqrt{r}$. Show that if the real world process for the short rate is the one assumed by CIR, the risk-neutral process has the same functional form. Derive the relationship between (a) the real-world reversion rate and the risk-neutral reversion rate and (b) the real-world reversion level and the risk-neutral reversion level.

31.15. In the two-factor extension of Vasicek given in Section 31.5, derive the differential equations which must be satified by a bond price, $P(t, T)$. Use this to derive differential equations that must be satisfied by $A(t, T)$, $B(t, T)$, and $C(t, T)$ in $P(t, T) = A(t, T)e^{-B(t,T)r - C(t,T)u}$. Show that the expressions given for $B(t, T)$ in equation (31.7) and $C(t, T)$ in equation (31.14) satisfy these equations. [*Hint*: Use equation (14A.10) to obtain the drift of $P(t, T)$ and set this drift equal to $rP(t, T)$.]

31.16. Use the result in Problem 31.7 to determine the best fit parameters for the Vasicek model using the same data as in Section 31.4 (see www-2.rotman.utoronto.ca/~hull/VasicekCIR). Verify that the regression approach in Section 31.4 and the maximum-likelihood approach give the same answer.

31.17. What is the result corresponding to that given in Problem 31.7. for the CIR model. Use maximum likelhood methods to estimate the a, b, and σ parameters for the CIR model using the same data as that used for the Vasicek model in Section 31.4 (see www-2.rotman.utoronto.ca/~hull/VasicekCIR). Setting the market price of risk equal to $\kappa\sqrt{r}$ use the market data in Table 31.1 to estimate the best fit κ.

CHAPTER

32

No-Arbitrage Models of the Short Rate

The disadvantage of the equilibrium models presented in Chapter 31 is that they do not automatically fit today's term structure of interest rates. By choosing the parameters judiciously, they can be made to provide an approximate fit to many of the term structures that are encountered in practice. But the fit is not an exact one. Most traders, when they are valuing derivatives, find this unsatisfactory. Not unreasonably, they argue that they can have very little confidence in the price of a bond option when the model used does not price the underlying bond correctly. A 1% error in the price of the underlying bond may lead to a 25% error in an option price.

A *no-arbitrage model* is a model designed to be exactly consistent with today's term structure of interest rates. The essential difference between an equilibrium and a no-arbitrage model is therefore as follows. In an equilibrium model, today's term structure of interest rates is an output. In a no-arbitrage model, today's term structure of interest rates is an input.

In an equilibrium model, the drift of the short rate is not usually a function of time. In a no-arbitrage model, the drift is, in general, dependent on time. This is because the shape of the initial zero curve governs the average path taken by the short rate in the future in a no-arbitrage model. If the zero curve is steeply upward-sloping for maturities between t_1 and t_2, then r has a positive drift between these times; if it is steeply downward-sloping for these maturities, then r has a negative drift between these times.

32.1 EXTENSIONS OF EQUILIBRIUM MODELS

It turns out that some equilibrium models can be converted to no-arbitrage models by including a function of time in the drift of the short rate. Here, we consider the Ho–Lee, Hull–White (one- and two-factor), Black–Derman–Toy, and Black–Karasinski models.

The Ho–Lee Model

Ho and Lee proposed the first no-arbitrage model of the term structure in a paper in 1986.[1] They presented the model in the form of a binomial tree of bond prices with two

---

[1] See T. S. Y. Ho and S.-B. Lee, "Term Structure Movements and Pricing Interest Rate Contingent Claims," *Journal of Finance*, 41 (December 1986): 1011–29.

Figure 32.1   The Ho–Lee model.

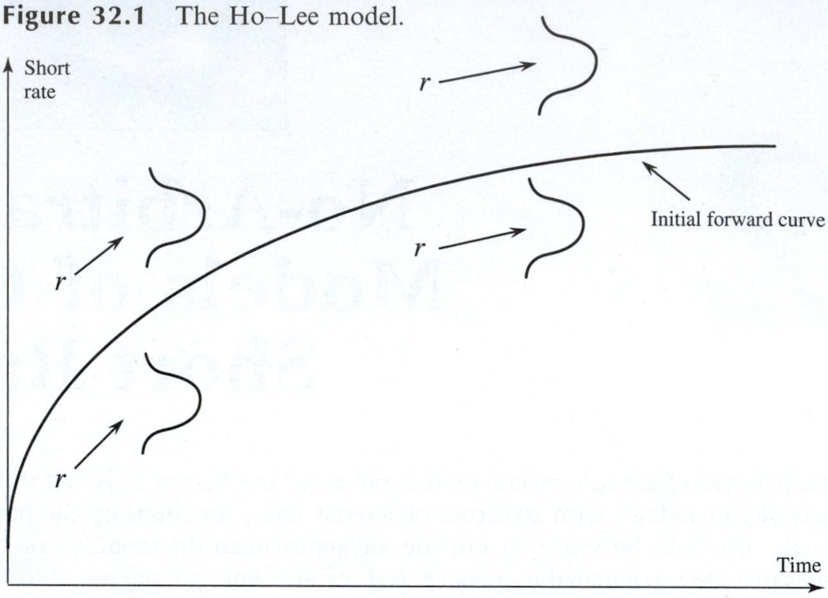

parameters: the short-rate standard deviation and the market price of risk of the short rate. It has since been shown that the continuous-time limit of the model in the traditional risk-neutral world is

$$dr = \theta(t)\,dt + \sigma\,dz \tag{32.1}$$

where σ, the instantaneous standard deviation of the short rate, is constant and $\theta(t)$ is a function of time chosen to ensure that the model fits the initial term structure. The variable $\theta(t)$ defines the average direction that r moves at time t. This is independent of the level of r. Ho and Lee's parameter that concerns the market price of risk is irrelevant when the model is used to price interest rate derivatives.

Technical Note 31 at www-2.rotman.utoronto.ca/~hull/TechnicalNotes shows that

$$\theta(t) = F_t(0, t) + \sigma^2 t \tag{32.2}$$

where $F(0, t)$ is the instantaneous forward rate for a maturity t as seen at time zero and the subscript t denotes a partial derivative with respect to t. As an approximation, $\theta(t)$ equals $F_t(0, t)$. This means that the average direction that the short rate will be moving in the future is approximately equal to the slope of the instantaneous forward curve. The Ho–Lee model is illustrated in Figure 32.1. Superimposed on the average movement in the short rate is the normally distributed random outcome.

Technical Note 31 also shows that

$$P(t, T) = A(t, T)e^{-r(t)(T-t)} \tag{32.3}$$

where

$$\ln A(t, T) = \ln \frac{P(0, T)}{P(0, t)} + (T - t)F(0, t) - \tfrac{1}{2}\sigma^2 t(T - t)^2$$

From Section 4.8, $F(0, t) = -\partial \ln P(0, t)/\partial t$. The zero-coupon bond prices, $P(0, t)$, are known for all t from today's term structure of interest rates. Equation (32.3) therefore gives the price of a zero-coupon bond at a future time t in terms of the short rate at time t and the prices of bonds today.

The Hull–White One-Factor Model

In a paper published in 1990, Hull and White explored extensions of the Vasicek model that provide an exact fit to the initial term structure.[2] One version of the extended Vasicek model that they consider is

$$dr = [\theta(t) - ar]\, dt + \sigma\, dz \tag{32.4}$$

or

$$dr = a\left[\frac{\theta(t)}{a} - r\right] dt + \sigma\, dz$$

where a and σ are constants. This is known as the Hull–White model. It can be characterized as the Ho–Lee model with mean reversion at rate a. Alternatively, it can be characterized as the Vasicek model with a time-dependent reversion level. At time t, the short rate reverts to $\theta(t)/a$ at rate a. The Ho–Lee model is a particular case of the Hull–White model with $a = 0$.

The model has the same amount of analytic tractability as Ho–Lee. Technical Note 31 shows that

$$\theta(t) = F_t(0, t) + aF(0, t) + \frac{\sigma^2}{2a}(1 - e^{-2at}) \tag{32.5}$$

Figure 32.2 The Hull–White model.

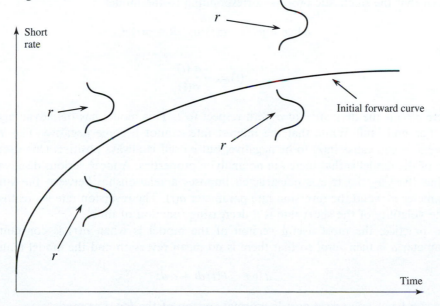

[2] See J. C. Hull and A. White, "Pricing Interest Rate Derivative Securities," *Review of Financial Studies*, 3, 4 (1990): 573–92.

The last term in this equation is usually fairly small. If we ignore it, the equation implies that the drift of the process for r at time t is $F_t(0, t) + a[F(0, t) - r]$. This shows that, on average, r follows the slope of the initial instantaneous forward rate curve. When it deviates from that curve, it reverts back to it at rate a. The model is illustrated in Figure 32.2.

Technical Note 31 shows that bond prices at time t in the Hull–White model are given by

$$P(t, T) = A(t, T)e^{-B(t,T)r(t)} \tag{32.6}$$

where

$$B(t, T) = \frac{1 - e^{-a(T-t)}}{a} \tag{32.7}$$

and

$$\ln A(t, T) = \ln \frac{P(0, T)}{P(0, t)} + B(t, T)F(0, t) - \frac{1}{4a^3}\sigma^2(e^{-aT} - e^{-at})^2(e^{2at} - 1) \tag{32.8}$$

As we show in the next section, European bond options can be valued analytically using the Ho–Lee and Hull–White models. A method for representing the models in the form of a trinomial tree is given later in this chapter. This is useful when American options and other derivatives that cannot be valued analytically are considered.

The Black–Derman–Toy Model

In 1990, Black, Derman, and Toy proposed a binomial-tree model for a lognormal short-rate process.[3] Their procedure for building the binomial tree is explained in Technical Note 23 at www-2.rotman.utoronto.ca/~hull/TechnicalNotes. It can be shown that the stochastic process corresponding to the model is

$$d \ln r = [\theta(t) - a(t) \ln r] \, dt + \sigma(t) \, dz$$

with

$$a(t) = -\frac{\sigma'(t)}{\sigma(t)}$$

where $\sigma'(t)$ is the derivative of σ with respect to t. This model has the advantage over Ho–Lee and Hull–White that the interest rate cannot become negative. The Wiener process dz can cause $\ln(r)$ to be negative, but r itself is always positive. One disadvantage of the model is that there are no analytic properties. A more serious disadvantage is that the way the tree is constructed imposes a relationship between the volatility parameter $\sigma(t)$ and the reversion rate parameter $a(t)$. The reversion rate is positive only if the volatility of the short rate is a decreasing function of time.

In practice, the most useful version of the model is when $\sigma(t)$ is constant. The parameter a is then zero, so that there is no mean reversion and the model reduces to

$$d \ln r = \theta(t) \, dt + \sigma \, dz$$

This can be characterized as a lognormal version of the Ho–Lee model.

---

[3] See F. Black, E. Derman, and W. Toy, "A One-Factor Model of Interest Rates and Its Application to Treasury Bond Prices," *Financial Analysts Journal*, January/February (1990): 33–39.

The Black–Karasinski Model

In 1991, Black and Karasinski developed an extension of the Black–Derman–Toy model where the reversion rate and volatility are determined independently of each other.[4] The most general version of the model is

$$d \ln r = [\theta(t) - a(t) \ln r] \, dt + \sigma(t) \, dz$$

The model is the same as Black–Derman–Toy model except that there is no relation between $a(t)$ and $\sigma(t)$. In practice, $a(t)$ and $\sigma(t)$ are often assumed to be constant, so that the model becomes

$$d \ln r = [\theta(t) - a \ln r] \, dt + \sigma \, dz \tag{32.9}$$

As in the case of all the models we are considering, the $\theta(t)$ function is determined to provide an exact fit to the initial term structure of interest rates. The model has no analytic tractability, but later in this chapter we will describe a convenient way of simultaneously determining $\theta(t)$ and representing the process for r in the form of a trinomial tree.

The Hull–White Two-Factor Model

In Section 31.4, we presented a two-factor equilibrium model which is an extension of Vasicek's model. Hull and White show how this model can be converted into a no-arbitrage model by adding $\theta(t)$ in the drift of r.[5]

This model provides a richer pattern of term structure movements and a richer pattern of volatilities than one-factor models of r. For more information on the analytical properties of the model and the way a tree can be constructed for it, see Technical Note 14 at www-2.rotman.utoronto.ca/~hull/TechnicalNotes.

32.2 OPTIONS ON BONDS

Some of the models just presented allow options on zero-coupon bonds to be valued analytically. For the Vasicek, Ho–Lee, and Hull–White one-factor models, the price at time zero of a call option that matures at time T on a zero-coupon bond maturing at time s is

$$L P(0, s) N(h) - K P(0, T) N(h - \sigma_P) \tag{32.10}$$

where L is the principal of the bond, K is its strike price, and

$$h = \frac{1}{\sigma_P} \ln \frac{L P(0, s)}{P(0, T) K} + \frac{\sigma_P}{2}$$

The price of a put option on the bond is

$$K P(0, T) N(-h + \sigma_P) - L P(0, s) N(-h)$$

---

[4] See F. Black and P. Karasinski, "Bond and Option Pricing When Short Rates are Lognormal," *Financial Analysts Journal*, July/August (1991): 52–59.

[5] See J.C. Hull and A. White, "Numerical Procedures for Implementing Term Structure Models II: Two-Factor Models," *Journal of Derivatives*, 2, 2 (Winter 1994): 37–48.

Technical Note 31 shows that, in the case of the Vasicek and Hull–White models,

$$\sigma_P = \frac{\sigma}{a}[1 - e^{-a(s-T)}]\sqrt{\frac{1 - e^{-2aT}}{2a}}$$

and, in the case of the Ho–Lee model,

$$\sigma_P = \sigma(s - T)\sqrt{T}$$

Equation (32.10) is essentially the same as Black's model for pricing bond options in Section 29.1 with the forward bond price volatility equaling $\sigma_P/\sqrt{T}$. As explained in Section 29.2, an interest rate cap or floor can be expressed as a portfolio of options on zero-coupon bonds. It can, therefore, be valued analytically using the equations just presented.

There are also formulas for valuing options on zero-coupon bonds in the Cox, Ingersoll, and Ross model, which we presented in Section 31.2. These involve integrals of the noncentral chi-square distribution.

Options on Coupon-Bearing Bonds

In a one-factor model of r, all zero-coupon bonds move up in price when r decreases and all zero-coupon bonds move down in price when r increases. As a result, a one-factor model allows a European option on a coupon-bearing bond to be expressed as the sum of European options on zero-coupon bonds. The procedure is as follows:

1. Calculate r^*, the critical value of r for which the price of the coupon-bearing bond equals the strike price of the option on the bond at the option maturity T.

2. Calculate prices of European options with maturity T on the zero-coupon bonds that comprise the coupon-bearing bond. The strike prices of the options equal the values the zero-coupon bonds will have at time T when $r = r^*$.

3. Set the price of the European option on the coupon-bearing bond equal to the sum of the prices on the options on zero-coupon bonds calculated in Step 2.

This allows options on coupon-bearing bonds to be valued for the Vasicek, Cox, Ingersoll, and Ross, Ho–Lee, and Hull–White models. As explained in Business Snapshot 29.2, a European swap option can be viewed as an option on a coupon-bearing bond. It can, therefore, be valued using this procedure. For more details on the procedure and a numerical example, see Technical Note 15 at www-2.rotman.utoronto.ca/~hull/TechnicalNotes.

32.3 VOLATILITY STRUCTURES

The models we have looked at give rise to different volatility environments. Figure 32.3 shows the volatility of the 3-month forward rate as a function of maturity for Ho–Lee, Hull–White one-factor and Hull–White two-factor models. The term structure of interest rates is assumed to be flat.

For Ho–Lee the volatility of the 3-month forward rate is the same for all maturities. In the one-factor Hull–White model the effect of mean reversion is to cause the

Figure 32.3 Volatility of 3-month forward rate as a function of maturity for (a) the Ho–Lee model, (b) the Hull–White one-factor model, and (c) the Hull–White two-factor model (when parameters are chosen appropriately).

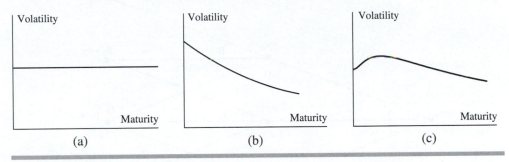

(a)   (b)   (c)

volatility of the 3-month forward rate to be a declining function of maturity. In the Hull–White two-factor model when parameters are chosen appropriately, the volatility of the 3-month forward rate has a "humped" look. The latter is consistent with empirical evidence and implied cap volatilities discussed in Section 29.2.

32.4 INTEREST RATE TREES

An interest rate tree is a discrete-time representation of the stochastic process for the short rate in much the same way as a stock price tree is a discrete-time representation of the process followed by a stock price. If the time step on the tree is Δt, the rates on the tree are the continuously compounded Δt-period rates. The usual assumption when a tree is constructed is that the Δt-period rate, R, follows the same stochastic process as the instantaneous rate, r, in the corresponding continuous-time model. The main difference between interest rate trees and stock price trees is in the way that discounting is done. In a stock price tree, the discount rate is usually assumed to be the same at each node or a function of time. In an interest rate tree, the discount rate varies from node to node.

It often proves to be convenient to use a trinomial rather than a binomial tree for interest rates. The main advantage of a trinomial tree is that it provides an extra degree of freedom, making it easier for the tree to represent features of the interest rate process such as mean reversion. As mentioned in Section 21.8, using a trinomial tree is equivalent to using the explicit finite difference method.

Illustration of Use of Trinomial Trees

To illustrate how trinomial interest rate trees are used to value derivatives, consider the simple example shown in Figure 32.4. This is a two-step tree with each time step equal to 1 year in length so that $\Delta t = 1$ year. Assume that the up, middle, and down probabilities are 0.25, 0.50, and 0.25, respectively, at each node. The assumed Δt-period rate is shown as the upper number at each node.[6]

---

[6] We explain later how the probabilities and rates on an interest rate tree are determined.

Figure 32.4 Example of the use of trinomial interest rate trees. Upper number at each node is rate; lower number is value of instrument.

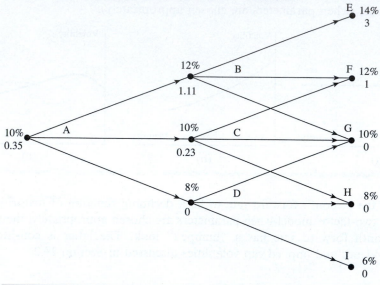

The tree is used to value a derivative that provides a payoff at the end of the second time step of

$$\max[100(R - 0.11), 0]$$

where R is the Δt-period rate. The calculated value of this derivative is the lower number at each node. At the final nodes, the value of the derivative equals the payoff. For example, at node E, the value is $100 \times (0.14 - 0.11) = 3$. At earlier nodes, the value of the derivative is calculated using the rollback procedure explained in Chapters 13 and 21. At node B, the 1-year interest rate is 12%. This is used for discounting to obtain the value of the derivative at node B from its values at nodes E, F, and G as

$$[0.25 \times 3 + 0.5 \times 1 + 0.25 \times 0]e^{-0.12 \times 1} = 1.11$$

At node C, the 1-year interest rate is 10%. This is used for discounting to obtain the value of the derivative at node C as

$$(0.25 \times 1 + 0.5 \times 0 + 0.25 \times 0)e^{-0.1 \times 1} = 0.23$$

At the initial node, A, the interest rate is also 10% and the value of the derivative is

$$(0.25 \times 1.11 + 0.5 \times 0.23 + 0.25 \times 0)e^{-0.1 \times 1} = 0.35$$

Nonstandard Branching

It sometimes proves convenient to modify the standard trinomial branching pattern that is used at all nodes in Figure 32.4. Three alternative branching possibilities are shown in Figure 32.5. The usual branching is shown in Figure 32.5a. It is "up one/straight along/ down one". One alternative to this is "up two/up one/straight along", as shown in

Figure 32.5 Alternative branching methods in a trinomial tree.

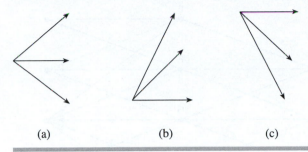

(a)   (b)   (c)

Figure 32.5b. This proves useful for incorporating mean reversion when interest rates are very low. A third branching pattern shown in Figure 32.5c is "straight along/down one/down two". This is useful for incorporating mean reversion when interest rates are very high. The use of different branching patterns is illustrated in the following section.

32.5 A GENERAL TREE-BUILDING PROCEDURE

Hull and White have proposed a robust two-stage procedure for constructing trinomial trees to represent a wide range of one-factor models.[7] This section first explains how the procedure can be used for the Hull–White model in equation (32.4) and then shows how it can be extended to represent other models, such as Black–Karasinski.

First Stage

The Hull–White model for the instantaneous short rate r is

$$dr = [\theta(t) - ar]\, dt + \sigma\, dz$$

We suppose that the time step on the tree is constant and equal to Δt.[8]

Assume that the Δt rate, R, follows the same process as r.

$$dR = [\theta(t) - aR]\, dt + \sigma\, dz$$

Clearly, this is reasonable in the limit as Δt tends to zero. The first stage in building a tree for this model is to construct a tree for a variable R^* that is initially zero and follows the process

$$dR^* = -aR^*\, dt + \sigma\, dz$$

This process is symmetrical about $R^* = 0$. The variable $R^*(t + \Delta t) - R^*(t)$ is normally distributed. If terms of higher order than Δt are ignored, the expected value of $R^*(t + \Delta t) - R^*(t)$ is $-aR^*(t)\Delta t$ and the variance of $R^*(t + \Delta t) - R^*(t)$ is $\sigma^2 \Delta t$.

[7] See J. C. Hull and A. White, "Numerical Procedures for Implementing Term Structure Models I: Single-Factor Models,"*Journal of Derivatives*, 2, 1 (1994): 7–16; and J. C. Hull and A. White, "Using Hull–White Interest Rate Trees," *Journal of Derivatives*, (Spring 1996): 26–36.

[8] See Technical Note 16 at www-2.rotman.utoronto.ca/~hull/TechnicalNotes for a discussion of how nonconstant time steps can be used.

Figure 32.6 Tree for R^* in Hull–White model (first stage).

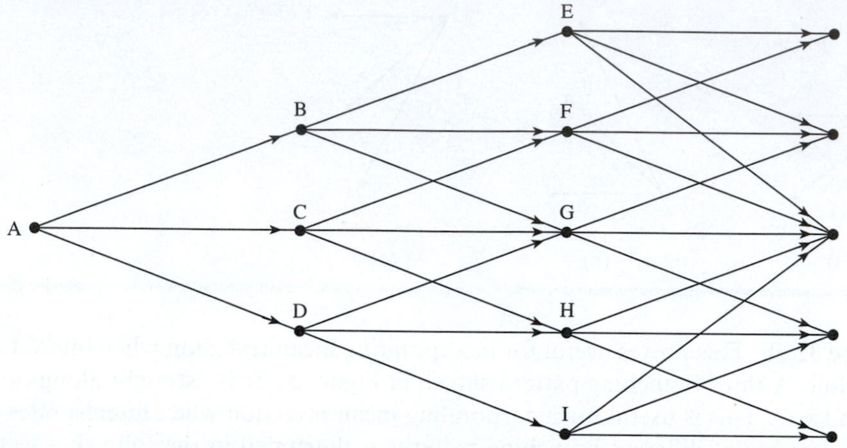

Node:	A	B	C	D	E	F	G	H	I
R^* (%)	0.000	1.732	0.000	−1.732	3.464	1.732	0.000	−1.732	−3.464
p_u	0.1667	0.1217	0.1667	0.2217	0.8867	0.1217	0.1667	0.2217	0.0867
p_m	0.6666	0.6566	0.6666	0.6566	0.0266	0.6566	0.6666	0.6566	0.0266
p_d	0.1667	0.2217	0.1667	0.1217	0.0867	0.2217	0.1667	0.1217	0.8867

The spacing between interest rates on the tree, ΔR, is set as

$$\Delta R = \sigma\sqrt{3\Delta t}$$

This proves to be a good choice of ΔR from the viewpoint of error minimization.

The objective of the first stage of the procedure is to build a tree similar to that shown in Figure 32.6 for R^*. To do this, it is first necessary to resolve which of the three branching methods shown in Figure 32.5 will apply at each node. This will determine the overall geometry of the tree. Once this is done, the branching probabilities must also be calculated.

Define (i, j) as the node where $t = i\,\Delta t$ and $R^* = j\,\Delta R$. (The variable i is a positive integer and j is a positive or negative integer.) The branching method used at a node must lead to the probabilities on all three branches being positive. Most of the time, the branching shown in Figure 32.5a is appropriate. When $a > 0$, it is necessary to switch from the branching in Figure 32.5a to the branching in Figure 32.5c for a sufficiently large j. Similarly, it is necessary to switch from the branching in Figure 32.5a to the branching in Figure 32.5b when j is sufficiently negative. Define j_{max} as the value of j where we switch from the Figure 32.5a branching to the Figure 32.5c branching and j_{min} as the value of j where we switch from the Figure 32.5a branching to the Figure 32.5b branching. Hull and White show that probabilities are always positive if j_{max} is set equal to the smallest integer greater than $0.184/(a\,\Delta t)$ and j_{min} is set equal to $-j_{max}$.[9] Define

---

[9] The probabilities are positive for any value of j_{max} between $0.184/(a\,\Delta t)$ and $0.816/(a\,\Delta t)$ and for any value of j_{min} between $-0.184/(a\,\Delta t)$ and $-0.816/(a\,\Delta t)$. Changing the branching at the first possible node proves to be computationally most efficient.

p_u, p_m, and p_d as the probabilities of the highest, middle, and lowest branches emanating from the node. The probabilities are chosen to match the expected change and variance of the change in R^* over the next time interval Δt. The probabilities must also sum to unity. This leads to three equations in the three probabilities.

As already mentioned, the mean change in R^* in time Δt is $-aR^* \Delta t$ and the variance of the change is $\sigma^2 \Delta t$. At node (i, j), $R^* = j \Delta R$. If the branching has the form shown in Figure 32.5a, the p_u, p_m, and p_d at node (i, j) must satisfy the following three equations to match the mean and standard deviation:

$$p_u \Delta R - p_d \Delta R = -aj \Delta R \Delta t$$

$$p_u \Delta R^2 + p_d \Delta R^2 = \sigma^2 \Delta t + a^2 j^2 \Delta R^2 \Delta t^2$$

$$p_u + p_m + p_d = 1$$

Using $\Delta R = \sigma \sqrt{3 \Delta t}$, the solution to these equations is

$$p_u = \tfrac{1}{6} + \tfrac{1}{2}(a^2 j^2 \Delta t^2 - aj \Delta t)$$

$$p_m = \tfrac{2}{3} - a^2 j^2 \Delta t^2$$

$$p_d = \tfrac{1}{6} + \tfrac{1}{2}(a^2 j^2 \Delta t^2 + aj \Delta t)$$

Similarly, if the branching has the form shown in Figure 32.5b, the probabilities are

$$p_u = \tfrac{1}{6} + \tfrac{1}{2}(a^2 j^2 \Delta t^2 + aj \Delta t)$$

$$p_m = -\tfrac{1}{3} - a^2 j^2 \Delta t^2 - 2aj \Delta t$$

$$p_d = \tfrac{7}{6} + \tfrac{1}{2}(a^2 j^2 \Delta t^2 + 3aj \Delta t)$$

Finally, if the branching has the form shown in Figure 32.5c, the probabilities are

$$p_u = \tfrac{7}{6} + \tfrac{1}{2}(a^2 j^2 \Delta t^2 - 3aj \Delta t)$$

$$p_m = -\tfrac{1}{3} - a^2 j^2 \Delta t^2 + 2aj \Delta t$$

$$p_d = \tfrac{1}{6} + \tfrac{1}{2}(a^2 j^2 \Delta t^2 - aj \Delta t)$$

To illustrate the first stage of the tree construction, suppose that $\sigma = 0.01$, $a = 0.1$, and $\Delta t = 1$ year. In this case, $\Delta R = 0.01\sqrt{3} = 0.0173$, j_{max} is set equal to the smallest integer greater than $0.184/0.1$, and $j_{min} = -j_{max}$. This means that $j_{max} = 2$ and $j_{min} = -2$ and the tree is as shown in Figure 32.6. The probabilities on the branches emanating from each node are shown below the tree and are calculated using the equations above for p_u, p_m, and p_d.

Note that the probabilities at each node in Figure 32.6 depend only on j. For example, the probabilities at node B are the same as the probabilities at node F. Furthermore, the tree is symmetrical. The probabilities at node D are the mirror image of the probabilities at node B.

Second Stage

The second stage in the tree construction is to convert the tree for R^* into a tree for R. This is accomplished by displacing the nodes on the R^*-tree so that the initial term structure of interest rates is exactly matched. Define

$$\alpha(t) = R(t) - R^*(t)$$

The $\alpha(t)$'s that apply as the time step Δt on the tree becomes infinitesimally small can be calculated analytically from equation (32.5).[10] However, we want a tree with a finite Δt to match the term structure exactly, so we use an iterative procedure to determine the α's.

Define α_i as $\alpha(i\,\Delta t)$, the value of R at time $i\,\Delta t$ on the R-tree minus the corresponding value of R^* at time $i\,\Delta t$ on the R^*-tree. Define $Q_{i,j}$ as the present value of a security that pays off \$1 if node (i,j) is reached and zero otherwise. The α_i and $Q_{i,j}$ can be calculated using forward induction in such a way that the initial term structure is matched exactly.

Illustration of Second Stage

Suppose that the continuously compounded zero rates in the example in Figure 32.6 are as shown in Table 32.1. The value of $Q_{0,0}$ is 1.0. The value of α_0 is chosen to give the right price for a zero-coupon bond maturing at time Δt. That is, α_0 is set equal to the initial Δt-period interest rate. Because $\Delta t = 1$ in this example, $\alpha_0 = 0.03824$. This defines the position of the initial node on the R-tree in Figure 32.7. The next step is to calculate the values of $Q_{1,1}$, $Q_{1,0}$, and $Q_{1,-1}$. There is a probability of 0.1667 that the $(1, 1)$ node is reached and the discount rate for the first time step is 3.82%. The value of $Q_{1,1}$ is therefore $0.1667e^{-0.0382} = 0.1604$. Similarly, $Q_{1,0} = 0.6417$ and $Q_{1,-1} = 0.1604$.

Once $Q_{1,1}$, $Q_{1,0}$, and $Q_{1,-1}$ have been calculated, α_1 can be determined. It is chosen to give the right price for a zero-coupon bond maturing at time $2\Delta t$. Because $\Delta R = 0.01732$ and $\Delta t = 1$, the price of this bond as seen at node B is $e^{-(\alpha_1 + 0.01732)}$. Similarly, the price as seen at node C is $e^{-\alpha_1}$ and the price as seen at node D is $e^{-(\alpha_1 - 0.01732)}$. The price as seen at the initial node A is therefore

$$Q_{1,1}e^{-(\alpha_1 + 0.01732)} + Q_{1,0}e^{-\alpha_1} + Q_{1,-1}e^{-(\alpha_1 - 0.01732)} \tag{32.11}$$

From the initial term structure, this bond price should be $e^{-0.04512 \times 2} = 0.9137$.

Table 32.1   Zero rates for example in Figures 32.6 and 32.7.

Maturity	Rate (%)
0.5	3.430
1.0	3.824
1.5	4.183
2.0	4.512
2.5	4.812
3.0	5.086

---

[10] To estimate the instantaneous $\alpha(t)$ analytically, we note that

$$dR = [\theta(t) - aR]\,dt + \sigma\,dz \quad \text{and} \quad dR^* = -aR^*\,dt + \sigma\,dz$$

so that $d\alpha = [\theta(t) - a\alpha(t)]\,dt$. Using equation (32.7), it can be seen that the solution to this is

$$\alpha(t) = F(0, t) + \frac{\sigma^2}{2a^2}(1 - e^{-at})^2.$$

Figure 32.7 Tree for R in Hull–White model (the second stage).

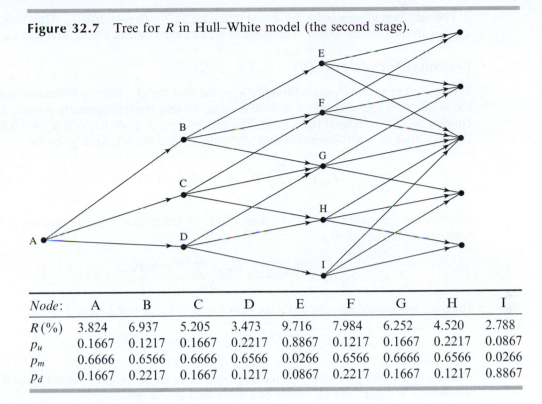

Node:	A	B	C	D	E	F	G	H	I
R (%)	3.824	6.937	5.205	3.473	9.716	7.984	6.252	4.520	2.788
p_u	0.1667	0.1217	0.1667	0.2217	0.8867	0.1217	0.1667	0.2217	0.0867
p_m	0.6666	0.6566	0.6666	0.6566	0.0266	0.6566	0.6666	0.6566	0.0266
p_d	0.1667	0.2217	0.1667	0.1217	0.0867	0.2217	0.1667	0.1217	0.8867

Substituting for the Q's in equation (32.11),

$$0.1604e^{-(\alpha_1+0.01732)} + 0.6417e^{-\alpha_1} + 0.1604e^{-(\alpha_1-0.01732)} = 0.9137$$

or

$$e^{-\alpha_1}(0.1604e^{-0.01732} + 0.6417 + 0.1604e^{0.01732}) = 0.9137$$

or

$$\alpha_1 = \ln\left[\frac{0.1604e^{-0.01732} + 0.6417 + 0.1604e^{0.01732}}{0.9137}\right] = 0.05205$$

This means that the central node at time Δt in the tree for R corresponds to an interest rate of 5.205% (see Figure 32.7).

The next step is to calculate $Q_{2,2}$, $Q_{2,1}$, $Q_{2,0}$, $Q_{2,-1}$, and $Q_{2,-2}$. The calculations can be shortened by using previously determined Q values. Consider $Q_{2,1}$ as an example. This is the value of a security that pays off \$1 if node F is reached and zero otherwise. Node F can be reached only from nodes B and C. The interest rates at these nodes are 6.937% and 5.205%, respectively. The probabilities associated with the B–F and C–F branches are 0.6566 and 0.1667. The value at node B of a security that pays \$1 at node F is therefore $0.6566e^{-0.06937}$. The value at node C is $0.1667e^{-0.05205}$. The variable $Q_{2,1}$ is $0.6566e^{-0.06937}$ times the present value of \$1 received at node B plus $0.1667e^{-0.05205}$ times the present value of \$1 received at node C; that is,

$$Q_{2,1} = 0.6566e^{-0.06937} \times 0.1604 + 0.1667e^{-0.05205} \times 0.6417 = 0.1998$$

Similarly, $Q_{2,2} = 0.0182$, $Q_{2,0} = 0.4736$, $Q_{2,-1} = 0.2033$, and $Q_{2,-2} = 0.0189$.

The next step in producing the R-tree in Figure 32.7 is to calculate α_2. After that, the $Q_{3,j}$'s can then be computed. The variable α_3 can then be calculated, and so on.

Formulas for α's and Q's

To express the approach more formally, suppose that the $Q_{i,j}$ have been determined for $i \leqslant m$ $(m \geqslant 0)$. The next step is to determine α_m so that the tree correctly prices a zero-coupon bond maturing at $(m + 1)\Delta t$. The interest rate at node (m, j) is $\alpha_m + j\,\Delta R$, so that the price of a zero-coupon bond maturing at time $(m + 1)\Delta t$ is given by

$$P_{m+1} = \sum_{j=-n_m}^{n_m} Q_{m,j} \exp[-(\alpha_m + j\,\Delta R)\Delta t] \tag{32.12}$$

where n_m is the number of nodes on each side of the central node at time $m\,\Delta t$. The solution to this equation is

$$\alpha_m = \frac{\ln \sum_{j=-n_m}^{n_m} Q_{m,j} e^{-j\Delta R\Delta t} - \ln P_{m+1}}{\Delta t}$$

Once α_m has been determined, the $Q_{i,j}$ for $i = m + 1$ can be calculated using

$$Q_{m+1,j} = \sum_k Q_{m,k} q(k, j) \exp[-(\alpha_m + k\,\Delta R)\,\Delta t]$$

where $q(k, j)$ is the probability of moving from node (m, k) to node $(m + 1, j)$ and the summation is taken over all values of k for which this is nonzero.

Extension to Other Models

The procedure that has just been outlined can be extended to more general models of the form

$$df(r) = [\theta(t) - af(r)]\,dt + \sigma\,dz \tag{32.13}$$

where f is a montonic function of r. This family of models has the property that they can fit any term structure.[11]

As before, we assume that the Δt period rate, R, follows the same process as r:

$$df(R) = [\theta(t) - af(R)]\,dt + \sigma\,dz$$

We start by setting $x = f(R)$, so that

$$dx = [\theta(t) - ax]\,dt + \sigma\,dz$$

The first stage is to build a tree for a variable x^* that follows the same process as x except that $\theta(t) = 0$ and the initial value is zero. The procedure here is identical to the procedure already outlined for building a tree such as that in Figure 32.6.

---

[11] Not all no-arbitrage models have this property. For example, the extended-CIR model, considered by Cox, Ingersoll, and Ross (1985) and Hull and White (1990), which has the form

$$dr = [\theta(t) - ar]\,dt + \sigma\sqrt{r}\,dz$$

cannot fit yield curves where the forward rate declines sharply. This is because the process is not well defined when $\theta(t)$ is negative.

As in Figure 32.7, the nodes at time $i\,\Delta t$ are then displaced by an amount α_i to provide an exact fit to the initial term structure. The equations for determining α_i and $Q_{i,j}$ inductively are slightly different from those for the $f(R) = R$ case. The value of Q at the first node, $Q_{0,0}$, is set equal to 1. Suppose that the $Q_{i,j}$ have been determined for $i \leqslant m$ ($m \geqslant 0$). The next step is to determine α_m so that the tree correctly prices an $(m+1)\Delta t$ zero-coupon bond. Define g as the inverse function of f so that the Δt-period interest rate at the jth node at time $m\,\Delta t$ is

$$g(\alpha_m + j\,\Delta x)$$

The price of a zero-coupon bond maturing at time $(m+1)\Delta t$ is given by

$$P_{m+1} = \sum_{j=-n_m}^{n_m} Q_{m,j} \exp[-g(\alpha_m + j\,\Delta x)\Delta t] \tag{32.14}$$

This equation can be solved using a numerical procedure such as Newton–Raphson. The value α_0 of α when $m = 0$, is $f\big(R(0)\big)$.

Once α_m has been determined, the $Q_{i,j}$ for $i = m + 1$ can be calculated using

$$Q_{m+1,j} = \sum_k Q_{m,k}\, q(k, j) \exp[-g(\alpha_m + k\,\Delta x)\Delta t]$$

where $q(k, j)$ is the probability of moving from node (m, k) to node $(m + 1, j)$ and the summation is taken over all values of k where this is nonzero.

Figure 32.8   Tree for lognormal model.

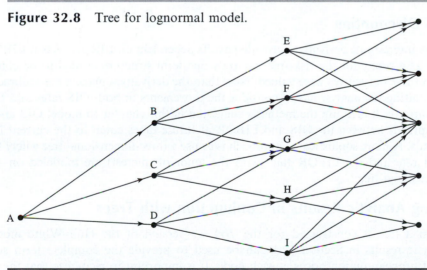

Node:	A	B	C	D	E	F	G	H	I
x	−3.373	−2.875	−3.181	−3.487	−2.430	−2.736	−3.042	−3.349	−3.655
$R\,(\%)$	3.430	5.642	4.154	3.058	8.803	6.481	4.772	3.513	2.587
p_u	0.1667	0.1177	0.1667	0.2277	0.8609	0.1177	0.1667	0.2277	0.0809
p_m	0.6666	0.6546	0.6666	0.6546	0.0582	0.6546	0.6666	0.6546	0.0582
p_d	0.1667	0.2277	0.1667	0.1177	0.0809	0.2277	0.1667	0.1177	0.8609

Figure 32.8 shows the results of applying the procedure to the Black–Karasinski model in equation (32.9):

$$d \ln(r) = [\theta(t) - a \ln(r)]\, dt + \sigma\, dz$$

when $a = 0.22$, $\sigma = 0.25$, $\Delta t = 0.5$, and the zero rates are as in Table 32.1.

Setting $f(r) = r$ leads to the Hull–White model in equation (32.4); setting $f(r) = \ln(r)$ leads to the Black–Karasinski model in equation (32.9). The main advantage of the $f(r) = r$ model is its analytic tractability.

Negative Rates

Traditionally the main disadvantage of Hull-White has been that it allows interest rates to become negative. Some analysts have been reluctant to use a model where there is any chance at all of negative rates and have therefore preferred $f(r) = \ln(r)$ even though it has no analytic tractability.

This aversion to models that give rise to negative rates has changed somewhat in recent years because, as mentioned in earlier chapters, negative interest rates have become a feature of financial markets in some countries. The Ho–Lee and Hull–White models are similar in spirit to the Bachelier normal model discussed in Section 29.2.[12] They can be used to value nonstandard deals in negative interest rate environments. An alternative is to use a "shifted Black–Karasinski" model. In this, $r + \alpha$ rather than r is assumed to follow the process in equation (32.9), so that

$$d \ln(r + \alpha) = [\theta(t) - a \ln(r + \alpha)]\, dt + \sigma\, dz$$

The short-term interest rate can then become (almost) as low as $-\alpha$.

OIS Discounting

Many interest rate derivatives provide payoffs dependent on LIBOR. When LIBOR was used as a proxy for the risk-free rate only one term structure needed to be considered when these derivatives were valued. Now than the derivatives market has embraced OIS discounting, an analyst has to consider the movements in both OIS rates and LIBOR. One approach is to use the methods suggested in this chapter to model OIS and to set the spreads between the OIS and LIBOR at future times equal to the current forward spreads. A more sophisticated approach is to use a three-dimensional tree where the OIS short rate and the LIBOR rate (with the tenor of interest) are modeled on a three-dimensional tree.[13]

Using Analytic Results in Conjunction with Trees

When a tree is constructed for the $f(r) = r$ version of the Hull–White model, the analytic results in Section 32.1 can be used to provide the complete term structure and European option prices at each node. It is important to recognize that the interest rate on the tree is the Δt-period rate R. It is not the instantaneous short rate r.

---

[12] There is a slight difference. Suppose that the tenor of the rate being considered is τ. In the Bachelier normal model, the rate is assumed to be normal when the compounding frequency used to measure the interest rate is τ. In Ho–Lee and Hull–White, the interest rate is also normal, but with continuous compounding.

[13] See J. C. Hull and A. White, "Multi-Curve Modeling Using Trees," In: *Challenges in Derivatives Markets*, edited by Kathrin Glau, Matthias Scherer, and Rudi Zagst, Springer Proceedings in Mathematics and Statistics, 2016. Also ssrn 2601457.

From equations (32.6), (32.7), and (32.8), it can be shown (see Problem 32.15) that

$$P(t, T) = \hat{A}(t, T)e^{-\hat{B}(t,T)R} \tag{32.15}$$

where

$$\ln \hat{A}(t, T) = \ln \frac{P(0, T)}{P(0, t)} - \frac{B(t, T)}{B(t, t + \Delta t)} \ln \frac{P(0, t + \Delta t)}{P(0, t)}$$

$$- \frac{\sigma^2}{4a}(1 - e^{-2at})B(t, T)[B(t, T) - B(t, t + \Delta t)] \tag{32.16}$$

and

$$\hat{B}(t, T) = \frac{B(t, T)}{B(t, t + \Delta t)} \Delta t \tag{32.17}$$

(In the case of the Ho–Lee model, we set $\hat{B}(t, T) = T - t$ in these equations.)

Bond prices should therefore be calculated with equation (32.15), and not with equation (32.6).

Example 32.1

Suppose zero rates are as in Table 32.2. The rates for maturities between those indicated are generated using linear interpolation.

Consider a 3-year ($= 3 \times 365$ days) European put option on a zero-coupon bond that will pay 100 in 9 years ($= 9 \times 365$ days). Interest rates are assumed to follow the Hull–White ($f(r) = r$) model. The strike price is 63, $a = 0.1$, and $\sigma = 0.01$. A 3-year tree is constructed and zero-coupon bond prices are calculated analytically at the final nodes as just described. As shown in Table 32.3, the results from the tree are consistent with the analytic price of the option.

This example provides a good test of the implementation of the model because the gradient of the zero curve changes sharply immediately after the expiration of

Table 32.2 Zero curve with all rates continuously compounded, actual/365.

Maturity	Days	Rate (%)
3 days	3	5.01772
1 month	31	4.98284
2 months	62	4.97234
3 months	94	4.96157
6 months	185	4.99058
1 year	367	5.09389
2 years	731	5.79733
3 years	1,096	6.30595
4 years	1,461	6.73464
5 years	1,826	6.94816
6 years	2,194	7.08807
7 years	2,558	7.27527
8 years	2,922	7.30852
9 years	3,287	7.39790
10 years	3,653	7.49015

Table 32.3 Value of a 3-year put option on a 9-year zero-coupon bond with a strike price of 63: $a = 0.1$ and $\sigma = 0.01$; zero curve as in Table 32.2.

Steps	Tree	Analytic
10	1.8468	1.8093
30	1.8172	1.8093
50	1.8057	1.8093
100	1.8128	1.8093
200	1.8090	1.8093
500	1.8091	1.8093

the option. Small errors in the construction and use of the tree are liable to have a big effect on the option values obtained. (The example is used in Sample Application G of the DerivaGem Applications software.)

Tree for American Bond Options

The DerivaGem software accompanying this book implements the normal and the lognormal model for valuing European and American bond options, caps/floors, and European swap options. Figure 32.9 shows the tree produced by the software when it is used to value a 1.5-year American call option on a 10-year bond using four time steps and the lognormal (Black–Karasinski) model. The parameters used in the lognormal model are $a = 5\%$ and $\sigma = 20\%$. The underlying bond lasts 10 years, has a principal of 100, and pays a coupon of 5% per annum semiannually. The yield curve is flat at 5% per annum. The strike price is 105. As explained in Section 29.1 the strike price can be a cash strike price or a quoted strike price. In this case it is a quoted strike price. The bond price shown on the tree is the cash bond price. The accrued interest at each node is shown below the tree. The cash strike price is calculated as the quoted strike price plus accrued interest. The quoted bond price is the cash bond price minus accrued interest. The payoff from the option is the cash bond price minus the cash strike price. Equivalently it is the quoted bond price minus the quoted strike price.

The tree gives the price of the option as 0.672. A much larger tree with 100 time steps gives the price of the option as 0.703. Note that the price of the 10-year bond cannot be computed analytically when the lognormal model is assumed. It is computed numerically by rolling back through a much larger tree than that shown.

32.6 CALIBRATION

Up to now, we have assumed that the volatility parameters a and σ are known. We now discuss how they are determined. This is known as calibrating the model.

The volatility parameters are determined from market data on actively traded options. These will be referred to as the *calibrating instruments*. The first stage is to choose a "goodness-of-fit" measure. Suppose there are n calibrating instruments. A popular goodness-of-fit measure is $\sum_{i=1}^{n}(U_i - V_i)^2$, where U_i is the market price of the ith calibrating instrument and V_i is the price given by the model for this instrument. The

Figure 32.9 Tree, produced by DerivaGem, for valuing an American bond option.

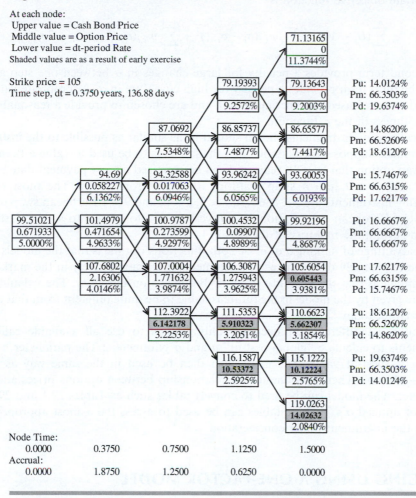

At each node:
Upper value = Cash Bond Price
Middle value = Option Price
Lower value = dt-period Rate
Shaded values are as a result of early exercise

Strike price = 105
Time step, dt = 0.3750 years, 136.88 days

Node Time:
0.0000 0.3750 0.7500 1.1250 1.5000
Accrual:
0.0000 1.8750 1.2500 0.6250 0.0000

objective of calibration is to choose the model parameters so that this goodness-of-fit measure is minimized.

The number of volatility parameters should not be greater than the number of calibrating instruments. If a and σ are constant, there are only two volatility parameters. The models can be extended so that a or σ, or both, are functions of time. Step functions can be used. Suppose, for example, that a is constant and σ is a function of time. We might choose times $t_1, t_2, \ldots, t_n$ and assume $\sigma(t) = \sigma_0$ for $t \leqslant t_1$, $\sigma(t) = \sigma_i$ for $t_i < t \leqslant t_{i+1}$ $(1 \leqslant i \leqslant n-1)$, and $\sigma(t) = \sigma_n$ for $t > t_n$. There would then be a total of $n + 2$ volatility parameters: $a, \sigma_0, \sigma_1, \ldots,$ and σ_n.

The minimization of the goodness-of-fit measure can be accomplished using the Levenberg–Marquardt procedure.[14] When a or σ, or both, are functions of time, a penalty function is often added to the goodness-of-fit measure so that the functions are

---

[14] For a good description of this procedure, see W. H. Press, B. P. Flannery, S. A. Teukolsky, and W. T. Vetterling, *Numerical Recipes: The Art of Scientific Computing*, 3rd edn. Cambridge University Press, 2007.

"well behaved". In the example just mentioned, where σ is a step function, an appropriate objective function is

$$\sum_{i=1}^{n}(U_i - V_i)^2 + \sum_{i=1}^{n} w_{1,i}(\sigma_i - \sigma_{i-1})^2 + \sum_{i=1}^{n-1} w_{2,i}(\sigma_{i-1} + \sigma_{i+1} - 2\sigma_i)^2$$

The second term provides a penalty for large changes in σ between one step and the next. The third term provides a penalty for high curvature in σ. Appropriate values for $w_{1,i}$ and $w_{2,i}$ are based on experimentation and are chosen to provide a reasonable level of smoothness in the σ function.

The calibrating instruments chosen should be as similar as possible to the instrument being valued. Suppose, for example, that the model is to be used to value a Bermudan-style swap option that lasts 10 years and can be exercised on any payment date between year 5 and year 9 into a swap maturing 10 years from today. The most relevant calibrating instruments are 5×5, 6×4, 7×3, 8×2, and 9×1 European swap options. (An $n \times m$ European swap option is an n-year option to enter into a swap lasting for m years beyond the maturity of the option.)

The advantage of making a or σ, or both, functions of time is that the models can be fitted more precisely to the prices of instruments that trade actively in the market. The disadvantage is that the volatility structure becomes nonstationary. The volatility term structure given by the model in the future is liable to be quite different from that existing in the market today.[15]

A somewhat different approach to calibration is to use all available calibrating instruments to calculate "global-best-fit" a and σ parameters. The parameter a is held fixed at its best-fit value. The model can then be used in the same way as Black–Scholes–Merton. There is a one-to-one relationship between options prices and the σ parameter. The model can be used to convert tables such as Tables 29.1 and 29.2 into tables of implied σ's.[16] These tables can be used to assess the σ most appropriate for pricing the instrument under consideration.

32.7 HEDGING USING A ONE-FACTOR MODEL

Section 29.5 outlined some general approaches to hedging a portfolio of interest rate derivatives. These approaches can be used with the term structure models in this chapter. The calculation of deltas, gammas, and vegas involves making small changes to either the zero curve or the volatility environment and recomputing the value of the portfolio.

Note that, although one factor is often assumed when pricing interest rate derivatives, it is not appropriate to assume only one factor when hedging. For example, the deltas calculated should allow for many different movements in the yield curve, not just those that are possible under the model chosen. The practice of taking account of changes that

---

[15] For a discussion of the implementation of a model where a and σ are functions of time, see Technical Note 16 at www-2.rotman.utoronto.ca/~hull/TechnicalNotes.

[16] Note that in a term structure model the implied σ's are not the same as the implied volatilities calculated from Black's model in Tables 29.1 and 29.2. The procedure for computing implied σ's is as follows. The Black volatilities are converted to prices using Black's model. An iterative procedure is then used to imply the σ parameter in the term structure model from the price.

cannot happen under the model considered, as well as those that can, is known as *outside model hedging* and is standard practice for traders.[17] The reality is that relatively simple one-factor models if used carefully usually give reasonable prices for instruments, but good hedging procedures must explicitly or implicitly assume many factors.

SUMMARY

When valuing derivatives, it is important that the model used be consistent with the initial term structure observed in the market. No-arbitrage models are designed to have this property. They take the initial term structure as given and define how it can evolve.

This chapter has provided a description of a number of one-factor no-arbitrage models of the short rate. These are robust and can be used in conjunction with any set of initial zero rates. The simplest model is the Ho–Lee model. This has the advantage that it is analytically tractable. Its chief disadvantage is that it implies that all rates are equally variable at all times. The Hull–White model is a version of the Ho–Lee model that includes mean reversion. It allows a richer description of the volatility environment while preserving its analytic tractability. Lognormal one-factor models avoid the possibility of negative interest rates, but have no analytic tractability.

FURTHER READING

Black, F., E. Derman, and W. Toy, "A One-Factor Model of Interest Rates and Its Application to Treasury Bond Prices," *Financial Analysts Journal*, January/February 1990: 33–39.

Black, F., and P. Karasinski, "Bond and Option Pricing When Short Rates Are Lognormal," *Financial Analysts Journal*, July/August (1991): 52–59.

Brigo, D., and F. Mercurio, *Interest Rate Models: Theory and Practice*, 2nd edn. New York: Springer, 2006.

Ho, T. S. Y., and S.-B. Lee, "Term Structure Movements and Pricing Interest Rate Contingent Claims," *Journal of Finance*, 41 (December 1986): 1011–29.

Hull, J. C., and A. White, "Bond Option Pricing Based on a Model for the Evolution of Bond Prices," *Advances in Futures and Options Research*, 6 (1993): 1–13.

Hull, J. C., and A. White, "Pricing Interest Rate Derivative Securities," *The Review of Financial Studies*, 3, 4 (1990): 573–92.

Hull, J. C., and A. White, "Using Hull–White Interest Rate Trees," *Journal of Derivatives*, Spring (1996): 26–36.

Rebonato, R., *Interest Rate Option Models*. Chichester: Wiley, 1998.

Practice Questions (Answers in Solutions Manual)

32.1. What is the difference between an equilibrium model and a no-arbitrage model?

32.2. Can the approach described in Section 32.2 for decomposing an option on a coupon-bearing bond into a portfolio of options on zero-coupon bonds be used in conjunction with a two-factor model? Explain your answer.

---

[17] A simple example of outside model hedging is in the way that the Black–Scholes–Merton model is used. The Black–Scholes–Merton model assumes that volatility is constant—but traders regularly calculate vega and hedge against volatility changes.

32.3. Suppose that $a = 0.1$, $b = 0.08$, and $\sigma = 0.015$ in Vasicek's model, with the initial value of the short rate being 5%. Calculate the price of a 1-year European call option on a zero-coupon bond with a principal of $100 that matures in 3 years when the strike price is $87.

32.4. Repeat Problem 32.3 valuing a European put option with a strike of $87. What is the put–call parity relationship between the prices of European call and put options? Show that the put and call option prices satisfy put–call parity in this case.

32.5. Suppose that $a = 0.05$, $b = 0.08$, and $\sigma = 0.015$ in Vasicek's model with the initial short-term interest rate being 6%. Calculate the price of a 2.1-year European call option on a bond that will mature in 3 years. Suppose that the bond pays a coupon of 5% semiannually. The principal of the bond is 100 and the strike price of the option is 99. The strike price is the cash price (not the quoted price) that will be paid for the bond.

32.6. Use the answer to Problem 32.5 and put–call parity arguments to calculate the price of a put option that has the same terms as the call option in Problem 32.5.

32.7. In the Hull–White model, $a = 0.08$ and $\sigma = 0.01$. Calculate the price of a 1-year European call option on a zero-coupon bond that will mature in 5 years when the term structure is flat at 10%, the principal of the bond is $100, and the strike price is $68.

32.8. Suppose that $a = 0.05$ and $\sigma = 0.015$ in the Hull–White model with the initial term structure being flat at 6% with semiannual compounding. Calculate the price of a 2.1-year European call option on a bond that will mature in 3 years. Suppose that the bond pays a coupon of 5% per annum semiannually. The principal of the bond is 100 and the strike price of the option is 99. The strike price is the cash price (not the quoted price) that will be paid for the bond.

32.9. Suppose $a = 0.05$, $\sigma = 0.015$, and the term structure is flat at 10%. Construct a trinomial tree for the Hull–White model where there are two time steps, each 1 year in length.

32.10. Calculate the price of a 2-year zero-coupon bond from the tree in Figure 32.4.

32.11. Calculate the price of a 2-year zero-coupon bond from the tree in Figure 32.7 and verify that it agrees with the initial term structure.

32.12. Calculate the price of an 18-month zero-coupon bond from the tree in Figure 32.8 and verify that it agrees with the initial term structure.

32.13. What does the calibration of a one-factor term structure model involve?

32.14. Use the DerivaGem software to value 1×4, 2×3, 3×2, and 4×1 European swap options to receive fixed and pay floating. Assume that the 1-, 2-, 3-, 4-, and 5-year interest rates are 6%, 5.5%, 6%, 6.5%, and 7%, respectively. The payment frequency on the swap is semiannual and the fixed rate is 6% per annum with semiannual compounding. Use the Hull–White model with $a = 3\%$ and $\sigma = 1\%$. Calculate the volatility implied by Black's model for each option.

32.15. Prove equations (32.15), (32.16), and (32.17).

Further Questions

32.16. Construct a trinomial tree for the Ho–Lee model where $\sigma = 0.02$. Suppose that the initial zero-coupon interest rate for a maturities of 0.5, 1.0, and 1.5 years are 7.5%, 8%, and 8.5%. Use two time steps, each 6 months long. Calculate the value of a zero-coupon bond with a face value of $100 and a remaining life of 6 months at the ends of the final nodes of the tree. Use the tree to value a 1-year European put option with a strike price of 95 on the bond. Compare the price given by your tree with the analytic price given by DerivaGem.

32.17. A trader wishes to compute the price of a 1-year American call option on a 5-year bond with a face value of 100. The bond pays a coupon of 6% semiannually and the (quoted) strike price of the option is $100. The continuously compounded zero rates for maturities of 6 months, 1 year, 2 years, 3 years, 4 years, and 5 years are 4.5%, 5%, 5.5%, 5.8%, 6.1%, and 6.3%. The best-fit reversion rate for either the normal or the lognormal model has been estimated as 5%.

A 1-year European call option with a (quoted) strike price of 100 on the bond is actively traded. Its market price is $0.50. The trader decides to use this option for calibration. Use the DerivaGem software with 10 time steps to answer the following questions:
(a) Assuming a normal model, imply the σ parameter from the price of the European option.
(b) Use the σ parameter to calculate the price of the option when it is American.
(c) Repeat (a) and (b) for the lognormal model. Show that the model used does not significantly affect the price obtained providing it is calibrated to the known European price.
(d) Display the tree for the normal model and calculate the probability of a negative interest rate occurring.
(e) Display the tree for the lognormal model and verify that the option price is correctly calculated at the node where, with the notation of Section 32.4, $i = 9$ and $j = -1$.

32.18. Use the DerivaGem software to value 1×4, 2×3, 3×2, and 4×1 European swap options to receive floating and pay fixed. Assume that the 1-, 2-, 3-, 4-, and 5-year interest rates are 3%, 3.5%, 3.8%, 4.0%, and 4.1%, respectively. The payment frequency on the swap is semiannual and the fixed rate is 4% per annum with semiannual compounding. Use the lognormal model with $a = 5\%$, $\sigma = 15\%$, and 50 time steps. Calculate the volatility implied by Black's model for each option.

32.19. Verify that the DerivaGem software gives Figure 32.9 for the example considered. Use the software to calculate the price of the American bond option for the lognormal and normal models when the strike price is 95, 100, and 105. In the case of the normal model, assume that $a = 5\%$ and $\sigma = 1\%$. Discuss the results in the context of the heavy-tails arguments of Chapter 20.

32.20. Modify Sample Application G in the DerivaGem Application Builder software to test the convergence of the price of the trinomial tree when it is used to price a 2-year call option on a 5-year bond with a face value of 100. Suppose that the strike price (quoted) is 100, the coupon rate is 7% with coupons being paid twice a year. Assume that the zero curve is as in Table 32.2. Compare results for the following cases:
(a) Option is European; normal model with $\sigma = 0.01$ and $a = 0.05$
(b) Option is European; lognormal model with $\sigma = 0.15$ and $a = 0.05$
(c) Option is American; normal model with $\sigma = 0.01$ and $a = 0.05$
(d) Option is American; lognormal model with $\sigma = 0.15$ and $a = 0.05$.

CHAPTER 33

HJM, LMM, and Multiple Zero Curves

The interest rate models discussed in Chapter 32 are widely used for pricing instruments when the simpler models in Chapter 29 are inappropriate. They are easy to implement and, if used carefully, can ensure that most nonstandard interest rate derivatives are priced consistently with actively traded instruments such as interest rate caps, European swap options, and European bond options. Two limitations of the models are:

1. Most involve only one factor (i.e., one source of uncertainty).

2. They do not give the user complete freedom in choosing the volatility structure.

By making the parameters a and σ functions of time, an analyst can use the models so that they fit the volatilities observed in the market today, but as mentioned in Section 32.6 the volatility term structure is then nonstationary. The volatility structure in the future is liable to be quite different from that observed in the market today.

This chapter discusses some general approaches to building term structure models that give the user more flexibility in specifying the volatility environment and allow several factors to be used. When OIS discounting is used, it is often necessary to develop a model describing the evolution of two (or more) yield curves (e.g., the LIBOR zero curve and the OIS zero curve). This chapter discusses how this can be done.

This chapter also covers the agency mortgage-backed security market in the United States and describes how some of the ideas presented in the chapter can be used to price instruments in that market.

33.1 THE HEATH, JARROW, AND MORTON MODEL

In 1990 David Heath, Bob Jarrow, and Andy Morton (HJM) published an important paper describing the no-arbitrage conditions that must be satisfied by a model of the yield curve.[1] To describe their model, we will use the following notation:

$P(t, T)$: Price at time t of a risk-free zero-coupon bond with principal \$1 maturing at time T

---

[1] See D. Heath, R. A. Jarrow, and A. Morton, "Bond Pricing and the Term Structure of Interest Rates: A New Methodology," *Econometrica*, 60, 1 (1992): 77–105.

Ω_t: Vector of past and present values of interest rates and bond prices at time t that are relevant for determining bond price volatilities at that time

$v(t, T, \Omega_t)$: Volatility of $P(t, T)$

$f(t, T_1, T_2)$: Forward rate as seen at time t for the period between time T_1 and time T_2

$F(t, T)$: Instantaneous forward rate as seen at time t for a contract maturing at time T

$r(t)$: Short-term risk-free interest rate at time t

$dz(t)$: Wiener process driving term structure movements.

Processes for Zero-Coupon Bond Prices and Forward Rates

We start by assuming there is just one factor and will use the traditional risk-neutral world. A zero-coupon bond is a traded security providing no income. Its return in the traditional risk-neutral world must therefore be r. This means that its stochastic process has the form

$$dP(t, T) = r(t)P(t, T)\,dt + v(t, T, \Omega_t)P(t, T)\,dz(t) \tag{33.1}$$

As the argument Ω_t indicates, the zero-coupon bond's volatility v can be, in the most general form of the model, any well-behaved function of past and present interest rates and bond prices. Because a bond's price volatility declines to zero at maturity, we must have[2]

$$v(t, t, \Omega_t) = 0$$

From equation (4.5), the forward rate $f(t, T_1, T_2)$ can be related to zero-coupon bond prices as follows:

$$f(t, T_1, T_2) = \frac{\ln[P(t, T_1)] - \ln[P(t, T_2)]}{T_2 - T_1} \tag{33.2}$$

From equation (33.1) and Itô's lemma,

$$d\ln[P(t, T_1)] = \left[r(t) - \frac{v(t, T_1, \Omega_t)^2}{2}\right]dt + v(t, T_1, \Omega_t)\,dz(t)$$

and

$$d\ln[P(t, T_2)] = \left[r(t) - \frac{v(t, T_2, \Omega_t)^2}{2}\right]dt + v(t, T_2, \Omega_t)\,dz(t)$$

so that from equation (33.2)

$$df(t, T_1, T_2) = \frac{v(t, T_2, \Omega_t)^2 - v(t, T_1, \Omega_t)^2}{2(T_2 - T_1)}\,dt + \frac{v(t, T_1, \Omega_t) - v(t, T_2, \Omega_t)}{T_2 - T_1}\,dz(t) \tag{33.3}$$

Equation (33.3) shows that the risk-neutral process for f depends solely on the v's. It depends on r and the P's only to the extent that the v's themselves depend on these variables.

---

[2] The $v(t, t, \Omega_t) = 0$ condition is equivalent to the assumption that all zero-coupon bonds have finite drifts at all times. If the volatility of the bond does not decline to zero at maturity, an infinite drift may be necessary to ensure that the bond's price equals its face value at maturity.

When we put $T_1 = T$ and $T_2 = T + \Delta T$ in equation (33.3) and then take limits as ΔT tends to zero, $f(t, T_1, T_2)$ becomes $F(t, T)$, the coefficient of $dz(t)$ becomes $-v_T(t, T, \Omega_t)$, and the coefficient of dt becomes

$$\frac{1}{2} \frac{\partial [v(t, T, \Omega_t)^2]}{\partial T} = v(t, T, \Omega_t) v_T(t, T, \Omega_t)$$

where the subscript to v denotes a partial derivative. It follows that

$$dF(t, T) = v(t, T, \Omega_t) v_T(t, T, \Omega_t) \, dt - v_T(t, T, \Omega_t) \, dz(t) \qquad \textbf{(33.4)}$$

Once the function $v(t, T, \Omega_t)$ has been specified, the risk-neutral processes for the $F(t, T)$'s are known.

Equation (33.4) shows that there is a link between the drift and standard deviation of an instantaneous forward rate. This is the key HJM result. Integrating $v_\tau(t, \tau, \Omega_t)$ between $\tau = t$ and $\tau = T$ leads to

$$v(t, T, \Omega_t) - v(t, t, \Omega_t) = \int_t^T v_\tau(t, \tau, \Omega_t) \, d\tau$$

Because $v(t, t, \Omega_t) = 0$, this becomes

$$v(t, T, \Omega_t) = \int_t^T v_\tau(t, \tau, \Omega_t) \, d\tau$$

If $m(t, T, \Omega_t)$ and $s(t, T, \Omega_t)$ are the instantaneous drift and standard deviation of $F(t, T)$, so that

$$dF(t, T) = m(t, T, \Omega_t) \, dt + s(t, T, \Omega_t) \, dz$$

then it follows from equation (33.4) that

$$m(t, T, \Omega_t) = s(t, T, \Omega_t) \int_t^T s(t, \tau, \Omega_t) \, d\tau \qquad \textbf{(33.5)}$$

This is the HJM result.

The process for the short rate r in the general HJM model is non-Markov. This means that the process for r at a future time t depends on the path followed by r between now and time t as well as on the the value of r at time t.[3] This is the key problem in implementing a general HJM model. Monte Carlo simulation has to be used. It is difficult to use a tree to represent term structure movements because the tree is usually nonrecombining. Assuming the model has one factor and the tree is binomial as in Figure 33.1, there are 2^n nodes after n time steps (when $n = 30$, 2^n is about 1 billion).

The HJM model in equation (33.4) is deceptively complex. A particular forward rate $F(t, T)$ is Markov in most applications of the model and can be represented by a recombining tree. However, the same tree cannot be used for all forward rates. Setting $s(t, T, \Omega_t)$ equal to a constant, σ, leads to the Ho–Lee model (see Problem 33.3); setting $s(t, T, \Omega_t) = \sigma e^{-a(T-t)}$ leads to the Hull–White model (see Problem 33.4). These are particular Markov cases of HJM where the same recombining tree can be used to represent the short rate, r, and all forward rates.

---

[3] For more details, see Technical Note 17 at www-2.rotman.utoronto.ca/~hull/TechnicalNotes.

Figure 33.1 A nonrecombining tree such as that arising from the general HJM model.

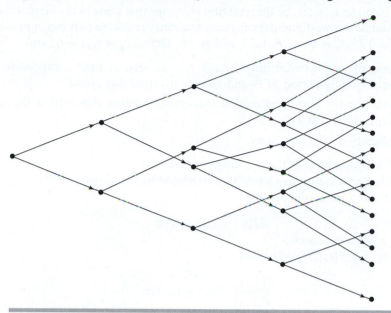

Extension to Several Factors

The HJM result can be extended to the situation where there are several independent factors. Suppose

$$dF(t, T) = m(t, T, \Omega_t)\, dt + \sum_k s_k(t, T, \Omega_t)\, dz_k$$

A similar analysis to that just given (see Problem 33.2) shows that

$$m(t, T, \Omega_t) = \sum_k s_k(t, T, \Omega_t) \int_t^T s_k(t, \tau, \Omega_t)\, d\tau \tag{33.6}$$

33.2 THE LIBOR MARKET MODEL

One drawback of the HJM model is that it is expressed in terms of instantaneous forward rates and these are not directly observable in the market. Another related drawback is that it is difficult to calibrate the model to prices of actively traded instruments. This has led Brace, Gatarek, and Musiela (BGM), Jamshidian, and Miltersen, Sandmann, and Sondermann to propose an alternative.[4] It is known as the *LIBOR market model* (LMM) or the *BGM model* and it is expressed in terms of the forward rates that traders use in conjunction with LIBOR discounting.

---

[4] See A. Brace, D. Gatarek, and M. Musiela "The Market Model of Interest Rate Dynamics," *Mathematical Finance* 7, 2 (1997): 127–55; F. Jamshidian, "LIBOR and Swap Market Models and Measures," *Finance and Stochastics*, 1 (1997): 293–330; and K. Miltersen, K. Sandmann, and D. Sondermann, "Closed Form Solutions for Term Structure Derivatives with LogNormal Interest Rate," *Journal of Finance*, 52, 1 (March 1997): 409–30.

The Model

Define $t_0 = 0$ and let $t_1, t_2, \ldots$ be the reset times for caps that trade in the market today. In the United States, the most popular caps have quarterly resets, so that it is approximately true that $t_1 = 0.25$, $t_2 = 0.5$, $t_3 = 0.75$, and so on. Define $\delta_k = t_{k+1} - t_k$, and

$F_k(t)$: Forward rate between times t_k and t_{k+1} as seen at time t, expressed with a compounding period of δ_k and an actual/actual day count

$m(t)$: Index for the next reset date at time t; this means that $m(t)$ is the smallest integer such that $t \leqslant t_{m(t)}$

$\zeta_k(t)$: Volatility of $F_k(t)$ at time t.

Initially, we will assume that there is only one factor.

As shown in Section 28.4, in a world that is defined by the numeraire $P(t, t_{k+1})$, $F_k(t)$ is a martingale and follows the process

$$dF_k(t) = \zeta_k(t)F_k(t)\,dz \tag{33.7}$$

where dz is a Wiener process.

The process for $P(t, t_k)$ has the form

$$\frac{dP(t, t_k)}{P(t, t_k)} = \cdots + v_k(t)\,dz$$

where $v_k(t)$ is negative because bond prices and interest rates are negatively related.

In practice, it is often most convenient to value interest rate derivatives by working in a world that is always defined by the numeraire equal to a bond maturing at the next reset date. We refer to this as a *rolling risk-neutral world* because the numeraire changes as we roll forward.[5] In this world we can discount from time t_{k+1} to time t_k using the zero rate observed at time t_k for a maturity t_{k+1}. We do not have to worry about what happens to interest rates between times t_k and t_{k+1}.

At time t, the rolling risk-neutral world is a world defined by the numeraire $P(t, t_{m(t)})$. Equation (33.7) gives the process followed by $F_k(t)$ in a world defined by the numeraire $P(t, t_{k+1})$. From Section 28.8, it follows that the process followed by $F_k(t)$ in the rolling risk-neutral world is

$$dF_k(t) = \zeta_k(t)[v_{m(t)}(t) - v_{k+1}(t)]F_k(t)\,dt + \zeta_k(t)F_k(t)\,dz \tag{33.8}$$

The relationship between forward rates and bond prices is

$$\frac{P(t, t_i)}{P(t, t_{i+1})} = 1 + \delta_i F_i(t)$$

or

$$\ln P(t, t_i) - \ln P(t, t_{i+1}) = \ln[1 + \delta_i F_i(t)]$$

Itô's lemma can be used to calculate the process followed by both the left-hand side and

---

[5] In the terminology of Section 28.4, this world corresponds to using a "rolling CD" as the numeraire. A rolling CD (certificate of deposit) is one where we start with \$1, buy a bond maturing at time t_1, reinvest the proceeds at time t_1 in a bond maturing at time t_2, reinvest the proceeds at time t_2 in a bond maturing at time t_3, and so on. (Strictly speaking, the interest rate trees we constructed in Chapter 32 are in a rolling risk-neutral world rather than the traditional risk-neutral world.) The numeraire is a CD rolled over at the end of each time step.

the right-hand side of this equation. Equating the coefficients of dz gives[6]

$$v_i(t) - v_{i+1}(t) = \frac{\delta_i F_i(t) \zeta_i(t)}{1 + \delta_i F_i(t)} \tag{33.9}$$

so that from equation (33.8) the process followed by $F_k(t)$ in the rolling risk-neutral world is

$$\frac{dF_k(t)}{F_k(t)} = \sum_{i=m(t)}^{k} \frac{\delta_i F_i(t) \zeta_i(t) \zeta_k(t)}{1 + \delta_i F_i(t)} dt + \zeta_k(t) \, dz \tag{33.10}$$

The HJM result in equation (33.4) is the limiting case of this as the δ_i tend to zero (see Problem 33.7).

Forward Rate Volatilities

The model can be simplified by assuming that $\zeta_k(t)$ is a function only of the number of whole accrual periods between the next reset date and time t_k. Define Λ_i as the value of $\zeta_k(t)$ when there are i such accrual periods. This means that $\zeta_k(t) = \Lambda_{k-m(t)}$ is a step function.

The Λ_i can (at least in theory) be estimated from the volatilities used to value caplets in Black's model (i.e., from the spot volatilities in Figure 29.3).[7] Suppose that σ_k is the Black volatility for the caplet that corresponds to the period between times t_k and t_{k+1}. Equating variances, we must have

$$\sigma_k^2 t_k = \sum_{i=1}^{k} \Lambda_{k-i}^2 \delta_{i-1} \tag{33.11}$$

This equation can be used to obtain the Λ's iteratively.

Example 33.1

Assume that the δ_i are all equal and the Black caplet spot volatilities for the first three caplets are 24%, 22%, and 20%. This means that $\Lambda_0 = 24\%$. Since

$$\Lambda_0^2 + \Lambda_1^2 = 2 \times 0.22^2$$

Λ_1 is 19.80%. Also, since

$$\Lambda_0^2 + \Lambda_1^2 + \Lambda_2^2 = 3 \times 0.20^2$$

Λ_2 is 15.23%.

Example 33.2

Consider the data in Table 33.1 on caplet volatilities σ_k. These exhibit the hump discussed in Section 29.2. The Λ's are shown in the second row. Notice that the hump in the Λ's is more pronounced than the hump in the σ's.

---

[6] Since the v's and ζ's have opposite signs, the bond price volatility becomes larger (in absolute terms) as the time to maturity increases. This is as expected.

[7] In practice the Λ's are determined using a least-squares calibration, as we will discuss later.

Table 33.1   Volatility data; accrual period = 1 year.

Year, k:	1	2	3	4	5	6	7	8	9	10
σ_k (%):	15.50	18.25	17.91	17.74	17.27	16.79	16.30	16.01	15.76	15.54
Λ_{k-1} (%):	15.50	20.64	17.21	17.22	15.25	14.15	12.98	13.81	13.60	13.40

Implementation of the Model

The LIBOR market model can be implemented using Monte Carlo simulation. Expressed in terms of the Λ_i's, equation (33.10) is

$$\frac{dF_k(t)}{F_k(t)} = \sum_{i=m(t)}^{k} \frac{\delta_i F_i(t) \Lambda_{i-m(t)} \Lambda_{k-m(t)}}{1 + \delta_i F_i(t)} \, dt + \Lambda_{k-m(t)} \, dz \tag{33.12}$$

so that from Itô's lemma

$$d \ln F_k(t) = \left[\sum_{i=m(t)}^{k} \frac{\delta_i F_i(t) \Lambda_{i-m(t)} \Lambda_{k-m(t)}}{1 + \delta_i F_i(t)} - \frac{(\Lambda_{k-m(t)})^2}{2} \right] dt + \Lambda_{k-m(t)} \, dz \tag{33.13}$$

If, as an approximation, we assume in the calculation of the drift of $\ln F_k(t)$ that $F_i(t) = F_i(t_j)$ for $t_j < t < t_{j+1}$, then

$$F_k(t_{j+1}) = F_k(t_j) \exp \left[\left(\sum_{i=j+1}^{k} \frac{\delta_i F_i(t_j) \Lambda_{i-j-1} \Lambda_{k-j-1}}{1 + \delta_i F_i(t_j)} - \frac{\Lambda_{k-j-1}^2}{2} \right) \delta_j + \Lambda_{k-j-1} \epsilon \sqrt{\delta_j} \right]$$

$$\tag{33.14}$$

where ϵ is a random sample from a normal distribution with mean equal to zero and standard deviation equal to one. In the Monte Carlo simulation, this equation is used to calculate forward rates at time t_1 from those at time zero; it is then used to calculate forward rates at time t_2 from those at time t_1; and so on.

Extension to Several Factors

The LIBOR market model can be extended to incorporate several independent factors. Suppose that there are p factors and $\zeta_{k,q}$ is the component of the volatility of $F_k(t)$ attributable to the qth factor. Equation (33.10) becomes (see Problem 33.11)

$$\frac{dF_k(t)}{F_k(t)} = \sum_{i=m(t)}^{k} \frac{\delta_i F_i(t) \sum_{q=1}^{p} \zeta_{i,q}(t) \zeta_{k,q}(t)}{1 + \delta_i F_i(t)} \, dt + \sum_{q=1}^{p} \zeta_{k,q}(t) \, dz_q \tag{33.15}$$

Define $\lambda_{i,q}$ as the qth component of the volatility when there are i accrual periods between the next reset date and the maturity of the forward contract. Equation (33.14) then becomes

$$F_k(t_{j+1}) = F_k(t_j)$$

$$\times \exp\left[\left(\sum_{i=j+1}^{k} \frac{\delta_i F_i(t_j) \sum_{q=1}^{p} \lambda_{i-j-1,q}\lambda_{k-j-1,q}}{1+\delta_i F_i(t_j)} - \frac{\sum_{q=1}^{p} \lambda_{k-j-1,q}^2}{2}\right)\delta_j + \sum_{q=1}^{p} \lambda_{k-j-1,q}\,\epsilon_q\sqrt{\delta_j}\right]$$

$$(33.16)$$

where the ϵ_q are random samples from a normal distribution with mean equal to zero and standard deviation equal to one.

The approximation that the drift of a forward rate remains constant within each accrual period allows us to jump from one reset date to the next in the simulation. This is convenient because as already mentioned the rolling risk-neutral world allows us to discount from one reset date to the next. Suppose that we wish to simulate a zero curve for N accrual periods. On each trial we start with the forward rates at time zero. These are $F_0(0)$, $F_1(0), \ldots,\ F_{N-1}(0)$ and are calculated from the initial zero curve. Equation (33.16) is used to calculate $F_1(t_1)$, $F_2(t_1), \ldots, F_{N-1}(t_1)$. Equation (33.16) is then used again to calculate $F_2(t_2)$, $F_3(t_2), \ldots, F_{N-1}(t_2)$, and so on, until $F_{N-1}(t_{N-1})$ is obtained. Note that as we move through time the zero curve gets shorter and shorter. For example, suppose each accrual period is 3 months and $N = 40$. We start with a 10-year zero curve. At the 6-year point (at time t_{24}), the simulation gives us information on a 4-year zero curve.

The drift approximation that we have used (i.e., $F_i(t) = F_i(t_j)$ for $t_j < t < t_{j+1}$) can be tested by valuing caplets using equation (33.16) and comparing the prices to those given by Black's model. The value of $F_k(t_k)$ is the realized rate for the time period between t_k and t_{k+1} and enables the caplet payoff at time t_{k+1} to be calculated. This payoff is discounted back to time zero, one accrual period at a time. The caplet value is the average of the discounted payoffs. The results of this type of analysis show that the cap values from Monte Carlo simulation are not significantly different from those given by Black's model. This is true even when the accrual periods are 1 year in length and a very large number of trials is used.[8] This suggests that the drift approximation is innocuous in most situations.

Ratchet Caps, Sticky Caps, and Flexi Caps

The LIBOR market model can be used to value some types of nonstandard caps. Consider ratchet caps and sticky caps. These incorporate rules for determining how the cap rate for each caplet is set. In a *ratchet cap* it equals the LIBOR rate at the previous reset date plus a spread. In a *sticky cap* it equals the previous capped rate plus a spread. Suppose that the cap rate at time t_j is K_j, the LIBOR rate at time t_j is R_j, and the spread is s. In a ratchet cap, $K_{j+1} = R_j + s$. In a sticky cap, $K_{j+1} = \min(R_j, K_j) + s$.

Tables 33.2 and 33.3 provide valuations of a ratchet cap and sticky cap using the LIBOR market model with one, two, and three factors, and LIBOR discounting. The principal is $100. The term structure is assumed to be flat at 5% per annum continuously compounded, or 5.127% annually compounded, and the caplet volatilities are

---

[8] See J. C. Hull and A. White, "Forward Rate Volatilities, Swap Rate Volatilities, and the Implementation of the LIBOR Market Model," *Journal of Fixed Income*, 10, 2 (September 2000): 46–62. The only exception is when the cap volatilities are very high.

Table 33.2 Valuation of ratchet caplets.

Caplet start time (years)	One factor	Two factors	Three factors
1	0.196	0.194	0.195
2	0.207	0.207	0.209
3	0.201	0.205	0.210
4	0.194	0.198	0.205
5	0.187	0.193	0.201
6	0.180	0.189	0.193
7	0.172	0.180	0.188
8	0.167	0.174	0.182
9	0.160	0.168	0.175
10	0.153	0.162	0.169

as in Table 33.1. The interest rate is reset annually. The spread is 25 basis points applied to the annually compounded rate. Tables 33.4 and 33.5 show how the volatility was split into components when two- and three-factor models were used. The results are based on 100,000 Monte Carlo simulations incorporating the antithetic variable technique described in Section 21.7. The standard error of each price is about 0.001.

A third type of nonstandard cap is a *flexi cap*. This is like a regular cap except that there is a limit on the total number of caplets that can be exercised. Consider an annual-pay flexi cap when the principal is $100, the term structure is flat at 5%, and the cap volatilities are as in Tables 33.1, 33.4, and 33.5. Suppose that all in-the-money caplets are exercised up to a maximum of five. With one, two, and three factors, the LIBOR market model gives the price of the instrument as 3.43, 3.58, and 3.61, respectively (see Problem 33.15 for other types of flexi caps).

Table 33.3 Valuation of sticky caplets.

Caplet start time (years)	One factor	Two factors	Three factors
1	0.196	0.194	0.195
2	0.336	0.334	0.336
3	0.412	0.413	0.418
4	0.458	0.462	0.472
5	0.484	0.492	0.506
6	0.498	0.512	0.524
7	0.502	0.520	0.533
8	0.501	0.523	0.537
9	0.497	0.523	0.537
10	0.488	0.519	0.534

Table 33.4   Volatility components in two-factor model.

Year, k:	1	2	3	4	5	6	7	8	9	10
$\lambda_{k-1,1}$ (%):	14.10	19.52	16.78	17.11	15.25	14.06	12.65	13.06	12.36	11.63
$\lambda_{k-1,2}$ (%):	−6.45	−6.70	−3.84	−1.96	0.00	1.61	2.89	4.48	5.65	6.65
Total volatility (%):	15.50	20.64	17.21	17.22	15.25	14.15	12.98	13.81	13.60	13.40

The pricing of a plain vanilla cap depends only on the total volatility and is independent of the number of factors. This is because the price of a plain vanilla caplet depends on the behavior of only one forward rate. The prices of caplets in the nonstandard instruments we have looked at are different in that they depend on the joint probability distribution of several different forward rates. As a result they do depend on the number of factors.

Valuing European Swap Options

There is an analytic approximation for valuing European swap options in the LIBOR market model.[9] Assume that LIBOR discounting is used. Let T_0 be the maturity of the swap option and assume that the payment dates for the swap are $T_1, T_2, \ldots, T_N$. Define $\tau_i = T_{i+1} - T_i$. From equation (28.23), the swap rate at time t is given by

$$s(t) = \frac{P(t, T_0) - P(t, T_N)}{\sum_{i=0}^{N-1} \tau_i P(t, T_{i+1})}$$

It is also true that

$$\frac{P(t, T_i)}{P(t, T_0)} = \prod_{j=0}^{i-1} \frac{1}{1 + \tau_j G_j(t)}$$

Table 33.5   Volatility components in a three-factor model.

Year, k:	1	2	3	4	5	6	7	8	9	10
$\lambda_{k-1,1}$ (%):	13.65	19.28	16.72	16.98	14.85	13.95	12.61	12.90	11.97	10.97
$\lambda_{k-1,2}$ (%):	−6.62	−7.02	−4.06	−2.06	0.00	1.69	3.06	4.70	5.81	6.66
$\lambda_{k-1,3}$ (%):	3.19	2.25	0.00	−1.98	−3.47	−1.63	0.00	1.51	2.80	3.84
Total volatility (%):	15.50	20.64	17.21	17.22	15.25	14.15	12.98	13.81	13.60	13.40

[9] See J. C. Hull and A. White, "Forward Rate Volatilities, Swap Rate Volatilities, and the Implementation of the LIBOR Market Model," *Journal of Fixed Income*, 10, 2 (September 2000): 46–62. Other analytic approximations have been suggested by A. Brace, D. Gatarek, and M. Musiela "The Market Model of Interest Rate Dynamics," *Mathematical Finance*, 7, 2 (1997): 127–55 and L. B. G. Andersen and J. Andreasen, "Volatility Skews and Extensions of the LIBOR Market Model," *Applied Mathematical Finance*, 7, 1 (March 2000), 1–32.

for $1 \leqslant i \leqslant N$, where $G_j(t)$ is the forward rate at time t for the period between T_j and T_{j+1}. These two equations together define a relationship between $s(t)$ and the $G_j(t)$. Applying Itô's lemma (see Problem 33.12), the variance $V(t)$ of the swap rate $s(t)$ is given by

$$V(t) = \sum_{q=1}^{p} \left[\sum_{k=0}^{N-1} \frac{\tau_k \beta_{k,q}(t) G_k(t) \gamma_k(t)}{1 + \tau_k G_k(t)} \right]^2 \tag{33.17}$$

where

$$\gamma_k(t) = \frac{\prod_{j=0}^{N-1}[1 + \tau_j G_j(t)]}{\prod_{j=0}^{N-1}[1 + \tau_j G_j(t)] - 1} - \frac{\sum_{i=0}^{k-1} \tau_i \prod_{j=i+1}^{N-1}[1 + \tau_j G_j(t)]}{\sum_{i=0}^{N-1} \tau_i \prod_{j=i+1}^{N}[1 + \tau_j G_j(t)]}$$

and $\beta_{j,q}(t)$ is the qth component of the volatility of $G_j(t)$. We approximate $V(t)$ by setting $G_j(t) = G_j(0)$ for all j and t. The swap volatility that is substituted into the standard market model for valuing a swaption is then

$$\sqrt{\frac{1}{T_0} \int_{t=0}^{T_0} V(t) \, dt}$$

or

$$\sqrt{\frac{1}{T_0} \int_{t=0}^{T_0} \sum_{q=1}^{p} \left[\sum_{k=0}^{N-1} \frac{\tau_k \beta_{k,q}(t) G_k(0) \gamma_k(0)}{1 + \tau_k G_k(0)} \right]^2 dt} \tag{33.18}$$

In the situation where the length of the accrual period for the swap underlying the swaption is the same as the length of the accrual period for a cap, $\beta_{k,q}(t)$ is the qth component of volatility of a cap forward rate when the time to maturity is $T_k - t$. This can be looked up in a table such as Table 33.5

The accrual periods for the swaps underlying broker quotes for European swap options do not always match the accrual periods for the caps and floors underlying broker quotes. For example, in the United States, the benchmark caps and floors have quarterly resets, while the swaps underlying the benchmark European swap options have semiannual resets. Fortunately, the valuation result for European swap options can be extended to the situation where each swap accrual period includes M subperiods that could be accrual periods in a typical cap. Define $\tau_{j,m}$ as the length of the mth subperiod in the jth accrual period so that

$$\tau_j = \sum_{m=1}^{M} \tau_{j,m}$$

Define $G_{j,m}(t)$ as the forward rate observed at time t for the $\tau_{j,m}$ accrual period. Because

$$1 + \tau_j G_j(t) = \prod_{m=1}^{M}[1 + \tau_{j,m} G_{j,m}(t)]$$

the analysis leading to equation (33.18) can be modified so that the volatility of $s(t)$ is obtained in terms of the volatilities of the $G_{j,m}(t)$ rather than the volatilities of the $G_j(t)$.

The swap volatility to be substituted into the standard market model for valuing a swap option proves to be (see Problem 33.13)

$$\sqrt{\frac{1}{T_0} \int_{t=0}^{T_0} \sum_{q=1}^{p} \left[\sum_{k=n}^{N-1} \sum_{m=1}^{M} \frac{\tau_{k,m} \beta_{k,m,q}(t) G_{k,m}(0) \gamma_k(0)}{1 + \tau_{k,m} G_{k,m}(0)} \right]^2 dt} \tag{33.19}$$

Here $\beta_{j,m,q}(t)$ is the qth component of the volatility of $G_{j,m}(t)$. It is the qth component of the volatility of a cap forward rate when the time to maturity is from t to the beginning of the mth subperiod in the (T_j, T_{j+1}) swap accrual period.

The expressions (33.18) and (33.19) for the swap volatility do involve the approximations that $G_j(t) = G_j(0)$ and $G_{j,m}(t) = G_{j,m}(0)$. Hull and White compared the prices of European swap options calculated using (33.18) and (33.19) with the prices calculated from a Monte Carlo simulation and found the two to be very close. Once the LIBOR market model has been calibrated, (33.18) and (33.19) therefore provide a quick way of valuing European swap options. Analysts can determine whether European swap options are overpriced or underpriced relative to caps. As we shall see shortly, they can also use the results to calibrate the model to the market prices of swap options. The analysis can be extended to cover OIS discounting.

Calibrating the Model

The variable Λ_j is the volatility at time t of the forward rate F_j for the period between t_k and t_{k+1} when there are j whole accrual periods between t and t_k. To calibrate the LIBOR market model, it is necessary to determine the Λ_j and how they are split into $\lambda_{j,q}$. The Λ's are usually determined from current market data, whereas the split into λ's is determined from historical data.

Consider first the determination of the λ's from the Λ's. A principal components analysis (see Section 22.9) on forward rate data can be used. The model is

$$\Delta F_j = \sum_{q=1}^{M} \alpha_{j,q} x_q$$

where M is the total number of factors (which equals the number of different forward rates), ΔF_j is the change in the jth forward rate F_j, $\alpha_{j,q}$ is the factor loading for the jth forward rate and the qth factor, x_q is the factor score for the qth factor. Define s_q as the standard deviation of the qth factor score. If the number of factors used in the LIBOR market model, p, is equal to the total number of factors, M, it is correct to set

$$\lambda_{j,q} = \alpha_{j,q} s_q$$

for $1 \leqslant j, q \leqslant M$. When, as is usual, $p < M$, the $\lambda_{j,q}$ must be scaled so that

$$\Lambda_j = \sqrt{\sum_{q=1}^{p} \lambda_{j,q}^2}$$

This involves setting

$$\lambda_{j,q} = \frac{\Lambda_j s_q \alpha_{j,q}}{\sqrt{\sum_{q=1}^{p} s_q^2 \alpha_{j,q}^2}} \tag{33.20}$$

Consider next the estimation of the Λ's. Equation (33.11) provides one way that they can be theoretically determined so that they are consistent with caplet prices. In practice, this is not usually used because it often leads to wild swings in the Λ's and sometimes there is no set of Λ's exactly consistent with cap quotes. A commonly used calibration procedure is similar to that described in Section 32.6. Suppose that U_i is the market price of the ith calibrating instrument (typically a cap or European swaption) and V_i is the model price. The Λ's are chosen to minimize

$$\sum_i (U_i - V_i)^2 + P$$

where P is a penalty function chosen to ensure that the Λ's are "well behaved." Similarly to Section 32.6, P might have the form

$$P = \sum_i w_{1,i}(\Lambda_{i+1} - \Lambda_i)^2 + \sum_i w_{2,i}(\Lambda_{i+1} + \Lambda_{i-1} - 2\Lambda_i)^2$$

When the calibrating instrument is a European swaption, formulas (33.18) and (33.19) make the minimization feasible using the Levenberg–Marquardt procedure. Equation (33.20) is used to determine the λ's from the Λ's.

Volatility Skews

Brokers provide quotes on caps that are not at the money as well as on caps that are at the money. In some markets a volatility skew is observed, that is, the quoted (Black) volatility for a cap or a floor is a declining function of the strike price. This can be handled using the CEV model. (See Section 27.1 for the application of the CEV model to equities.) The model is

$$dF_i(t) = \cdots + \sum_{q=1}^{p} \zeta_{i,q}(t)F_i(t)^\alpha \, dz_q \qquad \textbf{(33.21)}$$

where α is a constant $(0 < \alpha < 1)$. It turns out that this model can be handled very similarly to the lognormal model. Caps and floors can be valued analytically using the cumulative noncentral χ^2 distribution. There are similar analytic approximations to those given above for the prices of European swap options.[10]

Bermudan Swap Options

A popular interest rate derivative is a Bermudan swap option. This is a swap option that can be exercised on some or all of the payment dates of the underlying swap. Bermudan swap options are difficult to value using the LIBOR market model because the LIBOR market model relies on Monte Carlo simulation and it is difficult to evaluate early exercise decisions when Monte Carlo simulation is used. Fortunately, the procedures described in Section 27.8 can be used. Longstaff and Schwartz apply the least-squares approach when there are a large number of factors. The value of not exercising on a particular payment date is assumed to be a polynomial function of the

---

[10] For details, see L. B. G. Andersen and J. Andreasen, "Volatility Skews and Extensions of the LIBOR Market Model," *Applied Mathematical Finance*, 7, 1 (2000): 1–32; J. C. Hull and A. White, "Forward Rate Volatilities, Swap Rate Volatilities, and the Implementation of the LIBOR Market Model," *Journal of Fixed Income*, 10, 2 (September 2000): 46–62.

values of the factors.[11] Andersen shows that the optimal early exercise boundary approach can be used. He experiments with a number of ways of parameterizing the early exercise boundary and finds that good results are obtained when the early exercise decision is assumed to depend only on the intrinsic value of the option.[12] Most traders value Bermudan options using one of the one-factor no-arbitrage models discussed in Chapter 32. However, the accuracy of one-factor models for pricing Bermudan swap options has been a controversial issue.[13]

33.3 HANDLING MULTIPLE ZERO CURVES

The label "LIBOR Market Model" dates back to the time when LIBOR was used as a proxy for the risk-free rate. By modeling LIBOR, analysts were able to value all derivatives that provided payoffs dependent on LIBOR. There was assumed to be a single LIBOR zero curve and rates of all maturities could be determined, as indicated in Section 31.1, from the assumed behavior of the LIBOR short rate.

Since the 2007 to 2008 crisis, derivatives practitioners have switched to using OIS as a proxy for the risk-free rate and have built credit risk into their LIBOR estimates. Prior to the crisis, the 12-month LIBOR–OIS spread was sometimes greater and sometimes less than the 1-month LIBOR–OIS spread. Since the crisis, as indicated in Figure 33.2, this has not been the case. The 12-month spread has been greater than the 6-month spread, which has been greater than the 3-month spread, which in turn has been greater than the 1-month spread. This ranking is simply a reflection of the fact that the longer an unsecured loan is made to a AA-rated bank, the greater is the spread necessary to compensate for credit risk.

Analysts have to keep track of 1-month, 3-month, 6-month, and 12-month LIBOR forward rates, as well as OIS rates, in all the currencies in which they transact interest rate derivatives. The HJM or LMM models can be used to model OIS rates in the way described in this chapter. (The LIBOR market model should then be called the OIS market model.) Suppose that a derivative of interest has a payoff dependent on 3-month LIBOR. Once OIS rates have been modeled, one simple approach would be to assume that the future 3-month LIBOR–OIS spreads equal to forward spreads observed in the market today. An alternative is to base a model for forward spreads on one or more factors similarly to the models in equations (33.10) and (33.15) for forward interest rates, so that

$$\frac{dF_k(t)}{F_k(t)} = \cdots + \sum_{q=1}^{p} \zeta_{k,q}(t)\, dz_q$$

where, for the purposes of this equation, we define $F_k(t)$ as the forward spread between

---

[11] See F. A. Longstaff and E. S. Schwartz, "Valuing American Options by Simulation: A Simple Least Squares Approach," *Review of Financial Studies*, 14, 1 (2001): 113–47.

[12] L. B. G. Andersen, "A Simple Approach to the Pricing of Bermudan Swaptions in the Multifactor LIBOR Market Model," *Journal of Computational Finance*, 3, 2 (Winter 2000): 5–32.

[13] For opposing viewpoints, see "Factor Dependence of Bermudan Swaptions: Fact or Fiction," by L. B. G. Andersen and J. Andreasen, and "Throwing Away a Billion Dollars: The Cost of Suboptimal Exercise Strategies in the Swaption Market," by F. A. Longstaff, P. Santa-Clara, and E. S. Schwartz. Both articles are in *Journal of Financial Economics*, 62, 1 (October 2001).

Figure 33.2   Post-crisis LIBOR–OIS spreads for different tenors (basis points).

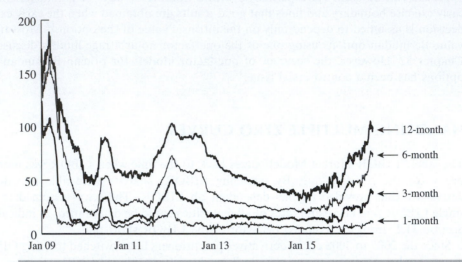

times t_k and t_{k+1} as seen at time t and $\zeta_{k,q}$ as the qth component of the volatility of this forward spread. All the results we have given in Section 33.2 for calculating the process followed by interest rates under the rolling risk-neutral measure then apply to spreads. Correlations between the factors driving OIS rates and the factors driving spreads can be built into the simulation model.

33.4   AGENCY MORTGAGE-BACKED SECURITIES

One application of the models presented in this chapter is to the agency mortgage-backed security (agency MBS) market in the United States.

An agency MBS is similar to the ABS considered in Chapter 8 except that payments are guaranteed by a government-related agency such as the Government National Mortgage Association (GNMA) or the Federal National Mortgage Association (FNMA) so that investors are protected against defaults. This makes an agency MBS sound like a regular fixed-income security issued by the government. In fact, there is a critical difference between an agency MBS and a regular fixed-income investment. This difference is that the mortgages in an agency MBS pool have prepayment privileges. These prepayment privileges can be quite valuable to the householder. In the United States, mortgages typically last for 30 years and can be prepaid at any time. This means that the householder has a 30-year American-style option to put the mortgage back to the lender at its face value.

Prepayments on mortgages occur for a variety of reasons. Sometimes interest rates fall and the owner of the house decides to refinance at a lower rate. On other occasions, a mortgage is prepaid simply because the house is being sold. A critical element in valuing an agency MBS is the determination of what is known as the *prepayment function*. This is a function describing expected prepayments on the underlying pool of mortgages at a time t in terms of the yield curve at time t and other relevant variables.

A prepayment function is very unreliable as a predictor of actual prepayment experience for an individual mortgage. When many similar mortgage loans are combined in the same pool, there is a "law of large numbers" effect at work and prepayments can be predicted more accurately from an analysis of historical data. As mentioned, prepayments are not always motivated by pure interest rate considerations. Nevertheless, there is a tendency for prepayments to be more likely when interest rates are low than when they are high. This means that investors require a higher rate of interest on an agency MBS than on other fixed-income securities to compensate for the prepayment options they have written.

Collateralized Mortgage Obligations

The simplest type of agency MBS is referred to as a *pass-through*. All investors receive the same return and bear the same prepayment risk. Not all mortgage-backed securities work in this way. In a *collateralized mortgage obligation* (CMO) the investors are divided into a number of classes and rules are developed for determining how principal repayments are channeled to different classes. A CMO creates classes of securities that bear different amounts of prepayment risk in the same way that the ABS considered in Chapter 8 creates classes of securities bearing different amounts of credit risk.

As an example of a CMO, consider an agency MBS where investors are divided into three classes: class A, class B, and class C. All the principal repayments (both those that are scheduled and those that are prepayments) are channeled to class A investors until investors in this class have been completely paid off. Principal repayments are then channeled to class B investors until these investors have been completely paid off. Finally, principal repayments are channeled to class C investors. In this situation, class A investors bear the most prepayment risk. The class A securities can be expected to last for a shorter time than the class B securities, and these, in turn, can be expected to last less long than the class C securities.

The objective of this type of structure is to create classes of securities that are more attractive to institutional investors than those created by a simpler pass-through MBS. The prepayment risks assumed by the different classes depend on the par value in each class. For example, class C bears very little prepayment risk if the par values in classes A, B, and C are 400, 300, and 100, respectively. Class C bears rather more prepayment risk in the situation where the par values in the classes are 100, 200, and 500.

The creators of mortgage-backed securities have created many more exotic structures than the one we have just described. Business Snapshot 33.1 gives an example.

Valuing Agency Mortgage-Backed Securities

Agency MBSs are usually valued by modeling the behavior of Treasury rates using Monte Carlo simulation. The HJM/LMM approach can be used. Consider what happens on one simulation trial. Each month, expected prepayments are calculated from the current yield curve and the history of yield curve movements. These prepayments determine the expected cash flows to the holder of the agency MBS and the cash flows are discounted at the Treasury rate plus a spread to time zero to obtain a sample value for the agency MBS. An estimate of the value of the agency MBS is the average of the sample values over many simulation trials.

Business Snapshot 33.1   IOs and POs

In what is known as a *stripped MBS*, principal payments are separated from interest payments. All principal payments are channeled to one class of security, known as a *principal only* (PO). All interest payments are channeled to another class of security known as an *interest only* (IO). Both IOs and POs are risky investments. As prepayment rates increase, a PO becomes more valuable and an IO becomes less valuable. As prepayment rates decrease, the reverse happens. In a PO, a fixed amount of principal is returned to the investor, but the timing is uncertain. A high rate of prepayments on the underlying pool leads to the principal being received early (which is, of course, good news for the holder of the PO). A low rate of prepayments on the underlying pool delays the return of the principal and reduces the yield provided by the PO. In the case of an IO, the total of the cash flows received by the investor is uncertain. The higher the rate of prepayments, the lower the total cash flows received by the investor, and vice versa.

Option-Adjusted Spread

In addition to calculating theoretical prices for mortgage-backed securities and other bonds with embedded options, traders also like to compute what is known as the *option-adjusted spread* (OAS). This is a measure of the spread over the yields on government Treasury bonds provided by the instrument when all options have been taken into account.

To calculate an OAS for an instrument, it is priced as described above using Treasury rates plus a spread for discounting. The price of the instrument given by the model is compared to the price in the market. A series of iterations is then used to determine the value of the spread that causes the model price to be equal to the market price. This spread is the OAS.

SUMMARY

The HJM and LMM models provide approaches to valuing interest rate derivatives that give the user complete freedom in choosing the volatility term structure. The LMM model has two key advantages over the HJM model. First, it is developed in terms of the forward rates that determine the pricing of caps, rather than in terms of instantaneous forward rates. Second, it is relatively easy to calibrate to the price of caps or European swap options. The HJM and LMM models both have the disadvantage that they cannot be represented as recombining trees. In practice, this means that they must usually be implemented using Monte Carlo simulation and require much more computation time than the models in Chapter 32.

Since the credit crisis that started in 2007, the OIS rate has been used as the risk-free discount rate for collateralized derivatives. This means that it is sometimes necessary to model the joint evolution of the OIS zero curve and the LIBOR–OIS spreads.

The agency mortgage-backed security market in the United States has given birth to many exotic interest rate derivatives: CMOs, IOs, POs, and so on. These instruments provide cash flows to the holder that depend on the prepayments on a pool of mortgages. These prepayments depend on, among other things, the level of interest rates. Because they are heavily path dependent, agency mortgage-backed securities usually have to be valued using Monte Carlo simulation. These are, therefore, ideal candidates for applications of the HJM and LMM models.

FURTHER READING

Andersen, L.B.G., "A Simple Approach to the Pricing of Bermudan Swaption in the Multi-Factor LIBOR Market Model," *The Journal of Computational Finance*, 3, 2 (2000): 5–32.

Andersen, L.B.G., and J. Andreasen, "Volatility Skews and Extensions of the LIBOR Market Model," *Applied Mathematical Finance*, 7, 1 (March 2000): 1–32.

Andersen, L.B.G., and V. Piterbarg, *Interest Rate Modeling*, Vols. I–III. New York: Atlantic Financial Press, 2010.

Brace A., D. Gatarek, and M. Musiela "The Market Model of Interest Rate Dynamics," *Mathematical Finance*, 7, 2 (1997): 127–55.

Duffie, D. and R. Kan, "A Yield-Factor Model of Interest Rates," *Mathematical Finance* 6, 4 (1996), 379–406.

Heath, D., R. Jarrow, and A. Morton, "Bond Pricing and the Term Structure of Interest Rates: A Discrete Time Approximation," *Journal of Financial and Quantitative Analysis*, 25, 4 (December 1990): 419–40.

Heath, D., R. Jarrow, and A. Morton, "Bond Pricing and the Term Structure of Interest Rates: A New Methodology," *Econometrica*, 60, 1 (1992): 77–105.

Hull, J.C., and A. White, "Forward Rate Volatilities, Swap Rate Volatilities, and the Implementation of the LIBOR Market Model," *Journal of Fixed Income*, 10, 2 (September 2000): 46–62.

Jamshidian, F., "LIBOR and Swap Market Models and Measures," *Finance and Stochastics*, 1 (1997): 293–330.

Jarrow, R.A., and S.M. Turnbull, "Delta, Gamma, and Bucket Hedging of Interest Rate Derivatives," *Applied Mathematical Finance*, 1 (1994): 21–48.

Mercurio, F., and Z. Xie, "The Basis Goes Stochastic," *Risk*, 25, 12 (December 2012): 78–83.

Miltersen, K., K. Sandmann, and D. Sondermann, "Closed Form Solutions for Term Structure Derivatives with Lognormal Interest Rates," *Journal of Finance*, 52, 1 (March 1997): 409–30.

Rebonato, R., *Modern Pricing of Interest Rate Derivatives: The LIBOR Market Model and Beyond*. Princeton Umiversity Press, 2002.

Practice Questions (Answers in Solutions Manual)

33.1. Explain the difference between a Markov and a non-Markov model of the short rate.

33.2. Prove the relationship between the drift and volatility of the forward rate for the multifactor version of HJM in equation (33.6).

33.3. "When the forward rate volatility $s(t, T)$ in HJM is constant, the Ho–Lee model results." Verify that this is true by showing that HJM gives a process for bond prices that is consistent with the Ho–Lee model in Chapter 32.

33.4. "When the forward rate volatility, $s(t, T)$, in HJM is $\sigma e^{-a(T-t)}$, the Hull–White model results." Verify that this is true by showing that HJM gives a process for bond prices that is consistent with the Hull–White model in Chapter 32.

33.5. What is the advantage of LMM over HJM?

33.6. Provide an intuitive explanation of why a ratchet cap increases in value as the number of factors increase.

33.7. Show that equation (33.10) reduces to (33.4) as the δ_i tend to zero.

33.8. Explain why a sticky cap is more expensive than a similar ratchet cap.

33.9. Explain why IOs and POs have opposite sensitivities to the rate of prepayments.

33.10. "An option adjusted spread is analogous to the yield on a bond." Explain this statement.

33.11. Prove equation (33.15).

33.12. Prove the formula for the variance $V(T)$ of the swap rate in equation (33.17).

33.13. Show that the swap volatility expression (33.19) in Section 33.2 is correct.

Further Questions

33.14. In an annual-pay cap, the Black volatilities for at-the-money caplets which start in 1, 2, 3, and 5 years and end 1 year later are 18%, 20%, 22%, and 20%, respectively. Estimate the volatility of a 1-year forward rate in the LIBOR Market Model when the time to the start of the period covered by the forward rate is (a) 0 to 1 year, (b) 1 to 2 years, (c) 2 to 3 years, and (d) 3 to 5 years. Assume that the zero curve is flat at 5% per annum (annually compounded). Use DerivaGem with LIBOR discounting to estimate flat volatilities for 2-, 3-, 4-, 5-, and 6-year at-the-money caps.

33.15. In the flexi cap considered in Section 33.2 the holder is obligated to exercise the first N in-the-money caplets. After that no further caplets can be exercised. (In the example, $N = 5$.) Two other ways that flexi caps are sometimes defined are:

(a) The holder can choose whether any caplet is exercised, but there is a limit of N on the total number of caplets that can be exercised.

(b) Once the holder chooses to exercise a caplet all subsequent in-the-money caplets must be exercised up to a maximum of N.

Discuss the problems in valuing these types of flexi caps. Of the three types of flexi caps, which would you expect to be most expensive? Which would you expect to be least expensive?

CHAPTER 34

Swaps Revisited

Swaps have been central to the success of over-the-counter derivatives markets. They have proved to be very flexible instruments for managing risk. Based on the range of different contracts that now trade and the total volume of business transacted each year, swaps are arguably one of the most successful innovations in financial markets ever.

Chapter 7 discussed how plain vanilla LIBOR-for-fixed interest rate swaps can be valued. The standard approach can be summarized as: "Assume forward rates will be realized." The steps are as follows:

1. Calculate the swap's net cash flows on the assumption that LIBOR rates in the future equal the forward rates calculated from instruments trading in the market today.

2. Set the value of the swap equal to the present value of the net cash flows.

This chapter describes a number of nonstandard swaps. Some can be valued using the "assume forward rates will be realized" approach; some require the application of the convexity, timing, and quanto adjustments we encountered in Chapter 30; some contain embedded options that must be valued using the procedures described in Chapters 29, 32, and 33.

34.1 VARIATIONS ON THE VANILLA DEAL

Many interest rate swaps involve relatively minor variations to the plain vanilla structure discussed in Chapter 7. In some swaps the notional principal changes with time in a predetermined way. Swaps where the notional principal is an increasing function of time are known as *step-up swaps*. Swaps where the notional principal is a decreasing function of time are known as *amortizing swaps*. Step-up swaps could be useful for a construction company that intends to borrow increasing amounts of money at floating rates to finance a particular project and wants to swap to fixed-rate funding. An amortizing swap could be used by a company that has fixed-rate borrowings with a certain prepayment schedule and wants to swap to borrowings at a floating rate.

Business Snapshot 34.1   Hypothetical Confirmation for Nonstandard Swap

Trade date:	4-January, 2016
Effective date:	11-January, 2016
Business day convention (all dates):	Following business day
Holiday calendar:	U.S.
Termination date:	11-January, 2021

Fixed amounts

Fixed-rate payer:	Microsoft
Fixed-rate notional principal:	USD 100 million
Fixed rate:	6% per annum
Fixed-rate day count convention:	Actual/365
Fixed-rate payment dates	Each 11-July and 11-January commencing 11-July, 2016, up to and including 11-January, 2021

Floating amounts

Floating-rate payer	Goldman Sachs
Floating-rate notional principal	USD 120 million
Floating rate	USD 1-month LIBOR
Floating-rate day count convention	Actual/360
Floating-rate payment dates	11-July, 2016, and the 11th of each month thereafter up to and including 11-January, 2021

The principal can be different on the two sides of a swap. Also the frequency of payments can be different. Business Snapshot 34.1 illustrates this by showing a hypothetical swap between Microsoft and Goldman Sachs where the notional principal is $120 million on the floating side and $100 million on fixed side. Payments are made every month on the floating side and every 6 months on the fixed side. These type of variations to the basic plain vanilla structure do not affect the valuation methodology. The "assume forward rates are realized" approach can still be used.

The floating reference rate for a swap is not always LIBOR. For instance, in some swaps it is the commercial paper (CP) rate or the OIS rate. A *basis swap* involves exchanging cash flows calculated using one floating reference rate for cash flows calculated using another floating reference rate. An example would be a swap where the 3-month OIS rate plus 10 basis points is exchanged for 3-month LIBOR with both being applied to a principal of $100 million. A basis swap could be used for risk management by a financial institution whose assets and liabilities are dependent on different floating reference rates.

Swaps where the floating reference rate is not LIBOR can usually be valued using the "assume forward rates are realized" approach. The forward rate is calculated so that swaps involving the reference rate have zero value. (This is similar to the way forward LIBOR is calculated when OIS discounting is used.)

Business Snapshot 34.2 Hypothetical Confirmation for Compounding Swap

---

Trade date:	4-January, 2016
Effective date:	11-January, 2016
Holiday calendar:	U.S.
Business day convention (all dates):	Following business day
Termination date:	11-January, 2021

Fixed amounts

Fixed-rate payer:	Microsoft
Fixed-rate notional principal:	USD 100 million
Fixed rate:	6% per annum
Fixed-rate day count convention:	Actual/365
Fixed-rate payment date:	11-January, 2021
Fixed-rate compounding:	Applicable at 6.3%
Fixed-rate compounding dates	Each 11-July and 11-January commencing 11-July, 2016, up to and including 11-July, 2020

Floating amounts

Floating-rate payer:	Goldman Sachs
Floating-rate notional principal:	USD 100 million
Floating rate:	USD 6-month LIBOR plus 20 basis points
Floating-rate day count convention:	Actual/360
Floating-rate payment date:	11-January, 2021
Floating-rate compounding:	Applicable at LIBOR plus 10 basis points
Floating-rate compounding dates:	Each 11-July and 11-January commencing 11-July, 2016, up to and including 11-July, 2020

34.2 COMPOUNDING SWAPS

Another variation on the plain vanilla swap is a *compounding swap*. A hypothetical confirmation for a compounding swap is in Business Snapshot 34.2. In this example there is only one payment date for both the floating-rate payments and the fixed-rate payments. This is at the end of the life of the swap. The floating rate of interest is LIBOR plus 20 basis points. Instead of being paid, the interest is compounded forward until the end of the life of the swap at a rate of LIBOR plus 10 basis points. The fixed rate of interest is 6%. Instead of being paid this interest is compounded forward at a fixed rate of interest of 6.3% until the end of the swap.

The "assume forward rates are realized" approach can be used at least approximately for valuing a compounding swap such as that in Business Snapshot 34.2. It is straightforward to deal with the fixed side of the swap because the payment that will be made at maturity is known with certainty. The "assume forward rates are realized" approach for the floating side is justifiable because there exist a series of forward rate agreements

(FRAs) where the floating-rate cash flows are exchanged for the values they would have if each floating rate equaled the corresponding forward rate.[1]

Example 34.1

A compounding swap with annual resets has a life of 3 years. A fixed rate is paid and a floating rate is received. The fixed interest rate is 4% and the floating interest rate is 12-month LIBOR. The fixed side compounds at 3.9% and the floating side compounds at 12-month LIBOR minus 20 basis points. All LIBOR forward rates are 5%. OIS rates are all 4% and are used for discounting. The notional principal is $100 million.

On the fixed side, interest of $4 million is earned at the end of the first year. This compounds to $4 \times 1.039 = \$4.156$ million at the end of the second year. A second interest amount of $4 million is added at the end of the second year bringing the total compounded forward amount to $8.156 million. This compounds to $8.156 \times 1.039 = \$8.474$ million by the end of the third year when there is the third interest amount of $4 million. The cash flow at the end of the third year on the fixed side of the swap is therefore $12.474 million.

On the floating side we assume all future interest rates equal the corresponding forward LIBOR rates. This means that all future interest rates are assumed to be 5% with annual compounding. The interest calculated at the end of the first year is $5 million. Compounding this forward at 4.8% (forward LIBOR minus 20 basis points) gives $5 \times 1.048 = \$5.24$ million at the end of the second year. Adding in the interest, the compounded forward amount is $10.24 million. Compounding forward to the end of the third year, we get $10.24 \times 1.048 = \$10.731$ million. Adding in the final interest gives $15.731 million.

The swap can be valued by assuming that it leads to an inflow of $15.731 million and an outflow of $12.474 million at the end of year 3. The value of the swap is therefore

$$\frac{15.731 - 12.474}{1.04^3} = 2.895$$

or $2.895 million. (This analysis ignores day count issues and makes the approximation indicated in footnote 1.)

34.3 CURRENCY SWAPS

Currency swaps were introduced in Chapter 7. They enable an interest rate exposure in one currency to be swapped for an interest rate exposure in another currency. Usually two principals are specified, one in each currency. The principals are exchanged at both the beginning and the end of the life of the swap as described in Section 7.7.

Suppose that the currencies involved in a currency swap are U.S. dollars (USD) and British pounds (GBP). In a fixed-for-fixed currency swap, a fixed rate of interest is specified in each currency. The payments on one side are determined by applying the

---

[1] See Technical Note 18 at www-2.rotman.utoronto.ca/~hull/TechnicalNotes for the details. The "assume forward rates are realized" approach works exactly if the spread used for compounding, s_c, is zero or if it is applied so that Q at time t compounds to $Q(1 + R\tau)(1 + s_c\tau)$ at time $t + \tau$, where R is LIBOR. If, as is more usual, it compounds to $Q[1 + (R + s_c)\tau]$, then there is a small approximation.

fixed rate of interest in USD to the USD principal; the payments on the other side are determined by applying the fixed rate of interest in GBP to the GBP principal.

In a floating-for-floating currency swap, the payments on one side are determined by applying USD LIBOR (possibly with a spread added) to the USD principal; similarly the payments on the other side are determined by applying GBP LIBOR (possibly with a spread added) to the GBP principal. In a cross-currency interest rate swap, a floating rate in one currency is exchanged for a fixed rate in another currency.

Floating-for-floating and cross-currency interest rate swaps can be valued using the "assume forward rates are realized" rule. Future LIBOR rates in each currency are assumed to equal today's forward rates. This enables the cash flows in the currencies to be determined. The USD cash flows are discounted at the USD zero rate. The GBP cash flows are discounted at the GBP zero rate. The current exchange rate is then used to translate the two present values to a common currency.

It is important to ensure that valuation procedures are such that transactions that could be negotiated today (at the midpoint of bid and offer) have zero value. The discount rates that are used are often adjusted to ensure that this is the case.[2]

34.4 MORE COMPLEX SWAPS

We now move on to consider some examples of swaps where the simple rule "assume forward rates will be realized" does not work. In each case, it must be assumed that an adjusted forward rate, rather than the actual forward rate, is realized. This section builds on the discussion in Chapter 30.

LIBOR-in-Arrears Swap

A plain vanilla interest rate swap is designed so that the floating rate of interest observed on one payment date is paid on the next payment date. An alternative instrument that is sometimes traded is a *LIBOR-in-arrears swap*. In this, the floating rate paid on a payment date equals the rate observed on the payment date itself.

Suppose that the reset dates in the swap are t_i for $i = 0, 1, \ldots, n$, with $\tau_i = t_{i+1} - t_i$. Define R_i as the LIBOR rate for the period between t_i and t_{i+1}, F_i as the forward value of R_i, and σ_i as the volatility of this forward rate. (The value of σ_i is typically implied from caplet prices.) In a LIBOR-in-arrears swap, the payment on the floating side at time t_i is based on R_i rather than R_{i-1}. As explained in Section 30.1, it is necessary to make a convexity adjustment to the forward rate when the payment is valued. The valuation should be based on the assumption that the floating rate paid is

$$F_i + \frac{F_i^2 \sigma_i^2 \tau_i t_i}{1 + F_i \tau_i} \tag{34.1}$$

and not F_i.

Example 34.2

In a LIBOR-in-arrears swap, the principal is $100 million. A fixed rate of 5% is received annually and LIBOR is paid. Payments are exchanged at the ends of

---

[2] If a bank's system does not value deals consistently with the market, its traders will be able to arbitrage the system.

years 1, 2, 3, 4, and 5. All LIBOR forward rates are 5% per annum (measured with annual compounding). All caplet volatilities are 22% per annum. OIS rates, which are used for discounting, are all 4% with annual compounding.

The forward rate for each floating payment is 5%. If this were a regular swap rather than an in-arrears swap, its value would (ignoring day count conventions, etc.) be exactly zero. Because it is an in-arrears swap, convexity adjustments must be made. In equation (34.1), $F_i = 0.05$, $\sigma_i = 0.22$, and $\tau_i = 1$ for all i. The convexity adjustment changes the rate assumed at time t_i from 0.05 to

$$0.05 + \frac{0.05^2 \times 0.22^2 \times 1 \times t_i}{1 + 0.05 \times 1} = 0.05 + 0.000115 t_i$$

The floating rates for the payments at the ends of years 1, 2, 3, 4, and 5 should therefore be assumed to be 5.0115%, 5.0230%, 5.0345%, 5.0460%, and 5.0575%, respectively. The net exchange on the first payment date is equivalent to a cash outflow of 0.0115% of $100 million or $11,500. Equivalent net cash flows for other exchanges are calculated similarly. The value of the swap is

$$-\frac{11,500}{1.04} - \frac{23,000}{1.04^2} - \frac{34,500}{1.04^3} - \frac{46,000}{1.04^4} - \frac{57,500}{1.04^5}$$

or about −$150,000.

CMS and CMT Swaps

A constant maturity swap (CMS) is an interest rate swap where the floating rate equals the swap rate for a swap with a certain life. For example, the floating payments on a CMS swap might be made every 6 months at a rate equal to the 5-year swap rate. Usually there is a lag so that the payment on a particular payment date is equal to the swap rate observed on the previous payment date. Suppose that rates are set at times $t_0, t_1, t_2, \ldots$, payments are made at times $t_1, t_2, t_3, \ldots$, and L is the notional principal. The floating payment at time t_{i+1} is

$$\tau_i L S_i$$

where $\tau_i = t_{i+1} - t_i$ and S_i is the swap rate at time t_i.

Suppose that y_i is the forward value of the swap rate S_i. To value the payment at time t_{i+1}, it turns out to be correct to make an adjustment to the forward swap rate, so that the realized swap rate is assumed to be

$$y_i - \frac{1}{2} y_i^2 \sigma_{y,i}^2 t_i \frac{G_i''(y_i)}{G_i'(y_i)} - \frac{y_i \tau_i F_i \rho_i \sigma_{y,i} \sigma_{F,i} t_i}{1 + F_i \tau_i} \qquad (34.2)$$

rather that y_i. In this equation, $\sigma_{y,i}$ is the volatility of the forward swap rate, F_i is the current forward interest rate between times t_i and t_{i+1}, $\sigma_{F,i}$ is the volatility of this forward rate, and ρ_i is the correlation between the forward swap rate and the forward interest rate. $G_i(x)$ is the price at time t_i of a bond as a function of its yield x. The bond pays coupons at rate y_i and has the same life and payment frequency as the swap from which the CMS rate is calculated. $G_i'(x)$ and $G_i''(x)$ are the first and second partial derivatives of G_i with respect to x. The volatilities $\sigma_{y,i}$ can be implied from swaptions; the volatilities $\sigma_{F,i}$ can be implied from caplet prices; the correlation ρ_i can be estimated from historical data.

Equation (34.2) involves a convexity and a timing adjustment. The term

$$-\frac{1}{2}y_i^2\sigma_{y,i}^2 t_i \frac{G_i''(y_i)}{G_i'(y_i)}$$

is an adjustment similar the one in Example 30.2 of Section 30.1. It is based on the assumption that the swap rate S_i leads to only one payment at time t_i rather than to an annuity of payments. The term

$$-\frac{y_i\tau_i F_i\rho_i\sigma_{y,i}\sigma_{F,i}\, t_i}{1 + F_i\tau_i}$$

is similar to the one in Section 30.2 and is an adjustment for the fact that the payment calculated from S_i is made at time t_{i+1} rather than t_i.

Example 34.3

In a 6-year CMS swap, the 5-year swap rate is received and a fixed rate of 5% is paid on a notional principal of $100 million. The exchange of payments is semiannual (both on the underlying 5-year swap and on the CMS swap itself). The exchange on a payment date is determined from the swap rate on the previous payment date. All LIBOR forward rates are 5% per annum with semiannual compounding. All options on 5-year swaps have a 15% implied volatility and all caplets with a 6-month tenor have a 20% implied volatility. The correlation between each cap rate and each swap rate is 0.7.

In this case, $y_i = 0.05$, $\sigma_{y,i} = 0.15$, $\tau_i = 0.5$, $F_i = 0.05$, $\sigma_{F,i} = 0.20$, and $\rho_i = 0.7$ for all i. Also,

$$G_i(x) = \sum_{i=1}^{10}\frac{2.5}{(1+x/2)^i} + \frac{100}{(1+x/2)^{10}}$$

so that $G_i'(y_i) = -437.603$ and $G_i''(y_i) = 2261.23$. Equation (34.2) gives the total convexity/timing adjustment as $0.0001197t_i$, or 1.197 basis points per year until the swap rate is observed. For example, for the purposes of valuing the CMS swap, the 5-year swap rate in 4 years' time should be assumed to be 5.0479% rather than 5% and the net cash flow received at the 4.5-year point should be assumed to be $0.5 \times 0.000479 \times 100{,}000{,}000 = \$23{,}940$. Other net cash flows are calculated similarly. Taking their present value assuming a 5% discount rate (i.e., a negligible difference between OIS and LIBOR), we find the value of the swap to be $159,811.

A constant maturity Treasury swap (CMT swap) works similarly to a CMS swap except that the floating rate is the yield on a Treasury bond with a specified life. The analysis of a CMT swap is essentially the same as that for a CMS swap with S_i defined as the par yield on a Treasury bond with the specified life.

Differential Swaps

A *differential swap*, sometimes referred to as a *diff swap*, is an interest rate swap where a floating interest rate is observed in one currency and applied to a principal in another currency. Suppose that the LIBOR rate for the period between t_i and t_{i+1} in currency Y is applied to a principal in currency X with the payment taking place at time t_{i+1}. Define V_i as the forward interest rate between t_i and t_{i+1} in currency Y and W_i as the forward exchange rate for a contract with maturity t_{i+1} (expressed as the number of units of currency Y that equal one unit of currency X). If the LIBOR rate in currency Y were applied to a principal in currency Y, the cash flow at time t_{i+1} would be valued on the assumption that the LIBOR rate at time t_i equals V_i. From the analysis in Section 30.3, a quanto adjustment is necessary when it is applied to a principal in currency X. It is correct to value the cash flow on the assumption that the LIBOR rate equals

$$V_i + V_i \rho_i \sigma_{W,i} \sigma_{V,i} t_i \tag{34.3}$$

where $\sigma_{V,i}$ is the volatility of V_i, $\sigma_{W,i}$ is the volatility of W_i, and ρ_i is the correlation between V_i and W_i.

Example 34.4

In a 3-year diff swap agreement with annual payments, USD 12-month LIBOR is received and sterling 12-month LIBOR is paid with both being applied to a principal of 10 million pounds sterling. All LIBOR forward rates in both currencies are 5% per annum (with annual compounding). The volatility of all 1-year forward rates in the United States is estimated to be 20%, the volatility of the forward USD/sterling exchange rate (dollars per pound) is 12% for all maturities, and the correlation between the two is 0.4.

In this case, $V_i = 0.05$, $\rho_i = 0.4$, $\sigma_{W,i} = 0.12$, $\sigma_{V,i} = 0.2$. The floating-rate cash flows dependent on the 1-year USD rate observed at time t_i should therefore be calculated on the assumption that the rate will be

$$0.05 + 0.05 \times 0.4 \times 0.12 \times 0.2 \times t_i = 0.05 + 0.00048 t_i$$

This means that the net cash flows from the swap at times 1, 2, and 3 years should be assumed to be 0, 4,800, and 9,600 pounds sterling for the purposes of valuation. Assuming the (OIS) discount rate is 4.8% (annually compounded), the value of the swap is therefore

$$\frac{0}{1.048} + \frac{4,800}{1.048^2} + \frac{9,600}{1.048^3} = 12,711$$

or 12,711 pounds sterling.

34.5 EQUITY SWAPS

In an equity swap, one party promises to pay the return on an equity index on a notional principal, while the other promises to pay a fixed or floating return on a notional principal. Equity swaps enable a fund managers to increase or reduce their exposure to an index without buying and selling stock. An equity swap is a convenient way of packaging a series of forward contracts on an index to meet the needs of the market.

The equity index is usually a total return index where dividends are reinvested in the stocks comprising the index. An example of an equity swap is in Business Snapshot 34.3. In this, the 6-month return on the S&P 500 is exchanged for LIBOR. The principal on either side of the swap is $100 million and payments are made every 6 months.

For an equity-for-floating swap such as that in Business Snapshot 34.3, the value at the start of its life is zero, assuming LIBOR discounting. This is because a financial institution can arrange to costlessly replicate the cash flows to one side by borrowing

---

Business Snapshot 34.3 Hypothetical Confirmation for an Equity Swap

Trade date:	4-January, 2016
Effective date:	11-January, 2016
Business day convention (all dates):	Following business day
Holiday calendar:	U.S.
Termination date:	11-January, 2021

Equity amounts

Equity payer:	Microsoft
Equity principal	USD 100 million
Equity index:	Total Return S&P 500 index
Equity payment:	$100(I_1 - I_0)/I_0$, where I_1 is the index level on the payment date and I_0 is the index level on the immediately preceding payment date. In the case of the first payment date, I_0 is the index level on 11-January, 2016
Equity payment dates:	Each 11-July and 11-January commencing 11-July, 2016, up to and including 11-January, 2021

Floating amounts

Floating-rate payer:	Goldman Sachs
Floating-rate notional principal:	USD 100 million
Floating rate:	USD 6-month LIBOR
Floating-rate day count convention:	Actual/360
Floating-rate payment dates:	Each 11-July and 11-January commencing 11-July, 2016, up to and including 11-January, 2021

---

the principal on each payment date at LIBOR and investing it in the index until the next payment date with any dividends being reinvested. A similar argument shows that the swap is always worth zero immediately after a payment date. (When OIS discounting is used, swapping OIS for the equity return should be assumed to have zero value.)

Between payment dates the equity cash flow and the LIBOR cash flow at the next payment date must be valued. The LIBOR cash flow was fixed at the last reset date and so can be valued easily. The value of the equity cash flow is LE/E_0, where L is the principal, E is the current value of the equity index, and E_0 is its value at the last payment date.[3]

34.6 SWAPS WITH EMBEDDED OPTIONS

Some swaps contain embedded options. In this section we consider some commonly encountered examples.

---

[3] See Technical Note 19 at www-2.rotman.utoronto.ca/~hull/TechnicalNotes for a more detailed discussion.

Accrual Swaps

Accrual swaps are swaps where the interest on one side accrues only when the floating reference rate is within a certain range. Sometimes the range remains fixed during the entire life of the swap; sometimes it is reset periodically.

As a simple example of an accrual swap, consider a deal where a fixed rate Q is exchanged for 3-month LIBOR every quarter and the fixed rate accrues only on days when 3-month LIBOR is below 8% per annum. Suppose that the principal is L. In a normal swap the fixed-rate payer would pay QLn_1/n_2 on each payment date where n_1 is the number of days in the preceding quarter and n_2 is the number of days in the year. (This assumes that the day count is actual/actual.) In an accrual swap, this is changed to QLn_3/n_2, where n_3 is the number of days in the preceding quarter that the 3-month LIBOR was below 8%. The fixed-rate payer saves QL/n_2 on each day when 3-month LIBOR is above 8%.[4] The fixed-rate payer's position can therefore be considered equivalent to a regular swap plus a series of binary options, one for each day of the life of the swap. The binary options pay off QL/n_2 when the 3-month LIBOR is above 8%.

To generalize, suppose that the LIBOR cutoff rate (8% in the case just considered) is R_K and that payments are exchanged every τ years. Consider day i during the life of the swap and suppose that t_i is the time until day i. Suppose that the τ-year LIBOR rate on day i is R_i so that interest accrues when $R_i < R_K$. Define F_i as the forward value of R_i and σ_i as the volatility of F_i. (The latter is estimated from spot caplet volatilities.) Using the usual lognormal assumption, the probability that LIBOR is greater than R_K in a world defined by a numeraire equal to a zero-coupon bond maturing at time $t_i + \tau$ is $N(d_2)$, where

$$d_2 = \frac{\ln(F_i/R_K) - \sigma_i^2 t_i/2}{\sigma_i \sqrt{t_i}}$$

The payoff from the binary option is realized at the swap payment date following day i. Suppose that this is at time s_i. The probability that LIBOR is greater than R_K in a world defined by a numeraire equal to a zero-coupon bond maturing at time s_i is given by $N(d_2^*)$, where d_2^* is calculated using the same formula as d_2, but with a small timing adjustment to F_i reflecting the difference between time $t_i + \tau$ and time s_i.

The value of the binary option corresponding to day i is

$$\frac{QL}{n_2} P(0, s_i) N(d_2^*)$$

where $P(0, t)$ as usual is the price of a risk-free zero-coupon bond maturing at time t. The total value of the binary options is obtained by summing this expression for every day in the life of the swap. The timing adjustment (causing d_2 to be replaced by d_2^*) is so small that, in practice, it is frequently ignored.

Cancelable Swap

A cancelable swap is a plain vanilla interest rate swap where one side has the option to terminate on one or more payment dates. Terminating a swap is the same as entering

---

[4] The usual convention is that, if a day is a holiday, the applicable rate is assumed to be the rate on the immediately preceding business day.

into the offsetting (opposite) swap. Consider a swap between Microsoft and Goldman Sachs. If Microsoft has the option to cancel, it can regard the swap as a regular swap plus a long position in an option to enter into the offsetting swap. If Goldman Sachs has the cancelation option, Microsoft has a regular swap plus a short position in an option to enter into the swap.

If there is only one termination date, a cancelable swap is the same as a regular swap plus a position in a European swaption. Consider, for example, a 10-year swap where Microsoft will receive 6% and pay LIBOR. Suppose that Microsoft has the option to terminate at the end of 6 years. The swap is a regular 10-year swap to receive 6% and pay LIBOR plus long position in a 6-year European option to enter into a 4-year swap where 6% is paid and LIBOR is received. (The latter is referred to as a 6 × 4 European swaption.) The standard market model for valuing European swaptions is described in Chapter 29.

When the swap can be terminated on a number of different payment dates, it is a regular swap plus a Bermudan-style swaption. Consider, for example, the situation where Microsoft has entered into a 5-year swap with semiannual payments where 6% is received and LIBOR is paid. Suppose that the counterparty has the option to terminate the swap on payment dates between year 2 and year 5. The swap is a regular swap plus a short position in a Bermudan-style swaption, where the Bermudan-style swaption is an option to enter into a swap that matures in 5 years and involves a fixed payment at 6% being received and a floating payment at LIBOR being paid. The swaption can be exercised on any payment date between year 2 and year 5. Methods for valuing Bermudan swaptions are discussed in Chapters 32 and 33.

Cancelable Compounding Swaps

Sometimes compounding swaps can be terminated on specified payment dates. On termination, the floating-rate payer pays the compounded value of the floating amounts up to the time of termination and the fixed-rate payer pays the compounded value of the fixed payments up to the time of termination.

Some tricks can be used to value cancelable compounding swaps. Suppose first that the floating rate is LIBOR, it is compounded at LIBOR, and LIBOR discounting is used. Assume that the principal amount of the swap is paid on both the fixed and floating sides of the swap at the end of its life. This is similar to moving from Table 7.1 to Table 7.2 for a vanilla swap. It does not change the value of the swap and has the effect of ensuring that the value of the floating side always equals the notional principal on a payment date. To make the cancelation decision, we need only look at the fixed side. We construct an interest rate tree as outlined in Chapter 32. We roll back through the tree in the usual way valuing the fixed side. At each node where the swap can be canceled, we test whether it is optimal to keep the swap or cancel it. Canceling the swap in effect sets the fixed side equal to par. If we are paying fixed and receiving floating, our objective is to minimize the value of the fixed side; if we are receiving fixed and paying floating, our objective is to maximize the value of the fixed side.

When the floating side is LIBOR plus a spread compounded at LIBOR, the cash flows corresponding to the spread rate of interest can be subtracted from the fixed side instead of adding them to the floating side. The option can then be valued as in the case where there is no spread.

When the compounding is at LIBOR plus a spread, an approximate approach is as follows:[5]

1. Calculate the value of the floating side of the swap at each cancelation date assuming forward rates are realized.

2. Calculate the value of the floating side of the swap at each cancelation date assuming that the floating rate is LIBOR and it is compounded at LIBOR.

3. Define the excess of step 1 over step 2 as the "value of spreads" on a cancelation date.

4. Treat the option in the way described above. In deciding whether to exercise the cancelation option, subtract the value of the spreads from the values calculated for the fixed side.

A similar approach can be used for OIS discounting if the spread between OIS and LIBOR is assumed to be equal to the forward spread.

34.7 OTHER SWAPS

This chapter has discussed just a few of the swap structures in the market. In practice, the range of different contracts that trade is limited only by the imagination of financial engineers and the appetite of corporate treasurers for innovative risk management tools.

A swap that was very popular in the United States in the mid-1990s is an *index amortizing rate swap* (also called an *indexed principal swap*). In this, the principal reduces in a way dependent on the level of interest rates. The lower the interest rate, the greater the reduction in the principal. The fixed side of an indexed amortizing swap was originally designed to mirror approximately the return obtained by an investor on an agency mortgage-backed security after prepayment options are taken into account. The swap therefore exchanged the return on the mortgage-backed security for a floating-rate return.

Commodity swaps are now becoming increasingly popular. A company that consumes 100,000 barrels of oil per year could agree to pay $8 million each year for the next 10 years and to receive in return $100,000S$, where S is the market price of oil per barrel. The agreement would in effect lock in the company's oil cost at $80 per barrel. An oil producer might agree to the opposite exchange, thereby locking in the price it realized for its oil at $80 per barrel. Energy derivatives such as this will be discussed in Chapter 35.

A number of other types of swaps are discussed elsewhere in this book. For example, asset swaps are discussed in Chapter 24, total return swaps and various types of credit default swaps are covered in Chapter 25, and volatility and variance swaps are analyzed in Chapter 26.

Bizarre Deals

Some swaps have payoffs that are calculated in quite bizarre ways. An example is a deal entered into between Procter and Gamble and Bankers Trust in 1993 (see Business

---

[5] This approach is not perfectly accurate in that it assumes that the decision to exercise the cancelation option is not influenced by future payments being compounded at a rate different from LIBOR.

Business Snapshot 34.4   Procter and Gamble's Bizarre Deal

A particularly bizarre swap is the so-called "5/30" swap entered into between Bankers Trust (BT) and Procter and Gamble (P&G) on November 2, 1993. This was a 5-year swap with semiannual payments. The notional principal was $200 million. BT paid P&G 5.30% per annum. P&G paid BT the average 30-day CP (commercial paper) rate minus 75 basis points plus a spread. The average commercial paper rate was calculated by taking observations on the 30-day commercial paper rate each day during the preceding accrual period and averaging them.

The spread was zero for the first payment date (May 2, 1994). For the remaining nine payment dates, it was

$$\max\left[0, \frac{98.5\left(\dfrac{\text{5-year CMT\%}}{5.78\%}\right) - (\text{30-year TSY price})}{100}\right]$$

In this, 5-year CMT is the constant maturity Treasury yield (i.e., the yield on a 5-year Treasury note, as reported by the U.S. Federal Reserve). The 30-year TSY price is the midpoint of the bid and offer cash bond prices for the 6.25% Treasury bond maturing on August 2023. Note that the spread calculated from the formula is a decimal interest rate. It is not measured in basis points. If the formula gives 0.1 and the CP rate is 6%, the rate paid by P&G is 15.25%.

P&G were hoping that the spread would be zero and the deal would enable it to exchange fixed-rate funding at 5.30% for funding at 75 basis points less than the commercial paper rate. In fact, interest rates rose sharply in early 1994, bond prices fell, and the swap proved very, very expensive (see Problem 34.9).

Snapshot 34.4). The details of this transaction are in the public domain because it later became the subject of litigation.[6]

SUMMARY

Swaps have proved to be very versatile financial instruments. Many swaps can be valued by (a) assuming that LIBOR (or some other floating reference rate) will equal its forward value and (b) discounting the resulting cash flows. These include plain vanilla interest swaps, most types of currency swaps, swaps where the principal changes in a predetermined way, swaps where the payment dates are different on each side, and compounding swaps.

Some swaps require adjustments to the forward rates when they are valued. These adjustments are termed convexity, timing, or quanto adjustments. Among the swaps that require adjustments are LIBOR-in-arrears, CMS/CMT, and differential swaps.

Equity swaps involve the return on an equity index being exchanged for a fixed or floating rate of interest. They are usually designed so that they are worth zero immediately after a payment date, but they may have nonzero values between payment dates.

---

[6] See D. J. Smith, "Aggressive Corporate Finance: A Close Look at the Procter and Gamble–Bankers Trust Leveraged Swap," *Journal of Derivatives* 4, 4 (Summer 1997): 67–79.

Some swaps involve embedded options. An accrual swap is a regular swap plus a large portfolio of binary options (one for each day of the life of the swap). A cancelable swap is a regular swap plus a Bermudan swaption.

FURTHER READING

Chance, D., and Rich, D., "The Pricing of Equity Swap and Swaptions," *Journal of Derivatives* 5, 4 (Summer 1998): 19–31.

Smith D. J., "Aggressive Corporate Finance: A Close Look at the Procter and Gamble–Bankers Trust Leveraged Swap," *Journal of Derivatives*, 4, 4 (Summer 1997): 67–79.

Practice Questions (Answers in Solutions Manual)

34.1. Calculate all the fixed cash flows and their exact timing for the swap in Business Snapshot 34.1. Assume that the day count conventions are applied using target payment dates rather than actual payment dates.

34.2. Suppose that a swap specifies that a fixed rate is exchanged for twice the LIBOR rate. Can the swap be valued using the "assume forward rates are realized" rule?

34.3. What is the value of a 2-year fixed-for-floating compounding swap where the principal is $100 million and payments are made semiannually? Fixed interest is received and floating is paid. The fixed rate is 8% and it is compounded at 8.3% (both semiannually compounded). The floating rate is LIBOR plus 10 basis points and it is compounded at LIBOR plus 20 basis points. The LIBOR zero curve is flat at 8% with semiannual compounding. The risk-free discount rate is 7.5% continuously compounded.

34.4. What is the value of a 5-year swap where LIBOR is paid in the usual way and in return LIBOR compounded at LIBOR is received on the other side? The principal on both sides is $100 million. Payment dates on the pay side and compounding dates on the receive side are every 6 months. The LIBOR zero curve is flat at 5% with semiannual compounding and is used for discounting.

34.5. Calculate the total convexity/timing adjustment in Example 34.3 of Section 34.4 if all cap volatilities are 18% instead of 20% and volatilities for all options on 5-year swaps are 13% instead of 15%. What should the 5-year swap rate in 3 years' time be assumed for the purpose of valuing the swap? What is the value of the swap?

34.6. Explain why a plain vanilla interest rate swap and the compounding swap in Section 34.2 can be valued using the "assume forward rates are realized" rule, but a LIBOR-in-arrears swap in Section 34.4 cannot.

34.7. In the accrual swap discussed in the text, the fixed side accrues only when the floating reference rate lies below a certain level. Discuss how the analysis can be extended to cope with a situation where the fixed side accrues only when the floating reference rate is above one level and below another.

Further Questions

34.8. LIBOR zero rates are flat at 5% in the United States and flat at 10% in Australia (both annually compounded). In a 4-year diff swap Australian LIBOR is received and 9% is paid with both being applied to a USD principal of $10 million. Payments are exchanged annually. The volatility of all 1-year forward rates in Australia is estimated to be 25%, the volatility of the forward USD/AUD exchange rate (AUD per USD) is 15% for all maturities, and the correlation between the two is 0.3. What is the value of the swap? Assume a USD discount rate of 4.7% continuously compounded.

34.9. Estimate the interest rate paid by P&G on the 5/30 swap in Section 34.7 if (a) the CP rate is 6.5% and the Treasury yield curve is flat at 6% and (b) the CP rate is 7.5% and the Treasury yield curve is flat at 7% with semiannual compounding.

34.10. Suppose that you are trading a LIBOR-in-arrears swap with an unsophisticated counter-party who does not make convexity adjustments. To take advantage of the situation, should you be paying fixed or receiving fixed? How should you try to structure the swap as far as its life and payment frequencies?

Consider the situation where all 12-month LIBOR forward rates are 10% per annum with annual compounding. All cap volatilities are 18%. Estimate the difference between the way a sophisticated trader and an unsophisticated trader would value a LIBOR-in-arrears swap where payments are made annually and the life of the swap is (a) 5 years, (b) 10 years, and (c) 20 years. Assume a notional principal of $1 million and no difference between risk-free discount rates and LIBOR.

34.11. Suppose that all 12-month LIBOR forward rates are 5% with annual compounding. The OIS zero curve is flat at 4.8% with continuous compounding. In a 5-year swap, company X pays a fixed rate of 6% and receives LIBOR. The volatility of the 2-year swap rate in 3 years is 20%.
(a) What is the value of the swap?
(b) Use DerivaGem to calculate the value of the swap if company X has the option to cancel after 3 years.
(c) Use DerivaGem to calculate the value of the swap if the counterparty has the option to cancel after 3 years.
(d) What is the value of the swap if either side can cancel at the end of 3 years?

34.12. How would you calculate the initial value of the equity swap in Business Snapshot 34.3 if OIS discounting were used?

35

Energy and Commodity Derivatives

The variable underlying a derivative is sometimes simply referred to as the *underlying*. Earlier parts of this book have focused on situations where the underlying is a stock price, a stock index, an exchange rate, a bond price, an interest rate, or the loss from a credit event. In this chapter, we consider a variety of other underlyings.

The first part of the chapter is concerned with situations where the underlying is a commodity. Chapter 2 discussed futures contracts on commodities and Chapter 18 discussed how European and American options on commodity futures contracts can be valued. As a European futures option has the same payoff as a European spot option when the futures contract matures at the same time as the option, the model used to value European futures options (Black's model) can also be used to value European spot options. However, American spot options and other more complicated derivatives dependent on the spot price of a commodity require more sophisticated models. A feature of commodity prices is that they often exhibit mean reversion (similarly to interest rates) and are also sometimes subject to jumps. Some of the models developed for interest rates can be adapted to apply to commodities.

The second part of the chapter considers weather and insurance derivatives. A distinctive feature of these derivatives is that they depend on variables with no systematic risk. For example, the expected value of the temperature at a certain location or the losses experienced due to hurricanes can reasonably be assumed to be the same in a risk-neutral world and the real world. This means that historical data is potentially more useful for valuing these types of derivatives than for some others.

35.1 AGRICULTURAL COMMODITIES

Agricultural commodities include products that are grown (or created from products that are grown) such as corn, wheat, soybeans, cocoa, coffee, sugar, cotton, and frozen orange juice. They also include products related to livestock such as cattle, hogs, and pork bellies. The prices of agricultural commodities, like all commodities, is determined by supply and demand. The U.S. Department of Agriculture publishes reports on inventories and production. One statistic that is watched for commodities such as corn and wheat is the *stocks-to-use ratio*. This is the ratio of the year-end inventory to the year's usage. Typically it is between 20% and 40%. It has an impact on price volatility. As the ratio for a commodity becomes lower, the commodity's price becomes more sensitive to supply changes, so that the volatility increases.

There are reasons for supposing some level of mean reversion in agricultural prices. As prices decline, farmers find it less attractive to produce the commodity and supply decreases creating upward pressure on the price. Similarly, as the price of an agricultural commodity increases, farmers are more likely to devote resources to producing the commodity creating downward pressure on the price.

Prices of agricultural commodities tend to be seasonal, as storage is expensive and there is a limit to the length of time for which a product can be stored. Weather plays a key role in determining the price of many agricultural products. Frosts can decimate the Brazilian coffee crop, a hurricane in Florida is likely to have a big effect on the price of frozen orange juice, and so on. The volatility of the price of a commodity that is grown tends to be highest at pre-harvest times and then declines when the size of the crop is known. During the growing season, the price process for an agricultural commodity is liable to exhibit jumps because of the weather.

Many of the commodities that are grown and traded are used to feed livestock. (For example, the corn futures contract that is traded by the CME Group refers to the corn that is used to feed animals.) The price of livestock, and when slaughtering takes place, is liable to be dependent on the price of these commodities, which are in turn influenced by the weather.

35.2 METALS

Another important commodity category is metals. This includes gold, silver, platinum, palladium, copper, tin, lead, zinc, nickel, and aluminum. Metals have quite different characteristics from agricultural commodities. Their prices are unaffected by the weather and are not seasonal. They are extracted from the ground. They are divisible and are relatively easy to store. Some metals, such as copper, are used almost entirely in the manufacture of goods and should be classified as consumption assets. As explained in Section 5.1, others, such as gold and silver, are held purely for investment as well as for consumption and should be classified as investment assets.

As in the case of agricultural commodities, analysts monitor inventory levels to determine short-term price volatility. Exchange rate volatility may also contribute to volatility as the country where the metal is extracted is often different from the country in whose currency the price is quoted. In the long term, the price of a metal is determined by trends in the extent to which a metal is used in different production processes and new sources of the metal that are found. Changes in exploration and extraction methods, geopolitics, cartels, and environmental regulation also have an impact.

One potential source of supply for a metal is recycling. A metal might be used to create a product and, over the following 20 years, 10% of the metal might come back on the market as a result of a recycling process.

Metals that are investment assets are not usually assumed to follow mean-reverting processes because a mean-reverting process would give rise to an arbitrage opportunity for the investor. For metals that are consumption assets, there may be some mean reversion. As the price of a metal increases, it is likely to become less attractive to use the metal in some production processes and more economically viable to extract the metal from difficult locations. As a result there will be downward pressure on the price. Similarly, as the price decreases, it is likely to become more attractive to use the metal in some production processes and less economically viable to extract the metal from difficult locations. As a result, there will be upward pressure on the price.

35.3 ENERGY PRODUCTS

Energy products are among the most important and actively traded commodities. A wide range of energy derivatives trade in both the over-the-counter market and on exchanges. Here we consider oil, natural gas, and electricity. There are reasons for supposing that all three follow mean reverting processes. As the price of a source of energy rises, it is likely to be consumed less and and produced more. This creates a downward pressure on prices. As the price of a source of energy declines, it is likely to be consumed more, but production is likely to be less economically viable. This creates upward pressure on the price.

Crude Oil

The crude oil market is the largest commodity market in the world, with global demand amounting to about 90 million barrels daily. Ten-year fixed-price supply contracts have been commonplace in the over-the-counter market for many years. These are swaps where oil at a fixed price is exchanged for oil at a floating price.

There are many grades of crude oil, reflecting variations in the gravity and the sulfur content. Two important benchmarks for pricing are Brent crude oil (which is sourced from the North Sea) and West Texas Intermediate (WTI) crude oil. Crude oil is refined into products such as gasoline, heating oil, fuel oil, and kerosene.

In the over-the-counter market, virtually any derivative that is available on common stocks or stock indices is now available with oil as the underlying asset. Swaps, forward contracts, and options are popular. Contracts sometimes require settlement in cash and sometimes require settlement by physical delivery (i.e., by delivery of oil).

Exchange-traded contracts are also popular. The CME Group and Intercontinental-Exchange (ICE) trade a number of oil futures and oil futures options contracts. Some of the futures contracts are settled in cash; others are settled by physical delivery. For example, the Brent crude oil futures traded on ICE have a cash settlement option; the light sweet crude oil futures traded on CME Group require physical delivery. In both cases, the amount of oil underlying one contract is 1,000 barrels. The CME Group also trades popular contracts on two refined products: heating oil and gasoline. In both cases, one contract is for the delivery of 42,000 gallons.

Natural Gas

The natural gas industry throughout the world went through a period of deregulation and the elimination of government monopolies in the 1980s and 1990s. The supplier of natural gas is now not necessarily the same company as the producer of the gas. Suppliers are faced with the problem of meeting daily demand.

A typical over-the-counter contract is for the delivery of a specified amount of natural gas at a roughly uniform rate over a 1-month period. Forward contracts, options, and swaps are available in the over-the-counter market. The seller of natural gas is usually responsible for moving the gas through pipelines to the specified location.

The CME Group trades a contract for the delivery of 10,000 million British thermal units of natural gas. The contract, if not closed out, requires physical delivery to be made during the delivery month at a roughly uniform rate to a particular hub in Louisiana. ICE trades a similar contract in London.

Natural gas is a popular source of energy for heating buildings. It is also used to produce electricity, which in turn is used for air-conditioning. As a result, demand for natural gas is seasonal and dependent on the weather.

Electricity

Electricity is an unusual commodity because it cannot easily be stored.[1] The maximum supply of electricity in a region at any moment is determined by the maximum capacity of all the electricity-producing plants in the region. In the United States there are 140 regions known as *control areas*. Demand and supply are first matched within a control area, and any excess power is sold to other control areas. It is this excess power that constitutes the wholesale market for electricity. The ability of one control area to sell power to another control area depends on the transmission capacity of the lines between the two areas. Transmission from one area to another involves a transmission cost, charged by the owner of the line, and there are generally some transmission or energy losses.

A major use of electricity is for air-conditioning systems. As a result the demand for electricity, and therefore its price, is much greater in the summer months than in the winter months. The nonstorability of electricity causes occasional very large movements in the spot price. Heat waves have been known to increase the spot price by as much as 1,000% for short periods of time.

Like natural gas, electricity has been through a period of deregulation and the elimination of government monopolies. This has been accompanied by the development of an electricity derivatives market. The CME Group now trades a futures contract on the price of electricity, and there is an active over-the-counter market in forward contracts, options, and swaps. A typical contract (exchange-traded or over-the-counter) allows one side to receive a specified number of megawatt hours for a specified price at a specified location during a particular month. In a 5×8 contract, power is received for five days a week (Monday to Friday) during the off-peak period (11 p.m. to 7 a.m.) for the specified month. In a 5×16 contract, power is received five days a week during the on-peak period (7 a.m. to 11 p.m.) for the specified month. In a 7×24 contract, it is received around the clock every day during the month. Option contracts have either daily exercise or monthly exercise. In the case of daily exercise, the option holder can choose on each day of the month (by giving one day's notice) whether to receive the specified amount of power at the specified strike price. When there is monthly exercise a

---

[1] Electricity producers with spare capacity sometimes use it to pump water to the top of their hydroelectric plants so that it can be used to produce electricity at a later time. This is the closest they can get to storing this commodity.

single decision on whether to receive power for the whole month at the specified strike price is made at the beginning of the month.

An interesting contract in electricity and natural gas markets is what is known as a *swing option* or *take-and-pay option*. In this contract, a minimum and maximum for the amount of power that must be purchased at a certain price by the option holder is specified for each day during a month and for the month in total. The option holder can change (or swing) the rate at which the power is purchased during the month, but usually there is a limit on the total number of changes that can be made.

35.4 MODELING COMMODITY PRICES

To value derivatives, we are often interested in modeling the spot price of a commodity in the traditional risk-neutral world. From Section 18.6, the expected future price of the commodity in this world is the futures price.

A Simple Process

A simple process for a commodity price can be constructed by assuming that the expected growth rate in the commodity price is dependent solely on time and the volatility of the commodity price is constant. The risk-neutral process for the commodity price S then has the form

$$\frac{dS}{S} = \mu(t)\, dt + \sigma\, dz \tag{35.1}$$

and

$$F(t) = \hat{E}[S(t)] = S(0)e^{\int_0^t \mu(\tau)d\tau}$$

where $F(t)$ is the futures price for a contract with maturity t and $\hat{E}$ denotes expected value in a risk-neutral world. It follows that

$$\ln F(t) = \ln S(0) + \int_0^t \mu(\tau)d\tau$$

Differentiating both sides with respect to time gives

$$\mu(t) = \frac{\partial}{\partial t}[\ln F(t)]$$

Example 35.1

Suppose that the futures prices of live cattle at the end of July 2017 are (in cents per pound) as follows:

August 2017	62.20
October 2017	60.60
December 2017	62.70
February 2018	63.37
April 2018	64.42
June 2018	64.40

These can be used to estimate the expected growth rate in live cattle prices in a risk-neutral world. For example, when the model in equation (35.1) is used, the expected growth rate in live cattle prices between October and December 2017, in a risk-neutral world is

$$\ln\left(\frac{62.70}{60.60}\right) = 0.034$$

or 3.4% per 2 months with continuous compounding. On an annualized basis, this is 20.4% per annum.

Example 35.2

Suppose that the futures prices of live cattle are as in Example 35.1. A certain breeding decision would involve an investment of $100,000 now and expenditures of $20,000 in 3 months, 6 months, and 9 months. The result is expected to be that an extra cattle will be available for sale at the end of the year. There are two major uncertainties: the number of pounds of extra cattle that will be available for sale and the price per pound. The expected number of pounds is 300,000. The expected price of cattle in 1 year in a risk-neutral world is, from Example 35.1, 64.40 cents per pound. Assuming that the risk-free rate of interest is 10% per annum, the value of the investment (in thousands of dollars) is

$$-100 - 20e^{-0.1\times0.25} - 20e^{-0.1\times0.50} - 20e^{-0.1\times0.75} + 300 \times 0.644e^{-0.1\times1} = 17.729$$

This assumes that any uncertainty about the extra amount of cattle that will be available for sale has zero systematic risk and that there is no correlation between the amount of cattle that will be available for sale and the price.

Mean Reversion

As already discussed, most commodity prices follow mean-reverting processes. They tend to get pulled back to a central value. A more realistic process than equation (35.1) for the risk-neutral process followed by the commodity price S is

$$d\ln S = [\theta(t) - a\ln S]\,dt + \sigma\,dz \tag{35.2}$$

This incorporates mean reversion and is analogous to the lognormal process assumed for the short-term interest rate in Chapter 32. Note that this process is sometimes written

$$\frac{dS}{S} = [\theta^*(t) - a\ln S]\,dt + \sigma\,dz$$

From Itô's lemma, this is equivalent to the process in equation (35.2) when $\theta^*(t) = \theta(t) + \frac{1}{2}\sigma^2$.

The trinomial tree methodology in Section 32.5 can be adapted to construct a tree for S and determine the value of $\theta(t)$ in equation (35.2) such that $F(t) = \hat{E}[S(t)]$. We will illustrate the procedure by building a three-step tree for the situation where the current spot price is $20 and the 1-year, 2-year, and 3-year futures prices are $22, $23, and $24, respectively. Suppose that $a = 0.1$ and $\sigma = 0.2$ in equation (35.2). We first define a variable X that is initially zero and follows the process

$$dX = -aX\,dt + \sigma\,dz \tag{35.3}$$

Using the procedure in Section 32.5, a trinomial tree can be constructed for X. This is shown in Figure 35.1.

The variable $\ln S$ follows the same process as X except for a time-dependent drift. Analogously to Section 32.5, the tree for X can be converted to a tree for $\ln S$ by displacing the positions of nodes. This tree is shown in Figure 35.2. The initial node corresponds to a price of 20, so the displacement for that node is $\ln 20$. Suppose that the displacement of the nodes at 1 year is α_1. The values of the X at the three nodes at the 1-year point are $+0.3464$, 0, and -0.3464. The corresponding values of $\ln S$ are $0.3464 + \alpha_1$, α_1, and $-0.3464 + \alpha_1$. The values of S are therefore $e^{0.3464 + \alpha_1}$, e^{α_1}, and $e^{-0.3464 + \alpha_1}$, respectively. We require the expected value of S to equal the futures price. This means that

$$0.1667e^{0.3464 + \alpha_1} + 0.6666e^{\alpha_1} + 0.1667e^{-0.3464 + \alpha_1} = 22$$

The solution to this is $\alpha_1 = 3.071$. The values of S at the 1-year point are therefore 30.49, 21.56, and 15.25.

At the 2-year point, we first calculate the probabilities of nodes E, F, G, H, and I being reached from the probabilities of nodes B, C, and D being reached. The probability of reaching node F is the probability of reaching node B times the probability of moving from B to F plus the probability of reaching node C times the probability of moving from C to F. This is

$$0.1667 \times 0.6566 + 0.6666 \times 0.1667 = 0.2206$$

Similarly the probabilities of reaching nodes E, G, H, and I are 0.0203, 0.5183, 0.2206, and 0.0203, respectively. The amount α_2 by which the nodes at time 2 years are

Figure 35.1   Tree for X. Constructing this tree is the first stage in constructing a tree for the spot price of a commodity, S. Here p_u, p_m, and p_d are the probabilities of "up", "middle", and "down" movements from a node.

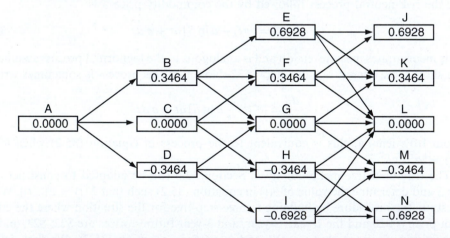

Node:	A	B	C	D	E	F	G	H	I
p_u:	0.1667	0.1217	0.1667	0.2217	0.8867	0.1217	0.1667	0.2217	0.0867
p_m:	0.6666	0.6566	0.6666	0.6566	0.0266	0.6566	0.6666	0.6566	0.0266
p_d:	0.1667	0.2217	0.1667	0.1217	0.0867	0.2217	0.1667	0.1217	0.8867

Figure 35.2 Tree for spot price of a commodity: p_u, p_m, and p_d are the probabilities of "up", "middle", and "down" movements from a node.

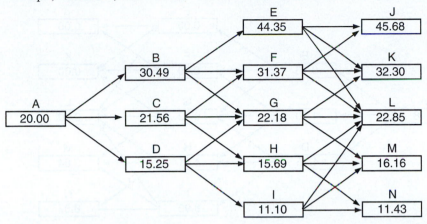

Node:	A	B	C	D	E	F	G	H	I
p_u:	0.1667	0.1217	0.1667	0.2217	0.8867	0.1217	0.1667	0.2217	0.0867
p_m:	0.6666	0.6566	0.6666	0.6566	0.0266	0.6566	0.6666	0.6566	0.0266
p_d:	0.1667	0.2217	0.1667	0.1217	0.0867	0.2217	0.1667	0.1217	0.8867

displaced must satisfy

$$0.0203e^{0.6928+\alpha_2} + 0.2206e^{0.3464+\alpha_2} + 0.5183e^{\alpha_2}$$

$$+ 0.2206e^{-0.3464+\alpha_2} + 0.0203e^{-0.6928+\alpha_2} = 23$$

The solution to this is $\alpha_2 = 3.099$. This means that the values of S at the 2-year point are 44.35, 31.37, 22.18, 15.69, and 11.10, respectively.

A similar calculation can be carried out at time 3 years. Figure 35.2 shows the resulting tree for S.

Example 35.3

Suppose that the tree in Figure 35.2 is used to price a 3-year American put option on the spot price of the commodity with a strike price of 20 when the interest rate (continuously compounded) is 3% per year. Rolling back through the tree in the usual way, we obtain Figure 35.3 showing that the value of the option is $1.48. The option is exercised early at nodes D, H, and I. To obtain a more accurate value, a tree with many more time steps would be used. The futures prices would be interpolated to obtain futures prices for maturities corresponding to the end of every time step on this more detailed tree.

Interpolation and Seasonality

When a large number of time steps are used, it is necessary to interpolate between futures prices to obtain a futures price at the end of each time step. When there is seasonality, the interpolation procedure should reflect this. Suppose there are monthly

Figure 35.3 Valuation of an American put option with a strike price of $20 using the tree in Figure 35.2.

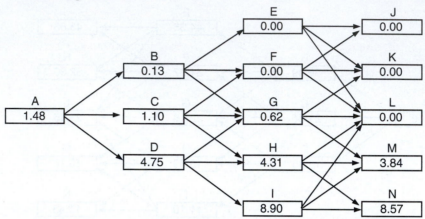

Node:	A	B	C	D	E	F	G	H	I
p_u:	0.1667	0.1217	0.1667	0.2217	0.8867	0.1217	0.1667	0.2217	0.0867
p_m:	0.6666	0.6566	0.6666	0.6566	0.0266	0.6566	0.6666	0.6566	0.0266
p_d:	0.1667	0.2217	0.1667	0.1217	0.0867	0.2217	0.1667	0.1217	0.8867

time steps. One simple way of incorporating seasonality is to collect monthly historical data on the spot price and calculate the 12-month moving average of the price. A *percentage seasonal factor* can then be estimated as the average of the ratio of the spot price for the month to the 12-month moving average of spot prices that is centered (approximately) on the month.

The percentage seasonal factors are then used to deseasonalize the futures prices that are known. Monthly deseasonalized futures are then calculated using interpolation. These futures prices are then seasonalized using the percentage seasonal factors and the tree is built. Suppose, for example, that the futures prices are observed in the market for September and December as 40 and 44, respectively, and we want to calculate a futures prices for October and November. Suppose further that the percentage seasonality factors for September, October, November, and December are calculated from historical data as 0.95, 0.85, 0.8 and 1.1, respectively. The deseasonalized futures prices are $40/0.95 = 42.1$ for September and $44/1.1 = 40$ for December. The interpolated deseasonalized futures prices are 41.4 and 40.7 for October and November, respectively. The seasonalized futures prices that would be used in tree construction for October and November are $41.4 \times 0.85 = 35.2$ and $40.7 \times 0.8 = 32.6$, respectively.

As has been mentioned, the volatility of a commodity sometimes shows seasonality. For example, the prices of some agricultural commodities are more volatile during the growing season because of weather uncertainty. Volatility can be monitored using the methods discussed in Chapter 23, and a percentage seasonal factor for volatility can be estimated. The parameter σ can then be replaced by $\sigma(t)$ in equations (35.2) and (35.3). A procedure that can be used to construct a trinomial tree for the situation where the volatility is a function of time is discussed in Technical Notes 9 and 16 at www-2.rotman.utoronto.ca/~hull/TechnicalNotes.

Jumps

Some commmodities, such as electricity and natural gas, exhibit price jumps because of weather-related demand shocks. Other commodities, particularly those that are agricultural, are liable to exhibit price jumps because of weather-related supply shocks. Jumps can be incorporated into equation (35.2) so that the process for the spot price becomes

$$d \ln S = [\theta(t) - a \ln S]\, dt + \sigma\, dz + dp$$

where dp is the Poisson process generating the percentage jumps. This is similar to Merton's mixed jump–diffusion model for stock prices, which is described in Section 27.1. Once the jump frequency and jump size probability distribution have been chosen, the average increase in the commodity price at a future time t that is as a result of jumps can be calculated. To determine $\theta(t)$, the trinomial tree method can be used with the futures prices for maturity t reduced by this increase. Monte Carlo simulation can be used to implement the model, as explained in Sections 21.6 and 27.1.

Other Models

More-sophisticated models are sometimes used for oil prices. If y is the convenience yield, then the proportional drift of the spot price is $r - y$, where r is the short-term risk-free rate and a natural process to assume for the spot price is

$$\frac{dS}{S} = (r - y)\, dt + \sigma_1\, dz_1$$

Gibson and Schwartz suggest that the convenience yield y be modeled as a mean-reverting process:[2]

$$dy = k(\alpha - y)dt + \sigma_2\, dz_2$$

where k and α are constants and dz_2 is a Wiener process, which is correlated with the Wiener process dz_1. To provide an exact fit to futures prices, α can be made a function of time.

Eydeland and Geman propose a stochastic volatility for gas and electricity prices.[3] This is

$$\frac{dS}{S} = a(b - \ln S)\, dt + \sqrt{V}\, dz_1$$

$$dV = c(d - V)dt + e\sqrt{V}\, dz_2$$

where a, b, c, d, and e are constants, and dz_1 and dz_2 are correlated Wiener processes. Later Geman proposed a model for oil where the reversion level b is also stochastic.[4]

[2] See R. Gibson and E. S. Schwartz, "Stochastic Convenience Yield and the Pricing of Oil Contingent Claims," *Journal of Finance*, 45 (1990): 959–76.

[3] A. Eydeland and H. Geman, "Pricing Power Derivatives," *Risk*, September 1998.

[4] H. Geman, "Scarcity and Price Volatility in Oil Markets," EDF Trading Technical Report, 2000.

35.5 WEATHER DERIVATIVES

Many companies are in the position where their performance is liable to be adversely affected by the weather.[5] It makes sense for these companies to consider hedging their weather risk in much the same way as they hedge foreign exchange or interest rate risks.

The first over-the-counter weather derivatives were introduced in 1997. To understand how they work, we explain two variables:

HDD: Heating degree days
CDD: Cooling degree days

A day's HDD is defined as

$$HDD = \max(0, 65 - A)$$

and a day's CDD is defined as

$$CDD = \max(0, A - 65)$$

where A is the average of the highest and lowest temperature during the day at a specified weather station, measured in degrees Fahrenheit. For example, if the maximum temperature during a day (midnight to midnight) is 68° Fahrenheit and the minimum temperature is 44° Fahrenheit, $A = 56$. The daily HDD is then 9 and the daily CDD is 0.

A typical over-the-counter product is a forward or option contract providing a payoff dependent on the cumulative HDD or CDD during a month. For example, a derivatives dealer could in January 2018 sell a client a call option on the cumulative HDD during February 2019 at the Chicago O'Hare Airport weather station with a strike price of 700 and a payment rate of $10,000 per degree day. If the actual cumulative HDD is 820, the payoff is $1.2 million. Often contracts include a payment cap. If the payment cap in our example is $1.5 million, the contract is the equivalent of a bull spread (see Chapter 12). The client has a long call option on cumulative HDD with a strike price of 700 and a short call option with a strike price of 850.

A day's HDD is a measure of the volume of energy required for heating during the day. A day's CDD is a measure of the volume of energy required for cooling during the day. Most weather derivative contracts are entered into by energy producers and energy consumers. But retailers, supermarket chains, food and drink manufacturers, health service companies, agriculture companies, and companies in the leisure industry are also potential users of weather derivatives. The Weather Risk Management Association (www.wrma.org) has been formed to serve the interests of the weather risk management industry.

In September 1999 the Chicago Mercantile Exchange (CME) began trading weather futures and European options on weather futures. The contracts are on the cumulative HDD and CDD for a month observed at a weather station. The contracts are settled in cash just after the end of the month once the HDD and CDD are known. One futures contract is on $20 times the cumulative HDD or CDD for the month. The CME now offers weather futures and options for many cities throughout the world.

---

[5] The U.S. Department of Energy has estimated that one-seventh of the U.S. economy is subject to weather risk.

35.6   INSURANCE DERIVATIVES

When derivative contracts are used for hedging purposes, they have many of the same characteristics as insurance contracts. Both types of contracts are designed to provide protection against adverse events. It is not surprising that many insurance companies have subsidiaries that trade derivatives and that many of the activities of insurance companies are becoming very similar to those of investment banks.[6]

Traditionally the insurance industry has hedged its exposure to catastrophic (CAT) risks such as hurricanes and earthquakes using a practice known as reinsurance. Reinsurance contracts can take a number of forms. Suppose that an insurance company has an exposure of $100 million to earthquakes in California and wants to limit this to $30 million. One alternative is to enter into annual reinsurance contracts that cover on a pro rata basis 70% of its exposure. If California earthquake claims in a particular year total $50 million, the cost to the company would then be only $15 million. Another more popular alternative, involving lower reinsurance premiums, is to buy a series of reinsurance contracts covering what are known as *excess cost layers*. The first layer might provide indemnification for losses between $30 million and $40 million; the next might cover losses between $40 million and $50 million; and so on. Each reinsurance contract is known as an *excess-of-loss* reinsurance contract. The reinsurer has written a bull spread on the total losses. It is long a call option with a strike price equal to the lower end of the layer and short a call option with a strike price equal to the upper end of the layer.[7]

Some payouts on CAT risks have been very high. Hurricane Andrew in 1992 caused about $15 billion of insurance costs in Florida. This exceeded the total of relevant insurance premiums received in Florida during the previous seven years. If Hurricane Andrew had hit Miami, it is estimated that insured losses would have exceeded $40 billion. Hurricane Andrew and other catastrophes have led to increases in insurance/reinsurance premiums.

The over-the-counter market has come up with a number of products that are alternatives to traditional reinsurance. The most popular is a CAT bond. This is a bond issued by a subsidiary of an insurance company that pays a higher-than-normal interest rate. In exchange for the extra interest the holder of the bond agrees to provide an excess-of-loss reinsurance contract. Depending on the terms of the CAT bond, the interest or principal (or both) can be used to meet claims. In the example considered above where an insurance company wants protection for California earthquake losses between $30 million and $40 million, the insurance company could issue CAT bonds with a total principal of $10 million. In the event that the insurance company's California earthquake losses exceeded $30 million, bondholders would lose some or all of their principal. As an alternative the insurance company could cover this excess cost layer by making a much bigger bond issue where only the bondholders' interest is at risk.

---

[6] The difference between a derivatives contract and an insurance contract is as follows. When entering into an insurance contract, an entity must have an exposure to the underlying risk. For a derivatives contract this is not necessary. For example, it is not possible for person A to insure person B's house against being burnt down. But it is possible to buy a put option on a stock when it is not owned.

[7] Reinsurance is also sometimes offered in the form of a lump sum if a certain loss level is reached. The reinsurer is then writing a cash-or-nothing binary call option on the losses.

35.7 PRICING WEATHER AND INSURANCE DERIVATIVES

One distinctive feature of weather and insurance derivatives is that there is no systematic risk (i.e., risk that is priced by the market) in their payoffs. This means that estimates made from historical data (real-world estimates) can also be assumed to apply to the risk-neutral world. Weather and insurance derivatives can therefore be priced by

1. Using historical data to estimate the expected payoff
2. Discounting the estimated expected payoff at the risk-free rate.

Another key feature of weather and insurance derivatives is the way uncertainty about the underlying variables grows with time. For a stock price, uncertainty grows roughly as the square root of time. Our uncertainty about a stock price in 4 years (as measured by the standard deviation of the logarithm of the price) is approximately twice that in 1 year. For a commodity price, mean reversion kicks in, but our uncertainty about a commodity's price in 4 years is still considerably greater than our uncertainty in 1 year. For weather, the growth of uncertainty with time is much less marked. Our uncertainty about the February HDD at a certain location in 4 years is usually only a little greater than our uncertainty about the February HDD at the same location in 1 year. Similarly, our uncertainty about earthquake losses for a period starting in 4 years is usually only a little greater than our uncertainty about earthquake losses for a similar period starting in 1 year.

Consider the valuation of an option on the cumulative HDD. We could collect 50 years of historical data and estimate a probability distribution for the HDD. This could be fitted to a lognormal or other probability distribution and the expected payoff on the option calculated. This would then be discounted at the risk-free rate to give the value of the option. The analysis could be refined by analyzing trends in the historical data and incorporating weather forecasts produced by meteorologists.

Example 35.4

Consider a call option on the cumulative HDD in February 2019 at the Chicago O'Hare Airport weather station with a strike price of 700 and a payment rate of \$10,000 per degree day. Suppose that the HDD is estimated from 50 years of historical data to have a lognormal distribution with the mean HDD equal to 710 and the standard deviation of the natural logarithm of HDD equal to 0.07. From equation (15A.1), the expected payoff is

$$10,000 \times [710N(d_1) - 700N(d_2)]$$

where

$$d_1 = \frac{\ln(710/700) + 0.07^2/2}{0.07} = 0.2376$$

$$d_2 = \frac{\ln(710/700) - 0.07^2/2}{0.07} = 0.1676$$

or \$250,900. If the risk-free interest rate is 3% and the option is being valued in February 2018 (one year from maturity) the value of the option is

$$250,900 \times e^{-0.03 \times 1} = 243,400$$

or \$243,400.

We might want to adjust the mean of the probability distribution of HDD for temperature trends. Suppose that a linear regression shows that the cumulative HDD for February is decreasing at the rate of 0.5 per year (perhaps because of global warming), so that the estimate of the mean HDD in February 2019 is only 697.[8] Keeping the estimate of the standard deviation of the natural logarithm of the payoff the same, this would reduce the value of the expected payoff to $180,400 and the value of the option to $175,100.

Finally, suppose that long-range weather forecasters consider it likely that February 2019 will be particularly mild. The estimate of the expected HDD might then be reduced even further making the option even less valuable.

In the insurance area, Litzenberger *et al.* have shown that there is (as one would expect) no statistically significant correlation between the returns from CAT bonds and stock market returns.[9] This confirms that there is no systematic risk and that valuations can be based on the actuarial data collected by insurance companies.

CAT bonds typically give a high probability of an above-normal rate of interest and a low probability of a big loss. Why would investors be interested in such instruments? The answer is that the expected return (taking account of possible losses) is higher than the return that can be earned on risk-free investments. However, the risk in CAT bonds can (at least in theory) be completely diversified away in a large portfolio. CAT bonds therefore have the potential to improve risk–return trade-offs.

35.8 HOW AN ENERGY PRODUCER CAN HEDGE RISKS

There are two components to the risks facing an energy producer. One is the risk associated with the market price for the energy (the price risk); the other is risk associated with the amount of energy that will be bought (the volume risk). Although prices do adjust to reflect volumes, there is a less-than-perfect relationship between the two, and energy producers have to take both into account when developing a hedging strategy. The price risk can be hedged using the energy derivative contracts. The volume risks can be hedged using the weather derivatives. Define:

Y: Profit for a month

P: Average energy prices for the month

T: Relevant temperature variable (HDD or CDD) for the month.

An energy producer can use historical data to obtain a best-fit linear regression relationship of the form

$$Y = a + bP + cT + \epsilon$$

where ϵ is the error term. The energy producer can then hedge risks for the month by taking a position of $-b$ in energy forwards or futures and a position of $-c$ in weather

---

[8] The mean decreased at 0.5 per year over the last 50 years and was 710 on average. This suggests that the mean was about 722.5 at the beginning of the 50 years and 697.5 at the end of the 50 years. A reasonable estimate for next year is 697.

[9] R. H. Litzenberger, D. R. Beaglehole, and C. E. Reynolds, "Assessing Catastrophe Reinsurance-Linked Securities as a New Asset Class," *Journal of Portfolio Management*, Winter 1996: 76–86.

forwards or futures. The relationship can also be used to analyze the effectiveness of alternative option strategies.

SUMMARY

When there are risks to be managed, derivatives markets have been very innovative in developing products to meet the needs of the market.

There are a number of different types of commodity derivatives. The underlyings include agricultural products that are grown, livestock, metals, and energy products. The models used to value them usually incorporate mean reversion. Sometimes seasonality is modeled explicitly and jumps are incorporated. Energy derivatives with oil, natural gas, and electricity as the underlying are particularly important and have been the subject of models that are as sophisticated as the most sophisticated models used for stock prices, exchange rates, and interest rates.

In the weather derivatives market, two measures, HDD and CDD, have been developed to describe temperature during a month. These are used to define payoffs on both exchange-traded and over-the-counter derivatives. As the weather derivatives market develops, contracts on rainfall, snow, and other weather-related variables may become more widely used.

Insurance derivatives are an alternative to traditional reinsurance as a way for insurance companies to manage the risk of a catastrophic event such as a hurricane or an earthquake. We may see other sorts of insurance, such as life and automobile insurance, being traded in a similar way in the future.

Weather and insurance derivatives have the property that the underlying variables have no systematic risk. This means that the derivatives can be valued by estimating expected payoffs using historical data and discounting the expected payoff at the risk-free rate.

FURTHER READING

On commodity derivatives

Clewlow, L., and C. Strickland. *Energy Derivatives: Pricing and Risk Management*. Lacima Group, 2000.

Edwards, D.W. *Energy, Trading, and Investing: Trading, Risk Management and Structuring Deals in the Energy Markets*. Maidenhead: McGraw-Hill, 2010.

Eydeland, A., and K. Wolyniec. *Energy and Power Risk Management*. Hoboken, NJ: Wiley, 2003.

Geman, H. *Commodities and Commodity Derivatives: Modeling and Pricing for Agriculturals, Metals, and Energy*. Chichester: Wiley, 2005.

Gibson, R., and E. S. Schwartz. "Stochastic Convenience Yield and the Pricing of Oil Contingent Claims," *Journal of Finance*, 45 (1990): 959–76.

Schofield, N. C. *Commodity Derivatives: Markets and Applications*. Chichester: Wiley, 2011.

On weather derivatives

Alexandridis, A. K., and A. D. Zapranis. *Weather Derivatives: Modeling and Pricing Weather Related Risk*. New York: Springer, 2013.

Cao, M., and J. Wei. "Weather Derivatives Valuation and the Market Price of Weather Risk," *Journal of Futures Markets*, 24, 11 (November 2004), 1065–89.

On insurance derivatives

Canter, M. S., J. B. Cole, and R. L. Sandor. "Insurance Derivatives: A New Asset Class for the Capital Markets and a New Hedging Tool for the Insurance Industry," *Journal of Applied Corporate Finance* (Autumn 1997): 69–83.

Froot, K. A. "The Market for Catastrophe Risk: A Clinical Examination," *Journal of Financial Economics*," 60 (2001): 529–71.

Litzenberger, R. H., D. R. Beaglehole, and C. E. Reynolds. "Assessing Catastrophe Reinsurance-Linked Securities as a New Asset Class," *Journal of Portfolio Management* (Winter 1996): 76–86.

Practice Questions (Answers in Solutions Manual)

35.1. What is meant by HDD and CDD?

35.2. How is a typical natural gas forward contract structured?

35.3. Distinguish between the historical data and the risk-neutral approach to valuing a derivative. Under what circumstance do they give the same answer?

35.4. Suppose that each day during July the minimum temperature is 68° Fahrenheit and the maximum temperature is 82° Fahrenheit. What is the payoff from a call option on the cumulative CDD during July with a strike of 250 and a payment rate of $5,000 per degree-day?

35.5. Why is the price of electricity more volatile than that of other energy sources?

35.6. Why is the historical data approach appropriate for pricing a weather derivatives contract and a CAT bond?

35.7. "HDD and CDD can be regarded as payoffs from options on temperature." Explain this statement.

35.8. Suppose that you have 50 years of temperature data at your disposal. Explain carefully the analyses you would carry out to value a forward contract on the cumulative CDD for a particular month.

35.9. Would you expect the volatility of the 1-year forward price of oil to be greater than or less than the volatility of the spot price? Explain your answer.

35.10. What are the characteristics of an energy source where the price has a very high volatility and a very high rate of mean reversion? Give an example of such an energy source.

35.11. How can an energy producer use derivatives markets to hedge risks?

35.12. Explain how a 5×8 option contract for May 2017 on electricity with daily exercise works. Explain how a 5×8 option contract for May 2017 on electricity with monthly exercise works. Which is worth more?

35.13. Explain how CAT bonds work.

35.14. Consider two bonds that have the same coupon, time to maturity, and price. One is a B-rated corporate bond. The other is a CAT bond. An analysis based on historical data shows that the expected losses on the two bonds as a function of time are the same. Which bond would you advise a portfolio manager to buy and why?

35.15. Consider a commodity with constant volatility σ and an expected growth rate that is a function solely of time. Show that, in the traditional risk-neutral world,

$$\ln S_T \sim \phi[\ln F(T) - \tfrac{1}{2}\sigma^2 T, \ \sigma^2 T]$$

where S_T is the value of the commodity at time T, $F(t)$ is the futures price at time 0 for a contract maturing at time t, and $\phi(m, v)$ is a normal distribution with mean m and variance v.

Further Questions

35.16. An insurance company's losses of a particular type are to a reasonable approximation normally distributed with a mean of $150 million and a standard deviation of $50 million. (Assume no difference between losses in a risk-neutral world and losses in the real world.) The 1-year risk-free rate is 5%. Estimate the cost of the following:

(a) A contract that will pay in 1 year's time 60% of the insurance company's losses on a pro rata basis

(b) A contract that pays $100 million in 1 year's time if losses exceed $200 million.

35.17. How is the tree in Figure 35.2 modified if the 1- and 2-year futures prices are $21 and $22 instead of $22 and $23, respectively. How does this affect the value of the American option in Example 35.3.

CHAPTER 36

Real Options

Up to now we have been almost entirely concerned with the valuation of financial assets. In this chapter we explore how the ideas we have developed can be extended to assess capital investment opportunities in real assets such as land, buildings, plant, and equipment. Often there are options embedded in these investment opportunities (the option to expand the investment, the option to abandon the investment, the option to defer the investment, and so on.) These options are very difficult to value using traditional capital investment appraisal techniques. The approach known as *real options* attempts to deal with this problem using option pricing theory.

The chapter starts by explaining the traditional approach to evaluating investments in real assets and shows how difficult it is to correctly value embedded options when this approach is used. It then explains how the risk-neutral valuation approach can be extended to handle the valuation of real assets and presents a number of examples illustrating the application of the approach in different situations.

36.1 CAPITAL INVESTMENT APPRAISAL

The traditional approach to valuing a potential capital investment project is the "net present value" (NPV) approach. The NPV of a project is the present value of its expected future incremental cash flows. The discount rate used to calculate the present value is a "risk-adjusted" discount rate, chosen to reflect the risk of the project. As the riskiness of the project increases, the discount rate also increases.

As an example, consider an investment that costs $100 million and will last 5 years. The expected cash inflow in each year (in the real world) is estimated to be $25 million. If the risk-adjusted discount rate is 12% (with continuous compounding), the net present value of the investment is (in millions of dollars)

$$-100 + 25e^{-0.12 \times 1} + 25e^{-0.12 \times 2} + 25e^{-0.12 \times 3} + 25e^{-0.12 \times 4} + 25e^{-0.12 \times 5} = -11.53$$

A negative NPV, such as the one we have just calculated, indicates that the project will reduce the value of the company to its shareholders and should not be undertaken. A positive NPV would indicate that the project should be undertaken because it will increase shareholder wealth.

The risk-adjusted discount rate should be the return required by the company, or the company's shareholders, on the investment. This can be calculated in a number of ways. One approach often recommended involves the capital asset pricing model (see the appendix to Chapter 3). The steps are as follows:

1. Take a sample of companies whose main line of business is the same as that of the project being contemplated.

2. Calculate the betas of the companies and average them to obtain a proxy beta for the project.

3. Set the required rate of return equal to the risk-free rate plus the proxy beta times the excess return of the market portfolio over the risk-free rate.

One problem with the traditional NPV approach is that many projects contain embedded options. Consider, for example, a company that is considering building a plant to manufacture a new product. Often the company has the option to abandon the project if things do not work out well. It may also have the option to expand the plant if demand for the output exceeds expectations. These options usually have quite different risk characteristics from the base project and require different discount rates.

To understand the problem here, return to the example at the beginning of Chapter 13. This involved a stock whose current price is $20. In three months the price will be either $22 or $18. Risk-neutral valuation shows that the value of a three-month call option on the stock with a strike price of 21 is 0.545. Footnote 1 of Chapter 13 shows that if the expected return required by investors on the stock in the real world is 10% then the expected return required on the call option is 55.96%. A similar analysis shows that if the option is a put rather than a call the expected return required on the option is −70.4%. These analyses mean that if the traditional NPV approach were used to value the call option the correct discount rate would be 55.96%, and if it were used to value a put option the correct discount rate would be −70.4%. There is no easy way of estimating these discount rates. (We know them only because we are able to value the options another way.) Similarly, there is no easy way of estimating the risk-adjusted discount rates appropriate for cash flows when they arise from abandonment, expansion, and other options. This is the motivation for exploring whether the risk-neutral valuation principle can be applied to options on real assets as well as to options on financial assets.

Another problem with the traditional NPV approach lies in the estimation of the appropriate risk-adjusted discount rate for the base project (i.e., the project without embedded options). The companies that are used to estimate a proxy beta for the project in the three-step procedure above have expansion options and abandonment options of their own. Their betas reflect these options and may not therefore be appropriate for estimating a beta for the base project.

36.2 EXTENSION OF THE RISK-NEUTRAL VALUATION FRAMEWORK

In Section 28.1 the market price of risk for a variable θ was defined as

$$\lambda = \frac{\mu - r}{\sigma} \tag{36.1}$$

where r is the risk-free rate, μ is the return on a traded security dependent only on θ, and σ is its volatility. As shown in Section 28.1, the market price of risk, λ, does not depend on the particular traded security chosen.

Suppose that a real asset depends on several variables θ_i ($i = 1, 2, \ldots$). Let m_i and s_i be the expected growth rate and volatility of θ_i so that

$$d\theta_i/\theta_i = m_i \, dt + s_i \, dz_i$$

where z_i is a Wiener process. Define λ_i as the market price of risk of θ_i. Risk-neutral valuation can be extended to show that any asset dependent on the θ_i can be valued by [1]

1. Reducing the expected growth rate of each θ_i from m_i to $m_i - \lambda_i s_i$

2. Discounting cash flows at the risk-free rate.

Example 36.1

The cost of renting commercial real estate in a certain city is quoted as the amount that would be paid per square foot per year in a new 5-year rental agreement. The current cost is \$30 per square foot. The expected growth rate of the cost is 12% per annum, the volatility of the cost is 20% per annum, and its market price of risk is 0.3. A company has the opportunity to pay \$1 million now for the option to rent 100,000 square feet at \$35 per square foot for a 5-year period starting in 2 years. The risk-free rate is 5% per annum (assumed constant). Define V as the quoted cost per square foot of office space in 2 years. Assume that rent is paid annually in advance. The payoff from the option is

$$100{,}000A \max(V - 35, \, 0)$$

where A is an annuity factor given by

$$A = 1 + 1 \times e^{-0.05 \times 1} + 1 \times e^{-0.05 \times 2} + 1 \times e^{-0.05 \times 3} + 1 \times e^{-0.05 \times 4} = 4.5355$$

The expected payoff in a risk-neutral world is therefore

$$100{,}000 \times 4.5355 \times \hat{E}[\max(V - 35, \, 0)] = 453{,}550 \times \hat{E}[\max(V - 35, \, 0)]$$

where $\hat{E}$ denotes expectations in a risk-neutral world. Using the result in equation (15A.1), this is

$$453{,}550[\hat{E}(V)N(d_1) - 35N(d_2)]$$

where

$$d_1 = \frac{\ln[\hat{E}(V)/35] + 0.2^2 \times 2/2}{0.2\sqrt{2}} \quad \text{and} \quad d_2 = \frac{\ln[\hat{E}(V)/35] - 0.2^2 \times 2/2}{0.2\sqrt{2}}$$

The expected growth rate in the cost of commercial real estate in a risk-neutral world is $m - \lambda s$, where m is the real-world growth rate, s is the volatility, and λ is the market price of risk. In this case, $m = 0.12$, $s = 0.2$, and $\lambda = 0.3$, so that the expected risk-neutral growth rate is 0.06, or 6%, per year. It follows that $\hat{E}(V) = 30e^{0.06 \times 2} = 33.82$. Substituting this in the expression above gives the expected payoff in a risk-neutral world as \$1.5015 million. Discounting at the

---

[1] To see that this is consistent with risk-neutral valuation for an investment asset, suppose that θ_i is the price of a non-dividend-paying stock. Since this is the price of a traded security, equation (36.1) implies that $(m_i - r)/s_i = \lambda_i$, or $m_i - \lambda_i s_i = r$. The expected growth-rate adjustment is therefore the same as setting the return on the stock equal to the risk-free rate. For a proof of the more general result, see Technical Note 20 at: www-2.rotman.utoronto.ca/~hull/TechnicalNotes.

risk-free rate the value of the option is $1.5015e^{-0.05 \times 2} = \$1.3586$ million. This shows that it is worth paying $1 million for the option.

36.3 ESTIMATING THE MARKET PRICE OF RISK

The real-options approach to evaluating an investment avoids the need to estimate risk-adjusted discount rates in the way described in Section 36.1, but it does require market price of risk parameters for all stochastic variables. When historical data are available for a particular variable, its market price of risk can be estimated using the capital asset pricing model. To show how this is done, we consider an investment asset dependent solely on the variable and define:

μ: Expected return of the investment asset

σ: Volatility of the return of the investment asset

λ: Market price of risk of the variable

ρ: Instantaneous correlation between the percentage changes in the variable and returns on a broad index of stock market prices

μ_m: Expected return on broad index of stock market prices

σ_m: Volatility of return on the broad index of stock market prices

r: Short-term risk-free rate

Because the investment asset is dependent solely on the market variable, the instantaneous correlation between its return and the broad index of stock market prices is also ρ. From a continuous-time version of the capital asset pricing model, which is presented in the appendix to Chapter 3,[2]

$$\mu - r = \frac{\rho \sigma}{\sigma_m}(\mu_m - r)$$

From equation (36.1), another expression for $\mu - r$ is

$$\mu - r = \lambda \sigma$$

It follows that

$$\lambda = \frac{\rho}{\sigma_m}(\mu_m - r) \tag{36.2}$$

This equation can be used to estimate λ.

Example 36.2

A historical analysis of company's sales, quarter by quarter, show that percentage changes in sales have a correlation of 0.3 with returns on the S&P 500 index. The volatility of the S&P 500 is 20% per annum and based on historical data the expected excess return of the S&P 500 over the risk-free rate is 5%. Equation (36.2) estimates the market price of risk for the company's sales as

$$\frac{0.3}{0.2} \times 0.05 = 0.075$$

---

[2] When the excess return on the asset is regressed against the excess on the market index, the slope of the regression, beta, is $\rho\sigma/\sigma_m$.

When no historical data are available for the particular variable under consideration, other similar variables can sometimes be used as proxies. For example, if a plant is being constructed to manufacture a new product, data can be collected on the sales of other similar products. The correlation of the new product with the market index can then be assumed to be the same as that of these other products. In some cases, the estimate of ρ in equation (36.2) must be based on subjective judgment. If an analyst is convinced that a particular variable is unrelated to the performance of a market index, its market price of risk should be set to zero.

For some variables, it is not necessary to estimate the market price of risk because the process followed by a variable in a risk-neutral world can be estimated directly. For example, if the variable is the price of an investment asset, its total return in a risk-neutral world is the risk-free rate. If the variable is the short-term interest rate r, Chapter 31 shows how a risk-neutral process can be estimated from the initial term structure of interest rates.

For commodities, futures prices can be used to estimate the risk-neutral process, as discussed in Chapter 35. Example 35.2 provides a simple application of the real options approach by using futures prices to evaluate an investment involving the breeding of cattle.

36.4 APPLICATION TO THE VALUATION OF A BUSINESS

Traditional methods of business valuation, such as applying a price/earnings multiplier to current earnings, do not work well for new businesses. Typically a company's earnings are negative during its early years as it attempts to gain market share and establish relationships with customers. The company must be valued by estimating future earnings and cash flows under different scenarios.

The real options approach can be useful in this situation. A model relating the company's future cash flows to variables such as the sales growth rates, variable costs as a percent of sales, fixed costs, and so on, is developed. For key variables, a risk-neutral stochastic process is estimated as outlined in the previous two sections. A Monte Carlo simulation is then carried out to generate alternative scenarios for the net cash flows per year in a risk-neutral world. It is likely that under some of these scenarios the company does very well and under others it becomes bankrupt and ceases operations. (The simulation must have a built in rule for determining when bankruptcy happens.) The value of the company is the present value of the expected cash flow in each year using the risk-free rate for discounting. Business Snapshot 36.1 gives an example of the application of the approach to Amazon.com.

36.5 EVALUATING OPTIONS IN AN INVESTMENT OPPORTUNITY

As already mentioned, most investment projects involve options. These options can add considerable value to the project and are often either ignored or valued incorrectly. Examples of the options embedded in projects are:

1. *Abandonment options.* This is an option to sell or close down a project. It is an American put option on the project's value. The strike price of the option is the

Business Snapshot 36.1   Valuing Amazon.com

One of the earliest published attempts to value a company using the real options approach was Schwartz and Moon (2000), who considered Amazon.com at the end of 1999. They assumed the following stochastic processes for the company's sales revenue R and its revenue growth rate μ:

$$\frac{dR}{R} = \mu \, dt + \sigma(t) \, dz_1$$

$$d\mu = \kappa(\bar{\mu} - \mu) \, dt + \eta(t) \, dz_2$$

They assumed that the two Wiener processes dz_1 and dz_2 were uncorrelated and made reasonable assumptions about $\sigma(t)$, $\eta(t)$, κ, and $\bar{\mu}$ based on available data.

They assumed the cost of goods sold would be 75% of sales, other variable expenses would be 19% of sales, and fixed expenses would be $75 million per quarter. The initial sales level was $356 million, the initial tax loss carry forward was $559 million, and the tax rate was assumed to be 35%. The market price of risk for R was estimated from historical data using the approach described in the previous section. The market price of risk for μ was assumed to be zero.

The time horizon for the analysis was 25 years and the terminal value of the company was assumed to be ten times pretax operating profit. The initial cash position was $906 million and the company was assumed to go bankrupt if the cash balance became negative.

Different future scenarios were generated in a risk-neutral world using Monte Carlo simulation. The evaluation of the scenarios involved taking account of the possible exercise of convertible bonds and the possible exercise of employee stock options. The value of the company to the share holders was calculated as the present value of the net cash flows discounted at the risk-free rate.

Using these assumptions, Schwartz and Moon provided an estimate of the value of Amazon. com's shares at the end of 1999 equal to $12.42. The market price at the time was $76.125 (although it declined sharply in 2000). One of the key advantages of the real-options approach is that it identifies the key assumptions. Schwartz and Moon found that the estimated share value was very sensitive to $\eta(t)$, the volatility of the growth rate. This was an important source of optionality. A small increase in $\eta(t)$ leads to more optionality and a big increase in the value of Amazon.com shares.

liquidation (or resale) value of the project less any closing-down costs. When the liquidation value is low, the strike price can be negative. Abandonment options mitigate the impact of very poor investment outcomes and increase the initial valuation of a project.

2. *Expansion options.* This is the option to make further investments and increase the output if conditions are favorable. It is an American call option on the value of additional capacity. The strike price of the call option is the cost of creating this additional capacity discounted to the time of option exercise. The strike price often depends on the initial investment. If management initially choose to build capacity in excess of the expected level of output, the strike price can be relatively small.

3. *Contraction options.* This is the option to reduce the scale of a project's operation. It is an American put option on the value of the lost capacity. The strike price is the present value of the future expenditures saved as seen at the time of exercise of the option.

4. *Options to defer.* One of the most important options open to a manager is the option to defer a project. This is an American call option on the value of the project.

5. *Options to extend life.* Sometimes it is possible to extend the life of an asset by paying a fixed amount. This is a European call option on the asset's future value.

Illustration

As an example of the evaluation of an investment with embedded options, consider a company that has to decide whether to invest $15 million to extract 6 million units of a commodity from a certain source at the rate of 2 million units per year for 3 years. The fixed costs of operating the equipment are $6 million per year and the variable costs are $17 per unit of the commodity extracted. We assume that the risk-free interest rate is 10% per annum for all maturities, that the spot price of the commodity is $20, and that the 1-, 2-, and 3-year futures prices are $22, $23, and $24, respectively.

Evaluation with No Embedded Options

First consider the case where the project has no embedded options. The expected prices of the commodity in 1, 2, and 3 years' time in a risk-neutral world are $22, $23, and $24, respectively. The expected payoff from the project (in millions of dollars) in a risk-neutral world can be calculated from the cost data as 4.0, 6.0, and 8.0 in years 1, 2, and 3, respectively. The value of the project is therefore

$$-15.0 + 4.0e^{-0.1 \times 1} + 6.0e^{-0.1 \times 2} + 8.0e^{-0.1 \times 3} = -0.54$$

This analysis indicates that the project should not be undertaken because it would reduce shareholder wealth by 0.54 million.

Use of a Tree

We now assume that the spot price of the commodity follows the process

$$d \ln S = [\theta(t) - a \ln S] \, dt + \sigma \, dz \tag{36.3}$$

where $a = 0.1$ and $\sigma = 0.2$. In Section 35.4, we showed how a tree can be constructed for commodity prices using the same example as the one considered here. The tree is shown in Figure 36.1 (which is the same as Figure 35.2). The process represented by the tree is consistent with the process assumed for S, the assumed values of a and σ, and the assumed 1-, 2-, and 3-year futures prices.

We do not need to use a tree to value the project when there are no embedded options. (We have already shown that the base value of the project without options is -0.54.) However, before we move on to consider options, it will be instructive, as well as useful for future calculations, for us to use the tree to value the project in the absence of embedded options and verify that we get the same answer as that obtained earlier.

Figure 36.1   Tree for spot price of a commodity: p_u, p_m, and p_d are the probabilities of "up", "middle", and "down" movements from a node.

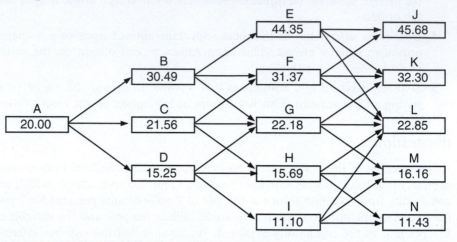

Node:	A	B	C	D	E	F	G	H	I
p_u:	0.1667	0.1217	0.1667	0.2217	0.8867	0.1217	0.1667	0.2217	0.0867
p_m:	0.6666	0.6566	0.6666	0.6566	0.0266	0.6566	0.6666	0.6566	0.0266
p_d:	0.1667	0.2217	0.1667	0.1217	0.0867	0.2217	0.1667	0.1217	0.8867

Figure 36.2 shows the value of the project at each node of Figure 36.1. Consider, for example, node H. There is a 0.2217 probability that the commodity price at the end of the third year is 22.85, so that the third-year profit is $2 \times 22.85 - 2 \times 17 - 6 = 5.70$. Similarly, there is a 0.6566 probability that the commodity price at the end of the third year is 16.16, so that the profit is -7.68 and there is a 0.1217 probability that the commodity price at the end of the third year is 11.43, so that the profit is -17.14. The value of the project at node H in Figure 36.2 is therefore

$$[0.2217 \times 5.70 + 0.6566 \times (-7.68) + 0.1217 \times (-17.14)]e^{-0.1 \times 1} = -5.31$$

As another example, consider node C. There is a 0.1667 chance of moving to node F where the commodity price is 31.37. The second year cash flow is then

$$2 \times 31.37 - 2 \times 17 - 6 = 22.74$$

The value of subsequent cash flows at node F is 21.42. The total value of the project if we move to node F is therefore $21.42 + 22.74 = 44.16$. Similarly the total value of the project if we move to nodes G and H are 10.35 and -13.93, respectively. The value of the project at node C is therefore

$$[0.1667 \times 44.16 + 0.6666 \times 10.35 + 0.1667 \times (-13.93)]e^{-0.1 \times 1} = 10.80$$

Figure 36.2 shows that the value of the project at the initial node A is 14.46. When the initial investment is taken into account the value of the project is therefore -0.54. This is in agreement with our earlier calculations.

Figure 36.2 Valuation of base project with no embedded options: p_u, p_m, and p_d are the probabilities of "up", "middle", and "down" movements from a node.

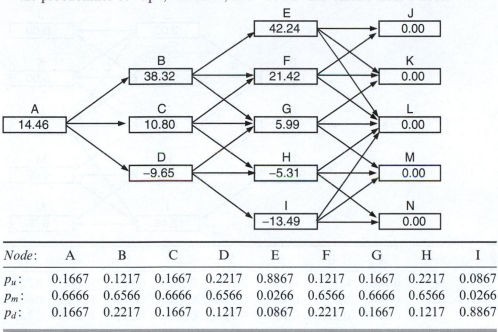

Node:	A	B	C	D	E	F	G	H	I
p_u:	0.1667	0.1217	0.1667	0.2217	0.8867	0.1217	0.1667	0.2217	0.0867
p_m:	0.6666	0.6566	0.6666	0.6566	0.0266	0.6566	0.6666	0.6566	0.0266
p_d:	0.1667	0.2217	0.1667	0.1217	0.0867	0.2217	0.1667	0.1217	0.8867

Option to Abandon

Suppose now that the company has the option to abandon the project at any time. We suppose that there is no salvage value and no further payments are required once the project has been abandoned. Abandonment is an American put option with a strike price of zero and is valued in Figure 36.3. The put option should not be exercised at nodes E, F, and G because the value of the project is positive at these nodes. It should be exercised at nodes H and I. The value of the put option is 5.31 and 13.49 at nodes H and I, respectively. Rolling back through the tree, the value of the abandonment put option at node D if it is not exercised is

$$(0.1217 \times 13.49 + 0.6566 \times 5.31 + 0.2217 \times 0)e^{-0.1 \times 1} = 4.64$$

The value of exercising the put option at node D is 9.65. This is greater than 4.64, and so the put should be exercised at node D. The value of the put option at node C is

$$[0.1667 \times 0 + 0.6666 \times 0 + 0.1667 \times (5.31)]e^{-0.1 \times 1} = 0.80$$

and the value at node A is

$$(0.1667 \times 0 + 0.6666 \times 0.80 + 0.1667 \times 9.65)e^{-0.1 \times 1} = 1.94$$

The abandonment option is therefore worth $1.94 million. It increases the value of the project from −$0.54 million to +$1.40 million. A project that was previously unattractive now has a positive value to shareholders.

Figure 36.3 Valuation of option to abandon the project: p_u, p_m, and p_d are the probabilities of "up", "middle", and "down" movements from a node.

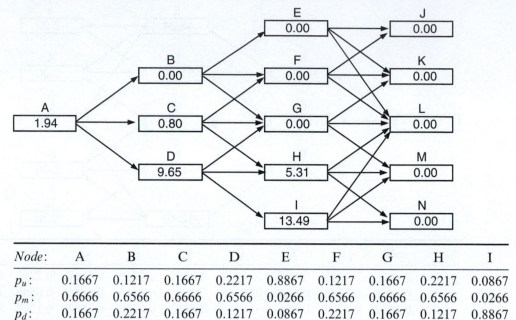

Node:	A	B	C	D	E	F	G	H	I
p_u:	0.1667	0.1217	0.1667	0.2217	0.8867	0.1217	0.1667	0.2217	0.0867
p_m:	0.6666	0.6566	0.6666	0.6566	0.0266	0.6566	0.6666	0.6566	0.0266
p_d:	0.1667	0.2217	0.1667	0.1217	0.0867	0.2217	0.1667	0.1217	0.8867

Option to Expand

Suppose next that the company has no abandonment option. Instead it has the option at any time to increase the scale of the project by 20%. The cost of doing this is $2 million. Production increases from 2.0 to 2.4 million units per year. Variable costs remain $17 per unit and fixed costs increase by 20% from $6.0 million to $7.2 million. This is an American call option to buy 20% of the base project in Figure 36.2 for $2 million. The option is valued in Figure 36.4. At node E, the option should be exercised. The payoff is $0.2 \times 42.24 - 2 = 6.45$. At node F, it should also be exercised for a payoff of $0.2 \times 21.42 - 2 = 2.28$. At nodes G, H, and I, the option should not be exercised. At node B, exercising is worth more than waiting and the option is worth $0.2 \times 38.32 - 2 = 5.66$. At node C, if the option is not exercised, it is worth

$$(0.1667 \times 2.28 + 0.6666 \times 0.00 + 0.1667 \times 0.00)e^{-0.1 \times 1} = 0.34$$

If the option is exercised, it is worth $0.2 \times 10.80 - 2 = 0.16$. The option should therefore not be exercised at node C. At node A, if not exercised, the option is worth

$$(0.1667 \times 5.66 + 0.6666 \times 0.34 + 0.1667 \times 0.00)e^{-0.1 \times 1} = 1.06$$

If the option is exercised it is worth $0.2 \times 14.46 - 2 = 0.89$. Early exercise is therefore not optimal at node A. In this case, the option increases the value of the project from -0.54 to $+0.52$. Again we find that a project that previously had a negative value now has a positive value.

Figure 36.4 Valuation of option to expand the project: p_u, p_m, and p_d are the probabilities of "up", "middle", and "down" movements from a node.

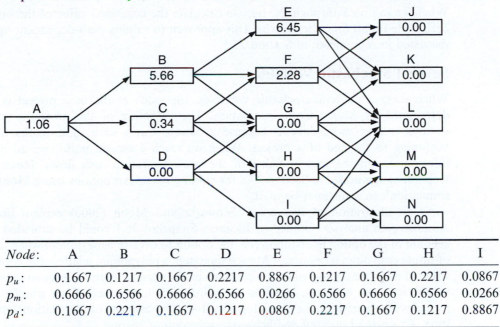

Node:	A	B	C	D	E	F	G	H	I
p_u:	0.1667	0.1217	0.1667	0.2217	0.8867	0.1217	0.1667	0.2217	0.0867
p_m:	0.6666	0.6566	0.6666	0.6566	0.0266	0.6566	0.6666	0.6566	0.0266
p_d:	0.1667	0.2217	0.1667	0.1217	0.0867	0.2217	0.1667	0.1217	0.8867

The expansion option in Figure 36.4 is relatively easy to value because, once the option has been exercised, all subsequent cash inflows and outflows increase by 20%. In the case where fixed costs remain the same or increase by less than 20%, it is necessary to keep track of more information at the nodes of Figure 36.4. Specifically, we need to record the following in order to calculate the payoff from exercising the option:

1. The present value of subsequent fixed costs
2. The present value of subsequent revenues net of variable costs.

Multiple Options

When a project has two or more options, they are typically not independent. The value of having both option A and option B, for example, is generally not the sum of the values of the two options. To illustrate this, suppose that the company we have been considering has both abandonment and expansion options. The project cannot be expanded if it has already been abandoned. Moreover, the value of the put option to abandon depends on whether the project has been expanded.[3]

These interactions between the options in our example can be handled by defining four states at each node:

1. Not already abandoned; not already expanded
2. Not already abandoned; already expanded

---

[3] As it happens, the two options do not interact in Figures 36.3 and 36.4. However, the interactions between the options would become an issue if a larger tree with smaller time steps were built.

3. Already abandoned; not already expanded

4. Already abandoned; already expanded.

When we roll back through the tree we calculate the combined value of the options at each node for all four alternatives. This approach to valuing path-dependent options is discussed in more detail in Section 27.5.

Several Stochastic Variables

When there are several stochastic variables, the value of the base project is usually determined by Monte Carlo simulation. The valuation of the project's embedded options is then more difficult because a Monte Carlo simulation works from the beginning to the end of a project. When we reach a certain point, we do not have information on the present value of the project's future cash flows. However, the techniques mentioned in Section 27.8 for valuing American options using Monte Carlo simulation can sometimes be used.

As an illustration of this point, Schwartz and Moon (2000) explain how their Amazon.com analysis outlined in Business Snapshot 36.1 could be extended to take account of the option to abandon (i.e. the option to declare bankruptcy) when the value of future cash flows is negative.[4] At each time step, a polynomial relationship between the value of not abandoning and variables such as the current revenue, revenue growth rate, volatilities, cash balances, and loss carry forwards is assumed. Each simulation trial provides an observation for obtaining a least-squares estimate of the relationship at each time. This is the Longstaff and Schwartz approach of Section 27.8.[5]

SUMMARY

This chapter has investigated how the ideas developed earlier in the book can be applied to the valuation of real assets and options on real assets. It has shown how the risk-neutral valuation principle can be used to value a project dependent on any set of variables. The expected growth rate of each variable is adjusted to reflect its market price of risk. The value of the asset is then the present value of its expected cash flows discounted at the risk-free rate.

Risk-neutral valuation provides an internally consistent approach to capital investment appraisal. It also makes it possible to value the options that are embedded in many of the projects that are encountered in practice. This chapter has illustrated the approach by applying it to the valuation of Amazon.com at the end of 1999 and the valuation of a project involving the extraction of a commodity.

FURTHER READING

Amran, M., and N. Kulatilaka, *Real Options*, Boston, MA: Harvard Business School Press, 1999.

---

[4] The analysis in Section 36.4 assumed that bankruptcy occurs when the cash balance falls below zero, but this is not necessarily optimal for Amazon.com.

[5] F. A. Longstaff and E. S. Schwartz, "Valuing American Options by Simulation: A Simple Least-Squares Approach," *Review of Financial Studies*, 14, 1 (Spring 2001): 113–47.

Copeland, T., and V. Antikarov, *Real Options: A Practitioners Guide*, New York: Texere, 2003.

Koller, T., M. Goedhart, and D. Wessels, *Valuation: Measuring and Managing the Value of Companies*, 5th edn. New York: Wiley, 2010.

Mun, J., *Real Options Analysis*, Hoboken, NJ: Wiley, 2006.

Schwartz, E. S., and M. Moon, "Rational Pricing of Internet Companies," *Financial Analysts Journal*, May/June (2000): 62–75.

Trigeorgis, L., *Real Options: Managerial Flexibility and Strategy in Resource Allocation*, Cambridge, MA: MIT Press, 1996.

Practice Questions (Answers in Solutions Manual)

36.1. Explain the difference between the net present value approach and the risk-neutral valuation approach for valuing a new capital investment opportunity. What are the advantages of the risk-neutral valuation approach for valuing real options?

36.2. The market price of risk for copper is 0.5, the volatility of copper prices is 20% per annum, the spot price is 80 cents per pound, and the 6-month futures price is 75 cents per pound. What is the expected percentage growth rate in copper prices over the next 6 months?

36.3. Show that if y is a commodity's convenience yield and u is its storage cost, the commodity's growth rate in the traditional risk-neutral world is $r - y + u$, where r is the risk-free rate. Deduce the relationship between the market price of risk of the commodity, its real-world growth rate, its volatility, y, and u.

36.4. The correlation between a company's gross revenue and the market index is 0.2. The excess return of the market over the risk-free rate is 6% and the volatility of the market index is 18%. What is the market price of risk for the company's revenue?

36.5. A company can buy an option for the delivery of 1 million units of a commodity in 3 years at $25 per unit. The 3-year futures price is $24. The risk-free interest rate is 5% per annum with continuous compounding and the volatility of the futures price is 20% per annum. How much is the option worth?

36.6. A driver entering into a car lease agreement can obtain the right to buy the car in 4 years for $10,000. The current value of the car is $30,000. The value of the car, S, is expected to follow the process $dS = \mu S\, dt + \sigma S\, dz$, where $\mu = -0.25$, $\sigma = 0.15$, and dz is a Wiener process. The market price of risk for the car price is estimated to be -0.1. What is the value of the option? Assume that the risk-free rate for all maturities is 6%.

Further Questions

36.7. Suppose that the spot price, 6-month futures price, and 12-month futures price for wheat are 250, 260, and 270 cents per bushel, respectively. Suppose that the price of wheat follows the process in equation (36.3) with $a = 0.05$ and $\sigma = 0.15$. Construct a two-time-step tree for the price of wheat in a risk-neutral world.

A farmer has a project that involves an expenditure of $10,000 and a further expenditure of $90,000 in 6 months. It will increase wheat that is harvested and sold by 40,000 bushels in 1 year. What is the value of the project? Suppose that the farmer can abandon the project in 6 months and avoid paying the $90,000 cost at that time. What is the value of the abandonment option? Assume a risk-free rate of 5% with continuous compounding.

36.8. In the example considered in Section 36.5:
   (a)   What is the value of the abandonment option if it costs $3 million rather than zero?
   (b)   What is the value of the expansion option if it costs $5 million rather than $2 million?

37

Derivatives Mishaps and What We Can Learn from Them

Since the mid-1980s there have been some spectacular losses in derivatives markets. The biggest losses have come from the trading of products created from subprime residential mortgages in the United States and were discussed in Chapter 8. Some of the other losses made by financial institutions are listed in Business Snapshot 37.1, and some of those made by nonfinancial organizations in Business Snapshot 37.2. What is remarkable about these lists is the number of situations where huge losses arose from the activities of a single employee. In 1995, Nick Leeson's trading brought a 200-year-old British bank, Barings, to its knees; in 1994, Robert Citron's trading led to Orange County, a municipality in California, losing about $2 billion. Joseph Jett's trading for Kidder Peabody lost $350 million. John Rusnak's losses of $700 million for Allied Irish Bank came to light in 2002. In 2006 the hedge fund Amaranth lost $6 billion because of trading risks taken by Brian Hunter. In 2008, Jérôme Kerviel lost over $7 billion trading equity index futures for Société Générale. The huge losses at UBS, Shell, and Sumitomo were also each the result of the activities of a single individual.

The losses should not be viewed as an indictment of the whole derivatives industry. The derivatives market is a vast multitrillion dollar market that by most measures has been outstandingly successful and has served the needs of its users well. The events listed in Business Snapshots 37.1 and 37.2 represent a tiny proportion of the total trades (both in number and value). Nevertheless, it is worth considering carefully the lessons that can be learned from them.

37.1 LESSONS FOR ALL USERS OF DERIVATIVES

First, we consider the lessons appropriate to all users of derivatives, whether they are financial or nonfinancial companies.

Business Snapshot 37.1   Big Losses by Financial Institutions

---

Allied Irish Bank

This bank lost about $700 million from speculative activities of one of its foreign exchange traders, John Rusnak, that lasted a number of years. Rusnak managed to cover up his losses by creating fictitious option trades.

Amaranth

This hedge fund lost $6 billion in 2006 betting on the future direction of natural gas prices.

Barings

This 200-year-old British bank was destroyed in 1995 by the activities of one trader, Nick Leeson, in Singapore, who made big bets on the future direction of the Nikkei 225 using futures and options. The total loss was close to $1 billion.

Enron's counterparties

Enron managed to conceal its true situation from its shareholders with some creative contracts. Several financial institutions that allegedly helped Enron do this have settled shareholder lawsuits for over $1 billion.

Kidder Peabody (see page 112)

The activities of a single trader, Joseph Jett, led to this New York investment dealer losing $350 million trading U.S. government securities. The loss arose because of a mistake in the way the company's computer system calculated profits.

Long-Term Capital Management (see page 34)

This hedge fund lost about $4 billion in 1998 as a result of Russia's default on its debt and the resultant flight to quality. The New York Federal Reserve organized an orderly liquidation of the fund by arranging for 14 banks to invest in the fund.

Midland Bank

This British bank lost $500 million in the early 1990s largely because of a wrong bet on the direction of interest rates. It was later taken over by the Hong Kong and Shanghai Banking Corporation (HSBC).

Société Générale (see page 18)

Jérôme Kerviel lost over $7 billion speculating on the future direction of equity indices in January 2008.

Subprime Mortgage Losses (see Chapter 8)

In 2007 investors lost confidence in the structured products created from U.S. subprime mortgages. This led to a "credit crunch" and losses of tens of billions of dollars by financial institutions such as UBS, Merrill Lynch, and Citigroup.

UBS

In 2011, Kweku Adoboli lost $2.3 billion by taking unauthorized speculative positions in stock market indices.

Business Snapshot 37.2   Big Losses by Nonfinancial Organizations

---

Allied Lyons
The treasury department of this drinks and food company lost $150 million in 1991 selling call options on the U.S. dollar–sterling exchange rate.

Gibson Greetings
The treasury department of this greeting card manufacturer lost about $20 million in 1994 trading highly exotic interest rate derivatives contracts with Bankers Trust. It later sued Bankers Trust and settled out of court.

Hammersmith and Fulham (see page 176)
This British Local Authority lost about $600 million on sterling interest rate swaps and options in 1988. All its contracts were later declared null and void by the British courts, much to the annoyance of the banks on the other side of the transactions.

Metallgesellschaft (see page 69)
This German company entered into long-term contracts to supply oil and gasoline and hedged them by rolling over short-term futures contracts. It lost $1.3 billion when it was forced to discontinue this activity.

Orange County (see page 92)
The activities of the treasurer, Robert Citron, led to this California municipality losing about $2 billion in 1994. The treasurer was using derivatives to speculate that interest rates would not rise.

Procter & Gamble (see page 769)
The treasury department of this large U.S. company lost about $90 million in 1994 trading highly exotic interest rate derivatives contracts with Bankers Trust. It later sued Bankers Trust and settled out of court.

Shell
A single employee working in the Japanese subsidiary of this company lost $1 billion dollars in unauthorized trading of currency futures.

Sumitomo
A single trader working for this Japanese company lost about $2 billion in the copper spot, futures, and options market in the 1990s.

Define Risk Limits

It is essential that all companies define in a clear and unambiguous way limits to the financial risks that can be taken. They should then set up procedures for ensuring that the limits are obeyed. Ideally, overall risk limits should be set at board level. These should then be converted to limits applicable to the individuals responsible for managing particular risks. Daily reports should indicate the gain or loss that will be experienced for particular movements in market variables. These should be checked against the actual gains and losses that are experienced to ensure that the valuation procedures underlying the reports are accurate.

It is particularly important that companies monitor risks carefully when derivatives are used. This is because, as we saw in Chapter 1, derivatives can be used for hedging, speculation, and arbitrage. Without close monitoring, it is impossible to know whether a derivatives trader has switched from being a hedger to a speculator or switched from being an arbitrageur to being a speculator. The Barings, Société Générale, and UBS losses are classic examples of what can go wrong. In each case, the trader's mandate was to carry out low-risk arbitrage or hedging. Unknown to their supervisors, the traders switched from being arbitrageurs or hedgers to taking huge bets on the future direction of market variables. Systems at their banks were so inadequate that nobody knew the full extent of what they were doing.

The argument here is not that no risks should be taken. A trader in a financial institution or a fund manager should be allowed to take positions on the future direction of relevant market variables. But the sizes of the positions that can be taken should be limited and the systems in place should accurately report the risks being taken.

Take the Risk Limits Seriously

What happens if an individual exceeds risk limits and makes a profit? This is a tricky issue for senior management. It is tempting to ignore violations of risk limits when profits result. However, this is shortsighted. It leads to a culture where risk limits are not taken seriously, and it paves the way for a disaster. In some of the situations listed in Business Snapshots 37.1 and 37.2, the companies had become complacent about the risks they were taking because they had taken similar risks in previous years and made profits.

A classic example here is Orange County. Robert Citron's activities in 1991–93 had been very profitable for Orange County, and the municipality had come to rely on his trading for additional funding. People chose to ignore the risks he was taking because he had produced profits. Unfortunately, the losses made in 1994 far exceeded the profits from previous years.

The penalties for exceeding risk limits should be just as great when profits result as when losses result. Otherwise, traders who make losses are liable to find a way of temporarily hiding their losses so that they can increase their bets in the hope that eventually a profit will result and all will be forgiven.

Do Not Assume You Can Outguess the Market

Some traders are quite possibly better than others. But no trader gets it right all the time. A trader who correctly predicts the direction in which market variables will move 60% of the time is doing well. If a trader has an outstanding track record (as Robert Citron did in the early 1990s), it is likely to be a result of luck rather than superior trading skill.

Suppose that a financial institution employs 16 traders and one of those traders makes profits in every quarter of a year. Should the trader receive a good bonus? Should the trader's risk limits be increased? The answer to the first question is that inevitably the trader will receive a good bonus. The answer to the second question should be no. The chance of making a profit in four consecutive quarters from random trading is 0.5^4 or 1 in 16. This means that just by chance one of the 16 traders will "get it right" every single quarter of the year. It should not be assumed that the trader's luck will continue and the trader's risk limits should not be increased.

Do Not Underestimate the Benefits of Diversification

When a trader appears good at predicting a particular market variable, there is a tendency to increase the trader's limits. We have just argued that this is a bad idea because it is quite likely that the trader has been lucky rather than clever. However, let us suppose that a fund is really convinced that the trader has special talents. How undiversified should it allow itself to become in order to take advantage of the trader's special skills? The answer is that the benefits from diversification are huge, and it may not be the best strategy to forego these benefits to speculate heavily on just one market variable.

An example will illustrate the point here. Suppose that there are 20 stocks, each of which have an expected return of 10% per annum and a standard deviation of returns of 30%. The correlation between the returns from any two of the stocks is 0.2. By dividing an investment equally among the 20 stocks, an investor has an expected return of 10% per annum and standard deviation of returns of 14.7%. Diversification enables the investor to reduce risks by over half. Another way of expressing this is that diversification enables an investor to double the expected return per unit of risk taken. The investor would have to be very good at stock picking to consistently get a better risk–return trade-off by investing in just one stock.

Carry out Scenario Analyses and Stress Tests

The calculation of risk measures such as value at risk and expected shortfall should always be accompanied by scenario analyses and stress testing to obtain an understanding of what can go wrong. They are very important. Human beings have an unfortunate tendency to anchor on one or two scenarios when evaluating decisions. In 1993 and 1994, for example, Procter & Gamble and Gibson Greetings may have been so convinced that interest rates would remain low that they ignored the possibility of a 100-basis-point increase in their decision making.

It is important to be creative in the way scenarios are generated and to use the judgment of experienced managers. One approach is to look at 20 or 30 years of data and choose the most extreme events as scenarios. Sometimes there is a shortage of data on a key variable. It is then sensible to choose a similar variable for which much more data is available and use historical daily percentage changes in that variable as a proxy for possible daily percentage changes in the key variable. For example, if there is little data on the prices of bonds issued by a particular country, historical data on prices of bonds issued by other similar countries can be used to develop possible scenarios.

37.2 LESSONS FOR FINANCIAL INSTITUTIONS

We now move on to consider lessons that are primarily relevant to financial institutions.

Monitor Traders Carefully

In trading rooms there is a tendency to regard high-performing traders as "untouchable" and to not subject their activities to the same scrutiny as other traders. Apparently Joseph Jett, Kidder Peabody's star trader of Treasury instruments, was often "too busy" to answer questions and discuss his positions with the company's risk managers.

All traders—particularly those making high profits—should be fully accountable. It is important for the financial institution to know whether the high profits are being made by taking unreasonably high risks. It is also important to check that the financial institution's computer systems and pricing models are correct and are not being manipulated in some way.

Separate the Front, Middle, and Back Office

The *front office* in a financial institution consists of the traders who are executing trades, taking positions, and so forth. The *middle office* consists of risk managers who are monitoring the risks being taken. The *back office* is where the record keeping and accounting takes place. Some of the worst derivatives disasters have occurred because these functions were not kept separate. Nick Leeson controlled both the front and back office for Barings in Singapore and was, as a result, able to conceal the disastrous nature of his trades from his superiors in London for some time. Jérôme Kerviel had worked in Société Générale's back office before becoming a trader and took advantage of his knowledge of its systems to hide his positions.

Do Not Blindly Trust Models

Some of the large losses incurred by financial institutions arose because of the models and computer systems being used. We discussed how Kidder Peabody was misled by its own systems on page 112.

If large profits are always reported when relatively simple trading strategies are followed, there is a good chance that the models underlying the calculation of the profits are wrong. Similarly, if a financial institution appears to be particularly competitive on its quotes for a particular type of deal, there is a good chance that it is using a different model from other market participants, and it should analyze what is going on carefully. To the head of a trading room, getting too much business of a certain type can be just as worrisome as getting too little business of that type.

Be Conservative in Recognizing Inception Profits

When a financial institution sells a highly exotic instrument to a nonfinancial corporation, the valuation can be highly dependent on the underlying model. For example, instruments with long-dated embedded interest rate options can be highly dependent on the interest rate model used. In these circumstances, a phrase used to describe the daily marking to market of the deal is *marking to model*. This is because there are no market prices for similar deals that can be used as a benchmark.

Suppose that a financial institution manages to sell an instrument to a client for $10 million more than it is worth—or at least $10 million more than its model says it is worth. The $10 million is known as an *inception profit*. When should it be recognized? There appears to be quite a variation in what different financial institutions do. Some recognize the $10 million immediately, whereas others are much more conservative and take reserves so that the profit (if it materializes) is recognized over the life of the deal.

Recognizing model-based inception profits immediately is very dangerous. It encourages traders to use aggressive models, take their bonuses, and leave before the model and the value of the deal come under close scrutiny. It is much better to recognize inception profits slowly, so that traders have the motivation to investigate the impact of several different models and several different sets of assumptions before committing themselves to a deal.

Do Not Sell Clients Inappropriate Products

It is tempting to sell corporate clients inappropriate products, particularly when they appear to have an appetite for the underlying risks. But this is shortsighted. The most dramatic example of this is the activities of Bankers Trust (BT) in the period leading up to the spring of 1994. Many of BT's clients were persuaded to buy high-risk and totally inappropriate products. A typical product (e.g., the 5/30 swap discussed on page 769) would give the client a good chance of saving a few basis points on its borrowings and a small chance of costing a large amount of money. The products worked well for BT's clients in 1992 and 1993, but blew up in 1994 when interest rates rose sharply. The bad publicity that followed hurt BT greatly. The years it had spent building up trust among corporate clients and developing an enviable reputation for innovation in derivatives were largely lost as a result of the activities of a few overly aggressive salesmen. BT was forced to pay large amounts of money to its clients to settle lawsuits out of court. It was taken over by Deutsche Bank in 1999.

Beware of Easy Profits

Enron provides an example of how overly aggressive deal makers can cost the banks they work for billions of dollars. Doing business with Enron seemed very profitable and banks competed with each other for this business. But the fact that many banks push hard to get a certain type of business should not be taken as an indication that the business will ultimately be profitable. The business that Enron did with banks resulted in shareholder lawsuits that were very expensive for the banks. In general, transactions where high profits seem easy to achieve should be looked at closely for hidden risks.

Investing in the AAA-rated tranches of the ABS CDOs that were created from subprime mortgages (see Chapter 8) seemed like a fantastic opportunity. The promised returns were much higher than the returns normally earned on AAA-rated instruments. Many investors did not stop to ask whether the extra returns reflected risks not taken into account by the rating agencies.

Do Not Ignore Liquidity Risk

Financial engineers usually base the pricing of exotic instruments and other instruments that trade relatively infrequently on the prices of actively traded instruments. For example:

1. A financial engineer often calculates a zero curve from actively traded government bonds (known as on-the-run bonds) and uses it to price government bonds that trade less frequently (off-the-run bonds).
2. A financial engineer often implies the volatility of an asset from actively traded options and uses it to price less actively traded options.

3. A financial engineer often implies information about the behavior of interest rates from actively traded interest rate caps and swap options and uses it to price nonstandard interest rate derivatives that are less actively traded.

These practices are not unreasonable. However, it is dangerous to assume that less actively traded instruments can always be traded at close to their theoretical price. When financial markets experience a shock of one sort or another there is often a "flight to quality." Liquidity becomes very important to investors, and illiquid instruments often sell at a big discount to their theoretical values. This happened in 2007–9 following the jolt to credit markets caused by lack of confidence in securities backed by subprime mortgages.

Another example of losses arising from liquidity risk is provided by Long-Term Capital Management (LTCM), which was discussed in Business Snapshot 2.2. This hedge fund followed a strategy known as *convergence arbitrage*. It attempted to identify two securities (or portfolios of securities) that should in theory sell for the same price. If the market price of one security was less that of the other, it would buy that security and sell the other. The strategy is based on the idea that if two securities have the same theoretical price their market prices should eventually be the same.

In the summer of 1998 LTCM made a huge loss. This was largely because a default by Russia on its debt caused a flight to quality. LTCM tended to be long illiquid instruments and short the corresponding liquid instruments (for example, it was long off-the-run bonds and short on-the-run bonds). The spreads between the prices of illiquid instruments and the corresponding liquid instruments widened sharply after the Russian default. LTCM was highly leveraged. It experienced huge losses and there were margin calls on its positions that it found difficult to meet.

The LTCM story reinforces the importance of carrying out scenario analyses and stress testing to look at what can happen in the worst of all worlds. LTCM could have tried to examine other times in history when there had been extreme flights to quality to quantify the liquidity risks it was facing.

Beware When Everyone Is Following the Same Trading Strategy

It sometimes happens that many market participants are following essentially the same trading strategy. This creates a dangerous environment where there are liable to be big market moves, unstable markets, and large losses for the market participants.

We gave one example of this in Chapter 19 when discussing portfolio insurance and the market crash of October 1987. In the months leading up to the crash, increasing numbers of portfolio managers were attempting to insure their portfolios by creating synthetic put options. They bought stocks or stock index futures after a rise in the market and sold them after a fall. This created an unstable market. A relatively small decline in stock prices could lead to a wave of selling by portfolio insurers. The latter would lead to a further decline in the market, which could give rise to another wave of selling, and so on. There is little doubt that without portfolio insurance the crash of October 1987 would have been much less severe.

Another example is provided by LTCM in 1998. Its position was made more difficult by the fact that many other hedge funds were following similar convergence arbitrage strategies to its own. After the Russian default and the flight to quality, LTCM tried to liquidate part of its portfolio to meet margin calls. Unfortunately, other hedge funds were facing similar problems to LTCM and trying to do similar trades. This exacerbated the situation, causing liquidity spreads to be even higher than they would otherwise have been and reinforcing the flight to quality. Consider, for example, LTCM's position in U.S. Treasury bonds. It was long the illiquid off-the-run bonds and short the liquid on-the-run bonds. When a flight to quality caused spreads between yields on the two types of bonds to widen, LTCM had to liquidate its positions by selling off-the-run bonds and buying on-the-run bonds. Other large hedge funds were doing the same. As a result, the price of on-the-run bonds rose relative to off-the-run bonds and the spread between the two yields widened even more than it had done already.

A further example is provided by the activities of British insurance companies in the late 1990s. These insurance companies had entered into many contracts promising that the rate of interest applicable to annuities would be the greater of the market rate and a guaranteed rate. The insurance companies stood to lose money if long-term interest rates fell below the guaranteed rate. For various reasons, they all entered into derivatives transactions to partially hedge their risks at about the same time. The financial institutions on the other side of the derivatives transactions hedged their risks by buying huge numbers of long-dated sterling bonds. As a result, bond prices rose and sterling long-term interest rates declined. More bonds had to be bought to maintain the dynamic hedge, sterling long-term interest rates declined further, and so on. The financial institutions lost money and insurance companies found themselves in a worse position on the risks that they had chosen not to hedge.

The key lesson to be learned from these stories is that there can be big risks in situations where many market participants are following the same trading strategy.

Do Not Make Excessive Use of Short-Term Funding for Long-Term Needs

All financial institutions finance long-term needs with short-term sources of funds to some extent. But a financial institution that relies too heavily on short-term funds is likely to expose itself to unacceptable liquidity risks.

Suppose that a financial institution funds long-term needs by rolling over commercial paper every month. Commercial paper issued on April 1 would be redeemed with the proceeds of a new commercial paper issue on May 1; this new commercial paper issue would be redeemed with the proceeds of a commercial paper issue on June 1; and so on. Provided that the financial institution is perceived as healthy, there should be no problem. But if investors lose confidence in the financial institution (rightly or wrongly), it becomes impossible to roll over commercial paper and the financial institution experiences severe liquidity problems.

Many of the failures of financial institutions during the credit crisis (e.g., Lehman Brothers and Northern Rock) were largely caused by excessive reliance on short-term funding. It is not surprising that the Basel Committee, which is responsible for regulating banks internationally, is introducing liquidity ratios which banks must satisfy.

Market Transparency Is Important

One of the lessons from the credit crunch of 2007 is that market transparency is important. During the period leading up to 2007, investors traded highly structured products without any real knowledge of the underlying assets. All they knew was the credit rating of the security being traded. With hindsight, we can say that investors should have demanded more information about the underlying assets and should have more carefully assessed the risks they were taking—but it is easy to be wise after the event!

The subprime meltdown of August 2007 caused investors to lose confidence in all structured products and withdraw from that market. This led to a market breakdown where tranches of structured products could only be sold at prices well below their theoretical values. There was a flight to quality and credit spreads increased. If there had been market transparency so that investors understood the asset-backed securities they were buying, there would still have been subprime losses, but the flight to quality and disruptions to the market would have been less pronounced.

Manage Incentives

A key lesson from the credit crisis of 2007 and 2008 is the importance of incentives. The bonus systems in banks tend to emphasize short-term performance. Some financial institutions have switched to systems where the payment for performance in a year is spread out over a number of future years and part of the bonus may be "clawed back" if it turns out that performance was not as good as originally thought. This has obvious advantages. It discourages traders from doing trades that will look good in the short run, but may "blow up" in a few years.

When loans are securitized, it is important to try and align the interests of the party originating the loan with the party who bears the ultimate risk so that agency costs are minimized. One way of doing this is for regulators to require the originator of a loan portfolio to keep a stake in all the tranches and other instruments that are created from the portfolio.

Never Ignore Risk Management

When times are good (or appear to be good), there is a tendency to assume that nothing can go wrong and ignore the output from stress tests and other analyses carried out by the risk management group. There are many stories of risk managers not being listened to in the period leading up to the credit crisis of 2007. Chuck Prince, CEO of Citigroup, said in a much quoted interview with the *Financial Times* in July 2007 (just before the credit crisis):

> When the music stops, in terms of liquidity, things will be complicated. But as long as the music is playing, you've got to get up and dance. We're still dancing.

No doubt he regretted the comment later. As it turned out, Citigroup's losses from the credit crisis were over $50 billion. Mr. Prince lost his job later in 2007.

37.3 LESSONS FOR NONFINANCIAL CORPORATIONS

We now consider lessons primarily applicable to nonfinancial corporations.

Make Sure You Fully Understand the Trades You Are Doing

Corporations should never undertake a trade or a trading strategy that they do not fully understand. This is a somewhat obvious point, but it is surprising how often a trader working for a nonfinancial corporation will, after a big loss, admit to not knowing what was really going on and claim to have been misled by investment bankers. Robert Citron, the treasurer of Orange County did this. So did the traders working for Hammersmith and Fulham, who in spite of their huge positions were surprisingly uninformed about how the swaps and other interest rate derivatives they traded really worked.

If a senior manager in a corporation does not understand a trade proposed by a subordinate, the trade should not be approved. A simple rule of thumb is that if a trade and the rationale for entering into it are so complicated that they cannot be understood by the manager, it is almost certainly inappropriate for the corporation. The trades undertaken by Procter & Gamble and Gibson Greetings would have been vetoed using this criterion.

One way of ensuring that you fully understand a financial instrument is to value it. If a corporation does not have the in-house capability to value an instrument, it should not trade it. In practice, corporations often rely on their derivatives dealers for valuation information. This is dangerous, as Procter & Gamble and Gibson Greetings found out. When they wanted to unwind their deals, they found they were facing prices produced by Bankers Trust's proprietary models, which they had no way of checking.

Make Sure a Hedger Does Not Become a Speculator

One of the unfortunate facts of life is that hedging is relatively dull, whereas speculation is exciting. When a company hires a trader to manage the risks in exchange rates, commodity prices, or interest rates, there is a danger that the following might happen. At first, the trader does the job diligently and earns the confidence of top management. The trader assesses the company's exposures and hedges them. As time goes by, the trader becomes convinced that he or she can outguess the market. Slowly the trader becomes a speculator. At first things go well, but then a loss is made. To recover the loss, the trader doubles up the bets. Further losses are made—and so on. The result is likely to be a disaster.

As mentioned earlier, clear limits to the risks that can be taken should be set by senior management. Controls should be put in place to ensure that the limits are obeyed. The trading strategy for a corporation should start with an analysis of the risks facing the corporation in foreign exchange, interest rate, commodity markets, etc. A decision should then be taken on how the risks are to be reduced to acceptable levels. It is a clear sign that something is wrong within a corporation if the trading strategy is not derived in a very direct way from the company's exposures.

Be Cautious about Making the Treasury Department a Profit Center

In the last 20 years there has been a tendency to make the treasury department within a corporation a profit center. This appears to have much to recommend it. The treasurer is motivated to reduce financing costs and manage risks as profitably as possible. The problem is that the potential for the treasurer to make profits is limited. When raising funds and investing surplus cash, the treasurer is facing an efficient market. The treasurer can usually improve the bottom line only by taking additional risks. The company's hedging program gives the treasurer some scope for making shrewd decisions that increase profits. But it should be remembered that the goal of a hedging program is to reduce risks, not to increase expected profits. As pointed out in Chapter 3, the decision to hedge will lead to a worse outcome than the decision not to hedge roughly 50% of the time. The danger of making the treasury department a profit center is that the treasurer is motivated to become a speculator. This is liable to lead to the type of outcome experienced by Orange County, Procter & Gamble, or Gibson Greetings.

SUMMARY

The huge losses experienced from the use of derivatives have made many treasurers very wary. Following some of the losses, some nonfinancial corporations have announced plans to reduce or even eliminate their use of derivatives. This is unfortunate because derivatives provide treasurers with very efficient ways to manage risks.

The stories behind the losses emphasize the point, made as early as Chapter 1, that derivatives can be used for either hedging or speculation; that is, they can be used either to reduce risks or to take risks. Most losses occurred because derivatives were used inappropriately. Employees who had an implicit or explicit mandate to hedge their company's risks decided instead to speculate.

The key lesson to be learned from the losses is the importance of *internal controls*. Senior management within a company should issue a clear and unambiguous policy statement about how derivatives are to be used and the extent to which it is permissible for employees to take positions on movements in market variables. Management should then institute controls to ensure that the policy is carried out. It is a recipe for disaster to give individuals authority to trade derivatives without a close monitoring of the risks being taken.

FURTHER READING

Dunbar, N. *Inventing Money: The Story of Long-Term Capital Management and the Legends Behind It*. Chichester, U.K.: Wiley, 2000.

Jorion, P. "How Long-Term Lost Its Capital," *Risk*, 12 (September 1999).

Jorion, P., and R. Roper. *Big Bets Gone Bad: Derivatives and Bankruptcy in Orange County*. New York: Academic Press, 1995.

Persaud, A. D. (ed.) *Liquidity Black Holes: Understanding, Quantifying and Managing Financial Liquidity Risk*. London, Risk Books, 2003.

Sorkin, A. R., *Too Big to Fail*. New York: Penguin, 2010.

Tett, G. *Fool's Gold: How the Bold Dream of a Small Tribe at J. P. Morgan Was Corrupted by Wall Street Greed and Unleashed a Catastrophe*. New York: Free Press, 2009.

Glossary of Terms

ABS *See* Asset-Backed Security.

ABS CDO Instrument where tranches are created from the tranches of ABSs.

Accrual Swap An interest rate swap where interest on one side accrues only when a certain condition is met.

Accrued Interest The interest earned on a bond since the last coupon payment date.

Adaptive Mesh Model A model developed by Figlewski and Gao that grafts a high-resolution tree on to a low-resolution tree so that there is more detailed modeling of the asset price in critical regions.

Agency Costs Costs arising from a situation where the agent (e.g., manager) is not motivated to act in the best interests of the principal (e.g., shareholder).

Agency Mortgage-Backed Security Mortgage-backed security where payments are backed by a government agency.

American Option An option that can be exercised at any time during its life.

Amortizing Swap A swap where the notional principal decreases in a predetermined way as time passes.

Analytic Result Result in the form of an equation.

Arbitrage A trading strategy that takes advantage of two or more securities being mispriced relative to each other.

Arbitrageur An individual engaging in arbitrage.

Asian Option An option with a payoff dependent on the average price of the underlying asset during a specified period.

Ask Price The price that a dealer is offering to sell an asset.

Asked Price *See* Ask Price.

Asset-Backed Security Security created from a portfolio of loans, bonds, credit card receivables, or other assets.

Asset-or-Nothing Call Option An option that provides a payoff equal to the asset price if the asset price is above the strike price and zero otherwise.

Asset-or-Nothing Put Option An option that provides a payoff equal to the asset price if the asset price is below the strike price and zero otherwise.

Asset Swap   Exchanges the coupon on a bond for LIBOR plus a spread.

As-You-Like-It Option   *See* Chooser Option.

At-the-Money Option   An option in which the strike price equals the price of the underlying asset.

Average Price Call Option   An option giving a payoff equal to the greater of zero and the amount by which the average price of the asset exceeds the strike price.

Average Price Put Option   An option giving a payoff equal to the greater of zero and the amount by which the strike price exceeds the average price of the asset.

Average Strike Option   An option that provides a payoff dependent on the difference between the final asset price and the average asset price.

Bachelier Normal Model   Model where a future interest rate is normally distributed.

Backdating   Practice (often illegal) of marking a document with a date that precedes the current date.

Back Testing   Testing a value-at-risk or other model using historical data.

Backward Induction   A procedure for working from the end of a tree to its beginning in order to value an option.

Barrier Option   An option whose payoff depends on whether the path of the underlying asset has reached a barrier (i.e., a certain predetermined level).

Base Correlation   Correlation that leads to the price of a 0% to X% CDO tranche being consistent with the market for a particular value of X.

Basel Committee   Committee responsible for regulation of banks internationally.

Basis   The difference between the spot price and the futures price of a commodity.

Basis Point   When used to describe an interest rate, a basis point is one hundredth of one percent (= 0.01%)

Basis Risk   The risk to a hedger arising from uncertainty about the basis at a future time.

Basis Swap   A swap where cash flows determined by one floating reference rate are exchanged for cash flows determined by another floating reference rate.

Basket Credit Default Swap   Credit default swap where there are several reference entities.

Basket Option   An option that provides a payoff dependent on the value of a portfolio of assets.

Bear Spread   A short position in a put option with strike price K_1 combined with a long position in a put option with strike price K_2 where $K_2 > K_1$. (A bear spread can also be created with call options.)

Bermudan Option   An option that can be exercised on specified dates during its life.

Beta   A measure of the systematic risk of an asset.

Bid–Ask Spread   The amount by which the ask price exceeds the bid price.

Bid–Offer Spread   *See* Bid–Ask Spread.

Bid Price   The price that a dealer is prepared to pay for an asset.

Bilateral Clearing   Arrangement between two parties to handle transactions in the OTC market, often involving an ISDA Master Agreement.

Binary Credit Default Swap Instrument where there is a fixed dollar payoff in the event of a default by a particular company.

Binary Option Option with a discontinuous payoff, e.g., a cash-or-nothing option or an asset-or-nothing option.

Binomial Model A model where the price of an asset is monitored over successive short periods of time. In each short period it is assumed that only two price movements are possible.

Binomial Tree A tree that represents how an asset price can evolve under the binomial model.

Bivariate Normal Distribution A distribution for two correlated variables, each of which is normal.

Black's Approximation An approximate procedure developed by Fischer Black for valuing a call option on a dividend-paying stock.

Black's Model An extension of the Black–Scholes–Merton model for valuing European options on futures contracts. As described in Chapter 18, it is used extensively in practice to value European options when the distribution of the asset price at maturity is assumed to be lognormal.

Black–Scholes–Merton Model A model for pricing European options on stocks, developed by Fischer Black, Myron Scholes, and Robert Merton.

Bond Option An option where a bond is the underlying asset.

Bond Yield Discount rate which, when applied to all the cash flows of a bond, causes the present value of the cash flows to equal the bond's market price.

Bootstrap Method A procedure for calculating zero rates or forward rates from market data. It involves using progressively longer maturity instruments.

Boston Option *See* Deferred Payment Option.

Box Spread A combination of a bull spread created from calls and a bear spread created from puts.

Break Forward *See* Deferred Payment Option.

Brownian Motion *See* Wiener Process.

Bull Spread A long position in a call with strike price K_1 combined with a short position in a call with strike price K_2, where $K_2 > K_1$. (A bull spread can also be created with put options.)

Butterfly Spread A position that is created by taking a long position in a call with strike price K_1, a long position in a call with strike price K_3, and a short position in two calls with strike price K_2, where $K_3 > K_2 > K_1$ and $K_2 = 0.5(K_1 + K_3)$. (A butterfly spread can also be created with put options.)

Calendar Spread A position that is created by taking a long position in a call option that matures at one time and a short position in a similar call option that matures at a different time. (A calendar spread can also be created using put options.)

Calibration Method for implying a model's parameters from the prices of actively traded options.

Callable Bond A bond containing provisions that allow the issuer to buy it back at a predetermined price at certain times during its life.

Call Option   An option to buy an asset at a certain price by a certain date.

Cancelable Swap   Swap that can be canceled by one side on prespecified dates.

Cap   *See* Interest Rate Cap.

Cap Rate   The rate determining payoffs in an interest rate cap.

Capital Asset Pricing Model   A model relating the expected return on an asset to its beta.

Capital Valuation Adjustment (KVA)   Valuation adjustment to reflect the cost of capital requirements.

Caplet   One component of an interest rate cap.

Case–Shiller Index   Index of house prices in the United States.

Cash Flow Mapping   A procedure for representing an instrument as a portfolio of zero-coupon bonds for the purpose of calculating value at risk.

Cash-or-Nothing Call Option   An option that provides a fixed predetermined payoff if the final asset price is above the strike price and zero otherwise.

Cash-or-Nothing Put Option   An option that provides a fixed predetermined payoff if the final asset price is below the strike price and zero otherwise.

Cash Settlement   Procedure for settling a futures contract in cash rather than by delivering the underlying asset.

CAT Bond   Bond where the interest and, possibly, the principal paid are reduced if a particular category of "catastrophic" insurance claims exceed a certain amount.

CCP   *See* Central Counterparty.

CDD   Cooling degree days. The maximum of zero and the amount by which the daily average temperature is greater than $65°$ Fahrenheit. The average temperature is the average of the highest and lowest temperatures (midnight to midnight).

CDO   *See* Collateralized Debt Obligation.

CDO Squared   An instrument in which the default risks in a portfolio of CDO tranches are allocated to new securities.

CDS   *See* Credit Default Swap.

CDS Spread   Basis points that must be paid each year for protection in a CDS.

CDX NA IG   Portfolio of 125 North American companies.

CEBO   *See* Credit Event Binary Option.

Central Clearing   The use of a clearing house for over-the-counter derivatives.

Central Counterparty   A clearing house for over-the-counter derivatives.

Cheapest-to-Deliver Bond   The bond that is cheapest to deliver in the CME Group bond futures contract.

Cholesky Decomposition   A method of sampling from a multivariate normal distribution.

Chooser Option   An option where the holder has the right to choose whether it is a call or a put at some point during its life.

Class of Options   *See* Option Class.

Clean Price of Bond   The quoted price of a bond. The cash price paid for the bond (or dirty price) is calculated by adding the accrued interest to the clean price.

Clearing House   A firm that guarantees the performance of the parties in a derivatives transaction (also referred to as a clearing corporation).

Clearing Margin   A margin posted by a member of a clearinghouse.

Cliquet Option   A series of call or put options with rules for determining strike prices. Typically, one option starts when the previous one terminates.

CMO   Collateralized Mortgage Obligation.

Collar   *See* Interest Rate Collar.

Collateral   Cash or securities posted by a company to provide its counterparty with protection against a default by the company.

Collateralization   A system for posting collateral by one or both parties in a derivatives transaction.

Collateralized Debt Obligation   A way of packaging credit risk. Several classes of securities (known as tranches) are created from a portfolio of bonds and there are rules for determining how the cost of defaults are allocated to classes.

Collateralized Mortgage Obligation (CMO)   A mortgage-backed security where investors are divided into classes and there are rules for determining how interest and principal repayments are channeled to the classes.

Combination   A position involving both calls and puts on the same underlying asset.

Commodity Futures Trading Commission   A body that regulates trading in futures contracts and swaps in the United States.

Commodity Swap   A swap where cash flows depend on the price of a commodity.

Compound Correlation   Correlation implied from the market price of a CDO tranche.

Compound Option   An option on an option.

Compounding Frequency   This defines how an interest rate is measured.

Compounding Swap   Swap where interest compounds instead of being paid.

Compression   Procedure where two or more derivatives counterparties restructure outstanding transactions to reduce principal amounts and capital requirements.

Conditional Value at Risk (C-VaR)   *See* Expected Shortfall.

Confirmation   Contract confirming verbal agreement between two parties to a trade in the over-the-counter market.

Constant Elasticity of Variance (CEV) Model   Model where the variance of the change in a variable in a short period of time is proportional to the value of the variable.

Constant Maturity Swap (CMS)   A swap where a swap rate is exchanged for either a fixed rate or a floating rate on each payment date.

Constant Maturity Treasury Swap   A swap where the yield on a Treasury bond is exchanged for either a fixed rate or a floating rate on each payment date.

Consumption Asset   An asset held for consumption rather than investment.

Contango   A situation where the futures price is above the expected future spot price (also often used to refer to the situation where the futures price is above the current spot price).

Continuous Compounding   A way of quoting interest rates. It is the limit as the assumed compounding interval is made smaller and smaller.

Control Variate Technique   A technique that can sometimes be used for improving the accuracy of a numerical procedure.

Convenience Yield   A measure of the benefits from ownership of an asset that are not obtained by the holder of a long futures contract on the asset.

Conversion Factor   A factor used to determine the number of bonds that must be delivered in the CME Group bond futures contract.

Convertible Bond   A corporate bond that can be converted into a predetermined amount of the company's equity at certain times during its life.

Convexity   A measure of the curvature in the relationship between bond prices and bond yields.

Convexity Adjustment   An overworked term. For example, it can refer to the adjustment necessary to convert a futures interest rate to a forward interest rate. It can also refer to the adjustment to a forward rate that is sometimes necessary when Black's model is used.

Copula   A way of defining the correlation between variables with known distributions.

Cornish–Fisher Expansion   An approximate relationship between the fractiles of a probability distribution and its moments.

Cost of Carry   The storage costs plus the cost of financing an asset minus the income earned on the asset.

Counterparty   The opposite side in a financial transaction.

Coupon   Interest payment made on a bond.

Covariance   Measure of the linear relationship between two variables (equals the correlation between the variables times the product of their standard deviations).

Covariance Matrix   *See* Variance–Covariance Matrix.

Covered Call   A short position in a call option on an asset combined with a long position in the asset.

Crashophobia   Fear of a stock market crash that some people claim causes the market to increase the price of deep-out-of-the-money put options.

Credit Contagion   The tendency of a default by one company to lead to defaults by other companies.

Credit Default Swap   An instrument that gives the holder the right to sell a bond for its face value in the event of a default by the issuer.

Credit Derivative   A derivative whose payoff depends on the creditworthiness of one or more companies or countries.

Credit Event   Event, such as a default or reorganization, triggering a payout on a credit derivative.

Credit Event Binary Option   Exchange-traded option that provides a fixed payoff if a reference entity suffers a credit event.

Credit Index   Index that tracks the cost of buying protection for each company in a portfolio (e.g., CDX NA IG and iTraxx Europe).

Credit Rating   A measure of the creditworthiness of a bond issue.

Credit Ratings Transition Matrix   A table showing the probability that a bond will move from one credit rating to another during a certain period of time.

Credit Risk   The risk that a loss will be experienced because of a default by a counterparty.

Credit Spread Option   Option whose payoff depends on the spread between the yields earned on two assets.

Credit Support Annex (CSA)   Part of ISDA Master Agreement dealing with collateral requirements.

Credit Valuation Adjustment   Adjustment to value of derivatives outstanding with a counterparty to reflect the counterparty's default risk.

Credit Value at Risk   The credit loss that will not be exceeded at some specified confidence level.

CreditMetrics   A procedure for calculating credit value at risk.

Cross Hedging   Hedging an exposure to the price of one asset with a contract on another asset.

Cumulative Distribution Function   The probability that a variable will be less than x as a function of x.

Currency Swap   A swap where interest and principal in one currency are exchanged for interest and principal in another currency.

CVA   *See* Credit Valuation Adjustment.

Day Count   A convention for quoting interest rates.

Day Trade   A trade that is entered into and closed out on the same day.

Debt (or Debit) Valuation Adjustment   Value to a company of the fact that it might default on outstanding derivatives transactions.

Default Correlation   Measures the tendency of two companies to default at about the same time.

Default Intensity   *See* Hazard Rate.

Deferred Swap   An agreement to enter into a swap at some time in the future (also called a forward swap).

Delivery Price   Price agreed to in a forward contract.

Delta   The rate of change of the price of a derivative with the price of the underlying asset.

Delta Hedging   A hedging scheme that is designed to make the price of a portfolio of derivatives insensitive to small changes in the price of the underlying asset.

Delta-Neutral Portfolio   A portfolio with a delta of zero so that there is no sensitivity to small changes in the price of the underlying asset.

DerivaGem   The software accompanying this book.

Derivative   An instrument whose price depends on, or is derived from, the price of another asset.

Deterministic Variable   A variable whose future value is known.

Diagonal Spread   A position in two calls where both the strike prices and times to maturity are different. (A diagonal spread can also be created with put options.)

Differential Swap   A swap where a floating interest rate in one currency is applied to a principal in another currency.

Diffusion Process   Model where value of asset changes continuously (no jumps).

Dirty Price of Bond   Cash price of bond.

Discount Bond   *See* Zero-Coupon Bond.

Discount Instrument   An instrument, such as a Treasury bill, that provides no coupons.

Diversification   Reducing risk by dividing a portfolio between many different assets.

Dividend   A cash payment made to the owner of a stock.

Dividend Yield   The dividend as a percentage of the stock price.

Dodd–Frank Act   An act introduced in the United States in 2010 designed to protect consumers and investors, avoid future bailouts, and monitor the functioning of the financial system more carefully.

Dollar Duration   The product of a bond's modified duration and the bond price.

DOOM Option   Deep-out-of-the-money put option.

Down-and-In Option   An option that comes into existence when the price of the underlying asset declines to a prespecified level.

Down-and-Out Option   An option that ceases to exist when the price of the underlying asset declines to a prespecified level.

Downgrade Trigger   A clause in a contract that states that collateral will be required or that the contract will be terminated if the credit rating of one side falls below a certain level.

Drift Rate   The average increase per unit of time in a stochastic variable.

Duration   A measure of the average life a bond. It is also an approximation to the ratio of the proportional change in the bond price to the absolute change in its yield.

Duration Matching   A procedure for matching the durations of assets and liabilities in a financial institution.

DV01   The dollar value of a 1-basis-point increase in all interest rates.

DVA   *See* Debt (or Debit) Valuation Adjustment.

Dynamic Hedging   A procedure for hedging an option position by periodically changing the position held in the underlying asset. The objective is usually to maintain a delta-neutral position.

Early Exercise   Exercise prior to the maturity date.

Effective Federal Funds Rate   Weighted average federal funds rate for brokered transactions.

Efficient Market Hypothesis   A hypothesis that asset prices reflect relevant information.

Electronic Trading   System of trading where a computer is used to match buyers and sellers.

Embedded Option   An option that is an inseparable part of another instrument.

Empirical Research Research based on historical market data.

Employee Stock Option A stock option issued by company on its own stock and given to its employees as part of their remuneration.

EONIA Overnight interest rate in the euro.

Equilibrium Model A model for the behavior of interest rates derived from a model of the economy.

Equity Swap A swap where the return on an equity portfolio is exchanged for either a fixed or a floating rate of interest.

Equity Tranche The tranche that first absorbs losses.

Equivalent Annual Interest Rate Interest rate with annual compounding.

Equivalent Martingale Measure Result Result that the processes for security prices are martingales when (a) they are measured in terms of a numeraire security and (b) the market price of risk is the volatility of the numeraire security.

ETP Exchange-traded product such as an exchange-traded fund (ETF).

Euribor Euro rate of interest at which banks in the Eurozone borrow from each other.

Eurocurrency A currency that is outside the formal control of the issuing country's monetary authorities.

Eurodollar A dollar held in a bank outside the United States.

Eurodollar Futures Contract A futures contract written on a Eurodollar deposit.

Euro LIBOR London interbank offered rate for euros.

European Option An option that can be exercised only at the end of its life.

EWMA Exponentially weighted moving average.

Exchange Option An option to exchange one asset for another.

Ex-dividend Date When a dividend is declared, an ex-dividend date is specified. Investors who own shares of the stock just before the ex-dividend date receive the dividend.

Exercise Limit Maximum number of option contracts that can be exercised within a five-day period.

Exercise Multiple Ratio of stock price to strike price at time of exercise for employee stock option.

Exercise Price The price at which the underlying asset may be bought or sold in an option contract (also called the strike price).

Exotic Option A nonstandard option.

Expectations Theory The theory that forward interest rates equal expected future spot interest rates.

Expected Shortfall Expected loss during N days conditional on being in the $(100 - X)\%$ tail of the distribution of profits/losses. The variable N is the time horizon and $X\%$ is the confidence level.

Expected Value of a Variable The average value of the variable obtained by weighting the alternative values by their probabilities.

Expiration Date The end of life of a contract.

Explicit Finite Difference Method   A method for valuing a derivative by solving the underlying differential equation. The value of the derivative at time t is related to three values at time $t + \Delta t$. It is essentially the same as the trinomial tree method.

Exponentially Weighted Moving Average Model   A model where exponential weighting is used to provide forecasts for a variable from historical data. It is sometimes applied to variances and covariances in value at risk calculations.

Exponential Weighting   A weighting scheme where the weight given to an observation depends on how recent it is. The weight given to an observation i time periods ago is λ times the weight given to an observation $i - 1$ time periods ago where $\lambda < 1$.

Exposure   The maximum loss from default by a counterparty.

Extendable Bond   A bond whose life can be extended at the option of the holder.

Extendable Swap   A swap whose life can be extended at the option of one side to the contract.

Factor   Source of uncertainty.

Factor analysis   An analysis aimed at finding a small number of factors that describe most of the variation in a large number of correlated variables (similar to a principal components analysis).

FAS 123   Accounting standard in United States relating to employee stock options.

FAS 133   Accounting standard in United States relating to instruments used for hedging.

FASB   Financial Accounting Standards Board.

Federal Funds Rate   Overnight interbank borrowing rate.

FICO   A credit score developed by Fair Isaac Corporation.

Financial Intermediary   A bank or other financial institution that facilitates the flow of funds between different entities in the economy.

Finite Difference Method   A method for solving a differential equation.

Flat Volatility   The name given to volatility used to price a cap when the same volatility is used for each caplet.

Flex Option   An option traded on an exchange with terms that are different from the standard options traded by the exchange.

Flexi Cap   Interest rate cap where there is a limit on the total number of caplets that can be exercised.

Floor   *See* Interest Rate Floor.

Floor–Ceiling Agreement   *See* Collar.

Floorlet   One component of a floor.

Floor Rate   The rate in an interest rate floor agreement.

Foreign Currency Option   An option on a foreign exchange rate.

Forward Contract   A contract that obligates the holder to buy or sell an asset for a predetermined delivery price at a predetermined future time.

Forward Exchange Rate   The forward price of one unit of a foreign currency.

Forward Interest Rate   The interest rate for a future period of time implied by the rates prevailing in the market today.

Forward Price   The delivery price in a forward contract that causes the contract to be worth zero.

Forward Rate   Rate of interest for a period of time in the future implied by today's zero rates.

Forward Rate Agreement (FRA)   Agreement that a certain interest rate will apply to a certain principal amount for a certain time period in the future.

Forward Start Option   An option designed so that it will be at-the-money at some time in the future.

Forward Swap   *See* Deferred Swap.

FRTB   *See* Fundamental Review of the Trading Book.

Fundamental Review of the Trading Book (FRTB)   New rules for calculating capital for market risk, due to be implemented in 2018–19.

Funding Valuation Adjustment (FVA)   Adjustment made to the price of a derivative for funding costs.

Futures Commission Merchants   Futures traders who are following instructions from clients.

Futures Contract   A contract that obligates the holder to buy or sell an asset at a predetermined delivery price during a specified future time period. The contract is settled daily.

Futures Option   An option on a futures contract.

Futures Price   The delivery price currently applicable to a futures contract.

Futures-Style Option   Futures contract on the payoff from an option.

FVA   *See* Funding Valuation Adjustment.

Gamma   The rate of change of delta with respect to the asset price.

Gamma-Neutral Portfolio   A portfolio with a gamma of zero.

GAP Management   Procedure for matching the maturities of assets and liabilities.

Gap Option   European call or put option where there are two strike prices. One determines whether the option is exercised. The other determines the payoff.

GARCH Model   A model for forecasting volatility where the variance rate follows a mean-reverting process.

Gaussian Copula Model   A model for defining a correlation structure between two or more variables. In some credit derivatives models, it is used to define a correlation structure for times to default.

Gaussian Quadrature   Procedure for integrating over a normal distribution.

Generalized Wiener Process   A stochastic process where the change in a variable in time t has a normal distribution with mean and variance both proportional to t.

Geometric Average   The nth root of the product of n numbers.

Geometric Brownian Motion   A stochastic process often assumed for asset prices where the logarithm of the underlying variable follows a generalized Wiener process.

Girsanov's Theorem   Result showing that when we change the measure (e.g., move from real world to risk-neutral world) the expected return of a variable changes but the volatility remains the same.

Greeks   Hedge parameters such as delta, gamma, vega, theta, and rho.

Guaranty Fund   Fund to which members of an exchange or CCP contribute. It may be used to cover losses in the event of a default.

Haircut   Discount applied to the value of an asset for collateral purposes.

Hazard Rate   Measures probability of default in a short period of time conditional on no earlier default.

HDD   Heating degree days. The maximum of zero and the amount by which the daily average temperature is less than 65° Fahrenheit. The average temperature is the average of the highest and lowest temperatures (midnight to midnight).

Hedge   A trade designed to reduce risk.

Hedge Funds   Funds that are subject to less regulation and fewer restrictions than mutual funds. But they cannot publicly offer their securities.

Hedger   An individual who enters into hedging trades.

Hedge Ratio   The ratio of the size of a position in a hedging instrument to the size of the position being hedged.

Historical Simulation   A simulation based on historical data.

Historical Volatility   A volatility estimated from historical data.

Holiday Calendar   Calendar defining which days are holidays for the purposes of determining payment dates in a swap.

IMM Dates   Third Wednesday in March, June, September, and December.

Implicit Finite Difference Method   A method for valuing a derivative by solving the underlying differential equation. The value of the derivative at time $t + \Delta t$ is related to three values at time t.

Implied Correlation   Correlation number implied from the price of a credit derivative using the Gaussian copula or similar model.

Implied Distribution   A distribution for a future asset price implied from option prices.

Implied Dividend Yield   Dividend yield estimated using put–call parity from the prices of calls and puts with the same strike price and time to maturity.

Implied Tree   A tree describing the movements of an asset price that is constructed to be consistent with observed option prices.

Implied Volatility   Volatility implied from an option price using the Black–Scholes or a similar model.

Implied Volatility Function (IVF) Model   Model designed so that it matches the market prices of all European options.

Inception Profit   Profit created by selling a derivative for more than its theoretical value.

Index Amortizing Swap   See indexed principal swap.

Index Arbitrage An arbitrage involving a position in the stocks comprising a stock index and a position in a futures contract on the stock index.

Index Futures A futures contract on a stock index or other index.

Index Option An option contract on a stock index or other index.

Indexed Principal Swap A swap where the principal declines over time. The reduction in the principal on a payment date depends on the level of interest rates.

Initial Margin The cash required from a futures trader at the time of the trade.

Instantaneous Forward Rate Forward rate for a very short period of time in the future.

Interest Rate Cap An option that provides a payoff when a specified interest rate is above a certain level. The interest rate is a floating rate that is reset periodically.

Interest Rate Collar A combination of an interest-rate cap and an interest rate floor.

Interest Rate Derivative A derivative whose payoffs are dependent on future interest rates.

Interest Rate Floor An option that provides a payoff when an interest rate is below a certain level. The interest rate is a floating rate that is reset periodically.

Interest Rate Option An option where the payoff is dependent on the level of interest rates.

Interest Rate Swap An exchange of a fixed rate of interest on a certain notional principal for a floating rate of interest on the same notional principal.

International Swaps and Derivatives Association Trade Association for over-the-counter derivatives and developer of master agreements used in over-the-counter contracts.

In-the-Money Option Either (a) a call option where the asset price is greater than the strike price or (b) a put option where the asset price is less than the strike price.

Intrinsic Value For a call option, this is the greater of the excess of the asset price over the strike price and zero. For a put option, it is the greater of the excess of the strike price over the asset price and zero.

Inverted Market A market where futures prices decrease with maturity.

Investment Asset An asset held by at least some individuals for investment purposes.

IO Interest Only. A mortgage-backed security where the holder receives only interest cash flows on the underlying mortgage pool.

ISDA *See* International Swaps and Derivatives Association.

Itô Process A stochastic process where the change in a variable during each short period of time of length Δt has a normal distribution. The mean and variance of the distribution are proportional to Δt and are not necessarily constant.

Itô's Lemma A result that enables the stochastic process for a function of a variable to be calculated from the stochastic process for the variable itself.

ITraxx Europe Portfolio of 125 investment-grade European companies.

Jump–Diffusion Model Model where asset price has jumps superimposed on a diffusion process such as geometric Brownian motion.

Jump Process Stochastic process for a variable involving jumps in the value of the variable.

Kurtosis A measure of the fatness of the tails of a distribution.

KVA *See* Capital Valuation Adjustment.

LEAPS Long-term equity anticipation securities. These are relatively long-term options on individual stocks or stock indices.

LIBOR London interbank offered rate. The rate offered by banks on Eurocurrency deposits (i.e., the rate at which a bank is willing to lend to other banks).

LIBOR Discounting Use of LIBOR rates as proxies for the risk-free rate when derivatives are valued.

LIBOR-in-Arrears Swap Swap where the interest paid on a date is determined by the interest rate observed on that date (not by the interest rate observed on the previous payment date).

LIBOR–OIS Spread Difference between LIBOR rate and OIS rate for a certain maturity.

Limit Move The maximum price move permitted by the exchange in a single trading session.

Limit Order An order that can be executed only at a specified price or one more favorable to the investor.

Liquidity Preference Theory A theory leading to the conclusion that forward interest rates are above expected future spot interest rates.

Liquidity Risk Risk that it will not be possible to sell a holding of a particular instrument at its theoretical price. Also, the risk that a company will not be able to borrow money to fund its assets.

Locals Individuals on the floor of an exchange who trade for their own account rather than for someone else.

Lognormal Distribution A variable has a lognormal distribution when the logarithm of the variable has a normal distribution.

Long Hedge A hedge involving a long futures position.

Long Position A position involving the purchase of an asset.

Lookback Option An option whose payoff is dependent on the maximum or minimum of the asset price achieved during a certain period.

Low Discrepancy Sequence *See* Quasi-random Sequence.

Maintenance Margin When the balance in a trader's margin account falls below the maintenance margin level, the trader receives a margin call requiring the account to be topped up to the initial margin level.

Margin The cash balance (or security deposit) required from a futures or options trader.

Margin Call A request for extra margin when the balance in the margin account falls below the maintenance margin level.

Margin Valuation Adjustment (MVA) Adjustment to the value of a derivative to reflect the cost of funds tied up in margin accounts.

Market-Leveraged Stock Unit (MSU)   A unit entitling the holder to receive shares of a stock at a future time. The number of shares received depends on the stock price.

Market Maker   A trader who is willing to quote both bid and offer prices for an asset.

Market Model   A model most commonly used by traders.

Market Price of Risk   A measure of the trade-offs investors make between risk and return.

Market Segmentation Theory   A theory that short interest rates are determined independently of long interest rates by the market.

Marking to Market   The practice of revaluing an instrument to reflect the current values of the relevant market variables.

Markov Process   A stochastic process where the behavior of the variable over a short period of time depends solely on the value of the variable at the beginning of the period, not on its past history.

Martingale   A zero drift stochastic process.

Maturity Date   The end of the life of a contract.

Maximum Likelihood Method   A method for choosing the values of parameters by maximizing the probability of a set of observations occurring.

Mean Reversion   The tendency of a market variable (such as an interest rate) to revert back to some long-run average level.

Measure   Sometimes also called a probability measure, it defines the market price of risk.

Mezzanine Tranche   Tranche which experiences losses after equity tranche but before senior tranches.

Minimum Variance Delta   Delta that takes the negative correlation between volatility and asset price into account.

Modified Duration   A modification to the standard duration measure so that it more accurately describes the relationship between proportional changes in a bond price and actual changes in its yield. The modification takes account of the compounding frequency with which the yield is quoted.

Money Market Account   An investment that is initially equal to $1 and, at time t, increases at the very short-term risk-free interest rate prevailing at that time.

Monte Carlo Simulation   A procedure for randomly sampling changes in market variables in order to value a derivative.

Mortgage-Backed Security   A security that entitles the owner to a share in the cash flows realized from a pool of mortgages.

MVA   *See* Margin Valuation Adjustment.

Naked Position   An unhedged position, e.g., a short position in a call option that is not combined with a long position in the underlying asset.

Netting   The ability to offset contracts with positive and negative values in the event of a default by a counterparty or for the purpose of determining collateral requirements.

Newton–Raphson Method   An iterative procedure for solving nonlinear equations.

NINJA Term used to describe a person with a poor credit risk: no income, no job, no assets.

No-Arbitrage Assumption The assumption that there are no arbitrage opportunities in market prices.

No-Arbitrage Interest Rate Model A model for the behavior of interest rates that is exactly consistent with the initial term structure of interest rates.

Nonstationary Model A model where the parameters are a function of time.

Nonsystematic Risk Risk that can be diversified away.

Normal Backwardation A situation where the futures price is below the expected future spot price.

Normal Distribution The standard bell-shaped distribution of statistics.

Normal Market A market where futures prices increase with maturity.

Notional Principal The principal used to calculate payments in a swap. The principal is "notional" because it is neither paid nor received.

Numeraire Defines the units in which security prices are measured. For example, if the price of IBM is the numeraire, all security prices are measured relative to IBM. If IBM is $80 and a particular security price is $50, the security price is 0.625 when IBM is the numeraire.

Numerical Procedure A method of valuing an option when no formula is available.

OCC Options Clearing Corporation. *See* Clearinghouse.

Offer Price *See* Ask Price.

OIS *See* Overnight Indexed Swap.

OIS Discounting Use of OIS rates as proxies for the risk-free rate when derivatives are valued.

OIS Rate Rate swapped for geometric average of overnight rates in an OIS.

Open Interest The total number of long positions outstanding in a futures contract (equals the total number of short positions).

Open Outcry System of trading where traders meet on the floor of the exchange

Option The right to buy or sell an asset.

Option-Adjusted Spread The spread over the Treasury curve that makes the theoretical price of an interest rate derivative equal to the market price.

Option Class All options of the same type (call or put) on a particular stock.

Option Series All options of a certain class with the same strike price and expiration date.

Out-of-the-Money Option Either (a) a call option where the asset price is less than the strike price or (b) a put option where the asset price is greater than the strike price.

Overnight Indexed Swap Swap where a fixed rate for a period (e.g., 1 month) is exchanged for the geometric average of the overnight rates during the period.

Overnight Rate One-day rate.

Over-the-Counter Market A market where traders deal directly with each other or through an interdealer broker. The traders are usually financial institutions, corporations, and fund managers.

Package A derivative that is a portfolio of standard calls and puts, possibly combined with a position in forward contracts and the asset itself.

Par Value The principal amount of a bond.

Par Yield The coupon on a bond that makes its price equal the principal.

Parallel Shift A movement in the yield curve where each point on the curve changes by the same amount.

Parisian Option Barrier option where the asset has to be above or below the barrier for a period of time for the option to be knocked in or out.

Path-Dependent Option An option whose payoff depends on the path followed by the underlying variable—not just its final value.

Payoff The cash realized by the holder of an option or other derivative at the end of its life.

PD Probability of default.

Perpetual Derivative A derivative that lasts forever.

Plain Vanilla A term used to describe a standard deal.

P-Measure Real-world measure.

PO Principal Only. A mortgage-backed security where the holder receives only principal cash flows on the underlying mortgage pool.

Poisson Process A process describing a situation where events happen at random. The probability of an event in time Δt is $\lambda \Delta t$, where λ is the intensity of the process.

Portfolio Immunization Making a portfolio relatively insensitive to interest rates.

Portfolio Insurance Entering into trades to ensure that the value of a portfolio will not fall below a certain level.

Position Limit The maximum position a trader (or group of traders acting together) is allowed to hold.

Practitioner Black–Scholes Model Model using implied volatilities and the Black–Scholes–Merton pricing formula.

Premium The price of an option.

Prepayment function A function estimating the prepayment of principal on a portfolio of mortgages in terms of other variables.

Principal The amount of a debt instrument that has to be repaid at maturity.

Principal Components Analysis An analysis aimed at finding a small number of factors that describe most of the variation in a large number of correlated variables (similar to a factor analysis).

Principal Protected Note A product where the return earned depends on the performance of a risky asset but is guaranteed to be nonnegative, so that the investor's principal is preserved.

Program Trading A procedure where trades are automatically generated by a computer and transmitted to the trading floor of an exchange.

Protective Put   A put option combined with a long position in the underlying asset.

Pull-to-Par   The reversion of a bond's price to its par value at maturity.

Put–Call Parity   The relationship between the price of a European call option and the price of a European put option when they have the same strike price and maturity date.

Put Option   An option to sell an asset for a certain price by a certain date.

Puttable Bond   A bond where the holder has the right to sell it back to the issuer at certain predetermined times for a predetermined price.

Puttable Swap   A swap where one side has the right to terminate early.

Q-Measure   Risk-neutral measure.

Quanto   A derivative where the payoff is defined by variables associated with one currency but is paid in another currency.

Quasi-random Sequences   A sequences of numbers used in a Monte Carlo simulation that are representative of alternative outcomes rather than random.

Rainbow Option   An option whose payoff is dependent on two or more underlying variables.

Range Forward Contract   The combination of a long call and short put or the combination of a short call and long put.

Ratchet Cap   Interest rate cap where the cap rate applicable to an accrual period equals the rate for the previous accrual period plus a spread.

Real Option   Option involving real (as opposed to financial) assets. Real assets include land, plant, and machinery.

Rebalancing   The process of adjusting a trading position periodically. Usually the purpose is to maintain delta neutrality.

Recovery Rate   Amount recovered in the event of a default as a percent of the face value.

Reference Entity   Company for which default protection is bought in a credit default swap.

Repo   Repurchase agreement. A procedure for borrowing money by selling securities to a counterparty and agreeing to buy them back later at a slightly higher price.

Repo Rate   The rate of interest in a repo transaction.

Reset Date   The date in a swap or cap or floor when the floating rate for the next period is set.

Restricted Stock Unit (RSU)   A unit entitling the holder to receive one share of a stock at a future time.

Reversion Level   The level to which the value of a market variable (e.g., an interest rate) tends to revert.

Reversion Rate   Rate at which the value of a market variable is pulled to the reversion level when there is mean reversion.

Rho   Rate of change of the price of a derivative with the interest rate.

Rights Issue   An issue to existing shareholders of a security giving them the right to buy new shares at a certain price.

Risk-Free Rate   The rate of interest that can be earned without assuming any risks.

Risk-Neutral Valuation   The valuation of an option or other derivative assuming the world is risk neutral. Risk-neutral valuation gives the correct price for a derivative in all worlds, not just in a risk-neutral world.

Risk-Neutral World   A world where investors are assumed to require no extra return on average for bearing risks.

Roll Back   *See* Backward Induction.

SABR Model   A stochastic volatility model designed to be consistent with the volatility smile for options with a particular maturity

Scalper   A trader who holds positions for a very short period of time.

Scenario Analysis   An analysis of the effects of possible alternative future movements in market variables on the value of a portfolio.

SEC   Securities and Exchange Commission.

Securitization   Procedure for distributing the risks in a portfolio of assets.

SEF   *See* Swap Execution Facility.

Self-financing Portfolio   Portfolio where there is no infusion or withdrawal of money.

Settlement Price   The average of the prices that a contract trades for immediately before the bell signaling the close of trading for a day. It is used in mark-to-market calculations.

Sharpe Ratio   Ratio of excess return over risk-free rate to standard deviation of the excess return.

Shifted Lognormal Model   Model where an interest rate plus a spread is lognormally distributed.

Short Hedge   A hedge where a short futures position is taken.

Short Position   A position assumed when traders sell shares they do not own.

Short Rate   The interest rate applying for a very short period of time.

Short Selling   Selling in the market shares that have been borrowed from another investor.

Short-Term Risk-Free Rate   *See* Short Rate.

Shout Option   An option where the holder has the right to lock in a minimum value for the payoff at one time during its life.

Simulation   *See* Monte Carlo Simulation.

SONIA   Overnight rate in sterling.

Specialist   An individual responsible for managing limit orders on some exchanges. The specialist does not make the information on outstanding limit orders available to other traders.

Speculator   An individual who is taking a position in the market. Usually the individual is betting that the price of an asset will go up or that the price of an asset will go down.

Spot Interest Rate   *See* Zero-Coupon Interest Rate.

Spot Price   The price for immediate delivery.

Spot Volatilities The volatilities used to price a cap when a different volatility is used for each caplet.

Spread Option An option where the payoff is dependent on the difference between two market variables.

Spread Transaction A position in two or more options of the same type.

Stack and Roll Procedure where short-term futures contracts are rolled forward to create long-term hedges.

Static Hedge A hedge that does not have to be changed once it is initiated.

Static Options Replication A procedure for hedging a portfolio that involves finding another portfolio of approximately equal value on some boundary.

Step-up Swap A swap where the principal increases over time in a predetermined way.

Sticky Cap Interest rate cap where the cap rate applicable to an accrual period equals the capped rate for the previous accrual period plus a spread.

Stochastic Process An equation describing the probabilistic behavior of a stochastic variable.

Stochastic Variable A variable whose future value is uncertain.

Stock Dividend A dividend paid in the form of additional shares.

Stock Index An index monitoring the value of a portfolio of stocks.

Stock Index Futures Futures on a stock index.

Stock Index Option An option on a stock index.

Stock Option Option on a stock.

Stock Split The conversion of each existing share into more than one new share.

Storage Costs The costs of storing a commodity.

Straddle A long position in a call and a put with the same strike price.

Strangle A long position in a call and a put with different strike prices.

Strap A long position in two call options and one put option with the same strike price.

Stressed ES Expected shortfall using data from a period of stressed market conditions.

Stressed VaR Value at risk calculated using data from a period of stressed market conditions.

Stress Test Test of the impact of extreme market moves on the value of a portfolio.

Strike Price The price at which the asset may be bought or sold in an option contract (also called the exercise price).

Strip A long position in one call option and two put options with the same strike price.

Strip Bonds Zero-coupon bonds created by selling the coupons on Treasury bonds separately from the principal.

Subprime Mortgage Mortgage granted to borrower with a poor credit history or no credit history.

Swap An agreement to exchange cash flows in the future according to a prearranged formula.

Swap Execution Facility Electronic platform for trading over-the-counter derivatives.

Swap Rate The fixed rate in an interest rate swap that causes the swap to have a value of zero.

Swaption An option to enter into an interest rate swap where a specified fixed rate is exchanged for floating.

Swing Option Energy option in which the rate of consumption must be between a minimum and maximum level. There is usually a limit on the number of times the option holder can change the rate at which the energy is consumed.

Synthetic CDO A CDO created by selling credit default swaps.

Synthetic Option An option created by trading the underlying asset.

Systematic Risk Risk that cannot be diversified away.

Systemic Risk Risk of the collapse of an entire financial system or market.

Tailing the Hedge A procedure for adjusting the number of futures contracts used for hedging to reflect daily settlement.

Tail Loss *See* Expected Shortfall.

Take-and-Pay Option *See* Swing Option.

TED Spread The difference between 3-month LIBOR and the 3-month T-Bill rate.

Tenor Frequency of payments.

Term Structure of Interest Rates The relationship between interest rates and their maturities.

Terminal Value The value at maturity.

Theta The rate of change of the price of an option or other derivative with the passage of time.

Time Decay *See* Theta.

Time Value The value of an option arising from the time left to maturity (equals an option's price minus its intrinsic value).

Timing Adjustment Adjustment made to the forward value of a variable to allow for the timing of a payoff from a derivative.

Total Return Swap A swap where the return on an asset such as a bond is exchanged for LIBOR plus a spread. The return on the asset includes income such as coupons and the change in value of the asset.

Traditional Risk-Neutral World Author's terminology for a world where the market price of risk is zero. Equivalently, it is a world defined by a numeraire equal to the money market account.

Tranche One of several securities that have different risk attributes. Examples are the tranches of a CDO or CMO.

Transaction Costs The cost of carrying out a trade (commissions plus the difference between the price obtained and the midpoint of the bid–offer spread).

Treasury Bill A short-term non-coupon-bearing instrument issued by the government to finance its debt.

Treasury Bond A long-term coupon-bearing instrument issued by the government to finance it debt.

Treasury Bond Futures   A futures contract on Treasury bonds.

Treasury Note   *See* Treasury Bond. (Treasury notes have maturities of less than 10 years.)

Treasury Note Futures   A futures contract on Treasury notes.

Tree   Representation of the evolution of the value of a market variable for the purposes of valuing an option or other derivative.

Trinomial Tree   A tree where there are three branches emanating from each node. It is used in the same way as a binomial tree for valuing derivatives.

Triple Witching Hour   A term given to the time when stock index futures, stock index options, and options on stock index futures all expire together.

Underlying Variable   A variable on which the price of an option or other derivative depends.

Unsystematic Risk   *See* Nonsystematic Risk.

Up-and-In Option   An option that comes into existence when the price of the underlying asset increases to a prespecified level.

Up-and-Out Option   An option that ceases to exist when the price of the underlying asset increases to a prespecified level.

Uptick   An increase in price.

Value at Risk   A loss that will not be exceeded at some specified confidence level.

Variance–Covariance Matrix   A matrix showing variances of, and covariances between, a number of different market variables.

Variance-Gamma Model   A pure jump model where small jumps occur often and large jumps occur infrequently.

Variance Rate   The square of volatility.

Variance Reduction Procedures   Procedures for reducing the error in a Monte Carlo simulation.

Variance Swap   Swap where the realized variance rate during a period is exchanged for a fixed variance rate. Both are applied to a notional principal.

Variation Margin   An extra margin required to bring the balance in a margin account up to the initial margin when there is a margin call.

Vega   The rate of change in the price of an option or other derivative with volatility.

Vega-Neutral Portfolio   A portfolio with a vega of zero.

Vesting Period   Period during which an option cannot be exercised.

VIX Index   Index of the volatility of the S&P 500.

Volatility   A measure of the uncertainty of the return realized on an asset.

Volatility Skew   A term used to describe the volatility smile when it is nonsymmetrical.

Volatility Smile   The variation of implied volatility with strike price.

Volatility Surface   A table showing the variation of implied volatilities with strike price and time to maturity.

Volatility Swap   Swap where the realized volatility during a period is exchanged for a fixed volatility. Both percentage volatilities are applied to a notional principal.

Volatility Term Structure   The variation of implied volatility with time to maturity.

Volcker Rule   A rule in the Dodd–Frank Act restricting the speculative activities of banks, proposed by former Federal Reserve Chairman, Paul Volcker.

Warrant   An option issued by a company or a financial institution. Call warrants are frequently issued by companies on their own stock.

Waterfall   Rules determining how cash flows from the underlying portfolio are distributed to tranches.

Weather Derivative   Derivative where the payoff depends on the weather.

Weeklys   Option created on a Thursday that expires on Friday of the following week.

Wiener Process   A stochastic process where the change in a variable during each short period of time of length Δt has a normal distribution with a mean equal to zero and a variance equal to Δt.

Wild Card Play   The right to deliver on a futures contract at the closing price for a period of time after the close of trading.

World Defined by Numeraire X   World where market price of risk equals the volatility of X.

Writing an Option   Selling an option.

XVA   Valuation adjustments such as FVA, CVA, DVA, MVA, and KVA are collectively known as XVAs.

Yield   A return provided by an instrument.

Yield Curve   *See* Term Structure.

Zero-Coupon Bond   A bond that provides no coupons.

Zero-Coupon Interest Rate   The interest rate that would be earned on a bond that provides no coupons.

Zero-Coupon Yield Curve   A plot of the zero-coupon interest rate against time to maturity.

Zero Curve   *See* Zero-Coupon Yield Curve.

Zero Rate   *See* Zero-Coupon Interest Rate.

DerivaGem Software

DerivaGem 4.00 accompanies this book. It enables readers to value many of the products that are discussed.

Getting Started

The most difficult part of using any software is getting started. Here is a step-by-step guide to using DerivaGem 4.00 for the first time.

1. Use the online access material that comes with this book to load DG400.xls, DG400 functions.xls, and DG400 applications.xls on to your computer. Open Excel file DG400.xls.

2. You will need to make sure that macros are enabled. If *Enable Editing* and *Enable Macros* appear at the top of the worksheet click on them. For some versions of Windows and Office, you may need to make sure that security for macros is set at medium or low.

3. Click on the *Equity_FX_Indx_Fut_Opts_Calc* worksheet at the bottom of the page.

4. Choose *Currency* as the Underlying Type and *Binomial: American* as the Option Type. Click on the *Put* button. Leave *Imply Volatility* unchecked.

5. You are now all set to value an American put option on a currency. There are seven inputs: exchange rate, volatility, domestic risk-free rate, foreign risk-free rate, time to expiration (years), exercise price, and time steps. Input these in cells D5, D6, D7, D8, D13, D14, and D15 as 1.61, 12%, 8%, 9%, 1.0, 1.60, and 4, respectively.

6. Hit *Enter* on your keyboard and click on *Calculate*. You will see the price of the option in cell D20 as 0.07099 and the Greek letters in cells D21 to D25. Part of your screen display should now be as shown on the following page.

7. Click on *Display Tree*. You will see the binomial tree used to calculate the option. This is Figure 21.6 in Chapter 21.

Next Steps

You should now have no difficulty valuing other types of option on other underlyings with this worksheet. To imply a volatility, check the *Imply Volatility* box and input the

Underlying Type:

Currency ▼

Exchange Rate ($ / foreign):	1.6100
Volatility (% per year):	12.00%
Risk-Free Rate (% per year):	8.00%
Foreign Risk-free Rate (% per year):	9.00%

Option Type:

Binomial: American ▼   ☐ Imply Volatility

Life (Years):	1.0000	⦿ Put
Strike Price:	1.6000	
Tree Steps:	4	○ Call

Ca**l**culate   Display Tree

Results:

Price:	0.07099
Delta (per $):	-0.4586061
Gamma (per $ per $):	2.4279267
Vega (per %):	0.0055861
Theta (per day):	-0.000129
Rho (per %):	-0.0065305

option price in cell D20. Hit *Enter* and click on *Calculate*. The implied volatility is displayed in cell D6.

Many different charts can be displayed below the results. To display a chart, you must first choose the variable you require on the vertical (Y) axis, the variable you require on the horizontal (X) axis, the range of X-values to be considered, and the number of X-values to be considered. Following that, you should click on *Draw Graph*.

Other points to note about the *Equity_FX_Indx_Fut_Opts_Calc* worksheet are:

1. For European and American equity options, up to 7 dividends on the underlying stock can be input in a table that pops up. Enter the time of each dividend (measured in years from today) in the first column and the amount of the dividend in the second column.

2. Up to 500 time steps can be used for the valuation of American options, but only a maximum of 10 time steps can be displayed.

3. Greek letters for all options other than standard calls and puts are calculated by perturbing the inputs, not by using analytic formulas.

4. For an Asian option the *Current Average* is the average price since inception. For a new deal (with zero time since inception), the current average is irrelevant.

5. In the case of a lookback option, *Minimum to Date* is used when a call is valued and *Maximum to Date* is used when a put is valued. For a new deal, these should be set equal to the current price of the underlying asset.

6. Interest rates are continuously compounded with an Actual/Actual day count.

The *Alternative Models* worksheet operates like the *Equity_FX_Indx_Fut_Opts_Calc* worksheet. Options can be valued using lognormal, CEV, Merton mixed jump–diffusion, variance-gamma, Heston, and SABR models. Choose chart where implied volatility is Y-axis and strike price is X-axis to display volatility smiles.

Monte Carlo Simulation

In the *Monte Carlo* worksheet, users can see how a number of different types of options are valued using the lognormal, Merton mixed jump–diffusion, and variance-gamma models. Up to 10,000 simulation trials can be used. Full results from ten trials are displayed. When the *Do AntiThetic* box is checked, these are averaged in pairs to produce five sample values. When it is not checked, there are ten sample values. Standard errors from both the full simulation and the ten displayed trials are shown.

Zero Curve

The *Zero_Curve* worksheet allows you to calculate OIS and Treasury zero curves as described in Section 4.7. Bond yields and OIS rates are input with a compounding frequency corresponding to the frequency of payments as in Tables 4.3 and 4.5. The calculated zero rates are continuously compounded. Accrual periods are assumed to be exact fractions of a year and day counts are Actual/Actual.

Swaps

The *Swap_Price* worksheet allows swaps to be valued using OIS discounting. Points on the OIS zero curve are input with continuous compounding. (The points could be transferred from the *Zero_Curve* worksheet.) LIBOR forward rates must also be input. These are forward rates for periods beginning at the specified time and ending one period later, with the length of the period corresponding to the settlement frequency. The forward rates are expressed with a compounding frequency corresponding to the settlement frequency. Thus in Example 7.1 the forward rate for time 0.25 would be 3.329% and the forward rate for time 0.75 would be 3.734%. The OIS zeros for times 0.25, 0.75, and 1.25 would be 2.8%, 3.2%, and 3.4%. The Swap End would be 1.25, the Swap Rate would be 3%, the Last Reset would be 2.9%, and the Settlement Frequency would be Semiannual. The software uses linear interpolation to determine any required zero rates and forward rates that have not been specified.

Bond Options

The general operation of the *Bond_Options* worksheet is similar to that of earlier worksheets. The alternative models are Black's model (see Section 29.1), the normal model of the short rate (see equation (32.4)), and the lognormal model of the short rate (see equation (32.9)). The first model can be applied only to European options. The other two can be applied to European or American options. The coupon is the rate paid per year and the frequency of payments can be selected as Quarterly, Semi-Annual or Annual. The zero-coupon yield curve is entered in the table labeled Term Structure. Enter maturities (measured in years) in the first column and the corresponding continuously compounded rates in the second column. DerivaGem assumes a piecewise linear zero curve similar to that in Figures 4.1 and 4.2. The strike price can be quoted (clean) or cash (dirty) (see Section 29.1). The quoted bond price, which is calculated by the software, and the strike price, which is input, are per $100 of principal.

Caps and Swaptions

The general operation of the *Caps_and Swap_Options* worksheet is similar to that of other worksheets. The worksheet is used to value interest rate caps/floors and swap options. Black's model for caps and floors is explained in Section 29.2 and Black's model for European swap options is explained in Section 29.3. The shifted lognormal model and the Bachelier (normal) model are also described in these sections. The frequency of payments can be selected as Monthly, Quarterly, Semi-Annual, or Annual. The software calculates payment dates by working backward from the end of the life of the instrument. The initial accrual period for a cap/floor may be a nonstandard length between 0.5 and 1.5 times a normal accrual period. OIS discounting is used. Data on LIBOR forward rates and OIS zero rates is input in the same way as for the *Swaps* worksheet. In the case of swap options, the forward LIBOR rates are used only to determine the forward swap rate. If the forward swap rate is known, it is sufficient to input a single forward LIBOR rate and set it as this rate.

CDSs

The CDS worksheet is used to calculate hazard rates from CDS spreads, and vice versa. Users must input a term structure of interest rates (continuously compounded) and either a term structure of CDS spreads or a term structure of hazard rates. The initial hazard rate applies from time zero to the time specified; the second hazard rate applies from the time corresponding to the first hazard rate to the time corresponding to the second hazard rate; and so on. The calculations are carried out assuming that default can occur only at points midway between payment dates. This corresponds to the calculations for the example in Section 25.2.

CDOs

The CDO worksheet calculates quotes for the tranches of CDOs from tranche correlations input by the user. The attachment points and detachment points for tranches are input by the user. The quotes can be in basis points or involve an upfront payment. In the latter case, the spread in basis points is fixed and the upfront payment, as a percent of the tranche principal, is either input or implied. (For example, the fixed spread for the equity tranche of iTraxx Europe or CDX NA IG is 500 basis points.) The number of integration points (see equation (25.12)) defines the accuracy of calculations and can be left as 10 for most purposes (the maximum is 30). The software displays the expected loss as a percent of the tranche principal (ExpLoss) and the present value of expected payments (PVPmts) at the rate of 10,000 basis points per year. The spread and upfront payment are

$$\text{ExpLoss} * 10{,}000/\text{PVPmts} \quad \text{and} \quad \text{ExpLoss} - (\text{Spread} * \text{PVPmts}/10{,}000)$$

respectively. The worksheet can be used to imply either tranche (compound) correlations or base correlations from quotes input by the user. For base correlations to be calculated, it is necessary for the first attachment point to be 0% and the detachment point for one tranche to be the attachment point for the next tranche.

How Greek Letters Are Defined

In the *Equity_FX_Index_Futures* worksheet, the Greek letters are defined as follows:

Delta: Change in option price per dollar increase in underlying asset

Gamma: Change in delta per dollar increase in underlying asset

Vega: Change in option price per 1% increase in volatility (e.g., volatility increases from 20% to 21%)

Rho: Change in option price per 1% increase in interest rate (e.g., interest increases from 5% to 6%)

Theta: Change in option price per calendar day passing.

For instruments dependent on interest rates, the Greek letters are defined as follows:

DV01: Change in option price per 1-basis-point upward parallel shift in the zero curve

Gamma: Change in DV01 for an upward parallel shift in the zero curve (Gamma is per % per %)

Vega: Change in option price when volatility parameter increases by 1% (e.g., volatility increases from 20% to 21%).

The Applications Builder

Once you are familiar with the Options calculator (DG300.xls), you may want to start using the Application Builder (DG300 applications.xls). You can also develop your own applications with DG300 functions.xls. This contains the functions underlying Deriva-Gem with VBA source code. The applications included with the software are:

A. Binomial Convergence. This investigates the convergence of the binomial model in Chapters 13 and 21.

B. Greek Letters. This provides charts showing the Greek letters in Chapter 19.

C. Delta Hedge. This investigates the performance of delta hedging as in Tables 19.2 and 19.3.

D. Delta and Gamma Hedge. This investigates the performance of delta plus gamma hedging for a position in a binary option.

E. Value and Risk. This calculates Value at Risk for a portfolio using three different approaches.

F. Barrier Replication. This carries out calculations for static options replication (see Section 26.16).

G. Trinomial Convergence. This investigates the convergence of a trinomial tree model.

Major Exchanges Trading Futures and Options

Australian Securities Exchange (ASX)	www.asx.com.au
BM&FBOVESPA (BMF)	www.bmfbovespa.com.br
Bombay Stock Exchange (BSE)	www.bseindia.com
Boston Options Exchange (BOX)	www.bostonoptions.com
Bursa Malaysia (BM)	www.bursamalaysia.com
Chicago Board Options Exchange (CBOE)	www.cboe.com
China Financial Futures Exchange (CFFEX)	www.cffex.com.cn
CME Group	www.cmegroup.com
Dalian Commodity Exchange (DCE)	www.dce.com.cn
Eurex	www.eurexchange.com
Hong Kong Futures Exchange (HKFE)	www.hkex.com.hk
IntercontinentalExchange (ICE)	www.theice.com
International Securities Exchange (ISE)	www.ise.com
Japan Exchange Group	www.jpx.co.jp
Kansas City Board of Trade (KCBT)	www.kcbt.com
London Metal Exchange (LME)	www.lme.co.uk
MEFF Renta Fija and Variable, Spain	www.meff.es
Mexican Derivatives Exchange (MEXDER)	www.mexder.com.mx
Minneapolis Grain Exchange (MGE)	www.mgex.com
Montreal Exchange (ME)	www.m-x.ca
NASDAQ OMX	www.business.nasdaq.com
National Stock Exchange, Mumbai (NSE)	www.nseindia.com
NYSE Euronext	www.nyse.com
Shanghai Futures Exchange (SHFE)	www.shfe.com.cn
Singapore Exchange (SGX)	www.sgx.com
Tokyo Financial Exchange (TFX)	www.tfx.co.jp
Zhengzhou Commodity Exchange (ZCE)	www.zce.cn

Table for $N(x)$ When $x \leqslant 0$

This table shows values of $N(x)$ for $x \leqslant 0$. The table should be used with interpolation. For example,

$$N(-0.1234) = N(-0.12) - 0.34[N(-0.12) - N(-0.13)]$$
$$= 0.4522 - 0.34 \times (0.4522 - 0.4483)$$
$$= 0.4509$$

x	.00	.01	.02	.03	.04	.05	.06	.07	.08	.09
−0.0	0.5000	0.4960	0.4920	0.4880	0.4840	0.4801	0.4761	0.4721	0.4681	0.4641
−0.1	0.4602	0.4562	0.4522	0.4483	0.4443	0.4404	0.4364	0.4325	0.4286	0.4247
−0.2	0.4207	0.4168	0.4129	0.4090	0.4052	0.4013	0.3974	0.3936	0.3897	0.3859
−0.3	0.3821	0.3783	0.3745	0.3707	0.3669	0.3632	0.3594	0.3557	0.3520	0.3483
−0.4	0.3446	0.3409	0.3372	0.3336	0.3300	0.3264	0.3228	0.3192	0.3156	0.3121
−0.5	0.3085	0.3050	0.3015	0.2981	0.2946	0.2912	0.2877	0.2843	0.2810	0.2776
−0.6	0.2743	0.2709	0.2676	0.2643	0.2611	0.2578	0.2546	0.2514	0.2483	0.2451
−0.7	0.2420	0.2389	0.2358	0.2327	0.2296	0.2266	0.2236	0.2206	0.2177	0.2148
−0.8	0.2119	0.2090	0.2061	0.2033	0.2005	0.1977	0.1949	0.1922	0.1894	0.1867
−0.9	0.1841	0.1814	0.1788	0.1762	0.1736	0.1711	0.1685	0.1660	0.1635	0.1611
−1.0	0.1587	0.1562	0.1539	0.1515	0.1492	0.1469	0.1446	0.1423	0.1401	0.1379
−1.1	0.1357	0.1335	0.1314	0.1292	0.1271	0.1251	0.1230	0.1210	0.1190	0.1170
−1.2	0.1151	0.1131	0.1112	0.1093	0.1075	0.1056	0.1038	0.1020	0.1003	0.0985
−1.3	0.0968	0.0951	0.0934	0.0918	0.0901	0.0885	0.0869	0.0853	0.0838	0.0823
−1.4	0.0808	0.0793	0.0778	0.0764	0.0749	0.0735	0.0721	0.0708	0.0694	0.0681
−1.5	0.0668	0.0655	0.0643	0.0630	0.0618	0.0606	0.0594	0.0582	0.0571	0.0559
−1.6	0.0548	0.0537	0.0526	0.0516	0.0505	0.0495	0.0485	0.0475	0.0465	0.0455
−1.7	0.0446	0.0436	0.0427	0.0418	0.0409	0.0401	0.0392	0.0384	0.0375	0.0367
−1.8	0.0359	0.0351	0.0344	0.0336	0.0329	0.0322	0.0314	0.0307	0.0301	0.0294
−1.9	0.0287	0.0281	0.0274	0.0268	0.0262	0.0256	0.0250	0.0244	0.0239	0.0233
−2.0	0.0228	0.0222	0.0217	0.0212	0.0207	0.0202	0.0197	0.0192	0.0188	0.0183
−2.1	0.0179	0.0174	0.0170	0.0166	0.0162	0.0158	0.0154	0.0150	0.0146	0.0143
−2.2	0.0139	0.0136	0.0132	0.0129	0.0125	0.0122	0.0119	0.0116	0.0113	0.0110
−2.3	0.0107	0.0104	0.0102	0.0099	0.0096	0.0094	0.0091	0.0089	0.0087	0.0084
−2.4	0.0082	0.0080	0.0078	0.0075	0.0073	0.0071	0.0069	0.0068	0.0066	0.0064
−2.5	0.0062	0.0060	0.0059	0.0057	0.0055	0.0054	0.0052	0.0051	0.0049	0.0048
−2.6	0.0047	0.0045	0.0044	0.0043	0.0041	0.0040	0.0039	0.0038	0.0037	0.0036
−2.7	0.0035	0.0034	0.0033	0.0032	0.0031	0.0030	0.0029	0.0028	0.0027	0.0026
−2.8	0.0026	0.0025	0.0024	0.0023	0.0023	0.0022	0.0021	0.0021	0.0020	0.0019
−2.9	0.0019	0.0018	0.0018	0.0017	0.0016	0.0016	0.0015	0.0015	0.0014	0.0014
−3.0	0.0014	0.0013	0.0013	0.0012	0.0012	0.0011	0.0011	0.0011	0.0010	0.0010
−3.1	0.0010	0.0009	0.0009	0.0009	0.0008	0.0008	0.0008	0.0008	0.0007	0.0007
−3.2	0.0007	0.0007	0.0006	0.0006	0.0006	0.0006	0.0006	0.0005	0.0005	0.0005
−3.3	0.0005	0.0005	0.0005	0.0004	0.0004	0.0004	0.0004	0.0004	0.0004	0.0003
−3.4	0.0003	0.0003	0.0003	0.0003	0.0003	0.0003	0.0003	0.0003	0.0003	0.0002
−3.5	0.0002	0.0002	0.0002	0.0002	0.0002	0.0002	0.0002	0.0002	0.0002	0.0002
−3.6	0.0002	0.0002	0.0001	0.0001	0.0001	0.0001	0.0001	0.0001	0.0001	0.0001
−3.7	0.0001	0.0001	0.0001	0.0001	0.0001	0.0001	0.0001	0.0001	0.0001	0.0001
−3.8	0.0001	0.0001	0.0001	0.0001	0.0001	0.0001	0.0001	0.0001	0.0001	0.0001
−3.9	0.0000	0.0000	0.0000	0.0000	0.0000	0.0000	0.0000	0.0000	0.0000	0.0000
−4.0	0.0000	0.0000	0.0000	0.0000	0.0000	0.0000	0.0000	0.0000	0.0000	0.0000

Table for $N(x)$ When $x \geqslant 0$

This table shows values of $N(x)$ for $x \geqslant 0$. The table should be used with interpolation. For example,

$$N(0.6278) = N(0.62) + 0.78[N(0.63) - N(0.62)]$$
$$= 0.7324 + 0.78 \times (0.7357 - 0.7324)$$
$$= 0.7350$$

x	.00	.01	.02	.03	.04	.05	.06	.07	.08	.09
0.0	0.5000	0.5040	0.5080	0.5120	0.5160	0.5199	0.5239	0.5279	0.5319	0.5359
0.1	0.5398	0.5438	0.5478	0.5517	0.5557	0.5596	0.5636	0.5675	0.5714	0.5753
0.2	0.5793	0.5832	0.5871	0.5910	0.5948	0.5987	0.6026	0.6064	0.6103	0.6141
0.3	0.6179	0.6217	0.6255	0.6293	0.6331	0.6368	0.6406	0.6443	0.6480	0.6517
0.4	0.6554	0.6591	0.6628	0.6664	0.6700	0.6736	0.6772	0.6808	0.6844	0.6879
0.5	0.6915	0.6950	0.6985	0.7019	0.7054	0.7088	0.7123	0.7157	0.7190	0.7224
0.6	0.7257	0.7291	0.7324	0.7357	0.7389	0.7422	0.7454	0.7486	0.7517	0.7549
0.7	0.7580	0.7611	0.7642	0.7673	0.7704	0.7734	0.7764	0.7794	0.7823	0.7852
0.8	0.7881	0.7910	0.7939	0.7967	0.7995	0.8023	0.8051	0.8078	0.8106	0.8133
0.9	0.8159	0.8186	0.8212	0.8238	0.8264	0.8289	0.8315	0.8340	0.8365	0.8389
1.0	0.8413	0.8438	0.8461	0.8485	0.8508	0.8531	0.8554	0.8577	0.8599	0.8621
1.1	0.8643	0.8665	0.8686	0.8708	0.8729	0.8749	0.8770	0.8790	0.8810	0.8830
1.2	0.8849	0.8869	0.8888	0.8907	0.8925	0.8944	0.8962	0.8980	0.8997	0.9015
1.3	0.9032	0.9049	0.9066	0.9082	0.9099	0.9115	0.9131	0.9147	0.9162	0.9177
1.4	0.9192	0.9207	0.9222	0.9236	0.9251	0.9265	0.9279	0.9292	0.9306	0.9319
1.5	0.9332	0.9345	0.9357	0.9370	0.9382	0.9394	0.9406	0.9418	0.9429	0.9441
1.6	0.9452	0.9463	0.9474	0.9484	0.9495	0.9505	0.9515	0.9525	0.9535	0.9545
1.7	0.9554	0.9564	0.9573	0.9582	0.9591	0.9599	0.9608	0.9616	0.9625	0.9633
1.8	0.9641	0.9649	0.9656	0.9664	0.9671	0.9678	0.9686	0.9693	0.9699	0.9706
1.9	0.9713	0.9719	0.9726	0.9732	0.9738	0.9744	0.9750	0.9756	0.9761	0.9767
2.0	0.9772	0.9778	0.9783	0.9788	0.9793	0.9798	0.9803	0.9808	0.9812	0.9817
2.1	0.9821	0.9826	0.9830	0.9834	0.9838	0.9842	0.9846	0.9850	0.9854	0.9857
2.2	0.9861	0.9864	0.9868	0.9871	0.9875	0.9878	0.9881	0.9884	0.9887	0.9890
2.3	0.9893	0.9896	0.9898	0.9901	0.9904	0.9906	0.9909	0.9911	0.9913	0.9916
2.4	0.9918	0.9920	0.9922	0.9925	0.9927	0.9929	0.9931	0.9932	0.9934	0.9936
2.5	0.9938	0.9940	0.9941	0.9943	0.9945	0.9946	0.9948	0.9949	0.9951	0.9952
2.6	0.9953	0.9955	0.9956	0.9957	0.9959	0.9960	0.9961	0.9962	0.9963	0.9964
2.7	0.9965	0.9966	0.9967	0.9968	0.9969	0.9970	0.9971	0.9972	0.9973	0.9974
2.8	0.9974	0.9975	0.9976	0.9977	0.9977	0.9978	0.9979	0.9979	0.9980	0.9981
2.9	0.9981	0.9982	0.9982	0.9983	0.9984	0.9984	0.9985	0.9985	0.9986	0.9986
3.0	0.9986	0.9987	0.9987	0.9988	0.9988	0.9989	0.9989	0.9989	0.9990	0.9990
3.1	0.9990	0.9991	0.9991	0.9991	0.9992	0.9992	0.9992	0.9992	0.9993	0.9993
3.2	0.9993	0.9993	0.9994	0.9994	0.9994	0.9994	0.9994	0.9995	0.9995	0.9995
3.3	0.9995	0.9995	0.9995	0.9996	0.9996	0.9996	0.9996	0.9996	0.9996	0.9997
3.4	0.9997	0.9997	0.9997	0.9997	0.9997	0.9997	0.9997	0.9997	0.9997	0.9998
3.5	0.9998	0.9998	0.9998	0.9998	0.9998	0.9998	0.9998	0.9998	0.9998	0.9998
3.6	0.9998	0.9998	0.9999	0.9999	0.9999	0.9999	0.9999	0.9999	0.9999	0.9999
3.7	0.9999	0.9999	0.9999	0.9999	0.9999	0.9999	0.9999	0.9999	0.9999	0.9999
3.8	0.9999	0.9999	0.9999	0.9999	0.9999	0.9999	0.9999	0.9999	0.9999	0.9999
3.9	1.0000	1.0000	1.0000	1.0000	1.0000	1.0000	1.0000	1.0000	1.0000	1.0000
4.0	1.0000	1.0000	1.0000	1.0000	1.0000	1.0000	1.0000	1.0000	1.0000	1.0000

Credits

Author Index

Subject Index

References to items in the Glossary of Terms are **bolded**.

851